CROSS AND TAPPER ON EVIDENCE

Twelfth edition

COLIN TAPPER, MA, BCL

Emeritus Professor of Law, University of Oxford

OXFORD

UNIVERSITY PRESS

OXFORD
UNIVERSITY PRESS

Great Clarendon Street, Oxford OX2 6DP
United Kingdom

Oxford University Press is a department of the University of Oxford.
It furthers the University's objective of excellence in research, scholarship,
and education by publishing worldwide. Oxford is a registered trade mark of
Oxford University Press in the UK and in certain other countries

© Oxford University Press 2010

The moral rights of the author have been asserted

First edition 1958
Second edition 1963
Third edition 1967
Fourth edition 1974
Fifth edition 1979
Sixth edition 1985
Seventh edition 1990
Eighth edition 1995
Ninth edition 1999
Tenth edition 2004
Eleventh edition 2007
This edition 2010
Reprinted 2013

Crown copyright material reproduced with the permission of the
Controller, HMSO (under the terms of the Click Use licence)

British Library Cataloguing in Publication Data
Data available

Library of Congress Cataloging in Publication Data
Data available

ISBN 978-0-19-957414-8

PREFACE TO THE 12TH EDITION

This is the latest, and will be the last, edition of this work to be written by Professor Cross, or edited by someone he taught in person. The book owes its conception, organization, and method to the outstanding talents and personality of its original author. It has been carried on by an editor whose first contact with the subject was as Professor Cross's pupil, working from the then just published first edition, and later as an academic collaborator and personal friend. As Professor Cross intimated in his first preface, the book was intended to bridge the gap between practitioners' books and elementary primers, in the form of a text more critical and comparative than the former, and more substantial than the latter. The law of evidence, while necessarily and essentially practical, draws its intellectual underpinning from philosophy and history, both areas of intense interest to Professor Cross. The book's practical usefulness stemmed from Professor Cross's early career as a solicitor, and his bluff distrust of cant and of technicality for its own sake. His disability, in addition to honing his incredible memory for detail, also compelled the development of reading and research patterns which his sighted successor has attempted to emulate, aided by the development of modern technology. The result has been a work which generated more practical application then Professor Cross may have initially contemplated, and that has affected the way in which the book has developed, in the sense of imposing greater commitment to comprehensive coverage.

Over its twelve editions the law of evidence has experienced significant change. It is now much less universal than it once was, in the sense that English law has divided ever more firmly between its applications in civil and criminal proceedings, and diverged more from the law in other common law jurisdictions, mainly as a result of increased, and persistent, statutory intervention, but also partly as a result of the influence of European attitudes and approaches, themselves transmitted through the mechanism of the European treaties and Court of Justice, and the European Court of Human Rights. It has also become much more intertwined with procedural law as the application of legal rules is expressed in a continuing, and less episodic, process.

An aim of this work has always been to reconcile the two different engines of development of the law in common law jurisdictions; on the one hand deep and tightly focussed examination in the decisions of the courts, and on the other in wider-ranging and more diffuse policies expressed in statutory intervention, complicated by the different processes, and use of language, in each. The work has aimed to draw principle and reduce anomaly from the one, and to explore the application and practical results of the other. A similar motivation has inspired the increasing activity of law-reforming bodies, and especially of the Law Commission.

This edition attempts to follow that tradition in stating the English law of Evidence as at the end of 2009. It continues to illustrate that law by reference to the law of other common law jurisdictions, and to an increasing extent the law of the civil law jurisdictions, mainly through the influence of the European Court of Human Rights. The principal domestic development has been the burgeoning of reported case law on the meaning and application of the provisions of the Criminal Justice Act 2003 in relation to bad character and hearsay. It is remarkable that despite the plethora of case law in the Court of Appeal there is still no decision from the ultimate domestic court of appeal in relation to the former, although the decision of the Supreme Court in *R v Horncastle* in relation to the latter shows the value of such support. That decision was itself driven by reaction to an earlier decision of the European Court of Human Rights, and much of the re-writing in this edition stems from a similar impetus. It has dictated substantial change in the parts of the book dealing with the burden and standard of proof, the privilege against self-incrimination, and hearsay. It has also had to be taken into account in the expanded section dealing with the new legislation, now the Coroners and Justice Act 2009, on the anonymity of witnesses. The chapters on character have had to be almost completely re-written on account of the weight of domestic case-law, and some evaluation has been attempted now that the changes have been in force for more than five years, although it cannot be claimed that they have yet bedded down. It really will require authoritative guidance from the Supreme Court before that happier state can be achieved. Domestic concerns have led to the inclusion of a short new section on evidence of mediators, and changes to sections dealing with evidence at inquests, and without prejudice privilege. The volume of new material to be accommodated, together with the need to restrain expansion has necessitated changes throughout the book. It may be true that a text of this sort needs to be comprehensive, readable, and concise; and that while any two can be achieved at the expense of the third, the achievement of all three is impossible: the editor can only say that he has tried to reconcile these conflicting goals.

The book will continue to be supported electronically as described a little more fully on the following 'Guide to the Online Resource Centre'. The website also now contains a new section on further reading. The editor thanks all of those who have contributed to the development of this work over the years, especially to students and colleagues whose contributions have averted errors and provided inspiration; and to successive publishers who have provided essential support, and welcome encouragement.

Colin Tapper
2010

EXTRACT FROM THE PREFACE TO THE FIRST EDITION

In the preface to the first edition of his *Law of Evidence*, the late S L Phipson said that he had endeavoured to supply students and practitioners with a work which would take a middle place between 'the admirable but extremely condensed *Digest* [*of the Law of Evidence*] of Sir James Stephen, and that great repository of evidentiary law, *Taylor on Evidence*'. Those words were written as long ago as 1892, and Phipson's book now has claims to be regarded as *the* great English repository of evidentiary law. I realize therefore that I am flying high when I say I hope to have supplied students and practitioners with a work which will take a middle place between those of Stephen and Phipson. The needs of students and practitioners are not, of course, identical; but I have catered for the students by including many more cases in the footnotes than any student could conceivably wish to consult. Nearly all the decisions that are really important from the student's point of view are mentioned in the text. Though I have primarily borne in mind the requirements of those who are working for a law degree, I trust that the book may not prove too long for those working for the professional examinations. The long book may often be tedious, but it is sometimes more digestible than the shorter one.

I have adopted the growing practice of citing a number of decisions of the courts of the Commonwealth. My citations are not intended to be exhaustive. I have, in the main, chosen Commonwealth decisions in which English cases have been discussed or which provide a neat illustration of what is pretty clearly English law.

I have laid myself open to the charge of having quoted at too great length from English judges and American writers. My answer is that I have endeavoured to meet the undoubted need for an up-to-date account of the theory of the subject—a need that is made plain by the fact that, in nine cases out of ten, any advocate can say whether evidence is admissible or inadmissible, but he is frequently at a loss to explain why this should be so. It is impossible to give a satisfactory account of the theory of our law of evidence without frequent reference to the ipsissima verba of the judges and the work of such great American exponents of the subject as Thayer, Wigmore, Morgan, and Maguire.

Rupert Cross
January 1958

GUIDE TO THE ONLINE RESOURCE CENTRE

This book is accompanied by an Online Resource Centre—an open-access website which has been designed to support the book. The ORC can be found at: www.oxfordtextbooks. co.uk/orc/tapper12e/

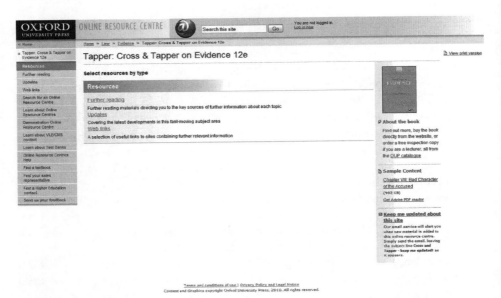

- Extensive twice-yearly updates to the text ensure the reader is kept up-to-date with the latest developments in this fast-moving subject area.
- An extensive selection of useful weblinks to sites containing further relevant information helps you to efficiently direct your online research.
- A useful list of further reading materials directs you to the key sources of further information about each topic.

OUTLINE CONTENTS

CONTENTS

TABLE OF CASES

TABLE OF STATUTES

AUSTRALIA

I

INTRODUCTION

The evidence of a fact is that which tends to prove it—something that may satisfy an inquirer of the fact's existence. Courts of law must decide on a basis of facts,[1] and such evidence as they will receive to find them is described as 'judicial evidence'.[2] It has been said that:[3]

[I]t is on the whole undesirable that the process of judicial decision-making on issues of fact should diverge more than it need from the process followed by rational, objective and fair-minded people called upon to decide issues of fact in other contexts where reaching the right answer matters.

After mentioning the development of the law of evidence in Section 1 of this chapter, the extent to which it applies to all of the different stages and matters considered by the courts, and to other tribunals, will be considered in Section 2. The main purposes and categories of evidence will be considered and exemplified in Section 3, together with the question of whether any broad general rules can usefully be elaborated. The fundamental principle is relevance, discussed in Section 4.

SECTION 1. THE DEVELOPMENT OF
THE LAW OF EVIDENCE

Although some of the modern rules of evidence can be traced back to the Middle Ages, their development really begins with the decisions of the common law judges[4] in the seventeenth and eighteenth centuries. Recent centuries have witnessed a number of

---

[1] See *R v Lawson* [2008] EWCA Crim 2948, *Re R (A Child)* (2008) 152(46) SJLB 29 (not upon speculation); *Mills v DPP* [2008] EWHC 3304 (Admin) (not inference from pre-trial conduct of proceedings); *Haringey LBC v Tshilumbe* [2009] EWHC 2820 (Admin) (not pre-trial exculpatory statement to legal adviser); *R v MacDonald* (2008) 233 CCC (3d) 1 (certainly not convict after rejecting all evidence tendered), but it need not necessarily be that tendered by a party on a particular issue, so long as the more general point has been raised, *Woodhouse School v Webster* [2009] EWCA Civ 91.

[2] In some contexts, *O'Brien v Moriarty (No 2)* [2006] IESC 6, [2006] 2 IR 415 (terms of reference of a Tribunal); *Nine Networks Australia Pty v McGregor* [2004] NTSC 27, 150 ACR 150 (prohibition of publication), 'evidence' may have a wider meaning. It does not extend to questions asked by counsel, *People (DPP) v Murphy* [2005] IECCA 1, [2005] 2 IR 125.

[3] Lord Bingham in *O'Brien v Chief Constable of South Wales Police* [2005] UKHL 26, [2005] 2 AC 534, [4]; cp Menashe (2008) E & P 32 for analysis of reasoning processes in other contexts.

[4] Civilian law was much less dominated by exclusionary rules, to some extent reflected in the approach of the European Court of Human Rights; for comparison with the common law, see Jussila (2004) 43 *Eur L* 31.

statutory reforms, but the older decisions of the common law judges still dictate the form in which much of the law of evidence must be stated, remaining largely a set of exclusionary rules,[5] declaring that certain matters which might well be accepted as evidence of a fact by other responsible inquirers will not be accepted by the courts; rules declaring, in other words, what is not judicial evidence. There are, however, also signs of an increasing tendency to develop guidelines relating to the weight of such evidence[6] and to elaborate rules relating to the circumstances in which its disclosure can be compelled,[7] and as to its authentication.[8] Three factors that have contributed to the largely exclusionary character of the law of evidence are the jury, the oath, and the common law's adversary[9] system of procedure,[10] to which cost may now be added, especially in relation to rules of disclosure.[11] Allowance must also be made for a deep-seated fear that evidence will be manufactured:[12]

[T]he presumption...is, that no man would declare anything against himself, unless it were true; but that every man, if he was in a difficulty, or in the view to any difficulty, would make declarations for himself.

A policy of piecemeal reform is liable to have particularly unfortunate results in relation to a subject which is so highly integrated, and the persistent application of that policy led one commentator to describe it as:[13]

Founded apparently on the propositions that all jurymen are deaf to reason, that all witnesses are presumptively liars and that all documents are presumptively forgeries, it has been added to, subtracted from and tinkered with for two centuries until it has become less of a structure than a pile of builders' debris.

Yet it must not be supposed that all assessments were equally critical. In *A-G v Horner (No 2)*,[14] Hamilton LJ was more sanguine:

I yield to authority on the law of evidence without reluctance, because I am satisfied that in the main the English rules of evidence are just, and I am satisfied also that there is no portion of the English law which ought more rigidly to be upheld. My experience is that the public have in the result derived great benefit from their strict application.

In 1964 in an attempt to make this branch of the law more coherent, the government referred the law of evidence in civil and criminal cases respectively to the Law Reform

---

[5] Thought by some to be inappropriate to the proceedings of international criminal tribunals, see Murphy (2008) 12 E&P 1.

[6] The tendency was first discerned long ago: 'People were formerly frightened out of their wits about admitting evidence lest juries should go wrong. In modern times we admit the evidence and discuss its weight' (Cockburn CJ in *R v Birmingham Overseers* (1861) 1 B & S 763, 767). See also Auld *Review of the Criminal Courts of England and Wales* (2001) ch 11, [78], and the recommendation of such an approach in Scotland, *L v L* 1997 SCLR 866, 871D.   [7] See Chapter VI.

[8] See Pattenden (2008) 12 E&P 273.

[9] Some of the worst effects in criminal cases may be alleviated by pressure towards pretrial disclosure and discussion between counsel and judge of the proper terms for direction: see e.g. *R v N* [1998] Crim LR 886, and by increasing use of model forms.

[10] Modern scholarship suggests that judicial control of lawyers also played its part: Langbein (1978) 45 *U Chi LR* 263.   [11] *Re M* [2007] EWCA Civ 589, [2007] FLR 1006, [14].

[12] *R v Hardy* (1794) 24 State Tr 199, 1093, Eyre CB.   [13] Harvey *The Advocate's Devil* (1958) 79.

[14] [1913] 2 Ch 140, 156.

Committee and the Criminal Law Revision Committee. The split reference, however, exacerbated the difference between the rules in civil and criminal proceedings.[15] Disquiet was expressed by the Roskill Fraud Trials Committee Report[16] about the extent of such divergence, especially in view of the more radical approach adopted in civil cases as a result of the Civil Evidence Act 1968.[17] The force of the law has been weakened in criminal proceedings by restriction of the grounds upon which an appeal may be allowed to cases in which the conviction is unsafe,[18] with the result that where the rules prescribe the inadmissibility of evidence on grounds other than irrelevance or unreliability, failure to observe those rules will no longer lead to the conviction being quashed. Deprived of incentive to appeal against such decisions, it may be that such rules will begin to decay. There remain significant differences between the rules applying to criminal and to civil proceedings.[19] Nor does their removal seem necessarily imminent, despite the current tendency to refer evidential reform to the Law Commission.[20] The common law rules of evidence were devised for jury trial, a procedure obsolescent in civil cases, although still[21] the mode of trial for serious criminal charges and, even in less serious ones, the fact that they are for the most part heard by lay magistrates may justify greater restriction of admissible evidence than for proceedings before a legally qualified judge sitting alone.[22] Subject to finding the proper balance between the rules governing civil and criminal cases, the law of evidence is a fit subject for codification. If this task is ever undertaken in England, there will be some useful precedents, mentioned here from time to time. There is the Indian Evidence Act 1872, drafted by Sir James Stephen, which still forms the basis of a number of Evidence Ordinances in the Commonwealth. In Canada[23] Australia,[24] and in New Zealand comprehensive Codes have been drafted, and in the latter two enacted.[25] In the United States, the Federal Rules of Evidence, approved by Congress in 1975, do not

[15] The distinction became still more important after the passage of the Human Rights Act 1998, and is not always easy to draw: *Clingham v Kensington and Chelsea Royal LBC* [2002] UKHL 39, [2003] 1 AC 787, [2002] 4 All ER 539, and more fully 156.

[16] (1986), paras 5.7 and 5.8.

[17] Now superseded by the Civil Evidence Act 1995, although the Criminal Justice Act 2003 has reduced the gap. [18] Criminal Appeal Act 1995, s 2, substituting new subs (1) in Criminal Appeal Act 1968, s 2.

[19] In criminal proceedings the standard of proof is higher, the accused is incompetent as a witness for the prosecution, unsworn evidence may be given by young children, special rules govern the competence and compellability of the accused's spouse, there is no issue estoppel, the reception of hearsay and opinion evidence remains more restricted, and the grounds for discretionary exclusion are broader.

[20] References to which often remain limited either to civil or to criminal proceedings.

[21] Although under pressure, and its ambit being reduced: see the Criminal Justice Act 2003, Pt 7; *R v SK* [2009] EWHC 2930 (Admin) (trial by judge alone after jury tampering).

[22] It has been suggested that because of the difficulty of handling exclusionary discretion in such a tribunal, there is uncertainty whether or not such a form of trial can be fair so as to comply with human rights law: see Keeley (2000) 164 JP 182.

[23] See draft Code of Evidence published by Law Reform Commission of Canada in 1976 and the Report of the Federal and Provincial Task Force on the Uniform Rules of Evidence (1982).

[24] See Law Reform Commission of Australia Report No 38 'Evidence' (1987).

[25] Although far-reaching Evidence Acts have been enacted for the Commonwealth, New South Wales and some other states. Reference will most often be made here to the Evidence Act 1995 (Commonwealth). Even there, however, the new legislation builds on the old concepts: see *O'Brien v Gillespie* (1997) 41 NSWLR 549. For an appraisal from an English point of view, see Dennis [1996] *Crim LR* 477, and from an Australian, Smith (1995) 18 *UNSWLR* 1; for comprehensive analysis, see Odgers *Uniform Evidence Law* (8th edn, 2008). In New Zealand see Evidence Act 2006.

amount to a complete code, nor are they binding upon the separate States, but they have been widely adopted by them, and in some constitute part of a code.[26]

Despite the best efforts of the Law Commission, reform of the law of evidence in criminal cases has been obstructed by the refusal of the legislature to authorize comprehensive and systematic empirical research into the operation of the jury system. It is, however, encouraging that the courts have continued to stress the importance of cooperation between judges and counsel in drafting directions to juries, assisted to a considerable extent by the work of the Judicial Studies Board in drafting standard directions.[27] It is likely that further comprehensive reform will[28] result from the projection into English law[29] of the European Convention on Human Rights,[30] despite formal insistence[31] that the Convention deals only with the fairness of trials[32] and not with the admissibility of evidence.[33] It cannot be excluded that a painful, and confusing, process of adjustment of the law of evidence will occur.[34] It is interesting that in an attempt to confine the problem the Court of Appeal took early steps to discourage gratuitous reliance upon the Convention,[35] and the Attorney-General went so far as to issue guidance to prosecutors as to how to refute arguments based upon it.[36] Nor are Convention Rights incapable of being displaced by a resolution of the

---

[26] Comparison with the law of evidence in the United States is complicated, especially in criminal cases, by the impact of the Constitution, although, somewhat paradoxically, in some respects its modern interpretation has augmented convergence with English law: see Imwinkelreid [1990] *Crim LR* 790.

[27] Although empirical research demonstrates the danger of directions to disregard being counterproductive, see e.g. Lee (2005) 28 *Int J of Law and Psychiatry* 589.

[28] For a full account of its implications, see Emmerson and Ashworth *Human Rights and Criminal Justice* (2nd edn, 2007). See also Gil Robles (Commissioner for Human Rights): Report of Visit to United Kingdom (2005) 41 EHRR SE9 113.

[29] Human Rights Act 1998. It does not apply to British facilities situated outside the EU, *R (Al-Saadoon v Secretary of State for Ministry of Defence)* [2009] EWCA Civ 7; [2010] 1 All E.R. 271.

[30] It should be noted that outside the strict province of community law, the authoritative source for construction of this Convention is the European Court of Human Rights, and not the European Court of Justice: *Kremzow v Austria* [1997] 3 CMLR 1289. The Commission has, however, signalled its intention to publish proposals on evidential safeguards: COM (2004) 328 final, 14. For detail of pressure on the European Court of Human Rights, see Lord Woolf's Review of Its Working Methods (2006) 42 EHRR SE12 121, and for convincing criticism of its application in this way, see Hoffmann (2009) 125 *LQR* 416.

[31] *Holland v HM Adv (DRA No 1 of 2005)* 2005 SCCR 417, [39] (PC).

[32] Such unfairness will not inevitably mandate referral of a conviction to the Court of Appeal, *Dowsett v Criminal Cases Review Commission* (2007) unreported QDD 8 June; nor necessarily give rise to a claim for damages: *(R)Greenfield v Secretary of State for Home Affairs* above. In Scotland, *Rose v HM Adv* [2003] SCCR 569 held that invocation of Art 6 in advance of trial required proof of more than a material risk of an unfair trial.

[33] In *R(Nasseri) v Home Secretary* [2007] EWHC 1548 (Admin) it was, however, held that parts of the Asylum Act 2004 were incompatible with the Convention because of discrepancy as to the admissibility of evidence. Otherwise mandatory Convention rules can sometimes be by-passed by reference to arbitration, see *Stretford v Football Association* [2006] EWHC 479 (Ch), [2006] All ER (D) 275; in other tribunals the Convention can be sustained by judicial review, *Heather Moore & Edgecombe Ltd v Financial Ombudsman Service* [2008] EWCA 642.

[34] As has been the case in Canada, New Zealand, and South Africa, where schemes of incorporation of human rights have also been introduced. For incisive analysis, see Marshall (2003) *Pub L* 236.

[35] See *R v Perry* (2000) The Times, 28 April, CA, [42]–[47] (criminal); *Walker v Daniels* [2000] 1 WLR 1382, [2000] CPLR 462 (civil). And to the escalating body of authority, see *R v Home Secretary, ex p Carroll* [2001] EWCA Civ 1224, [2002] 1 WLR 545, [73]. See also exhortation to restrain applications for abuse of process on evidential grounds, *R v Childs* [2002] EWCA Crim 2578, [11].

[36] *Points for Prosecutors* (2000). It predictably provoked response, see, e.g., Cape (2000) *Legal Action* (November) 29.

United Nations.[37] Where English law is clear and emphatic, foreign persuasive authority is unlikely to be regarded as shaking it.[38] Nevertheless, in the criminal context,[39] it is well to heed the words of Sachs J in the South African case of *S v Coetzee*:[40]

...the more serious the crime and the greater the public interest in securing convictions of the guilty, the more important do constitutional protections of the accused become.

The advent in 1999 of the Civil Procedure Rules may transform the operation of the rules of evidence in civil proceedings, since the whole aim of the new rules was to draft in less technical language than that of the old Rules so as to emphasize judicial flexibility and to simplify and expedite the administration of justice. To those ends far-reaching powers were conferred to exclude admissible evidence[41] and to limit cross-examination.[42] It remains to be seen how far this will be taken.

The subsequently introduced Criminal Procedure Rules 2005 were perhaps less radical in their approach,[43] but made some attempt to correct a perceived bias of the criminal justice system in favour of the accused, by explicit recognition of the interests of the public in convicting the guilty, and increasingly catering for the victims of crime.[44]

SECTION 2. RANGE OF THE LAW OF EVIDENCE[45]

The law of evidence comprises a wide diversity of topics and rules.[46] Some deal with essentially procedural matters, such as the ability to secure the disclosure of relevant evidence, or rules about forms in which questions may be put to a witness; some deal with witnesses, such as the rules relating to their competency and the extent to which their evidence requires corroboration; some deal with the admissibility of particular sorts of evidence, such as that of character or of potentially unreliable evidence such as hearsay; and some deal with questions of proof, such as rules about judicial notice or the standard required. These various categories overlap and interlock, and can be combined in different ways. There is no type of proceeding to which all of the rules of evidence apply; different patterns exist for civil and criminal, for public and private, and for higher and lower court proceedings. The most significant difference is probably that between the rules which apply to judicial proceedings in the courts, and those which apply to fact-finding in other tribunals.

---

[37] *R (Al Jedda) v Secretary of State for Defence* [2005] EWHC 1809 (Admin), [2001] HRLR 1.

[38] See *Myles v DPP* [2004] EWHC 594, [2004] 2 All ER 402.

[39] Even more strongly in relation to terrorism, see Gearty, Dickson, and Flynn [2005] *EHRLR* 1, 11, and 29.   [40] 1997 (3) SA 527, [220].

[41] Rule 32.1(2).   [42] Rule 32.1(3).

[43] They should be applied as strictly as possible: *R(Robinson) v Sutton Coldfield Mag Ct* [2006] EWHC 307 (Admin), [2006] 4 All ER 1029, [13].

[44] Overriding objective [1.1(2)]. Such an approach may also be discerned in judicial decisions deploring undue technicality favouring the defence: *Cox v DPP* [2005] EWHC 2694 (Admin) [10]; *R (P) v South and South East Hampshire Youth Court* [2005] EWHC 2694 (Admin).

[45] For elaborate statutory recognition of the need for different rules in different situations, see in Australia, Evidence Act (Cwth) 1995, ss 4, 5, 8, and 9; for exegesis, *Epeabaka v Minister for Immigration and Multicultural Affairs* (1997) 150 ALR 397.

[46] For a more detailed analysis, see Tapper in Birks (ed) *Pressing Problems in the Law 1: Criminal Justice and Human Rights* (1995).

PROCEEDINGS IN COURTS

The fullest range of the rules of evidence applies to proceedings in courts,[47] but there remain important variations of pattern between different types of jurisdiction, different types of court, and at different stages in the proceedings.

Different types of jurisdiction[48]

Notwithstanding many assertions of the common character of the law of evidence in civil and criminal proceedings,[49] it is obvious, even to those making them, that many of the rules are different,[50] and that the same ones are often applied differently.[51] In *R v Christie*,[52] Lord Reading, having stated the theoretical similarity, went on to say that in practice 'it is desirable in certain circumstances to relax the strict application of the law of evidence'. He meant the need to temper strictness when it was applied to the accused in a criminal case, and in particular preservation of the accused from the effect of admitting evidence more prejudicial to him than probative of the prosecution case. The Criminal Justice Act 2003 preserved the distinction but moved in the opposite direction, allowing broader admissibility of the accused's bad character in criminal than in civil proceedings.[53] Even here the matter is not straightforward, for strictly that should lead less to discrimination between civil and criminal proceedings, and more between rules applying to the accused in criminal proceedings, and those applying to others. This leads to difficulty when the true adversary is not the prosecutor, but a co-defendant, for whom similar solicitude should be shown, leading to further modification in the rules.[54] Another factor that contributes, perhaps even more strongly,[55] to variation between the rules applying in criminal and civil proceedings is difference between the forms of procedure and methods of trial. In criminal cases, pleading is generally oral, and there are commonly no interim applications. In civil cases, there is hardly ever a jury. Here too the consequences of such differences find statutory expression, for example in the different methods of reforming

---

[47] Although some rules can be waived by the parties, and there is statutory provision in some jurisdictions for the rules of evidence to be disapplied on application by a party, see *Harrington-Smith v Western Australia (No 8)* [2004] FCA 338, 207 ALR 483. In Canada, see *Minister of National Revenue v Mitchell* [2001] 1 SCR 910, 935.

[48] See Cooper (2006) 156 NLJ 310 for a neat demonstration of the differences between the rules applying to expert witnesses in civil, family, and criminal proceedings.

[49] The High Court of Australia denied in *Chief Executive Officer of Customs v Labrador Liquor Wholesale Pty Ltd* [2003] HCA 49, 216 CLR 161 that characterization of proceedings as 'criminal' or 'civil' was determinative of the evidential rules to be applied; cp in Canada *Martineau v Minister of National Revenue* 2004 SCC 81, [2004] 3 SCR 737.

[50] Thus the persuasive burden of negating self-defence is borne by the prosecution on a charge of murder, but of establishing it by the defence on a civil claim for battery: *Ashley v Chief Constable of Sussex Police* [2006] EWCA Civ 1085, 103(32) LSG 20, [33].

[51] See e.g. *Halford v Brookes* [1992] PIQR P175, in which civil proceedings were brought for damages for murder and Rougier J rehearsed a number of differences between the proceedings before him and earlier criminal proceedings, which had resulted in the acquittal of one of the defendants.

[52] [1914] AC 545, 564.

[53] As emphasized in *R v Weir* [2005] EWCA Crim 2866, [2006] 2 All ER 570, [35].

[54] See e.g. *Murdoch v Taylor* [1965] AC 574, [1965] 1 All ER 406.

[55] In Ireland, so strong as to prevent discovery rules applying to criminal proceedings despite explicit reference to criminal proceedings in the relevant provision: *People v Sweeney* [2001] 4 IR 102.

the hearsay rule to be found in the Civil Evidence Act 1995 and the Criminal Justice Act 2003.[56] For some differences it is hard to find any rational explanation.[57]

A now powerful stimulus to the distinction between different forms of evidence is that made in Art 6 of the European Convention on Human Rights between the general right to a fair trial[58] encapsulated in sub-clause (1), and the more specific rights in the next two sub-clauses, which are explicitly limited to those charged with criminal offences. It appears generally accepted in European human rights jurisprudence that a more protective regime applies in criminal cases.[59] For this purpose, English[60] courts have found that confiscation proceedings,[61] restoration proceedings,[62] civil recovery proceedings,[63] civil contempt proceedings,[64] determinations of fact under s 4A of the Criminal Procedure Act 1964 in the case of those found unfit to plead,[65] the imposition of antisocial behaviour orders,[66] sexual offences prevention orders,[67] bail proceedings,[68] proceedings for condemnation of goods seized by Customs,[69] disciplinary proceedings of the SFA,[70] those for breach of prison rules,[71] and for revocation of a prisoner's licence[72] are not criminal,[73] although sometimes the criminal standard of proof,[74] or the criminal rules for the admission of hearsay[75] are nevertheless applied. On the other hand, a formal police caution[76] and proceedings for the recovery of a penalty for non-payment of tax[77] have been regarded as criminal.

---

[56] See further Chapters XII–XIV.

[57] Such as the old rule allowing dying declarations as an exception to the hearsay rule only in criminal proceedings, or the exclusion in South Africa of that rule from admiralty proceedings: see *Cargo Laden and Lately Laden on Board the MV Thalassini Avgi v MV Dimitris* 1989 (3) SA 820.

[58] The European Court of Human Rights has denied that extradition proceedings amount to trials for this purpose: *Kirkwood v United Kingdom* (1984) 6 EHRR 373.

[59] *Dombo Beheer BV v Netherlands* (1993) 18 EHRR 213, [32].

[60] And also Scottish: see *McIntosh v Lord Adv* [2001] UKPC D1, [2003] 1 AC 1078, [2001] 2 All ER 638. The European Court of Human Rights regards the definition in the Convention as autonomous, and holds that classification under domestic law is not the sole criterion, taking into account also the nature of the conduct, and the severity of the penalty: see *Hurter v Switzerland* (2005) 44 EHRR 201 (disciplinary tribunal).

[61] Under either the Criminal Justice Act 1988, s 72AA, *R v Rezvi* [2002] UKHL 1, [2003] 1 AC 1099, [2002] 1 All ER 801; or the Drug Trafficking Act 1994, s 4(3), *R v Benjafield* [2002] UKHL 2, [2003] 1 AC 1099, [2002] 1 All ER 815. See, in Australia, *R v Lam* [2000] WASCA 115, 111 ACR 576.

[62] *Gora v Customs and Excise Comrs* [2003] EWCA Civ 525, [2004] QB 93.

[63] *Director of the Assets Recovery Agency v Ashton* [2006] EWHC 1064 (Admin), [2006] ACD 78.

[64] *Coca-Cola Co v Aytacli* [2003] EWHC 91 (Ch), (2003) 26(3) IPD 26016, [49].

[65] *R v H* [2003] UKHL 1, [2003] 1 All ER 497.

[66] *R(McCann) v Crown Court at Manchester* [2002] UKHL 39, [2003] 1 AC 787, [2002] 4 All ER 593. In contrast to binding-over proceedings, which the European Court of Human Rights has determined to be criminal, *Steele v United Kingdom* (1998) 28 EHRR 603, cf the position in Australia, *Laidlaw v Hulett* [1998] 2 Qd 45, and in Canada *R v CJC* (1999) 140 CCC (3d) 159.

[67] *Cleveland Police v H* [2009] EWHC 3231 (Admin).

[68] *R(Thomas) v Greenwich Magistrates' Court* [2009] EWHC 1180 (Admin).

[69] *Mudie v Customs and Excise Comrs* [2003] EWCA Civ 237, [2003] QB 1238.

[70] *R(Fleurose) v Securities and Futures Authority* [2001] EWCA Civ 2015, [2002] IRLR 297.

[71] *R v Home Secretary, ex p Carroll* [2001] EWCA Civ 1224, [2002] 1 WLR 545; *Matthewson v Scottish Ministers* 2001 GWD 23–875.

[72] *R v Parole Board, ex p West* [2002] EWHC 769 (Admin), for fuller discussion of evidence before the Parole Board see Jackson [2007] *Crim LR* 417.

[73] For a definition, see *Customs and Excise Comrs v City of London Magistrates' Court* [2000] 4 All ER 763, [2000] 1 WLR 2020, [17], Lord Bingham CJ, and for academic discussion see Ashworth (2000) 116 LQR 225.

[74] See further 156.

[75] *R v Chal* [2007] EWCA Crim 2647.

[76] *R(Aru) v Chief Constable of Merseyside* [2004] EWCA Civ 199, [2004] 1 WLR 1697.

[77] *King v Walden* [2001] STC 822, [2001] BPIR 1012.

In general, the courts are concerned with a *lis*, a dispute between the parties before them,[78] which is resolved by the adversarial process so typical of the common law. There are other aspects of their jurisdiction which are of a different character. Interim applications often have to be heard urgently without recourse to the full panoply of evidential rules, often admitting hearsay, and even when such an application is treated as the trial of the claim, the more relaxed rules to the admission of hearsay may still be applied.[79] If interim proceedings, such as a care order in respect of a child, involve making serious allegations against a party, and may lead to important consequences for that party, however, it seems that he is entitled to have the matter determined by evidence tendered on oath.[80] In proceedings for judicial review, cross-examination on affidavits is allowed only exceptionally.[81] In *Scott v Scott*,[82] Viscount Haldane singled out the paternal jurisdiction exercised in relation to wards of court and lunatics. In *Official Solicitor of the Supreme Court v K*,[83] the House of Lords considered how far the ordinary principles of judicial inquiry were to apply to such proceedings. In particular, the House considered whether it was open to the judge to find facts relevant to the exercise of his discretion upon a basis of hearsay.[84] Lord Devlin distinguished between dispensable rules and those so fundamental as necessarily to be applied in all judicial proceedings, so constituting rules of natural justice. He emphasised that many of the rules of evidence fell into the former category:[85]

There are also rules of less importance designed to aid in the administration of justice and to regulate procedure. They are rules of convenience rather than of principle; and the rule against hearsay... is among them. No one would suggest that it is contrary to natural justice to act on hearsay.

The particular application to hearsay has been overtaken by statute, but the general principle remains that the precise mixture of rules is not fixed, but determined by the nature of the jurisdiction. As Lord Evershed said[86] in the same case:[87]

[I]t [is] not enough to say that the proceeding is a judicial proceeding. It is necessary to define or to have in mind what is the true character of this judicial proceeding and what is its end or purpose.

This view has prevailed for rules of evidence in all proceedings where the welfare of a child is paramount, for example under the provisions of the Children Act 1989,[88] although

---

[78] In principle, the same rules apply to class actions as to those involving only the parties before the court: *Syndicat National des Employés et al v Public Curator* [1996] 3 SCR 211.

[79] Cp *Rose v Information Services Ltd* [1987] FSR 254 (where they were) with *Re A Debtor (No 87 of 1993)* [1996] 1 BCLC 55 (where they were not). In *Lichter and Schwarz v Rubin* [2008] EWHC 450 (Ch) it was suggested that the further before proceedings the application was heard, the more likely such relaxation.

[80] This accounts for the refusal to permit hearsay in summary contempt proceedings: see *R v Shokoya* (1992) The Times, 10 June. But see, in Canada, *R v Budreo* (1996) 104 CCC (3d) 245 for relaxation of the rules relating to standard of proof in relation to a preventive order against a paedophile.

[81] *R v Arts Council of England, ex p Women's Playhouse Trust* (1997) The Times, 20 August; *R(PG) v Ealing LBC* [2002] EWHC 250 (Admin), [2002] ACD 48, [30].

[82] [1913] AC 417.

[83] [1965] AC 201, [1963] 3 All ER 191.

[84] The same principle leads to modification of legal professional privilege in wardship proceedings: *Re A* [1991] 2 FLR 473; or of estoppel in guardianship, JEN v MEN [2005] IEHC 385, [2007] 3 IR 517.

[85] 238, 208.   [86] With whom Lord Reid expressly agreed.   [87] 217, 195.

[88] *Re L (a minor)* [1997] AC 16, [1996] 2 All ER 78, but see also the minority view of Lords Nicholls and Mustill 33B, 91A (immunity claimed on the grounds of legal professional privilege); *Re B (minors) (care proceedings) (evidence)* [1997] Fam 117, [1997] 2 All ER 29 (relaxation of rules relating to issue estoppel).

special care may be required in evaluating hearsay emanating from a child in a pre-trial interview.[89] Similarly, in care proceedings, the court is prepared to take a more robust view of the refusal of a parent to testify than in criminal proceedings against the parent.[90] It has been said that:[91]

The strict rules of evidence applicable in a criminal trial, which is adversarial in nature, are to be contrasted with the partly inquisitorial approach of the court dealing with children cases in which the rules of evidence are considerably relaxed.

So too there are implied exceptions to the hearsay and opinion rule in proceedings to disqualify a director under the Company Directors Disqualification Act 1986.[92]

Many administrative functions involving fact-finding used to be performed by ordinary courts. Most of these are now performed by special administrative tribunals, although some remain with ordinary courts. Here courts sometimes apply a different set of rules of evidence, including at least one set permitting the admission of hearsay, whether in the Crown courts[93] or before magistrates.[94] Similarly, when magistrates act in committal proceedings, the rules of evidence differ from those that apply at a summary trial.[95] Although extradition proceedings have always had more in common with committal than trial, the Extradition Act 2003, under which evidence and proof is becoming increasingly vestigial,[96] takes a further step away from the analogy and procedures for trial. It has been said that, in conducting judicial proceedings with a strong administrative element, a judge is entitled to take into account material which would be accepted by a responsible administrator.[97] This has been continued into the admissibility of evidence in judicial review of administrative decisions.[98]

Different types of court

Occasionally legislation establishes totally new courts, and sometimes explicitly abridges the rules of evidence to be applied in them. Thus, when the Industrial Court was set up under the Industrial Relations Act 1971, it was provided that 'it should not be bound by

---

[89] See *C v Minister of Community Welfare* (1989) 52 SASR 304.

[90] *Re O* [2003] EWHC 2011 (Fam), [2004] 1 FLR 161; cf *Re U* [2006] EWHC 372 (Fam), [2006] 2 FLR 690, [31].   [91] By Butler-Sloss P in *Re T* [2004] EWCA Civ 558, [2004] 2 FLR 838, [28].

[92] *Secretary of State for Business Enterprise and Regulatory Reform v Aaron* [2008] EWCA Civ 1146.

[93] *Kavanagh v Chief Constable of Devon and Cornwall* [1974] QB 624, [1974] 2 All ER 697. The position with regard to cross-examination was less certain, but in *R v Crown Court at Aylesbury, ex p Farrer* (1988) The Times, 9 March, it was held that the court had no power to order a licensing authority to call a witness to give oral evidence as opposed to the admission of hearsay. The position is the same in Canada, see *R v Zeolkowski* [1989] 1 SCR 1378.   [94] *Westminster City Council v Zestfair Ltd* (1989) 88 LGR 288.

[95] Compare *R v Horsham Justices, ex p Bukhari* (1982) 74 Cr App Rep 291 (no discretion to exclude admissible evidence in committal proceedings) with *R v Sang* [1980] AC 402, [1979] 2 All ER 1222 (discretion at summary trial affirmed); *R v Crown Prosecution Service, ex p Warby* (1994) 158 JP 190 (magistrates not entitled to consider claim to public policy immunity at committal proceedings) with *R v South Worcestershire Magistrates, ex p Lilley* [1995] 4 All ER 186, [1995] 1 WLR 1595 (so entitled at summary trial). They are not, however, at liberty simply to disregard the rules of evidence in committal proceedings: *R v Bedwellty Justices, ex p Williams* [1997] AC 225, [1996] 3 All ER 737.

[96] For the position in Canada see *Ferras v USA* 2006 SCC 33, [2006] 2 SCR 77.

[97] *R v Sanghera* [1983] 2 VR 130, 131, McGarvie J.

[98] *R v Home Secretary ex p Rahman* [1998] QB 136, [1997] 1 All ER 796. See also *R v Ealing LBC* (n81), where the Court was prepared to admit evidence and allow cross-examination, even in the absence of explicit authorization in the relevant r 54 of the CPR.

any enactment or rule of law relating to the evidence which is admissible in proceedings in other courts'.[99] Sometimes the statute simply provides for rules of evidence to be made by secondary means, as in the case of the Special Immigration Appeals Commission,[100] where those rules specified[101] that the Commission 'may receive evidence that would not be admissible in a court of law'.

Such provisions are, however, to be construed narrowly, and it has been said in Australia that:[102]

the rules of evidence should not be treated as excluded from the proceedings of a court unless the words are clear or the context compelling.

Even in the extreme case of the Commission, the House of Lords has held that the generality of the words quoted above are to be qualified to the extent that evidence obtained by torture remains inadmissible.[103]

It is perhaps surprising that so little formal recognition is given to the difference in the practical approach to the law of evidence in criminal proceedings between magistrates' courts, especially those comprising lay magistrates, and the higher criminal courts.[104] Similar practical differences occur between cases tried by judge alone and cases tried by judge and jury.[105]

Different stages of proceedings

Even if the ordinary higher courts alone are considered, deviations are still to be found between the rules that apply to fact-finding at different stages.[106] Thus variations apply, before trial, to issues of fact on a plea in a criminal case or about the admissibility of evidence, and, after trial, about questions of sentence or on appeal.

Pre-trial[107]

At pre-trial[108] such scanty authority as exists conflicts as to whether the courts should try to follow the rules for trials so far as possible.[109] In relation to affidavits and witness

---

    99   Industrial Relations Act 1971, Sch 3, 18(5).
    100   Special Immigration Appeals Act 1997, s 5 (a court by virtue of s 1(3) inserted by the Anti-Terrorism, Crime and Security Act 2001, s 35).
    101   Special Immigration Appeals Commission (Procedure) Rules SI 2003 1034 r 44(3).
    102   *Geschke v Del-Monte Home Furnishers Ltd* [1981] VR 856, 863; see also *Pearce v Button* (1986) 65 ALR 83, 90, 97, and 102, in which the court said that it will be slow to apply the rule to admit hearsay in respect of a central issue.
    103   *A v Secretary of State for the Home Department (No 2)* [2005] UKHL 71, [2006] 2 AC 221.
    104   See Darbyshire [1997] *Crim LR* 105, 627.
    105   See *Balchin v Chief Constable of Hampshire* [2001] EWCA Civ 538.
    106   For example, even the test of relevancy may apply differently to an issue at the stage of discovery and at trial, see *The Captain Gregos* (1990) The Times, 21 December.
    107   For detailed analysis see Pattenden 125 LQR 79 (2009).
    108   The Criminal Procedure Rules now permit the judge to allow limited written submissions only at this stage: *R v K* [2006] EWCA Crim 835.
    109   Disclosure may be more limited, see *R v Manchester Crown Court, ex p Brokenbrow* (1991) The Times, 31 October, *Fiona Trust Holding Corp v Privalov* [2007] EWHC 39 (Comm), and the without prejudice rule does not apply to directions hearings as it does at trial, *Carman v Cronos Group UK* [2006] EWHC 1324, [2006] BPIR 1055; but in preliminary decisions in child care cases the normal rules as to burden of proof and

statements in civil proceedings, it is uncertain how far inadmissible evidence can be relied upon as a source of belief.[110] In criminal proceedings, formal rules can be relaxed for preliminary issues such as the extension of custody limits, so long as they are determined fairly,[111] as also in determining facts relevant to the question of disclosure of evidence to the defence.[112] Then, in *R v Podola*,[113] a full Court of Criminal Appeal overruled *R v Sharp*,[114] in favour of the view that the burden of proving unfitness to plead was, like the substantive defence of insanity, on the accused who raised it rather than the prosecution.[115] If raised by the prosecution, it must be proved by them beyond reasonable doubt.[116]

So far as issues of fact relevant to the admissibility of evidence are concerned, the general rule is that such questions should be tried by the judge on the voir dire,[117] at a trial within the trial.[118] It would, however, be unrealistic for such evidence to be considered in total isolation from that already adduced at the trial proper,[119] and perhaps confusing if a different standard of proof were to be required at the two different stages.[120]

Most such trials have dealt with the admissibility of confessions, and it is well established in such cases that the prosecution must prove admissibility beyond reasonable doubt,[121]

allocation of persuasive and evidential burdens have been applied, see *Re O and N* [2002] EWCA Civ 1271, [2002] 3 FCR 418. In Australia, see *Casley-Smith v FS Evans & Sons Pty* (1988) 49 SASR 339.

[110] Cp *Savings and Investment Bank Ltd v Gasco Investments (Netherlands) BV* [1984] 1 All ER 296, [1984] 1 WLR 271 (disregarded) and *Deutsche Ruckversicherung v Walbrook Insurance Co Ltd* [1994] 4 All ER 181, [1995] 1 WLR 1017 (considered).

[111] *Wildman v DPP* [2001] EWHC Admin 14, (2001) 165 JP 453, [24].

[112] *R v Law* (1996) The Times, 15 August; or in the Court of Appeal, if it first arises at that stage, *R v Botmeh and Alami* [2001] EWCA Crim 2226, [2002] 1 Cr App Rep 345.

[113] [1960] 1 QB 325, [1959] 3 All ER 418, where expert witnesses were called on each side and cross-examined, and the accused also testified and was cross-examined. In Scotland in *Russell v HM Adv* 1946 JC 37, a similar issue of fact was determined by judge, and not by jury. See also *Jessup v Mahon* 1989 SCCR 600.

[114] (1958) 41 Cr App Rep 197.

[115] This was regarded as analogous to other pretrial issues such as autrefois convict or autrefois acquit in *R v Martin Coughlan* [1976] Crim LR 631, where an accelerated procedure for reading statements was also approved. In the United States, such allocation has been held not to violate the constitutional guarantee of due process: *Medina v California* 505 US 1244 (1992).

[116] *R v Robertson* [1968] 3 All ER 557, 52 Cr App Rep 690.

[117] Or in the case of committal proceedings by the magistrates, *R v Ormskirk Magistrates, ex p Davies* (1994) 158 JP 1145. It seems discretionary whether or not reasons for the decision are pronounced: *Wallace and Fuller v R* [1997] 1 Cr App Rep 396, PC.

[118] At which cross-examination will in appropriate cases be permitted, and to facilitate which the judge should not rely upon material withheld from the defence on grounds of public interest, *R v Ali and Hussein (No 2)* [2008] EWCA Crim 146. In the United States only, the rules of privilege apply at this stage: see Federal Rules of Evidence, rr 104(a), 1101(d)(1); *Bourjaily v US* 483 US 471 (1987).

[119] *R v Tyrer* (1989) 90 Cr App Rep 446.   [120] *R v Quidley* 232 CCC (3d) 255 (2008).

[121] Now as a result of the Police and Criminal Evidence Act 1984, s 76(2), in this respect re-enacting the common law, see *R v Sartori, Gavin and Phillips* [1961] Crim LR 397. The position is the same in Canada, *R v LTH* 2008 SCC 49, [2008] 2 SCR 739; in New Zealand, *R v McCuin* [1982] 1 NZLR 13, and there uniquely among evidentiary matters, see *R v Dobler* [1993] 1 NZLR 431, 438. In Scotland, the rule is the same for confessions, *HM Adv v Jenkinson* 2002 SCCR 43, 46F, but the balance of probabilities standard applies to both prosecution and defence in relation to facts relevant to the admissibility of hearsay under the Criminal Procedure (Scotland) Act 1995, s 259(8). In the United States (*Bourjaily v US* (n118)), the standard is merely proof on the balance of probabilities, as it is generally believed to be in Australia: *Wendo v R* (1963) 109 CLR 559, and applied to showing that a witness was an accomplice in *R v He and Bun* [2001] VSCA 58, 122 ACR

and that witnesses, including the accused,[122] can be called[123] and cross-examined. Where the burden on a preliminary question is borne by the accused in criminal proceedings, the standard of proof is the balance of probabilities just as it is at the trial proper.[124] The issue of the rules that apply at this stage of judicial proceedings has been examined very thoroughly in the United States.[125] While it appears that here the rules are more similar to those at trial,[126] there are some indications of difference. Thus the court has taken[127] the view that the proponent, there the prosecution, need make out only a prima facie case to show that a tape recording satisfy the condition of originality. A similarly reduced onus has been applied to jurisdictional questions,[128] and there is a special statutory regime for extradition cases.[129] It must also often be the case, just because the purpose of the preliminary issue is to determine the admissibility of a disputed piece of evidence or the competency of a witness, that the rules at the preliminary stage must be different from those operating at the trial so as to allow the piece of evidence to be perused, or the witness examined.[130] How much further the rules are different is obscure in the modern English law.[131] It is sometimes suggested[132] that a distinction is required between preliminary issues of authenticity, which require only a prima facie case to be established in advance, and those of admissibility, which require proof at least on the balance of probabilities at that stage. Different considerations may also apply when the rules for the inadmissibility of evidence are discretionary.[133]

---

487. In Canada it depends upon whether the evidence is likely to have a conclusive effect upon guilt, *R v Arp* [1998] 3 SCR 339, [71].

[122] *R v Cowell* [1940] 2 KB 49, [1940] 2 All ER 599.

[123] Under the Youth Justice and Criminal Evidence Act 1999, s 54(2), it is for the party calling the witness, including the prosecution, to establish competency on the balance of probabilities.

[124] *R v Mattey and Queeley* [1995] 2 Cr App Rep 409; *R v Zardad* [2007] EWCA Crim 279.

[125] See Maguire and Epstein (1927) 36 *Yale LJ* 1101; Saltzburg (1974) 27 *Stan LR* 271. Rule 104(a) of the US Federal Rules provides that the judge is not bound by any of the rules of evidence except those relating to privileges in deciding such questions.

[126] In Canada, in *R v Guttman* (2000) 145 CCC (3d) 81, it was held that issues could be resolved only by evidence, and not by speculation.

[127] *R v Robson and Harris* [1972] 2 All ER 699, [1972] 1 WLR 651; and for identification of the persons before the court, *Pattison v DPP* [2005] EWHC 2938, [2006] 2 All ER 317.

[128] In England, see *Vitkovice Horni a Hutni Tezirvisto v Korner* [1951] AC 869, 883, and in Australia, *Empire Shipping Co Inc v Owners of the Ship 'Shin Kobe Matu'* (1991) 104 ALR 489.

[129] Extradition Act 2003 s 84: see *India v Rajarathinam* [2006] EWHC 2919.

[130] A procedure endorsed, though not implemented, in *R v Yacoob* (1981) 72 Cr App Rep 313, 317, in relation to calling the witness on the preliminary question of her competency at the trial. It was pointed out in *R v Ferguson* (1996) 112 CCC (3d) 342, 361c, that, as witnesses could be called in criminal trials either by prosecution or defence, it would be odd to have a different burden of proof of facts relating to competency depending upon which it was to be. In *R v Parrott* [2001] 1 SCR 178, it was held better to call a witness of dubious competence on the voir dire than for expert evidence to be received, at least in the absence of evidence that to call the witness would itself cause harm.

[131] In *Duke of Beaufort v Crawshay* (1866) LR 1 CP 699, an affidavit that would have been inadmissible at trial seems to have been admitted at this preliminary stage. There is also some suggestion that the rules permitting expert evidence of mental condition may apply less stringently on a preliminary issue than at the trial: see *R v Ward* (1992) 96 Cr App Rep 1, 66, and *R v Heaton* [1993] Crim LR 593.

[132] For example, its canvassing by the Supreme Court of Canada in *R v Evans* [1993] 3 SCR 653, citing McCormick (4th edn, 1992) Vol 2, 54.

[133] See *R v Sparkes* (1996) 88 ACR 194 (evidence obtained during hypnosis).

Post-trial

There are also significant differences in relation to the mixture of rules that apply to issues of fact determined after the trial has concluded, either in relation to the order, or on appeal.[134]

Order

In criminal cases, issues of fact often arise in relation to the basis for sentencing the accused,[135] or making some other order,[136] which can be done only on the basis of evidence before the court.[137] If there is a contested trial, to the extent that the relevant matters have emerged during the hearing, sentencing may be conducted on the basis of the judge's[138] assessment of those matters,[139] although the accused may not be sentenced on the basis of aggravating factors that could have constituted a separate, and more serious, charge.[140] Such uncharged crimes may nevertheless rebut extraneous mitigating factors advanced by the defence.[141] If the accused pleads guilty,[142] there may be discrepancy between the basis for that plea[143] and the Crown case. Thereupon, the defence must clearly[144] reject the Crown case, and it is not enough for the accused to tender a more moderate version

---

[134] These are not mutually exclusive and fresh evidence can be adduced even though relevant only to sentence: see, in Australia, *R v Rostom* [1996] 2 VR 97, and in Canada, *R v Levesque* [2000] 2 SCR 487.

[135] See Thomas (ed) *Current Sentencing Practice* Pt L2; NZLC No 76 (2001) *Proof of Disputed Facts on Sentence*. In Canada, the Supreme Court has pronounced it commonplace that the strict rules for trial do not apply at a sentencing hearing (*R v Gardiner* (1982) 140 DLR (3d) 612, 648), and, more dubiously, that there is no difference between the situation in Australia, Canada, and England: *R v Brown* [1991] 2 SCR 518, 522.

[136] *R v Thompson and Smith* [1997] 1 Cr App Rep (S) 289, the Drug Trafficking Act 1994, s 2(8)(b), explicitly applied the civil standard of proof in respect of confiscation orders in drug trafficking cases. See also *DB Deniz Nakliyati TAS v Yugopetrol* [1992] 1 All ER 205, [1992] 1 WLR 437, applying trial rules to a post-trial application for inspection of a third party's bank account under the Bankers' Books Evidence Act 1879, s 7. In *Re Westmid Packing Services Ltd, Secretary of State for Trade and Industry v Griffiths* [1998] 2 All ER 124, Lord Woolf deplored the development of special evidential rules to deal with the issue of disqualification of a director found unfit to direct a company.

[137] *R v Lee* [2006] EWCA Crim 835; *R v Hylands* [2004] EWCA Crim 2999, [2005] 2 Cr App R (S) 25. See also, in Australia, *R v Nemer* [2003] SASC 375, 143 ACR 50.

[138] In the United States it was in *Cunningham v California* (2007) 127 S Ct R 856 held unconstitutional for such facts to be determined by judge rather than jury.

[139] The prosecution should not advert in opening to any facts that are not to be proved by evidence, even if their only relevance is as to sentence: *R v Hobstaff* (1993) 14 Cr App Rep (S) 605. But at some stage evidence will be required to justify an order, such as a restriction order: *R v Reynolds* (1999) 164 JP 220; or sometimes to refuse one, such as payment of costs: *Mooney v Cardiff Justices* (22 October 1999, unreported) QBD. Even where evidence has been heard at an earlier stage, it may be necessary to reopen it at the stage of making a final order: *Re M and M-C* [2002] EWCA Civ 499, [2002] 2 FCR 377; *R(Gillan) v DPP* [2007] EWHC 380 (Admin), [2007] 1 WLR 2214.

[140] *R v Davies* [1998] 1 Cr App Rep (S) 380 (rape must be charged to justify aggravation on basis of lack of consent); *R v Eubank* [2001] EWCA Crim 891, [2002] 1 Cr App Rep (S) 11 (possession of firearms in course of robbery).

[141] *R v Twisse* [2001] 2 Cr App Rep (S) 9, [8]; the same is true in Australia: *R v Daniels* (1999) 8 Tas R 397.

[142] The prosecution should not agree to an unreal set of facts as part of a plea-bargaining arrangement with the defence, without reference to the judge: *R v Beswick* [1996] 1 Cr App Rep (S) 343.

[143] Rejection of which by the Court must be indicated to the accused, *R v Lucien*{2009} EWCA Crim 2004, [12].

[144] *R v Tolera* [1999] 1 Cr App Rep 29; conversely the prosecution must make it clear that it does not accept the defence's version in the pre-sentence report: *R v Welby* [2000] Crim LR 59.

in the course of preparation of a pre-sentence report[145] submitted by the prosecution.[146] Such a version may be rejected even in the absence of prosecution evidence to 'gainsay' it.[147] This report is intended to be used at the sentencing stage, despite much of it being hearsay.[148] This seems immaterial so long as the facts are not disputed,[149] but if they are, it is necessary to prove them by evidence admissible under the rules for trial,[150] and if not, it cannot be remedied on appeal.[151] Issues relevant to sentence may be insufficiently, or not at all relevant to any issue before the jury.[152] There,[153] a special Newton hearing,[154] taking its name from the leading case, should[155] be held,[156] and the possibility of such a hearing is mandated by the European Convention on Human Rights.[157] Findings of fact for these purposes must not be inconsistent with the finding of the jury or the basis of a plea.

The accused is entitled to testify,[158] so where facts are within the knowledge of the accused but not of the prosecution, he should be called to give evidence; and if he fails to do so, adverse inferences may be drawn.[159] So too if an inference is to be drawn as to the facts

---

[145] See Criminal Justice Act 2003, ss 156–158.

[146] In cases tried on indictment where the accused has a criminal record, a statement of his previous convictions and antecedents is prepared by the police in the form of a proof of evidence: *Practice Note* [1993] 4 All ER 863. In *R v Butterwasser* [1948] 1 KB 4, [1947] 2 All ER 415, Lord Goddard CJ drew attention to the practice of substituting for the normal trial oath the special voir dire oath for such evidence given at the sentencing stage.

[147] *R v Hogg and Rolls* [2008] EWCA Crim 240, [43], where this terminology was deprecated.

[148] In the analogous case in domestic proceedings in the magistrates' courts of a report by a probation officer on the means of the parties, received to help in determining the amount of an order, after a decision on the merits, it is expressly provided by statute that the ordinary exclusionary rules of evidence do not apply: see Magistrates' Courts Act 1980, s 72(5). The position is the same in Canada: see *Albright v R* [1987] 2 SCR 383 explicitly approving this work, and permitting the proof of previous convictions by hearsay.

[149] *R v Marquis* (1951) 35 Cr App Rep 33.

[150] Where hearsay is now admissible by discretion in the interests of justice. In the somewhat similar situation of a report by a court welfare officer to a court considering a family matter relating to children, hearsay may be included, but any critical issue should be decided by original evidence: see *Thompson v Thompson* [1986] 1 FLR 212n, approved by the Court of Appeal in *H v H and C, K v K* [1990] Fam 86, [1989] 3 All ER 740. See also Children Act 1989, s 7, as amended.

[151] *A-G's Reference (No 95 of 1998)* (1999) The Times, 21 April, although it may be challenged on a confiscation proceeding arising from the same conviction, *R v Knaggs* [2009] EWCA Crim 1363.

[152] This may increasingly be the case in offences of strict liability after *R v Sandhu* [1997] Crim LR 288 (evidence of mental state irrelevant to guilt); see commentary by Thomas to *R v Hill* [1997] Crim LR 459. Even if the jury reports its finding on such facts, the judge is not bound to accept it: *R v Mills* [2003] EWCA Crim 2397.

[153] *R v Tolera* [1999] 1 Cr App Rep 29 (discrepancy with basis for plea of guilty); *R v Finch* (1992) 14 Cr App Rep (S) 226 (different sentencing issues). See also *R v Winter* [1997] 1 Cr App Rep (S) 331 (discrepancy between basis for pleading guilty and evidence in contested trial of co-accused).

[154] It is not treated as a contested hearing for legal aid purposes: *R v Legal Aid Board, ex p Graham Dobson & Co* [1996] 40 LS Gaz R 25.

[155] Unless the basis of plea is patently untenable, *R v Taylor* [2006] EWCA Crim 3132, [2006] 2 Cr App R 222 (although even then counsel must be allowed to make submissions).

[156] *R v Newton* (1982) 77 Cr App Rep 13. This procedure applies equally to appeals to the Crown Court: *R v Williams* (1983) The Times, 26 April. See, in Canada, *R v Gauthier (No 2)* (1996) 108 CCC (3d) 231.

[157] *R(Hammond) v Secretary of State for Home Department* [2005] UKHL 69, [2006] 1 AC 603, [16].

[158] *R v Jenkins* (1990) 12 Cr App Rep (S) 582, even where he has already testified at the trial as he may wish to add to that testimony on the different issues relevant to sentence, although in Australia it was held, in *R v Ford* (1994) 75 ACR 398, that the court should not admit self-serving hearsay inconsistent with the verdict at trial.   [159] *R v Underwood* [2004] EWCA Crim 2256, [2005] 1 Cr App R 178, [7].

of the offence, either from the facts as stated by the prosecution on a plea of guilty or from the evidence at the trial,[160] any matters upon which it is proposed to rely for the purposes of sentencing should be indicated to the accused in advance,[161] and supported by evidence, including the calling of witnesses,[162] if the facts are disputed. Recent legislation appears to have restricted the circumstances under which anything other than offences for which the accused has been previously convicted, or those which the accused has asked to be taken into consideration, can be used to assess the appropriate sentence,[163] thus avoiding anything like the application of the similar facts rule at the sentencing stage.[164] It has been held in Australia that cautious use of statistical material is more readily admissible at this stage than at the trial proper.[165] It is immaterial that the evidence relied upon for sentencing was erroneously admitted at the trial,[166] and even though it favours the accused.[167]

The burden and standard of proof for fact-finding at this stage varies. In Canada, the Supreme Court has rejected the American view that a lesser standard is appropriate,[168] in favour of adherence to the ordinary criminal standard of proof beyond reasonable doubt, resting upon the prosecution, on the basis that, in the words of Stephen, the question of sentence is the gist of criminal proceedings, being to them 'as the bullet is to the powder'.[169] In England,[170] it is now quite clear that at this stage the normal trial rules of incidence and onus of proof apply both in relation to matters of aggravation, which the prosecution must prove, and to matters of mitigation, which the defence must establish.[171] Only in the case of purely extraneous matters,[172] falling outside the scope of a Newton enquiry, has the

[160] Although at this stage the accused may contest irrebuttably presumed facts, *Goldsmith v DPP* [2009] EWHC 3010 (Admin).   [161] *R v Lester* (1975) 63 Cr App Rep 144.

[162] *R v Robinson* (1969) 53 Cr App Rep 314; *R v Hearne* [1976] Crim LR 753.

[163] Doubts have even been expressed about the application of such provisions to cases where there are specimen counts: *R v Perkins* [1994] Crim LR 141; *R v Kidd* [1998] 1 All ER 42, [1998] 1 WLR 604.

[164] It must surely be the case that, if such offences have not been admitted by the accused, they must be proved according to the ordinary rules and under the ordinary conditions: see *Anderson v DPP* [1978] AC 964, [1978] 2 All ER 512; *R v Marshall* [1989] Crim LR 819.

[165] *R v Henry* [1999] NSWCCA 111, 106 ACR 149. In England, this will be truer in a case where the court seeks to lay down guidelines under the procedure prescribed by Pt 12, c 1, Criminal Justice Act 2003.

[166] Although it has been held in Canada that an expert cannot base his opinion at this stage on a document ruled inadmissible at the trial: *R v Archer* (2005) 193 CCC (3d) 376.

[167] *Flewitt v Horvath* [1972] RTR 121, in which the evidence admitted at the trial was hearsay, and wrongly taken into account by the magistrates in determining not to disqualify the accused driver; see also *James v Morgan* [1988] RTR 85, in which hearsay evidence that the accused's drink had been 'laced' by his friends was rejected on the same issue. By contrast, the Supreme Court of the United States has held it an unconstitutional denial of due process to exclude hearsay favouring the accused at the sentencing stage: *Green v Georgia* 442 US 95 (1979).

[168] In *Williams v New York* 337 US 241 (1949). A disturbing side-effect is that the discrepancy permits American courts to sentence on the basis of guilt in respect of crimes for which the accused has been acquitted at the very same trial: *United States v Watts; United States v Putra* 519 US 148 (1997); cf *R v Gillespie* [1998] Crim LR 139.

[169] *R v Gardiner* (n135), quoting Sir James Fitzjames Stephen (1863) *Cornill Magazine* 189, endorsed in Criminal Code, s 724(3)(e) as amended.

[170] Subject to specific statutory provision, for example Proceeds of Crime Act 2002, s 8; and see *R v Silcock and Levin* [2004] EWCA Crim 408, [60]; *Re O'Donoghue* [2004] EWHC 176 (Admin).

[171] *R v Davies* [2008] EWCA Crim 1055, [14]. In Australia, intrinsic matters of mitigation are to be proved on the preponderance of probability by the defence: *R v Olbrich* [1999] HCA 270, 199 CLR 270.

[172] Or under statutory provisions, see *R v Barwick* [2000] 1 Cr App Rep (S)129, [2001] Crim LR 52, CA, imposing a burden of satisfying the court of the paucity of realizable assets for the purposes of a confiscation order under the provisions of s 73(6) of the Criminal Justice Act 1988.

accused any burden of persuasion, and then only[173] on the preponderance of probabilities.[174] It is far from clear whether this will survive challenge on the basis of Art 6 of the
European Convention on Human Rights.[175]

Appeal

The final situation[176] to be mentioned here concerns rules to be applied to evidence
adduced[177] on an appeal.[178] More stringent conditions apply where it is sought to reopen a
concluded appeal;[179] but less stringent where it is sought to amend a judgment before final
order.[180] There are provisions on both civil[181] and criminal[182] appeals for allowing fresh
evidence to be heard. In each case, the relevant provisions narrow, rather than broaden,
the range of material that may be adduced compared with that admissible in the court
below.[183] There are, however, differences between the limitations upon the receipt of fresh
evidence to be received in the two types of proceedings. It seems that avoidance of injustice
to the accused may more readily override the need to achieve finality.[184]

Civil proceedings

Rules of evidence are often relaxed in civil proceedings by agreement between the parties.
In one case, no objection was taken to the admission of a hearsay report in a local newspaper to show what had taken place at the trial, no proper note having been taken.[185] The
appellate court may take into account evidence of events between the original trial and
the appeal being heard,[186] as it may if the subsequent events have destroyed the whole

---

[173] Even stricter rules apply to judicial review: *Dwr Cymru Cyfyngedig v Environment Agency of Wales*
[2003] EWHC 336 (Admin), [2003] 16 LS Gaz R 27. For rules applying to fresh evidence in the Constitutional
Court of South Africa, see *S v Shaik* 2008 (2) SA 208; in the Supreme Court of Canada, *R v Trotta* 2007 SCC
49, [2007] 3 SCR 453; in criminal proceedings in Ireland, *People v O'Regan* [20077] IESC 38, [2007] 3 IR 805;
and in criminal proceedings in Scotland, *Couborough v HMA* [2008] HCJAC 13, 2008 SCCR 317.

[174] *R v Guppy and Hirst* (1994) 16 Cr App Rep (S) 25.

[175] It went without question in *Cuscani v United Kingdom* (2003) 36 EHRR 2 that a sentencing hearing
was subject to all parts of Art 6.

[176] The two may overlap as in *Graham v HMA* [2005] HCJAC 75, 2005 SCCR 544, where sentence was
based on belief that the accused would continue his medication, and then amended after fresh evidence that
he had subsequently ceased to do so.

[177] Similarly, restrictive principles have been applied to discovery for the purposes of an appeal: *R v
Secretary of State for Home Department, ex p Gardian* [1996] Imm AR 6; and in Queensland, to setting aside
a judgment obtained by fraud: see *Brough v Abel* [1987] 1 Qd R 138.

[178] Removal from a register was not regarded as an appeal for these purposes in *Betterment Properties
(Weymouth) Ltd v Dorset County Council* [2008] EWCA Civ 22.

[179] *Re Uddin* [2005] EWCA Civ 52, [2005] 3 All ER 550, explaining this aspect of the jurisdiction set out in
Taylor v Lawrence [2002] EWCA Civ 90, [2003] QB 528, and now encapsulated in CPR 52.17.

[180] *Fisher v Cadman* [2005] EWHC 2424.

[181] Now only by specific order by way of exception to the normal refusal of such evidence: CPR
52.11(2)(b).   [182] Criminal Appeal Act 1968, s 23.

[183] Although CPR 52.11 contains no such explicit limitation to evidence that would have been admissible
at the trial as does s 23(2)(a), such limitation may be implied. As it may in relation to s 23(1), see *R v Lattimore*
(1975) 62 Cr App Rep 53, 56. Even though s 29(4) of the Extradition Act 2003 refers to 'unavailable' evidence,
it is construed to require the conditions for the admissibility of fresh evidence, *Hungary v Fenyvesi* [2009]
EWHC 231 (Admin).

[184] *Braddock v Tillotson's Newspapers Ltd* [1950] 1 KB 47, [1949] 2 All ER 306, 54, 311.

[185] *Re Cowburn, ex p Firth* (1882) 19 Ch D 419, 424.

[186] *Rushmoor Borough Council v Richards* (1996) 160 LG Rev 460 (appeal by way of rehearing); *Khan v
Secretary of State for the Home Department* [2003] EWCA Civ 530 (review of appellate tribunal).

common basis on which the trial was conducted.[187] Although the range of considerations is now wider on account of the overriding objectives of the Civil Procedure Rules,[188] a good starting point is still to be found,[189] after a trial on the merits,[190] in the classic statement of the conditions[191] to be applied[192] in such cases[193] by Denning LJ in *Ladd v Marshall*:[194]

[F]irst, it must be shown that the evidence could not have been obtained with reasonable diligence for use at the trial: second, the evidence must be such that, if given, it would probably have an important influence on the result of the case, although it need not be decisive: third, the evidence must be such as is presumably to be believed, or in other words, it must be apparently credible, though it need not be incontrovertible.

The first condition will normally[195] not be satisfied if the evidence could have been secured before the trial through disclosure,[196] although the court may permit fresh evidence to be taken to replace that contained in a note which has been lost by accident.[197] This condition also covers a case where a witness who can be found could not reasonably have been expected to testify to the desired effect,[198] especially as the new system of procedure, in its attempt to reduce cost, would not want to encourage great expense to pre-empt all possible contingencies, however unlikely.[199] Evidence wrongly held inadmissible at trial may also be regarded as satisfying the first condition.[200]

---

[187] *Mulholland v Mitchell* [1971] AC 666, [1971] 1 All ER 307. In such a case, there is an obligation of disclosure to the other side: *Vernon v Bosley (No 2)* [1999] QB 18, [1997] 1 All ER 614.

[188] *Gillingham v Gillingham* [2001] EWCA Civ 906, [2001] 4 CPLR 355; *Evans v Tiger Investments* [2002] EWCA Civ 161, [2002] 2 BCLC 185, [23]. In *Lifely v Lifely* [2008] EWCA Civ 904 it was suggested that impropriety in obtaining such evidence might prejudice its admissibility.

[189] More as principle than rule, and as a guide to achieving the overriding objectives specified in the CPR, see *Daly and Daly v Sheikh* [2004] EWCA Civ 119, [42]. The same approach applies in the County Court: see *Hertfordshire Investments v Bubb* [2000] 1 WLR 2318.

[190] See *AIB Finance Ltd v Debtors* [1997] 4 All ER 677; *Canada Trust Co v Stolzenberg (No 4)* (1998) The Times, 14 May. A summary judgment under the Civil Procedure Rules, Pt 24 seems like one under the old RSC Ord 14 to remain a decision on the merits: see *Ramanathan Rudra v Abbey National plc* (1998) 76 P & CR 537. Similar, if slightly less rigorous, principles apply in relation to appeals from interlocutory decisions: *Electra Private Equity Partners v KPMG Peat Marwick* [1999] EWCA Civ 1247; [2001] 1 BCLC 589; see also *Al-Koronky v Timelife Entertainment Group Ltd* [2006] EWCA Civ 1123, [2006] CPR 47.

[191] In *Lattimer v Cumbria County Council* [1994] PIQR P395, Staughton LJ suggested absence of delay as a fourth implicit condition.

[192] In some jurisdictions especially, the conditions are to be applied in a balanced way, and failure in the first not to preclude consideration of the others: *R v Immigration Appeal Tribunal, ex p Azkhosravi* [2001] EWCA Civ 977, [23].

[193] And in other similar exercises of case management: see *Ahmed v Coleman and Hill* [2002] EWCA Civ 935, [43].

[194] [1954] 3 All ER 745, [1954] 1 WLR 1489, 748, 1491. Expressly approved by the House of Lords in *Skone v Skone* [1971] 2 All ER 582, [1971] 1 WLR 812; 586, 815, and in *Langdale v Danby* [1982] 3 All ER 129, [1982] 1 WLR 1123; 137, 1133.

[195] Even after the advent of the CPR, *Marchmont Investments Ltd v BFOSA* [2007] EWCA Civ 677.

[196] *Turnbull & Co v Duval* [1902] AC 429, although this will not necessarily bar admissibility in a case where a party has been misled into believing that disclosure would be ineffective (*Skone v Skone* (n194), 587, 816) or where the relevant overlooked document was in the possession of the other party, who had failed to disclose it: *Gillingham v Gillingham* (n188). [197] *Re Cowburn, ex p Firth* (n185), 426.

[198] A subsequent admission that evidence at trial was false is not sufficient to satisfy the condition if that confession is then withdrawn: *Sun Bank plc v Wootten* [2004] EWCA Civ 1423.

[199] *Saluja v Gill* [2002] EWHC 1435 (Ch), [39].

[200] *Re Multicultural Media Centre for the Millennium Ltd* [2001] EWCA Civ 1687.

The second represents a compromise between two formulations suggested in *Brown v Dean*, the stronger expressed by Lord Loreburn LC, that 'if believed it would be conclusive',[201] the weaker by Lord Shaw, that it be 'so gravely material and so clearly relevant…that it should have been before the jury'.[202] It will be hard to satisfy if the evidence relates to a matter already taken into account hypothetically in the assessment of damages.[203] The test is more stringent when the fresh evidence relates solely to credit,[204] but it may nevertheless be admitted even then in an exceptional case;[205] and less stringent when required to overturn a summary judgment.[206] It should be noted, more especially in the light of the CPR, that the force of evidence is to be assessed according to the case advanced at trial, and not on the basis of a reformulation for the purposes of the appeal,[207] although events occurring after trial may constitute fresh evidence.[208] The hurdle is highest of all in elation to orders, for example of adoption, which can be set aside only in the most exceptional circumstances.[209]

The third relates to cogency and is really implicit in the second. In particular, it seems that fresh evidence is unlikely to be admitted if it amounts to no more than a witness wishing to renege on the evidence he gave at the trial,[210] although exceptionally it may.[211]

The rule in *Ladd v Marshall* is designed to ensure that litigation is not unduly prolonged, but as such, is subservient to the principle that a litigant should not succeed by fraud, and in such a case, fresh evidence may be admitted notwithstanding the restrictions imposed by the rule,[212] thus avoiding the need to institute fresh litigation to set aside the judgment.[213] Conversely, these conditions are necessary rather than sufficient, and even when satisfied will not suffice if there has been a deliberate tactical decision to proceed in the absence of the relevant evidence, amounting to abuse of process.[214]

Criminal proceedings

In criminal proceedings, the situation is different, first, because of the importance of securing justice for the accused,[215] and second, because of the width of the power to order

---

[201] [1910] AC 373, 374.   [202] Ibid 376.

[203] See *Hunt v Severs* [1993] QB 815, [1993] 4 All ER 180 referring to dicta of Lord Wilberforce in *Mulholland v Mitchell* (n187).

[204] *Braddock v Tillotson's Newspaper Ltd* [1950] 1 KB 47, [1949] 2 All ER 306; 57, 313.

[205] *Meek v Fleming* [1961] 2 QB 366, [1961] 3 All ER 148; 379, 154, Holroyd Pearce LJ. Willmer LJ thought it enough that such evidence be of vital significance, and Pearson LJ that it need merely be material. A fortiori if it goes in part to issue, but predominantly to credit: *Burke v Giumba* [2002] EWCA Civ 1003.

[206] *Cotton (TA Allmat Enterprises) v Rickard Metals Inc* [2008] EWHC 824 (QB).

[207] *Singh v Singh* [2002] EWCA Civ 992.

[208] *Lincoln v Comr of Police for the Metropolis* [2001] EWCA Civ 2110, [27].

[209] *Webster v Norfolk County Council* [2009] EWCA Civ 59.

[210] *Sadrolashrafi v Marvel International Food Logistics Ltd* [2004] EWHC 777 (original testimony knowingly false).

[211] As in *Daly and Daly v Sheikh* [2002] EWCA Civ 1630 (plausible explanation for a mistake).

[212] See *Meek v Fleming* (n205), endorsed by *Brady(Inspector of Taxes) v Group Lotus Car Companies plc* [1987] 3 All ER 1050. See also after the CPR, *Saluja v Gill* (n199), [59].

[213] *Zincroft Civil Engineering Ltd v Sphere Drake Insurance plc* (1996) The Times, 13 December.

[214] *Khetani v Kanbi* [2006] EWCA Civ 1621, (2006) 150 SJLB 1603, [29].

[215] Said in *Hughes v Singh* (1989) unreported CA; The Times, 21 April to be the overriding consideration. See also, in Canada, *R v Warsing* [1998] 3 SCR 579. The rule is nevertheless available also to the prosecution: *R v Gilfoyle* [1996] 3 All ER 883, [1996] 1 Cr App Rep 302; even apart from rebutting fresh evidence adduced by the defence: *R v Hanratty* [2002] EWCA Crim 1141, [2002] 3 All ER 534.

a new trial.[216] Thus s 23(1) of the Criminal Appeal Act 1968[217] conferred wide discretion,[218] to adduce fresh evidence,[219] and s 23(2) imposed a more circumscribed duty to consider certain specified factors.[220]

The current test was said in *Dial and Dottin v Trinidad*[221] to be clear and simple:

Where fresh evidence is adduced on a criminal appeal it is for the Court of Appeal, assuming always that it accepts it, to evaluate its importance in the context of the remainder of the evidence in the case. If the Court concludes that the fresh evidence raises no reasonable doubt as to the guilt of the accused it will dismiss the appeal. The primary question is for the Court itself and is not what effect the fresh evidence would have had on the mind of the jury. That said, if the Court regards the case as a difficult one, it may find it helpful to test its view 'by asking whether the evidence, if given at the trial, might reasonably have affected the decision of the trial jury to convict' (*Pendleton* [19]). The guiding principle remains that stated by Viscount Dilhorne in *Stafford* (906) and affirmed by the House in *Pendleton*:

While...the Court of Appeal and this House may find it a convenient approach to consider what a jury might have done if they had heard the fresh evidence, the ultimate responsibility rests with them and them alone for deciding the question [whether or not the verdict is unsafe].

Justice must prevail.[222] Here, it seems to connote that the evidence should have been admissible at the trial; that there should be good reason why it was not adduced; and that it should have been capable of affecting the decision at trial.

- *Admissible*—The court will not normally[223] admit evidence that could not have been adduced at trial,[224] such as hearsay[225] or expert evidence on matters not requiring such expertise,[226] but is not bound by a decision of inadmissibility at trial.[227] It will

---

[216] Criminal Appeal Act 1968, s 7. Although it has been emphasized that the issues are distinct: *R v Pendleton* [2001] UKHL 66, [2002] 1 All ER 524, [20]. In some cases, fresh evidence is so cogent that there is no need to order a new trial: *R v Cash* [2004] EWCA Crim 666, (2004) 148 SJLB 416.

[217] As amended by Criminal Appeal Act 1995, s 4.

[218] So wide as to justify reception in exceptional cases even after a plea of guilty: *R v Foster* [1985] QB 115, [1984] 2 All ER 679; or on the factual basis for sentence: *R v Frankum* (1983) 5 Cr App Rep (S) 259. It extends to evidence held inadmissible at trial if on appeal believed admissible: *R v Gilfoyle* (n215), and 899, 321 was said 'to be confined only by the requirement that the court must be satisfied that it is necessary or expedient in the interests of justice to require the evidence to be given'.

[219] This will normally be evidence of fact rather than of opinion, as suggested by the wording of the provision, because the issue should normally have been raised at the trial, and because experts are more fungible: *R v Jones* [1997] 1 Cr App Rep 86.

[220] The duty is merely to consider the factors, and even if they are not satisfied the court may still admit the evidence: *R v Harris* [2001] EWCA Crim 252.

[221] [2005] UKPC 4, [2005] 1 WLR 1660; fully endorsed as a statement of English law in *R v Harris* [2005] EWCA Crim 1980, [2006] 1 Cr App R 55.   [222] *R v Gilfoyle* (n215) 899, 321.

[223] Although exceptionally it may: *R v D* [1996] QB 283 (finding in a related case).

[224] *R v Thomas* [1996] Crim LR 654, disapproving *R v Beckford and Daley* [1991] Crim LR 833 to the extent of any inconsistency.

[225] *R v Dallas* [1971] Crim LR 90; *R v Lattimore* (n183), 56, although hearsay may be used to determine what fresh evidence should be produced: *R v Callaghan* [1988] 1 All ER 257, [1988] 1 WLR 1. See also, in Australia, *R v Scoullar* (1995) 76 ACR 487.

[226] *R v H (JR) (Childhood Amnesia)* [2005] EWCA Crim 1828, [2006] 1 Cr App R 195 (some did).

[227] *R v Gilfoyle* (n215), although it is not enough that an adverse inference could have been drawn at trial on account of failure to disclose the evidence sought to be admitted on appeal, *R(Tinnion) v Reading Crown Court* [2009] EWHC 2930 (Admin).

also insist upon the observation of procedural requirements applied by statute to the admission of evidence at trial.[228] Even when otherwise admissible, fresh evidence may be refused if regarded as clearly[229] incapable of belief.[230]

- ***Reason for failing to adduce***—Evidence must be adduced to show why the evidence was not adduced at trial.[231] It is not normally[232] enough that the evidence was not called at trial for tactical reasons,[233] although in one case it was enough that it was felt that the witnesses would not be believed.[234] Nor will it be easy to evade such disqualification by alleging the incompetence of counsel.[235] In the case of fresh expert evidence, it will usually be necessary to show some subsequent development in expertise,[236] or a different set of facts upon which it should be based,[237] rather than that the expert called at trial proved unconvincing.[238] Conversely, it will normally be a sufficient reason to allow fresh evidence if it can be shown that it was not called at trial because wrongly not disclosed in advance,[239] or because of the dishonesty of a legal adviser.[240] It is also enough that neither side appreciated its significance before the trial[241] or if it relates to the overall conduct of the trial and emerges only later.[242] Where there is a dispute

---

228 *R v Conway* (1979) 70 Cr App Rep 4, in which the procedure of first putting an inconsistent statement to a witness before contradicting him, prescribed by the Criminal Procedure Act 1865, s 4, was insisted upon. See also, in Canada, *R v Rogers* (2000) 144 CCC (3d) 568, in which the rules of compellability, and for disclosure of medical reports on third parties, were applied at this stage.

229 Where there is doubt as to credibility, this should normally be resolved only after hearing the witness *de bene esse*, *R v Sales* [2000] 2 Cr App Rep 431, approved in *Shaw v R* [2002] UKPC 53, [30].

230 *R v Clarke* [2004] UKPC 5, 148 SJLB 146. For a recent English case in which the evidence was also rejected as incapable of belief, see *R v Thackery* [2005] EWCA Crim 828.

231 *Dosoruth v Mauritius* [2004] UKPC 45. In the case of a new witness, the court will require an affidavit sworn by a solicitor explaining the circumstances in which the witness came to be discovered: *R v Gogana* (1999) unreported CA, The Times, 12 July; *R v James* (2000) unreported, CA, 28 March.

232 *R v Solomon* [2007] EWCA Crim 2633 constituted an exception.

233 *R v Hampton and Brown* [2004] EWCA Crim 2139, (2004) 148 SJLB 971; *R v Shickle* [2005] EWCA Crim 1881 (not to raise diminished responsibility as a defence); *R v O'Connor* [2004] EWCA Crim 1295, (2004) 148 SJLB 693 (witness expected to be hostile). It would be different if the medical situation were not clear at the time of the trial: *R v Huckerby* [2004] EWCA Crim 3251, (2004) 148 SJLB 693 (effects of PTSD).

234 *R v Clark* [1999] Crim LR 573 (about police misconduct, in the light of a subsequent enquiry into the practices of this unit).

235 See e.g. *R v Clarke* [2005] EWCA Crim 2514 (unless the lawyer kept the client in ignorance of the evidence, *R(Adams) v Secretary of State for Justice* [2009] EWCA Civ 1291; although some other jurisdictions are more accommodating: United States, *Strickland v Washington* (1984) 466 US 668, 694; Canada, *R v GDB* 2000 SCC 22, [2000] 1 SCR 520.   236 *R v Yaqoob* [2005] EWCA Crim 2169 (no such development).

237 *R v Jenkins* [2004] EWCA Crim 2047, which may include a case where misdiagnosis before trial has prevented a possible defence from being raised at all, *R v Sultan* [2008] EWCA Crim 6.

238 *R v Kai-Whitewind* [2005] EWCA Crim 1092, [2005] 2 Cr App Rep 457, although in New Zealand held sufficient not to have called a supporting foreign expert where the only local expert unexpectedly reneged on his witness statement under cross-examination: *R v Cassidy* [1995] 3 NZLR 184.

239 *R v Cannings* [2004] EWCA Crim 1, [2004] 1 WLR 2607, [16]; *R v Heron* [2005] EWCA Crim 3245, although it is not enough that it was not disclosed by the accused to his counsel.

240 *R v Santharatnam* [2007] EWCA Crim 2687, [24].

241 *R v Harris* (n220). In *R v Moyle* [2008] EWCA Crim 3059, the evidence was of mental defect, which had itself dictated the decision not to call it at trial. In Canada, see *R v Pietrangelo* (2008) 233 CCC (3d) 338.

242 In Canada, evidence of a juror's affair during the trial with the accused fell into this category: *R v Budai* (2000) 144 CCC (3d) 1. But in Australia not if it consists of events occurring after sentence, *R v Courtney* [2007] NSWCCA 195, 172 ACR 195.

about counsel's instructions to call the evidence at trial, the accused should usually be allowed to tender fresh evidence himself on appeal on that issue.[243]

- *Cogency*[244]—The evidence must be such that it might reasonably[245] have affected the decision of the trial court to convict.[246] Where the evidence goes to the credibility of a prosecution witness, it will not be admitted when it was already clear at the trial that the witness was unreliable,[247] nor simply because a witness subsequently thinks himself to have given unreliable evidence.[248] If, however, it shows an apparently credible witness in a totally false light, it may be admissible.[249]

- Once admitted, fresh evidence is to be considered as part of the evidence in the case as a whole, and in the case of a joint trial, in relation to the conviction of all of the accused,[250] although this might cause more difficulty in a case where some of those so tried had been acquitted.

PROCEEDINGS IN OTHER TRIBUNALS[251]

A very wide variety of proceedings of a quasi-judicial, administrative, and legislative nature require authoritative fact-finding.[252] Many are susceptible to control by courts of law.[253] It is sometimes a matter of dispute how far and how many of the rules of evidence apply, or should apply, in such proceedings,[254] and on occasion, even where the rules do not apply, an analogous approach may be adopted under a different rubric.[255] Rules of

---

[243] *R v Ebanks* [2006] UKPC 16, [2006] 1 WLR 1827, [19].

[244] For discussion of the cogency required of fresh evidence in criminal cases, see: in Australia, *Gallagher v R* (1986) 160 CLR 392 and *Mickelberg v R* (1989) 167 CLR 259; in Canada, *Palmer v R* [1980] 1 SCR 759 and *Stolar v R* [1988] 1 SCR 480; and in New Zealand, *R v Dunsmuir* [1996] 2 NZLR 1.

[245] It will not normally be appropriate, especially in the case of defence evidence, for the appellate court to go further, and determine the matter itself, rather than remit it for re-trial by a jury, see *Bain v R* [2007] UKPC 9.

[246] *R v Pendleton* (n216), [19]; the same test is applied in Australia, *Mickelberg v R* (n244), and in Canada, *Palmer v R* [1980] 1 SCR 759.

[247] *R v Stone* [2005] EWCA Crim 105 (in which evidence from a self-confessed criminal and drug addict at trial was subsequently retracted); in Canada in *R v Hanemaayer* (2008) 234 CCC (3d) 3 a subsequent third party confession showed an identifying complainant to have been mistaken.

[248] *R v Khan* [2006] EWCA Crim 8. Except perhaps where the witness was an expert whose evidence was central to the prosecution case, *R v George* [2007] EWCA Crim 2722.

[249] *R v Cooper* [2005] EWCA Crim 1094 (evidence of statements by such witnesses that they had 'stitched up' the accused at trial).   [250] *R v Ali and Ali* [1999] Crim LR 663.

[251] Tribunals are occasionally regarded as courts for the purposes of the European Convention on Human Rights: see e.g. *R(Roberts) v Parole Board* [2005] UKHL 45, [2005] 2 AC 738, [13].

[252] But not always provision of reasoning for such decisions, see *Cheatle v General Medical Council* [2009] EWHC 645 (Admin).

[253] Even when the decision on such an administrative matter turns on questions of fact, it is still sufficient to satisfy the provisions of the European Convention on Human Rights that an appeal is allowed only on an issue of law: *Begum v Tower Hamlets LBC* [2003] UKHL 5, [2003] 1 All ER 731; see also *Tehrani v United Kingdom Central Council for Nursing, Midwifery and Health Visiting* [2001] IRLR 208.

[254] Sometimes, general revision of the rules of evidence will provide explicitly for application outside ordinary courts, thus the Civil Evidence Act 1995, s 11 applies its hearsay provisions to civil proceedings before any tribunal in which 'the strict rules of evidence apply'; see also in Scotland, Civil Evidence (Scotland) Act 1988, s 9.

[255] See *R(Ullah) v Secretary of State for the Home Department* [2003] EWCA Civ 1366, in which immigration issues were said not to involve the determination of civil rights and obligations, but where any trial still needed to be 'fair'.

evidence from civil and criminal proceedings may be combined.[256] Because the concerns
and purposes of these bodies vary so widely few general principles could be discerned.[257]
In any given tribunal, the rules may, as in the case of courts, vary according to the gravity
of the issue involved.[258] Conversely, even the same issue may be decided upon a different
basis before a tribunal rather than a court.[259] Similarly, when formal rules of evidence
apply to a non-judicial tribunal, to an arbitration for example, a more tolerant attitude
to the enforcement of the rules is likely to be exhibited,[260] and a different attitude taken
towards associated procedures, such as disclosure from third parties.[261]

Many of the bodies charged with these functions are statutory, and it is not uncommon for express provision to relate to applicable[262] procedure.[263] Sometimes, a lengthy
code is embodied in secondary legislation.[264] Where the inquiry is formal, the statute
may expressly import the rules of evidence applicable in ordinary courts.[265] Thus the
Race Relations Act 1976 regulates compulsory provision of information and disclosure of documents by reference to civil proceedings in the High Court.[266] It is, however, more common for the provision to exclude the strict application of the rules of
evidence that apply in ordinary courts, although this may still leave their application

---

[256] See *Haikel v General Medical Council* [2002] UKPC 37, [13], in which professional disciplinary proceedings are described as 'hybrid' for these purposes. In New Zealand, see *Gurusinghe v Medical Council of
New Zealand* [1989] 1 NZLR 139.

[257] The whole system is currently in flux following the passage of the Tribunals, Courts and Enforcement
Act 2007, which is in the process of superimposing a unified structure, including power under s 22 to specify
practice and procedure. So far the rules so made for both levels of tribunal have specified an identical,
and flexible, procedure permitting deviation from the rules of evidence in civil court proceedings, see The
Tribunal Procedure (Upper Tribunal) Rules 2008 (SI 2008/2698), para 15(2), but preserving immunities and
privileges, ibid para 16(3).

[258] In *R v Wolverhampton Coroner, ex p McCurbin* [1990] 2 All ER 759, [1990] 1 WLR 719, it was held
that, in the Coroners' Court, unlawful killing must be established beyond reasonable doubt, but death by
misadventure only on the balance of probabilities; for a slightly different approach to this issue in Australia,
see *Anderson v Blastriki* [1993] 2 VR 89.

[259] As in *R v Maidstone Crown Court, ex p Olson* (1992) 136 SJLB 174, in which a licensing authority
needed to determine an allegation of indecent assault only on the balance of probabilities, and was not
bound by the applicant's acquittal of that very offence; see in Canada, *Cambie Hotel (Nanaimo) Ltd v General
Manager of the Liquor Control and Licensing Branch* (2006) 265 DLR (4th) 657.

[260] See *Re Enoch and Zaretzky, Bock & Co's Arbitration* [1910] 1 KB 327.

[261] *BNP Paribas v Deloitte Touche LLP* [2003] EWHC 2874 (Comm).

[262] Sometimes by secondary legislation made under the powers conferred on the Lord Chancellor by
the Tribunals and Inquiries Act 1992, s 9.

[263] Although there is little unanimity of approach to strictness of construction cp *AI v Secretary of State
for the Home Department* [2007] EWCA Civ 386 [31] and *R (R) v Special Educational Needs & Disability
Tribunal* [2008] EWHC 473 (Admin) [23].

[264] See e.g. General Medical Council Preliminary Proceedings Committee and Professional Conduct
Committee (Procedure) Rules Order of Council (SI 1988/2255). The rules cannot be disregarded by mere
implication from the common law: see *Macharia v Immigration Appeal Tribunal* [2000] Imm AR 190, [17].

[265] If so, it is essential that the issue of admissibility in the ordinary courts be considered: *Re Flynn*
2002 SCLR 76. In Canada, a reference simply to 'all relevant evidence' has been held to exclude hearsay: *R v
Zeolkowski* (n93). Thus it was held in *R(Paul) v Inner London Coroner* [2007] EWCA Civ 1259, [2008] 1 All ER
981 that a coroner may admit hearsay only in accordance with rule 37 of the Coroners' Rules.

[266] Section 50(3)(a). See also Osteopaths Act 1993, s 26(3), where the procedure of the place where the
tribunal sits is to be applied; cf *McAllister v General Medical Council* [1993] AC 388, [1993] 1 All ER 982, in
which the Privy Council determined that the law of England applied to proceedings of the Council wherever
it sat.

optional.[267] Sometimes the statute contents itself with bestowing a power to prescribe rules of evidence to apply.[268] In *R v Deputy Industrial Injuries Comr, ex p Moore*,[269] despite such a power, no regulations had been made under it. It was said that the existence of the power indicated that Parliament did not intend the strict rules of evidence to apply.[270] It would, however, be rash to construe the non-existence of such a power as indicating any intention at all. Failure to specify the preservation of basic procedural rights, such as that to an oral hearing, is not alone to be regarded as amounting to implied exclusion.[271] The precise pattern of rules depends upon a very wide range of factors defining the nature of the proceedings:[272]

[T]here are degrees of judicial hearing, and those degrees run from the borders of pure administration to the borders of the full hearing of a criminal cause or matter in the Crown Court. It does not profit one to try to pigeon-hole the particular set of circumstances either into the administrative pigeon-hole or into the judicial pigeon-hole. Each case will inevitably differ, and one must ask oneself what is the basic nature of the proceeding.

Flexibility is the essence of the matter. The precise concatenation of rules of evidence and procedure should be adapted to the purposes of the proceedings, and to their circumstances. Not all situations can be anticipated, and perceptions of fairness are in constant flux.[273] Where the procedure is in some sense judicial, it is common to invoke the rules of natural justice, but this carries the matter little further:[274]

Natural justice requires that the procedure before any tribunal which is acting judicially shall be fair in all the circumstances, and I would be sorry to see this fundamental general principle degenerate into a series of hard and fast rules. For a long time the courts have, without objection from Parliament, supplemented procedure laid down in legislation where they have found that to be necessary for this purpose.

Even if it were possible, it would not be appropriate to specify here all of the various mixtures of rules of evidence that apply in all fact-finding tribunals. It is, however, worth giving a few examples of some of the main rules that have been controverted. The rules involved have principally been those dealing with the calling of witnesses, the administration of an oath, the right to cross-examine, the admissibility of hearsay, public interest immunity, and the need to disclose. Where the European Convention on Human Rights is engaged, the proceedings will be judged as a whole, and it is likely to be premature to attempt to determine in advance whether any evidential rules will preclude the possibility

---

[267] See, in Australia, *De Domenico v Marshall* [1999] ACTSC 1, 153 FLR 437.

[268] See e.g. Regulation of Investigatory Powers Act 2000, s 69(2)(g); occasionally overlaid by a few compulsory rules, see Social Security Act 1998, s 16(5) (privilege against self-incrimination), as continued by Social Security Contributions (Transfer of Functions) Act 1999, s 16(6) (7).

[269] [1965] 1 QB 456, [1965] 1 All ER 81.   [270] 474, 85.   [271] *R(West) v Parole Board* (n72), [29].

[272] *R v Commission for Racial Equality, ex p Cottrell and Rothon* [1980] 3 All ER 265, [1980] 1 WLR 1580. Proceedings are not converted from judicial to administrative just because the tribunal dismisses a claim without consideration of the merits: *Barber v Staffordshire County Council* [1996] 2 All ER 748.

[273] *R(Roberts) v Parole Board* (n251), [43], [48].

[274] *Wiseman v Borneman* [1971] AC 297, [1969] 3 All ER 275; 308, 277, Lord Reid. In Australia, in *Hempel v A-G* (1987) 77 ALR 641, it was held to be consistent with natural justice in extradition proceedings to cast the onus of proof upon the party resisting extradition, and not allow him to cross-examine witnesses, or even an oral hearing.

of a fair hearing.[275] Sometimes, however, the consequences may be so unfair that some procedures may be declared to be incompatible with the Convention.[276]

It is clear that the nature of the issues of fact to be decided[277] and the consequences[278] of a finding must have an important bearing on the nature of the rules that govern that finding.[279] Thus in *R v Board of Visitors of Hull Prison, ex p St Germain (No 2)*,[280] where the board of visitors was adjudicating upon allegations of very serious offences, guilt of which would involve substantial loss of liberty, the requirements were very stringent. Nevertheless, they differed significantly from those that would have operated in a court. Thus while the court thought it necessary to allow the accused to call witnesses and to cross-examine, it nevertheless permitted discretion to the chairman to limit the number of witnesses upon proper grounds, and to insist upon cross-examination being channelled through himself.[281] In view of the notorious difficulty of some of the issues involved, questions of identification at a distance for example, the court was reluctant to permit disposal simply on the basis of hearsay,[282] but here too its solution was not exclusion, as it might have been at common law, but rather to give the accused an adequate opportunity to deal with it.[283] This decision may be compared with that in *R v Commission for Racial Equality, ex p Cottrell and Rothon*,[284] in which questions of the right to cross-examine and to rely upon hearsay were also raised. Here, however, the point arose in relation to the issue of a non-discrimination notice by the Commission for Racial Equality within the statutory framework of the Race Relations Act 1976. The allegations did not involve the commission of a criminal offence, nor did an adverse determination involve loss of liberty, or, at least in the absence of a series of further steps, interference with the discriminator's business. It was for these reasons that

---

[275] *R(Roberts) v Parole Board* (n251), [19].

[276] *R(Wright) v Secretary of State for Health* [2009] UKHL 3.

[277] Where there is no *lis*, as in an inquiry, the terms of reference will determine issues of relevance: *Mount Murray Country Club v Macleod* [2003] UKPC 53, [2003] STC 1525, [27]. See also Willmott (2003) 12 Nott LJ 34, on the extent to which witnesses are entitled to legal representation at such an inquiry.

[278] Such consequences may themselves sometimes be informal, such as community reaction to disclosure that someone is a suspected sexual offender: see e.g. *R v Dyfed Police Public Protections Group* (16 October 2000, unreported) QBD.

[279] In *R v Milk Marketing Board, ex p Austin* (1983) The Times, 21 March, QB, where a tribunal decision could deprive a man of his livelihood, the full criminal standard of proof was required.

[280] [1979] 3 All ER 545, [1979] 1 WLR 1401.

[281] This course was also required by the Court of Appeal in *Chilton v Saga Holidays plc* [1986] 1 All ER 841, in which, although the rules for the arbitration of small claims authorized an informal and equal approach to be adopted, they were nevertheless held not to permit the Registrar to disallow cross-examination by a legally represented party, the other party not being so represented.

[282] By contrast, *R (Sim) v Secretary of State for the Home Department* [2003] EWHC 152 (Admin), [2003] 2 WLR 1374 held it compatible with the European Convention on Human Rights that the Parole Board could decide recall for an extended sentence on the basis of hearsay, partly because such a decision would be subject to judicial review; see *R (P) v Parole Board* [2003] EWHC 1391 (Admin) for such a review upholding the use of hearsay for this purpose; see also *Brooks v Parole Board* [2003] EWHC 1458 (Admin), in which the matter determined by hearsay was absolutely central to the decision. The United States has now abandoned its old rule that such an issue could not be decided solely on the basis of hearsay: *Johnson v United States* 628 F 2d 187, 190 (1980).

[283] A similar approach was taken to hearsay in the form of a scientific certificate in *R v Governor of Swaleside Prison, ex p Wynter* (1998) 10 Admin LR 597, and to evidence of breach of licence in *R(Headley) v Parole Board* [2009] EWHC. 663 (Admin).

[284] [1980] 3 All ER 265, [1980] 1 WLR 1580; see also *R v Haringey London Borough Leader's Investigative Panel, ex p Edwards* (1983) The Times, 22 March.

the court distinguished the prison visitors' case, and decided that the scheme of the Act neither required to be supplemented by an automatic right to cross-examine, nor excluded the admission of hearsay. Indeed, since the statute made it proper for the Commission to delegate its investigatory functions, the court thought it right for the Commission to act upon the basis of the hearsay necessarily contained in reports by those carrying out such functions. Such statutory support is not, however, necessary. In cases where the statute provides little more than a requirement that a tribunal shall act upon the basis of evidence, the general view is that this entitles it, in the absence of special considerations, to act upon any material, including hearsay, which is logically probative:[285]

[T]echnical rules of evidence form no part of the rules of natural justice. The requirement that a person exercising quasi-judicial functions must base his decision upon evidence means no more than that it must be based on material which tends logically to show the existence or non-existence of facts relevant to the issue to be determined, or to show the likelihood or unlikelihood of the occurrence of some future event the occurrence of which would be logically probative. It means that he must not spin a coin or consult an astrologer; but he may take into account any material which as a matter of reason, has some probative value in the manner mentioned above. If it is capable of having any probative value, the weight to be attached to it is a matter for the person to whom Parliament has entrusted the responsibility of deciding the issue. The supervisory jurisdiction of the High Court does not entitle it to usurp this responsibility and to substitute its own view for his.

Disciplinary proceedings seem close to the model of a criminal trial,[286] normally requiring strict proof;[287] similar identification[288] and adverse inference directions;[289] in some cases, the rule excluding evidence of similar facts seems to have been applied;[290] they are subject to a similar approach to the use of fresh evidence at the appellate stage,[291] and generally to proceedings for abuse of process.[292] Nevertheless, facts have been permitted to be proved

---

[285] *R v Deputy Industrial Injuries Comr, ex p Moore* [1965] 1 QB 456, [1965] 1 All ER 81; 488, 94, Diplock LJ. See also *Minister for Immigration and Ethnic Affairs v Pochi* (1980) 31 ALR 666.

[286] Although in Australia, in *McCarthy v Law Society of New South Wales* (1997) 43 NSWLR 42, held to be comprehended within the description 'civil proceedings' for the purpose of admitting an inspector's report into evidence. See *Carroll v Disciplinary Tribunal of Law Society of Ireland (No 2)* [2003] IR 284 for a full explanation of the rules of evidence in disciplinary proceedings in Ireland.

[287] Although nowadays in England cast in terms of the amount of evidence needed to satisfy the civil standard, see *R(IPCC) v Hayman* [2008] EWHC 2191 (Admin), [20]. In Australia, the enhanced civil standard has been required: *Kerin v Legal Practitioners' Complaints Committee* (1996) 67 SASR 149; while in Ireland, a distinction is drawn between the higher standard required by a disciplinary tribunal and the lower required for one determining unfair dismissal in regard to the same facts: *Georgopoulus v Beaumont Hospital Board* [1998] 3 IR 132; in New Zealand, see *Z v Dental Complaints Assessment Committee* [2008] NZSC 55, [2009] 1 NZLR 1.

[288] *R v Cardinal Newman's School, Birmingham, ex p S* (1997) The Times, 26 December.

[289] *Secretary of State for Health v C (Tribunal: Failure to Draw Inference)* [2003] EWCA Civ 10, [2003] 2 FCR 274.

[290] *Lanford v General Medical Council* [1990] 1 AC 13, [1989] 2 All ER 921; *Re College of Physicians and Surgeons of Ontario and K* (1987) 36 DLR (4th) 707; in *Secretary of State for Schools and Families v X* [2009] EWHC 524 (Admin) despite previous acquittal.

[291] *E v Secretary of State for Home Department* [2004] EWCA Civ 49, [2004] QB 1044, [82], subject to discretion to depart from strict application of *Ladd v Marshall*.

[292] *Re Saluja* [2006] EWHC 2784 (Admin). It will rarely amount to abuse of process to adjudicate upon a matter previously determined by some other tribunal, even one acting inquisitorially, *Independent Police Complaints Commission v Chief Constable of West Mercia* [2007] EWHC 1035 (Admin).

by reference to criminal convictions otherwise inadmissible at law,[293] or even acquittals;[294] there is no absolute entitlement to cross-examine,[295] and a legal assessor is not a judge under a duty to direct on criminal principles.[296] Because the issues in such an enquiry[297] differ from those in a criminal trial, there is no scope for double jeopardy,[298] estoppel,[299] or pleas of autrefois acquit or convict.[300] As the issue departs further and further from the model of a criminal prosecution,[301] so the likelihood of importing rules of evidence that apply there diminishes,[302] or their application is applied in a more relaxed fashion.[303] Thus the wholly inquisitorial procedure before a coroner is inimical to the application of the rules of evidence,[304] which accordingly do not apply to such proceedings,[305] although the inquest must still be fair, and such fairness may import certain evidential requirements,[306] such as the desirability of disclosing material in advance,[307] calling witnesses where evidence is likely to be controversial,[308] and sometimes even applying the criminal standard of

[293] *Re Del Core and Ontario College of Pharmacists* (1985) 19 DLR (4th) 68; cf *Hill v Clifford* [1907] 2 Ch 236.

[294] *Z v Dental Complaints Assessment Committee* (n287) and a fortiori in licensing applications: *McCool v Rushcliffe Borough Council* [1998] 3 All ER 889.

[295] *Shakespeare v British Coal Corp* (1988) The Times, 5 April; *R v Governor of Swaleside Prison, ex p Wynter* (n283).   [296] *Gopakumar v General Medical Council* [2008] EWCA Civ 309.

[297] Especially at the early stages of a developing process, see *R (S) v Swindon Borough Council* [2001] EWHC Admin 334, [34]. If, however, the issues are identical, these rules may apply: see *Lennon v Birmingham City Council* [2001] EWCA Civ 435, [2001] IRLR 826.

[298] *R(Redgrave) v Comr of Police of Metropolis* [2003] EWCA Civ 04, [2003] 1 WLR 1136.

[299] Nor between different tribunals: *Bramwell v Repatriation Commission* (1998) 158 ALR 623.

[300] Principles of fairness might nevertheless play a part: see *AA v General Medical Council* [2002] 3 IR 1.

[301] The seriousness of the consequences may require some evidential safeguards: see, in Ireland, *Gallacher v Revenue Comrs (No 2)* [1995] 1 IR 55, in which an internal enquiry into an employee's conduct was accordingly prevented from relying on hearsay.

[302] Some provisions of the ECHR may nevertheless have an influence, as in *R (D) v Secretary of State for Home Department* [2003] EWHC 155 (Admin), [2003] 1 FLR 979, where Art 8 was held to dictate the calling of expert evidence to assist with the largely administrative decision of whether or not to separate a mother and child in prison.

[303] *Kerr v Department for Social Development* [2004] UKHL 23, [2004] 4 All ER 385 (allocation of burden of proof).

[304] *R v South London Coroner, Ex parte Thompson* (1982) 126 SJ 625, 'It should not be forgotten that an inquest is a fact-finding exercise and not a method of apportioning guilt. The procedure and rules of evidence which are suitable for one are unsuitable for the other.' Here too the rules differ with the circumstances and require more elaboration where the relevant death occurs in custody, when the death is to be investigated 'fully, fairly and fearlessly': Bingham MR in *R v HM Coroner for North Humberside and Scunthorpe, ex p Jamieson* [1995] QB 1, [1994] 3 All ER 972. The Coroner may still prevent the jury bringing in a perverse verdict, *R(Bennett) v HM Coroner for Inner South London* [2007] EWCA Civ 617.

[305] *R v West London Coroner, ex p Gray* [1988] QB 467, [1987] 2 All ER 129; *McKerr v Armagh Coroner* [1990] 1 All ER 865, [1990] 1 WLR 649; *R O'Connor v HM Coroner for District of Avon* [2009] EWHC 854 (Admin), [2009] 4 All ER 1020. Although the Coroners' Rules import some evidential rules, such as the means of adducing hearsay, see *R(Paul and Ritz Hotel Ltd) v Assistant Deputy Coroner of Inner West London* [2007] EWHC 2721 (Admin).

[306] Some in favour of the witnesses, such as tendering evidence anonymously where necessary: *A v Inner South London Coroner* [2004] EWHC 1592 (Admin), (2004) 168 JP 511.

[307] See in Ireland *Ramseyer v Mahon* [2005] IESC 82, [2006] 1 IR 216.

[308] *R(Bentley) v HM Coroner District of Avon* [2001] EWHC (Admin) 170 (fairness a dynamic concept); *R(Nicholls) v HM Coroner for the City of Liverpool* [2001] EWHC Admin 922 (verdict quashed because coroner refused to call expert witness); *R(Stanley) v Coroner for Inner North London* [2003] EWHC 1180 (Admin) (argument to be addressed on admissibility of deceased's convictions, and reasons given for decision).

proof.[309] More wholesale importation of evidential rules was proposed in the Counter-Terrorism Bill 2008.

In the case of local inquiries in planning matters, Lord Diplock refused even to adopt the terminology of natural justice as suggesting that 'the prototype is only to be found in procedures followed by English courts of law'.[310] Instead, he referred simply to the need for the procedure to be fair.[311] So far from finding that rights to cross-examine constitute one of the ingredients of a fair procedure, he suggested that they might make it unfair:[312]

To 'over-judicialise' the inquiry by insisting on observation of the procedures of a court of justice which professional lawyers alone are competent to operate effectively in the interests of their clients would not be fair.

He also drew attention to the totally different conditions of a planning inquiry in relation to the nature of the issues, the number of interested parties, and of their witnesses, and the length of the proceedings.[313] He felt that in determining even so apparently straightforward a matter as the fairness of allowing cross-examination, a multitude of factors needed to be considered, such as, in the case of an expert opinion witness, the nature of the topic on which the opinion was expressed, the qualifications of the witness and competence of the cross-examiner, and the inspector's view of whether his report would be more useful if cross-examination were allowed.

In general, powers to compel attendance and to administer an oath require to be endowed by statute,[314] though it is possible for a tribunal recognized by law, even though not set up by statute, to secure a subpoena to secure the attendance of a witness.[315] The power to administer an oath does not preclude the reception of unsworn testimony, if appropriate.[316] The application of spousal immunities may depend upon how close the issues are to an accusation of crime.[317] In principle, public interest immunity applies to tribunals,[318] but in some cases it has been thought desirable to make explicit provision.[319] In those cases where a witness can be compelled to give evidence, the normal range of privileges[320] will

---

[309] Restated in *R(Cash) v County of Northamptonshire Coroner* [2007] EWHC 1354 (Admin), [2007] 4 All ER 903, [28].

[310] *Bushell v Secretary of State for the Environment* [1981] AC 75, [1980] 2 All ER 608; 95, 612.

[311] In *R (B) v Merton LBC* [2003] EWHC 1689 (Admin), [2003] 4 All ER 280, fairness was all that was required of a local council official investigating a claim by an asylum seeker to be a child.

[312] 97, 614.

[313] In Scotland, in *Errington v Wilson* 1995 SC 550, even in so administrative a matter as ordering the destruction of food unfit for human consumption, cross-examination was required because there was no special urgency, the owner's rights would be affected, and the issue depended entirely on the evaluation of expert evidence.

[314] But not in New Zealand for the use of video linkage by tribunals just as by courts: *B v Dentists' Disciplinary Tribunal* [1994] 1 NZLR 95.

[315] *Currie v Chief Constable of Surrey* [1982] 1 All ER 89, [1982] 1 WLR 215, QB. It has even been held that the powers of some tribunals to call witnesses of their own volition may be wider than those enjoyed by a court: see *Kesse v Secretary of State for Home Department* [2001] EWCA Civ 177, [37].

[316] *General Medical Council v Spackman* [1943] AC 627, [1943] 2 All ER 337.

[317] See *Australian Federal Police Comr v McMillan and Hordes* (1987) 24 ACR 278.

[318] In *R(Roberts) v Parole Board* (n251), the issue related only to the use of the special advocate procedure to deal with it.

[319] Town and Country Planning (Enforcement) (Inquiries Procedure) Rules 1981, SI 1981/1743, r 11(4).

[320] Including without prejudice privilege: *Independent Research Services v Catterall* [1993] ICR 1.

presumably apply in the absence of specific statutory provision,[321] since it would be odd for a court to be in a weaker position than a tribunal in securing relevant evidence.[322] On the other hand, hearings before tribunals often do not involve an adversarial element, and even if they do, are not properly categorized in many cases as 'litigation' for the purposes of the litigation branch of legal professional privilege.[323] It may, however, be preferable to save any desired exclusionary privilege when the ordinary rules are relaxed. It may further be noted that the nature of the issue before a tribunal may dictate the application of different, and more restrictive, rules as to the admissibility of fresh evidence on appeal,[324] and that the privacy of some tribunals, such as arbitrations, may allow greater relaxation than would be proper in a public court.[325]

It need hardly be added that the purposes and position of legislative committees are so far removed from those of a court that quite different sets of rules apply,[326] including some abrogating protection so well established in the ordinary courts as that of the privilege not to disclose communications between solicitor and client.

It may also be the case that where the inquiry is essentially governmental, for example in England[327] under the Tribunals of Inquiry (Evidence) Act 1921, there may be no need to claim immunity on the basis of public policy.[328]

The appellate process often takes the form of judicial review of the original decision, and in such cases, there are strict limitations upon the admissibility of fresh expert evidence,[329] although even outside those limits expert reports seeking merely to explain the issues at stake might still be admissible.[330] In general, the admissibility of fresh evidence before appellate tribunals applies the rules for courts set out in *Ladd v Marshall*, as discussed above.[331]

---

[321] *AM & S Europe v EC Commission* [1983] QB 878, [1983] 1 All ER 705; 896, 720; but see *Parry-Jones v Law Society* [1969] 1 Ch 1, [1968] 1 All ER 177; 9, 180.

[322] *Southampton University v Kelly* (2005) unreported EAT 14 November, [22]; see also, in New Zealand, *Health and Disability Comr v Medical Practitioners Disciplinary Tribunal* [1999] 2 NZLR 616, 628; but see, in Canada, *Workers' Compensation Board of Prince Edward Island v Queens Regional Authority* (1999) 174 DLR (4th) 537.

[323] The issue was discussed at some length in *Three Rivers District Council v Bank of England (No 4)* [2004] EWCA Civ 218, [2004] 2 WLR 1065, [31]–[38], and the concept of 'quasi-litigation' aired, see further 451.

[324] Sometimes implemented by secondary legislation: see Immigration and Asylum Application Rules 2003, r 21. For the vexed issue of fresh evidence on judicial review in such cases, see *E v Secretary of State for Home Department* (n291).

[325] *Associated Electric and Gas Insurance Services Ltd v European Reinsurance Co of Zurich* [2003] UKPC 11, [2003] 1 All ER (Comm) 253, [2003] 1 WLR 1041, [20].

[326] See May *Treatise on the Law, Privileges and Usages of Parliament* (23rd edn, 2004), *First Report of Select Committee on Procedure* (1978); for Australia, see *Parliamentary Committees: Powers Over and Protection Afforded to Witnesses* (Parl Pap No 168, 1972); and for Canada, see *Witnesses Before Legislative Committees* (Ontario Law Reform Committee, 1981). See also Harders (1993) 67 *ALJ* 109.

[327] See also, under comparable legislation in Ireland, *O'Callaghan v Mahon* [2005] IESC 9, [2006] 2 IR 32; and in the Isle of Man, *Mount Murray Country Club Ltd v Macleod (The Assessor of Income Tax)* [2003] UKPC 53, [2003] STC 1525.

[328] For a general discussion of the evidential rules relating to such bodies, see Hallett *Royal Commissions and Boards of Enquiry* (1982). The evidential rules relating to inquiries by bodies like Royal Commissions have been much debated in the Commonwealth: see e.g. *Bisaillon v Keable* [1983] 2 SCR 60; *Bercove v Hermes (No 3)* (1983) 51 ALR 109.

[329] *R v Secretary of State for the Environment, ex p Powis* [1981] 1 All ER 788, [1981] 1 WLR 584.

[330] *Lynch v General Dental Council* [2003] EWHC 2987 (Admin), [2004] 1 All ER 1159.

[331] *Montes v Secretary of State for Home Dept* [2004] EWCA Civ 324, [2004] 2 All ER 463.

SECTION 3. PURPOSES AND CATEGORIES OF JUDICIAL EVIDENCE

Judicial evidence is used to prove either facts in issue, or facts from which facts in issue may properly be inferred. It comprises the testimony of witnesses, hearsay, documents, and things. The first part of this section will consider the main categories of facts in issue, and different sorts of circumstantial evidence. The second part will explain different types of judicial evidence.

OBJECTS OF PROOF

The objects of proof are either facts in issue or facts, relevant to facts in issue, of which circumstantial evidence is the clearest example.

Facts in issue

There are two principal types of facts in issue: those that are in issue as a matter of substantive law; and those that are in issue as a matter of the law of evidence itself.[332]

The main facts in issue are all those facts that the claimant[333] in a civil action, or the prosecutor in criminal proceedings, must prove in order to succeed, together with any further facts that the defendant or accused must prove in order to establish a defence.

Most cases involve more than one issue. In criminal cases:[334]

...whenever there is a plea of not guilty, everything is in issue, and the prosecution has to prove the whole of their case, including the identity of the accused, the nature of the act and the existence of any necessary knowledge or intent.

Failure to discriminate clearly between different issues is one of the most potent, and least recognized, sources of confusion and difficulty in the law of evidence. It is especially acute in criminal proceedings just because no formal pleadings are made or required in advance, although the general nature of the defence must be disclosed.

Matters in issue on account of the law of evidence itself include the competence or credibility of a witness and the admissibility or cogency of certain items of evidence.

Thus in *R v Yacoob*,[335] the competence of the witness depended upon whether or not she was married to the accused. Similarly, it may be relevant to know of the existence of a relationship that would tend to make a witness biased in favour of a party calling him. He may thus be asked about the relationship in cross-examination and, if denied, the relationship may be proved by the opposite party.[336]

Facts relating to the admissibility or authenticity of an item of evidence may be in issue, as when an apparent confession to the police is alleged to have been obtained by

---

[332] In *R v Robertson; R v Golder* [1987] QB 920, [1987] 3 All ER 231; 927, 236, the Lord Chief Justice distinguished them as 'restricted' and 'extended'.

[333] This term must be taken to include the applicant or petitioner where appropriate, and the word 'defendant' must be taken to include the respondent.

[334] Lord Goddard CJ, in *R v Sims* [1946] KB 531, [1946] 1 All ER 697; 539, 701.

[335] (n130).   [336] *Thomas v David* (1836) 7 C & P 350.

oppression, or to have been altered subsequently. The cogency of a piece of evidence may also become a subordinate fact, for example when a challenge is mounted to the accuracy of a new device for measuring the speed of a motor car.[337]

Facts as evidence of other facts: circumstantial evidence

If evidence were admissible only if going directly to facts in issue, or direct evidence, many claims would fail. Resort must usually be made to 'circumstantial evidence', that is, any fact from the existence of which the judge or jury may infer the existence of a fact in issue.[338] A typical instance is afforded by the statement of a witness at a trial for murder that he saw the accused carrying a bloodstained knife at the door of the house in which the deceased was found mortally wounded. The prosecutor invites the jury, first, to assume that the witness is speaking the truth, and second, to infer that the accused inflicted the mortal wound with the knife. Conduct on other occasions may amount to important circumstantial evidence.[339] The absence of any evidence of a fact to be used circumstantially may be fatal.[340]

Evidentiary facts may be proved by testimony, hearsay, documents, things, and other evidentiary facts. An example of the proof of one such fact by another is afforded by the statement of a witness at a trial for murder that he saw blood on the coat pocket in which the accused's knife was found. The jury is asked, first, to assume that the witness is telling the truth, second, to infer that the blood on the pocket came from the knife, and finally, to infer that the blood was on the knife because the accused stabbed the deceased with that weapon. This process might be prolonged still further, but as the number of steps that have to be taken from the first evidentiary fact to the ultimate inference of a fact in issue increases, the weaker becomes the former as a means of proving the latter and the opportunities of adducing evidence in favour of a contrary conclusion are increased.[341] The line between circumstantial evidence and speculation is neither clear nor sharp.[342]

The common fear of manufactured evidence applies, perhaps even more strongly, to circumstantial evidence: 'Circumstantial evidence may sometimes be evidence, but it must always be narrowly examined, if only because evidence of this kind may be manufactured to cast suspicion on another.'[343]

No useful purpose is served by a comparison of the merits of direct and circumstantial evidence.[344] Circumstantial evidence may be so strong as to lead to the exclusion of fresh

---

337 *Kent v Stamps* [1982] RTR 273.

338 This definition was explicitly approved by Gleeson CJ in the High Court of Australia in *Festa v R* [2001] HCA 72, 208 CLR 593, [5].

339 As in *Benhams Ltd v Kythira Investments Ltd* [2004] EWHC 2973 (in the absence of any documentary evidence, it furnished the basis for proof of the contract upon which the claim was based).

340 *R v NW et al* [2008] EWCA Crim 2 (charge of money laundering in the absence of any proof that the property did represent the proceeds of crime).

341 'Arguments upon evidence are generally arguments from effects to causes; and in proportion as the number of possible causes of a given effect increases, the force of the argument is diminished. It is impossible to fix the precise point at which the argument becomes so weak as not to be worth noticing' (Stephen *General View of the Criminal Law* (1st edn) 307).

342 See e.g. the difference of opinion in *Richard Evans Ltd v Astley* [1911] AC 674.

343 *Teper v R* [1952] AC 480, 489.

344 'It has been said that circumstantial evidence is to be considered as a chain, and each piece of evidence as a link in the chain, but that is not so, for then, if any one link break, the chain would fall. It is more like the case of a rope comprised of several cords. One strand of the cord might be insufficient to sustain the weight,

evidence to contradict the conclusion it indicates,[345] although its strength should not be exaggerated in any direction to the jury.[346]

Examples of circumstantial evidence

This section adopts one of Wigmore's classifications of circumstantial evidence.[347] His terms 'prospectant', 'concomitant', and 'retrospectant' are strange, but stress the main ways in which the relevance of one fact to another may be established. When considering the illustrations below, it should be noted that the classes of witness allowed to give evidence at common law trials were severely restricted until the mid-nineteenth century. Those 'interested' in the outcome of the proceedings were generally unable to testify before the Evidence Act 1843 came into force; parties in civil cases, and their spouses, were made competent only by the Evidence Acts of 1851 and 1853, respectively; and, as a general rule, the accused and his spouse were unable to give evidence at a criminal trial before 1898.[348] Circumstantial evidence was once all that was available on points upon which direct evidence would probably be given today.

Prospectant evidence

The basic argument for the reception of this kind of evidence is that the occurrence of an act, state of mind, or state of affairs in the past justifies an inference that the act was done, or that the state of mind or affairs existed at the moment of time into which the court is inquiring.

Continuance

If the speed at which someone was driving at a particular time is in issue, evidence of the rate at which he was travelling a few moments earlier is admissible;[349] in cases turning on mental incapacity, evidence of its existence at a time earlier than that with which the court is concerned is likewise admissible.[350] Evidence has been received of a person's theological opinions four years before the time at which their nature was in issue;[351] similarly, the fact that someone was alive at an antecedent date may support an inference that he was alive at a subsequent date.[352] Evidence of this sort is given so frequently that it is sometimes said that continuance in general, and the continuance of life in particular, is

---

but three stranded together may be quite of sufficient strength. Thus it may be in circumstantial evidence-there may be a combination of circumstances, no one of which would raise a reasonable conviction or more than a mere suspicion; but the three taken together may create a conclusion of guilt with as much certainty as human affairs can require or admit of' (*per* Pollock CB in *R v Exall* (1866) 4 F & F 922, 929). See also *Thomas v R* [1972] NZLR 34.

[345] *R v Probyn* [2005] EWCA Crim 2347; *R v Pinnock* [2006] EWCA Crim 3119.

[346] *People v Cahill* [2001] 3 IR 494.

[347] Wigmore *A Treatise on the Anglo-American System of Evidence* (Tillers revn, 1983) vol 1A, [43].

[348] During the previous 25 years, the total exclusion had been relaxed by sundry statutes applying to specific offences.

[349] *Beresford v St Albans Justices* (1905) 22 TLR 1. Compare *R v Horvath* [1972] VR 533; and see *R v Martin* (1981) 4 ACR 302.   [350] *Owners of Strata Plan No 23007 v Cross* [2006] FCA 900, 233 ALR 296.

[351] *A-G v Bradlaugh* (1885) 14 QBD 667, 711.

[352] In *Chard v Chard* [1956] P 259, [1955] 3 All ER 721, Sachs J inferred the continuance of life of a woman aged 26 for a further 16 years.

the subject of a rebuttable presumption of law; the question is simply one of relevance and weight.[353]

Course of business

To prove postage, evidence may be given that a letter was copied in an office letter book, and that, according to the practice of the office, all letters dealt with in this way were posted immediately.[354] Proof of postage is evidence of delivery to the addressee.[355] It seems, however, that these two steps cannot be combined and proof of a practice of postage accepted as evidence of receipt by the intended recipient.[356]

Habit[357]

The fact that someone was in the habit of acting in a given way is relevant to the question whether he acted in that way on the occasion into which the court is inquiring. Thus, in *Joy v Phillips, Mills & Co Ltd*,[358] a claim was made for workmen's compensation in respect of the death of a stable boy caused by a kick from a horse. The deceased was found near the horse, holding a halter that there was no occasion for him to use at that time of day. It was held that the defendant might call evidence of the boy's practice of teasing the horse as tending to negate the applicant's claim that the accident arose out of and in the course of the deceased's employment. Phillimore LJ said:[359]

wherever an inquiry has to be made into the cause of the death of a person and, there being no direct evidence, recourse must be had to circumstantial evidence, any evidence as to the habits and ordinary doings of the deceased which may contribute to the circumstances by throwing light upon the probable cause of death is admissible, even in the case of a prosecution for murder.

Motive or plan

Facts that supply a motive for a particular act, such as that a man engaged to another woman on the basis that he was already a widower murdered his wife, may even be used to prove commission of the act so motivated,[360] are among the items of circumstantial evidence most often admitted. Conversely, facts that tend to show a total absence of motive may be adduced, as where the lack of financial embarrassment on his part is proved by someone accused of arson with intent to defraud an insurance company.[361] It is, however, easy to attach too much weight to evidence of motive: 'Almost every child has something to gain by the death of his parents, but rarely on the death of a parent is parricide even

---

[353] 'Nothing can be more absurd than the notion that there is to be any rigid presumption of law on such questions of fact, without reference to accompanying circumstances, such, for instance, as the age or health of the party. There can be no such strict presumption of law. I think that the only questions in such cases are, what evidence is admissible? and what inference may fairly be drawn from it?' (*per* Denman CJ in *R v Harborne Inhabitants* (1835) 2 Ad & El 540, 544–5).

[354] *Trotter v Maclean* (1879) 13 Ch D 574, (proof of postage evidence of delivery to addressee).

[355] *Watts v Vickers* (1916) 86 LJKB 177. See Interpretation Act 1978, s 7, as to service by post.

[356] *Bogdal v Hall* [1987] Crim LR 500 (although this decision may merely express scepticism of the efficiency of the computerized operation of public bureaucracy, at least to the prejudice of the accused).

[357] This section was explicitly approved in *R v Watson* (1996) 108 CCC (3d) 310, 325a.

[358] [1916] 1 KB 849; *Lahrs v Eichsteadt* [1961] Qd R 457. It is not always easy to distinguish between the proof of isolated acts and of habit; the fact that the evidence amounted to no more than the former may have accounted for its exclusion in *Manenti v Melbourne Tramways* [1954] VLR 115.

[359] [1916] 1 KB 849, 854.   [360] *Plomp v R* (1963) 110 CLR 234.

[361] *R v Grant* (1865) 4 F & F 322.

suspected.'[362] So far as lack of motive is concerned, 'there is a great difference between absence of proved motive and proved absence of motive'.[363]

Facts, such as the purchase of poison by someone who is accused of murder,[364] which suggest the existence of a plan or design, or preparation for a given course of action, may always be proved, and this evidence is of considerable weight because it calls for an explanation of his conduct from the person against whom it is given. When it consists of declarations of an intention to act in a particular way, the hearsay rule has to be borne in mind. If the declarations are made by a party, they may often be brought within the category of admissions and received in criminal proceedings under a well-recognized exception embodied in s 76 of the Police and Criminal Evidence Act 1984, and in civil proceedings by virtue of s 1 of the Civil Evidence Act 1995. Even if the declarations are not those of a party, they are admissible in civil cases under the Act of 1995, and perhaps now in criminal cases under an exception to the hearsay rule in the Criminal Justice Act 2003. Relevance and weight nevertheless remain highly contestable.

Knowledge or capacity

Facts that tend to prove or negative a person's capacity to do an act into which the court is inquiring may be highly relevant. Thus, the accused's knowledge of the effects of certain drugs, his skill in their application, and his ability to procure them, would be admissible evidence at his trial for murder by means of their use, and the absence of any of these factors would likewise be admissible on his behalf.[365] An unusual decision relating to the knowledge of the accused occurred in *R v Potamitis*,[366] in which the accused was charged with an elaborate fraud to which his defence was that, although he was the person to whom the money was passed, he had been acting as the innocent dupe of a third-party fraudster. It transpired that all of the detail of the fraud had previously occurred in crimes for which the accused's cousin had been convicted, whom the accused had subsequently visited in prison. Despite the apparent relevance of such evidence, it was excluded, it is submitted wrongly, because of the danger of inference of guilt by association.

Concomitant evidence

The general argument for the reception of evidence of this type is that circumstances existing contemporaneously with the transaction into which the court is inquiring render the facts alleged by one or other of the parties more or less probable. It is best illustrated by what is usually described as evidence of opportunity, but reference will also be made to the reception of res gestae, the general question of the use of standards of comparison, and use of samples.

Opportunity

The presence of the accused at the time and place of an alleged crime is something that must be proved by the prosecution on practically every criminal charge, and the

---

[362] Best *Principles of the Law of Evidence* (12th edn) 384.
[363] Channell J in *R v Ellwood* (1908) 1 Cr App Rep 181, 182.   [364] *R v Palmer* (1856) 5 E&B 1024.
[365] In the United States, such knowledge is often subsumed under a broadened category of opportunity: see *United States v Green* 648 F 2d 587 (1981), 592.
[366] [1994] Crim LR 434.

establishment of an alibi[367] is conclusive in favour of innocence.[368] Any evidence that tends to prove either of the above facts is therefore admissible, and, if the defence consists of an allegation that other named persons committed the crime, their alibis in turn become relevant and admissible as part of the case for the prosecution.[369] It is, however, regarded as too remotely relevant that such persons advance a false alibi.[370] Because of the difficulties that an alibi defence sprung for the first time at the trial could create, special rules providing for advance notice were devised.[371] Section 6A(2) of the Criminal Procedure and Investigations Act 1996 now[372] requires advance disclosure of the names and addresses of alibi witnesses if known and, if not, any information in the possession of the defence that might help to find them.[373]

If a false alibi is tendered,[374] the judge should direct the jury in accordance with the standard Judicial Studies Board terms,[375] which stress that a false alibi may be advanced in support of a true defence.

Opportunity is often an important feature when adultery is alleged. In *Woolf v Woolf*,[376] the Court of Appeal decided that the fact that a couple occupied the same bedroom must be treated as clear evidence of adultery in all but the most unusual circumstances. There is, however, no irrebuttable presumption of law to this effect, even if the evidence of opportunity is accompanied by evidence of inclination arising from the previous association of the parties.[377]

Res gestae

A fact may be relevant to a fact in issue because it throws light on it by reason of proximity in time, place, or circumstance. This is frequently expressed by the statement that the relevant fact is part of the res gestae, although it is difficult not to sympathize with Sir Frederick Pollock when he described this as an unmeaning term that 'merely fudges the truth that there is no universal formula for all the kinds of relevancy'.[378] The doctrine is

---

[367]   An unsupported denial of presence at the scene of the crime does not amount to an alibi: *R v Mussell and Dalton* [1995] Crim LR 887. See also Criminal Procedure and Investigations Act 1996, s 5(8).

[368]   On the whole subject, see Gooderson *Alibi*. The fact that the defence of alibi is raised does not mean that a judge should never leave some other defence, such as self-defence, to the jury: *R v Bonnick* (1977) 66 Cr App Rep 266.

[369]   *R v Dytche* (1890) 17 Cox CC 39.   [370]   *R v Steel* as reported in (1981) 73 Cr App Rep 173, 186.

[371]   First by the Criminal Justice Act 1967, s 11.

[372]   Inserted by s 33(2) of the Criminal Justice Act 2003.

[373]   Whether or not the prosecution should be permitted to put in an alibi notice as part of its case will depend upon the circumstances: see *R v Rossborough* (1985) 81 Cr App Rep 139. See also Tosswill [1978] *Crim LR* 276; and in Australia, *R v Hunt* (1994) 76 ACR 363.

[374]   In Canada, it has been said that the prosecution should be slow to tender evidence that an alibi is false on account of the prejudice that is likely to arise from the mere suggestion of concoction: *R v Campbell* (1999) 139 CCC (3d) 258.

[375]   In cases where an alibi is controverted, the judge must avoid leaving the impression that he regards it as false just because he has given such a direction: *R v McPherson* [2001] EWCA Crim 2019. See also, in Canada, *R v Hibbert* [2002] SCC 59, [2002] 2 SCR 445, where it should not be glossed by reference to consciousness of guilt or of fault, *R v Babinski* (2005) 193 CCC (3d) 172.

[376]   [1931] P 134; but see *Ross v Ross* [1930] AC 1, as applied in *Webster v Webster* [1945] NZLR 537.

[377]   *England v England* [1953] P 16, [1952] 2 All ER 784.

[378]   Pollock-Holmes *Correspondence* vol 2, 285. Lord Tomlin suspected it of being 'A phrase adopted to provide a respectable legal cloak for a variety of cases to which no formula of precision can be applied' (*Homes v Newman* [1931] 2 Ch 112, 120); 'If you wish to tender inadmissible evidence, say it is part of the

mainly concerned with the admissibility of statements made contemporaneously with the occurrence of some act or event into which the court is inquiring.[379] The relevant degree of contemporaneity may depend upon the particular issues raised by the parties. Thus in *Ratten v R*,[380] it was the 15-minute period during which the deceased must have been shot, within which the accused denied that the telephone call in question had been made.[381]

Standards of comparison

Whenever it is necessary to determine whether someone's conduct complies with some objective standard, as where negligence is alleged, evidence is admissible to show how others might be expected to behave in similar circumstances. This may comprise evidence of moral standards or of professional practice. Thus, in *Fraser v Thames Television Ltd*,[382] witnesses were allowed to testify that they would never use ideas for programmes without the consent of their originators. Similarly, in *G & K Ladenbau (UK) Ltd v Crawley and de Reya*,[383] a number of solicitors testified to their individual practice in conducting searches of registers during the course of conveyancing transactions. In *Banque Keyser Ullmann SA v Skandia (UK) Insurance Co Ltd*,[384] the evidence related to the practice common in the London insurance market when an underwriter learned of deception practised by a broker upon his principal. Where the practice of a particular branch of a trade is in question, evidence may be tendered of the practice in closely related branches.[385]

No special rules apply to such cases beyond those that require the evidence tendered to be more than remotely relevant to the issue, and unlikely to raise a number of collateral questions. It is, however, essential that the point in dispute should concern some matter as to which the argument from analogous situations to the situation under inquiry is likely to be of real assistance to the court.

Samples

It is common practice in other situations, for example financial auditing, where facts need to be established, to take samples from which inferences are drawn to facts relating to the whole from which the samples were taken.[386] It is rare to find explicit examples of this in the law of evidence,[387] although it is intrinsic in the means of establishing identity by reference to fingerprints or the use of DNA. In view of the complexity of some cases, and the

---

res gestae' (Lord Blackburn). Stone spoke of the law as to res gestae as 'the lurking place of a motley crowd of conceptions in mutual conflict and reciprocating chaos' (55 LQR 66).

[379] See further, 569. [380] [1972] AC 378.

[381] Although in *Teper v R* [1952] AC 480, it might be thought that insufficient attention was paid to the fact that the accused's alibi was inconsistent not only with his presence on the scene at the time of setting the fire, but also with his presence there at the time at which the utterance in question was made.

[382] [1984] QB 44, [1983] 2 All ER 101. [383] [1978] 1 All ER 682, [1978] 1 WLR 266.

[384] [1990] 1 QB 665, [1987] 2 All ER 923, expressly approving the statement in *Cross*.

[385] *Noble v Kennoway* (1780) 2 Doug KB 510 (practice in Labrador trade to prove practice in Newfoundland trade); *Fleet v Murton* (1871) LR 7 QB 126 (practice in colonial fruit trade to prove practice in London fruit trade).

[386] Such a technique is sometimes regulated by explicit legal provision as in Sale of Goods Act 1979, s 15.

[387] But see *Carnegie v Findlay* 2000 SCCR 873, in which, despite only testing three packages from twelve apparently identical ones, guilt was established for an offence depending upon more than three of the packages containing the relevant substance.

proliferation of documents, it is apprehended that more attention will in future need to be
devoted to the development of rules to govern such practices.

Retrospectant evidence

In general

In its most general form, the argument for the reception of this kind of evidence is the converse of that which demonstrates the relevance of prospectant evidence: the subsequent
occurrence of an act, state of mind, or state of affairs justifies an inference that the act was
done, or the state of mind or affairs existed, in the past. Thus, a driver's excessive speed
may be proved to support the conclusion that he was going too fast a short distance further
back.[388] A classic and simple example is provided by *Gumbley v Cunningham*,[389] in which
the House of Lords permitted an inference to be drawn from the proportion of alcohol
in the accused's blood some four hours after an accident to what it must have been at the
time of the accident, given the normal rate of elimination. A person's anterior intention
may also be proved by his subsequent acts, although this general principle of relevancy has
often had to give way to precedent, based on the dread of manufactured evidence, as in
advancement cases.[390]

Similarly, the court may be invited to infer that an event occurred from events that followed it in the ordinary course of business, as when an indorsed cheque is produced by
the drawer to show that a payment was made.[391] Employees usually claim arrears of pay
shortly after their employer has defaulted, so failure to make such a claim is some evidence
that none was due.[392] Quite apart from any question of the course of business, delay in
taking action may always have to be explained in order to prevent the conclusion that the
circumstances of which complaint is ultimately made did not justify such action.[393]

Omnia praesumuntur rite esse acta

Proof that someone acted as holder of a public office is evidence of his title to do so.[394] On
a charge of assaulting a police officer in the course of his duty, formal proof of his appointment is not essential, as evidence that he acted as a police officer will suffice.[395] Similarly,
if a solicitor claims damages for words spoken of him in the way of his profession, it is
unnecessary for him to produce his practising certificate, or an extract from the roll of
solicitors, provided there is evidence that he acted as a solicitor.[396] The principle applies
to corporations, so proof that a company has acted as such is evidence that it was duly
incorporated.[397] As has been truly said, 'The wheels of business will not go round unless it
is assumed that that is in order which appears to be in order.'[398] Much trouble and expense

---

[388] *R v Dalloz* (1908) 1 Cr App Rep 258; cf *Beresford v St Albans Justices* (n349).

[389] [1989] AC 281, [1989] 1 All ER 5.   [390] See *Warren v Gurney* [1944] 2 All ER 472, 473.

[391] *Egg v Barnett* (1800) 3 Esp 196.

[392] *Sellen v Norman* (1829) 4 C & P 80. But see *Bogdal v Hall* (n356), in which failure to complain of non-
receipt of social security cheques was not accepted as proof of their receipt.

[393] This theory underlay the law relating to complaints by those alleging rape.

[394] For a full citation of authorities, see Phipson *Law of Evidence* (17th edn) [6.29].

[395] *R v Gordon* (1789) 1 Leach 515.

[396] *Berryman v Wise* (1791) 4 Term Rep 366. See now Solicitors Act 1974, s 18 and s 63, rendering authorized Law Society lists admissible evidence.

[397] *R v Langton* (1876) 2 QBD 296. For companies incorporated under the Companies Act 2006,
see s 15(4).   [398] Lord Simonds in *Morris v Kanssen* [1946] AC 459, [1946] 1 All ER 475; 586, 592.

is saved when the courts act on this assumption. The maxim *omnia praesumuntur rite esse acta* must, however, be used with care in criminal cases. It cannot be relied upon to prove the existence of facts central to an offence.[399] Nor should it be relied upon to presume a fact contrary to the liberty of the subject, such as that a prisoner is being held in lawful custody.[400] The presumption cannot be invoked to support the conclusion that a breathalyser was approved by the Secretary of State in accordance with statutory requirements from the mere fact that an instrument of that type was issued to the police.[401]

Those who are concerned to establish that things were done in the right order in the absence of affirmative evidence to that effect may be able to rely on an extension of the principle *ut res magis valeat quam pereat* even when it is clear that the maxim *omnia praesumuntur rite esse acta* is inapplicable because the evidence shows that at least one act was performed prematurely. Thus, in *Eaglehill Ltd v J Needham (Builders) Ltd*,[402] a notice of dishonour of a bill of exchange that plainly could not be met because it was drawn on a company which had since gone into liquidation was mistakenly posted on 30 December, the day before, instead of the day after, the bill was presented. The notice was received on 31 December and it was presumed that the bill had already been dishonoured on that day because, if two acts are done, one of which ought to be done after the other, it is presumed that they were done in the right order.[403]

Mechanical instruments

The same factors justify the presumption that mechanical instruments were in order when they were used. In the absence of evidence to the contrary, the courts will presume that stopwatches, speedometers,[404] traffic lights,[405] and approved breathalysers[406] were in order at the material time.[407] The court will be reluctant to limit the range of evidence admissible to challenge the reliability of such an instrument in the absence of clear statutory authority to do so.[408] Although in *Castle v Cross*[409] the court omitted the qualification that the instrument must be one of a kind as to which it is common knowledge that they

---

[399] *Scott v Baker* [1969] 1 QB 659, [1968] 2 All ER 993; *Dillon v R* [1982] AC 484, [1982] 1 All ER 1017. But see, in Australia, *Cassell v R* [2000] HCA 8, (2000) 201 CLR 189, in which the majority of the High Court was prepared to presume the validity of a session of a government commission when the accused was charged with providing false evidence to the commission.   [400] *Dillon v R* (n399).

[401] *Scott v Baker*(n399), although there were then so many cases that formal proof of approval of that device was no longer required: *R v Jones* [1969] 3 All ER 1559, [1970] 1 WLR 16.

[402] [1973] AC 992, [1972] 3 All ER 895.

[403] In *Cooper v Chief Comr of Land Tax* (1988) 12 NSWLR 660, this was restricted to cases where the order of events was necessary to the efficacy of the acts.

[404] *Nicholas v Penny* [1950] 2 KB 466, [1950] 2 All ER 89; *Skalde v Evans* [1966] SASR 176; *Re Appeal of White* (1987) 9 NSWLR 427; *R v Amyot* [1968] 2 OR 626.

[405] *Tingle Jacobs & Co v Kennedy* [1964] 1 All ER 888n, [1964] 1 WLR 638n. See also *S v Lund* 1987 (4) SA 548.   [406] *R v Skinner* [2004] EWHC 2914 (Admin), [2005] RTR 17.

[407] Presumptions of correct setting and calibration are preserved by the Criminal Justice Act 2003, s 129(2).

[408] *Cracknell v Willis* [1988] AC 450, [1987] 3 All ER 801, overruling *Hughes v McConnell* [1986] 1 All ER 268, [1985] RTR 244 (although it may be reluctant to permit evidence to attack the approval of a class of device where that is required: *DPP v Memery* [2002] EWHC 1720 (Admin, [2003] RTR 249)). Conversely, the court will allow oral evidence as to the correct operation of a machine to compensate for a technical failure to comply with the statutory procedure for putting an automatic printout into evidence: *Greenaway v DPP* [1994] RTR 17.

[409] [1985] 1 All ER 87, [1984] 1 WLR 1372.

are more often than not in working order, it is submitted that some such qualification is necessary. As Lord Griffiths observed in *Cracknell v Willis*,[410] 'trial by machine' is an entirely novel concept and should be introduced with a degree of caution. Such caution is accorded by not applying this presumption to instruments in respect of which there is no common knowledge that they are more often than not in working order. If there is no such knowledge, evidence should be adduced,[411] though in the case of commonly used instruments, it may come from a regular operator, not necessarily from a technical expert,[412] and is not required if the output of the machine is not itself put in evidence.[413]

Possession as evidence of ownership

A further rebuttable presumption of law is that of lawful origin. It lies at the root of the substantive law of acquisitive prescription:[414]

Modern possession and user, being prima facie evidence of property and right, the judges attached to them an artificial weight, and held that uninterrupted, uncontradicted, and unexplained, they constituted proof from which a jury ought to infer a prescriptive right, coeval with the time of legal memory.

Quite apart from any question of prescriptive right, possession is always treated as prima facie evidence of ownership of real,[415] or personal,[416] property. As Wills put it in a well-known passage:[417]

The acts of enjoyment from which the ownership of real property may be inferred, are very various, as for instance, the cutting of timber, the repairing of fences or banks, the perambulation of boundaries of a manor or parish, the taking of a wreck on the foreshore, and the granting to others of licences or leases under which possession is taken and held; also the receipt of rents from tenants of the property; for all these acts are fractions of that sum total of enjoyment which characterises dominium.

Silence: failure to explain, to give evidence, or to call a witness.[418]

General considerations. As a matter of everyday lay reasoning, the evidence against a man may be greatly strengthened by his failure to give a prompt explanation of conduct proved or alleged against him, or by the inadequacy of his explanation; those negative facts can therefore be regarded as a species of retrospectant evidence. A belated explanation may be

---

[410] 459, 806.

[411] As formerly required in the case of computers, affirmed in *R v Shephard* [1993] AC 380, [1993] 1 All ER 225, 386, 230. See also *Leonard v Newell* [1983] Tas R 78 (requirement of expert evidence of operation of local radar); *Chiou Yaou Fa v Morris* (1987) 46 NTR 1 (requirement of expert evidence of operation of satellite navigation system); *State Insurance Comr v Whyatt* (1984) 37 SASR 454 (breathalyser not sufficiently reliable).   [412] *R v Shephard* (n411).

[413] *Prince v DPP* [1996] Crim LR 343 (breathalyser output used as justification for securing blood test).

[414] Best *Principles of the Law of Evidence* (12th edn) 322.

[415] *Doe d Graham v Penfold* (1838) 8 C & P 536.   [416] *Robertson v French* (1803) 4 East 130.

[417] *Law of Evidence* (3rd edn) 62.

[418] Heydon (1974) 1 Monash ULR 53. The diversity of situations compendiously lumped together under the rubric 'the right to silence' was emphasized by Lord Mustill in *R v Director of Serious Fraud Office, ex p Smith* [1993] AC 1, 30, 31, 463, 464, who distinguished no fewer than six. It does not apply in its compendious form in civil proceedings: Megaw LJ in *Jefferson Ltd v Bletcha* [1979] 1 WLR 898, 904; not even when they arise from the same facts as criminal: *Re Priority Stainless (UK) Ltd, Secretary of State for Trade and Industry v Crane and Burton* [2001] 2 BCLC 222, [9](i).

suspicious, first, because delay in giving it may have been due to the fact that it had to be contrived, and second, because it may have impeded its investigation.

However, people react to charges in different ways so all inferences from silence should be cautious. The silent party may have been confused or surprised; he may have considered the allegation to be unworthy of an answer; or he may have wished to conceal matters concerning himself or others that are irrelevant to the case before the court. He may also have wished to have legal advice about speaking, or if he has received legal advice not to speak, to act upon it. This suggests that, before a person's silence is taken to count against him, the circumstances must have been such that an explanation was called for, and there must have been no apparent reason, apart from a consciousness of guilt, for its absence.[419]

Such conflicting considerations have cause particular concern in criminal proceedings, and have led to the development of special rules in relation to police investigation, including the necessity to explain the nature of the offence under investigation, and to give a warning of the effects of the suspect's response or lack of it. Such warnings may then themselves have second-order effects in determining the inferences to be drawn from silence after they have been given.[420]

It is proposed here to consider first the inferences that may be drawn in civil proceedings, where there has been less direct statutory intervention than in criminal, distinguishing failure to explain from failure to testify or to call witnesses at trial. The position in criminal proceedings will then be considered, taking into account the greater degree of statutory intervention,[421] and distinguishing similarly between different sorts of failure.

Civil proceedings: failure to explain

A thin stream of civil cases adhered to the proposition that failure to answer an allegation is capable of amounting to evidence against the silent party.[422] If two cars are involved in a collision, and a passenger in one of them claims damages from both drivers, it has been said that 'proof of the collision is held to be sufficient to call on the two defendants for an answer'.[423] The principle underlying the cases in which reliance has been placed on

---

[419] See *Weissensteiner v R* (1993) 178 CLR 217, where the High Court of Australia analysed similar factors in relation to the failure of the accused to testify; now somewhat qualified in the later case of *RPS v R* [2000] HCA 3, (2000) 199 CLR 620. See also the full explanation of the reasons for reluctance to draw inferences from the accused's failure to testify, or to call witnesses, in *Dyers v R* [2002] HCA 45, (2000) 210 CLR 285.

[420] See *Bruce v R* (1987) 74 ALR 219, in which the High Court of Australia pointed out that an explanation could have been given before the accused was cautioned; but see also *R v McCarthy* [1992] 2 NZLR 550 explaining that the accused may often be in a similar position, even though not yet formally cautioned.

[421] Though full consideration of the most important provisions is postponed until later chapters.

[422] *Hayslep v Gymer* (1834) 1 Ad & El 162 (failure to deny claim of gift); *Bessela v Stern* (1877) 2 CPD 265 (failure to deny oral claim of promise to marry). Failure to answer isolated letters is less likely to have the same effect: *Wiedemann v Walpole* [1891] 2 QB 534 (letter alleging promise of marriage); *Thomas v Jones* [1921] 1 KB 22 (letter alleging paternity); *Great Future International Ltd v Sealand Housing Corp* [2004] EWHC 124 (Ch), [30].

[423] *Baker v Market Harborough Industrial Co-operative Society* [1953] 1 WLR 1472, 1476, Denning LJ. See also *Bray v Palmer* [1953] 2 All ER 1449, [1953] 1 WLR 1455 and *France v Parkinson* [1954] 1 All ER 739, [1954] 1 WLR 581. The effect of these decisions is that if two cars are in collision on crossroads of equal status, and there is no further evidence, the correct inference is that both parties were negligent. *Hummerstone v Leary* [1921] 2 KB 664 is a decision to the same effect; but it was pointed out in *Nesterczuk v Mortimore* (1965) 115 CLR 140 that all these decisions are explicable on narrower grounds and the High Court of Australia held that the trial judge had rightly dismissed both claim and counterclaim where one of the two cars involved in a collision must have swerved and there was no evidence which one. An inference of joint negligence

the maxim *res ipsa loquitur* is based on the importance of the absence of an explanation. In *Ellor v Selfridge & Co* the claimants were hit by a van that mounted the pavement, and Scrutton LJ said:[424]

The fact that in the present case the van appeared upon the pavement, where it had no business to be, and injured the plaintiffs on the pavement, and the further fact that the defendants offered no explanation why their van was there seems to be more consistent with negligence than with the exercise of reasonable care.

In cases of racial discrimination, it is rarely possible to prove more than discrimination and difference of race; if this is done, then in the absence of any credible explanation, it is permissible to infer that the discrimination was made upon racial grounds.[425]

Civil proceedings: failure to testify[426]

In *McQueen v Great Western Rly Co*,[427] the claimant claimed that his goods had been lost owing to the crime of one of the defendant's servants. All he could prove was that the goods were delivered to the company, and placed on a truck in a siding to which the public had access, after which they disappeared. The defendant's failure to explain the loss was held not to make the plaintiff's evidence sufficient to sustain his case. As Cockburn CJ said:[428]

If a prima facie case is made out, capable of being displaced, and if the party against whom it is established might by calling particular witnesses and producing particular evidence displace that prima facie case, and he omits to adduce that evidence, then the inference fairly arises, as a matter of inference for the jury and not a matter of legal presumption, that the absence of that evidence is to be accounted for by the fact that even if it were adduced it would not displace the prima facie case. But that always presupposes that a prima facie case has been established; and unless we can see our way clearly to the conclusion that a prima facie case has been established, the omission to call witnesses who might have been called on the part of the defendant amounts to nothing.

Very soon after the parties were enabled to testify in most civil cases by the Evidence Act 1851, Alderson B recognized that the failure of one of them to deny a fact that it is in his power to deny 'gives colour to the evidence against him'.[429] Parties were made compellable as well as competent by that legislation, and it might have been argued that, in those

---

may not be justified where the collision was not head-on but between rear portions of two vehicles: *Wotta v Haliburton Oil Well Cementing Co Ltd* [1955] 2 DLR 785.

[424] (1930) 46 TLR 236.

[425] See *North West Thames Regional Health Authority v Noone* [1988] ICR 813.

[426] Failure to adduce real evidence is analogous. In the case of its destruction by the prosecution, it may be possible to stay for abuse of process, see Epp (1999) 3 E & P 165. Destruction before the commencement of civil proceedings may lead to striking out only if it amounts to an attempt to pervert the course of justice: *Douglas v Hello! Ltd* [2003] EWHC 55 (Ch), [2003] 1 All ER 1087 (note), [2003] EMLR 601, [86], endorsing *British and America Tobacco Australia Services Ltd v Cowell and McCabe* [2002] VSCA 197 [195], [197]; if the destruction takes place after the commencement of proceedings, then the claim may be struck out only if such destruction would prevent the possibility of a fair trial on the relevant issues, ibid [99].

[427] (1875) LR 10 QB 569.

[428] 574. See also *Hughes v Liverpool City Council* (1988) The Times, 30 March; *Wisniewski v Central Manchester Health Authority*, [1998] PIQR P324, [1998] LlR Med 223.

[429] *Boyle v Wiseman* (1855) 10 Exch 647, 651. Adverse inference may be made even more readily when a party walks out of the hearing so as not to testify: *Gayle v Gayle* [2001] EWCA Civ 1910, [13]. Failure to attend at all is the most extreme case, but may be explicable: see *Re Abiola* [2004] EWHC 709 (Ch).

circumstances, it was incumbent on a party to call his opponent, rather than to rely on inferences from his silence; in *Halford v Brookes*,[430] it was argued that the effect was rather to make it clear that a party to civil proceedings enjoyed no right of silence, and that inferences could be drawn even more readily in civil proceedings. The strength of such inference was examined by the House of Lords in *R v IRC, ex p TC Coombs & Co*:[431]

In our legal system generally, the silence of one party in face of the other party's evidence may convert that evidence into proof in relation to matters which are, or are likely to be, within the knowledge of the silent party and about which that party could be expected to give evidence. Thus, depending on the circumstances, a prima facie case may become a strong or even an overwhelming case. But, if the silent party's failure to give evidence (or to give the necessary evidence) can be credibly explained, even if not entirely justified, the effect of his silence in favour of the other party may be either reduced or nullified.

This makes it clear, first, that a prima facie case must be established;[432] second, that it applies to partial as well as total failure to testify; and third, that the inference may be rebutted by a plausible explanation for silence.[433] The effect can be to convert a prima facie case into proof of even the most serious matter, such as murder[434] or equitable fraud,[435] or one having very serious consequences, such as a child being taken into care.[436] Refusal to attend for cross-examination on an affidavit may also ground an adverse inference, and reduce the weight to be attached to the affidavit.[437]

Adverse inferences may be drawn, as when a party to a civil case fails to call a witness who might have been expected to give evidence favourable to him,[438] and a joint judgment delivered in the Supreme Court of Victoria on an appeal in a civil case tried with a jury would probably be approved here too:[439]

[W]here a party without explanation fails to call as a witness a person whom he might reasonably be expected to call, if that person's evidence would be favourable to him, then, although the

---

[430] [1991] 3 All ER 559, [1991] 1 WLR 428, CA.

[431] [1991] 2 AC 283, [1991] 3 All ER 623; 300, 636. See also Privy Council in *Gibbs v Rea* [1998] AC 786.

[432] Cf the dissent of Dixon CJ in *Insurance Comr v Joyce* (1948) 77 CLR 39, 61. Much more attention has been paid to this question in Australia, where it is referred to as the rule in *Jones v Dunkel* (1959) 101 CLR 298, and appears to have survived non-reference to it in the Evidence Act (Cwth) 1995: see *Australian Securities Commission v AS Nominees* (1995) 133 ALR 1. In trial by judge alone, the judge should instruct himself explicitly: *Transport Industries Insurance Ltd v Longmuir* [1997] 1 VR 125, 143.

[433] In *Killick v Pountney* [2000] WTLR 41, the possibility of alternative explanations was sufficient to displace any adverse inference, and in *Re U* (n90), [31], counsel's advice.

[434] As in *Halford v Brookes* (n51), and *Francisco v Diedrick* (1998) The Times, 3 April.

[435] *Donovan Crawford v Financial Institutions Services Ltd* [2005] UKPC 40. In *Bastion Holdings Ltd v Jorril Financial Inc* [2007] UKPC 60 refusal to attend for judicially ordered cross-examination on such a matter amounted to contempt, and justified the judge in refusing to hear argument on the point.

[436] *Re O* (n90).

[437] *Comet Products UK Ltd v Hawkex Plastics Ltd* [1971] 2 QB 67, [1971] 1 All ER 1141; *Great Futures International Ltd v Sealand Housing Corp* (n422). In *Bastion Holdings Ltd v Jorril Financial Inc* [2007] UKPC 60 refusal to attend for judicially ordered cross-examination amounted to contempt, and justified the judge in refusing to hear argument on the point.

[438] This may be most necessary when the party failing to call the witness bears the onus of proving a negative: see, in Australia, *Sims v Celcast Pty Ltd* (1998) 71 SASR 142, 151. In *Buksh v Miles* (2008) 296 DLR (4th) 608 it was suggested that such inferences were over-claimed, and should be restricted to situations where the uncalled evidence would have been more favourable than that actually tendered.

[439] Newton and Norris JJ in *O'Donnell v Reichard* [1975] VR 916, 929. An adverse inference need not necessarily be drawn: *Flack v Chairperson, National Crime Authority* (1997) 150 ALR 153.

jury may not treat as evidence what they may as a matter of speculation think that that person would have said if he had been called as a witness, nevertheless it is open to the jury to infer that that person's evidence would not have helped the party's case; if the jury draw that inference, then they may properly take it into account *against the party in question* for two purposes, namely (a) in deciding whether to accept any particular evidence, which has in fact been given, either for or against that party, and which relates to a matter with respect to which the person not called as a witness could have spoken; and (b) in deciding whether to draw inferences of fact, which are open to them upon evidence which has been given, again with respect to matters to which the person not called as a witness could have spoken.

Criminal proceedings: failure to explain at common law

As long ago as 1820, Abbot CJ said:[440]

No person is to be required to explain or contradict until enough has been proved to warrant a reasonable and just conclusion against him, in the absence of explanation or contradiction; but when such proof has been given, and the nature of the case is such as to admit of explanation or contradiction if the conclusion to which the prima facie case tends to be true, and the accused offers no explanation or contradiction, can human reason do otherwise than adopt the conclusion to which the proof tends?

In those days, the accused was incompetent to give evidence on his own behalf, but the explanation might have been given by other witnesses, or it might have been advanced out of court.[441] Much depended upon the circumstances, and in particular whether denial of an accusation was to be expected.[442] If it was, then silence might be regarded as demeanour indicating acceptance of the charge.[443] Such an inference was much less eligible when the parties were not on equal terms, and especially in the case of police interrogation.[444] Arcane distinctions were drawn between the use of silence to indicate acceptance of an allegation,[445] directly to show consciousness of guilt,[446] to strengthen other prosecution evidence,[447] and to weaken other defence evidence.[448]

A particularly common situation arises when one suspected of handling is found in possession of recently stolen goods. If he fails to give a credible explanation of how he came by them, the jury is entitled to infer that he either stole them or handled them contrary to s 22 of the Theft Act 1968. The absence of an explanation is equally significant whether the case is being considered as one of theft or handling, but it is used more often in the latter. Where the only evidence on a charge of handling is that the defendant was in possession

---

440   *R v Burdett* (1820) 4 B & Ald 95, 120. See also *Purdie v Maxwell* [1960] NZLR 599; *Sanders v Hill* [1964] SASR 327; *R v Lepage* [1995] 1 SCR 654.

441   Although an English court would almost certainly agree with the decision of the Cape Provincial Court in *S v Kibido* 1988 (1) SA 802 that the failure of an unrepresented defendant to put his defence to particular witnesses in cross-examination should ground no adverse inference; and less certainly with the view expressed in Canada in *R v Raj* (2001) 157 CCC (3d) 572 criticizing the cross-examination of a represented accused about his failure to instruct his counsel to cross-examine on a particular matter.

442   See *R v Cramp* (1880) 14 Cox CC 390 (in which it was); *R v Mitchell* (1892) 17 Cox CC 503 (in which it was not).   443   *R v Christie* (n52).

444   *Hall v R* [1971] 1 All ER 322 (even though before caution); *R v Chandler* [1976] 3 All ER 105, [1976] 1 WLR 585 (in which the presence of the suspect's solicitor at a police interview was regarded as evening the terms).   445   As in *Parkes v R* [1976] 3 All ER 380, [1976] 1 WLR 1251.

446   As in *R v Ryan* (1964) 50 Cr App Rep 144, but see the criticism of this reasoning by the High Court of Australia in *Petty and Maiden v R* (1991) 173 CLR 95.   447   As in *R v Sullivan* (1966) 51 Cr App Rep 102.

448   As in *R v Gilbert* (1977) 66 Cr App Rep 237.

of stolen goods, a jury may infer guilty knowledge or belief (a) if he offers no explanation to account for his possession; or (b) if the jury are satisfied that the explanation he does offer is untrue. If, however, the explanation offered is one that leaves the jury in doubt as to whether he knew or believed the goods were stolen,[449] they should be directed that the case has not been proved.[450] What constitutes recent possession within the meaning of the above doctrine is a question of fact depending on the circumstances of the particular case,[451] but it must be emphasized that, even if no explanation is given by the handler, 'the jury are entitled, but not compelled to convict'.[452] In the absence of further incriminating circumstances, an inference is not warranted that someone in possession of goods obtained by means of blackmail or deception[453] knew of the unlawful obtaining, even if no explanation is forthcoming. On the other hand, the mere fact that a reasonable explanation is forthcoming does not mean that the jury must be directed to acquit.[454] The inference of guilty knowledge is warranted in the case of recently stolen goods because theft is by far the most common means of unlawful acquisition.[455] Now that theft and handling, unlike the former larceny and receiving, are not mutually exclusive offences because most handlers by receiving become thieves through a later appropriation, it is probably safer to convict of theft, where both offences are charged and the evidence justifies the conclusion that one or other of them was committed.[456]

Adverse comment may sometimes be made[457] of the accused's[458] failure to call witnesses, and it has been said that such a direction may now more readily be made after the passage of section 35,[459] and in cases where there are multiple defendants running cutthroat defences.[460] It may then be useful to remind the jury about the burden and standard of proof, and to discuss any judicial comment in advance with counsel.[461]

Criminal proceedings: the effect of statutory provision upon failure to explain

Where the law imposes a duty to provide an explanation, as in some statutory offences, the inference to be drawn from failure to reply may be strengthened.[462] As noted above, the

---

[449] Or that they were stolen at all: *R v Irwin* [1997] CLY 1110.

[450] *R v Aves* [1950] 2 All ER 330: this is the effect of *R v Schama; R v Abramovitch* (1914) 84 LJKB 396 (the leading case); see also *R v Garth* [1949] 1 All ER 773; *R v Raviraj* (1986) 85 Cr App Rep 93.

[451] *R v Marcus* (1923) 17 Cr App Rep 191. The circumstances of the receipt may be relied on as proof that the goods were stolen: *R v Sbarra* (1918) 87 LJKB 1003; *R v Fushillo* (1940) 27 Cr App Rep 193; *R v Guidice* [1964] WAR 128. The accused's demonstrably false testimony is evidence to the same effect: *R v Young* (1952) 36 Cr App Rep 200. The circumstance of statements by third parties that the goods were stolen, even though believed and acted upon by the accused, is inadmissible to show that the goods were in fact stolen, but it is admissible to show that the accused believed that they had been: *R v Hulbert* (1979) 69 Cr App Rep 243; *R v Korniak* (1983) 76 Cr App Rep 145. It might, in some circumstances, be very difficult to draw the inference against a particular one of several cohabiting parties: see *R v Myall* (1986) 43 SASR 258.

[452] Lord Goddard CJ in *R v Cohen* [1951] 1 KB 505, [1951] 1 All ER 203; 508, 206.

[453] Theft Act 1968, s 24(4).   [454] *R v Ately* (1985) 9 NSWLR 226.

[455] *DPP v Nieser* [1959] 1 QB 254, [1958] 3 All ER 662, where it was said that one way of supporting an inference that the accused knew of the unlawful obtaining would be to prove an association with the obtainer showing that they were in each other's confidence.

[456] *Stapylton v O'Callaghan* [1973] 2 All ER 782.

[457] Sometimes by the Judge but not counsel, *R v Whitton* [1998] Crim LR 492.

[458] Defence counsel may comment adversely on the failure of the prosecution to call a witness, see in Canada *R v Trakas* (2008) 233 CCC (3d) 172.   [459] *R v Shakeel Khan* [2001] EWCA Crim 486, [18].

[460] *R v Campbell* [2009] EWCA Crim 1076, [31].   [461] *R v Shakeel Khan* (n459), [19].

[462] *Secretary of State for the Environment, Transport and the Regions v Holt* [2000] RTR 309.

particular problems of alibis advanced for the first time at the trial was dealt with by statutory intervention, and more general recommendations allowing adverse inference from failure to mention when questioned matters later relied upon in evidence were made by the Criminal Law Revision Committee,[463] although its recommendations in this respect led to the jettisoning of the Committee's whole report at that time.

Nevertheless, the recommendations were ultimately accepted, and constitute the substance of s 34 of the Criminal Justice and Public Order Act 1994.[464] The Act also permits adverse inference from failure to explain ostensibly incriminating real evidence[465] or presence in a particular place.[466] In this way, statute has intervened to supplement common sense in the two common situations, of late excuses and late explanations. It should be noted that it also supplements,[467] rather than supplants, the common law, which may still be invoked in these situations.

Criminal cases: the effect of statutory provision upon failure to testify[468]

Bentham expressed a commonly held view in observing that 'Innocence claims the right of speaking as guilt invokes the privilege of silence.'[469] The problem could arise in relation to failure to testify only after the accused became a competent witness. The Criminal Evidence Act 1898 thus both permitted the accused to testify for himself generally in criminal cases,[470] and regulated permissible comment.[471]

The position in England[472] is largely[473] governed by s 35 of the Criminal Justice and Public Order Act 1994:

(1) At the trial of any person[474] for an offence, subsections (2) and (3) below apply unless—

    (a) the accused's guilt is not in issue; or

---

463 In its 11th report, *Evidence (General)* Cmnd 4991 (1973), paras 28–52.

464 Discussed in more detail below. Preceded in Northern Ireland by the Criminal Evidence (NI) Order 1988 (SI 1988/1987 (NI 20)); see Jackson [1991] *Crim LR* 404; (1993) 44 *NILQ* 103. See, generally, Pattenden (1998) 2 *E&P* 141; Mirfield *Silence, Confessions and Improperly Obtained Evidence* (1997) 238–81.

465 Section 36.   466 Section 37.

467 Criminal Justice and Public Order Act 1994, ss 34(5), 36(6), and 37(5).

468 There is here no explicit preservation of the pre-existing common law: see generally Pattenden (1997) 2 *E&P* 141. Similar considerations might apply to deliberate destruction of real evidence to prevent the proof of a claim: see, in Canada, *R v Bero* (2000) 151 CCC (3d) 545.   469 *Treatise on Evidence*, 241.

470 In those jurisdictions where there is still the right to make an unsworn statement, adverse comment may be made upon the choice to give evidence in such form: *Fox v R* [2002] UKPC 13, [2002] 2 AC 284. In *R v Hines* (2001) 154 CCC (3d) 158, it was decided that the prosecution could not cross-examine the accused about his refusal to testify in separate proceedings against others charged in connection with the same incident.

471 Section 1(b). For the position in Canada in the light of the Charter on failure to testify, see *R v Noble* [1997] 1 SCR 874, and on failure to call witnesses, *R v Dupuis* (1995) 98 CCC (3d) 496, *R v Carey* (1996) 113 CCC (3d) 74, and *R v S (G)* [1995] 2 SCR 411.

472 See in Scotland. *Larkin v HMA* [2005] HCJAC 28, 2005 SCCR 302; in Australia the High Court held in *CTM v R* [2008] HCA 25 that failure to testify prevented satisfaction of an evidential burden by the defence, even though the prosecution had itself tendered the accused's explanation in the video-recorded evidence of his police interview.

473 A residual power at common law allows gaps to be filled, exercised in *R v Reid and Rowe* [2006] EWCA 2900, [12] in relation to a refusal to undergo further cross-examination.

474 The original restriction to persons aged over 14 was removed by s 35 of the Crime and Disorder Act 1998.

(b) it appears to the court that the physical or mental condition of the accused makes it undesirable for him to give evidence;

but subsection (2) below does not apply if, at the conclusion of the evidence for the prosecution, his legal representative informs the court that he will give evidence or, where he is unrepresented, the court ascertains from him that he will give evidence.

(2) Where this subsection applies, the court shall, at the conclusion of the evidence for the prosecution, satisfy itself (in the case of proceedings on indictment, in the presence of the jury) that the accused is aware that the stage has been reached at which evidence can be given for the defence and that he can, if he wishes, give evidence, and that, if he chooses not to give evidence, or having been sworn, without good cause refuses to answer any question, it will be permissible for the court or jury to draw such inferences as appear proper from his failure to give evidence or his refusal, without good cause to answer any question.

(3) Where this subsection applies, the court or jury, in determining whether the accused is guilty of the offence charged, may draw such inferences as appear proper from the failure of the accused to give evidence or his refusal, without good cause, to answer any question.

(4) This section does not render the accused compellable to give evidence on his own behalf, and he shall accordingly not be guilty of contempt of court by reason of failure to do so.

(5) For the purposes of this section a person who, having been sworn, refuses to answer any question shall be taken to do so without good cause unless—

(a) he is entitled to refuse to answer the question by virtue of any enactment, whenever passed or made, or on the ground of privilege; or

(b) the court in the exercise of its general discretion excuses him from answering it.

The Court of Appeal set out to provide authoritative guidance on the general approach to the interpretation of this provision in *R v Cowan*.[475] It took a broad view of its application, and declined the invitation apply its provisions only in exceptional cases. In particular, it rejected argument that such a course should be adopted because the provisions effectively forced the accused to testify; *reversed* the onus of proof; and encroached upon legal professional privilege by requiring reasons for failure to testify,[476] which might involve the revelation of legal advice. It pointed out that the Act explicitly preserves the accused's right not to testify;[477] that s 38(3) provides that failure to testify is not alone to constitute a basis for conviction, but requires supplementation by other evidence, to which any adverse inference drawn under these provisions merely adds weight; and that nothing asked of counsel is a matter of confidence. These arguments seem somewhat formal, since it is accepted by the court that the whole aim of the Act is to bring pressure upon the accused to testify; that it is designed to ease proof of guilt when the accused fails to do so; and that, apart from the

---

[475] [1996] QB 373, [1995] 4 All ER 939.

[476] *Practice Note* [1995] 2 All ER 499, [1995] 1 WLR 657, [3] requires the judge to enquire whether or not the client has been advised of his position under the Act.

[477] Section 35(4), as noted above, by way of departure from the draft bill. In Northern Ireland, where the original form was enacted, the House of Lords has held that a witness called by the judge under the relevant provision and thereby made available for cross-examination did not 'fail to give evidence' for the purposes of drawing adverse inferences: *R v Bingham and Cooke* [1999] 1 WLR 598.

provisions of the Act, legal advice as to the tactics to be employed by the defence is at the very centre of the protection provided by legal professional privilege. The court apparently thought that some protection would be provided as a result of its view that not only the judge, but also the jury, would have to be satisfied that there was a case to answer, before any inference could be drawn from the accused's failure to testify.[478] But since that question can be answered by the jury only in the course of its final consideration of its verdict, this seems artificial, and unlikely to occur.[479] It has nevertheless been held to be fatal not to give such a direction.[480]

The only substantial exception now[481] recognized by the Act relates to those whose physical and mental condition appear to be such as to make it undesirable for them to testify. This provision too has been given a restrictive interpretation,[482] and in *R v Friend*[483] a person aged only 15 years, but with a mental age of 9, was held not to come within it. The court appeared to have been influenced by the protective measures nowadays employed to ease the ordeal of testifying, evidence of the accused's above-average performance on a suggestibility test, and his apparently cunning behaviour after the commission of the crime in an attempt to conceal or withhold incriminating evidence. The court seemed to come close to equating the operation of this exclusion with cases where the accused was unfit to plead. It was nevertheless prepared to concede a very wide discretion to the judge, upon the basis that:[484]

It cannot be said that he applied the wrong test if only because there is no right test. Indeed we do not consider it appropriate to spell out a test to be applied in such a situation.

The court took refuge from the obvious implication of unreviewable palm tree justice in its observation that only *proper* inferences could be drawn, and that any medical evidence adduced in support of the contention[485] that it was undesirable for any inference to be drawn could be relied upon for the purpose of determining what inference was proper.

It should be noted that even where so strict a view determines that an adverse inference is possible, the judge still retains overriding discretion to decline to direct the jury to draw it if the accused has good cause not to testify.[486] Here too, in *R v Cowan*, the court rejected any attempt to develop the notion of a good cause[487] in such a way as to cramp the exercise

---

[478] Although a statutory exception has been provided for a limited range of cases by s 6(2) of the Domestic Violence, Crime and Victims Act 2004.

[479] It would, in effect, require the jury to reason that with the inference from failure there was proof beyond reasonable doubt that the accused was guilty, but that without it there would not have been; and that it must thus pronounce a verdict of not guilty upon a person it believes beyond reasonable doubt to be guilty.   [480] In *R v El-Hannachi* [1998] 2 Cr App Rep 226; *R v Birchall*, [1999] Crim LR 311.

[481] Since the exception for those aged under 14 was removed by s 35 of the Crime and Disorder Act 1998.   [482] The risk of self-harm was held insufficient in *R v Tabbakh* [2009] EWCA Crim 464.

[483] [1997] 2 All ER 1011, [1997] 1 WLR 1433.

[484] 1020f, 1442H. Its only gloss is that: 'A physical condition might include the risk of an epileptic attack; a mental condition, a latent schizophrenia where the experience of giving evidence might trigger a florid state.' In *R v Lee* [1998] 6 CL 102, it was suggested that the fact that giving evidence might itself further impair the accused's mental state, or that he might be prone to embarrassing outbursts, might be relevant factors to consider.

[485] The judge need not raise the issue of his own motion and may decide it on a voir dire, but it does require a proper evidential basis: *R v A* [1997] Crim LR 883.   [486] Section 35(3).

[487] Note that s 35(5) otherwise limits the exception to statutory rule and privilege.

of the discretion. It was particularly scathing of the suggestion that an accused person with a long record would have good cause not to testify, arguing that to accept it would be to prefer those with records over those who had none. This does not seem to meet the point that the latter would have no incentive not to testify on this account. Of the other contentions raised, it did not dismiss out of hand suggestions that a weak prosecution case,[488] other evidence contradicting the prosecution case, a particular likelihood of the accused being an unimpressive witness,[489] an abnormal medical condition,[490] or fear, duress, or desire to protect others, could be taken into account, although it was not inclined to consider them expansively,[491] and in general[492] required an evidential basis[493] for considering them at all.

Since nothing appears to the contrary,[494] and s 1(b) of the Criminal Evidence Act 1898 has been repealed,[495] it may be assumed that comment, now including either a direction or an invocation to draw an adverse inference, will continue to be allowed to the judge and to counsel for a co-accused,[496] and now permitted also by counsel for the prosecution.

It should be noted that it is incumbent upon the judge to ensure that the accused understands the danger of adverse inference upon failure to testify,[497] and to direct the jury of its strength.[498] In *R v Cowan*, the Court of Appeal rehearsed,[499] and recommended, the specimen direction advised by the Judicial Studies Board.[500] In particular, it required the judge to tell the jury that the accused was entitled not to testify, that any adverse inference was not alone sufficient,[501] that the jury must itself determine that the prosecution had

[488] This does, however, seem to have been so dismissed by the Court of Appeal in *R v Byrne* (1995) LEXIS, 21 November.

[489] As being nervous, inarticulate, or generally unlikely to perform well.

[490] Falling short of the requirement of s 35(1)(b).

[491] Reiterated in *R v Napper* [1996] Crim LR 591 in rejecting an argument that, because the accused had been interviewed by the police soon after the events in relation to only one of eight incidents, it was a good reason not to testify that the accused's memory might not have been refreshed.

[492] 380E, 944d. *Cowan* does seem to recognize the possibility of exceptional cases without an evidential basis.

[493] Counsel's argument is not to be regarded as sufficient to raise them; see also *R v Charisma* [2009] EWCA Crim 2345, (2009) 173 JP 633.

[494] It is interesting, but probably not significant, that no explicit reference is made to direction or comment, but only to permissible inference by court or jury.

[495] See Sch XI. But not s 80(8) of the Police and Criminal Evidence Act 1984, which prohibits comment by the prosecution upon the failure of the accused's spouse to testify. It is unclear how this provision will apply if husband and wife are co-defendants. A lenient view seems now to be taken of such failure: see *R v Whitton* (n457); cf *R v Naudeer* [1984] 3 All ER 1036.

[496] For the permitted purport of any such comment in Australia see *R v Tran and To* [2006] SASC 276, 164 ACR 541; and in Canada, *R v Oliver and Morrison* (2005) 194 CCC (3d) 92.

[497] Section 35(2). Even if the accused has absconded during the trial: *R v Gough* [2001] EWCA Crim 2545, [2002] 2 Cr App Rep 121, [16] (although there the irregularity of erroneously giving such a direction was not held to be fatal in view of the strength of the prosecution case).

[498] *R v Paton* [2007] EWCA Crim 1572, where an appeal was allowed because *no* direction as to an adverse inference had been given.

[499] 380G, 944f.

[500] No self-direction is required by justices who refrain from drawing an adverse inference: *Radford v Kent County Council* (1998) 162 JP 697.

[501] Although the wording of the provision appears not to preclude a conviction based on a combination of pretrial silence and refusal to testify, it was said obiter in *R v Knight* [2003] EWCA Crim 1977, [2004] 1 WLR 340, [12], that adverse inference under s 35 precludes further adverse inference under s 34.

established a case to answer irrespective of failure to testify and, perhaps most importantly, that the jury must draw an adverse inference only if, after hearing all of the evidence, it concluded that 'the silence can only sensibly be attributed to the defendant's having no answer or none that would stand up to cross-examination'.[502] It is significant that in two of the three cases dealt with under *R v Cowan*, the appeal was allowed on account of failure to remind the jury of this last factor.[503] This formulation makes it quite clear that the adverse inference is as to the accused's guilt at large, and is in no way limited to disbelief of any particular defence. It was, however, held in *Murray v DPP* that, because of the complexity of issues in a criminal trial, it is necessary to consider the precise impact of the inference separately in respect of each of them in the light of the surrounding evidence.[504] Failure to testify has thus had an adverse effect on a challenge to evidence of identification,[505] an attempt to bolster the credibility of extra-testimonial statements,[506] and a defence based on lack of intent.[507] In *R v Becouarn*,[508] the House of Lords held it not to be unfair to direct the jury that it could draw an adverse inference if it considered the accused to have no answer to the prosecution case, or none that would stand up to cross-examination, even though an unrevealed subsidiary reason might be fear of exposing his criminal record. It rejected any suggestion of a direction, along the lines of that in relation to lies,[509] that there might be other reasons, as too vague, perhaps counterproductive,[510] and overprotective. The House enthusiastically adopted a 'tit-for-tat' rationale on the facts, on the basis that if the accused were going to allege his deliberate false identification by prosecution witnesses, then his own record should be revealed. As there noted,[511] this situation is perhaps less likely to arise now that the Criminal Justice Act 2003 has come into force, since there are now many other gateways to cross-examination of the accused on his record, although attack on another person's character remains among them.

It is not yet clear whether the position at common law that adverse comment could be made more than once without necessary impropriety[512] still applies.

It has long been common for the prosecution to put into evidence any transcripts of the accused's interviews with the police.[513] If the accused refrains from testifying in such a situation, the trial judge should direct the jury to consider the contents of such a transcript in its finding of fact.[514]

It is worth considering how far the current position is likely to be affected by the incorporation into English law of the provisions of the European Convention on Human

---

[502] This reflects Lord Mustill's words in *Murray v DPP* [1994] 1 WLR 1, 99 Cr App Rep 396.

[503] Although in each of them accompanied by another failure, different in each case.

[504] In *R v Cowan*, this view is supported by reference to the judgment of Kelly LJ in *R v McLernon* (1990) 10 NIJB 91, 102 in relation to the comparable provision in Northern Ireland. For general appraisal of the law in Northern Ireland, see Jackson [1995] Crim LR 587.   [505] *Elliott v DPP* [1996] CLY 1387.

[506] *R v Burnham* [1995] Crim LR 491.   [507] *R v Callender* [1998] Crim LR 337.

[508] [2005] UKHL 55, [2005] 4 All ER 673.   [509] See further, 266.

[510] By stimulating speculation by the jury of an even worse record or reason.   [511] [27].

[512] *R v Sparrow* [1973] 2 All ER 129, [1973] 1 WLR 488. But a sense of proportion is required, and appeals were allowed where the judge commented in *Waugh v R* [1950] AC 203 on the accused's failure to testify on nine separate occasions, and in *R v Berry* [1993] Crim LR 973 on no fewer than 12 occasions.

[513] Although the evidential basis for admissibility has never been fully explained. The current practice seems to be to serve a hearsay notice under the Criminal Justice Act 2003, which raises a hornet's nest of evidential problems.   [514] *R v Hampson* [2004] EWCA Crim 3100.

Rights.[515] Although these do not in terms endorse the right to silence, or a privilege against self-incrimination, it has nevertheless been proclaimed in *Murray v United Kingdom*:[516]

…that there can be no doubt that the right to remain silent under police questioning and the privilege against self-incrimination are internationally recognised standards which lie at the heart of the notion of a fair procedure under Article 6.

and that:

it is self-evident that it is incompatible with the immunities under consideration to base a conviction solely or mainly on the accused's silence or on a refusal to answer questions *or to give evidence himself.*

In that case, the court refused to condemn the Northern Ireland version of this legislation, largely upon the basis that the accused retained the right to refuse to testify, that the prosecution had to make out a prima facie case otherwise than upon silence, and that the justification for drawing the inferences was made in a reasoned opinion by an experienced judge, itself subject to review. It should also be noted that there was a very strong case against the accused, fully supported by direct oral testimony and convincing real evidence, of the commission of brutal terrorist offences.

It is far from obvious in a case where silence played a more prominent role,[517] or where a jury trial took place in which the jury's use of adverse inferences was as little susceptible of appeal as the judge's discretion to permit such inference under the abdication from control indicated by the dicta in *R v Friend*,[518] that the decision would remain unscathed. It may well prove to be the case that the introduction of the European Convention on Human Rights will necessitate some reshaping of this area of the law of evidence.

Criminal proceedings: the effect of lies

In *R v Nash*,[519] the appellant was charged with the murder of her child, whose body was found in a well. She had been seen near the well with the child, for whom she could not find a home, and she also told lies concerning the child's whereabouts. When affirming the conviction, Lord Coleridge CJ said 'the facts which are proved call for an explanation, and beyond the admittedly untrue statements, none was forthcoming'.[520] There the effect of silence as to the true explanation was magnified in its significance by the fact of advancing a false one. This important consideration was elaborated by Lord Devlin delivering the decision of the Privy Council in *Broadhurst v R*:[521]

There is a natural tendency for the jury to think that if an accused is lying, it must be because he is guilty, and accordingly to convict him without more ado. It is the duty of the judge to make it clear to them that this is not so. Save in one respect, a case in which an accused gives untruthful evidence is no different from one in which he gives no evidence at all. In either case the burden remains on the prosecution to prove the guilt of the accused. But if on the proved facts two

---

[515] See Munday [1996] Crim LR 370, upon which the editor has here relied.

[516] (1996) 22 EHRR 29, [60] (emphasis supplied), citing *Funke v France* (1993) 16 EHRR 297.

[517] For example, by operating in addition to more than one form of pretrial silence, perhaps cumulatively constituting a case to answer.

[518] [1997] 2 All ER 1011, [1997] 1 WLR 1433.

[519] (1911) 6 Cr App Rep 225.   [520] 228.

[521] [1964] AC 441, [1964] 1 All ER 111; 447, 119, 120.

inferences may be drawn about the accused's conduct or state of mind, his untruthfulness is a factor which the jury can properly take into account as strengthening the inference of guilt. What strength it adds depends, of course, on all the circumstances and especially on whether there are reasons other than guilt that might account for such untruthfulness.

This dictum appears to apply outside the area of evidential support[522] and identification,[523] and to permit, if not to require, some explicit direction as to the strength of any such inference in the light of the circumstances of the case.[524] One such circumstance may be that where the alternative charges are murder and manslaughter, the lies may be explicable by reference to either, and will thus be unhelpful in relation to a charge of murder.[525]

In many cases where the prosecution seeks to rely upon inferences from silence, lies may come into play either because the accused alleges that he had mentioned a relevant fact at an early stage, and the prosecution contends that the allegation is a lie,[526] or where the accused supplements or amends his initial account to accommodate subsequently established facts about which he had hitherto been silent, and it is alleged that the later account is a lie.[527] The latter situation does not require a specific direction, since it will be central to the issues in the case,[528] but the former may require a special direction that there are more reasons for lying than consciousness of guilt.[529]

Fingerprints, bodily samples, and tracker dogs[530]

Fingerprints[531] The matching of fingerprints can be very strong retrospectant circumstantial evidence, and convictions have long been upheld when there was no other evidence of identity.[532] Establishing a match is a matter for expert opinion,[533] although it is for the jury to decide whether or not to accept it.[534] Although there is now no binding rule as to the number of similarities required to suggest a match, the Court of Appeal has intimated that if there are fewer than eight the prosecution should not tender the evidence, and that the judge would be likely to use his discretion to exclude it.[535]

Subject to this point, it seems that no special rules apply to the admissibility of fingerprint evidence. In *Callis v Gunn*,[536] such evidence was held to be admissible even though the accused had not been cautioned when asked by a police officer for his prints. The procedure for taking fingerprints is governed by the Police and Criminal Evidence Act 1984.[537]

---

[522] Below, 239.   [523] Below, 713.

[524] *R v Bey* [1993] 3 All ER 253, [1994] 1 WLR 39; *R v Sharp* [1994] QB 261, [1993] 3 All ER 225; *R v Goodway* [1993] 4 All ER 894, 98 Cr App Rep 11. See also, in Australia, *R v Renzella* [1997] 2 VR 88.

[525] *R v Richens* [1993] 4 All ER 877, 98 Cr App Rep 43; *R v Taylor* [1998] Crim LR 822.

[526] *R v Robinson* [1996] Crim LR 417.   [527] *R v Hill* [1996] Crim LR 419.

[528] But even there it has, in Australia, been held to be fortified by failure to testify to explain the lie: *Murphy v R* (1994) 62 SASR 121.   [529] See the analysis in *R v Burge and Pegg* [1996] 1 Cr App Rep 163.

[530] For a case combining bodily samples and fingerprints, see *R v Smith* (1998) 71 SASR 543.

[531] See Campbell [1985] *Crim LR* 195. For a different approach to earprints see *R v Kempster* [2008] EWCA Crim 975.

[532] *R v Castleton* (1909) 3 Cr App Rep 74; cf *R v Court* (1960) 44 Cr App Rep 242 (fingerprints on car windscreen insufficient evidence of possession on receiving charge). See also, in Canada, *R v Lepage* (n440).

[533] *R v O'Callaghan* [1976] VR 676.

[534] In *R v Buisson* [1990] 2 NZLR 542, it was emphasized that such comparison could not be made by the jury alone.

[535] *R v Buckley* (1999) 163 JP 561, setting out the criteria relevant to the exercise of the discretion in this area.

[536] [1964] 1 QB 495, [1963] 3 All ER 677.   [537] As amended by Criminal Justice Act 2003, s 9.

Bodily samples

Scientific advance has supplemented the possibility of identification by fingerprints with newer methods. First, blood testing was employed to help determine paternity.[538] Although it gradually became more refined, this technique suffered from defects. It involved what some regarded as a peculiarly objectionable intrusion upon their bodily integrity,[539] and in most cases, it operated only negatively to rebut a purported identification. Its use in paternity cases was thus often controversial, since it might seem capable only of bastardizing, but not of legitimizing, a child. Nevertheless its usefulness was recognized, and its use regulated, by the Family Law Reform Act 1969.[540]

The situation has been transformed by the continuing[541] development of DNA testing of bodily samples.[542] This technique has the advantage that it can use any tissue carrying the relevant genetic code, that the sample need be neither large nor recent, and, most significantly of all, that it furnishes effectively[543] conclusive positive proof of identity, or of family relationship,[544] to such an extent that refusal of a test has supplanted the use of the presumption of legitimacy. It can be of great assistance to any innocent suspect,[545] especially as it has been held that failure to match is powerful evidence for the jury to consider.[546] On the other hand, it has the disadvantage that it is a complex matter to perform the test, and there are plenty of opportunities for errors of evaluation[547] and calculation,[548] although the technology[549] and systems for its use[550] are constantly improving. The

---

[538] See SI 2008/972 for the current regulations.

[539] See *S v S* [1972] AC 24, [1970] 3 All ER 107; and after the advent of DNA testing, *Re F(a minor)* [1993] Fam 314, [1993] 3 All ER 596. Cf *JPD v MG* [1991] IR 47.   [540] Sections 20–25.

[541] *R v Murrin* (1999) 181 DLR (4th) 320 (progress from nuclear to mitochondrial DNA); *R v Reed and Reed* [2009] EWCA Crim 2698 (definitive explanation of the use and limits of low copy number DNA, following doubt in Northern Ireland in *R v Hoey* (2007) NICC 49).

[542] An enormous literature has been created dealing with this problem: for comparatively recent accounts, see Redmayne [1998] *Crim LR* 437; Hunter, ibid, 478.

[543] Given the virtual certainty of there being some supporting non-statistical evidence, see *R v Doheny and Adams* [1997] 1 Cr App Rep 369, 373E.

[544] It is, however, for the trier of fact to make this determination, and not for the expert witness presenting the evidence, to express an opinion upon it: *R v Doheny and Adams* (n543), and see also in Australia, *R v Humphrey* (1999) SASC 67, 72 SASR 558. There are statutory restrictions on the use of samples taken for the purposes of criminal proceedings to determine paternity in civil proceedings, see *Lambeth LB v S,C,V and J* [2006] EWHC 326 (Fam), [2007] 1 FLR 152.

[545] Exculpatory significance may even be attached to the voluntary supply of samples to be tested: see *R v SCB* (1997) 119 CCC (3d) 530. There is, however, some danger that this may attempt to be exploited by those who are DNA-aware: see *R v Malkinson* [2006] EWCA Crim 1891, (2006) 150 SJLB 1288, [36].

[546] *R v Mitchell* [2004] EWCA Crim 1928, (2004) 101(29) LSG 29.

[547] For problems where the potential suspects all come from an unusual and isolated racial group, see Hunter [1998] *Crim LR* 478; for those where the purpose of the test has been misunderstood by the testers, see *Re F (Children) (DNA Evidence)* [2007] EWHC 3235 (Fam), [2008] 1 FLR 348.

[548] In Canada, a voir dire may be held to resolve such problems: *R v Johnston* (1992) 69 CCC (3d) 395. Its use was deprecated in Australia in *R v Jarrett* (1994) 62 SASR 443. Problems persist in some jurisdictions, see e.g. *Pringle v R* [2003] UKPC 9, [10]–[24].

[549] The use of short tandem repeats (STRs) has now enabled identification without even the potential to reveal any personal characteristics of the person identified, see Sinha (2001) 15 *Int Rev of Law and Computers* 73.

[550] See Squibb-Williams (2004) 154 NLJ 1693. Use is assisted by the ability to establish continuity of the evidence as the trial proceeds if objection is made on that ground: *R v Philips* [2004] EWC A Crim 2288, (2004) 148 SJLB 1033.

statistical significance of the evidence has proved difficult to explain to a jury,[551] and has been far from clarified by attempts to employ Bayesian analysis,[552] resulting in some disarray in the admission of such evidence.[553] The Family Law Reform Act 1969 has now been amended[554] to allow for the use of this new technique.[555] The new provisions permit tests to be ordered not only upon the application of the parties, but also by the court of its own motion. If the court's direction to submit to such a test is refused, s 23 permits the court to draw any inference from such refusal as seems proper in the circumstances.[556]

These provisions apply only to civil proceedings in which parentage is in issue, but there seems no reason why such tests should not be used with the consent of the parties in other civil, or in criminal, proceedings. The Royal Commission on Criminal Justice considered the question of DNA matching techniques, and recommended the reclassification as 'non-intimate' of samples taken by plucking hair[557] or by oral swabbing. It recommended also the retention of DNA records of those convicted of criminal offences for investigative processes, and of a wider group for the purposes of statistical matching.[558] Although it was never regarded as unfair in principle to use DNA gathered for one purpose to be used for another,[559] it was thought appropriate to put the procedure on a statutory basis. Some difficulty was experienced in the construction of the rules relating to the taking and destruction of such materials,[560] and a revised statutory basis has now been provided.[561] This too has attracted criticism,[562] partly on the basis of its discrimination between the retention of samples of those who have been suspected, charged, and then acquitted of criminal offences, and the absence of any power to take and retain samples from others who have never even been suspected. Such criticism involves the paradox that the elimination of the discrimination would be achieved completely only by the extension of powers to take and retain samples from the entire population, which some proponents of human rights might regard as an unacceptable intrusion into personal

---

[551] See *R v Deen* (1994) The Times, 10 January, in which the equation of the odds against an innocent person having the relevant string of DNA with the odds against the accused, who has the string, being innocent was described as the prosecutor's fallacy. In Australia, however, in *R v Berry* [2007] VSCA 202, 176 ACR 195 it was held to be within the competence of the jury to resolve conflicting expert evidence as to the significance of DNA evidence.

[552] In *R v Adams* [1996] 2 Cr App Rep 467, it was decisively rejected in favour of a direction in terms of the random occurrence ratio. For the position in Australia, see *R v Mitchell* (1997) 130 ACTR 48; in Canada, see *R v Legere* (1994) 95 CCC (3d) 139.

[553] It was accepted in *JPD v MG* (n539) and *Welch v HM Adv* 1986 JC 13; but rejected in *R v Tran* (1990) 50 ACR 233 and *R v Lucas* [1992] 2 VR 109.

[554] By s 23 of the Family Law Reform Act 1987, and by s 82(3) of the Child Support, Pensions and Social Security Act 2000. The relevant regulations have also been amended so as now to refer to 'scientific', rather than 'blood', tests: SI 2001/773. For the position in Scotland, see *Cameron v Carr* 1997 SCLR 1164, construing the relevant legislation.

[555] In *F v Child Support Agency* [1999] 2 FCR 385, an adverse inference from refusal of such a test together with hearsay evidence from the mother was enough to rebut the presumption of legitimacy.

[556] See James [2009] *Fam L* 147.

[557] Other than pubic hair. See also *R v Cooke* [1995] 1 Cr App Rep 318.

[558] Cm 2263 (1993) paras 2.25–2.38, recommendations 13, 14, and 19–21.

[559] *R v Kelt* [1994] 2 All ER 780, [1994] 1 WLR 765; see also, in Australia, *King v R* (1966) 16 WAR 540.

[560] See *R v Nathaniel* [1995] 2 Cr App Rep 565; *A-G's Reference (No 3 of 1999)* [2001] 2 AC 91, [2001] 1 All ER 577. For similar difficulty in Canada, see *R v RC* 2005 SCC 61 [2005] 3 SCR 99.

[561] Section 82 of the Criminal Justice and Police Act 2001, amending s 64 of the Police and Criminal Evidence Act 1984.

[562] Nuffield Council on Bioethics, *The Forensic Use of Bio-information: Ethical Issues* (2007).

privacy. It further seems to have motivated the European Court of Human Rights in *S and Marper v United Kingdom*.[563]

Tracker dogs[564]

If, after being taken to the scene of a crime, a dog picks up a scent and leads those in charge of him to the accused, a useful piece of retrospectant circumstantial evidence may have been brought into existence. Such evidence has been received in Scotland,[565] Northern Ireland,[566] New Zealand,[567] Canada,[568] and the United States,[569] but rejected in South Africa[570] and Mauritius.[571] Here the Court of Appeal also accepted the principle of admitting such evidence in *R v Pieterson and Holloway*.[572] In each such case, however, it is necessary to lay an adequate foundation by way of adducing sufficient evidence of the training, skills, and habits of the particular dog and its handler. Evidence or judicial notice of the fact that each human being has a different scent that is liable to be picked up by a well-trained dog might be desirable. The person giving such evidence must not express his opinion about what the dog was thinking at the material time.[573] It is also necessary to direct the jury to the special need for care,[574] given that the dog cannot be cross-examined.[575]

MEANS OF PROOF

Testimony

To revert to the principal items of judicial evidence, 'testimony' is the statement of a witness in court[576] offered as evidence of the truth of that which is stated. Many of the rules of evidence, such as those concerned with the oath, the competency of witnesses, and their cross-examination, are designed to ensure that testimony shall be as reliable as possible. There is a sense in which testimony is the only item of judicial evidence. A hearsay statement, if oral, has to be narrated to the court; if it is contained in a document, the document has usually, although not invariably, to be produced to the court and identified by a witness. The same is true of things.[577] In all of the above cases, however, testimony is used for a widely different purpose from that of inducing the court to accept the witness's direct

---

[563] Grand Chamber 4 December 2008, explicitly rejecting the contrary view of the House of Lords in *R (Marper) v Chief Constable of South Yorkshire* [2002] EWCA Civ 1275, [2003] 1 All ER 148.

[564] See McCormick [1985] *Crim LR* 202. In *Pierce v Minister of Community Welfare* (1987) 27 ACR 119, evidence derived from observation of the manipulation by a child of anatomically explicit dolls was analogized to that obtained from the observation of tracker dogs.   [565] *Paterson v Nixon* 1960 JC 42.

[566] *R v Montgomery* [1966] NI 120.

[567] *R v Lindsay* [1970] NZLR 1002; *R v McCartney* [1976] 1 NZLR 472.

[568] *R v Klymchuk* (2005) 203 CCC (3d) 341 (negative evidence).

[569] *Roberts v Maryland* 469 A 2d 442 (1983).   [570] *R v Trupedo* [1920] AD 58.

[571] *Dulip v R* [1990] Maur 149. I am indebted for this reference to Mr David Kell.

[572] [1995] 1 WLR 293, [1995] 2 Cr App Rep 11.   [573] *R v Te Whiu and Buckton* [1964] NZLR 748.

[574] *R v Benecke* [1999] NSWCCA 163, (1999) 106 ACR 282.

[575] Although absence of a formal warning may not be fatal to a conviction if the dog's reliability has been established, and the need for caution is implicit in other more general directions: *R v Sykes* [1997] Crim LR 752.   [576] Or through a video link.

[577] See *R v Forrester* [1985] 2 NZLR 85, in which the jury was not entitled to take into account real evidence that it discovered for itself in an exhibit handed to it in the course of a trial.

statement concerning a relevant fact, and that is why hearsay statements, documents, and things, although normally proved by a witness,[578] may properly be regarded as separate items of judicial evidence.

The general rule is that a witness can give evidence only of facts of which he has personal knowledge, something that he has perceived with one of his five senses. The only exception to the general rule is the expert witness testifying to matters calling for expertise. Parts of his testimony may be based on information derived from textbooks or on what he has learned from other people.[579] The party against whom testimony is given has a right to cross-examine the witness and this right, coupled with the personal knowledge rule, lay at the root of the ban on hearsay evidence. The probative value of a statement is diminished if it is not made by a witness when giving evidence in the proceedings.

Hearsay

A litigant may endeavour to prove a fact in issue by direct testimony, that is, by swearing to it himself or calling a witness to swear to it, but it sometimes happens that the best he, or his witness, can do is to depose to what someone else was heard to say on the subject, and the rule against hearsay must then be borne in mind. In spite of the etymological ineptitude, the rule applies to what people wrote as well as to what they were heard to say, and to what the witness himself said out of court as well as to what he proves to have been said by others, whether they are or are not called as witnesses.

It is ironic that the first statutory formulation of the hearsay rule appeared in the legislation designed[580] to abolish it in civil proceedings, the Civil Evidence Act 1995. Section 1(2) accordingly states:

In this Act—

(a) 'hearsay' means a statement made otherwise than by a person while giving oral evidence in the proceedings which is tendered as evidence of the matters stated; and

(b) references to hearsay include hearsay of whatever degree.

The definition conflates two historically different rules, the first relating to statements made by non-testifying third parties, and the second to previous statements of a testifying witness.[581] In both, the aim was to prevent reliance upon such statements as proof of the truth of any matter asserted by them. Where it was not intended to use them for that purpose, but merely because of the circumstantial relevance of the fact of their having been made, then they were untouched by the exclusionary rule. So, if the issue were whether or not a third party had threatened one accused of crime, for the purposes of establishing a defence of duress, evidence of such a threat was held not to fall within the rule.[582] As may be imagined, admissibility for one purpose, but not for another, created serious analytic problems relating to the scope and effect of the rule.[583] Criminal

---

[578] The only exception is a public document that proves itself, i.e. may simply be handed to the judge.

[579] See Criminal Justice Act 2003, s 127.

[580] Law Com No 216 *The Hearsay Rule in Civil Proceedings* (Cm 2321, 1993).

[581] Sometimes described as the rule against narration, or the rule against self-corroboration.

[582] *Subramaniam v Public Prosecutor* [1956] 1 WLR 965.

[583] Eliciting from Lord Reid in *Myers v DPP* [1965] AC 1001, [1964] 2 All ER 881; 1019, 884 the lament that 'it is difficult to make any general statement about the law of hearsay which is entirely accurate'.

proceedings retain more of the exclusionary rule and its definition is somewhat more expansive:[584]

A matter stated is one to which this Chapter applies if (and only if) the purpose, or one of the purposes, of the person making the statement appears to the court to have been—

(a) to cause another person to believe the matter, or

(b) to cause another person to act or a machine to operate on the basis that the matter is as stated.

It still remains uncertain how far this approach will resolve the complexities and difficulties experienced in interpreting the common law.

Hearsay will now be admissible to a greater or lesser extent in both civil and criminal proceedings.[585] It is, however, often regarded as less convincing in principle on account of the lack of opportunity to cross-examine a non-testifying third party, or in the case of a consistent out-of-court statement, on account of the ease of fabrication and multiplication. Such considerations lead to expedients such as greater discretion in relation to admission,[586] and special rules relating to the assessment of weight.

Documents

The contents of a document may be incorporated in the evidence of a witness who swears, for instance, that he entered into a written contract, and the court may be referred to them because they contain admissible hearsay statements, as when an entry made by a registrar of births, deaths, and marriages is produced to prove one of these occurrences. Strictly speaking, the contents of a document need not be treated as a separate item of judicial evidence, although it is convenient to do so because they are governed by special rules.

A document may be put in evidence either as a chattel—a substance such as a paper or parchment bearing an inscription—or else as a statement—the inscription on the substance. This distinction was very clearly expressed by Hoffmann J in *Huddleston v Control Risks Information Services Ltd*[587] in distinguishing between the application of the Supreme Court Act 1981 to 'property' and to 'documents':

...a written instrument or any other object carrying information such as a photograph, tape recording or computer disk can be both 'property' for the purposes of s 33(1) and a 'document' for the purposes of s 33(2). Whether for the purposes of a particular case it is the one or the other depends on the nature of the question which it is said may arise.

When treated as a chattel, there is no doubt that it constitutes real evidence, as when a deed alleged to have been stolen is produced to the court in order to show that it bears the fingerprints of the accused. When treated as a statement, a document constitutes testimonial evidence in the vast majority of cases; it may be used as circumstantial evidence, as when

---

[584] Criminal Justice Act 2003, s 115(3), adopting the recommendation of the Law Commission in Law Com No 245 *Evidence in Criminal Proceedings: Hearsay and Related Topics* (Cm 3670, 1997).

[585] See further below Chapters XIII–XIV.

[586] Civil Evidence Act 1995, s 6(2)(a) (discretion); Criminal Justice Act 2003, ss 114(1)(d), 114(2), 126 (discretion).

[587] [1987] 2 All ER 1035, [1987] 1 WLR 701; 1037, 703.

ancient leases are tendered to prove that the lessor, through whom the claimant seeks a prescriptive title, was in possession of the locus in quo:[588]

Ancient documents coming out of proper custody, and purporting on the face of them to show exercise of ownership, such as a lease or licence, may be given in evidence…as being in themselves acts of ownership and proof of possession.

Although it is produced and identified by a witness, the document is not incorporated in his testimony as having been written or read by him, neither are its contents tendered as proof of anything they may assert. It is offered to the court as the kind of document that would only have been executed by someone in possession. In other words, its existence is a relevant fact proved by real evidence—the production of a material object for examination by the court.

Things or real evidence

Things are an independent species of evidence as their production calls upon the court to reach conclusions on the basis of its own perception, and not on that of witnesses directly or indirectly reported to it. If a witness swears that he saw a knife, and that it bore bloodstains, the court is asked to assume that both statements are true; if the witness swears that the bloodstained knife he produces is the one he saw on a particular occasion, only one assumption has to be made by the court in order to reach a conclusion as to the condition of the knife.

Although it was devised by Bentham and adopted by Best, 'real evidence' is not a term that has received the blessing of common judicial usage. It is clear that it covers the production of material objects for inspection by the judge or jury in court, but obscure how much further the term should be extended.

Material objects

If the condition of a material object is among the facts in issue, the object may be produced to the judge and jury for them to form their own opinion on the matter.[589] Indeed, failure to produce such an object may be the subject of observation by the judge,[590] and, if its value is in issue, a presumption adverse to his case operates against a party who fails to produce the thing.[591] Loss or destruction of evidence by the prosecution,[592] even when innocent, may ground a stay of proceedings for abuse of process,[593] or be found to render a trial unfair under the provisions of Art 6 of the European Convention on Human Rights.[594] In

---

[588] *Malcomson v O'Dea* (1863) 10 HL Cas 593, 614, Willes J. For a modern Canadian example, see *R v Emes* (2001) 157 CCC (3d) 124 (presence of personal documents in apartment to show occupation).

[589] Although any experiment to be performed upon it must be conducted in the presence of the parties, so that they may make submissions: *R v Higgins* (1989) The Times, 16 February.

[590] *R v Francis* (1874) LR 2 CCR 128, 133, Lord Coleridge CJ. In Canada, in *R v Fournier* (2000) 145 CCC (3d) 420, [55] the court went so far as to say that the Crown, having destroyed the evidence, 'must either prove the total absence of relevance of the material evidence destroyed or lost, or the absence of gross or unacceptable negligence'.   [591] *Armory v Delamirie* (1722) 1 Stra 505.

[592] As may planting it, *R v Sheri* (2004) 185 CCC (3d) 155.

[593] *R (Ebrahim) v Feltham Magistrates' Court* [2001] EWHC Admin 130, [2001] 1 WLR 1293. For fuller discussion, see Martin (2005) 9 E&P 158. See, in the US, the distinction between destruction of exculpatory and of neutral evidence: *Arizona v Youngblood* (1988) 488 US 51.

[594] *Papageorgiou v Greece* (2004) 38 EHRR 30; cf *Sofri v Italy* [2004] Crim LR 846.

exceptional circumstances, the court will accept secondary evidence of real objects rather than requiring their physical production, for example photographs of aircraft parts.[595] If an object is fungible, replicas may be examined, but they must be identical in all relevant respects.[596]

Real evidence may be used as a means of proving facts in issue; it may also be used in an endeavour to establish relevant facts, as when a knife found in the hands of a person accused of murder is produced in order to show the jury that it bears the stains of blood. But although the production of exhibits is a common enough occurrence, the above example shows that real evidence is of little value unless accompanied by testimony identifying it as the object the qualities of which are in issue, or relevant to the issue. It is of great value so far as it goes, but it rarely goes very far.

Appearance of persons

A person's physical characteristics are frequently included among the possible items of real evidence, and these may often serve as a valuable means of proof. For instance, the fact that the accused is left-handed, tall or short, strong or weak, or has a distinctive voice,[597] may frequently render it more or less probable that he committed the crime charged; a physical deformity such as a rupture may lead almost inevitably to the conclusion that a man was not guilty of rape;[598] and the resemblance that a child produced to the court bears to its alleged father or mother may be some, although very weak, evidence of parentage.[599] If, at the hearing of a claim for damages for personal injuries, the court examines those injuries or their effects, it may be said to be receiving real evidence,[600] but great caution is exercised in allowing wounds to be exhibited owing, no doubt, to the prejudice that might be excited.[601] Again, the court is acting on real evidence when it determines the age of a child by inspection,[602] which may include inspection of photographs.[603]

---

[595] *R v Uxbridge Justices, ex p Sofaer* (1986) 85 Cr App Rep 367. See also *Tudhope v Stewart* 1986 JC 88; *Dyk v Protec Automotive Repairs* (1997) 151 DLR (4th) 374.

[596] *R v Devichand* [1991] Crim LR 446, in which the weight of tins of paint was relevant, but the tins shown to the jury bore a different price tag from those in issue, and because this might have influenced the jury the conviction was quashed.　　　　　　　　　　　　　　[597] *Bulejcik v R* (1996) 185 CLR 375, Aus HC.

[598] 1 Hale, PC, 635–6.

[599] *Burnaby v Baillie* (1889) 42 Ch D 282; *Slingsby v A-G* (1916) 33 TLR 120, 122, in which Lord Loreburn regarded such evidence as of some weight, and Lord Shaw regarded it as worthless except where there was a difference in colour between the alleged parent and child (see *MacLeod v Hill* [1976] 2 WWR 593); *Russell v Russell and Mayer* (1923) 129 LT 151, 153, in which the evidence was admitted, but spoken of as unsafe and conjectural; *C v C and C* [1972] 3 All ER 577, [1972] 1 WLR 1335 (photographic evidence of resemblance of child to alleged father admissible).

[600] And where the court proposes to rely upon such observations, they should be drawn to the attention of counsel so as to permit representations to be made: see *Angaston and District Hospital v Thamm* (1987) 47 SASR 177.

[601] See *Gray v La Fleche, Saskatchewan Power Corp* (1962) 31 DLR (2d) 189, showing that the fact that liability is admitted makes a difference. In *Niznik v Johnson* (1961) 28 DLR (2d) 541, motion pictures were shown to the court in order to establish the fact that the claimant's manifestations of pain in court were faked. See also *Stevens v William Nash Ltd* [1966] 3 All ER 156, [1966] 1 WLR 1550 and *Draper v Jacklyn* [1970] SCR 92.

[602] Children and Young Persons Act 1933, s 99. In *R v Colgan* [1959] SRNSW 96, it was held that, subject to the judge's discretion, it was proper to allow the jury to see a girl alleged to be mentally defective with whom the accused was charged with having had intercourse, although the girl was not called as a witness.

[603] *R v Land* [1998] 1 Cr App Rep 301.

Demeanour of witnesses[604]

If a witness gives his evidence in a forthright way, unperturbed by cross-examination,[605] the court will no doubt be more disposed to believe him than would be the case with a halting and prevaricating witness. So far as its bearing on the facts in issue is concerned, this type of demeanour is analogous to the answers given by a witness who is being cross-examined as to credit, and may rightly be regarded as evidence in the case.[606]

When the court acts on the remarks or behaviour of a witness as constituting a contempt, it may be said to accept real evidence because it is not asked to do more than act on its powers of perception in determining the existence of a fact in issue—the contemptuous conduct. If the personality of a witness is in issue in a case, such as his suitability to care for a child[607] or to direct a company,[608] the court may attach some weight to its assessment of him in giving evidence.

View[609]

A view is an observation undertaken out of court during the course of a trial. When that which is shown at the view is something that might have been produced as an exhibit had it been convenient to do so, as when omnibuses are examined in the yard of the court[610] or the tribunal visits a place so that witnesses can show where they were standing at the relevant time,[611] the court is being asked to act on real evidence. Although in *Goold v*

---

604 For a sceptical appraisal, see Law Com No 245 (1997) paras 3.09–3.12. Evidence of demeanour out of court was rejected in *R v Keast* [1998] Crim LR 748, but that of demeanour in court but out of the witness box accepted in Australia in *R v Martin (No 4)* [2000] SASC 436, 78 SASR 140; while in Canada in *R v RIL* (2005) 197 CCC (3d) 169 it was held that the trial judge was wrong to refuse to admit the demeanour of a complainant on a pre-trial video-recording which was significantly different from her demeanour in court. An appellate court may take the view that the judge has not sufficiently checked his favourable view of a witness on account of demeanour by reference to the totality of the evidence: see *Sheikh v Law Society* [2006] EWCA Civ 1577, (2006) 103(47) LSG 27, [96]. In Australia in *R v Barrett* [2007] VSCA 95, 171 ACR 315 a warning against attaching too much importance to it was suggested.

605 It is disputed whether demeanour is more important in relation to cross-examination than as to examination in chief or re-examination, see *Attorney-General for the Sovereign Base Areas of Akrotiri and Dhekelia v Steinhoff* [2005] UKPC 31, [19], [32].

606 If the inference might be controversial, there is something to be said for drawing the matter to the attention of the parties in case they wish to make submissions about it: see *Newell v Cronje* 1985 (4) SA 692; *In the Marriage of Zantiotis* (1993) 113 FLR 182. In *Coombs v Bessel* (1994) 4 Tas 149, an appeal was allowed because what the trial judge had regarded as unsatisfactory demeanour in testifying transpired to be the result of a medical condition.

607 *Re N-BCM* [2002] EWCA Civ 1052 (although there not to the extent of being preferred to the contrary unanimous view of three experts).

608 *Secretary of State for Trade and Industry v Reynard* [2002] EWCA Civ 497.

609 See generally Justice Heydon in *Evans v R* [2007] HCA 50, approving Ormerod [2000] Crim LR 452.

610 *London General Omnibus Co Ltd v Lavell* [1901] 1 Ch 135, in which, however, the Court of Appeal regarded the evidence as insufficient; too much importance has been attached to the dicta of Lord Alverstone CJ in this case, see *R v De Grey, ex p Fitzgerald* (1913) 109 LT 871. Where relevant, musical or dramatic performances may be given in or out of court.

611 *Karamat v R* [1956] AC 256, [1956] 1 All ER 415, in which the view was treated as a substitute for, or supplementary to, photographs and plans. See also Megarry J in *Tito v Waddell* [1975] 3 All ER 997, [1975] 1 WLR 1303 at 1002, 1307.

Evans & Co[612] Hodson LJ regarded a view of a factory to observe the reconstruction of an accident as no more than a means of interpreting evidence given in court,[613] Denning LJ regarded it as a species of real evidence, a view subsequently endorsed by the Court of Appeal. In *Buckingham v Daily News Ltd*,[614] it held that the trial judge had rightly taken into account his opinion of the working of the machine formed at a view. Parker LJ said that the occurrences at the view were part of the evidence: it was as if the machine had been brought into the well of the court and the claimant had there demonstrated what had occurred on the occasion under inquiry. It is for this reason important[615] that such a demonstration[616] should take place in the presence of judge,[617] parties,[618] accused,[619] and, where there is one, jury. Such a demonstration may be distinguished from a visit to a relevant public place to appreciate better the evidence adduced in court. Even in such a case, however, it has been said to be better for the judge to give prior warning to the parties of any such proposed visit.[620] The purpose of such a warning is to give the parties an opportunity to suggest possibly misleading features, such as a change since the events in question, or allow the parties to answer points raised by the judge at such a view.[621] Such a visit by the jury in the absence of the judge is also undesirable since it is so highly likely that questions will be asked and things said transforming the character of the visit into something more akin to a demonstration.[622] In some cases, a demonstration may be too graphic and justice better served by the use of expert evidence,[623] informed outside the court by experimentation.[624]

As with other types of real evidence, there is no intrinsic objection to the reception of photographs, or in the case of demonstrations, film, or video recordings. Thus the recording of the route taken by a car was admitted in *R v Thomas*.[625] The main consideration is relevancy. In the case of inanimate objects, it is important to film them as close to the relevant happening as possible, so as to minimize the possibility of material change. In the case of demonstrations involving animate bodies, such as an allegedly obscene dance, it

---

[612] [1951] 2 TLR 1189.

[613] A view also held in Australia: see *Railways Comr v Murphy* (1967) 41 ALJR 77.

[614] [1956] 2 QB 534, [1956] 2 All ER 904; see also *Webster v Burns* [1964] NZLR 749.

[615] In *Hoekstra v HM Adv* 2002 SLT 599, 2002 SCCR 135, it was held not to be essential for the accused to be present at every visit where the jury had to visit in groups for logistical reasons.

[616] See *R v Harbour* [1995] 1 NZLR 440 for an apt illustration of the fine line between a simple view and a demonstration.

[617] *Tameshwar v R* [1957] AC 476, [1957] 2 All ER 683; *R v Hunter* [1985] 2 All ER 173, [1985] 1 WLR 613.

[618] *Salsbury v Woodland* (n620); and for the precise conduct of any visit to be settled in advance, *M v DPP* (2009) unreported DC 26 February. [1970] 1 QB 324, [1969] 3 All ER 863.

[619] *R v Ely Justices, ex p Burgess* (1992) 157 JP 484.

[620] Lord Widgery in *Salsbury v Woodland* [1970] 1 QB 324, [1969] 3 All ER 863; 344, 874.

[621] See *Parry v Boyle* (1986) 83 Cr App Rep 310.

[622] *R v Hunter* (n617). See also, in Australia, *Grosser v South Australian Police* (1994) 63 SASR 243, where the evidence was rejected for this reason.

[623] Or even non-expert experimentation, see *R v Collins* (2001) 160 CCC (3d) 85 (police evidence of ricochetting of bullets on water).

[624] *R v Sutherland* (1996) 112 CCC (3d) 454 (preferred to computer simulation of the trajectory of a bullet). For consideration of the increased use of computer animation as an aid to proceedings in court, see Narayanan et al (1999) 8 *Inf and Comm Tech Law* 151.

[625] [1986] Crim LR 682.

is exceedingly unlikely that a sufficiently accurate or trustworthy reconstruction can be made, because,[626]

...it would be almost impossible to analyse motion by motion those slight differences which may in the totality result in a scene of quite a different character from that performed on the night in question.

No such objection would apply to a film of the very dance that was the subject of the charge.[627]

If considered, not as real evidence, but as a species of testimony by conduct, the evidence is equally objectionable as hearsay.[628] Such an objection can, however, be overcome if such a reconstruction can be brought within an exception to the hearsay rule, as in *Li Shu-ling v R*,[629] in which the accused's re-enactment of his crime could be considered to come within the exception for confessions.

Automatic recordings

Recordings have become increasingly important on account of the increased use of electronic apparatus for such purposes as recording interviews with suspects by the police and with victims of abuse by social workers, monitoring telephone calls, conducting continuous video surveillance,[630] and generally conducting business. Most discussion once centred on the admissibility of tape recordings,[631] but this has been supplemented by a burgeoning stream of authority[632] on the admissibility of other media such as film, video-tape, and computer output.[633] It even extends to new ways of extracting information from them, such as lip-reading from a CCTV recording.[634] The relevance of what was recorded and the operation of other exclusionary rules may determine ultimate admissibility. Thus, if a recording were obtained illegally[635] or in breach of public policy,[636] it might be rejected

---

[626] *R v Quinn and Bloom* [1962] 2 QB 245, [1961] 3 All ER 88; 259, 93. See also in Canada, *R v MacDonald and Varcoe* (2000) 146 CCC (3d) 525 (video reconstruction of arrest rejected). Cf *R v Fernandes* (1996) 133 FLR 477 (upside-down signature accepted).

[627] As in *S v W* 1975 (3) SA 841.

[628] This was the essence of the objection to the admission of a video recording of an interview between a child and a social worker in a sexual abuse case involving the use of anatomically accurate dolls: *Re E; Re G* (1986) 136 NLJR 843.

[629] [1989] AC 270, [1988] 3 All ER 138. See also Children Act 1989, s 7, as amended.

[630] This practice has become sufficiently common to have elicited judicial requests for authoritative regulation to govern the procedure: *R v Caldwell, R v Dixon* (1993) 99 Cr App Rep 73; *R v Roberts* [1998] Crim LR 682.

[631] Many of the relevant authorities were cited in *R v Maqsud Ali; R v Ashiq Hussain* [1966] 1 QB 688, [1965] 2 All ER 464.

[632] And commentary, see e.g. Goldstein [1987] *Crim LR* 384, Munday (1995) 159 *JP* 547, Elliott [1998] *Crim LR* 159, and Murphy (1999) 13 *Int J Law and Comp Tech* 383.

[633] A concern is that the transition from analogue to digital technology increases the possibility of undetectable interference, see further Fifth Report of the House of Lords Committee on Science and Technology, *Digital Images as Evidence* (3 February 1998).

[634] Subject to suitable directions, *R v Luttrell* [2004] EWCA Crim 1344, [2004] 2 Cr App R 520.

[635] Although this is usually a matter of discretion, and one unlikely to be exercised in favour of exclusion, see *R v Senat, R v Sin* (1968) 52 Cr App Rep 282 (private act for prosecution); *R v Khan* [1997] AC 558, [1996] 3 All ER 289 (official act for prosecution); *Jones v University of Warwick* [2003] EWCA Civ 151, [2003] 3 All ER 760, [2003] 1 WLR 954 (private act for civil suit).   [636] *R v Migliorini* (1981) 38 ALR 356.

on these grounds,[637] but not because it was a recording. If the matter recorded is itself in issue,[638] then the recording is capable of constituting real evidence of it.[639] It is incumbent on the prosecution to disclose such evidence to the defence as soon as possible,[640] and to account satisfactorily for failing to adduce at the trial[641] any video recording that may be relevant.[642] If only part of the original recording has been retained, a court may treat that as a very material factor influencing the exercise of any discretion to exclude the part that is tendered[643] or to stay for abuse of process.[644] It seems, however, that where a compilation of incidents is made there is no need to disclose the context of each component, at least in the absence of specific objection.[645]

At a trial by jury, the party relying on a recording or film must satisfy the judge that there is a prima facie case that it is authentic, and it must be sufficiently intelligible to be placed before the jury.[646] The evidence must define and describe the provenance and history of the recording up to the moment of its production in court.[647] There is no need to account for the absence of the original if the copy is shown to be authentic.[648] Where it is helpful, a copy in the shape of a transcript of a sound recording,[649] or even of a summary,[650]

[637] Or, on a discretionary basis, if the relevant procedural rules have been disregarded; see in civil proceedings: *Rall v Hume* [2001] EWCA Civ 146, [2001] 3 All ER 248; and in criminal, Criminal Justice Act 2003, s 132(5)(a).

[638] This should be distinguished from the situation in which the recording is testimonial, for example in the case of child witnesses. For an unusual intermediate situation, see *Bulejcik v R* (n597), where the identity of a participant in a recorded conversation was in issue, and the jury wished to have for comparison in the jury room a recording that had been made of the accused's unsworn statement made before them in the courtroom.

[639] *R v Governor of Brixton Prison, ex p Levin* [1997] AC 741, [1997] 3 All ER 289. In *R v Nikolovski* [1996] 3 SCR 1197, the trial judge's identification of the accused from a video recording of the robbery was upheld over failure by the victim to make a dock identification.

[640] *R v Secombes* [2007] EWCA Crim 158, [21].

[641] It is permissible to withhold information about it from the accused, or even from his solicitor, during the process of investigation: *R v Imran and Hussein* [1997] Crim LR 754, despite ss 34–38 of Criminal Justice and Public Order Act 1994.

[642] So to fail might amount to abuse of process: for the principles, see *R(Ebrahim) v Feltham Magistrates' Court* (n593). For a survey of recent case law, including a number of otherwise unreported cases, see Dodd (2001) 165 JP 316.   [643] *R v Curran and Torney* [1983] 2 VR 133.

[644] *R v Brooks* [2004] All ER (D) 84.

[645] *Newman v Commissioner of Metropolitan Police* (2009) unreported QBD 25 March.

[646] In *R v Briddick* [2001] EWCA Crim 984, an expert in video enhancement was permitted to testify to the inference he drew from an enhanced version of the film, even though that version was neither shown in court nor viewed by the jury out of court, and to be supported by copies of stills from the enhanced version. It may sometimes, on account of its low quality, be admissible only for general and not detailed purposes, such as identification of participants: *R v Williams and Best* [2006] EWCA Crim 2148.

[647] *R v Robson and Harris* [1972] 2 All ER 699, [1972] 1 WLR 651; *Butera v DPP* (1987) 164 CLR 180, 184. It is not, however, necessary in every case to prove every part of the recording authentic in every detail to the standard of scientific certainty: *R v Chen* [1993] 2 VR 139. But no serious danger of distortion should remain: *R v Penney* (2002) 163 CCC (3d) 329 (rejecting edited video of seal culling).

[648] *Kajala v Noble* (1982) 75 Cr App Rep 149.

[649] It is acceptable for such a transcript to be authenticated not by the typist, but by a police officer who was present at the interview, and who has compared the transcript with the recording.

[650] This appears to have occurred by agreement in *R v Aitken* (1991) 94 Cr App Rep 85, and was approved in *R v Riaz, R v Burke* (1991) 94 Cr App Rep 339. Although the use of a summary may avoid the tedium of listening to a full recording, it is dangerous to rely upon it when there is a suggestion of ambiguity, as in *R v Brown* [1995] Crim LR 494, in which much depended upon whether the absence of punctuation in the summary reflected the sense of the breaks in the recorded speech.

may be adduced in evidence to help the jury.[651] It should be noted that while a literal transcription of a tape in a language understood by the jury may sometimes help it to understand the sounds recorded on the tape,[652] it is more common to permit the jury to receive a
written translation in cases where a foreign language was used.[653] If such a transcript is put
in evidence, the court will, of course, have to be satisfied of its accuracy. Such a translation
cannot help the jury to understand the sounds, and experts must testify to its accuracy.[654]
Provided that this has been done, there is no objection to the receipt of such translations
by the jury.[655] In such a case, the judge has a discretion to permit the jury to be supplied
with the transcript, but solely to help it to understand the tape recording, which itself
remains the only evidence of what was said.[656] For this reason, the jury may be permitted recourse to the tape during its deliberations at the discretion of the judge,[657] but not
normally to a transcript, least of all over the objection of the defence.[658] Such use should
normally take place in open court, certainly if that is the first occasion on which the tape
is actually played, but access to the tape in the jury room may sometimes be allowed.[659]
Where a video recording has been received under the provisions of the Youth Justice and
Criminal Evidence Act 1999,[660] it is a matter for the discretion of the judge whether it
should be replayed to the jury.[661] In exercising that discretion, the judge should consider
any possible distortion occasioned by hearing part of the evidence twice in what might
well be an especially dramatic form, and in particular should not normally allow a replay
at the instance of the prosecution, in the absence of a request from the jury.[662] Any such

[651] This applies equally to the soundtrack of a video recording: see *Re G* [1987] 1 WLR 1461, 1472.
The use of video recording and transcript is likely to shorten the presentation of the relevant evidence
significantly.

[652] As in *Hopes and Lavery v HM Adv* 1960 JC 104, in which a typist who prepared a transcript after famil-
iarizing herself with the contents of the recording by playing it over many times was permitted to testify to
the authenticity of her transcription.

[653] In *R v Duffy* [1999] 1 Cr App Rep 307, this analogy was used to admit evidence from his social worker
of the meaning of sounds made by a disabled person in seeking to express himself in English, which no one
else could understand; cf *R v Imrie* (1916) 12 Cr App Rep 282. This problem was eliminated by s 30 of the
Youth Justice and Criminal Evidence Act 1999.

[654] Expert evidence of the nature of non-verbal sounds is also admissible: see *R v Chan* (1993) 87 CCC
(3d) 25.

[655] *R v Maqsud Ali, R v Ashiq Hussain* [1966] 1 QB 688, [1965] 2 All ER 464. The same view has prevailed in
Australasia, see *Butera v DPP* (1987) 164 CLR 180; *R v Menzies* [1982] 1 NLZR 40, and in Canada, see *Papalia
v R* [1979] 2 SCR 256.

[656] *R v Rampling* [1987] Crim LR 823; see also *R v Rowbotham* (1988) 41 CCC (3d) 1, 48. In Australia, the
jury has been provided with the transcript of an electronic diary: *Markovina v R* (1996) 16 WAR 354. There
seems to be no objection to a witness using a tape to help refresh his memory in an appropriate case: see *R v
Sitek* [1988] 2 Qd R 284.

[657] *R v Riaz, R v Burke* (1991) 94 Cr App Rep 339. An exception occurs, however, if the prosecution and
defence have agreed on a summary of the tape that omits a disputed passage; it is not then open to the jury
by listening to the full tape to make its own determination of what it contains: *R v Hagan* [1997] 1 Cr App
Rep 464.   [658] *R v Coshall* [1995] 12 LS Gaz R 34, CA; *R v Boakes* [1996] CLY 1393.

[659] *R v Tonge* (1993) 157 JP 1137, and even though there the judge felt that he had to impose the condition
that the jury should not attempt to decipher passages regarded as indecipherable for the purposes of preparing the transcript.   [660] Sections 27, 28.

[661] This discretion may be exercised to prevent a video recording from being played as part of the closing
address of the defence: *R v Eldridge and Salmon* [1999] Crim LR 166.

[662] *R v M* [1996] 2 Cr App Rep 56.

replay should normally be in court,[663] the jury should be specially warned not to accord the evidence disproportionate weight, and should be reminded of the cross-examination and re-examination of the complainant.[664] Such guidance is, however, designed to achieve justice, and may be departed from if appropriate.[665] Since the rule allowing jury access to recordings has also been extended to those that have not been tendered in evidence, but merely referred to by the defence to demonstrate impropriety in initial interviewing and inconsistency with evidence in court, it is even more important in such cases to ensure that the jury is directed clearly of the limited purposes for which such recordings can be used.[666]

While the use of such transcripts is clearly a great convenience to the jury, some doubt has been expressed as to how far the recording may be supplemented by evidence explaining it. In the case of videotapes, a number of cases has accepted the principle of permitting a witness to testify to the identity of the accused and the person shown on the film.[667] This seems correct in principle, since evidence is readily admitted when required to supplement the production of an exhibit, and in these cases, the testimony of a witness who knows the accused well and has observed his personal characteristics and body movements in everyday life[668] is likely to be helpful to the jury, which will only have seen the accused at the trial. In *Taylor v Chief Constable of Cheshire*,[669] this was taken a step further in allowing evidence of the commission of an offence by the accused to be tendered by witnesses who had seen a video recording of an incident, even though the video recording had accidentally been erased before the trial. The court took the view that their evidence was just as much direct evidence of the commission of the offence as would have been that of someone observing an event through binoculars: in other words, the recording was simply an extension of the human senses.[670] It should, perhaps, be remembered that in *Maqsud Ali* the actual recording was unintelligible to the jury, and it is perhaps not going too far

[663] Although this may be relaxed when the recording is of the events in issue, so long as the jury is clearly instructed what use it may make of the tape: *R v Briggs* [2002] EWCA Crim 612, [44], to that extent qualifying remarks in *R v Imran and Hussain* [1997] Crim LR 754. See also *R v Hagan* [1997] 1 Cr App Rep 464. The general rule is the same in Australia, see *R v H* [1999] 2 Qd 283, and in Canada, see *R v Lalande* (1999) 138 CCC (3d) 441.

[664] *R v Rawlings*; *R v Broadbent* [1995] 1 All ER 580, [1995] 2 Cr App Rep 222. This applies even if the video has not been replayed, but lengthy extracts read out by the judge from the transcript: *R v McQuiston* [1998] 1 Cr App Rep 139. It seems, however, that it is not fatal not to remind the jury of cross-examination in such a case if in the judge's view no purpose would be served by it, and the jury does not request it: *R v Saunders* [1995] 2 Cr App Rep 313; cf *R v O* [1996] 3 NZLR 295, requiring the jury to be provided with transcripts of cross-examination relating to the video, if provided with a transcript of it.

[665] *R v Horley* [1999] Crim LR 488. For the view in Australia, see *Gately v R* [2007] HCA 55. See also the plaintive words of Judge Edwards in [2001] *Crim LR* 1002.

[666] *R v Atkinson* [1995] Crim LR 490 (although failure to do so as not there fatal).

[667] *Kajala v Noble* (1982) 75 Cr App Rep 149; *R v Caldwell*; *R v Dixon* (1993) 99 Cr App Rep 73. See also *R v Smith* (1983) 33 SASR 558; *R v Sitek* (n656) (in which the issue was not the identity but the actions of the accused); *Steele v HM Adv* 1992 JC 1. For discussion of the use of expert evidence of facial mapping in conjunction with CCTV film, see Bromby (2003) 153 NLJ 302.

[668] In *R v Clare, R v Peach* [1995] 2 Cr App Rep 333, this was extended to the case of a police witness testifying to the identity of the accused where his familiarity was derived from another, and clearer, video recording taken elsewhere the same day.

[669] [1987] 1 All ER 225, [1987] 1 WLR 1479.

[670] It has even been held in Scotland, in the case of tape-recorded interviews with suspects at police stations, that the evidence of the recording and of the memory of those present are equally primary evidence of what was said: *HM Adv v Swift* 1983 SCCR 204, 207.

to assimilate a situation in which the actual recording is unavailable. Although objection to the evidence in *Taylor* contended that it was hearsay, this cannot be sustained, since the recording was automatic, and the only human mind through which the information passed was that of the witnesses, who were present and available for cross-examination.[671] The argument that such cross-examination might be less effective in the absence of the recording seems speculative, and in principle to go more to weight than to admissibility.

Exactly the same principles apply to more complex automatic recordings, such as those of a radar trace of the movements of a ship.[672] The former special rules relating to computer output have been repealed.[673] It might be supposed that, in the case of any new and unfamiliar form of automatic recording, the court will require more in the way of foundation testimony to prove the ordinary working of the device.[674] Thus in *R v Cochrane*,[675] it was not enough to produce witnesses who knew nothing at all about the working of the relevant computer, or even where it was located. On the other hand, once a device has become familiar and is widely regarded as reliable, in the absence of any evidence of malfunctioning, and despite the operator's knowledge being defective in some respects,[676] his testimony may well be sufficient.[677]

SECTION 4. RELEVANCE, ADMISSIBILITY, AND WEIGHT OF EVIDENCE[678]

The main general rule governing the entire subject is that all evidence that is sufficiently relevant to an issue before the court is admissible and all that is irrelevant, or insufficiently relevant,[679] should be excluded.[680]

The affirmative aspect of this rule (the exceptions to which constitute much of the law of evidence) and its negative aspect (to which there are no exceptions at common law)[681]

---

[671] Evidence of what appeared on the visual display of a breath-testing device was accepted as being real evidence in *Owen v Chesters* [1985] RTR 191, and in *Gunn v Brown* 1986 SLT 94.

[672] *The Statue of Liberty* [1968] 2 All ER 195, [1968] 1 WLR 739. Modern examples include satellite photographic images, see Purdy and Macrory (2003) 153 NLJ 337, and access records for databases available over the Internet: *R (O'Shea) v Coventry Magistrates Court* [2004] EWHC 905, [2004] ACD 50. Such recording remains outside the definition of hearsay in s 115 of the Criminal Justice Act 2003, which is cast in terms of statements or representations *of a person*.

[673] In civil proceedings, by Civil Evidence Act 1995, Sch 2; in criminal proceedings, by the Youth Justice and Criminal Evidence Act 1999, s 60.

[674] But see *Castle v Cross* [1985] 1 All ER 87, [1984] 1 WLR 1372, and compare *Mehesz v Redman* (1980) 21 SASR 569; *Holt v Auckland City Council* [1980] 2 NZLR 124. Section 129(2) of the Criminal Justice Act 2003 preserves the presumption that a mechanical device has been properly set or calibrated.

[675] [1993] Crim LR 48.   [676] *Haggis v DPP* [2003] EWHC 2481 (Admin), [2004] 2 All ER 382.

[677] As in *R v Shephard* (n411); see also *Marac Financial Services v Stewart* [1993] 1 NZLR 86.

[678] See Eggleston *Evidence, Proof and Probability* (2nd edn, 1983), especially ch 6, together with the same author's earlier papers in Glass (ed) *Seminars on Evidence*, ch 3; and 4 *Melb ULR* 180; ALRC Res Paper No 7 'Relevance'; see also James in (1940) 29 *Cal LR* 689.

[679] See *R v Byrne* (n488), [31]; *R v Yaeck* (1991) 68 CCC (3d) 545, 565, citing and applying this passage.

[680] See Goddard LJ in *Hollington v F Hewthorn & Co Ltd* [1943] KB 587, [1943] 2 All ER 35, 594, 39.

[681] Some statutory rules provide for the admission of evidence of dubious logical relevance, for example s 6 of the Criminal Procedure Act 1865 (permitting any criminal conviction to be put to a witness in cross-examination with a view to attacking credibility), see further, 357; Theft Act 1968, s 27(3) (inferring guilty knowledge from previous convictions), see further, 411. See also the proposal of the Royal Commission on

must be considered separately. When this has been done, the distinction between the relevancy, admissibility, and weight of evidence will be examined.

THE ADMISSIBILITY OF RELEVANT EVIDENCE

The first and most important rule of the law of evidence, though one that is not always perceived or observed, is that evidence is admissible only if it is indeed relevant to an issue between the parties.[682]

Definition of 'relevance'

It is difficult to improve[683] upon Stephen's definition of relevance when he said that the word 'relevant' means that:[684]

…any two facts to which it is applied are so related to each other that according to the common course of events one either taken by itself or in connection with other facts proves or renders probable the past, present, or future existence or non-existence of the other.

In this sense, relevance is an absolute concept: either proof of one fact makes the existence of another more probable or it does not.[685] It is, however, often regarded as variable,[686] and evidence regarded as more or less relevant.[687] This seems to relate more to the cogency of the evidence,[688] given its relevance, but it secures a place in the exposition of the subject because the qualification of sufficiency appears to relate to it. As explained in *R v Wilson*, this often allows a balancing process to be performed:[689]

[L]ack of relevance can be used to exclude evidence not because it has absolutely no bearing upon the likelihood or unlikelihood of a fact in issue but because the connection is considered

---

Criminal Justice Cm 2263 (1993) [8.34] and rec 194 to admit evidence of the accused's previous convictions even though he has not testified, the evidence is inadmissible in chief, and hence at least as prejudicial as probative.

[682] Buxton LJ in *XXX v YYY* [2004] EWCA Civ 231, [2004] IRLR 471, [16]. The way in which it is relevant may sometimes be crucial, *Evans v R* [2007] HCA 50, [25].

[683] It is more helpful than the rather circular definition approved in *R v Robinson* [2005] EWCA Crim 1940, [2006] 1 Cr App R 221, [19] as evidence 'such that a jury properly warned could place some weight on it'.

[684] *Digest of the Law of Evidence* (12th edn) art 1. This definition was approved in *R v Nethercott* [2001] EWCA Crim 2535, [2002] 2 Cr App Rep 117, and used to justify the admission of conduct subsequent to that charged in the indictment by reference to the word 'past'.

[685] It should be noted that for the purpose of determining relevance each piece of evidence is to be considered independently, and a piece of evidence remains relevant however many other pieces of evidence are tendered to prove exactly the same fact: see *Conway v R* [2000] FCA 461, (2000) 172 ALR 185, [181]. Relevance is a logical and not a pragmatic concept.

[686] In *R v Robinson* (n683), [15] the Court of Appeal cited without criticism the trial judge's application of different thresholds to defence and prosecution evidence.

[687] Although the distinction is not sharp, see e.g. *R v Faal* [1999] Crim LR 833, where the evidence was possession of £115 in cash on arrest some four weeks after the last of three alleged offences of drug dealing.

[688] In Canada, in particular, it is stressed that relevance is independent, and requires no minimum threshold of cogency, see e.g. *Morris v R* [1983] 2 SCR 190, 203.

[689] [1991] 2 NZLR 707, 711. See also, in Canada, *R v Hunter* (2001) 155 CCC (3d) 225, in which the absence of context was such as to make an apparently incriminating snatch of overheard conversation too speculative to be admitted.

to be too remote. Once it is regarded as a matter of degree, competing policy considerations can be taken into account. These include the desirability of shortening trials, avoiding emotive distractions of marginal significance, protecting the reputations of those not represented before the Courts and respecting the feelings of a deceased's family. None of these matters would be determinative if the evidence in question were of significant probative value.

It should be stressed that merely because evidence is admissible, it will not necessarily be admitted, since the judge now has in civil proceedings an explicit general[690] power to exclude pursuant to his case management role.[691] It has, however, been said that the power should be used with great circumspection.[692]

Exceptions

The general rule that all relevant evidence is admissible is subject to numerous exceptions because 'our law...undoubtedly excludes evidence of many matters which anyone in his own daily affairs of moment would regard as important in coming to a decision'.[693] The following four exceptions are frequently stressed, but there are many others.

Hearsay[694]

Hearsay used to be the leading example, but it is now universally admissible by statute in civil proceedings,[695] and may always be admitted as a matter of discretion in criminal, if it would not be contrary to the interests of justice to do so.[696]

Opinion

Witnesses are generally not allowed to inform the court of the inferences they draw from facts perceived by them, but must confine their statements to an account of such facts.

It frequently happens that a bystander has a complete and full view of an accident. It is beyond question that, while he may inform the court of everything that he saw, he may not express an opinion on whether either or both of the parties were negligent.[697]

Opinion is often said to be excluded because it is irrelevant, but something more will have to be said on this subject in Chapter XI; expert witnesses may testify to their opinion on matters involving their expertise.

Character

Any evidence of the bad character of the accused might well be regarded as relevant, but it is still in principle excluded in criminal cases if it falls outside the, now admittedly wide, categories specified in the Criminal Justice Act 2003.[698]

---

690   Exclusionary discretion is more circumscribed in criminal cases, see further Chapter IV.
691   CPR 32.1(2).   692   *Great Future International Ltd v Sealand Housing Corp* (n422), [24].
693   Darling J in *R v Bond* [1906] 2 KB 389, 410. See also the remarks of Hamilton LJ, 2 above.
694   See further Chapters XII–XIV.   695   Civil Evidence Act 1995, s 1(1).
696   Criminal Justice Act 2003, s 114(1)(d).
697   Goddard LJ in *Hollington v F Hewthorn & Co Ltd* [1943] KB 587, [1943] 2 All ER 35; 595, 40. See also *R v Cahill* [1998] 4 VR 1, in which the victim of an attempted rape was not permitted to testify to her belief that her assailant intended to rape her, but was required to confine her evidence to facts, such as his attempt to remove her clothes.
698   Section 101(1), 'admissible if, *but only if…*'.

Conduct on other occasions

It might be thought that the fact that someone behaved in a particular way on one occasion is relevant to the question of whether he behaved in a similar fashion on the occasion that is being considered by the court, merely by reason of the general tendency of human behaviour to repeat itself. Nevertheless, evidence may generally not be given of a party's misconduct on other occasions if its sole purpose is to show that he is a person likely to have conducted himself in the manner alleged by his adversary on the occasion that is under inquiry:[699] 'You must not prove, for example, that a particular engine driver is a careless man in order to prove that a particular accident was caused by his negligence.'[700] Nor is it enough that a witness has been shown to be truthful in relation to some persons to show that the witness is likely to be truthful in relation to others, even in relation to allegations of the same sort made in the same statement.[701]

Multiple relevance and admissibility

An item of evidence may be relevant for more than one reason. In other words, the major premise of a syllogism may be altered, although the minor premise and conclusion remain the same. Thus in *R v Mackie*,[702] the accused's previous violence to a young child was admissible to show the child's reasonable fear of the accused, and hence how he came to run away from him, but was inadmissible to show the accused's disposition towards the child to show that he was likely to have been violent on this occasion. In such a case, the judge must direct the jury accordingly. Some scepticism may, however, reasonably be expressed as to how effectively such directions can prevent the evidence from being used for the wrong purpose.[703] Indeed, in some cases, the danger has been recognized as being so great as to require the principle of multiple admissibility to be overridden, and the evidence excluded altogether, though only as a matter of discretion.[704] These remarks must also be understood to be subject to the operation of some rules, such as that excluding evidence the admission of which would be likely to damage the interests of the state, which override arguments for admission based on any type of relevancy.

Wigmore described the principle involved as one of 'multiple admissibility'.[705] The term is not particularly well chosen, because it suggests that evidence may be admissible

---

[699] But it is sometimes possible: see *R v Nethercott* (n684), where the conduct was subsequent to that alleged in the indictment; in *Birmingham City Council v Dixon* [2009] EWHC 761 (Admin) subsequent conduct was also held relevant for the purposes of an ASBO, and in *R v Wilson* [2008] EWCA Crim 1754 it was regarded as relevant that a series of similar crimes terminated as soon as the accused had been arrested.

[700] Stephen J in *Brown v Eastern and Midlands Rly Co* (1889) 22 QBD 391, 393. The context makes it plain that Stephen J was concerned with conduct on other occasions as proof of disposition. See also *R v Westfield Freezing Co* [1951] NZLR 456.

[701] *R v T* [2006] EWCA Crim 2006, [2007] 1 Cr App R 43, although in Australia in *R v RGP* [2006] VSCA 259 a pattern of previous false confessions was admitted to show the falsity of the instant confession.

[702] (1973) 57 Cr App R 453.

[703] Some of the strongest expressions have been made by American judges. Justice Jackson described it as 'unmitigated fiction' in *Krulewitch v United States* 336 US 440 (1949), 453; Judge Learned Hand as 'a mental gymnastic' in *Nash v United States* 54 F 2d 1006 (1932), 1007; Judge Jerome Frank as 'a judicial lie' in *United States v Grunewald* 233 F 2d 556 (1956), 574; while Traynor CJ remarked that a jury 'cannot segregate evidence into separate intellectual boxes', in *People v Aranda* 407 P 2d 265 (1965), 272.

[704] *R v Shepherd* (1980) 71 Cr App Rep 120; *R v Watts* [1983] 3 All ER 101, 77 Cr App Rep 126 at 104, 129, in which Lord Chief Justice Lane said that the jury was required 'to perform difficult feats of intellectual acrobatics' that were 'practically impossible'.

[705] I Wigmore [13].

for more than one purpose.[706] This is undoubtedly true, but the point of the rule under consideration is that evidence may be admissible for one purpose although it is inadmissible for another. It might be better to refer to it as a situation of 'limited admissibility'.[707] The application of the doctrine is fraught with danger, but the total exclusion of the evidence could be productive of even greater injustice.[708]

THE INADMISSIBILITY OF IRRELEVANT, AND INSUFFICIENTLY RELEVANT, EVIDENCE

Illustrations

A few illustrations may be given of the exclusion of evidence that is irrelevant, or insufficiently relevant, to any issue[709] before the court.

Insufficient relevance

In *Hart v Lancashire and Yorkshire Rly Co*,[710] the fact that the defendant's method of changing the points was altered after an accident was held to be inadmissible as evidence that the accident was caused by the defendant's negligence. According to Bramwell B:

People do not furnish evidence against themselves simply by adopting a new plan in order to prevent the recurrence of an accident. Because the world gets wiser as it gets older, it was not therefore foolish before.

A more generous view was taken in *R v Greenwood*[711] in favour of the defence, where the evidence against the accused consisted of confessions to the murder of a woman. At first instance, he was prevented from adducing evidence of past violence towards the victim

---

[706] A criticism explicitly endorsed in *R v Georgiev* [2001] VSCA 18, [54].

[707] As does Vol 1 of the new edition of Wigmore (1996), [13].

[708] 'No doubt it renders the administration of justice more difficult when evidence which is offered for one purpose or person, may incidentally apply to another; but that is an infirmity to which all evidence is subject, and exclusion on such a ground would manifestly occasion greater mischief than the reception of the evidence' (Tindall CJ in *Willis v Bernard* (1832) 8 Bing 376, 383). 'It often happens, both in civil and criminal cases, that evidence is tendered on several alternative grounds, and yet it is never objected that if on any ground it is admissible, that ground must not prevail, because on some other ground it would be inadmissible and prejudicial. In such cases it is usual for the judge (not always very successfully) to caution the jury against being biased by treating the evidence in the objectionable sense' (*per* Jelf J in *R v Bond* (n693), 389). For an application in the context of statutory rules, see *R v Wall* [1983] NZLR 238, and for belated correction on realizing the alternative basis in Australia, see *Engbretson v Bartlett* [2007] VSC 163, 172 ACR 304.

[709] The more objective the issue, the less subjective evidence relating to the parties is likely to be relevant, *R v Bannister* [2010] RTR 4, (2009) 153(30) SJLB 30 (driver's skill on charge of dangerous driving).

[710] (1869) 21 LT 261, 263. Cf *State Electricity Commission of Victoria v Gray* [1951] VLR 104, 116 (change in lighting system after accident admissible to show warning could have been given before accident) and *Anderson v Morris Wools Pty Ltd* [1965] Qd R 65 (evidence of alteration of machine after accident admissible to show precaution that might have been taken). The US Federal Rules, r 407 reads: 'When, after an event, measures are taken which, if taken previously, would have made the event less likely to occur, evidence of the subsequent measures is not admissible to prove negligence or culpable conduct in connection with the event. This rule does not require the exclusion of evidence of subsequent measures when offered for another purpose, such as proving ownership, control, or feasibility of precautionary measures, if controverted, or impeachment.' Such evidence is also admissible in Canada: *Winsor v Marks & Spencer Canada Ltd* (1995) 129 DLR (4th) 189.

[711] [2004] EWCA Crim 1388, [2005] 1 Cr App R 99.

from her ex-lover. This was overturned on appeal on the basis that there was sufficient relevance in demonstrating the existence of an alternative possible criminal, even without showing him to have been in the vicinity at the relevant time.

Juristic relevance is a matter of degree and it is as idle to enquire as it is impossible to say whether, when the evidence was rejected in the above two cases, it was because it was altogether irrelevant or merely because it was too remotely relevant. Sometimes a balance must be struck between the probative force of the evidence and external pressure vitiating its use,[712] such as the time likely to be taken in resolving collateral issues, the danger of manufacture, and sensitivity to private and public sentiment. These will be considered in turn.

Multiplicity of issues[713]

Rolfe B once pertinently observed that:[714]

...if we lived for a thousand years instead of about sixty or seventy, and every case was of sufficient importance, it might be possible, and perhaps proper...to raise every possible inquiry as to the truth of statements made...In fact mankind finds it to be impossible.

Evidence that might even be highly relevant in a protracted academic investigation is treated as too remote from the issue in a forensic inquiry because the body that has to come to the conclusion is controlled by the time factor, not to mention considerations such as the danger of distracting the jury,[715] and the undesirability of pronouncing upon matters that are not being litigated. Thus, in *JP Morgan Chase Bank v Springwell Navigation Corp*,[716] it was accepted that while similar transactions with other members of a family were relevant to show that a transaction of that sort had been made with this member, nevertheless, because of the difficulty of establishing the facts in those other examples or of limiting evidence adduced upon them, there would be such a serious danger of disrupting the trial for marginal gain that the evidence should not be admitted.

Danger of manufactured evidence

The courts rightly take the view that the degree to which an item of evidence is relevant to an issue diminishes in proportion to the likelihood of its having been manufactured, but it is open to question whether people are as prone to manufacture evidence as some judgments suggest,[717] and the bogey has led to certain exclusionary rules, the mechanical application of which may lead to the rejection of evidence of real probative value.

It certainly played a large part in the development of the rule excluding hearsay, and especially the rule excluding evidence of previous consistent statements of a witness. The dread of manufacture retarded and complicated reform of this branch of the law to no

---

[712] In *Ashmore v Corp of Lloyd's* [1992] 2 All ER 486, [1992] 1 WLR 446; 493, 454, the House of Lords encouraged judicial intervention upon these lines.

[713] The extent to which the rules of relevance may be moulded to meet the exigencies of other facts has been examined quite independently in two essays: from a theoretical point of view, by Dworkin in Tapper (ed) *Crime, Proof and Punishment* (1981), and from a more practical point of view, by Mr Justice Fox in Waller and Campbell (eds) *Well and Truly Tried* (1982).   [714] *A-G v Hitchcock* (1847) 1 Exch 91, 105.

[715] 'The fewer and simpler the issues left to the jury, the less chance there is of a miscarriage of justice' (*per* Byrne J in *R v Patel* [1951] 2 All ER 29, 30).

[716] [2005] EWCA Civ 1602.   [717] See the remarks of Eyre CJ, 2 above.

small extent.[718] Even now it has prevented statutory reform in criminal proceedings from being so comprehensive as that enacted for civil.[719]

Sensitivity

In *Vernon v Bosley*,[720] the trial judge disallowed cross-examination of a divorced woman about an extramarital affair of her ex-husband when she was to be called as a witness by him in a claim in which one of the elements was the collapse of their marriage. He took the view that the distress and embarrassment would outweigh its value. While reversing him on its application in that case, the Court of Appeal nevertheless enunciated as a general principle that:

...the degree of relevance needed for admissibility is not some fixed point on a scale, but will vary according to the nature of the evidence and in particular the inconvenience, expense, delay or oppression which would attend its reception.... For example, having to answer a question may involve a witness in breaking a confidence imposed by his religion, profession or conscience.

Control of such weighing was equated for appellate purposes with that applicable to the exercise of discretion by the trial judge.[721]

Prejudice

Where evidence of at best marginal relevance is tendered, the court will be astute to determine that it is of no, or insufficient, relevance when its admission is likely to be highly prejudicial to the accused. Thus in *R v Byrne*,[722] the principal evidence for the prosecution was a particularly graphic account that the accused had murdered the victim, but because of a previous acquittal, it had to be tendered on a charge of manslaughter. Although it may have been of marginal relevance in showing the accused's presence, its prejudicial effect was regarded as far too great for it to be admitted. Similarly, in *R v Sandhu*,[723] in which the accused was charged with an offence of strict liability, evidence of his malicious intent was too prejudicial to be regarded as sufficiently relevant; so in *R v B*[724] was evidence that the accused had failed to reveal that he was HIV-positive, where his defence to a charge of rape was consent.

Apparent exceptions

A few exceptions to the general prohibition on irrelevant evidence have been suggested, but it is submitted that none of them is substantial so far as English law is concerned.

Facts affecting the admissibility of evidence

Phipson said that Thayer was inaccurate when he asserted that 'without any exception, nothing that is not logically relevant is admissible', because numerous facts are legally

---

[718] The House of Lords has suggested that such caution has proved justifiable in the light of cases of miscarriages of justice: see *R v Kearley* [1992] 2 AC 228, [1992] 2 All ER 345; 258, 366.

[719] See further Chapters XII–XIV.   [720] [1994] PIQR P337.

[721] See further 191.   [722] [2002] EWCA Crim 632.

[723] [1997] Crim LR 288.

[724] [2006] EWCA Crim 2945, (2006) 150 SJLB 1392. The evidence in fact seems relevant in the other direction since consent would be less likely if the condition had been revealed.

admissible although they have no logical bearing on the issue the court has to decide.[725] He referred to such facts as that a witness was not sworn in a particular way, that a hearsay declarant was dead at the date of the trial, and that due search had been made for a lost document. It seems, however, that the criticism is purely semantic, because it assumes that by 'logically relevant', Thayer meant relevant to the main facts in issue. His statement might equally well be taken to mean that nothing is admissible that is not relevant, either to the main facts in issue or else to such subordinate facts as those relating to the credibility and admissibility of evidence, in which case the relevance of the facts mentioned by Phipson is obvious enough.

Curative admissibility[726]

It is sometimes said that, if irrelevant evidence is adduced by one party, his opponent may seek to dispel its effect by calling irrelevant evidence himself. Whatever the position may be in certain American jurisdictions, this principle (which Wigmore described as one of 'curative admissibility') is not recognized by the English courts. Thus, in *R v Cargill*,[727] on a charge of unlawful intercourse with a girl aged between 13 and 16, the prosecutrix swore that she had been chaste before the accused seduced her. This was irrelevant because absence of consent, and hence the girl's character, is immaterial in such a case, but it did not entitle the accused to call evidence concerning the girl's behaviour with other men because the court was not prepared to say that, if the prosecution introduced a matter irrelevant to the issue, the defence was entitled to call evidence with regard to that irrelevant issue.

Conditional admissibility[728]

One fact may be relevant to another only if it is taken together with some further matter, and it may well be the case that this can be proved only by a witness who will be called after the one who testifies to the fact the relevancy of which is being considered. In such circumstances, the court allows the evidence to be given conditionally on its turning out to be relevant. If it proves to be irrelevant, the judge will tell the jury to disregard it. An excellent example is provided by the rules governing the admissibility of statements made in the presence of a party. These have probative value only in the light of the conduct of the person to whom they were made. If A confronts B and alleges that he has committed a crime against him, and B is later tried for that offence, evidence of what A said will usually be relevant only if B's conduct is something other than a stalwart denial of the charge; there is no doubt that A's statement may always be proved in the first instance, although

---

[725] *Manual of Law of Evidence* (7th edn) 28; Thayer *Preliminary Treatise on Evidence at the Common Law* 266. The view taken in the text is followed by the editor of *Phipson's Manual* (12th edn) 25.

[726] I Wigmore, [15].

[727] [1913] 2 KB 271. See also *Ready v Brown* (1968) 118 CLR 165. On the other hand, in *Barry v News Group Newspapers Ltd* 1999 SLT 590, it was held in Scotland that if irrelevant evidence were adduced, cross-examination to show it was a lie was permitted in an effort to discredit the witness's testimony as to relevant matters; for a similar rule in Australia, see *R v Maslen and Shaw* (1995) 79 ACR 199.

[728] I Wigmore, [14]; Phipson *Law of Evidence* (17th edn) [7.11], citing *Haig v Belcher* (1836) 7 C & P 389. The same notion is involved in the statement that evidence will be received *de bene esse*, for the origin of which see FDM in 62 *LQR* 38, and Plucknett in 68 *LQR* 130.

the judge may subsequently be obliged to tell the jury to disregard it altogether.[729] Such a state of affairs is better regarded as a concession to the fact that the evidence in a case often emerges slowly, and from the mouths of many witnesses, rather than an exception to the rule prohibiting the reception of irrelevant, or insufficiently relevant, matter. It seems that this factor may have motivated the analogical extension of the relevant provision of s 74 of Police and Criminal Evidence Act 1984[730] by Lord Steyn[731] to evidence tendered to show the guilt of a co-accused on a different count with which he had been charged, to rebut a submission of no case when proof of the count relating to the accused depended upon the co-accused's guilt of the crime on his own count. It may be thought that the composite nature of the issue, and the likelihood of prejudice, renders such an extension problematic.[732]

Inextricable matter

In a few cases, relevant and admissible evidence is so closely linked to irrelevant evidence that it is impracticable to sever the irrelevant evidence from the relevant, and in such a case, the irrelevant evidence is admitted so long as its admission is unlikely to be harmful.[733] Thus in a money laundering case admissions relating to the vulnerability of the victims was allowed, even though there was no evidence that the accused knew of it.[734]

RELEVANCE AND ADMISSIBILITY

Although there are no real exceptions to this rule, the existence of important exceptions to the rule that all sufficiently relevant evidence is admissible renders it essential to draw a sharp distinction between the relevancy and admissibility of evidence. The former is a concept arrived at inductively from experience, and its applicability can be tested deductively by the construction of a syllogism. It is not primarily dependent on rules of law.[735] The admissibility of evidence, on the other hand, depends first on the concept of relevancy of a sufficiently high degree, and second, on the fact that the evidence tendered does not infringe any of the exclusionary rules that may be applicable to it.[736] To quote Wigmore:[737] 'Admissibility signifies that the particular fact is relevant and something more,—that it

[729] *R v Christie* (n52). Such a direction may be exceedingly difficult to phrase: see *Hoch v R* (1988) 165 CLR 292.   [730] For fuller discussion of this provision, see 113.
[731] In *R v Hayter* [2005] UKHL 6, [2005] 2 All ER 209, [28] citing this passage.
[732] This extension was explicitly rejected in the minority judgments, and not explicitly endorsed by the other Lords constituting the majority.
[733] Even in the case of inextricable inadmissible evidence, a conviction will not necessarily be quashed if it is left in, so long as a sufficiently firm direction is given to the jury: *R v Flicker* [1995] Crim LR 493 (impossible to edit out from a vital statement an incidental reference to the accused's previous record).
[734] *R v Burdett* [2009] EWCA Crim 2541.
[735] Thayer sometimes wrote as though the doctrine of precedent was wholly inapplicable to questions of relevance (see (1900) 14 *Harv LR* 139, answering Fox 14 *Harv LR* 39). Wigmore, on the other hand, said 'So long as courts continue to declare in judicial rulings what their notions of logic are, just so long will there be rules of law which must be observed' (I Wigmore (Tillers revn) 691). For once, the truth really does lie between the two views, and Thayer conceded as much when he said decisions concerning relevance may 'stand as a precedent to half settle other cases'.
[736] In the United States, it has been held constitutional for states to draft legislation making relevant evidence inadmissible, even in the case of evidence relevant to the defence in a criminal case: *Montana v Egelhoff* 116 S Ct 2013 (1996) (evidence of voluntary drunkenness).   [737] I Wigmore (Tillers revn) 689.

has also satisfied all the auxiliary tests and extrinsic policies.' It is especially important not to smuggle new rules of inadmissibility into the law under the guise of axioms of relevance. The facts of every case are always complex, and it is inherently unlikely that any absolute general rules of relevance will be of legal significance. Thus a purported rule that evidence of the 'lifestyle' of the accused is never relevant to a charge of possession of drugs, but only to one of possession with intent to supply, has had to be rejected.[738] Although the distinction between relevancy and admissibility is expressly recognized in many English judgments, an oversimplification of Stephen's has exercised a somewhat baneful influence, and, by way of reaction perhaps, demands are sometimes made for the recognition of further basic concepts in the law of evidence.

STEPHEN'S TERMINOLOGY

In his *Digest of the Law of Evidence*, Stephen attempted to state the rules concerning the matters that may be proved in court wholly in terms of relevancy. The result was that he had to explain the rejection of hearsay on the ground that it was irrelevant or deemed to be irrelevant, while its reception under exceptions to the hearsay rule was based on the fact that it was relevant or deemed to be so. Other exclusionary rules were likewise said to involve the rejection of evidence that is irrelevant or deemed to be irrelevant. The objection to this mode of expression is that much of the evidence that English law rejects is highly relevant, and no one would now wish wholeheartedly to adhere to the terminology of the *Digest*, although its influence has been considerable.

Confusion between relevance and admissibility, or more accurately irrelevance and inadmissibility, was induced in *R v Kearley*[739] by counsel's concession that the admissibility of one of a number of solicitations for the supply of drugs by different people should be considered in isolation from the others, and that if it were inadmissible because irrelevant, then so must they be. This seems to rest on the implicit assumption that such inadmissibility connotes zero relevance, whereas the better view is that it connotes no more than insufficient relevance to be admissible when considered alone. While it is true that multiplication of zero can never increase the value of evidence, it is also true that, at some point, multiplication of an insufficient value is likely to increase the value of the evidence sufficiently to justify admissibility.

The demand for more basic concepts

It has been said that, in addition to recognizing the separate concepts of relevancy and admissibility, two further concepts of 'materiality' and 'receivability' should be introduced.[740] If this were done: 'relevant' would imply that the evidence tendered tends to prove the fact it purports to establish; 'materiality' would mean direct relevance to a fact in issue; 'admissibility' would denote that the evidence did not infringe an exclusionary rule; while 'receivability' would mean that the evidence was relevant, material, and admissible.

---

[738] *R v Guney* [1998] 2 Cr App Rep 242, 267A, disapproving dicta in *R v Halpin* [1996] Crim LR 112.
[739] [1992] 2 AC 228.
[740] Montrose (1954) 70 *LQR* 527. The concept of materiality is employed by Wigmore, that of receivability is canvassed by Professor Montrose.

These additional concepts have never been employed in practice, and it is dubious that their adoption would make the law any clearer.

Admissibility and weight of evidence

Questions concerning the admissibility of evidence must be distinguished from those relating to its weight. The former is a matter of law for the judge (although it may sometimes depend upon a preliminary finding of fact by him); the weight of evidence, on the other hand, is a question of fact, although, in cases tried with a jury, the summing-up frequently contains observations on the cogency of certain matters, and the judge can always withdraw an issue from the jury because the proponent has not adduced sufficient evidence in support of his claim. The distinction between admissibility and weight does not require further elaboration, but it is not clear-cut. The weight of evidence may affect its admissibility, as this is to some extent dependent on the degree of relevancy of the matter under consideration.[741] The law tends towards a broad basis of admissibility.[742] As a practical test it has been proposed, somewhat circularly, that evidence should be inadmissible for the defence in a criminal case on account of lack of weight only if 'no reasonable jury, properly directed as to its defects, could place any weight on it'.[743]

---

[741] *R v Quinn and Bloom* (n626). This is a complicating factor in the modern law relating to the admissibility of 'similar fact' evidence in criminal cases: see further, 378.

[742] 'People were formerly frightened out of their wits about admitting evidence lest juries should go wrong. In modern times, we admit the evidence and discuss its weight' (Cockburn CJ in *R v Birmingham Overseers* (n6), 767).

[743] *R v Robinson* (n683) [19], although a higher, but unspecified, standard was envisaged for prosecution evidence.

II

MATTERS NOT REQUIRING PROOF AND JUDICIAL FINDINGS AS EVIDENCE

The general rule is that all of the facts in or relevant to the issue in a given case must be proved by evidence—testimony, hearsay statements, documents, or things. While the question of which facts are in issue in any given proceedings is really a matter of substantive law, such rules occasionally masquerade as rules of evidence. This is the case with 'irrebuttable' presumptions, as for example s 50 of the Children and Young Persons Act 1933,[1] which says that it shall be conclusively presumed that no child under the age of ten can be guilty of any offence. Similarly it is not uncommon for a statute to dispense with proof of a disputable matter, thus s 79(1) of the Animal Health Act 1981 dispenses with proof of the appointment or handwriting of certain officials for the purposes of the Act. If a claimant or prosecutor fails to prove an essential fact, his opponent may succeed on a submission that there is no case to answer, although the evidence was readily available, for the court rarely exercises its discretion to allow a witness to be recalled.[2]

The general rule is subject to exceptions. Sometimes, the judge, or trier of fact, is entitled to find a fact of his own motion.[3] He may take judicial notice of it. In others, a party may formally admit a relevant matter. Even if not, a matter may still be determined against him because the law prevents him from contesting it. He is then 'estopped', as when the same matter has been determined against him and in favour of his opponent by a binding and conclusive judgment of a court. It is convenient to consider also in this chapter the whole question of the status of judicial findings in other proceedings. Each of these topics: judicial notice, formal admissions, estoppel, and evidence of judicial findings will be considered in turn, the second very briefly.

---

[1] As amended by the Children and Young Persons Act 1963, s 16.

[2] See *R v Pilcher* (1974) 60 Cr App Rep 1; *R v Gainsborough Justices, ex p Green* (1983) 78 Cr App Rep 9; and in Australia, *Bulecjik v R* (1996) 185 CLR 375, 408. For a rare exception, see *James v South Glamorgan County Council* (1994) 99 Cr App Rep 321.

[3] But should not on the basis of mere allegation unsupported by evidence, and without furnishing any opportunity for rebuttal: *Vogon International Ltd v Serious Fraud Office* [2004] EWCA Civ 104, [30].

SECTION 1. JUDICIAL NOTICE[4]

When a court takes judicial notice of a fact, in civil or criminal proceedings,[5] it declares that it will find the fact, or direct the jury to do so, although it has not been established by evidence. If, for instance, the date of Christmas should be in issue, or otherwise relevant, it will not be necessary for the proponent to call evidence that the relevant date is 25 December, because this is a matter of which judicial notice is taken.[6] There are two classes of case in which the court will act[7] in this way:[8]

Judicial notice refers to facts which a judge can be called upon to receive and to act upon either from his general knowledge of them, or from inquiries to be made by himself for his own information from sources to which it is proper for him to refer.

Statutes sometimes provide for judicial notice of certain facts. It will be convenient to illustrate the application of the doctrine by reference to facts that are judicially noticed without inquiry, facts judicially noticed after inquiry, and some which are noticed by statutory provision. Various theoretical questions are raised at the end.

FACTS JUDICIALLY NOTICED WITHOUT INQUIRY

It is pointless to try to list all cases in which courts have taken judicial notice of facts without inquiry. Their general justification is that the fact in question is too notorious[9] for serious dispute.[10] Examples include rulings that a fortnight is too short a period for

---

[4] For theoretical discussion, see Thayer *Preliminary Treatise on Evidence at the Common Law* ch 7; Morgan *Some Problems of Proof Under the Anglo-American System of Litigation* 36; McConville (1979) 1 *Liverpool LR* 62; Carter in Waller and Campbell (eds) *Well and Truly Tried* (1982).

[5] The court has discretion, and if the facts to be noticed would constitute a major part of the prosecution's case, may instead require evidence: see *R v Zundel* (1987) 35 DLR (4th) 338.

[6] The date of Good Friday is less notorious, and an Australian court was prepared to receive evidence from witnesses: *Pikos v Bezuidenhout* [2004] QCA 178, 145 ACR 544, although authoritative sources might seem available.

[7] There may be grounds also for distinguishing cases in which the court will take notice on its own motion, and those where it requires application: see *Dosoruth v Mauritius* [2004] UKPC 45, (2004) 148 SJLB 971.

[8] *Commonwealth Shipping Representative v P&O Branch Services* [1923] AC 191, 212. Morgan (n4) says the party seeking judicial notice of a fact 'has the burden of convincing the judge (a) that the matter is so notorious as not to be the subject of dispute among reasonable men, or (b) the matter is capable of immediate accurate demonstration by resort to readily accessible sources of indisputable accuracy'. Davis (see, for example, (1955) 55 *Columbia LR* 945) promoted a distinction between judicial notice of adjudicative and legislative facts, accepted by the Canadian Law Reform Committee in its draft Code, though it is more common to restrict judicial notice to adjudicative facts. See US Federal Rule 201; in Australia, in *Woods v Multi-Sport Holdings Pty Ltd* [2002] HCA 9, (2002) 208 CLR 460, [65] McHugh J explained the more generous scope of judicial notice, apt for the establishment of legislative facts, like greater use of statistical sources. In *R v Henry* [1999] NSWCCA 111, (1999) 106 ACR 149, [63], a similar approach was adopted with respect to facts relevant to establishing guidelines for sentencing. In Canada, see *R v Spence* 2005 SCC 71, [2005] 3 SCR 458.

[9] It may have become notorious, even if only to a limited class, including the magistrates, by constant reference: *Whitfield v DPP* [2006] EWHC 1414 (Admin), (2006) 150 SJLB 665 (contents of booklet habitually used by police as checklist for procedure to be applied in drink driving cases).

[10] Care may be needed against moving from an indisputable fact to a disputable gloss, as in *R v Hill* (2005) 221 CCC3d 472 (from fact that drug trade existed in British Columbia, to its aggravation by lenient

human gestation,[11] that the advancement of learning is among the purposes for which the University of Oxford exists,[12] that cats are kept for domestic purposes,[13] that men and women sharing a bed are likely to have sexual intercourse,[14] that criminals have unhappy lives,[15] that the reception of television is a common feature of English domestic life enjoyed mainly for domestic purposes,[16] and that sporting celebrities seek endorsement.[17] The court may be taken to know the meaning of ordinary expressions in the English language,[18] and that the value of money has declined since 1189,[19] but not, in Australia, of the relationship between the availability of alcohol and its consumption.[20] Judicial notice has been taken of the fact that a postcard might be read by anyone,[21] but not that husbands read their wives' letters.[22] These conclusions were reached without reference to extraneous sources of information, but sometimes judicial notice has been taken only after such reference.

FACTS JUDICIALLY NOTICED AFTER INQUIRY

These include cases in which the court acts on information supplied by a Secretary of State on what may loosely be described as political matters; inquiries into historical facts; various customs; and matters of professional practice.

The sources consulted by the judge may include reports of previous cases, certificates from various officials, works of reference,[23] and oral statements of witnesses.

What was once a notorious fact may become one of which notice will be taken only after the court's memory has been refreshed. In *Hoare v Silverlock*,[24] for instance, the claimant had applied to a benevolent society for assistance, and alleged defamation by reference to the truth of the fable about the frozen snake. Erle J said:[25]

I may take judicial notice that the words 'frozen snake' have an application very generally known indeed, which application is likely to bring into contempt a person against whom it is directed.

Nowadays a fact-finder would require a good deal of instruction about Aesop's fables.

---

sentencing); or from the danger of transmitting HIV to a partner by unprotected sexual relations, to the accused's knowledge that he was thereby endangering her life: *Mutemeri v Cheesman* [1998] 4 VR 484.

[11] *R v Luffe* (1807) 8 East 193.

[12] *Re Oxford Poor Rate Case* (1857) 8 E & B 184 (university premises within special rating provisions).

[13] *Nye v Niblett* [1918] 1 KB 23 (cats protected by the Malicious Damage Act 1861).

[14] *Woolf v Woolf* [1931] P 134.   [15] *Burns v Edman* [1970] 2 QB 541, [1970] 1 All ER 886.

[16] *Bridlington Relay Ltd v Yorkshire Electricity Board* [1965] Ch 436, [1965] 1 All ER 264.

[17] *Irvine v Talksport Ltd* [2003] EWCA Civ 423, [2003] 2 All ER 881.

[18] *Chapman v Kirke* [1948] 2 KB 450, [1948] 2 All ER 556; 454, 557. See, in Australia, *Bendixen v Coleman* (1943) 68 CLR 401. Expert evidence may be needed for unusual usage, as in 'rap': *Confetti Records v Warner Music UK Ltd* [2003] EWHC 1274 (Ch).

[19] *Bryant v Foot* (1868) LR 3 QB 497. See, in Australia, *In the marriage of Monticone* (1989) 98 FLR 460.

[20] *Executive Director of Health v Lily Creek International Pty Ltd* [2000] WASCA 258, (2000) 22 WAR 510, [72].   [21] *Huth v Huth* [1915] 3 KB 32.

[22] *Theaker v Richardson* [1962] 1 All ER 229, [1962] 1 WLR 151.

[23] Such works must be 'authoritative': see *Casley-Smith v FS Evans & Son Pty (No 4)* (1988) 49 SASR 339; and may not be consulted by the jury on its own initiative: *R v Wallace* [1990] Crim LR 433 (consultation of dictionary not sufficiently material).   [24] (1848) 12 QB 624.

[25] 633.

Political matters

In *Duff Development Co Ltd v Government of Kelantan*,[26] the government of Kelantan applied for an order against the enforcement of an arbitration award on the ground that Kelantan was an independent sovereign state. The Secretary of State for the Colonies, in reply to an inquiry, wrote that Kelantan was a sovereign state and the Sultan its ruler. The House of Lords held this conclusive because:[27]

It has for some time been the practice of our courts, when such a question is raised, to take judicial notice of the sovereignty of a state, and for that purpose (in case of any uncertainty) to seek information from a Secretary of State; and when information is so obtained the court does not permit it to be questioned by the parties.

The source of information to which the court resorts is treated as one of indisputable accuracy to avoid conflict between the courts and the executive.[28] As ever when courts renounce their powers of determining facts on the basis of evidence, the practice may be represented as something like submission to official dictatorship, but it is difficult to see an alternative means to determining the sovereignty of a foreign state, the membership of a diplomatic suite, the extent of territorial waters, or the existence of a state of war.[29] Moreover, the courts form their own opinion of the effect of the Secretary of State's answer and they may differ *inter se* on this point.[30]

Historical facts

In *Read v Bishop of Lincoln*,[31] the question was whether the mixing of communion wine with water and various other practices were contrary to the law of the church. It was held, against an objection to their doing so, that the courts might consider historical and ritualistic works on the subject. In the course of his speech in the House of Lords, Lord Halsbury made it clear that the judge can rely on his own historical learning, although 'where it is important to ascertain ancient facts of a public nature the law does permit historical works to be referred to'.[32] If questions concerning the tenets of a political creed were to arise, the English courts would, like Australian courts, consult the appropriate literature.[33] A similar practice would no doubt be adopted to decide general scientific or

---

[26] [1924] AC 797. See also *Taylor v Barclay* (1828) 2 Sim 213 (non-recognition of South American republic); *The Fagernes* [1927] P 311 (extent of territorial waters); *Engelke v Musmann* [1928] AC 433 (membership of diplomatic suite); *R v Bottrill, ex p Kuechenmeister* [1947] KB 41, [1947] 2 All ER 434 (continuance of war with Germany). [27] Lord Cave, 805.

[28] So, in Zimbabwe, the courts refused to take notice of the shortage there of foreign currency: *Chiraga v Msimuko* 2004 (1) SA 98.

[29] See cases cited in (n26) and *Preston v Preston* [1963] P 141, [1962] 3 All ER 1057 at 149, 1060f. Judicial notice will not be taken of a particular event, such as the date of a military operation, in a modern war: *Commonwealth Shipping Representative v P&O Branch Services* [1923] AC 191.

[30] *Carl Zeiss Stiftung v Rayner and Keeler Ltd (No 2)* [1967] 1 AC 853, [1966] 2 All ER 536. In *A-G v Tse Chu-Fai* (1998) 153 ALR 128, the High Court of Australia, faced with a difficult question relating to the effects of the transition of sovereignty in Hong Kong, explicitly affirmed its own ultimate right of decision, but found the view of the government helpful in determining a question of construction.

[31] [1892] AC 644.

[32] 653. In Canada, in *Law Society of British Columbia v Gravelle* (2001) 200 DLR (4th) 82, such consultation was allowed in relation to a disputed fact, despite expert evidence tendered to the contrary.

[33] *Australian Communist Party v Commonwealth* (1951) 83 CLR 1.

aesthetic questions. The courts have taken notice of what people must have at the time have believed about such matters as the likelihood of a war.[34]

Custom

In general, courts cannot treat facts as proved on the basis of the evidence in previous cases,[35] but this does not apply to the proof of custom, for it has been recognized that eventually, having had its existence before them in other cases, are entitled to say that they will take judicial notice of a custom and will not continue to require proof.[36] This recognition was made by Bray J while upholding a county court judge's right to take judicial notice of the custom whereby a domestic servant might terminate her employment within its first month by less than a full month's notice, but the doctrine so enunciated lies at the root of the recognition of a vast number of mercantile customs.[37] It is not easy to say when a custom has been recognized often enough to become the subject of judicial notice.

Professional practice

In *Davey v Harrow Corp*,[38] Lord Goddard CJ said:[39]

Where a boundary hedge is delineated on an ordnance survey map by a line, that line indicated the centre of the existing hedge. That is in accordance with the practice of the ordnance survey and courts can take notice of that practice as at least prima facie evidence of what a line on the map indicates.

Judicial notice will likewise be taken of the practice of conveyancers.

STATUTORY PROVISIONS

The doctrine of judicial notice may assist the proof of documents.[40] Subject to the presumption of due execution arising from the production of a document more than twenty years old from the proper custody, the due execution of a document, i.e. the fact that it was signed or sealed by the person by whom it purports to be signed or sealed, must be proved before the court will receive it in evidence.[41] This could lead to endless trouble with various documents in constant use, and numerous statutes provide for judicial notice being taken of signatures attached to official documents.[42] Former difficulties in the proof of statutes, like showing that the document before the court reproduced the Act duly passed by both Houses of Parliament, have been resolved by what is now s 3 of the Interpretation Act 1978. Its effect, when read together with the second Schedule and s 9 of the repealed

---

[34] *Monarch Steamship Co Ltd v Karlshamns Oljefabriker A/B* [1949] AC 196, [1949] 1 All ER 1; 234, 20, Lord Du Parcq.   [35] *Roper v Taylor's Central Garages (Exeter) Ltd* [1951] 2 TLR 284.

[36] *George v Davies* [1911] 2 KB 445, 448.   [37] *Brandao v Barnett* (1846) 12 Cl & Fin 787.

[38] [1958] 1 QB 60, 69.   [39] *Re Rosher* (1884) 26 Ch D 801.

[40] See European Communities Act 1972, s 4(2), for judicial notice by the English courts of community treaties and decisions of community courts, and Patents Act 1977, s 91, for judicial notice of the European Patent Convention.

[41] This was ameliorated in civil proceedings by s 9 of the Civil Evidence Act 1995, which vastly simplified the proof of public and business documents, dispensing with the need to prove signatures upon provision of an appropriate certificate. Although greater scope was given for authentication of documents in criminal proceedings by s 133 of the Criminal Justice Act 2003, there is no exact equivalent of s 9.

[42] See the Evidence Act 1845, s 2.

Interpretation Act 1889, is that every Act passed after 1850 shall be a public Act, and judicially noticed as such in the absence of an express provision to the contrary. Judicial notice has always been taken of a public Act of Parliament, so no evidence has ever been required concerning its passage through Parliament or its contents. Local by-laws must be formally proved.[43]

It is unfortunate that there is no express provision for the taking of judicial notice of statutory instruments because, even in recent times, courts have varied in their insistence on the production of a Stationery Office copy[44] and it is obscure whether proof by this method is authorized in the case of all statutory instruments.[45] It is, however, clear that proof of a statutory instrument is not required once constant reliance upon it has made it a matter of which judicial notice may be taken.[46] It has been sensibly suggested that no objection should be taken to informal proof of such instruments, unless there is some reason to doubt their accuracy.[47]

THEORETICAL QUESTIONS

The principal theoretical questions raised by the practice of taking judicial notice concern its relationship to the reception of evidence, the use that a judge can make of his personal knowledge, the rationale of the practice, and its tacit application.

Judicial notice and the reception of evidence

No problem arises with regard to the distinction between receiving evidence and taking judicial notice of a fact when judicial notice depends upon notoriety without need for inquiry by the judge. The judge is then acting on his own knowledge, a completely different procedure from assessing evidence. The processes converge when the judge makes inquiries before deciding to take judicial notice. If treatises are consulted, it is hard to say whether evidence is being received under an exception to the rule against hearsay or whether the judge is equipping himself to take judicial notice.[48] When the certificate of a Minister is sought on the question of foreign sovereignty, it was said both that evidence is not being taken and that the best evidence was being received.[49] Speaking of the class of case in which assessors may be consulted under statutory provisions, Lord Denning said:[50]

The court must possess itself of necessary information. Some judges may have it already because of their previous experience. Others may have to acquire it for the first time, but in either case

---

43 See *Donnelly v Carmichael* 1995 JC 215.

44 See *Palastanga v Solman* [1962] Crim LR 334. See also, in Canada, *R v Schaeffer* (2005) 251 DLR (4th) 156.   45 But see *R v Clarke* [1969] 2 QB 91, [1969] 1 All ER 924.

46 *R v Jones* [1969] 3 All ER 1559, 54 Cr App Rep 63; the same is true in Scotland: see *Valentine v McPhail* 1986 JC 131.   47 *R v Tang* [1995] Crim LR 813.

48 The distinction can be of practical importance only in proceedings before a jury. If evidence is being taken, the judge must place it before the jury. If judicial notice is taken, he can direct the jury to find the fact judicially noticed.

49 Contrast Lord Finlay and Lord Sumner in *Duff Development Co Ltd v Government of Kelantan* (n26), 813, 824, respectively.

50 *Baldwin and Francis Ltd v Patent Appeal Tribunal* [1959] AC 663, 691. In *R v HM Coroner for Surrey, ex p Wright* [1997] QB 786, [1997] 1 All ER 823 (assessor sitting with a coroner could cross-examine witnesses, but not tender evidence).

the information they glean is not evidence strictly so-called. When an assessor explains the technicalities, he does not do it on oath, nor can he be cross-examined, and no one ever called the author of a dictionary to give evidence. All that happens is that the court is equipping itself for its task by taking judicial notice of all such things as it ought to know in order to do its work properly.

The convergence of judicial notice and the reception of evidence is more marked when sworn testimony is heard before taking judicial notice. In *McQuaker v Goddard*,[51] the trial judge held that, in the absence of any evidence of scienter, those in control of a zoo had no case to answer for personal injuries caused by a bite from a camel because camels are *mansuetae naturae*. He reached this conclusion after consulting books about camels and hearing witnesses, some of whom spoke of the wild habits of camels but the more expert of whom deposed to their tameness. The judge's decision was affirmed by the Court of Appeal, Clauson LJ being careful to point out that, when hearing witnesses, the judge had not been taking evidence. The witnesses were simply assisting him in 'forming his view as to what the ordinary course of nature in this regard in fact is, a matter of which he is supposed to have complete knowledge'.[52] It seems that, even where the processes of taking judicial notice and receiving evidence approximate most closely, they remain essentially different: because: first, when the judge decides to take judicial notice of a fact after hearing witnesses, he may withdraw that fact from the jury although the witnesses differ; and second, the judge's decision constitutes a precedent.

If the processes of taking judicial notice and receiving evidence of a fact are essentially different, no evidence should be admissible in rebuttal of a fact that is judicially noticed. This seems the case in spite of occasional remarks suggesting that taking judicial notice is merely the equivalent of prima facie proof. Such remarks reflect the extreme generality of the facts of which judicial notice may be taken. Judicial notice that the seal or signature on a document is that of a particular court or official merely means that the seal or signature is recognized as similar to that of the court or official, and evidence of forgery in a particular case, although plainly admissible, does not rebut the fact of which judicial notice is taken.[53] Similarly, evidence that a particular practice was not followed on a particular occasion would not rebut the existence of the practice of which judicial notice is taken, nor, strictly speaking, would evidence of a change of practice, for judicial notice is simply taken of the current practice at a particular time.[54] There are, of course, many cases of judicial notice in which there can be no question of evidence in rebuttal, as when judicial notice is taken of the facts stated in the certificate of a government department.

Personal knowledge[55]

The general rule is that neither judge nor juror may act on his personal knowledge of facts,[56] even if acquired only from previous cases heard in the same court.[57] Nor may the court

---

[51] [1940] 1 KB 687, [1940] 1 All ER 471; cf *Turner v Coates* [1917] 1 KB 670 (both decided under common law liability for animals).

[52] 700. The ambiguity of this distinction between taking judicial notice and receiving evidence has been reflected in the need to give alternative bases for judgment in *Tutin v Mary Chipperfield Promotions Ltd* (1980) 130 NLJ 807. [53] *Holland v Johns* (1917) 23 CLR 149, 154.

[54] See, in Canada, *Media Health and Pharmaceutical Services Inc v Bramble* (1999) 175 DLR (4th) 385.

[55] See Manchester (1979) 42 MLR 22. [56] *Palmer v Crone* [1927] 1 KB 804.

[57] *Jarvis v DPP* [1996] RTR 192 (that a particular police station had only one breath-testing device).

take steps to acquire such knowledge in private, and in cases where the jury is permitted to disperse during a trial, it should be warned not to do so.[58] If the jury defies the judge's instruction not to visit the site of a crime to conduct its own observations, it may be enough to invalidate a conviction.[59] Justices may not apply scientific instruments[60] to exhibits in private,[61] nor may jurors conduct experiments in the jury room,[62] or precipitate serious possibility that they may have done so.[63] This rule has reference to particular facts.[64] When taking judicial notice, a judge frequently makes use of his general knowledge,[65] and justices can certainly make use of their knowledge of local conditions,[66] although in *Bowman v DPP*[67] this was distinguished from judicial notice, and warning recommended to facilitate comment by an opponent, absence of which might be fatal.[68] Distinction from the private reception of evidence is sometimes hard to draw. In *R v Field Justices, ex p White*,[69] for instance, the issue was whether cocoa must necessarily contain a quantity of foreign ingredients, not a matter of general notoriety nor even capable of being put beyond dispute by reference to appropriate sources of information. Nevertheless, some of the justices had acquired such knowledge in the navy, and the Divisional Court did not dispute the propriety of their making use of it. Wills J, a distinguished mountaineer, said:

In the nature of things, no one in determining a case of this kind, can discard his own particular knowledge of a subject of this kind. I might as well be asked to decide a question as to the sufficiency of an alpine rope without bringing my personal knowledge into play.

In *Reynolds v Llanelly Associated Tinplate Co*, in which the Court of Appeal held that the trial judge had gone too far in making use of his personal knowledge of the prospects of employment of a workman of a particular age and skill, Lord Greene said:[70]

The practice of county court judges of supplementing evidence by having recourse to their own local knowledge and experience has been criticised, praised as most beneficial, objected to and encouraged in different decisions.

---

[58] *R v Oliver* [1996] 2 Cr App Rep 514.

[59] *R v Morrison and Sutton* [1997] CLY 1331, although if a juror visits the scene of the crime in private, the irregularity will not be fatal provided it is unrelated to any issue in the case: *R v Smyth* (1998) The Times, 16 September.

[60] Although the use of such things as magnifying glasses or rulers is not excluded: *R v Maggs* (1990) 91 Cr App Rep 243. See, in Australia, *Marika v Manley* (1998) 101 ACR 345 (magistrate wrongly took into account an alcohol test that he had ordered to be conducted on the accused in the courtroom before him).

[61] *R v Tiverton Justices, ex p Smith* [1981] RTR 280.

[62] *R v Stewart and Sappleton* (1989) 89 Cr App Rep 273.

[63] *R v Cadman* [2008] EWCA Crim 1418; and should be warned against it; *R v Taka* [1992] 2 NZLR 129, 132.

[64] Although the distinction is sometimes hard to draw, and it is difficult to reconcile the result in *Jarvis* above with that in *Mullen v Hackney LBC* [1997] 2 All ER 906, [1997] 1 WLR 1103, in which the court was prepared to take judicial notice of the past behaviour of the defendant in relation to undertakings to the court, even though there was no evidence to that effect, and indeed, some to the contrary.

[65] But in *Donnelly v Carmichael* 1995 JC 215, it was held improper for a judge to supplement partial evidence of a location, which should have been fully proved, with his local knowledge about it.

[66] *Ingram v Percival* [1969] 1 QB 548, [1968] 3 All ER 657 (extent of tidal water); *Kent v Stamps* [1982] RTR 273 (topography of road); *Paul v DPP* (1989) 90 Cr App Rep 173 (residential character of area).

[67] [1991] RTR 263.

[68] As in *Norbrook Laboratories (GB) Ltd v Health and Safety Executive* [1998] EHLR 207.

[69] (1895) 64 LJMC 158; cf *R v Tager* [1944] AD 339.

[70] [1948] 1 All ER 140, 142, where a number of the relevant authorities are cited.

It was cited in *Wetherhall v Harrison*,[71] where a Divisional Court distinguished between the use of their private knowledge by judges and arbitrators, on the one hand, and by justices and jurors,[72] on the other. The latter are not trained to exclude certain matters from their consideration and, in any case, as a cross-section of the community they should pool their general knowledge. The issue had been whether a motorist whose roadside breath test had proved positive had simulated a fit in order to prevent a specimen of his blood from being taken. One of the justices was a doctor and communicated to the other members of the bench his views about the possible effects on the accused of the prospect of having his blood taken. They also made use of their wartime experience of the effect of inoculations on certain people. The accused was held to have had reasonable excuse for not providing a specimen and the Divisional Court held that the conduct of the justices had been proper, for there had been no question of one of their number giving evidence to the others. This may be contrasted with the decision in *R v Ficker*,[73] a case involving tyres where one of the jurors was a tyre specialist, and seems to have used his specialist knowledge to introduce wholly different lines of argument from those advanced by counsel, and the verdict was quashed on the basis that he had, in effect, being giving evidence.[74] There is now further danger that some of the jurors may be tempted to supplement the evidence in the case by private research on the Internet.[75]

Nor should it be forgotten that some judges, like those in the Patent Court, are selected just because they have some technical expertise, and may probably take notice of a wider range of matters, although their not having such expertise does not mean that they can take notice that there is none.[76] This is also true in the case of expert assessors to a tribunal, and who should provide their advice in public at the close of the evidence, and before submissions, so that the parties can respond.[77] In such cases, it has been said that the distinction between general and particular knowledge tends to break down, and that it should be drawn between the specialist knowledge reasonably to be expected of someone selected for his expertise, and that which is not.[78]

[71] [1976] QB 773, [1976] 1 All ER 241.

[72] The extent to which the issue can be ventilated in relation to jurors is limited by the strict restriction on evidence of what has taken place in the jury room: Contempt of Court Act 1981, s 8; see, in Australia, *R v Vjestica* [2008] VSCA 47, 182 ACR 350. [73] (1999) 96(30) LSG 29.

[74] In such a situation, it was said in *Mangano v Farleigh Nettheim* (1965) 65 SRNSW 228 that any juror with special knowledge should testify.

[75] Condemned in *R v Karakaya* [2005] EWCA Crim 346, [2005] 2 Cr App R 77; *R v Marshall and Crump* [2007] EWCA Crim 35, [15] (recommending more specific direction to jury).

[76] *Hauni-Werke Korber & Co KG's Application* [1982] RPC 327.

[77] *Watson v General Medical Council* [2005] EWHC 1896, (Admin), [2005] LIR Med 435. This accords with the position in the United States under FRE 201(e). See also *Thomas v Thomas* [1961] 1 All ER 19 (magistrates not to act on knowledge of party derived from past cases without giving opportunity to rebut; cf *Mullen v Hackney LBC* [1997] 2 All ER 906, county court judge was permitted, it is submitted inadvisedly, so to act); and, in Australia, *In the marriage of Dean* (1988) 94 FLR 32 (judge not to consult book on valuation of business without affording opportunity to make submissions).

[78] *Checkpoint Ltd v Strathclyde Pension Fund* [2003] EWCA Civ 84, [2003] L&TR 22, [31].

Rationale

There are at least two reasons for having a doctrine of judicial notice. In the first place, it expedites the hearing of many cases. Much time would be wasted if every fact that was not admitted had to be the subject of evidence that would, in many instances, be costly and difficult to obtain. Secondly, the doctrine tends to produce uniformity of decision on matters of fact where a diversity of findings might sometimes be distinctly embarrassing. It was used to promote such consistency in the application to flick knives of the definition of offensive weapons in *R v Simpson*.[79] It has been said that the basic essential is that the fact judicially noticed should be of a class that is so generally known as to give rise to the presumption that all persons are aware of it.[80] No doubt this is the justification for taking judicial notice in the vast majority of cases, but it is not always so. It would be idle to pretend that the particulars with regard to the behaviour of camels[81] in *McQuaker v Goddard* could be presumed to be generally known.

Tacit applications

Tacit applications of the doctrine of judicial notice are more numerous and more important than express ones. A great deal is taken for granted or assumed in determining relevance, as when persons accused of drugs dealing were found in possession of scales or wraps, or that the accused became confused when charged; such facts are relevant only provided there is a common practice to use such things in the commission of the crime, or provided that the guilty tend more than the innocent to become confused when charged, but no one ever thinks of calling evidence on such a subject.

SECTION 2.   FORMAL ADMISSIONS

A party may admit facts for the purposes of the trial, thus saving his adversary time and expense. In civil proceedings, he may seek to avert the costs of proving facts not so admitted.[82] The Civil Proceedings Rules specify the procedure for making formal admissions, and encourage their use as a form of saving costs. Such formal admissions are binding only for the purposes of the particular case in which they are made[83] and must be distinguished from informal admissions that are received under an exception to the rule against hearsay discussed in Chapter XIV.[84] Unlike formal admissions, informal admissions are an item of evidence. Their maker may endeavour to explain them away at the trial at which they are proved.

Under s 10 of the Criminal Justice Act 1967, formal admissions of any facts of which oral evidence may be given[85] may be made by or on behalf of the prosecution or defendant

---

[79] [1983] 3 All ER 789, [1983] 1 WLR 1494, citing this passage. Followed in relation to butterfly knives in *DPP v Hynde* [1998] 1 All ER 649, [1998] 1 WLR 1222.

[80] *Holland v Jones* (1917) 23 CLR 149, 153, Isaacs CJ; *Auckland City Council v Hapimana* [1976] 1 NZLR 731.   [81] That they require help in the act of copulation.

[82] CPR 14 and 14.1.A.

[83] Although they can be withdrawn with the permission of the court pursuant to CPR 14.1(5) upon the principles laid down in *Braybrook v Basildon and Thurrock University NHS Trust* [2004] EWHC 3352, [45]; see Williams (2006) 156 *NLR* 542.

[84] *Sowerby v Charlton* [2005] EWCA Civ 1610, [2006] 1 WLR 568; for cases outside the range of the amended rule, see *White v Greensand Homes Ltd.* [2007] EWCA Civ 643, [2007] 1 CLC 1001, [29].

[85] So not if the evidence would be inadmissible: see *R v Coulson* [1997] Crim LR 886.

before or at any criminal proceedings, and may, with the leave of the court, be withdrawn.[86] They may be reduced to writing, and provided to the jury.[87] A potentially troubling feature of s 10 is that it appears to make no allowance for the possibility of the co-accused raising inconsistent defences, and one position being the subject of admission by the prosecution, which would then appear to be conclusively binding, at least against it,[88] for the purpose of the proceedings. It is extremely doubtful that such a procedure would be regarded as fair under the European Convention on Human Rights, since the prejudiced accused would have conclusively presumed against him a matter upon which the prosecution relied, simply because it was prepared to admit its truth as against his co-accused.

Another form of formal admission needs to be made in order to justify the delivery of a police caution,[89] or warning.[90]

SECTION 3. ESTOPPEL[91]

When an estoppel binds a party to litigation, he is prevented from placing reliance on, or denying the existence of, certain facts. This justifies the treatment of estoppel as an exclusionary rule of evidence. So regarded, it is less rigorous than the rules governing the exclusion of evidence on the ground of public policy because estoppels operate only if they are pleaded, but, like the exclusion of evidence on that ground, and unlike the exclusion of evidence under the rule relating to hearsay, estoppels operate without reference to the purpose for which reliance is placed on a particular fact. From the point of view of the party in whose favour they operate, an estoppel can be regarded as something that renders proof of certain facts unnecessary. The only form of estoppel that needs to be discussed here is estoppel by record.

The principles underlying estoppel by record[92] are 'interest rei publicae ut sit finis litium'—it is for the common good that there should be an end to litigation—and 'nemo debet bis vexari pro eadem causa'—no one should be sued twice on the same ground. The practical consequence is that, generally speaking, the order of a court of competent jurisdiction[93] is conclusive.[94] An application may be made to have it set aside if it was

---

[86] For the correct practice, see *R v Kolton* [2000] Crim LR 761.

[87] *R v Pittard* [2006] EWCA Crim 2028, [24].

[88] It would require some schizophrenia to avoid prejudice to the co-accused also.

[89] *R (Wyman) v Chief Constable of Hampshire Constabulary* [2006] EWHC 1904 (Admin), (2006) 150 SJLB 665, [11].   [90] *R (R) v Durham Constabulary* [2005] UKHL 21, [2005] 2 All ER 369, [46].

[91] It was suggested in *Specialist Group International Ltd v Deakin* [2001] EWCA Civ 777, [10] that the word 'finality' be substituted for 'estoppel' as being more generally understood by laymen. In the United States the term 'preclusion' is used, see *San Remo Hotel v County of San Francisco* 545 US 323 (2005).

[92] Spencer-Bower *Res Judicata* [1.10] (4th edn, 2008, by Handley). Letters patent may constitute estoppel by record between the Crown and the grantee (*Cropper v Smith* (1884) 26 Ch D 700), but the only estoppel worth discussion here is estoppel by a judgment or res judicata. Estoppel by record is a misnomer because the doctrine applies to judgments that are not those of a court of record (see Lord Guest in *Carl Zeiss Stiftung v Rayner and Keeler Ltd (No 2)* (n30); 933, 564).

[93] *Butland v Powys County Council* [2009] EWHC 151 (Admin).

[94] Even if made only because a claim has been withdrawn, rather than litigated out: see e.g. *Barber v Staffordshire County Council* [1996] 2 All ER 748; or the order is made by consent: see, in Australia, *Somanader v Minister for Immigration* [2000] FCA 1192, 178 ALR 677, but not if it has been struck out overseas for public policy reasons, *Relfo Ltd v Varsani* 2009] EWHC 2297 (Ch).

obtained by fraud,[95] and fraud or collusion in the obtaining of a judgment may be proved by a stranger to the proceedings.[96] These matters belong to the law of procedure, but the conclusive effects of judgments on the whole world as well as the parties to civil litigation do bear upon the law of evidence. After they have been considered, reference will be made to the position in criminal proceedings.

The present concern is with the extent to which judgments constitute an estoppel preventing any evidence from being given to contradict them.[97] The extent to which they can be regarded as prima facie evidence of the facts upon which they were founded (to be discussed in the final section of this chapter) is another matter. An estoppel can be raised on a foreign judgment, whether national[98] or supranational,[99] even one itself denying fraud in obtaining a prior foreign judgment.[100] It may, however, sometimes be more difficult to discern the precise issues in such cases.[101] In the case of two inconsistent foreign judgments each pronounced by a court of competent jurisdiction, the earlier prevails.[102]

CONCLUSIVE EFFECT OF JUDGMENTS ON THE WHOLE WORLD—JUDGMENTS *IN REM*

A judgment is conclusive as against all persons of the existence of the state of things that it actually effects when the existence of that state is in issue or relevant to it.[103] Examples include an action for malicious prosecution in which the record of the criminal court would be conclusive of the acquittal of the claimant,[104] or an action by a surety against the principal debtor in which a judgment obtained against the surety by the creditor would be conclusive of the fact that it was obtained and the amount for which it was pronounced.[105] These examples may seem trivial, but the conclusiveness of a judgment with regard to the state of things that it actually effects is of great importance if it is *in rem*.

A judgment *in rem* is:[106]

A judgment of a court of competent jurisdiction determining the status of a person or thing, or the disposition of a thing (as distinct from a particular interest in it of a party to the litigation).

---

[95] In *R v Calcedo* [1986] VR 499, an acquittal obtained by a plea bargain from which the accused subsequently resiled failed to ground an estoppel. In Ireland, it has been held that misconduct that was known to the prejudiced party and deliberately not raised cannot be relied upon: *Tobin v Twomey Services Ltd v Kerry Foods Ltd* [1999] 3 IR 483.   [96] *R v Duchess of Kingston* (1776) 20 State Tr 355.

[97] A clear distinction between effect as estoppel and as precedent was made by the New Zealand Court of Appeal in *Wire Supplies Ltd v Commissioner of Taxation* [2007] NZCA 244, [2007] 3 NZLR 458, [32].

[98] *DSV Silo-und Verwaltungsgesellschaft mbH v Owners of the Sennar* [1985] 2 All ER 104, [1985] 1 WLR 490 (Dutch Court).   [99] *Iberian (UK) Ltd v BPB Industries plc* [1997] ICR 164 (European Court).

[100] *House of Spring Gardens Ltd v Waite* [1991] 1 QB 241, [1990] 2 All ER 990. More readily on substantive than purely procedural decisions, especially if interim: *Desert Sun Loan Corp v Hill* [1996] 2 All ER 847.

[101] The matter is fully treated in textbooks on the conflict of laws; see, for example, Dicey, Morris, and Collins *Conflict of Laws* (14th edn, 2006) ch 14.

[102] *Showlag v Mansour* [1995] 1 AC 431, [1994] 2 All ER 129.

[103] Stephen *Digest of the Law of Evidence* (12th edn) art 41. This article was adopted by Lord Goddard CJ in *Hollington v Hewthorn & Co Ltd* [1943] KB 587, [1943] 2 All ER 35; 594, 39.

[104] *Purcell v Macnamara* (1807) 9 East 157.   [105] *Re Kitchin, ex p Young* (1881) 17 Ch D 668, 673.

[106] *Halsbury's Laws of England* (4th edn) 194, as adopted in *Lazarus-Barlow v Regent Estates Co Ltd* [1949] 2 KB 465, [1949] 2 All ER 118; 475, 122, by the Master of the Rolls who added 'such a judgment is conclusive evidence for and against all persons whether parties, privies or strangers, of the matters actually decided'.

Allen v Dundas[107] is a simple illustration of the effect of such a judgment so far as the whole world is concerned. The defendant was indebted to P, and, on P's death, X obtained probate of what purported to be P's will. The defendant paid X the amount of P's debt, and, when the grant of representation was set aside in favour of the claimant because the will was a forgery, it was held that the defendant was not liable to pay the debt over again to the claimant. Everyone was bound to give credit to the probate (a judgment *in rem*) until it was vacated, which meant that the claimant was estopped from denying X's executorship at the material time. Other examples of judgments *in rem* are provided by the condemnation of a ship by a prize court, which precludes everyone from denying the non-neutral nature of the cargo,[108] a determination that a street is a highway,[109] and a decree of nullity or divorce.[110] Just occasionally, difficulty may be experienced in determining exactly what matters the judgment comprises.[111]

EFFECT OF JUDGMENTS ON PARTIES TO CIVIL CASES

Whether a judgment is *in rem* within the meaning of the above definition or *in personam*— a term that can be taken to comprise all judgments that are not *in rem*—its effect on the parties and those claiming through them is much wider than its effect in litigation between strangers.[112] This is because the rule is that parties and their privies[113] are estopped from denying not merely the state of affairs established by the judgment, that A has been adjudged liable to B in the sum of a thousand pounds, for example, or that C is divorced, but also the grounds upon which that judgment was based, that A broke a contract with B, or that C committed adultery.

Cause of action estoppel

Estoppel by record *inter partes*, or '*estoppel per rem judicatam*' as it is usually called, is of two kinds. The first, usually called 'cause of action estoppel', is dependent on the merger of the cause of action in the judgment. Although its bearing on the substantive law is of great importance, this kind of estoppel does not call for detailed consideration here. Once it appears that the same cause of action was held to lie or not to lie in a final[114]

---

[107] (1789) 3 Term Rep 125.   [108] *Geyer v Aguilar* (1798) 7 Term Rep 681.

[109] *Wakefield Corp v Cooke* [1904] AC 31.

[110] *Salvesen v Austrian Property Administrator* [1927] AC 641; *Callaghan v Hanson-Fox* [1992] Fam 1, [1992] 1 All ER 56.

[111] See *Neil Pearson & Co Pty Ltd v Comptroller of Customs* (1995) 127 FLR 350 (whether previous decision established that goods dutiable or that persons importing them liable to pay duty for doing so) incorporating extensive discussion of the principles of estoppel generally.

[112] Although where there is substantial overlap of fact the earlier decision, while not grounding an estoppel, may nevertheless furnish a good starting point, deviation from which might require strong reasons, *AA(Somalia) v Secretary of State for Home Department* [2007] EWCA Civ 1040.

[113] The expression is a rough equivalent for those claiming through the original party. Privies are said to be either 'in estate'—lessor and lessee or vendor and purchaser, for instance; 'in blood'—ancestor and heir; or 'in law'—testator and executor or intestate and administrator, for instance.

[114] A judgment of the English court upholding a European patent (UK) is final, even though revocation proceedings remain possible in the European Patent Office (EPO), *Unilin Beheer BV v Berry Floor NV* [2007] EWCA Civ 364; although a revocation decision in the EPO is not final for these purposes in the English courts, *Buehler AG v Chronos Richardson Ltd* [1998] 2 All ER 960, and nor are opposition proceedings in the Trade Marks registry, *Special Effects Ltd v L'Oreal SA* [2007] EWCA Civ 1.

judgment between the same parties,[115] or their privies, litigating in the same capacity, provided the judgment was not obtained by fraud,[116] there is an end of the matter: 'If one party brings an action against another for a particular cause and judgment is given on it, there is a strict rule of law that he cannot bring another action against the same party for the same cause.'[117] The effect can be draconian. Thus, in *Conquer v Boot*,[118] judgment for the claimant for damages for breach of warranty to build a house in a workmanlike manner was held to bar a claim for damages subsequently occurring in consequence of the breach of warranty.[119] This form of estoppel has survived, and may even have been fortified by, the introduction of the CPR.[120] Nor can it be precluded by splitting an action into different parts as between different courts.[121] Of course, this applies only to litigation[122] arising out of the same facts.[123] If the facts change,[124] then a judgment arising out of the earlier facts raises no estoppel.[125] Nor can there be an estoppel in respect of an issue withdrawn only after the decision relied upon to estop.[126] There has nonetheless been a tendency to extend the idea underlying cause of action estoppel to claims that, although not the subject of formal adjudication, could have been brought forward as part of the cause of action in the proceedings, which resulted

---

[115] In *Prospere v Prospere* [2007] UKPC 2 there were two previous judgments, one between the claimant and a third party, the other between the defendant and the same third party, and only the former, despite being merely a default judgment, created an estoppel. In exceptional circumstances, the practical effect may also be to prevent a third party's action succeeding: see *Mulkerrins v PriceWaterhouseCoopers* [2003] UKHL 41, [2003] 4 All ER 1, [45].

[116] *Cinpres Gas Injection Ltd v Melea Ltd* [2008] EWCA Civ 9. Minor delinquencies may not be fatal, *Director of the Assets Recovery Agency v Kean* [2007] EWHC 112 (Admin).

[117] Lord Denning MR in *Fidelitas Shipping Co Ltd v V/O Exportchleb* [1966] 1 QB 630, [1965] 2 All ER 4; 640, 8. As explained by Lord Goff in *Indian Endurance* [1993] AC 410, [1993] 1 All ER 998; 417, 1004, the doctrine of merger prevents further action when the claimant has succeeded, and it was to bolster that in cases involving foreign litigation that s 34 of the Civil Jurisdiction and Judgments Act 1982 was passed, whereas cause of action and issue estoppel operate where the claimant had failed in the earlier proceedings.

[118] [1928] 2 KB 336. See also, in Australia, *Chamberlain v Deputy Comr of Taxation* (1988) 164 CLR 502, (doctrine of res judicata applied rigidly to prevent recovery of the balance of tax outstanding after a claim had been understated by a factor of ten as a result of omitting a last digit of zero).

[119] Distinguished in *Purser & Co (Hillingdon) Ltd v Jackson* [1977] QB 166, [1976] 3 All ER 641, submission to arbitration and award held to apply only to the matters covered by the submission).

[120] *Lennon v Birmingham City Council* [2001] EWCA Civ 435, [35]. It was also there said, [36], that it was equally unaffected by the passage of the Human Rights Act 1998.

[121] *Fraser v HLMAD Ltd* [2006] EWCA Civ 738, [2007] 1All ER 383, in which the claimant unsuccessfully sought to proceed in an employment tribunal up to the statutory maximum, and in the High Court for any excess.

[122] It does not apply to informal adjudication, such as a formal police caution: *Abraham v Metropolitan Police Comr* [2001] 1 WLR 1257.

[123] But it does apply despite purely formal differences, e.g. where one action *in rem* against a ship and the second *in personam* against owners: *Indian Endurance (No 2)* [1998] AC 878, [1997] 4 All ER 380; and still more surprisingly in patent proceedings when the patent raising the estoppel had subsequently been revoked retrospectively in proceedings brought by a stranger to the original proceedings: *Coflexip SA v Stolt Offshore MS Ltd* [2004] EWCA Civ 213, [2004] FSR 34.

[124] Or had already changed before a judgment given in ignorance of the change: *Powell v Wiltshire* [2004] EWCA Civ 534, [2005] QB 117. Change of time is not enough, even in the case of a continuing obligation, *Onwuama v Ealing LBC* [2008] EWHC 1704 (QB).

[125] *Thyssen-Bornemisza v Thyssen-Bornemisza* [1986] Fam 1, [1985] 1 All ER 328.

[126] *Blackburn Chemicals Ltd v Bim Kemi AB* [2004] EWCA Civ 1490, [2005] UKCLR 1.

in the judgment alleged to constitute an estoppel.[127] In the frequently quoted words of Wigram VC:[128]

...where a given matter becomes the subject of litigation in, and of adjudication by, a court of competent jurisdiction, the court requires the parties to that litigation to bring forward their whole case, and will not (except under special circumstances) permit the same parties to open the same subject of litigation in respect of matter which might have been brought forward as part of the subject in contest, but which was not brought forward, only because they have, from negligence, inadvertence, or even accident, omitted part of their case. The plea of res judicata applies, except in special cases, not only to points upon which the court was actually required by the parties to form an opinion and pronounce a judgment, but to every point which properly belonged to the subject of litigation, and which the parties, exercising reasonable diligence, might have brought forward at the time.

This dictum has been applied in the Court of Appeal,[129] the Privy Council,[130] the House of Lords,[131] and in other jurisdictions.[132] It has been extolled and applied in the field of personal injuries:[133]

It is a salutary rule. It avoids unnecessary proceedings involving expense to the parties, and waste of court time which could be available to others; it prevents stale claims being brought long after the event, which is the bane of this type of litigation; it enables the defendant to know the extent of his potential liability in respect of any one event; this is important for insurance companies who have to make provision for claims and it may also affect their conduct of negotiations, their defence and any question of appeal.

It has, however, never been quite free from criticism,[134] and despite the desirability of preventing a party from splitting his claim in the hope of securing some forensic advantage, its basis has been increasingly questioned. It may have the effect of preventing a party from pursuing an otherwise justifiable cause of action and, especially after the passage of the Human Rights Act 1998, there is increased awareness of potential breach of Art 6 of the European Convention on Human Rights entitling access to the courts.[135] Its rationale sits somewhat uneasily between private law, so far as it is designed to prevent a party from being continually harassed by different proceedings in respect of the same situation, and public law, so far as it regards the involvement of the courts in such attempts as an abuse of their process.

---

[127] Especially in intellectual property cases: see *Poulton v Adjustable Cover and Boiler Block Co* (1908) 25 RPC 661 (patent); *Parmenter v Malt House Joinery* [1993] FSR 680 (registered design); *Hormel Foods Corp v Antilles Landscape NV* [2005] EWHC 13 (Ch), [2005] RPC 85 (trademark).

[128] *Henderson v Henderson* (1843) 3 Hare 100, 114.

[129] *Greenhalgh v Mallard* [1947] 2 All ER 255. And applied by the Court of Appeal to industrial tribunals, *Divine-Bortey v Brent LBC* [1998] ICR 886.

[130] *Brisbane City Council v A-G for Queensland* [1979] AC 411, [1978] 3 All ER 30.

[131] *Arnold v National Westminster Bank Ltd* [1991] 2 AC 93, [1991] 3 All ER 41.

[132] See e.g. in South Africa *Van Rensburg v Myburgh* 2007 (6) SA 287.

[133] *Talbot v Berkshire County Council* [1994] QB 290, [1993] 4 All ER 9; 297, 15.

[134] See Lord Devlin in *Connelly v DPP* [1964] AC 1254, 1356f; and in Australia, Deane and Gaudron JJ in *Rogers v R* (1994) 181 CLR 251, 275.

[135] See Lord Millett in *Johnson v Gore Wood & Co* [2002] 2 AC 1, [2001] 1 All ER 481; 59D, 525j. Although such is the vagueness and qualification of human rights law that it is far from clear that the rule could not be justified.

Nor is it at all obvious that it has the clear link expressed by Wigram VC to the doctrine of res judicata. As noted by the Privy Council in *Associated Electric and Gas Insurance Services Ltd v European Reinsurance Company of Zurich*:[136]

[T]hat principle relates to issues that might have been raised but were not and therefore depends not upon matters of decision but upon matters which might have been decided but were not.

The position was authoritatively reviewed by the House of Lords in *Johnson v Gore Wood & Co*.[137] The claimant was the alter ego of a company, and both he and the company alleged loss on account of the defendant's negligence. The company sued, and despite some discussion of joining both corporate and personal claims in the same proceedings, the company's suit went ahead alone, and was settled. When the claimant subsequently initiated his personal proceeding, he was met by the argument that to do so would amount to an abuse of process of the sort indicated by the rule in *Henderson v Henderson*. This claim failed at first instance, but succeeded in the Court of Appeal. The categorization of the rule as a form of abuse of process first appeared in 1947,[138] and was endorsed by Lord Wilberforce as its true basis in 1979.[139] The advantage of such a categorization is that it widens the scope of the rule from one limited to previous adjudication to one like that in issue where not only had the issue not been raised in the previous proceedings, but neither had it been adjudicated,[140] since the proceedings had been settled before reaching that stage. This flexible[141] approach was adopted by the House which considered it sufficient, without any additional element of collateral attack[142] or unjust harassment, for relitigation[143] to amount to abuse, although the mere fact that an issue *could* have been raised did not mean that it necessarily *should* have been raised. Lord Bingham reformulated the rule in saying:[144]

[I]t is in my view preferable to ask whether in all the circumstances a party's conduct is an abuse than to ask whether the conduct is an abuse and then, if it is, to ask whether the abuse is excused or justified by special circumstances.

---

136 [2003] UKPC 11, [2003] 1 All ER (Comm) 253, [16]. See also Lord Bingham in *Barrow v Bankside Agency Ltd* [1996] 1 All ER 981, [1996] 1 WLR 257; 983h, 260: 'The rule is not based on the doctrine of res judicata in a narrow sense, nor even on any strict doctrine of issue or cause of action estoppel. It is a rule of public policy based on the desirability, in the general interest as well as that of the parties themselves, that litigation should not drag on for ever and that a defendant should not be oppressed by successive suits when one would do.'   137 (n135).

138 Somervell LJ in *Greenhalgh v Mallard* (n129).

139 *Brisbane City Council v A-G for Queensland* (n130), 425G. In *Anju Tannu v Shiraz Salerhal Moosajee* [2003] EWCA Civ 815, an appeal was allowed because the trial judge had applied the rule too rigidly without considering whether there was an abuse.

140 In *R (East Hertfordshire DC) v First Secretary of State* [2007] EWHC 834 a decision arrived at by default on account of lack of evidence was not regarded as adjudication. Conversely, failure to amend but instead to initiate separate proceedings precipitated the application of *Henderson v Henderson* in *Hossain v Sonali Bank* [2007] EWHC 1431 (QB).

141 It is not, however, a discretion, although the appellate court might still review on a *Wednesbury* basis, *Aldi Stores v WSP Group plc* [2007] EWCA Civ 1260, [16]; *Stuart v Goldberg* [2008] EWCA Civ 2, [24].

142 Even collateral attack will not necessarily amount to abuse of process: see *Arthur JS Hall & Co v Simons* [2002] 1 AC 615, [2000] 3 All ER 673, 679G and 703E, 681d and 703f.

143 In *Ruttle Plant Hire Ltd v Secretary of State for Environment, Food and Rural Affairs* [2007] EWHC 1773 (TCC) late amendment was distinguished from re-litigation.   144 31E.

It is interesting that on these facts Lord Millett thought it more an abuse for the defendant to raise the issue of abuse of process than for the claimant to pursue his personal suit. It should be noted that the Court is invested with sufficient power to strike out any statement of case on such a basis.[145]

The old rule could have worked great hardship on defendants who let judgment go against them by default, and had been held to have no application to those judgments, the rules of cause of action estoppel being very narrowly applied in such cases.[146] Nor is the rule to be applied so strictly to pre-trial applications.[147] Similarly, the court has been astute to refuse to apply the doctrine of cause of action estoppel when its strict application would lead to injustice, and an increase rather than a decrease in litigation.[148] Delay[149] in bringing a second action alone is not enough to trigger the rule in *Henderson v Henderson*,[150] and it may sometimes even be acceptable to keep two separate actions in being so as to avoid a limitation defence, especially where the party so doing is willing to consolidate them.[151]

The rule has been extensively discussed in Australia, where a distinction is drawn between different types of defence.[152] It has further been held there to depend upon its being unreasonable not to have raised the issue in the earlier litigation.[153] It seems that a similar approach is now being adopted here in the aftermath of *Johnson v Gore Wood*, with the result that estoppel has been refused when both parties agreed not to raise an issue,[154] but allowed when one party so delayed a claim that he was prevented from raising it in the original action.[155]

---

[145] CPR 3.4.

[146] *New Brunswick Rly Co v British and French Trust Corp Ltd* [1939] AC 1, [1938] 4 All ER 747; *Kok Hoong v Leong Cheong Kweng Mines Ltd* [1964] AC 993, [1964] 1 All ER 300; *Pugh v Cantor Fitzgerald* [2001] EWCA Civ 307 reaffirmed this approach after the adoption of the CPR. There is no estoppel by record where an action is dismissed for want of prosecution (*Pople v Evans* [1969] 2 Ch 255, [1968] 2 All ER 743) or where proceedings are withdrawn (*Owens v Minoprio* [1942] 1 KB 193, [1942] 1 All ER 30). It does, however, apply where an issue has been argued, and finally decided, even though the litigant appeared in person: *Item Software (UK) Ltd v Fassihi* [2002] EWHC 3116, [2003] IRLR 769; but not in Ireland, where the litigant's absence was due to a failure by his insurers, *Foley v Smith* [2004] IR 538.

[147] *Woodhouse v Consignia plc* [2002] EWCA Civ 275, [2002] 2 All ER 737, [56].

[148] *Sajid v Sussex Muslim Society* [2001] EWCA Civ 1684.

[149] Misconduct of the opposing party is not generally very relevant to a claim of abuse of process by the other, *Walbrook Trustees (Jersey) Ltd v William Fattal* [2008] EWHC 991 (Ch).

[150] *Stuart v Goldberg* (n141).   [151] *Rosenberg v Nazarov* [2008] EWHC 812 (Ch), [76].

[152] See the thorough discussion of the rule by the High Court of Australia in *Port of Melbourne Authority v Anshun Pty Ltd (No 2)* (1981) 147 CLR 589, in which the defendant in negligence proceedings claimed contribution from a co-defendant, but failed to claim an indemnity, and was held to be estopped. In *Heid v Connell Investments Pty* (1987) 9 NSWLR 628, there was some suggestion that the rule applies more naturally to defendants than to claimants, not least in respect of a different cause of action; and in *Bryant v Commonwealth Bank of Australia* (1995) 130 ALR 129, it was applied in respect of counterclaims based on defences that had been withdrawn from the original action.

[153] *Gibbs v Kenna* [1999] 2 VR 19, especially [28], listing factors relevant to that determination.

[154] *Kennecott Utah Copper Corp v Minet Ltd* [2003] EWCA Civ 905, [2004] 1 All ER (Comm) 60.

[155] *Basso v Estry* [2005] APP LR 11/03. See also *Barnes v Handf Aceptances Ltd* [2005] EWCA Civ 314 (claim based on prolix amendment rejected in earlier proceedings).

Issue estoppel

Lord Denning MR regarded this form as an extension of the first:[156]

Within one cause of action, there may be several issues raised which are necessary for the determination of the whole case. The rule then is that, once an issue has been raised and distinctly determined between the parties, then, as a general rule, neither party can be allowed to fight that issue all over again.

He suggested that the dicta in *Henderson v Henderson* might also apply to issue estoppel, but it may be better to regard the latter as restricted to issues actually determined in the former litigation, for there may be many reasons why a litigant did not raise a particular issue, and it would be unjust to prevent him from raising it in later proceedings.[157] On the other hand, when an issue has been determined, even by way of concession on an appeal, there is less reason to take a strict view, and every reason to uphold the estoppel.[158]

Issue estoppel started late and developed gradually. The basic principles were first clearly stated by Diplock LJ in *Mills v Cooper*,[159] and subsequently endorsed by the House of Lords in *Hunter v Chief Constable of West Midlands*.[160] The House of Lords rejected Lord Denning's attempt in the Court of Appeal to eliminate the requirements of privity and mutuality on the basis that it is unjust that a party against whom an issue has been determined after a full opportunity to contest it, should be permitted to raise precisely the same issue again in subsequent proceedings involving another. The House of Lords preferred to decide the case upon an issue upon which the Court of Appeal had been unanimous: that it amounted to an abuse of the process of the court to launch a collateral attack upon a decision of a court of competent jurisdiction,[161] by raising an issue for a second time.[162] The House noted that this involved recognizing a difference between the operation of the doctrine in England and in North America.[163] The conditions were concisely reformulated by Lord Brandon in *DSV Silo-und Verwaltungsgesellschaft mbH v Owners of The Sennar*:[164]

In order to create an estoppel of that kind, [issue estoppel per rem judicatam] three requirements have to be satisfied. The first requirement is that the judgment in the earlier action relied on as

---

[156]   *Fidelitas Shipping Co Ltd v V/O Exportchleb* (n117); 640, 8; see also the judgments of Diplock LJ in the same case and in *Thoday v Thoday* [1964] P 181, [1964] 1 All ER 341. In Canada judicial review is immune to res judicata but not to issue estoppel, *Mohl v University of British Columbia* (2006) 265 DLR (4th) 109.

[157]   *Carl-Zeiss-Stiftung v Rayner and Keeler Ltd (No 2)* (n30), 555 and 916, 947, and 573, Lords Reid and Upjohn, respectively. In Canada, confusion between cause of action and issue estoppel has led to an appeal being allowed: *Furlong v Avalon Bookkeeping Services Ltd* (2004) 243 DLR (4th) 153.

[158]   *Khan v Goleccha International Ltd* [1980] 2 All ER 259, [1980] 1 WLR 1482; 267, 1491, distinguishing *Jenkins v Robertson* (1867) LR 1 Sc & Div 117, and restricting it to cause of action estoppel proper.

[159]   [1967] 2 QB 459, [1967] 2 All ER 100; 468, 104.

[160]   [1982] AC 529, [1981] 3 All ER 727; 541, 733.

[161]   It is not enough to attack an informal process, such as a police caution, even though it is in some respects similar: *Abraham v Metropolitan Police Comr* [2001] 1 WLR 1257, [15].

[162]   Although this alone may be insufficient, see *Arthur JS Hall & Co v Simons* (n142), 100 and *Bragg v Oceanus Mutual* [1982] 2 Lloyd's Rep 132 (good reasons to present the issue differently on the second occasion).

[163]   See e.g. in the United States, *Bernhard v Bank of American National Trust and Savings Association* 122 P 2d 892 (1942); *Bruszewski v United States* 181 F 2d 419 (1950); *Blonder-Tonque Laboratories Inc v University of Illinois* 402 US 313 (1971); and in Canada, *Royal Bank of Canada v McArthur* (1985) 19 DLR (4th) 762.

[164]   (n98); 110, 499.

creating an estoppel must be (a) of a court of competent jurisdiction, (b) final and conclusive and (c) on the merits. The second requirement is that the parties (or privies) in the earlier action relied on as creating an estoppel and those in the later action in which that estoppel is raised as a bar must be the same. The third requirement is that the issue in the later action in which the estoppel is raised as a bar must be the same issue as that decided by the judgment in the earlier action.

It will generally be irrelevant that the earlier decision was wrong,[165] since as Lord Hoffmann has said:[166]

The whole point of an issue estoppel on a question of law is that the parties remain bound by an erroneous decision,

In other words, the predominant purpose is to prevent re-litigation of an issue already determined[167] in the absence of special circumstances making it just to do so.[168]

It was further accepted in *Johnson v Gore Wood*[169] that considerations of abuse of process might apply as much to issue as to cause of action estoppel, and in such cases might diminish the importance of the technical conditions set out by Lord Brandon, although they continue to apply where no abuse of process can be demonstrated.[170]

Each of the requirements listed by Lord Brandon will be considered in turn.

Previous judgment

This must first be one of a court[171] of competent jurisdiction. This issue was analysed most clearly by Steyn J in *Speedlink Vanguard v European Gateway*.[172] In that case, a collision at sea had been considered by a court of formal investigation, set up under the Merchant Shipping Act 1894. The court found negligence in the navigation of one of the ships, and it was argued that this finding estopped its being controverted in subsequent proceedings for damages in Admiralty. It was held that, as such, a court of formal investigation acts primarily in an investigative role so far as the cause of the collision is concerned, and in an adjudicative capacity only so far as the certification of the relevant mariners is concerned; similarly, it can be regarded as a court of competent jurisdiction only for its findings in the latter, and not in the former, respect. In similar vein, it has been held that neither purely administrative decisions, whether of magistrates[173] or of administrative tribunals,[174] nor

---

[165] But not in Australia that it was procedurally unfair, especially in the absence of a positive ruling on the relevant point, *Applicants M16 of 2004 v Minister for Immigration* [2005] FCA 1641, 228 ALR 519, [67].

[166] *Watt v Ahsan* [2007] UKHL 51, [33].

[167] *Phosphate Sewage Co Ltd v Molleson* (1879) 4 App Cas 801, 814, approved unanimously by the House of Lords in *Hunter v Chief Constable of West Midlands* (n160), 545, and applied by the Court of Appeal in *Taylor Walton v Laing* [2007] EWCA Civ 1146 (re-litigation of the same unchanged issue against a different party).

[168] *Arnold v National Westminster Bank* (n131). See also *Paulik v Slovakia* (2008) 46 EHRR 142 (later DNA test showed paternity judgment wrong).

[169] (n135), 31A, 498b; see *Koulias v Makris* [2005] UKHC 526 (Ch) (abuse of process for sister to bring claim identical to one by her brother that had failed, after a previous indication that she would not do so).

[170] See e.g. *Sweetman v Nathan* [2002] EWHC 2458 (QB).

[171] Or exceptionally a tribunal with fully adjudicative powers: *Lennon v Birmingham City Council* [2001] EWCA Civ 435, [24].   [172] [1987] QB 206, [1986] 3 All ER 554.

[173] Failure by examining magistrates to commit can raise no estoppel: *R (Redgrave) v Metropolitan Police Comr* [2003] EWCA Civ 4, [2003] 1 WLR 1136; see also in Australia, *Wiest v DPP* (1988) 81 ALR 129.

[174] *R v Secretary of State for the Environment, ex p Hackney LBC* [1983] 3 All ER 358, [1983] 1 WLR 524; but see, in Australia, *Secretary of Department of Aviation v Ansett Transport Industries Ltd* (1987) 72 ALR 188.

mere exercises of discretion,[175] can raise an estoppel. If, however, an inferior tribunal has an adjudicative function, its decisions may ground an estoppel, provided that it is acting within such jurisdiction,[176] or even if it wrongly so determines.[177] It should be noted further that a partly inquisitorial procedure will not by itself prevent a court from being one of competent jurisdiction.[178]

A second condition is that the previous judgment must have been final. Matrimonial decisions apart,[179] a decision of an inferior court will operate as an estoppel in the High Court, but the decision must be one from which there could have been an appeal.[180] The mere fact that there was no appeal does not prevent a judgment from being final. A judgment can be final in this context even though made on an interlocutory application.[181] Where a decision is taken on a provisional basis, it will not support issue estoppel if one of the parties failed to anticipate that it would be made on the basis of a full hearing. It seems that a decision about the admissibility of evidence, or the credibility of a witness,[182] made by the judge on a voir dire may also amount to a final decision, at least when the jury returns its verdict after considering the evidence so admitted.[183] If, on the other hand, the jury disagrees, and a retrial is ordered, no rulings made at the first trial can raise an issue estoppel at the retrial,[184] even on substantial issues.[185] Where a decision by a supranational body[186] or a foreign tribunal[187] is subject to revocation by a national court, it cannot raise an estoppel.[188]

The third condition relating to the prior judgment is that it should have been made 'on the merits', a phrase explained by Lord Diplock in *DSV Silo-und Verwaltungsgesellschaft mbH v Owners of The Sennar*:[189]

What it means in the context of judgments delivered by courts of justice is that the court has held that it has jurisdiction to adjudicate on an issue raised in the course of action to which the particular set of facts give rise, and that its judgment on that cause of action is one that cannot

---

[175] *Mullen v Conoco Ltd* [1998] QB 382.

[176] *Crown Estate Comrs v Dorset County Council* [1990] Ch 297, [1990] 1 All ER 19. It is immaterial that the judgment is obtained by consent, and not yet entered into the court's records: *Marks v National & General Insurance Co Ltd* (1993) 114 FLR 416.   [177] *Watt v Ahsan* (n166).

[178] In *DSV Silo-und Verwaltungsgesellschaft mbH v Owners of The Sennar* (n98), the Dutch court's procedure in the decision creating the estoppel was partly inquisitorial.

[179] And it seems matters determined on bankruptcy petitions that are liable to be set aside at a full hearing before a final order is made: *Eberhardt & Co Ltd v Mair* [1995] 3 All ER 963, [1995] 1 WLR 1180.

[180] *Concha v Concha* (1886) 11 App Cas 541.

[181] *Midland Bank Trust Co Ltd v Green* [1981] AC 513, [1981] 3 All ER 153. Cf, in Australia, *Re Martin* (1966) 141 ALR 117, in which an interlocutory decision did raise an estoppel, and *Wilson v Union Insurance Co* (1992) 112 FLR 166, in which it did not. See, in New Zealand, *Joseph Lynch Land Co Ltd v Lynch* [1995] 1 NZLR 37.   [182] *MY(Turkey) v Secretary of State for Home Affairs* [2008] EWCA Civ 477.

[183] *Hunter v Chief Constable of West Midlands* (n160); 542, 734. But see, in Canada, *Duhamel v R* [1984] 2 SCR 555, in which a ruling on the first voir dire in the accused's favour, crystallized by an acquittal, created no estoppel in respect of a second voir dire in respect of the same confession.

[184] *Bobolas v Economist Newspaper* [1987] 3 All ER 121, [1987] 1 WLR 1101.

[185] And certainly not rulings on the admissibility of evidence during a voir dire at the first aborted trial: *R v Blair* (1985) 1 NSWLR 584.

[186] *Buehler AG v Chronos Richardson Ltd* [1998] 2 All ER 960 (decision of Opposition Division of the European Patent Office).

[187] *Svenska Petroleum Exploration AB v Government of Lithuania* [2005] EWHC 1529.

[188] (n186).   [189] (n98); 106, 494.

be varied, re-opened or set aside by the court that delivered it or any other court of co-ordinate jurisdiction although it may be subject to appeal to a court of higher jurisdiction.

So expressed this condition seems to add little to the others,[190] although it may be the most appropriate explanation for disregarding matters pronounced upon by way of *obiter dicta*.[191]

Same parties acting in the same capacity

In *Townsend v Bishop*,[192] the claimant was injured in a collision with the defendant's lorry when he was driving his father's car. The claimant's father sued for damages to the car, when the defendant's plea that it was caused by the contributory negligence of the claimant who was acting as his father's agent succeeded. It was held that the claimant was not estopped from denying his contributory negligence in an action in which he claimed damages for personal injuries. This was simply because the parties to the two actions were different. If allowance is made for the notion of privity under which one party may be estopped because the person through whom he derives his right would be estopped, the question of identity of parties is not usually likely to cause trouble;[193] the unusual case of *Carl Zeiss Stiftung v Rayner and Keeler Ltd (No 2)*,[194] shows that the requirements of identity and privity are narrowly construed by the English courts. In a previous action brought in the West German courts, it had been held that the claimants, a body known as the Council of Gera, had no right to represent the Stiftung. The Stiftung then brought an action in the English courts by an English firm of solicitors, and it was held by a majority of the House of Lords that, although the solicitors were instructed by the Council of Gera, no estoppel precluded either the solicitors or the Stiftung from alleging that the action was duly authorized because the parties to the two proceedings were not identical and because there was no privity between the Council of Gera and the solicitors. Representation of a common principal does not lead of itself to privity.[195] Nor are directors, managers, or employees bound by litigation against a company.[196] The strength of this view was re-emphasized

---

[190] It does not, e.g., exclude a consent judgment: *Palmer v Durnford Ford* [1992] QB 483, [1992] 2 All ER 122.

[191] See *Penn-Texas Corp v Murat Anstalt (No 2)* [1964] 2 QB 647, [1964] 2 All ER 594; 660, 597; *Green v Martin* (1986) 63 ALR 627.

[192] [1939] 1 All ER 805. See also *Gleeson v J Wippel & Co Ltd* [1977] 3 All ER 54, [1977] 1 WLR 510; *Ramsay v Pigram* (1967) 118 CLR 271; *Bryan v Kildangan Stud Unlimited Liability Co* [2005] IEHC 144, [2005] 1 IR 587.

[193] In *Bank of Montreal v Mitchell* (1997) 143 DLR (4th) 697, principals were estopped from contesting the result of claims being struck out in litigation involving their agents, which they had deliberately refused to join.   [194] (n30).

[195] Lord Wilberforce, unlike the other members of the House, tended to think that the only ground on which it could be held that there was no estoppel was that the West German judgment was not final. From a realistic point of view, he thought the parties were the same (the Council of Gera) and the issues raised in the causes of action were the same (passing off). There is American authority in favour of this more flexible approach.

[196] *Shears v Chisholm* [1994] 2 VR 535; *Keller v Glenco Enterprises Ltd* (2008) 290 DLR (4th) 712. Nor liquidators in their personal capacity: *Brien v Australasian Memory Pty Ltd* (1997) 142 FLR 242; nor shareholders: *Belton v Carlow County Council* [1997] 1 IR 172; nor, in Canada, other plaintiffs represented by the same firm with the same arguments by the determination of a foreign class action to which other Canadians were party: *Currie v McDonald's Restaurants of Canada* (2005) 250 DLR (4th) 224; and in South Africa *Rail Commuters Action Group v Transnet Ltd* 2006 (6) SA 69.

by the House of Lords in *Inntrepreneur Pub Co v Crehan*,[197] in which Park J's decision to try an issue relating to the legality of an agreement by one pub chain was held not to have been precluded by the European Commission's decision to the contrary in relation to a similar agreement made by another pub chain in relation to a different tenant.

In the field of public law, although in principle estoppels may bind the Crown,[198] it was held in *R (Nahar) v Social Security Comrs*[199] that the Crown is not indivisible, and litigation against one department cannot raise an estoppel against another.

Where the same issue arises in new litigation between co-defendants to previous litigation, they are bound by issue estoppel arising from those proceedings, even though in the previous litigation they did not raise the issue so decided against each other.[200]

Same issues

A strict construction of the requirement concerning identity of parties and their capacity can be justified on the ground that no one ought to be wholly precluded from arguing a point by a decision taken in proceedings at which he was not represented. It is open to question whether the requirement with regard to identity of issues should be applied so strictly, for it is undesirable that there should be conflicting decisions on what is in substance the same issue of fact, even though there is a technical ground for treating it as different from that which was the subject of earlier litigation. Where new legislation has supervened, it is harder to contend that an issue remains the same.

Some cases favour a narrow and some a broad approach to this question. In *Hoystead v Taxation Comr*,[201] the Privy Council held that a taxing authority was estopped from making an assessment for the year 1920–21 by a previous judgment relating to the assessment for the year 1918–19. In *Society of Medical Officers of Health v Hope (Valuation Officer)*,[202] on the other hand, the House of Lords held that a local valuation officer was not estopped from assessing the Society's premises for rates by a decision on a previous year's assessment that the Society was exempt. The question in these cases was basically whether one year's assessment raises a different issue from another year's assessment, although the same legal point is involved, and special rules may be applicable to tax cases.

The issue has arisen most often,[203] and proved most contentious, in 'running down' cases, where a collision occurs between two cars, injuring an innocent third party, most often a passenger in one of the cars. The question is whether apportionment on an issue

---

[197] [2006] UKHL 38, [2006] 4 All ER 465.

[198] *Robertson v Minister of Pensions* [1949] 1 KB 227, [1948] 2 All ER 767; 231, 770.

[199] [2001] EWHC Admin 1049, [2002] 2 FCR 442, [43]–[69]; so too adverse determinations in confiscation proceedings do not bar action by the Assets Recovery Agency: *Director of Assets Recovery Agency v Olupitan* [2006] EWHC 1906 (Admin).

[200] *Sweetman v Nathan* (n170), [59]. It is not, however, enough that a party merely interpleaded in the earlier litigation: *Gribbon v Lutton* [2001] EWCA Civ 1956, [2002] QB 902, [48] and [90].

[201] [1926] AC 155, not followed in *Mohamed Falil Abdul Carffoor (Trustees of the Abdul Caffoor Trust) v Income Tax Comr, Columbo* [1961] AC 584, [1961] 2 All ER 436, but accepted as still good authority in *Aston-Barrett v Universal Island Records Ltd* [2006] EWHC 1009 (Ch), [2006] EMLR 21.

[202] [1960] AC 551, [1960] 1 All ER 317. Lord Keith of Avonholm also held, 569, that an estoppel could not bind the rating officer as he was carrying out a statutory duty; this could hardly prevent a cause of action estoppel from arising. On the whole question of estoppel against statutes, see Andrews (1966) 29 MLR 1.

[203] The cases down to 1957 are discussed by Street, 73 LQR 358.

between the first two parties governs that between them when a third party's claim is being determined.[204]

The broad view gained strength,[205] and found expression in *Wall v Radford*.[206] This involved a successful action by an innocent passenger against her driver as first defendant and the other culpable driver as second defendant,[207] with contribution held equal between the two defendants. The first defendant then sued the second defendant in respect of her own injuries, and the second defendant sought to estop her from claiming more than 50 per cent on the basis of the earlier finding. After examining the older, and Commonwealth, authority, Popplewell J conceded that the duties to a passenger and to other road users were technically different as a matter of law, but thought them identical as a matter of fact. On the facts, he found that there was no difference between the driver's negligence in respect of her own passenger, and her contributory negligence in respect of her own injuries. He encapsulated this view by remarking:[208]

...although a *separate* duty is owed to another driver from that owed to a passenger that does not mean in the instant case that the duty is in any way *different*.

Even when the issues are identical, differences in the onus of proof may sometimes prevent an estoppel from arising, so civil proceedings are not necessarily estopped by an acquittal in respect of the same matter.[209] Similarly, in *Re Norris*,[210] the House of Lords was not prepared to allow an estoppel to be raised on the basis of a confiscation order made in criminal proceedings, to which the claimant was not a party, although present as a witness, and against whose interest a presumption arose.[211] A claimant might, however, be estopped from denying facts relied on by the defence as justification if he were to sue the Crown for damages for an assault by a police officer if those facts had been the subject of a criminal conviction for some such offence as drunkenness or using insulting words on the occasion in question.[212] In such a case, the heavier burden borne by the prosecutor on a criminal charge could not possibly operate adversely to the claimant.

Pleading

In *Vooght v Winch*,[213] it was held that the party alleging the existence of an estoppel by record must plead the former judgment, otherwise it merely constitutes evidence in his favour to be considered by the jury. If, nevertheless, it is prepared to decide in favour of the opposite party, it may do so, although it may often be disposed to act as the tribunal did on

[204] Sometimes the issue is first litigated between the drivers directly, as in *Wood v Luscombe* [1966] 1 QB 169, [1964] 3 All ER 972, and sometimes between the innocent third party and one of the drivers, as a contribution point, as in *Bell v Holmes* [1956] 3 All ER 449, [1956] 1 WLR 1359.

[205] For example, *Wood v Luscombe* [1966] 1 QB 169, [1964] 3 All ER 972.

[206] [1991] 2 All ER 741. See also *North West Water Ltd v Binnie & Partners* [1990] 3 All ER 547.

[207] Not, in fact, the driver of the car collided with.   [208] 750. Original emphasis.

[209] See *Halford v Brookes* [1991] 3 All ER 559, [1991] 1 WLR 428.

[210] [2001] UKHL 34, [2001] 3 All ER 961, [2001] 1 WLR 1389.

[211] The House also intimated, [29], that had it not so decided, it would have been necessary to consider the possible impact of the Human Rights Act 1998.

[212] It would, however, be necessary for the normal conditions to be satisfied: *Hunter v Chief Constable of West Midlands* (n160).

[213] (1819) 2 B & Ald 662. An estoppel may be pleaded in a second action, although the claim form was issued before judgment in the first: *Morrison Rose & Partners v Hillman* [1961] 2 QB 266, [1961] 2 All ER 891.

the former occasion. The rules of procedure are, of course, less strict than they used to be, but it was still generally maintained under the old law that all estoppels should be specially pleaded.[214] The rule that, when a judgment was not pleaded, it might, nevertheless, be treated as evidence of the facts upon which it was based in later proceedings between the same parties is hard to reconcile on principle with the common law rule that the judgment is not admissible as evidence of these facts in proceedings between parties, or between one party to the earlier litigation and a stranger, but it will be shown in the next section that the latter rule is questionable.

EFFECT OF JUDGMENTS ON PARTIES TO CRIMINAL CASES

In criminal[215] proceedings, the rule against double jeopardy[216] has played a role roughly equivalent to that played by cause of action estoppel in civil proceedings, and will be mentioned first. Exceptions to the doctrine will be set out in the second section. Although issue estoppel, as such, has been held inapplicable in English criminal law,[217] some aspects of abuse of process bear resemblance to it, and this will constitute the third section of this part.

Double jeopardy: autrefois acquit and autrefois convict

These pleas in bar, in their strict[218] form, most resemble cause of action estoppel. It has now been accepted that, in *Connelly v DPP*, Lord Devlin stated the law correctly:[219]

For the doctrine of autrefois to apply it is necessary that the accused should have been put in peril of conviction for the same offence as that with which he is then charged. The word 'offence' embraces both the facts which constitute the crime and the legal characteristics which make it an offence. For the doctrine to apply it must be the same offence both in fact and in law.

The accused had had his conviction for murder in the course of an armed robbery quashed on appeal, and was subsequently charged with robbery, patently a different charge from one of murder, and one that did not require the prosecution as part of its argument to prove that he had committed the murder.[220] Although that case involved what was argued to be equivalent to an acquittal, exactly the same approach has been endorsed in relation to a previous conviction.[221] This has been held quite consistent with the European Convention

---

214 Odgers *On Civil Court Actions* (24th edn, 1996) 13.26. Estoppel does not figure among the examples of matters required by Practice Direction 16, [10.2] to be included in the particulars of claim, but this is not, of course, decisive.

215 Extradition is subject to a special statutory regime under the Extradition Act 2003 s 80, see *Bohning v USA* [2005] EWHC 2613 (Admin), [2006] 3 All ER 394; and also in Ireland, *Att-Gen v Abimbola* [2007] IESC 56, [2008] 2 IR 302.

216 For historical background, see Friedland *Double Jeopardy* (1969); for the basis for reform of the modern law, see Law Commission No 267 *Double Jeopardy and Prosecution Appeals* (Cm 5048, 2001).

217 *DPP v Humphrys* [1977] AC 1, [1976] 2 All ER 497, but it can apply to habeas corpus proceedings despite their 'criminal' character: *R v Governor of Brixton Prison, ex p Osman* [1992] 1 All ER 108, [1991] 1 WLR 281.

218 Given the development of abuse of process it seems unlikely that double jeopardy will be extended, *R v IK et al* [2007] EWCA Crim 971, [23] (not to earlier proceedings themselves not strictly criminal).

219 (n134); 1339, 433H.   220 There was no doubt that the murder had occurred.

221 *R v Beedie* [1998] QB 356, [1997] 2 Cr App Rep 167; 360F, 170E (accused convicted of regulatory offence for poor maintenance of a gas fire causing user's death, subsequently indicted for manslaughter).

on Human Rights.[222] It should be noted, however, that even on the strict view, acquittal of a more serious offence implies acquittal of less serious offences of which the accused could have been convicted on the same indictment.[223] It has similarly been held that where the *actus reus* and *mens rea* of one count in the indictment is the same as that in another, even a technical acquittal on the former will bar prosecution for the latter, and that it is irrelevant that the accused at the time of acquittal forswore any intention subsequently to plead autrefois acquit.[224]

Exceptions

It must first be noted that the doctrine applies only to valid[225] and final decisions.[226] Two statutory exceptions to the doctrine, relating to acquittals will be described and their compatibility with human rights law considered.

Tainted acquittals

This exception,[227] contained in ss 54 to 57 of the Criminal Procedure and Investigations Act 1996, was designed to deal with burgeoning intimidation of jurors or witnesses. It may be invoked when a conviction of an administration of justice offence[228] relates to the relevant acquittal. Application may then be made to quash the acquittal: then if without the offence, the accused would not otherwise have been acquitted, and providing that it would not be contrary to the interests of justice to do so,[229] the Court of Appeal will quash the acquittal; and proceedings can then be instituted against the accused for the offence of which he was originally acquitted.

This provision has been little used,[230] and the Law Commission has made a number of suggestions for its reform, including extending the range of offences against the administration of justice,[231] relaxing the requirement that there have been a conviction,[232]

---

[222] *R v Young* [2005] EWCA Crim 2963 (guilty of wounding with intent, and acquitted of intent to murder; subsequent charge of murder when victim died).

[223] For example, acquittal of murder implies acquittal of manslaughter in respect of the same incident. See also in Australia *Gilham v R* [2007] NSWCCA 323, 178 ACR 72 (a factually difficult case where acceptance of a plea of manslaughter implied acquittal of the charge of murder).

[224] *R v G* [2001] EWCA Crim 1215, [2001] 1 WLR 1727; *R (A) v S Staffs Mag Ct* [2006] EWHC 1200.

[225] So not to cases where the court had no jurisdiction: *R v West* [1964] 1 QB 15, [1962] 2 All ER 624 (purported trial of indictable offence by magistrates); or adopted an invalid procedure: *Crane v DPP* [1921] 2 AC 299 (two defendants purportedly tried together without joinder); or the offence was a continuing one and different dates were particularized, *Clare County Council v Floyd* [2007] 2 IR 671.

[226] So not to retrials where part of the regular process of appeal, such as those ordered by the Divisional Court after an appeal from magistrates by way of case stated, or by the Court of Appeal under the provisions of the Criminal Appeal Act 1968, s 7, as amended. Finality refers to only the expiration of normal processes, and is not precluded by the possibility of an appeal out of time, or of a conviction being reopened after review by the Criminal Cases Review Commission. Nor does the rule apply in respect of withdrawn summary prosecutions: *Islington LBC v Michaelides* [2001] EWHC Admin 468. In the United States, however, the rule does apply to an interim judicial ruling that there is no evidence to justify a conviction: *Smith v Massachusetts* (2005) 543 US 462.

[227] The original recommendation was made by the Royal Commission on Criminal Justice (Cm 2263, 1993) [10–74].   [228] As defined in s 54(6).

[229] Section 55 contains these and the further conditions that the accused has been given a reasonable opportunity to make representations to the court, and that it appears to the court that the administration of justice conviction will stand.

[230] At the time of Law Com WP 156 *Double Jeopardy* (1999), it had never been invoked: [6.1] n 1.

[231] Law Com 267 recs 10 and 11.   [232] Rec 12.

changing the standard of proof of causation,[233] and removing the burden of showing that a retrial would be in the interests of justice.[234] These recommendations have, however, yet to be enacted.[235]

New evidence

This exception, contained in Pt 10 of the Criminal Justice Act 2003, was largely inspired by disquiet over the Stephen Lawrence case,[236] and implements a rather broader version[237] of the recommendations of the Law Commission.[238] The core justification is that in cases where compelling new evidence comes to hand after an acquittal to show that the accused indeed committed the crime, it is unjust that the acquittal should stand. The primary consideration against reform is the value of finality, and the principle that once a person has been acquitted, he is entitled not to be harassed by being charged with, and tried again for, the same offence.[239] As might be expected, the result has been compromise, with a limited power to retry after an acquittal, subject to a number of explicit safeguards. The power is limited first in the range of offences for which it is available,[240] and second in the number of times it can be invoked in any given case.[241] The procedure is for a prosecutor to apply[242] to the Court of Appeal[243] for an order quashing the acquittal, and ordering a retrial. The Court of Appeal must be satisfied that there is new and compelling evidence, and that it is in the interests of justice to do so:

78 (1) The requirements of this section are met if there is new and compelling evidence against the acquitted person in relation to the qualifying offence.

(2) Evidence is new if it was not adduced in the proceedings in which the person was acquitted (nor, if those were appeal proceedings, in earlier proceedings to which the appeal related).

(3) Evidence is compelling if—
(a) it is reliable,
(b) it is substantial, and
(c) in the context of the outstanding issues, it appears highly probative of the case against the acquitted person.

...

---

[233] Rec 14.   [234] Rec 15.

[235] They were not included in the Criminal Justice Act 2003.

[236] *The Stephen Lawrence Inquiry* (Cm 4262, 1999).

[237] Derived in part from Home Affairs Committee *Third Report: The Double Jeopardy Rule* HC Session 1999–2000, 17 May 2000 and Auld *Review of the Criminal Courts of England and Wales* (2001) paras 627–34.

[238] Law Com 267 above recs 1–9. For discussion and comparison with the position elsewhere, see Dennis [2000] *Crim LR* 933, [2001] *Crim LR* 339; Roberts (2002) 65 *Mod LR* 393, (2002) 6 *E&P* 197; Hamer [2009] *Crim LR* 63.

[239] The Law Commission strengthened its commitment to this concept, influenced by the discussion of its constitutional importance by Roberts in his *Mod LR* article (n238). Other subsidiary arguments against the exception relate to the distress to the accused at a retrial and the encouragement of efficient investigation.

[240] CJA 2003, ss 75(1), (8), Sch 5 Pt 1; 29 qualifying offences are listed in Sch 5, all of them serious offences, together with some inchoate forms. The Law Commission recommended using the procedure only in cases of murder, which would have reduced its impact much further.   [241] CJA 2003, s 76(5); only once.

[242] Subject to the consent of the Director of Public Prosecutions: CJA 2003, s 63(3).

[243] By analogy with the admission of fresh evidence on appeal.

79 (1) The requirements of this section are met if in all the circumstances it is in the interests of justice for the court to make the order under section 77.

(2) That question is to be determined having regard in particular to—

(a) whether existing circumstances make a fair trial unlikely;

(b) for the purposes of that question and otherwise, the length of time since the qualifying offence was allegedly committed;

(c) whether it is likely that the new evidence would have been adduced in the earlier proceedings against the acquitted person but for a failure by an officer or by a prosecutor to act with due diligence or expedition;

(d) whether, since those proceedings or, if later, since the commencement of this part, any officer or prosecutor has failed to act with due diligence or expedition.

It is only to be expected that so novel a provision, not reproducing exactly the recommendations of any one body, should present difficulties of interpretation. Some attempt at resolution has been attempted in respect of those that could be anticipated. Thus it seems that evidence is not to be regarded as unavailable at an earlier trial if, although known to the prosecution, it was not used because it was then inadmissible.[244] There remains plenty of room for elaboration of the new term 'compelling',[245] but the Law Commission's view, which appears to have had some influence, was very much that the concept should be forward-looking, and related to the potential impact of the evidence upon a retrial[246] in the light of the issues which were truly open. It is to be noted that the evidence must *be* reliable, not merely potentially reliable.[247]

So far as the interests of justice test is concerned, CJA 2003, s 79 is closer to the drafting of the Law Commission,[248] in particular in not making the due diligence of the original investigator an absolute condition, but rather listing it as a factor to be taken into account. It has now been held[249] not to be a bar to the provision's application that the accused may have been induced to provide the compelling evidence because of his accurate belief at the time that he was no longer at risk. Among other safeguards for the accused against harassment, the most unusual is probably the provision in s 85 that, in the normal[250] case, the consent of the Director of Public Prosecutions[251] must be obtained on written application before engaging in such investigative practices as questioning, searching, or taking fingerprints or a sample.[252] A further safeguard for the purposes of ensuring the fairness of any retrial is the imposition of reporting restrictions at the stage of application.[253]

---

[244] CJA 2003, s 78(5), apparently adopting rec 6 in LC 267.

[245] In *R v A* [2008] EWCA Crim 2908 it was enough that the evidence related to the comparative credibility of different witnesses.

[246] In *R v Miell* [2007] EWCA Crim 3130 a subsequent confession was insufficient because it was inconsistent with other evidence, and 'manifestly untruthful'.

[247] In *R v B (J)* [2009] EWCA Crim 1036, [9] not extended to evidence of a co-accused with a motive to lie. See also *R v G and B* [2009] EWCA Crim 1207.   [248] Rec 4.

[249] *R v Dunlop* [2006] EWCA Crim 1354, [2007] 1 WLR 1657.

[250] CJA 2003, s 86 provides for different procedures to apply in cases of urgency.

[251] For this purpose, CJA 2003, s 78 disapplies the usual provision to allow the functions of the DPP to be exercised by a Crown Prosecutor.   [252] CJA 2003, s 85.

[253] CJA 2003, ss 82, 83. Section 84 requires that any retrial be subject to a two-month time limit: see *R v Dunlop* (n249).

Issue estoppel in criminal cases and abuse of process[254]

Three of the Law Lords who heard *Connelly v DPP*[255] asserted that issue estoppel would be applicable on appropriate facts in an English criminal case.[256] Lord Devlin thought this undesirable if only because of the difficulty of ascertaining what precise issues are determined in criminal proceedings in which there are no pleadings, nothing but a general jury verdict, and no reasoned judgments. There was the further problem of mutuality. If issue estoppel binds the Crown, it is hard to see why it should not also bind the accused. It was so held by Lawson J in *R v Hogan*,[257] where it was possible to ascertain what issues had been determined by the jury at the first trial. Hogan had unsuccessfully relied on self-defence when tried for causing grievous bodily harm with intent. He was then tried for murder after his victim had died. It was held that he was estopped from denying that he intentionally caused grievous bodily harm to the deceased without lawful excuse. The result was that the only live issues were causation and provocation (inapplicable at the first trial). Hogan was nonetheless acquitted.

Hogan was overruled by the House of Lords in *DPP v Humphrys*[258] when the House unanimously declared that issue estoppel does not apply in English criminal proceedings. Humphrys was acquitted of driving a motor vehicle on 18 July 1972 while disqualified from doing so. The only issue at that first trial was whether a constable was correct in identifying him as the man he had stopped after seeing him drive a motorcycle that day. Humphrys had testified to not having driven a motor vehicle at any time during 1972, and was subsequently charged with perjury. Evidence tending to show that he had driven his motorcycle at various times during 1972 was tendered at that second trial and, after the judge had ruled against issue estoppel, the same constable gave the same evidence as on the former occasion, namely identifying Humphrys as the driver stopped by him on 18 July. Humphrys was convicted, his appeal to the Court of Appeal was allowed because the constable's evidence was precluded by issue estoppel, but the House of Lords restored the conviction. Differing views were expressed on the question whether a judge had power to stop proceedings for perjury based exclusively on evidence that had not been accepted at an earlier trial for another offence of which the accused was acquitted. It was also held that, even if issue estoppel does apply in English criminal law, it would have been inapplicable in Humphrys' case because no estoppel is created by a judgment obtained by fraud (including wilfully false evidence).[259]

It is thus unlikely that much more will be heard about issue estoppel in English criminal proceedings;[260] however, both in *Connelly* and in *Humphrys*, the House of Lords

---

[254] Issue estoppel remains part of the criminal law in Canada: *Mahalingan v R* 2008 SCC 63, [2008] 3 SCR 316 but not of Australia: *Rogers v R* (n134); New Zealand: *R v Davis* [1982] 1 NZLR 584; or Ireland: *Lynch v Judge Carroll Moran* [2006] IESC 31, [2006] 3 IR 389. See also Lanham [1970] *Crim LR* 428, containing some criticisms of *Sambasivam v Malaya Federation Public Prosecutor* and *G(an infant) v Coltart*; and cf Mirfield [1980] *Crim LR* 336 presenting a powerful case for issue estoppel in criminal proceedings.

[255] (n134).   [256] Although they opined it inapplicable to the instant case.

[257] [1974] QB 398, [1974] 2 All ER 142.   [258] (n217).

[259] See also, in Australia, *McCleary v DPP(Cwth)* (1998) 20 WAR 288, 315; and in New Zealand, *R v Moore* [1999] 3 NZLR 385. The Supreme Court has redefined its retention of issue estoppel in Canada in *Mahalingan v R* (n254) while denying the possibility of giving it retrospective effect.

[260] But see *R v Pervez and Khan* [1983] Crim LR 108 and commentary. It also seems in effect to have been used in *R v Johannes* [2001] EWCA Crim 2825, where the Court of Appeal was not prepared to allow a finding on a drug-trafficking confiscation issue inconsistent with a finding on a Newton hearing for sentencing.

detected and defined a role for the concept of abuse of process. It was decided as long ago as 1861 that it would be improper to prosecute the accused for a different and more serious offence based upon the same facts[261] that had led to conviction for a lesser.[262] In *Connelly*, this rule was adopted as an abuse of process:[263]

It would be an abuse if he [the prosecutor] could bring up one offence after another based on the same incident, even if the offences were different in law, in order to break down the defence.

It may[264] be an abuse of process for a private prosecution to be brought after the accused has accepted a written caution, but it is not where a fixed penalty notice is issued in respect of a lesser offence when the accused is charged with a more serious offence arising from the same facts.[265]

It was recognized, however, that this general rule could be overridden, but only in special circumstances related to the facts of the individual case:[266]

But a second trial on the same or similar facts is not always and necessarily oppressive, and there may be special circumstances which make it just and convenient in that case. The judge must then, in all the circumstances of the particular case, exercise his discretion as to whether or not he applies the general rule.

These remarks received support in *Humphrys*, and were applied in *R v Beedie*[267] to prevent prosecution for a different offence arising out of the same facts, despite the rejection of autrefois convict. Just what will count as special circumstances remains little explored, although Lord Devlin seemed to have in mind cases where the defence acquiesced in the separation of charges.[268] It seems that it will not be enough simply that the acquittal is inadvertent, and of a technical character,[269] nor that the law has changed after the decision in the first trial.[270] It should be noted that a change of fact that occurs after the first trial, such as the death of the victim, is sufficient to rebut any suggestion that a subsequent charge of an offence of homicide amounts to abuse of process.[271]

It is now worth considering two further aspects of abuse of process in this context, which to some extent pull in opposite directions, but have both been resolved in their different ways to favour the interests of the prosecution.

---

[261] A prosecution for perjury in respect of a denial at trial resulting in an acquittal was held covered in Australia: *R v Carroll* [2002] HCA 55, 213 CLR 635. Anything else would lead to the prospect of an infinite regress.

[262] *R v Elrington* (1861) 1 B & S 688; see also *R v Forest of Dean Justices, ex p Farley* [1990] RTR 228, in which the premise was that the first decision would be a conviction. There is a parallel to the rule in *Henderson v Henderson* (1843) 3 Hare 100 in civil cases: (n128).

[263] Lord Pearce, 1367, 451B.

[264] Depending upon the terms of the caution: *Jones v Whalley* [2006] UKHL 41, [2007] 1 AC 63.

[265] *R v Gore and Mather* [2009] EWCA Crim 1424, [2009] 2 Cr App R 445.

[266] Lord Devlin, 1360, 446D.

[267] (n221). A similar application occurred before the decision in *Humphrys* in *R v Riebold* [1965] 1 All ER 653, [1965] 1 WLR 674.

[268] See also Law Com 267 [2.18] mentioning the unreported case of *A-G for Gibraltar v Leoni*, in which it was intimated that it would apply to permit a charge of possessing cannabis after a successful prosecution for jettisoning a cargo, before that cargo had been recovered and identified for bringing the possession charges.

[269] *R v Martello* (4 April 2000, unreported), CA; cf *R v G* [2001] EWCA Crim 1215.

[270] *R v N* [1998] Crim LR 886.   [271] *R v Young* (n222).

Collateral attack on previous decisions[272]

This aspect of abuse of process came into prominence in the decision of the House of Lords in *Hunter v Chief Constable of the West Midlands Police*.[273] This was part of the notorious saga of the 'Birmingham Six', and in particular an attempt by the alleged bombers in a civil suit to secure damages from the police for alleged assaults to induce them to confess, which allegations had been rejected on a voir dire in the criminal proceedings arising from the bombing. Unsurprisingly, this claim met with distaste from the courts, and in the House of Lords, Lord Diplock, speaking for the whole House, impugned it on the basis that:[274]

The abuse of process which the instant case exemplifies is the initiation of proceedings in a court of justice for the purpose of mounting a collateral attack upon a final decision against the intending plaintiff which has been made by another court of competent jurisdiction in previous proceedings in which the intending plaintiff had a full opportunity of contesting the decision in the court by which it was made.

It is noteworthy that Lord Diplock regarded this form of abuse of process as more a matter of rule than discretion,[275] that he regarded the relevant issue as the one decided on the voir dire,[276] and that he attached considerable importance to the motivation of the plaintiffs for bringing the action.[277] In *DPP v Humphrys*,[278] Lord Hailsham LC applied much the same reasoning to a case in which it was the prosecution seeking to go behind an acquittal:

[W]here the evidence is substantially identical with the evidence given at the first trial without any addition and the Crown is in substance simply seeking to get behind a verdict of acquittal, the second charge is inadmissible both on the ground that it infringes the rule against double jeopardy, and on the ground that it is an abuse of the process of the court.

This reasoning does not apply when proceedings for the more serious offence have become time-barred, even though the more minor offence which is not so barred depends on much the same facts.[279]

It is worth noting here that it may also amount to abuse of process to attack a finding in previous civil proceedings, even though such an attack is mounted by way of defence,[280] and even though the parties to those proceedings are different.[281] It is, however, likely to be harder to establish abuse in such a case, given the lower standard of proof required in civil proceedings,[282] especially in a case where the subsequent proceedings preclude striking out, or judgment in default, and the evidence is under the control of the court.[283] The matter is further complicated when one set of proceedings, although nominally civil, arises from and incorporates facts amounting to criminal offences, as in the case of antisocial

---

[272] See Zaltzman [1999] *Crim LR* 886.   [273] (n160).   [274] 541B, 733b.   [275] 536D, 729g.

[276] 542D, 734b. He regarded the subsequent reventilation of the same issue before the jury as no more than corroborative, and the decision of the court of the accused's guilt as simply rendering the ruling on the voir dire final, at least once the time limit for an appeal had passed.   [277] 541F, 733f.

[278] (n217); 41D, 523h. See also Lord Salmon, 46D, 527d; and Lord Edmund Davies, 55B-F, 535d-h.

[279] *R v J* [2002] EWCA Crim 2983, [2003] 1 All ER 518.

[280] *Reichel v McGrath* (1889) 14 App Cas 665. It is less likely to be considered an abuse when it is the prosecution which attacks the civil finding: see *R v SL* [2006] EWCA Crim 1902, [2007] 1 WLR 3092, and in Australia, *Roberts v Western Australia* [2005] WASCA 37, 152 ACR 346.

[281] *Perotti v Bennett* [2003] EWHC 2497 (Ch).

[282] And the fact that Civil Evidence Act 1968, s 11 makes such previous findings no more than presumptive.

[283] *Secretary of State for Trade and Industry v Bairstow* [2003] EWCA Civ 321, [2004] Ch 1, [41].

behaviour orders. It seems that the inclination of the court is likely to be to look at the substance rather than the form, and to determine whether or not the subsequent proceedings do involve a direct attack upon the findings in the former.[284]

Reuse of evidential material in previous decisions resulting in acquittal

This can arise in a number of ways, but it is perhaps worth distinguishing between, first, those where the previous acquittal arose from the exclusion of a piece of evidence that is then subsequently tendered in a prosecution for another offence, where the grounds for inadmissibility remain much the same and, second, those where the facts constituting the offence of which the accused has been acquitted are themselves relevant to a subsequent charge, on the assumption that the accused was in fact guilty of the offences of which he had been acquitted.

Sambasivam v Malaya Federation Public Prosecutor[285] is the leading example, in this jurisdiction,[286] of the former category. The appellant had been charged with the two offences, of carrying a firearm and of being in possession of ammunition. He was acquitted of the second, but a new trial was ordered with regard to the first. At the second trial, the prosecution relied upon a statement in which the appellant said that he was both carrying a firearm and in possession of ammunition. He was convicted of carrying a firearm, but the Judicial Committee advised that his conviction should be quashed because the assessors had not been told that the prosecution had to accept that the part of the statement dealing with the ammunition must be regarded as untrue. Lord Macdermott said:[287]

The effect of a verdict of acquittal pronounced by a competent court on a lawful charge and after a lawful trial is not completely stated by saying that the person acquitted cannot be tried again for the same offence. To that it must be added that the verdict is binding and conclusive in all subsequent proceedings between the parties to the adjudication, the maxim 'res judicata pro veritate accipitur' is no less applicable to criminal than to civil proceedings. Here, the appellant having been acquitted at the first trial on the charge of having ammunition in his possession, the prosecution was bound to accept the correctness of that verdict and was precluded from taking any step to challenge it at the second trial. And the appellant was no less entitled to rely on his acquittal so far as it might be relevant in his defence.

The case fell outside the plea of autrefois acquit and there could have been no question of issue estoppel, but the knowledge that part of the accused's statement must be regarded as untrue might well have affected the assessors' attitude to the other parts.[288] It does not, however, follow that simply because the accused was acquitted of earlier charges of a similar nature to that which he now faces, on the basis of evidence adduced by the same witness, that he may necessarily adduce evidence of his acquittal.[289] If the

---

[284] See *Daar v Chief Constable of Merseyside Police* [2005] EWCA Civ 1774.

[285] [1950] AC 458, 479.

[286] In Australia, see *Rogers v R* (n134), which rationalized the decision on the basis of abuse of process in order to distinguish a contrary ruling in Canada in *Duhamel v R* (n183). It applies only to findings of fact, and not to exercises of discretion: *R v Edwards* (1997) 94 ACR 204.   [287] As defined in s 54(6).

[288] See also *R v Hay* (1983) 77 Cr App Rep 70, in which the same confession was to two less connected crimes than in *Sambasivam*.

[289] See *R v Doosti* (1985) 82 Cr App Rep 181, in which the evidence was of the finding of drugs in the same room by the same policeman.

acquittal can be explained on some basis other than disbelief of the witness's evidence it is irrelevant,[290] or similarly if it might result from an honest mistake as in a case of misidentification.[291]

An early example of the second sort was provided by *R v Ollis*.[292] The accused had been charged and acquitted of obtaining a cheque by false pretences on 5 July, the alleged false pretence being that a cheque drawn by the accused and given to Ramsey would be honoured. Ollis was then charged with obtaining money by means of worthless cheques on 24 June, 26 June, and 6 July respectively. He was convicted of these offences after Ramsey had given evidence concerning the incident of 5 July to the same effect as that given at the hearing, which had resulted in an acquittal. The conviction was affirmed by a majority of the Court for Crown Cases Reserved. The court was unanimously of the opinion that the fact that he had been acquitted on the charge to which Ramsey deposed was immaterial; the judges differed over the question of the admissibility of the evidence under the similar fact rule. On the basis of the facts and judgments, however, it is difficult to escape the conclusion that Ramsey's evidence was tendered in order to show that Ollis was acting dishonestly on 5 July, in which case it went to show that he was at least guilty of an attempt to obtain by false pretences, an offence of which he was in danger of being convicted at his previous trial.

An attempt to reconcile these cases was made in *G (an Infant) v Coltart*.[293] G, a domestic servant, was convicted of stealing goods from Mrs T, her mistress. Her defence was that she intended to return the goods to Mrs T. In order to rebut this, the prosecution had adduced evidence that G had taken goods from Mrs Doig, a guest of Mrs T, and not returned them although told that she was going to South Africa. G had, however, been acquitted of stealing these goods at the instance of the prosecution on the mistaken assumption that the absence of Mrs Doig in South Africa was fatal to their case.[294] It was held that the conviction of stealing from Mrs T must be quashed because it was not open to the prosecution to invite the court to make an inference that G was guilty of an offence of which she had been acquitted. As in *Sambasivam v Malaya Federation Public Prosecutor*, *Coltart* decided that the prosecution may not, in case B, rely on evidence that is relevant only on the assumption that the accused was guilty of the offence of which he was acquitted in case A.[295] What is alleged to have been wrongly challenged in the second case is the innocence of the accused in the first.[296]

---

[290]   *R v H* (1989) 90 Cr App Rep 440, in which the question arose in relation to earlier proceedings for the same series of offences on some of which the accused had been acquitted and on some of which the jury had failed to agree. It is also irrelevant in the hands of the prosecution: see *R v Verney* (1993) 87 CCC (3d) 363.

[291]   *R v Hendrie; R v Paramasivan* (1994) The Times, 27 July.

[292]   [1900] 2 QB 758; cf *R v Norton* (1910) 5 Cr App Rep 197. For a more recent Australian example, see *R v Patton* [1998] 1 VR 7.   [293]   [1967] 1 QB 432, [1967] 1 All ER 271.

[294]   It is noteworthy that this was not a result arrived at after a trial on the merits, and in *R v M(RA)* (1994) 94 CCC (3d) 459, it was applied where the acquittal was part of a plea bargain.

[295]   See also *Re Mulligan, ex p Isidoro* [1979] WAR 198, in which the acquittal occurred after a licence had been refused in respect of the facts constituting the offence, and the appeal against the refusal was bound to give credit for the acquittal.

[296]   Although the issue seems not to have been raised in these terms, in *Re H (minors) (sexual abuse: standard of proof)* [1996] AC 563, [1996] 1 All ER 1, the outcome that the accused's previous acquittal of sexual abuse could not be relied upon to show the risk of his causing harm is consistent with the result of this rule;

Salmon LJ attempted to reconcile these decisions, and chose to do so, rather in the face of the facts of *Ollis*, and the reasoning of the court,[297] on a different basis:[298]

> But it seems to me that the distinction between that case and the present one is that in the present case the only relevance of the evidence tendered was to prove guilt in the Doig case, whereas in *R v Ollis* the prosecution were able to say; we are not alleging let alone relying on the defendant's guilt in respect of the first cheque; we are relying on the fact that the first cheque was not met only to show what the defendant's knowledge or state of mind was when he gave the other three cheques.

In other words, that evidence is no less admissible in the second case because it tends to show that the accused was guilty in the first provided that, in tendering it, the prosecution is not in effect denying the validity of the acquittal. This attempted reconciliation did not arouse universal approval,[299] was criticized by the Law Commission,[300] and rejected by the House of Lords in *R v Z*.[301] In *Z*, the accused was charged with the rape of a woman, and his defence was consent. He had previously been charged with the rape of different women, and had on each occasion alleged consent. He had been once convicted, and three times acquitted. It was accepted that the circumstances of all of the incidents were sufficiently similar to satisfy the similar facts rule, but on the basis only that the accused had indeed been guilty of the offences of which he had been acquitted. The House of Lords refused to apply *Sambasivam* so as to prevent the use of the evidence of the circumstances of the earlier incidents. Lord Hutton regarded the distinction drawn in *G v Coltart* 'a difficult one to maintain'.[302] Instead, he sought to base the rule in *Sambasivam* more clearly on double jeopardy. It should be remembered that there some of the ammunition was actually in the gun, so the acquittal in respect of that[303] ammunition really would have been inconsistent with guilt of the possession of the gun. He refused to apply the rule where no element of double jeopardy, in the sense of inconsistency of verdict, was involved, as in the case before him. It is interesting that he reserved his view of the continuing validity of the decision in *Hay*, where it will be recalled there was no connection between the offences, but the link consisted only in the evidence adduced to prove them. This reservation of view thus leaves scope for the distinction advanced above between cases in which the intention is to use a previous acquittal as if it were evidence of guilt, and cases in which it is instead sought to use evidence in a second case, the exclusion of

---

although the actual reasoning was not, since it seems that the facts of the crime for which the accused had been acquitted would have been admissible, if supported by other evidence, to show risk.

[297] See the cogent criticism in Andrews and Hirst *Criminal Evidence* (4th edn, 2001), 22.13.

[298] (n293), 440.   [299] See e.g. Hirst [1991] *Crim LR* 510.

[300] *Double Jeopardy* Con Pap 156 (1999) Pt VIII.

[301] [2000] 2 AC 483, [2000] 3 All ER 385. For criticism, see Tapper (2001) 117 *LQR* 1, Mirfield, ibid, 194; for support, see Roberts [2000] *Crim LR* 952.

[302] 499E. In Australia, in *R v Garrett* (1977) 139 CLR 437, in which the accused had been acquitted on an earlier occasion of raping the same woman, the court was equally prepared to reject the fineness of the distinction between using the evidence depending on whether it could be used only because of, or irrespective of, guilt on the earlier occasion, but the High Court resolved the issue in favour of the accused, and prevented use in such circumstances.

[303] In fact, not all of the ammunition had been in the gun.

which in the first had resulted in acquittal.[304] In the latter case, it is evidence as to which a particular finding of inadmissibility has been made that it is sought to use again, without any need to speculate about the possibility of implied double jeopardy, or the strength of the link between the evidence and the verdict in the earlier case.

It should also be noted that all of the members of the House were prepared for discretionary exclusion of evidence derived from a previous acquittal, on the basis of an assumption of the accused's guilt. It was accepted in Z[305] that there may be circumstances in which, even in cases where the evidence is simply of the contrary of the facts that the previous acquittal suggests, as it was there, it may be unfair to use the evidence even when there is no question of double jeopardy. It is submitted that a combination of the facts of Z and *Garrett* may be used as an illustration. Suppose that all of the earlier incidents had involved the same complainant, without much extrinsic evidence; surely a time would come, after repeated acquittals, when the evidence of those acquittals would not be accepted as evidence to support a further charge?

R v Z was argued, and decided, upon considerations of domestic English law, and no reference was made to its compatibility in this respect with the European Convention on Human Rights. It is instructive to observe that there an acquittal seems to be accorded more respect, and in *Minelli v Switzerland*, the court went so far as to assert:[306]

[T]he presumption of innocence will be violated if, without the accused's having previously been proved guilty according to law...a judicial decision concerning him reflects an opinion that he is guilty. This may be so even in the absence of any formal finding: it suffices that there is some reasoning suggesting that the court regards the accused as guilty.

This view has been maintained, and in *Rushiti v Austria*:[307]

[F]ollowing a final acquittal, even the voicing of suspicions regarding an accused's innocence is no longer admissible.

In cases such as Z, in which the evidence is to be used as similar fact evidence, there is more than a suggestion of guilt, since under a ruling in *R v H*[308] it must be taken to be true for the purposes of considering the test for its admissibility as similar fact evidence. This seems more like a presumption of guilt in the case of an acquittal than a presumption of innocence. It must be far from certain whether it is compatible with Art 6(2) of the European Convention on Human Rights. It has, however, been held here that the Convention jurisprudence is limited to compensation cases.[309]

---

[304] This is consistent with the view of the Court of Appeal in *R v Terry* [2004] EWCA Crim 3252, [2005] QB 996, in which the broad views expressed in *Sambasivam* and *Hay* were heavily qualified.

[305] Most clearly by Lord Hobhouse, 510C, 408d.

[306] (1983) 5 EHRR 554, [37]. This view is, if anything, strengthened by the reason for distinguishing it stated in *Nolkenbockhoff v Germany* (1987) 13 EHRR 360, and in *Englert v Germany* (1987) 13 EHRR 392.

[307] (2001) 33 EHRR 1331, [31]; re-affirmed in *Geerings v Netherlands* (2008) 46 EHRR 1212, [49]. In Australia in *R v Glennon (No 3)* [2005] VSCA 262, 158 ACR 74, [15] a strict warning against any such reasoning was recommended.

[308] [1995] 2 AC 596, [1995] 2 All ER 865; 612C, 877b.

[309] *R v Terry* (n304), [53] (although neither *Minelli* nor *Rushiti* were among the cases considered); see also recognition of the problem obiter by Lord Mance at [125] in his minority view in *R v Briggs-Price* [2009] UKHL 19, [2009] 1 AC 1026.

SECTION 4. JUDICIAL FINDINGS AS EVIDENCE OF THE FACTS UPON WHICH THEY WERE BASED[310]

The problem here[311] is whether and to what extent a judgment can be treated as evidence of the facts upon which it was founded when the proceedings in which this question is raised are between a party and a stranger, or two strangers. If A is convicted of murder and he sues B for libel in describing him as a killer, would the conviction be admissible evidence in support of pleas of justification on B's part? *Hollington v F Hewthorn & Co Ltd*[312] confirmed the preponderantly negative view.[313]

In that case, the conviction of one of the defendants for careless driving was held inadmissible evidence of his negligence in civil proceedings for damages against him and his employer. The main reasons were that the conviction merely proved the opinion of another court, acting on unknown evidence; and amounted to hearsay as it would have been treated as the equivalent of an assertion of negligence by a non-witness; but these points are indefensible technicalities.[314]

Rationalise it how one will, the decision in this case offends one's sense of justice. The defendant driver had been found guilty of careless driving by a court of competent jurisdiction. The onus of proof of culpability in criminal cases is higher than in civil; the degree of carelessness required to sustain a conviction of careless driving is, if anything, greater than that required to sustain a civil action for negligence. Yet the fact that the defendant driver had been convicted of careless driving at the same time and place of the accident was held not to amount to even prima facie evidence of his negligent driving at that time and place.

It is not easy to escape the implication in the rule in *Hollington v Hewthorn* that, in the estimation of lawyers, a conviction by a criminal court is as likely to be wrong as right.[315]

The rule in *Hollington v F Hewthorn & Co Ltd* has since been overruled so far as it governs proof of convictions and findings of adultery and paternity in civil proceedings, by the Civil Evidence Act 1968,[316] and so far as it governs proof of convictions in criminal proceedings, by the Police and Criminal Evidence Act 1984.[317] Despite having been regarded by Lord Hoffmann as having taken technicality too far,[318] it remains valid in respect of other findings,[319] and in civil[320] or arbitral[321] proceedings. It has, however,

---

[310] The common law is fully discussed in Cowan and Carter *Essays on the Law of Evidence* Essay 6 and V Wigmore [1671(a)].

[311] It has become less important now that hearsay is more readily admissible.

[312] (n103).   [313] But see the discrepant affirmative holding in *Re Crippen's Estate* [1911] P 108, 115.

[314] The rule originated in the days when interested witnesses, parties, and their spouses were incompetent in civil proceedings and may have been based on the possibility that the conviction would have been obtained by evidence which would have been inadmissible in the subsequent civil proceedings.

[315] Fifteenth Report of the Law Reform Committee, [3].

[316] Sections 11, 13 (as amended). The rule has been retained in statutory form in Australia by the Evidence Act 1995, s 91; for an example of the operation of the old rule, see *R v Burnett* (1994) 76 ACR 148.

[317] Section 74.   [318] *Arthur JS Hall v Simons* (n142); 702.

[319] Such as acquittals: see *Hui Chi Ming v R* [1992] 1 AC 34, [1991] 3 All ER 897; and still more mere observations by the judge: see, in Australia, *National Mutual Life Ass of Australia v Grosvenor Hill (Qld)* [2001] FCA 237, (2001) 183 ALR 700.

[320] *Secretary of State for Trade and Industry v Bairstow* (n283), [26].

[321] *Hayter v Nelson* [1990] 2 Lloyd's Rep 265, 271.

been suggested[322] that the House of Lords might at some stage reconsider the matter in the light of the modern emphasis on fairness and the abuse of process, especially where the prejudiced party had a full opportunity to contest the finding against him in the earlier proceedings. Some statutes also make specific provision for the use of convictions, or other judicial findings, as evidence of their underlying facts.[323] These provisions will be discussed in the first two parts of this section. The remaining parts will consider the status of evidence of acquittals, and of other findings.

THE CIVIL EVIDENCE ACT 1968, SS 11–13[324]

Previous convictions in subsequent civil proceedings

Section 11 (1) of the Civil Evidence Act 1968, provides that:

(1) In any civil proceedings the fact that a person has been convicted of an offence by or before any court in the United Kingdom or by a court martial there or elsewhere shall...be admissible in evidence for the purpose of proving, where to do so is relevant to any issue in those proceedings, that he committed that offence...but no conviction other than a subsisting one[325] shall be admissible in evidence by virtue of this section.

Section 11(2) provides that:

In any civil proceedings in which by virtue of this section a person is proved to have been convicted of an offence by or before any court in the United Kingdom or by a court martial there or elsewhere (a) he shall be taken to have committed that offence unless the contrary is proved; and (b) without prejudice to the reception of any other admissible evidence for the purpose of identifying the facts upon which the conviction was based, the contents of any document which is admissible as evidence of the conviction and the contents of the information, complaint, indictment or charge sheet on which the person in question was convicted shall be admissible in evidence for that purpose.

Practice Direction 16, [10.1] under the Civil Procedure Rules requires a party who intends to rely on s 11 to state that intention in his particulars of claim, to give details of the conviction, and to indicate the issue to which it is relevant. On facts such as those of *Hollington v F Hewthorn & Co Ltd*, once the conviction has been proved, and the negligence in respect of which the driver was convicted identified, the court will be bound to find in favour of the claimant unless the driver or his employer disproves negligence on the balance of probabilities.[326]

---

[322] By Toulsen J in *Lincoln National Life Insurance Co v Sun Life Assurance Co of Canada* [2004] EWHC 343 (Comm), [92].

[323] See, for example, Company Directors Disqualification Act 1986; for exegesis see *Official Receiver v Stojevic* [2007] EWHC 1186 (Ch).

[324] The provisions with regard to previous convictions must be read subject to the Rehabilitation of Offenders Act 1974.

[325] See *Re Raphael, Raphael v D'Antin* [1973] 3 All ER 19, [1973] 1 WLR 998. A conviction subject to appeal is subsisting; the civil court has power to adjourn the case pending the appeal, but sometimes that will be undesirable, even though for tactical reasons the convicted party refuses to testify. *Re U* [2006] EWHC 372 (Fam), [2006] 2 FLR 690 (in which the matter was nevertheless determined independently of the effect of s 11).

[326] *Stupple v Royal Insurance Co Ltd* [1971] 1 QB 50, [1970] 3 All ER 230. Although the conviction alone will not establish the quantum of damage: *Microsoft Corp v Alibhai* [2004] EWHC 3282.

Various observations have been made about the weight to be attached to the conviction in the subsequent civil proceedings in which it is proved.[327] Lord Denning MR and Buckley LJ took different views on this subject in *Stupple v Royal Insurance Co Ltd*.[328] The claimant had been convicted of robbery from a bank, indemnified by the defendants. Money found in the claimant's possession was paid over to the defendants under the Police (Property) Act 1897.[329] The claimant sought this sum and the defendants counterclaimed for the balance of their indemnity. The Court of Appeal upheld judgment for the defendants. Lord Denning said:[330]

I think that the conviction does not merely shift the burden of proof. It is a weighty piece of evidence of itself. For instance, if a man is convicted of careless driving on the evidence of a witness, but that witness dies before the civil action is heard (as in *Hollington v Hewthorn & Co Ltd*) then the conviction itself tells in the scale in the civil action. It speaks as clearly as the witness would have done, had he lived. It does not merely reverse the burden of proof. If that was all it did, the defendant might well give his own evidence, negativing want of care and say: 'I have discharged the burden. I have given my evidence and it has not been contradicted.' In answer to the defendant's evidence the plaintiff can say: 'But your evidence is contradicted by the convictions.'

Buckley LJ said:[331]

In my judgment, proof of conviction under this section gives rise to the statutory presumption laid down in s 11(2)(a) which, like any other presumption, will give way to evidence establishing the contrary on the balance of probability without itself affording any evidential weight to be taken into account in determining whether that onus has been discharged.

It is submitted that the approach of Buckley LJ is to be preferred. The assessment of the weight of the conviction would be a difficult task. As Buckley LJ pointed out, the propriety of the conviction is irrelevant in the civil action: the claimant would not discharge the onus cast upon him by s 11(2)(a) by proving that every witness who had given evidence against him at the criminal trial was guilty of perjury. He has to adduce sufficient evidence to satisfy the civil court that he was not negligent and, in spite of Lord Denning's suggestion to the contrary, his own testimony without more will generally not suffice.[332] The House of Lords has affirmed that the burden is the ordinary civil one, but nonetheless characterized as 'uphill' the task of a defendant[333] to persuade the court of the contrary of

---

[327] Cp *Wauchope v Mordecai* [1970] 1 All ER 417, [1970] 1 WLR 317; *Taylor v Taylor* [1970] 2 All ER 609, [1970] 1 WLR 1148.

[328] [1971] 1 QB 50, [1970] 3 All ER 230. See the note by Zuckerman (1971) 87 *LQR* 21.

[329] Now repealed, and its functions replaced by the Proceeds of Crime Act 2002.

[330] 72. If available, the transcript or proof of evidence of the deceased witness in the criminal case would be admissible under the Civil Evidence Act 1995.

[331] 76. This view was followed in *Wright v Wright* (1971) 115 Sol Jo 173. For an argument in support of Lord Denning based on the statutory wording, see Phipson *Law of Evidence* (17th edn), [43–88].

[332] *Ludgate v Lovett* [1969] 2 All ER 1275, [1969] 1 WLR 1016 (negligent bailee); see also 15th Report of the Law Reform Committee, [25]. Indeed, Lord Denning's view might itself attach too much weight to an unsupported plea of guilty for the purposes of a substantial consequential civil claim: see e.g. *Jacobsen v Suncorp Insurance & Finance (No 2)* [1992] 1 Qd 385.

[333] The House regarded it as difficult to conceive of a claimant seeking to rely upon his own conviction. It is not, however, impossible: for example, if a salesman is dismissed for not visiting his sales area, he might want to put in evidence his conviction for a motoring offence in the area at the relevant time in a claim for unfair dismissal. Any attempt by a claimant to do so by way of collateral attack upon the conviction will run the risk of being struck out as an abuse of the process of the court: *Smith v Linskells* [1996] 2 All ER 353, [1996] 1 WLR 763.

a verdict beyond reasonable doubt.[334] Any such attempt must be timely, and the chances of its success substantial in view of the time and expense it is likely to consume.[335]

As the conviction constitutes the basic fact of a presumption, it should be capable of supporting other evidence where support is required; it is stated by s 11(1) to be 'admissible in evidence for the purpose of proving that [the accused] committed the offence'. In *Mash v Darley*,[336] a Divisional Court treated the respondent's conviction of unlawful intercourse with the applicant as corroboration of her evidence in affiliation proceedings. The decision could hardly have stood with *Hollington v F Hewthorn & Co Ltd*, but it may well have been resuscitated by the 1968 Act.

As long as convictions are not conclusive evidence of the guilt of the person convicted, it is possible for him to obtain a retrial of the issues raised in the criminal proceedings in a subsequent civil action for defamation by suing anyone suggesting that he were guilty of the offence. Even if the civil action were decided in his favour, the validity of the conviction would, of course, be unaffected. The Law Reform Committee took the view that, as a matter of substantive law, no one ought to be at risk of incurring civil liability for stating that the claimant[337] was guilty of an offence of which he had been convicted; and conversely, no one ought to be entitled, without incurring civil liability, to state that the claimant was guilty of an offence of which he had been acquitted.[338] The Committee therefore recommended that, in defamation actions, where the statement complained of alleges that the claimant has been guilty of a criminal offence, proof that he has been convicted of that offence should be conclusive evidence of his guilt, and proof that he was acquitted should be conclusive evidence of his innocence. The first, but not the second, of these recommendations was accepted. Section 13(1) of the Civil Evidence Act 1968 now[339] provides that:

(1) In an action for libel or slander in which the question whether the plaintiff did or did not commit a criminal offence is relevant to an issue arising in the action, proof that, at the time when the issue falls to be determined, he stands convicted of that offence shall be conclusive evidence that he committed that offence...

Findings of adultery and paternity

Section 12(1) of the Civil Evidence Act 1968, as amended by s 29 of the Family Law Reform Act 1987, now provides that:

In any civil proceedings—(a) the fact that a person has been found guilty of adultery in any matrimonial proceedings; and (b) the fact that a person has been found to be the father of a child in relevant proceedings before any court in England and Wales or has been adjudged to be the

---

[334] *Hunter v Chief Constable of West Midlands* (n160); 544, 735, 736. In some cases where little or no new evidence is to be adduced, leave to defend might be refused as an abuse of process, as in *Brinks Ltd v Abu-Saleh* [1995] 4 All ER 65, [1995] 1 WLR 1478, but this is somewhat incompatible with the drafting of s 11, and the general rule would allow challenge by a defendant: *J v Oyston* [1999] 1 WLR 694; see also *McCauley v Hope* [1999] 1 WLR 1977, [2000] RTR 70, discussed by McLaren in (1999) 147 NLJ 228.

[335] *Raja v Van Hoogstraten* [2005] EWHC 1315, (2006) 150 SJLB 855.

[336] [1914] 1 KB 1 affirmed on other grounds [1914] 3 KB 1226.

[337] The wording has been limited by s 12 of Defamation Act 1996 to actions brought by the person in question, so as not to impede unduly the investigation and reporting in the media of alleged improprieties by police or other third parties in the process of investigation and trial of a third party.

[338] Fifteenth Report of the Law Reform Committee, [26]–[33].

[339] As amended by s 12 of Defamation Act 1996.

father of a child in affiliation proceedings before any court in the United Kingdom; shall...be admissible in evidence for the purpose of proving, where to do so is relevant to any issue in those civil proceedings, that he committed the adultery to which the finding relates or, as the case may be, is (or was) the father of that child...

Section 12(2), as also so amended, now provides that:

In any civil proceeding in which by virtue of this section a person is proved to have been found guilty of adultery as mentioned in subsection (1)(a) above, or to have been found or adjudged to be the father of a child as mentioned in subsection 1(b) above—(a) he shall be taken to have committed the adultery to which the finding relates, or, as the case may be, to be (or have been) the father of that child, unless the contrary is proved...[340]

'Matrimonial proceedings' means, for the purposes of s 12(5)(a), 'Any matrimonial cause in the High Court or a county court in England or Wales, or in the High Court in Northern Ireland, any consistorial action in Scotland, or any appeal arising out of such cause or action', while 'relevant proceedings' for the purposes of s 12(2)(b) has been defined in an expanded form by s 29(4) of the Family Law Reform Act 1987 to include any public proceedings involving an adjudication of paternity.[341]

PREVIOUS CONVICTIONS IN CRIMINAL CASES[342]

Although there was very little authority on the point, it seems that the principle of *Hollington v F Hewthorn & Co Ltd* applied to criminal cases.[343] For example, the conviction of a principal was inadmissible as evidence of the commission of the main crime at the trial of an accessory,[344] and the conviction of the thief was inadmissible as evidence that the goods received were stolen at the trial of the handler.[345] One of the oldest justifications for the rule applied in such cases, as it would have been possible for the principal or thief to have been convicted on evidence inadmissible against the accessory or handler, such as evidence of their spouses. The matter was made explicit in s 74 of the Police and Criminal Evidence Act 1984, which largely followed the recommendation of the 11th Report of the Criminal Law Revision Committee.[346] It provides[347] that:

(1) In any proceedings the fact that a person other than the accused has been convicted[348] of an offence by or before any court in the United Kingdom or by a Service court outside the United Kingdom shall be admissible in evidence for the purpose of proving that that person committed that offence, where evidence of his having done so is admissible.

(2) In any proceedings in which by virtue of this section a person other than the accused is proved to have been convicted of an offence by or before any court in the United Kingdom

---

[340] On the balance of probabilities, *Sutton v Sutton* [1969] 3 All ER 1348, [1970] 1 WLR 183.
[341] Section 12(5).   [342] See Munday [1990] *Crim LR* 236.
[343] *R v Shepherd* (1980) 71 Cr App Rep 120.   [344] *R v Xaki* 1950 (4) SA 332.
[345] *R v Turner* (1832) 1 Mood CC 347; *R v Lee* 1952 (2) SA 67; see also *Taylor v Wilson* (1911) 76 JP 69 and *R v Hassan* [1970] 1 QB 423, 426. For a learned discussion of the English position before the passage of s 74, see Brooking LJ in *R v Welsh* [1999] 2 VR 62. See also *R v Kirkby* [2000] 2 Qd 57.
[346] Cmnd 4991.
[347] As amended by the Criminal Justice Act 2003 Sch 37 [85] to accommodate the new provisions of Pt 11 relating to the extended admissibility of evidence of the accused's bad character.
[348] It is immaterial that the conviction is based upon a plea of guilty, even one based upon hearsay, and perhaps double hearsay: *R v Pigram* [1995] Crim LR 808.

or by a Service court outside the United Kingdom, he shall be taken to have committed that offence unless the contrary is proved.

(3) In any proceedings where evidence is admissible of the fact that the accused has committed an offence, if the accused is proved to have been convicted of the offence:

(a) by or before any court in the United Kingdom; or

(b) by a Service court outside the United Kingdom, he shall be taken to have committed that offence unless the contrary is proved.

The proceedings referred to are defined as criminal proceedings.[349] It was necessary to depart slightly from the draft bill in the 11th Committee's Report because its recommendation of statutory reform of the similar facts rule was not implemented. It is, perhaps, somewhat surprising to find this section so retained in view of the failure[350] of the Criminal Justice Act 2003 to admit out-of-court statements of one co-accused's evidence against the other, at least as a matter of rule.[351] Nor despite some[352] dicta to the contrary does the wording of s 74 itself leave much room for discretionary exclusion.[353] This has always caused judicial disquiet. It first surfaced in *R v O'Connor*[354] in which the conviction of another for the very conspiracy charged against the accused was adduced in evidence. The other conspirator had first admitted conspiring with the accused, and had then pleaded guilty to that charge. No other person was alleged to have been involved. Since the other conspirator was not called to give evidence for either prosecution or defence, the accused was put in the difficult position of having damning evidence against him, based upon the statements of a third party, without being able to cross-examine that third party. These are the very dangers that the hearsay rule is designed to avert. So uneasy was the court that it invoked its discretionary powers under s 78 of the Police and Criminal Evidence Act 1984 to exclude on the basis of the adverse effect of the evidence upon the fairness of the proceedings.[355] If the conviction relates to a conspiracy to which there were alleged to have been other parties, the court has felt more ready to admit the evidence of the conviction.[356]

The court has seemed most uneasy when the conviction follows a plea[357] rather than a contested trial, since there may be undisclosed reasons for pleading guilty beyond guilt itself.[358] One problem is that while a conviction following a contested trial may be more

---

[349] Section 82(1). But a similar result has been achieved in disciplinary tribunals by invocation of the rule forbidding collateral attacks upon convictions: *Re A Solicitor* (1996) The Times, 18 March. They do not exclude a retrial: *R v Harris* 19 April 2000, unreported) CA [23].

[350] In this respect, following the recommendation of the Law Commission in Law Com No 245 (Cm 3670, 1997) [8.96].

[351] They may be admitted under s 114 as a matter of discretion, but it has now been held in *R v Smith* [2007] EWCA Crim 2105, [25, 26] that the operation of that discretion is similar to that of the exclusionary discretion in s 78 of the Police and Criminal Evidence Act 1984.

[352] *R v Wardell* [1997] Crim LR 450; but see also *R v Mahmood* [1997] 1 Cr App Rep 414, *R v Stewart* (1998) unreported CA, 27 November.   [353] *R v Smith* (n351), [12].

[354] (1986) 85 Cr App Rep 298.

[355] Although under the bill as introduced this would have had to have been the statutory retention of the common law discretion to exclude evidence more prejudicial than probative.

[356] *R v Robertson; R v Golder* [1987] QB 920, [1987] 3 All ER 231; *R v Lunnon* (1988) 88 Cr App Rep 71.

[357] In *R v Marlow* [1997] Crim LR 457, the brief report even seems to go so far as to suggest that such evidence falls outside s 74 altogether, which in view of the wording of the section can only be shorthand for an indication of the way in which the judge's discretion is most likely to be exercised.

[358] *R v Lee* [1996] Crim LR 825.

reliable than a simple out-of-court assertion to the same effect, a plea involving an assertion may easily be less reliable, just because of possible ulterior motives. The major difficulty, however, is that evidence of a conviction is likely to be extremely powerful, and may
effectively shut off issues which the instant jury is to try.[359] This, at first led to an artificially
restricted view of what a conviction admitted under s 74 could be used to prove,[360] but it
was decided in *R v Downer*[361] that the decisive question is the relevance of the conviction
under s 74, and that there is no further test of relevance of the detail to prove it furnished
under s 75.[362]

This makes it more, rather than less, important that the trial judge be meticulous in his
direction to the jury of precisely what use it is permitted to make of a conviction proved
under s 74,[363] and certainly that it is capable of being disproved.[364]

The relevant convictions may be of third parties, and used only to show the character
of such third parties when relevant to the accused's guilt.[365] In *R v Hayter*,[366] unease was
reflected in a split decision of the House of Lords. The majority was prepared to extend the
principle of s 74 to a case where the guilt of one co-accused was necessary to the conviction
of another, and the jury was allowed to use its provisional determination of that, based
solely on the relevant co-accused's confession, to constitute a case to answer against the
co-accused. The majority[367] felt that the hearsay rule was not infringed since the confession was being used only indirectly through the determination of the co-accused's guilt,
while the minority[368] felt that any such distinction lacked substance. It is certainly true
that the majority position more accurately reflects the policy of s 74 than does that of the
minority.

Two more technical questions that have been resolved in these cases are that the 'matters in issue' to which reference is made extend beyond essential ingredients of the crime
charged to more evidential issues,[369] and are by no means restricted to cases in which
the conviction relates to offences in which the accused played no part at all; reference to
a 'conviction' applies to situations in which the third party has been found guilty, but has
yet to be sentenced.[370] It is unsatisfactory to have a situation in which the instincts of the
judiciary so conflict with the clear terminology of the relevant provision that resort is
made to amelioration by way of discretion. It is to be hoped that an opportunity may still[371]
be taken to reconsider the anomaly between the generally restricted ambit of hearsay in
criminal proceedings against the interests of the accused, and its implicit admission by
way of proof of the convictions of third parties.

---

[359] *R v Smith* (n351).   [360] See *R v Lunnon* (n356) and *R v Curry* [1988] Crim LR 527.
[361] [2009] EWCA Crim 1361.   [362] *R v Hinchcliffe* [2002] EWCA Crim 837.
[363] *R v Kempster* (1989) 90 Cr App Rep 14. In *R v Humphreys and Tully* [1993] Crim LR 288, an appeal
was allowed even though the conviction did not expressly implicate the accused in the relevant conspiracy,
just because the trial judge had not sufficiently balanced the possible prejudice to the accused against such
relevance.
[364] *R v Dixon* (2000) unreported CA, 3 October [16].
[365] *R v Warner and Jones* (1992) 96 Cr App Rep 324.   [366] [2005] UKHL 6, [2005] 2 All ER 209.
[367] Lord Brown with whom Lord Bingham agreed, and Lord Steyn with whom both agreed in
substance.
[368] Lords Rodger and Carswell.
[369] *R v Robertson* (n354), 927, 236, now overtaken by the explicit statutory excision referred to above.
[370] *R v Golder* (n356); 931, 240.
[371] There is a faint hint in *R v Dixon* (n364), [17], that an appeal to the law of human rights might provide
an opportunity.

It should be noted that s 74(3), which deals with previous convictions of the accused, is concerned exclusively with the means of proof, and does not furnish an independent route to admissibility.[372]

ACQUITTALS

So far as the previous acquittal of a party is concerned, it may, of course, be proved when it is a fact in issue, as would be the case in an action for malicious prosecution.[373] Use[374] in evidence of the underlying facts against the accused despite his acquittal has also been permitted,[375] and even in such a case evidence of the fact of acquittal said to be inadmissible.[376] There is a variety of reasons why an acquittal should not be admitted as evidence of innocence in subsequent civil proceedings. Chief amongst these is the fact that the standard of proof is different, so that an acquittal means only that the case against the accused has not been proved beyond reasonable doubt. It seems quite clear that acquittals are admissible as evidence of innocence in neither subsequent civil[377] nor criminal[378] proceedings. It should be noted, however, that it is more doubtful how far evidence throwing doubt on the validity on an acquittal[379] is admissible in subsequent proceedings under the European Convention on Human Rights, since any such use might be thought to infringe the presumption of innocence in Art 6.[380] It seems that the closer the connection between the subsequent proceedings and the criminal proceedings resulting in an acquittal, and the more explicit the linkage between the evidence offered in the latter proceedings and that in the criminal, the greater the risk of exclusion,[381] but this has been held not to bar in all cases civil proceedings in respect of conduct that has previously resulted in the defendant's acquittal when tried for the same conduct in previous criminal proceedings,[382] not

---

[372] *R v Harris* (n349), [21].

[373] Nor is it an abuse of process to do so despite the issue of an ASBO in respect of the matters relied upon in contradiction of the acquittal: *Daar v Chief Constable of Merseyside Police* (n284).

[374] But not disclosure by the police on the basis of mere suspicion that the acquittal may have been unjustified, *R (S) v Chief Constable of West Mercia* [2008] EWHC 2811 (Admin).

[375] As authorized by *R v Z* [2000] 2 AC 483, [2000] 3 All ER 385. In Scotland, there is statutory authorization for such use: Criminal Procedure (Scotland) Act 1995, s 119, applied in *Diamond v HM Adv* 1999 SCCR 411; in Ireland, in *People (DPP) v O'S* [2006] IESC 12, [2006] 3 IR 57 subsequent acquittal of acts relied upon as similar facts in an earlier trial led to the conviction being quashed. In Canada, however, even a co-accused may not cross-examine another about offences of which he had been acquitted with a view to showing that he had in fact been guilty: *R v Akins* (2002) 164 CCC3d 289.

[376] *R v Fair* [2007] EWCA Crim 597; a similar view was taken by the High Court of Australia in *Washer v Western Australia* [2007] HCA 48, 234 CLR 492; but see *R v Boulton* [2007] EWCA Crim 597, [42]. For criticism see Tapper (2008) 12 *E&P* 53.

[377] *TD Radcliffe & Co v NFU Mutual Insurance Society* [1993] CLY 708. In Australia, see *S & Y Investments (No 2) Pty Ltd v Commercial Union Assurance Co of Australia Ltd* (1986) 82 FLR 130; in Canada, *Rizzo v Hanover Insurance Co* (1993) 103 DLR (4th) 577.

[378] *Hui Chi-ming v R* [1992] 1 AC 34, [1991] 3 All ER 897. See also *R v Terry* (n304); *R v Ebcin* [2005] EWCA Crim 2006.

[379] Even though technical, *Hussein v United Kingdom* (2006, unreported) 5 April (non-attendance of witness).

[380] Evidence throwing doubt on an acquittal was, however, held compatible with the European Convention in *R v Terry* (n304), [53].

[381] *Hammern v Norway; O v Norway, Y v Norway* (11 February 2003, unreported) ECHR. For commentary, see Hickman and Saifee [2003] *EHRLR* 539.

[382] *Ringvold v Norway* (11 February 2003, unreported) ECHR.

even when the evidence relied upon had been held inadmissible in the previous criminal proceedings.[383]

OTHER FINDINGS

Judicial findings

Hollington v F Hewthorn & Co Ltd could probably be cited as authority for the proposition that all judicial findings are inadmissible as evidence of the facts found in subsequent proceedings that are not between the same parties or their privies. From this, it follows that judicial findings in cases falling outside ss 11–13 of the Civil Evidence Act 1968 are still, subject to other statutory provisions,[384] no evidence of the facts found.[385] For example, in an action for damages for negligence brought by a passenger injured in a bus accident, a finding of negligence in an earlier action brought by another passenger in respect of the same accident would be inadmissible. Nor is a finding in a civil case admissible in a subsequent criminal case[386] at common law,[387] rendering a stay unnecessary.[388] It has also been held that a matter falling outside the explicit terms of s 75, even though as closely associated with a conviction as a confiscation order under the Drug Trafficking Act 1994,[389] is not capable of proof under these provisions if tendered to show the amounts of the drug involved in the offence.[390] It was further argued in *McIlkenny v Chief Constable of West Midlands*[391] that an issue determined on the voir dire[392] remains governed by the rule in *Hollington v F Hewthorn & Co*, since the relaxation in s 11 of the Civil Evidence Act 1968 is restricted to the use of convictions as evidence of the commission of the offences charged. A number of answers to this problem were propounded. Lord Denning MR was prepared to disregard *Hollington v F Hewthorn & Co* as having been wrongly decided.[393] Goff LJ and the House of Lords were able to avoid a direct decision on this point. Goff LJ clearly thought the voir dire outside the provisions of the statute.[394] The view of the House of Lords is less clear. It seems to have regarded the decision on the voir dire as so vital on the facts to the ultimate decision of guilt[395] that evidence of the conviction amounted to evidence of the

---

[383] *Serious Organised Crime Agency v Olden* [2009] EWHC 610 (QB).

[384] See Phipson *Law of Evidence* (17th edn) [43–86] n 526.

[385] But see *Birmingham City Council v H* [2005] EWHC 2885, in which it was clearly contemplated that findings relating to a first child in adoption proceedings in relation to a second child could, in the absence of strong contradictory evidence, be relied upon in care proceedings in the case of a third child.

[386] Or appeal: *R v D* [1996] QB 283, [1996] 1 All ER 881.

[387] Although in *R v Hogart* [2007] EWCA 338, [20] such findings were held admissible under s 117 of the Criminal Justice Act 2003 to prove misconduct for the purpose of s 101(1)(d).

[388] *Rudman v Wasy* [2008] 3 NZLR 404.   [389] Now Proceeds of Crime Act 2002.

[390] *R v Boam* [1998] Crim LR 205.

[391] [1980] QB 283, [1980] 2 All ER 227, and on appeal as *Hunter v Chief Constable of West Midlands* (n160).

[392] The same might apply to a factual issue decided only for the purposes of sentencing: see *Federal Police Comr v Hatfield* (1992) 59 ACR 392.

[393] 319, 237. A view shared in Western Australia: see *Mickelberg v Director of Perth Mint* [1986] WAR 365.   [394] 325, 241.

[395] Cf *R v Vuckov and Romeo* (1986) 40 SASR 498, in which an evidential issue arising on the voir dire was held to be sufficiently close to the issue of guilt to justify cross-examination under the local equivalent to s 1(3)(i) of the Criminal Evidence Act 1898.

factual basis of that holding under the terms of s 11.[396] Sir George Baker, the only judge to have addressed the question in any detail, held that the rule in *Hollington v F Hewthorn & Co* did not apply to such holdings because they were never expressly considered, and fell outside the policy of the rule, being readily identifiable issues, the subject of public reasoning by the judge, and determined according to the criminal standard of proof.[397]

Evidence of findings in other jurisdictions remains subject to the rule in *Hollington v F Hewthorn & Co*, and is, as such,[398] inadmissible as evidence of the underlying facts.

Inquisitions

Hearsay is now generally admissible in civil proceedings under the provisions of the Civil Evidence Act 1995, subject only to various procedural safeguards,[399] although the objection to evidence of the opinion of a different tribunal continues to apply,[400] and an attack is not necessarily abuse of process.[401] Those safeguards may, however, be dispensed with under the provisions of s 9.

This common law exception to the combined operation of the hearsay and opinion rules covered a heterogeneous mass of cases ranging from extracts from the Domesday Book to a return by a bishop to a writ from the Exchequer directing him to ascertain the vacancies and advowsons in his diocese.[402]

---

[396] 542, 731, although it is also said, at 543, 734, that *Hollington v F Hewthorn & Co* is generally considered to have been wrongly decided, which seems more consonant with Lord Denning's view.

[397] At 342, 255. See also *R v Fatu* [1989] 3 NZLR 419.

[398] *Calyon v Michailaidis* [2009] UKPC 34, [32]; perhaps hinting that the position might be different in a case where the earlier court had made a considered and well-articulated finding of fact.

[399] See further Chapter XIII.

[400] *Secretary of State for Trade and Industry v Bairstow* (n283), [26]. Unless it falls within an implied exception to the rule, *Secretary of State for Business Enterprise and Regulatory Reform v Aaron* [2008] EWCA Civ 1146 (Directors' disqualification proceedings).

[401] *Conlon and Harris v Simms* [2006] EWCA Civ 1749.

[402] *Irish Society v Bishop of Derry* (1846) 12 Cl & Fin 641.

III

BURDENS AND PROOF

When an issue of fact has to be proved in a court of law, it is necessary to consider the burdens borne by the parties. Their allocation helps to determine which party should begin calling evidence, discussed further in Chapter VI, and by extension, how to decide upon a submission that there is no case to answer. The terminology and techniques relating to burden of proof are most appropriate to the determination of past fact. They are far less well suited for application to the burden of persuasion on issues involving significant reliance upon judgment or discretion,[1] or those where it is one of the assessment of future risk,[2] or heavily dependent upon expert opinion,[3] or where the procedure is more inquisitorial than adversarial,[4] or where no issue of fact arises at all.[5] It may, however, be possible to require satisfaction of an evidential burden sufficient to raise the relevant issue.[6]

The nature of a burden in the law of evidence is obscured by the use of the term in a number of different senses discussed in the first section below. The two principal senses are the burden of adducing evidence and the burden of proving facts. In relation to each, questions arise as to its incidence and discharge. The second section considers the allocation of the burden in these two senses, at common law and under statutory provisions, and the effects of presumptions of law or agreement of the parties. These matters now require re-examination in the light of the Human Rights Act 1998, and especially its guarantee of the presumption of innocence in Art 6(2).[7] The third section, dealing with the discharge, is principally concerned with the extent of the two burdens, and the way in which the burden of proof has to be explained to the jury.

The key to clarity in this whole area lies in the precise definition and discrimination of the issues to be tried, and of the facts upon the determination of which they depend. Unfortunately, this is hindered by the absence of formal particulars of claim or developed pre-trial proceedings in criminal cases, and more generally by the lack of an agreed terminology. These factors have contributed to some confusion in the authorities, for

---

[1] See e.g. *R (McCann) v Crown Court at Manchester* [2002] UKHL 39, [2003] 1 AC 787, Lord Steyn, [37]; and in relation to abuse of process, *R v S* [2006] EWCA 756, [2006] 2 Cr App R 341, [20]. See in Australia *Leach v R* [2007] HCA 3, 230 CLR 1, [47].

[2] See e.g. *Fernandez v Government of Singapore* [1971] 2 All ER 691, [1971] 1 WLR 987; *Secretary of State for the Home Department v Rehman* [2001] UKHL 47, [2003] 1 AC 153, Lord Hoffmann, [56]. Special considerations apply to proof of the conditions banning the use of evidence obtained by torture in a tribunal otherwise dispensed from constraint in its use of evidence, and where security considerations impede access to factual material: see *A v Secretary of State for Home Department* [2005] UKHL 71, [2006] 2 AC 221, [55].

[3] See e.g. *R (O) v Harrow Crown Court* [2003] EWHC 868 (Admin), [2003] 1 WLR 2756, [33].

[4] See e.g. *R (D) v The Mental Health Review Tribunal* [2005] EWHC 587, [2005] ACD 92, especially [82].

[5] See e.g. *Kadre v France* [2005] EWHC 1712, [2006] ACD 26.

[6] *Thompstone v Tameside and Glossop Acute Services NHS Trust* [2006] EWHC 2904 (QB), [52].

[7] Article 6.2, although explicitly unqualified, has been interpreted as subject to exceptions: see *Salabiaku v France* (1988) 13 EHRR 379, accepted by the House of Lords in *R v Lambert* [2001] UKHL 37, [2002] 2 AC 545.

example on such issues of whether burdens of proof can shift, and as to the precise effect of presumptions.

SECTION 1. NATURE OF THE BURDEN

Thayer claimed that the phrase 'burden of proof' is used in two clearly separable senses.[8]
    Thayer's first sense was:

The peculiar duty of him who has the risk of any given proposition on which parties are at issue—who will lose the case if he does not make this proposition out, when all has been said and done.

This nearly corresponds to the persuasive burden, or burden of proof in the strict sense, discussed below. The correspondence is not complete because no allowance is made for the fact that the burden in question is confined to particular issues.[9] Most cases involve more than one issue, and the burden of proof upon different issues may be variously distributed between the parties—a fact that can be readily appreciated by considering a contractual claim where the terms are disputed and a defence of infancy is also raised; or for the tort of negligence defended by claiming contributory negligence; or a criminal charge on which insanity is pleaded. Owing to possible multiplicity of issues, a party may have 'the risk' of a given proposition and yet not lose the case if he fails on it; an example would be a contractual claim defended on both infancy and duress: the defendant bears the burden of proof on each of these issues, but failure on either does not itself entail the loss of the case.
    Thayer's second sense of the phrase 'burden of proof' was:[10]

The duty of going forward in argument or in producing evidence, whether at the beginning of a case, or at any later moment throughout the trial or discussion.

This corresponds in part to the evidential burden discussed below, but it is much broader because, in addition to advancing argument as well as adducing evidence, it covers not merely the legal obligation to demonstrate sufficient evidence to raise an issue of fact, but also the tactical obligation to lead counter-evidence. To anticipate, Thayer's second sense of the term 'burden of proof' conflates the evidential burden with the 'provisional' or 'tactical' burden.
    Just because Thayer failed to distinguish between the strict senses of the legal and evidential burden as described below, and the burdens that arise as between different issues, or as a matter of tactics in the course of a trial, his successors, both in commentary,[11] and in judgments,[12] have had to refine his terminology.

---

    8 *Preliminary Treatise on Evidence at the Common Law* 355.
    9 Although surprisingly little attention ever seems to be bestowed upon the critical matter of the precise discrimination of issues.   10 Ibid.
    11 See Glanville Williams *Criminal Law: The General Part* (2nd edn, 1961) ch 23; Adams in Clark (ed) *Essays on Criminal Law in New Zealand* (1971); Bob Williams, (2003) 25 *Syd LR* 165 (endorsed by the New Zealand Court of Appeal in *Ithaca (Custodians) Ltd v Perry Corp* [2004] 1 NZLR 731).
    12 Glanville Williams's distinction between the persuasive and evidential burdens was adopted in the judgment of the Court of Criminal Appeal delivered by Edmund Davies J in *R v Gill* [1963] 2 All ER 688, [1963] 1 WLR 841, and was reaffirmed after the passage of the Human Rights Act 1998 in *R v Lambert* (n7) by Lord Slynn, [1], by Lord Steyn, [37], by Lord Hope, [90], by Lord Clyde, [130], and by Lord Hutton, [182]. In that respect, the House was unanimous. The distinction between the two principal burdens is frequently mentioned by Australian, Canadian, and American judges.

THE TWO PRINCIPAL SENSES OF BURDEN

It is essential to understand that these two senses apply to individual issues, and not to the case as a whole. On any one issue, there can be only one evidential and one persuasive burden, and each can be borne by only one party.[13]

Persuasive burden

The persuasive burden is the obligation of a party to meet the requirement that a fact in issue be proved (or disproved) either by a preponderance of the evidence or beyond reasonable doubt, as the case may be. The words in brackets are intended to cover the case in which a party has to negate a particular fact, as the complainant has to negate consent on a charge of rape. The words are also apt to cover a case in which a party has to negate a particular fact if his opponent adduces sufficient evidence of its existence. For example, where self-defence is claimed as a defence, if there is sufficient evidence to raise a reasonable doubt in the minds of a reasonable jury, it is incumbent on the prosecution to prove beyond reasonable doubt that the accused was not acting in self-defence.

Wigmore spoke of the 'risk of non-persuasion'. Williams subsequently[14] sharpened this to the 'persuasive burden' by way of contrast to the 'the evidential burden'. This terminology is clear, and clearly preferable to such alternatives as the 'legal burden'. Nor is it satisfactory that some judgments simply refer to this one as the 'burden of proof'[15] or the 'probative burden',[16] even though the discharge of the other principal burden, the evidential burden, proves nothing.[17]

In a wholly exceptional civil case, and only after raising the matter with counsel, upon demonstration that an issue of any sort is found to be too evenly balanced to determine the matter one way or the other, then the issue must be determined by the incidence of the persuasive burden,[18] as the House of Lords has recognized:[19]

No judge likes to decide cases on burden of proof if he can legitimately avoid having to do so. There are cases, however, on which owing to the unsatisfactory state of the evidence, or otherwise, deciding on the burden of proof is the only just cause for him to take.

In criminal cases also, it can happen that where the evidence is equivocal between two co-accused, each of whom alleges that the crime was committed by the other, then both must normally be acquitted,[20] even though it is abundantly clear that the crime must have been committed by one or the other of them.[21]

---

[13] *King v R* [2003] HCA 42, 215 CLR 150, [18].

[14] *Criminal Law (The General Part)* (1st edn, 1953) ch 23.

[15] Devlin J in *Hill v Baxter* [1958] 1 QB 277, 284; *Bratty v A-G for Northern Ireland* [1963] AC 386, at 407, [1961] 3 All ER 523; 407, 414, 530.

[16] *DPP v Morgan* [1976] AC 182, [1975] 2 All ER 347; *R v Bennett* (1978) 68 Cr App Rep 168.

[17] *Jayasena v R* [1970] AC 618, [1970] 1 All ER 219.

[18] *Stephens v Cannon* [2005] EWCA Civ 222, [2005] CP Rep 31, [46]; but not in relation to preliminary issues such as the identification of the perpetrator of injuries to a child, where the ultimate issue is as to the child's welfare, *Re D (Children)* [2009] EWCA Civ 472, [12].

[19] *Rhesa Shipping Co SA v Edmunds* [1985] 2 All ER 712, [1985] 1 WLR 948; 718, 955, 956; see also *Pickford v Imperial Chemical Industries plc* [1998] 3 All ER 462 [1998] 1 WLR 1189; 472, 1200A; and in Ireland *Quinn v Mid Western Health Board* [2005] IESC 19, [2005] 4 IR 1, [59].

[20] In the absence of evidence of complicity between them.

[21] *R v Abbott* [1955] 2 QB 497, 503; see further 166.

The adverse effects of this in the case of homicide of a child or vulnerable adult by one or other of several persons in the same household has been alleviated by the creation of a new offence, afforced by the permission of adverse inferences from silence to help to establish a case to answer in respect of a conjoined charge of murder or manslaughter.[22]

Evidential burden

An 'evidential burden' is not a burden of proof. It determines whether an issue *should be left to the trier of fact*, while the 'persuasive burden' determines *how the issue should be decided*.

The terminology of 'evidential burden' was used by Bridge and Williams, and has become increasingly common,[23] despite the view of one Judge that every such use leads to error.[24] Failure to demonstrate such sufficient[25] evidence varies in its effect according to the form and stage of the relevant proceedings. In civil proceedings failure to adduce sufficient evidence which if believed would not suffice to establish a fact in issue as more probable than not will lead to failure on that issue. In criminal proceedings by jury the position is more varied. Where the definition of a crime requires an issue to be determined beyond reasonable doubt by the Crown, it satisfies its evidential burden on that issue by adducing sufficient evidence, which if believed, is capable of establishing the issue beyond reasonable doubt; failure to do so, exposes it to the danger of the defence succeeding on a submission of no case to answer.[26] On issues where the operation of a presumption prevents the accused from succeeding on a submission of no case even though the prosecution has adduced no explicit evidence, for example that an alleged *actus reus* was not accidental, or that there was no *mens rea* because of duress, it does not necessarily follow that the issue must be left to the jury at the end of the case in the absence of further evidence.

Where, unusually, the accused bears the persuasive burden of establishing an extrinsic defence or mitigation, such as insanity or diminished responsibility, he must adduce sufficient evidence which if believed is capable of rendering the relevant defence or mitigation more probable than not; failure to do so will permit the trial judge to withdraw consideration of the issue from the jury. In the more common situation where the prosecution bears a persuasive burden of rebutting an extrinsic defence or mitigation, such as self-defence or provocation, the defence must adduce sufficient evidence which, if believed, is capable of raising a reasonable doubt as to the guilt of the accused as charged on account of the relevant defence or mitigation, which the trial judge must then direct the jury to consider, and which the prosecution must rebut beyond reasonable doubt.

It is somewhat dubious whether the terminology of burden is appropriate in the third of these scenarios, since such an issue should be left to the jury whether the evidence sufficient to raise it has been adduced by prosecution or defence,[27] and even when the accused would prefer the issue not to be so left, for example where on a charge of murder he runs

---

[22] Domestic Violence, Crime and Victims Act 2004 ss 5 and 6, responding to proposals in Law Com No 282; for exegesis, see *R v Ikram* [2008] EWCA Crim 586.

[23] LEXIS reveals that the phrase has been used in some two thousand cases since 1945.

[24] Browne-Wilkinson VC in *Brady v Group Lotus Car Companies plc* [1987] 2 All ER 674 at 686, 687.

[25] Not so implausible as to be incapable of belief, even if uncontradicted, *Godwin v DPP* (1992) 96 Cr App Rep 244.

[26] See further 187.   [27] See *Palmer v R* [1971] AC 814, [1971] 1 All ER 1077; 823, 1088.

a defence of alibi, but the prosecution evidence raises the possibility of provocation.[28] It is also worth remarking that Professor Glanville Williams once justified the imposition of an evidential burden upon the accused as follows:[29]

The object of placing the evidential burden on the defendant is twofold: (1) to save the prosecution the trouble of meeting the defence unless it is first raised by the defendant, with sufficient evidence in support of it to be left to a jury, and (2) (particularly where the matter relates to the defendant's state of mind) to force the defendant to go into the witness box and give evidence, if he wishes to deny a state of mind or other fact that would normally be inferred from the circumstantial evidence.

It might be thought that subsequent statutory change[30] has made these arguments redundant, and that there is a case for reconsidering the whole justification and terminology of evidential burdens.

Illustrations of confusion[31]

The principal source of confusion is to suppose the evidential burden one of proof upon which the jury requires direction, and apparently so endemic for counsel sometimes to concede satisfaction of the evidential burden to avoid it.[32] Two other major sources of confusion in this part of the law are: first, failure to agree upon the discrimination of separate issues to which the rules are to apply; second, failure to distinguish explicitly between the persuasive and evidential burden. One example will be given of each.

In *DPP v Morgan*,[33] the accused were charged with rape. Their defence was that the victim consented, or at least that they believed her to be consenting. The trial judge directed the jury that it was for the prosecution to show that the act took place and to negate consent, but, in effect, that it was then for the accused to adduce some evidence to show that his belief in the victim's consent was reasonable. This view was upheld by the Court of Appeal, where Bridge J distinguished between cases in which the definition of the offence specified a particular mental state, where the prosecution bore both legal and evidential burdens of showing it, and cases where there was no such definition, when the issue of reasonable belief arose as a separate issue, and the evidential burden of establishing it was on the accused. The House of Lords accepted Bridge J's analysis, but allowed the appeal because a majority took the view that in rape there was only one issue as to the accused's mental state,

---

[28] *Kwaku Mensah v R* [1946] AC 83 (provocation); *DPP(Jamaica) v Bailey* [1995] 1 Cr App R 257 (self-defence); *Shaw v R* [2002] 1 Cr App R 10 (special statutory defence). These decisions of the Privy Council are to be preferred to contrary dicta in *R v Campbell* (1986) 84 Cr App R 255 (diminished responsibility), which relied heavily upon the phraseology of the Homicide Act 1957, and failed to take into account that of s 4 of the Criminal Procedure (Insanity) Act 1964. It was said in Canada in *R v Marshall* (2005) 200 CCC3d 179 that the judge should make it clear that the accused did not wish the issue to be raised.

[29] *Criminal Law: The General Part* (2nd edn, 1961), [289].

[30] The Criminal Justice Act 2003, Pt 5 has further ensured disclosure of defences, and the Criminal Justice and Public Order Act 1994, s 35 has imposed pressure upon the accused to testify.

[31] Sometimes extending to the drafting of official forms: see *Gayle v Gayle* [2001] EWCA Civ 1910, [17].

[32] See *R v Malinina* [2007] EWCA Crim 3228, where the Court of Appeal repeatedly refers to the evidential burden as one of proof.

[33] [1976] AC 182, [1975] 2 All ER 347. For similar confusion in relation to causing death, see *R v Mellor* [1996] 2 Cr App Rep 245.

to which the prosecution bore both burdens. The difficulty was simply whether there was one issue, or two, as to the accused's *mens rea*.[34]

In *Woolmington v DPP*,[35] the accused was charged with murdering his wife from whom he was separated, and testified that he had shot and killed her accidentally by threatening to shoot himself while endeavouring to induce her to return to live with him. Swift J directed the jury that:

> If the Crown satisfy you that this woman died at the prisoner's hands, then he has to show that there are circumstances to be found in the evidence which has been given from the witness box in this case which alleviate the crime, so that it is only manslaughter, or which excuse the homicide altogether by showing that it was a pure accident.

Woolmington was convicted, but his appeal allowed by the House of Lords because the jury had been misdirected.

The actual decision turned on the point that the direction suggested that, the killing having been admitted, the persuasive burden of disproving malice aforethought shifted to the accused, but Lord Sankey's speech in the House of Lords also shows that, even in cases in which the defence consists of something other than a denial of an essential element of the prosecution's case, a plea of provocation or self-defence for instance, the accused does not, as was formerly believed, bear a persuasive as well as an evidential burden.[36] It confusingly elides the distinction between discharge of an established evidential burden upon the prosecution, for which the presumption that a man intends the natural consequences of his acts may suffice, and imposition of an evidential burden upon the accused to establish a defence.

OTHER SENSES AND SHIFTING OF BURDEN

The definitions of the two principal senses of burden render it difficult to speak meaningfully of the shifting of either of them. The evidential burden can be defined as the obligation to show, if called upon to do so, that there is sufficient evidence to raise an issue as to the existence or non-existence of a fact in issue. The persuasive burden can be defined as the obligation of a party to meet the requirement of a rule of law that a fact in issue must be proved or disproved. The question whether there is sufficient evidence to raise the issue of the existence of a particular fact can be answered only after both parties have called their

---

[34] Exactly the same problem arose in discrimination (but not victimization, *Oyarce v Cheshire CC* [2008] EWCA Civ 434, [2008] 4 All ER 907) cases as between the commission of apparently discriminatory acts, and their justification, which required resolution by a convoluted route involving the European Burden of Proof Directive OJ 1998 L 14, statutory amendment so as to comply; see e.g. s 63A inserted into the Sex Discrimination Act 1975, and exegesis by the Court of Appeal in *Wong v Igen Ltd* [2005] EWCA Civ142, [2005] 3 All ER 812; see also *EB v BA* [2006] EWCA Civ 132, *Madarassy v Nomura Int plc* [2007] EWCA Civ 33; *Appiah v Bishop Douglass Roman Catholic High School Governors* [2007] EWCA Civ 10.

[35] [1935] AC 462. For some amplification of the facts given in the official Report, see (1992) 142 NLJ 330. See also, in Australia, *He Kaw Teh v R* (1985) 157 CLR 523.

[36] Although the Law Commission has now proposed that the persuasive burden of proving duress be placed upon the accused: *Murder, Manslaughter and Infanticide* (Law Com 304, 2006), [6.141]. See also, in the United States, *Dixon v US* unreported 22 June 2006. [1935] AC 462.

evidence and, when there is a jury, the answer must be given by it after instruction from the judge. Writing about a criminal trial by jury, Williams has said:[37]

[T]he evidential burden governs what the judge does in leaving the question to the jury or withdrawing it from them, the persuasive burden governs what he says in directing the jury how to reach their verdict.

The concept of the evidential burden is the product of trial by jury and the possibility of withdrawing an issue from that body. Unlike the concept of the persuasive burden, it is not a logical necessity of litigation about questions of fact: 'If it were to be said of any issue, that it was not covered by an evidential burden, the only effect would be to remove the judge's filtering power in respect of that issue.'[38] It is accordingly difficult not to sympathize with Browne-Wilkinson V-C, who preferred the expression not to be used in civil proceedings since it was so apt to be applied to the tactical burden as discussed below.[39]

It is true that, when dissenting in *DPP v Morgan*,[40] Lord Simon of Glaisdale spoke of the shifting of the evidential burden 'backwards and forwards in the course of a trial', but he was attempting to justify the view of the Court of Appeal that, as a matter of law, someone charged with rape bears the evidential burden on the issue of his mistaken belief that the woman was consenting to intercourse.[41] The decision turned on the substantive law, but, so far as the evidential burden was concerned, the majority of the House of Lords appears to have accepted the argument of counsel for the appellant summarized by Lord Cross:[42]

If [the Crown] adduces evidence to show that intercourse took place and that the woman did not consent to it then in the absence of any evidence from the defendant the jury will certainly draw the inference that he was aware that she was not consenting. So as a practical matter he is bound—if he wishes to raise the point—to give evidence to the effect that he believed that she was consenting and as to his reason for that belief; and the weaker those reasons are the more likely the jury is to conclude that he had no such belief. But the issue as to the accused's belief in the woman's consent is before the jury from the beginning,[43] and is an issue in respect of which the evidential burden is on the Crown from the first to last. There is never any question of any evidential burden with regard to it being on the accused or of the judge withdrawing it from the jury.

It remains to be seen what judges, and others, really have in mind when they refer to the shifting of a burden.[44] Three possibilities are worthy of consideration. The first is that the

---

[37] (1977) 127 NLJ 156.   [38] Ibid, 158.

[39] *Brady v Group Lotus Car Companies plc* [1987] 2 All ER 674, 686, 687, approved by the Court of Appeal [1987] 3 All ER 1050, 1056.

[40] [1976] AC 182, 217. See also *Dunlop Holding Ltd's Application* [1979] RPC 523, where Buckley and Bridge LJJ take a similar view, although Waller LJ analyses the situation entirely in terms of the distribution of persuasive and evidential burdens.

[41] Even if that were law, it would not have justified the trial judge's action in leaving to the jury the question whether the accused had reasonable grounds for their belief, although it might have justified the withdrawal of the issue of the accused's belief from the jury on the ground of insufficiency of supporting evidence.

[42] [1976] AC 182, 200. Section 1(2) of the Sexual Offences (Amendment) Act 1976 declared that the presence or absence of reasonable grounds for an alleged belief in the victim's consent is a factor to be taken into account by the jury in conjunction with any other relevant evidence when considering whether the accused had such a belief: see now Sexual Offences Act 2003, s 1(2), (3).

[43] The definition of rape then being unlawful sexual intercourse with a non-consenting woman, knowing that she does not consent or being reckless as to whether she does so.

[44] For a judge's own explanation, see Mustill LJ in *Brady v Group Lotus Car Companies plc* [1987] 3 All ER 1050, 1058.

burden has been attenuated to refer only to the tactical desirability of adducing evidence in order to avoid an adverse decision of the issue by the trier of fact.[45] The second is that the burden has been expanded to apply outside the confines of a single issue, and to refer instead to the fluctuation of fortunes in a multiple-issue case, considering the ultimate effect of the sequential resolution of each successive issue. The third uses 'burden' as defined above, but directs attention to cases in which the allocation of one of the burdens is made conditional upon the proof of some other fact. The first two are considered below, and the third in the next section in relation to the allocation of the burden of proof.

The tactical burden

A tactical burden is one that is borne by the opponent of an issue after the proponent has discharged his evidential burden. The opponent must, in the words of Lord Denning, 'call evidence or take the consequences which may not necessarily be fatal'.[46] An example is provided by any criminal case in which the prosecution relies on the *actus reus* as evidence of *mens rea*. By not calling evidence on the subject, the accused runs the risk of an adverse finding with regard to his mental state if the jury accepts the Crown's version of his external conduct. The degree of risk run by an opponent who does not adduce evidence on a particular issue varies from case to case. In civil proceedings, the proponent's evidence may be so weighty that a verdict or decision in his favour will be demanded by common sense and a judge would be justified in directing a jury or himself accordingly.[47] In criminal cases tried with a jury,[48] the situation is complicated by the rule that there cannot be a directed verdict of guilty, but judges sometimes allude to a shifting of the burden of proof on account of the strength of the evidence adduced by the accused on issues as to which he bears the evidential and persuasive burdens.[49]

If a fact in issue may be inferred from the proof of another particular fact in a commonly recurring situation, the language of presumption is often employed. The fact that is proved can be referred to as the basic fact, and the fact inferred as the presumed fact. In other words, the party proving the basic fact is likely to win on the issue to which the presumed fact relates in the absence of evidence to the contrary adduced by the other. According to older classifications, presumptions having this limited effect are described as 'presumptions of fact', such as the presumption of continuance,[50] the presumption of guilty knowledge arising from the possession of recently stolen goods[51] and the presumption of unseaworthiness in the case of a vessel that founders shortly after leaving port.[52] These are all inferences that may be drawn by the tribunal of fact. It is not obliged to draw them as a matter of law even if there is no further evidence, although there may be occasions on which a civil jury should be directed that they ought to draw the inference as

---

[45] For a very clear example, see *R v SK* (2003) 177 CCC3d 90.

[46] (1945) 61 LQR 380. He referred to the burden as 'provisional'.

[47] *Ajum Goolam Hosen & Co v Union Marine Insurance Co* [1901] AC 362; cf *Pickup v Thames and Mersey Marine Insurance Co Ltd* (1878) 3 QBD 594.

[48] The Queen's Bench Divisional Court frequently remits a case to magistrates on an appeal by the prosecutor on the ground that the weight of the evidence adduced by him was such that there was a case to answer.   [49] *R v Matheson* [1958] 2 All ER 87, [1958] 1 WLR 474.

[50] See 31.   [51] See 42.

[52] *Ajum Goolam Hossen & Co v Union Marine Insurance Co* [1901] AC 362.

reasonable men, and, in civil cases, a verdict, or even the decision of a judge sitting alone, might be set aside if the inference were not drawn.

The ultimate burden

The 'ultimate burden' is a phrase appropriate only to a case involving more than one issue:[53]

Where the ultimate decision of a case depends on the determination of a number of separate issues, the burden on the ultimate issue needs to be distinguished from the burden on the separate issues.

The ultimate burden is thus the burden borne by the party against whom the persuasive burden on a particular issue has been discharged. Lord Denning illustrates his meaning by reference to a claim brought by the holder against the acceptor of a bill of exchange. The ultimate decision depends on whether the claimant is a holder in due course. He might begin by proving that he was the holder of a bill signed by the defendant as acceptor. He will succeed on his claim unless the defendant makes good some such defence as fraud in the negotiation of the bill. In his turn, the defendant will succeed unless the claimant makes good a reply such as value in good faith subsequent to the fraud: 'This shifting to and fro is often described as shifting of the burden of proof and so it is, but it is a shifting of the ultimate burden.' [54] No doubt such progression towards Lord Denning's ultimate burden is what judges sometimes have in mind when they say that burdens have 'shifted',[55] but the concept is subject to the same objections as those advanced above against the tactical burden, and more particularly that the expression 'burden of proof' is meaningless unless it is used with reference to a particular issue. The interaction of persuasive, evidential, tactical, and ultimate burdens was conveniently illustrated in *Ratford v Northavon District Council*.[56] The authority levied a rate upon the receivers of a company occupying rateable property in their area. It was held that, provided there was some reasonable basis for supposing a person to be in occupation of such property, the authority was entitled to levy a rate upon them. In proceedings for non-payment, the authority bore both evidential and persuasive burdens of showing that the rate had been duly made, demanded, and not paid. The non-payer would then lose unless he satisfied the evidential and persuasive burden upon the next issue, that of showing a valid reason why he had not paid. In this case, the receivers adduced evidence showing that, although empowered to do so, they had not in fact taken possession of the relevant premises. Once this had been done, and the evidential burden upon that issue satisfied, the only sense in which a burden could further shift was in the tactical sense, but its ultimate determination would decide the whole case. On this point, the court endorsed the remarks of Donaldson LJ in *Forsythe v Rawlinson*[57] that it was like all burdens of proof in litigation a swinging burden in the sense that:[58]

As the evidence of varying weight develops before the magistrates, the eventual burden of proof will, in accordance with ordinary principles of evidence, remain with or shift to the person who will fail without further evidence.

---

[53] Denning (1945) 61 *LQR* 380.

[54] For a case in which the burden of proof was said to shift in this way, see *Medawar v Grand Hotel Co* [1891] 2 QB 11; for a case of this type disposed of without any reference to the shifting of the burden of proof, see *Neal v Fior* [1968] 3 All ER 865, [1968] 1 WLR 1875.

[55] See Mustill LJ in *Brady v Group Lotus Cars Companies Ltd* [1987] 3 All ER 1050, 1058.

[56] [1987] QB 357, [1986] 3 All ER 193.   [57] [1981] RVR 97.   [58] 202.

SECTION 2.   ALLOCATION OF THE BURDEN[59]

Burdens are generally allocated as a matter of common law, either unconditionally, or sometimes conditionally upon the proof of certain facts, as in the case of true presumptions, although occasionally unconditional allocation borrows the language of presumption. Allocation may also be a matter of explicit provision, either by way of statutory provision,[60] itself either general or specific, or by agreement of the parties. These different modes of allocation will be considered in turn, and although all are capable of applying in either of the two principal senses of persuasive or evidential burden, by far the greater attention has been paid to the allocation of the persuasive burden.

UNCONDITIONAL ALLOCATION AT COMMON LAW

Evidential burden

The general rule is that the party bearing the persuasive burden on an issue also bears the evidential burden. This means that, in a criminal case, the prosecution must normally adduce evidence fit to be left to a jury of the essential ingredients of the offence charged. It is not enough to adduce evidence that would be sufficient on one of two mutually exclusive hypotheses, and leave the jury to choose between them.[61] The general rule also means that the defence bears an evidential burden on the issue of insanity, by virtue of the common law, and on sundry other issues by virtue of statutory provision, on which the persuasive burden is placed upon the defence by way of exception to the rule in *Woolmington v DPP*.[62] In these cases, it must adduce evidence sufficient, if believed, to satisfy the jury of the existence of the defence on the balance of probabilities.[63] It seems that on issues arising out of special pleas, the accused will bear an evidential burden, for example in relation to unfitness to plead[64] or autrefois convict[65] or acquit, where the persuasive burden is on the accused, and perhaps even in cases where the persuasive burden is borne by the prosecution.[66]

While the prosecution bears the persuasive burden of disproving a number of general common law defences, the accused bears the burden of adducing sufficient evidence to raise the issue of their existence.[67] Even in the absence of explicit provision, statutes are

---

[59] See generally Bob Williams in Waller and Campbell (eds) *Well and Truly Tried* (1982).

[60] Now subject to adjustment in the light of the provisions of the European Convention on Human Rights.

[61] *Tsang Ping-Nam v R* [1981] 1 WLR 1462.   [62] [1935] AC 462.

[63] *R v Dix* (1981) 74 Cr App Rep 306, (some medical evidence must be adduced before the defence of diminished responsibility can be left to the jury); *R v Bown* [2003] EWCA Crim 1989 (some evidence of a good reason for having a bladed knife needed to be adduced before the issue could be so left).

[64] *R v Podola* [1960] 1 QB 325; but see *R v Bradley (No 2)* (1986) 85 FLR 111 for doubts in Australia.

[65] *R v Coughlan and Young* (1976) 63 Cr App Rep 33.

[66] See *R v Graham* (1983) 11 ACR 21 (plea to the jurisdiction of the court).

[67] *Mancini v DPP* [1942] AC 1, [1941] 3 All ER 272 (provocation); *Chan Kau v R* [1955] AC 206, [1955] 1 All ER 266 (provocation and self-defence); *R v Lobell* [1957] 1 QB 547, [1957] 1 All ER 734 (self-defence); *DPP v Walker* [1974] 1 WLR 1090 (necessity for self-defence); *R v Gill* [1963] 2 All ER 688, [1963] 1 WLR 841 (duress); *R v Bone* [1968] 2 All ER 644, [1968] 1 WLR 983 (duress).

frequently construed to place an evidential, if not a persuasive, burden on a particular issue on the accused.[68]

Although there is little direct English authority on the point, it seems that where the accused bears an evidential, but not a persuasive burden, he may discharge it by adducing evidence of a reasonable possibility of the existence of the defence.[69] It is hardly surprising that there should be no direct authority because judicial generosity, or perhaps fear of a successful and unmeritorious appeal, leads to disinclination to withdraw issues of which there is some defence evidence from the jury.[70] This disinclination may also have accounted for the previous dearth of authority on the question of whether the accused bears an evidential burden in respect of all defences that are more than mere denials of an allegation necessary to the prosecution's case. This issue has, however, been ignited by the impact of Art 6(2) of the European Convention on Human Rights, largely in the context of the construction of statutory provisions, to be discussed further later in this chapter.

In civil cases, the nature of the defence will usually be raised in the particulars of claim and case for the defence from which the allocation of the respective burdens can be deduced. Where this does not occur, the principles that apply are similar to those in criminal cases. The proponent of a claim has an evidential burden, which will not normally be shifted to the defence at common law, even in cases where strong evidence will be required for the defence to succeed on that issue.[71] Although the proponent of a proposition may bear the persuasive burden of proving an issue to the satisfaction of the court, he is not necessarily bound to anticipate every possible defeasing defence, especially when it could easily have been stated.[72] Thus in *Dunlop Holdings Ltd's Application*,[73] the opponents of a claim to patent a wheel had the burden of proving that the wheel had been in prior use. They were not, however, bound to anticipate a contention that such prior use had been secret. It was for the applicant to raise the issue by adducing some evidence, or at least by cross-examining the opponents' witnesses so as to show that the use had been in secret. Until this had been done, proof of prior use without more was sufficient to entitle the opponents to succeed, though if the issue had been so raised they would have had to prove that the use was not secret upon the balance of probabilities.

There can be no doubt that the imposition of an evidential burden upon the defence in a criminal case is compatible with the provisions of Art 6(2) of the European Convention on

---

[68] See e.g. *R v John* [1974] 2 All ER 561, [1974] 1 WLR 624. In Canada, where the Charter invalidates the allocation of the persuasive burden to the accused, it has been held that any such attempt can be read down to allocate an evidential burden only to the accused: *R v Laba* [1994] 3 SCR 965.

[69] See Lord Devlin in *Jayasena v R* [1970] AC 618, 624, and *R v Newcastle-upon-Tyne Justices, ex p Hindle* [1984] 1 All ER 770 (drink imbibed after accident but before breath test); see also *R v Thornton* (1967) unreported, a Northern Irish case discussed by Comerton (1968) 19 NILQ 60.

[70] For a rare exception, see *R v Bianco* [2001] EWCA Crim 2516, despite the fact that the issue withdrawn was the only substantial one in the case, and its withdrawal precipitated a change of plea. Cf *Coca-Cola Co v Aytacli* [2003] EWHC 91 (Ch), [2003] 11 LS Gas R 31, for withdrawal of the same issue for failure to meet the evidential burden in civil contempt proceedings.

[71] See e.g. *Sheppard v Secretary of State for the Home Department* [2002] EWCA Civ 1921, in which the claimant had suffered very severe injuries in custody, but despite strong dicta in some European human rights cases, it was still not sufficient to transform the burden on the defence from a tactical to an evidential burden.

[72] Rule 16(5) of the Civil Procedure Rules both requires a statement of case by the defence, and specifies what it should include.   [73] [1979] RPC 523.

Human Rights, since it is not a burden of proof, but, at most, one of adducing evidence.[74] Most dispute in this area relates to the compatibility with Art 6(2) of the imposition of a persuasive burden. A similar approach has been widely applied elsewhere in the Commonwealth to the interpretation of similar constitutional guaranties.[75]

Persuasive burden[76]

Wigmore truly said 'There are merely specific rules for specific classes of case resting for their ultimate basis upon broad reasons of expedience and fairness',[77] but this does not often lead to difficulty in ascertaining the party upon whom the persuasive burden rests, for a fundamental requirement of any judicial system is that the person who desires the court to take action must prove his case to its satisfaction.[78] This means that, as a matter of common sense, it normally[79] rests upon the claimant in a civil suit or the prosecutor in criminal proceedings.

The rule is sometimes expressed in terms of such maxims as *omnia praesumuntur pro negante*, and *ei incumbit probatio qui dicit, non qui negat*, but this does not mean that the onus of proof cannot lie upon a party who makes a negative allegation. If so, the application of the rule would depend upon the language chosen to state a case. Even though a positive averment can always be converted into a negative statement by appropriate linguistic manipulation, there are numerous instances in which a claimant or prosecutor assumes the persuasive burden of proving a negative.[80] Absence of consent must be established by the Crown on a charge of rape or assault,[81] as must absence of reasonable belief that a female victim is over the statutory age;[82] where lack of consent[83] or want of due notice of a particular fact[84] is alleged in a civil action, these matters must be proved by the claimant. In the leading case of *Abrath v North Eastern Rly Co*,[85] Bowen LJ said that: 'If the assertion of a negative is an essential part of the plaintiff's case, the proof of the assertion still rests upon the plaintiff.'

Difficulty may sometimes arise with regard to the question of whether an assertion is essential to a party's case or to his adversary's. In *Joseph Constantine Steamship Line Ltd v Imperial Smelting Corp Ltd*,[86] the charterers of a ship claimed damages from the owners

---

[74] See e.g. *R v Lambert* (n7). For interaction with the New Zealand Bill of Rights see *R v Hansen* SC 58/2005, [2007] 3 NZLR 1.

[75] See *Vasquez v R* [1994] 1 WLR 1304 (Bermuda); *Yearwood v R* [2001] UKPC 31 (Grenada); *R v Stone* [1999] 2 SCR 290 (Canada), although there subject to some dissent; *State v Manamela* 2000 (3) SA 1 (South Africa).

[76] See, in relation to criminal cases, Roberts [1995] *Crim LR* 783.   [77] IX Wigmore 278.

[78] *Dickinson v Minister of Pensions* [1953] 1 QB 228, [1952] 2 All ER 1031; 232, 1033; *Schaffer v Weast* 546 US 49 (2005), [5].

[79] Exceptionally the burden of proving a counter-claim in an employment dispute rests upon the counter-claimant if the employment were fiduciary, *Environmental Recycling Technologies PLC v Daley* [2009] EWCA Civ 612.

[80] Although it is difficult to prove the negation of some facts, modern technology can sometimes make it as easy to prove a negative as a positive: see e.g. *United States v Greenlee* 517 F 2d 889 (1975).

[81] *R v Donovan* [1934] 2 KB 498.   [82] *R v K* [2001] UKHL 41, [2002] 1 AC 462.

[83] *Toleman v Portbury* (1870) LR 5 QB 288.   [84] *Williams v East India Co* (1802) 3 East 192.

[85] (1883) 11 QBD 440, 457 (absence of reasonable cause in action for malicious prosecution); affirmed by the House of Lords (1886) 11 App Cas 247.

[86] [1942] AC 154, [1941] 2 All ER 165. For an illustration in criminal law, see *R v Anwoir* [[2008] EWCA Crim 1354, [2008] 4 All ER 582 (knowledge of form of criminal source in money laundering).

for failure to load. The owners pleaded frustration by destruction of the ship owing to an explosion, and the only question of fact was whether this had been caused by their fault. As the evidence was scanty, it became necessary to determine which of the parties bore the persuasive burden with regard to this matter. If the rule were that charterparties cease to be binding when the vessel, without default of either party, is disabled by an overpowering disaster, the negation of fault would be essential to the defendant's case; on the other hand, proof of fault would be essential to the claimant's case, if the rule were that charterparties cease to be binding when the vessel is disabled by an overpowering disaster, provided that disaster is not brought about by the fault of either party. The House of Lords decided the latter to be the correct formulation, and accordingly held that the claimant has the persuasive burden of proving fault when frustration is stated as a defence to a contractual claim. Their Lordships' speeches referred to principles, such as the difficulty of proving a negative and the presumption of innocence, but, as Stone has shown, general considerations of public policy probably constituted the decisive factor.[87] If such considerations are the guide where there is no governing precedent, it is obviously futile to seek for any set formula determining what facts are essential to a party's case and hence the incidence of the persuasive burden of proof can be ascertained only by consulting precedents in various branches of the substantive law. In the case of bailment, for example, it is settled that the bailee has the onus of proving that the goods were lost without his fault,[88] and at a criminal trial, the accused has the persuasive burden on a plea of insanity.[89] No a priori tests could have produced these results; it is pointless to collect numerous isolated precedents.

The terminology of presumption

The burden of proof is sometimes allocated[90] by way of the terminology of presumption. Such terminology strictly applies when proof of one fact affects the burden relating to another, and consideration of that is postponed to the next part of this section. Sometimes, however, there is no basic fact at all, and the presumption does no more than express the incidence of the relevant burden.[91] Typical examples are provided by the presumption of innocence, and the presumption of sanity in criminal cases.

---

[87] It seems to be the case that frustration occurs more often than not without fault on anyone's part, and absence of fault is undoubtedly difficult to prove. Hence 'a rule requiring the defendant pleading frustration to negative fault will then ex hypothesi do injustice to the great majority of defendants. While, on the other hand, a rule requiring the plaintiff to prove fault will ex hypothesi do injustice to only a small minority of plaintiffs' ((1944) 60 LQR 278).

[88] *Hunt and Winterbotham (West of England) Ltd v BRS (Parcels) Ltd* [1962] 1 QB 617, [1962] 1 All ER 111; *Houghland v RR Low (Luxury Coaches) Ltd* [1962] 1 QB 694, [1962] 2 All ER 159.

[89] *McNaghten's Case* (1843) 10 Cl & Fin 200; *R v Smith* (1910) 6 Cr App Rep 19. For criticism, see Williams *Criminal Law: The General Part* (2nd edn) 516; and for penetrating analysis, see Jones (1995) 111 *LQR* 475. Under s 2(2) of the Homicide Act 1957, it is for the accused to prove diminished responsibility: see *R v Dunbar* [1958] 1 QB 1, and in Canada in *R v LB* 237 CCC3d 215 infanticide was also so treated. The allocation of both evidential and persuasive burden in that situation was upheld as compatible with the European Convention in *R v Ali* [2002] QB 1112, [2001] 1 All ER 1014, and by contrast to *R v Lambert*, decided in the same judgment below, no appeal was heard by the House of Lords.

[90] Or its allocation so explained; commonly in the jurisprudence of the ECHR, see e.g. *Salabiaku v France* (1988) 13 EHRR 379.

[91] The language of presumption is sometimes used to establish an issue conclusively with no possibility of rebuttal of the presumed fact once the basic fact is found, as in s 76 of the Sexual Offences Act 2003, where lack of consent, or belief in it, is so presumed upon a finding of impersonation. For fuller discussion of the various presumptions in this legislation, see McEwan (2005) 9 *E&P* 1.

Presumption of innocence[92]

When it is said that an accused person is presumed to be innocent, all that is generally[93] meant is that the prosecution is obliged to prove the case against him beyond reasonable doubt. This is a fundamental rule of criminal procedure,[94] and is expressed in terms of a presumption of innocence so frequently as to render criticism somewhat pointless; yet it sometimes leads to serious confusion of thought.[95] *Coffin* has been universally condemned: it could hardly have been pronounced if the court had not been misled by the verbal dissimilarity between the rule that the prosecution bears the persuasive burden of proof and the presumption of innocence.[96] In directing the jury it might be better to regard the rule not so much as a presumption of innocence, as the absence of a presumption of guilt.[97]

Article 6(2) of the European Convention on Human Rights is cast in terms of presumption in this general sense, and has generated an enormous body of law, mainly concerned with the construction of statutory provisions, to be discussed later in this chapter. It has, however, been determined that it does not preclude refusal to allow withdrawal of an unequivocal plea of guilty,[98] nor to refusal of compensation upon a conviction being quashed despite the Court being unconvinced of the appellant's innocence.[99]

Presumption of sanity

In criminal cases, the presumption of sanity is no more than a conclusion that must be drawn until the contrary is proved, for the McNaghten Rules have decreed:[100]

> …that the jurors ought to be told in all cases that every man is presumed to be sane and to possess a sufficient degree of reason to be responsible for his crimes until the contrary be proved to their satisfaction.

The McNaghten Rules apply to criminal charges,[101] and the presumption of sanity that they prescribe must be distinguished from the same presumption in some other branches

---

92 Allen *Legal Duties* 253; for invaluable empirical research, see Ashworth and Blake [1996] *Crim LR* 306.

93 For a broader approach to this concept, see Healy [1987] Crim LR 355, 364, 365. In *Broderick v DPP* [2006] IESC 34, [2006] 1 IR 629 (provision of bail). See also *Matijasevic v Serbia* 48 EHRR 876 (2006) (extension of pre-trial detention).

94 Its strength is indicated in the construction by the Privy Council of the local constitution in *Vasquez v R* [1994] 3 All ER 674, [1994] 1 WLR 1304 so as to strike down statutory provisions clearly imposing a persuasive burden on the defence. But see *Khan v State of Trinidad and Tobago* [2003] UKPC 79, [2005] 1 AC 374, in which it did not prevent the redefinition of murder so as to eliminate an issue as to the accused's *mens rea* by reintroducing the felony murder rule. Its effect can be by-passed by the use of serious crime prevention orders under the Serious Crime Act 2007.

95 Thus, in *Coffin v United States* 156 US 432 (1895), the presumption was regarded as itself an item of evidence: see Thayer *Preliminary Treatise on Evidence at the Common Law* App B.

96 It required the House of Lords in *R v JTB* [2009] UKHL 20, [2009] 1 AC 1310 to hold that s 34 of the Crime and Disorder Act 1998 abolished both rule and presumption of doli incapax of child.

97 See Wigmore (1981) vol 9 [2511].

98 *Revitt v DPP* [2006] EWHC 2266 (Admin), [2006] 1 WLR 3172, [13].

99 *R (Allen) v Secretary of State for Home Affairs* [2008] EWCA Civ 808, [2009] 1 Cr App R 36.

100 See Jones (1995) 111 LQR 475. The rules are not universally accepted in the United States, see *Clark v Arizona* 548 US 735 (2006).

101 A further issue may then arise under the provisions of the Criminal Procedure (Insanity and Unfitness to Plead) Act 1991, s 4A as to whether the accused did the relevant act, and in this case, it seems that he has an

of the law. If a rational will is produced, and shown to have been duly executed, the jury ought to be told to find in favour of the testator's competence.[102] The persuasive burden rests on the party who propounds the will, but the rule that he does not have to adduce evidence of capacity in the first instance is sometimes said to raise a presumption of sanity in testamentary cases. This presumption is dependent on the proof of a basic fact—the execution of a rational will—therefore it is an illustration of the proper use of the term.

Other examples

Allowance must be made for a number of presumptions without basic facts; for example, Lord Kilmuir and Lord Denning spoke of 'the presumption of mental capacity' in *Bratty v A-G for Northern Ireland*[103] simply as a compendious way of expressing the fact that the accused bears the evidential burden on the issue of non-insane automatism. Although it is common enough to speak of a presumption that mechanical instruments were in working order as a means of indicating the fact that an evidential burden is borne by the party denying that this was the case,[104] it can hardly be said that any basic fact is involved.

Statutes sometimes use the same technique, thus s 5(5) of the Dangerous Dogs Act 1991 presumes that a dog is a member of a prohibited breed unless the accused shows the contrary by evidence the court considers sufficient.[105] Thus the effect of this section as against the accused is a precise counterpart of the operation of the presumption of sanity in criminal cases.

CONDITIONAL ALLOCATION AT COMMON LAW: PRESUMPTIONS

The structure of all true presumptions requires first the proof of a basic fact or facts. Different consequences then follow so far as the establishment of the presumed fact is concerned. At its weakest, the only effect of proving the basic fact is that the presumed fact *may* be found by the trier of fact. In other words, the logical inference of the presumed fact from proof of the basic fact attracts a measure of formal endorsement, and casts at most a tactical burden of rebuttal.[106] Such presumptions have no effect upon the burden of proof in either of its two principal senses, and need here no further consideration.[107] Two

---

evidential burden to adduce 'objective' evidence of such defences as accident, mistake, or self-defence even though they involve some consideration of his mental state that in general is no longer in issue at that stage: *R v Antoine* [2001] AC 340, [2000] 2 All ER 208. The defence of provocation falls on the intent side of the line: *R v Grant* [2001] EWCA Crim 2611, [2002] QB 1030, [45].

[102] See *Sutton v Sadler* (1857) 3 CBNS 87; see also *Griffiths v Cork* [2007] EWHC 1827 (Ch) (deed).

[103] [1963] AC 386, 407, and 413, respectively. In Australia, see *R v Falconer* (1990) 171 CLR 30. It seems similarly tacitly to be presumed that an act is done without duress, provocation, or in self-defence, until the contrary is suggested. See, in New Zealand, *R v* (presumption of knowledge of nature of thing possessed).

[104] See 37 above.

[105] In *Bates v United Kingdom* [1996] EHRLR 312, this technique was held compatible with Art 6.2 of the ECHR.

[106] For examples, see (nn47–51). The most plausible reason for such formal recognition is that it preempts legalistic argument among the jurors that the prosecution charged with proving something has failed to do so because it has proved only something else.

[107] In traditional terminology, these would be described as presumptions of fact.

possibilities remain, one relating to the evidential, and one to the persuasive, burden.[108] If, after proof of the basic fact, the presumed fact must be taken to be established in the absence of evidence to the contrary, then an evidential burden has been cast upon the opponent of the presumed fact and the presumption can reasonably be described as an evidential presumption.[109] On the other hand, if, after proof of the basic fact, the presumed fact must be taken to be established unless the trier of fact is persuaded to the appropriate standard of the contrary, then a persuasive burden has been cast upon the opponent of the presumed fact, and the presumption can reasonably be described as a persuasive presumption. It is more accurate to speak of a shift in the burden of proof in the case of these stronger presumptions because they affect what the judge does in leaving an issue to the jurors or withdrawing it from them, and may determine the manner in which he must direct the jury at the end of the case.[110]

It would be unreasonable to expect neat precision in this area of the law. Indeed, it has been the subject of an extraordinary catalogue of complaints such as that:[111]

Every writer of sufficient intelligence to appreciate the difficulties of the subject-matter has approached the topic of presumptions with a sense of hopelessness, and has left it with a feeling of despair.

There are a number of reasons for this. The precise delimitation and distinction of basic fact and presumed fact is assumed by the approach indicated above, but often not realized in practice.[112] This can mean that the same evidence rebuts both basic fact and presumed fact; for example, in the case of the presumption of death, evidence that the subject has been seen alive by one of his family may rebut both one of the basic facts of the presumption, that he has not been seen alive, and the presumed fact, that he is dead.[113] This could cause serious problems where the persuasive burden of proving the basic fact of the presumption is on the proponent of death, and the persuasive burden of rebutting the presumed fact of death upon his opponent.

Nowadays, presumptions have much less importance than they did when the exclusionary rules were very much more restrictive, and the range of accessible evidence more limited. Many of them reflect the evidential value of their basic facts. In the absence of further evidence, it would be highly unreasonable not to infer legitimacy from a child's birth in wedlock, but once DNA evidence is available, it has been held in breach of the European Convention not to use it.[114] On the other hand, a presumption may have the effect of increasing the probative value of the basic fact where there is no evidence contradicting such inferences as might be drawn from it. In the case of the presumption of death, for example, there is no special magic in seven years' absence so far as the ordinary tests of probative value are concerned. Someone who has been absent, unheard of by those who would be likely to have heard from him, for six-and-a-half years is, for all practical purposes, just as likely to be dead as someone who has been absent in similar circumstances

---

[108] In traditional terminology, these would be described as rebuttable presumptions of law.

[109] See Williams *Criminal Law: The General Part* (2nd edn, 1961) 877ff.

[110] When a statute speaks of a shifting of the burden of proof, it is usually in relation to a rebuttable presumption of law created by the statute (see Bills of Exchange Act 1882, s 30 (2)).

[111] Morgan (1937) 12 *Wash LR* 255.

[112] For a convincing demonstration of this, see Treitel (1954) 17 MLR 530.

[113] See *Prudential Assurance Co v Edmonds* (1877) 2 App Cas 487.

[114] *Tavli v Turkey* (2009) 48 EHRR 225, [35].

for seven years; but seven years' absence brings into play a rebuttable presumption of law, while absence for a shorter period merely gives rise to a more or less cogent tactical presumption of fact that the person in question is dead. Reflections of this nature have led to the remark that 'presumptions of law are nothing else than natural inferences or presumptions of fact which the law invests with an artificial or preternatural weight'.[115] This is often true, but some presumptions are clearly designed merely to resolve an impasse either of proof or procedure. Thus the statutory presumption contained in s 184(1) of the Law of Property Act 1925 provides that where two or more persons have died in circumstances rendering it uncertain which of them survived the other, such deaths shall (subject to any order of the court), for all purposes affecting the title to property, be presumed to have occurred in order of seniority, and accordingly the younger shall be deemed to have survived the elder. In such a case, the evidential value of the basic fact is non-existent, and the whole effect of the presumption is expended on the allocation of the burden of proof.

It is, however, sometimes suggested that presumptions have an evidential effect in excess of the true probative worth of their basic fact, and quite independent of their effect in allocating the burden of proof.[116] It is submitted, however, that Lord Reid's words in *S v S* of the effect of the presumption of legitimacy are of more general application:[117]

Once evidence has been led it must be weighed without using the presumption as a makeweight in the scale of legitimacy. So even weak evidence against legitimacy must prevail if there is no other evidence to counter-balance it. The presumption will only come in at that stage in the very rare case of the evidence being so evenly balanced that the court is unable to reach a decision on it.

The danger of attaching such artificial weight to presumptions was highlighted by the House of Lords in *Royal Bank of Scotland v Etridge (No 2)*,[118] in which it was recognized that, in the vast majority of cases, evidence is tendered on both sides, and the great likelihood is that a court will not at the end of the day be unable to make up its mind as to whether or not a fact has been established as more likely than not, as Lord Hobhouse asserted:[119]

Where the relevant question is one of fact and degree and of the evaluation of evidence, the language of presumption is likely to confuse rather than assist and this is borne out by experience.

If this is correct, and if the artificial force of presumptions is achieved by allocation of burden, it is hardly surprising to find that it is affected by other policies also directed to that end.[120] This is most obvious in criminal cases, especially in view of the decision of the House of Lords in *Woolmington v DPP*,[121] and now in the application of Art 6(2) of the European Convention, to be discussed in the next section.

---

[115] Gulson *Philosophy of Proof* (2nd edn) 371.

[116] See Lord Denning in *Stupple v Royal Insurance Co Ltd* [1971] 1 QB 50, [1970] 3 All ER 230 at 72, 235–6, discussed in more detail above, 120. It is, however, possible that the difference between Lord Denning and Buckley LJ in that case related only to the probative worth of the basic fact.

[117] [1972] AC 24, [1970] 3 All ER 107; 41, 109.   [118] [2001] UKHL 44, [2002] 2 AC 773.

[119] [105]. It is interesting that in *Fontaine v Insurance Corp of British Columbia* [1998] 1 SCR 424, the Supreme Court of Canada expressed similar sentiments in relation to the presumption of res ipsa loquitur, taken as a model in *Etridge*; but see *George v Eagle Air Services* [2009] UKPC 21.

[120] For an interesting suggestion that presumptions should be classified on the basis of the policies they are designed to promote, see Cohen (1981) 45 *Albany LR* 1079.   [121] [1935] AC 462.

ALLOCATION BY STATUTORY PROVISION

It is common for statutes to provide explicitly for the allocation of the burden of proof,[122] although none seems so far ever to have distinguished in terms between evidential and persuasive burdens.[123] It has also been determined that it is possible for a statute to allocate the burden of proof implicitly.[124] The application of Art 6(2) of the European Convention on Human Rights may, in some cases, permit an apparent explicit allocation of a persuasive burden upon the accused to be read down to the allocation only of an evidential burden,[125] and to have a decisive influence on whether a persuasive or evidential burden is to be implied. Such an implicit allocation can be divined only by a process of statutory interpretation, and the common law developed certain principles that were subsequently encapsulated in a series of more general statutory provisions relating to summary proceedings.[126] It was at one time thought that these general statutory provisions for summary trials diverged in their effects from their counterparts at common law, perhaps because the accused could not before 1898 generally testify in his own defence, and perhaps because trial on indictment led to more serious consequences, thus justifying the imposition of a more onerous burden upon the prosecution. It is now clear that the rules are the same for both types of proceedings.[127] The accused has been a competent witness in his own defence since 1898, and it can be argued that since so many statutory offences are triable either upon indictment or summarily,[128] it would be confusing, impractical, and undesirable to apply different burdens in respect of the same offence depending upon how it came to be tried, especially if this were to involve offering advantages in the more expensive and time-consuming proceedings upon indictment. The principal distinction is now between those statutes that make explicit, and those that leave implicit, allocation of the burden of proof, and they will be addressed in turn. Care is needed in cases involving joint trials in respect of different, but related, offences in determining against which of the co-accused the allocation of the burden applies.[129]

Explicit allocation by statutory provision

Statutes sometimes provide that certain facts shall be deemed to exist until the contrary is proved. The precise wording varies from statute to statute,[130] and in a sense brings into

---

[122] Especially under the influence of various EU Directives in employment cases, see Sandison and Dallimore 92 *Emp LJ* 4 (2008).

[123] Although s 118 of the Terrorism Act 2000 and s 75 of the Sexual Offences Act s 75 achieve exactly that effect.

[124] *R v Hunt* [1987] AC 352, [1987] 1 All ER 1; although a court will be most reluctant to do so without very clear wording: see e.g. *R (P) v Liverpool Magistrates' Court* [2006] EWHC 887 (Admin), [2006] ACD 73, [24].

[125] Under the provisions of the Human Rights Act 1998, s 3(1).

[126] Culminating in the Magistrates' Courts Act 1980, s 101. Similar provisions abound in Commonwealth jurisdictions.

[127] See Lord Sankey's claim in *Woolmington v DPP* [1935] AC 462, 482 that the rules are the same 'No matter what the charge or where the trial': see, 139.

[128] With various permutations of options and consents by prosecution and defence.

[129] See *R v Hill* [2004] 2 NZLR 145.

[130] And even within a given statute, see e.g. Criminal Law (Consolidation) (Scotland) Act 1995 which in relation to sexual offences alone used four different formulations: s 1 (accused to prove); s 5 (defence if reasonable cause); s 8(4) (deemed); s 10(4) (proved to the satisfaction of the court).

play principles of implicit allocation, especially now that even the most explicit allocation of persuasive burden seems capable of being read down into the allocation of an evidential burden. It is, however, welcome that at last Parliament has used explicit means to distinguish between its intention to impose a persuasive or an evidential burden.[131] It seems constitutionally proper for Parliament to assume this task in the first instance, albeit that in the light of the Human Rights Act 1998 it may sometimes fail to be decisive. It may be helpful to give examples of apparent attempts to impose different burdens.

Evidential

Although the precise term is not used, it seems clear[132] that s 118(2) of the Terrorism Act 2000 was designed to impose an explicit evidential burden on the accused, while leaving the persuasive burden on the prosecution in certain cases where a given provision required the accused to 'prove' something:[133]

If the person adduces evidence which is sufficient to raise an issue with respect to the matter the court or jury shall assume that the defence is satisfied unless the prosecution proves beyond reasonable doubt that it is not.

Persuasive

In *R v DPP (ex p Kebilene)*,[134] the House of Lords was provided with, and accepted, an agreed list of provisions imposing a persuasive burden on the accused. Such provisions extended from the end of the nineteenth century. Given the provision of the Terrorism Act 2000 converting some apparent such provisions into evidential burdens, it is perhaps most useful to give as an example a section not so converted, thus s 18(2) provides in relation to a charge of money laundering that:

It is a defence for a person charged under subsection (1) to prove that he did not know and had no reasonable cause to suspect that the arrangement related to terrorist property.

As noted above, one of the features distinguishing an evidential from a persuasive burden is that only the latter is a burden of *proof*, as opposed to one of adducing evidence. This undoubtedly adds force to the argument that use of the verb 'to prove' naturally imposes a persuasive burden, but it has been held that the more equivocal verb 'to show' may also be taken to impose a persuasive burden.[135]

---

[131] It was extremely uncertain under the old law whether a variation of form even within the same section necessarily led to a different allocation: cf *Polychronakis v Richards and Jerrom Ltd* [1998] Env LR 346 (in which it did) with *R v Gibson* (2000) The Times, 3 March, CA (in which it did not). Where a statute, such as s 16(6) of the Finance Act 1994, referred in terms to the allocation of 'the burden of proof', this has been construed as allocating the persuasive burden: see *Golobkewska v Comrs of Customs and Excise* [2005] EWCA Civ 607.

[132] *R v G* [2009] UKHL 13, [2009] 2 Cr App R 60, [63] ('familiar' per Lord Rodger); *Bree* [2007] EWCA Crim 804, (s 75(1) of the Sexual Offences Act 2003).

[133] Section 118(4) contains a similar form of words for specified cases where the primary provision was for assumptions to be made. For a similar result, achieved by a different formulation, see s 53(3) of the Regulation of Investigatory Powers Act 2000.

[134] [2000] 2 AC 326, [1999] 4 All ER 801.

[135] *R v S* [2002] EWCA Crim 2558, [2003] 1 Cr App Rep 602, [20].

No burden

The Employment Rights Act 1996, s 98(4)(b),[136] which replaced earlier legislation, is concerned with the determination of the question of whether or not the dismissal of an employee was unfair. The employer must first show a proper reason, and then the question of fairness:

... shall be determined in accordance with equity and the substantial merits of the case.

It seems that this form of words was intended to leave the persuasive burden neutral between the parties,[137] the evidential burden presumably being satisfied by adduction of a reason sufficient to satisfy the earlier parts of s 98. An interesting, and perhaps unintended, result of this technique is to effect a change in the standard of proof. As will be seen in the next section of this chapter, the normal standard of proof in civil proceedings is proof on the balance of probabilities. It is fundamental to that standard that it involves weighing the evidence to see if the required standard has been achieved.

If it has not, the party bearing the persuasive burden loses, however little evidence his opponent has adduced. The effect of this change is that the only standard against which evidence can be weighed is that adduced by the opponent; in other words, if neither party bears the persuasive burden, then, if the case is to be decided at all, the party who adduces the greater amount wins, however little evidence he has adduced. In future, in this area, a party will win if he has adduced more evidence than his opponent, even though it may not, seen objectively, make his contention more probable than not. This is highly unsatisfactory, and the result may be that, in an effort to avoid it, cases will be fought out whenever possible on the question of the reason for dismissal, where the persuasive burden is borne by the employer,[138] although the nature of the issue may make that very difficult.[139]

Implicit allocation by statutory provision

A statute may allocate the burden of proof without explicit reference, and such statutes may concern civil[140] or criminal liability, and evidential[141] or persuasive burdens. The most contentious issue relates to the imposition of a burden upon the accused in criminal proceedings. As noted above, the general rule is that the prosecution bears both the evidential and persuasive burden in relation to issues necessary for the imposition of criminal liability. This general position was graphically expressed by the House of Lords in *Woolmington v DPP*:[142]

... throughout the web of the English Criminal Law one golden thread is always to be seen, that it is the duty of the prosecution to prove the prisoner's guilt subject to what I have already said

---

136 For an Australian example, see *RA v R* [2007] NSWCCA 251, 175 ACR 221, [11].

137 983 H of C Official Report (5th series) col 512.

138 Section 98(1) ('show').   139 See Freedland (1972) 1 ILJ 20.

140 For example, the Factories Act 1961, s 29(1), construed in *Nimmo v Alexander Cowan & Sons Ltd* [1968] AC 107, [1967] 3 All ER 187. It should be noted that Art 6(2) of the Human Rights Convention applies in terms only to those charged with a criminal offence, although, as noted above, it uses its own autonomous means of distinguishing civil and criminal proceedings, since to leave it solely to domestic law might lead to the erosion of the protection intended to be afforded.

141 In *Director of Assets Recovery Agency v Green* [2006] EWHC 3168, an evidential burden was cast upon the agency to show that the seized property did represent the proceeds of crime.

142 [1935] AC 462, 481, 482.

as to the defence of insanity and subject also to any statutory exception...No matter what the charge or where the trial, the principle that the prosecution must prove the guilt of the prisoner is part of the common law of England and no attempt to whittle it down can be entertained.

It should be noted that Lord Sankey allowed for the defence of insanity, and for statutory exception. The question has arisen of how to construe the reference to statutory exception. A number of considerations were elaborated at common law, and even expressed in general statutory form, but the whole area has been transformed, by the impact, in the wake of the Human Rights Act 1998, of Art 6(2) of the European Convention on Human Rights:

Everyone charged with a criminal offence shall be presumed innocent until proved guilty according to law.

This discussion will accordingly comprise first, a brief account of the development of the common law, and then an assessment of the impact of Art 6(2). It is worth noting that the impact of that Article extends beyond the construction of statutory provisions, into the area of crimes at common law, but it is convenient to consider both here, given that similar principles apply, and the latter area is by far the more extensive.[143]

Common law development

The common law attached importance, first to the distinction between exceptions and provisos, a matter that received some statutory endorsement, and second to the effect of the defendant's peculiar knowledge of material facts. These matters will be set out, together with subsequent development before the passage of the Human Rights Act 1998.

Exceptions and provisos

There was an old rule of pleading dating back to the seventeenth century according to which an indictment had to negate exceptions, but not provisos. In the words of Lord Mansfield: '[I]t is a known distinction that what comes by way of proviso in a statute must be insisted upon by way of defence by the party accused; but, where exceptions are in the enacting part of a law, it must appear in the charge that the defendant does not fall within any of them.'[144] But it did not follow from the fact that the prosecutor had to negate exceptions in the indictment that he bore any kind of burden with regard to them at the trial. This was the main point at issue in the leading case of *R v Turner*,[145] in which the validity of information under the game laws was challenged on *certiorari* before the King's Bench. The accused was prosecuted for having pheasants and hares in his possession without the necessary qualifications or authorization. Ten possible qualifications were mentioned in the relevant statute and the court held that, although the existence of any one of them was an exception, a fact that necessitated the reference to want of qualification in the information, it was unnecessary for the prosecution to adduce evidence on the subject. Lord Ellenborough made the point that proof of qualification was 'easy on the one side' whereas proof of total disqualification was 'almost impossible on the other'.

---

[143] For criticism of the confusion and inconvenience of attempting to keep these separate, see Lord Hope in *R v Lambert* (n7), [83].

[144] *R v Jarvis* (1756) 1 East 643n.   [145] (1816) 5 M & S 206.

Facts peculiarly within the knowledge of the accused

Bayley J's general justification of this result was treated as specially significant:[146]

If a negative averment be made by one party, which is peculiarly within the knowledge of the other, the party within whose knowledge it lies, and who asserts the affirmative, is to prove it and not he who asserts the negative.

It is important to grasp the limited extent of Bayley J's dictum. It is a rule of statutory interpretation confined to cases in which the affirmative of negative averments is peculiarly within the knowledge of the accused. There is nothing in the nature of a general rule that the burden of establishing any defence based on facts peculiarly within his knowledge is borne by him. Were there such a rule, someone charged with murder would bear the burden of proving many facts connected with provocation or self-defence, or even the burden of disproving an intention to kill, for few things can be more especially within a person's peculiar knowledge than his state of mind. The existence of such a rule was emphatically repudiated by the Court of Criminal Appeal in *R v Spurge*, a case in which a mechanical defect was the accused's answer to a charge of dangerous driving.[147] The most that can be said by way of generalization is that a party's knowledge of essential facts may lessen the amount of evidence required to discharge an evidential burden borne by his adversary.[148] To quote Lord Mansfield:[149]

It is certainly a maxim that all evidence is to be weighed according to the proof which it was in the power of one side to produce, and in the power of the other to have contradicted.

The mere fact that a matter is peculiarly within the knowledge of one party does not necessarily connote that it will be within his power to prove it.[150] It might well be thought that whether or not a matter is peculiarly within the knowledge of a party should go to the allocation of an evidential burden, and whether or not it is easy for a party to prove should go to the allocation of a persuasive burden. Nevertheless, in consequence of Bayley J's rule of statutory interpretation, the prosecution has been relieved of the necessity of negating numerous necessary qualifications.[151] Some of these holdings have been criticized as unjustifiable extensions of the decision in *R v Turner* from statutes containing a number of qualifications under which the acts charged would be lawful to issues concerning a single negative, which would be as easy to prove by prima facie evidence as the affirmative, and to those of which the accused has no peculiar knowledge. Suppose, for example, that a motorist is charged with driving without a licence. In practice, the only persons so charged are those who are unable to produce a licence on demand; yet the relevant register

---

[146] 5 M & S 211; applied in *General Accident, Fire and Life Assurance Corp v Robertson* [1909] AC 404, 413.

[147] [1961] 2 QB 205, [1961] 2 All ER 688 (the appeal was dismissed because the accused was negligent).

[148] See *Dunlop Holding Ltd's Application* [1979] RPC 523, 544, Buckley LJ.

[149] *Blatch v Archer* (1774) 1 Cowp 53, 65. See also *R v Burdett* (1820) 4 B & Ald 95, at 140, cited in *Joyce v DPP* [1946] AC 347, 380; Stephen *Digest of the Law of Evidence* (12th edn) art 104, applied in *R v Kakelo* [1923] 2 KB 793, 795, and cited in *R v Cohen* [1951] 1 KB 505, [1951] 1 All ER 203.

[150] See *R v DPP, ex p Kebilene* [2000] 2 AC 326, [1999] 4 All ER 801; 386C, 848j *per* Lord Hope.

[151] *Apothecaries' Co v Bentley* (1824) 1 C & P 538 (practising certificate); *R v Scott* (1921) 86 JP 69 (cocaine seller's licence); *Williams v Russell* (1933) 149 LT 190 (insurance certificate); *R v Oliver* [1944] KB 68, [1943] 2 All ER 800 (sugar-dealing licence); *John v Humphreys* [1955] 1 All ER 793, [1955] 1 WLR 325 (driving licence); *R v Ewens* [1967] 1 QB 322, [1966] 2 All ER 470 (prescription for drugs).

is accessible to the prosecution, and held in a form in which a negative is proved by the very same means as a positive.

General statutory provision

Statutory guidance for the construction of statutes creating summary offences achieved its present form in s 101 of the Magistrates' Courts Act 1980, which provides:

Where the defendant to an information or complaint relies for his defence on any exception, exemption, proviso, excuse or qualification, whether or not it accompanies the description of the offence or matter of complaint in the enactment creating the offence or on which the complaint is founded, the burden of proving the exception, exemption, proviso, excuse or qualification shall be on him; and this notwithstanding that the information or complaint contains an allegation negativing the exception, exemption, proviso, excuse or qualification.

There has been comparatively little authority on the construction of this section.[152] Its concentration on the form of the statutory decision, and its apparently exclusive concern with the allocation of the persuasive burden,[153] have largely been overtaken by subsequent case law, and by the passage of the Human Rights Act 1998.

Nimmo v Alexander Cowan & Sons Ltd,[154] a Scottish appeal to the House of Lords in civil proceedings, was concerned with the construction of s 29(1) of the Factories Act 1961, under which a place at which any person has to work 'shall, so far as is reasonably practicable, be made and kept safe for any person working therein'. Contraventions of the Act are made summary offences by s 155(1) and this accounts for the references that were made to the Scottish equivalent of s 101 of the Magistrates' Courts Act 1980. The issue was whether it was necessary for the claimant, a workman who had sustained injuries at his place of work, to plead and prove that it was reasonably practicable to keep the premises safe or whether it lay upon the defendant, his employer, to prove the contrary. By a majority of three to two, the House held that the defendant had to plead and prove impracticability. The minority, Lords Reid and Wilberforce, took the view that the words 'so far as is reasonably practicable' are an integral part of the definition of the offence, but two members of the majority, Lords Guest and Pearson, considered that they were a qualification or excuse.[155] The status of the decision as a binding authority on the construction of s 101 of the Magistrates' Courts Act 1980 is debatable, but the importance of some observations of Lord Pearson is beyond dispute. He said that while exceptions, exemptions, and provisos would be easily recognizable from the use of such words as 'except' or 'provided always', the words 'excuse or qualification' showed an intention to direct attention to the substance rather than the form of the enactment. It therefore seemed that, at any rate when the form of words did 'not speak for itself', the

---

[152] A claim of right was held outside its New Zealand equivalent in *R v Gorrie* [2007] NZCA 144, [2008] 3 NZLR 620.

[153] *Gatland v Metropolitan Police Comr* [1968] 2 QB 279, [1968] 2 All ER 100; *Assistant Registrar of Companies v Moses* [2002] 3 NZLR 129.

[154] [1968] AC 107, [1967] 3 All ER 187. Applied in *Bilton v Fastnet Highlands Ltd* 1998 SLT 1323.

[155] The third member of the majority, Lord Upjohn, did not base his opinion on the construction of the equivalent to s 101, but he was generally in agreement with Lord Pearson's speech. The assumption that the incidence of the burden of proof should be the same in civil proceedings and at a summary trial was questioned by Adams *Criminal Onus and Exculpations* (New Zealand 1968) [125], and has been rejected both in Australia, by the High Court in *Chugg v Pacific Dunlop Ltd* (1990) 170 CLR 249, and in New Zealand, by the Court of Appeal in *R v Rangi* [1992] 1 NZLR 385.

courts could have regard to the object of the statute creating the offence charged when considering the applicability of s 101.[156]

Later developments

The aspect of this area of the law changed dramatically as a result of two cases, one in the Court of Appeal[157] and the other in the House of Lords.[158] The accused in *R v Edwards*[159] had been convicted of selling intoxicating liquor by retail without holding a Justices' licence so authorizing him. The prosecution had adduced ample evidence from which sales might be inferred, but none as to the absence of a licence. In the Court of Appeal Lawton LJ recognized the force, on the particular facts, of the point taken with regard to peculiar knowledge, despite criticism of some of the arguments enunciated by Bayley J in *R v Turner*, but concluded:[160]

In our judgment this line of authority establishes that over the centuries the common law, as a result of experience and the need to ensure that justice is done both to the community and to defendants, has evolved an exception to the fundamental rule of our criminal law that the prosecution must prove every element of the offence charged. This exception, like so much else in the common law, was hammered out on the anvil of pleading. It is limited to offences arising under enactments which prohibit the doing of an act save in specified circumstances or by persons of specified classes or with specified qualifications or with the licence or permission of specified authorities. Whenever the prosecution seeks to rely on this exception, the court must construe the enactment under which the charge is laid. If the true construction is that the enactment prohibits the doing of acts, subject to provisos, exceptions and the like, then the prosecution can rely upon the exception.

This part of the judgment concludes with the clearly expressed opinion that the burden borne by the accused in cases covered by the statement was persuasive.

Lawton LJ's reformulation of the common law rules with regard to exceptions had the two great merits of avoiding problems with regard to the meaning of 'peculiar knowledge' and of equiparating the law governing trials on indictment with that applicable to summary trials.[161] Moreover, the reference to the court's duty to construe the statute under which the charge is laid left room for a consideration of the object of the legislation before concluding that it prohibits the doing of acts subject to provisos, exceptions, and the like.[162]

The whole matter was reviewed by the House of Lords in *R v Hunt*.[163] The accused was charged with unlawful possession of a controlled drug. The prosecution proved that the substance in question contained the relevant drug, but did not specify its proportion. Regulations made under the Act defined exempted substances to include those with a specified very small proportion of the otherwise illicit drug. It was argued that, since the prosecution had not shown the proportion to exceed that low threshold, there was no case

---

[156] See (1976) 92 LQR 402, 418.   [157] *R v Edwards* [1975] QB 27, [1974] 2 All ER 1085.

[158] *R v Hunt* [1987] AC 352, [1987] 1 All ER 1. The speech of Lord Griffiths, in whose reasoning Lords Keith and Mackay explicitly concurred, is taken to express the decision of the House.

[159] [1975] QB 27, [1974] 2 All ER 1085. For criticism, see Zuckerman (1976) 92 *LQR* 401.

[160] [1975] QB 27, 39–40.

[161] A cynic might suspect that elimination of any inducement for the choice of trial on indictment by way of the provision of a more favourable burden of proof was a hidden reason for the decision.

[162] In accordance with the views of Lords Pearson and Guest in *Nimmo v Alexander Cowan & Sons Ltd* [1968] AC 107, [1967] 3 All ER 187.   [163] [1987] AC 352, [1987] 1 All ER 1.

to answer. This view was rejected[164] by both Crown Court and Court of Appeal. The House of Lords was invited to review the whole area, and to overrule *Edwards* on the basis that it was inconsistent with the decision in *Woolmington*. The Misuse of Drugs Act 1971, s 5(2), under which the accused was charged, did not in terms contain a proviso or exception, but was made subject to the relevant regulations. The regulations[165] did not themselves individually refer to exceptions or provisos, but were generally headed 'Exemptions from Certain Provisions for the Misuse of Drugs Act 1971', and were made under a power[166] to 'except' from the provisions of the Act by regulation. It should also be noted that the Act provides a number of defences capable of applying to an offence under s 5(2) whereby a persuasive burden is explicitly cast upon the accused.[167]

The House of Lords endorsed the decision and reasoning in *Edwards*, while widening its scope to apply not only to provisions within the linguistic boundaries of exceptions and provisos,[168] but to those creating exemptions from otherwise generally applicable provisions.[169] It accepted *Nimmo v Alexander Cowan & Sons Ltd*,[170] in suggesting that:[171]

...if the linguistic construction of the statute did not clearly indicate on whom the burden should lie the court should look to other considerations to determine the intention of Parliament, such as the mischief at which the Act was aimed and practical considerations affecting the burden of proof and, in particular, the ease or difficulty that the respective parties would encounter in discharging the burden.

Especial stress was laid upon the final consideration, regarded as making it generally unlikely that Parliament would impose onerous burdens upon defendants.

Despite its result, the reasoning of the House of Lords in *Hunt* was widely attacked by commentators.[172] It was claimed that the principle of *Woolmington* had been eroded by breaking down the strict limitation upon the exceptions to the general rule that the prosecution always bears the burden of proof in criminal cases, and substituting for it considerations of policy determined by judges upon only the very vaguest of criteria.[173]

IMPACT OF HUMAN RIGHTS ACT 1998[174]

The Human Rights Act 1998 has had some impact upon this topic. The general approach will first be mentioned, then its effect on the evidential and persuasive burdens, and finally

---

[164] Although for different reasons.   [165] Misuse of Drugs Regulations 1973, SI 1973/797.

[166] Misuse of Drugs Act 1971, s 7.

[167] Which had also been held immaterial in cases governed by *Edwards*: see *Guyll v Bright* (1986) 84 Cr App Rep 260.

[168] No attention was paid to r 6(C) of the Indictment Rules 1971, excusing reference to exceptions etc. in the statement of the offence in the indictment, presumably because of r 8, which provides that nothing in the rules affects the law of evidence.

[169] This also seems to be the position in Australia: see *He Kaw Teh v R* (1985) 157 CLR 523; *DPP v United Telecasters Ltd* (1990) 168 CLR 594; *Chugg v Pacific Dunlop Ltd* (1990) 170 CLR 249.

[170] [1968] AC 107, [1967] 3 All ER 187.   [171] 374, 11.

[172] See Healy [1987] Crim LR 355; Smith (1987) 38 *NILQ* 223; Mirfield [1988] Crim LR 19 and [1988] Crim LR 233. It also attracted some support: see Zuckerman (1987) 103 *LQR* 170; Birch [1988] Crim LR 221.

[173] But nevertheless applied in the contentious context of the Hunting Act 2004 s 1 and Sch 1 in *DPP v Wright* [2009] EWHC 105(Admin).

[174] See Tadros and Tierney (2004) 67 MLR 402; Dennis [2005] Crim LR 901. Very similar situations have arisen under other constitutional documents in different jurisdictions, see above 130, although their relevance to modern English law was marginalized in *Sheldrake* [2004] UKHL 43, [2005] 1 AC 264 [33], [58].

the factors relevant to reading the allocation of the latter down to the allocation of the former.[175]

Extent

As early as 2002,[176] the Court of Appeal began a judgment with the lament that 'Once again this court has to consider whether a reverse burden of proof provision in a statute creating offences is compatible with the presumption of innocence enshrined in Article 6(2) of the ECHR.' Nor has this problem been easy to solve, as *Sheldrake v Director of Public Prosecutions*[177] illustrates, not only in the fact that the decision was not unanimous, but more in its cavalier, and in this respect unanimous, disregard of the determined attempt of the Court of Appeal to clarify the law by convening a full court to review all of the previous decisions, and to restate the relevant principles. It is complicated by arising in many different contexts, and as Lord Rodger pointed out[178] in *Sheldrake*, by attempting to solve problems in the application of Art 6, which has been elaborated in a predominantly civilian procedural context, by the use of concepts unique to common law procedure.

Although the prime area of application is as stated above, its ramifications extend more widely, even into civil proceedings when the issues closely mirror criminal,[179] into defences at common law,[180] and into post-trial procedures.[181] The House of Lords[182] has now robustly determined,[183] without even finding the need to hear supporting argument, that Art 6 regulates procedure only,[184] that it remains possible for a legislature to impose absolute or strict liability without reference to it. In so doing it rejected any contrary interpretation of a difficult paragraph in *Salabiaku v France*:[185]

If, as the Commission would appear to consider paragraph 2 of article 6 merely laid down a guarantee to be respected by the courts in the conduct of legal proceedings, its requirements would in practice overlap with the duty of impartiality imposed by paragraph 1. Above all, *the national legislature would be free to strip the trial court of any genuine power of assessment and deprive the presumption of innocence of its substance, if the words 'according to law' were construed exclusively with reference to domestic law.* Such a situation could not be reconciled with the object and purposes of article 6, which, by protecting the right to a fair trial and in particular the right to be presumed innocent, is intended to enshrine the fundamental principle of the rule of law.

Article 6(2) does not therefore regard presumptions of fact or of law provided for in the criminal law with indifference. It requires states to confine them within reasonable limits which take into account the importance of what is at stake and maintain the rights of the defence.

---

[175] In this context, it now seems unlikely that a declaration of incompatibility will be made.

[176] *Davies v Health and Safety Executive* [2002] EWCA Crim 2949, [1], emphasis supplied.

[177] (n174): a joint appeal with *Attorney-General's Reference (No 4 of 2002)*.   [178] [71].

[179] As in situations like that in *Nimmo v Alexander Cowan & Sons Ltd* [1968] AC 107, [1967] 3 All ER 187 before the Act, or in *Sheppard v Secretary of State for the Home Dept* [2002] EWCA Civ 1921 after it.

[180] See *R v Lambert* (n7), [83]; see also *R v Bianco* [2001] EWCA Crim 2516 (both duress).

[181] See *R (Henry) v Parole Board* [2004] EWHC 784; *R v Briggs-Price* [2009] UKHL 19, [2009] 1 AC 1026 (confiscation).   [182] Reference to the European Court of Human Rights is pending.

[183] *R v G* [2008] UKHL 37, [2009] 1 AC 92.

[184] Accepting the views expressed in *R v Daniel* [2002] EWCA Crim 959, [2003] 1 Cr App R 99, [34], citing Roberts (2002) 118 LQR 41, 50. See also *Barnfather v Islington LBC* [2003] EWHC 418 (Admin), [2003] 1 WLR 2318, *R v Deyemi and Edwards* [2007] EWCA Crim 2060, [2008] 1 Cr App R 345, [27]; Ashworth (2006) 10 E&P 241, 252–7.   [185] (1988) 13 EHRR 379, [28], emphasis supplied.

Their Lordships seem[186] to have been divided between giving up altogether any attempt to construe this passage,[187] and interpreting the limit narrowly to refer to offences incompatible with other articles of the Convention.[188] The odd result is that despite the diminished importance attached to drafting in the modern law it is possible to draft an offence in terms of strict liability, so as to be able to deal less favourably with the accused than if a defence were allowed, so evading breach of the Convention.[189]

It seems now to have become settled that the presumption of innocence in Art 6(2), at least when applied to the determination of guilt of a criminal offence requires proof beyond reasonable doubt, and to that extent will prevail over contrary domestic statutory provision of a lower standard.[190]

Procedure

It was argued in *R v Director of Public Prosecutions, ex p Kebilene*[191] that the issue of compatibility with Art 6(2) could arise only after the completion of the trial, but the argument was rejected[192] on the basis that such a view would contradict the whole premise of the provisions of the Human Rights Act 1998, which clearly contemplates review of the compatibility of legislation abstracted from the facts of particular cases.

In *Sheldrake*, Lord Bingham explained that the procedure is simple:[193]

[T]he first question for consideration in each case is whether the provision in question does, unjustifiably infringe the presumption of innocence. If it does the further question arises whether the provision can and should be read down in accordance with courts' interpretive obligation under s.3 of the Human Rights Act 1998 so as to impose an evidential and not a legal burden on the defendant.

Evidential burden

There can be no doubt that the imposition of an evidential burden alone is not regarded either as prejudicing the presumption of innocence or as being incompatible with Art 6(2), despite its imposition on the accused entailing that his failure to adduce evidence must lead to what might be the only live issue in the case being determined against him.[194] This position was explicitly determined in *R v Bianco*,[195] and resolved in terms of the compatibility there of imposing an evidential burden to raise the issue of duress upon the defence. It was unanimously accepted by all of the members of the House of Lords in *Sheldrake*.

---

[186] Despite the disagreement between Lord Hoffmann and Lord Hope, Baroness Hale, at [41] and Lord Mance, at [63] agreed with both, while Lord Carswell expressed no view.

[187] Lord Hoffmann, at [6].   [188] Lord Hope, at [28].

[189] See Lord Rodger in *Sheldrake* (n174), [71], justifying his rejected converse conclusion.

[190] *R v Briggs-Price* (n181), [79], [95], [152] (so reading down (or up) s 2(8) Drug Trafficking Act 1994).

[191] [2000] 2 AC 326, [1999] 4 All ER 801.   [192] See Lord Hope, 383G, 846h.

[193] [1]. 'Legal' in the last line equates to 'persuasive' in the terminology adopted here. Despite the disavowal mentioned in fn 174 above, this procedure is strikingly similar to that adopted in Canada in *R v Oakes* [1986] 1 SCR 103.

[194] The position is the same in South Africa and received full consideration by the Constitutional Court in *S v Singo* 2002 (4) SA 858.

[195] [2001] EWCA Crim 2516, [15].

In part, this is explained by increasing realization of the sometimes vestigial notion of the burden upon the defence in these situations, which was characterized, it is submitted helpfully, by the Court of Appeal in *R v S*:[196]

The appellant, as was common ground, had raised matters—which could not, at this stage, be dismissed as wholly and obviously without foundation—which were capable of giving rise to a defence under s 92(5) of the 1994 Act.

It is finally worth mentioning that in *R v Drummond*[197] the Court of Appeal rejected any suggestion that an evidential burden on the accused could be discharged only by producing evidence on a number of specified matters, since it was feared that that would reduce the difference between persuasive and evidential burdens to vanishing point.

Persuasive burden

The core of the problem is to determine the extent to which a persuasive burden may be cast upon the accused without breach of the Convention. The first question must therefore involve the determination of whether or not a persuasive burden has been cast upon the accused by the relevant provision. This is not entirely a linguistic matter, and may involve consideration of the proportionality of doing so in the light of the purpose of the statute.[198]

In this respect, the new law, applying the Human Rights Act 1998, reflects the position arrived at under the old law in *R v Hunt*.[199] It is interesting to compare a post-Human Rights Act decision in *DPP v Barker*,[200] which refused to read down the accused's persuasive burden on an exception to criminal liability based on a licence with that in the pre-*Hunt* decision in *R v Edwards*, in which exactly the same result had been achieved.[201] It is clear that neither the common law allocation of the persuasive burden by use of the word 'prove' in a statutory provision, nor the formulation of such a provision as an exception or proviso will any longer be decisive. Nor, as *Attorney-General's Reference (No 4 of 2002)* shows, will the deliberate decision of the legislature to discriminate between the ascription of persuasive and evidential burdens.[202] Although *Sheldrake* distinguishes the two steps of first determining that the allocation of a persuasive burden on the accused does infringe the presumption of innocence, and only then whether and to what extent it would be proportionate and reasonable to do so by casting such a burden, the two questions involve much the same range of policies and factors, and it is hard to see much utility in keeping them separate.[203] The factors mentioned below may be relevant in either enterprise.

Relevant factors

It is helpful to start by rehearsing the values in issue. The importance of the presumption of innocence was explained by the Supreme Court of Canada in *R v Whyte*:[204]

It is not a concern that an accused must disprove an element or provide an excuse: rather it is the risk that an accused may be convicted where a reasonable doubt may exist. When that possibility exists, there is a breach of the presumption of innocence.

---

[196] [2002] EWCA Crim 2558, [2003] 1 Cr App Rep 602. [7]. In *Lambert* (n7), opinions differed, cf Lord Steyn, [39] with Lord Hutton, [191], but see also a rather stricter view, [192], and even within the same speech, cf Lord Hope, [90] and [91].   [197] [2002] EWCA Crim 527, [35].

[198] *Lambert* (n7), [77].   [199] [1987] AC 352, [1987] 1 All ER 1.

[200] [2004] EWHC 2502; cf *R (Grundy) v Halton Division Magistrates' Court* [2003] EWHC 272 (Admin), (2003) 167 JP 387, in which reading down did occur in a different licensing situation.

[201] [1975] QB 27, [1974] 2 All ER 1085; 40D, 1095f.   [202] [50].

[203] Lord Bingham himself seemed to accept this, [41].   [204] [1988] 2 SCR 3, 18.

The House of Lords in *Lambert* put that into the context of the allocation to the accused of a persuasive burden:[205]

It necessarily involves the risk that, if the jury are faithful to the judge's direction, they may convict where the accused has not discharged the legal burden resting on him but left them unsure on that point. This risk is not present if only an evidential burden is created.

Unfortunately, the guidance offered by *Sheldrake* is unstructured, some of it derived only from expressions of approval or disapproval of earlier decisions, as Lord Bingham acknowledged:[206]

The justifiability of any infringement of the presumption of innocence cannot be resolved by any rule of thumb, but on examination of all the facts and circumstances of the particular provision as applied in the particular case.

So intuitive and incoherent an *ex post facto* approach, bereft of appeal to rule or principle, hardly seems likely to enshrine the rule of law as *Salabiaku* claimed Art 6 to have intended. Some decisions are accepted in *Sheldrake* without any supporting argument, for example the allocation of the persuasive burden to the defence on the issue of insanity.[207] It is surely arguable that to charge someone with murder, an essential ingredient of which is *mens rea*, and then to prescribe conviction even though the jury regards the accused as likely as not to be insane, requires considered, and considerable, justification.

There are, however, clues in Lord Bingham's speech to factors that are relevant to the infringement of the presumption of innocence by the allocation of a persuasive burden to the accused, and its alleviation by reading down the provision so as to allocate a merely evidential burden.

First, allocation of a persuasive burden seems to be regarded as more easily justified in predominantly regulatory areas of law,[208] often those concerned with the protection of consumers. This refers back to reservations about the ill-effects of the *Woolmington* principle stated in earlier decisions of the House of Lords.[209] In the case of regulatory offences, it was explained in Canada in *R v Wholesale Travel Group*:[210]

Regulatory legislation involves the shift of emphasis from the protection of individual interests and the deterrence and punishment of acts involving moral fault to the protection of the public and social interests. While criminal offences are usually designed to condemn and punish past, inherently wrongful conduct, regulatory measures are generally directed to the prevention of future harm through the enforcement of minimum standards of conduct and care.

Similar, and often overlapping, considerations apply in consumer and employee protection cases, where the accused voluntarily engages in an activity that he knows at the outset is made conditional upon the observation of detailed rules and prescriptions.[211]

---

[205] Lord Steyn, [38].   [206] [21].

[207] *H v United Kingdom* App No 15023/89 (1990, 4 April); mirrored in the United Kingdom in relation to diminished responsibility in *R v Ali* [2002] QB 1112, [2001] 1 All ER 1014, [19], conjoined in the Court of Appeal with *Lambert*.

[208] [6]. Although there is scope for disagreement as to when an offence is regulatory in nature, as demonstrated by the judgments in the Divisional Court in *Sheldrake* [2003] EWHC 273 Admin), [2004] QB 487, Clarke LJ, [80], that being in charge of a car while over the limit was not, and Henriques J, [130], that it was.

[209] *R v Warner* [1969] 2 AC 256, [1968] 2 All ER 356, Lord Pearce, 307, 386; *Sweet v Parsley* [1970] AC 132, [1969] 1 All ER 347, Lord Reid, 150, 351.

[210] [1991] 3 SCR 154. See also *R v 1260448 Ontario Inc* (2003) 180 CCC3d 254.

[211] Lord Bingham, [27], rehearsed the reasoning of Lord Nicholls in this respect in *R v Johnstone* [2003] UKHL 28, [2003] 3 All ER 884.

The question is sometimes presented in terms of the blameworthiness[212] of the conduct proved against the defendant, so that the more blameworthy it is on the basis of the prosecution evidence, the more justifiable is the allocation of a burden of some sort to the defendant.[213] This emerges from Lord Bingham's reconciliation of the difference in results in *Lambert* and *Johnstone*, in the former of which the prosecution needed to show no more than what might have been innocent possession of drugs in the former, while in the latter it needed to show trading in counterfeit goods with intent to gain.[214] The principle emerges perhaps more clearly from a comparison of *Kebilene*, in which the prosecution needed to show no more than reasonable suspicion that an article was possessed for the purposes of terrorism, and *R v Matthews*,[215] in which it needed to show knowing possession of a bladed article in a public place. It might be thought that such blameworthiness would be reflected in the seriousness of the crime, or the severity of the penalty capable of being imposed. These factors are, however, more often regarded as having the opposite effect, and making it less rather than more likely that a persuasive burden will be regarded as having been successfully transferred to the accused. The presumption of innocence is a prime example of the constitutional protection of the accused, which Sachs J considered[216] it especially important to preserve 'the more serious the crime and the greater the public interest in securing convictions'.

If neither the form of drafting, nor the seriousness of the offence charged, nor the maximum penalty, is to determine the justifiability of allocating a persuasive burden to the accused, what is? This may perhaps be gleaned from Lord Bingham's reasons for approving of such an allocation in *Sheldrake*, but disapproving of it in *Attorney-General's Reference (No 4 of 2002)*. It seems that it is for the judge to determine for himself quite apart from the considerations mentioned above what is the essential nature[217] of the offence. In *Sheldrake*, while accepting that the reason for the offence was to prevent the risk of a person driving while being drunk in charge of a car,[218] Lord Bingham thought this not part of its essential nature, which he seems to have derived from the *statutory* history of the provision, and the light that threw on its form of expression. It is not easy to reconcile such an approach with his general rejection of form as a guide, nor with the implicit rejection of *parliamentary* history in *Attorney-General's Reference (No 4 of 2002)*.[219] He seems also at one point[220] to regard the difficulty of disproof by the prosecution as a relevant factor, despite its having been pointed out in so many cases that this is always true of issues of intent. In the case of a presumption, he rejected the view that the allocation of a persuasive burden could be justified only when the presumed fact flowed inexorably from the proved fact,[221] arguing

---

212 [6], qualified by 'moral', [26], [47], [49], [51].

213 This reasoning has also been applied in Scotland: see *McLean v Carnegie* [2005] SCCR 549, [9].

214 It might be countered that, if the accused did not believe the goods to be counterfeit, there would not be any blameworthiness in trading them for gain. It is hard to see how giving credit for the possibility of establishing the defence being will not always prevent the prosecution evidence from demonstrating blameworthiness.

215 [2003] EWCA Crim 813, [2004] QB 690.   216 See 5.

217 Variously described elsewhere as its 'gist', 'gravamen' or 'grain'.   218 [40].

219 And perhaps even more spectacularly in Lord Bingham's apparent approval of *R v A (No 2)*, in which form and both statutory and parliamentary history had been disregarded. In *R v Keogh* [2007] EWCA Crim 528, [2007] 3 All ER 789, [22], a White Paper preceding the legislation was used to show that it was not intended to impose more than an evidential burden.   220 [41].

221 That is the basic fact in the terminology adopted here.

that the greater the connection, the less need for the presumption, and that it is very rare for there to be no rational connection between proved and presumed fact.

In *Attorney-General's Reference (No 4 of 2002)*, the offence was defined in s 11(1) of the Terrorism Act 2000 as being, or professing to be, a member of a proscribed organization, and a defence was provided in s 11(2) broadly for cases where the organization was not proscribed at the time of joining or professing to be a member, and inactivity after that time. Lord Bingham accepted the parallel of form with *Sheldrake*, but, notwithstanding the total absence of any reference to a presumption, went on to consider whether the allocation of a persuasive burden upon the accused to bring himself within the s 11(2) defence was proportionate and justifiable.[222] Apart from the possibility of convicting in the absence of blameworthiness, Lord Bingham attached some importance to the difficulty of disproof of activity after the relevant date. It is not easy to reconcile the lines of argument in the two conjoined decisions, at least so far as the allocation of a *persuasive* burden[223] is concerned. In both, the party allocated the burden of proof or disproof has an equally difficult task to discharge it. Some importance was also attached to the severity of the penalty, although once again this found little favour in many of the cases endorsed by Lord Bingham.[224]

In *R v Keogh*[225] the Court of Appeal explained that the essential nature of an offence is not to be distilled entirely from the prosecution case, but may incorporate some matters of denial by the defence in order to establish exactly the mischief at which the legislation was directed.

One quite separate factor, not relevant here, is that increasingly English legislation implements Directives of the European Union, and sometimes the terms of the Directive, including its recitals, give some indication[226] of the allocation and nature of the burden it is appropriate to impose.

A further question concerns the weight of the factors requisite for allocating a persuasive burden to the accused: must it render such an allocation necessary, compelling, balanced, or reasonable? The earlier cases provided no very clear answer,[227] but the issue was resolved in clarion terms[228] by Lord Chief Justice Phillips in *R v Keogh*:[229]

[T]he most critical question is whether the reverse burden of proof is a necessary element in the operation of ss 2 and 3. If it is not, we cannot see how placing such a burden on the defendant can be justified.

He was influenced in answering this question by the fact that parallel provisions[230] in the relevant legislation dealing with the same mental elements in other classes of person apparently found that this would not present the prosecution with an impossible task.

---

[222] [50].

[223] In *R v Clarke* [2008] EWCA Crim 651, the allocation of persuasive burden was justified by *Turner*-like considerations more appropriate for allocation of an evidential burden.

[224] Although the severity of the penalty for the offence in *Johnstone* (n211) is ascribed, [30], more to financial than moral considerations. [225] (n219) [19].

[226] It need not be mandatory: *R (Hoverspeed Ltd) v Comrs of Customs and Excise* [2002] EWCA Civ 1804, [2003] 2 All ER 553, [35]. See also *R v Gibson* (2000) The Times, 3 March, in which the implementation of a directive was fortified by reference to a previous statutory formulation.

[227] See the wide variety of formulations used by Lord Bingham in *Sheldrake* (n174).

[228] The relevant part of his judgment is headed 'NECESSITY'. [229] [26].

[230] In *R (Griffin) v Richmond Magistrates' Court* [2008] EWHC 84 (Admin), [2008] 1 Cr App R 453 such parallels led to the opposite conclusion.

Conclusion

The result of this interaction of EU and common law has been unfortunate. For decades, the common law was flawed by failure to appreciate the difference between evidential and persuasive burdens, and handicapped by the reluctance of the legislature to specify clearly where such burdens fell. It would indeed be apt to describe the old law as a semantic lottery.[231] The result of judicial intervention under the old law in *R v Hunt*, and under the new law in *Sheldrake*, was to substitute a judicial lottery, in which everything depended upon an individual judge's intuitive reaction to each individual situation, detached from the wording of the provision in question or the intention of Parliament in enacting it. It is submitted that the rule of law is better served by decisions like that in *R v Keogh*, leaving the substance of the law to be determined in advance by the elected legislature, and in particular, now that it has started to do so, to encourage it to continue clearly to define and allocate each burden by the use of consistent and transparent terminology.

THE INTERPRETATION OF AGREEMENTS AFFECTING THE BURDEN OF PROOF

The incidence of the burden of proof may be determined by the agreement of the parties in civil cases,[232] in which case there can be little doubt that the burden in question would generally be taken to be persuasive. This has been discussed in cases concerned with the construction of contracts for the carriage of goods by sea, and insurance against various types of loss.

Perils of the sea—*The Glendarroch*

If a claimant seeks damages from shipowners for breach of contract to carry goods safely, and the defendants rely on a clause exempting them from loss or damage occasioned to the goods by a peril of the sea, they must prove that the latter occurred, and alone[233] caused the damage in question; if the claimant relies upon a proviso to the exemption clause relating to negligence on the part of the defendants, the persuasive burden of proving negligence rests on him. These points were established in the leading case of *The Glendarroch*, in which the ship on which the goods had been placed struck a rock, and Lord Esher said:[234]

The plaintiffs would have to prove the contract and the non-delivery. If they leave that in doubt, of course they fail. The defendants' answer is 'Yes; but the case was brought within the exception—within its ordinary meaning'. That lies upon them. Then the plaintiffs have a right to say there are exceptional circumstances, viz that the damage was brought about by the negligence of the defendants' servants, and it seems to me that it is for the plaintiffs to make out the second exception.

---

231 See Lord Nicholls in *Ghaidan v Godin-Mendoza* [2004] UKHL 30, [2004] 2 AC 557 [31] (ironically criticizing excessive reference to form in the light of the court's wide interpretation of s 3 of the Human Rights Act 1998).

232 *Levy v Assicurazioni Generali* [1940] AC 791, [1940] 3 All ER 427. It seems also that, in Scotland, a concession as to the incidence of the burden of proof cannot be withdrawn, at least when it has been acted upon to the detriment of the other party: *John Thorburn & Sons v Border Harvesters Ltd* 1992 SLT 549.

233 Such provisions are sometimes expressly controlled by statute: see Merchant Shipping Act 1995, Sch 6, art 18.

234 [1894] P 226, 231; contrast *Slattery v Mance* [1962] 1 QB 676, [1962] 1 All ER 525. In the case of insurance of a ship against fire, the insurer must establish scuttling on the balance of probabilities. See also *Doats v Weekes* (1986) 82 FLR 334.

Insurance exceptions

This case was followed by Bailhache J in *Munro, Brice & Co v War Risks Association*,[235] which was concerned with an insurance policy covering the loss of a ship through the perils of the sea, subject to an exception in respect of enemy action. He held that the defendants bore the persuasive burden of proving that the ship was lost in consequence of the latter, with the result that the claimants succeeded on their claim as the ship had not been heard of after she set sail, and there was no evidence of the cause of her disappearance. The law on this point cannot, however, be regarded as completely settled, for, in the earlier case of *Hurst v Evans*,[236] Lush J had decided that, where an insurance policy against loss of jewellery contained an exception in respect of theft by the claimant's servants, it was incumbent on the claimant to negative loss from this cause. This is not the kind of problem that can be solved by logical argument, for there is no difference between a clause that is construed to read 'The insurers shall be liable for loss except that which occurs in specified circumstances' and a rule that says 'the insurers shall be liable for loss arising from all causes other than those specified',[237] but it is submitted that practical considerations as well as previous authority[238] favour the view of Bailhache J. He said that if he had been asked to advise on evidence in *Hurst v Evans*, it would not have occurred to him to suggest that the claimant should call all his servants, one after the other, to swear that they had not stolen the jewels: 'The procession would be a long one if Messrs Whiteley were the claimants.'[239]

SECTION 3. DISCHARGE OF THE BURDEN

Once the party who bears the evidential burden has discharged it by adducing evidence sufficient to justify consideration of a particular issue, it becomes necessary for the party bearing the persuasive burden on that issue, the proponent, to persuade the trier of fact that it should be decided in his favour. If his evidence is less persuasive than that of his opponent, he must inevitably fail; if it is more persuasive, the question is whether he must equally inevitably succeed. The answer to that question demands consideration of the requisite standard of proof, how it should be explained to the jury, and the treatment of precisely quantifiable evidence. It is logical first to consider the standard required to discharge an evidential burden.

DISCHARGE OF EVIDENTIAL BURDEN[240]

No clear formulae have been established for the standard required to discharge an evidential burden and, as this is not a matter upon which it can ever be necessary for a judge to direct a jury, there is no reason why it ever should attract such formulae.[241] Some indication

---

[235] [1918] 2 KB 78.   [236] [1917] 1 KB 352.
[237] Cf the arguments of Stone in (1944) 60 *LQR* 278.
[238] *Gorman v Hand-in-Hand Insurance Co* (1877) IR 11 CL 224; his dictum was approved by Donaldson J in *M Golodetz & Co Inc v Czarnikow-Rionda Co* [1979] 2 All ER 726, 743.   [239] [1918] 2 KB 78, 86.
[240] See Wood (1961) 77 *LQR* 491, and Glass (1981) 55 *ALJ* 842.
[241] Said in *R v Bonnick* (1977) 66 Cr App Rep 266, 269 to be one for the trial judge to resolve 'by applying common sense to the evidence in the particular case'.

may be gleaned from appellate decisions on whether a verdict should be quashed as unsafe. When an evidential burden is borne by the Crown, Lord Devlin has said that it must be discharged by 'such evidence as, if believed, and if left uncontradicted and unexplained, could be accepted by the jury as proof'.[242] 'Proof' in this context must mean proof beyond reasonable doubt, and, in spite of occasional suggestions to the contrary,[243] the standard must, at least from the theoretical point of view, be higher than that required to discharge an evidential burden borne by a party to civil proceedings. In *R v Pacey*,[244] it was held that the prosecution failed to discharge its evidential burden by inviting the jury to draw factual inferences contrary to the testimony of the sole prosecution witness, and in *Chappell v DPP*,[245] that the failure of the defence to deny a possible inference was insufficient. Nor is it sufficient for the prosecution to rely alone upon evidence of a sort that experience shows to be unreliable even if honestly tendered,[246] for example some forms of identification evidence.[247] Sometimes, lay evidence will not be enough without professional support.[248] A final consideration here is that the only evidence must not be equivocal between two co-accused, at least in the absence of some further showing of complicity between them.[249]

When the accused bears the evidential burden alone, it is necessary for there to be only such evidence as would, if believed and uncontradicted, induce a reasonable doubt in the mind of a reasonable jury as to whether his version might be true, for example as to whether he was provoked[250] or in a state of automatism.[251] Lord Morris of Borth-y-Gest said in *Bratty v A-G for Northern Ireland*:[252]

There was no sufficient evidence, fit to be left to a jury, on which a jury might conclude that the appellant had acted unconsciously and involuntarily or which *might leave a jury in reasonable doubt whether this might be so.*

---

242 *Jayasena v R* [1970] AC 618, 624.

243 *R v Smith* (1865) 34 LJMC 153: *Wilson v Buttery* [1926] SASR 150, 154.

244 (1994) The Times, 3 March. See also *CTM v R* [2008] HCA 25 (not by out of court statement not testified to), *R v Parkinson* [1990] 1 Qd R 382, (not normally by reliance upon a previous inconsistent statement rejected by the sole testifying witness). For civil proceedings, see *Nelson v Carillion Services* [2003] EWCA Civ 544, [2003] ICR 1256, [28] 'more than a credible suggestion'; and to rebut a submission of no case in the absence of election, a prima facie case sufficient to call for an explanation: *Graham v Chorley Borough Council* [2006] EWCA Civ 92, [2006] CPR 24.

245 (1988) 89 Cr App Rep 82.

246 This qualification is required to resolve any conflict with the decision in *R v Galbraith* [1981] 2 All ER 1060, [1981] 1 WLR 1039.

247 *R v Turnbull* [1977] QB 224, [1976] 3 All ER 549; *Reid v R* [1990] 1 AC 363, [1993] 4 All ER 95n; *Daley v R* [1994] AC 117, [1993] 4 All ER 86. See also below Chapter XVI.

248 *R v Morris* [1998] 1 Cr App Rep 386 (medical evidence needed to establish that non-physical assault could have physical result).

249 *R v Aston; R v Mason* (1991) 94 Cr App Rep 180; see further 166.

250 See *R v Cambridge* [1994] 2 All ER 760, [1994] 1 WLR 971, in which it is submitted that the Court of Appeal went too far in apparently requiring the defence to go so far as to adduce sufficient evidence for a reasonable jury to conclude that there was provocation. But in that case, the only issue was whether the defence should have been left at all, so since in the instant case it was held that the evidence was sufficient, this reference to the amount of evidence can be regarded as *obiter dicta*.

251 *A-G's Reference (No 2 of 1992)* [1994] QB 91, [1993] 4 All ER 683.

252 [1963] AC 386, 419 (emphasis supplied). See also *R v DPP, ex p Kebilene* [2000] 2 AC 326, [1999] 4 All ER 801, Lord Hope, 379A, 842e. But see Lord Woolf CJ in *R v Lambert* (n7), at 9, apparently discerning a difference between raising a doubt and raising an issue. See, in Canada, *R v St Pierre* [1995] 1 SCR 791.

In the words of Lord Devlin in the same case, the evidence must be enough to 'suggest a reasonable possibility'. There must be some evidence,[253] derived either from the prosecution[254] or adduced by the defence; it is not enough to rely upon an out-of-court self-serving statement,[255] matters raised in cross-examination while theoretically possible have been said to be unlikely to be sufficient in the tactical absence of testimony from the accused,[256] and it is probably not enough to give equivocal evidence from which the jury is invited to draw a medical inference, itself contradicted by the evidence of a doctor.[257] It was expressed in S in terms of the burden being discharged if the matters raised could not at the relevant stage 'be dismissed as wholly and obviously without foundation'.[258] Conversely, it has been said that evidence is insufficient to discharge the burden only if it is 'wholly incredible, or so tenuous or uncertain that no reasonable jury could accept it'.[259]

Where the accused bears both the legal and evidential burdens, for example in relation to insanity and related defences such as diminished responsibility, it is necessary for him to go further and to adduce evidence such as might satisfy a jury on the balance of probabilities. Thus in R v Dix,[260] it was held incumbent upon the accused to adduce some medical evidence[261] before the defence of diminished responsibility could be left to the jury.

It is incumbent upon the judge to leave to the jury all issues arising from the evidence, even when not explicitly relied upon by the defence for tactical reasons.[262] Such cases clearly raise complications so far as the analysis of evidential burden is concerned,[263] but it has been held that the standard here is similarly that the evidence must be more than speculative[264] and such as a reasonable jury might accept.[265] Thus, in a case of murder, the House of Lords has held that there was no need for the judge to put an issue of provocation to the jury, when the accused consistently denied any suggestion of loss of self-control, and

---

[253] In the context of a costs application, it was said that to surmount this threshold the evidence must not lack real substance: R v Secretary of State for Environment, ex p Wakefield Metropolitan Borough Council (1996) 75 P&CR 78. In Canada, it has been said to require an air of reality: R v Park [1995] 2 SCR 836.

[254] As in R v McDonald [1991] Crim LR 122, in which the issue of provocation was held to have been raised solely by a self-serving letter from the accused put in by the prosecution.

[255] R v Newcastle-upon-Tyne Justices, ex p Hindle [1984] 1 All ER 770. But the exculpatory part of a mixed statement will be sufficient to raise an issue, even though likely ultimately to carry little weight: R v Duncan (1981) 73 Cr App Rep 359; Western v DPP [1997] 1 Cr App Rep 474; but see Lord Steyn in R v Lambert (n7), [39].

[256] R v Bonnick (1977) 66 Crim App Rep 266, 269.   [257] R v Bailey (1983) 77 Cr App Rep 76.

[258] (n135), [7].   [259] Von Starck v R [2000] 1 WLR 1270, PC, Lord Clyde, 1275E.

[260] (1981) 74 Cr App Rep 306.

[261] It is, however, rare for the court to prescribe a particular type of evidence that must be adduced to discharge a burden: see e.g. Almighty Marketing Ltd v Milk Link Ltd [2005] EWHC 2584, [22].

[262] R v Coutts [2006] UKHL 39, [2006] 4 All ER 353, further elucidated in R v Foster [2007] EWCA Crim 2869, [2008] 1 Cr App R 470. See also, in Australia, Gilbert v R [2000] HCA 15, 201 CLR 414; in Canada, R v Cinous 2002 SCC 29, [2002] 2 SCR 3; and in Ireland, R v Cronin [2006] IESC 9, [2006] 4 IR 329 (normally unconstitutional).

[263] See Doran [1991] Crim LR 878.

[264] There is certainly no obligation upon the judge to speculate in such a way himself when there is nothing in the evidence to raise the issue (R v Walch [1993] Crim LR 714), especially when the accused has deliberately abstained from testifying: R v Hillier; R v Farrer (1993) 97 Cr App Rep 349, and conversely, the defence does not necessarily become less speculative because the victim has not testified, Booth v DPP [2008] EWHC 956 (Admin), [16]; but see R v Watson [1992] Crim LR 434, in which the defence did seem very speculative (but the resultant outcome might be explicable on a policy view). It may indeed be grounds for appeal that magistrates have so speculated: DPP v Ambrose [1992] RTR 285.

[265] R v Cambridge, above (n250).

there was no evidence of any provoking words or conduct outside the general relationship of the parties.[266]

For the sake of theoretical completeness, it may be added that when, in a civil case, the party with the persuasive burden on a particular issue also bears the evidential burden, it is discharged by the adduction of sufficient evidence to satisfy a reasonable trier of fact on the balance of probabilities.[267] If the party bearing the evidential burden does not bear the persuasive burden, the former is discharged by the adduction of sufficient evidence to leave the mind of a reasonable trier of fact in a state of equilibrium. If an issue is not pleaded in a civil case, the court should decide it only if it is satisfied that all of the facts are before it.[268]

Discharge of persuasive burden[269]

A number of different issues need to be separated. First, dispute as to the number of different standards recognized by the law, and if more than one, what factors determine the choice between them; and second dispute as to the way in which the different standards should be stated by the judge, and, where required, in direction of the jury, bearing in mind the different ways in which cases are fragmented in terms of multiplicity of issues, parties and evidence, and the difficulty of assimilating precise numerical evidence with incommensurable human recollection.

Number of standards

Although in *R v Hepworth and Fearnley*[270] Lord Goddard CJ confessed that he had some difficulty in understanding how there are or can be two standards of proof, presumably on the basis that the trier of fact after assessing the evidence either did or did not believe it proved that the fact had occurred, a distinction had already become well established between the standard of proof on the balance of probabilities which applied to proponents of issues in civil proceedings, and to the accused[271] in the rare situation of his bearing a

---

[266] *R v Acott* [1997] 1 All ER 706, [1997] 1 WLR 306 (unemployed middle-aged man living with, and dependent upon, demanding aged mother). There is still less need in the converse situation for the judge to put an unraised complete defence of self-defence, when a partial defence such as provocation has been relied upon: see *DPP v Walker* [1974] 1 WLR 1090, 1094E.

[267] Here too it is not discharged by honest, but unreliable evidence, in the absence of corroboration: *Lyon v Maidment* [2002] EWHC 1227 (QB), [23]; or by the exhibition of an anonymous letter from a third party to an affidavit sworn by the defendant: *Barclays Bank plc v Anderson* (1987) The Times, 10 March; but see in Ireland, *Anheuser Busch Inc v Controller of Patents* [1996] 2 IR 242. Occasionally, judges express reluctance to decide a civil case for failure to discharge an evidential burden: see e.g. Pumphrey J in *Stoddard International v William Lomas Carpets* [2001] FSR 44, [70].

[268] *Pickering v Deacon* [2003] EWCA Civ 554.

[269] For an historical account, see Shapiro *Beyond Reasonable Doubt and Probable Cause* (1991); for penetrating analysis, see Redmayne (1999) 62 MLR 167; Laudan *Truth, Error and Criminal Law* (2006). For the standard of proof at a trial within a trial, see 183.

[270] [1955] 2 QB 600, 603.

[271] It seems that the burden on the defence will never be more than the balance of probabilities: see *R v G* [2001] EWCA Crim 2308, in which the difference was decisive in relation to the imposition of a disqualification order from working with children under s 28 of the Criminal Justice and Court Services Act 2000. The jury must be unanimous that the burden has been discharged by the accused in order to acquit: *R v Siloata* [2005] 2 NZLR 145.

persuasive burden in criminal proceedings, and the standard of proof beyond reasonable doubt borne by the prosecution in the usual situation of its bearing the persuasive burden on an issue.

The distinction was stated clearly by Denning J in *Miller v Minister of Pensions*:[272]

Proof beyond a reasonable doubt does not mean proof beyond the shadow of a doubt. The law would fail to protect the community if it admitted fanciful possibilities to deflect the course of justice. If the evidence is so strong against a man as to leave only a remote possibility in his favour, which can be dismissed with the sentence 'of course it is possible but not in the least probable' the case is proved beyond reasonable doubt, but nothing short of that will suffice.

When speaking of the degree of cogency that evidence must reach in order that it may discharge the persuasive burden in a civil case, His Lordship said:

That degree is well settled. It must carry a reasonable degree of probability, but not so high as is required in a criminal case. If the evidence is such that the tribunal can say: 'we think it more probable than not', the burden is discharged, but if the probabilities are equal it is not.

The exclusivity of these standards was approved in the House of Lords by Lord Tucker:[273]

I am quite unable to accede to the proposition that there is some intermediate onus between that which is required in criminal cases and the balance of probability which is sufficient in civil actions.

The distinction of standards reflects perception that both belief and disbelief in the existence of a fact exist on a continuum of certainty, and that some facts are believed or disbelieved with a greater degree of certainty than others. Unfortunately, the existence of this continuum has created doubt, ironically enough also generated by words of Denning LJ:[274]

It is of course true that by our law a higher standard of proof is required in criminal cases than in civil cases. But this is subject to the qualification that there is no absolute standard in either case. In criminal cases the charge must be proved beyond reasonable doubt, but there may be degrees of proof within that standard... So also in civil cases the case must be proved by a preponderance of probability, but there may be degrees of probability within that standard. The degree depends on the subject-matter. A civil court, when considering a charge of fraud, will naturally require for itself a higher degree of probability than that which it would require when asking if negligence is established. It does not adopt so high a degree as a criminal court, even when it is considering a charge of a criminal nature; but still it does require a degree of probability which is commensurate with the occasion.

That passage was also approved in the House of Lords, this time by Lord Pearce:[275]

I entirely agree with judgment of Denning LJ in *Bater v Bater*, approved in *Hornal v Neuberger Products Ltd*.

---

[272] [1947] 2 All ER 372, 373–4. For an earlier statement, see *Cooper v Slade* (1858) 6 HL Cas 746, 772. The propriety of summing-up in terms of probability and possibility was questioned in *R v McKenna* (1964) 81 (Pt 1) WN NSW 330; but the reference to probabilities can be regarded as a direction to use common sense (*R v Coe* [1967] VR 712).

[273] In *Dingwall v J Wharton (Shipping) Ltd* [1961] 2 Lloyds Rep 213, 216.

[274] *Bater v Bater* [1951] P 35, 36–7.   [275] [1966] AC 643, [1966] 1 All ER 524; 673, 539G.

Although this has never here[276] been taken to suggest the existence in any criminal cases of a higher standard of proof than beyond reasonable doubt, such considerations have sometimes led to questioning of the division between the two standards, which it could be regarded as eliding. Subsequently, different members of the House of Lords thought that the reasoning in *Bater v Bater* made the standards 'virtually indistinguishable',[277] and the difference between them, 'largely a matter of words',[278] or 'largely illusory'.[279] Even Lord Nicholls, in re-asserting the distinction between the standards, thought that, sometimes at least, the result of their application would be 'much the same'.[280]

Such elision caused consternation in some family law cases involving children, where it was repudiated by Dame Butler-Sloss P.[281] The whole position also attracted further analysis and clarification in the House of Lords. Lord Hoffmann said in *Secretary of State for the Home Department v Rehman*:[282]

…a 'high civil balance of probabilities' is an unfortunate mixed metaphor. The civil standard of proof always means more likely than not. The *only* higher degree of probability required by the law is the criminal standard. But, as Lord Nicholls of Birkenhead explained *In re H (Minors) (Sexual Abuse: Standard of Proof)* [1996] AC 563, 586, some things are inherently more likely than others. It would need more cogent evidence to satisfy one that the creature seen walking in Regent's Park was more likely than not to have been a lioness than to be satisfied to the same standard of probability that it was an Alsatian. On this basis, cogent evidence is generally required to satisfy a civil tribunal that a person has been fraudulent or behaved in some other reprehensible manner. But the question is always whether the tribunal thinks it more probable than not.

Lord Hoffmann reverted to the matter in *Re B (children) (sexual abuse: standard of proof)*.[283] He argued that confusion in the form of escalation of the normal civil standard of the balance of probabilities had occurred in situations where the conduct alleged was particularly grave, or inherently improbable, or the consequences of so finding especially serious. He distinguished three categories:[284]

First, there are cases in which the court has for one purpose classified the proceedings as civil (for example, for the purposes of art 6 of the European Convention for the Protection of Human Rights and Fundamental Freedoms 1950 (as set out in Sch 1 to the Human Rights Act 1998) but nevertheless thought that, because of the serious consequences of the proceedings, the criminal standard of proof or something like it should be applied. Secondly, there are cases in which it has been observed that where some event is inherently improbable, strong evidence may be needed to persuade a tribunal that it more probably happened than not. Thirdly there are cases in which the judges are simply confused about whether they are talking about the standard of proof or about the role of inherent probabilities in deciding whether the burden of proving a fact to a given standard has been discharged.

---

[276] But see in Canada *R v RLR* (1988) 65 CR (3d) 235, 242.

[277] *R (McCann) v Crown Court at Manchester* [2002] UKHL 39, [2003] 1 AC 787, [37] (Lord Steyn).

[278] *Khawaja v Secretary of State* [1984] AC 74, [1983] 1 All ER 765; 112, 783 (Lord Scarman).

[279] *B v Chief Constable of Avon and Somerset Constabulary* [2001] 1 All ER 562, [2001] 1 WLR 340; 572, 354 (Lord Bingham).

[280] *Re H (minors) (sexual abuse: standard of proof)* [1996] AC 563, [1996] 1 All ER 1, 586, 16.

[281] *Re U (a child) (serious injury: standard of proof)* [2004] EWCA Civ 567, [2005] Fam 134, [13].

[282] [2001] UKHL 47, [2003] 1 AC 153, [55], emphasis supplied.

[283] [2008] UKHL 35, [2009] 1 AC 11; re-affirmed by the Supreme Court in *S-B Children* [2009] UKSC 17, [12].

[284] [5].

The third of these probably accounts for the view in some jurisdictions that there is a standard intermediate between proof beyond reasonable doubt and on the preponderance of probability, since such a third standard is commonly expressed in terminology more appropriate to the evidence itself than to the standard at which it is to be appraised. Thus a third standard in the United States has been described as: proof by 'clear, strong and cogent' evidence, and regarded as lying midway between proof on a preponderance of probability and proof beyond reasonable doubt.[285] Similar phrases have often been used in English law to describe the quality of evidence generally required on particular issues.[286] The European Court of Human Rights is essentially a court of review, and references there to the need for a 'satisfactory and convincing' explanation seem to refer more to the force of legal argument than to proof of facts.[287]

Very occasionally reference has been made to other enunciated[288] standards, for example certainty[289] or absolute impossibility,[290] only to be rejected.

It may be worth noting that although few statutes prescribe standards of proof; those that do, make no reference to more than two.[291] It may be concluded that English law recognizes only two standards, and that they are distinct from each other.[292]

Choice of standards

The ascription of standard is very occasionally made explicitly by statutory provision,[293] or by Royal Warrant,[294] and sometimes implicitly, as in s 60 of the Value Added Tax Act 1994 in distinguishing 'criminal liability' and 'civil penalty'.[295] It remains to consider the factors which contribute to the ascription to an issue of a particular standard in the more common case when the court has to decide for itself. In this endeavour it is well to remember that burdens of proof apply to issues of fact, and not to the outcomes of proceedings as a whole, nor to individual pieces of evidence contributing to the determination of such issues. It may be noted also that burdens of proof apply best to determination of past fact, rather

---

[285] Morgan *Problems of Proof in the Anglo-American System of Trials* 82; Uniform Rules 1.04; see *Addington v Texas* 441 US 418 (1979), although there is still a presumption that the civil standard will be on the balance of probabilities: *Grogan v Garner* 498 US 279 (1991). See *Cooper v Oklahoma* 517 US 348 (1996) for unease in casting such a burden on the accused in a criminal case, even on a procedural issue (competence to stand trial).

[286] As early as 1784, in *Countess Dowager Shelburne v Earl of Inchiquin* (1784) 1 Bro CC 338, 341, it was said that a claim for rectification needed to be established by 'strong irrefragable evidence'.

[287] See Thienal (2007) 50 *German Yearbook of International Law*, 543, 582 quoted in Pattenden 125 *LQR* 79, n 147.

[288] In *R v Askeland* [1983] Tas NC 224 an otherwise unenunciated standard intermediate between the traditional two was held to apply to the voluntariness of a confession.

[289] *Cooper v Slade* (1858) 6 HL Cas 746, 772 (pleading).

[290] *Preston-Jones v Preston-Jones* [1951] AC 391, [1951] 1 All ER 124 (by counsel, to rebut presumption of legitimacy).

[291] e.g. Family Law Reform Act 1969 s 26 (to rebut presumption of legitimacy).

[292] Said by the House of Lords in *Re Doherty* [2008] UKHL 33, [2008] 4 All ER 992, [23] to be 'indisputable'.

[293] (n291).

[294] *Judd v Minister of Pensions and National Insurance* [1966] 2 QB 580, [1965] 3 All ER 642.

[295] See *1st Indian Cavalry Club Ltd v Comrs of Customs and Excise* [1998] SCLR 47 (where the Court was assisted by reference to Hansard).

than to that of future risk, as clearly explained by Lord Diplock in relation to the standard of the balance of probabilities:[296]

It is a convenient and trite phrase to indicate the degree of certitude which the evidence must have induced in the mind of the court as to the existence of facts, so as to entitle the court to treat them as data capable of giving rise to legal consequences. But the phrase is inappropriate when applied not to ascertaining what has already happened but to prophesying what, if it happens at all, can only happen in the future. There is no general rule of English law that when a court is required, either by statute or common law, to take account of what may happen in the future and to base legal consequences on the likelihood of its happening, it must ignore any possibility of something happening merely because the odds upon it happening are fractionally less than evens.

The problem is still worse in criminal cases where it is hardly intelligible to direct a jury to determine whether it is satisfied beyond reasonable doubt that something is more probable than not.[297]

The ascription of the appropriate standard is a matter of policy, and it is at this point that the seriousness of the consequences of finding a particular issue proved fall to be considered. Ascription may vary even within different provisions of the same statute,[298] or be influenced by analogy with a different provision.[299] The basic distinction between the standard borne by the prosecution in criminal proceedings and that borne by the defence, or by the parties in civil proceedings, depends upon a number of factors, including that of minimizing the risk of convicting the innocent, and of imposing upon them the consequences of conviction, both punitive and social. It is sometimes expressed in terms of favouring the liberty of the subject. Thus civil contempt, sanctioned by imprisonment, has been regarded as of a criminal character, and so attracts the standard of proof beyond reasonable doubt,[300] as has binding over, even though commenced by complaint.[301] Similar analysis motivated the decision of the House of Lords in *R (McCann) v Manchester Crown Court*[302] that although civil in character both under domestic and European human rights law, an application for an ASBO, breach of which might lead to imprisonment, should attract the higher standard, and that to avoid confusion it was better to use the terminology of application of the criminal standard. It should be noted that this was applied only to the issue of whether the accused had indulged in anti-social behaviour, and not to the necessity of protecting the public, which, although also required, was held to be an exercise of judgment to which the ascription of any burden of proof was inappropriate. Some incursions on civil liberty[303] have been said to be subject to the ordinary civil standard, but enhanced, according to the older understanding of the effect of *Bater v Bater*, so as to equate the criminal. It has now been suggested that the criminal standard should, as in *McCann*, be made

---

[296] *Fernandez v Government of Singapore* [1971] 2 All ER 691, [1971] 1 WLR 987; 696g, 933H.

[297] *Chief Constable of Lancashire v Potter* [2003] EWHC 2272 (Admin), [33].

[298] *Re O (Minors) (Care: Preliminary Hearing)* [2003] UKHL 18, [2004] 1 AC 523, [18] (Children Act 1989).

[299] *Re A Solicitor* [1993] QB 69, [1992] 2 All ER 335 (standard in Bar Code adopted for solicitors).

[300] *Re Bramblevale* [1970] Ch 128, [1969] 3 All ER 1062; *Nelson v Nelson* 1988 SCLR 663; *Re Kerrison* (1990) 101 ALR 525.   [301] *Percy v DPP* [1995] 3 All ER 124, [1995] 1 WLR 1382.

[302] [2002] UKHL 39, [2003] 1 AC 787, [2002] 4 All ER 593, [37].

[303] *Khawaja v Secretary of State* [1984] AC 74, [1983] 1 All ER 765; 113, 114, 784 (determination of status of immigrant so as to imprison); *B v Chief Constable of the Avon and Somerset Constabulary* [2001] 1 All ER 562, [2001] 1 WLR 340 (sex offender order); *Gough v Chief Constable of the Derbyshire Constabulary* [2002] EWCA Civ 351, [2002] QB 1213 (football attendance banning order).

explicit in such cases.[304] The Court of Appeal has since agreed in relation to applications for a civil injunction in terms identical to those of an ASBO, and apparently used as an alternative to it.[305] The civil standard has hitherto been applied[306] to granting injunctions under the Protection from Harassment Act 1997. It remains to be seen whether this, or *McCann*, will be applied in respect of non-molestation orders, now that breach has been made criminal.

Although the ascription of the higher standard to issues in criminal proceedings has been influenced by the role there of punishment, that is not alone a sufficient criterion, and the factual basis for punitive damages in civil proceedings remains at the level of the balance of probabilities.[307] So also do some professional disciplinary proceedings.[308]

Some procedural issues determining judicial consequences, eschewing a trial at which their factual underpinnings can be questioned, may also require satisfaction of the criminal standard.[309]

Although it seemed sometimes to have been thought that cases involving the protection of children and allocation of care for them might be regarded as to be so similarly subjected to the higher standard, this reasoning was explicitly rejected in *Re U (A Child)*:[310]

There would appear to be no good reason to leap across a division, on the one hand between crime and preventative measures taken to restrain defendants for the benefit of the community and, on the other hand, wholly different considerations of child protection and child welfare nor to apply the reasoning in *McCann's* case... to public, or indeed to private, law cases concerning children.

Conversely, it also seemed that some legislative provisions at least implicitly permitted, or even required, the application of a lower standard than the balance of probability. Thus s 31 of the Children Act 1989 sets as threshold conditions for making a child protection order that a child 'is suffering, or is likely to suffer, significant harm'. The first of these alternatives is as noted above to be determined according to the ordinary civil standard of the balance of probabilities. The more difficult issue relates to the alternative. In *Re H (Minors) (Sexual Abuse: Standard of Proof)*[311] a father was accused of sexual abuse by one of four children, tried, and acquitted. The local authority nevertheless sought an order under s 31 on the basis that, given the difference between the civil and criminal standards of proof, it was *likely* that the other three children would suffer significant harm, although the evidence that they would, was based only on the allegations by the first child, which had been insufficient to prove guilt in the criminal proceedings. The application was dismissed even though the trial judge thought it a real possibility that the allegations were true. While the House of Lords accepted that likely does not mean probable,[312] a majority insisted that a finding of likelihood could be made only upon the basis of facts shown to be more probable than not, and not upon the basis of unproved allegations or speculation:[313]

[U]nresolved judicial doubts and suspicions can no more form the basis of a conclusion that the second threshold condition in section 31(2)(a) has been established than they can form the basis of a conclusion that the first has been established.

---

[304] *Re Doherty* [2008] UKHL 33, [49] although Lord Brown refused to apply this standard to the issue of release on licence of a mandatory life sentence prisoner.
[305] *Birmingham City Council v Shafi and Ellis* [2008] EWCA Civ 1186, [64].
[306] *Hipgrave and Hipgrave v Jones* [2004] EWHC 2901 (QB), [2005] 2 FLR 174.
[307] *John v MGN Ltd* [1997] QB 586, [1996] 2 All ER 35; 619B, 58b.
[308] *R (IPCC) v Hayman* [2008] EWHC 2191 (Admin), [20] (police); *Hutchinson v General Dental Council* [2008] EWHC 2896 (Admin), [24] (dentists).
[309] *Ricci Burns Ltd v Toole* [1989] 3 All ER 478, [1989] 1 WLR 993 (grant of summary judgment).
[310] (n281), [13].   [311] [1996] AC 563, [1996] 1 All ER 1.   [312] 585, 15f.   [313] 589, 19g.

Exactly the same analysis was subsequently adopted[314] by the Court of Appeal in relation to the welfare conditions which must be satisfied in order to make an order once the threshold condition has been proved to the ordinary civil standard.

It should be noted that just as some issues are more difficult to establish to the required standard because of their unusual nature or rarity, so too others are easier to establish at a given standard because they are commonplace and often found to exist. Thus in other sections of the Children's Act 1989 no more than 'reasonable suspicion' is required, for example to justify launching an enquiry, and less cogent evidence is required to establish that. As Lord Nicholls stressed:[315]

What the evidence is required to establish depends upon the issue the court has to decide.

So far as the exclusivity of the two standards is concerned it must also be remembered that the factual basis for most violations of the criminal law can also give rise to civil proceedings, and there is then a real danger to the credibility of the administration of justice if that basis is held to have been established for the purposes of one, but not for the other.[316] If the commission of a criminal act is an issue in civil proceedings[317] the court is placed in a dilemma in which it must abandon either consistency of standard of proof as between two different proceedings relating to the same issue, or abandon it as between two different issues arising in the same proceedings. In *Hornal v Neuberger Products Ltd*,[318] the Court of Appeal recognized that the earlier English cases conflicted, and concluded, in apparently general terms, that proof on a preponderance of probability will suffice when the commission of a crime is alleged in a civil action. The claimant claimed damages for breach of warranty and fraud on the ground that the defendant had falsely stated that a machine sold by him to the claimant had been reconditioned. So far as the alleged breach of warranty was concerned, the trial judge held that the words were spoken by the defendant, but the claim failed because he considered that the parties did not intend them to have contractual effect. The judge proceeded to award damages for fraud, although he said that he was merely satisfied on the balance of probability, and not beyond reasonable doubt, that the statement was made. If the statement had in fact been made, the defendant would have been guilty of obtaining money by false pretences, for it was beyond dispute that he knew that the machine had not been reconditioned. The Court of Appeal dismissed the appeal mainly because:[319]

... it would bring the law into contempt if a judge were to say that on the issue of warranty he finds that the statement was made, and on the issue of fraud he finds it was not made.

---

[314] *Re M and R (minors) (sexual abuse: expert evidence)* [1996] 4 All ER 239, [1996] 2 FLR 195, and said by the Court of Appeal, in *Re G (a child) (non-accidental injury: standard of proof)* [2001] 1 FCR 96, [13], to have become the basis of the approach by judges at all levels in family cases, and to be applied equally in civil cases.

[315] 589, 19h.

[316] [51]. Similar reasoning in child protection cases, but as between the satisfaction of the different conditions in s 31, was applied in *Re H* above (n311), 591, 21c; and as between s 1 and s 31 in *M and R* (n314), [248].

[317] It is not necessarily in issue just because criminality is a *possible* explanation of the civil wrong, *Blue Station Ltd v Kamyab* [2007] EWCA Civ 1073, [12].

[318] [1957] 1 QB 247, [1956] 3 All ER 970.

[319] 258, 973, respectively, Denning LJ. See also remarks of Sholl J in *McClelland v Symons* [1951] VLR 157, 166.

Yet this would have been the result of holding that the claim for damages for fraud had to be established beyond reasonable doubt.

Although there were several previous decisions that were not discussed by the Court of Appeal, *Hornal's Case* settled the English law at the time, and may now be explained under the modern interpretation of *Bater v Bater* propounded by Lord Hoffmann in *Re B*.[320] An allegation of criminal conduct, even of murder,[321] need be established only on a pre-ponderance of probability in a civil action.[322] When the commission of a crime is alleged in civil proceedings, the stigma attaching to an affirmative finding might be thought to justify the imposition of a strict standard of proof; but the person against whom crim-inal conduct is alleged is adequately protected by the consideration that the antecedent improbability of his guilt is 'a part of the whole range of circumstances which have to be weighed in the scale when deciding as to the balance of probabilities'.[323] A civil court may thus discriminate between evidence proving the commission of the same crime by dif-ferent individuals.[324] It may finally be noted that where proceedings are civil, there is no infringement of the European Convention just because what is alleged might have been charged as a crime, nor does it amount to an abuse of process to bring such proceedings, even though a deliberate decision had been made by public authorities initiating the pro-ceedings not to bring criminal proceedings.[325]

Explanation of standards

It will be convenient first to consider the general problems involved in the choice of the language to describe the burden, and then to go on to consider the special problems pre-sented by fragmented cases, and by the need to explain how precisely defined evidence, such as the result of mathematical calculations of probabilities, is to be assimilated to ordinary testimonial narration of what a human being remembers having perceived.

General formulation

Some of the difficulty is created by the words in which the standard is formulated. In ordinary civil cases, it is usually expressed as involving the 'preponderance of probability',

---

[320] (n283).

[321] *Re Dellow's Will Trusts, Lloyds Bank Ltd v Institute of Cancer Research* [1964] 1 All ER 771, [1964] 1 WLR 451; *Nishina Trading Co Ltd v Chiyoda Fire and Marine Insurance Co Ltd* [1969] 2 QB 449, [1969] 2 All ER 776 (theft proved on balance). See also, in England, *Francisco v Diedrick* (1998) The Times, 3 April; in Scotland, *Mullan v Anderson* 1993 SLT 835 (murder in civil proceedings for assault), departing from and disapproving of any intimation to the contrary in *Halford v Brookes* [1992] PIQR P175; in Australia, *G v M* (1995) 126 FLR 355 (sexual abuse in custody proceedings); and in New Zealand, *Real Estate Institute of New Zealand Inc v Private Sale Co (Auckland Central) Ltd* [1996] 2 NZLR 371 (statutory crime relating to trading in civil proceedings for injunction).

[322] In *SW v A City Council* [2009] EWCA Civ 644 the court held it compatible that a rape had been found to have been committed on the balance of probabilities for the purposes of care proceedings, but that the perpetrator had been acquitted in criminal proceedings.

[323] Morris LJ (n318). It is particularly unlikely to be a suitable issue for summary judgment: see *Allied Dunbar Assurance plc v Ireland* [2001] EWCA Civ 1129; although in a very strong case, a declaratory judg-ment of the commission of criminal offences may be made under CPR 40.20: *Financial Services Authority v Rourke* [2002] CPR 14.

[324] *Re G (a minor)* [1987] 1 WLR 1461 (more required to show father guilty of sexual abuse of child than would have been required for another).

[325] *Re D* (2004) unreported QBD, 7 December (proceedings by the Assets Recovery Agency under the Proceeds of Crime Act 2002).

the 'balance of probabilities', or the 'preponderance of evidence'. It might be argued that the last of these seems to involve no more than that the evidence, taking into account its cogency,[326] adduced by the proponent of an issue exceed that adduced by its opponent.[327] It is more common, however, to regard all of these terms as synonymous, and as connoting not merely relative preponderance over the evidence of the opponent but satisfaction of a prescribed level of probability.[328] In *Home Secretary v Rehman*, Lord Hoffmann was most emphatic:[329]

The civil standard of proof always means more likely than not.

The House of Lords has also pronounced any other view as contrary to common sense, since a judge should not be forced to find proved an occurrence that he regards on the evidence as extremely improbable.[330]

[The trial judge] adopted an erroneous approach to this case by regarding himself as compelled to choose between two theories, both of which he regarded as extremely improbable, or one of which he regarded as extremely improbable and the other of which he regarded as virtually impossible. He should have borne in mind, and considered carefully in his judgment, the third alternative which was open to him, namely that the evidence left him in doubt...and that, in these circumstances, the shipowners had failed to discharge the burden of proof which was upon them.

Similarly in *Re M (Children)* the trial judge was wrong to find one party responsible for abuse of the child while saying that she could not rule out its perpetration by another.[331]

The problem of formulation is still more acute in criminal cases where a direction has to be given to the jury. In 1949, Lord Goddard CJ said:[332]

Once a judge begins to use the words 'reasonable doubt' and to try to explain what is a reasonable doubt and what is not, he is much more likely to confuse the jury than if he tells them in plain language, 'It is the duty of the prosecution to satisfy you of the prisoner's guilt'.

This formulation failed to solve the problem, and Lord Goddard made another attempt at clarification in *R v Hepworth and Fearnley*, saying:[333]

One would be on safe ground if one said in a criminal case to a jury: 'you must be satisfied beyond reasonable doubt', and one could also say, 'you the jury, must be completely satisfied', or better still, 'you must feel sure of the prisoner's guilt'.

---

[326] *Isik v Clegg* [2007] EWHC 2552 (QB), [46].

[327] Some support for this view can be gleaned from the speech of Viscount Simon in *Hickman v Peacey* [1945] AC 304, [1945] 2 All ER 215; 318, 220, and from that of Lord Reid in *S v S* [1972] AC 24, [1970] 3 All ER 107; 41, 109. It seems that even a very weak case may be pushed over the threshold by the failure of the opponent to adduce any relevant evidence: *Francisco v Diedrick* (1998) The Times, 3 April, or refusal to cooperate in providing a sample: *Secretary of State for Work and Pensions v Jones* [2003] EWHC 2163 (Fam), [2004] 1 FLR 282; for a similar view in Ireland, see *Anheuser-Busch Inc v Controller of Patents* [1996] 2 IR 242. The burden is not necessarily discharged merely because a defence has been struck out, *Culla Park Ltd v Richards* [2007] EWHC 1687 (QB), [12].

[328] See also *Briginshaw v Briginshaw* (1938) 60 CLR 336. The same view prevails in the United States: see Devitt and Blackman *Federal Jury Practice and Instructions* (3rd edn, 1977) [71.14]—'To establish by a preponderance of evidence means to prove that something is more likely so than not so.'   [329] [55].

[330] *Rhesa Shipping Co SA v Edmunds* [1985] 2 All ER 712, [1985] 1 WLR 948; 718, 956. Lord Brandon attributed the contrary view to an unjudicial dictum of Mr Sherlock Holmes.

[331] [2008] EWCA Civ 1261.   [332] *R v Kritz* [1950] 1 KB 82, [1949] 2 All ER 406; 90, 410.

[333] [1955] 2 QB 600, [1955] 2 All ER 918; 603, 920.

In spite of this approval of three different ways of saying the same thing, including the reference to the time-honoured standard of proof beyond reasonable doubt, the Court of Criminal Appeal and the Court of Appeal had to express their disapproval of the trial judge's summing-up concerning the standard of proof in a number of subsequent cases,[334] and similar difficulties have been experienced in other common law jurisdictions.[335] It is not enough to direct the jury simply to decide which of two conflicting witnesses for defence and prosecution they believe to be telling the truth,[336] or whether an issue had been shown to be 'more than likely',[337] or 'reasonably certain'.[338] It is hardly surprising that the English courts[339] and the Judicial Committee of the Privy Council[340] are against any set form of words:[341]

If the jury are made to understand that they have to be satisfied and must not return a verdict against the defendant unless they feel sure, and that the onus is all the time on the prosecution and not on the defence, then whether the judge uses one form of language or another is neither here nor there.

The Court of Appeal has recommended that judges stop trying to define that which it is impossible to define,[342] and 'to keep the direction on this important matter short and clear'.[343] The current direction recommended by the Judicial Studies Board refers only to the jury's being sure, and if any reference has been made during the trial to 'beyond reasonable doubt' for a direction informing the jury that that is the same thing.[344] It is unwise to go further,[345] for example in attempting to distinguish being sure from being certain.[346]

Where there are 'cut-throat' mutually inconsistent defences, the temptation to say that one of the accused cannot be acquitted unless the jury is satisfied of the guilt of the other should be resisted, since it would be wrong to suggest that the accused has to satisfy the jury of anything.[347]

---

[334] *R v Jones* [1961] Crim LR 322; *R v Johnson* [1961] 3 All ER 969, [1961] 1 WLR 1468; *R v Head and Warrener* (1961) 45 Cr App Rep 225; *R v Attfield* [1961] 3 All ER 243, [1961] 1 WLR 1135; *R v Stafford and R v Luvaglio* [1968] 3 All ER 752n; *R v Gray* (1973) 58 Cr App Rep 177; *R v Sweeney* (1983) The Times, 22 October.

[335] *People (A-G) v Byrne* [1974] IR 1; *Murray v R* [2002] HCA 26, 211 CLR 193; *Victor v Nebraska* 511 US 1 (1994); *R v Lifchus* [1997] 3 SCR 320, unleashing a veritable torrent of more than 350 reported cases, many in the Supreme Court of Canada; *R v Wanhalla* [2007] 2 NZLR 573 (survey of many common law jurisdictions by full CA).

[336] Or for magistrates to appear to be deciding upon such a basis: *Ukpabi v DPP* [2008] EWHC 952 (Admin); see also *R v CLY* 2008 SCC 2, [2008] 1 SCR 5; *R v E* (1995) 89 ACR 325.

[337] *R (Bhoti) v Secretary of State for Home Department* [2003] EWHC 1628 (Admin); nor for magistrates to find against the accused 'on balance', *R (Ahmad) v Bradford Magistrates* [2008] EWHC 2934 (Admin).

[338] *Gilmour v HMA* [2007] HCJAC 48, [2007] SCCR 417, [122].

[339] *R v Allan* [1969] 1 All ER 91, [1969] 1 WLR 33.

[340] *Walter v R* [1969] 2 AC 26; the direction upheld in this case is criticized in (1969) 32 MLR 217, but it was also upheld, with a preference for the time-honoured formula of 'beyond reasonable doubt' in *Ferguson v R* [1979] 1 All ER 877, [1979] 1 WLR 94.   [341] Lord Diplock [1969] 2 AC 26, 30.

[342] *R v Yap Chuan Ching* (1976) 63 Cr App Rep 7.   [343] *R v Penny* (1991) 94 Cr App Rep 345, 350.

[344] *R v Adey* (3 March 1998, unreported) CA.

[345] But cf the definition proposed in the United States by the Federal Judicial Center, approved in *Victor v Nebraska* (n335).

[346] *R v Stephens* [2002] EWCA Crim 1529, except perhaps very rarely to distinguish between scientific certainty and being sure: *R v Bracewell* (1978) 68 Cr App Rep 44.

[347] *R v O'Rourke* (1993) 15 Cr App Rep (S) 650.

It is vitally important for the judge to direct the jury both as to the allocation and standard of the burden of proof,[348] but in very exceptional cases, the Court of Appeal may nevertheless apply the proviso despite failure to direct the jury on either the allocation,[349] or
standard,[350] of proof. In both of these cases, however, the decision was assisted by the
fact that the failure to direct on the one question was compensated by a full and proper
direction on the other. It is hard to conceive of circumstances in which the proviso would
be applied if there were no proper direction on either.[351] It is not, however, necessary for
magistrates to provide an explicit exposition of the tests they are applying when they have
been addressed on those tests, and seem clearly to be applying them.[352]

From time to time, it has been suggested that further precautionary instructions are
required in criminal cases, but the House of Lords has refused to lay down a rule that, in
addition to directing the jury that the prosecution bears the burden of proving the accused's
guilt beyond reasonable doubt, the judge must, where the evidence is purely circumstantial, direct them to acquit unless the facts are not only consistent with the accused's guilt,
but also inconsistent with any other rational conclusion.[353] Such a requirement was at one
time assumed to exist by the Canadian courts on the authority of *Hodge's Case*.[354] In that
case, great stress was properly placed on the destructive effect on the cumulative force of
circumstantial evidence pointing to guilt, of one rational hypothesis of innocence; the
direction to the jury was, rightly it is submitted, treated by the House of Lords as no more
than a formula, suitable in some cases, for instructing the jury that they must be satisfied
of the accused's guilt beyond reasonable doubt.[355]

A rule is very properly prescribed for the direction that must be given on issues on
which the accused bears the persuasive burden. To repeat the words of Humphreys J:[356]

In any case where, either by statute or at common law, some matter is presumed against an
accused person 'unless the contrary is proved', the jury should be directed that it is for them to
decide whether the contrary is proved, that the burden of proof required is less than that required
at the hands of the prosecution in proving the case beyond a reasonable doubt, and that the burden may be discharged by evidence satisfying the jury of that which the accused is called upon
to establish.

In this context, the word 'satisfy' connotes satisfaction on the balance of probabilities.[357]
It is sometimes questioned whether, in a comparatively brief summing-up, it is possible
to make clear to a jury the distinction between the standard to be applied on issues on

---

[348] In *R v Gibson* (1983) 77 Cr App Rep 151, an appeal was allowed because the direction as to allocation
and standard had been given only once.   [349] *R v Donoghue* (1987) 86 Cr App Rep 267.

[350] *R v Edwards* (1983) 77 Cr App Rep 5.

[351] The Supreme Court of the United States regards the matter as so important as to exclude the doctrine of harmless error: *Sullivan v Louisiana* 508 US 275 (1993). But see in Canada, *R v Parnell* (1995) 98
CCC (3d) 83.

[352] *R (McCubbin) v DPP* [2004] EWHC Admin 2504; cf *Evans v DPP* [2001] EWHC Admin 369 (in which
the stated reasons suggested that the civil standard had been applied).

[353] *McGreevy v DPP* [1973] 1 All ER 503, [1973] 1 WLR 276.   [354] (1838) 2 Lew CC 227.

[355] See also, in Australia, *Knight v R* (1992) 175 CLR 495; in New Zealand, *Police v Pereira* [1977] 1 NZLR
547; in Canada, *Monteleone v R* [1987] 2 SCR 154.

[356] *R v Carr-Briant* [1943] KB 607, 612 above; see also *Public Prosecutor v Yuvaraj* [1970] AC 913; *Sodeman
v R* [1936] 2 All ER 1138 (insanity); *R v Dunbar* [1958] 1 QB 1, [1957] 2 All ER 737 (diminished responsibility); *R v Podola* [1960] 1 QB 325, [1959] 3 All ER 418 (fitness to plead); *R v Milnes and Green* (1983) 33 SASR
211 (pardon).   [357] The Judicial Studies Board suggests 'probable', glossed as 'more likely than not'.

which the prosecution bears the persuasive burden and that to be applied when this burden is borne by the accused. If there is any difficulty in this regard, it is a further argument against placing the persuasive burden on the accused on any issue in a criminal case.

A still more esoteric question has been raised: can there be satisfaction beyond reasonable doubt of the guilt of the accused when there is no such satisfaction with regard to any of the evidentiary facts? On this, the full court of South Australia has expressed itself as follows:[358]

There is a clear distinction between drawing an inference of guilt from a combination of several proved facts, none of which by itself would support the inference, and drawing an inference of guilt from several facts whose existence is in doubt. In the first place [sic] the combination does what each fact taken in isolation could not do; in the second case the combination counts for nothing.

In the second case, much would depend upon the degree of doubt entertained about the existence of the several facts the existence of which was doubtful. An accumulation of evidentiary facts, each of which is proved on a balance of probabilities, may suffice to dispel all doubt about the existence of the fact to be proved. The South Australian court concluded that facts from which inferences are to be drawn must be 'clearly proved'.

These remarks were subsequently considered by the High Court of Australia in *R v Chamberlain (No 2)*[359] and by the Supreme Court of Canada in *R v Morin*.[360] The majority of the High Court in *Chamberlain* seemed to have taken the view that no inferences could be drawn from facts that were not themselves proved beyond reasonable doubt,[361] and that the jury should be so directed, but Deane J adopted a more discriminating approach, distinguishing between primary and intermediate facts.[362] The Supreme Court of Canada was divided on this question in *Morin*, but it was the minority[363] that took the view of the majority in the High Court of Australia, and even they qualified it by stressing that no fact was to be considered in isolation, but only in the light of all of the surrounding facts. Deane J and the majority[364] in *Morin* felt that this was to intrude too far into the jury's fact-finding process. They accepted that, if guilt depends upon a chain of elements, each corresponding to a different piece of evidence, then the jury must be, and must be instructed to be, satisfied beyond reasonable doubt that the required elements have been established. This does not, however, imply that no inferences can be drawn from facts less well established if they are not synonymous with essential elements of the offence.[365] Egglestone rightly points out that any other view would make nonsense of the rules relating to corroboration. As Deane J put it:[366]

There is certainly no requirement of the law that the members of the jury must examine separately each item of evidence adduced by the prosecution and reject it unless they are satisfied beyond reasonable doubt that it is correct. Nor is it the law that a jury is in all circumstances

---

[358] *R v Van Beelen* [1972] 4 SASR 353, 374; criticized by Egglestone *Evidence, Proof and Probability* (3rd edn), 122.

[359] (1984) 153 CLR 521. [360] (1988) 66 CR (3d) 1.

[361] See Gibbs CJ and Mason J, 538, 539; Murphy J and Brennan J, 599. [362] 626, 627.

[363] Wilson and Lamer JJ.

[364] Sopinka J, with whom Dickson CJC, McIntyre and La Forest JJ concurred.

[365] Or at any stage constitute single links in a chain of reasoning to the inference of such an essential element, as for example in *Re H* (n311). [366] 626. See also *Thomas v R* [1972] NZLR 34.

precluded from drawing an inference from a primary fact unless that fact is proved beyond reasonable doubt.

These views have now prevailed,[367] although it may be sensible for the trial judge to refrain from stressing the different standards applicable to individual pieces of evidence,[368] and to the issues of fact they constitute.[369]

It must finally be emphasized that the summing-up is to be considered as a whole, and that a minor isolated slip is not necessarily sufficient to contaminate a direction that is overwhelmingly correct.[370]

Fragmented cases[371]

Litigation is often complex on account of fragmentation between different parties, different causes of action, different occurrences of such causes, different defences, and different pieces of evidence. Criminal litigation is further complicated by the delegation of the determination of issues of fact to a jury, which is a collective body of lay people acting upon the direction of the judge. The issues to be put are often complex in the ways mentioned above, and yet the judge has to direct the jury in its capacity as trier of fact, in the most simple and effective way. This tension is difficult to resolve. Its resolution in terms of direction as to the application of the rules as to burden of proof is best considered by separating out the different complicating factors.

Different defendants

If there are different defendants, the evidence may implicate one or the other or both in the commission of the relevant crime. It may be quite conclusive so far as the commission of the crime is concerned, but quite inconclusive so far as the identity of the criminal is concerned, for example in a case where it is apparent that the deceased was killed by one of two accused, but the evidence is entirely neutral between them.[372] It is clear that, in this situation, it is immaterial that the evidence indicates that one or other of them must have committed the crime, and the jury must be directed that it may convict either of them only on the basis that all of the ingredients of the crime have been established to the appropriate criminal standard in relation to that particular one.

Different offences[373]

It is necessary to distinguish between different situations. Sometimes the indictment will specify different crimes, but occasionally the law permits conviction of a different,

---

[367] *Shepherd v R* (1990) 170 CLR 573, in which Dawson J ascribes the problem to the available nomenclature; *Edwards v R* (1993) 178 CLR 193. See also *Stratford v Ministry of Transport* [1992] 1 NZLR 486; *Mackenzie v R* (1993) 18 CR (4th) 133.

[368] In *R v Billingham and Billingham* [2009] EWCA Crim 19, [2009] 2 Cr App R 341 it was noted that even the Judicial Studies Board had become confused in its model direction in this respect.

[369] *R v IK* [2004] SASC 280, 147 ACR 237.

[370] *Walters v R* [1969] 2 AC 26; reaffirmed by the Court of Appeal in *R v Stephens* [2002] EWCA Crim 1529, [16].

[371] For a helpful account of many of these situations, see Smith [1988] *Crim LR* 335.

[372] As in *R v Aston; R v Mason* (1991) 94 Cr App Rep 180, as noted above the Domestic Violence, Crime and Victims Act 2004 has refrained from dealing with this problem by transferring the burden of proof (see Law Com 279 (2003) paras 5.3–5.27).

[373] See further Hirst (2000) 4 *E&P* 31.

and lesser offence, upon an indictment for another.[374] If the crimes arise out of the same incident but are quite distinct, say an assailant charged with theft and indecent assault, then the position is the same as with the co-defendants, and the jury should be directed to convict only in respect of an offence in respect of which a sufficient majority is convinced to the required standard. Where the crimes are not distinct, but are perhaps connected in having a similar *actus reus*, but different *mens rea*,[375] as in the case of murder and manslaughter, the situation is different. Here it seems that if the evidence is capable of supporting a verdict for either offence, then the jury is entitled to return a verdict of the lesser,[376] so long as a sufficient majority is satisfied to the requisite high standard, that the accused was at least guilty of that, notwithstanding that a substantial[377] minority would find the accused guilty of the more serious[378] offence, or that the jury may have different reasons for preferring the lesser offence.[379] This has led to disharmony between different Commonwealth courts. In *A-G for Hong Kong v Yip Kai-foon*,[380] the Privy Council determined that it was wrong for the jury to be directed that once it had been convinced to the criminal standard that, the accused was guilty of one or the other, then it could decide as a matter of probability which was the more likely. It should rather have been directed to try the more serious crime first, applying the ordinary criminal standard, and only if that were to result in acquittal should the lesser offence be considered. In relation to that, the jury should again be directed to apply the ordinary criminal standard, and to convict only if persuaded to the appropriate standard in relation to all of the essential ingredients of that lesser offence.[381] Such a process of reasoning requires the jury to accept as true the state of facts consistent with acquittal, perhaps contrary to its actual opinion. It was rejected by the High Court of Australia in *R v Gilson*[382] on the basis that it did not erode the principle of *Woolmington* to permit the jury to determine between the two eligible crimes on a basis of reasonable probability.[383]

Different defences

In much the same way as different offences may be spelled out of the evidence as to one count in an indictment, so they may be spelled out of different defences to that count. Thus a count of murder may be met by a defence of diminished responsibility or by one of

---

[374] See Criminal Appeal Act 1968, s 3, and the impact of the amendment to s 2 by the Criminal Appeal Act 1995, as explained in *R v Graham* [1997] 1 Cr App Rep 302. The situation in which this occurs because of the establishment of a mitigating defence is considered below.

[375] Or as in *R v Sharpe* 219 CCC3d 187 (2007) different sexual offences to which different defences applied according to timing.

[376] See *R v Sinha* [1995] Crim LR 68, in which the accused's intention was to pervert the course of justice in whatever tribunal might be seised of the matter.

[377] Otherwise enough to acquit.

[378] Or one committed by different means, such as by inciting and encouraging another to act: *Swindall v Osborne* (1864) 2 Car & Kir 230; *Du Cros v Lambourne* [1907] 1 KB 40; *R v Giannetto* [1997] 1 Cr App Rep 1. See also, in Canada, *Thatcher v R* [1987] 1 SCR 652.

[379] *R v Jones* (1999) The Times, 17 February.

[380] [1988] AC 642, [1988] 1 All ER 153. See also *R v Foreman* [1991] Crim LR 702.

[381] The Privy Council endorsed the decisions in *R v Griffiths* (1974) 60 Cr App Rep 14 and *R v Cash* [1985] QB 801, [1985] 2 All ER 128 that it was not necessary in relation to a charge of handling to show that it was committed 'otherwise than in the course of stealing'.   [382] (1991) 172 CLR 353.

[383] Here it need be no more than a matter of relative probability. The English view could lead to conviction by the jury for the offence that it believed it less likely that the accused had committed.

provocation seeking to reduce the verdict to one of manslaughter.[384] The question arises as to the proper direction when the evidence is capable of proving one of a number of defences, or one of a number of components of a defence. In *R v More*,[385] the question arose in relation to the defence of duress, which has three elements, and it was held that, as it was a matter of defence, the jury should be directed that it was sufficient to defeat it that the requisite majority failed to accept all three elements, so it was immaterial that different members might reject different elements. Here it is submitted that it is necessary to distinguish between cases in which the persuasive burden of establishing the defence is on the accused, as in diminished responsibility, and those in which the persuasive burden of disproving the defence is on the prosecution. In the former case, if there is no sufficient agreement as to any essential element, then the defence has not been proved, and the accused should be convicted; in the latter case, the prosecution has not disproved the defence, and the accused should be acquitted.[386] The question is more complicated still if both diminished responsibility and provocation are raised in the same case, given the differential distribution of persuasive burden. In such a case, there seems no alternative but to prescribe a sequential procedure.[387] Occasionally, where different occurrences of a given offence have not been separately particularized, different defences may be appropriate to the different occurrences, and an appeal allowed for that reason.[388]

Different counts

It is not at all uncommon for an indictment to contain a number of similar counts reflecting a succession of different incidents related by some common factors making joint trial appropriate.[389] In such a case, there is no doubt at all that the jury must be directed to consider each count separately[390] and to find the accused guilty only of those for which all the ingredients have been proved to the appropriate criminal standard.

Different evidence

Sometimes even within a single count there may be evidence of more than one occurrence of one of the ingredients of the offence, or of alternative means by which it may have been committed. For example, in one of the earliest cases to consider this problem, a number of false statements were alleged in support of a charge of procuring the execution of a valuable security by deception.[391] The Court of Appeal there took the view that it was wrong to prescribe too closely how the jury should reason, and that provided each juror was satisfied to the required standard that deception had been practised, it

---

384 In relation to diminished responsibility, the evidential and persuasive burdens are both borne by the accused, but as noted above, the persuasive burden to disprove a defence may remain on the prosecution, for example in relation to provocation.

385 [1987] 3 All ER 825, [1987] 1 WLR 1578. 4) *NLJ*, 24 June.

386 But see Smith [1988] Crim LR 335, 340, by whom it is argued that, in the latter case, there is a disagreement, justifying a retrial.

387 It is submitted that the accused should be permitted to elect which the jury should consider first: cf the procedure adopted by Devlin J in *R v Roberts* (1953) unreported, described in (1994) *NLJ*, 24 June.

388 As in *R v Turner* (30 November 1999, unreported), CA. See also, *WGC v R* [2007] HCA 58, [138].

389 See Indictment Rules 1971, r 9.

390 Although evidence of one may be admissible in considering another, see further Chapter VIII.

391 *R v Agbim* [1979] Crim LR 171. See also *R v Ryder* [1995] 2 NZLR 271.

was immaterial that different jurors might have relied upon different statements. This does seem to contravene the *Woolmington* principle, and in a subsequent case in which the jury explicitly asked whether it needed to agree on a particular ingredient, and was accordingly told that it need not, this was held to be a misdirection.[392] *Agbim* was distinguished on the basis that, in that case, there had been only one deception alleged in the indictment, although a number of different allegedly deceptive statements had been adduced as evidence of that one piece of deception. This appeared to make all turn upon the precise drafting of the particulars of the offence in the indictment.[393] If more than one statement were specified, then the jury must agree that one in particular was false, but if only one deceptive statement were specified, then the fact that its deceptive quality was to be derived from one of a number of allegedly false supporting statements was immaterial, and the jury need not agree upon the falsity of any one of them. This seems a very fine distinction[394] now that it has been decided that the direction in *Brown* is appropriate despite the separate incidents relied upon to establish one count not being separately particularized.[395] Thus in *R v Smith*,[396] it was held in a case of affray that, while there was no need for the jury to agree on any separate incident in a course of continuing conduct,[397] once it was established that there were two separate courses of conduct,[398] then the jury did have to be instructed that it must be unanimous in relation to the same one of the two courses.[399] A conviction is more likely to be quashed in this situation when the prosecution has refused to divulge to the defence its intention to rely upon an alternative means of commission.[400]

Even if a number of alternative allegations are made in the particulars, it is not always necessary to direct the jury of the need for unanimity in respect of one,[401] as this may

---

[392] *R v Brown* (1983) 79 Cr App Rep 115. In *R v Keeton* [1995] 2 Cr App Rep 241, it was held that this form of direction was exceptional, and confined to cases in which there was a real risk of confusion as a result of the prosecution's advancing alternative bases for liability. In New Zealand, a majority of the Court of Appeal has expressed its dissatisfaction with the confusion caused by *Brown* to the extent of being prepared to depart from it if necessary: *R v Mead* [2002] 1 NZLR 594; in Canada, in *Thatcher* [1987] 1 SCR 652, 697, the majority of the Supreme Court withheld its approval.

[393] See *R v D* [2001] 1 Cr App Rep 194, in which the prosecution resisted precise specification of any one of five different forms of indecency on any particular occasion. For a somewhat similar decision in Australia, see *KBT v R* (1997) 191 CLR 417.

[394] Cp *R v Chargot Ltd* [2008] UKHL 73, [2008] 1 WLR 1 (one offence of creating risk under s 3 of the Health and Safety at Work Act 1974, so no need for *Brown* direction as to supplied particulars) with *R v Beckingham* [2006] EWCA Crim 773 (duty to take care to protect health under s 7 of the Act, where there was a need to give a *Brown* direction in respect of a specific dereliction).

[395] *R v Houlden* (1993) 99 Cr App Rep 244.

[396] [1997] 1 Cr App Rep 14; see also *R v Boreman* [2000] 1 All ER 307, [2000] 2 Cr App Rep 17; *R v Kyte* [2001] EWCA Crim 3 (both cases involved two quite separate means of committing murder).

[397] See also *R v Young* (1992) 97 Cr App Rep 280.

[398] Cf *R v Phillips* (1987) 86 Cr App Rep 18, in which only one conspiracy was alleged, and it was not necessary to direct the jury that it had to agree with which other person the accused conspired; *R v Ibrahima* [2005] EWCA Crim 1436 (one possession of drugs, and unnecessary to decide to whom and on what basis it was to be supplied).

[399] But see *R v Morton* [2003] EWCA Crim 1501, in which two men were charged with murder, as the result of an incident in which they were both involved, and it was held immaterial which was principal and which accessory, so no *Brown* direction was required, despite the acquittal of one.

[400] As in *R v Carr* [2000] 2 Cr App Rep 149 (murder by kick or punch).

[401] *R v Price* [1991] Crim LR 465.

be accomplished implicitly by the prescription of a staged approach.[402] This may not be appropriate where the particulars specify two inconsistent methods of committing an offence, for example direct commission and procuring commission by another.[403] The current position appears to be that if, but only if, there is a serious possibility of confusion, then such a direction is required,[404] although a defect in it may not necessarily be fatal.[405]

Mathematics and the standards of proof[406]

Since the standard of proof is concerned with the question of the amount of evidence that is required to persuade the trier of fact, there is an understandable tendency to attempt to apply the techniques of mathematics to its assessment. The temptation to count is an old one,[407] which still persists in some corroboration requirements, as will be seen in Chapter V. It has appealed most to those of a theoretical disposition. Bentham was attracted to it, influenced by the observation that wagering and insurance both attach numerical values to probabilities.[408] As the number of ways in which modern technology can assist judicial enquiry grows, it has become increasingly necessary for courts to adopt methods of combining evidence of mathematical precision with less exact sources of information.[409] It is also common knowledge that many important decisions in fields such as business, national defence, and the formation of economic policy are increasingly taken upon the basis of the mathematical modelling of probabilities and decision theory. Whatever the reason, there has been a burgeoning of attention on the question of the possibility of applying mathematical techniques to law.[410] Much of this debate is, to say the least, remote from the practical concerns of trial lawyers. It has been said that:[411]

The concept of 'probability' in the legal sense is certainly different from the mathematical concept; indeed, it is rare to find a situation in which the two usages co-exist although, when they do,

---

[402]   R v More [1987] 3 All ER 825, [1987] 1 WLR 1578; R v Flynn (1985) 82 Cr App Rep 319; R v Rowe [1990] Crim LR 344.

[403]   In R v Tirnaveanu [2007] EWCA Crim 1239, [2007] 4 All ER 301, [49], this was unexceptionable as the jury must have believed that if one of the methods had not been employed then the other must have been, although if this is not the case, then it seems that the jury should be directed to acquit in the absence of agreement as to method: see obiter dicta of Lamer J differing from the majority in Thatcher v R [1987] 1 SCR 652.

[404]   R v Mitchell (1994) 26 HLR 394.   [405]   R v Connolly and Kennett [2007] EWCA Crim 790, [47].

[406]   For practical guidance see Aitken and Taroni (2008) 12 E&P 181, and for critical analysis see Pundik ibid 303.   [407]   It appears in late Roman Law, Corpus Juris 4.20.9 (AD 334).

[408]   Treatise on Judicial Evidence (1825) ch 17.

[409]   DNA analysis presents particular problems, and has been used as a stalking horse in an attempt to encourage the use of Bayes theorem as a means of combination, but use of the theorem seems inappropriate for jury trial, and has been roundly condemned by the English courts: see R v Adams [1996] 2 Cr App Rep 467; R v Adams (No 2) (1997) The Times, 3 November; and R v Doheny and Adams [1997] 1 Cr App Rep 369. For recent debate, see 3 Int J of Evidence & Proof 1, and 4 id 246, 260 (1999, 2000). See also Redmayne (2002) 65 MLR 19.

[410]   Such techniques are canvassed in Cohen The Probable and The Provable (2nd edn, 1991); Eggleston Evidence, Proof and Probability (2nd edn, 1983); Finkelstein and Fairley (1970) 83 Harv LR 489; Tribe (1971) 84 Harv LR 1329, see also 1801 and 1810 for continuation of debate; Glanville Williams [1979] Crim LR 297, 340; Cohen [1980] Crim LR 91, and see 103 for a rejoinder by Glanville Williams; and Jackson (1980) 31 NILQ 223. The subject has generated massive theoretical attention in the United States: see the report of a symposium in (1986) 66 Boston ULR 377 running to more than five hundred pages, and another in (1991) 13 Cardozo LR 253, running to more than eight hundred.

[411]   Re JS (a minor) [1981] Fam 22, [1980] 1 All ER 1061; 29, 1066. See also R v Shepherd (1988) 85 ALR 387, 392 by Roden J: 'Degrees of probability and degrees of proof with which juries are concerned are rarely capable of expression in mathematical terms.'

the mathematical probability has to be taken into the assessment of probability in the legal sense and given its appropriate weight.

In that case, the Court of Appeal refused to 'transmute a mathematical probability into a forensic certainty' by determining the paternity of a child upon the basis of statistical blood grouping evidence, at least in the absence of a full investigation of all the surrounding circumstances.[412] One of the problems is that the proper foundation for the application of the mathematical techniques is rarely present. A striking example of this, and one that sparked off much American interest, is provided by *People v Collins*.[413] In that case, the trial judge admitted statistical evidence in an attempt to identify the accused with the perpetrators of the robbery in question. There was evidence that the guilty couple possessed six characteristics. A statistician was allowed to testify that the likelihood of their all being present in any couple was, upon certain assumptions, 12 million to one against. The accused couple possessed these six characteristics, and were found guilty. As was pointed out on appeal, this procedure was quite inappropriate. There was no basis for the assumptions of the likelihood of each of the characteristics occurring independently, and there was no ground for supposing that they were independent; indeed, there was every ground for supposing that they were not.[414] It will be extremely rare for the information required to make such estimates of probability to be available to a court. Nor should the court attempt to manufacture its own statistics where there is no evidence at all. A cautionary example here is provided by the opinion of Murphy J in *TNT Management Pty Ltd v Brooks*.[415] The claimant sought damages in respect of a road accident in which both drivers had been killed, and there was little evidence which was to blame. Murphy J took the view that it was too little. He was, however, prepared to uphold the claim on the basis that there were three possibilities: both to blame, claimant to blame, or defendant to blame. Since two of these favoured the claimant's claim and only one opposed it, the balance of probabilities was satisfied. It is not clear why he excluded the possibility of neither to blame. Quite apart from that, the procedure is obviously prone to cause injustice, for example in a case where only one of three injured employees caused the damage by his negligence in the course of his employment, but it is unknown which of them it was. In such a case, the odds of any one being an innocent victim are also two to one on, with the startling consequence that all three can succeed, although the whole calculation presupposes that one of them is not, in fact, entitled to do so.

If part of the difficulty is that there is usually an insufficient evidential basis for the mathematical exegesis, another is that the mathematical techniques are themselves controversial. Thus the statistical appendix to the judgment in *Collins*, which purported to substitute an accurate statistical analysis for the faulty methods proposed by the trial

---

[412] See also *McTear v Imperial Tobacco Ltd* 2005 2 SC 1, 2005 GWD 20–365, in which the court refused to find a causal link in the instant case between the consumption of cigarettes and the onset of lung cancer.

[413] 438 P 2d 33 (1968). For a further example scathingly analysed by Justice Posner, see *United States v Veysey* 334 F3d 600 (CA7, 2003).

[414] Exactly the same flaw appeared in the expert reasoning in the English case of *R v Clark* [2003] EWCA Crim 1020, in which it was assumed that two cot deaths in the same family were independent for the purposes of calculating the probabilities. In Australia see *R v Matthey* [2007] VSC 398, 177 ACR 470.

[415] (1979) 53 ALJR 267, the rest of the court decided the case upon the quite different basis that the evidence adduced was just sufficient to prove negligence.

judge, has itself been attacked as being mathematically unsound,[416] and the inapplicability of classical Pascalian probability to law is the whole theme of Cohen's book.

There will, of course, be some statistical evidence that does have a satisfactory foundation, and some issues to which that evidence is relevant. Such evidence will not automatically be excluded on the basis that it falls short of absolute scientific certainty.[417] Blood group evidence may be of that character. If a question arises as to the paternity of a child, it may be possible to establish that, if the husband of the mother is not the father, then it could be one in ten of the population. In such a case, the court must be wary of the alluring precision of the figures, and must not be seduced from the path of weighing together all of the circumstances; for example, the terms of the relationship between husband and wife, the opportunities and inclinations of the wife for extramarital intercourse, and the motives of the parties in making any allegations.[418] It will be a rare case where mathematical techniques will make a decisive contribution to the resolution of forensic uncertainty;[419] so trial judges must be circumspect in their directions.[420]

---

[416] Fairley and Mosteller (1974) 41 *U Chi LR* 242.

[417] *S v S* [1972] AC 24, [1970] 3 All ER 107; *R v Bracewell* (1978) 68 Cr App Rep 44.

[418] In *R v Chedzey* (1987) 30 ACR 451, in which there was little other evidence to show that the accused was the maker of a malicious telephone call, the court refused to uphold a conviction based on evidence that the automatic tracking procedure was 99.96 per cent accurate.

[419] But not unknown; fingerprint or other forensic matching is often decisive: see further 50.

[420] See *R v Smith* (1998) 104 ACR 1, in which the trial judge weakened a strong case with plenty of other evidence by remarking that the DNA evidence was enough in itself to prove the case beyond reasonable doubt.

IV

THE FUNCTIONS OF THE
JUDGE AND JURY

A due appreciation of the respective functions of the judge[1] and jury[2] is essential to a proper understanding of the law of evidence, notwithstanding reduced incidence of jury trial, largely because of its influence on the conceptual basis and concepts of the common law. The general rule of separation of functions of judge and jury is discussed in Section 1, and some of the more direct methods of judicial control are considered in Section 2. No discussion of the law of evidence in criminal cases will, however, be completely satisfactory until we have some idea of the extent to which the average jury understands the directions that the law requires the judge to give, and whether jurors are as imperceptive, ignorant, or prejudiced as some of the rules of evidence suppose. Many such issues could be resolved satisfactorily only by controlled, and secret, monitoring of the deliberations of real juries in real cases. Unfortunately,[3] such monitoring would amount to contempt of court,[4] and that view has been held compatible with the European Convention on Human Rights.[5] Any discussion with a third party before verdict is liable to result in a conviction being quashed.[6] Recourse must, at present,[7] be had to simulations and generally less reliable methods of obtaining the information needed to provide a basis for understanding and improving the law of evidence.[8] The government seems to have accorded low priority to reform of s 8.[9]

---

[1] Who must be, and be seen to be, completely independent of the parties: *Morrison v AWG Group Ltd* [2006] EWCA Civ 6, [2006] 1 All ER 967.

[2] To whom are often assimilated magistrates as triers of fact, as in *R v Uddin* [2006] EWHC 1523 (Admin), [14].

[3] But for support for the current rule, see Zander (2005) The Times, 19 April.

[4] Contempt of Court Act 1981, s 8, invoked in *Attorney-General v Seckerson* [2009] EWHC 1023 (Admin).

[5] *R v Mirza* [2004] UKHL 2, [2004] 1 AC 1118; *Attorney-General v Scotcher* [2005] UKHL 36, [2005] 3 All ER 1. A juror will not, however, be in contempt if he discloses deliberations only to the court, whether directly or indirectly.   [6] *R v F* [2009] EWCA Crim 8051.

[7] Although the very first recommendation of the Royal Commission on Criminal Justice Cm 2263 (1993) was that s 8 be amended to permit proper scientific research into the working of juries.

[8] For a rich source of references to studies in many different jurisdictions, see Young [2003] *Crim LR* 665.

[9] The Department of Constitutional Affairs issued a consultation paper *Jury Research and Impropriety* in 2005, but no final report has yet been published.

SECTION 1. THE GENERAL RULE

The general rule is that questions of domestic[10] law, and procedural issues,[11] must be determined by the judge and questions of fact[12] by the jury, as stated by Lord Bingham in *R v Wang*:[13]

The judge directs, or instructs, the jury on the law relevant to the counts in the indictment, and makes clear that the jury must accept and follow his legal rulings. But he also directs the jury that the decision of all factual questions, including the application of the law as expounded to the facts as they find them to be, is a matter for them alone.

In South Africa it has been held an abuse of process to call expert witnesses on issues of law,[14] although it cannot be denied that it is often difficult to distinguish issues of fact upon which experts may testify from those of law where they may not.[15]

There are, nevertheless, some special cases as well as exceptions to the general rule.

SOME SPECIAL CASES

Construction

The meaning of an ordinary word of the English language is not a question of law. The proper construction of a statute is a question of law.[16]

Lord Reid said this on the hearing of an appeal in a criminal case from a Divisional Court, but his remarks also apply to trial by jury.[17] The appeal concerned the meaning of 'insulting behaviour' in s 5 of the Public Order Act 1936. Lord Reid continued:

If the context shows that a word is used in an unusual sense the court will determine in other words what that unusual sense is. But here there is in my opinion no question of the word 'insulting' being used in an unusual sense. It is for the tribunal which decides the case to consider, not as law but as fact, whether in the whole circumstances the words of the statute do or do not as a matter of ordinary usage of the English language cover or apply to the facts which have been proved.

Concern has been expressed lest this gives the jury too free a hand, but account must be taken of a number of limiting factors. The proper construction of a statute may require a

---

[10] See ch 16 below for proof of foreign law.   [11] *R v Currie* [2007] EWCA Crim 926.

[12] On the breathtaking assumption that a clear distinction is feasible either as a matter of theory, or of application; for discussion of the complexities, see *Smith v R* [2000] 1 WLR 1644, PC. This problem accounts for much of the current concern with the complexity of jury direction: see Auld *Review of the Criminal Courts of England and Wales* (2001) ch 11, paras 41–55, although the more radical revision there recommended was rejected by the government in *Justice for All* (2002) para 4.50.

[13] [2005] UKHL 9, [2005] 1 All 782, [8]; cf, in Canada, *R v Gunning* 2005 SCC 27, [2005] 1 SCR 627.

[14] *De Klerk v Scheepers* 2005 (5) SA 244 (former head of state as to effect of new constitution).

[15] *R (LB of Hackney) v Rottenberg* [2007] EWHC 166 (Admin) [20] (whether noise amounted to statutory nuisance); *Homepace Ltd v Sita South East Ltd* [2008] EWCA Civ 1 [30] (construction of contractual words by expert arbitrator).

[16] *Brutus v Cozens* [1973] AC 854, 861. Conversely, the effect of a judgment is not a matter of fact: *Customs and Excise Comrs v DFS Furniture Co Ltd* [2004] EWCA Civ 243.

[17] *R v Kirk* [2006] EWCA Crim 725 ('obscene'), and such an allocation was held compatible with Art 10 of the European Convention.

judge to do more than decide whether words are used in an unusual sense, and if so, what that sense is.[18] He may have to choose between a variety of possible meanings, including ordinary meanings, of which there are sometimes more than one, and this will result in a direction on the law. Even when the sole question is the ordinary meaning of a word, the fact that it is a matter for the jury does not mean that it has an unfettered choice, for Lord Reid recognized the possibility of an appeal on the ground that 'no tribunal acquainted with the ordinary use of the language could reasonably reach that decision'. The judge may therefore direct the jury that it is not open to it to give a particular meaning to ordinary words because that would be perverse.[19]

Defamation

Endeavours to restrict the role of the jury in cases of criminal libel were the precipitating cause of Fox's Libel Act 1792. It provides that, in criminal prosecutions for libel, the jury shall, after direction by the judge on the law, give a general verdict upon the whole matter. In consequence of this statute, it has come to be the practice for the judge to determine whether the document in question is capable of bearing the meaning alleged by the prosecution, while the jury decides whether it does in fact amount to a criminal libel. This has been said to be because the intention of the parties is always a question for the jury, and the meaning of the document is part of that intention;[20] the same procedure is adopted in civil cases, in which the intention of the parties is, to say the least, not so important as on a criminal charge.[21] It is therefore best to regard the established practice as a compromise. Now that the Civil Procedure Rules allow summary judgment in all cases, it has been determined that the judge can, even in defamation cases, pre-empt a jury trial if he takes the view that a particular decision would be perverse.[22]

EXCEPTIONS

Reasonableness

The reasonableness of a particular belief or course of conduct is essentially a question of fact, and, as such, normally has to be determined by the jury,[23] but, in certain civil cases, it must be decided by the judge, although he may leave subsidiary issues upon which the

---

[18] Although in the case of ordinary words, the judge is expected to employ his own knowledge, he may consider evidence to determine whether and what unusual sense is being employed: *Marquis Camden v IRC* [1914] 1 KB 641, 650.

[19] See *R v Bown* [2003] EWCA Crim 1989, [2004] 1 Cr App Rep 151.

[20] Lord Abinger CJ in *Morrell v Firth* (1838) 3 M & W 402, 404–5.

[21] *Nevill v Fine Arts and General Insurance Co* [1897] AC 68.

[22] *Alexander v Arts Council of Wales* [2001] EWCA Civ 514, [2001] 4 All ER 205 (no viable issue of malice), explaining *Safeway Stores plc v Tate* [2001] QB 1120, [2001] 4 All ER 193 (issue of defamatory meaning not excluded). But if his doing so is resisted, the party so resisting cannot then on appeal seek to argue that the decision of jury so secured is indeed perverse: *McPhilemy v Times Newspapers* [2001] EWCA Civ 871. If there is a disputed issue of fact, any evaluation must still be made by the jury: *Spencer v Sillitoe* [2003] EWHC 1651 (QB).

[23] But not when it is part of a duty of care, breach of which constitutes the crime charged, *R v Evans* [2009] EWCA Crim 650 (gross negligence manslaughter).

question of reasonableness ultimately depends to the jury. In a claim for malicious prosecution, the question of whether the defendant had a reasonable and probable cause for
initiating the criminal proceedings must be answered by the judge.[24] It is also the duty of
the judge to determine whether the terms of a covenant in restraint of trade are reasonably
necessary for the protection of the covenantee;[25] he may require the jury to find relevant
facts concerning the information on which the defendant acted in the first case,[26] and the
nature of the covenantee's business in the second.

Facts affecting the admissibility of evidence[27]

There are always some conditions precedent to the admissibility of evidence. Thus, an
oath, or its equivalent, and competency, are conditions precedent to admitting viva voce
evidence; a search, to secondary evidence of lost writings; and stamping, to certain written
instruments;[28] and consanguinity or affinity in the declarant, to declarations of deceased
relatives.[29] The judge alone has to decide whether the condition has been fulfilled. If the
proof is by witnesses, he must decide on their credibility. If counter-evidence is offered, he
must receive it before he decides; he has no right to ask the opinion of the jury on the fact
of a condition precedent.[30]

Other examples of the application of the rule are afforded by cases in which the accused
objects to the reception of a confession on the ground that it does not satisfy the conditions
of s 76 of the Police and Criminal Evidence Act 1984, or a witness claims privilege.[31] In all
such instances, the judge, and not the jury, must determine disputed facts, and the entirely
separate nature of these preliminary or incidental issues was emphasized by the old practice under which witnesses who deposed to them were required to take a different oath,
known as the 'voir dire', from that sworn by those giving evidence which was to be submitted to the jury. The trial of the incidental issues is often called 'a trial within a trial'.

It is sometimes impossible to decide the question of admissibility without disclosing
the evidence on which the dispute turns. If it is alleged that a confession was made under
pressure, the question can often be settled only by considering the terms of the accused's
statements, and the jury could scarcely help being influenced by them even if they were
to conclude that the surrounding circumstances rendered the confession inadmissible.[32]
As Lord Mustill stated in *Wallace and Fuller v R*,[33] the tasks of judge and jury in relation to disputed confessions, although theoretically distinct, are in practice very similar.

---

[24] *Herniman v Smith* [1938] AC 305, [1938] 1 All ER 1 (malicious prosecution); *Ward v Chief Constable of West Midlands* (1997) The Times, 13 December (false imprisonment).

[25] *Dowden and Pook Ltd v Pook* [1904] 1 KB 45.

[26] Although not where those facts themselves involve issues of law: *Ward v Chief Constable of West Midlands Police* (n24).

[27] See also Chapter I, Section 2. For thorough, if, from the English point of view, rather elaborate, discussions of this subject, see Maguire and Epstein (1926) 40 *Harv LR* 392, and Morgan (1929) 43 *Harv LR* 165. See
also Morgan *Some Problems of Proof*, ch 3.

[28] For an example, see *Bartlett v Smith* (1843) 11 M & W 483.

[29] Admissible under a common law exception to the rule against hearsay on genealogical issues (now
applicable only in criminal cases).

[30] *Doe d Jenkins v Davies* (1847) 10 QB 314, 323, Lord Denman CJ.

[31] *Stace v Griffith* (1869) LR 2 PC 420, 427–8.

[32] Lord Goddard CJ in *R v Reynolds* [1950] 1 KB 606, [1950] 1 All ER 335; 608, 336.

[33] [1997] 1 Cr App Rep 396, 407F.

The Privy Council has since decided that in cases involving a factual dispute[34] between prosecution and defence no reference should be made in the presence of the jury to the substance of the matter determined on the voir dire, or even its result.[35] It is, however, desirable that brief reasons be given in the absence of the jury to facilitate appeal.[36]

Given the validity of the reasons for the rule, its application has given rise to three practical difficulties: whether the evidence of facts constituting a condition precedent to admissibility should invariably be heard in the absence of the jury; the course to be adopted when the facts are identical with the facts in issue; and the distribution of the functions between judge and jury in relation to confessions.

Absence of the jury

Two settled rules in criminal proceedings are first, that the accused must be present throughout the entire trial of an indictable offence,[37] and second, that all the evidence should generally be given in the presence of the jury. Some qualifications are obviously necessary so far as the second of these rules is concerned, otherwise the accused might be prejudiced, and there is no doubt that the judge has power[38] to dismiss the jury while hearing arguments on the admissibility of evidence or while holding a trial within a trial.

The first rule requires the judge to hear all evidence in court, although occasionally in the absence of the jury, when an exception to the second rule applies.[39] It has accordingly been held that the judge should neither retire to his private room in order to question a child to determine its competence,[40] nor receive there the maker of a statement admitted as hearsay on the basis of being kept away by fear, to determine the true reason for his failure to testify.[41]

The second rule gives rise to difficulty where there is dispute about the competence of a witness, or as to a condition for admissibility of evidence. The orthodox rule prescribes that, in such a case, the jury should stay to hear what it will eventually have to consider in assessing the evidence. In the case of a child, the practice of inquisition[42] by the judge in the presence of the jury to determine competency was justified in *R v N*[43] as follows:

One reason is that although the trial judge must decide whether the evidence of the child should be admitted in the first place, if it is admitted, it is in the end for the jury to decide whether to attach any weight to it. Therefore the jury should see and observe the basic enquiry into the child's competence as a potential witness: it is an important part of the relevant material which

---

[34] But not if the dispute is as to the effect of agreed facts, *Foster and Williams v R* [2007] UKPC 20, [29].

[35] *Mitchell v R* [1998] AC 695, [1998] 2 Cr App Rep 35; 704B, 43C.

[36] *Thongjai v R* [1998] AC 54, at 59D. The same reasoning was applied in Australia in *Webb v R* (1994) 13 WAR 257.

[37] *Lawrence v R* [1933] AC 699, 708. There are exceptions, for example in cases in which the accused renders his continued presence in court impossible by his violence: see *R v Browne* (1906) 70 JP 472.

[38] Even over the objection of the defence, see *R v Hendry* (1988) 88 Cr App Rep 187, overruling, on this point, *R v Anderson* (1929) 21 Cr App Rep 178. See also *R v Davis* [1990] Crim LR 860.

[39] See *R v Preston* [1994] 2 AC 130, [1993] 4 All ER 638, in which the House of Lords deprecated the course of a trial in which considerable periods were spent in argument before the judge from which both the accused and his solicitors were excluded.   [40] *R v Dunne* (1929) 99 LJKB 117, under the old law.

[41] *R v Setz-Dempsey* (1994) 98 Cr App Rep 23. The witness offered an innocent and wholly different explanation for his late arrival.

[42] That is, a non-adversarial procedure in which counsel are not involved.

[43] (1992) 95 Cr App Rep 256. See also *R v Reynolds* (1950) 34 Cr App Rep 60; *R v Khan* (1981) 73 Cr App Rep 190, under the old law.

should be disclosed to them. Another reason is that the child is likely to be damaged by constant reiteration of the same material before different groups of people at court; first the judge and counsel and then, again, before the judge, counsel, and the assembled jury, as well, in each case, as other officials of the court and members of the public.

Sometimes the evidence relating to competence is that of a third party. The same principles apply, and in some cases where such evidence has been tendered on the preliminary issue in the absence of the jury, it has been repeated in open court at the trial proper.[44] The advantage is that the jury is not then exposed to possibly prejudicial material in relation to a witness or evidence held incompetent or inadmissible. It was, however, held in *R v Robinson*[45] that such evidence could be admitted on a voir dire to determine the competence of a witness for the prosecution, but should not be called at the trial,[46] as the effect of the evidence would be merely to bolster the testimony of the witness. It is hard to reconcile this view with the preceding cases, none of which was cited to the court.

It is submitted that the best view is that such evidence should normally be tendered in the presence of the jury, but if it is likely to be especially prejudicial, the judge should have a discretion to hear it on a voir dire, and the trial then continue according to the ordinary rules as to the admissibility of evidence impugning or supporting the credit of a witness or piece of evidence.[47]

Identity of preliminary fact with fact in issue

In principle, as once stated by Lord Denman CJ:[48]

...neither the admissibility nor the effect of the evidence is altered by the accident that the fact which is for the judge as a condition precedent is the same fact which is for the jury in the issue.

This course has two disadvantages when the preliminary question of fact to be determined by the judge as a condition precedent is identical with the issue that has ultimately to be decided by the jury. First, it means that the judge has to sum up to the jury on an issue that he has already decided; second, it may mean that all the evidence given on the voir dire will have to be repeated, certainly when the trial within a trial is held in the absence of the jury. So, sometimes, courts rejected contrary evidence, and allowed evidence to be adduced once those tendering it had adduced sufficient evidence for it to be considered by the jury.[49]

On practical grounds, that course may be preferable, but there are cases, such as those involving the reception of documentary evidence in which all that the judge can require, as a condition precedent to the admissibility of a copy, is prima facie evidence of the existence of a genuine original.[50]

---

[44] *R v Mackenzie* (1993) 96 Cr App Rep 98; *R v Dunphy* (1993) 98 Cr App Rep 393. See also *R v Setz-Dempsey* (1994) 98 Cr App Rep 23.

[45] (1994) 98 Cr App Rep 370.   [46] At least in the absence of a specific attack on the witness.

[47] This passage has been endorsed in Canada in *R v Ferguson* (1996) 112 CCC (3d) 342, 357. In the United States, r 104(c) of the United States Federal Rules reads: 'Hearings on the admissibility of confessions shall in all cases be conducted out of the hearing of the jury. Hearings on other preliminary matters shall be so conducted when the interests of justice require.'   [48] (1847) 10 QB 314, 323–4.

[49] As in *Hitchins v Eardley* (1871) LR 2 P & D 248.

[50] See e.g. *Stowe v Querner* (1870) LR 5 Exch 155.

A similar situation would arise in a case in which the defendant contends that the document on which the claimant is relying is forged. So too the question whether a tape recording was the original: being one that must ultimately be determined by the jury, the judge need do no more than decide whether there is sufficient evidence to leave the issue to it.[51]

Such cases must be carefully distinguished from those in which the preliminary issue is whether a document has been lost, or which of two originals is the proper one to place before the jury; there the question of fact to be decided by the judge is not the same as that which has to be decided by the jury.[52] Then the judge must hear evidence on both sides on the voir dire and come to a definite decision on the preliminary issue instead of being content with prima facie evidence from the party arguing for admissibility.

Confessions

If disputed, it is for the judge to decide whether there is prima facie evidence that a confession was made, leaving the jury to determine whether it was in fact made.[53] In respect of many other issues relating to the admissibility of confessions, the common law has been superseded by the provisions of s 76 of the Police and Criminal Evidence Act 1984, to be explained in more detail in Chapter XIV. Only the division of responsibilities between judge and jury will be considered here. It is for the prosecution to prove beyond reasonable doubt that the confession has not been obtained by oppression,[54] or in consequence of anything likely to make it unreliable.[55] These issues must, as a result of the wording of the relevant provision[56] of the Police and Criminal Evidence Act 1984, be resolved by a trial within a trial before a confession can be admitted into evidence.[57] This represents a change in English[58] law,[59] and can lead to a 'pantomime',[60] if the accused chooses to withhold his attack upon it until the trial. The judge can still achieve much the same result as under the old law by exercising his discretion at common law[61] to direct the jury to disregard the confession, or to discharge it.[62] In most cases, the accused will seek determination of the admissibility of a confession at a trial on the voir dire. If he does not do so, there is now a statutory power for the court to initiate such a trial of its own motion.[63] In *R v Brophy*,[64] the House of Lords decided that if the accused should, on the voir dire, adduce

---

[51] *R v Robson: R v Harris* [1972] 2 All ER 699, [1972] 1 WLR 651.

[52] *Boyle v Wiseman* (1855) 11 Exch 360.

[53] *R v Roberts* [1954] 2 QB 329, [1953] 2 All ER 340; *Ajodha v The State* [1982] AC 204, [1981] 2 All ER 193; *R v Mulligan* [1955] OR 240; *R v Gleeson* [1975] Qd R 399.   [54] Section 76(2)(a).

[55] Section 76(2)(b).   [56] Section 76. The same applies to s 78 in relation to exclusion by discretion.

[57] *R v Sat-Bhambra* (1988) 88 Cr App Rep 55, 62. The same applies to summary trial before magistrates: *R v Liverpool Juvenile Court, ex p R* [1988] QB 1, [1987] 2 All ER 668; but not to a preliminary examination: *R v Oxford City Justices, ex p Berry* [1988] QB 507, [1987] 1 All ER 1244.

[58] It was already the case at common law in South Africa: see *S v Nieuwoudt (No 3)* 1985 (4) SA 510.

[59] For the previous position, see *Ajodha v The State* [1982] AC 204, [1981] 2 All ER 193; 223, 202.

[60] As it was judicially described in *R v Millard* [1987] Crim LR 196.

[61] Expressly preserved by the Police and Criminal Evidence Act 1984, s 82(3).

[62] *R v Sat-Bhambra* (n57).

[63] Police and Criminal Evidence Act 1984, s 76(3), following the recommendation of the Criminal Law Revision Committee, Cmnd 4991, para 54, and following the old rule, see *Ajodha v The State* [1982] AC 204, at 222, [1981] 2 All ER 193, 202. It is the same in Australia: see *McPherson v R* (1981) 55 ALJR 594.

[64] [1982] AC 476, [1981] 2 All ER 705, although it is not clear that in *Brophy* there was an extrajudicial confession confirmed on the voir dire, this ought, in principle, to be immaterial.

evidence of the truth of a charge against him, such a confession would, nevertheless, be inadmissible at his trial if he should plead not guilty at that stage. Where such evidence is led by the prosecution, there is an unedifying conflict between the decision of the Court of Criminal Appeal in *R v Hammond*[65] that such evidence could be elicited on the voir dire, and the decision of the majority of the Privy Council in *Wong Kam-ming v R* that it could not. Now that one of the conditions for excluding a confession is the existence of circumstances likely to render a confession unreliable, the case for excluding the evidence has, if anything, become even stronger.[66] The statute does not, however, deal with any of the other matters that exercised the courts in these cases. One of these is the extent to which statements made by the accused on the voir dire could be used against him, either as an admission or as a previous inconsistent statement. The view that prevailed before the Act was that, if the confession were held to be inadmissible, then no later use could be made of admissions relevant to the issue of admissibility that had been made by the accused on the voir dire. In *R v Brophy*, the House of Lords regarded this as fundamental:[67]

If such evidence, being relevant, were admissible at the substantive trial, an accused person would not enjoy the complete freedom that he ought to have at the voir dire to contest the admissibility of his previous statements. It is of the first importance for the administration of justice that an accused person should feel completely free to give evidence at the voir dire of any improper methods by which a confession or admission has been extracted from him, for he can almost never make an effective challenge of its admissibility without giving evidence himself. He is thus virtually compelled to give evidence at the voir dire, and if his evidence were admissible at the substantive trial, the result might be a significant impairment of his so-called right to silence at the trial.

This ban on the use of a statement made on the voir dire applied both to use in chief by the prosecution as an admission, or use in cross-examination as a previous inconsistent statement to impeach the accused's credit, whether the trial was by judge alone or by judge and jury.[68] The force of this reasoning seems undiminished by the passage of the 1984 Act. It is not quite so clear that it is equally unaffected by the statutory language. It should be noted that most of s 76 follows the recommendations and draft provisions proposed by the Criminal Law Revision Committee in its 11th Report.[69] The question of the use of admissions made by the accused on the voir dire had not by 1972 come into much prominence,[70] and was not considered by the Committee, so its draft bill contained no explicit provision on the matter. The problem is created by the impact of s 76(1), which in effect provides that a confession may not be given in evidence unless the prosecution is able to negate the circumstances mentioned in s 76(2). An admission made by the accused on the voir dire would not appear either to have been obtained by oppression or in circumstances likely to render it unreliable. It would thus seem to be admissible under s 76(1) as a

---

65 [1941] 3 All ER 318, 28 Cr App Rep 84, supported in this view by the Supreme Court of Canada in *De Clercq v R* [1968] SCR 902; by the Queensland Court of Appeal in *R v Semyraha* [2000] QCA 303; and by Lord Hailsham in *Wong Kam-ming v R* [1980] AC 247, [1979] 1 All ER 939.

66 *Wong Kam-ming* was endorsed on this point by *R v Davis* [1990] Crim LR 860.

67 (n64); 481, 709.   68 482, 710. For criticism of this result, see Pattenden (1983) 32 *ICLQ* 812.

69 Cmnd 4991, paras 53–69, and draft bill, cl 2.

70 The question had been aired in Australia in an article by Neasey (1960) 34 *ALJ* 110 and see *R v Monks* (1955), an unreported Tasmanian case referred to in the article; *R v Gray* [1965] Qd R 373; *R v Wright* [1969] SASR 256; *R v Banner* [1970] VR 240.

matter of ordinary statutory interpretation. It is, however, submitted that there is nothing in the policy of the new Act that justifies such a departure from the existing position,[71] and that a court will be tempted to exclude any such admissions in most ordinary cases as a matter of its discretionary control of a criminal trial.[72] It must, however, be accepted that this is an unsatisfactory solution, and one explicitly rejected by the House of Lords in *Brophy*.[73] It has, however, now been accepted, at least where the dispute is essentially between co-accused, in relation to the analogous use of a retracted guilty plea.[74]

It should be noted that the drafting of s 76(2)(b) prevents[75] this problem from being eliminated by the simple expedient of admitting the disputed confession at the trial whenever the accused admits its truth at the voir dire.[76]

To the extent that prohibition of reference to statements made on the voir dire has been justified by its impact upon the accused's right to silence at the trial,[77] it has been weakened by the abridgement of that right by the passage of s 35 of the Criminal Justice and Public Order Act 1994. It has been suggested[78] that the discretionary solution advanced above is thus now less eligible, and justification for such prohibition found only in protection of the accused from inhibition in making a justified challenge to an alleged confession.

The resolution of this question must also determine the case in which the admission is used as a previous inconsistent statement in order to discredit the accused's testimony. In *Brophy*, the House of Lords felt that there was no difference between this situation and that where the evidence was led by the prosecution. It was settled in the old law that the terms of the excluded confession could not be used for this purpose,[79] and in *Wong Kam-ming*,[80] the same reasoning was applied to admissions made on the voir dire. No explicit reference has been made to this situation in any subsequent official proposals for reform.[81]

It had also become quite settled in the old law that, when the admissibility of the confession had been challenged unsuccessfully on the voir dire, counsel retained the right to cross-examine at the trial proper the witnesses who had previously given evidence at the voir dire.[82] It should be noted that the judge retains his control over the evidence ultimately to be submitted to the jury throughout the trial. Accordingly, if having admitted a confession on evidence given in the absence of the jury, the judge concludes, in the light of subsequent evidence, that the confession ought not to have been admitted, he may either

---

[71] It should be noted that, in *R v Mushtaq* [2005] UKHL 25, [2005] 3 All ER 885, Lord Hutton, [16], adopted the view, apparently without doubt, that nothing against his interests said by the defendant on a voir dire will ever be admitted at the trial.

[72] Expressly preserved by Police and Criminal Evidence Act 1984, s 82(3). It might alternatively choose to exercise the statutory discretion provided by s 78.

[73] 483, 710. But see *Burns v R* (1975) 132 CLR 258, 263.

[74] *R v Johnson* [2007] EWCA Crim 1651. In *R v Darwish* [2006] 1 NZLR 688 applied also to statements on bail applications.   [75] In its distinction between hypothetical and actual reliability.

[76] *R v Cox* [1991] Crim LR 276.

[77] See the last sentence of the extract from *Brophy*, quoted above (n67).

[78] By Mirfield who first exposed the problem in [1995] Crim LR 612, 617. See also his *Silence, Confessions and Illegally Obtained Evidence* (1997), 71–5.   [79] *R v Treacy* [1944] 2 All ER 229, 30 Cr App Rep 93.

[80] (n65); 259, 945.

[81] Neither in the 1984 nor 2003 legislation, nor in related reports. The full range of authority both in the Commonwealth and United States was rehearsed in *R v Ram* [2007] NZCA 166, [2007] 3 NZLR 322.

[82] *R v Murray* [1951] 1 KB 391, [1950] 2 All ER 925. See also *Jackson v R* (1962) 108 CLR 591; *People (A-G) v Ainscough* [1960] IR 136 (unrepresented accused, having cross-examined on the voir dire, must be told of his right to cross-examine again at the trial).

direct the jury to disregard it or, where there is no other sufficient evidence against the accused, direct an acquittal or, presumably, direct a new trial,[83] although the circumstances in which he will decide to take any of these courses are likely to be rare, especially now that this is no more than a matter of the judge's residual discretion.[84] In *R v Mushtaq*,[85] the House of Lords decided, by a majority,[86] that even after the trial judge has determined on a voir dire that a confession is admissible, this conclusion remains in issue at the trial, and that the jury should not rely upon a confession, even if they believe it to be true, if they also find that the conditions laid down in s 76(2) have not been negated beyond reasonable doubt. Although earlier authority had vacillated on this issue,[87] and despite different views being adopted in other common law jurisdictions,[88] the majority felt that the emphasis placed by the European Court of Human Rights on the privilege against self-incrimination was decisive: in short, that it would be incompatible with the Convention for a court to prevent the jury from disregarding a confession it believed had been obtained in breach of the conditions of s 76, and further that it should be positively directed so to disregard it. It was nevertheless claimed, somewhat hollowly, that this did not impinge on the general principle of division of functions between judge and jury in this area, that admissibility is for the judge, and reliability for the jury.

It was also established in *Wong Kam-ming v R* that even when a confession was admitted after a voir dire, other admissions made at it by the accused could not be led against him. The problem is similar to that discussed above in relation to cases in which the confession was excluded after a voir dire, except that even under the old law the argument for exclusion was recognized as weaker when the confession was admitted.[89] The statutory interpretation argument also applies more strongly in favour of admissibility. If, as submitted above, exclusion can now, after the statute, only be by way of discretion, then that discretion may be more rarely exercised in favour of the accused when the confession has been admitted after a voir dire. If so, this will be consistent with the general admission of such statements to impeach the credit of the accused by putting them to him in cross-examination. This use of statements made by the accused at the voir dire, and inconsistent with his testimony at the trial, was allowed by the Privy Council in *Wong Kam-ming* in cases in which the confession was admitted.[90] Under the new provisions, and in the light of the effect of the Criminal Justice and Public Order Act 1994 mentioned above, this reasoning will be stronger still.

It will have been noted that a distinction has been drawn between cases in which the accused denies that any confession was made, and those in which he asserts that it was made only as a result of improper pressure. In the latter case alone is there an issue to be tried on the voir dire; in real life, the situation will be less clear-cut. The accused may both deny some material parts of the confession, and assert that the whole was obtained by

---

[83] Only the first two possibilities were mentioned by Lord MacDermott in *R v Murphy* [1965] NI 138, 144. See also *Cornelius v R* (1936) 55 CLR 235.

[84] See 181.   [85] (n71); endorsed by the Privy Council in *Charles v R* [2007] UKPC 47, [14].

[86] Lord Hutton dissented.

[87] Cf *R v Bass* [1953] 1 QB 680 (direction to disregard); *Chan Wei Keung v R* [1967] 2 AC 160 (direction that goes only to weight).

[88] See, in Australia, *Basto v R* (1954) 91 CLR 628; in Canada, *R v McAloon* [1959] OR 441; in the United States, *Lego v Toomey* (1972) 404 US 477.   [89] (n65); 258, 944.

[90] 260, 946, subject only to the provisions of the Criminal Procedure Act 1865, s 4, discussed in Chapter VI.

improper pressure, or he may admit having signed a statement but complain that he was wrongly induced to do so. These more complicated situations were considered in *Ajodha v The State*.[91] The Privy Council held there to be no difference between obtaining a confession by improper means, and so inducing its acknowledgement. In both it was appropriate to hold a trial on the voir dire. The only situation in which there is no issue to be tried on the voir dire is that in which the accused simply denies making or acknowledging the statement.[92] If the accused denies having made a statement, and there is[93] also an issue of mistreatment by the police to force him to confess,[94] he is entitled to have the latter determined first on a voir dire.[95]

Occasionally the voir dire is conducted only after the prosecution has opened its case at the trial proper. In such a case, it seems that the trial judge may evaluate the evidence given on the voir dire in the light of the evidence thus far tendered or elicited at the trial proper.[96]

The burden and standard of proof[97]

As noted in Chapter III, decisions on the question of which party bears the burden of establishing a particular issue are generally decisions on the substantive law. Decisions as to which party bears the burden of establishing a fact constituting a condition precedent to the admissibility of an item of evidence belong to the law of evidence. There is, however, very little authority on the subject, no doubt because, as a matter of common sense, the conditions of admissibility have to be established by those alleging that they exist.

It is settled that the burden of proving the facts constituting the condition precedent to the admissibility of confessions[98] and dying declarations[99] is borne by the person seeking to tender them in evidence. These items of evidence are admissible as exceptions to the rule against hearsay, and it is reasonable to suppose that the burden of establishing the facts rendering hearsay admissible is always borne by the party tendering the evidence.

It was held in *R v Yacoob*[100] that the persuasive burden of establishing the competence of its witnesses beyond reasonable doubt is borne by the prosecution, although the evidential burden of raising the issue is naturally upon the accused. In the case of a claim to privilege by a witness, the burden of establishing the privilege would presumably be borne by the party calling the witness. In England, it has been held that there is no burden on disputed issues of fact when the question of the exclusion of evidence by discretion is being tried on a voir dire,[101] although the reasoning is questionable.[102]

---

[91] [1982] AC 204, [1981] 2 All ER 193.   [92] See also *MacPherson v R* (1981) 147 CLR 512, 37 ALR 81.
[93] Which need not be raised by evidence adduced by the accused, but may arise from the prosecution's own evidence, or be put in cross-examination to prosecution witnesses.
[94] Or otherwise to incriminate himself: *Timothy v State* [2001] 1 WLR 485, PC (reveal whereabouts of weapon).   [95] *Thongjai v R* (n36).
[96] *R v Tyrer* (1989) 90 Cr App Rep 446.
[97] For comprehensive discussion, and a different solution, see Pattenden 125 *LQR* 79 (2009).
[98] Police and Criminal Evidence Act 1984, s 76(2). A statute putting the persuasive burden in respect of one aspect of this matter onto the accused has been condemned as unconstitutional in South Africa: *S v Zuma* 1995 (2) SA 642.   [99] *R v Jenkins* (1869) LR 1 CCR 187, 192.
[100] (1981) 72 Cr App Rep 313.
[101] *Re Saifi* [2001] 4 All ER 168, [2001] 1 WLR 1135, [59]. In Australia, it is borne by the defence: *MacPherson v R* (n92), 519 (threats); *R v Gudgeon* (1995) 133 ALR 379, 390 (deception).
[102] Pattenden (n97).

As also noted in Chapter III, there are two standards of proof according to which facts may have to be established: proof on a balance of probabilities, the standard appropriate to civil cases, and proof beyond reasonable doubt, the standard demanded of the prosecution in criminal cases. Where the issue is one that must be decided once and for all by the judge, it would seem proper to hold that, in criminal cases when the evidence is tendered by the prosecution, such fact must be proved beyond reasonable doubt, but when tendered by the defence[103] or in civil cases when tendered by either party, the preliminary fact must be proved to the satisfaction of the judge on a preponderance of probability. The English rules on confessions,[104] and the authorities on dying declarations[105] and proof of handwriting tendered for comparative purposes,[106] bear out the above views, at least so far as the standard of proof demanded of the prosecution on the voir dire is concerned.

It has, however, been held in Australia with regard to both confessions[107] and dying declarations,[108] and generally in Scotland,[109] that the prosecution needs to establish facts justifying admissibility only on the balance of probabilities. The English rule at least has the merit of ensuring that the utmost care is taken before a confession is placed before the jury, and this is particularly important because, in many cases, to admit a confession is virtually to ensure the conviction of the accused.[110] Where the judge merely has to be satisfied that there is prima facie evidence—for example, that a confession was made, that a previous consistent statement amounted to a complaint, or that a tape recording was the original—he need hear evidence only from the party tendering the confession, previous consistent statement, or tape recording. In *R v Robson*,[111] the Court of Appeal regarded this as equivalent to a requirement that such evidence need reach only the standard of the balance of probabilities for fear of usurping the function of the jury. It is submitted that the better view is that the requirement is no different from that applying to the satisfaction of an evidential burden, namely whether the evidence, if believed by the jury, would be sufficient to prove the matter asserted to the standard required to satisfy the legal burden, namely beyond reasonable doubt, when borne by the prosecution in a criminal case. This involves no usurpation of the function of the jury since the jury is free not to believe the evidence, and may well not do so after taking into account its contravention by the other side. Such a view is in complete harmony with the ordinary rules on the discharge of an evidential burden, the determination of whether or not there is a case to answer, and the proper distribution of functions between judge and jury.[112]

103 This view was approved in *R v Mattey and Queeley* [1995] 2 Cr App Rep 409.

104 Police and Criminal Evidence Act 1984, s 76. See also *R v Pickett* (1975) 31 CRNS 239.

105 *R v Jenkins* (n99); in *R v Booker* (1924) 88 JP 75, the words used were: 'If it appears to the satisfaction of the judge'.

106 *R v Ewing* [1983] QB 1039, [1983] 2 All ER 645, overruling *R v Angeli* [1978] 3 All ER 950, [1979] 1 WLR 26. See also *R v Mazzone* (1985) 43 SASR 330; *R v Sim* [1987] 1 NZLR 356.

107 *Wendo v R* (1963) 109 CLR 559; *R v Clark* (1984) 11 ACR 257. The Federal position in the United States is the same for all preliminary matters: *Bourjaily v United States* 483 US 171, 175 (1987).

108 *R v Donohoe* [1963] SRNSW 38.   109 *Platt v HM Adv* 2004 JC 113, [2004] SCCR 209.

110 A similar view has been taken in Canada to reinforce the protection offered to a juvenile suspect, *R v LTH* 2008 SCC 49, [2008] 2 SCR 739; and to avoid confusion, *R v Quidley* 232 CCC3d 255.

111 (n51).

112 See *Timm v R* [1981] 2 SCR 315, applying this principle to the question of whether a complaint was made by the victim of a rape (but distinguishing the questions of whether it was spontaneous or recent).

SECTION 2. JUDICIAL CONTROL OF THE JURY

The exceptions to the general rule that questions of fact must be determined by the jury are one facet of the subject of judicial control of that body. This section is concerned with direct methods of control by means of withdrawing an issue[113] from the consideration of the jury,[114] by exercising discretion to exclude otherwise admissible evidence, by summing-up, and by setting aside verdicts on appeal.

WITHDRAWAL OF AN ISSUE FROM THE JURY

Before an issue can be submitted to the jury, the judge must be satisfied that there is sufficient evidence in support of the proponent's[115] contention for its consideration, and, if he is of the opinion that the evidence is insufficient, he must decide the issue in favour of the opponent. He could also at common law invite the jury to stop the case, but this practice may not, in a joint case, be compatible with art 6 of the European Convention of Human Rights, and should be resorted to only in the most exceptional circumstances.[116] Very occasionally, the tendered evidence may be so tainted as to attract findings of abuse of process,[117] contempt of court,[118] or prosecution for perjury.

The standard for intervention is always high, and in a civil case, a judge should not strike out a claim[119] simply because it seems very weak and unlikely to succeed, but only on the basis that it has no chance of success,[120] which will rarely be the case in an uncertain or developing area of law.[121] The issue should be determined on the basis of actual rather than assumed facts,[122] rarely on the basis of affidavits in the absence of

---

[113] If a fair trial is impossible on account of abuse of process, all of the issues will be effectively withdrawn from the jury: see *R (Ebrahim) v Feltham Magistrates' Court* [2001] EWHC Admin 130, [2001] 2 Cr App Rep 427. Even if a claim is so speculative for its pursuit to amount to abuse of process, it will nevertheless not be struck out if disclosure might reveal evidence to sustain it: *Arsenal FC v Elite Sports Distribution Ltd* [2002] EWHC 3057 (Ch), [2003] FSR 26. It was stressed in *R v Childs* [2002] EWCA Crim 2578, [11] that abuse of process should not lightly be alleged, sanctioned by liability for wasted costs.

[114] Under the Civil Procedure Rules, in which case management has high priority, the judge is accorded extensive powers of deciding which issues are worthy of trial, which can be settled summarily and of striking out before trial, although in that case, he must bear mind that the evidence may develop at the trial: *Royal Brompton Hospital NHS Trust v Hammond (No 5)* [2001] EWCA Civ 550, [2001] BLR 297; but it is not enough to prevent summary judgment that the opponent merely hopes that something may emerge on discovery or by cross-examination: *Parks v Clout* [2003] EWCA Civ 893.

[115] The proponent is the party bearing the evidential burden on that issue, usually the claimant in a civil case, and the prosecutor on a criminal charge, but not necessarily so.

[116] *R v C et al* [2007] EWCA Crim 854.

[117] See e.g. *Johnson v Perot Systems Europe* [2005] EWHC 2450 (QB), [24].

[118] Although committal should not be ordered in the absence of the alleged contemnor, *Raja v Van Hoogstraten* [2004] EWCA Civ 964, [2004] 4 All ER 793, [94].

[119] Nor allow summary judgment on it: *Getronics Holdings EMEA BV v Logistics and Transport Consultancy* [2004] EWHC 808.

[120] *Chan U Seek v Alvis Vehicles Ltd* [2003] EWHC 1238. The standard may have become higher after the passage of the Human Rights Act 1998; cf under the older law *Metropolitan Rly Co v Jackson* (1877) 3 App Cas 193, 207. The test was satisfied in *Moshen Salamony v Balfour Beatty Construction Co* [2004] EWHC 41 (Ch), in which the evidence was totally inconsistent with the pleaded case.

[121] *Barrett v Enfield LBC* [2001] 2 AC 550, [1999] 3 All ER 193; 557, 197; see also in New Zealand *Hobson v Att-Gen* [2007] 1 NZLR 374.   [122] *Richards v Hughes* [2004] EWCA Civ 266, [2004] PNLR 45.

cross-examination,[123] and on the basis of objective legal appraisal, rather than assessment of the possible subjective reaction of the jury.[124] It should not be considered before any evidence has been tendered.[125] Where the outcome depends upon the credibility of testimony[126] or the authenticity of documents,[127] the issue should normally go to trial,[128] especially where there is a conflict of expert evidence,[129] even if rebuttal is hindered by delay in launching the proceedings.[130] Failure to adopt approved procedure should rarely be sanctioned by withdrawal of an issue.[131] In general, issues should not be withdrawn when crucial evidence remains in dispute,[132] unless it is tainted,[133] or so weak that no reasonable jury could accept it.[134]

When a judge comes to the conclusion that evidence in support of the contention of the proponent of an issue is insufficient, the course that he should adopt will vary. Sometimes he should discharge the jury and enter judgment for the opponent of the issue, as in a civil suit in which there is insufficient evidence in support of the claimant's allegation of negligence;[135] sometimes he should direct the jury to return a verdict in favour of the opponent, as in a criminal case where the prosecution's evidence is insufficient. There may be other issues to be left to the jury, as on a criminal charge when the judge rules that there is insufficient evidence of insanity (an issue of which the accused is the proponent), and it is none the less necessary for the jury to decide whether the prosecution has established the accused's guilt in other respects. Whichever of these courses is adopted, the judge is obviously exercising considerable control over the jury, for he is either totally withdrawing facts from its consideration, or else directing it to come to a certain conclusion, whatever its own view may be.

The test to determine whether there is sufficient evidence in favour of the proponent of an issue, is for the judge to inquire whether there is[136] evidence that, if untainted[137] and uncontradicted,[138] would justify men of ordinary reason and fairness in affirming

---

123   *Microsoft Corporation v P$ Com Ltd* [2007] EWHC 746 (Ch).

124   *R v Gallo* [2005] EWCA Crim 242, [22].   125   *R v N Ltd* [2008] EWCA Crim 1223.

126   *Hayter v Fahie* [2008] EWCA Civ 1336 (summary judgment).

127   *Beirsdorf AG v Ramlort Ltd* [2004] EWHC 117, [2005] ETMR 15 (Ch) (allegation that documents supporting defence had been forged); *Comfort v Lord Chancellor's Dept* [2004] EWCA Civ 349 (authenticity of notes of meeting).

128   Lying as to some parts of the incident is not necessarily enough to justify withdrawal, *Wasim Ul-Haq v Shah* [2008] EWHC 1896 (QB).   129   As in *Yousif v Jordan* [2003] EWCA Civ 1852.

130   *R v B* [2005] EWCA Crim 29.

131   *Obasa v LB of Islington* [2004] EWCA 1237, [27] (fair chance to rebut allegation of want of prosecution required before striking out); *Armstrong v Times Newspapers Ltd* [2005] EWCA Civ 1007, [2005] EMLR 33, [82] (failure to put allegations to claimant should not bar defence of privilege in defamation proceedings).

132   *Ezsias v North Glamorgan NHS Trust* [2007] EWCA Civ 330.

133   As in *R v OB* [2008] EWCA Crim 238; *R v Hudson* [2007] EWCA Crim 2083 (deliberately false confession designed to secure co-accused).

134   As in *R v Robson* [2006] EWCA Crim 2754 (some counts).

135   Even in this kind of case, it may be desirable to have the damages assessed by the jury.

136   The circumstances in which the prosecution will be permitted to re-open its case are now wider than used to be the case; cp *R v Johnson* [2001] EWCA Crim 2312 and *Malcolm v DPP* [2007] EWHC 363, [2007] 3 All ER 578.

137   A judge should be slow to regard the evidence of a witness as wholly tainted for these purposes: *R v Dixon* [2002] EWCA Crim 1464.

138   For this purpose, contradiction in another part even of the proponent's own evidence is irrelevant, since the jury may accept some, but not all, of any witness's evidence: *Naxakis v Western General Hospital* [1999] HCA 22, (1999) 197 CLR 269.

the proposition that the proponent is bound to maintain, having regard to the degree of proof demanded by the law with regard to the particular issue.[139] This test is easy to apply when the evidence is direct, for, unless their cross-examination were utterly shattering, the question whether witnesses are to be believed must be left to the jury, but it is necessarily somewhat vague when circumstantial evidence has to be considered. In that case, little more can be done than inquire whether the proponent's evidence warrants an inference of the facts in issue, or whether it merely leads to conjecture concerning them,[140] but conversely if the opponent's opposition is itself conjectural his application must be dismissed.[141] At this stage, the submission should succeed only if the circumstantial evidence raises no hypothesis consistent with guilt.[142]

Although it is sometimes the judge's duty to withdraw an issue from the jury of his own motion,[143] questions of the sufficiency of evidence are usually raised on a submission of no case to answer made by the opponent of the issue.[144] The judge must rule in favour of the submission if there is insufficient evidence to prove an essential element in the proponent's[145] case,[146] or if the evidence that has been adduced is so tenuous that no jury properly directed could convict upon it,[147] although in relation to possible defences it may be preferable to delay a ruling until after the evidence has been adduced.[148] It is not alone enough that an alleged victim fails to testify,[149] or is shown to have been lying,[150] nor when any weakness in the proponent's case depends upon matters within the exclusive jurisdiction of the jury, such as the reliability of witnesses,[151] inconsistency

---

[139] *Bridges v North London Rly Co* (1874) LR 7 HL 213, 233, Brett J. The last 17 words that appeared in the first edition were reinstated out of deference to Edwards: see (1970) 9 Western Australian Law Review 169.

[140] The judge may determine whether any necessary inference can be drawn from primary facts, even in jury cases such as malicious prosecution: *Menagh v Chief Constable of Merseyside* [2003] EWHC 412 (QB). Mere improbability is not enough: *Rafidain Bank v Agom Universal Sugar Trading Co Ltd* [1987] 3 All ER 859, [1987] 1 WLR 1606. See also *Caswell v Powell Duffryn Associated Collieries Ltd* [1940] AC 152, [1939] 3 All ER 722; 169, 733.   [141] *L v DPP* [2009] EWHC 238 (Admin).

[142] See *R v Danells* [2006] EWCA Crim 628; in Scotland, *Smith v HM Adv* [2008] HCJAC 7, 2008 SCCR 255; and in Australia, *Torrance v Cornish* (1985) 79 FLR 87; *R v Haas* (1986) 22 ACR 299. Certainly not the converse that it should succeed unless all inferences inconsistent with guilt have been negated: *R v Morgan* [1993] Crim LR 870. For full discussion by the Supreme Court of Canada, see *R v Charemski* [1998] 1 SCR 679.

[143] Which can be exercised at any time, even after the defence has tendered its evidence: *R v Brown* [2002] EWCA Crim 961, [2002] 1 Cr App Rep 46.   [144] See Pattenden [1982] *Crim LR* 558.

[145] No element of balancing between plaintiff and defendant is apposite, *Zahoor v Masood* [2009] EWCA Civ 650.

[146] An unconvincing denial by the accused will be insufficient in the absence of any positive evidence of the commission of the crime charged: *R v Belau* [2004] EWCA Crim 2229.

[147] The prosecution case will rarely be withdrawn in case of disputed diminished responsibility, despite unanimity of expert medical evidence in favour of the defence, *R v Khan* [2009] EWCA Crim 1569, [2010] 1 Cr App R 74, [42].   [148] *R v McAuley* [2009] EWCA Crim 2130; (2009) 173 JP 585, [15].

[149] *R v PS* [2007] EWCA Crim 2058.   [150] *R v Bradley* (2009) unreported CA, 9 Oct.

[151] *R v Galbraith* [1981] 2 All ER 1060, [1981] 1 WLR 1039; *Haw Tua Tau v Public Prosecutor* [1982] AC 136, [1981] 3 All ER 14; 151, 19; *R v Fulcher* [1995] 2 Cr App Rep 251. Cp *R v Boakes* [1996] CLY 1393, in which the witness should have been determined by the judge to be too incredible for her evidence to be left to the jury at all, *R v Pepperman* [2007] EWCA Crim 1552 (where the refusal to withdraw was upheld, but the witness's testimony was then regarded as so weak as to necessitate quashing the subsequent conviction). Similar principles apply to committal for extradition: *R v Governor of Pentonville Prison, ex p Osman* [1989] 3 All ER 701, [1990] 1 WLR 277; 721, 299; *R v Governor of Pentonville Prison, ex p Alves* [1993] AC 284, [1992] 4 All ER 787.

between them,[152] or the resolution of equivocal evidence.[153] Any apparent contradiction between these rules was resolved by Lord Mustill in *Daley v R*,[154] on the basis that while the honesty of a witness should properly remain to be decided by the jury, there were situations,[155] such as identification,[156] in which the evidence even of an honest witness might be regarded as tenuous. Similar considerations may also apply where the maker of a confession suffers from a serious mental defect.[157] The Royal Commission on Criminal Justice recommended[158] that the rule in *Galbraith* be reversed, and that the trial judge have the general power to withdraw an issue from the jury when he consider the evidence demonstrably unsafe or unsatisfactory, or too weak. If he rules against the submission, the issue must be determined by the jury, but, even when the opponent calls no evidence, its decision will not necessarily be in favour of the proponent. The jury may disbelieve the testimony given on his behalf, or, if it does accept it, it may not be prepared to draw the requisite inference.

There are certain practical differences in the procedure that ought to be followed by the judge according to the class of case that he is trying.

Civil cases tried by a judge alone

A submission that there is no case to answer may be made by one of the parties to proceedings before a judge alone,[159] but even under the current[160] Rules of Civil Procedure,[161] the judge is unlikely to rule on the submission unless the party making it elects not to

---

[152] *R v Fletcher* [2005] EWCA Crim 3518, [20]; cf in Australia *Doney v R* (1990) 171 CLR 207, 214.

[153] Even when that of experts: *R v Cutts* [2003] EWCA Crim 28. See also *R v O'Driscoll* [2003] EWCA Crim 2369, in which a second trace of unidentifiable DNA was found on a glove used in the commission of a crime in addition to that of the accused.

[154] [1994] AC 117, [1993] 4 All ER 86; 129, 94.

[155] The Law Commission in Law Com 245 *Evidence in Criminal Proceedings: Hearsay and Related Topics* Cm 3670 (1997) paras 11.26–11.32, rec 47, draft bill, cl 14 suggested that the admission of hearsay by the prosecution should be another.

[156] As in *R v Turnbull* [1977] QB 224, [1976] 3 All ER 549, and in *Daley* itself. See also *Mezzo v R* (1986) 30 DLR (4th) 161. This may more often apply when the events occurred many years before: *R v Robson and Wilson* [2006] EWCA Crim 2754.

[157] As in *R v MacKenzie* (1993) 96 Cr App Rep 98; *R v Wood* [1994] Crim LR 222. The defect must have the effect of making the confession unconvincing: *R v Bailey* [1995] 2 Cr App Rep 262. See also *R v Heaton* [1993] Crim LR 593, where expert evidence of mental handicap was itself not sufficiently cogent to be admitted on the voir dire. In Australia, the court may also consider whether the mental defect contributed to the decision to make any statement at all: *R v Pfitzner* (1996) 85 ACR 120.

[158] Cm 2263 (1993) para 4.42, rec 86.

[159] Although such a submission will rarely succeed in proceedings before a tribunal: *Logan v Customs and Excise Comrs* [2003] EWCA Civ 1068, [2004] ICR 1, or at the preliminary fact-finding stage in a child-welfare case, *Re R (A Child)* [2008] EWCA Civ 1619, (2008) 152 (46) SJLB 29, or at a subsequent remedies stage, *Abegaze v Shrewsbury College of Arts and Technology* [2009] EWCA Civ 96. Similar reluctance extends to the judge striking out a claim of his own volition under CPR 3.4: *National Westminster Bank plc v Rabobank Nederland* [2006] EWHC 2959 (Comm Ct).

[160] The CPR do not govern striking out in family proceedings: see Burrows (2005) 35 Fam L 149.

[161] For judicial reluctance to use summary judgment under CPR Pt 24 as a substitute for trial, see *Derkson v Pillar* [2002] EWHC 3050; but it cannot be ruled out automatically, even when testimony is available to contest it: *Miller v Garton Shires* [2006] EWCA Civ 1386, [20]. A conditional order may sometimes amount to a satisfactory compromise, as in *Homebase Ltd v LSS Services Ltd* [2004] EWHC 3182, [32].

call evidence,[162] even in a case of civil contempt.[163] At least two considerations justify this requirement. In the first place, the judge has to determine the facts as well as the law, and he ought not to be asked to express an opinion on the evidence until it is complete.[164] No one would ask a jury, at the end of a claimant's case, to say what verdict they would be prepared to give if the defendant called no evidence.[165] Secondly, the parties might be put to extra expense if the judge were to rule in favour of the submission before the evidence was complete, for, if the Court of Appeal were to decide against his ruling, a new trial would be necessary so that the party who made the submission could call his evidence. In making his determination after the election, the judge should apply the ordinary civil standard of the balance of probabilities to the issues in the case.[166] If, exceptionally, the defendant were not put to his election, the standard would be whether or not the claimant had put up a prima facie case.[167] Very occasionally, the Court of Appeal may substitute for that of the trial Judge its own view that the evidence tendered by the proponent of an issue is incredible for the purpose of withdrawal.[168]

Civil cases tried with a jury

Neither of these considerations apply to civil cases tried with a jury. Accordingly, it has been held that the judge has discretion in such cases, and may rule on the submission without requiring election.[169] If the judge decides in favour of the submission, there would have to be a new trial if his ruling were reversed on appeal, but this would also be the case if he deferred his ruling until the evidence was completed, for the verdict of the jury would have to be obtained in either event.

Whether a civil case is tried with a jury or not, it seems that, if a judge rules that there is a case to answer and the defendant gives evidence, the defendant's liability must be judged on the whole of the evidence and an appeal may be dismissed, although the Court

---

[162] *Alexander v Rayson* [1936] 1 KB 169, emphatically reaffirmed by the Court of Appeal after the CPR in *Benham Ltd v Kythira Investments* [2003] EWCA Civ 1794, [32]. It is only in the most exceptional circumstances that a new trial will be ordered by the Court of Appeal after an election: *Portland Manufacturers Ltd v Harte* [1977] QB 306, [1976] 1 All ER 225. In Australia, it has become discretionary whether to allow a submission without an election: *J-Corp Pty Ltd v ABLFUW* (1992) 38 FCR 458, 111 ALR 377; the timing may differ according to whether it is made upon the basis of a pure matter of law or of the unreliability of the evidence: *Hall v Hall* (1994) 5 Tas R 1; election is less likely to be required in cases of allegations of fraud; the issue is unaffected by documents having been tendered in cross-examination of the claimant's witnesses, *Tru Floor Service Pty Ltd v Jenkins (No 2)* [2006] FCA 632, 232 ALR 532; and the submission may succeed in some respects while failing in others, *Cahill v Construction Forestry Mining and Energy Union (No 2)* [2008] FCA 1292, 250 ALR 223.

[163] *Barclays De Zoete Wedd Securities Ltd v Nadir* (1992) The Times, 25 March.

[164] Thus in 'split-hearing' cases under s 31 of the Children Act 1989, the result of the fact-finding hearing should not pre-empt the subsequent assessment stage, *Re L (A Child)* [2009] EWCA Civ 1008.

[165] Romer LJ [1936] 1 KB 169, 178.

[166] There is no need to go through a two-step process of first deciding whether there is a case to answer, and then whether it succeeds: *Miller v Cawley*. In the very exceptional case when no election is required, the judge should accept the submission only if the claim has no possibility of success. For complications caused by different tests conditional upon election to call being made or not, see, in Ireland, *O'Donovan v The Southern Health Board* [2001] 3 IR 385.

[167] *Graham v Chorley Borough Council* [2006] EWCA Civ 92, [2006] CPR 24, [30].

[168] As in *Lexi Holdings PLC v Shaid Luqman* [2007] EWCA Civ 1501.

[169] *Young v Rank* [1950] 2 KB 510, [1950] 2 All ER 166, in which the authorities are reviewed by Devlin J.

of Appeal is of opinion that the judge should have ruled in favour of the submission when it was made.[170]

Criminal cases tried with a jury

In criminal cases tried with a jury, the accused is never put to his election whether or not to call evidence before a ruling is made on his submission that there is no case to answer.[171] Even where the accused bears the evidential burden in respect of a special defence, he may rely upon its having been raised by evidence adduced by the prosecution as part of its case.[172] Although very scanty evidence can discharge the accused's evidential burden,[173] if it really is insufficient the judge is entitled, and sometimes bound,[174] notwithstanding the European Convention on Human Rights, to withdraw the defence from consideration by the jury.[175] If the ruling is in favour of the submission, the jury is directed to acquit,[176] Section 58 of the Criminal Justice Act 2003 now allows a prosecution appeal against such a ruling, and is frequently successful.[177] If the submission fails, the accused calls his evidence in the ordinary way. Contrary to what was once decided by the Court of Criminal Appeal,[178] it has been said that, on an appeal against conviction, the Court of Criminal Appeal considers the evidence as a whole, and can therefore dismiss the appeal, although it may be of opinion that the judge ought to have ruled that there was no case to answer at the close of the prosecution's evidence if, as sometimes happens, the accused is incriminated by his own evidence.[179] But this does not apply to a case in which the Court of Appeal is of opinion that there is no case to answer and the trial judge allows the case to go to the jury only in fairness to a co-accused, who incriminates the accused.[180] If the submission succeeds in respect of one jointly tried co-accused, it may become necessary to reconsider evidential rulings already made in the case of the other.[181]

The judge may always discharge the jury, even against the wishes of the accused,[182] prosecution, or both.[183]

---

[170] *Payne v Harrison* [1961] 2 QB 403, [1961] 2 All ER 873.

[171] Except in the special circumstances set out in s 6(4) of the Domestic Violence, Crime and Victims Act 2004, which prevents such a submission before the close of all of the evidence.

[172] Even when only by the exculpatory part of a mixed statement: *R v Duncan* (1981) 73 Cr App Rep 359; *R v Hamand* (1985) 82 Cr App Rep 65.

[173] *R v A* [2008] EWCA Crim 1759.   [174] See e.g. *R v Madden and Rose* [2004] EWCA Crim 764.

[175] *R v Bianco* [2001] EWCA Crim 2516; *R v Miao* [2003] EWCA Crim 3486, (2004) 101(5) LS Gaz R 28. He may not direct a verdict of guilty.

[176] *DPP v Stonehouse* [1978] AC 55, [1977] 2 All ER 909; 94, 940.

[177] See *R v P (JM)* [2007] EWCA Crim 3216; *R v A* (n173).   [178] *R v Joiner* (1910) 4 Cr App Rep 64.

[179] *R v Power* [1919] 1 KB 572; *Att-Gen for Jersey v O'Brien* [2006] UKPC 14, [2006] 1 WLR 1485; but see *R v Smith* [2000] 1 All ER 263, holding that even a subsequent admission of guilt under cross-examination would fail to sustain the conviction if there had been no case to answer when the prosecution case closed, although *Power* had apparently not been cited to the court. This may reflect the changed atmosphere after the passage of the Human Rights Act 1998. For criticism, see Tunkel (1999) 149 *New LJ* 1089.

[180] *R v Abbott* [1955] 2 QB 497, [1955] 2 All ER 899; applied in *R v Lane* (1985) 82 Cr App Rep 5. See the discussion of the earlier authorities in Wood (1961) 77 *LQR* 491.

[181] See *R v Christofides* [2001] EWCA Crim 906.

[182] Although he should be wary of overriding a decision of experienced counsel not to submit, *Western Australia v Montani* [2007] WASCA 259, 182 ACR 155.

[183] *R v Azam* [2006] EWCA Crim 161, [48].

Magistrates

A submission of no case may be made in proceedings before magistrates,[184] although it should not be used to impeach the particularity of the indictment.[185] Modern readiness to permit the prosecution to re-open its case may, however, reduce the incidence of such submissions.[186] Similarly magistrates in committal proceedings may entertain a submission that a trial would amount to abuse of process, but should be very cautious in doing so, especially when there is no evidence of malpractice by the prosecution.[187] In the case of an exhibit, any submission should be made as soon as the exhibit is produced, and should normally be justified by cross-examination or producing evidence.[188] If the proceedings are criminal, there is no question of the accused being put to his election,[189] nor need the magistrates give reasons for rejecting the submission, even after the implementation of the Human Rights Act 1998.[190] They may also defer any final decision on the application of exclusionary discretion until the close of the case.[191] If the proceedings are civil, the party making the submission may be put to his election. If the magistrates rule against the submission, they should give the party making it a further opportunity to address them on the facts.[192] This is because a finding that there is a case to answer is not a decision of the whole case against the party making the submission. It is perfectly proper for magistrates to hold that there is a case to answer and decide the issue in favour of the party making the submission. They may come to the conclusion that the evidence of the opposite party is not to be believed.[193]

DISCRETION TO EXCLUDE EVIDENCE[194]

If the judge has not altogether dictated the decision on an issue by withdrawing it from the trial[195] or by directing a verdict, the next most powerful way in which he can affect its decision is by overriding the rules governing the admission of evidence relevant to that issue. Although initially inimical to judicial instinct,[196] such discretion was recognized by

---

[184] Exceptionally, a special defence may be raised as a preliminary issue, but the magistrates should be particularly cautious before excluding it from consideration: *A v DPP* (2000) 164 JP 317 (duress).

[185] *Dacre Son and Hartley Ltd v North Yorkshire County Council* [2004] EWHC 2783 (Admin), (2005) 169 JP 59, [40].

[186] (n147).

[187] *R (HM Customs and Excise) v Nottingham Magistrates' Court* [2004] EWHC 1922 (Admin), [55].

[188] *R v Pydar Justices, ex p Foster* (1995) 160 JP 87.

[189] An unsuccessful submission that there was no sufficient case to answer does not deprive the accused of his right to give evidence at committal proceedings: *R v Horseferry Road Magistrates' Court, ex p Adams* [1978] 1 All ER 373, [1977] 1 WLR 1197.

[190] *Moran v DPP* [2002] EWHC 89 (Admin), (2002) 166 JP 467.

[191] *J v DPP* [2004] EWHC 1470 (Admin), [8].

[192] *Mayes v Mayes* [1971] 2 All ER 397, [1971] 1 WLR 679. The same applies to a special immigration adjudicator: *Kriba v Secretary of State for Home Department* 1998 SLT 1113.

[193] *De Filippo v De Filippo* (1963) 108 Sol Jo 56.

[194] This has become a prominent issue reflecting a fundamental shift away from rigid exclusionary rules. For fuller examination, see Pattenden *Judicial Discretion and Criminal Litigation* (1990); Livesey [1968] *CLJ* 291; Weinberg (1975) 21 *McGill LJ* 1; Cross (1979) 30 *NILQ* 289; Tapper [2009] *CLJ* 67.

[195] Abuse of process should be argued before discretionary exclusion, *Re Saluja* [2006] EWHC 2784 (Admin), [104].

[196] See e.g. *R v Inhabitants of Eriswell* (1790) 3 Term Rep 707, 711; *R v Cargill* (1913) 8 Cr App Rep 224, 229 (expressly disavowed in *R v Funderburk* [1990] 2 All ER 482, [1990] 1 WLR 587; 492, 599, so far as it suggested

the House of Lords in *R v Christie*,[197] and since then, there have been many dicta concerning the judge's power to exclude admissible evidence because its reception would create undue prejudice or be unfair in some other respect.[198] In *R v Sang*,[199] the House of Lords affirmed the existence of a discretion to control the use of evidence so as to ensure a fair trial, and that general matter was put upon a statutory footing by s 78 of the Police and Criminal Evidence Act 1984. Since then, for criminal proceedings, the Criminal Justice Act 2003 has enacted an explicit inclusionary discretion in respect of hearsay,[200] and the Court of Appeal has intimated[201] its readiness to consider the admission of evidence of the bad character of the accused more as a matter for the impression of the trial judge than as one for the application, or formulation, of rules by the Court of Appeal. For civil proceedings, an explicit exclusionary discretion now appears as r 32.1, as introduced as part of the new rules in 1997. The implications of that affirmation and those statutory provisions require exploration. First, the very nature of discretionary control must be examined.

Nature of the discretion

Not for the first, or last, time in the exposition of the law of evidence, it is necessary to beware of the danger inherent in the loose use of terminology: in this case, the use of the word 'discretion' in many different senses,[202] and ambiguity in the verb 'may', which sometimes connotes 'must'.[203] It is particularly important to distinguish between the idea that the judge has the responsibility of deciding upon the application to the facts before him of an inherently vague term, and the idea that he is free to act in any way he chooses upon the facts that he finds to exist.[204] The difference is that, in the former case, the judge must act in a particular way once he has found the facts, and in the latter, he is still free to choose which action to take after finding them. In many practical situations, the dichotomy may not appear so clear, the distinction has not always been present in the mind of judges, the terminology of discretion has been used undiscriminatingly to apply to both, and in *Renda* it was suggested that much the same tests should be applied by an appellate court.[205] Nevertheless, the distinction has been taken. Thus, in considering Lord Edmund Davies' speech in *D v National Society for the Prevention of Cruelty to Children*,[206] Cross deplored 'the use of the word "discretion" to describe the judge's

countenancing injustice); exactly the same sentiments prevented the adoption of the United States Model Code: see Wigmore (1942) 28 *ABA Jo* 23.

[197] (1914) 10 Cr App Rep 141, 149.

[198] See *Festa v R* [2001] HCA 72, 208 CLR 593, Gleeson CJ, [22] for a very clear distinction between the discretion to exclude on the basis of prejudice, and other forms of discretionary exclusion; in Australia, a common law discretion to exclude to secure a fair trial outside the limited area of confessions has been clearly recognized: see *R v Juric* [2002] VSCA 77, 129 ACR 408, [50].

[199] [1980] AC 402, [1979] 2 All ER 1222.   [200] S 114(1)(d).

[201] *R v Renda* [2005] EWCA Crim 2826, [2006] 2 All ER 553, [3].

[202] Pattenden (n194) distinguishes a number of senses.

[203] See Jervis CJ's intervention in argument in *Macdougall v Paterson* (1851) 11 CB 755, 766: 'The word "may" is merely used to confer the authority: and the authority *must* be exercised if the circumstances are such to call for its exercise.' (original emphasis), endorsed by the High Court of Australia in *Leach v R* [2007] HCA 3, 230 CLR 1, [38].

[204] Dworkin, in *Taking Rights Seriously* (1977), 31–3, describes these as weak and strong senses of discretion.   [205] Namely review on a *Wednesbury* basis.

[206] [1978] AC 171, [1977] 1 All ER 589; 246, 618.

duty to perform the contemplated balancing act'.[207] Nor has such criticism been limited to academic commentators. In *R v Viola*, the Court of Appeal said of the court's earlier judgment in *R v Mills*,[208] on the issue of allowing questions to be asked under the old law in cross-examination about the complainant's sexual history, that:[209]

...it is wrong to speak of a judge's 'discretion' in this context. The judge has to make a judgment whether he is satisfied or not in the terms of s 2 [of the Sexual Offences (Amendment) Act 1976]. But once having reached that judgment on the particular facts, he has no discretion. If he comes to the conclusion that he is satisfied it would be unfair to exclude the evidence, then the evidence has to be admitted and the questions have to be allowed.

Exactly the same view of the operation of s 78 of the Police and Criminal Evidence Act 1984 appeared in *R v Hasan*:[210]

Although it is formally cast in the form of a discretion ('the court may') the objective criterion whether 'the evidence would have such an adverse effect on the fairness of the proceedings' in truth imports a judgment whether in the light of the statutory criterion of fairness the court ought to admit the evidence.

One practical consequence of making this distinction is simply that the grounds upon which an appellate court will review a discretion, although now much more extensive than was once the case,[211] are still not so extensive as those in which it will reverse the incorrect application of a rule.[212] Nor will it even consider exercising an exclusionary discretion for the first time on appeal when the matter has not been put to the trial judge.[213] In general terms, the exercise of a discretion will stand so long as the judge 'does not err in law, takes into account all relevant matters and excludes consideration of irrelevant matters',[214] a

---

[207] (1979) 30 NILQ 289, 294.   [208] (1978) 68 Cr App Rep 327.

[209] [1982] 3 All ER 73, [1982] 1 WLR 1138; 77, 1142; same tests should be applied by an appellate court. See also *R v Murakami* [1951] SCR 801, 803; *R v Blick* [2000] NSWCCA 61, [20].

[210] [2005] UKHL 22, [2005] 2 AC 467, [53]. See also *R v Chalkley* [1998] QB 848, [1998] 2 All ER 155; 874D, 178d, in which the court was quite explicit in stating that 'the task of determining admissibility under s 78 does not strictly involve an exercise of discretion', and that view was then reinforced by comparison with what the court regarded as a genuine discretion to prevent abuse of process.

[211] *Evans v Bartlam* [1937] AC 473, [1937] 2 All ER 646 is often seen as the turning point. See also *House v R* (1936) 55 CLR 499. Under Pt 52 of the Civil Procedure Rules, an appellate court will generally proceed by way of review, but has the power to do so by rehearing, in which case it can exercise its own discretion: see e.g. *Audergon v La Baguette Ltd* [2002] EWCA Civ 10, [2002] CPR 27.

[212] *Charles Osenton & Co v Johnston* [1942] AC 130, [1941] 2 All ER 245, in which it was said that there is a presumption that the discretion has been exercised correctly; see also *Piglowska v Piglowski* [1999] 3 All ER 632, [1999] 1 WLR 1360, 643–5, 1372–5 (HL). In *Cookson v Knowles* [1979] AC 556, [1978] 2 All ER 604; 566, 607, Lord Diplock explicitly distinguished between the role of an appellate court in relation to rule and discretion. For a similar view in the context of criminal proceedings, see *R v Chung* (1991) 92 Cr App Rep 314, 323.

[213] *R v Goldenberg* (1988) 88 Cr App Rep 285, 289, although it seems immaterial that the first reference to the discretion at the trial was too late for its valid exercise: *R v Kempster* [1989] 1 WLR 1125, 90 Cr App Rep 14. The same view prevails in relation to appeals from the magistrates by way of case stated, and it is immaterial there that the clerk wrongly advised that no discretion was available: *Braham v DPP* (1994) 159 JP 527. As noted in *R v Mullen* [2000] QB 520, [1999] 2 Cr App Rep 143, the application of the discretion on appeal must necessarily be made on a different basis from that which operated at the trial. It seems that the parties can, however, invest the appellate court with authority to exercise its discretion when the trial judge has failed to do so, *R v Cheb Miller* [2007] EWCA Crim 1891, [6].

[214] *R v Scarrott* [1978] QB 1016, [1978] 1 All ER 672; 1028, 681; applied to the statutory s 78 discretion in *R v Rankin* (1995) The Times, 5 September; *R v Webster* (12 December 2000, unreported) CA, [20].

task much facilitated by the use of standard directions. In criminal cases, it has been held that the appellate court will not intervene unless no reasonable trial judge could have so exercised his discretion,[215] although there is also evidence of the possibly less stringent standard of its having been 'incumbent' on the trial judge to exercise his discretion to exclude.[216] Where a list of factors has been enumerated for consideration by the trial judge in the exercise of a broad discretion, the prospects of a successful appeal may be still more thin,[217] at least so long as he duly takes them into account. If he fails to do so, the chances of successful challenge are immensely enhanced.[218] There may, however, be less reluctance to intervene when the trial judge's view was clearly obiter, and designed merely to bolster exclusion by rule,[219] or perhaps where the appeal is made by the prosecution against the exercise of the discretion *to exclude* by a magistrate.[220] The appellate court may also be more inclined to overturn the exercise of an inclusionary discretion, such as that conferred by ss 114(1)(d) or 116(2)(e) of the Criminal Justice Act 2003.[221] It was particularly odd to find the Court of Appeal in *R v Smith*[222] reversing the trial Judge's application of the inclusionary discretion in s 114(1)(d) despite having taken all of the relevant factors in s 114(2) into account because his assessment had been tainted by flaws in his exercise of the s 78 exclusionary discretion. A further consequence is that it becomes much more difficult for even consistent practice to mature into a rule. It might have been thought that requirement[223] for a court to give reasons for a ruling under the bad character provisions of the Criminal Justice Act 2003 had been designed to alleviate this problem, but the decision in *Renda*, both to criticize the failure to observe this requirement[224] and to affirm the 'case-sensitive' nature of the decision,[225] seems to contradict any such view, although in *R v Reed and Williams* the issue was regarded as unresolved.[226] It is hoped that the House of Lords may adopt a construction more conducive to the development of a body of cohesive rules in this area.

In some situations, the nature of the rule of evidence that is in question is defined in such terms that it is difficult to discern any possible role for the application of an exclusionary discretion.[227] Sometimes the rule is drafted in much more rigid terms, and in such cases, it is feasible to construct guidelines for the exercise of a discretion designed to avoid injustice.[228]

If the distinction mentioned above is accepted, it is tolerably clear that the exercise of a discretion can only be to exclude otherwise admissible evidence. It cannot be used to

---

215 *R v Quinn* [1995] 1 Cr App Rep 480, 489C; *R v Dures* [1997] 2 Cr App Rep 247, 262A. For a rare case in which this rigorous standard was reached, see *R v Miller* [1998] Crim LR 209 (trial judge considered the wrong Code of Practice).   216 *R v Duffy* [1999] 1 Cr App R 307.

217 *Yates v Thakeham Tiles Ltd* [1995] PIQR P135.

218 See *Stanoevsky v R* [2001] HCA 4, (2001) 202 CLR 115.

219 As in *R v Samuel* [1988] QB 615, [1988] 2 All ER 135; 630, 147.

220 As in *DPP v Clarkson* [1996] CLY 1124.   221 Cf *R v Radak* [1999] 1 Cr App Rep 187.

222 [2007] EWCA Crim 2105.   223 Section 110.   224 *Osbourne*, [60].   225 [3].

226 [2007] EWCA Crim 3083, [37]; cp *R v McMinn* [2007] EWCA 3024, [5] (there merely implicit).

227 It is arguable that this was the situation with regard to the old similar fact rule. The High Court of Australia took a similar view in relation to the exclusion in that jurisdiction by discretion of confessions that have passed the local test for exclusion by rule: see Brennan J in *Collins v R* (1980) 31 ALR 257, 315.

228 *R v Britzman* [1983] 1 All ER 369, [1983] 1 WLR 350; 373, 355. This course is favoured by Pattenden.

admit otherwise inadmissible evidence, as remarked by Lord Reid in *Myers v DPP*:[229]

It is true that a judge has discretion to exclude legally admissible evidence if justice so requires, but it is a very different thing to say that he has a discretion to admit legally inadmissible evidence.

Some exclusionary rules are, however, phrased in such vague terms that judges occasionally appear to suppose that they are exercising an inclusionary discretion, but such cases are best explained as ones in which the vague question is resolved in such a way that the exclusionary rule does not apply.[230] This is becoming increasingly true of the discretion to exclude evidence leading to unfairness of the proceedings, enacted as s 78 of the Police and Criminal Evidence Act 1984.[231] It may be that, in that context, some influence is exerted on account of the less onerous burden of negating the factual basis for triggering the discretion now recognized to rest upon the prosecution.[232] The influence of the burden of proof that, in Australia,[233] is still stronger also explains the insistence there[234] that the weighing of proof and prejudice in relation to similar fact evidence should remain a matter of law rather than discretion.

A true inclusionary discretion is sometimes conferred by statute, as where s 6(2)(a) of the Civil Evidence Act 1995 empowers the court to admit previous consistent statements of witnesses even though the conditions for their admissibility prescribed by the Act have not been fulfilled,[235] and where ss 114(1)(d) and 116(2)(e) of the Criminal Justice Act 2003 permit discretionary acceptance of hearsay in the interests of justice. It is noteworthy that the Law Commission regarded the introduction of such an inclusionary discretion as an essential feature of its proposals for the reform of the hearsay rule in criminal cases.[236] Much will depend upon the willingness of the court to employ that discretion, since it clearly has the potential to undermine the more detailed exceptions to the hearsay rule comprising the majority of the provisions of that part of the Act. Fortunately, the latest indications are that the court is anxious to avoid that result.[237] The Act further complemented the previous discretion to exclude prosecution evidence with a new discretion to exclude even defence evidence where its probative value is substantially outweighed by the danger that it would result in an undue waste of time.[238]

---

[229] [1965] AC 1001, [1964] 2 All ER 881; 1024, 887. But see *R v Greasby* [1984] Crim LR 488.

[230] For example, *R v Dodd* (1981) 74 Cr App Rep 50; *R v Miller* [1997] 2 Cr App Rep 178. See also *R v Wilson* (1987) 32 ACR 286, 293.

[231] See e.g. *R v Gillard and Barrett* (1990) 92 Cr App Rep 61, 65, in which the court warns of *fettering* the operation of the discretion by too readily *excluding* confessions under s 76, a sentiment that makes sense only if the discretion is regarded as inclusionary: *R v Armas-Rodriguez* [2005] EWCA Crim, [14]–[17].

[232] *Re Saifi* [2001] 4 All ER 168, [2001] 1 WLR 1135, [59]. See further below, 663.

[233] Section 138 of the Evidence Act 1995 enacts an inclusionary discretion in relation to improperly obtained evidence, with the accused bearing the burden of establishing the necessary factual basis for its application should he wish to invoke it: *R v Coulstock* (1998) 99 ACR 143.

[234] See the powerful arguments of McHugh J in *Pfennig v R* (1995) 182 CLR 461, 515.

[235] On the court's discretion with regard to affidavits, see *Rossage v Rossage* [1960] 1 All ER 600, [1960] 1 WLR 249, and *Re J (an infant)* [1960] 1 All ER 603, [1960] 1 WLR 253; *Savings and Investment Bank Ltd v Gasco Investments (Netherlands) BV (No 2)* [1988] Ch 422, [1988] 1 All ER 975.

[236] *Evidence in Criminal Proceedings: Hearsay and Related Topics* Law Com No 245 Cm 3670 (1997) paras 8.133–8.149; recs 28–30.

[237] See e.g. *R v O'Hare* [2006] EWCA Crim 2512, [30]; *R v Z* [2009] EWCA 20, [20].

[238] Section 126(1)(b).

It is interesting to note that, in proceedings where the general exclusionary rules of evidence do not apply, for example in some tribunals,[239] there is no room for an exclusionary discretion. Where statute has sought to extend the range of material available to the tribunal, it is not for the tribunal to cut it down as it chooses by the exercise of any such discretion.[240] Nor is there much room for the exercise of an exclusionary discretion when the function of a court is merely to establish the existence of a case to answer, as in committal[241] proceedings, although extradition,[242] where the situation is similar, is now dealt with differently.[243]

Discretion to exclude relevant evidence in criminal proceedings

The existence of a discretion at common law[244] has been recognized in criminal cases in the highest appellate tribunals since *R v Christie*.[245] The general question was again certified in *R v Sang*:[246]

Does a trial judge have a discretion to refuse to allow evidence, being evidence other than evidence of admission, to be given in any circumstances in which such evidence is relevant and of more than minimal probative value?

Their Lordships were unanimous in agreeing to an answer that distinguished two situations:[247]

(1) A trial judge in a criminal trial has always a discretion to refuse to admit evidence if in his opinion its prejudicial effect outweighs its probative value.

(2) Save with regard to admissions and confessions and generally with regard to evidence obtained from the accused after commission of the offence, he has no discretion to refuse to admit relevant admissible evidence on the ground that it was obtained by improper or unfair means. The court is not concerned with how it was obtained. It is no ground for the exercise of discretion to exclude that the evidence was obtained as the result of the activities of an agent provocateur.

Strictly speaking, the *ratio decidendi* is expressed by the last sentence of this answer.[248] Nevertheless, the rest of it has had a very powerfully persuasive effect. In a subsequent case, Lord Roskill asserted not only that *Sang* settled existing doubts, but that it would be a retrograde step to 'enlarge the now narrow limits of that discretion or to engraft an exception'.[249] It is useful first to examine these limits.

Two situations seem to be distinguished: those in which the court is concerned to afford the accused a trial the outcome of which is likely to be reliable, and those in which it is

---

[239] See Chapter I, Section 2.   [240] *Rosedale Mouldings Ltd v Sibley* [1980] ICR 816, 822.
[241] Now excluded by the Criminal Justice and Public Order Act 1994, Sch 1, para 26: see, in Canada, *R v Hynes* 2001 SCC 82, [2001] 3 SCR 623.
[242] There is no explicit exclusion in relation to extradition proceedings.
[243] See Lord Hoffmann in *R v Governor of Brixton Prison, ex p Levin* [1997] AC 741, [1997] 3 All ER 289; 748, 295, pointing out that the discretion would need to be applied to the committal or extradition proceedings rather than to the ultimate trial, and that the evidence triggering such discretion would have to 'outrage civilised values': *Re Proulx* [2001] 1 All ER 57, applying this dictum in an extradition case.
[244] Fuller discussion of the statutory discretion superimposed upon the existing law by s 78 of the Police and Criminal Evidence Act 1984 is deferred until the end of this section.
[245] (n197); e.g. *Selvey v DPP* [1970] AC 304, [1968] 2 All ER 497; 341, 510.   [246] (n199); 431, 1225.
[247] 437, 1231.   [248] See Lord Diplock, 431, 1226; and Lord Scarman, 456, 1246.
[249] *Morris v Beardmore* [1981] AC 446, [1980] 2 All ER 753; 469, 767.

concerned to afford him fair treatment.[250] In the former case, the accused is to be protected, by the exclusion from his trial of evidence that might produce an unreliable result; in the latter case, he is to be protected by the exclusion from his trial of evidence that has been obtained by improper methods, however reliable the result might be. Confessional material straddles the two categories,[251] especially in view of s 76(2)(b) of the Police and Criminal Evidence Act 1984, which excludes confessions obtained:

...in consequence of anything said or done which was likely, in the circumstances existing at the time, to render unreliable any confession which might be made by him [the accused] in consequence thereof...

The section itself recognizes that a confession obtained in such circumstances might in fact be reliable, or even true. It is also obvious that a confession can be unreliable for many other reasons, for example that the person who confesses is mentally handicapped,[252] or confesses to something of which he has no knowledge.[253]

A number of recent decisions has considered the relationship between the court's discretion to exclude evidence and its duty to prevent abuse of its process. This relationship has been confused both by a change in the terminology describing the grounds upon which the Court of Appeal may allow appeals,[254] and the implementation of the Human Rights Act 1998. Sometimes the evidential basis justifying a stay may unfortunately be established only after the proceedings are under way, although they may then afford grounds for discretionary exclusion.[255]

In *R v Chalkley and Jeffries*,[256] in which the accused sought to appeal against a conviction on a plea of guilty, itself precipitated by a ruling that recordings had not been obtained improperly by the police, the court distinguished sharply between cases in which the conviction was unsafe in the sense that the impropriety might have affected the reliability of the outcome of the trial, and those in which there was no such risk, which ought to be considered in the context of an abuse of process where the court should assess such factors as the seriousness of the crime, and the degree of the impropriety. It should be noted, however, that this did not constitute *ratio decidendi*, since the Court of Appeal found that there had been no significant impropriety in obtaining the evidence, and specifically reserved its view on the effect that the then impending implementation of the Human Rights Act 1998 might have on the position.

---

[250] See *R v Benbrika* [2008] VSC 80, 182 ACR 205 for an unusual form of overlap.

[251] For an unusual example, see *R v Gudgeon* (n101), in which the accused sought to have a confession in earlier proceedings, induced only by the admission of inadmissible prosecution evidence, excluded by discretion from a retrial.

[252] See *R v Miller* [1986] 3 All ER 119, [1986] 1 WLR 1191, and the statutory recognition of such a possibility by the prescription of a special direction in s 77 of the Police and Criminal Evidence Act 1984; both were considered in *R v Bailey* (n157). See also *R v Elleray* [2003] EWCA Crim 553, [2003] 2 Cr App Rep 165.

[253] See *Comptroller of Customs v Western Electric Co* [1966] AC 367, [1965] 3 All ER 599; 371, 601.

[254] Criminal Appeal Act 1968, s 2(1), amended by the Criminal Justice Act 1995 to substitute 'unsafe' for 'unsafe or unsatisfactory': see Smith [1995] *Crim LR* 520. It was accepted in *R v Harmes and Crane* [2006] EWCA Crim 928, [54] that, in stay cases, the appellate court was not limited to review, as in s 78 cases, but could substitute its own view for that of the trial judge.

[255] *R v Looseley, A-G's Ref (No 3 of 2000)* [2001] UKHL 53, [2001] 4 All ER 897, Lord Hoffmann, [44], and Lord Hutton, [104] stressing that then the principles relating to a stay are to be applied.

[256] [1998] QB 848, [1998] 2 All ER 155.

Soon afterwards, in *R v Mullen*,[257] it was decided that, at least in cases where the abuse of process made it unfair for a trial to have been held at all, the outcome of such a trial could be regarded neither as 'safe'[258] nor 'fair'.[259] This view has prevailed,[260] although the circumstances in which such an abuse of process exists have been held to be extremely limited, restraint has been urged in making such claims,[261] and doubt expressed,[262] as to whether they can ever encompass questions of the wrongful admission of evidence. In such cases, the courts have expressed a clear preference for the application of s 78 of the Police and Criminal Evidence Act 1984. There is no discretion at common law to exclude evidence adduced by a co-defendant.[263]

It will be convenient to consider the application of the common law discretion to exclude separately in relation to each such category, then to consider the statutory discretion conferred by s 78 of the Police and Criminal Evidence Act 1984, and finally, discretion as applied to confessional statements.

Reliable outcome

The two major subcategories in relation to which the discretion operated under the old law in pursuance of a fair trial were evidence of the accused's discreditable extrinsic conduct, and cross-examination of the accused as to the otherwise-excluded matters under s 1(f) of the Criminal Evidence Act 1898. These rules have now been superseded by the provisions of the Criminal Justice Act 2003,[264] the principal aim of which is to increase the admissibility of evidence of the accused's bad character, including restriction of discretionary exclusion.[265] Thus, s 101(3) provides for exclusion explicitly on the basis of unfairness,[266] but applies in terms only to two[267] of the seven gateways to admission of the accused's[268] bad character opened by s 101. It can be argued that even in the other five other cases there should still be discretion to do so. If so, reliance might be placed upon s 112(3)(c), which

---

[257] [2000] QB 520, [1999] 2 Cr App Rep 143. Where the prosecution services blatantly infringed the accused's human rights so as to have him deported to England to stand trial for an offence of which there was no doubt that he could be proved to be guilty. Although even here the House of Lords disallowed a claim for compensation: *R (Mullen) v Secretary of State for Home Affairs* [2004] UKHL 17, interestingly distinguishing between convictions quashed for defects of trial and of treatment.

[258] For the purposes of s 2(1) of the Criminal Appeal Act 1968, as amended.

[259] For the purposes of Art 6 of the European Convention on Human Rights.

[260] *R v Togher* [2001] 3 All ER 463, [2001] 1 Cr App Rep 457. Lord Woolf CJ was at pains to stress harmony with the position under the European Convention.

[261] *R v Childs* (n113), [11].

[262] *DPP v Jimale* [2001] Crim LR 138, Buxton LJ, [25]. But see *R v Brown* [2006] EWCA Crim 141, in which a conviction was set aside for abuse of process when improperly obtained confessions precipitated a plea of guilty.

[263] *R v Robinson* [2005] EWCA Crim 1940, [2006] 1 Cr App R 221, [17] (admissibility is set at so low a threshold as to collapse into relevance).   [264] See further Chapters VII and VIII.

[265] Despite the absence of any formal abolition of discretionary exclusion; see further 383 below.

[266] Although cast in terms of a *duty* to exclude if the evidence would operate so unfairly that the court ought not to admit it.

[267] Section 101(1)(d) (an important matter in issue between the defendant and prosecution, which applies both to evidence in chief and in cross-examination), and s 101(1)(g) (retaliation for an attack by the accused on another person's character).

[268] In relation to the bad character of non-defendants, the Act in s 100(4) requires the leave of the court to be obtained, but abstains from specifying the criteria to be employed, so the effect might be functionally equivalent to an exclusionary discretion.

excludes the effect of that part of the Act from exclusion of evidence for any reason other than that the evidence is of bad character.[269] It is thus possible that some of the old law relating to discretionary exclusion will continue to apply in this way.

Quite apart from that possibility, the Criminal Justice Act 2003 failed to repeal[270] s 27(3) of the Theft Act 1968, which provides for the admission of various types of evidence of bad character in relation to specific situations. Evidence of the accused's previous convictions of offences involving fraud or dishonesty is admissible in chief on the issue of guilty knowledge, but it has been held that the judge has an exclusionary discretion when there is a danger that the jury may consider such evidence also on the question of possession.[271] The convictions that may be proved on a handling charge are restricted to those of handling and theft. The reason for applying discretion in these cases is simply that the statute gives a blanket power to the judge to admit the evidence for the stated purpose without expressing any restriction at all. In some circumstances, this can lead to prejudice, and so the court exercises discretion to prevent it. Exactly the same rationale applies to evidence of the bad character of the accused admitted under most of the gateways in s 101 of the Criminal Justice Act 2003. The analogy could become the stimulus for discretionary control by the judges for the same reason as that previously expressed in *Selvey v DPP*, in which Lord Guest said:[272]

If I had thought that there was no discretion in English Law for a judge to disallow admissible evidence, as counsel for the Crown argued, I should have striven hard and long to give a benevolent construction to s 1, proviso (f)(ii).

A problem here is one common to all attempts to replace, or even to supplement, rules with discretion, namely the unpredictability of its exercise. Awareness of such problems has in the past fostered attempts to improve predictability by the creation of guidelines for the exercise of the discretion.[273] On the other hand, the very flexibility bestowed by the conferment of discretion has sometimes been positively welcomed by the judiciary, and again in *Selvey*, Lord Guest asserted that:[274]

If it is suggested that the exercise of this discretion may be whimsical and depend on the individual idiosyncracies of the judge, this is inevitable where it is a question of discretion, but I am satisfied that this is a lesser risk than attempting to shackle the judge's power within a straight jacket.

If it is decided that the Criminal Justice Act 2003 leaves room for such an exclusionary discretion, it will be interesting to see how far it is exercised on a basis similar to that

---

[269] Both para 393 of the official explanatory note, and an oral assurance by the government's spokeswoman in the House of Lords, Official Report vol 654, col 1988 (19 November 2003), affirm that this provision was intended to preserve the operation of the statutory exclusionary discretion on the basis of unfairness contained in s 78 of the Police and Criminal Evidence Act 1984.

[270] Contrary to the recommendation of the Law Commission in Law Com 273 *Evidence of Bad Character in Criminal Proceedings* (Cm 5257, 2001), [11.55], rec 15.

[271] *R v Perry* [1984] Crim LR 680; *R v Wilkins* [1975] 2 All ER 734, 60 Cr App Rep 300. Under the old provisions, *R v List* [1965] 3 All ER 710, [1966] 1 WLR 9; *R v Herron* [1967] 1 QB 107, [1966] 2 All ER 26.

[272] [1970] AC 304, [1968] 2 All ER 497; 351, 519.

[273] A broadly similar approach by way of the factors governing leave to adduce evidence of bad character was favoured in this context by the Law Commission: see *Evidence of Bad Character in Criminal Proceedings* (n270), [7.19], rec 13.

[274] [1970] AC 304, [1968] 2 All ER 497; 352, 520.

under the old law.[275] Guidance was there provided by the Court of Appeal.[276] Those decisions resulted in the enumeration[277] of a number of points for the judge to bear in mind in this area: first, that the primary purpose of cross-examination to bad character is to show that the accused is unworthy of belief, and not that he has a disposition to the commission of crimes of the relevant type; second, that any such cross-examination should not be unduly prolonged for fear of diverting the jury; third, that similarities of defence thereby revealed may be relevant; fourth, the fact that the underlying facts indicate particularly prejudicial matters should be balanced against the gravity of the attack on the prosecution witness; fifth, that any objection to revelation of the underlying facts of the relevant convictions should be taken as early as possible; sixth, that unless objection is taken at the time, it will be difficult to contend later that the discretion was wrongly exercised, and in any case, an appellate court will interfere with its exercise only upon established principles; and seventh, that the judge must stress in summing-up that the convictions go only to credit and not to issue.

It should be noted that a similar direction has been approved by majorities in the High Court of Australia,[278] the Supreme Court of Canada,[279] and the Court of Session in Scotland.[280] In *Phillips v R*, the majority[281] was concerned that the discretion should be unfettered by rules,[282] and attached weight to the fact that, since in the case before them the convictions were for offences of dishonesty, they would not be particularly prejudicial on a charge of rape.[283] In his dissenting judgment, Deane J raised the interesting point that the nature of the imputation, namely that the victim and the accused had been associated in the misuse of drugs, reflected equally badly on both of them, so there was no upset balance to redress.[284] In Canada, as in the United States, once the accused chooses to testify, he enjoys no such special regime of protection as that once conferred by the Criminal Evidence Act 1898, s 1(f). In such circumstances, a majority[285] of the Supreme Court of Canada regarded such discretionary protection as nevertheless available. In Scotland, the legislation is in the English form, but used to be interpreted differently,[286] and the situation is complicated by statutory restriction on the use of previous convictions in court.[287] In *Leggate*, however, the rule, and apparently[288] its discretionary gloss, was assimilated to that applied in England.

---

[275] Although the very different form and spirit of the bad character provisions of the Criminal Justice Act 2003 will militate against any striking similarity.

[276] *R v Burke* (1985) 82 Cr App Rep 156; *R v Powell* [1986] 1 All ER 193, [1985] 1 WLR 1364; *R v Owen* (1985) 83 Cr App Rep 100; *R v McLeod* [1994] 3 All ER 254, [1994] 1 WLR 1500.

[277] In *McLeod* (n276).   [278] *Phillips v R* (1985) 159 CLR 45.   [279] *Corbett v R* [1988] 1 SCR 670.

[280] *Leggate v HM Adv* 1988 JC 127, 144.   [281] Mason CJ, Wilson, Brennan, and Dawson JJ.

[282] Deane J also agreed on this point.

[283] Even though it had been accomplished by breaking into a dwelling house.

[284] For an analysis stressing this factor, see Seabrooke [1987] *Crim LR* 231.

[285] Dickson CJC, Beetz, Lamer, and La Forest JJ (agreeing on this point).

[286] *O'Hara v HM Adv* 1948 JC 90.

[287] Criminal Procedure (Scotland) Act 1995, s 101, 166(3). See also Sexual Offences (Procedure and Evidence) (Scotland) Act 2002, s 10.

[288] Although no reference was made to the most recent English authority, and the tenor of the decision, which applied the discretion to exclude such cross-examination, might suggest that practice will continue to diverge.

It must be emphasized that this discretion is based upon the need for a fair trial to be conducted. That this may differ from the rationale of fair treatment of the individual concerned is illustrated by cases in which there is more than one accused. In such a case, courts have not exercised discretion to intervene so as to prevent one of several co-accused from adducing evidence of the bad character of another.[289]

In some cases, the injustice of not disallowing cross-examination in these circumstances can be alleviated by the operation of a different discretion to permit separate trials—but not in all.[290]

The existence of such residual discretion at common law to exclude any otherwise admissible evidence if its admission would be prejudicial to a fair trial was reaffirmed by the Privy Council in *Scott v R; Barnes v R*,[291] in relation to depositions of deceased persons identifying the accused.[292] Another example of the operation of this branch of the discretion was seen in relation to the exclusion of excessively inflammatory evidence, such as gruesome pictures[293] or unduly vivid terminology.[294] It seems, however, not to have been regarded as inimical to a fair trial that the prosecution come innocently into the possession of material that would be privileged in the hands of the accused.[295]

Fair treatment

Two apparent examples of a discretion to exclude evidence pursuant to a desire to achieve the fair treatment of the accused seemed to be those designed to protect him from compulsory self-incrimination, and from the use of improper methods to procure evidence against him.[296] This whole area was reviewed by the House of Lords in *R v Sang*.[297] The accused was charged with conspiracy to utter forged banknotes. He argued that he had been entrapped by the activities of an agent provocateur, and that evidence obtained as the result of such activities could be excluded by the trial judge at his discretion on the basis that it had been obtained by unfair methods. If this argument were correct, it would in effect have endowed the judge with the discretion to allow a defence of entrapment in the circumstances of that case, since there was too little other evidence to secure a conviction. The House of Lords had no doubt that, whatever the extent of this discretion, it did not go so far as that.

---

[289] For evidence in chief, see Devlin J in *R v Miller* [1952] 2 All ER 667, 36 Cr App Rep 169; 669, 171; for evidence in cross-examination, see the majority of the House of Lords in *Murdoch v Taylor* [1965] AC 574, [1965] 1 All ER 406.

[290] *R v Varley* [1982] 2 All ER 519, 75 Cr App Rep 242; 522, 246. For discussion of this discretion elsewhere see, in Australia, *R v Darby* (1982) 148 CLR 668; in Canada, *Guimond v R* [1979] 1 SCR 960.

[291] [1989] AC 1242, [1989] 2 All ER 305.

[292] In England, such matters would now be governed by the provisions of the Criminal Justice Act 2003 on hearsay; see further Chapter XIV.

[293] See *R v Jenkins* [2002] EWCA Crim 749, [3]; *R v Murphy* (1987) 37 ACR 118; *R v Baker* [1989] 3 NZLR 635; cf *R v Muchikekwanape* (2002) 166 CCC3d 144, [43].   [294] See *R v Millar* (1989) 71 CR (3d) 78.

[295] See *R v Tompkins* (1977) 67 Cr App Rep 181; *R v Cottrill* [1997] Crim LR 56; *R (HM Customs & Excise) v Nottingham Magistrates' Court* (n187), [55].

[296] Including improper methods of bringing the accused into the jurisdiction: *R v Horseferry Road Magistrates Court, ex p Bennett* [1994] 1 AC 42, [1993] 3 All ER 138; *R v Mullen* [2000] QB 520, [1999] 2 Cr App Rep 143.   [297] (n199).

There was less unanimity on the precise ambit of the discretion, though all of their Lordships subscribed to the answer to the certified question quoted above.[298] The difficulty resides in the precise delineation between the general denial of a discretion to exclude evidence obtained by improper means, and the exclusion from that denial of evidence obtained from the accused after the commission of the offence. It seems that Lord Fraser understood the exclusion to extend to evidence obtained from the premises of the accused.[299] He also expressed the view that the decision left judges with a discretion to exclude in accordance with their individual views of what is unfair, oppressive, or morally reprehensible. It is hard to reconcile that view of the discretion with Lord Diplock's view that there is no discretion to exclude evidence discovered as a result of an illegal search.[300] It is also difficult to be sure exactly what relation there is between the discretion as applied to confessions and that applying to improperly obtained evidence. Lord Diplock explained the cases of *R v Barker*[301] and *R v Payne*[302] on the basis of an analogy between the two situations.[303] In the former, incriminating books of account of impeccable reliability were regarded[304] as obtained by deception; in the latter, the accused was persuaded by deceptive means to submit to a medical examination, once again yielding perfectly reliable evidence. It seems then that the analogy is achieved by explaining the confession rule not on considerations of unreliability, but on those restricting self-incrimination.[305]

Inconsistencies in the reasoning immediately attracted the attention of academic commentators.[306] The lack of guidance was also recognized by the Court of Appeal, which remarked that the limited exception to the general denial of exclusionary discretion in respect of improperly obtained evidence had not been fully considered, although it was clear that where it existed one of its purposes was to control the police:[307]

As there was no deliberate misconduct by the officer, this hardly seems to be a case in which the Court should seek to discipline the police, even though there may be cases where the exclusion of the evidence for disciplinary purposes may be justified.

Subsequent English case law failed to take matters very much further before the advent of the statutory discretion in s 78 of the Police and Criminal Evidence Act 1984.[308] In other jurisdictions, very different approaches are adopted.[309] They will be discussed more fully in Chapter X. It is sufficient to note here that the Canadian approach was, before the enactment of the Charter, arguably more restrictive than that illustrated in *Sang*,[310] and

---

[298] 214.
[299] 450, 1241.   [300] 436, 1230.   [301] [1941] 2 KB 381, [1941] 3 All ER 33.
[302] [1963] 1 All ER 848, [1963] 1 WLR 637.   [303] 436, 1229.   [304] But see 506 n312.
[305] Lord Diplock, 436, 1230, Lord Fraser, 449, 1241, and Lord Scarman, 456, 1247.
[306] See commentary in [1979] *Crim LR* 656; Cross [1979] 30 *NILQ* 289; Polyviou in Tapper (ed) *Crime, Proof and Punishment* (1981); Pattenden *Judicial Discretion and Criminal Litigation* (1990).
[307] *R v Trump* (1979) 70 Cr App Rep 300, 303. A similarly disciplinary discretion was mentioned in *R v Heston-Francois* [1984] QB 278, [1984] 1 All ER 785.
[308] Many of the cases concerned breath-testing; cf *Trump* (n307), in which there was discretion to exclude the evidence (although it was held right not to exercise it) and *Winter v Barlow* [1980] RTR 209, in which there was held to be no discretion.
[309] See Pattenden (1980) 29 *ICLQ* 664; (1981) 13 MULR 31.
[310] *R v Wray* [1971] SCR 272. The court is still prepared to admit evidence secured by illegal searches when satisfied that exclusion would discredit the administration of justice more than admission: see e.g. *R v Caslake* [1998] 1 SCR 51.

the Irish,[311] Scottish,[312] and Australian, more expansive. In the leading Australian case, it was denied that the discretion:[313]

...takes as its central point the question of unfairness to the accused. It is, on the contrary, concerned with the broader question of high public policy, unfairness to the accused being only one factor which, if present, will play its part in the whole process of consideration.

The High Court also explained that the reason for this was that:[314]

...it is not fair play that is called in question in such cases but rather society's right to insist that those who enforce the law themselves respect it, so that a citizen's precious right to immunity from arbitrary and unlawful intrusion into the daily affairs of private life may remain unimpaired.

The High Court has also expressed the view that, in the case of entrapment involving the commission of crime by the authorities, the discretion passes beyond that of merely excluding particular pieces of evidence, and extends to the exclusion of any evidence of a crime so committed:[315]

...a trial judge possesses a discretion to exclude, on public policy grounds, evidence of an offence or of an element of an offence in circumstances where its commission has been brought about by unlawful conduct on the part of law enforcement officers.

The Police and Criminal Evidence Act 1984, s 78[316]

In England, the position was overtaken by the passage of s 78 of the Police and Criminal Evidence Act 1984, which provides:[317]

(1) In any proceedings the court may refuse to allow evidence on which the prosecution proposes to rely to be given if it appears to the court that, having regard to all the circumstances in which the evidence was obtained, the admission of the evidence would have such an adverse effect on the fairness of the proceedings that the court ought not to admit it.

(2) Nothing in this section shall prejudice any rule of law requiring a court to exclude evidence.

(3) This section shall not apply in the case of proceedings before a magistrates' court inquiring into an offence as examining justices.

This section was introduced at a very late stage, and replaced a clause introduced in the House of Lords on the motion of Lord Scarman, which would have spelled out a clear reverse onus exclusionary rule, linked explicitly to the Codes of Practice issued under the Act. An important difference is that, under s 78, the criteria for exclusion are much more

---

[311] *The People (A-G) v O'Brien* [1965] IR 142.   [312] *Lawrie v Muir* 1950 JC 19.

[313] *Bunning v Cross* (1978) 141 CLR 54, 74; affirmed as being of quite general application in *Cleland v R* (1983) 151 CLR 1. See also *R v Ireland* (1970) 126 CLR 321; *Pollard v R* (1992) 176 CLR 177; *Foster v R* (1993) 113 ALR 1; *Ridgeway v R* (1995) 184 CLR 19.

[314] (n313), 75.

[315] *Ridgeway* (n313), 35, 36. The result in *Ridgeway* was subsequently overturned by statute, and that statute's application to this discretion upheld as constitutional in *Nicholas v R* [1998] HCA 9, (1998) 193 CLR 173. For discussion of the policy and background, see Bronitt and Roche (2000) 4 *E&P* 77.

[316] See further Grevling (1997) 113 *LQR* 667; Ormerod and Birch [2004] *Crim LR* 50th Ann Edn 138.

[317] Section 78(3) was added by the Criminal Procedure and Investigations Act 1996, Sch 1, para 26.

vague.[318] It is interesting that s 78 uses the phrase 'evidence on which the prosecution proposes to rely'. This may be construed more widely than Lord Scarman's phrase, which was 'evidence (other than a confession) proposed to be given by the prosecution'.[319] Section 78 is wider in abstaining from any explicit exclusion of confessions,[320] and in perhaps extending to evidence assisting the prosecution, but tendered by, say, a co-accused. It remains uncertain what sorts of impropriety will prevail. The provenance of s 78 made it doubtful whether mere breach of one of the Codes of Practice would necessarily suffice, since this was explicitly and separately mentioned in Lord Scarman's provision, but was omitted here. It is noteworthy also that, while Lord Scarman's version referred to 'the fair administration of the criminal law', s 78 as enacted refers to 'the fairness of the proceedings'.[321] The former phrase would more easily have been capable of being construed in the spirit of *Bunning v Cross*. It was previously held that the point should be taken before evidence is adduced,[322] but in *R v Lashley*,[323] the Court of Appeal failed to use this as its principal ground for disapproving the trial judge's holding that the point should not be raised until the close of the case for the prosecution.

It should be noted that s 78 applies only to criminal proceedings,[324] from which committal proceedings have now been excluded.[325] In the case of summary trial by magistrates it is desirable that the evidence first be received, and then only if found unacceptable, and if necessary to avoid prejudice, the case be adjourned to a separate bench.[326] Since its enactment, s 78 has become the focus of attempts to secure the exclusion by discretion of evidence, both real and confessional, which has been unfairly obtained.[327] It is used both in conjunction with other discretions,[328] and as a discretionary backstop to the exclusionary rules.[329] It has even been suggested that it can be used to dilute the strict application of statutory provisions.[330] Its advent[331] transformed judicial practice. Whereas in *Sang* the

[318] Permitting analogy to breaches of the Codes of Practice in the case of those not formally subject to them: *R v Ristic* [2004] EWCA Crim 2107 (prison officer not engaged in investigation of offences).

[319] In *R v Cottrill* (n295), it was applied in a case in which the prosecution's reliance was conditional upon the accused's disavowal of the statement, which did not materialize.

[320] Although its interpretation in relation to confessions may be different: see *R v McCarthy* [1996] Crim LR 818.

[321] Although it should be noted that the fact that the surrounding ss 77 and 79 refer to 'a trial' has been held to indicate a more extended meaning of 'proceedings': see *R v King's Lynn Justices, ex p Holland* [1993] 2 All ER 377, [1993] 1 WLR 324; 379, 326.

[322] *R v Sat-Bhambra* (1989) 88 Cr App R 55, at 62. It could perhaps be argued that this is to read 'rely' as if it were synonymous with 'adduce'.

[323] [2005] EWCA Crim 2016, [12], perhaps undermining the point by stressing discretion.

[324] This will also have the consequential effect of exempting extradition proceedings as a result of the operation of the Extradition Act 1989, s 9(2): see *R v Governor of Brixton Prison, ex p Levin* [1997] AC 741, [1997] 3 All ER 289, Lord Hoffmann, 748H, 295a.

[325] Section 78(3), inserted by the Criminal Procedure and Investigation Act 1996, Sch 1, para 26.

[326] *DPP v Lawrence* [2007] EWHC 2154, [2008] 1 Cr App R 147, [26].

[327] For some early empirical evidence of its use, see Hunter [1994] *Crim LR* 558.

[328] In *R v Brigden* [2009] EWCA Crim 1690 to supplement that in s 101(3) of the Criminal Justice Act 2003 which does not extend to objection to the admission of evidence of the bad character of a co-accused.

[329] For attacks upon the breadth of its interpretation in this context, see Robertson (1989) 139 *NLJ* 1223; Gelowitz (1990) 106 *LQR* 327.

[330] *R v O'Connor* (1986) 85 Cr App R 298, 303 (s 74 of the Police and Criminal Evidence Act 1984); *R v Soroya* [2006] EWCA Crim 1884, [28] (s 41 of Youth Justice and Criminal Evidence Act 1999).

[331] As in Canada and New Zealand the enactment of the new constitutional provisions of the Charter and Bill of Rights: see, in Canada, *R v Collins* [1987] 1 SCR 265, 286, 287; in New Zealand, *Ministry of Transport v Noort* [1992] 3 NZLR 260, 271.

House of Lords was referred to only one appellate case in which the discretion to exclude operated on the basis of the evidence having been obtained unfairly, it has now been exercised to such effect in hundreds of cases.[332] Some general points have become clear: first, the discretion is at least as broad as the discretion at common law;[333] second, as part of a codifying provision, it will not be construed as subject to any common law restrictions expressed in *Sang*;[334] third, the circumstances to be taken into account in assessing its exercise are not limited to those that would be admissible, or likely to be admitted, in evidence;[335] fourth, impropriety is not a necessary condition to its exercise;[336] fifth, oppression is not a sufficient condition for its exercise;[337] sixth, it is the reality of unfairness rather than its appearance that is decisive;[338] seventh, and more controversial, fairness to other accused,[339] the prosecution,[340] or public[341] should be taken into account as well as fairness to the defence;[342] and eighth, not all unfairness in the proceedings will suffice to trigger the discretion, since the section refers to the exclusion only of matters having *such* an adverse effect, implying that some adverse effects are tolerable.[343] It seems that the exclusion of real evidence by reference to this discretion will still be exercised relatively rarely in serious[344] cases. Purely technical,[345] or even numerous and culpable,[346] breaches of the Codes of Practice, or even of the European Convention on Human Rights after 1998,[347] seem unlikely alone to suffice, sometimes not even in the case of a young person.[348] Indeed, the

---

[332] See Hunter (n327), 558 n2; as of 2009, over fifteen hundred cases recorded electronically: a number unlikely to include many more in which the provision was used successfully at trial.

[333] *R v Khan* [1997] AC 558, [1996] 3 All ER 289; 578E, 298f. Although this is immaterial, since the common law discretion is preserved by s 82(3) of the Police and Criminal Evidence Act 1984. In *R v Caldwell and Dixon* (1993) 99 Cr App Rep 73, that provision was invoked by the defence in relation to questionable procedures relating to identification.

[334] *R v Fulling* [1987] QB 426, [1987] 2 All ER 65; 432, 69.

[335] *R v Bailey* (n157), 271F.   [336] *Fulling* (n334); *R v O'Leary* (1988) 87 Cr App Rep 387.

[337] *R v Chalkley* [1998] QB 848, [1998] 2 All ER 155; 874A, 178a.

[338] *R v Ryan* [1992] Crim LR 187; but cf *R v Gall* (1989) 90 Cr App Rep 64. In this respect, the concept of unfairness coheres both with that at common law (*R v Christou* [1992] QB 979, [1992] 4 All ER 559) and with that under the European Convention on Human Rights (*R v Khan* [1997] AC 558, [1996] 3 All ER 289), since it has been held that its meaning cannot change according to its context.

[339] (1990) 91 Cr App Rep 371, 376. But not all disparity between the co-accused is necessarily unfair: *R v McNab* [2001] EWCA Crim 1605, [2002] 1 Cr App R (S) 72 (one accused interrogated under different provisions applicable in Scotland).

[340] See *R v Walsh* (1989) 91 Cr App Rep 161, 163, in which fairness under s 78 seems to subsume fairness required under s 58.

[341] *R v Smurthwaite and Gill* [1994] 1 All ER 898, 903.

[342] *R v Warner; R v Jones* (1992) 96 Cr App Rep 324, 330. This may be intended to act as a counterweight to the availability of reliance upon the discretion only to the defence, and may induce a more expansive approach to initial admissibility of prosecution evidence.

[343] *R v Walsh* (n340), 163.

[344] But perhaps more readily in less serious ones: see *Matto v Wolverhampton Crown Court* [1987] RTR 337 (illegally secured breath test); but even then not if the breach is purely technical: *DPP v Kennedy* [2003] EWHC 2583 (Admin), (2003) 168 JP 185.

[345] *R v McCarthy* [1996] Crim LR 818, disapproving of *R v Fennelley* [1989] Crim LR 142 in relation to deficiencies in the information provided prior to a search.

[346] *R v Stewart* [1995] Crim LR 500 (unauthorized entry to premises by electricity officials).

[347] *R v Bailey* [2001] EWCA Crim 733.

[348] *R (DPP) v BE* [2002] EWHC 2976, (2002) 167 JP 144, in which the magistrates were held to have been wrong to exclude a breath test on a 16-year-old in breach of Code C because of the absence of an appropriate adult; cf, in Australia, *R v KS* [2003] VSC 418, in which the youth of a person whose cell conversation was legally recorded precipitated its discretionary exclusion.

use of physical force,[349] or its threat,[350] has been held insufficient. On the other hand, especially after the implementation of the Human Rights Act 1998, where the accused is mentally handicapped and provided the assistance neither of an appropriate adult in breach of Code C, nor of legal advice, the discretion to exclude has been exercised.[351]

It should be noted that there was some doubt how far s 78 affected the principle, expressed in *Sang*, that the substantive rule that entrapment[352] is no defence could not be undermined by the use of an evidential discretion.[353] In *R v Smurthwaite and Gill*,[354] it was accepted that s 78 had introduced some discretion to exclude evidence in this situation, and indicated that its exercise should take into account how far the officer was acting as an agent provocateur, how active or passive his role, the nature of the entrapment,[355] how reliable its recording, and whether or not the officer, being undercover, had attempted to circumvent the restrictions on questioning imposed by the Code of Practice.[356] The matter was further considered by the House of Lords in *Looseley*, in which, although it was recognized that the primary remedy should be a stay, it was accepted that discretionary evidential exclusion on the same basis might sometimes be appropriate.[357]

These situations extend to those in which the accused are deceived into producing evidence against themselves, either by the interception of communications, or by some form of trick,[358] or both. They do not extend to those in which use is made of some extrinsic form of compulsory process, so long as it is not abused.[359] Nor do they extend to the situation in which the accused is tricked into coming within the jurisdiction of the court.[360] It

---

[349] *R v Hughes* (1994) 99 Cr App Rep 160 (pinching his nose to compel the accused to disgorge the contents of his mouth).

[350] *R v Cooke* [1995] 1 Cr App Rep 318 (three policemen in full riot gear to overcome the accused's initial refusal to provide a hair sample).

[351] *R v Aspinall* [1999] 2 Cr App Rep 115.

[352] In *R v Edwards* [1991] Crim LR 45, a somewhat restrictive view of the concept of entrapment was adopted.

[353] Compare *DPP v Marshall* [1988] 3 All ER 683, *R v Harwood* [1989] Crim LR 285, and *London Borough of Ealing v Woolworths plc* [1995] Crim LR 58, with *R v Gill and Ranuana* [1989] Crim LR 358. For a useful survey of the law in a number of common law jurisdictions, see Roser (1993) 67 *ALJ* 722.

[354] (1994) 98 Cr App Rep 437, which asserts an indicative rather than definitive intent. See also *R v Governor of Pentonville Prison, ex p Chinoy* [1992] 1 All ER 317.

[355] See, in Australia, *R v Venn-Brown* [1991] 1 Qd R 458; in Canada, *Mack v R* [1988] 2 SCR 903; in New Zealand, *R v O'Shannesy* [1973] 1 CRNZ 1, in which the preceding considerations are also applied.

[356] This falls far short of excluding all statements made to undercover policemen: *R v Lin* [1995] Crim LR 817. But see *R v Smith* (1994) 75 ACR 327 for a decision in Australia that approaches such a view.

[357] (n255), [16], Lord Nicholls, [43] Lord Hoffmann, [104] Lord Hutton, and [120] Lord Scott.

[358] This seems the most acceptable explanation of *R v Nathaniel* [1995] 2 Cr App Rep 565, in which compelling DNA evidence crucial to a very serious charge was excluded, apparently because of an assurance to the accused that a sample was required only for one particular charge, and that it would be destroyed if he were acquitted, even though the retention of the sample had been the result of an innocent mistake. For extensive discussion of police trickery in Australia, see *Em v R* [2007] HCA 46, 232 CLR 67.

[359] *R v Saunders* [1996] 1 Cr App Rep 463 (examination by compulsory process under ss 432(2) and 442 of the Companies Act 1985). An indication of permissible limits is seen in the trial judge's discretionary exclusion of answers obtained *after* the accused had been charged, and in the holding in *R v Smith* [1994] 1 WLR 1396, 99 Cr App Rep 233, that the discretion should have been exercised when the accused was under the mistaken belief that his interrogation related only to a non-criminal issue. See also *R v Crown Court at Southwark, ex p Bowles* [1998] AC 641, [1998] 2 All ER 193 (investigation into whether a person had benefitted from criminal conduct under Criminal Justice Act 1988, s 93H).

[360] *R v Latif* [1996] 1 All ER 353, [1996] 1 WLR 104. This was treated as a by-product of holding that this conduct did not amount to an abuse of process; for comparison with *Ridgeway* (n313), see Grevling, (1996)

seems that undercover police operations that provide an opportunity for the commission of crime,[361] or the disposal of its fruits,[362] will not necessarily attract the operation of the discretion. It is important though that such an operation be reliably recorded, and that the situation not be treated as an expedient to evade the conditions for police questioning set out in the Codes of Practice.[363] Sometimes illegal or deceptive conduct is undertaken to obtain a recording that may itself be incriminating, or even amount to a full confession. In *R v Khan*,[364] the police illegally[365] installed a listening device on private premises, yet the House of Lords approved the trial judge's refusal to exclude the incriminating material so obtained in his discretion under s 78.[366] In the sphere of trickery, while it has been thought appropriate to apply the discretion to a full confession secured only after deception addressed, after the accused's arrest, to his legal adviser,[367] a different view has been taken of a surreptitious recording of a conversation in a police station, even though suspicion was lulled[368] by an elaborate charade enacted by the investigating and custody officers,[369] and of a recording of an incriminating telephone call obtained by an elaborate trick involving cooperation between an accomplice and customs officers.[370] Nor is it appropriate to apply the discretion to earlier acts of third parties that led to the interception being arranged.[371] These results seem to accord with those arrived at in England under the common law discretion,[372] although a different view is taken in some overseas

---

112 LQR 401. In *Sammak v R* (1993) 2 Tas SR 339, breach of a temporal condition to jurisdiction was not sufficient to trigger exclusion.

[361] *Williams v DPP* [1993] 3 All ER 365 (a van full of cigarettes apparently left unattended).

[362] *R v Christou* (n338) (a shop apparently prepared to deal in stolen goods). Cf *R v Stead* (1992) 62 ACR 40 (apparently willing participant in stripping down stolen cars).

[363] *R v Bryce* [1992] 4 All ER 567, 95 Cr App Rep 320 (an apparently genuine purchaser of a stolen car). See also *R v Okafor* [1994] 3 All ER 741, 99 Cr App Rep 97 (plain-clothes customs officer apparently ignorant of illicit contents of package).

[364] (n333). For a similar result in Australia, in relation to the illegal installation of a video camera, see *R v McNamara* (1994) 73 ACR 539.

[365] Probably in breach of both civil and criminal law, but in conformity with Home Office guidelines!

[366] And also failed to stay the proceedings as an abuse of process: see further Tapper (1997) 1 *Int J of Ev & Proof* 162.

[367] *R v Mason* [1987] 3 All ER 481, [1988] 1 WLR 139. See also *R v De Silva* [2002] EWCA Crim 2673, [2003] 2 Cr App Rep 74, in which evidence from telephone calls made only on the basis of a promise of cooperation in return for promised treatment, which was then withheld, was regarded for that reason as inadmissible, although the rest of the evidence was so strong that the ultimate outcome was unaffected.

[368] Amazingly successfully, despite a warning from the accused's solicitor of the exact stratagem likely to be employed.

[369] *R v Bailey* [1993] 3 All ER 513, 97 Cr App Rep 365. This may be regarded as going further than *R v Jelen and Katz* (1989) 90 Cr App Rep 456 (in which the deception was practised by a third party); *R v Ali (Shaukat)* (1991) The Times, 19 February (in which the recording was surreptitiously made in the police station but without any specific deception or charade); or *R v Roberts* [1997] 1 Cr App Rep 217 (in which the recording was made in a cell bugged without the knowledge of either the accused or the co-accused, who the police knew would be likely to try to provoke a confession). Where the interception was made under the provisions of the Interception of Communications Act 1985, a still more complicated situation arose, but it was held that it did not enlarge the scope of discretionary exclusion under s 78: *R v Preston* [1994] 2 AC 130, [1993] 4 All ER 638; 169, 669. See also *R v Effik: Mitchell* [1995] 1 AC 309, [1994] 3 All ER 458. The relevant provision is now the Regulation of Investigatory Powers Act 2000.

[370] *R v Maclean: R v Kosten* [1993] Crim LR 687.   [371] *R v Dixon: R v Mann* [1995] Crim LR 647.

[372] Such as those in *R v Mills: R v Rose* [1962] 3 All ER 298, [1962] 1 WLR 1152 (conversation in police cell overheard without any deception beyond setting up a tape recorder without prior warning); *R v Buchan* [1964] 1 All ER 502, [1964] 1 WLR 365 (accused believed, and police knew he believed, that confession was

jurisdictions,[373] and, at least in one case, in which the police took a more active role in encouraging an informer to elicit confessions from a cell mate upon whom he had deliberately been foisted, by the European Court of Human Rights.[374]

It should also be noted that the new statutory discretion to preserve the fairness of the proceedings in s 78 has, perhaps surprisingly, been held even to permit the exclusion of evidence of convictions obtained in other proceedings, despite their clearly satisfying the relevant statutory conditions.[375] It is also interesting to note that s 78 now seems to have eclipsed the common law discretion to such an extent that a hearsay statement otherwise admissible under the common law res gestae rule was said to be subject to exclusion by reference to it, because its maker would not be available for cross-examination.[376]

It is ironic that the very presence of s 78, irrespective of its incidence of use in particular contexts, has been used both by English courts to justify an expansive view of domestic legislation,[377] and by the European Court of Human Rights as a sufficient guarantee of a fair trial as to militate against the success of appeals based on breach of the European Convention.[378]

Confessions

The final area in which the discretion must be considered is that relating to confessional statements, which was at first carefully distinguished from those cases mentioned above concerned with real evidence, but to which it was explicitly applied by the High Court of Australia in *Cleland v R*,[379] and to which the operation of the statutory discretion in s 78 of the Police and Criminal Evidence Act 1984 has been held to apply.[380] As noted earlier, it has hitherto been possible to explain the exclusion of some confessional statements either on the basis of the need for a fair trial—in which case, the unreliability of such statements, and perhaps the question of self-incrimination, will be emphasized— or on the basis of the need for fair treatment—in which case, the protection of the accused, and perhaps of the community's self-respect, will become more prominent.

---

not being recorded); *R v Maqsud Ali* [1966] 1 QB 688, [1965] 2 All ER 464 (presence in secretly bugged room in police station); *R v Stewart* [1970] 1 All ER 689n, [1970] 1 WLR 907 (conversation in cell overheard by officer posing as prisoner); *R v Keeton* (1970) 54 Cr App Rep 267 (accused's telephone call to wife overheard by police switchboard operator).

[373] See, in Australia, *Pavic v R; R v Swaffield* (1998) 192 CLR 159 (statements recorded by co-accused fitted out by police, but acting on his own initiative; statements recorded by undercover police officer in course of investigations into another suspected offence), in which earlier authority is extensively reviewed; in Canada, *Rv Hebert* [1990] 2 SCR 151 (policeman posing as fellow prisoner and asking questions), *R v Broyles* [1991] 3 SCR 595 (friend acting under instructions of police, and functional equivalent of interrogation), and *R v Liew* [1999] 3 SCR 227 (undercover policeman eliciting statement in prison) where the evidence was excluded; but in the United States, *Illinois v Perkins* 496 US 292 (1990) (undercover policeman and friend of prisoner eliciting statement in prison), in which the evidence was admitted. Cf *Pfennig* as to another incident (fellow prisoners not acting under police instructions and not clear whether questioning took place), in which the evidence was not excluded.

[374] *Allan v United Kingdom* (2002) 36 EHRR 12.

[375] Police and Criminal Evidence Act 1984, s 74, see further, above, 124.

[376] *A-G's Ref (No 1 of 2003)* [2003] 2 Cr App Rep 453.

[377] *A-G's Ref (No 3 of 1999)* [2001] 2 AC 91, [2001] 1 All ER 577; *R v Hasan* [2005] UKHL 22, [2005] 2 AC 467, [62].   [378] *Khan v United Kingdom* (2001) 31 EHRR 1016, [39].

[379] (n313), subject only to the unlikelihood of being able to make out a case for the application of the discretion if the rules for admissibility had been satisfied. See also *Seymour v A-G for Commonwealth* (1984) 53 ALR 513, for a full discussion.   [380] *R v Mason* (n367); 484f, 144.

The Police and Criminal Evidence Act 1984, s 76 changed the basis of rules relating to the admissibility of confessions. Quite apart from the application to confessions of s 78, it also retained the court's general discretion to exclude in s 82(3):

Nothing in this Part of this Act shall prejudice any power of a court to exclude evidence (whether by preventing questions from being put or otherwise) at its discretion.

It is thus necessary to see what discretion existed before 1984. It was recognized when the rule excluding involuntary statements was put into its traditional form in *Ibrahim v R*.[381] In *R v Voisin*,[382] the exclusionary discretion was considered in relation to the Judges' Rules, which had been devised to govern questioning by the police. The court was unwilling to concede the force of law to the Rules, but recognized the discretion of the judge to exclude statements 'obtained from prisoners, contrary to the spirit' of the Rules. Some stress was laid upon the use of the discretion to exclude statements that had not been made voluntarily, or which were unreliable, but a residual category of unfairness was also mentioned. By 1964, when a new set of Judges' Rules was produced,[383] oppression had been added as a second ground of mandatory exclusion. Perhaps the most common argument advanced for the exercise of the exclusionary discretion in relation to confessions was that they had been obtained after breaches of the Judges' Rules. After a few early successes, such arguments began to fall on stonier ground. The nadir of this aspect of the exclusionary discretion was reached in *R v Prager*. In that case, the Court of Appeal seemed to submerge any breach of the Judges' Rules within the ordinary voluntariness test for exclusion by rule:[384]

Their non-observance may, and at times does, lead to the exclusion of an alleged confession; but ultimately all turns on the judge's decision whether, breach or no breach, it has been shown to have been made voluntarily.

This proved to be an ephemeral stage in the development of this discretion, which was reaffirmed by the Court of Appeal.[385] It should be noted that it was immaterial whether a breach of the Judges' Rules themselves was alleged, or breach of the principles accompanying the Rules,[386] or of the administrative guidelines published by the Home Office for the use of the police.[387] The essence of this discretion was concern for the fair treatment of the accused,[388] and governed by the principles that inspired the exclusionary rule itself, as Lord Hailsham expressed them in *Wong Kam-ming v R*:[389]

This is not only because of the potential unreliability of such statements, but also, and perhaps mainly, because in a civilised society it is vital that persons in custody or charged with offences should not be subjected to ill-treatment or improper pressure in order to extract confessions.

The exercise of the discretion before 1984 was accordingly not limited to breaches of the rules and their direct accompaniments, but was equally inspired by other similar factors, such as the detention of the accused in excess of the period permitted by statute,[390] or in

---

[381] [1914] AC 599, 609. [382] [1918] 1 KB 531.

[383] *Practice Note* [1964] 1 All ER 237, [1964] 1 WLR 152.

[384] [1972] 1 All ER 1114, [1972] 1 WLR 260; 1118, 266.

[385] *R v MacIntosh* (1982) 76 Cr App Rep 177. [386] *R v Gowan* [1982] Crim LR 821.

[387] *R v Westlake* [1979] Crim LR 652; but see *R v King* [1980] Crim LR 40.

[388] Although it was implausibly ascribed to the balance of probative force and prejudicial effect in *R v Ovenell* [1969] 1 QB 17, [1968] 1 All ER 933; 26, 939. [389] (n65); 261, 946.

[390] *R v Hudson* (1980) 72 Cr App Rep 163.

breach of other statutory requirements.[391] It was also unsurprising to find that discretion remained a second string for the exclusion of statements obtained after oppressive behaviour. Before 1984, voluntariness had often been treated as a rather rigid and technical concept, thus permitting some scope for the exercise of an exclusionary discretion in cases falling outside its confines. In *R v Hudson*, the existence of such a discretion was accepted quite unequivocally.[392]

The statutory discretion in s 78 has been exercised in relation to confessional statements in two main areas: first, in respect of conduct clearly falling outside the exclusionary provisions of s 76 of the Police and Criminal Evidence Act 1984;[393] second, as a buttress to those provisions.[394]

Statutory exclusion of confessions on the basis of potential unreliability is limited to those made 'in consequence of anything said or done' by an interlocutor.[395] It is clear that this cannot apply to one who spontaneously blurts out a confession,[396] and has been held not to apply where the effective cause[397] of confessing is some defect inherent in the speaker,[398] rather than proper questioning by the police. Even in cases in which the police act improperly, for example by interviewing a juvenile in the absence of an appropriate adult,[399] it seems that a confession will be excluded under the s 78 discretion only when deliberate advantage has been taken of the juvenile.[400] In the case of a deranged person,[401] or one suffering from some other disability,[402] a court is likely to exclude a confession under s 78,[403] at least in the absence of an appropriate adult.[404] It should, however, be noted that a direction warning of a special need for caution in cases substantially relying upon

---

[391]   *R v Platt* [1981] Crim LR 622 (breach of s 62 of Criminal Law Act 1977 in not informing parent of accused child's arrest).   [392]   170. See also *R v Wilson* [1981] 1 NZLR 316.

[393]   See *R v Howden-Simpson* [1991] Crim LR 49, in which the Court of Appeal quite explicitly stated that, although a threat was not enough to make a confession potentially unreliable, it was enough to trigger the discretion; see further Chapter XIV.

[394]   Both in New Zealand and in the state of Victoria, where broadly similar provisions have been in force for many years, it has been held that there is still scope for an exclusionary discretion alongside: see *R v Phillips* [1949] NZLR 316, 345; *R v Lee* (1950) 82 CLR 133, 150.

[395]   In most Commonwealth jurisdictions, a 'voluntariness' test applies, but it tends to be interpreted less technically than was the case in England, so, e.g. in Australia, in extreme cases of impairment, a confession may be excluded by rule, while in some cases, it is a matter for discretion: see *Sinclair v R* (1947) 73 CLR 316; *McDermott v R* (1948) 76 CLR 501, 507; *Murphy v R* (1989) 167 CLR 94; *R v Parker* (1990) 47 ACR 281; in New Zealand, see *R v Cooney* [1994] 1 NZLR 38.

[396]   Or to a case in which a confession is made to a solicitor, and passed to the prosecution in error without any suggestion of impropriety on the part of prosecution or police: *R v Cottrill* [1997] Crim LR 56.

[397]   Although this again will not be allowed to degenerate into technicality: *R v Barry* (1991) 95 Cr App Rep 384, 389.   [398]   *R v Goldenberg* (1989) 88 Cr App Rep 285.

[399]   Contrary to Code of Practice, C. 13.1.

[400]   Compare *R v Fogah* [1989] Crim LR 141 with *R v Maguire* (1989) 90 Cr App Rep 115.

[401]   *R v Miller* (n252); *R v Moss* (1990) 91 Cr App Rep 371.

[402]   *R v Clarke* [1989] Crim LR 892 (deafness); *R v Li* [1993] 2 VLR 80 (foreigner unable to understand without interpreter). For special discretion in relation to aborigines in Australia, see *Kiah v R* [2001] NTCCA 1, (2001) 160 FLR 26.

[403]   Since a plea of guilty was disregarded in *R v Swain* [1986] Crim LR 480 and the conviction quashed, it would be odd if the court had no power to exclude evidence of the overturned plea as a confession at a retrial, should one have been ordered; as in *R v Aspinall* [1999] 2 Cr App Rep 115. For full consideration of discretion in this context in Australia, see *R v Pfitzner* (1996) 66 SASR 161.

[404]   See *R v Utip* [2003] EWCA 1256, in which the presence of such an adult and a solicitor, and a decision by the only psychiatrist involved that the accused was fit to be interviewed, contributed to the decision not to exclude a confession from a mentally ill person.

confessions by the mentally handicapped made otherwise than in the presence of independent persons has now been prescribed for such cases by s 77 of the Police and Criminal Evidence Act 1984.[405] Such a provision clearly contemplates that some such confessions will be admitted. A different aspect of unfairness may arise if the accused is induced to confess by being led to believe that what he says will be 'off the record', but is then confronted with his statement at the last minute.[406] A number of cases are concerned with access to legal advice during an interview. There is some presumption that its denial[407] will trigger the discretion to exclude,[408] but it is rebutted where such access is unlikely to have made any difference.[409] Conversely, access to legal advice[410] may serve to neutralize breaches of the Code,[411] and a court is likely to be highly sceptical of any suggestion that such access actually induced a false confession.[412]

The second area of application of s 78 to confessional statements is when it is used as a secondary argument in favour of discretionary exclusion, if a principal argument based upon exclusion by rule should fail.[413] In many cases, such a claim is linked to a breach of the Codes of Practice issued pursuant to s 66 of the Police and Criminal Evidence Act 1984. It is now clear that breach of the Code is neither a necessary, nor a sufficient,[414] condition for discretionary exclusion of a confession under this provision. It has indeed been held that the wording of s 78 itself indicates that some breaches may not lead to exclusion.[415] On the other hand, although police impropriety is not a necessary condition for the application of s 78, it seems that it is a powerful factor inclining the court to infer from such unfair treatment that the fairness of the proceedings has also been sufficiently adversely affected.[416]

It must be stressed that the discretion to exclude operates only in respect of confessional statements.[417] It is not available to exclude statements made by witnesses, however oppressively they may have been induced by the police. That is a matter going only to weight.[418]

---

[405] Omission of which may be fatal to conviction: see *R v Bailey* (n157).

[406] As in *R v Woodall* [1989] Crim LR 288.

[407] Especially in respect of an interview at which such access is denied after a less productive one at which it was granted: see *R v Marshall* (1992) The Times, 28 December.

[408] *R v Walsh* (n340), 163. In Trinidad, despite a constitutional right to be informed of a right to such access, breach does not automatically lead to exclusion, although there, the discretion was itself, somewhat mysteriously, said to be neither presumptively exclusionary nor inclusionary: *Mohammed (Allie) v State* [1999] 2 AC 111.   [409] *R v Dunford* (1990) 91 Cr App Rep 150.

[410] Despite some well-founded doubts as to its competence in many cases: see Royal Commission on Criminal Justice Res St Nos 2 and 16 (1992); *R v Paris* (1992) 97 Cr App Rep 99, 110; *R v Glaves* [1993] Crim LR 685.   [411] *R v Dunn* (1990) 91 Cr App Rep 237; *R v Hoyte* [1994] Crim LR 215.

[412] See *R v Francis* [1992] Crim LR 372.

[413] See e.g. *R v Alladice* (1988) 87 Cr App Rep 380; *R v Delaney* (1988) 88 Cr App Rep 338; *R v McGovern* (1990) 92 Cr App Rep 228 (in which both parts of s 76 were also invoked); *R v Barry* (n397).

[414] *R v Parris* (1988) 89 Cr App Rep 68, 72, in which the trial judge seems to have regarded it as the former, and the Court of Appeal negated, in addition, the latter. For the situation in Australia, see *Pollard v R* (1992) 176 CLR 177. It seems quite likely that in England, as much as in Australia, there may be more inclination to exclude when the breach of the Code has led to a failure to record the confession: see *R v Cvitko* [2001] SASC 72, (2001) 159 FLR 403.   [415] *R v Walsh* (n340), 165.

[416] *R v Alladice* (1988) 87 Cr App Rep 380, 386. For the converse view that punctilious observation of the Code of Practice militates against a finding of unfairness, see *Re Walters* [1987] Crim LR 577.

[417] Including exculpatory parts of mixed statements, acceptance of which might be misleading, *People v O'Neill* [2007] IECCA 8. [2007] IR 564.   [418] *R v Austin* (1982) Lexis Transcript, 18 June.

The Royal Commission on Criminal Justice[419] was generally well disposed towards the use of the discretionary exclusion of evidence in criminal proceedings, and recommended[420] the adoption in England of a rule corresponding to r 403 of the US Federal Rules of Evidence.[421] It is arguable that many of the considerations taken into account in that rule are already present in the assessment of the relevance of evidence in England,[422] but that the intervention of the judge to exclude unnecessarily cumulative evidence may intrude upon the function of the jury since it cannot be known which pieces of admissible evidence a jury will accept, nor how much weight it will attach to them.[423] It seems, in any event, that the judge may already have power to achieve these ends by the operation of time limits upon the processes of examination, cross-examination, and re-examination of witnesses.[424]

Discretion to exclude relevant evidence in civil proceedings[425]

This topic may now have been transformed by r 32.1.2 of the Civil Procedure Rules, which starkly provides that: 'The court may use its power under this rule to exclude evidence that would otherwise be admissible.' This is supplemented by the conferment of far-reaching powers to determine relevance. All will depend upon how this new discretion is exercised, and guidance has been sparse. There have been bland assertions that it should be exercised in support of dealing with the case justly,[426] less readily in trial by jury,[427] and with great circumspection so as to achieve the overriding objectives.[428] On the other hand, it has been said that, where a witness refuses to testify, it may be employed to exclude a prepared hearsay statement.[429] It was also held in *Jones v University of Warwick*,[430] in which a film had been made illegally, that its exclusion will not simply depend upon whether or not it has been disclosed to the other party, or withheld by way of an ambush defence. There, the exercise of the discretion was influenced by the distorting effect that exclusion would create, given that the case needed to be tried, and taking into account both the amount of the claim, and the degree of illegality. It may be useful to explain what has hitherto been the practice, pending further development.

Consideration was given to the existence of such a discretion in cases in which evidence had been unlawfully obtained, and in cases in which information was being

---

[419] Cm 2263 (1993).   [420] [8.13], rec 181.

[421] 'Although relevant, evidence may be excluded if its probative value is substantially outweighed by the danger of unfair prejudice, confusion of the issues, or misleading the jury, or by considerations of undue delay, waste of time, or needless presentation of cumulative evidence.' For exegesis see *Holmes v South Carolina* 547 US 319 (2008).

[422] Section 126(1)(b) of the Criminal Justice Act 2003 also enacts a new discretion to exclude hearsay on the basis of undue waste of time.

[423] See above, 189. But see *DPP v Wilson* [2001] EWHC Admin 198, (2001) 165 JP 715, [44] endorsing the use of cumulative evidence in English law.

[424] *Vernon v Bosley* [1995] 2 FCR 78, on the assumption that it applies in criminal proceedings as well as in civil.

[425] See Pattenden (1997) 1 *E&P* 361; and from an Australian perspective, Forbes (1988) 62 ALJ 211. For judicial consideration of the application of the various discretions operative there in criminal proceedings to civil, see *Southern Equities Corp Ltd v Bond* [2001] SASC 70, (2001) 78 SASR 554.

[426] *Grobbelaar v Sun Newspapers Ltd* (1999) The Times, 12 August.

[427] *Watson v Chief Constable of Cleveland* [2001] EWCA Civ 1547, [23]–[24].

[428] *Great Future International Ltd v Sealand Housing Corp* [2002] EWCA Civ 1183, [24].

[429] *Polanski v Condé Nast Publications Ltd* [2003] EWCA Civ 1573, [2004] 1 All ER 1220, [23].

[430] [2003] EWCA Civ 151, [2003] 3 All ER 760.

withheld from the court.[431] There seem to be no English cases asserting a discretion to exclude, pursuant to the fair-trial categorization, on the basis that the evidence will be more prejudicial than probative in revealing evidence of extrinsic discreditable acts.[432] It was explicitly rejected in *Bradford City Metropolitan Council v K*.[433] In some cases, while accepting this view as technically correct, the court has softened its impact, either by suggesting the possibility of discounting weight,[434] or by subsuming such matters into the initial determination of relevance.[435]

It was denied, in *Ibrahim v R*,[436] that there was any discretion to exclude improperly obtained statements in civil proceedings. In *Helliwell v Piggott-Sims*, in which the Court of Appeal assumed the evidence to have been obtained by improper means, the same view was repeated:[437]

…in criminal cases the judge may have a discretion. That is shown by *Kuruma v R*.[438] But so far as civil cases are concerned, it seems to me that the judge has no discretion. The evidence is relevant and admissible. The judge cannot refuse it on the ground that it may have been unlawfully obtained in the beginning.

The other context in which the question has been raised is in relation to claims of privilege, which will be dealt with in detail in Chapters IX and X. If an established privilege already exists, no question of discretion arises because, in the words of Lord Wilberforce: 'to substitute for the privilege a dependence on the courts' discretion would substantially be to the defendant's detriment'.[439] It arises only when a witness makes an unsuccessful claim to be privileged from answering a question: does the judge then have a residual discretion not to allow the question to be put? In *D v National Society for the Prevention of Cruelty to Children*, Lord Simon was quite clear that in such a case 'it must be law, not discretion,

---

[431] In Scotland, there is no common law discretion to exclude otherwise admissible evidence in civil proceedings: *McVinnie v McVinnie* 1995 SLT 81, a decision of Sheriff MacPhail, endorsed by the Outer House in *Glaser v Glaser* 1997 SLT 456; but see also *Lobban v Phillip* 1995 SCLR 1104.

[432] Such a discretion was denied in Australia: see *Polycarpou v Australian Wire Industries Pty Ltd* (1995) 36 NSWLR 49, in which all of the authorities were reviewed by Kirby P. Statutory exclusionary discretions are now provided for civil proceedings by the Evidence Act 1995 (Cwth) ss 135 and 138, and a discretion to limit the use of evidence by s 136. It may be noted that the corresponding r 403 of the US Federal Rules does apply to civil proceedings. Although the terminology of discretion was employed in this context in *Berger v Raymond & Son Ltd* [1984] 1 WLR 625, it seems likely that it was used no more than loosely to characterize those elements of the exclusionary rule of an essentially indeterminate nature or perhaps to prevent prejudice in the case of surprise or unduly lengthening the proceedings by adducing evidence of dubious relevance, which might include evidence of previous judicial findings of misconduct: see *Al-Hawaz v Thomas Cook Group Ltd* LEXIS 27 October 2000. See further below 356.

[433] [1990] Fam 140, although in terms applying only to the civil jurisdiction of magistrates the language is general, and contains no hint of restriction to lower courts.

[434] *Re C (minors)* [1993] 4 All ER 690, 694.

[435] *Vernon v Bosley* (n424), in which Hoffmann LJ explicitly equates considerations relating to such an assessment with the operation of the discretion.

[436] (n381); 610, 878. In some jurisdictions, such a discretion has been recognized where the grounds amount to breach of an explicit constitutional provision: see e.g. *Lotter v Arlow* 2002 (6) SA 60.

[437] *Helliwell v Piggott-Sims* [1980] FSR 356, 357, echoing similar sentiments expressed in *R v Christie* [1914] AC 545, [1914–15] All ER Rep 63, Lord Moulton, 559, 69 and Lord Reading, 564, 71. See also *ITC Film Distributors v Video Exchange Ltd* [1982] Ch 431, [1982] 2 All ER 241.

[438] [1955] AC 197.

[439] *Rank Film Distributors Ltd v Video Information Centre* [1982] AC 380, [1981] 2 All ER 76; 442, 81.

which is in command'.[440] Unfortunately, Lord Hailsham took the opposite view, accepting the views expressed in the 16th report of the Law Reform Committee on privilege in civil proceedings:[441]

Privilege in the main is the creation of the common law whose policy, pragmatic as ever, has been to limit to a minimum the categories of privileges which a person has an absolute right to claim, but to accord to the judge a wide discretion to permit the witness, whether a party to the proceedings or not, to refuse to disclose information where disclosure would be a breach of some ethical or social value and non-disclosure would be unlikely to result in serious injustice in the particular case in which it is claimed.

The position has been reconsidered in subsequent authority, although the issue has, at best, arisen on the periphery of a claim based on resistance to discovery. Since discovery is an equitable remedy, it always has a discretionary element.[442] It is far from clear that the same principles apply to prevent evidence from being adduced. Thus in *McGuiness v A-G of Victoria*, Sir Owen Dixon, in refuting a claim that the rules limiting discovery applied to evidence, said: 'The answer is that it is not a rule of evidence but a practice of refusing in an action for libel...to compel discovery of the name of...informants.'[443] It might be argued that this passage relates only to the question of total immunity as a matter of law, and does not touch the question of discretionary exclusion. When the issue arose during a trial, a judge always had control over the propriety of the proceedings before him, and could certainly disallow vexatious or irrelevant questions. It is possible that the dicta in the authorities cited to justify the Law Reform Committee's view in its report relied upon that power.[444] At first instance, in *Granada*, Megarry VC urged separate consideration of the position, first, in interlocutory proceedings, second, at the trial, and third, in deciding upon a remedy.[445] In the Court of Appeal, Lord Denning rejected this view and asserted that the same principles applied at each stage.[446] In the House of Lords, it is less clear how far the decision that the court has a discretion extends beyond the precise question of pretrial disclosure. The better view is that it did extend to evidence at the trial. Lord Wilberforce referred to the duty as one to disclose to a court,[447] not as one to disclose to an opponent. Then, in his final summary of his reasons, after asserting that the court undoubtedly had a discretion, he went on to consider those parts of Megarry VC's reasons that explicitly related to a discretion in relation to evidence, and not to the discretion in relation to a remedy that he had carefully segregated.[448] It seems that the principle upon

---

440   [1978] AC 171, [1976] 2 All ER 993 239, 613. The House was numerically equally divided on this point. Lord Edmund Davies delivered a speech to the same effect as Lord Simon; Lord Diplock did not mention the matter; and Lord Kilbrandon contented himself with agreeing with Lord Hailsham. In *British Steel Corp v Granada Television Ltd* [1981] AC 1096, [1981] 1 All ER 417; 1113, 431, Megarry VC thought the balance favoured Lord Hailsham's view.

441   Para 1, citing *A-G v Clough* [1963] 1 QB 773, [1963] 1 All ER 420 and *A-G v Mulholland* [1963] 2 QB 477, [1963] 1 All ER 767, which, however, do not entirely justify the statement. See also para 51.

442   In *British Steel Corp v Granada Television Ltd* [1981] AC 1096, [1981] 1 All ER 417; 1174, 459, Lord Wilberforce said 'the remedy (*being equitable*) is discretionary' (emphasis supplied).

443   (1940) 63 CLR 73, 104, a passage quoted with approval by Viscount Dilhorne in *Granada* (n442).

444   As decided in *Re Buchanan* (1964) 65 SRNSW 9.

445   [1981] AC 1096, [1981] 1 All ER 417; 1111, 427.   446   1129, 441.

447   1168, 455.   448   1175, 460.

which the discretion was to be exercised was that stated by the House of Lords in *Science Research Council v Nassé*, namely:[449]

...to consider fairly the strength and value of the interest in preserving confidentiality and the damage which may be caused by breaking it; then to consider whether the objective, to dispose fairly of the case, can be achieved without doing so.

It is probably now too late to argue that this process related only to the determination of the initial obligation to answer, rather than to that of determining whether the obligation should be overridden in the circumstances of a particular case at the discretion of the judge.[450] In the particular case of the disclosure of the source of information contained in a publication, the matter came to be regulated, not by judicial discretion, but by a statutory rule that disclosure may be compelled only in the interests of justice or national security, or for the prevention of disorder or crime.[451] It was faintly suggested that an inclusionary discretion might exist in some cases, but this was rejected in relation to the discretionary admission of hearsay in proceedings involving children, both in the higher,[452] and lower,[453] courts. It is also significant that, in *Savings and Investment Bank Ltd v Gasco Investments (Netherlands) BV (No 2)*,[454] in which the Court of Appeal held contempt proceedings to be civil for the purposes of the admission of hearsay, it asserted not that such hearsay could be excluded at the court's discretion, but rather that it would be unlikely to be accorded sufficient weight to satisfy the heavy burden of proof.

It seems that the judge has a discretion to impose strict time limits upon the examination, cross-examination, and re-examination of a witness, which in effect amounts to a discretion to exclude at least some unnecessarily cumulative evidence.[455] It was, however, suggested by Butler Sloss LJ in *Re M and R (minors)*[456] that further review should take place with a view to instituting an exclusionary discretion at least in non-adversarial proceedings.[457] The new Civil Procedure Rules seem to have been designed specifically to respond more generally to this problem.[458]

THE SUMMING-UP

It is difficult to estimate the amount of control that a judge exercises over a jury by means of his summing-up,[459] for, quite apart from the legal rules that govern the matter, juries expect and receive considerable guidance with regard to the evidence submitted

---

[449] [1980] AC 1028, [1979] 3 All ER 673; 1067, 681. Although in terms limited to questions arising in relation to discovery, it should be noted that this passage is justified by reference to cases such as *Mulholland* and *Clough*, in which no question of discovery arose.   [450] As argued by Cross (1979) 30 *NILQ* 289.

[451] Contempt of Court Act 1981, s 10.   [452] *H v H* [1990] Fam 86, [1989] 3 All ER 740; 107; 754.

[453] *Bradford City Metropolitan Council v K* (n433).   [454] [1996] 4 All ER 239, [1996] 2 FLR 195.

[455] *Vernon v Bosley* (n424), 340.   [456] [1996] 4 All ER 239, 255.

[457] A view rejected by Pattenden and Forbes (n425) on the basis that relevance is a sufficiently flexible concept to achieve anything not achievable by the residuary powers of the judge to regulate proceedings before him.

[458] The generally enhanced powers of case management may also have the effect of reducing the need to exercise such a discretion: see *Hawaz v Cook* (27 October 2000, unreported) for an example of how determinations of relevance can lead to the exclusion of evidence.

[459] Self-direction in trial by judge alone was analysed in Australia by the High Court in *AK v Western Australia* [2008] HCA 8.

to them, and this guidance may be expressed in emphatic terms.[460] The legal rules on the subject have never been precisely formulated, but it seems that a judge must always put defences raised by the evidence to the jury[461] in his own words rather than merely repeating or referring to the arguments of counsel,[462] must not interrupt his rehearsal of the evidence with one-sided and unfair comment,[463] and can never be justified in directing a jury that they must accept his view of disputed facts,[464] although he may, in a civil case, and sometimes should, tell them they ought to do so as reasonable men.[465] If a party tenders no evidence on a contested issue, the judge may instruct the jury to draw the most favourable inference possible from the evidence tendered by the other.[466] Physical attack on the judge by a defendant does not prevent him from resuming upon his recovery.[467]

In a criminal case, the overriding duty of the judge[468] is to put the defence[469] fairly and adequately to the jury,[470] which in almost every case will involve a summing-up explaining the constituents of the offences charged,[471] and the relevance to them of the evidence that has been adduced[472] in a structured way,[473] but normally[474] without dictating the form or order of their reasoning.[475] In a joint trial he should deal with inconsistencies between the co-defendants.[476] It is not enough to leave the rehearsal of the facts to the speeches of counsel, supplemented by transcripts of interviews with the police.[477] The judge must not direct the jury to convict,[478] and must leave to the jury

---

[460] For general statements, see *Clouston & Co Ltd v Corry* [1906] AC 122, 130, Lord James of Hereford, and *R v Lawrence* [1982] AC 510, [1981] 1 All ER 974; 519F, 977e, Lord Hailsham LC.

[461] *R v Keith Keba Badjan* (1966) 50 Cr App Rep 141. In a complex case, a draft direction should be shown to counsel for comment before being delivered: *R v Taylor* [2003] EWCA Crim 2447.

[462] See in New Zealand *R v Shipton* [2007] 2 NZLR 218, [38].

[463] *R v Spencer* [1995] Crim LR 235.

[464] *Dublin Wicklow and Wexford Rly Co v Slattery* (1878) 3 App Cas 1155, 1186.

[465] See e.g. *Pickup v Thames and Mersey Marine Insurance Co* (1878) 3 QBD 594, 600.

[466] *Ross v Associated Portland Cement Manufacturers Ltd* [1964] 2 All ER 452, [1964] 1 WLR 768.

[467] *R v Russell* [2006] EWCA Crim 470.

[468] Although he is entitled to take into account in tailoring his summary the closing speeches of counsel: *Rv Ghani* [2003] EWCA Crim 2461, [8].

[469] If there are multiple defendants then the defences of all should be put similarly, see e.g. *R v Clothier* [2004] EWCA Crim 2629, [28].

[470] *R v Spencer* [1987] AC 128, [1986] 2 All ER 928; 142G, 938c. In Australia, even when the trial is by judge alone, he is required to direct himself explicitly: *Fleming v R* [1999] HCA 68, (1999) 197 CLR 250; in Canada, the trial judge sitting alone should also normally deliver reasons for his decision: *R v Sheppard* [2002] SCC 26, [2002] 1 SCR 869.

[471] *R v Brower* [1995] Crim LR 746. For this reason, it will rarely be possible to uphold a decision where the judge has proceeded on a false view of the law, since incorrect issues of fact will almost certainly have been left to the jury: *Mohammed and Richardson v State* [2001] UKPC 21.

[472] *R v Martins; R v Katthoeffer* [1996] CLY 1419.

[473] *R v Robson* (n51); *R v Sampson* [2007] EWCA Crim 1238, [57].

[474] For an exceptional case where the jury should first have been directed to consider conflicting medical evidence see *R v Schmidt* [2009] EWCA Crim 838.

[475] *R v Norris* [2007] NSWCCA 235, 176 ACR 42, [58].

[476] *R v Greenwood* [2009] EWCA Crim 549, [15].

[477] *R v Amado-Taylor* [2000] 2 Cr App Rep 189.

[478] *R v Wang* (n13).

any defence that is raised,[479] unless, in an exceptional case, there is no evidence at all to support it.[480]

He should also direct the jury on any other defence for which there is evidence, even if the defence has not raised it.[481] It is even enough if the only evidence in support is the exculpatory part of a pre-trial mixed statement.[482] He ought also to direct the jury whenever it might otherwise fall into error.[483] Where potentially prejudicial evidence[484] has been admitted, the judge must direct the jury on its potentially probative value, which is then for the jury to determine.[485] Admission of, or reference to, such evidence in error after a decision to exclude it, will usually be incorrigible.[486] The judge may comment quite robustly on the evidence, but must not direct the jury to accept it,[487] even in the case of uncontradicted medical evidence.[488] He must direct the jury in a balanced way,[489] without giving the impression of favouring one side rather than the other,[490] by not publicly attacking one side's counsel,[491] without assuming disputed facts,[492] and cannot content himself by simply reiterating the incantation that it is for the jury to decide the facts.[493] This is especially important if the jury has sought further guidance.[494] The judge's direction must be full[495] as well as fair.[496]

[479] Although even then a conviction may be upheld if the failure could have made no possible difference to the outcome: *R v Van Dongen* [2005] EWCA Crim 1728, [2005] 2 Cr App R 632, relying on *Franco v R* (n481).

[480] As in *R v Briley* [1991] Crim LR 444. The same applies to a coroner who is bound to leave to the jury only those verdicts for which there is evidence: *R v Coroner for the East Riding of Yorkshire* [2001] EWHC Admin 352.

[481] *Franco v R* [2001] UKPC 38 (provocation); *DPP v Bailey* [1995] 1 Cr App Rep 257 (self-defence); *Shaw v R* [2001] UKPC 26, [2001] 1 WLR 1519 (special statutory defence); whatever the judge's own view whether or not it would reasonably make any difference. See also in Australia *Fingleton v R* [2005] HCA 34, 227 CLR 166, [83].

[482] *R v Silverman* (1987) 86 Cr App Rep 213; *R v Bass* [1992] Crim LR 647.

[483] *R v Paton* [2007] EWCA Crim 1572, [32] (inference from accused's silence); *R v Ahmed* [2006] EWCA Crim 1636, [16] (use of co-accused's guilty plea); *Rodden v R* [2008] NSWCCA 53, 182 ACR 227 (proper use of tape recording).

[484] Which, when equivocal, should be taken at its most prejudicial: *R v Docherty* [1999] Cr App Rep 274.

[485] *R v Bethelmie* (1995) The Times, 27 November.

[486] As in *R v Lawson* [2005] EWCA Crim 84, approved by the Privy Council in *R v Mitcham* [2009] UKPC 5.

[487] The Royal Commission on Criminal Justice Cmnd 2263 (1993) para 8.23 suggests that the judge should not express any view as to the credibility of a witness.

[488] *R v Lanfear* [1968] 2 QB 77, [1968] 1 All ER 683.

[489] It is inappropriate to direct the jury in the form of a rhetorical question: *R v Lloyd* [2000] 2 Cr App Rep 355.

[490] *R v Copsey* [2008] EWCA Crim 2403, [23].

[491] *R v Cole* [2008] EWCA Crim 3234, [15].   [492] *R v RIL* (2005) 197 CCC3d 166.

[493] *R v Baird* [2007] EWCA Crim 2887, [25].

[494] *Mears v R* (1993) 97 Cr App Rep 239. Although even then he need not remind the jury of cross-examination as well as evidence in chief, unless it has also been requested: *R v Morgan* [1996] Crim LR 600.

[495] Although a minor omission even of a crucial detail is unlikely to be fatal if it is clear that the jury has disbelieved the whole story of which it is a part: *R v Williams* [2001] EWCA Crim 932, (2001) 98(19) LSG 36. On the other hand, an accumulation of errors can suffice: *R v Erskine and Dale* [2001] EWCA Crim 2513. So too, especially where the accused has not testified, should points in response to cross-examination be summarized: *R v Ojinnaka* [2003] EWCA Crim 3183, [100].

[496] *R v Marashi* [2001] EWCA Crim 2448.

The judge must instruct the jury on all matters of law, including the effect of any relevant presumption of law and of the onus of proof.[497] He should direct the jury that they must find a fact in issue proved if they are satisfied as to the existence of another fact, which under a rebuttable presumption triggers proof of the fact in issue in the absence of further evidence. As mentioned above,[498] the law attaches what may be an artificial probative value to certain facts, and the direction instructs the jury of the legal consequences of finding these facts to exist.

Directing the jury in criminal cases has now become so important, and so complex[499] a task that the Judicial Studies Board has provided model directions for judges to use.[500] Although it is not necessarily fatal for the judge to depart from the phraseology of model directions,[501] it may be dangerous, and defeat the whole purpose of instilling consistency of content and terminology.[502] In cases of disputed direction the issues should be raised in closing argument, and the judge indicate his intended approach.[503] The summing-up should come last, and counsel should not be permitted any further address to the jury, even to clear up errors.[504]

In civil cases tried without a jury, the judge should explain the reasons for his decision, including those relating to the credibility of witnesses,[505] sufficiently for it to be understandable why he has reached his decision, although he need not mention every argument put to him by counsel. This not only clarifies the law, and makes the decision more acceptable to the parties, but also establishes a basis for discerning whether leave should be given for an appeal.[506] It also accords better with Art 6 of the European Convention on Human Rights.[507] Counsel should raise any problems with any such explanation so that the judge can deal with them, rather than nurse a grievance and merely apply to appeal.[508]

In general the summing-up must be considered as a whole[509] and in the light of all of the evidence in the case, rather than by minute dissection of isolated passages divorced from their context.[510]

---

[497] *R v Zarrabi* (1985) The Times, 23 February, in which a conviction was quashed because the judge directed only upon the standard, and not upon the incidence of the burden, of proof.

[498] 133.

[499] Especially in cases involving more than one defendant: see *R v Ashton* [1992] Crim LR 667; *R v Lummes and Adams* [2001] EWCA Crim 72; *R v Kinneir* [2002] EWCA Crim 902; or more than one issue, see e.g. *R v Ogundipe* [2001] EWCA Crim 2576, in which there were issues of alibi, lies, and identification all requiring special directions.

[500] Although there is now some disquiet that the plethora of model directions may themselves be confusing and cause injustice: see *R v Sylvester* [2002] EWCA Crim 1327, [14].

[501] It may sometimes be desirable in order to focus on the facts of the case, and to eliminate speculative issues that do not really arise in the instant case: *R v Maturine* [2006] EWCA Crim 1543, [30].

[502] See *R v Kennedy and Hill* [2001] EWCA Crim 998, [36].

[503] *R v Graham* [2007] EWCA Crim 1499, [17].   [504] *R v JDC* (2002) 172 CCC3d 268.

[505] *Baird v Thurrock BC* [2005] EWCA Civ 1499, [18] (inconsistency with evidence from others); *Whitehead Mann Ltd v Cheverney Consulting Ltd* [2006] EWCA Civ 1303, [47] (self-inconsistency). See also *Re F (Children)* [2006] EWCA Civ 792, [2006] 2 FCR 837.

[506] *English v Emery Reimbold and Strick Ltd* [2002] EWCA Civ 605, [2002] 3 All ER 385, [19].

[507] See e.g. *Ruiz Torija v Spain* (1994) 19 EHRR 553, [29].

[508] *Re S (Children)* [2007] EWCA Civ 694, [25].

[509] Including retraction of part in further direction, see in Australia *R v TP* [2007] QCA 169, 172 ACR 23.

[510] *R v Noden* [2007] EWCA Crim 2050, [32]. See also in Canada *Daley v R* 2007 SCC 53 [2007] 3 SCR 523, [31].

APPEALS

Criminal cases[511]

Statement of the law in this area has been simplified[512] by the Criminal Appeal Act 1995,[513] which now[514] provides that:[515]

(1) Subject to the provisions of this Act, the Court of Appeal—
    (a) shall allow an appeal against conviction if they think that the conviction is unsafe; and
    (b) shall dismiss such an appeal in any other case.

The term 'unsafe' is not defined, and as the Act is intended to codify the law, it is permissible to refer to the pre-existing law in relation to any doubtful term.[516] It can hardly be denied, in the light of serious controversy in relation to the use of this word in the previous legislation, that its meaning was doubtful,[517] and reference to that law would accord with the government's expressed intention of restating the existing practice of the Court of Appeal.[518] This view was confirmed in *R v Togher*,[519] in which Lord Woolf CJ not only affirmed a broad approach to the meaning of 'unsafe', but declared[520] that it would be very rare[521] for its interpretation to differ from that of an unfair trial for the purposes of Art 6 of the European Convention on Human Rights.[522] There might nevertheless remain some difficulty in reconciling the emphasis within the European jurisprudence of fairness to the accused with the English view also taking account of fairness to the prosecution.[523]

---

[511] The system of appeal and review is currently under review by the Law Commission which published a consultation paper 'The High Court's Jurisdiction in Relation to Criminal Proceedings' (Law Com CP 184) in 2007, and expects to publish a final report in 2010. See generally Pattenden [2009] *Crim LR* 15.

[512] See Smith [1995] *Crim LR* 920 for discussion of the impact of the new legislation in an article described as 'penetrating' by Lord Bingham CJ in *R v Graham* [1997] 1 Cr App Rep 302, 308B.

[513] A recent Consultation Paper, *Quashing Convictions* (Office for Criminal Justice Reform, 2006) recommended further tightening, but the relevant clause in the Criminal Justice and Immigration Bill 2007 was withdrawn.

[514] As amended by the Criminal Justice Act 2003 s 316(3) inserting s 3A (power to substitute conviction following guilty plea), and by the Criminal Justice and Immigration Act 2008 s 42, inserting s 16C (expanding grounds to dismiss cases referred by Criminal Cases Review Commission.

[515] By substituting the new provision into s 2 of the Criminal Appeal Act 1968, replacing the old subs (1), and the proviso to it.   [516] *Bank of England v Vagliano Bros* [1891] AC 107, 144.

[517] As it remains in Australia, where the same formula still applies: see *Tran v R* [2000] FCA 1888, (2000) 180 ALR 62.

[518] See Hansard Vol 256, para 24 (6 March 1995) (Home Secretary on Second Reading); Standing Committee B (21 March 1995) (Minister of State at col 26). In *Dookran v R* [2007] UKPC 15 the old terminology of 'lurking doubt' was still approved.

[519] (n260), preferring the approach in *R v Mullen* [2000] QB 520, to that in *R v Chalkley and Jeffries* [1998] QB 848, [1998] 2 All ER 155.

[520] [33], reiterating his own view previously expressed in *R v Francom* [2001] 1 Cr App Rep 17, and pointing out that the passage of the Human Rights Act 1998 had caused the contrary view expressed by the Court of Appeal in *R v Davis* [2001] 1 Cr App Rep 115, [65] and by the ECHR itself in *Condron v United Kingdom* (2001) 31 EHRR 1, [65] to have been overtaken.

[521] For a recent example see *R v Ali and Hussain (No 2)* [2008] EWCA Crim 1466; and for extended analysis Taylor and Ormerod [2004] *Crim LR* 266.

[522] Which might, in practice, still bring about the liberalization of the previous law recommended by the Royal Commission on Criminal Justice Cm 2263 (1993) ch 10, para 3.

[523] See above, 205. It is not fatal to the success of an appeal that the point was deliberately not taken for tactical reasons at the trial: *Popat v Barnes* [2004] EWCA Civ 820, (2004) 148 SJLB 1061, [10].

It has indeed been held that such considerations do have a role to play when the appeal is based upon an argument that the trial amounted to an abuse of process.[524] The application of these rules remains doubtful,[525] although the Privy Council has said that it is correct to take into account the inevitability of conviction even if the relevant defect in the trial court's procedure had not occurred.[526]

It should also be noted that, contrary to some earlier suggestions,[527] *Togher* is also clear authority that it is immaterial for the purposes of an appeal[528] that the invalidating factor had precipitated a plea of guilty. Thus in *R v Montague-Darlington*,[529] the prosecution wrongly withheld sensitive material that, had the defence been aware of its existence, would have precluded a plea of guilty, on the basis that the prosecution should either have disclosed the material or abandoned the prosecution, and on the assumption that it would have done the latter, it was held that a trial, which would almost certainly not have taken place had the law been properly applied, could not be fair. Similarly, in *R v Smith*,[530] an admission of guilt under cross-examination after the wrongful rejection of a submission of no case did not make the conviction safe.

The 1995 legislation[531] also makes provision, even after an appeal has been disposed of, for a further appeal to be considered on the basis of fresh evidence or new arguments, upon a reference back to the Court of Appeal by the Criminal Cases Review Commission, provided only that the Commission take the view that there be a realistic possibility of the conviction or verdict not being upheld. It seems that such a reference may be made at any time, and the appeal considered on the basis of the state of the law at the time of the further review, not at that of the original trial; so, in theory, it is now possible for changes in the law of evidence to be given retrospective effect.[532]

No formal amendment[533] has been made to s 7 of the Criminal Appeal Act 1968 relating to the power to order a retrial, which remains open-endedly to depend upon the court's perception of the requirements of the 'interests of justice'. Section 4 of the Criminal Appeal Act 1995 does, however, accept the recommendation[534] of the Royal Commission in changing the definition of the fresh evidence that the court is empowered to receive from 'likely to be credible' to 'capable of belief'. This appears to have been an attempt to ameliorate the test and, despite the logical and linguistic difficulty in doing so,[535] this seems likely to be how it will be interpreted.[536] Although the Royal Commission disapproved[537] of the decision in *Stafford v DPP*,[538] that the appellate court should be guided by its own view of fresh evidence rather than its assessment of the view that a jury might

---

524 *R v Alfrey* [2005] EWCA Crim 3232.

525 Especially where an intermediate court has not considered the correct factors: see *Howse v R* [2005] UKPC 30, in which the Privy Council was split.

526 *Singh v State* [2005] UKPC 35, [2005] 4 All ER 781.   527 In *R v Rajcoomer* [1999] Crim LR 728.

528 Different considerations apply to awarding compensation: *R v Home Secretary, ex p Mullen* [2002] EWHC 230 (Admin), [2002] 3 All ER 293.   529 [2003] EWCA Crim 1542.

530 [2000] 1 All ER 263.   531 Criminal Appeal Act 1995, Pt II, as amended by s 16C (n515).

532 *R v Johnson* [2001] 1 Cr App Rep 408, [26].

533 Despite the view of the Royal Commission on Criminal Justice that there should be greater readiness to order retrials: Cm 2263, ch 10, para 65.

534 Chapter 10, para 60, rec 322.   535 As explained by Smith [1995] *Crim LR* 920, at 928.

536 In the older test, 'likely to be credible' was often construed as if it read 'likely to be credited', and it is submitted that the new test is likely to be read as 'likely to be capable of belief'.

537 Chapter 10, para 62.

538 [1974] AC 878, [1973] 3 All ER 762. See also *R v McMahon* (1978) 68 Cr App Rep 18.

take, no recommendation was made to that effect, and no action has been taken to change the law. While upholding the formal reasoning in *Stafford*, however, the House of Lords glossed it in *R v Pendleton*[539] by emphasizing that the task of an appellate court is to determine the safety of the conviction rather than the guilt of the accused,[540] and that it would normally be wise for the court to test its own provisional view by reference to whether the fresh evidence might reasonably have affected the decision of the jury.[541] It trenchantly asserted that:[542]

Trial by jury does not mean trial by jury in the first instance and trial by Judges of the Court of Appeal in the second.

The Criminal Justice Act 2003 for the first time contained provisions permitting the prosecution to appeal against interlocutory rulings at the trial, including appeals against evidentiary rulings. Although the latter have not yet been brought into force, it was held in *R v Y*[543] that there is some overlap between the two sets of provisions, and that if evidentiary rulings relate to proof of counts in the indictment, then they relate to such counts sufficiently to come within that batch of provisions which are in force.

Civil cases

The system of appeals in civil cases has been transformed[544] by the new regime introduced in 2000. The first version of the Civil Procedure Rules mainly continued the previous system pending full consideration of the Bowman Report.[545] The fruits of that consideration are now expressed largely in Pt 52 of the Civil Procedure Rules.[546]

The principal change is to the focus of appeal from rehearing to review,[547] as appears in CPR 52.11, which must be set out in full:

(1) Every appeal will be limited to a review of the decision of the lower court unless—
   (a) a practice direction makes different provision for a particular category of appeal; or
   (b) the court considers that in the circumstances of an individual appeal it would be in the interests of justice to hold a re-hearing.

---

[539] [2001] UKHL 66, [2002] 1 All ER 524, [2002] 1 WLR 72.

[540] As to which the possibility of a retrial is logically irrelevant.

[541] See *R v Purdy* [2007] EWCA Crim 295 for a striking example.

[542] [17]. See also *A-G for Jersey v O'Brien* (n179), *Bain v R* [2007] UKPC 9. And in Australia *Weiss v R* [2005] HCA 81, 224 CLR 300; while in *R v Munro* [2008] 2 NZLR 87 the Court of Appeal undertook a comparative survey of the position in all of the major common law jurisdictions.

[543] [2008] EWCA Crim 10, [22], followed in *R v O* [2008] EWCA Crim 463. The relevant criteria relating to a possible re-trial were briefly considered in *R v A* [2008] EWCA Crim 2186.

[544] Described by Brooke LJ in *Tanfern Ltd v Cameron-MacDonald* [2000] 2 All ER 801, [2000] 1 WLR 1311, [50] as 'the most significant changes in the arrangements for civil appeals in this country for over 125 years' (i.e. since the Judicature Act). Reform in relation to appeals in family proceedings is still awaited.

[545] *Review of the Court of Appeal (Civil Division)* Lord Chancellor's Dept 1997.

[546] See also the Access to Justice Act 1999.

[547] Although in relation to some cases involving essentially judgments on matters of fact, and when no fresh evidence is allowed on the appeal, it is unlikely that review and rehearing will differ very much: *Assicurazioni Generali Spa v Arab Insurance Group (BSC)* [2002] EWCA Civ 1642, [2003] 1 All ER (Comm) 140, [2003] 1 WLR 577. It is also worth noting that where the Access to Justice Act 1999 has provided a system of appeals, as in relation to those from county courts, the operation of such a system is preferred to judicial review: see *R (Sivasubramaniam) v Wandsworth County Court* [2002] EWCA Civ 1738, [2003] 2 All ER 160, [2003] 1 WLR 475.

(2) Unless it orders otherwise, the appeal court will not receive—
   (a) oral evidence; or
   (b) evidence which was not before the lower court.

(3) The appeal court will allow an appeal where the decision of the lower court was—
   (a) wrong; or
   (b) unjust because of a serious procedural or other irregularity in the proceedings of the lower court.

(4) The appeal court may draw any inference of fact which it considers justified on the evidence.

(5) At the hearing of the appeal a party may not rely on a matter not contained in his appeal notice unless the appeal court gives permission.

It should be noted that the court is given a discretion to receive fresh evidence,[548] and it seems likely[549] that it will proceed on a similar basis to that which formerly applied, often categorized as the rule in *Ladd v Marshall*.[550] It has been said to be unlikely that the overriding objectives of the Civil Procedure Rules will alter this very much.[551] The court will normally accept the decisions of the trial judge on issues of primary fact,[552] but will be more ready to reverse when they consist of inferences from those facts,[553] especially when derived from materials equally available to the appellate tribunal. These grounds must be distinguished from those closer to review of discretion which apply to findings of fact based upon balancing different factors.[554] Where the original trier of fact has wrongly rejected evidence, the issue is whether on the evidence that remains the decision can be maintained.[555] Where an expert tribunal exists to determine issues of primary fact, an appellate court is likely to be more prepared to refer back disputed issues of fact than to determine the matter for itself, when there was some legal flaw in the originals finding.[556]

In relation to the grounds of appeal, it appears from *Tanfern v Cameron-MacDonald* that wrong includes the exercise of discretion outside the boundaries of reasonable disagreement.[557] It should also be noted that the irregularity mentioned in para 3(b) must both be serious and have causative effect, but that the effect need not itself have been an incorrect determination of the outcome of the case.

---

[548] Although the Court of Appeal may be reluctant to exercise such a power, and in *Madarassy v Nomura International* [2006] EWHC 748 (QB), in effect delegated it to a lower court.

[549] See *Hertfordshire Investments Ltd v Bubb* [2000] 1 WLR 2318; *Hamilton v Al Fayed* (21 December 2000, unreported).

[550] [1954] 3 All ER 745, [1954] 1 WLR 1489; see further 18.

[551] *Prentice v Hereward Housing Association* [2001] EWCA Civ 437, [2001] 2 All ER (Comm) 900, [25].

[552] For reasons summarized by Lord Hoffmann in *Biogen Inc v Medeva plc* [1997] RPC 1, 47, especially where they reject any suggestion of fraud or dishonesty: *Ryan v Jarvis* [2005] UKPC 27, at [27].

[553] *Assicurazioni* above (n547), [14]–[17], specifically approved by the House of Lords in *Datec Electronic Holdings Ltd v United Parcels Service Ltd* [2007] UKHL 23; [2007] 4 All ER 765 [46].

[554] *Assicurazioni* above (n547) [16].

[555] *HK v Secretary of State for Home Department* [2006] EWCA Civ 1037, [46].

[556] *TG (Central African Republic) v Secretary of State for Home Department* [2008] EWCA Civ 997, [5].

[557] Above (n544), [32], citing *G v G (minors: custody appeal)* [1985] 2 All ER 225, 1 WLR 647, HL; 229, 652. In *Rowland v Bock* [2002] EWHC 692 (QB), [2002] 4 All ER 370, it was the decision to disallow evidence to be tendered by video link for what were regarded as insufficient reasons.

V

WITNESSES

The most common vehicle for proof is the evidence of witnesses, and this chapter considers some special considerations relating to them. It will first give a brief description of the development of this branch of the law, and set out the standard incidents of testimony; it will then go on to discuss factors peculiar to particular categories of witness, such as children, spouses, and offenders; the final section will deal with the nature of supporting evidence.

SECTION 1. STANDARD CASE

This section first sets out to sketch the way in which this aspect of the subject has changed over time, and will then deal with the procedures for taking testimony in the standard case and in particular appropriate measures for dealing with witnesses who are fearful.

HISTORICAL OVERVIEW

It is no exaggeration to say that the old common law in this area was predominantly a law of witnesses, mainly concerned with their qualification to testify. Witnesses were divided into two classes: those who were not permitted, and those who could be compelled, to testify. The obligation was to testify generally, but might be mitigated by a privilege of not answering certain types of question.[1] The death knell of that old system was sounded by Bentham, and its execution mainly accomplished by the passage of the Evidence Act 1843, which abolished the largest and most technical of the categories of those who were disqualified, namely those with an interest in the outcome. A few categories remained subject to the old rules of disqualification, such as parties, including the accused in a criminal case and spouses. These exclusions were mitigated by legislative enactment,[2] often by introducing a distinction between the competence of witnesses to testify and their compulsion to do so,[3] or by requiring corroboration in some relevant respect.[4] The common law similarly reflected the older system of disqualification by developing

---

[1] What remains of this mitigation is discussed in Chapter IX.

[2] Principally, the Evidence Act 1851 (parties in civil cases), the Evidence Amendment Act 1853 (spouses in civil cases), the Evidence Further Amendment Act 1869 (parties and spouses in breach of promise and adultery cases), and the Criminal Evidence Act 1898 (accused and spouse in criminal cases).

[3] For example, Evidence Amendment Act 1853, s 3.

[4] For example, Evidence Further Amendment Act 1869, s 2.

mandatory rules as to corroboration for certain categories of witness and situation.[5] To these were added further analogous categories, but often on a less mandatory basis. It was hardly surprising that the technicality of the distinctions between the various components of this patchwork grated upon the judges, and that moves toward rationalization and reform were undertaken in most common law jurisdictions, sometimes by legislation[6] and sometimes by judicial innovation.[7] This movement has owed something to the decline in jury trial in civil cases, and much to a desire for greater flexibility in the form of direction to the jury in criminal. More generous perception of the capabilities of witnesses, especially of children, and a feeling that some distinctions were demeaning,[8] have also contributed.

The current general position is that all who can give relevant testimony may be compelled by witness summons to attend at the court to testify,[9] and in trial by jury, its instruction as to the approach they should adopt to such testimony,[10] tailored to the facts of the particular trial, untrammelled by technical rules. This fabric has become overlaid by the development of special procedures for special situations, and special types of witness.[11] It must now, after the passage of the Human Rights Act 1998, also ensure that trials are fair.[12]

OATHS[13]

The old law developed from the notion that only those prepared to testify on oath on the Gospel were competent witnesses, but other forms of oath and affirmation were gradually permitted. The present law is contained in the Oaths Act 1978, which consolidated earlier enactments. Section 1 of the Act prescribed the form in which an oath should be administered to Christians and Jews. It also allowed for the administration of an oath in other forms to those with other religious beliefs.[14] In such cases, the Act was merely directive, requiring only that the form of the oath should be regarded by both court and witness as

---

[5] Such as complainants in sexual cases.

[6] For example, the abolition of corroboration requirements in civil proceedings in Scotland by the Civil Evidence (Scotland) Act 1988, s 1.

[7] For example, the abolition of corroboration requirements in the cases of accomplices in Canada by the Supreme Court of Canada in *Vetrovec v R* [1982] 1 SCR 811.

[8] Especially that which treated complainants in sexual cases, overwhelmingly female, as being peculiarly unreliable.

[9] Except foreign officers of foreign corporations, *Masri v Consolidated Contractors Int Co SAL* [2009] UKHL 43.

[10] In trial by judge alone, the proper approach to fact-finding, especially in relation to the determination of the credibility of witnesses, was helpfully summarized by Goff LJ in *Armagas Ltd v Mundogas SA* [1985] 1 Lloyd's Rep 1, 57 (in a passage omitted from other reports).

[11] Especially in the Youth Justice and Criminal Evidence Act 1999; cf, the Vulnerable Witnesses (Scotland) Act 2004.

[12] Thus in *Cuscani v United Kingdom* (2003) 36 EHRR 11, it was held that proceedings would be unfair in the absence of an interpreter.

[13] See 11th Report of the Criminal Law Revision Committee 1972 (Cmnd 4991) paras 279–81, which, so far unavailingly, recommended abolition of an oath in favour of a declaration, and more generally Australian Law Reform Commission Research Paper No 6 'Sworn and Unsworn Evidence'.

[14] But they are not available as a matter of right, and a witness who refuses to swear in the normal form, or to affirm, is not entitled to give unsworn evidence: *Vitalis v CPS* [1995] CLY 1186.

binding.[15] Taking an oath without religious belief does not prevent its being binding.[16] Under s 5, anyone objecting to being sworn is permitted to make a solemn affirmation, and such an affirmation may be required of any person in relation to whom it is not reasonably practicable to administer an oath in the manner appropriate to his religious belief.[17] An affirmation has the same force and effect as an oath, which means that a false affirmer may be punished as a perjurer.

In a few of the special categories to be mentioned in the next section, there is no need for a witness to be sworn. In criminal proceedings, ss 55 and 56 of the Youth Justice and Criminal Evidence Act 1999 provide for unsworn testimony from witnesses under the age of 14, and in general terms, for competent witnesses who fail to qualify to give sworn testimony under the provisions of s 55(2). More general provision for the admissibility of video-recorded evidence, which need not have been made on oath, is authorized by s 137(5) of the Criminal Justice Act 2003.[18] Unsworn expert testimony has been admitted on appeal under the wide discretion afforded by s 23(1)(c) of the Criminal Appeal Act 1968.[19] Other cases in which a witness need not be sworn depend, at present, on the common law. Someone who simply produces a document pursuant to a witness summons does not have to be sworn if there is another witness who can identify the document.[20] This means that the person producing it cannot be cross-examined. Another person who need not be sworn is the advocate giving evidence of the terms of a compromise reached between the parties to litigation in which he acted for one of them. It is customary for his statement to be made from the well of the court[21] but the matter is dependent on convention and there is really no authority on the question of whether he can insist on his right not to take the oath.[22]

The common law right of the accused to make an unsworn statement was abolished by s 72 of the Criminal Justice Act 1982, in accordance with the recommendations of the Criminal Law Revision Committee.[23]

PROCEDURE

The complex functions of trial are in England expressed in a predominantly oral procedure in both criminal and civil cases, in which the cross-examination of witnesses plays a key role. The relevant procedure must contain rules for the competence and attendance

---

[15] *R v Chapman* [1980] Crim LR 42 (witness not holding the book when swearing); *R v Kemble* [1990] 3 All ER 116, [1990] 1 WLR 1111 (Muslim swearing on New Testament); *R v Majid* [2009] EWCA Crim 2563, [19] (Muslim affirming). See, in Australia, *McShane v Higgins* [1997] 2 Qd R 373; *R v T* (1998) 71 SASR 265.

[16] Section 4(2).

[17] In very exceptional circumstances, it has been held not to be unfair for a witness to be cross-examined as to his reasons for preferring to affirm rather than swear: *R v Mehrban* [2001] EWCA Crim 2627, [2002] 1 Cr App Rep 561; *R v Wiebe* (2006) 205 CCC3d 326. In *R v Robinson* (2005) 198 CCC3d 105, it was held not to be contrary to the Canadian Charter of Rights to require such a choice.   [18] See further below, 233.

[19] *R v Flynn and St John* [2008] EWCA Crim 970, [2008] 2 Cr App R 266, [15].

[20] *Perry v Gibson* (1834) 1 Ad & El 48.

[21] *Hickman v Berens* [1895] 2 Ch 638. But see *Pioneer Concrete Gold Coast Pty Ltd v Cassidy (No 2)* [1969] Qd R 290.

[22] There are obvious objections to an advocate acting as a witness in a case in which he is professionally engaged (*R v Secretary of State for India in Council, ex p Ezekiel* [1941] 2 KB 169, [1941] 2 All ER 546), but he is nevertheless competent.   [23] Cmnd 4991, paras 102–6.

of witnesses; attempt to secure that their testimony is reliable; attempt to overcome any reluctance to testify, for example by providing in appropriate cases for witness immunity, anonymity, or other special measures; and, when all else fails, substitute pre-recorded statements for testimony. These will be mentioned in turn.

The procedure for determining whether or not a witness is competent, and if so whether or not the evidence should be given sworn or unsworn, may occasion certain problems. In criminal proceedings, the position and procedure for determining competence and eligibility to swear is now governed by ss 55 and 56 of the Youth Justice and Criminal Evidence Act 1999. It is worth noting that, in both respects, it is for the party calling the witness to establish on the balance of probabilities[24] that the witness is competent, or eligible to be sworn. These sections provide that the question can be raised by any party,[25] that the issue shall be determined in the presence of the parties but in the absence of the jury, and that expert evidence is admissible.[26] In civil proceedings, although a party wishing to call a witness to testify[27] can compel him to do so by the use of a witness summons,[28] this has become subject to a greater measure of control by the court.[29] The rule of compellability applies to parents in child care proceedings, despite the fact that in such cases the privilege against self-incrimination is also abrogated.[30] In the case of a young child being sworn in civil proceedings,[31] the judge will normally conduct a voir dire in which the child will be examined.[32] In criminal proceedings attendance, and production of documents, can be compelled by means of the Criminal Procedure (Attendance of Witnesses) Act 1965.[33] Testimony can then be required, its refusal sanctioned by summary proceedings for contempt of court,[34] and witnesses remanded in custody pending its conclusion.[35] The normal[36] punishment is a custodial sentence,[37] even where the refuser is the victim of the relevant crime.[38] The accused will not be liable for contempt for refusal to testify at his

[24] Including the prosecution, contrary to the common law rule as to proof of other facts relevant to the admission of evidence: see, 183.   [25] Or by the court of its own motion.

[26] There is no indication of abrogation of the common law rule that the party whose competence is in issue shall be permitted to testify on that very issue: see *R v Yacoob* (1981) 72 Cr App Rep 313.

[27] Or to produce documents, although the old rules as to specification of such documents continue to apply, unaffected by the expansion of third party disclosure in CPR 31.17: *Tajik Aluminium Plant v Hydro Aluminium AS* [2005] EWCA Civ 1218, [2005] 4 All ER 1218; or to be cross-examined on an affidavit: *Kensington International Ltd v Congo* [2006] EWHC 1848 (Comm).

[28] This too is under the control of the court, and such a summons may be set aside, for example in the case of an expert when the fee cannot be paid: see *Brown v Bennett* [2001] EWCA Civ 1352.

[29] See especially CPR 34.1. A confidentiality agreement may be a material consideration: *South Tyneside BC v Wickes Building Supplies Ltd* [2004] EWHC 2428, [2004] NPC 164.

[30] *Re Y and K* [2003] EWCA Civ 669, [35].

[31] This was the old procedure in criminal proceedings, so now that the rules which formerly obtained in criminal proceedings have been imported, it seems likely that the procedure for implementing them will be imported also.   [32] *R v Hayes* [1977] 2 All ER 288, [1977] 1 WLR 234.

[33] Or in the case of evidence before magistrates under the Magistrates' Courts Act 1980, s 97, but the evidence must be material: see *Cunliffe v Hastings Magistrates' Court* [2006] EWHC 2081 (Admin). See also *Practice Note* [2001] 3 All ER 94 for operation of rules as to contempt in case of refusal.

[34] *R v Popat* [2008] EWCA Crim 1921, explaining the interaction with arrest warrants.

[35] *TH v Crown Court Wood Green* [2006] EWHC 268 (QB), (2006) 156 NLJ 1722.

[36] But circumstances vary greatly, and in some cases, a partial failure to respond in cross-examination will be visited by no sanction at all: see e.g. *R v McLennan* [1999] 2 Qd R 297.

[37] *R v Montgomery* [1995] 2 Cr App Rep 23.

[38] *R v Holt* (1996) 161 JP 96; for similar procedure in Australia, see *R v Razzak* [2006] NSWSC 1366, 166 ACR 132. Where the production of real evidence would require an intrusive physical examination of

own trial;[39] but if he chooses to testify, he must answer all questions,[40] presumably upon pain of being in contempt, and certainly upon pain of having adverse inferences drawn from his refusal.[41] Witnesses should rarely, if ever, be prevented from testifying, if willing to do so.[42]

If the prosecution changes its mind after notification to the defence as to whether or not it intends to call a witness, it does not necessarily amount to abuse of process,[43] but proper provision must be made for the defence to be able to react to the change.[44]

Despite judges always having had a wide general power over the procedure to be adopted before them, including alteration to the arrangement of their court in the interests of doing justice,[45] neither they,[46] nor administrators,[47] have the power to amend the rules of admissibility of testimony. The Youth Justice and Criminal Evidence Act 1999, Pt II provided explicitly for a number of special measures,[48] including screening,[49] testimony by live link,[50] excluding the general public from the courtroom, video recording both of evidence in chief and cross-examination, and permitting the intervention of interpreters[51] and intermediaries.[52] Video linkage is now more widely available in courtrooms,[53] and its

a complainant, it is extremely unlikely that refusal would be visited by such a sanction: see *R v B* [1995] 2 NZLR 172.

[39] Criminal Justice and Public Order Act 1994, s 35(4). [1995] 2 NZLR 172. In Scotland, under s 259(2)(e) of the Criminal Procedure (Scotland) Act 1995, hearsay can sometimes be used in case of such refusal, but its conditions are strictly construed: *MacDonald v HM Adv* 1999 SCCR 146.

[40] Other than those he is excused from answering on the basis of privilege: see further Chapter IX.

[41] Criminal Justice and Public Order Act 1994, s 35(5); *R v Ackinclose* [1996] Crim LR 747.

[42] *S v AC and TC* [2006] JCA 151, considering and approving English authority in relation to the stress involved in testifying.

[43] *R v Drury* [2001] EWCA Crim 975 (failure to call); *R v Carr* [2008] EWCA Crim 1283 (decision to call).   [44] *Khurshied v Peterborough Borough Council* [2009] EWHC 1136 (Admin).

[45] See e.g. *R v Smellie* (1919) 14 Cr App Rep 128 (screening); *Re S* [2007] EWCA Civ 589 (veiled witness); *R v Yam* [2008] EWCA Crim 269 (exclusion of press). A judge who makes, or refuses to make such a decision is in no way disqualified from going on to hear the case: *KL v DPP* [2001] EWHC Admin 1112; exercise of such discretion will rarely be overturned by an appellate court, *R v Giga* [2007] EWCA Crim 345, [35].

[46] *R v Ukpabio* [2007] EWCA Crim 2108, [15].

[47] *R v Rochester* [2008] EWCA Crim 678, [2008] 2 Cr App R 112, [32].

[48] Implemented by SI 2002/1687, 1688, and amended by ch 3 of the Coroners and Justice Act 2009. Such measures remain within the control of the judge, and may be changed in the interests of case management, especially to move in the direction of oral testimony, *R v Sirrs and Povey* [2006] EWCA Crim 3185, [106].

[49] Section 23, which descends to considerable detail, although departure is not necessarily fatal so long as the trial is fair, especially if the departure is accepted at the time by the defence: *A-G for the Sovereign Base Areas of Akrotiri and Dhekelia v Sreinhoff* [2005] UKPC 31 (applying English law).

[50] Section 24: see further, 242. The provisions are extended more generally by Pt 8 of the Criminal Justice Act 2003.

[51] Guaranteed by Art 6(3)(e) of the European Convention on Human Rights. It is not necessarily a breach of a party's human rights that there is no complete interpretation of all of the proceedings: *Daniels v Governor of Holloway Prison* [2005] EWHC 148. The matter is currently under review by the European Commission: see *Proposal for a Council Framework Decision on certain procedural rights in criminal proceedings* (2004) COM 328 final. Defective interpretation may make a trial unfair under purely domestic law, as in *R v Belo* [2007] EWCA Crim 374.

[52] The accused is entitled to be heard on whether such measures should be adopted: *R (Hillman) v Richmond Magistrates Court* [2003] EWHC 2660 (Admin).

[53] Some research indicates that the form of video linkage can make a 20% difference to perceived credibility, White (2007) 104.38 *LSG* 11. Evidence by telephone has occasionally been accepted in Australia as an alternative, although it has been recognized that it makes issues of credibility even more difficult to resolve: *Re Marriage of S and R* (1998) 149 FLR 149.

use in criminal proceedings can be ordered either under ss 16[54] or 17[55] of the Youth Justice and Criminal Evidence Act 1999 and is encouraged as a means of saving costs in civil proceedings[56] under the Civil Procedure Rules,[57] but the court is not so far prepared to allow its use merely for the convenience of parties who could easily attend in person,[58] although it is prepared to accede to a wide range of reasons[59] in the interests of doing justice. It is not to be regarded as being intrinsically unfair to the accused to allow it, nor necessarily to prevent testing the witness's credibility, although no doubt the English courts will be as cautious as are those in Australia not to open any floodgates.[60] Litigants may also be encouraged to attend by allowing them to be accompanied and represented by layman acting as a 'Mackenzie friend'.[61]

The aim is to secure reliable testimony, and while an oath and opportunity for cross-examination[62] are important, a number of other supplementary rules have developed. Witnesses testify as individuals even though called by a party, and should not collaborate,[63] be coached[64] nor rehearsed,[65] nor shown the witness statements of others before testifying.[66] Police witnesses are, however, allowed to confer with each other in the aftermath of an incident, even one in which the behaviour of the police is in issue.[67] This has been criticized,[68] and may sometimes be inconsistent with the requirements of the European Convention of Human Rights,[69] and may well be changed.[70] Some degree of prior familiarization with court procedures is unexceptionable,[71] and proposals have been made to improve the documentation of initial interviews with potential witnesses.[72] Intimidation of witnesses is clearly prone to create unreliability, which explains the availability of two

---

[54] On grounds of youth or incapacity.   [55] On grounds of fear or distress.

[56] See *Black v Pastouna* [2005] EWCA Civ 1389, [14].

[57] CPR 32.3, but it remains a matter for decision by the court in the light of all of the circumstances.

[58] *Yamaichi International Europe v Anthony* [1999] CL 345.

[59] Including the refusal of the witness to come to England on account of liability to be arrested on a warrant for extradition for trial in a different overseas jurisdiction: *Polanski v Condé Nast Publications Ltd* [2005] UKHL 10, [2005] 1 All ER 945 (party witness) or to avoid potential liability to tax, *Ian McGlinn v Waltham Contractors Ltd* [2006] EWHC 2322, [2006] BLR 489 (party witness); *Bank of Credit and Commerce International v Rahim* [2005] EWHC 528 (Ch) (non-party witness).

[60] In the United States, the Supreme Court rejected a new draft r 26b of the Criminal Procedure Rules to liberalize the use of video links as an unconstitutional abridgement of the accused's right to confront his accusers. For an Australian view, see *R v Ngo* [2003] NSWCCA 82.

[61] See Millward (2008) 158 NLJ 1133.   [62] See further, 313.

[63] *R v O'B* [2008] EWCA Crim 238, [19]; *R v AP* [2009] EWCA Crim 1327.

[64] Defined in Australia as suggesting an answer to a question: *Australian Automotive Repairers' Association (Political Action Committee) Inc v NRMA Insurance Ltd* [2004] FCA 369, 207 ALR 389, [1].

[65] *R v Arif* (1993) unreported, The Times 17 June.   [66] *R v Richardson* [1971] 2 QB 484, 490.

[67] *R v Bass* [1953] 1 QB 680, [1953] 1 All ER 1064, 686, 1067. See also in Australia *Heanes v Herangi* [2007] WASC 175, 175 ACR 175.

[68] *Saunders and Tucker v Independent Police Complaints Commission* [2008] UKHC 2372 (Admin), [14].

[69] Cf *Ramsahai v Netherlands* (2006) 43 EHRR 39 (in the context of Art 2 in relation to a police killing).

[70] *Saunders* (1996) 23 EHRR 313, [1998] 1 BCLC 362 [62].

[71] *R v Momodou* [2005] EWCA Crim 177, [2005] 2 All ER 571, [61] (criminal proceedings); *Ultraframe (UK) Ltd v Fielding* [2005] EWHC 1638 (Ch), [29] (civil proceedings).

[72] Wolchover and Heaton-Armstrong (2008) *Counsel* February 8 (advocating video-recording of initial police interviews); Roberts [2008] *Crim LR* 831 (describing pilot experiments with pre-trial witness interviewing); Dumont and Mathers (2007) 157 *NLJ* 574 (attendance notes in civil cases in light of *Supple v Pender* [2007] EWHC 829 (Ch)).

forms of contempt and a separate criminal offence for witness intimidation.[73] If witnesses may have been encouraged by a party to testify falsely so as to exonerate the accused, or there is good reason to suspect such a practice,[74] the police must be free to investigate, and to interview those witnesses, without automatically rendering any subsequent trial unfair.[75]

Despite some alleviation where special measures have been introduced.[76] witnesses are becoming increasingly reluctant to testify, especially in criminal cases.[77] Pressure may be relieved by taking a limited view of the evidence required of witnesses. Thus not only must evidence be relevant, but it is permissible for the judge to accept the assessment of counsel, instructed by the witness, of such relevance.[78] Similarly, in relation to oral evidence required by a foreign court, witnesses should be protected by a narrow specification of the issues to which the evidence is alleged to be relevant.[79] Nor does such relevance extend to documents that can be used only in cross-examination.[80] Where evidence may be material, however, the police must allow access by the defence to potential witnesses.[81] To encourage testimony,[82] some attempt has been made to mitigate the perceived legal and personal dangers of testifying in person, although any such measures risk diminishing reliability. In particular mitigation of legal risk has dictated some measure of witness immunity; and mitigation of personal risk, some measure of witness anonymity.

Protection is provided for witnesses, including expert witnesses,[83] by immunity from legal[84] process in respect of testimony or closely associated documentation,[85] including

---

[73] Clearly set out in *R v AS* [2008] EWCA Crim 138, [18].

[74] Pressure to testify falsely is itself a criminal offence: see *R v Patrascu* [2004] EWCA Crim 2417.

[75] *R v Higgins* [2003] EWCA Crim 2943.

[76] Home Office Research Study 283 *Are Special Measures Working? Evidence from surveys of vulnerable and intimidated witnesses* (2004). A Consultation Paper *Securing the Attendance of Witnesses in Court* was issued by the government on 3 October 2003. A Witness Charter to support witnesses is also planned, and special witness care units have been set up in each police area. For possible extension of special measures to civil proceedings see Pemberton (2009) 39 *Fam L* 244.

[77] It may also happen in civil cases, and it has been held that a witness summons will normally be appropriate even in cases in which damage might be caused to a third party on account of such reluctance: *Tilbury Consulting Ltd v Margaret Gitins (HMIT)* (15 August 2003, unreported) Sp Comm of Income Tax.

[78] *R v W (G) and W (E)* [1997] 1 Cr App Rep 166. Even if technically relevant, it would be wrong for the prosecution to call a witness in one case in the hope of securing evidence that could be used against that witness in a pending prosecution of him: see e.g. *R v Cadagan* (1998) 165 DLR (4th) 747.

[79] *First America Corp v Sheik Zayed Al-Nahyan* [1998] 4 All ER 439.

[80] *R v H (L)* [1997] 1 Cr App Rep 176; still less when the subject matter of the cross-examination has become irrelevant: *McKenna Breen v James* [2002] EWHC 1291 (QB).

[81] *Connolly v Dale* [1996] 1 Cr App Rep 200.

[82] In *R v Davis* [2006] EWCA Crim 115, [2006] 4 All ER 648 [10], said by the President of the Criminal Division of the Court of Appeal to threaten the rule of law: 'Without witnesses, justice cannot be done.'

[83] *X (Minors) v Bedfordshire CC* [1995] 2 AC 633.

[84] They may still be liable to professional disciplinary proceedings: *GMC v Meadow* [2006] EWCA Civ 1390; for wasted costs: *Sulaman v Axa Insurance plc* [2009] EWCA Civ 1331(party lying), *Williams v Calvin Jarvis (Lex Komatsu)* [2009] EWHC 1837 (QB) (irresponsible experts); to civil public proceedings for contempt in respect of false statements of truth, *KJM Superbikes Ltd v Hinton* [2008] EWCA Civ 1280; and to criminal proceedings for perjury in respect of false testimony; or as false complainants of crime for malicious prosecution. A third party costs order may, however, be excluded by witness immunity considerations, *Oriakhel v Vickers* [2008] EWCA Civ 748.

[85] *Darker v Chief Constable of West Midlands Police* [2001] 1 AC 435; but not for proceedings against them for antecedent acts about which they subsequently testify, *Reynolds v City of Kingston Police Services Board*

complaint to the police,[86] although it may not prevail to support a striking out application.[87] It can be argued that, in view of the special duty of the expert, a high standard of care should be expected, but on the other hand, expert witnesses in the absence of such immunity might be difficult to persuade to testify. It should be noted that the police are under no actionable duty of care to protect witnesses,[88] nor does the fact that the police have failed to protect a witness put them in breach of article 2 of the European Convention of Human Rights.[89]

Reluctance to testify is, however, widely believed to be dictated more by the desire to preserve personal safety.[90] It has been found necessary to supplement the usual protection afforded to all by the criminal law, with special legislation penalizing the intimidation of witnesses,[91] and common law measures to preserve witnesses from psychological pressure.[92] Nevertheless the general rule was that witnesses should testify openly in person. It applied in both criminal[93] and in civil[94] proceedings, and was endorsed by the European Court of Human Rights.[95] Finally, it was upheld by the House of Lords in *R v Davis*[96] in this very context. Such was the concern for the effect on witness reluctance to testify that remedial legislation was introduced within three weeks,[97] and subsequently enacted little more than a month after the decision in *Davis* in the form of the Criminal Evidence (Witness Anonymity) Act 2008,[98] enabling the court to make witness anonymity orders under specified conditions, and now repealed and largely re-enacted in the Coroners and Justice Act 2009:

88 Conditions for making order

(1) This section applies where an application is made for a witness anonymity order to be made in relation to a witness in criminal proceedings.

(2) The court may make such an order only if it is satisfied that Conditions A to C below are met.

(3) Condition A is that the proposed order is necessary—

(a) in order to protect the safety of the witness or another person or to prevent any serious damage to property, or

---

(2007) 280 DLR (4th) 311 (Ont CA). See also, *Karling v Purdue* [2005] SCLR 43; cf in South Africa *Black v Joffe* 2007 (3) SA 171.

[86] *Buckley v Dalziel* [2007] EWHC 1025 (QB); *Westcott v Westcott* [2007] EWHC 2501 (QB).

[87] *Walsh v Staines* [2007] EWHC 1814 (Ch).

[88] *Brooks v Metropolitan Police Comr* [2005] UKHL 24, [2005] 2 All ER 489, [33].

[89] *Van Colle v Chief Constable of Hertfordshire* [2008] UKHL 50, [2009] 1 AC 225.

[90] As dramatically demonstrated in *Van Colle* above.

[91] Criminal Justice and Public Order Act 1994, s 51; Youth Justice and Criminal Evidence Act 1999 s 36 (prohibition of cross-examination of sexual complainant by accused in person). Civil proceedings may be struck out for witness intimidation, *Force One Utilities Ltd v Hatfield* [2009] IRLR 45 (EAT).

[92] *R v Smellie* (1919) 14 Cr App Rep 128 (screen between accused and witness).

[93] *R v Lord Saville of Newdigate* (n111); *R v Scott* [2004] EWCA Crim1835.

[94] *Re W (Care Proceedings: Witness anonymity)* [2002] EWCA Civ 1626, [2003] 1 FLR 329, CA.

[95] *Doorson v The Netherlands* (1996) 22 EHRR 330; *Visser v The Netherlands* [2002] Crim LR 495.

[96] [2008] UKHL 36; [2008] 1 AC 1128.

[97] A similar pattern of judicial decision and legislative reversal has occurred in New Zealand, see *R v Hines* [1997] 3 NZLR 529 and New Zealand Evidence Act 2006 ss 108–19.

[98] For procedural amendment see Consolidated Criminal Practice Direction (Amendment No. 21) [2009] 1 *Cr App R* 70 (dated 28 August 2008).

(b) in order to prevent real harm to the public interest (whether affecting the carrying on of any activities in the public interest or the safety of a person involved in carrying on such activities, or otherwise).

(4) Condition B is that, having regard to all the circumstances, the effect of the proposed order would be consistent with the defendant receiving a fair trial.

(5) Condition C is that the importance of the witness's testimony is such that in the interests of justice the witness ought to testify and—
   (a) the witness would not testify if the order were not made, or
   (b) there would be real harm to the public interest if the witness were to testify without the proposed order being made.

(6) In determining whether the proposed order is necessary for the purpose mentioned in subsection (3)(a), the court must have regard (in particular) to any reasonable fear on the part of the witness—
   (a) that the witness or another person would suffer death or injury, or
   (b) that there would be serious damage to property,

(7) if the witness were to be identified.

89 Relevant considerations

(1) When deciding whether Conditions A to C in section 4 are met in the case of an application for a witness anonymity order, the court must have regard to—
   (a) the considerations mentioned in subsection (2) below, and
   (b) such other matters as the court considers relevant.

(2) The considerations are—
   (a) the general right of a defendant in criminal proceedings to know the identity of a witness in the proceedings;
   (b) the extent to which the credibility of the witness concerned would be a relevant factor when the weight of his or her evidence comes to be assessed;
   (c) whether evidence given by the witness might be the sole or decisive evidence implicating the defendant;
   (d) whether the witness's evidence could be properly tested (whether on grounds of credibility or otherwise) without his or her identity being disclosed;
   (e) whether there is any reason to believe that the witness—
      (i) has a tendency to be dishonest, or
      (ii) has any motive to be dishonest in the circumstances of the case,
      having regard (in particular) to any previous convictions of the witness and to any relationship between the witness and the defendant or any associates of the defendant;
   (f) whether it would be reasonably practicable to protect the witness's identity by any means other than by making a witness anonymity order specifying the measures that are under consideration by the court.

So short a period of gestation has unsurprisingly left its product undeveloped and defective.[99] An attempt to pre-empt[100] some of the problems was taken by the Court of Appeal in

---

[99] Condition C in s 88 amends the initial formulation; the drafting of condition B was described in *Mayers* (n101) at [36] as odd, and at [113] contemplates parliamentary extension to deal with the problem of anonymous hearsay.

[100] Facilitated by s 11 of the original Act, which made its application retrospective.

R v Mayers.[101] Unfortunately, in some respects the reasoning is obscure, for example none of the considerations in s 5 is said to be decisive in determining the satisfaction of any of the conditions in s 4,[102] but it is hard to accept that inability to test a prosecution witness's evidence properly can ever be compatible with a fair trial.[103] Although the Court emphasized the rigour of Condition C in requiring that the witness *will not* testify as opposed to being reluctant to do so,[104] this was immediately diluted by permitting such refusal to be inferred,[105] and the formulation may well encourage expressions of refusal which will be difficult to refute. It is also difficult to square the then requirement in Conditions A and C for necessity with the Court's acceptance in one of the cases that there was plenty of other evidence without that of the relevant witness, and with the more general view that the more support there was elsewhere for the relevant witness the more likely the application was to be granted, when one would think that might often tend against necessity.[106] Most difficulty was exposed by the fourth of the cases in which some of the witnesses not only insisted on anonymity but were also too frightened to testify at all, leading to the invocation of the appropriate exception to the hearsay rule.[107] The definition of a witness in the Act is, however, limited to witnesses who propose to testify, and the Court felt unable to extend it. It also, somewhat summarily, dismissed the view that the terminology of the Criminal Justice Act could be satisfied by identifying the witness to the judge. The Court justified this part of its judgment by reference to the difficulty of satisfying the requirement of the Criminal Justice Act for testing the credibility of hearsay, which sits none too well with the general policy of anonymity orders. An order may be made under this provision despite the possibility that the identity of the witness may already be known, so as to prevent public confirmation.[108] It should be noted that the Act requires, and *Mayers* stresses, the importance of prosecution disclosure, so as to ensure so far as possible the credibility of anonymous witnesses.

The issue of anonymity is not only different from that of the admission of hearsay, but also from that of disclosure of evidence,[109] and that of provision of special advocates.[110] The new legislation applies only to criminal proceedings, and leaves the common law position unaffected elsewhere. Anonymity is rarely sought in private civil proceedings, but may be of great significance in quasi-judicial enquiries, such as those into terrorism. It was in such a context that it was held that soldier witnesses could remain anonymous in the 'Bloody Sunday' enquiry,[111] and that anonymity is justified by *increased* personal danger as a result of testifying.[112]

At common law open identification of witnesses was not an absolute rule, and, could be departed from if there were objective evidence[113] of there being a reasonable chance or serious possibility of any[114] witness being harmed if his identity should be

---

[101] [2008] EWCA Crim 1418, [2009] 2 All ER 145a compendium of four cases decided by a five-judge Court presided over by the Lord Chief Justice, see further Bagshaw (2009) 13 *E&P* 137.   [102] [19].

[103] See [22].   [104] [26].   [105] [27].

[106] It is unclear in which direction this condition points.

[107] Criminal Justice Act 2003 s 116(2)(e), see further 608.

[108] *R v Powar and Powar* [2009] EWCA Crim 594, [2009] 2 Cr App R 120, [79].

[109] Rules of public interest immunity are expressly excluded by s 1(3) from the otherwise general abolition of the common law relating to witness anonymity in criminal proceedings by s 1(2).

[110] See further 485.   [111] *R (A) v Lord Saville of Newdigate* [2000] 1 WLR 1855.

[112] *Re Officer L* [2007] UKHL 36, [2007] 1 WLR 2135.

[113] Perhaps established on a voir dire: *Scott* (n93), [17].

[114] In criminal proceedings for the defence as much as for the prosecution.

revealed.[115] The policy arguments[116] for any such departure are conceptually difficult, since to justify departure, the evidence must be important, but the European Court of Human Rights in particular is especially reluctant to allow reliance upon such evidence to be decisive.[117] So too the more serious the charge, the more necessary that the court be fully informed, but equally the more necessary that parties be able to test the evidence by fully informed cross-examination. For this reason, the rule may more readily be disregarded in proceedings in which there is no provision for cross-examination.[118] If anonymous testimony is permitted, the judge should direct the jury to take special care, and not to be prejudiced in any way by the anonymity.[119] The situation may also be alleviated by other measures such as clearing the courtroom,[120] permitting testimony in a remote location,[121] using screens, restricting reporting, and insisting upon the fullest disclosure of material liable to discredit any anonymous witness.[122] Ex post facto protection may be offered through special witness protection schemes.[123]

As noted above, the last resort is to permit the use of hearsay. Section 116(2)(e) of the Criminal Justice Act 2003 is designed to permit its use where potential witnesses fail to testify through fear. It should be noted that in this, as in other cases where documentary statements are permitted to stand as evidence, the words of the statement should represent the words of the witness, and not the ideas of a lawyer,[124] or the unchecked version of an interpreter.[125] In criminal proceedings, more extensive and elaborate provision has been made for directions that video-recorded evidence of witnesses, apart from the accused, should be admitted as evidence in chief of the truth of the matters stated.[126] The conditions for so directing are set out in the later provisions of s 137:

...

(3) A direction under subsection (1)(f)—
   (a) may not be made in relation to a recorded account given by the defendant;
   (b) may be made only if it appears to the court that—
      (i) the witness's recollection of the events in question is likely to have been significantly better when he gave the recorded account than it will be when he gives oral evidence in the proceedings, and
      (ii) it is in the interests of justice for the recording to be admitted, having regard in particular to the matters mentioned in subsection (4).

---

[115] *Family of Derek Bennett v Officer A et al* [2004] EWCA Civ1439, [30]. Similar principles apply in Scotland: see *HM Adv v Smith* [2000] SCCR 910.

[116] See Royal Commission on Criminal Justice Cm 2263 ch 8, paras 36–47, recs 196–207.

[117] Its jurisprudence was extensively reviewed in *R v Davis* (n82), [75]–[90]. By contrast, in competition proceedings the European Court of Justice has permitted the admission of anonymous documents.

[118] *R (Al Fawwaz) v Governor of Brixton Prison* [2001] UKHL 69, [2002] 1 AC 556, [2002] 1 All ER 545, [87].   [119] *Scott* (n93), [24].

[120] *R v Richards* [1999] Crim LR 764. This may be ordered despite the opposition of the accused, *R v Wang Yam* [2008] EWCA Crim 269.   [121] *R v Lord Saville of Newdigate* (n111).

[122] See further, 237 for statutory provisions for such special measures in Youth Justice and Criminal Evidence Act 1999 (ss 19–31), and for restrictions on reporting (ss 44–52).

[123] For the effects of the Irish scheme see *People v Gilligan* [2005] IESC 78, [2006] 4 IR 362.

[124] *Alex Lawrie Factors Ltd v Morgan* [2001] CPR 2; *Aquarius Financial Enterprises Inc v Certain Underwriters at Lloyds* [2001] 2 Ll R 542.   [125] *R v Raynor* (2000) 165 JP 149, [13].

[126] Criminal Justice Act 2003, s 137(1) (still uncommenced).

(4) Those matters are—

  (a) the interval between the time of the events in question and the time when the recorded account was made;

  (b) any other factors that might affect the reliability of what the witness said in that account;

  (c) the quality of the recording;

  (d) any views of the witness as to whether his evidence in chief should be given orally or by means of the recording.

Further provision has been made for witnesses[127] to make video recordings of accounts of events forming part of an indictable criminal offence when still fresh in the witness's memory, subject to a number of conditions, and for such recordings to stand as evidence in chief of those matters, subject to the witness testifying at trial to their truth.[128]

Although there is special provision for the exclusion of unreliable hearsay in criminal proceedings,[129] the general rule is that the credibility of a witness[130] is a matter for the jury. Except in special situations to be mentioned below, evidence in chief going only to credibility, even expert evidence, is inadmissible.[131] In civil proceedings tried by judge alone, the credibility of witnesses should not be determined in isolation from the totality of the evidence.[132]

SECTION 2. SPECIAL CATEGORIES

As indicated above, in a number of cases, special rules have been devised to cater for special categories of witness:[133] sometimes special rules of competence and compulsion; sometimes rules requiring supporting evidence; and sometimes rules of practice dictating the form of direction to be given to the jury when considering such evidence. To an extent, experience of the operation of these rules in special categories can be used to evaluate the possibility of using them more generally.

CHILDREN[134]

It is not long since the evidence of children was regarded with such suspicion as to justify strict tests of competence, to require corroboration in some cases, and a particularly

---

[127] Other than the defendant.

[128] Criminal Justice Act 2003 ss 137, 138 (not, at the time of editing, yet brought into force).

[129] Criminal Justice Act 2003, s 125, emphasized in this context in *R v Horncastle* [2009] EWCA Crim 964, [73]–[75], [2009] UKSC 14, [36]–[37]; and s 126 (expressly preserving the exclusionary effects 78 of the Police and Criminal Evidence Act 1986).

[130] Including hearsay, although expert evidence on the reliability of confessions made under certain conditions of stress has been held admissible: *R v Blackburn* [2007] EWCA Crim 2290 [28].

[131] See *R v W* [2003] EWCA Crim 3490, [24].

[132] *Jakto Transport Ltd v Hall* [2005] EWCA 1327, [29].

[133] Many of them categorized as 'vulnerable': see e.g. Vulnerable Witnesses (Scotland) Act 2004; distinguished in the Youth Justice and Criminal Evidence Act 1999 for the purposes of special measures between those eligible on account of age or incapacity (s 16), or of fear or distress about testifying (s 17).

[134] The maximum age for the purposes of special measures was increased to 18 by s 98 of the Coroners and Justice Act 2009.

emphatic warning of the dangers of convicting on the basis of such evidence. The child was required to testify in much the same way as any other witness in open court, and exposed to the ordinary rigour of cross-examination. This situation aroused serious concern, both for the well-being of children required to undergo such ordeals, and for the administration of justice, if, as a result of failures so induced, the guilty should not be convicted. That situation has changed dramatically,[135] principally as a result of legislative intervention.[136] It is useful to examine the rules relating to the compellability and competence of children; special pre-trial procedures for securing their evidence; the manner in which their evidence may be given; some special considerations relating to the support it may be given; and the way in which the jury should be directed in assessing its weight.

Compellability

One focus of concern has been the possibility of harm being caused to a child witness. The evidence is necessarily inconclusive since much of the work has been done in sexual abuse cases, in which it is extremely difficult to distinguish between the trauma of the crime and of the trial.[137] If a child is a ward of court, leave is required before the child can be interviewed,[138] although the police may otherwise interview any child in the course of investigation of a serious crime, notwithstanding parental objection, since the interests of the child are not then paramount.[139] Leave is not required to call a child as a witness in criminal proceedings, whether application is made before or after the wardship order, and whether for prosecution or defence.[140] Competent children are, in principle, compellable witnesses, even when they are parties to care proceedings, but it will rarely be appropriate to compel them to give evidence.[141] Child defendants are as entitled as any others to the provision of legal assistance.[142] Where concurrent criminal and civil proceedings arise from the same facts it is imperative that both courts liaise as to timing.[143]

---

[135] In some jurisdictions, such as Australia, evidential rules (see *In the marriage of N and E* (1994) FLR 99) and discretions (see *In the marriage of Parker and Williams* (1993) 117 FLR 1) can be disregarded in favour of children.

[136] Largely in the Youth Justice and Civil Evidence Act 1999, although not all of its provisions have been brought into force. For judicial affirmation of preference for legislative intervention, see *R v FAR* [1996] 2 Qd 49, Fitzgerald P, 51.

[137] See Spencer and Flin *The Evidence of Children* (2nd edn, 1993), ch 13, in which the evidence is examined.

[138] *Practice Direction* [1988] 1 All ER 223, [1987] 1 WLR 1739; as modified by *Practice Direction* [1988] 2 All ER 1015, [1988] 1 WLR 989. Prior application may be waived for interview by the police in an emergency, so long as proper procedures for all juveniles are observed: *Re R; Re G* [1990] 2 All ER 633, [1990] 2 FLR 347.

[139] *Chief Constable of Greater Manchester v KI and KF* [2007] EWHC 1837 (Fam), [2008] 1 FLR 504.

[140] *Re K* [1988] Fam 1, [1988] 1 All ER 214 (before and for prosecution); *Re R* [1991] Fam 56, [1991] 2 All ER 193, (after and for defence). A fortiori if the child is not a ward: *R v Highbury Corner Magistrates' Court, ex p Deering* [1997] 1 FLR 683.

[141] *LM v Medway Council* [2007] EWCA Civ 9, [2007] 1 FLR 1698, [44], [59].

[142] *R v Blackburn* (n130), [53].   [143] *SW v A City Council* [2009] EWCA Civ 644.

Competence[144]

This is governed for the purposes of criminal proceedings in England[145] by the provisions of the Youth Justice and Criminal Evidence Act 1999. It provides in s 53 that:[146]

(1) At every stage in criminal proceedings all persons are *(whatever their age)* competent to give evidence.

...

(3) A person is not competent to give evidence in criminal proceedings if it appears to the court that he is not a person who is able to—
    (a) understand questions put to him as a witness, and
    (b) give answers to them which can be understood.

Thus children will be presumed[147] to be able to perform *both* of these feats, subject to s 54:

(1) Any question whether a witness in criminal proceedings is competent to give evidence in the proceedings, whether raised—
    (a) by a party to the proceedings, or
    (b) by the court of its own motion, shall be determined by the court in accordance with this section.

(2) It is for the party calling the witness to satisfy the court that, on a balance of probabilities, the witness is competent to give evidence in the proceedings.

(3) In determining the question mentioned in subsection (1) the court shall treat the witness as having the benefit of any direction under section (19) which the court has given, or proposes to give, in relation to the witness.

(4) Any proceedings held for the determination of the question shall take place in the absence of the jury (if there is one).

(5) Expert evidence may be received on the question.

(6) Any questioning of the witness (where the court considers that necessary) shall be conducted by the court in the presence of the parties.

These provisions continue the progress made by previous statutory provision,[148] and appear to resolve a number of matters that had created doubt,[149] or dissent,[150] under the old law. When the issue is raised, the burden of showing the child to be competent rests

---

[144] An incompetent child's statement may occasionally be received under s 114 of the Criminal Justice Act 2003 as in *R v SJ* [2009] EWCA Crim 1869, or as part of the res gestae, as in *R v Cooper* [2007] ACTSC 74, 175 ACR 94.

[145] A similar approach applies in Australia under the provisions of the Commonwealth Evidence Act 1995.   [146] Emphasis supplied.

[147] In Australia, the similarly framed Evidence Act 1995 has explicitly been so construed: *R v Brooks* (1998) 44 NSWLR 121.

[148] Notably by the Criminal Justice Acts of 1988 and 1991.

[149] For example, whether there was a presumptive minimum age for competence: see e.g. *DPP v M* [1998] QB 913, [1997] 2 All ER 749 (child aged four); *R v DP* [2007] VSCA 219, 176 ACR 382 (child aged three). In one recent case a child of four was cross-examined as to events which had occurred when the child was two, (2009) 39 *Fam L* 608.

[150] For example, that expert evidence was inadmissible in the case of 'normal' children: see e.g. *R v Robinson* [1994] 3 All ER 346 (bottom 1 per cent of 15-year-olds). In Canada, there seems to be some discrepancy in the admission of expert testimony as between trial by jury and trial by judge alone: cf *R v Tayebi: R v Talbot* (2002) 161 CCC3d 197, 256.

on the proponent of competence, and is likely to be resolved informally in advance of trial.[151] Issues of credibility have no bearing on the decision, which depends entirely on understanding.[152] It is interesting to note that it seems, as a result of s 54(3), that the determination of whether or not a child can understand a question may be informed by evidence facilitated by an intermediary whose function is to enable such understanding.[153] A decision as to competence can be informed by expert evidence. In many cases, it will be necessary to make a preliminary decision on competence in relation to pre-recorded testimony, but this should be kept under review, and a finding of competence may be rescinded in the light of defective performance in cross-examination.[154]

Once a child has testified, it will be rare for the court to intervene to prevent consideration by the jury, for example on the basis of inconsistency or vagueness.[155] It should be noted that, in the case of child defendants, separate issues arise as to whether the child has sufficient understanding to participate more generally in the trial.[156]

Pre-trial procedure[157]

Although the provisions of the Youth Justice and Criminal Evidence Act 1999[158] have primary relevance for procedure at trial, the new regime also affects pre-trial procedure. It has in particular taken over much of the previous law relating to the use in evidence of pre-recorded videos, while making a number of changes, largely recommended by a governmental interdepartmental working party.[159] In response to criticism of the old law based on the initial failure to implement in full the recommendations of the Pigot Report,[160] it added provision for the pre-recording of cross-examination, although this has now been discarded because of difficulty over pre-trial disclosure, and consultation on possible replacement is in train.[161] Pre-recording evidence in chief[162] represents so different a regime from that which obtained at common law that the relevant provision[163] is reproduced here in full:

27 Video recorded evidence in chief

(1) A special measures direction may provide for a video recording of an interview of the witness to be admitted as evidence in chief of the witness.

---

[151] In *R v M* [2008] EWCA Crim 2751, [26] (proper for judge to decide on the basis of his own impression after seeing the video recording that the child was incompetent).

[152] *R v MacPherson* [2005] EWCA Crim 3605, [2006] 1 Cr App R 459.

[153] If the court directs under s 19 that such an intermediary is to be provided under s 29.

[154] *R v Powell* [2006] EWCA Crim 3, [2006] 1 Cr App R 468.

[155] See e.g. *R v H* [2006] EWCA Crim 853, (2006) 150 SJLB 571.

[156] Cf *SC v United Kingdom* (2004) 40 EHRR 10 (Crown Court); *R (TP) v West London Youth Court* [2005] EWHC 2583 (Admin) (Youth Court).

[157] For a fuller account see Hoyano and Keenan *Child Abuse* (2008) pts III and IV.

[158] As amended by ch 3 of the Coroners and Justice Act 2009.

[159] *Speaking Up For Justice* (1998). The whole area is currently under further review, see *Improving the Criminal Trial Process for Young Witnesses* (February, 2009).

[160] *Report of the Advisory Group on Video-Recorded Evidence* (1989).

[161] See Birch and Powell *Meeting the Challenge of Pigot: Pre-Trial Cross-Examination under s 28 of the Youth Justice and Criminal Evidence Act 1999* (2004); Cooper [2005] *Crim LR* 456.

[162] Supplemented by Crown Court (Special Measures Directions and Directions Prohibiting Cross-Examination) Rules 2002, SI 2002/1688.

[163] As amended.

(2) A special measures direction may, however, not provide for a video recording, or a part of such a recording, to be admitted under this section if the court is of the opinion, having regard to all the circumstances of the case, that in the interests of justice the recording, or that part of it, should not be so admitted.

(3) In considering for the purposes of subsection (2) whether any part of a recording should not be admitted under this section, the court must consider whether any prejudice to the accused which might result from that part being so admitted is outweighed by the desirability of showing the whole, or substantially the whole, of the recorded interview.

(4) Where a special measures direction provides for a recording to be admitted under this section, the court may nevertheless subsequently direct that it is not to be so admitted if—

    (a) it appears to the court that—

        (i) the witness will not be available for cross-examination (whether conducted in the ordinary way or in accordance with any such direction), and

        (ii) the parties to the proceedings have not agreed that there is no need for the witness to be so available; or

    (b) any rules of court requiring disclosure of the circumstances in which the recording was made have not been complied with to the satisfaction of the court.

(5) Where a recording is admitted under this section—

    (a) the witness must be called by the party tendering it in evidence, unless—

        (i) a special measures direction provides for the witness's evidence on cross-examination to be given in any recording admissible under section 28, or

        (ii) the parties to the proceedings have agreed as mentioned in subsection (4)(a)(ii); and

    (b) the witness may not without the permission of the court give evidence in chief otherwise than by means of the recording as to any matter which, in the opinion of the court, is dealt with in the witness's recorded testimony.

(6) Where in accordance with subsection (2) a special measures direction provides for part only of a recording to be admitted under this section, references in subsections (4) and (5) to the recording or to the witness's recorded testimony are references to the part of the recording or testimony which is to be so admitted.

(7) The court may give permission for the purposes of subsection (5)(b) if it appears to the court to be in the interests of justice to do so, and may do so either—

    (a) on an application by a party to the proceedings or

    (b) of its own motion.

(8) [repealed]

(9) The court may, in giving permission for the purposes of subsection (5)(b), direct that the evidence in question is to be given by the witness by means of a live link;

(9A) If the court directs under subsection (9) that evidence is to be given by live link, it may also make such provision in that direction as it could make under section 24(1A) in a special measures direction.

(10) [repealed]

(11) Nothing in this section affects the admissibility of any video recording which would be admissible apart from this section.

It cannot be denied that the provisions of the full Act are complex,[164] and require great care in their implementation.[165] Much of this complexity has been dictated by attempts to ensure that the legislation is compatible with the European Convention on Human Rights, and in particular with its assertion of the right of the accused to a fair trial in Art 6.[166] The Coroners and Justice Act 2009 has now introduced[167] a new s 33A into the Youth Justice and Criminal Evidence Act 1999 permitting the use of live link facilities to accused children. Pre-recorded evidence in chief was to be the primary rule,[168] although in the case of child witnesses not in need of special protection, this primary rule could be displaced if the court was satisfied that applying it would not be likely to maximize the quality of the witness's evidence,[169] although the dangers of absence of cross-examination should not be ignored.[170] In the case of a handicapped child complaining of sexual assault, it has even been held that, in exceptional cases, irrelevant material need not be excised from the recording if its presence is necessary to allow the recording to be understood.[171]

Procedures for interviewing children and creating such a video recording were examined by the Butler Sloss Report,[172] and recommendations were included in official guidelines.[173] Now required in criminal cases, their use has also become common[174] in civil cases,[175] although conflict between therapeutic and forensic considerations should always be borne in mind.[176] It was held in *R v Dunphy*[177] that such guidelines had deliberately not been given the same force as a code of practice, and a fortiori that departure from them would not automatically amount to a ground for quashing a conviction. It is important

---

[164] Hoyano [2000] Crim LR 250 (fig 2 deploys 30 boxes with 38 linking arrows to represent the special measures directions of the Act applying to children.

[165] See Cooper and Roberts *Special Measures for Vulnerable and Intimidated Witnesses: An Analysis of Crown Prosecution Service Monitoring Data* (CPS, 2005); Roberts, Cooper, and Judge (2005) 9 *E&P* 269; Burton, Evans and Sanders (2007) 11 *E&P* 1. For criticism of the machinery of implementation see Spencer (2008) Archbold News July 7.

[166] Thus the European Court of Human Rights in *PS v Germany* (2003) 36 EHRR 61 held it contrary to Art 6 for legislation to prevent cross-examination of a child complainant of sexual abuse in person by the alleged abuser, despite evidence that such a procedure might damage the child; cf *SN v Sweden* [2002] Crim LR 831 to somewhat different effect. For an overview of the impact of human rights on special measures directions, with appropriate reference to the position in other jurisdictions, see Hoyano [2001] *Crim LR* 948.

[167] Including by s 33B the presence of a 'supporter'.

[168] Supplemented where necessary by evidence taken by live link: s 21(3).

[169] Section 21(4)(c). If a child refuses to be cross-examined after a special measures direction and after having made a recording for use in evidence in chief, the court now appears to have a discretion under s 27(4) nevertheless to allow that recording to stand as evidence in chief.

[170] Stressed in *B v Torbay CC* [2007] 1 FLR 203.

[171] *R (CPS) v Brentford Youth Court* [2003] EWHC 2409 (Admin), (2003) 167 JP 614.

[172] (1988) Cmnd 412.

[173] Currently *Achieving the Best Evidence in Criminal Proceedings: Guidance for Vulnerable and Intimidated Witnesses, Including Children*. Failure to follow the guidelines weakens the weight of the evidence, but does not eliminate it completely: *Re B and O (Children)* [2006] EWCA Civ 773, [2006] 2 FCR 773.

[174] *LM v Medway Council* [2007] EWCA Civ 9, [2007] 1 FLR 1698, [56].

[175] Recordings taken for the purpose of criminal proceedings are discoverable in subsequent civil proceedings: *Re M (minors) (care proceedings: police videos)* [1995] 2 FLR 571.

[176] *Re D (minors) (child abuse: interviews)* [1998] 2 FLR 11; *D v B (Flawed Sexual Abuse Inquiry)* [2006] EWHC 2987 (Fam) is a particularly disturbing example. See Boulter (2001) 45 *Sol Jo* 412 for an account of an apparently successful experiment to mitigate this problem.   [177] (1994) 98 Cr App Rep 393.

to observe the general rule that evidence of a child be adduced in chief and not led,[178] although minor departure is sometimes tolerated.[179] There are, however, a number of reported cases that illustrate the pressures sometimes exerted on children to testify on tape in a particular way when the guidelines are not observed.[180] A pre-recorded video should not be tendered if it has subsequently been retracted.[181] It is desirable that the filming be done in such a way as not to deprive the court of a full opportunity of observing the demeanour of the child.[182] Ultimately, the test for admission is that set out in s 27:[183] in brief, that a properly directed jury could be sure that any defect was not such as to prevent the witness from giving an accurate and credible account.[184]

The issue of pre-recording is somewhat problematic. The essence of the problem is tension between on the one hand, the desire to terminate the child's direct involvement with the legal process, especially where the child is an alleged victim of sexual abuse, so as to proceed with therapeutic measures that, if conducted earlier, might taint the forensic value of the child's evidence; on the other, the need for a fair trial at which all of the material then available to the accused can be deployed in his defence.[185] The preparation of what are usually difficult cases from an evidential point of view—with events taking place in private, with people unable, or very reluctant, to speak freely about what has occurred, the emotional intensity and often antagonism of those closely concerned, the need to consult doctors and obtain medical, often psychiatric opinion, the frequent involvement of social services committed to a culture of confidentiality, and sometimes the legal complexities of the use to be made of background circumstances and personal records—all contribute to the likelihood of delay in formulating charges, in mounting a defence, and then in negotiating so as to avoid a court appearance if at all possible. If corners are cut in attempting to produce a video recording that can stand as evidence in chief too fast and at too early a stage,[186] it is almost inevitable that justice will fail to be seen to be done.[187] Conversely, delay between the incident and the making of a recording, and then further delay before trial and cross-examination in person, may also cause problems of inconsistency.[188]

---

[178] See further below.

[179] As in *R v Deacon; R v Seymour* [2002] EWCA Crim 1460, (2002) 166 JP 792; see also in Australia, *R v Morris* (1995) 78 ACR 465; in Canada, *R v CCF* [1997] 3 SCR 1182; and in New Zealand, *R v E* [2008] 3 NZLR 145.

[180] See e.g. *Re A and B (minors) (investigation of alleged abuse)* [1995] 3 FCR 389; *Re N (a minor)* [1996] 4 All ER 225, [1996] 1 WLR 153; *L (a child) v Reading Borough Council* [2001] EWCA Civ 346, [2001] 1 WLR 1575. See also, in the United States, *Idaho v Wright* 497 US 805 (1990); and, in Australia, *R v NRC* [1999] 3 VR 537 (five-year-old child interviewed on forty separate occasions in an effort to secure accusations against father).

[181] *R v Parker* [1996] Crim LR 511. But cf *R v D* [1996] QB 283, in which testimony that was subsequently recanted by a child was not regarded as thereby removed from possible acceptance by the jury, although in such a case a particularly careful warning is required: *R v Walker* [1996] Crim LR 742.

[182] *R v P (indecent assault)* [1998] CLY 882 (not filmed full face).

[183] Although s 78 of Police and Criminal Evidence Act 1984 might yield a very similar result.

[184] *R v K* [2006] EWCA Crim 472, [23].

[185] See *R (DPP) v Redbridge Youth Court* [2001] EWHC Admin 209, [2001] 4 All ER 411 for discussion of how these should be weighed in this context, and where the burden of persuasion should lie.

[186] See Keenan et al [1999] *Crim LR* 863.

[187] For an account of the pros and cons of pre-recorded cross-examination, see Hoyano (n157), 265–71.

[188] As in *R v Powell* (n154).

It seems[189] that, where a recording has been played[190] to the jury in court, a transcript may be supplied to the jury to assist it to follow the tape,[191] but while it is very exceptionally permissible for the transcript to be allowed to be taken into the jury room,[192] this should normally be at the request of the jury itself,[193] not against the wishes of the defence in a criminal case,[194] and the judge should warn the jury not to attach more weight to the transcript than to the rest of the evidence given in the ordinary way.[195]

Trial

Two aspects of the position at trial should be mentioned, both of them concerned to minimize the stress upon child witnesses:[196] first, there are special relaxations of the hearsay rule; second, there are provisions for evidence in chief to be given in a less stressful manner.

Hearsay

In criminal proceedings in England,[197] the ordinary law of hearsay applies to children, just as it does to any other witnesses,[198] subject only to the provisions discussed above for the reception of videotaped pre-trial interviews to stand for evidence in chief.[199]

In some civil proceedings,[200] special provision[201] is made for the reception of hearsay, which will often emanate from witnesses less than 18 years of age.[202] In general, the court attaches less weight to hearsay than to direct evidence, and some emphasis has been put

---

[189] No explicit alteration is made to the old law in this respect by the Youth Justice and Criminal Evidence Act 1999.

[190] It may be replayed at the jury's request and the judge's discretion if an issue as to the manner of giving the evidence requires further examination, but subject only to a strict direction as to weight by the judge: *R v Mullen* [2004] EWCA Crim 602, [2004] 2 Cr App R 290.

[191] *R v Welstead* [1996] 1 Cr App Rep 59; approved and applied in Australia in *R v Lyne* [2003] VSCA 118. See, in Canada, *R v Schell* (2004) 188 CCC3d 254, [90].

[192] *R v Rawlings*; *R v Broadbent* [1995] 1 All ER 580, [1995] 1 WLR 178; *R v M* [1996] 2 Cr App Rep 56. For the position in Australia, see *Gately v R* [2007] HCA 55.

[193] And then only after ascertaining that the reason for the request is justified: *R v W* [2004] EWCA Crim 2979, [30].   [194] *R v Coshall* [1995] 12 LS Gaz R 34.

[195] *R v Morris* [1998] Crim LR 416. Section 32 of the Youth Justice and Criminal Evidence Act 1999 requires a general direction that the very making of a special measures direction should not itself redound to the prejudice of the accused.

[196] Although sometimes other considerations prevail, as in *R v Smolinski* [2004] EWCA Crim 1270, [2004] 2 Cr App R 661, [9], in which, despite exposing children to the ordeal of a trial, it was determined that it was generally preferable to do so rather than first attempt to secure a stay for abuse of process because of delay.

[197] But not in Canada, where the otherwise mandatory evidentiary requirement of showing necessity is relaxed in the case of children: *R v WJF* [1999] 3 SCR 569; and the same seems to apply to reliability: see *R v Dubois* (1997) 118 CCC3d 544.

[198] See further Chapters XII–XIV, more liberal now under the new statutory regime.

[199] Although strictly this is in derogation not of the hearsay rule but of the rule against narrative. In New Zealand, cross-examination is regarded as so important that, even when there is a sufficient reason for the child not to be present to be cross-examined, a conviction obtained upon the basis of a pre-trial statement has been quashed: *R v J* [1998] 1 NZLR 20.

[200] Any proceedings in connection with the upbringing, maintenance, or welfare of a child.

[201] Children (Admissibility of Hearsay) Order 1993 (SI 1993/621), made under the Children Act 1989, s 96(3).

[202] In Scotland, it is even unnecessary for the child to be competent at the time of making the statement: *T v T* 2000 SCLR 1057, Lord Rodger, departing from an *obiter dictum* of Lord Hope in *Sanderson v McManus* 1997 SCLR 281.

upon the need to look at the evidence 'anxiously and consider carefully the extent to which it can properly be relied upon'.[203] On the other hand, some judges have been reluctant to receive direct evidence from children, even when tendered, if they think it unnecessary.[204] Section 125 of the Criminal Justice Act 2003 conferred a new power in criminal proceedings for stopping a case in which the evidence against the accused consists of statements not made in oral evidence, and is so unconvincing as to render a conviction on its basis unsafe. To the extent that children are less likely to testify in person, this provision may bite more in relation to them than in relation to adults.

Reduction of stress[205]

Courts always had some discretion to conduct their own proceedings in the manner most conducive to the administration of justice, and often used it to try to reduce stress upon child witnesses, for example by permitting them to give their evidence screened from the accused.[206] These powers have been augmented by statutory provision, for example by prohibiting the reporting of proceedings in such a way as to reveal the identity of a child concerned in them,[207] and since 1998 by the provisions of the European Convention on Human Rights.[208] One of the most notable innovations has been a power to give leave for the testimony of a child or mentally disordered defendant to be given[209] in a remote location by live link.[210] This is a departure from the norm that requires reasoned justification, but remains a matter within the discretion of the court.[211] Opinions vary as to whether it is more conducive to convictions on the basis that the witnesses are more willing to testify under such conditions, or less conducive on the basis that the emotional impact of such testimony is diluted. These links are available for the conduct of cross-examination,[212] to which similar considerations apply. A further measure designed to reduce stress has been

---

[203] Butler Sloss LJ in *R v B County Council, ex p P* [1991] 2 All ER 65, [1991] 1 WLR 221; 72, 230, endorsing Neill LJ in *Re W (minors) (wardship evidence)* [1990] 1 FLR 203, 227.

[204] *Nottinghamshire County Council v P* [1993] 1 FCR 180, 188. It has been suggested that evidence of children in care proceedings should receive special attention, Davis (2007) 37 *Fam L* 65, Pemberton (2009) *Fam L* 244.

[205] Many of the special measures provided in Pt II of the Youth Justice and Criminal Evidence Act 1999 have been designed with this aim.

[206] See also Home Office Circular 61/1990 encouraging this practice in magistrates' courts. In *R v Levogianmis* [1993] 4 SCR 475, it was held compatible with the Canadian Charter of Rights and Freedoms. It may cause identification problems: see *BH v Williams* 2005 SCCR 234.

[207] Children and Young Persons Act 1933, ss 39 and 49 (as substituted by Youth Justice and Criminal Evidence Act 1999, Sch 2 para 3); for civil proceedings, see CPR 39.2. It is also now the practice not to reveal the addresses of witnesses in court.

[208] Which has become the primary source in respect of restraint of publicity, see *Re S (A child)* [2004] UKHL 47, [2005] 1 AC 593, [23].

[209] Criminal Justice Act 2003, s 51, extended to child defendants by s 47 of the Police and Justice Act 2006.

[210] In *R (D) v Camberwell Youth Court* [2005] UKHL 4, [2005] 1 All ER 999, it was held that such provisions comply with Art 6. In *White v Ireland* [1995] 2 IR 268, the practice was held compatible with the Irish Constitution; in *R v L (DO)* [1993] 4 SCR 419, with the Canadian Charter of Rights and Freedoms; and in *Maryland v Craig* 497 US 836 (1990), with the confrontation clause in the Sixth Amendment to the Constitution of the United States. CPR 32.1 has endowed the judge in civil proceedings with a wide discretion over the form of evidence, and CPR 32.3 explicitly permits the use of video links.

[211] *R (H) v Thames Youth Court* [2002] EWHC 2046 (Admin), (2002) 166 JP 711.

[212] Not only in cases where evidence has been tendered in chief by this method, but also in those where a videotaped interview has been used as evidence in chief.

the prohibition of cross-examination in person of a child by the unrepresented accused.[213] It should also be remembered that, in sexual cases, cross-examination is restricted by s 41 of the Youth Justice and Criminal Evidence Act 1999.[214]

The Youth Justice and Criminal Evidence Act 1999 further provides dispensing with wigs and gowns,[215] for the exclusion of persons from the court,[216] for provision of physical aids to communication,[217] and for the use of intermediaries to assist understanding both by the witness of the question, and by the court of the answer.[218] These provisions have been held quite compatible with Art 6 of the European Convention, and because of their flexibility, in no way prejudicial to a fair trial.[219]

A system whereby vulnerable witnesses, and especially children, could be accompanied by a suitable person[220] to provide emotional support had developed long before 1999.[221]

Supporting evidence

In criminal proceedings, it used to be the case that special provisions applied to the support, or corroboration, of the evidence of children. None of the few provisions that require more than one witness now seem particularly likely to involve child witnesses.[222] In criminal proceedings, the evidence of children under the age of 14 is to be given unsworn.[223] Such evidence may corroborate other evidence of the same sort.[224] No special requirements for the support or the corroboration of the evidence of children have ever existed in English civil law.

Although the Youth Justice and Criminal Evidence Act 1999 specifically allows expert evidence on the issues of competence, and whether or not a witness can be sworn, it does not purport to change the general rule in English law that the evaluation of the evidence of normal witnesses is the exclusive function of the jury, and

---

[213] The Youth Justice and Criminal Evidence Act 1999, ss 34–39 (as amended by the Coroners and Justice Act 2009), now regulates this system. The principal amendment is the insertion into s 24 of an entitlement to the presence of a 'supporter' for line-link testimony and cross-examination).   [214] See further 332.

[215] YJCEA 1999, s 26.

[216] YJCEA 1999, s 25. Although special provision is made for the presence of persons from the media of communications, any reporting of the proceedings is governed by separate rules. It would only be in the most exceptional circumstances that the accused would be excluded from the court: see, in Australia, *R v WS* [2000] SASC 294, 116 ACR 328.

[217] YJCEA 1999, s 30.

[218] YJCEA 1999, s 29. Normally such an intermediary will be quite independent of any of the parties to the dispute, and will in all cases be required to declare that he will perform his functions faithfully: s 29(5). It is arguable that a more rigorous set of regulations would help the appearance of justice being done. For full discussion, see Ellison [2002] *Crim LR* 114.

[219] *R (D) v Camberwell Youth Court* (n210).

[220] Preferably a trained professional, completely independent of the parties. See *Achieving the Best Evidence in Criminal Proceedings: Guidance for Vulnerable and Intimidated Witnesses, Including Children* (Draft 2000) ch 4, para 4.2.

[221] See *R v Smith* [1994] Crim LR 458.

[222] Especially after the repeal by s 33 of the Criminal Justice and Public Order Act 1994 of a number of such requirements, which previously existed under the Sexual Offences Act 1956.

[223] YJCEA 1999, s 55(2)(a).

[224] Criminal Justice Act 1988, s 34(3) as amended by the Criminal Justice and Public Order Act 1994.

that expert evidence as to the credibility of witnesses, including 'normal' children,[225] is unlikely to be helpful.[226] It is certainly rarely uncontentious.[227] It remains the case that evidence in chief of truthfulness in relation to others is inadmissible to support credibility.[228]

Direction

Even when corroboration was not strictly required in the old law, there was sometimes either a mandatory requirement or a rule of practice requiring that the jury be warned of the danger of convicting on the basis of the uncorroborated evidence of a child. Such requirement was abrogated by s 34(2) of the Criminal Justice Act 1988, and any lingering vestige eliminated by the extension of such abolition in cases of children to all remaining such requirements[229] in s 32 of the Criminal Justice and Public Order Act 1994.[230] These provisions apply to proceedings before magistrates as much as to those in the higher courts.

The judge must direct the jury in a balanced way, and is free to mention both the weaknesses and strengths in general of the evidence of children.[231] Although not absolutely mandatory, some warning of the difficulties faced by the defence when charged with the sexual abuse of those who were then children, when the trial took place many years later, is desirable.[232] As noted above,[233] it may also be necessary to instruct the jury very carefully as to the permissible use of transcripts,[234] or replays, of pre-recorded video interviews, especially where there have been allegations of departure from the relevant guidelines.[235]

The Youth Justice and Criminal Evidence Act 1999 provides both that evidence given under any of the special measures that may be ordered is entitled to the weight appropriate to the circumstances,[236] and that the jury must be warned against drawing any prejudicial inference adverse to the accused from the fact that the special measures have been ordered.[237]

---

[225] *R v Robinson* (n150); *Re M and R (minors) (sexual abuse: expert evidence)* [1996] 4 All ER 239. See, also in Scotland, *HM Adv v Grimmond* 2001 SCCR 708; in New Zealand, *R v Aymes* [2005] 2 NZLR 376; in Australia, *Farrell v R* [1998] HCA 50, 198 CLR 286; and in Canada, *R v DD* 2000 SCC 43, [2000] 2 SCR 275.

[226] *R v Pendleton* [2001] UKHL 66, [2002] 1 All ER 524, [45]. Cf *R v JH; R v TG* [2005] EWCA Crim 1828, [2006] 1 Cr App R 195: *R v S; R v W* [2006] EWCA Crim 1404 (expert evidence of childhood amnesia).

[227] For stark disagreement, see *Re A and B (minors) (investigation of alleged abuse)* [1995] 3 FCR 389.

[228] *R v T* [2006] EWCA Crim 2006. In Canada the credibility of children has been made subject to different criteria from that of adults, *R v HC* [2009] ONCA 56, 241 CCC3d 45.

[229] Principally for accomplices and victims of sexual offences.

[230] Embodying the recommendations of Law Commission No 202 (Cm 1620, 1991) *Corroboration of Evidence in Criminal Trials.*

[231] *R v L* [1999] Crim LR 489. Cf, in Australia, *Reference of A Question of Law (No 1 of 1999)* [1999] WASCA 53, 106 ACR 408; while in Canada, it would seem that a jury could be directed to ignore inconsistencies to a greater extent in the evidence of a child than in that of an adult: *R v RAN* (2001) 152 CCC3d 464.

[232] *R v E (sexual abuse: delay)* [1996] 1 Cr App Rep 88.   [233] 241.

[234] *R v McQuiston* [1998] 1 Cr App Rep 139 recommended the reading out of transcripts, even when the video is not replayed. See also *R v Springer* [1996] Crim LR 903.   [235] *R v Hanton* [2005] EWCA 2009.

[236] YJCEA 1999, s 31(4).

[237] YJCEA 1999, s 32. The judge has the duty to decide what warning, if any, is necessary.

OTHERWISE INCAPACITATED WITNESSES

Most of the changes described above in relation to children made by the Youth Justice and Criminal Evidence Act 1999 have been applied[238] to otherwise incapacitated witnesses as defined by s 16(2):

The circumstances falling within this subsection are—

(a) that the witness—

(i)   suffers from mental disorder within the meaning of the Mental Health Act 1983, or

(ii) otherwise has a significant impairment of intelligence and social functioning;

(b) that the witness has a physical disability or is suffering from a physical disorder.

The provision in s 30 for a special measures direction allowing the use of communication devices may be specially useful in some forms of incapacity,[239] although great care is necessary to avoid injustice.[240] It is worth noting some special points relating to competence, the admission of hearsay, and the appropriate direction to the jury.

Competence

A person is presumed capable of participating in a trial and testifying,[241] and bears the persuasive burden of rebuttal.[242] Even before the implementation of the YJCEA 1999, it had been thought fit to apply the test of competence set out in s 53 to a very old witness, not strictly as a test of competence,[243] since there could be no question of her giving oral testimony, but rather as a test of the admissibility of a hearsay statement, tendered under s 23 of the Criminal Justice Act 1988, and subject to the discretionary control of s 26.[244] If expert evidence of the witness's mental state is admitted, it should not be taken in the presence of the jury over the objection of the accused.[245] It may then be necessary to allow

---

[238] Extended to incapacitated defendants under s 33A of the Youth Justice and Criminal Evidence Act 1999 inserted by s 47 of the Police and Justice Act 2006. In some jurisdictions, application of similar special measures primarily applicable to children is made on a discretionary basis: see, in Ireland, *O'Sullivan v District Judge Hamill and DPP* [1999] 2 Ir 9. Here, as for children, it has been suggested that the application of special measures be extended to defendant witnesses.

[239] For an example of the sort of difficulties that may occur, see *R v Cacic* [2001] VSC 483, 124 ACR 598 (evidence from wheelchair-bound witness whose tongue had been surgically removed, of the physical movements of the accused at the relevant time). To facilitate testimony by disabled witnesses in person, a pilot scheme involving social workers liasing with counsel has been launched in Liverpool: see Silverman, The Times, 25 January 2005 (Law) 8.

[240] See the scepticism of Butler-Sloss P toward the technique of 'facilitated communication' in *Re D (evidence: facilitated communications)* [2001] 1 FLR 148.

[241] In Canada, in *Bilawchuk v Wawryko* (2002) 215 DLR (4th) 385, it seems to have been accepted that dispensation from discovery could be ordered if there were sufficient evidence that a party would suffer psychiatric injury by compliance. Compulsory testing for fitness to participate was held contrary to the ECHR in *MG v Germany* (2009) 48 EHRR SE5.

[242] *Phillips v Symes* [2004] EWHC Civ 654, [2006] 34 All ER 838; in *R v Cash* [2004] EWCA Crim 666, (2004) 148 SJLB 416, fresh evidence was allowed on appeal to show incompetence unsuspected at the time of trial. See, in Canada, *R v Peepeetch* (2003) 177 CCC3d 37; the ability to instruct counsel to cross-examine is there regarded as an indication of competence to testify: *R v Morrissey* (2003) 177 CCC3d 428.

[243] See also, in Canada, *R v AA* (2001) 155 CCC3d 279, in which the court is careful to distinguish between capacity to testify and capacity to consent to sexual intercourse.

[244] *R v D* [2002] EWCA Crim 990, [2003] QB 90.

[245] *R v Deakin* [1994] 4 All ER 769. In this case, the expert evidence was directed exclusively to the competence of the witness, leaving credibility alone to the jury.

access to the witness by the defence for the purposes of assessment.[246] Temporary incapacity occasioned by illness or intoxication would presumably lead to an adjournment when appropriate.

Hearsay

Under the provisions of c 2 of Pt 11 of the Criminal Justice Act 2003,[247] permitting the use of hearsay, one of the conditions specified by s 116(2)(b) is that the witness be unfit to attend as a witness because of his bodily or mental condition. It was held in *R v Setz-Dempsey*[248] in relation to similar earlier legislation that a mentally ill witness who was physically able to attend, and had indeed testified to a certain extent, was nevertheless unfit to attend for the purpose of admitting his earlier statements.[249]

The admission of hearsay in the case of the incapacitated has been held both in England,[250] and in Scotland,[251] compatible with Art 6 of the European Convention on Human Rights.

Direction

Section 77 of the Police and Criminal Evidence Act 1984 imposes an obligation[252] upon the court to warn the jury of special need for care in convicting upon the confession of a mentally handicapped person, obtained by the police otherwise than in the presence of an independent person.[253] The section further provides that the reason for such need should also be explained. Apart from this provision, no special rule applied to the evidence of those with a mental handicap, even though in one case the witnesses were patients in a special hospital for the criminally insane, and the allegations were made against nurses in the hospital.[254] It is noteworthy, however, that the judge still thought it appropriate to direct the jury that one such witness could not corroborate another, and specified the reasons for the evidence of such witnesses being suspect. This direction was commended by the House of Lords. It does not justify the uncritical acceptance of the evidence of a psychotic,[255] or leaving the evidence of a witness suffering from psychiatric disorder to the jury without any warning at all;[256] indeed, in such a case, a particularly careful warning may be required.[257]

---

[246] As held in New Zealand in *R v Griffin* [2001] 3 NZLR 577.   [247] See generally, 606.

[248] (1994) 98 Cr App Rep 23.

[249] Subject to the then current statutory discretions in ss 25 and 26. See also, in Canada, *R v Pearson* (1994) 95 CCC (3d) 365, in which a hearsay statement was admitted to supplement the evidence of a mentally handicapped witness.   [250] *R v D* (n181).

[251] *HM Adv v Nulty* [2000] SCCR 431.

[252] Although where other similar warnings have been given, abstention from a s 77 warning will not necessarily be fatal, *R v Qayyum* [2006] EWCA Crim 1127.

[253] The Code of Practice for Police Questioning provides that a mentally handicapped person shall be interviewed in the absence of an independent person only in cases of urgency as specified in [11.1]. A family member has been held not sufficiently independent: *R v Bailey* [1995] 2 Cr App Rep 262.

[254] *R v Spencer* [1987] AC 128, [1986] 2 All ER 928. For similar approaches elsewhere, see, in Australia, *Bromley v R* (1986) 161 CLR 315, and in New Zealand, *R v Harawira* [1989] 2 NZLR 714.

[255] *Re A and B (minors) (investigation of alleged abuse)* [1995] 3 FCR 389.

[256] *R v Cooper* [1995] CLY 1095. See also now Youth Justice and Criminal Evidence Act 1999, s 31(4); and in Australia, see *R v Latcha* (1998) 104 ACR 390 (mentally incapacitated complainant of sexual offence).

[257] *R v Yammine and Chami* [2002] NSWCCA 289, 132 ACR 44.

SPOUSES AND OTHERS[258]

When interest was the principal ground for disqualification, there was no need for special rules relating to the evidence of spouses, ex-spouses, or close relations. After 1843, when interest ceased to be a principal ground for disqualification, special rules of spouse competence and compellability were created. It is here necessary to consider the rules relating to competence, to compellability, to their specific application to spouses of a co-accused, and to ex-spouses, and very briefly to mention the claims to special consideration of other relationships.

Competence

Subject to comparatively unimportant exceptions, which were confined to criminal cases, a party's spouse was incompetent as a witness for or against him at common law.[259] The incompetence extended to spouses of either sex and to testimony concerning events occurring before, as well as during, the marriage.[260] It was immaterial that the marriage was contracted after the occurrence of the relevant events,[261] or even after the commencement of proceedings,[262] and whatever the motive for marrying.

The one clear exception to the common law rule related to criminal charges involving personal violence by the accused against his or her spouse, and was established in *Lord Audley's Case*,[263] in which a wife was held competent to testify against her husband who was charged as accessory to her rape. The decision was based on necessity. Were the law otherwise, the injured spouse would frequently have had no remedy. In *R v Sergeant*,[264] it was said that a wife was in all cases a competent witness for her husband when admissible against him, and there was no reason to doubt that this doctrine applied to all the exceptions to the common law rule of the incompetence of spouses, and to husbands as well as to wives.

After a long, complicated, and thoroughly unsatisfactory process of development, the modern law on this topic has been greatly simplified by the Police and Criminal Evidence Act 1984, s 80.[265] Most difficulty has been experienced in criminal proceedings. Spouses have been competent and compellable witnesses in civil proceedings since 1853,[266] and are now competent in criminal proceedings under the Youth Justice and Criminal Evidence Act 1999, s 53.

It is desirable[267] that the court explain to a competent, but non-compellable, spouse the precise nature of that situation, so as to inform the witness's choice whether or not to testify.[268] The choice is particularly important because it is exhausted once a witness has

---

[258] See Creighton [1990] *Crim LR* 34.

[259] *Bentley v Cooke* (1784) 3 Doug KB 422; *Davis v Dinwoody* (1792) 4 Term Rep 678. The rule has even defied the 'principled' exception to hearsay in Canada, *R v Couture* 2007 SCC 28, [2007] 2 SCR 517.

[260] *Pedley v Wellesley* (1829) 3 C & P 558.

[261] *Hoskyn v Metropolitan Police Comr* [1979] AC 474, [1978] 2 All ER 136.

[262] See *S v Leepile (No 3)* 1986 (2) SA 352.

[263] (1631) 3 State Tr 401, followed in *R v Azire* (1725) 1 Stra 633. [264] (1826) Ry & M 352.

[265] Similar reform has been undertaken in other jurisdictions, see e.g. Criminal Procedure (Scotland) Act 1975, s 143; Evidence Act (Cwth) 1995, ss 18, 19.

[266] As a result of the Evidence Further Amendment Act 1853, as further amended.

[267] Although omission is not fatal: *R v Nelson* [1992] Crim LR 653.

[268] *R v Acaster* (1912) 7 Cr App Rep 187; *R v Pitt* [1983] QB 25, [1982] 3 All ER 63. See also *Bates v HM Adv* 1989 SLT 701.

decided to testify. There is then no further chance of refusing, and if a witness resiles from his proof, he is liable to be treated as hostile, and to be cross-examined on any previous statement he may have made, a procedure explained more fully in the next chapter. In several reported cases, the accused has been found guilty despite, or perhaps because, a spouse witness for the prosecution has attempted to shield him, and then been treated as hostile.[269] It is noteworthy that, notwithstanding the recommendation of the Criminal Law Revision Committee[270] the prohibition[271] on comment upon the accused's spouse's failure to testify be lifted, it was instead re-enacted.[272] It is still more surprising that this provision has now been re-enacted yet again,[273] despite the ban on comment upon the accused's similar failure having been lifted by the Criminal Justice and Public Order Act 1994.[274]

Compellability[275]

Most of the remaining problems now relate more to compellability than to competence, and it is useful to set out the relevant provisions in full:

80 Compellability of accused's spouse

(2) In any proceedings the wife or husband of a person charged in the proceedings shall, subject to subsection (4) below, be compellable to give evidence on behalf of that person.

(2A) In any proceedings the wife or husband of a person charged in the proceedings shall, subject to subsection (4) below, be compellable—

(a) to give evidence on behalf of any other person charged in the proceedings but only in respect of any specified offence with which that other person is charged; or

(b) to give evidence for the prosecution but only in respect of any specified offence with which any person is charged in the proceedings.

(3) In relation to the wife or husband of a person charged in any proceedings, an offence is a specified offence for the purposes of subsection (2A) above if—

(a) it involves an assault on, or injury or a threat of injury to, the wife or husband or a person who was at the material time under the age of 16;

(b) it is a sexual offence alleged to have been committed in respect of a person who was at the material time under that age; or

(c) it consists of attempting or conspiring to commit, or of aiding, abetting, counselling, procuring or inciting the commission of, an offence falling within paragraph (a) or (b) above.

(4) No person who is charged in any proceedings shall be compellable by virtue of subsection (2) or (2A) above to give evidence in the proceedings.

---

[269] *Hoskyn v Metropolitan Police Comr* (n261); *R v Pitt* (n268); *R v Nelson* (n267).

[270] Eleventh Report 1972 (Cmnd 4991), para 154.

[271] The Criminal Evidence Act 1898, s 1(b). Although curable by direction, *R v Davey* [2006] EWCA Crim 565.

[272] Police and Criminal Evidence Act 1984, s 80(8).

[273] By the Youth Justice and Criminal Evidence Act 1999, s 67(1), and Sch 4 para 14, as a new s 80A of the Police and Criminal Evidence Act 1984.

[274] Section 35(3).

[275] This topic has been simplified by the provisions of Sch 4, para 13 of the Youth Justice and Criminal Evidence Act 1999, amending s 80 of the Police and Criminal Evidence Act 1984.

(4A) References in this section to a person charged in any proceedings do not include a person who is not, or is no longer, liable to be convicted of any offence in the proceedings (whether as a result of pleading guilty or for any other reason).

(5) In any proceedings a person who has been but is no longer married to the accused shall be...compellable to give evidence as if that person and the accused had never been married.

(6) Where in any proceedings the age of any person at any time is material for the purposes of subsection (3) above, his age at the material time shall for the purposes of that provision be deemed to be or to have been that which appears to the court to be or to have been his age at that time.

(7) In subsection (3)(b) above 'sexual offence' means an offence under the Protection of Children Act 1978 or Part I of the Sexual Offences Act 2003.

Since it was not thought universally desirable to apply to spouse witnesses the general rule of the common law that competence implies compellability,[276] many of the old problems that formerly related to spouse competence reappeared in relation to spouse compellability for the prosecution.[277] It should be noted that in England[278] a spouse's hearsay statement may be received in the interests of justice under the inclusionary discretion introduced by s 114(1)(d) of the Criminal Justice Act 2003, notwithstanding the wishes of its maker without infringing spousal non-compellability.[279] The Act deals with three situations: offences involving assault or injury to the spouse; offences of a similar character against children; and sexual offences against children. Each requires separate consideration.

Assault on spouse

At the time of the Criminal Law Revision Committee's report, it was thought that, in cases of violence against them, spouses were compellable at common law.[280] The policy underlying such a rule was accepted by the Criminal Law Revision Committee.[281] This position was overturned by the decision of the House of Lords in *Hoskyn v Metropolitan Police Comr.*[282] In that case, the accused was charged with wounding a woman. They were married two days before the trial,[283] and the wife was compelled to testify over her objection. Her evidence was unhelpful to the prosecution, but it secured leave to treat her as a hostile witness and the accused was convicted. His appeal to the Court of Appeal was rejected on the authority of *Lapworth*. The House of Lords allowed the appeal overruling *Lapworth* on the ground that it was inconsistent both with the common law,[284] and also with the analogy of the position in statutory offences scheduled to

---

[276] *Ex p Fernandez* (1861) 10 CBNS 3.

[277] It has been held to be desirable, but not necessary, to inform a spouse witness that she is not compellable: *R v Nelson* (n267) (in which the prosecution went on to have her treated as a hostile witness).

[278] But not in Canada, see *R v Couture* (n259).

[279] *R v L* [2008] EWCA Crim 973, [2009] 1 WLR 626.

[280] As decided in *R v Lapworth* [1931] 1 KB 117.   [281] Cmnd 4991, [149].

[282] [1979] AC 474, [1978] 2 All ER 136.

[283] There is still no power to prevent a marriage even with a prisoner on remand, despite the object being to prevent the spouse being compelled to give evidence: *R v Registrar General for Births, Marriages and Deaths, ex p Crown Prosecution Service* [2002] EWCA Civ 1661, [2003] QB 1222.

[284] As expounded in *R v Inhabitants of All Saints, Worcester* (1817) 6 M & S 194, 200 by Bayley J, and as interpreted by Taylor *On Evidence* (9th edn, 1895), 892.

the Criminal Evidence Act 1898.[285] Neither ground was very plausible. As Lord Edmund Davies pointed out in his dissent,[286] *R v Inhabitants of All Saints, Worcester* was decided on the basis not of non-compellability, but of privilege. *Leach v R* can be criticized on many grounds.[287] The House of Lords also doubted the policy underlying the law as understood in *Lapworth* and as accepted by the Criminal Law Revision Committee. That policy was simply that to allow the spouse a choice would often, in effect, be to subvert the rule of criminal law that the consent of a spouse is no defence to a charge of assault upon that spouse. It may also be argued that, where one spouse has used such violence against the other as to be charged with it, there can be little confidence that the victim's choice not to testify has been inspired by marital affection rather than by fear. The argument on the other side is that it is generally unsatisfactory to compel witnesses to testify against their will, and repugnant to compel a wife to testify unwillingly against her husband. The Act reflects the policy applied in *Lapworth* and recommended by the Criminal Law Revision Committee. A difference between the Committee's draft bill and the Act is that the former referred only to assault or threat of violence, while the latter refers to assault, injury, or threat of injury. It is perhaps clearer from the terminology of the Act that a case such as *R v Verolla*,[288] in which the accused was charged with attempting to murder his wife by poisoning her, would still be covered, although in view of the inclusion of s 80(3)(c), which covers that situation exactly, there would be no need to rely upon s 80(3)(a). The explicit reference to threat of violence also removed the difficulty found at common law in relation to competence in *R v Yeo*,[289] in which a wife was held not competent to testify against her husband who was charged with sending a letter threatening to murder her. On the other hand, it seems clear that a wife would still not be compellable if her husband should be prosecuted for living on her immoral earnings.[290] It remains unclear whether a spouse would be compellable upon a charge, such as arson, which had in the circumstances put the other in fear.[291] On balance, the wording seems not apt to go quite so far. 'Injury' is less redolent of intent than 'violence', so it is possible that a spouse will be compellable for the prosecution in respect of offences in which injury is caused recklessly or negligently. Retention of the concept of assault means that a wife is compellable in the prosecution of her husband for buggering her, presumably irrespective of her consent at the time, although it is hard to imagine any circumstances in which such a charge would be brought to trial if the wife were unwilling to testify.[292] Indeed, empirical evidence suggests that, in practice, it is extremely rare for a prosecution to be

---

285   As decided in *Leach v R* [1912] AC 305.

286   It may be noted that Lord Edmund Davies had been chairman of the Criminal Law Revision Committee at the time of the 11th Report.

287   For some of them, see Zuckerman (1979) 94 *LQR* 321.

288   [1963] 1 QB 285, [1962] 2 All ER 426.   289   [1951] 1 All ER 864n.

290   Assuming the absence of assault, injury, or threat of injury. Under the old law, she was not even competent: *DPP v Blady* [1912] 2 KB 89; although in the United States, compellability has been achieved at common law: *Wyatt v United States* 362 US 525 (1960).

291   See *R v Sillars* [1979] 1 WWR 743; *R v Czipps* (1979) 101 DLR (3d) 323.

292   *R v Blanchard* [1952] 1 All ER 114, 35 Cr App Rep 183.

brought for a violent assault if the spouse is reluctant to cooperate, thus rendering compellability something of a dead letter.[293]

Assaults on children

The next category—offences involving assault, injury or threat of injury to children under the age of 16—had no predecessor at common law. It too was foreshadowed in the Criminal Law Revision Committee's Report. There is, however, one important difference. The Committee's recommendation was that the scope of the offences should be limited to those against children who were also members of the same household as the accused.[294] It was felt that the basic reason for enacting compellability in such cases was to try to secure the availability of some evidence where otherwise there might be none, and some cases, for example of cruelty to children too young to testify, might otherwise have to go unpunished. This would be most likely to occur in cases where the child was a member of the same household as the accused. The Act has, it is submitted rightly, adopted the more expansive policy of protecting children generally.

Sexual offences[295] against children

The Act also implemented the Committee's recommendation[296] that no distinction be drawn between offences involving injury to children and those of sexual offences. Here too consent is irrelevant. This means that the accused's wife is compellable against him if he kissed a 15-year-old, however much encouragement was offered, but not if he raped and murdered a 16-year-old. If the potential availability of evidence is an important consideration, cases of homicide might seem eligible for addition to the category under which the spouse is compellable.

Application to spouse of co-accused

It should be noted that both the general provision as to competence, and these exceptional cases of compellability, apply to the spouse of a co-accused exactly as to the spouse of a sole accused.[297] The Act also simplified the law in relation to the competence and compellability of a spouse witness for the defence.

The result of the new provisions upon spouse compellability can be expressed in the form of a table, first supposing A and B to be jointly tried for a non-sexual offence against neither a spouse nor a child, and then supposing them to be jointly tried for an assault on Mrs A.

---

[293] Cretney and Davis (1997) 37 *Brit Jo of Criminology* 75, but see also the policy of the Crown Prosecution Service, as stated on its website, to use evidence other than that of the victim to prosecute cases of domestic violence. For comparative comment on this possibility, see also Ellison (2002) 65 *MLR* 834.

[294] Para 151, draft bill, cl 9(3)(a).   [295] As defined in s 80(7).

[296] Para 150, draft bill, cl 9(3)(b).

[297] I am grateful to Mr James Goudkamp for pointing out to me that these provisions run counter to the general principle of not fettering the defence of a co-accused, and are difficult to justify.

	For Prosecution		For Defence	
	Against A	Against B	For A	For B
General Case				
Mrs A	No	No	Yes	No
	(s80(2A)(b))	(s80(2A)(b))	(s80(2))	(s80(2A)(a))
Mrs B	No	No	No	Yes
	(s80(2A)(b))	(s80(2A)(b))	(s80(2A)(a))	(s80(2))
Assault on Mrs A				
Mrs A	Yes	Yes	Yes	Yes
	(s80(2A)(b))	(s80(2A)(b))	(s80(2A)(a))[298]	(s80(2A)(a))
Mrs B	No	No	No	Yes
	(s80(2A)(b))	(s80(2A)(b))	(s80(2A)(a))	(s80(2))

These results accord with the recommendations of the Criminal Law Revision Committee.[299]

Ex-spouses

In the case of criminal proceedings, the Act follows the recommendation of the Criminal Law Revision Committee[300] in providing that:[301]

In any proceedings a person who has been but is no longer married to the accused shall be … compellable to give evidence as if that person and the accused had never been married.

This changed the position at common law in respect of voidable marriages.[302] Parties to a void marriage are regarded as strangers to each other for these purposes.[303] The existing law, whereby a marriage is treated as subsisting for these purposes notwithstanding that the parties are living apart, even pursuant to a judicial order for separation or non-cohabitation,[304] was retained. Nor does there seem likely to be much basis for excluding the evidence of such a witness upon the basis of its making the proceedings unfair,[305] although an unsuccessful attempt to do so has been made.[306]

Other relationships

Little consideration was given in this country to claims in respect of other relationships, but s 84 of the Civil Partnerships Act 2004 has now assimilated civil partners to spouses.

---

[298] In all cases because the assault is a specified offence against Mrs A under s 80(3)(a).

[299] Cmnd 4991, [155], draft bill, cll 9(2) and 9(3).   [300] Cmnd 4991, [156], draft bill, cl 9(4).

[301] Section 80(5), as amended by Youth Justice and Criminal Evidence Act 1999, s 67(1) and Sch 4.

[302] *R v Algar* [1954] 1 QB 279, [1953] 2 All ER 1381.

[303] So a party to a polygamous marriage, bigamous in England, is competent and compellable: *R v Khan* (1986) 84 Cr App Rep 44.   [304] *Moss v Moss* [1963] 2 QB 799, [1963] 2 All ER 829.

[305] An English court might, however, in appropriate circumstances, like the Canadian court, instruct the jury in relation to the likelihood of bias: see *R v KA* (1999) 137 CCC3d 554.

[306] *R v Mathias* [1989] Crim LR 64, unaffected on this point by the appellate proceedings (1989) 137 NLJ 1417.

In *R v W*,[307] the prosecution declined to call a mother to testify against her child who was charged with a violent assault upon her, and even suggested that her res gestae statements incriminating the child might be excluded on a discretionary basis under s 78 of the Police and Criminal Evidence Act 1984, because no cross-examination of her would then be possible. *R v C* shows some reluctance to compel heterosexual partners to testify against each other in cases of assault, after apparent reconciliation.[308]

OFFENDERS

This generic term comprehends those who have been convicted of crime in the past, those who are now charged with committing crimes, and those who have been concerned in the commission of the crime with which the accused is charged.[309] The principal concern is with issues relating to the competence of the accused and co-accused to testify. A second issue is that of support for this category of witness. It is now possible to present this more simply following the abolition of formal corroboration rules in relation to the evidence of accomplices by s 32(1) of the Criminal Justice and Public Order Act 1994:[310]

Any requirement whereby at a trial on indictment it is obligatory for the court to give the jury a warning about convicting the accused on the uncorroborated evidence of person merely because that person is—

(a) an alleged accomplice of the accused,...

is hereby abrogated.

What remains is an open-ended discretion to direct the jury appropriately as to credibility,[311] to be discussed later in this chapter.

Competence of the accused[312]

It is helpful to consider separately the competence of the accused as a witness for the prosecution, for himself and for a co-accused.

As a witness for the prosecution

The general rule is[313] that the accused is not a competent witness for the prosecution in any criminal case. The rule is the result of the common law, which, so far as this point is concerned, was not modified by the Criminal Evidence Act 1898, because that statute conferred competence on the accused only as a witness for the defence.

Where several people are charged in the same indictment, there are various devices by which the prosecution can render one of them competent and compellable against

---

[307] [2003] EWCA Crim 1286, [2003] 2 Cr App Rep 453. [308] [2007] EWCA Crim 3463.

[309] In Canada, an overlapping selection of witnesses is categorized as 'unsavoury', and a special direction is regarded as appropriate: see e.g. *R v Khela* 2009 SCC 4; *R v Smith* 2009 SCC 5.

[310] Following the recommendation of the Law Commission, (Cm 1620, 1991) Law Com No 202.

[311] *R v Causley* [1999] Crim LR 572.

[312] Likely to be construed strictly so as to permit even a policy-making director to be compelled to testify for the prosecution against the firm whose policy he makes: see *Penn-Texas Corp v Murat Anstalt* [1964] 1 QB 40, [1963] 1 All ER 258, distinguishing between officer and corporation in the context of compulsory process. See also *R v NM Peterson & Sons* [1980] 2 SCR 679, to the same effect in Canada. See also the definition of a person charged in criminal proceedings in the Youth Justice and Criminal Evidence Act 1999, s 53(5).

[313] This rule has been retained as the one exception to the provision of general competence by s 53(4) of the Youth Justice and Criminal Evidence Act 1999.

the others. A *nolle prosequi* may be filed with reference to his case; it may be stated that no evidence will be offered against him when he will be acquitted; an order for separate trials may be obtained; or he may plead guilty.[314] In this last event, it is a matter for the discretion of the court whether or not the witness should be sentenced before being called on behalf of the prosecution.[315] In such a case, the increased flexibility of any direction to the jury in the modern law may militate in favour of sentencing after the testimony has been given.

It was said in *R v Pipe*[316] that an accomplice[317] against whom proceedings are pending must not, as a matter of practice, be called on behalf of the prosecution unless it is made plain that the proceedings will be discontinued. No doubt the ban would apply to a case in which proceedings, though not actually pending, were likely, but the judgment of Lawton LJ in *R v Turner*[318] suggested that the matter was basically one of judicial discretion. An accomplice who had turned 'King's evidence' was, together with his family, accorded police protection, an advantage that he might have lost had he not testified in accordance with statements previously made by him. This whole area has been largely[319] codified,[320] enabling specified prosecutors to grant immunity, guarantees of confidentiality, and reduced or reviewed sentences, both in respect of crimes in which the subject was involved and in which he was not.[321]

As a witness for himself

The effect of s 1 of the Criminal Evidence Act 1898 is that the accused is a competent witness on his own behalf at every stage[322] of a criminal trial. Doubts have been raised whether that which an accused person says when testifying on his own behalf may be used against a co-accused, whether the statement was made in chief or in cross-examination.

Evidence in chief

In *R v Rudd*,[323] the leading case on the availability of the testimony of one of several accused given on his own behalf as evidence for the prosecution, the Court of Criminal

---

[314] Even if the witness is also unreliable, he may still be called by the prosecution, although in that case an especially strong direction is likely to be necessary: *R v Cairns et al* [2002] EWCA Crim 2838, [2003] 1 WLR 796.

[315] *R v Palmer* (1993) 99 Cr App Rep 83, reconsidering *R v Payne* [1950] 1 All ER 102. See also Gooderson (1953) 11 CLJ 279. For the form of direction in such a case in Scotland, see *Dickson v HM Adv* 2004 SLT 843, 2004 SCCR 426.

[316] (1966) 51 Cr App Rep 17.

[317] Presumably including an accessory after the fact: see *R v Bleich* (1983) 150 DLR (3d) 600.

[318] (1975) 61 Cr App Rep 67, applied *R v Governor of Pentonville Prison, ex p Schneider* (1981) 73 Cr App Rep 200; but see *R v Treadaway* [1997] CLY 1134, in which the evidence of two 'supergrasses' was held insufficient to sustain a conviction because it was manifestly tainted. See also *R v Weightman* [1978] 1 NZLR 79; *R v Brown* (1983) 74 FLR 97.

[319] The old common law could still apply outside the confines of the statutory conditions.

[320] Serious Organized Crime and Police Act 2005 ss 71–75.

[321] As fully explained, at least in the latter respects, in *R v P: R v Blackburn* (n130).

[322] Even after a plea of guilty, he may give evidence in mitigation of sentence: *R v Wheeler* [1917] 1 KB 283. The accused may also give evidence on the voir dire: *R v Cowell* [1940] 2 KB 49, [1940] 2 All ER 599.

[323] (1948) 32 Cr App Rep 138. To the same effect are *R v Hunting and Ward* (1908) 1 Cr App Rep 177; *R v Paul* [1920] 2 KB 183, 14 Cr App Rep 155; and *R v Garland* (1941) 29 Cr App Rep 46n. See also *Young v HM Adv* 1932 JC 63, in which the earlier English and Scottish authorities are reviewed.

Appeal held that the trial judge had rightly refrained from telling the jury to disregard the evidence implicating the appellant given by his co-accused. Humphreys J said:

While a statement made in the absence of the accused person by one of his co-defendants cannot be evidence against him,[324] if the co-defendant goes into the witness box and gives evidence in the course of a joint trial, then what he says becomes evidence for all the purposes of the case including the purpose of being evidence against his co-defendant.

These remarks were well supported by authority, if not entirely to the extent suggested by Humphreys J,[325] and it is submitted that they are sound in principle because it is the common lot of a party to litigation to have adverse as well as favourable testimony given by his own witnesses, and, not infrequently, by himself. Any hesitancy sprang from a failure to distinguish between one co-accused's out-of-court testimonial assertions or unsworn statements in court,[326] which were certainly not evidence against the other, and his sworn evidence in court, which is analogous to that of any other witness.

Evidence elicited in cross-examination

In principle, there can be no doubt that what a witness says in cross-examination may be relied on by the person responsible for the cross-examination as evidence in his favour. This would mean that anything that one accused says when he is being cross-examined by the prosecution may be treated as evidence against the other; but principle sometimes has to give way to considerations of policy, and, if it is sound policy to prohibit the prosecution from calling accused persons to testify against each other, it is pertinent to remember that the policy is liable to be circumvented whenever the prosecution is allowed to rely on the statements of an accused elicited in cross-examination as evidence against his co-accused. To some extent, it is only proper that this permission should be accorded, but it is arguable that the court went too far in *R v Paul*.[327] Paul, Goldberg, and others were jointly charged with an offence. Goldberg was told that he need not give evidence, but nonetheless went into the witness box, and declared that he was guilty. This was all he said in chief, but the Court of Criminal Appeal held that the judge had rightly allowed the prosecution to cross-examine him on Paul's alibi—a subject on which his evidence assisted the Crown. This case was criticized by Lord Justice General Clyde in *Young v HM Advocate*.[328] The court has discretion with regard to the cross-examination it will permit, and Lord Clyde considered that it should have been exercised in favour of Paul. It is, however, possible to exaggerate the criticisms because, had the accused pleaded guilty immediately, he would have been compellable for the prosecution, although it is true that his evidence could not then have been obtained by means of leading questions and other forms of pressure permissible in cross-examination.

---

[324] Because of the hearsay rule, but see *Mawaz Khan v R* [1967] 1 AC 454, [1967] 1 All ER 80, in which such a statement was regarded as original evidence.

[325] His Lordship said, 140, that it had been the invariable rule to state the law in the same way.

[326] As noted 225 no unsworn statement may now be made.   [327] (n323).

[328] 1932 JC 63, although some of the views there expressed were regarded as outmoded in *Todd v HM Adv* 1984 JC 13.

As a witness for the co-accused

The general rule is that the accused is a competent but not a compellable witness for any-one[329] being tried jointly with him. This is the effect of s 1 of the Criminal Evidence Act 1898.[330] It means that, if A and B are being tried together, B may call upon A to testify for him provided A is willing to do so. Within the meaning of the Criminal Evidence Act 1898, a prisoner who has pleaded guilty is not a 'person charged' because he is not concerned in any issue before the jury; he is therefore both competent and compellable for a co-accused.[331] For the same reason, someone who was originally jointly indicted with the accused, but has been acquitted or directed to be tried separately, is both competent and compellable for the accused.[332] It is not a sufficient ground to sever a trial that one co-accused will be deprived of the evidence of the other, if the other chooses not to give evidence.[333] An accused who gives evidence[334] is liable to be cross-examined by his co-accused as well as by the prosecution, even if his evidence was in no way adverse to the accused,[335] although he will enjoy some protection under s 104(1) of the Criminal Justice Act 2003 against cross-examination as to bad character so as to undermine credibility if he does not give evidence undermining the cross-examiner's defence.

Supporting evidence

As stated above, the law in this respect has been greatly simplified by abolition of the formal rules relating to corroboration of the evidence of accomplices. This was successfully accomplished by judicial decision in Canada,[336] and bypassed here in relation to those not strictly accomplices,[337] or to accomplices when called by the defence.[338] It seems likely that the approach taken in those English cases will now be extended to the evidence of all witnesses involved in some way in the commission of the crime with which the accused is charged. In England, the judge has always had considerable power to comment upon the evidence when summing-up to the jury.[339] This power must be exercised so as to present the case fairly. It is particularly important to bring out matters that might not be obvious to the jury. In these cases, it usually will be obvious that a co-accused testifying on his own behalf is quite likely to be trying to minimize his own involvement, in some cases at the expense of his co-accused.[340] What might be less obvious to the jury is that a witness

---

[329] Including a co-accused spouse, Youth Justice and Criminal Evidence Act 1999, s 53(1), Police and Criminal Evidence Act 1984, s 80(4) as substituted by Youth Justice and Criminal Evidence Act 1999, s 67(1), Sch 4, paras 12, 13.   [330] See *R v Payne* (1872) LR 1 CCR 349 as to incompetence before the Act.

[331] *R v Finch* [2007] EWCA Crim 36, [2007] 1 WLR 1685, [15] (although it may be tactically unwise to attempt to compel testimony from a reluctant witness).

[332] *R v Conti* (1973) 58 Cr App Rep 387 (directed acquittal); *R v Richardson* (1967) 51 Cr App Rep 381 (separate trials).

[333] *R v Kerry and Staveley* [1995] Crim LR 899, because to allow this would offer an opportunity for tactical manipulation, see *R v Taylor* [2007] 2 NZLR 250 for a similar result in New Zealand.

[334] In *Kaste and Mathison v Norway* (2009) 48 EHRR 45 a non-testifying co-accused whose deposition had been adduced against a co-accused was held liable to cross-examination despite his choice not to testify.   [335] *R v Hilton* [1972] 1 QB 421, [1971] 3 All ER 541.

[336] *Vetrovec v R* (n7). For subsequent development of the law relating to appropriate direction of the jury, see *R v Brooks* 2000 SCC 11, [2000] 1 SCR 237; *R v Kehler* 2004 SCC 11, [2004] 1 SCR 328.

[337] *R v Beck* [1982] 1 All ER 807, [1982] 1 WLR 461.   [338] *R v Loveridge* (1983) 76 Cr App Rep 125.

[339] See e.g. *R v Sparrow* [1973] 2 All ER 129, 135, [1973] 1 WLR 488, 495.

[340] See e.g. *R v Knowlden and Knowlden* (1983) 77 Cr App Rep 94 (decided in 1981); *R v Lovell* [1990] Crim LR 111.

testifying for the prosecution might still have reason to minimize his involvement,[341] and might, because of that involvement, be able to lie more convincingly on account of being able to conceal a small, but effective, amount of falsity in a substantial quantity of demonstrable truth.[342]

It seems that there is now no obligation but merely a discretion to warn the jury to proceed on the basis of such a witness with caution. In the case of a co-defendant, it has been reaffirmed that the normal practice will be to direct the jury to approach his evidence with caution in view of the fact that he has an interest of his own to serve.[343] If, however, a co-accused is seeking to support the evidence of the other co-accused, it will be unnecessary, and wrong, to give such a direction.[344] It has also been held by the Privy Council that it is incumbent on the trial judge to go beyond a merely general direction to exercise caution, and more specifically to identify the reasons for regarding the evidence of criminals testifying to cell confessions as tainted by self-interest, and to warn them to treat such evidence with caution,[345] although failure in these respects is mot necessarily fatal.[346]

Although in an extreme case witnesses may have been so tainted as to make a prosecution an abuse of process, and the police should not normally make offers of immunity from prosecution to potential witnesses, there is no obligation, independent of the normal rules for investigation of offences and disclosure of evidence, requiring the recording of all contact by the police with the sort of witnesses discussed here.[347] An appeal was, however, allowed in *R v Kappler*,[348] when the prosecution wrongfully presented a witness as independent.

COMPLAINANTS OF SEXUAL OFFENCES[349]

The two respects in which such complainants were regarded as a special category were that they were treated differently in some respects when testifying, and a rule of practice required a special corroboration warning. They have now become entitled[350] to the operation of special measures if not otherwise eligible.[351]

---

[341] For example, if not yet sentenced, or to justify the grant of immunity, *Eiley v R* [2009] UKPC 40. For that reason, it is essential that the facts be brought to the attention of the jury, but if they are, the question becomes one simply of weight: *Chan Wai-Keung v R* [1995] 2 All ER 438, [1995] 1 WLR 251.

[342] It was for that reason above all that the old law distinguished between accomplices called for the prosecution and for the defence.

[343] *R v Jones; R v Jenkins* [2003] EWCA Crim 1966, [2004] 1 Cr App Rep 60, [45]–[46] affirming *R v Cheema* (1994) 98 Cr App Rep 195, and denying any general principle of refraining from such a direction when the co-accused testify in support of 'cut-throat' defences.

[344] *R v Burley, Molnar and Stanton* [2001] EWCA Crim 731, para [28].

[345] *Benedetto v R* [2003] UKPC 27, [2003] 1 WLR 1545, [35].

[346] *R v Cundell* [2009] EWCA Crim 2072.

[347] Either under the domestic or ECHR jurisprudence: *R v Reed* [2003] EWCA Crim 2667.

[348] [2006] EWCA Crim 1224.

[349] See Ellison [2003] *Crim LR* 760 for a suggestion of adopting similar special protection in domestic violence cases, perhaps encouraging prosecution in the absence of testimony from the victim. It has also been suggested that cross-examination in person of an alleged victim by an alleged assailant be prohibited generally, including in civil proceedings: *Re H,L and R* [2006] EWHC 3099. See also *FU v RU* [2008] 1 NZLR 816.

[350] Including the mandatory application of video-recording provision unless the court finds that it would be unlikely to maximize the quality of the complainant's evidence.

[351] Youth Justice and Criminal Evidence Act 1999 s 22A, introduced by Coroners and Justice Act 2009 s 101.

Testimony

As noted above, the Youth Justice and Criminal Evidence Act 1999 provides, in s 16, for special measures directions in relation to all children aged under 17, thus extending to all those in that category who are complainants of sexual offences, and in s 17(4) makes further presumptive provision for such complainants over that age:

Where the complainant in respect of a sexual offence is a witness in proceedings relating to that offence (or to that offence and any other offences), the witness is eligible for assistance in relation to those proceedings by virtue of this subjection unless the witness has informed the court of the witness's wish not to be so eligible by virtue of this subsection.

As a result of abuse under the old law,[352] the Act also makes special provision to protect a complainant of a sexual offence[353] from cross-examination in person by the accused:[354]

No person charged with a sexual offence may in any criminal proceedings cross-examine in person a witness who is the complainant, either—

(a) in connection with that offence; or

(b) in connection with any other offence (of whatever nature) with which that person in charged in the proceedings.

One further mainly procedural point is that in the more limited subclass of 'rape offences'[355] publication of the name and address of a complainant will normally be suppressed, as an incentive to the reporting and prosecution of such offences.[356] The accused may apply to the judge to exercise his discretion to lift the ban, so as to seek witnesses or otherwise avoid prejudice, but it is rare for the judge to do so.

Supporting evidence[357]

Here too the law has undergone considerable simplification as a result of the abolition of the requirement of corroboration of evidence of victims of sexual offences.[358] It has since been made clear that,[359] while the legislation does not prohibit a cautionary direction, it will be strongly discouraged[360] in all but the most extreme cases,[361] some evidential

---

[352] See also *Speaking Up For Justice* (1998). For a similar response in Scotland, see Sexual Offences (Procedure and Evidence) Act 2002, s 1, inserting a new s 288C in the Criminal Procedure (Scotland) Act 1995.

[353] Although here a different range of offences from that applicable above; cf s 35(3) (cross-examination) with s 62(1) (eligibility for special measures).   [354] Section 34.

[355] As defined in the Sexual Offences (Amendment) Act 1976, s 7(2), as further amended.

[356] Sexual Offences (Amendment) Act 1976, s 4, following the recommendation of the Advisory Group on the Law of Rape (1975) Cmnd 6352. See also Adler *Rape on Trial* (1987) pp 56–64.

[357] See Lewis [2006] *Crim LR* 889, (2006) 10 *E&P* 157.

[358] By s 32(1)(b) of the Criminal Justice and Public Order Act 1994 upon the recommendation of the Law Commission in Law Com No 202 (Cm 1620, 1991). Corroboration requirements have also been abolished in Australia: see Evidence Act (Cwth) 1955, s 164. In *R v Gilbert* [2002] UKPC 17, [2002] 2 AC 531, it was even held that, since the old rule was merely a rule of practice, it may be changed by judicial decision to reflect more modern views. Although similar abolition in Ireland is differently drafted, it is to be interpreted in the same way as in England: *People v JEM* [2001] 4 Ir 385.

[359] *R v Makanjuola; R v Easton* [1995] 3 All ER 730, [1995] 1 WLR 1348 .

[360] In *R v L* [2005] EWCA Crim 3119, it was not enough to quash a conviction that undisclosed evidence would have shown some inconsistency in the complainant's evidence. See also in Australia, *Rolfe v R* [2007] NSWCCA 155, 173 ACR 168.

[361] Although, in such an extreme case, an appeal may be allowed if no sufficient direction is given: *R v Rutter* [2005] EWCA Crim 712 (complainants of substantial bad character and with many convictions for offences involving dishonesty).

basis[362] will be required to justify such a direction, and that its permissible terms are quite fluid, but need to be adapted to the circumstances of the case.[363] A claim, existing or potential, by the complainant witness for compensation does not disqualify the witness's testimony, but does require direction to the jury.[364] The form of direction should be discussed in advance between judge and counsel, and no appeal against the form of the direction will succeed unless it is *Wednesbury* unreasonable.[365] The change in the law has made no difference to the admissibility of a recent complaint to support the consistency of the complainant, which is now evidence of its truth.[366]

If it becomes clear only after the trial[367] that the complainant's evidence was unreliable, this may lead to the verdicts being set aside,[368] but the mere fact of long delay preventing the accused from any convincing rebuttal of the complainant's unsupported evidence is not alone sufficient reason.[369] The judge should direct the jury in a balanced way both of justifiable reasons for delay,[370] and any contrary argument, including difficulties caused by delay,[371] perhaps in connection with burden and standard of proof.[372] There remains strong concern that evidential problems contribute to the low conviction rate in respect of allegations of rape.[373] The government accordingly launched[374] a consultation process on increasing the admissibility of expert evidence to the mental state of complainants so as to rebut suggestions that their behaviour after the event was inconsistent with the commission of the offence,[375] and on abolition of the requirement that to be admissible a complaint should have been made at the first reasonable opportunity.[376] A special cross-government initiative has been announced, one facet of which anticipates further reform in this area.[377]

---

[362] It is as yet uncertain what will be required: see Lewis (1997) 7 *King's College LJ* 140. The fact that in only one of six counts relying on the witness's evidence the jury had convicted was held not to be a sufficient basis in *R v H* [2001] EWCA Crim 1922.

[363] An important factor may relate to any long delay between the events and the complaint, especially if there is a claim that memory has been recovered by psychological prompting: see, in Australia, *Robinson v R* [1999] HCA 42, (1999) 197 CLR 162; *Crampton v R* [2000] HCA 60, 206 CLR 161. For academic controversy about this issue, see Lewis and Mullis (1999) 115 *LQR* 265, and reply by Redmayne (2000) 116 *LQR* 265.

[364] *R v Sutton* [2005] EWCA Crim 190, [78]; a false complaint may amount to a criminal offence, *R v Carrington-Jones* [2007] EWCA Crim 2551.

[365] Which, in *R v H*, (n362) was held compatible with the European Convention on Human Rights.

[366] Criminal Justice Act 2003 s 120; cf, in Australia, *Crofts v R* (1996) 88 ACR 232.

[367] Section 125 of the Criminal Justice Act 2003 confers power to stop a case based on unconvincing evidence not tendered by testimony at earlier stages.

[368] *R v PFS* [2002] EWCA Crim 3435.

[369] *R v Hooper* [2003] EWCA Crim 2427, rejecting any such interpretation of the decision in *R v B* [2003] EWCA Crim 319, [2003] 2 Cr App Rep 197, a rejection confirmed in *R v Swales* [2004] EWCA Crim 1050, and *R v Evans* [2004] EWCA Crim 1441, [2004] 2 Cr App R 621. For extended consideration, see Lewis, *Delayed Prosecution for Childhood Sexual Abuse* (2006).

[370] *R v Doody* [2008] EWCA Crim 2557, [11]–[13].

[371] *R v Rutter* (n361).   [372] See *R v Sutton* (n364), [60].

[373] See Kelly, Lovett and Regan *A Gap or a Chasm? Attrition in Reported Rape Cases* HO *Res St* 196 (2005).

[374] *Convicting Rapists and Protecting Victims—Justice for Victims of Rape* (Office for Criminal Justice Reform 2006).

[375] As in some states in the United States, ibid Annex E; and now in Scotland, Criminal Procedure (Scotland) Act 1995 s 275, inserted by the Vulnerable Witnesses (Scotland) Act 2005, s 5; see also *HM Adv v A* 2005 SLT 975, 2005 SCCR 593. See further Ellison (2005) 9 *E&P* 239.

[376] Amending Criminal Justice Act 2003 s 120(7)(d); see further, 301.

[377] *Cross-government Action Plan on Sexual Violence and Abuse* (April, 2007).

OTHER WITNESSES AND SPECIAL SITUATIONS

While the preceding parts of this section cover the majority of the cases in which rules of competence, compellability, and support were invoked, there remains a miscellaneous ragbag of further situations in which some of them arose. It may also be noted that, at least in the non-technical sense, there has been some demand for greater support in particularly contentious situations, such as that relating to the evidence of eyewitnesses and of policemen reporting an oral confession, especially when it was subsequently denied to have been made. The most significant subgroup is the class for which some such requirement has been made by direct statutory provision. Some of the latter will be described very briefly in the first part, and then a few other situations that have been mooted will be mentioned.

Statutory provision

The Law Commission largely confined its investigation to corroboration at common law.[378] Most statutory provisions have been cast in terms of requiring some corroborative evidence, rather than a warning against convicting in its absence.

Statutes requiring two or more witnesses[379]

Some statutes have provided that the accused could be convicted[380] only on the oath of two or more credible witnesses. These included s 1 of the Treason Act 1795, penalizing the compassing of the death or restraint of the monarch, and s 168(5) of the Representation of the People Act 1983 (now repealed), dealing with impersonation at elections. These provisions are of no practical importance from the point of view of the general law of evidence, and their repeal was recommended in the 11th Report of the Criminal Law Revision Committee.

Section 89 of the Road Traffic Regulation Act 1984

Under s 89 of the Road Traffic Regulation Act 1984,[381] a person charged with the offence of driving a motor vehicle at a speed greater than the maximum allowed shall not be liable to be convicted solely on the evidence of one witness to the effect that, in the opinion of the witness, the person charged was driving the vehicle at such greater speed. The effect of this provision is that, where the evidence is that of the opinion of witnesses concerning the speed at which the accused was travelling, there must be two or more of them, and it has been held that their opinion must concern the accused's speed over the same stretch of road at the same time.[382] There may, however, be a conviction on the evidence of one witness if it amounts to something more than his opinion. In *Nicholas v Penny*,[383] a police officer's evidence that he followed the accused in a police car and

---

378 Except where there was significant overlap, as in relation to a requirement of corroboration or a warning in some provisions in the Sexual Offences Act 1956, which have now been removed: Criminal Justice and Public Order Act 1994, s 33.

379 The same rule applies to an attempt to commit such an offence: Criminal Attempts Act 1981, s 2(1)(g), as amended.

380 The Criminal Procedure (Insanity and Unfitness to Plead) Act 1991, s 1 is unusual in requiring two witnesses before a jury may *acquit*.

381 Re-enacting earlier legislation.   382 *Brighty v Pearson* [1938] 4 All ER 127.

383 [1950] 2 KB 466, [1950] 2 All ER 89, in which earlier decisions are reviewed.

consulted its speedometer, which showed an excessive speed, was held to be sufficient. The speedometer reading is prima facie evidence of the speed recorded, although it is, of course, always open to the accused to raise a doubt about whether the instrument was working properly.[384] The reading is evidence of a fact, and not a statement of opinion. As a general rule, the opinion of witnesses who are not experts is excluded, but it is admissible in a number of cases in which its exclusion would be absurd. Estimates of the speed at which a vehicle was travelling are among these cases, but the fact that such estimates are more liable to be inaccurate than testimony concerning direct perception amply justifies the provisions of s 89 of the Road Traffic Regulation Act 1984. Where the opinion is not based upon an estimation from observation of the vehicle in motion, but upon calculation from real evidence, such as skid marks and the effects of impact, there is not the same danger, and a generous view has been taken allowing such evidence to supplement the testimony of the expert deriving the appropriate inference from it.[385]

Perjury

Section 13 of the Perjury Act 1911 provides:

A person shall not be liable to be convicted of any offence against this Act, or of any offence declared by any other Act to be perjury or subornation of perjury, or to be punishable as perjury or subornation of perjury solely upon the evidence of one witness as to the falsity of any statement alleged to be false.

This confirmed the common law as settled in *R v Muscot*,[386] but the reason for the rule given in that case—'else there is only oath against oath'—is questionable because it would justify a requirement of corroboration in any number of situations in which it never was necessary as matter of law or practice. There is historical basis for the rule in the fact that perjury was originally punished in the Star Chamber, the procedure of which court was, to some extent, influenced by the civil law that usually applied the principle that the testimony of one witness was insufficient. The requirement of corroboration in the case of perjury and kindred offences may also be justified on the ground that nothing must be allowed to discourage witnesses from testifying, and the fact that a conviction for perjury might be secured on the oath of one witness could have this effect. A second witness to the falsity of the impugned statement is not, however, essential. A letter, the authenticity of which is duly proved or admitted, and which might be construed as a subornation to someone else to commit perjury in relation to the same matter, will suffice.[387] If all that is proved is that the accused contradicted the impugned statement, there is not enough evidence to support a conviction, for nothing more is established than that one of two allegations made by the accused is untrue. Additional evidence, such as the repetition of the contradiction of the impugned statement on a number of occasions to different people, will, however, be sufficient.[388]

---

[384] If no reason is adduced for doubting such a reading, the trier of fact must accept it as corroboration: *Burton v Gilbert* (1983) 147 JP 441.   [385] *Crossland v DPP* [1988] 3 All ER 712.

[386] (1713) 10 Mod Rep 192, and extended it to a wider range of offences: see *R v Barker* [1986] 1 NZLR 252.

[387] *R v Threlfall* (1914) 10 Cr App Rep 112.

[388] *R v Hook* (1858) Dears & B 606. See also *R v Atkinson* (1934) 24 Cr App Rep 123 and *R v Stokes* [1988] Crim LR 110.

Although it is necessary for the judge to give an appropriate direction to the jury,[389] it is noted that only the falsity of the statement need be corroborated.[390] It is, however, sufficient for this purpose that two different witnesses heard the same admission of falsity by the accused.[391]

The Criminal Law Revision Committee recommended, as did the Law Commission, that the requirement of corroboration should be confined to perjury in judicial proceedings and should not, like the present law, apply to such other offences under the Act of 1911 as the making of false statutory declarations.[392] This is because the encouragement of people to testify without fear of too easy a prosecution is regarded as the justification of the requirement of corroboration. This recommendation has not yet been implemented.

Claims against the estates of deceased persons

A claim against the estate of a deceased person will not generally be allowed on the unsupported evidence of the claimant, but there is no rule of law against allowing it[393] in England. The absence through death of one of the parties to the transaction calls for caution in such a case, but claims have been allowed where there was no corroboration.[394]

The sovereign and diplomats

The sovereign is not a compellable witness,[395] although it seems that this immunity may be incompatible with the European Convention on Human Rights.[396] The same applies to heads of other sovereign states,[397] because they are not subject to legal process. Under various statutes, diplomatic and consular officials, and officials of, and other persons connected with, certain international organizations enjoy total or partial immunity from compellability to give evidence.[398]

Experts

While, in most cases, parties have no choice of witnesses, this is not usually the case with expert opinion witnesses, and it is appropriate to modify the rules relating to

---

[389] *R v Hamid* (1979) 69 Cr App Rep 324; *R v Carroll* (1993) 99 Cr App Rep 381.

[390] *R v O'Connor* [1980] Crim LR 43; strictly interpreted in Canada: see *R v Neveu* (2003) 184 CCC3d 18. If the falsity of the statement is not an issue, or is formally admitted by the accused, no reference need be made to s 13: see *R v Rider* (1986) 83 Cr App Rep 207. See also *R v Willmot* [1987] 1 Qd R 53, in which the falsity of the statement was admitted under oath in the earlier proceedings.

[391] *R v Peach* [1990] 2 All ER 966, [1990] 1 WLR 976, contrary to the view expressed in para 192 of the 11th Report of the Criminal Law Revision Committee (1972) Cmnd 4991.   [392] Ibid, para 191.

[393] *Re Cummins, Cummins v Thompson* [1972] Ch 62, [1971] 3 All ER 782; see note in 87 LQR 268.

[394] It is required by statute in some Canadian jurisdictions: see *Ken Ertel Ltd v Johnson* (1986) 25 DLR (4th) 233.

[395] *R v Mylius* (1911) The Times, 2 February; cf *President of the Republic of South Africa v South African Rugby Football Union* 2000 (1) SA 1; *Clinton v Jones* 520 US 681 (1997).

[396] See *Bricmont v Belgium* (1990) 12 EHRR 217, [85] (in which the breach did not impair a fair trial since there was other evidence).

[397] Although in *State of Darussalam v Prince Jefri Bolkiah* [2008] EWHC 1247 (Ch) a sovereign was summoned for cross-examination pending a claim for immunity.

[398] See, in particular, Diplomatic Privileges Act 1964 (c 81), s 2(1), Sch 1, arts 1, 31(2), 37(1), (2); Consular Relations Act 1968 (c 18), s 1(1), Sch 1, arts 1(1), 44, 58(2); International Organisations Act 1968 (c 48); Diplomatic and Other Privileges Act 1971 (c 64), s 4; International Organisations Act 1981 (c 9); Arms Control and Disarmament (Privileges and Immunities) Act 1988 (c 2). The assistance of G V Hart, sometime secretary of the Criminal Law Revision Committee, on this subject is acknowledged.

compellability where it is the case that there is a range of witnesses competent to provide the evidence required, and there are good reasons[399] for the proposed expert to decline.[400] If this were not so, the burden upon the most popular experts could easily become intolerable.

Bankers

Reference must finally be made to the limited immunity enjoyed by bankers under the Bankers' Books Evidence Act 1879. Section 6 provides that:[401]

A banker or officer of a bank shall not, in any legal proceeding to which the bank is not a party, be compellable to produce any banker's book the contents of which can be proved under this Act, or to appear as a witness to prove the matters, transactions and accounts therein recorded, unless by order of a judge made for special cause.

The object of this statute is to save the time of bankers and protect them and their customers from the inconvenience of producing the originals of their books. Although it is sufficient to produce a copy of a public document to the court, the original of a private document has normally to be produced. Bankers' books, apart from those of the Bank of England, rank as private documents, but the Act of 1879 provides for their proof by means of a copy. There are various safeguards that it is not necessary to mention here, beyond saying that the authenticity of the copy can usually be established by affidavit, thus sparing any bank official the necessity of attending court.

Other possible cases

In *The People (A-G) v Casey (No 2)*,[402] Kingsmill-Moore J speaking for the Supreme Court of Eire said:

The category of circumstances and special types of case which call for special directions and warnings from the trial judge cannot be considered as closed. Increased judicial experience and, indeed, further psychological research, may extend it.

The case before the court concerned the reliability of evidence of visual identification and it was said that, in all such cases, whether or not there was a plurality of witnesses, the jury's attention should be drawn to the necessity for caution, because there have been cases in the past in which responsible witnesses to identification have been subsequently proved to have been mistaken.

The words of Kingsmill-Moore J were repeated with approval by the Lord Chancellor in *DPP v Kilbourne*;[403] although the problem of identification has been dealt with by the English courts in a different way. The precautions mentioned in *R v Turnbull*[404] must be observed, but they do not prescribe an invariable requirement of corroborative evidence or a warning to the jury of the danger of convicting in its absence. Indeed, the Report of the Devlin Committee on *Evidence of Identification in Criminal Cases*, which preceded

---

[399] Such as the disruption of other work, or not to be paid: *Brown v Bennett* (2000) The Times, 2 November.
[400] *Society of Lloyd's v Clementson (No 2)* [1996] CLC 1205.
[401] See also Companies Act 1989, s 69.
[402] [1963] IR 33, 38.   [403] [1973] AC 729, 740.   [404] [1977] QB 224, [1976] 3 All ER 549.

the decision in *R v Turnbull*, spoke of the declining belief in the value of a requirement of corroboration and said that the law on the subject had become too technical.[405]

The tide of judicial feeling seems to be running strongly against the ritualistic observation of rigid rules in this area, and for this reason, new categories of witnesses[406] or further areas for the application of rules or practices of requiring an inflexible warning are highly unlikely to open up.[407] The question was considered by the Royal Commission on Criminal Justice in relation in particular to the corroboration of confessions made to the police.[408] The majority view was that such confessions should continue to be admissible despite the absence of supporting evidence,[409] but that a warning should be given, tailored to the facts of the particular case and referring to the reasons that sometimes account for false confessions being made, and to any particular reasons raised by the defence in the particular case. It was felt that the jury should be directed to look for supporting evidence, but that it should be supporting evidence in the looser *Turnbull* sense rather than that which passed the old stricter tests.[410] The Law Commission also resiled[411] from a provisional view that unsupported hearsay alone should be insufficient to sustain a conviction,[412] a view strongly shared by the Supreme Court in *R v Horncastle*.[413]

SECTION 3. THE NATURE OF SUPPORTING EVIDENCE

Even under the old law, it was said that 'corroboration' was not a technical term, but simply meant 'confirmation' or 'support'.[414] Nevertheless, much of the momentum for reform was sustained by the technicality with which the old law of corroboration was engulfed, principally in the definition of what amounted to corroboration, and in the obligation upon the judge to direct the jury in detail as to what could and could not amount to corroboration.

It seems that the rigidity and technicality of the old law has now been replaced by more rational and relevant construction of what amounts to support. It remains worth distinguishing between support provided from the source requiring support, and support in

---

[405] Paras 4.36 and 4.53. See Chapter XVI, Section 2, below for an account of the report and evidence of identification generally.

[406] The House of Lords has refused to erect patients in a secure mental hospital into such a category: *R v Spencer* (n254); and in Australia, it has been denied in respect of witnesses at a relevant time under the influence of drugs: *R v Southon* [2003] SASC 205, 139 ACR 250.

[407] In *Nembhard v R* [1982] 1 All ER 183, 74 Cr App Rep 144, extension of the old corroboration requirement to dying declaration cases was denied.

[408] Cm 2263 (1993) paras 4.56–4.87, recs 89, 90. See also Res St No 13.

[409] Though Res St No 13 showed that this would be likely to occur in no more than 5 per cent of cases.

[410] In Australia, warnings in relation to the *making* of disputed and uncorroborated confessions to the police were required at common law: *R v McKinney and Judge* (1991) 171 CLR 468; and may now be required under the provisions of the Evidence Act (Cwth) 1995, s 165. For the interaction of the two, see *R v Beattie* (1996) 40 NSWLR 155. See generally Pattenden (1991) 107 *LQR* 317. For the position in Ireland, see *People (DPP) v Connolly* [2003] 2 IR 1.

[411] *Evidence in Criminal Proceedings: Hearsay and Related Topics* Law Com 245 Cm 3670 (1997) [5.41].

[412] *Evidence in Criminal Proceedings: Hearsay and Related Topics* Law Com Consultation Paper 138 (1995) [9.5], rec 14. [413] (n129).

[414] *DPP v Hester* [1973] AC 296, [1972] 3 All ER 1056, 325, 1073.

some fashion from the accused against whom it is required. A final part of this section will deal with procedural considerations.

SUPPORT FROM THE SOURCE REQUIRING IT

One of the most fundamental tenets of the old law was that, in order to amount to corroboration, the evidence had to emanate from a source independent of the witness to be corroborated,[415] or in still more extreme a form, from a different type of source from the witness to be corroborated.[416] This led to difficult distinctions depending upon whether the evidence did, or did not, emanate from an independent source, regardless of the strength of the evidence.[417] A modern direction should deal only with the strength of the support offered by the evidence.

In *R v Makanjuola*,[418] in the course of its general explanation of the impact of the abolition of the old corroboration requirement, the Court of Appeal explicitly upheld the continued admissibility of recent complaints, which are now evidence of the truth of what they assert.[419] In such a case, evidence of the distress of the complainant is admissible, and not necessarily to be regarded as of little weight, provided that the jury is satisfied that it is not feigned.[420] It was not, even under the old law, automatically excluded as a form of implied previous consistent statement.[421] It has, in Scotland, been held that it is sometimes so delayed that no reasonable jury could regard it as supportive.[422] It should also be emphasized that the mere absence of a motive to lie does not support the truth of whatever is asserted.[423]

SUPPORT FROM THE OBJECT AGAINST WHOM IT IS REQUIRED

The question of how far the conduct of the accused constituted corroboration of the evidence against him was a matter of some debate under the old law. It was considered, in previous editions of this work, under the heads of the admission of the party against whom corroboration is required, lies told by him, his failure to give evidence, his silence when charged out of court, his failure to provide a sample of real evidence, and his conduct on an occasion previous to that with which the trial is concerned. It is worth retaining that division of topics, although their substance has, in some of these situations, been much affected by specific provision in the Criminal Justice and Public Order Act 1994.[424] In

---

[415] *R v Baskerville* [1916] 2 KB 658.

[416] See the discussion of the position relating to children in *DPP v Hester* (n414); and that relating to accomplices in *DPP v Kilbourne* (n403).

[417] Contrast *R v Willoughby* (1988) 88 Cr App Rep 91 (allegation that assailant had spots *was not* corroborated by accused having spots) with *R v McInnes* (1989) 90 Cr App Rep 99 (allegation that assailant had sweet papers in his car *was* corroborated by accused having car littered with sweet papers).

[418] (n359). See, in Australia, *Crofts v R* (1996) 88 ACR 232.   [419] Criminal Justice Act 2003, s 120.

[420] *R v Romeo* [2003] EWCA Crim 2844, [2004] 1 Cr App R 417, [13]. Although it is not always crucial to warn the jury about this: *R v Parkin and Irwin* [2004] EWCA Crim 2975, [10]. Such evidence is still more readily admitted in non-sexual situations: *R v Townsend* [2003] EWCA Crim 3173, [15].

[421] *R v Kennedy* [2004] EWCA Crim 374.   [422] *McCrann v HM Adv* 2003 SCCR 722.

[423] *R v Jovanovic* (1997) 42 NSWLR 520, in which it was held the judge should have intervened to prevent this line of cross-examination.

[424] Quite different from that specifically withdrawing an obligation to give a corroboration warning.

some situations, they can overlap,[425] in which case the various suggested directions may conflict.[426]

Admission of defendant or accused

Statements intended as mitigation or exculpation in court may be held to support the case against their maker. In *R v Dossi*[427] for instance, it was held that the accused's admission in evidence that he had platonically fondled the child who gave sworn testimony to the effect that he had indecently assaulted her could be treated as some corroboration of her statement. As Atkin LJ said: 'The question of corroboration often assumes an entirely different aspect after the accused person has gone into the witness box and has been cross-examined.'[428] Whether anything that emerges in the course of the evidence of the defendant or accused does support his opponent's witnesses is, of course, a question of fact dependent on the circumstances of the particular case. Much may depend upon the issues that remain contested, and the extent of any admission.[429]

Lies of defendant or accused[430]

As a matter of common sense, to tell a lie may indicate consciousness of guilt[431] and so support contrary testimony. In *Tumahole Bereng v R*,[432] however, Lord MacDermott said that a prisoner does not corroborate an accomplice merely by giving evidence that is not accepted and must therefore be regarded as false:

Corroboration may well be found in the evidence of an accused person, but that is a different matter, for there confirmation comes, if at all, from what is said, and not from the falsity of what is said.

There is nothing in the context that suggests that this dictum is applicable only to the testimony of an accomplice. To quote from a South Australian judgment in affiliation proceedings:[433]

The court cannot, as is sometimes suggested, prefer the evidence of the mother to that of the defendant and then use its disbelief of his evidence as the basis of an inference to be used in corroboration of the mother's testimony.

---

[425] *R v Napper* (1995) 161 JP 16 (with direction as to adverse inference from failure to testify); *R v O (A)* [2000] Crim LR 617; *R v Rodrigues* [2001] EWCA Crim 444; *R v Sylvester; R v Walcott* [2002] EWCA Crim 1327; *R v Stanislas* [2004] EWCA Crim 2266 (with direction as to adverse inference from pretrial silence).

[426] It is particularly disturbing that a different approach seems to be taken to the identity of the issue with the resolution of the need for a direction, apparently taking the view that such identity does remove the justification for a *Lucas* direction that favours the accused: see *R v Harron* [1996] 2 Cr App Rep 457; but does not remove the justification for a s 34 direction that is adverse to the accused: see *R v Gowland-Wynn* [2001] EWCA Crim 2715, [2002] 1 Cr App Rep 41. For full elaboration, see Grevling in Mirfield and Smith (eds) *Essays for Colin Tapper* (2003) 1.

[427] (1918) 13 Cr App Rep 158; *Goguen and Goguen v Bourgeois and Bourgeois* (1957) 6 DLR (2d) 19. See also *R v Simpson* [1994] Crim LR 436, in which minor sexual activity was admitted during interview about a range of offences, some much more serious, which were then charged.   [428] 162.

[429] See Munday [1985] *Crim LR* 190, pointing out that in *R v Tragen* [1956] Crim LR 332 Lord Goddard CJ seems to have taken a different view of facts superficially similar to those in *Dossi* (1918) 13 Cr App Rep 158, 87 LJKB 1024.   [430] See Heydon (1973) 89 *LQR* 552.

[431] This terminology has been condemned as misleading and prejudicial in Canada in *R v White* (1998) 2 SCR 72, [20], and in Australia, in *Zoneff v R* [2000] HCA 28, (2000) 200 CLR 234, [15].

[432] [1949] AC 253, 280.   [433] Napier J in *Pitman v Byrne* [1926] SASR 207, 211.

Any suggestion[434] that this meant that lies told in court could, for this reason, never be relied upon to support evidence against the accused has been rejected both in the Commonwealth,[435] and in England, where in *R v Lucas* it was said that:[436]

To be capable of amounting to corroboration the lie told out of court must first of all be deliberate. Secondly, it must relate to a material issue. Thirdly the motive for the lie must be a realisation of guilt and a fear of the truth. The jury should in appropriate cases be reminded that people some-times lie, for example, in an attempt to bolster up a just cause, or out of shame or out of a wish to conceal disgraceful behaviour from their family. Fourthly the statement must be clearly shown to be a lie by evidence other than that of the accomplice who is to be corroborated, that is to say by admission or by evidence from an independent witness.

It was regarded as sensible to apply exactly the same principles to lies told in court, and provided that the conditions can be satisfied there seems no reason to suppose that they cannot also be applied to the adoption of lies told by others.[437] If the lie is being used only as part of the background of the case, for example to discredit the witness, there is no need for such a direction.[438] Nor is it necessarily negligent for counsel not to seek such a direc-tion.[439] There must be some evidential support for the allegation that a lie has been told.[440] Such a direction is, however, complex,[441] and might confuse the jury if it were given when it is unnecessary,[442] as in the ordinary case in which little more than a conflict of testimony occurs between the testimony of the accused[443] and of other evidence.[444] It will be rare for an appeal to be allowed on the basis that such a direction was given unnecessarily.[445] In *R v Burge and Pegg*,[446] the Court of Appeal suggested four possible occasions for the direction: first, that in which the defence relies on alibi;[447] second, that in which the judge suggests that the jury should look for support for a piece of evidence and refer it to lies told by the accused; third, when the prosecution relies on the lies as an independent part

---

[434] *R v Chapman and Baldwin* [1973] QB 774, [1973] 2 All ER 624.

[435] *R v Collings* [1976] 2 NZLR 104; *R v Perera* [1982] VR 901.

[436] *R v Lucas* [1981] QB 720, [1981] 2 All ER 1008, rejecting the construction of *Chapman* (n434). See *Edwards v R* (1993) 178 CLR 193 for careful analysis of this direction by the High Court of Australia; and in New Zealand, see *R v Marshall* [2004] 1 NZLR 793.

[437] See *R v Perera* (n435).

[438] *R v Smith* [1995] Crim LR 305; see elaboration of this point in Australia, see *Zoneff* (n431), [50]. The same distinction is made in Scotland: see *Bovill v HM Adv* 2003 SLT 930, 2003 SCCR 182.

[439] *Popat v Barnes* [2004] EWCA Civ 820, (2004) 148 SJLB 1061, [13].

[440] *R v Garaxo* [2005] EWCA Crim 1170 (in which both sides alleged lies by the other).

[441] Especially where the lie can relate to either of two alternative verdicts: see *Meko v R* [2004] WASCA 159, 146 ACR 130.

[442] Although in Australia the direction, when necessary, must be given even though not sought by coun-sel: *Rv Ali* [2002] VSC 194, 135 ACR 426; and by the judge, not simply left to counsel: *R v Martin* [2002] QCA 443, 134 ACR.

[443] This may become more common if the Criminal Justice and Public Order Act 1994 has its desired effect of promoting statements by the accused both before and at the trial. It makes no difference that another witness whose account coheres with that of the accused can be shown to be lying: *R v Ball* [2001] EWCA Crim 3037.

[444] See *R v Barnett* [2002] EWCA Crim 454, [2002] 2 Cr App Rep 168; *Rahming v R* [2002] UKPC 23, [12].   [445] See e.g. *R v Mongon* [2004] EWCA Crim 2312, [13].

[446] [1996] 1 Cr App Rep 163, 173D.

[447] Although even here there is no invariable requirement: *R v Harron* (n426). It is immaterial that the lie relates to the reason for a former admittedly false alibi: *R v Peacock* [1998] Crim LR 681.

of its case;[448] fourth, when the judge thinks it possible that the jury will do so.[449] It seems discretionary whether such a direction should be given in relation to a co-accused when such directions have to be given in relation to his co-accused.[450] Where the lie has little relevance to silence, which is itself ambiguous as between two exculpatory defences, the judge should attempt to combine the terms of a *Lucas* direction with one dictated by s 34.

It has been suggested that the need for the direction is stronger in cases where the alleged lie was made under compulsion in other proceedings.[451] If there are unrelated lies, then the direction should be applied to both sets of circumstances separately.[452] If, on the other hand, there are separate issues, and the lies more relevant to one than to the other, this too should be made clear.[453]

Here, as elsewhere, it is submitted that the best solution is to mould the direction closely to the facts of the case, and to resist the temptation to resort to rules of thumb that will do no more than replace old technicalities with new.

Failure to adduce evidence

Under the old law, the failure of the accused to testify could not amount to corroboration of the evidence against him.[454] The position was changed by s 35 of the Criminal Justice and Public Order Act 1994.[455] Since s 38(3) prevents conviction solely upon an inference from failure to testify, its effect was affirmed in *R v Cowan*[456] as being:

> that the court or jury may regard the inference from failure to testify as, in effect, a further evidential factor in support of the prosecution case.

The court was quite clear that the inference was in no way exceptional, and that the trial judge had considerable flexibility in tailoring his direction to the facts of the case,[457] although it recommended starting from the Judicial Studies Board's specimen direction.[458] Although it has been claimed[459] that this is different from inviting the jury to infer that the accused who fails to testify is guilty, the difference is barely discernible once a prima facie case has been established.

---

[448] See *R v Goodway* [1993] 4 All ER 894, 98 Cr App Rep 11, which, in its reference to *R v Dehar* [1969] NZLR 763, recognized that even in this situation it might not be necessary to give a full *Lucas* direction. In Australia, a distinction is drawn between lies that go to credit only, and do not require a special direction, and those that are in effect implied admissions, and do: see *Edwards v R* (n436); but for condemnation of the confusion this is capable of causing, see also *Zoneff v R* (n431). The same distinction is made in New Zealand: see *R v Oakes* [1995] 2 NZLR 673, 684.

[449] See *R v Richens* [1993] 4 All ER 877, 886. This aspect of *Goodway* (n448) has been rejected in Australia: *R v Renzella* (1996) 88 ACR 65.

[450] Cf *R v Burley, Molnar and Stanton* (n344), [32] (should); *R v Edwards and Gordon* [2004] EWCA Crim 2102, [56] (should not).   [451] *R v Faryab* [1999] BPIR 569.

[452] Ibid.

[453] *R v Woodward* [2001] EWCA Crim 2051, [37] (lies more relevant to causation than to absence of provocation).

[454] *R v Jackson* [1953] 1 All ER 872, [1953] 1 WLR 591. See, in Australia, *Weissensteiner v R* (1993) 178 CLR 217; and for continuing difficulty, see *R v Peel* [1999] 2 Qd R 400.

[455] Following the recommendation of the Criminal Law Revision Committee's 11th Report *Evidence (General)* (Cmnd 4991, 1972) [111]. The same reasoning would apply a fortiori to failure to call a spouse.

[456] [1996] QB 373, [1995] 4 All ER 939; 379C, 943c.

[457] Especially in its endorsement of the opinions expressed by Kelly LJ in relation to its Northern Ireland predecessor in *R v McLernon* (1990) 10 NIJB 91, 102.

[458] Set out in *Cowan* 1996] QB 373, [1995] 4 All ER 939, 380G, 944f.

[459] By Lord Slynn in *Murray v United Kingdom* (1996) 22 EHRR 29, 160.

Failure to call witnesses to support a party's case, coupled with the absence of any plausible explanation for that failure, has been held to detract from the party's credibility, and to justify the rejection of his account.[460] It is scarcely necessary to add that failure to cross-examine a witness does not amount to support of the witness's evidence.[461]

Silence when charged

There is a broad principle of common sense that was stated by Cave J in the course of his judgment in *R v Mitchell*:[462]

Undoubtedly, when persons are speaking on even terms, and a charge is made, and the person charged says nothing, and expresses no indignation, and does nothing to repel the charge, that is some evidence to show that he admits the charge to be true.

But what if the persons in question are not speaking on even terms?

Silence in the face of police questioning[463] is governed by the Criminal Justice and Public Order Act 1994.[464] In the case of failure to mention facts subsequently relied upon, the accused need mention only those that it is reasonable to expect that he would mention. Given the failure to require more disclosure of the case against the accused than emerges from the arrest or charge, it is still unclear quite what will be regarded as a reasonable excuse. The Court of Appeal seems to be opposed to laying down any fixed rules,[465] and to prefer to leave it all to the judgment of the trial court in the light of particular facts. In Northern Ireland, it was held that the failure to provide access to a legal adviser was insufficient to prevent inference from silence prior to his arrival,[466] but such failure may itself be in breach of Art 6 of the European Convention on Human Rights,[467] more especially because of the inference from silence permitted by the relevant legislation.[468] It is possible that it was the incorporation of the Convention that has now led to the introduction of legislation to exclude such an inference when no opportunity of access to a solicitor has been allowed.[469]

It is further provided that this ground for adverse inference is additional to any existing power, so those cases in which it has been established that the parties are on even

---

[460] *TK (Burundi) v Secretary of State for Home Affairs* [2009] EWCA Civ 40.

[461] *Dingwall v J Wharton (Shipping) Ltd* [1961] 2 Lloyd's Rep 213, 219. Not even under the Criminal Justice and Public Order Act 1994.

[462] (1892) 17 Cox CC 503. In Scotland, this extends to failure to contradict an allegation made in the accused's presence to a third party: *McDonnell v HM Adv* 1997 SCCR 760.

[463] Or others charged with the duty of investigating offences: for further exegesis, see below, 649.

[464] Section 34 (failure to mention facts later relied on in defence); s 36 (failure to account for objects, marks, and substances believed by the police to be incriminating); and s 37 (failure to account for presence in a particular place believed by the police to be incriminating). See further below Chapter XIV, Section 2, 'Silence'.

[465] *R v Condron and Condron* [1997] 1 WLR 827, [1997] 1 Cr App Rep 185; *R v Argent* [1997] 2 Cr App Rep 27; *R v Roble* [1997] Crim LR 449.

[466] *R v Quinn* (LEXIS) 17 September 1993.

[467] Right to fair trial. [468] *Murray v United Kingdom* (n459).

[469] The Youth Justice and Criminal Evidence Act 1999, s 58. The explanatory notes explicitly refer to *Murray* (n459), and the Act is prefaced by an annotation that, in the view of the Lord Chancellor, its provisions are compatible with rights under the Convention. The provision qualifies ss 34, 36, 37, and 38 of the Criminal Justice and Public Order Act 1994.

terms, despite one of them being a member of the police force, will continue to have the same effect.[470]

It should also be noted that any adverse inference must be proper. Given that it is expressly provided that such an inference may contribute to the establishment of a prima facie case, it seems that it is capable of supporting the elements of the prosecution case in general, and is not limited to weakening the defence evidence of the matter relied upon at the trial.[471]

In the cases of failure to explain objects, substances and marks or presence in a particular place, it is incumbent upon the police officer to make his belief in the incriminating nature of the relevant thing apparent to the accused, and explain in clear terms what the consequences of failure will be. Here the adverse inference even more clearly goes directly to guilt, since it is the prosecution evidence[472] that is strengthened by the accused's failure to explain.

Failure to provide a sample of real evidence

Since no one is obliged to provide a sample of real evidence,[473] it might be thought that refusal to do so should not be regarded as supportive of other evidence. This seemed not to be the case. It was held in *R v Smith*[474] that the accused's arbitrary refusal to provide a sample of his hair, after being told that the hair to which it was to be matched had been found at the scene of a robbery, could corroborate the testimony of a witness treated as an accomplice. In affiliation proceedings, similar reasoning was applied in *McVeigh v Beattie*[475] to the refusal by a putative father to take a blood test[476] at the direction of the court. It should perhaps be noted that in both of these cases the person who refused to provide the sample was at the time in receipt of legal advice. The matter has also been altered by more general statutory provision. Section 62(10) of the Police and Criminal Evidence Act 1984 expressly permitted inferences from failure to provide an intimate sample to be used to corroborate relevant evidence. In the case of fingerprints and non-intimate samples, no such provision is made, but there is power to require the provision of such evidence in the absence of consent, upon satisfaction of the relevant conditions.[477]

---

[470] As in *R v Chandler* [1976] 3 All ER 105, [1976] 1 WLR 585, in which the accused was accompanied by a solicitor.

[471] For more extensive, and persuasive, discussion, see Mirfield *Silence, Confessions and Improperly Obtained Evidence* (1997) ch 9.

[472] Although it is not a formal condition that the matter be put in evidence by the prosecution, it would be most exceptional if this did not occur.

[473] Apart from special situations governed by statute, such as alcohol samples from drivers, and powers of the police and prison authorities mentioned below.   [474] (1985) 81 Cr App Rep 286.

[475] [1988] Fam 69, [1988] 2 All ER 500.

[476] In New Zealand, refusal of a blood sample for DNA analysis has been held to be a basic human right such that no adverse inference may be drawn from it: *R v Martin* [1992] 1 NZLR 313.

[477] Police and Criminal Evidence Act 1984, ss 61 (fingerprints) and 63 (non-intimate samples); the distinction between intimate and non-intimate samples was amended by the Criminal Justice and Public Order Act 1994, s 58 (principally to transfer dental impressions and mouth swabs to the non-intimate category). See also further amendment by Criminal Evidence (Amendment) Act 1997, principally to extend the powers to create DNA databases to those convicted before 1995, and those detained after acquittal or being found unfit to plead on account of mental impairment.

Conduct on other occasions

Such evidence is now to be much more freely admitted under the provisions of c 1 of Pt 11 of the Criminal Justice Act 2003.[478] It may be relevant, either directly by showing it to be more likely that the accused committed the offence in issue on account of his propensity to do so, or indirectly by showing the accused either to have made a true confession, or a false denial, of having committed another offence.

FUNCTIONS OF JUDGE AND JURY[479]

The aim of reforming this part of the law was largely to rid it of its cumbersome and counterproductive technicality. Two of the most unpopular parts of the old law were the constraint on the form of words[480] used in directing the jury, and insistence on a review of the evidence applying the old rigid categorization to it.

It was accepted under the old law to be desirable for the judge to discuss with counsel, in the absence of the jury and before closing speeches, the form in which he should direct the jury.[481] This view was endorsed by the Law Commission in its Report, for application to the new law:[482]

it would be beneficial if it were provided that, in any case that involved issues of fact or the credibility of evidence that needed or might need special treatment in the summing-up, the judge should before final speeches discuss those issues with counsel in the absence of the jury. The purpose of that discussion would be if possible to agree on the terms of the summing-up, and if not so possible at least to clarify, and to assist the judge on, the points of disagreement. The discussion would not be intended to be elaborate and should not in any event be used as an excuse for the introduction by counsel of arguments or submissions that are not warranted by the present law.

The Law Commission recommended the issue of a Practice Direction to this effect,[483] and further reinforcement has been provided by the Court of Appeal.[484] It is to be hoped that directions will now more often be tailored to the circumstances of the case, subject only to the requirement that they be fair. This process should be assisted by the terms of the model directions in this area published by the Judicial Standards Board.[485] It need hardly be added that, in a case of a warning being given to himself in the case of trial by judge alone, he must not then disregard it.[486]

---

[478] See further Chapter VIII.

[479] For judicial discussion, see *R v Gill* [2003] VSC 317, 142 ACR 22; and for academic, Hartshorne (1998) 2 *Int J of Ev & Pr* 1.

[480] See *R v Chambers* (1993) The Times, 7 May; *R v Fullerton* [1994] Crim LR 63 (in both descending even to the order in which points were to be put in the direction).

[481] *R v Ensor* [1989] 2 All ER 586, 593, [1989] 1 WLR 497, 505; *R v Nagy* [1990] Crim LR 187; *R v Royle*; *R v Hall* [1993] Crim LR 57.

[482] (Cm 1620, 1991) Law Com No 202, [4.29]. In Canada, where a similar change to that proposed by the Law Commission was accomplished by judicial decision, this consequence has also been accepted: *Bevan v R* [1993] 2 SCR 599.

[483] [4.30].   [484] *R v Makanjuola and Easton* (n359); *R v Haynes* [2004] EWCA Crim 390, [12].

[485] See especially model directions 21 (corroboration); 27 (lies); 38–44 (various silence directions).

[486] *Miles v Cain* (1989) The Times, 15 December (an unusual civil trial for rape).

VI

THE COURSE OF EVIDENCE

This chapter concerns the principal rules governing examination in chief, cross-examination and re-examination of witnesses. Such an account is not entirely satisfactory because it is concerned with regulations that are either matters of common knowledge or else can be thoroughly mastered only by experience, but the rules with which it deals have been highly characteristic of the English law of evidence. The elucidation of facts by means of questions put by parties or their representatives to witnesses mainly summoned by them, and called mainly in the order of their choice, before a judge, acting as umpire rather than inquisitor,[1] has been an essential feature of the English 'adversarial' or 'accusatorial' system of justice. Not only is an appreciation of this procedure desirable for its own sake, but it is necessary for a proper understanding of such matters as the law concerning the admissibility of the convictions, character, and credibility of parties and witnesses, governed by the terms of the Criminal Justice Act 2003, considered in the two following chapters. It must be recognized, however, that there is an increasing call,[2] to some extent driven by the soaring size[3] and cost of litigation, for greater intervention by the judge by way of management of the progress of a case, both at the pre-trial and trial stages. It should also be remarked that technicality has sought to be reduced by the specification and application of the overriding objectives of both Civil and Criminal Procedure Rules.

Section 1 deals with some procedural matters that appear to be essential to the exposition of the subject covered in this and subsequent chapters.

SECTION 1. MISCELLANEOUS PROCEDURAL MATTERS

EVIDENCE BEFORE TRIAL

Enormous changes have occurred, and still are occurring,[4] in both civil and criminal proceedings. In each area, the situation has been transformed over the past three decades, with important repercussions for the law of evidence in its traditional sense. In

---

[1] *R v Whybrow and Saunders* (1994) 144 NLJ 124.

[2] See, in relation to civil proceedings, Report by Lord Woolf *Access to Justice* (1996) Sec II, followed by the Civil Procedure Act 1997, leading to the Civil Procedure Rules (CPR); and the Auld *Review of the Criminal Courts of England and Wales* (2001) followed by the Criminal Justice Act 2003 ss 69–73, leading to the Criminal Procedure Rules.   [3] Leading to the phenomenon of 'mega-litigation', see Sackville (2008) 27 CJQ 244.

[4] The CPR undergo very frequent amendment.

part, these have been exacerbated by an increasing overlap between civil and criminal proceedings, especially in the area of commercial fraud. It has become increasingly difficult to isolate pre-trial proceedings[5] from those at the trial, and civil proceedings from criminal.[6]

Civil cases[7]

There are two main areas of pre-trial activity in civil litigation:[8] the first broadly concerned with the identification and preservation of relevant materials,[9] the second with their provision in the form in which they are to be used at trial. It is first necessary to mention these two important and burgeoning areas, however briefly. In addition, evidence may be taken before trial and read at the trial when it is given by affidavit, on commission, under letters of request, in answer to requests for further information, or by way of perpetuation of testimony.

Disclosure and inspection[10]

The principal means of identifying relevant material used to be by the system of compulsory revelation known as discovery, originally developed by the Court of Chancery, and available in the Supreme Court as a whole since the Judicature Act.[11] This spawned a whole panoply of parasitic procedures, largely as a result of judicial innovation as described by Hoffmann J in *Arab Monetary Fund v Hashim (No 5)*:[12]

The last 20 years have seen a judge-made revolution in English civil procedure. Under pressure from the increase in cases of commercial fraud, the courts have provided plaintiffs with remedies and investigative powers which previously, if they existed at all, were available only to the police. In many large cases involving allegations of fraud and embezzlement, the greater part of the early interlocutory stages of the action is concerned with endeavours to trace assets against which claims can be made. The function of the judge at this stage is not so much to decide or even define the issues between the parties as to supervise an investigation by the plaintiff. On the plaintiff's application, usually in the first instance ex parte, the judge issues orders freezing assets, appointing receivers of companies, requiring defendants to permit searches for evidence, demanding documents and information from third parties.

---

[5] Which increasingly involve formal hearings.

[6] For consideration of the procedural implications of this overlap in the United States, see *Degen v United States* 517 US 820 (1996).

[7] Which in this context encompass proceedings for judicial review, *R (Corner House Research) v BAE Systems plc* [2008] EWHC 246 (Admin), [2008] CPR 365, [18], illustrating the purposive interpretation of the CPR adopted by the Court.

[8] Quite apart from the increasing obligations to provide more material relating to the claim before issuing proceedings governed by the plenitude of pre-action protocols designed to avoid litigation wherever possible. Some, but not all, of these procedures are imported into arbitration by s 44 of the Arbitration Act 1996: see *Assimina Maritime Ltd v Pakistan National Shipping Corp* [2004] EWHC 3005 (Comm), [2005] 1 Lloyd's Rep 525.

[9] Including the identity of parties, their assets, and the subject matter of the dispute as well as testimonial material. Increased powers in these respects have been conferred by Civil Procedure Act 1997, s 7.

[10] See generally the CPR, Pt 31.

[11] On an automatic basis since 1964. Including judicial review in the case of 'hard-edged' issues of fact: *R (Al-Sweady) v Secretary of State for Defence* [2009] EWHC 2387 (Admin), [19].

[12] [1992] 2 All ER 911, 913.

The area is now largely[13] governed by Civil Procedure Rules, r 31.6 of which provides:

Standard disclosure requires a party to disclose only—

    (a) the documents[14] on which he relies; and

    (b) the documents which[15]—

        (i)   adversely affect his own case;

        (ii) adversely affect another party's case; or

        (iii) support another party's case; and

    (c) the documents which he is required to disclose by a relevant practice direction.[16]

Such disclosure must be supported by a statement certifying that the duty to search and disclose has been duly carried out.[17] Disclosure can be ordered in advance of proceedings,[18] and from third parties,[19] and where necessary, under special conditions designed to maintain confidentiality.[20] Under the old law, it had been possible to secure disclosure of the

---

[13] Although significant, and in some respects wider, disclosure under less exacting conditions may be obtained under s 7 of the Data Protection Act 1998. It also operates against a background of greater disclosure as part of the statement of case under CPR Pt 16. An attempt to impose blanket rules of non-disclosure in patent cases was rebuffed by a majority of the Court of Appeal in *Nichia Corporation v Argos Ltd* [2007] EWCA Civ 741, [2008] CPR 735.

[14] Including content in electronic form and meta-data, *Hellard and Goldfarb v Money and Robbins* [2008] EWHC 2275 (Ch), [2008] BPIR 1487; see further 276, and Chapter XV.

[15] So normally the cases should have been developed in advance of disclosure: *Scottish & Newcastle plc v Raguz* [2004] EWHC 1835 (Ch), [18].

[16] Considerable guidance is supplied by pre-action protocols, and the rule has been supplemented by PD 31. The formulation was taken from that originally devised for Queensland: see Davies (1993) 5 *J Jud Admin* 201, 213. Specific disclosure may also be available under CPR 31.12, even before standard disclosure has been sought: *Dayman v Canyon Holdings Ltd* (2006) unreported Ch, 11 January.

[17] CPR 31.10(6), and PD 31 Annex. Such a certificate will normally be accepted, and only if there is strong evidence that it is unreliable will a court go behind it: *Henderson v Overall* (13 December 2001, unreported), QB. This should help prevent the development here of meta-discovery, cp Starks (2008) 29.10 *The Company Lawyer* 309. Full disclosure is especially important when making an ex parte application, *R (Lawer) v Restormel Borough Council* [2007] EWHC 2299 (Admin).

[18] CPR 31.16; on similar terms to those that would apply had proceedings commenced, thus requiring careful consideration of the probable heads of claim: see *Black v Sumitomo Corp* [2001] EWCA Civ 1819, [2002] 1 WLR 1562, [76]. Any such claim must be exceptional, *Trouw UK Ltd v Mitsui & Co plc* [2007] EWHC 863 (Comm): based on more than mere speculation: *Snowstar Shipping Co v Graig Shipping plc* [2003] EWHC 1367 (Comm); but need be no more than 'arguable': *Rose v Lynx Express* [2004] EWCA Civ 447, [2004] BCC 714, [26]. To the extent that proceedings, parties, or documents must be shown to be *likely* to commence, be involved or be relevant, it seems that the jurisdictional threshold will require only a low level of likelihood ('may well'): *Three Rivers District Council v HM Treasury* [2002] EWCA Civ 1182, [2002] 4 All ER 881, [2003] 1 WLR 210, [22]. For a convenient summary of the conditions, see Collins J in *Meretz Investments NV v First Penthouse Ltd* [2003] EWHC 2324 (Ch), [52]. Earlier disclosure may be appropriate in family proceedings for substantial ancillary relief: *OS v DS* [2004] EWHC 2376 (Fam), [2005] 1 FLR 675.

[19] CPR 31.17, under which the court must be especially careful to be sure that the documents exist: *Re Howglen* [2001] 1 All ER 376. It should be noted that in the case of litigation involving a department of government, other departments are not regarded as third parties: *R v Blackledge* [1996] 1 Cr App Rep 326. In cases of doubt as to the identity of the parties or the scope of the proceedings, an application under CPR 31.17 may be used as an alternative to one under CPR 31.16: *Moresfield Ltd v Banners & Banners* [2003] EWHC 1602 (Ch). Conversely, third parties have little power to seek non-disclosure, *Ashley v Chief Constable of Sussex Police* [2008] EWHC 3151 (Admin).

[20] *Ixis Corporate and Investment Bank v Westlb AG* [2007] EWHC 1852 (Comm). A court is unlikely to order disclosure of confidential medical records of a third party: *A v X & B* [2004] All ER (D) 517, or, in advance, the medical records of a party, *OCS Group Ltd v Wells* [2008] EWHC 919 (QB).

identities, and other relevant material,[21] of third parties 'mixed up' in the illegal activities of others,[22] or even where disclosure was necessary to reveal such illegality.[23] This jurisdiction was specifically preserved by the new rules,[24] and has, if anything, been subsequently extended.[25] Ultimately, the decision to order disclosure rests upon judicial discretion, and there has been more than the usual reluctance for appellate courts to interfere, at least until the new rules have bedded down,[26] although it will do so if a case management decision will lead to fundamental unfairness.[27]

These obligations apply to disclosure only when the relevant documents are within the control of the party,[28] and to inspection when there is no right to withhold it.[29] Confidentiality may be necessary,[30] but is unlikely to be a sufficient reason for non-disclosure.[31] The form of disclosure should be discussed between the parties,[32] and there is some indication that executable code may be required.[33]

This original exercise of judicial innovation was supplemented by statutory provision. It is not now uncommon for public regulators to be furnished with a statutory code of powers to secure disclosure of information to assist their activities,[34] or even for a special code

---

[21] *R (Mohamed) v Secretary of State for Foreign Affairs* [2008] EWHC 2048 (Admin), CPR 31.16. is limited to documentation.

[22] *Norwich Pharmacal Co v Customs and Excise Comrs* [1974] AC 133, [1973] 2 All ER 943; see in Canada *Isofoton SA v Toronto Dominion Bank* (2007) 282 DLR (4th) 325; in Australia, *Wyeth v Secretary, Dept. of Health and Ageing* [2009] FCA 313, 255 ALR 352.

[23] *P v T Ltd* [1997] 4 All ER 200, [1997] 1 WLR 1309; although this was not taken so far as to amount to a general means of securing discovery from known third parties: *Axa Equity and Law Life Assurance Society v National Westminster Bank* [1998] CLC 1177, [1998] PNLR 433.

[24] CPR 31.18. See also *BNP Paribas v TH Global Ltd* [2009] EWHC 37 (Ch).

[25] Although not so far in relation to advance discovery as to dispense with the need to show a strong evidential basis for suspicion: *Parker v CS Structured Credit Fund* [2003] EWHC 391 (Ch), [2003] 1 WLR 1680; and only ever as a last resort: *Mitsui Ltd v Nexen Petroleum UK Ltd* [2005] EWHC 625, [2005] 3 All ER 511, [24].

[26] *Bermuda International Securities v KPMG* [2001] EWCA Civ 269, [2001] CPR 73, [26].

[27] *Watford Petroleum Ltd v Inter-Oil Trading SA* [2003] EWCA Civ 1417, in which an order made *ex parte* would have required the delivery of witness statements in advance of the disclosure of documents establishing the nature of the case that those statements were advanced to meet.

[28] Rule 31.8. There is an obligation upon a party not to destroy documents that it might be required to disclose: *Rockwell Machine Tool Co v Barrus* [1968] 2 All ER 98n, [1968] 1 WLR 693; and this includes electronic messages: *Douglas v Hello! Ltd* [2003] EWHC 55 (Ch), [2003] 1 All ER 1087, [35]. Communications data must also be retained for a year under the Data Retention (EC Directive) Regulations 2009. A party may be sanctioned for contempt in deliberately retaining a device in breach of a court order so as to destroy information contained in it: *LTE Scientific Ltd v Thomas* [2005] EWHC 7 (QB). Recoverable deleted electronic documents are subject to disclosure: 31 PD 2.1A. In the United States, in *Coleman (Parent) Holdings v Morgan Stanley* (2005) Fl Cir Ct, 1 March, a fine of $850m was levied upon a bank unable to disclose its electronic documents.

[29] Rule 31.3(1)(b). In many cases, because private privilege or public interest immunity may be invoked, although even then the existence rather than the content of the privileged information may be subject to disclosure: *Pearson Education Ltd v Prentice Hall India Private Ltd* [2005] EWHC 636 (QB), [2006] FSR 8, [40]; as a last resort in cases of doubt about the grounds for withholding disclosure the maker of the disclosure statement may be cross-examined, *West London Pipeline & Storage Ltd v Total UK Ltd* [2008] EWHC 1296 (Comm). See further Chapters IX and X, Section 1.

[30] *Comfort v Department of Constitutional Affairs* (2005) 102(35) LSG 42, [27], [31] (solicitor's note of evidence given in open court).   [31] *Law Society v Karim* (2005) unreported Ch, 5 July.

[32] PD 31, para 2.A.3.

[33] *R (Eisai Ltd) v National Institute for Clinical Excellence* [2007] EWCA Civ 438, [66] (an analogous situation).   [34] See e.g. Financial Services and Markets Act 2000, Pt XI.

to be established for the disclosure of a category of information.[35] By far the most important type is information in electronic form.[36] Proportionality is the key and sometimes
the cost of disclosing vast quantities of electronic information will more than outweigh
the matters at stake.[37] Although it is for the possessor to determine what search is reasonable in the first instance, this should be discussed between the parties, and is subject to
determination, and not merely review, by the Court if the parties disagreee.[38]

Under s 236 of the Insolvency Act 1985,[39] anyone[40] thought capable of providing information relating to an insolvent company may be required either to submit documents, or
to attend for oral examination.[41] This provision may not, however, be used to the prejudice
of third parties by being invoked against intermediate institutions, which had themselves
come into the possession of the evidence only by the exercise of statutory compulsion, at
least not without notice to the affected party.[42] Nor should liquidators voluntarily disclose
evidence coming to them under these compulsory powers to third parties for the purpose
of legal proceedings,[43] or seek to exercise such powers for the collateral purposes.[44] The
fact that information was obtained by the exercise of compulsory powers is not, however,
enough in itself to bar compulsory disclosure under the provisions of the Civil Procedure
Rules. Nor is it necessarily enough that disclosure or inspection would expose the dis-
closer to liability under foreign law.[45] It has further been held that since disclosure helps to

---

[35] See e.g. Regulation of Investigatory Powers Act 2000, Pt III (encrypted data); Children Act Guidance
And Regulations Vol 1 (forthcoming).

[36] Constituting some 90 per cent of all documents, the vast majority of which achieve no other form. In
2005, it was estimated that 22.2b business email messages were created every day. For fuller consideration of
preservation and disclosure of documents in electronic form, see the Cresswell Report *Electronic Disclosure*
(2004), the adoption of its recommendations as a new [2A] of CPR PD31; for an empirical survey of reactions
and suggestions for further reform, see KPMG *e-Disclosure* (2007). Cf comparable amendments in the US to
rr 16, 26, 33, and 34 of the Federal Rules of Civil Procedure, which came into force on 1 December 2006.

[37] In *Hands v Morrison Construction Services* [2006] EWHC 2018 (Ch), the court ordered disclosure of
175 lever-arch files of hard copy, whereas the electronic information would have filled 850,000 such files.
Part of the problem is that only part of the storage is relevant, but it cannot easily be isolated without disclosure of the whole: see, in Australia, *Sony Music Entertainment (Australia) Ltd v University of Tasmania*
[2003] FCA 532, 198 ALR 367.

[38] *Digicel (St Lucia) Ltd v Cable & Wireless plc* [2008] EWHC 2522 Ch, [2009] 2 All ER 1094, [52] in the
course of a very helpful exposition of the operation of the CPR in this area.

[39] See also Insolvency Rules 1986, SI 1986/1925, r 9.5.

[40] Including foreign nationals holding documents overseas: *Re Mid-East Trading Ltd* [1998] 1 All
ER 577.

[41] Although this is a drastic power and will not be sanctioned except within strict limits, especially in
relation to attendance for oral examination: *Cloverbay Ltd v Bank of Credit and Commerce International*
[1991] Ch 90, [1991] 1 All ER 894. These limits seem to be stricter in England than in Australia: see *England
v Purves* [1999] 2 BCLC 256.

[42] *Morris v Director of the Serious Fraud Office* [1993] Ch 372, [1993] 1 All ER 788 (evidence acquired by
the application of Criminal Justice Act 1987, s 2); *Marcel v Metropolitan Police Comr* [1992] Ch 225, [1992] 1
All ER 72 (evidence acquired under Police and Criminal Evidence Act 1984, s 18); *Soden v Burns* [1996] 3 All
ER 967 (evidence acquired by Board of Trade Inspectors under Companies Act 1985, s 432).

[43] Not even to defendants in criminal proceedings: *Re Barlow Clowes Gilt Managers Ltd* [1992] Ch 208,
[1991] 4 All ER 385. Since they are, however, partly aimed at prosecution, it is immaterial that the information is passed from the DTI to a separate prosecuting authority: *R v Brady* [2004] EWCA Crim 1763, [2004]
3 All ER 520, [27] (there s 235 material).

[44] Although the ambit of the powers of a liquidator were broadly construed by the House of Lords in
allowing the appeal in *Re Pantmaenog Timber Co Ltd* [2003] UKHL 49, [2004] 1 AC 158.

[45] *Morris v Banque Arabe et Internationale d'Investissement SA* [2002] BCC 407.

ensure that a trial is fair, it receives strong support from Art 6 of the European Convention on Human Rights, and should be disallowed only in exceptional cases.[46]

Rule 31.22 encapsulates the old common law rule[47] that material supplied under such provision[48] is to be used 'without the leave of the court'[49] only for the purposes of the proceedings[50] for which it was supplied.[51] In some cases, the material so supplied will have been included in the papers filed in earlier[52] proceedings,[53] but although special rules may apply to this situation, and it may be preferable for the application for disclosure of such material for the purposes of other proceedings to be made to the judge in the earlier proceedings, the same principles apply for the purposes of the application of discretion as under CPR 31.12(1).[54] That discretion is likely to involve a difficult balancing exercise, especially where the earlier disclosure has been made in sensitive family proceedings.[55] It must be exercised bearing in mind the overriding objective, which may sometimes lead to greater disclosure than under the old law,[56] and, it seems, more readily when issues of proportionality,[57] or public interest,[58] arise. It may be necessary to take the requirements of article 8 of the European Convention if Human Rights into account in assessing proportionality of disclosure.[59]

---

[46] Even in delicate family disputes: *Re B (disclosure to other parties)* [2001] 2 FLR 1017, thus endorsing the similar view expressed by Lord Mustill in *Re D (minors) (adoption reports: confidentiality)* [1996] AC 593, [1995] 4 All ER 385, 615D, 393a under the pre-1998 law. It should, however, be noted that Art 8 may sometimes pull, perhaps less strongly, in the opposite direction.

[47] *Riddick v Thames Board Mills Ltd* [1977] QB 881, [1977] 3 All ER 677: see *SmithKline Beecham plc v Apotex* [2003] EWHC 127, (2003) 26(5) IPD 26031.

[48] This extends to cases where the material is supplied without an order, but in situations where an order could be made: *Bourns Inc v Raychem Corp* [1999] 3 All ER 154.

[49] See *Marlwood Commercial Inc v Kozeny* [2004] EWCA Civ 798, [2004] 3 All ER 648; *Dadourian Group Int Inc v Simms* [2006] EWCA Civ 1745 (in which such leave was given for use in contempt proceedings).

[50] Including arbitrations: *Glidepath BV v John Thompson* [2005] EWHC 818, [2005] 2 All ER (Comm) 833.

[51] For a systematic, and devastating, critique, see Gibbons *Subsequent Use of Documents Disclosed in Civil Proceedings* Oxford DPhil thesis (2002).

[52] Or in parallel proceedings in other jurisdictions, see *Dendron Gmbh v Regents of the University of California* [2004] EWHC 589 (Pat), [2005] 1 WLR 200.

[53] Where the document has been read in open court, or referred to by the judge after exercising the modern practice of reading materials in advance: *SmithKline Beecham Biologicals SA v Connaught Laboratories Inc* [1999] 4 All ER 498; any restriction is discharged, although the court still has power to impose a restriction: CPR 31.22(2). For the applicable principles, see *Lilly Icos Ltd v Pfizer Ltd* [2002] EWCA Civ 02, [2002] 1 All ER 842, [2002] 1 WLR 2253; and for those in which such a restriction can be lifted, see *SmithKlineBeecham plc v Generics (UK) Ltd* [2003] EWCA Civ 1109, [2003] 4 All ER 1302. For such disclosure to a third party, see *Law Debenture Trust Corp (Channel Islands) v Lexington Insurance Co* [2003] EWHC 2297 (Comm), (2003) 153 NLJ 1551.   [54] *Nayler v Beard* [2001] EWCA Civ 1201, [2001] 2 FLR 1346, [26].

[55] See *Medway v Doublelock* [1978] 1 All ER 1261, [1978] 1 WLR 710. It seems that its principles still apply even in the aftermath of the Human Rights Act 1998: see *Nayler v Beard* (n54), *Clibbery v Allan* [2002] EWCA Civ 45, [2002] 1 All ER 865. For detailed consideration of the restrictions on disclosure in family cases, see *Kent County Council v B* [2004] EWHC 411 (Fam), [2004] 2 FLR 142. Such disclosure may be restricted to professional advisers, as in *Samuel R v W Primary Care Trust* [2004] EWHC 2085 (Fam), or extended to Mackenzie friends: *Re O* [2005] EWCA Civ 759, [2006] Fam 1. For restriction in Canada see *Juman v Doucette* 2008 SCC 8, [2008] 1 SCR 157.   [56] See *IRC v Exeter City AFC* [2004] BCC 519.

[57] *Tweed v Parades Commission for Northern Ireland* [2006] UKHL 53, [2007] 2 WLR 1.

[58] *Sitauk Group Holdings Ltd v Serruys* [2009] EWHC 869 (QB); [2009] STC 1595, [23].

[59] *Webster v Ridgeway Foundation School Governors* [2009] EWHC 1140 (QB).

Failure to comply with an order for disclosure may be sanctioned by striking out a claim, debarring a defence or refusing to allow a counter-claim,[60] but an opportunity to explain any apparent failure should be provided;[61] contempt of court proceedings may also be appropriate.[62] A court may order return of any materials seized in advance of trial without authorization.[63]

Lord Woolf identified[64] excessive disclosure as one of the two principal defects of the old system of procedure. It is still too early to assess how far this will be overcome by the CPR.

Exchange of witness statements[65]

In civil cases at common law,[66] the traditional position was that all the evidence was normally given viva voce at the trial, but here too the position underwent a revolution. As Lord Donaldson MR said in *Mercer v Chief Constable of Lancashire*:[67]

Over the last quarter of a century there has been a sea change in legislative and judicial attitudes towards the conduct of litigation…. The most important change has been the requirement that, save in exceptional cases, witness statements be exchanged prior to the trial.

This system of advance provision of evidence began in limited areas, but was gradually extended to embrace the whole range of legal proceedings.[68] It formed the model for the more extensive system established by the CPR. Rule 32.1 invests the court with considerable powers to control evidence at trial:

(1) The court may control the evidence by giving directions as to—
    (a) the issues on which it requires evidence;
    (b) the nature of the evidence which it requires to decide those issues; and
    (c) the way in which the evidence is to be placed before the court.

(2) The court may use its power under this rule to exclude evidence that would otherwise be admissible.

CPR 32 goes on to provide for the service of witness statements,[69] and for their standing at trial as evidence in chief.[70] The normal requirement is that the witness should still attend,[71] and may then, with the permission of the court, amplify his statement or give evidence as to any new matters that have arisen since the statement was served on the other parties.[72] Provision is also made for witness statements to be admitted, without the attendance of the

---

[60] *Fairacres Ltd v Abdul Mohamed* [2008] EWCA Civ 1637.

[61] *Rahamim v Reich* (2009) unrep Ch 10 February.

[62] *Marketmaker Technology (Beijing) Co Ltd v CMC Group plc* [2009] EWHC 1445 (QB).

[63] *L v L* [2007] EWHC 140 (QB), [2007] 2 FLR 171.   [64] *Access to Justice* [13.1].

[65] See generally the CPR Pt 32, and PD 32.

[66] But not in Chancery, where it was more often prepared before the hearing and sealed up in the form of an affidavit to be revealed only at the trial.

[67] [1991] 2 All ER 504, [1991] 1 WLR 367, 508, 509, 373.

[68] The terms of the rule were unlimited, and accorded a literal construction in *Richard Saunders & Partners v Eastglen Ltd* [1990] 3 All ER 946. It applied also to proceedings in the county court: CCR Ord 20, r 12A. A similar approach was taken to proceedings for committal for contempt: *Re B* [1996] 1 WLR 627. There is now a move to reduce the length of such statements.

[69] CPR 32.4. Or in some cases witness summaries, r 32.9.   [70] CPR 32.5.   [71] CPR 32.5(1).

[72] CPR 32.5(3).

witness, as hearsay, upon giving proper notice.[73] It is necessary that a witness statement be made in the witness's own words,[74] verified by a statement that it is true,[75] sanctioned by discretion to exclude,[76] or by the possibility of proceedings for contempt.[77] The form of such a statement is prescribed by PD 32. Failure to observe the correct form, or the time-table dictated by the court,[78] may result in the evidence being excluded, but the court has a discretion, and will be reluctant to exclude in a situation where the effect will be to non-suit the party in default,[79] or where no prejudice is occasioned by the late statement.[80]

Affidavits[81]

If the court so orders[82] or permits, evidence may be given by affidavit.[83] The statements in the affidavit are, of course, not subject to cross-examination, and are sometimes based on the knowledge, information, or belief of the deponent but, in appropriate cases, he may be obliged to attend for cross-examination.[84]

One of the changes made here by the CPR is that interim orders can, and usually must,[85] be supported not only by affidavits, but by witness statements, or the facts stated in the application for the order or in the statement of case filed in the proceedings, provided that there is a statement of truth.[86]

Commissions[87]

It will now much less often be necessary for a deposition to be taken, even when the witness is overseas.[88] Provision is nevertheless made under the CPR for depositions to be taken,[89] when appropriate.[90] The evidence will be taken before an examiner,[91] so far as possible in

---

[73] CPR 33.2(2). Such a statement may be admitted as hearsay at the behest of an opposing party if the party serving the statement decides not to rely upon it, or to call the witness: *Society of Lloyds v Jaffray* (2000) The Times, 9 June.

[74] *Aquarius Financial Enterprises Inc v Certain Underwriters at Lloyds* [2001] 2 LlR 542, [49].

[75] CPR 32.8.   [76] CPR 22.1, 22.3.

[77] CPR 32.14; even after settlement, *Kirk v Walton* [2008] EWHC 1780 (QB).

[78] Although the timing may be adjusted, as in *Roberts v Williams* [2005] EWCA Civ 1086, [2005] CPR 44.

[79] *Primus Telecommunications Netherlands BV v Pan European Ltd* [2005] EWCA Civ 273. A severe sanction in costs may suffice: *Parnall v Hurst* [2003] WTLR 997, The Times, 10 July.

[80] *LTE Scientific Ltd v Thomas* [2004] EWCA Civ 1622, [25].

[81] See generally CPR 32.15. Affirmations are assimilated by PD 32.1.7.

[82] Or if otherwise required by statute, rule, or practice direction.

[83] CPR 32.15, PD 32 [1.6], and is required to be in the cases specified in PD 32 [1.4].

[84] Even before the trial: *Watford Petroleum Ltd v Interoil Trading SA* (n27), [11], especially if affidavits conflict, *Western Broadcasting Services v Seaga* [2007] UKPC 19, [17]; in New Zealand see *Siemer v Stiassny* [2007] NZCA 117, [2008] 1 NZLR 150.   [85] CPR 32.6.

[86] PD 32, [1.3].

[87] Now governed by CPR 34, and PD 34. The procedure within the EU has been simplified by the Council Regulation on Taking of Evidence EC No 1206/2001, which was brought into force by the Civil Procedure (Amendment No 4) Rules 2003, SI 2003/2113, with effect from 1 January 2004.

[88] Because of the more ready acceptance of hearsay and video linking and conferencing: see, in New Zealand, *B v Dentists' Disciplinary Tribunal* [1994] 1 NZLR 95, reviewing the position in the whole common law world.   [89] CPR 34.8. Depositions may also be taken in England for use either here, or overseas.

[90] Normally when the witness is unable to attend court. They may also be restrained, *Benfield Holdings Ltd v Elliott Richardson* [2007] EWHC 171 (QB).

[91] Who can even be the trial judge himself: *Peer International Corp v Termidor Music Publishers Ltd* [2005] EWHC 1048 (Ch), [2006] CPR 2.

the same way as in a court,[92] including provision for cross-examination. The deposition so produced may then be adduced in evidence upon appropriate notice, unless the court orders otherwise.[93]

The procedure for supplying evidence for use in foreign courts is now governed by Pt II of CPR 34.[94]

Letters of request[95]

Letters of request may be issued to courts outside the jurisdiction of the High Court asking one of their judges to take the evidence of a specific person within the jurisdiction of the local court.[96] The depositions are remitted to the High Court, and may be read at the trial.[97] Documents may be requested under the inherent jurisdiction of the court,[98] provided that they are specified with particularity similar to that required in relation to a subpoena duces tecum, and that the request is in the interests of justice, and not unfair.[99]

Further information[100]

The old system of interrogatories has been replaced with a simplified procedure for securing further information by way of request and response, the latter of which must be supported by a statement of truth under Pt 22 of the Civil Procedure Rules, and which is subject to restrictions on use for the purposes of other proceedings.[101]

Criminal cases

Here[102] also radical change has occurred in pre-trial procedural provision,[103] in particular to the situations in which disclosure must be made by one side to the other before the trial.[104] This will be mentioned first, and then the section will go on to consider the various

---

[92] CPR 34.9.   [93] CPR 34.11.

[94] By operation of the Civil Procedure (Amendment) Rules 2002, SI 2002/2058; revoking the old RSC Ord 70.

[95] See the CPR 34, especially 34.13, PD 34, 5, now see 33rd amendment to CPR; for exegesis of principle see *First American Corp v Sheikh Zayed Al-Nahyan*, [1998] 4 All ER 439, [1999] 1 WLR 1154. The court will treat both incoming and outgoing letters of request on the same basis: *Charman v Charman* [2005] EWCA Civ 1606, [2006] 1 WLR 1053, [29]. For the position in the United States, see *Intel Corp v Advanced Micro Devices* 542 US 241, 124 S Ct R 2466 (2004).

[96] It is for the recipient court to determine whether to reply, for example if the request has become stale: *R v Central Criminal Court, ex p Hunt* (1995) The Times, 21 February.   [97] CPR 34.11.

[98] See also CPR 34.8(4). Powers may also be accorded by other legislation, see Financial Services and Markets Act 2000 Pt IX construed in *R (Amro International SA) v Financial Services Authority* [2009] EWHC 2242, (Admin).

[99] *Honda Kaishu v KJM Superbikes Ltd* [2007] EWCA Civ 313, [2007] CPR 28.

[100] See generally CPR 18.   [101] CPR 18.2, and PD 18.

[102] The situation elsewhere was summarized by Lord Collins in *HM Adv v Murtagh* [2009] UKPC 35, [76], [77]. See also in Canada *R v McNeill* 2009 SCC 3, [2009] 1 SCR 66.

[103] Although the new Criminal Procedure Rules have so far made little change in relation to disclosure.

[104] Different rules apply to other tribunals, for example there is no duty upon the Police Complaints Authority to disclose material to complainants when determining whether or not to discipline a police officer against whom a complaint has been made: *R (Green) v Police Complaints Authority* [2004] UKHL 6, [2004] 2 All ER 209.

provisions permitting evidence recorded before the trial to be used at it. Agreed statements of fact may be received under s 9 of the Criminal Justice Act 1967. Statements secured at the instance of liquidators of a company under the provisions of s 236 of the Insolvency Act 1986, or by officers of the Serious Fraud Office or Serious Organised Crime Agency under the provisions of s 2 of the Criminal Justice Act 1987 or s 62 of the Serious Organised Crime and Police Act 2005, may be required for use in evidence, as may evidence secured under various other statutory provisions.

Disclosure[105]

A fair criminal trial requires sufficient disclosure to inform the accused of the case he has to meet, and to enable him to give instructions to meet it.[106] The Criminal Procedure and Investigations Act 1996[107] replaced the common law[108] with a new statutory scheme.[109] It was designed to alleviate the burdens of disclosure perceived to lie upon the police and prosecution under the old law, which it was felt were being exploited by those accused of crime.[110] Because of continuing dissatisfaction with the operation of the scheme,[111] further changes both in practice[112] and of the statutory rules have since been implemented for subsequent[113] investigations.[114] It is proposed here first to outline the statutory procedure, then to consider the nature of the material to which it applies, its effects, and its evaluation, especially in the light of the European Convention on Human Rights. The section will finally consider other possible means of securing pre-trial disclosure.

[105] For further detail see the official protocols for disclosure in the Crown Court and in the Magistrates' Court, and the *Attorney-General's Guideline on Disclosure* (April 2005). See the extensive and learned discussion of the history of this topic in *R v Sobh* [1994] 1 VR 41. Disclosure is not available for extradition proceedings: *R (USA) v Tollman* [2006] EWHC 2256 (Admin), (2006) 156 NLR 1440, [85]. In Australia see *R v Law* [2008] NTCCA 4, 182 ACR 312, [48]–[89].

[106] *A v United Kingdom* (2009) 49 EHRR 29, (2009) 26 BHRC 1; *Secretary of State for the Home Department v AF (No 3)* [2009] UKHL 28, [64].

[107] Parts I and II, and its accompanying regulations, and Code of Practice, SI 1997/1033. See also *Attorney-General's Guidelines: Disclosure of Information in Criminal Proceedings* (2005). Similar development has taken place in Scotland: see *Sinclair v HM Adv* [2005] UKPC D2, 2005 1 SC (PC) 28, [29].

[108] With the sole exception of the rules relating to material subject to restriction on grounds of public policy, s 21(2). See further Chapter X. Although it does not explicitly concern itself with the period between arrest and committal, it has effectively supplanted the common law there also: *R v DPP, ex p Lee* [1999] 2 All ER 737; *A-G's Guidelines* (2002) [34]. Some failures to disclose prior to charge can render subsequent charge an abuse of process: see *DPP v Ara* [2001] EWHC Admin 493, [2001] 4 All ER 559, [2002] 1 WLR 815 (refusal to disclose record of interview alleged to justify possibility of caution).

[109] Universally and compulsorily for trials on indictment, and voluntarily (s 6) for summary trials.

[110] Home Office Consultation Paper *Disclosure* (Cm 2864, 1995) ch 1. See Ley (1995) 145 NLJ 1124 for suggestions of manipulation of the common law rules by the prosecution.

[111] See *Thematic Review of the Disclosure of Unused Material* (CPS, 2000), Introduction to *Attorney-General's Guidelines* on disclosure of information in criminal proceedings (2002) [4], *Justice for All* (2002) [4.46]; but see also Plotnikoff and Woolfson 'A fair balance'? *Evaluation of the operation of disclosure law*, Home Office RDS Occ Pap 76 (2001), and for an egregious example, *Murphy v DPP* [2006] EWHC 1753 (Admin).

[112] *Disclosure: A Protocol for the Control and Management of Unused Material in the Crown Court* (2006).

[113] After 4 April 2005.

[114] Criminal Justice Act 2003, Pt 5, and Sch 36, Pt 3, with its Code of Practice (SI 2005/985).

Outline of provisions

The broad scheme of the legislation requires the investigator of crime to record[115] and retain[116] relevant[117] material;[118] it then imposes an initial[119] obligation[120] upon the prosecution to disclose[121] in a usable form,[122] to the defence,[123] material that it is not proposed to use,[124] but which might reasonably be considered capable of undermining[125] the case for the prosecution, or of assisting the case for the accused,[126] and a schedule listing other unused non-sensitive material;[127] then for the accused to disclose specified details of the defence;[128] then for both parties to make continuing disclosure of any material, not so far disclosed by them, which in the light of disclosure by the other, or for some other reason, appear to fulfil the relevant conditions;[129] finally, in the event of a dispute, for the defence to raise it, and the court to dispose of it.[130]

Nature of material to be disclosed

Under the previous criteria for prosecution disclosure as set out in *R v Keane*,[131] three categories were required to be disclosed: relevant evidence; evidence raising a new issue;

---

[115] S 23(1)(b).

[116] S 23(1)(c). Although an innocent failure to do so will not necessarily constitute abuse of process: *R v R* [2001] EWCA Crim 2844 [39]–[41]; despite breach of a relevant Code of Practice: *R v Parker* [2002] EWCA Crim 90.

[117] Including relevance to collateral issues such as entrapment: *R v Nicholls* [2005] EWCA Crim 1797, [24].

[118] Other provisions have more limited scope, e.g. Magistrates Courts (Advance Information) Rules 1985, which are restricted to statements, held to include video recordings: *R v Calderdale Magistrates' Court, ex p Donahue and Cutler* [2001] Crim LR 141; but to exclude DNA profiles: *R (DPP) v Croydon Magistrates' Court* [2001] EWHC Admin 552, [2001] Crim LR 980. A wholly different regime applies in the case of summary offences: see *R v Stratford Justices, ex p Imbert* [1999] 2 Cr App Rep 276. Cf *Sangster and Dixon v R* [2002] UKPC 58 (retrial for failure to disclose CCTV recordings where issue of identification); *Aylesbury Vale DC v Khan* [2005] EWHC 841 (Admin) (no duty to disclose CCTV recordings of alleged unlicensed plying for hire); see, in Ireland, *Dunne v DPP* [2002] 2 IR 305.   [119] Before 2003 called 'primary' disclosure.

[120] But only after committal papers have been served. S 47 and Sch I make substantial and significant alterations to committal procedures, and the use of material employed in them.

[121] There is no obligation to disclose to the defence information known to the accused, but not to his advisers: *R v Denton* [2002] EWCA Crim 272, [62].

[122] *Griffiths v DPP* [2007] EWHC 619 (Admin). In *R v Oszenaris* (2008) 236 CCC3d 476 asserted computer illiteracy rightly failed to secure supply in hard copy.

[123] Ss 5A–5D as inserted by Criminal Justice Act 2003, s 33(1) provide for disclosure to a co-accused.

[124] Material that it is proposed to use must be provided to the defence within 42 days under the current scheme for indictable-only offences under s 51 of the Crime and Disorder Act 1998, Sch 3 and the regulations made thereunder, although this time limit may be extended, even retrospectively: *R (Fehily at al) v Governor of Wandsworth Prison* [2002] EWHC 1295 (Admin), [2003] 1 Cr App Rep 153.

[125] S 3. For criticism of the uncertain criterion of 'undermining', see Sharpe (1999) 63 J Cr L 67. The term was retained in Pt 5 of the Criminal Justice Act 2003.

[126] The test was made objective, and expanded to include unused material assisting the defence by s 32 of the Criminal Justice Act 2003. This includes material assisting the case of the accused against other co-defendants.   [127] S 4.

[128] S 5 formerly required disclosure merely of the nature of the defence, although already construed as going beyond the legal nature of the defence, and to encompass some factual detail (see *R v Tibbs* [2000] 2 Cr App Rep 309), but vast expansion in the detail required is now imposed under the Criminal Justice Act 2003, s 33, as indicated below. The judge has no power to insist that such a statement be signed by the accused: *R (Sullivan) v Maidstone Crown Court* [2002] EWHC 967 (Admin), [2002] 4 All ER 427.

[129] Ss 6B and 7A.   [130] S 8.   [131] (1994) 99 Cr App Rep 1.

and evidence that might realistically lead to either of the preceding categories. It seems that the decision to use the phrase 'might undermine the prosecution case' was designed to narrow the notion of relevance.[132] Its width can also be assessed by reference to the definition of material to be disclosed at the secondary stage, which includes anything that might reasonably be expected to assist the accused's defence as disclosed. Some amplification was provided by the *Attorney-General's Guidelines of 2000*, which, in general terms, regard anything that has an adverse effect on the strength of the prosecution's case as undermining it, for example by the use that might be made of it in cross-examination,[133] or by its capacity to indicate the possibility of exclusion of evidence,[134] a stay of proceedings, or incompatibility with the protections provided by the European Convention on Human Rights.[135] Attention is drawn to the capacity of material that does not appear undermining when seen in isolation, to do so when considered in combination with other material. In some cases, a more generous interpretation of the duty to disclose has been applied where the accused has not been represented by counsel.[136] As noted above, one of the changes made by the Criminal Justice Act 2003 was to make the definition of 'undermining' objective, and to make explicit the need for the prosecution to disclose material that assists the case for the defence.[137]

The court has discretion as to the form in which disclosure is made, and where the public interest requires, it may impose conditions, such as the provision of transcripts of tapes, where copying for improper purposes might otherwise occur.[138]

Shortly before the Criminal Procedure and Investigations Act 1996 was brought into force, the House of Lords considered the prosecution's obligation to disclose material going to the credibility of its own, or the defence's probable witnesses. In *R v Brown*,[139] it was held that there was no obligation to disclose in advance evidence that damaged the credibility of a defence witness.[140] This seems entirely in accordance with the policy underlying the new legislation. On the other hand, where the credibility[141] of prosecution witnesses is important, the failure to disclose material capable of impugning their

---

[132] *Disclosure* [26]; 567 HL Official Report cols 1437–8.

[133] See e.g. *R v K* [2002] EWCA Crim 2878, in which this was decisive. See, in Australia, *Grey v R* [2001] HCA 65.

[134] As in *R v Langley* [2001] EWCA Crim 732, [2001] Crim LR 651(evidence to support claim to exclude confession on a voir dire).   [135] Para 36. Illustrated by examples in paras 37 and 38.

[136] *Murphy v R* [2002] UKPC 3.

[137] S 27. Thus endorsing the decision of the House of Lords in *R v Mills and Poole* [1998] AC 382, [1997] 3 All ER 780, and of the Court of Appeal in *R v Guney* [1998] 2 Cr App Rep 242 under the old law. It need not support the defence in the way the defence probably envisages: *R v West* [2005] EWCA Crim 517, [8].

[138] *R v X JJ, ex p J and S* [2000] 1 All ER 183, [2000] 1 WLR 1215. Costs can escalate if electronic forms are not used, as in Canada in *R v Hallstone Products Ltd* (1999) 140 CCC3d 145, in which the cost of providing hard copies of unused material ran to C\$340,000.

[139] [1998] AC 367, [1997] 3 All ER 769. This also accords with the decision in *R v Imran and Hussain* [1997] Crim LR 754 that there is no obligation to disclose evidence to a suspect at an early stage that might indicate which parts of a potential statement could be demonstrated to be lies. In Scotland the practice is to disclose, *HM Adv v Murtagh* (n102), [70], perhaps indicating some doubt about the continuing validity of the decision in *Brown*.

[140] The defence will be supplied with a copy of a police note listing the accused's criminal convictions immediately after committal: *Practice Note (crime: antecedents)* [1997] 4 All ER 350.

[141] Including expertise: *R v Luttrell* [2004] EWCA Crim 1344, [2004] 2 Cr App R 520, [62].

credibility is likely[142] to be decisive,[143] whether the failure is deliberate[144] or accidental.[145] Thus there will be an obligation to disclose any form of witness training,[146] or the offer of a reward.[147] It is not however necessary to disclose the whole of a witness's criminal history, since in this context there is some tension between rights to a fair trial under article 6 of the European Convention and privacy rights under article 8. Thus in *HM Adv v Murtagh*,[148] decided non-parochially, it was held that only those parts truly[149] relevant to credibility need be disclosed.

At no stage is the prosecution bound to disclose material held not to be in the public interest to disclose,[150] including the uncensored originals of foreign letters of request,[151] or which is barred by s 17 of the Regulation of Investigatory Powers Act 2000.[152] This should be decided on a case-by-case basis, and not by the application of blanket rules.[153] It is sometimes possible for the substance of the information to be presented in the form of an admission that does not prejudice the public interest.[154]

It should be noted that the new legislation relates only to disclosure of information in the possession of the prosecutor,[155] or inspected by him.[156] It leaves unaffected the more restricted[157] common law in relation to third-party disclosure,[158] and the procedure for

---

[142] Unless the witness is peripheral to the prosecution case, as in *R v Makin* [2004] EWCA Crim 1607, (2004) 148 SJLB 821, [29]; or in the case of a co-defendant, if disclosure would add little to the strength of his case: *R v Ebcin* [2005] EWCA Crim 2006, [20].

[143] If disclosed it might sometimes have suggested a different defence theory, as indicated in *R v Cormack* [2004] EWCA Crim 1117, (2004) 148 SJLB 511.

[144] As may have been the case in *R v Kelly* [2002] EWCA Crim 2957 (a case concerning police behaviour in 1949).   [145] *R v Bishop* [2003] EWCA Crim 3628.

[146] *R v Salisbury* (2004) unreported Cr Ct, 18 June.

[147] *R v Allan* [2004] EWCA Crim 2236, (2004) 148 SJLB 1032, [139].   [148] (n102), [30].

[149] But to be generously construed by the prosecutor in making his initial determination.

[150] It may be expected that, under the new law, the court will remain astute to detect cases in which the defence has been specially manufactured to justify disclosure, or more accurately abandonment of the prosecution in lieu of non-disclosure: see *R v Turner* [1995] 3 All ER 432, [1995] 1 WLR 264. The prosecution will itself be under an obligation to disclose in a hearing to determine whether public policy immunity should be granted, and its failure to do so may be fatal to a conviction, as in *R v Gell* [2003] EWCA Crim 123, in which the court was for this reason compelled to overturn a conviction following a guilty plea.

[151] *Evans v Serious Fraud Office* [2002] EWHC 2304 (Admin), [2003] 1 WLR 299.

[152] Ss 3(2), 7A(9). See also the regulation of disclosure of surveillance authorization by s 91(10) of the Police Act 1997, as explained in *R v GS* [2005] EWCA Crim 887, and of confidential or sensitive material by Youth Justice and Criminal Evidence Act 1999, s 37(5)(d).

[153] *R v Heggart* (30 November 2000, unreported) CA (not automatic suppression of names and addresses of 999 callers to police).

[154] As in *R v Hansford* [2006] EWCA Crim 1225, (2006) 150 SJLB 740 (in which a first admission had to be amended in the light of further information that became available).

[155] In Canada irrespective of the means by which the information was obtained, *Minister of Justice v Khadr* 2008 SCC 28, [2008] 2 SCR 125.

[156] S 7A(6). In *R v M* [2000] Ll Med Rep 304, 306, the Court of Appeal expressed surprise that the prosecution had not sought to obtain relevant material; cp *R (Siddall) v Secretary of State for Justice* [2009] EWHC 482 (Admin).

[157] Although some assistance may sometimes be derived from the *Norwich Pharmacal* procedure, 274, 275.

[158] See *R v Alibhai* [2004] EWCA Crim 681; *DPP v Wood* [2006] EWHC 32 (Admin), (2006) 170 JP 177, [43]; at the time of editing, under further review by the Home Office. For comparable problems in New Zealand, see *R v B (No 2)* [1995] 2 NZLR 752, and cf *R v Moore* [2001] 2 NZLR 761.

determining its materiality.[159] It can operate in only the most limited way in relation to material held outside the European Union.[160]

Defence disclosure was vastly expanded under the Criminal Justice Act 2003 by the insertion of five new sections into the legislation.[161] Section 6A removes the previous qualification that the obligation is to disclose merely the *general nature* of the defence,[162] and in addition requires for the first time that points of law to be taken and the authority to be relied upon for them be disclosed.[163] It also requires the disclosure in addition to the names and addresses of alibi witnesses, of their date of birth.[164] Section 6C makes the highly significant change of extending the so-expanded disclosure requirements relating to alibi witnesses to all witnesses intended to be called by the defence. Section 6D goes still further in requiring disclosure of details relating to all experts from whom opinions were sought for possible use by the defence at trial. The aim is to prevent 'shopping around' for expert evidence, despite little evidence that this occurs, and risk of inhibiting defence recourse to expert opinion.[165]

Effect

The Court of Appeal indicated its readiness to support robust case-management by trial judges under the Criminal Procedure Rules in *R v Lee*[166] but not at the expense of proper and timely disclosure by the prosecution, as in *R v Phillips*,[167] where the defence was unable to secure such access to transcripts of evidence tendered at a relevant earlier trial in respect of this very incident of the person alleged to have been a joint offender with the current accused. The effects of both non-disclosure[168] and disclosure must be considered. If the prosecution fails in its obligation to make primary disclosure, it runs the risk[169] of any conviction[170] being overturned[171] as unsafe,[172] as at common law; if it fails even to purport to comply, no obligation upon the defence to disclose arises. Failure to disclose may

---

[159] See *R v Whittle* [1997] 1 Cr App Rep 166.

[160] *R v Khyam* [2008] EWCA Crim 1612, [37]; *R v RF* [2009] EWCA Crim 678, [2010] *Crim LR* 148. Within the European Union some assistance may be derived under a European evidence warrant.

[161] To replace s 5(6)–(9) in the old legislation, so far only the first and fifth have been brought into force.

[162] S 6A(1)(a). Provision is also made for the expansion of the detail required by Home Office regulation: s 6A(2)(d). See also *R v Bryant* [2005] EWCA Crim 2079, [12].   [163] S 6A(1)(d).

[164] S 6A(2)(a).   [165] For this and other criticism, see Zander (2002) 146 *Sol Jo* 824.

[166] [2007] EWCA Crim 764.   [167] [2007] EWCA Crim 1042.

[168] Widely construed here to include defective disclosure.

[169] Failure to disclose does not necessarily render a trial unfair: see e.g. *R v Sirrs and Povey* [2006] EWCA Crim 3185, [123] not even in jurisdictions where there are strong constitutional guaranties of human rights: see *Ferguson v A-G for Trinidad and Tobago* [2001] UKPC 3. Unfairness is to be determined in the light of all of the evidence, including fresh evidence, available to the court making the determination: *R v Craven* [2001] 2 Cr App Rep 12; it is, however, wrong for a court to pre-empt the function of the jury by taking the view that failure to disclose could have made no difference: *R v Mills and Poole* [2003] EWCA Crim 1753, [2003] 1 WLR (2931). It will rarely be a ground for a stay that evidence has been innocently destroyed before trial: *R v Winzar* [2002] EWCA Crim 2950.

[170] Even after a guilty plea: *R v Early* [2002] EWCA Crim 1904, [2003] 1 Cr App R 288, [74].

[171] *R v Hadley* [2006] EWCA Crim 2554, [37]; sometimes by way of a second appeal following the intervention of the Criminal Cases Review Committee, as in *R v Clark* [2003] EWCA Crim 1020, [2003] 2 FCR 447; sometimes because of refusal to adjourn, as in *S v DPP* [2006] EWHC 1207 (Admin), (2006) 170 JP 107.

[172] Although a trial made unfair by lack of disclosure may nevertheless not necessarily make a conviction unsafe, even when the unfairness has been established by a decision in that very matter from the European Court of Human Rights, as in *R v Lewis* [2005] EWCA Crim 859.

be regarded as providing a tenable claim of abuse of process.[173] Delay in compliance will amount to abuse of process, only if as a result the accused is denied a fair trial.[174] In the case of the defence, disclosure under ss 5, 6, or 6A is required as a condition precedent to an application under s 8 for further or better disclosure by the prosecution. A substituted s 11(5) also permits comment[175] upon non-disclosure by the defence where disclosure is required, and allows adverse inferences to be drawn.[176] These are not to amount to the sole evidence to justify conviction,[177] but may apparently help to constitute a case to answer. It seems that they will justify a direct conclusion of guilt, and that their effect will not simply be to negate the defences that were not raised or sufficiently supported.[178]

Where information has been disclosed in criminal proceedings, the question has arisen of the extent to which it can be used for collateral purposes outside those proceedings, for example to found a civil claim for defamation. To the extent that the disclosure is of material not intended to be used by the prosecution pursuant to the Criminal Procedure and Investigations Act 1996, such collateral use is regulated by s 17. The effect of that section is broadly to ban the collateral use of such material,[179] unless it has been read out in open court. It should also be noted that material first disclosed under compulsion in other proceedings may be required to be disclosed to the police for the purposes of criminal proceedings.[180]

Evaluation[181]

The motivation for the Criminal Procedure and Investigations Act 1996 was to withhold some relevant material from disclosure in advance to the defence, yet in *Edwards v United Kingdom*[182] the European Court on Human Rights had pronounced disclosure of all material evidence to the accused to be a requirement of a fair trial pursuant to Art 6 of the Convention. It remains the case that the prosecution often fails to comply with this duty,[183]

---

[173] As in *R v Matthew Smith* [2004] EWCA Crim 2212, [19]. Although, in such a case, the effect should be so drastic as to make it almost impossible that in its absence the proceedings could be fair: *R v Hall* [2005] EWCA Crim 747.

[174] S 10. See *R v Boksh* [2003] EWCA Crim 1145.

[175] By the court, or by any other party, and in the latter case the requirement to secure the leave of the court has been greatly reduced; cf Criminal Procedure and Investigations Act 1996, s 11(4).

[176] In terminology resembling comparable parts of the Criminal Justice and Public Order Act 1994.

[177] S 11(9).

[178] By analogy with the construction of the similar phraseology of s 35 of the Criminal Justice and Public Order Act 1994 in *R v Cowan* [1999] 2 AC 177, [1996] QB 373, [1995] 4 All ER 939.

[179] Except after application to, and with the leave of, the court, s 17(4), even in civil proceedings: *Taylor v Serious Fraud Office* [1999] 2 AC 177, [1998] 4 All ER 801. Although it is not improper for an indication of the content of the information to be disclosed, sufficient to stimulate the issue of a witness summons in civil proceedings: *Preston Borough Council v McGrath* (12 May 2000, unreported) CA.

[180] *A Chief Constable v A County Council* [2002] EWHC 2198 (Fam), [2003] 1 FLR 579.

[181] For discussion of disclosure in the United States, see *Brady v Maryland* 373 US 83 (1963); *Kyles v Whitley* 514 US 419 (1995). For the impact of Charter considerations on disclosure obligations in Canada, see *R v Chaplin* [1995] 1 SCR 727 (onus in relation to suspected wiretapping); *R v O'Connor* [1995] 4 SCR 411 (medical records of complainants); *R v Carosella* [1997] 1 SCR 80 (destruction of records to pre-empt disclosure); *R v La* [1997] 2 SCR 680 (lost records).

[182] (1992) 15 EHRR 417. For further consideration of the impact of the ECHR, see Plowden and Kerrigan (2001) 151 NLJ 735, 820. See also *Atlan v United Kingdom* (2002) 34 EHRR 833; *Dowsett v United Kingdom* [2003] Crim LR 890, ECHR.

[183] For recent examples see *Tucker v Crown Prosecution Service* [2008] EWCA Crim 3063; *R v Zengeya* [2009] EWCA Crim 1369; see also Edwards [2007] Crim LR 665.

and trial courts to enforce it.[184] Conversely, it was intended to put pressure upon the defence to provide more detail of its intended defence in advance, and to employ failure satisfactorily to comply to help construct a prima facie case, yet in *Saunders v United Kingdom*[185] the use of compulsorily acquired material was also regarded as derogating from a fair trial. While it is not impossible to reconcile the current state of the law with those decisions, the introduction of the European Convention on Human Rights seems likely to lead, at the very least, to a restrictive interpretation of these provisions.[186]

It should also be noted that some commentators take the view that, without a wholesale, and most unlikely, change of attitude on the part of police, prosecution, defence, and judiciary, the disclosure regime in criminal cases is likely to prove patchy in operation, and unsatisfactory in effect.[187] Issues may also arise here, as in Canada, of the cost of disclosure, especially by third parties.[188]

Other means

The courts are astute to prevent the prosecution from obtaining the effect of compulsory disclosure of evidence in advance by other means, except where expressly contemplated by statutory provision. Thus in *R v Crown Court at Southwark, ex p Bowles*,[189] the House of Lords condemned an attempt to secure disclosure of material from a third party with a view to its use in subsequent criminal proceedings, by use of an application[190] for the information to determine whether a person had benefited from criminal conduct. It should also be noted that a witness summons under s 2 of the Criminal Procedure (Attendance of Witnesses) Act 1965[191] can be addressed only to documents that are likely to be material evidence, and thus not to those that may lead to the discovery of such evidence, or which could be used only in cross-examination.[192]

Coroners

When depositions are taken by a coroner, there does not appear to be any statutory provision for their being read at any trial that takes place on the coroner's inquisition; in *R v Cowle*,[193] it was held that the deposition of a dead deponent might be read if it was signed by him and the coroner, and the accused had had an opportunity of cross-examination.

---

[184] For recent example see *Swash v DPP* [2009] EWHC 803, (Admin).
[185] (1996) 23 EHRR 313. As seems now to have been recognized by the interpolation of cl 58 into the Youth Justice and Criminal Evidence Act 1999.
[186] Although, needless to say, the Home Secretary has certified his view that the Criminal Justice Act 2003 (including its expansive amendments to defence disclosure requirements) is compatible with Convention rights.
[187] See Redmayne [2004] *Crim LR* 441; Zander (2006) 156 *NLJ* 618 ('Mission Impossible').
[188] *Tele-Mobile Co v R* 2008 SCC 12, [2008] 1 SCR 305.   [189] [1998] AC 641, [1998] 2 All ER 193.
[190] Under Criminal Justice Act 1988, s 93H.
[191] As amended by Criminal Procedure and Investigations Act 1996 s 66: see Corker (1999) 149 *NLJ* 1006.
[192] *R v Reading Justices, ex p Reading County Council* [1996] 1 Cr App Rep 239. In some jurisdictions, legislation prevents access to confidential third party records, and in Canada, in *R v Mills* [1999] 3 SCR 668, it was even held compatible with the Canadian Charter. See also in Ireland *JF v Reilly* [2007] IESC 32, [2008] 1 IR 753.
[193] (1907) 71 JP 152, contra *R v Butcher* (1900) 64 JP 808. See also *R v Black* (1909) 74 JP 71 and *R v Marriott* (1911) 75 JP 288. In Australia, there is discretion to reject such a deposition: *R v Collins* [1986] VR 37.

Letters of request[194]

Given that hearsay was made more widely admissible in criminal cases under the provisions of the Criminal Justice Act 1988,[195] provision has been made for information[196] to be secured for the purposes of criminal proceedings by the issue of letters of request.[197] Such evidence may be secured before proceedings have been instituted, if they are then likely to be so instituted, and the procedure may also be invoked by the accused, although in his case only if proceedings have been instituted. Evidence may also be secured from abroad by video link, even in the absence of extradition from the jurisdiction concerned.[198]

Statements under s 9 of the Criminal Justice Act 1967[199]

Agreed statements may be admitted under these provisions, but it is arguable that there is such a discrepancy between the detail of the rules that govern the recording of statements made by the accused, and the informality that obtains in this context, that reform is required.[200]

Statements under s 236 of Insolvency Act 1986

Section 236 allows the liquidators of a company to invoke the assistance of the court to conduct a compulsory investigation so as to assist with the recovery of assets. The threat of such an investigation may be sufficient to induce witnesses to provide evidence on a voluntary basis to the liquidators. This was the situation in *R v Clowes*,[201] in which the question arose of whether the transcripts of such interviews could be secured for use by the defendants in subsequent criminal proceedings. Since the transcripts were not merely relevant but also admissible,[202] it was held that their production could be compelled.[203] Although it was recognized that this would, to some extent, impinge upon the confidentiality of such statements, it was nevertheless held that, on balance, the interests of justice in enabling the accused to present a defence to a serious charge should prevail.

---

[194] See also draft proposals for a European Evidence Warrant (COM 2003 688 fin); for exegesis, see Garlick and Leaf (2004) 154 *NLJ* 858.

[195] Expanded by the provisions of the Criminal Justice Act 2003: see further below 644.

[196] See *R (on the application of Evans) v Serious Fraud Office* (n151).

[197] Crime (International Co-operation) Act 2003, ss 7–9. This legislation also provides in ss 13–19 for the converse situation in which evidence is required for a criminal court overseas, and even for the mutual international transportation of prisoners to testify: ss 47–48. For procedural guidance, see *Energy Financing Team Ltd v Director of Serious Fraud Office* [2005] EWHC 1626 Admin, [2005] 4 All ER 285, [24]. Allowance must be made for the application of art 8 of the European Convention, *Hafner v Westminster Magistrates' Court* [2008] EWHC 524 (Admin).

[198] *R v Forsyth* [1997] 2 Cr App Rep 299. See also, in Australia, *R v Kim* (1998) 104 ACR 233.

[199] See further 622.   [200] Heaton-Armstrong and Wolchover [1992] *Crim LR* 160.

[201] [1992] 3 All ER 440. See also *Re Barlow Clowes Gilt Managers Ltd* (n43).

[202] As a result of s 24 of the Criminal Justice Act 1988, then in force, see further 610, thus enabling the contrary decision in *R v Cheltenham Justices, ex p Secretary of State for Trade* [1977] 1 All ER 460, [1977] 1 WLR 95 to be distinguished.

[203] So long at least as they were at least conditionally required with a view to being adduced as evidence of their contents, and not simply to being used for purposes of contradiction in cross-examination.

Statements under s 2 of the Criminal Justice Act 1987 and s 62 of the Serious Organised Crime and Police Act 2005

These provisions permit compulsory interrogation by officials of the Serious Fraud Office of those believed to be in possession of information relevant to the investigation of serious fraud. The legislation further provides that evidence so obtained shall not be generally admissible in evidence in subsequent criminal proceedings,[204] but may be used as a previous inconsistent statement.[205] Such statements may be obtained even after criminal proceedings have been commenced,[206] and the trial judge has no power to regulate the process of securing them.[207]

These provisions constituted the basis, and justification, for a potentially massive expansion of powers to secure advance disclosure both from suspects and third parties in a very wide range of serious crime cases.[208] Misgivings have been expressed about the paucity of parliamentary scrutiny,[209] especially in the light of the width of the powers and the narrowness of the exceptions.[210] The accuracy of the sanguine view of the government that the powers will not be abused remains to be seen.

Miscellaneous statutory provisions

Under ss 42 and 43 of the Children and Young Persons Act 1933, the deposition of a child or young person may be taken out of court, and used at the preliminary examination or trial of a person for an offence under the Act.[211] The conditions are that the child's attendance in court would cause serious danger to his life or health, and that the accused should have had an opportunity of cross-examining him.[212] These provisions were not regarded as affording sufficient protection for young children, and have now been supplemented by various special measures under the Youth Justice and Criminal Evidence Act 1999.[213]

It should be noted that the Family Proceedings Rules[214] no longer require application to the court by a party to disclose for the purposes of criminal, or disciplinary,[215] proceedings any documents adduced in care proceedings under the Children Act 1989.

THE RIGHT TO BEGIN

The claimant, prosecutor, or their respective advocates open every case in the sense that they explain the issues to the court, but questions sometimes arise concerning the right to begin calling evidence.

---

[204] It is admissible on charges ancillary to the power itself under s 2(14) of the Act. Nor need material obtained under these powers be disclosed to the defence while the investigation is continuing: *R v Serious Fraud Office, ex p Maxwell* (1992) The Times, 9 October.

[205] S 2(8)(b), and now only if evidence is given relating to it, or a question asked about it, by the party against whom it is to be used: s 8(AA) inserted by Youth Justice and Criminal Evidence Act 1999, s 59, Sch 3, [20].

[206] *R v Director of Serious Fraud Office, ex p Smith* [1993] AC 1, [1992] 3 All ER 456.

[207] *R v Nadir* [1993] 4 All ER 513, [1993] 1 WLR 1322.   [208] Defined in s 61.

[209] Less than three hours.

[210] Effectively for legal professional privilege and 'banking business', s 64.

[211] See Spencer and Tucker (1987) NLJ 816.

[212] See also Children and Young Persons Act 1963, as to committal proceedings in the case of sexual offences.   [213] See generally 237.

[214] Rule 10.20A.   [215] *Re A (a minor) (disclosure of medical records to GMC)* [1999] 1 FCR 30.

The Crown will almost always have the right to begin in criminal cases in which there is a plea of not guilty,[216] because there will be some issue upon which the evidential, if not the legal, burden will be borne by the prosecution; as there can be formal admissions and agreed statements of fact under s 10 and s 9 of the Criminal Justice Act 1967, respectively, there can be exceptional cases in which the accused has the right to begin.

In civil cases, the judge now has wide powers to regulate the way in which evidence is presented,[217] and it has become increasingly common to dispense with an opening address on the basis that the judge will have read the papers in advance.[218] Under the old law, the claimant had the right to begin unless the defendant had the burden of proof on every issue,[219] and, in this context, 'burden of proof' was taken to mean 'evidential burden'.[220]

THE ADVOCATES' SPEECHES

The judge's decision on who is to begin the case may affect the order in which the advocates' speeches are made to the court. Under the old civil procedure, if the claimant begins, he will open the case to the court,[221] call his witnesses and sum up if the defendant does not call witnesses. The defendant will then reply and thus secure the last word. If the defendant calls witnesses, the claimant will not sum up at the conclusion of his case, but the defendant will open his case, call his witnesses and sum up, leaving the claimant with the right of reply. The foregoing procedure will be reversed if the defendant begins.

In criminal cases tried on indictment, the prosecutor opens and calls his evidence. If the accused does not call evidence, the prosecutor sums up, leaving the accused with the right of reply.[222] If the accused calls evidence,[223] the prosecutor's closing speech is made after the close of the evidence for the defence, with the result that the accused has the right of reply.[224] In both civil and criminal cases, the above procedure may be interspersed with a submission that there is no case to answer, arguments about the admissibility of evidence,[225] or arguments on points of law.

---

[216] Where a special plea is raised, such as autrefois convict, and there is a dispute of fact, the accused would begin. A plea of guilty does not admit everything on the depositions: *R v Riley* [1896] 1 QB 309, 318; *R v Maitland* [1964] SASR 332, according to which an accused pleading guilty should call evidence as to disputed facts.   [217] CPR 32.1.

[218] See Harrison (2002) 152 *NLJ* 473.   [219] Ord 35, r 7(6).

[220] *Mercer v Whall* (1845) 5 QB 447; *Re Parry's Estate, Parry v Fraser* [1977] 1 All ER 309, [1977] 1 WLR 93n; *Pontifex v Jolly* (1839) 9 C & P 202, showing that an amendment will not be allowed for the sole purpose of altering the right to begin. See *W Lusty & Sons Ltd v Morris Wilkinson & Co (Nottingham) Ltd* [1954] 2 All ER 347, [1954] 1 WLR 911, showing that, where a claim is admitted in court, the defendant may begin calling evidence on his counterclaim. See also *Seldon v Davidson* [1968] 2 All ER 755, [1968] 1 WLR 1083.

[221] He must not allude to facts with regard to which he cannot call evidence: *Faith v M'Intyre* (1835) 7 C & P 44; *R v O'Neill* (1950) 34 Cr App Rep 108.

[222] Wrongfully allowing a closing speech to the prosecutor is not necessarily fatal, *R v Rabani* [2008] EWCA Crim 2030.

[223] Held in Tasmania in *R v Ferguson* [2000] TASSC 151, 117 ACR 44 to include putting a document to a prosecution witness in the course of cross-examination.

[224] Criminal Procedure (Right of Reply) Act 1964. For summary trial, see Magistrates' Courts Rules 1981, rr 13 and 14. For consideration of the history of the rule, see *R v Carter* (1997) 19 WAR 8. It is submitted that the trial judge has some discretion as to the order of speeches as between counsel for co-accused in a joint trial: see, in Australia, *DPP's Ref under s 693A of the Criminal Code: Re Y* (1997) 19 WAR 47.

[225] If, as will usually be the case, counsel knows that objection will be taken to an item of evidence, he should not refer to it in opening, and the objection should be raised when the evidence is about to be

THE CALLING OF WITNESSES AND THE ROLE OF THE JUDGE

It was said in the first paragraph of this chapter that the essential feature of the English adversary or accusatorial system of justice is the questioning of witnesses by the parties or their representatives, mainly summoned by them,[226] and called in the order of their choice before a judge acting as umpire rather than as inquisitor.[227]

Most of the qualifications relate to criminal proceedings. In civil cases, the parties could always call as many or as few witnesses able to give admissible evidence as they chose, in the order that commended itself to them,[228] and the judge can call witnesses only with their consent.[229] The judge is, however, entitled, and sometimes bound, to put leading questions to witnesses after they have been examined, and cross-examined.[230] Nor in the case of late-filed material is he entitled to depart from an indication that he will treat such material with caution.[231]

In criminal cases, the prosecution is obliged to call[232] certain witnesses and to have others available to be called by the defence; there is a restriction on the order in which defence witnesses may be called and the judge may[233] call a witness without the consent of the parties.

The advent of the Criminal Procedure and Investigations Act 1996 has changed the situation relating to the tendering of witnesses and statements to the defence completely. It is now settled that the prosecution discharges its obligation to the defence by reading a committal statement.[234] If a witness is, in the opinion of the prosecutor, incapable of belief, there is no need to use the statement for committal purposes, or to call the witness at trial. It seems that the prosecutor will not reasonably consider a statement unworthy of belief simply because it is inconsistent with the majority of the evidence supporting the prosecution case.[235] Nor will it be enough that the statement might help the accused to

given: *R v Cole* (1941) 28 Cr App Rep 43; *R v Zielinski* (1950) 34 Cr App Rep 193. This procedure can be applied to civil cases tried with a jury. The point is not very important when there is no jury.

[226] In family cases with a public law element the Court of Appeal may require the calling of potentially decisive expert evidence, *Re L (A Child)* [2008] EWCA Civ 1388, [2009] 1 FLR 1152, [11].

[227] Re-emphasized in *R v Grafton* [1993] QB 101, [1992] 4 All ER 609; 104, 610, 611.

[228] *Briscoe v Briscoe* [1968] P 501, [1966] 1 All ER 465. Cf *Vernon v Bosley* [1995] 2 FCR 78; and risks as to costs. Under CPR 32.1, the discretion of the judge has become still wider.

[229] *Re Enoch and Zaretsky, Bock & Co's Arbitration* [1910] 1 KB 327; but such consent is unnecessary on motions to commit for contempt: *Yianni v Yianni* [1966] 1 All ER 231n, [1966] 1 WLR 120. Exceptionally in child care proceedings it seems from *Re X (Children)* [2008] EWHC 242 (Fam), [2008] 3 All ER 958 that under the new regime the Judge can compel a witness to be called in the absence of consent, either of the witness or his counsel, and even though the witness being a party seeks to withdraw from the proceedings.

[230] *Currey v Currey* [2004] EWCA Civ 1799, [2005] 1 FLR 952, [20] (bound if necessary in order to promote the best interests of a child).   [231] *Re B-L* [2004] EWCA Civ 786, [14].

[232] Or recall: see, in Hong Kong, *HKSAR v Wai* (21 March 2003, unreported), CA.

[233] And should do so, rather than stay the proceedings, where the witness is material, and there are good reasons for neither side wishing to call him: *R v Haringey Justices, ex p DPP* [1996] QB 351, [1996] 1 All ER 828. The same applies to a tribunal in immigration proceedings: *Kesse v Home Secretary* [2001] EWCA Civ 177, [2001] Imm AR 366. In New Zealand, a full Court of Appeal has said this to be justified in only the most exceptional circumstances: *R v Bishop* [1996] 3 NZLR 399; and the rule appears to be the same in Australia: see *R v Griffis* (1996) 67 SASR 170. An example of such circumstances is provided by *R v Wilson* [1998] 2 Qd 599 (unrepresented accused charged with murder, and refusing to call expert evidence as to his mental condition at the time). In Canada, the judge is required to enquire why such a witness is not being called by the prosecution: *R v Cook* (1996) 107 CCC (3d) 334.   [234] *R v Armstrong* [1995] Crim LR 831.

[235] *R v Russell-Jones* [1995] 3 All ER 239, [1995] 1 Cr App Rep 538.

manufacture a false defence.[236] In neither case is the prosecution itself under an obligation to call the witness.[237] On the other hand, if witnesses are worthy of belief, named in the indictment, assist the prosecution case, and are present in court, then the prosecution is not at liberty simply to close its case, and to refuse to call or tender them.[238] Nevertheless, if the prosecution case is sufficiently established by other witnesses, it is not absolutely essential that the victim of a crime testify.[239] Conversely, it does not necessarily amount to abuse of process if the prosecution calls a witness, despite having informed the defence that it does not intend to do so.[240]

The restriction upon the order in which defence witnesses may be called relates to the accused himself. In *R v Morrison*,[241] Lord Alverstone CJ said:

In all cases I consider it most important for the prisoner to be called before any of his witnesses. He ought to give his evidence before he has heard the evidence and cross-examination of any witnesses he is going to call.

It has since been said that there are rare exceptions to this rule under which a formal witness, or one about whose evidence there is no controversy, might, with the leave of the court, give evidence before the accused.[242] A majority of the Criminal Law Revision Committee thought the rule a good one, but the Committee unanimously recommended that the discretion to allow for exceptions should be unlimited.[243] This general rule, and the unfettered discretion to depart from it, achieved statutory form in the Police and Criminal Evidence Act 1984, s 79.

In civil and criminal proceedings, the parties must, as a general rule, call all their evidence before the close of their cases.[244] In civil proceedings, if evidence emerges afterwards that could not have been foreseen to be necessary,[245] the case may have to be remitted for retrial with a different judge.[246]

In criminal proceedings, it was once said that leave to call evidence in rebuttal after the close of the case[247] should be given only 'if any matter arises ex improviso which no

---

[236] *R v Brown* [1998] 2 Cr App Rep 364.

[237] *R v Nugent* [1977] 3 All ER 662, [1977] 1 WLR 789. See also, in Australia, *Lewis v R* (1998) 20 WAR 1; in New Zealand, *R v Wilson* [1997] 2 NZLR 500. In Canada, it is impermissible for the judge to inhibit adverse comment by the defence on a late reversal of a decision by the prosecution to call a witness, by threatening to remind the jury that the defence could have called the witness if it chose to do so: *R v Jolivet* [2000] 1 SCR 751.

[238] *R v Wellingborough Magistrates' Court, ex p François* (1994) 158 JP 813; if the statement is served on the defence only as unused prosecution material there is no need for the prosecution to call the witness: *R v Richardson* (1993) 98 Cr App R 174.   [239] *Swanston v DPP* (1997) 161 JP 203.

[240] *R v Drury* [2001] EWCA Crim 975, distinguishing *R v Bloomfield* [1997] 1 Cr App Rep 135. This also applies where the decision to call the witness is taken after an adjournment, but before the prosecution has closed its case: *DPP v Jimale* [2001] Crim LR 138.   [241] (1911) 6 Cr App Rep 159, 165.

[242] *R v Smith* [1968] 2 All ER 115, [1968] 1 WLR 636.   [243] Eleventh Report, [107].

[244] Although, in civil cases, the court has a general discretion in the interests of justice to allow evidence that ought to have been disclosed to be adduced at any time before judgment: *Stocznia Gdanska SA v Latvian Shipping Co* [2001] 1 LlR 537; but not after a draft has been circulated to the parties: *Gravgaard v Aldridge and Brownlee* [2004] EWCA Civ 1529, [2005] PNLR 19, [28].

[245] *R (Richards) v Pembrokeshire CC* [2004] EWCA Civ 813; but not where abstention was made for purely tactical reasons: *Choudhoury v Ahmed* [2005] EWCA Civ 1102.

[246] *Butcher v Rowe* [2004] EWCA Civ 1794.

[247] The judge should inform an unrepresented accused of the need to call his witnesses: *Tiwari v State* [2002] UKPC 29.

human ingenuity can foresee',[248] but this formulation of what is universally considered to be a rule of practice rather than law has now been overtaken. In *R v Khan* [2008] EWCA Crim 1112 the Court of Appeal took a much more relaxed approach to the admissibility of evidence after the jury had retired, and, contrary to many of the earlier authorities, appears to have taken the view that it will be prevented only if its admission would make the trial unfair. This seems more practicable and more just. The court will normally allow evidence in rebuttal to be called in order to make good a purely technical omission,[249] especially if earlier objection had deliberately been eschewed for tactical reasons,[250] provided that to do so is not unfair.[251] It would, however, be wrong to allow the Crown to split its case as it wished, especially if in so doing, the accused might be compelled to testify in reply, and be exposed to cross-examination.[252]

A stronger rule prevents further evidence[253] from being received[254] after the jury has retired.[255] The jury should be discharged if further evidence emerges after its retirement, unless the defence is prepared for the evidence to be disregarded, and the jury to continue upon that basis.[256] In Ireland, however, the Supreme Court has held that the judge has a discretion to allow a witness to be called up to the time when the jury returns its verdict.[257] The English rule nevertheless makes for tidiness because the witness who was called would have to be cross-examined, and the process might lead to suggestions that further witnesses should be called.

At a trial on indictment, the rule prevents the judge from calling a witness after the jury has retired. Up to that point, he has a discretion to do so, although it has been stressed that there must be good reason for such an interference with the adversarial process and reference has even been made to the *ex improviso* rule in this context.[258] The Court of Appeal will be extremely reluctant to interfere with the discretion of the trial judge, and, in *R v Roberts*,[259] remarked that it knew of no case in which an appeal had been allowed because the trial judge had refused to exercise it to call a witness.

---

[248] Tindal CJ in *R v Frost* (1839) 4 State Tr NS 85, 376.

[249] *Yearly v Crown Prosecution Service* [1997] CLY 1101; *Hammond v Wilkinson* 165 JP 786, [2001] Crim LR 323 (failure to prove statutory instrument).

[250] *R (Lawson) v Stafford Magistrates' Court* [2007] EWHC 2490, (Admin).

[251] *R v Hinchcliffe* [2002] EWCA Crim 837.

[252] See *John v R* [1985] 2 SCR 476; *R v Chin* (1985) 157 CLR 671, in which the principle was extended to matters introduced for the first time in cross-examination.

[253] Still more a letter to the judge from one of the litigants, *Diedrichs-Sturland v Talanga Stiftung* [2006] UKPC 38.

[254] In *R v Karakaya* [2005] EWCA Crim 346, [2005] 2 Cr App R 77, the extraneous material had been downloaded by a juror from the Internet.

[255] *R v Davis* (1975) 62 Cr App Rep 194; as to proceedings before justices, see *Pheland v Back* [1972] 1 All ER 901, [1972] 1 WLR 273. The rule is not so rigid in Australia: see *R v Delon* (1992) 29 NSWLR 29, in which a view was taken after the jury had retired.

[256] *R v Kaul and Collin* [1998] Crim LR 135.

[257] *The People (A-G) v O'Brien* [1963] IR 65. This rule was also recommended in England by the Criminal Law Revision Committee in its 11th Report *Evidence (General)* (Cmnd 4991, 1972), [216].

[258] *R v Cleghorn* [1967] 2 QB 584, [1967] 1 All ER 996, in which the conviction was quashed and stress was placed on the fact that, in *R v Tregear* [1967] 2 QB 574, [1967] 1 All ER 989, the judge was in effect requested by the defence to call the witness in question. For the position in Australia, see *R v Apostilides* (1984) 154 CLR 563; for that in Canada, see *R v Finta* [1994] 1 SCR 701, 855.

[259] (1984) 80 Cr App Rep 89, 96.

The power to call a witness in criminal cases serves as a reminder that the English judge is more than an umpire in the strict sense of the word, and nowadays much more than he was fifty years ago.[260] It is true that he must not descend into the dust of the arena,[261] for example by conducting the trial, and intervening in the addresses of counsel and the examination of witnesses so as to appear to have determined issues before hearing evidence.[262] Even after re-examination, his power to ask questions must be restricted to clarification, and not amount to cross-examination.[263] He may nevertheless intervene to exclude clearly inadmissible evidence, despite the absence of any objection by counsel.[264] We have seen that he may exert a very considerable influence over the jury,[265] he has a discretion to exclude certain types of evidence,[266] and he can question witnesses in the cause of clarification.[267] His position was well summed up in the following passage from a judgment of Denning LJ:[268]

In the system of trial which we have evolved in this country, the judge sits to hear and determine the issues raised by the parties, not to conduct an investigation or examination on behalf of society at large as happens, we believe, in some foreign countries. Even in England, however, a judge is not a mere umpire to answer the question 'How's that?' His object, above all, is to find out the truth, and to do justice according to law…

SECTION 2.   EXAMINATION IN CHIEF

The object of examination in chief is to obtain testimony in support of the version of the facts in issue or relevant to the issue for which the party calling the witness contends. Generally speaking, such witnesses may not be asked leading questions, and special rules apply to the extent to which use may be made of out-of-court statements, including those used to refresh the memory of the witness. A party may call someone else to contradict his witness who has given unfavourable evidence with regard to a fact in issue or relevant to the issue, but he may discredit his witness only if the judge considers that witness to be hostile. Leading questions, refreshing memory, previous statements of witnesses consistent with their present testimony, and unfavourable or hostile witnesses will be considered in turn.

---

[260] *Almeida v Opportunity Equal Partners Ltd* [2006] UKPC 44, [94], approving dicta of Kirby ACJ in *Galea v Galea* (1990) 19 NSWLR 263.

[261] *R v Grafton* (n227).

[262] For example, *R v Michel* [2009] UKPC 41; *Southwark LBC v Kofi-Adu* [2006] EWCA Civ 281, [2006] HLR 33.

[263] *R v Wiggan* (1999) The Times, 22 March, although a lenient view may be taken of the distinction: see *Cairnstores v Aktiebolaget Hassle* [2002] EWCA Civ 1504, [2003] FSR 23; and it will take a very strong case to amount to a breach of the European Convention on Human Rights: see *CG v United Kingdom* (2002) 34 EHRR 31. The judge may cross-examine if a child witness would otherwise refuse to continue testifying: *R v Cameron* [2001] EWCA Crim 562, [2001] Crim LR 587. For the position in Australia, see *R v Esposito* (1998) 45 NSWLR 442, 472.   [264] *R v Hook* (1994) 158 JP 1129.

[265] Chapter IV.   [266] Chapter IV, Section 2.

[267] *Manning v King's College Hospital NHS Trust* [2009] EWCA Civ 832; *R v Denton* [2007] EWCA Crim 1111.

[268] *Jones v National Coal Board* [1957] 2 QB 55, 63.

LEADING QUESTIONS[269]

A leading question is one that either suggests the answer desired, or assumes the existence of disputed facts as to which the witness is to testify.[270] An example of the first type would be the following question put to one of the claimant's witnesses in a running-down case: 'Did you see another car coming very fast from the opposite direction?' It should be split up into something such as the following: 'Did you notice any other traffic? Which direction was it coming from? At what sort of speed?' A typical example of the second type of leading question would be: 'What did you do after Smith hit you?', if it were put to the claimant in a claim for assault before he had deposed to being hit by Smith.

The answers to leading questions are not inadmissible in evidence, although the method by which they were obtained may rob them of all, or most, of their significance.[271] Leading questions are objectionable because of the danger of collusion between the person asking them and the witness, or the impropriety of suggesting the existence of facts that are not in evidence.[272] Account must also be taken of human laziness—it is easy to say 'yes' or 'no' on demand, and most leading questions can be answered in this way, even if the same is true of some questions that are not leading. There is, however, no doubt that leading questions save time: they are often an indispensable prelude to further interrogation and a travesty could be made of any examination in chief by overemphatic insistence on the prohibition. There are, therefore, numerous recurring situations to which it does not apply. If no objection is taken to a leading question, any answer amounts to evidence in the case, but may be regarded as being of diminished weight.[273]

It is said on good authority[274] that leading questions may always be put in cross-examination. No doubt this is true so far as questions suggesting the desired answer are concerned; those that suggest the existence of unproved facts might well be disallowed, even in cross-examination, and in *R v MacDonnell*,[275] it was said that questions put to a prisoner in cross-examination ought to be put in an interrogative form: they should commence 'Did you?' and not 'You did'. The judge has a wide discretion in these matters,[276] and it is difficult to say more than that leading questions will usually be disallowed in chief, or in re-examination, although they will generally be permitted in cross-examination.[277]

---

[269] This discussion was approved in *R v Saunders* (1985) 15 ACR 115.

[270] This is, in effect, the definition in Stephen *Digest of the Law of Evidence* (12th edn) art 140, and in Australia, in the Dictionary to the Evidence (Cwth) Act 1995. The alternative is to describe questions of type (b) as improper rather than leading.

[271] *Moor v Moor* [1954] 2 All ER 458, [1954] 1 WLR 927. Caution as to relaxation in the case of child witnesses was expressed in *R v E* NZCA 404, [2008] 3 NZLR 145, [67].

[272] This may be especially acute where a prosecution witness is being examined on the basis of a witness statement suspected to have been tailored to the prosecution's requirements, as exemplified in Canada in *R v Rose* (2001) 153 CCC3d 225.   [273] Ibid; *Gabrielsen v Farmer* [1960] NZLR 832, 834.

[274] *Parkin v Moon* (1836) 7 C & P 408.   [275] (1909) 2 Cr App Rep 322.

[276] *Bastin v Carew* (1824) 1 Ry & M 126.

[277] In some cases, the effective role of witnesses may vary, and the right to ask leading questions will vary accordingly: see e.g. *Peabody Donation Fund (Governors) v Sir Lindsay Parkinson* [1983] CLY 1660 (unaffected on this point by subsequent proceedings); in Australia, *Rawcliffe v R* [2000] WASCA 239, (2000) 22 WAR 490.

Refreshing memory

Traditionally, a most important feature of an English trial, civil or criminal, has been its 'orality'. Much greater weight has been attached to the answers given by witnesses in court on oath or affirmation than to written statements previously made by them. This position has been sapped by legislative encroachment. All previous statements of witnesses, whether made orally or in writing, are now admissible, with the leave of the court, as evidence of the facts stated in civil cases under the Civil Evidence Act 1995;[278] some persistence of faith in orality is shown by the fact that the Act still requires the leave of the court[279] to put in a previous statement[280] made by a witness who is called to testify. Preference for orality has been even stronger in criminal cases,[281] and was invoked to water down the originally radical proposals to admit documentary hearsay proposed by the Roskill Committee;[282] similar considerations motivated the Law Commission to reject the general admissibility of previous statements in criminal proceedings as in civil.[283] The Criminal Justice Act 2003 largely accepts these recommendations, and seeks to clarify and expand the situations in which previous statements are admitted as evidence of their truth. It takes a generally relaxed view of the use of previous statements to refresh the memory of a testifying witness.[284]

Out of court

For all its apparent orality, an examination in chief is rarely conducted 'out of the blue'. The witness has usually given a statement (commonly called his 'proof of evidence') to the solicitor for the party calling him or, if he is a prosecution witness in a criminal case, he will have made a signed statement to the police. It is on the basis of these documents that the questions put to the witness in chief will be framed. The statement will frequently have been made a considerable time before the trial, and the witness may or may not have retained a copy of it. In these circumstances, it is inevitable and desirable that the witness should read his proof shortly before the hearing, or even be taken through it by the person to whom it was made. If it were to transpire that there had been anything in the nature of 'coaching' by such person, or some kind of pre-trial confabulation between the witnesses,[285] the judge should inform the jury, and condemn the practice, even though in exceptional circumstances, despite being weakened, the evidence might remain admissible.[286] It was, however, once suggested that it is objectionable for prosecution witnesses to be provided with copies of their statements to the police, to be read or gone through shortly before the trial,[287] but it would have been difficult to justify or enforce a special rule for this particular case, and, if the statement were an elaborate one the rule would

---

[278] Subject only to the notice and competence requirements of ss 1 and 5. See further, 587.

[279] S 6(2)(a), or to rebut a suggestion of fabrication, s 6(2)(b).   [280] See also CPR 32.5.

[281] The reasons for this were eloquently elaborated by the High Court of Australia in *Butera v DPP* (1987) 164 CLR 180, 189.

[282] Report of the Departmental Inquiry on Fraud Trials (1986).

[283] Law Com 245 *Evidence in Criminal Proceedings: Hearsay and Related Topics* (Cm 3670, 1997), [10.34].   [284] S 120(3). See further, 297.

[285] See Stephenson [1990] *Crim LR* 302.

[286] *R v Arif* (1993) The Times, 17 June; *R v Skinner* (1993) 99 Cr App Rep 212.

[287] *R v Yellow and Thay* (1932) 96 JP 826.

have been absurd. The practice has since been held to be perfectly proper,[288] although it is desirable for the defence to be notified of what has taken place.[289] The defence is free to cross-examine on a document[290] used in this way, just as if refreshment had taken place in court.[291] No other conditions concerning the documents that may be used to refresh memory out of court have been laid down.[292]

In court

The conditions for refreshment of memory in criminal proceedings are set out in s 139(1) of the Criminal Justice Act 2003:[293]

> (1) A person giving oral evidence in criminal proceedings about any matter may, at any stage in the course of doing so, refresh his memory of it from a document made or verified by him at an earlier time if—
> (a) he states in his oral evidence that the document records his recollection of the matter at that earlier time, and
> (b) his recollection of the matter is likely to have been significantly better at that time than it is at the time of his oral evidence.

The statutory relaxation of the hearsay rule in both civil and criminal proceedings has had a dramatic effect on the status of documents so used. Different considerations apply, however, according to whether the refreshing document was or was not made by the testifying witness himself.

Made by witness

Where the memory-refreshing document was made by the witness himself, it will be admissible as evidence of its truth in civil proceedings with the leave of the court.[294] In criminal proceedings, the conditions are specified in the Criminal Justice Act 2003, s 120:[295]

> (3) A statement made by a witness in a document—
> (a) which is used by him to refresh his memory while giving evidence,
> (b) on which he is cross-examined, and
> (c) which as a consequence is received in evidence in the proceedings,
>
> is admissible as evidence of any matter stated of which oral evidence by him would be admissible.

---

[288] *R v Richardson* [1971] 2 QB 484, [1971] 2 All ER 773. Nor need the judge give any special direction to the jury: *Rooke v Auckland City Council* [1980] 1 NZLR 680. For criticism, see Howard [1972] *Crim LR* 351.

[289] *Worley v Bentley* [1976] 2 All ER 449; *R v Westwell* [1976] 2 All ER 812. It is still more desirable for such refreshment to take place in court wherever feasible: *R v Tyagi* (1986) The Times, 21 July.

[290] Even those otherwise subject to legal professional privilege: *Mancorp Pty Ltd v Baulderstone Pty Ltd* (1991) 57 SASR 87 (in which many English authorities are considered).

[291] *Owen v Edwards* (1983) 77 Cr App Rep 191. But not in Scotland: *Hinshelwood v Auld* 1926 JC 4; *Deb v Normand* 1996 SCCR 766. See also *Mather v Morgan* [1971] Tas SR 192; *R v Pachonick* [1973] 2 NSWLR 86; *R v Kingston* [1986] 2 Qd R 114.

[292] Thus no question was even raised in *R v South Ribble Magistrates, ex p Cochrane* [1996] 2 Cr App Rep 544 about such a document needing to be contemporaneous.

[293] S 139(2) applies a similar approach to transcripts of sound recordings.

[294] Evidence Act 1995, s 6(2)(a).

[295] It was said in *R v Pashmfouroush* [2006] EWCA Crim 2330, [25] that the effect of cross-examination on such a statement remains governed by the old common law rules.

(4) A previous statement by the witness is admissible as evidence of any matter stated of which oral evidence by him would be admissible, if—

(a) any of the following three conditions is satisfied, and

(b) while giving evidence the witness indicates that to the best of his belief he made the statement, and that to the best of his belief it states the truth.

...

(6) The second condition is that the statement was made by the witness when the matters stated were fresh in his memory but he does not remember them, and cannot reasonably be expected to remember them, well enough to give evidence of them in the proceedings.

Little change seems to have been intended to the circumstances in which refreshment of memory has hitherto been permitted, including the more relaxed modern view of freshness,[296] as elaborated in the first two conditions set out in *R v Da Silva*:[297]

(1)...the witness indicates that he cannot now recall the details of events because of the lapse of time since they took place, (2) that he made a statement much nearer the time of the events and that the contents of the statement represented his recollection at the time he made it...

It is, however, possible, now such a statement in a document is to become evidence of the truth of its contents, that the rather casual attitude to refreshment by reference to copies of original documents[298] will be reconsidered.[299]

CJA 2003, s 120(3) appears to be intended to preserve the common law rule that, where cross-examination on a document used to refresh memory strays outside the part so used, the testifying witness may require the whole of the document[300] to be put in evidence. It is drafted widely enough to allow the admission into evidence of documents used to refresh memory and subjected to cross-examination on the basis that they were concoctions.[301] So the common law condition, that the cross-examination be on a part not relied upon, no longer seems to apply.

It may be remarked here that the condition in s 120(4)(b)[302] seems oddly phrased. If a witness is unable to remember particular details, it is very hard to see how he can conscientiously affirm that he believes to be true a statement of the very details he can no longer remember. Perhaps the solution lies in the different terminology of s 139, under which

---

[296] In *R v McAfee* [2006] EWCA Crim 2330, [35] a delay of four-and-a-half months in compiling the statement from which memory was refreshed was allowed, although in Australia, the same phrase in s 66 of the Evidence Act (Cwth) 1995 has been interpreted as relating to temporality rather than vividness, and was said in *Graham v R* [1998] HCA 1, (1998) 195 CLR 606 to be likely to be measured in hours and days rather than years. See also *Papakosmas v R* [1999] HCA 37, (1999) 196 CLR 297. In Canada in *R v Duong* (2007) 217 CCC3d 143 refreshment seems to have waxed and waned during the trial.

[297] [1990] 1 All ER 29, 33c.

[298] See *Horne v MacKenzie* (1839) 6 Cl & Fin 628; *Topham v M'Gregor* (1844) 1 Car & Kir 320; *R v Cheng* (1976) 63 Cr App Rep 20; *A-G's Reference (No 3 of 1979)* (1979) 69 Cr App Rep 411.

[299] In *R v Fliss* [2002] SCC 16, [2002] 1 SCR 535, the Supreme Court of Canada held that it would not bring the administration of justice into disrepute to allow a police witness to refresh his memory of the accused's confession from a transcript of a tape recording that would itself have been inadmissible as unauthorized, even though he was unable to recall any of the detail without such refreshment.

[300] The explanatory note to this section seems to be in error in referring to the 'statement' rather than to the 'document' being put in evidence in this situation.

[301] As in *R v Sekhon* (1987) 85 Cr App Rep 19.

[302] Which applies also to statements identifying or describing persons objects or places, and to complaints of the commission of offences.

the witness need testify only that the document containing the statement was made at an earlier time, and that such earlier recollection is more likely to be accurate than his current one. In those circumstances, the statement here can be argued to be equivalent to an assertion that he has no reason to believe the statement to be false, although it is submitted that it would have been clearer to have used some such phrase.

Made by another

It has never been necessary that the memory-refreshing document should originally have been made by the witness,[303] and the common law made such a document capable of becoming evidence in the case when cross-examination upon it took place outside the parts referred to by the testifying witness;[304] the effect of this rule was explicitly preserved in the Evidence Act 1995, s 6(4). There is no comparable explicit provision in the Criminal Justice Act 2003.[305] This could create some difficulty in view of the explicit abolition by s 118(2) of all of the common law rules governing the admissibility[306] of hearsay, apart from those preserved by the section. It might, however, be argued that this rule is unaffected by that provision on the basis that it is not a rule governing the admissibility of hearsay. This would accord with the status of such a document at common law where although evidence in the case, it was not to be used for the truth of its contents, but merely to support the oral evidence of the witness made after refreshing his memory.[307] The retention of such a result would, however, run counter to the general simplifying thrust of this statutory reform of the hearsay rule, and would result in an anomaly with the situation in which the document is made by the testifying witness. It is submitted that the best solution is to admit such a statement for its truth,[308] either under the general provisions for the hearsay evidence of unavailable witnesses,[309] or, if for some reason or another those conditions cannot be satisfied, then under the residual discretion in s 114(1)(d).

There now seems even stronger reason to retain the rule that any document used to refresh memory should be handed to the opposite party for inspection with a view to cross-examination,[310] and to be made available to the jury.[311]

PREVIOUS CONSISTENT STATEMENTS

The general rule at common law[312] was that a witness could not be asked in chief[313] whether he had formerly made a statement consistent with his present testimony. He could not

---

[303] *Dyer v Best* (1866) 4 H & C 189. Although the witness must have checked it while the facts were still fresh in his mind: *R v Eleftheriou and Eleftheriou* [1993] Crim LR 947.

[304] *Gregory v Tavernor* (1833) 6 C & P 280. It has been held to apply just as much to documents used to refresh memory out of court: *Owen v Edwards* (n291). See also *R v Kingston* [1986] 2 Qd R 114.

[305] Despite the express reference in s 139(1) to the possibility of using the statement of another if verified by the witness at the time. [306] Not limited to rules of inadmissibility.

[307] *R v Virgo* (1978) 67 Cr App Rep 323. [308] When appropriate.

[309] S 116. See further below Chapter XIV. [310] *Beech v Jones* (1848) 5 CB 696.

[311] *R v Bass* [1953] 1 QB 680, [1953] 1 All ER 1064; *R v Fenlon and Neal* (1980) 71 Cr App Rep 307312.

[312] This statement of the common law was explicitly adopted in *R v Gregson* [2003] EWCA Crim 1099, [2003] 2 Cr App Rep 521, [20].

[313] Nor as a general rule in cross-examination where the witness is not adverse to the cross-examiner: *R v Evans and Caffrey* [2001] EWCA Civ 730.

narrate such statement[314] if it was oral, or refer to it if it was in writing (save for the purpose of refreshing his memory), and other witnesses could not be called to prove it.[315] The rule against hearsay as defined here prohibited the reception of the statement as evidence of the facts stated, but there was an independent common law ban on proof of the previous oral or written statements of the witness as evidence of his consistency.[316]

In this case, the reason given for the ban (sometimes loosely described as 'the rule against narrative' or 'the rule against self-corroboration') was the ease with which evidence of this nature can be manufactured.[317] But, generally speaking, this can be apposite only when the witness is a party and the ease with which evidence can be fabricated is a matter that should affect only its weight. A more convincing reason is that, in an ordinary case, the evidence would be superfluous, for the assertions of a witness are to be regarded in general as true, until there is some particular reason for impeaching them as false.[318] The necessity of saving time by avoiding superfluous testimony and sparing the court a protracted inquiry into a multitude of collateral issues that might be raised about such matters, as the precise terms of the previous statement seems sound.[319] This is why the leave of the court is required for the admission of such statements in civil cases, and in criminal proceedings, the Criminal Justice Act 2003, s 126(1)(b) bestows a new discretion to exclude out-of-court statements where 'the undue waste of time, substantially outweighs the case for admitting it, taking account of the weight of the evidence'. The Criminal Justice Act 2003 also differs from the Civil Evidence Act 1995 by specifying a number of situations in which previous statements may be received.[320] These largely correspond, although sometimes with important changes, to situations in which such statements were admissible to show consistency at common law. Unless such an exception applies, the reception of these statements may cause such prejudice as to cause a conviction to be quashed.[321] That dealing with refreshing memory has already been mentioned, and to the extent that it is not wholly an exception to the hearsay rule, that dealing with res gestae statements will be considered

---

314 The rule probably did not apply to the tendering of real evidence, such as an offer to supply tissue for DNA testing, as in *R v B (SC)* (1997) 119 CCC3d 530.

315 The two preceding statements were adopted as an accurate statement of the law by the Privy Council in *White v R* [1999] 1 AC 210.

316 For this reason, the Civil Evidence Act 1995 not only abolished the hearsay rule in s 1, but also made separate provision for the admission of previous statements in s 6; a precedent followed by the Criminal Justice Act 2003, Pt 11, c 2, which makes its general provision in s 114, but contains a separate s 120 dealing with previous statements of witnesses. See also in Scotland, Civil Evidence (Scotland) Act 1988, ss 2, 3. In Canada, it has also been held that a party may not adduce in chief previous inconsistent statements of his witness together with reasons for resiling from such statements as a means of bolstering the witness: *R v Pinkus* (1999) 140 CCC3d 309.

317 191, Humphreys J. See too Swinfen-Eady LJ in *Jones v South Eastern and Chatham Rly Co's Managing Committee* (1918) 87 LJKB 775, 778.   318 *Pothier on Obligations* (1806 edn) vol 2, 289.

319 This reason was explicitly approved by the Law Commission in Law Com No 245 *Evidence in Criminal Proceedings: Hearsay and Related Topics* (Cm 3670, 1997) [10.12]. See also 'Generally speaking, as is well known, such confirmatory evidence is not admissible, the reason presumably being that all trials, civil and criminal, must be conducted with an effort to concentrate evidence on what is capable of being cogent': Lord Radcliffe in *Fox v General Medical Council* [1960] 3 All ER 225, 230.

320 And may only be received unless all parties agree, or the inclusionary discretion of s 114(1)(d) of the Criminal Justice Act 2003 is applied. Any issue of the survival of the common law after the passage of the 2003 Act was categorized as 'arid' in *R v Openshaw* [2006] EWCA Crim 556, [2006] 2 Cr App Rep 405, [18].

321 See *R v B* [2003] EWCA Crim 1204, in which a complainant in a sexual abuse case wrote a letter to herself describing the incident, but it could be brought within none of the accepted exceptions.

in Chapter XII. Some mention will be made of the other specific provisions, dealing with evidence of complaints, previous statements to rebut suggestions of fabrication, those of identification and description, and the position with regard to statements made to the police upon being taxed with an offence, and finally of the attitude of the law of evidence towards statements induced by special means adopted in an effort to ensure truth, such as the administration of a 'truth drug' or hypnosis.

Complaints[322]

An ancient common law rule required evidence that the victim should have raised 'hue and cry' at the time, if her appeal of rape were to succeed. This rule was elaborated over the years, and extended to other sexual offences[323] and to male complainants.[324] It became an extremely technical rule,[325] was widely regarded as anomalous[326] and unsatisfactory,[327] and was abrogated in some common law jurisdictions.[328]

The Criminal Justice Act 2003, accepting the view that sexual cases should be tried so far as possible in the same way as others, has instead broadened the reception of complaints to embrace the whole range of offences. As set out above,[329] previous statements of witnesses affirmed as true[330] are permitted in three situations,[331] of which the third is set out in s 120:[332]

(7) The third condition is that—
    (a) the witness claims to be a person against whom an offence has been committed,
    (b) the offence is one to which the proceedings relate,
    (c) the statement consists of a complaint made by the witness (whether to a person in authority or not) about conduct which would, if proved, constitute the offence or part of the offence,
    (d) the complaint was made as soon as could reasonably be expected after the alleged conduct,
    (e) the complaint was not made as a result of a threat or a promise, and (f) before the statement is adduced the witness gives oral evidence in connection with the subject matter.

(8) For the purposes of subsection (7) the fact that the complaint was elicited (for example by a leading question) is irrelevant unless a threat of promise was involved.

---

[322] See further Lewis (2006) 10 E&P 104.

[323] Or perhaps limited to them, since hue and cry was required in ancient times in all appeals of felony.

[324] *Chesney v Newsholme* [1908] P 301; *R v Camelleri* [1922] 2 KB 122.

[325] See *R v Osborne* [1905] 1 KB 551.   [326] See *R v Newsome* (1980) 71 Cr App Rep 325.

[327] In *Commonwealth v Cleary* (1898) 172 Mass 175, Justice Holmes described it as 'a perverted survival'; in *R v H* [1997] 1 NZLR 673, 697, it was described as 'indefensible and its continued application unconscionable'.   [328] For example, Canadian Criminal Code, s 275.

[329] 298.

[330] If a complaint is inconsistent with the prosecution case, it may be admissible as part of the events, but not then under this exception as a recent complaint: see *R v Kennedy* [2004] EWCA Crim 374, [26].

[331] It should be noted that in *R v Xhabri* [2005] EWCA Crim 3135, [2006] 1 All ER 776, [36], despite finding these conditions satisfied, the Lord Chief Justice was prepared to admit a complaint under the inclusionary discretion in s 114(1)(d) even if they had not been.

[332] In *R v Openshaw* (n320), [24] the Court of Appeal stressed that the provisions of s 120(7) are new and freestanding, and not in principle to be interpreted so as to comply with the old law so far as possible. For construction of similar provisions in New Zealand see *R v Barlieu* [2008] NZCA 180, [2009] 1 NZLR 170.

Four questions remain: what is to count as a 'complaint'; how soon must it be made; to what extent need it be spontaneous; how should the jury be directed?

Nature

This has rarely caused difficulty,[333] although some statements were rejected under the old law as 'conversation'[334] or 'narrative'.[335] It is not decisive that the complaint is denied by the person to whom it is alleged to have been made,[336] or even by the complainant by the time of trial.[337] To some extent, s 120(8) is apt to amend the old common law on this point, on which it was sometimes held[338] that an affirmative reply to a leading question disqualified the answer from being a complaint.

Contemporaneity

Under the old law, where the complaint always related to a sexual offence,[339] a certain amount of delay until a suitable recipient was encountered was accepted,[340] The phrase 'as soon as could be reasonably expected' had indeed been used to express the position at common law.[341] Sometimes contemporaneity is critical to weight, and in such a case, a particularly careful direction to the jury may be required.[342] Subsequent complaints are admissible, but might be excluded as a matter of discretion if they have no additional significance from the first.[343] It seems likely that, as in Australia,[344] the trial judge's assessment of this issue will be accorded considerable weight.

Spontaneity

In explanation of the ruling in *R v Osborne*, it was in *R v Norcott* affirmed that:[345]

The court is concerned to see that in the present case the statement made by the girl was spontaneous in the sense that it was her unassisted and unvarnished statement of what happened.

In its rejection of statements made as a result of a threat[346] or promise, but its tolerance of leading questions, the Criminal Justice Act 2003 appears to have adopted this approach.[347]

---

[333] In *R v G* [2004] EWCA Crim 3022, the court dismissed any suggestion that the complaint was so recent as to amount to part of the facts of the offence. It is possible that some evidence relevant to the existence of a complaint may be too prejudicial to the accused to be admitted, as in *R v Mustafa* [2005] SASC 66, 151 ACR 580.

[334] *R v Merry* (1900) 19 Cox CC 442.

[335] *De B v De B* [1950] VLR 242; but see *R v Robertson* [1991] 1 Qd R 262, 276.

[336] As in *R v Lee* (1911) 7 Cr App Rep 11.

[337] As in *R v Walker* [2001] 2 NZLR 289, but cf *McDonald v HM Adv* 2004 SCCR 100, 2003 GWD 40–1074; this situation will clearly arise more often under the new law where it is not limited to showing consistency.

[338] As in *R v Osborne* (n325).

[339] There may be more difficulty when a continuing series of offences extending over a considerable period is alleged, as in *R v S* [2004] EWCA Crim 1320, [2004] 3 All ER 689; *R v HG* [2007] VSCA 55, 171 ACR 55 (exacerbated by unspecificity).

[340] See *R v Valentine* [1996] 2 Cr App Rep 213. But delay in complaining to such a person once encountered has been criticized: *R v Peake* (1974) 9 SASR 458 (although not there decisively).

[341] In *R v Lillyman* [1896] 2 QB 167, 171; but it had been restrictively interpreted: *R v Birks* [2002] EWCA Crim 3091, [2003] 2 Cr App Rep 122.   [342] *R v Hartley* [2003] EWCA Crim 3027.

[343] *Openshaw* (n320), [23].   [344] *R v M* [2000] QCA 20, (2000) 109 ACR 530.

[345] [1917] 1 KB 347, 350.   [346] For an example, see *S v T* 1963 (1) SA 484 (A).

[347] In the official note to this provision, the requirement is described as being that the complaint should be 'voluntary'.

There is no reason to suppose that, as in Australia,[348] a letter of complaint would not be sufficiently spontaneous.[349]

Direction

Under the old law, the judge was faced in these cases with the difficult task of directing the jury to regard an admissible complaint as indicating the consistency of the witness without its being used either as proof of the truth of its contents, or even as corroboration of them.[350] Given the rationale for such admission being the expectation that such a complaint would be made, questions were also raised as to the appropriate direction when there was no such complaint, and if there were, why a false complaint should have been made. Although the former problem no longer applies, the very admission of complaints may lead to the exacerbation of difficulty in the latter respects. It is, however, submitted that there is no logical reason for according any significance to the absence of complaint, which may have any number of plausible explanations,[351] and still less to accord making one the sort of tendentious fortification of the witness's credibility mentioned above; it was nevertheless endorsed by the Court of Appeal in *R v B*.[352] The view may, however, be taken that, if the jury is likely to reason in this way, it should be given some direction as to its legitimacy when appropriate.[353]

It is in any event submitted that, given the statutory endorsement of the admissibility of an elicited complaint, the jury may well still, and perhaps now more often, need careful direction on any reduction in its weight as a result.[354] Where the earlier complaint is introduced at the instigation of the defence in order to demonstrate inconsistency, there is less need for a direction.[355]

Previous[356] consistent statements admitted to rebut suggestion of fabrication

Such an exception existed at common law, and has been accepted by modern statutory enactment. In civil proceedings, s 6(2) of the Civil Evidence Act 1995 provides that:

A party who has called or intends to call a person as a witness in civil proceedings may not in those proceedings adduce evidence of a previous statement made by that person, except—

(a) with the leave of the court, or

(b) for the purpose of rebutting a suggestion that his evidence had been fabricated.

---

[348] *R v S* (1998) 103 ACR 101.

[349] See the remarkably lenient admission of a very late letter to a third party under the old law in *R v NK* [1999] Crim LR 980.

[350] See *R v Croad* [2001] EWCA Crim 644.

[351] See criticism of this sort of inference by the High Court of Australia in *Kilby v R* (1973) 129 CLR 460.

[352] [2003] EWCA Crim 951, [2003] 1 WLR 2809, endorsing *R v T* [1998] 2 NZLR 257, 265, and rejecting *Palmer v R* (1998) 193 CLR 1. See also, in Canada, *R v FS* (2000) 144 CCC3d 466.

[353] See, in Australia, *Doggett v R* [2001] HCA 46, 208 CLR 343 (delay of complaint); *R v PLK* [1999] 3 VR 567 (motive to lie). It should be noted that special statutory provisions relating to such directions apply in different states in Australia (including Victoria and Western Australia).

[354] See *R v A* [2007] EWCA Crim 1779, [2007] All ER (D) (May) where the Court seems to revert to the old law in requiring a direction that the statement is not corroborative of the complainant's testimony because it is not independent.

[355] *R v JF* [2004] EWCA Crim 3156, [21].

[356] Previous to the statement alleged to have been fabricated, *R v Ellard* 2009 SCC 27.

In criminal proceedings, the Criminal Justice Act 2003, s 120(2) provides:

If a previous statement by the witness is admitted as evidence to rebut a suggestion that his oral evidence has been fabricated, that statement is admissible as evidence of any matter stated of which oral evidence by the witness would be admissible.

In both cases, the principal change is that a statement so admitted is now accepted for the proof of its contents. No alteration seems to have been intended by the Law Commission to the law relating to the conditions of the admission of such a statement, but in *R v Athwal*[357] the Court of Appeal took the view that the prior issue of admissibility must now also be governed by the new statutory provisions. In civil proceedings where the basic rule is of the admissibility of hearsay, there is no problem; in criminal proceedings where statutory provision is required,[358] it is to be found in the inclusionary discretion of s 114(1)(d). This then requires further reference to the conditions mentioned in s 114(2), and in *R v Athwal* while noting that s 120(2) makes no reference to fabrication being recent, the Court of Appeal said:[359]

The mere fact that the witness has said substantially the same thing on a previous occasion will not generally be a sufficient basis to adduce the previous statement when the truthfulness of his evidence is put in issue. There must be something more—for example, the absence on the earlier occasion of a factor, say personal dislike, which is being advanced as a possible explanation for the falsity of his evidence in court. However, when circumstances have changed in such a way, it may not matter that they changed last week, last month or last year, provided that there is a qualitative difference in circumstances, but substantial similarity between the two accounts. There is no margin in the length of time. The touchstone is whether the evidence may fairly assist the jury in ascertaining where the truth lies. It is for the trial judge to preserve the balance of fairness and to ensure that unjustified excursions into self-corroboration are not permitted, whether the witness was called by the prosecution or the defence.

The question whether a situation has arisen in which a previous statement may be proved under this head is, both in civil and criminal cases, largely a matter for the judge's decision. It is difficult to improve on the following observations of Dixon CJ:[360]

In as much as the rule forms a definite exception to the general principle excluding statements made out of Court and admits a possibly self-serving statement made by the witness, great care is called for in applying it. The judge at the trial must determine for himself, upon the conduct of the trial before him, whether a case for applying the rule of evidence has arisen—and must exercise care in assuring himself not only that the account given by the witness in his testimony is attacked on the ground of recent invention or reconstruction or that a foundation for such an attack has been laid—but also that the contents of the statement are in fact to the like effect as his account given in his evidence and that having regard to the time and circumstances in which it was made it rationally tends to answer the attack.

---

[357] [2009] EWCA Crim 789, [55].   [358] By s 114 of the Criminal Justice Act 2003.

[359] [58]. For the position elsewhere, see *Coyle v HM Adv* 1994 JC 239 (Scotland); *Flanagan v Fahy* [1918] 2 IR 361 (Eire); *Tome v United States* 513 US 150 (1995) (United States); *R v Stirling* 2008 SCC 10, [2008] 1 SCR 272 (Canada); *R v Fraser* (1995) 65 SASR 260, 85 ACR 385 (Australia).

[360] *Nominal Defendant v Clements* (1960) 104 CLR 476, 479. This statement was itself cited in *(R v Athwal*, [39].

The rationale of the exception requires that there be independent evidence of the statement's having been made.[361] Generally speaking, the previous statement will be put to the witness in re-examination,[362] but circumstances are conceivable in which he would be asked about it in chief. This might be done when the cross-examination of a previous witness had contained a suggestion of fabrication by himself and the succeeding witness, or at a criminal trial when something of the sort had been suggested at the proceedings before the magistrates.

Identification[363]

Although previous statements identifying persons, and especially the accused, have been admitted from time immemorial,[364] some difficulty was experienced in admitting components of identity, such as the race of the criminal,[365] and photofit representations,[366] or sketches derived from descriptions.[367] Still more difficulty was experienced in relation to the identification of objects, and in particular, identification by quickly forgotten details such as the registration numbers of cars.[368]

For this reason, the Criminal Justice Act 2003, s 120(5) makes the previous statement of a witness identifying or describing a person, object, or place admissible as evidence of its truth, subject only to the witness affirming having made the statement, and his current belief in its truth.[369]

Statements on arrest[370]

As explained more fully below,[371] inculpatory statements by the accused in the form of admissions or confessions have always been admitted as evidence of the truth of their contents.[372] At a later date, it became clear that, where a statement[373] was partly inculpatory and partly exculpatory, or 'mixed',[374] the exculpatory part was also admissible as

---

[361] *Pearse v Sommers* (1992) 28 NSWLR 492; but see *R v DJT* [1998] 4 VR 784, 794, in which the court refused to follow *Pearse*, holding that the statement could be proved in the absence of independent evidence, although apparently accepting that this would reduce its weight.

[362] For an illustration of the difficulty created by premature tendering, see *R v AER* (2001) 156 CCC3d 335. 　　　　　　　　　　　　　　　　　　　　　[363] See further Chapter XVI.

[364] *R v Fannon* (1922) 22 SRNSW 427, 430.

[365] Cf *Sparks v R* [1964] AC 964 (in which the identifying witness had not testified on account of incompetence).

[366] Comprising individual components: see *R v O'Brien* [1982] Crim LR 746, although finally resolved in favour of admission in *R v Cook* [1987] QB 417, [1987] 1 All ER 1049.

[367] *R v Smith* [1976] Crim LR 511, although the difficulty was resolved in favour of admission.

[368] See e.g. *Jones v Metcalfe* [1967] 3 All ER 205, [1967] 1 WLR 1286, in which Diplock LJ castigated exclusion of such evidence as absurd. 　　　　　　　　　　　　　　　　　[369] See 298.

[370] Occasionally difficult to distinguish from part of the res gestae, see in Canada *R v QD* (2005) 199 CCC3d 490, For an illuminating account, see Hall (2001) 10 *Arch News* 5. 　　　　　　[371] Chapter XIV.

[372] Subject to disproof of certain defeasing conditions, although if they apply, the whole statement including the exculpatory parts is inadmissible, *People v O'Neill* [2007] IECCA 8, [2007] 4 IR 564. They may occasionally be relevant for other reasons, as in *R v Edgar* (2000) 142 CCC3d 401 (to establish accused's disturbed mental state at time of arrest).

[373] The same rules govern re-enactments, *Mahmood v Western Australia* [2008] HCA 1, 232 CLR 397.

[374] This classification depends upon the circumstances of the case, and is sometimes difficult to determine: see e.g. *R v Tozer* [2002] 1 NZLR 193. Such determination is to be made by the judge, *McGirr v HM Adv* [2007] HCJAC 7.

evidence of its truth.[375] This could lead to the anomalous situation of the accused's arguing that part of such a statement were adverse.[376] This has required a restrictive interpretation of 'adverse' in this context.[377] *R v Finch*[378] canvassed, but did not decide, the difficult issue of when there is one mixed statement, or the conjunction of two discrete statements, one inculpatory and one exculpatory. It is submitted that this should depend upon whether the exculpatory part is necessary to understand the extent of the inculpatory part.

Even wholly exculpatory statements made by the accused when taxed with a crime were, however, also admitted:[379]

A statement made voluntarily by an accused person to the police is evidence in the trial because of its vital relevance as showing the reaction of the accused when first taxed with incriminating facts.

If an exculpatory statement has no such relevance, perhaps because it was made only after careful consideration and upon legal advice, it can now be admitted only under the inclusionary discretion in s 114(1)(d) of the Criminal Justice Act 2003 if it is in the interests of justice to do so, which will rarely be the case.[380]

Statements validated by scientific means

Wigmore once said that 'if ever there is devised a psychological test for the valuation of witnesses, the law will run to meet it'. Three possibilities that have been considered involve the use of lie detectors, truth drugs, and hypnosis. None has, in fact, been received with any enthusiasm at all. Evidence of the use of a lie detector has been rejected by the Supreme Court of Canada, whether the relevant subject testifies,[381] or chooses not to do so.[382] In *Phillion*, the accused had been given a truth drug, and the evidence of the psychiatrist who administered it was admitted at the trial. The admissibility of that evidence was not in issue before the Supreme Court, and in any event did not consist of statements of fact relevant to the issues made under the influence of the drug. That situation did, however, arise in New Zealand in *R v McKay*.[383] The evidence was rejected because it infringed the rules excluding previous consistent statements and hearsay, because it would distort the process

---

[375] Authoritatively affirmed in *R v Aziz* [1996] AC 41, [1995] 3 All ER 149, but only when the confession was adduced by the prosecution. See also, in Scotland, *McCutcheon v HM Adv* 2002 SCCR 101. In Australia, in *Middleton v R* (1998) 19 WAR 179, a majority decided that the accused could, by cross-examination of a police officer, rely upon the exculpatory parts of an earlier mixed statement, not adduced by the prosecution, which had relied upon a later, and more inculpatory, mixed statement. In Canada the jury should not be directed that the exculpatory part is likely to be less weighty than the inculpatory part, *R v Rojas* 2008 SCC 56, [2008] 3 SCR 111, [39] (explicitly departing from the English view expressed in *R v Duncan* (1981) 73 Cr App R 359, 365).

[376] As in *R v Garrod* [1997] Crim LR 445; but see the *R v Papworth and Doyle* [2007] EWCA Crim 3031, [13]–[15].   [377] *R v Papworth and Doyle* [2007] EWCA Crim 3031, [13]–[15].

[378] [2007] EWCA Crim 36, [2007] 1 WLR 1685, [12].

[379] *R v Storey* (1968) 52 Cr App Rep 334, 337. For cogent criticism of the result, see Birch [1997] *Crim LR* 416. In Canada, the court has been readier to admit such an exculpatory statement when one of the elements of the offence charged is the absence of excuse: see *R v Crossley* (1997) 117 CCC3d 533.

[380] *R v Finch* [2007] EWCA Crim 36, [2007] 1 WLR 1685, [15].   [381] *R v Béland* [1987] 2 SCR 398.

[382] *Phillion v R* [1978] 1 SCR 18, not accepting the contrary decision in *R v Wong* [1977] 1 WWR 1, but following the then majority view in the United States, stemming from *Frye v United States* 293 F 1013 (1923). 'Failure' may affect the admissibility of a subsequent confession: see *R v McIntosh* (1999) 141 CCC3d 97; *R v Oickle* 2000 SCC 38, [2000] 2 SCR 3 (although there a majority favoured admission).

[383] [1967] NZLR 139.

of trial, and because it was unreliable.[384] In Scotland, facilities for taking such a statement have been refused, once again because it would involve distortion of the trial process.[385] The evidence of statements made during, and indeed after, a hypnotic trance that had been induced, apparently inadvertently, by a police interrogator was rejected by the Supreme Court of Canada in *Horvath v R*, largely on grounds of unreliability.[386] Despite arguments[387] in favour of the admission of such statements, it is submitted that the unproven reliability of these techniques, together with the danger of the jury's attributing more weight to such unfamiliar scientific evidence than it deserves, justify the English courts in following the example of their counterparts in the rest of the common law world[388] in excluding such statements unless a convincing case can be made for their reliability, as by following Home Office guidelines.[389] Similar considerations would presumably apply to any other memory-enhancing therapy.[390]

Not only has no special provision been made for the admissibility of such statements by the Criminal Justice Act 2003, but by the operation of s 114, any such admission could only be by the operation of the inclusionary discretion, and would thus become subject to the rigour of the conditions imposed by s 114(2), including those relating to reliability.

UNFAVOURABLE AND HOSTILE WITNESSES[391]

A party calling a witness to prove certain facts may be disappointed by his failure to do so, and his difficulties may be increased by the witness's manifest antipathy to his cause. This lies at the root of the distinction between unfavourable and hostile witnesses. An unfavourable witness is one called by a party to prove a particular fact in issue or relevant to the issue who fails to prove such fact, or proves an opposite fact. A hostile witness is one who is not desirous of telling the truth at the instance of the party calling him,[392] and serious and otherwise inexplicable inconsistency, which may amount merely to an omission, between a previous statement and the oral evidence may be sufficient to demonstrate it.[393] It will be convenient to state the common law with regard to unfavourable and hostile witnesses separately, and then to mention the relevant statutory provisions—s 3 of the Criminal

---

[384] See Mathieson [1967] Crim LR 645.   [385] *Meehan (petitioner)* 1970 JC 11.

[386] [1979] 2 SCR 376. See also, in Canada, *R v Trochym* 2007 SCC 6, [2007] 1 SCR 239 (presumption of inadmissibility); in Australia, *R v Geering* (1984) 39 SASR 111 and cf *Van Vliet v Griffiths* (1978) 19 SASR 195.

[387] See e.g. Haward and Ashworth [1980] *Crim LR* 469, and Harnon [1982] *Crim LR* 340. For an excellent exposition of the problems, see Elliott in Campbell and Waller (eds) *Well and Truly Tried* (1982), and, from a psychological standpoint, Gudjonsson *The Psychology of Interrogations, Confessions and Testimony* (1993).

[388] Although, in Tasmania, doubts have been aired as to the need to adopt so strict a view: *R v Roughley* (1995) 5 Tas 8; *R v Sparkes* (5 March 1998, unreported), Tas CCA.

[389] *R v Mayes and McIntosh* [1995] CLY 930, although disclosure of a defective session arriving at inconsistent conclusions from the testimony of the witness was regarded as a material irregularity in *R v Browning* [1995] Crim LR 227 (in which the Home Office guidelines are conveniently summarized). See *R v McFelin* [1985] 2 NZLR 750; *R v Jenkyns* (1993) 32 NSWLR 712 for safeguards elsewhere.

[390] See *R v Tillott* (1995) 38 NSWLR 1 (EMDR, which can have this effect) in which many different codes and guidelines for the forensic use of hypnosis are discussed. In *R v JAT* (1998) 103 ACR 345, such evidence was held admissible despite failure to meet one of the conditions set out in the California guidelines (accurate recording of the memory prior to the therapy).   [391] See Pattenden (1992) 56 *J Cr L* 414.

[392] Stephen *Digest of the Law of Evidence* (12th edn) art 147; endorsed in *R v Pryce* (1988) 86 Cr App Rep 111, and further approved in *R v Jobe* [2004] EWCA 3155, [65]. See also Pattenden (n391), in which a broader definition is suggested, allowing both for animus against the party calling the witness and absence of desire to tell the truth as alternatives.   [393] *R v Jobe* (n392), [68].

Procedure Act 1865, s 6 of the Civil Evidence Act 1995, and s 119 of the Criminal Justice Act 2003—but something must first be said of the prohibition against a party impeaching his own witness.

The prohibition against impeaching a party's own witness[394]

A party against whom a witness is called may impeach him in various ways.[395] He may cross-examine him by means of leading questions, ask him about his previous inconsistent statements, and prove them if they are denied—a matter that is now covered by statute; he may cross-examine him with regard to his discreditable conduct in the past with a view to showing bad character, or he may ask the witness about his previous convictions or the existence of bias, and prove these two matters by other evidence if they are denied. Finally, a party may call evidence to show that the opponent's witness is not to be believed on oath. The prohibition against a party impeaching his own witness means that there is a general rule preventing a litigant from taking any of the above steps with regard to witnesses called by him.[396] It is for the judge to determine whether, and to what extent, a witness is unfavourable to the party calling him, and no such determination should be made before the witness has been sworn and given a chance to come up to his proof.[397] Such procedure renders a voir dire generally unnecessary[398] on this issue, although where a previous inconsistent statement is relevant to such a determination, it should not be revealed to the jury before the witness has been adjudged hostile.[399] It seems that a party may nevertheless invite the court to disregard his witness's evidence, even though it is consistent with the initial presentation of the case, and in accord with the witness's proof, if the course of the trial has indicated that the party's case would, by that stage, be better served by so disregarding the evidence.[400]

Various reasons have been given for the general rule. It is said that a party ought not to have the means of discrediting his witness, or that he guarantees the trustworthiness of the evidence he adduces, or that it would be unfair to subject the witness to two cross-examinations. None of these is very convincing, and even though the rule seems to work well enough in ordinary circumstances as applied to unfavourable witnesses, it would be ludicrous to apply it to a hostile witness in its full rigour.[401]

---

394 III Wigmore [896 f]. See also Bryant (1982) 32 *Univ of Tor LJ* 412, (1983) 33 *Univ of Tor LJ* 108.

395 Below Chapter VII.

396 Even when done under the guise of examination in chief: *R v Situ* (2005) 200 CCC (3d) 9.

397 *R v Darby* [1989] Crim LR 817; although this is a matter for the judgment of the court: see *R v Birkby* [1994] 2 NZLR 38. It may be necessary to make the determination after the witness has been cross-examined by the opponent, and before re-examination, as in *R v Ethier* (2005) 197 CCC3d 435.

398 Although permissible: see *R v Jones* [1998] Crim LR 579 (in which in contrast to the situation in relation to those apparently hostile, a potentially unfavourable witness may be asked whether the previous statement is true). In Australia, where a voir dire on this point is more common, the opposing party must be permitted to cross-examine on the point: *R v Ashton* (1999) 108 ACR 200. See also *R v Coventry* (1997) 7 Tas R 199.

399 *R v Darby* (n397). See also *Price v Bevan* (1978) 8 SASR 81; *R v Hadlow* [1992] 2 Qd R 440.

400 *Anonima Petroli Italiana SpA v Marlucidez Armadora SA (The Filiatra Legacy)* [1991] 2 Lloyd's Rep 337, 362.

401 The rule was abrogated by r 607 of the United States Federal Rules (following the Model Code and Uniform Rules), but the Criminal Law Revision Committee was in favour of its retention (11th Report, [162]).

Unfavourable witnesses[402]

At common law, a party was allowed to contradict his own witness by calling other evidence[403] if he was unfavourable, but this did not amount to a modification of the prohibition against discrediting his witness, because it did not involve resort to any of the methods mentioned at the beginning of the last section. In *Ewer v Ambrose*,[404] someone whom the defendant called to prove a partnership proved the contrary, and it was held that the defendant could rely on the testimony of other witnesses in support of the existence of the partnership. In the words of Holroyd J:

If a witness proves a case against the party calling him, the latter may show the truth by other witnesses. But it is undoubtedly true, that if a party calls a witness to prove a fact, he cannot, when he finds the witness proves the contrary, give general evidence to show that the witness was not to be believed on his oath, but he may show by other evidence that he is mistaken as to the fact which he is called to prove.

This last kind of evidence would necessarily concern the issue more directly than evidence with regard to the witness's credibility, and, in order to appreciate the enormity of the injustice that might be occasioned by rejecting it, a case may be supposed in which a party has four witnesses to support his version of the facts. If he happened to begin by calling a witness who disproved his case, he would be deprived of the testimony of the other three. If he called these before the one who disproved his case, it would have been a question for the jury upon the evidence whether they gave credit to the three or the one. The order in which the witnesses happen to be called ought not to make any difference.[405] If a party thus contradicts part of the testimony of an unfavourable witness, he is not precluded from relying on the rest of that testimony.

Hostile witnesses[406]

The judge may allow the examination in chief of a hostile witness to be conducted in the manner of a cross-examination, to the extent to which he considers it necessary for the purpose of doing justice.[407] If the witness is not compellable, the possibility of being cross-examined as a hostile witness should be explained before the witness is sworn.[408] The witness may be asked leading questions, challenged with regard to his means of knowledge of the facts to which he is deposing, or tested on such matters as the accuracy of his memory and perception; the party by whom he is called cannot ask about his previous bad

---

[402] 'Unfavourable' is used in this sense also in s 38 of the Evidence Act (Cwth) 1995: *R v Souleyman* (1996) 40 NSWLR 712.

[403] If the original evidence takes the form of an interrogatory the conflicting testimony may even come from the very same witness: see *Mundy v Bridge Motors Pty Ltd* (1987) 45 SASR 125.

[404] (1825) 3 B & C 746. If the prosecution calls a witness to identify the accused and he fails to do so, he is not contradicted by evidence that he did identify the accused given by a police officer who saw him do so at a parade: *R v Osborne and Virtue* [1973] QB 678, [1973] 1 All ER 649; although the officer's evidence gives rise to hearsay problems not as yet fully considered in the English cases.

[405] This is the basis of the judgment of Littledale J in *Ewer v Ambrose* (1825) 3 B & C 746 . See also *Bradley v Ricardo* (1831) 8 Bing 57. For a modern Australian example, see *Graham v Police* [2001] SASC 93, (2001) 122 ACR 152.

[406] This procedure has survived the passage of s 119 of the Criminal Justice Act 2003, *R v Gibbons* [2008] EWCA Crim 1574, [11].   [407] *Bastin v Carew* (n276).

[408] *R v Pitt* [1983] QB 25, [1982] 3 All ER 63, although failure to do so is not necessarily fatal: *R v Nelson* [1992] Crim LR 653.

conduct and convictions, nor can he adduce evidence of the witness's doubtful veracity. This is the result of the common law, but it used not to be clear whether a statement inconsistent with his present testimony could be proved against a hostile witness—a matter that became increasingly important with the growth of the practice among attorneys of taking a proof of the evidence that a person was prepared to give.[409] As Erle CJ observed:[410]

There are treacherous witnesses who will hold out that they can prove facts on one side in a cause and then, for a bribe or for some other motive, make statements in support of the opposite interest. In such cases the law undoubtedly ought to permit the party calling the witness to question him as to the former statement, and ascertain, if possible, what induces him to change it.

In *R v Fraser and Warren*,[411] Lord Goddard CJ said that if, in a criminal case, counsel for the prosecution has a statement contradicting a Crown witness who says, at the trial, that he is unable to identify the accused, he should at once show the statement to the judge and ask for leave to cross-examine the witness, but it is doubtful whether the mere existence of an inconsistency between a witness's previous statement and his testimony at the trial will necessarily lead the judge to allow the witness to be treated as hostile. In a civil case, the mere fact that the witness is the other litigant does not mean that he may be treated as hostile.[412] Although the matter has been much more fully discussed in the Commonwealth than in this country, there seems to be no doubt that, in deciding whether to allow the witness to be treated as hostile, the judge may have regard to the witness's demeanour, the terms of any inconsistent statement, and the circumstances in which it was made.[413] As the matter is largely dependent on assessment of fact, the judge's decision will seldom be reversed by an appellate tribunal.[414]

Now that such a statement is admissible for the truth of its contents, it is perhaps more likely that an English court will accept the idea of calling a witness known to be hostile[415] for the sole purposes of cross-examining by reference to such a previous inconsistent statement.[416] In *R v Mohamed Khan*[417] this possibility was regarded as a good reason for

---

[409] See, for example, the difference of opinion in *Wright v Beckett* (1834) 1 Mood & R 414.

[410] *Melhuish v Collier* (1850) 15 QB 878, 890.

[411] (1956) 40 Cr App Rep 160. See also *R v Pitt* [1983] QB 25, [1982] 3 All ER 63; *R v Mann* (1972) 56 Cr App Rep 750.   [412] *Price v Manning* (1889) 42 Ch D 372.

[413] *The People v Hannigan* [1941] IR 252; *R v Hunter* [1956] VLR 31 (citing *R v Harris* (1927) 20 Cr App Rep 144, 146 and doubting whether *Coles v Coles and Brown* (1866) LR 1 P & D 70 supports the view that demeanour alone can be considered); *R v Hayden and Slattery* [1959] VLR 102; *McLellan v Bowyer* (1962) 106 CLR 94; *Wawanesa Mutual Insurance Co v Hanes* (1961) 28 DLR (2d) 386.

[414] *Rice v Howard* (1886) 16 QBD 681. In a sufficiently strong case, a new trial could be ordered by an appellate tribunal (see the review of the authorities by the High Court of Australia in *McLellan v Bowyer* (n413)).

[415] The prosecution should not normally call a witness it regards as unreliable: *R v Russell Jones* [1995] 1 Cr App Rep 538; but see *R v Jobe* (n392) in which the witness was believed to be likely to be favourable to the prosecution in some respects, although known to be a friend of the accused.

[416] See a similar change in approach in the light of rather less apt legislation in Australia: *R v Adam* [2001] HCA 57, 207 CLR 96. Even before the change, the practice was sometimes allowed in England: see *R v Honeyghon and Sayles* [1999] Crim LR 221; support may be garnered from *A-G's Ref (No 1 of 2003)* [2003] EWCA Crim 1286, [2003] 2 Cr App Rep 453, [19], although, in *R v Smith* [2003] EWCA Crim 1240, [23–24], it was said that the prosecution should not call a witness who had made two previous inconsistent statements, with a view to cross-examining him as hostile on the one favourable to the prosecution if he should testify in the terms of the other. See generally Munday [1989] *Crim LR* 866 for general comparative discussion of the problem.

[417] [2009] EWCA Crim 86, [15]. See also *R v Olamoe* [2005] 3 NZLR 80.

disallowing the use of a hearsay statement by the defence from a witness whom they had reason to believe would be hostile in court.[418]

Where a witness has been declared hostile, the judge should direct the jury that if there is a serious conflict with the witness's oral evidence, the jury may reject it altogether.[419] It may also be necessary in a less extreme case to warn the jury about the reliability of the witness,[420] even after reversion to the original version.[421]

Statutory provision

Section 22 of the Common Law Procedure Act 1854 was passed in order to settle the law in civil cases with regard to proof of inconsistent statements by a party's own witness. As was pointed out five years later in *Greenough v Eccles*,[422] the terms of the section were confusing so far as unfavourable witnesses were concerned, but they were re-enacted in s 3 of the Criminal Procedure Act 1865.

This governs a party's right to impeach a hostile witness in civil and criminal cases alike at the present day.[423] It reads as follows:

A party producing a witness shall not be allowed to impeach his credit by general evidence of bad character, but he may, in case the witness shall, in the opinion of the judge, prove adverse, contradict him by other evidence, or, by leave of the judge, prove that he has made at other times a statement inconsistent with his present testimony; but before such last-mentioned proof can be given the circumstances of the supposed statement, sufficient to designate the particular occasion, must be mentioned to the witness, and he must be asked whether or not he has made such statement.

The prohibition on general evidence of bad character applies to hostile and unfavourable witnesses alike. This part of the section is declaratory of the common law and means that the witness cannot be asked about his bad conduct on former occasions or his previous convictions, in order that he may be discredited, while the party calling him cannot adduce evidence of his mendacious disposition.[424] In *Greenough v Eccles*, it was decided that 'adverse' means hostile, so the concluding portions of the section are unambiguous so far as the proof of such a witness's previous statements is concerned.

The section gives rise to two remaining questions—its effect on the old law concerning unfavourable and hostile witnesses, and the evidential value of the inconsistent statements that are proved or admitted under the Act.

Unfavourable witnesses

The words 'he may, in case the witness shall, in the opinion of the judge, prove adverse, contradict him by other evidence' suggest that a party cannot do this when his witness

---

[418]   More reluctance was shown in *R v C* [2007] EWCA Crim 3463, [12] in relation to calling a reconciled sexual partner as a witness for the prosecution in a case of violent assault.

[419]   *R v Middleton* [2005] EWCA Crim 692, [24] (no reference to s 119).

[420]   *R v Ugorji* [1999] 9 Arch News 3. See also *R v Maw* [1994] Crim LR 841.

[421]   *R v Greene* [2009] EWCA Crim 2282, [80].   [422]   (1859) 5 CBNS 786.

[423]   See *R v Booth* (1981) 74 Cr App Rep 123 (leave required before accused could put inconsistent statement to his own hostile witness).

[424]   See e.g. *R v Hutchison* (1990) 53 SASR 94, 95, 96; cf Pattenden, (n391).

is merely unfavourable and not, in the opinion of the judge, hostile. If this is so, the section has altered the common law as illustrated by cases such as *Ewer v Ambrose*.[425] It appears to be universally agreed that this is not the effect of the section, and, as long ago as 1859, Cockburn CJ said of the identical provision in the Common Law Procedure Act 1854:[426]

There has been a great blunder in the drawing of it, and on the part of those who adopted it...Perhaps the better course is to consider the second part of the section as altogether superfluous and useless.

The alternative, and probably the sounder method, of ignoring the implications of the section is that adopted by Williams and Willes JJ:[427]

We think the preferable construction is, that in case the witness shall, in the opinion of the judge, prove 'hostile', the party producing him may not only contradict him by other witnesses, as he might heretofore have done, and may still do, if the witness is unfavourable, but may also, by leave of the judge, prove that he has made inconsistent statements.

Whatever means may be adopted in order to reach it, the conclusion is that an unfavourable witness can be contradicted with regard to facts in issue or relevant to the issue, but he cannot be cross-examined or discredited in any other way.

Hostile witnesses

Section 3 of the 1865 Act has not affected the common law according to which the judge has a discretion to allow a hostile witness to be examined by means of leading questions or with reference to a previous statement,[428] for this does not amount to impeachment of credit 'by general evidence of bad character'. In *R v Thompson*,[429] the accused was convicted of incest with his daughter who was called as a witness by the prosecution. After answering some formal questions, she said that she did not wish to give evidence. The judge allowed her to be treated as hostile, with the result that she was examined on a statement she had made to the police and by means of leading questions. The Court of Appeal held that the judge had acted properly and affirmed the conviction. The witness did not deny making the statement to the police but, even if she had done so, it is doubtful whether s 3 would have applied to the case, for the girl's statement was not 'inconsistent with her present testimony'. If the section does not apply in such circumstances, it is questionable whether the statement can be proved,[430] unless the refusal to testify further were on account of fear.[431]

---

[425] (n405).   [426] *Greenough v Eccles* (1859) 5 CBNS 786, 28 LJCP 160, 806.

[427] The quotation is from 28 *LJCP* 160, 163.

[428] *Clarke v Saffery* (1824) Ry & M 126; *Bastin v Carew* (n276).

[429] (1976) 64 Cr App Rep 96. See also *R v Lawrie* [1986] Qd R 502; *R v Hadlow* [1992] 2 Qd R 440.

[430] See *R v Booth* (1981) 74 Cr App Rep 123.

[431] And so admissible under Criminal Justice Act 2003, s 116(2)(e), or perhaps by discretion under s 114(1)(d).

Evidential value of previous inconsistent statements

At common law,[432] no previous inconsistent statement of an unfavourable or hostile witness was admitted for the truth of its contents.[433] Modern legislation for both civil[434] and criminal[435] proceedings has retained the conditions for admission set out above, but has changed the law to allow them to prove the truth of their contents. Inconsistency between statements in and out of court must, of course, affect the weight to be attached to both.[436]

SECTION 3. CROSS-EXAMINATION AND RE-EXAMINATION

The object of cross-examination is twofold: first, to elicit information concerning the facts in issue or relevant to the issue that is favourable to the party on whose behalf the cross-examination is conducted;[437] second, to cast doubt upon the accuracy of the evidence in chief given against such party.[438] So far as cross-examination to the issue is concerned, the ordinary rules with regard to the admissibility of evidence apply so that the prosecution cannot cross-examine the accused on the contents of an inadmissible confession,[439] and the rule against hearsay applies in the same way to answers given by a witness in cross-examination as it does to those given by him in chief.[440] The exclusionary force of the rule has, however, been much diminished by modern statutory reform.[441] Now that witness statements stand for evidence in chief, cross-examination has become even more important as a means for evaluating credibility.[442]

---

[432] The rule was changed by legislative provision in Australia: Evidence Act (Cwth) 1995, s 60; in the United States: Federal Rules of Evidence, s 801(d)(1). In Canada, it was changed by judicial fiat: *R v B (KG)* [1993] 1 SCR 740.

[433] Unless readopted by the witness under cross-examination, and even then it would be regarded as of reduced weight: *R v Allen* (10 November 2000, unreported), CA.

[434] Civil Evidence Act 1995, s 6(3), (5).   [435] Criminal Justice Act 2003, s 119.

[436] Even under the old law it had been held that the evidence of a hostile witness need not be wholly disregarded: *R v Goodway* [1993] 4 All ER 894, 899. A situation in which inconsistency remains seems to require stronger direction than one in which it has been resolved, as in *R v Allen* (n433).

[437] If, after cross-examination by counsel, his instructions are withdrawn, there is no right to conduct a second cross-examination: *Sharma v Sood* [2006] EWCA Civ 1480.

[438] It was held in Australia in *R v Maslen and Shaw* (1995) 79 ACR 199 that this could be accomplished by showing the accused to have been lying in respect of an irrelevant matter to which he had mistakenly been permitted to testify.

[439] *R v Treacey* [1944] 2 All ER 229, 30 Cr App Rep 93; endorsed in *Wong Kam-Ming v R* [1980] AC 247, [1979] 1 All ER 939; 259, 945. See also *R v Brophy* [1982] AC 476, [1981] 2 All ER 705, in which it was apparently regarded as too obvious to need separate explanation. In Canada, it was said in *R v C (G)* (1996) 110 CCC (3d) 233 to be beyond dispute that cross-examination as to tactics at the voir dire was forbidden; and in New Zealand, *R v Ram* [2007] NZCA 166, [2007] 3 NZLR 322. See also *R v Neville* [1985] 2 Qd R 398, in which cross-examination was forbidden on a previous inconsistent statement that had formed the foundation of a charge of which the witness had been acquitted.

[440] There is a danger that, if a witness is cross-examined on the statements of a third party, the jury may think that the statement is evidence against the witness: see *R v Clarke and Hewins* [1999] 6 Arch News 2, [13], summarizing the effect of *R v Windass* (1989) 89 Cr App R 258 (girlfriend's diary); *R v Hickey* (1997) unreported CA 30 July; *R v Gray and Evans* [1998] Crim LR 570 (in both last two, statements by co-accused).

[441] Civil Evidence Act 1995; Criminal Justice Act 2003, Pt II, c 2. See further Chapters XIII–XIV.

[442] *Watford Petroleum Ltd v Interoil Trading SA* (n27), [10].

Any matter upon which it is proposed to contradict the evidence in chief[443] given by the witness must normally be put to him[444] so that he may have an opportunity of explaining the contradiction;[445] failure to do so does not, however, concede the truth of the evidence in chief, but it is not an inflexible rule,[446] and has been held to be unsuitable to proceedings before lay justices,[447] and less applicable to parties, including the complainant, in a sexual case.[448] Failure to put the evidence to the witness does not make it inadmissible, but does make it desirable for the witness to be recalled, so as to have an opportunity to comment on it.[449] In criminal proceedings, material proposed to be put to the accused in cross-examination should normally have been led by the prosecution as part of its case in chief,[450] although this is not strictly necessary in relation to other witnesses.[451] It has been held in Australia[452] that the determination of whether or not the rule has been broken will vary according to the remedy sought, so that where it is procedural, for example whether to permit a witness to be recalled, the question is for the judge, but where it is substantial, for example the weight[453] of the evidence in issue, it should be for the jury.

Leading questions may be employed in cross-examination,[454] but whether this is directed to the issue or the credit of the witness, the judge has a discretion under which he may disallow questions that he considers to be improper[455] or oppressive,

---

[443] Normally only that part of a lengthy statement which it is proposed to contradict, so as not to prolong the proceedings or confuse the jury: *R v Clarke and Hewins* (n440), [8]; cf *R v Antar* [2004] EWCA Crim 2708, [30]. In Canada, cross-examination must not be made conditional upon adducing evidence of the matters to be put to a witness: *R v Lyttle* 2004 SCC 5, [2004] 1 SCR 193. For the proper conduct of cross-examination by the prosecution in a criminal case see *Libke v R* [2007] HCA 30, 230 CLR 559, per Heydon J.

[444] Although this may in some circumstances be implicit, or accomplished by raising an eyebrow: see *R v Lovelock* [1997] Crim LR 821. It is not necessary that, where the cross-examiner has already testified in-chief, he should confine cross-examination to such evidence: *Jones v Havering LBC* (29 April 2003, unreported), EAT.

[445] *Browne v Dunn* (1893) 6 R 67; *R v Fenlon and Neal* (n311). See also *Allied Pastoral Holdings Pty Ltd v Comr of Taxation* [1983] 1 NSWLR 1; *Machado v Berlet* (1986) 32 DLR (4th) 634, applying the rule to a video recording of the claimant.

[446] *AB (Turkey) v Secretary of State for the Home Department* [2007] EWCA Civ 1535, [21]. Not even in Australia, where it is taken very seriously: see in civil proceedings, *Brockway v Pando* [2000] WASCA 192, (2000) 22 WALR 405, [55]; in criminal, *MWJ v R* [2005] HCA 74, 80 ALJR 329 (especially when the failure is by the accused). Icn Canada, see *R v Marshall* (2005) 200 CCC3d 179, [52]–[63].

[447] *O'Connell v Adams* [1973] RTR 150. See also, in Australia, *Garrett v Nicholson* [1999] WASCA 32, (1999) 21 WALR 226, 239.

[448] *R v A* [2008] EWCA Crim 1759; *R v Grant* (1989) 49 CCC (3d) 410; *R v Howes* [2000] VSCA 159, (2000) 116 ACR 249, 255, 256.

[449] *R v Cannan* [1998] Crim LR 284.

[450] Especially if prejudicial: see *Randall v R* [2001] UKPC 19. In most common law jurisdictions outside North America cross-examination of the accused is restricted by statutory provision (see Chapter VIII for the English rules). In those jurisdictions that pursue a more open policy, some restriction is imposed at common law: see e.g. in Canada, *R v Stewart* (1991) 62 CCC (3d) 289.

[451] *R v Kepple* [2007] EWCA Crim 1339, [27].   [452] *Beattie v Ball* [1999] 1 VR 1.

[453] It is unlikely to be decisive, *R v Rajakaruna (No 2)* [2006] VSCA 277, 168 ACR 1, [50], [51].

[454] *Parkin v Moon* (n274).

[455] In *Jabarianha v R* [2001] SCC 75, [2001] 3 SCR 430, the Supreme Court of Canada thought it improper to cross-examine a defence witness, who was confessing to the crime for which the accused was being tried, as to his knowledge of the operation of the privilege against self-incrimination, which would, under the local law, prevent the use against him of his answer, if he were subsequently tried for the offence.

and this would include leading questions of the second kind mentioned above,[456] or questions requiring the accused to speculate about matters of which he has no first-hand knowledge.[457]

Cross-examination by the accused in person has been regulated by the Youth Justice and Criminal Evidence Act 1999.[458] This unconditionally excludes cross-examination by the accused in person in the case of complainants in sexual cases,[459] and child witnesses in certain prescribed cases,[460] and permits the court to exclude such cross-examination upon application, or on its own initiative, in any criminal case:[461]

…if it appears to the court—

(a) that the quality of the evidence given by the witness on cross-examination—
   (i) is likely to be diminished if the cross-examination (or further cross-examination) is conducted by the accused in person, and
   (ii) would be likely to be improved if a direction were given under this section, and
(b) that it would not be contrary to the interests of justice to give such a direction.

A range of factors is prescribed for the court to take into account in making its determination, including the views of the witness.[462] It is worth noting here also that the court may direct examination of vulnerable witnesses through an intermediary under certain conditions.[463]

The judge has a residual discretion to regulate the proceedings before him and this may be used to curb excessive cross-examination.[464] Such a power should, however, be exercised sparingly,[465] and only as a last resort if counsel abuse the restraint expected of them.[466] The judge may also curb cross-examination if the witness becomes too ill,[467] or

---

[456] 295. For egregious examples, see *Randall v R* (n450). See also the Code of Conduct of the Bar (5th edn, 1990) paras 610(e) and (g). In New Zealand, the use of hypothetical questions has been regulated: see *Practice Note* [1985] 1 NZLR 386.

[457] For example, why the prosecution witnesses should be telling lies: *Palmer v R* (1997) 186 CLR 499; whether other witnesses were telling the truth: *R v Foley* [2000] 1 Qd 290; or to explain discrepancies in the prosecution case: *R v Tombran* (2000) 142 CCC3d 380.

[458] Youth Justice and Criminal Evidence Act 1999, P II, c II, Crown Court Rules 1982, rr 24B–24D inserted by Crown Court (Amendment) Rules 2000 (SI 2000/2093), and Crown Court r 24E inserted by Crown Court (Special Measures and Directions Prohibiting Cross-examination) Rules 2002 (SI 2002/1688). This supplements the residual power of the judge to control cross-examination of a complainant by the accused in person at common law: *R v Brown* (n236).   [459] S 34.

[460] S 35.   [461] S 36(2).

[462] S 36(3). Provision is also made by s 37(5)(d) for rules of court to be drafted to regulate the disclosure to a party of confidential or sensitive material.

[463] Youth Justice and Criminal Evidence Act 1999, s 29; for appraisal, and some scepticism about the likelihood of the effectiveness of such measures, see Ellison (2001) 21 *Legal Studies* 353.

[464] CPR 32.3; for exegesis, see *Three Rivers DC v Bank of England* [2005] EWCA Civ 889, [2005] CF Rep 46. Reasonable notice of any such order should be given: *Hayes v Transco* [2003] EWCA Civ 1261.

[465] And undue restriction may be regarded as a serious procedural irregularity justifying a retrial: *Hayes v Transco plc* (n464).

[466] *Wakeley v R* (1990) 64 ALJR 321, in which the High Court refers to *R v Kalia* (1974) 60 Cr App Rep 200 and *R v Maynard* (1979) 69 Cr App Rep 309. In Canada, an appeal has been allowed despite there being an overwhelming case against the accused because of the prejudice caused by abusive cross-examination: *R v R (AJ)* (1994) 94 CCC (3d) 168.

[467] *R v M* [2008] EWCA Crim 2787; *R v Cameron* (2006) 208 CCC3d 481 (following a four-month adjournment).

distressed,[468] for it to continue, and may leave the case to the jury subject to an appropriate warning after such truncation. He may also curb cross-examination of one co-accused if the answers are likely to prejudice another.[469]

All witnesses are liable[470] to be cross-examined[471] except one who is called for the sole purpose of producing or verifying a document, and one who is not examined in chief because he has been called by mistake.[472] A witness who does not come within these excepted categories is liable to be cross-examined,[473] not merely by the opponent of the party calling him, but also by all other parties.[474] Refusal to attend for cross-examination may, when it impedes the course of justice, be sanctioned by withdrawing the original evidence from consideration,[475] or preventing further argument from the refusing party.[476] Fairness may demand that if a witness for one side is required to attend for cross-examination, so should those for the party so requiring.[477] All parties have the right to cross-examine witnesses not called by them, whether or not the witness is himself a party, whether or not the witness has given evidence against the party seeking to cross-examine him,[478] and even though the witness is a co-accused.[479] Of course, it would be wrong to allow a party to endeavour to discredit a witness who had not given evidence against him, but so far as cross-examination to the issue is concerned, it is difficult to disagree with the following statement of a South African judge: 'An accused ought, if a fair trial is what is aimed at, to be at liberty to cross-examine a co-accused or any witness not called by him who may not have inculpated him in any way in order to establish facts which might tend

---

[468] *R v Wyatt* [1990] Crim LR 343. See, in Canada, *R v Wyatt* (1997) 115 CCC (3d) 288, in which the witness became distressed very early in the cross-examination, and the conviction was quashed.

[469] *R v Lewis* [2007] EWCA Crim 2912, [26].

[470] The judge has a discretion to refuse cross-examination if, in his view, there is no relevant matter upon which the witness can contribute, as in *R v Mahmood* [2005] EWCA Crim 3426.

[471] Although in civil proceedings, under the CPR, at anything other than a trial, held in *Dorsett v Grant* [2000] CLYB 340 to include disposal hearings such as the quantification of damages, their presence for such purpose must be requested; but is unlikely to be refused when they testify to 'hard-edged questions of fact', *R (Al-Sweady) v Secretary of State for Defence* (n11) (judicial review).

[472] *Wood v Mackinson* (1840) 2 Mood & R 273; *Fernandes v Governor of Brixton Prison* [2004] EWCA Crim 2207, [41]. The position of a witness called by the judge is not altogether clear. In *R v Tregear* (n258), 580, the judge said that counsel for the prosecution and defence should both have an opportunity of examining and cross-examining the witness he was calling. It has been held in South Australia that there is no absolute right to cross-examine a witness on a voir dire: *R v Henderson and Panagaris* (1984) 14 ACR 274.

[473] Although cross-examination can, in civil proceedings, be restricted to issues raised by the witness's affidavit: *Re Stardella Ltd* (22 October 2000, unreported), Ch.

[474] *Allen v Allen* [1894] P 248, 254; *Dryden v Surrey County Council and Stewart* [1936] 2 All ER 535, 537–8 (adversity of interest enough); *Re Baden's Deed Trusts, Baden v Smith* [1967] 3 All ER 159, [1967] 1 WLR 1457; unless his having been called by a formal opponent has merely pre-empted his being called by the party seeking to cross-examine: *Governors of Peabody Donation Fund v Sir Lindsay Parkinson & Co Ltd* (n277) (not reported on this point in subsequent proceedings).

[475] *R v Duong* (n296), [30]. See also *Cadogan Petroleum plc v Tolley* [2009] EWHC 2527 (Ch) (deployment in chief of previous cross-examination).

[476] *Bastion Holdings Ltd v Jorril Financial Inc* [2007] UKPC 60, [45].

[477] *Re Bangla Television Ltd* [2009] EWHC 2530 (Ch).

[478] In *Douglas v Hello! Ltd (No 5)* [2003] EWCA Civ 332, [2003] CPR 42, a party was entitled to cross-examine its own uncalled witness under CPR 33.4 when its opponent sought to rely upon some of that witness's statements as hearsay.

[479] *R v Fenlon and Neal* (n311); *R v Hilton* [1972] 1 QB 421, [1971] 3 All ER 541; *Murdoch v Taylor* [1965] AC 574, especially Lord Morris, 584; *R v Hadwen* [1902] 1 KB 882; *State v Langa* 1963 (4) SA 941; *Nyense v R* [1962] R & N 271; but see *Gemmel and McFadyen v MacNiven* 1928 JC 5.

to support an alibi.'[480] The absence of a right to discredit in such a situation led the other member of the court to prefer to speak of the accused having a right to put questions to, rather than cross-examine his co-accused.

The Human Rights Act 1998 has placed more emphasis upon the need to ensure that a trial is fair in all of its aspects, including that of cross-examination. This may sometimes lead to further restraint upon cross-examination: for example, cross-examination by reference to a medical report on one of several co-defendants in relation to a non-medical matter.[481]

The matters that call for further treatment at this stage are the previous contradictory statements of witnesses under cross-examination (a subject that may conveniently be followed by some general remarks concerning cross-examination on documents), and the outline of the rule that a witness's answers to questions that are collateral to the issue must be treated as final. More detail upon these matters, and in relation to impugning the credit of a witness is postponed until the next chapter. A final brief part mentions re-examination.

PREVIOUS INCONSISTENT[482] STATEMENTS[483]

The proof of previous statements[484] of a witness under cross-examination that are inconsistent with his evidence in chief is governed by ss 4 and 5 of the Criminal Procedure Act 1865,[485] but their evidential effect is now dependent on the Civil Evidence Act 1995 and the Criminal Justice Act 2003. Under the CPR, a testifying witness may always be cross-examined on his witness statement, whether he referred to it in chief or not.[486] It seems that they are not to be regarded as being used *against* the witness for the purposes of being excluded under provisions abrogating the privilege against self-incrimination.[487] It has similarly been held that no leave is required to cross-examine the accused on discrepancy between his disclosed defence statement, or even a communication from his solicitor to the Crown Prosecution Service offering a guilty plea,[488] and his testimony.[489]

---

[480] Harcourt J in *State v Langa* 1963 (4) SA 941, 945. A similar view was adopted in *R v Evans and Caffrey* [2001] EWCA Civ 730 (cross-examination permitted by one co-defendant of prosecution witness, principally testifying against the other, to elicit more exculpatory evidence than tendered in chief). On the whole subject, see Carvell [1965] *Crim LR* 419.

[481] See remarks in *R v Reid* [2001] EWCA Crim 1806, [2002] 1 Cr App Rep 234, [25]. See also, in Canada, *R v Shearing* [2002] SCR 33, 2002 SCC 58, in which the Supreme Court of Canada was required to consider the propriety under the Canadian Charter of cross-examining a complainant of a sexual offence about the omission of any reference to the event in her personal diary, which was in the possession of the defence.

[482] There is no English authority on what constitutes an inconsistency for this purpose: see *Carbury v Measures* (1904) 4 SRNSW 569 and V Wigmore [1040], and for modern confusion see *R v A* (n448). There is Victorian authority for the sound view that, if the statement is both consistent and inconsistent, the whole must go in: *R v Titijewski* [1970] VR 371, citing *R v Riley* (1866) 4 F & F 964.

[483] See generally Bryant (1984) 62 *Crim BR* 43.

[484] The statement may be proved in the form of an audio-visual tape: see *R v Andrews* [1987] 1 Qd R 21; but cf *R v Parks* (1993) 84 CCC (3d) 353, requiring a transcript.

[485] These sections apply to civil as well as criminal cases (s 1), and they re-enact ss 23 and 24 of the Common Law Procedure Act 1854. [486] Rule 32.11.

[487] *Re K* [1994] 3 All ER 230, [1994] 1 WLR 912.

[488] *R v Hayes* [2004] EWCA Crim 2844, [2005] 1 Cr App R 557, [23]. [489] *R v Tibbs* (n128).

Criminal Procedure Act 1865, s 4

Under s 4 of the Criminal Procedure Act 1865:

If a witness, upon cross-examination as to a former statement made by him relative to the subject matter of the indictment or proceeding, and inconsistent with his present testimony, does not distinctly admit that he has made such statement, proof may be given that he did in fact make it; but before such proof can be given, the circumstances of the supposed statement, sufficient to designate the particular occasion, must be mentioned to the witness, and he must be asked whether or not he has made such statement.

This is, almost, if not entirely, declaratory of the common law.[490] The importance of designating the occasion is that it ensures fairness in that the witness then has an opportunity to deny the matter more convincingly.[491] It has been held, in relation to a somewhat similar provision in Scotland,[492] that where the statement has been reduced to writing, there is no obligation to put the whole document to the witness.[493] At that time, such a statement was not admitted as proof of its contents. As a result of modern statutory intervention, it is now admitted[494] for any relevant purpose in both civil[495] and criminal[496] proceedings, whether or not explicitly retracted.[497] The relevance of a matter may change during the course of the proceedings in the light of the evidence.[498]

Criminal Procedure Act 1865, s 5

Section 5 of the Act of 1865 applies to cases in which the previous statement is in writing:

A witness may be cross-examined as to previous statements made by him in writing or reduced into writing relative to the subject matter of the indictment or proceeding, without such writing being shown to him; but if it is intended to contradict such witness by the writing, his attention must, before such contradictory proof can be given, be called to those parts of the writing which are to be used for the purpose of so contradicting; provided always, that it shall be competent for the judge, at any time during the trial, to require the production of the writing for his inspection, and he may thereupon make such use of it for the purposes of the trial as he may think fit.

---

[490] See the judgment of Parke B in *Crowley v Page* (1837) 7 C & P 789. The only doubtful point seems to have concerned the position when the witness did not clearly deny or admit the statement. See *R v Hart* (1957) 42 Cr App Rep 47, 50, which confirms that the section is in no way confined to previous statements on oath.

[491] Such an objection was decisive in the important decision of the High Court of Australia in *Nicholls v R* [2005] HCA 1, 219 CLR 196 in relation to the local re-enactment of this provision.

[492] Criminal Procedure (Scotland) Act 1995, s 263(4).   [493] *Leckie v HM Adv* 2002 SCCR 493.

[494] Although subject to discretionary exclusion under s 78 of the Police and Criminal Evidence Act 1984, *R v Coates* [2007] EWCA Crim 1471, [2008] 1 Cr App R 52, [42]. It will rarely be necessary to give a formal direction under s 34 of the Criminal Justice and Public Order Act 1994 in relation to any 'fact' in the inconsistent testimony at trial, *R v Maguire* [2008] EWCA Crim 1028, [9]–[11].

[495] Civil Evidence Act 1995, s 6.

[496] Criminal Justice Act 2003, s 119. The difficulty of directing the jury about this was noted in *R v Billingham* [2009] EWCA 19, [2009] 2 Cr App R 341, [62], and failure to do so held not to be crucial.

[497] *R v Joyce and Joyce* [2005] EWCA Crim 1785.

[498] As in *R v Kiffin* [2005] EWCA Crim 1105, [31].

The witness can be asked whether he made a statement[499] and be cross-examined on the general nature of its contents without being shown the document.[500] The cross-examiner is not obliged to put it in evidence, even if he shows it to the witness, but he must do so if he wishes to use the document as a contradictory statement,[501] and the witness must be given an opportunity of explaining the contradiction.[502] Here, too, the document is now by statute admitted as evidence of the truth of its contents.[503]

A cross-examiner cannot make the contents of a document evidence in a case simply by requiring the person under cross-examination to read it aloud. Thus in *R v Gillespie and Simpson*,[504] the manageress and cashier of a store were charged with theft and false accounting, the case against them being that they had accounted for sums less than those shown to have been received by documents prepared by salesgirls. Some of the girls gave evidence, but documents prepared by others were handed to the accused in cross-examination with a request, notwithstanding their dissent from what was said in the documents, to read them aloud. This was duly done and the judge referred to the documents in his summing-up. The procedure was held to have been improper by the Court of Appeal, which quashed the convictions:[505]

As it seems to this court, if a document is produced to a witness and the witness is asked; 'Do you see what that document purports to record?' the witness may say 'I see it, I accept it as true' in which case the contents of the document become evidence: or he may say: 'I see what is there written, I do not accept it as true', whereupon that which is purported to be recorded in the document is not evidence against that person who has rejected the contents; it becomes what one might call non-evidence, the document itself being nothing but hearsay.

CROSS-EXAMINATION ON DOCUMENTS GENERALLY[506]

There are, however, situations in which a document may become evidence of the facts stated in it by virtue of the common law rules[507] concerning cross-examination. If, at the trial, a party calls for and inspects a document held by his adversary, he is bound to put it in evidence if required to do so, provided the document was not being used to refresh the memory of one of the adversary's witnesses. If the document was being used for this purpose, neither the inspection, nor cross-examination on such parts of the document as

---

[499] In contrast to s 4, it need not be an *inconsistent* statement: see *R v Manapouri* [1995] 2 NZLR 407.

[500] Wrottesley *The Examination of Witnesses* (2nd edn) 61 f. Cross-examining counsel must have the document with him even if he does not intend to contradict the witness with it: *R v Yousry* (1914) 11 Cr App Rep 13; *R v Anderson* (1929) 21 Cr App Rep 178. It is not a condition of use that previous consistent statements also be tendered: *R v Bartlett* [1996] 2 VR 687 (construing a similar provision in Victoria).

[501] *R v Riley* (n482); *R v Wright* (1866) 4 F & F 967.

[502] Even if this means recalling a witness before the Court of Appeal if the statement has been made after the trial: *R v Conway* (1979) 70 Cr App Rep 4.   [503] 313.

[504] (1967) 51 Cr App Rep 172, applied in *R v Cooper* (1985) 82 Cr App Rep 74; *R v Cross* (1990) 91 Cr App Rep 115.   [505] Winn LJ.

[506] Where a document is proposed to be put to a witness in cross-examination, he should normally be given advance notice so that he is better prepared to respond: *Watford Petroleum Ltd v Interoil Trading SA* (n27) [20].

[507] They can no longer have this effect by this route in criminal proceedings in England: Criminal Justice Act 2003, s 118(2).

were used to refresh memory, makes it evidence in the case, although cross-examination on other parts will have this effect.

In *Stroud v Stroud*,[508] a divorce case in which a doctor was giving evidence on behalf of the wife, the husband's counsel called for, and inspected medical reports from, other doctors that were in the hands of the doctor who was testifying, although he was not referring to them for any purpose. Wrangham J held that the reports were thus made evidence in the case at the option of the wife. Unfortunately, Wrangham J did not say, any more than do any of the older authorities on cross-examination on documents, whether or not they were used to refresh memory,[509] or for what purpose the reports could have been made evidence in the case. They might have contained matter consistent with the doctor's testimony or inconsistent with the evidence of one of the husband's witnesses, or their contents might have been received as hearsay statements in support of the wife's case.

In Australia, it has been held that a document called for in cross-examination may become evidence of the facts stated in it at the option[510] of the party thus obliged to produce it, although the rule against hearsay would have prevented him from relying on the document for this purpose in the first instance. Thus in *Walker v Walker*,[511] a wife was applying for a maintenance order against her husband. She made a statement in chief with regard to his income, and was cross-examined concerning her means of knowledge of this matter. She mentioned a letter received by her father from an accountant who had been making enquiries. Counsel for the husband called for the letter, and it was held that he had rightly been obliged to put it in evidence at the request of the wife's counsel. A majority of the High Court was also of the opinion that the trial judge had been correct in treating the letter as some evidence of the husband's means.

FINALITY OF ANSWERS TO COLLATERAL QUESTIONS

The general rule

There is a sound general rule, based on the desirability of avoiding a multiplicity of issues,[512] that the answers given by a witness to questions put to him in cross-examination concerning collateral facts[513] must be treated as final. They may or may not be accepted by the jury, but the cross-examiner must take them for better or worse, and cannot contradict them by other evidence.[514]

---

508   [1963] 3 All ER 539, [1963] 1 WLR 1080. The headnote to *Senat v Senat* [1965] P 172, [1965] 2 All ER 505 suggests that that case conflicts with *Stroud v Stroud*, but this is doubtful because the diaries with which *Senat's case* were concerned were used to refresh memory.

509   *Wharam v Routledge* (1805) 5 Esp 235; *Wilson v Bowie* (1823) 1 C & P 8; *Calvert v Flower* (1836) 7 C & P 386; *Palmer v Maclear and M'Grath* (1858) 1 Sw & Tr 149.

510   It was settled in *R v Vella* [2006] VSCA 248, 167 ACR 66, [23] that this option persists after the end of the cross-examination.

511   (1937) 57 CLR 630. The rule was not applied to criminal proceedings in *R v Weatherstone* (1968) 12 FLR 14, and was recommended for abolition by the Australian Law Reform Commission: Interim Report No 26 (1985) [617]. For a consideration of the limits of the decision in *Walker v Walker*, see *O'Brien v Clegg* [1951] Qd R 1. The rule has also been limited in Canada: see *Bank of Scotland v Nel* [1999] 2 FCR 417.

512   And secondarily upon considerations of fairness to the witness: *Natta v Canham* (1991) 104 ALR 143.

513   In *R v Fahy* [2002] EWCA Crim 525, [15], the court favoured limitation of such cross-examination.

514   Nor should he suggest to the witness that he can: *S v Damalis* 1984 (2) SA 105.

As relevance is a matter of degree, it is impossible to devise an exhaustive means of determining when a question is collateral for the purpose of the rule under consideration. Pollock CB said in the leading case of *A-G v Hitchcock*:[515]

The test whether a matter is collateral or not is this: if the answer of a witness is a matter which you would be allowed on your own part to prove in evidence—if it have such a connection with the issues, that you would be allowed to give it in evidence—then it is a matter on which you may contradict him.

The defendant was charged with using a cistern for making malt without complying with various statutory requirements. One Spooner gave evidence of the use of the cistern and was asked in cross-examination on behalf of the defendant whether he had not told Cook that the excise officers had offered him £20 to say that the cistern had been used. Spooner denied that he had ever made such a statement, and it was held that the defendant could not ask Cook to narrate the alleged conversation. If Cook had been able to prove that Spooner had actually received a bribe from the excise officers, his testimony would have been admissible, because it would have tended to show bias under an exception to the rule prohibiting contradictory evidence on collateral issues.[516]

It seems that the general rule is necessarily circular, and would be just as well expressed in terms of sufficient relevance to justify rebuttal, especially in relation to cases where the witness is a participant in the events in issue.[517]

The Australian case of *Piddington v Bennett and Wood Pty Ltd*[518] prompts speculation on the merits of the finality rule. One of the claimant's witnesses in a running-down claim was asked, in cross-examination, how he accounted for his presence at the scene of the accident, and he said that he had been to the bank on behalf of the named person. A new trial was ordered on the ground that the judge had wrongly allowed the bank manager to give evidence to the effect that no business was done on that day on behalf of the man named by the witness. Similar speculations are prompted by the Irish case of *R v Burke*,[519] in which a witness was giving evidence through an interpreter. He was cross-examined about his knowledge of English, and it was held that evidence could not be given to contradict his statement that he was ignorant of the language. No doubt the questions of how a witness came to be where he was and whether an interpreter was really necessary were collateral, but the first could have been a step towards challenging the witness's presence at the accident,[520] and the second casts doubt on the honesty of the whole of his testimony. The indubitable value of the finality rule should not derogate from the undesirability of a closed list of exceptions to it.

---

[515] (1847) 1 Exch 91, 99. Pollock CB was really saying no more than that a witness may be contradicted on matters relevant to the issue: see Ogilvy-Thompson JA in *S v Sinkankanka* 1963 (2) SA 531, 539. See also *Palmer v Trower* (1852) 8 Exch 247.

[516] For a clear, recent restatement by the Supreme Court of Canada of the effect of this rule prohibiting rebuttal of other types of attack on credibility, see *Kranse v R* [1986] 2 SCR 466, softened to some extent in *R v Aalders* [1993] 2 SCR 482.

[517] For McHugh J's view that the rule should be applied flexibly, see, for criminal proceedings, *Palmer v R* (1998) 193 CLR 1, 22, and for civil, *Goldsmith v Sandilands* (2002) HCA 31 (2002) 190 ALR 370, [3]. This view was adopted in New Zealand in *R v M* [1996] 3 NZLR 502. See also Seabrooke [1999] *Crim LR* 387.

[518] (1940) 63 CLR 533.   [519] (1858) 8 Cox CC 44.

[520] This has been held to go to the issue in Nova Scotia: *Tzagarakis v Stevens* (1968) 69 DLR (2d) 466, a decision that seems to follow from *Toohey v Metropolitan Police Comr* [1965] AC 595, [1965] 1 All ER 506.

Exceptions to the general rule

The nature of the cross-examination will sometimes entitle the party calling the witness to call another to testify to matters that could not have been deposed to in the absence of the cross-examination. For example, if the claimant in a running-down case is cross-examined in such a way as to suggest that he has suppressed information about a later accident in which he sustained injuries, his solicitor may be called to prove the prompt disclosure of those injuries. The point is directly relevant to the amount of damages claimed,[521] but cases of this sort do not constitute a real exception to the rule that a witness's answers to collateral questions or questions concerning credit only are final.

There are three well-recognized exceptions: the fact that a witness has been convicted of a crime; the fact that he is biased in favour of the party calling him; and the fact that he has previously made a statement inconsistent with his present testimony.[522] Nothing more need be said about the third exception, and both of the other two will be discussed in the following chapter.

RE-EXAMINATION[523]

The subject of re-examination can be disposed of briefly. Leading questions may not be put, any more than they may be put in chief;[524] previous consistent statements can be put to the witness only if rendered admissible by the terms of the cross-examination, or under the Civil Evidence Act 1995, s 6, or to refresh memory.[525] The most important rule is that the re-examination must be confined to matters arising out of the cross-examination, and new matter may be introduced only by leave of the judge. Thus in *Prince v Samo*,[526] a claim for malicious arrest arising out of the non-payment of a loan alleged by the claimant to be a gift, the claimant had given evidence at the trial of one of the defendant's witnesses for perjury. The claimant's attorney was present at the trial, and he was called as a witness on behalf of his client in the present proceedings. The attorney could not be asked in chief about statements made by the claimant at the earlier trial on account of the rule against hearsay, and the prohibition on evidence of a witness's prior consistent statements; he was asked in cross-examination whether the claimant had not said, in the course of his evidence in the previous proceedings, that he had repeatedly been insolvent. It was held that he could not be asked in re-examination about other portions of the claimant's earlier evidence, which had no connection with the statement concerning his insolvency. The rule is sound in principle because it prevents the reception of inadmissible evidence in

---

[521] *Drakos v Smith* [1958] VLR 536; the solicitor's evidence was also admissible on the ground that it rebutted the cross-examiner's allegation of recent invention. Had the defendant been in a position to rebut the claimant's denials of his failure to disclose the later accident, no doubt he would have been allowed to call a witness to do so.

[522] See *R v Aldridge* (1990) 51 ACR 281 for a neat exploitation of this exception to evade the result in *Hitchcock* (n515) in a somewhat similar situation.

[523] Yet another stage of repeated cross-examination about a matter raised in re-examination was permitted in Australia in *R v Cheshire* (1994) 76 ACR 261.

[524] The two situations were explicitly equated in *Rawcliffe v R* [2000] WASCA 239, (2000) 22 WAR 490; in *Hannes v DPP (Cth) (No 2)* [2006] NSWCCA 373, 165 ACR 151 the questions assumed the accused's guilt.

[525] *R v Harman* (1984) 148 JP 289.   [526] (1838) 7 Ad & El 627.

re-examination,[527] under the guise of dealing with points emerging from the cross-examination, and any hardship that the rule may occasion can be mitigated at the discretion of the judge. It is nowadays likely to be exercised to promote 'the best chances of learning the truth',[528] and in *R v Sutton*,[529] refreshment of memory was permitted on re-examination in relation to matters omitted from evidence in chief more it seemed because of their intrinsic relevance than as a response to cross-examination. It is not a decisive objection that the matter had been deliberately omitted from evidence in chief, unless the withholding were designed with a view to production at a later stage or so to prejudice the prosecution, if its relevance is substantially enhanced by matters adduced in cross-examination.[530]

The terms of the cross-examination may, however, let significant and prejudicial evidence in through the re-examination, although such evidence would not be admissible in chief. Perhaps the most striking example is provided by a case in which it was held that a suggestion to a child witness in cross-examination that her testimony was activated by hatred for the accused would permit re-examination to show that such hatred was derived from the witness's belief that the accused had attempted to murder someone.[531]

---

[527] See e.g. *Petty and Maiden v R* (1991) 173 CLR 95, in which it was employed to prevent cross-examination on the accused's failure in committal proceedings to raise a defence advanced only in the course of presenting the defence case at trial.   [528] *R v Richardson* (n288).

[529] (1991) 94 Cr App Rep 70.   [530] *R v JF* (n355), [20].

[531] *R v Phair* [1986] 1 Qd R 136. See also *R v Nation* [1954] SASR 189; *Wojcic v Incorporated Nominal Defendant* [1969] VR 323; *R v Singleton* [1986] 2 Qd R 535.

VII

CHARACTER IN GENERAL

Evidence of the character of parties, witnesses and, sometimes, third parties is central to the law of evidence. It is often crucial, especially in criminal cases.[1] It developed first at common law, especially after the Evidence Act 1843, which changed focus from the incompetence of witnesses to the inadmissibility of evidence. The one major area of incompetence to have survived into the late nineteenth century was that of the accused in criminal proceedings, and it was not until the accused generally became a competent witness under the provisions of the Criminal Evidence Act 1898 that it was necessary[2] to provide special rules relating to cross-examination of the accused. Evidence of character[3] has never been a model of coherence or clarity either at common law[4] or under statute.[5] It is complex,[6] both in the connotation and means of proof of the concept of character, and in the variety of contexts in which it arises. The concept embraces both disposition, commonly described as propensity, to act in a relevant way, and sometimes the means of proof of such relevant disposition, either through reputation, the expressed belief of others of the subject's disposition,[7] or of acts of the subject from which such disposition may be inferred. It may be relevant in any form of proceedings, and at any stage of a trial. Because cross-examination of the accused was not generally permitted before 1898 the rules relating to the admissibility of the bad character of the accused in such cross-examination developed quite separately from, and later than, those relating to the admissibility of such evidence either in chief, or in rebuttal of evidence of good character adduced by the accused. The rules relating to its admissibility in civil proceedings were also quite different from those in criminal, notwithstanding that most crimes also involve civil wrongs, and that there is sometimes the possibility of using findings in one set of proceedings in the other. It need hardly be added that such complexity has been aggravated by long and piecemeal development over the centuries, often by courts

---

[1] Thus in *R v Bailey* [1924] 2 KB 300, the use of such evidence contributed to the conviction of the accused on counts for which it was ultimately conceded there had been no case to answer.

[2] Although one of the expedients tried in an effort to secure passage of the general statute making the accused a competent witness specified no special rules for his cross-examination, and more limited statutes making the accused a competent witness omitted any such provision, e.g. Criminal Law Amendment Act 1885. It is, however, worth noting that even when permitted to do so counsel often refrained from conducting such cross-examination, to the regret of some: see Stephen 'Prisoners as Witnesses' (1886) 20 *Nineteenth Century* 453, 469.

[3] Described as, 'far the most difficult of all the topics we have discussed' by the Criminal Law Revision Committee in its 11th Report (Cmnd 4991, [70]).

[4] Described as 'a pitted battlefield' by Lord Hailsham LC in *R v Boardman* [1975] AC 421, [1974] 3 All ER 887; 445, 898.

[5] Described as 'a nightmare of construction' by Lord Lane LCJ as in *R v Anderson* [1988] QB 678, [1988] 2 All ER 549; 686, 554.   [6] For a fuller account, see earlier editions of this work.

[7] Which in defamation may also be itself a fact in issue.

at first instance, by points taken *ex improviso* rather than anticipated in advance, by confusion over the scope of discretionary control, by convoluted statutory amendment,[8] and by the intensely practical focus of this part of the law, to some extent resisting rationalization.

Radical surgery was undertaken for criminal proceedings in Pt 11 of the Criminal Justice Act 2003 in relation to the rules relating to the admissibility of evidence of bad character, and especially that of the accused. It is proposed to devote this chapter *mainly* to character at common law and in civil proceedings, and to postpone to the next the major impact of the provisions of the Criminal Justice Act 2003 upon the bad character of the accused. The qualification is necessary because some provisions of the Criminal Justice Act[9] also extend to the bad character of witnesses other than the accused, and others are intimately connected with evidence of good character. It is proposed to consider here, in separate sections, evidence of the character of parties other than that of the bad character of the accused;[10] evidence of the character of witnesses other than the accused; and evidence of the character of third parties, although, as will be discovered, it is not possible to confine them in watertight compartments.

SECTION 1. THE CHARACTER OF PARTIES

As explained in Chapter V, parties to civil proceedings have been generally competent to testify since 1843, and the accused became similarly competent in 1898. It is thus the case that the character of a party may be relevant either to issue or to credit.[11] It is necessary to distinguish between civil proceedings and criminal on account of the statutory abolition by the Criminal Justice Act 2003 of the common law rules of admissibility of bad character for the purposes of criminal, which, as noted above, relate not only to the bad character of the accused but also to that of other witnesses. It is proposed here to adopt an extended view of the identity of parties to include those closely associated with them, such as employees or directors for whom corporate parties are vicariously liable, and in criminal proceedings, to include the character of the prosecutor,[12] and of any co-accused. The primary focus of this section is upon character as going to issue, although to the extent that the parties testify, or otherwise put their credit in issue, it is capable also of going to credibility.

CIVIL PROCEEDINGS

Evidence of character may be relevant in civil proceedings in different ways. Quite apart from its possible relevance as 'similar fact' evidence, it may itself be in issue, as in defamation cases, or it may be used to impugn the credibility of a party witness.

---

[8] See Tapper in Tapper (ed) *Crime, Proof and Punishment* (1981), 303.

[9] S 100 is wholly devoted to the bad character of non-defendants.

[10] Except the use of such bad character in rebuttal of evidence of good character of the accused, and of attack upon the character of a co-accused.

[11] And often both: see Gummow J in *DF Lyons Pty Ltd v Commonwealth Bank of Australia* (1990) 100 ALR 468.

[12] Itself construed in an extended sense to include the complainant or victim, even though not formally a party to the criminal proceedings, even as prosecutor.

Good character

The general good character of a party may not be adduced, unlike that of the accused in criminal proceedings. This was clearly stated by Eyre CB in *A-G v Bowman*,[13] a suit for a penalty, and elaborated by Baron Martin in *A-G v Radloff*:[14]

In criminal cases evidence of the good character of the accused is most properly and with good reason admissible in evidence, because there is a fair and just presumption that a person of good character would not commit a crime; but in civil cases such evidence is with equal good reason not admitted, because no presumption would fairly arise, in the very great proportion of cases, from the good character of the defendant, that he did not commit the breach of contract or of civil duty alleged against him.

As one would expect, exactly the same rule applies to evidence of good character of the claimant.[15]

If a party testifies,[16] his credibility comes into play, but there is a general rule against adducing evidence to bolster the credibility of a testifying witness in advance of any rebuttable attack upon it. This partly accounts for the common law rule against the use of previous consistent statements to support oral testimony, which certainly applied to party witnesses.[17] Nevertheless, it often happens that the credit of a party witness is implicitly bolstered by his clothing or reference to his occupation or rank, as noted by Pearce LJ in *Meek v Fleming*:[18]

It is clear that he [the trial judge] reasonably considered that the defendant's rank and status were relevant on credibility in a case where there was oath against oath, and where there was a question of the defendant's conduct in the course of duty.

Indeed, in that case, the matter was considered sufficiently important to order a new trial because steps had been taken to conceal the defendant's demotion within the police force for misconduct.[19]

Occasionally, where a party's character has been attacked, it has been held that his good character can be proved in rebuttal.

Bad character

A claimant's character may be directly in issue on the question of liability in a claim for defamation when justification is pleaded, and the question of whether specific acts, rumours, or reputation can be received will depend upon the claims in the particular case,[20] sometimes extending to subsequent material.[21] The claimant's character is also relevant to the amount of damages recoverable in such proceedings. *Plato Films Ltd v Speidel*[22] approved earlier decisions in deciding that evidence in mitigation must be confined to reputation, and might not consist of rumours or testimony concerning specific acts. In part, this was because of

---

[13] (1781) 2 Bos & P 532n.   [14] (1854) 10 Exch 84, 97.

[15] *Cornwell v Richardson* (1825) 1 Ry & M 305. See also *Deep v Wood* (1983) 143 DLR (3d) 246.

[16] The same is true if a hearsay statement is admissible under s 5(2) of the Civil Evidence Act 1995.

[17] As in *Gillie v Posho* [1939] 2 All ER 196, PC.

[18] [1961] 2 QB 366, [1961] 3 All ER 148; 376, 152. See also remarks of Dillon LJ in *Orchard v South Eastern Electricity Board* [1987] QB 565, [1987] 1 All ER 95; 578, 104.

[19] The case was treated as one turning solely on credibility: see Pearson LJ, 383, 156.

[20] *Maisel v Financial Times Ltd* (1915) 84 LJKB 2145.   [21] *Desmond v Bower* [2009] EWCA Civ 667.

[22] [1961] AC 1090, [1961] 1 All ER 876. See also, in Ireland, *Browne v Tribune Newspapers Ltd* [2001] 1 IR 521.

the unfairness of expecting a claimant to be in a position to defend his whole life's actions without notice, and in part, because of the inconvenience of prolonging trials by establishing the facts of numerous incidents. Some, however,[23] considered it unfair to exclude in the assessment of damages evidence of the commission-specific facts of the very type of which his reputation for non-performance constitutes the foundation of the claim for defamation. So far as inconvenience was a factor, it now seems that the case-management approach of the Civil Procedure Rules will enable at least some evidence of specific facts to be adduced in these circumstances.[24] It is clear that evidence of reputation must relate to the segment of the complainant's life to which the defamation relates, and some of their Lordships pointed to the difficulty of drawing a sharp distinction between evidence of specific acts and evidence of reputation. Although evidence of specific acts is not admissible to show that they were performed, it may be admissible to show that the complainant has the reputation of being a man who is in the habit of performing such acts.[25] Such matters as rumours and specific acts may be put to the complainant in cross-examination as to credit, but his answers are final in accordance with the general rule, and the judge must endeavour to separate the issue of credibility from that concerning the quantum of damages when he sums up to the jury.[26]

In a claim for defamation, the complainant's previous convictions for offences relevant to the alleged defamation may be proved in mitigation of damages,[27] as well as in cross-examination, to credit:[28]

They are the raw material upon which bad reputation is built up. They have taken place in open court. They are matters of public knowledge. They are acted on by people generally as the best guide to his reputation and standing.

They are also, in defamation cases, conclusive evidence of the accused having committed the offence of which he has been convicted.[29]

Although some early civil cases[30] rejected similar fact evidence as res inter alios acta, it was soon accepted that the rule of exclusion was certainly no stricter than that in criminal cases.[31]

The general tendency was indeed for continuing relaxation. Lord Reid doubted whether the same considerations that then justified the rule in criminal cases applied in the civil

---

[23] Including the Porter Committee in 1948, the Faulks Committee in 1975, and the Neill working group of the Supreme Court Procedure Committee in 1991. This led to the inclusion of a draft clause abolishing the rule in *Scott v Sampson* in the bill, although it failed to be enacted as part of the Defamation Act 1996.

[24] *Burstein v Times Newspapers Ltd* [2001] 1 WLR 579, applied and explained in *Turner v News Group Newspapers Ltd* [2006] EWCA Civ 540, [2006] 4 All ER 613.

[25] *Waters v Sunday Pictorial Newspaper Ltd* [1961] 2 All ER 758, [1961] 1 WLR 967.

[26] *Hobbs v CT Tinling & Co Ltd* [1929] 2 KB 1.

[27] Similarly, the character of a complainant of sexual harassment may be relevant to the detriment suffered: see *Snowball v Gardner Merchant Ltd* [1987] ICR 719.

[28] *Goody v Odhams Press Ltd* [1967] 1 QB 333, [1966] 3 All ER 369, 340, 372.

[29] Civil Evidence Act 1968, s 13. Acquittals are, however, no evidence of innocence.

[30] *Spencely v De Willott* (1806) 7 East 108 (usurious contracts); *Holcombe v Hewson* (1810) 2 Camp 391 (bad beer).

[31] *Blake v Albion Life Assurance Society* (1878) 4 CPD 94 (fraudulent trading). See also *Thorpe v Greater Manchester Chief Constable* [1989] 2 All ER 827, [1989] 1 WLR 665 (certificate of the results of disciplinary proceedings involving acts of similar misconduct by the relevant policemen). In Australia, the standard in both criminal and civil proceedings was changed by s 97 of the Evidence Act (Cwth) 1995 to 'significant probative value': see *Jacara Pty Ltd v Perpetual Trustees WA Ltd* [2000] FCA 1886, 180 ALR 569 for full analysis. In Canada, see *G (JRI) v Tyhurst* (2003) 226 DLR (4th) 447.

law.[32] The most authoritative statement of the position was made by Lord Denning MR in *Mood Music Publishing Co Ltd v de Wolfe Publishing Ltd*:[33]

The criminal courts have been very careful not to admit such evidence unless its probative value is so strong that it should be received in the interests of justice; and its admission will not operate unfairly to the accused. In civil cases the courts will admit evidence of similar facts if it is logically probative, that is if it is logically relevant in determining the matter which is in issue; provided that it is not oppressive or unfair to the other side; and also that the other side has fair notice of it and is able to deal with it.

This passage could have been interpreted as applying in civil cases a similar sort of balancing approach to the rules for admissibility of similar fact evidence as then applied in criminal cases.[34] The matter has now been clarified by the House of Lords in *O'Brien v Chief Constable of South Wales*,[35] in which it was explained that there is a two-stage test:[36] first, one of admissibility depending on the probative force of the evidence of other misconduct; second, one of discretionary exclusion, now that such exclusion has been explicitly provided for by the Civil Procedure Rules.[37]

Lord Denning's view that simple[38] relevance was sufficient to satisfy the first stage was approved.[39] Fraudulent representations to the purchasers of shares,[40] however, and forgeries of the signatures of some other members of the same family, were even then regarded as sufficiently relevant.[41] As in criminal cases, the estimation of probative force is a complex one, depending upon the precise circumstances of the case and the issues being contested.[42] It seems that, where relevant to issue, the disposition of a party may be proved by previous convictions,[43] or findings in other civil proceedings.[44]

---

[32] *Cummings (McWilliams) v Sir William Arrol & Co* [1962] 1 All ER 623, [1962] 1 WLR 295, 630, 305.

[33] [1976] Ch 119, [1976] 1 All ER 763; 127, 766. It is, however, interesting to note that, in the more recent copyright case of *Stoddard International plc v William Lomas Carpets Ltd* [2001] FSR 44 Ch, [31], the issue of copying is discussed in terms of 'striking similarity', which was the terminology once used as signifying a different standard from simple relevance in criminal proceedings.

[34] In *Jones v Greater Manchester Police Authority* [2001] EWHC Admin 189, [2002] ACD 4, the formal categorization of restraint proceedings under ss 1 and 2 of the Crime and Disorder Act 1998 as civil rather than criminal was disregarded so far as the admissibility of evidence of similar events to show disposition was concerned.   [35] [2005] UKHL 26, [2005] 2 AC 534 (Ho (2006) 26 OJLS 131).

[36] In *Silversafe Ltd v Hood* [2006] EWHC 1849 (Ch), [2006] STI 1988, [37], it was emphasized that the court should be slow to make a pre-emptive decision on admissibility in advance of the trial.

[37] CPR 32.1(2).   [38] Unenhanced, [53].

[39] Casting doubt on some earlier cases that had taken a rather more restricted approach, such as *Thorpe* (n31) (police misconduct as in *O'Brien* itself (n35)); *Macintyre v Chief Constable of Kent* [2002] EWCA Civ 1087, [2003] EMLR 194 (other television programmes in the same series as the one to which the claim related). See also similar decisions elsewhere: *Laubscher v National Foods Ltd* 1986 (1) SA 553; *Durrani v Augier* (2000) 190 DLR (4th) 183; *Kurgiel v Mitsubishi Motors Australia Ltd* (1990) 54 SASR 125; *Jacara Pty Ltd v Perpetual Trustees WA Ltd* [2000] FCA 886, 180 ALR 569.

[40] *MacDonald v Canada Kelp Co Ltd* (1973) 39 DLR (3d) 617.

[41] *Berger v Raymond & Son Ltd* [1984] 1 WLR 625.

[42] They must be sufficiently formulated before disclosure of other similar material will be required: *Cheshire Building Society v Dunlop Haywards (DHL) Ltd (2007)* [2007] EWHC 403 (QB).

[43] *Thorpe* (n31) and, in Canada, in *Statton v Johnson* (1999) 172 DLR (4th) 535 (reference to comparative convictions for speeding offences was accepted to show which of two parties was likely to have been driving at the time of a road accident caused by excessive speed). Or conversely, in cases of malicious prosecution by acquittals: see, in Australia, *Grivas v Brooks* (1997) 69 SASR 532.

[44] *Cheshire Building Society v Dunlop Haywards (DHL) Ltd (2007)* [2008] EWHC 51 (Comm), [53]–[57].

Although in some situations a civil court may have to consider exclusion on the grounds of prejudice, especially where exceptionally there is a jury, the relevant factors are now more likely to be those set out in r 1(2) of the Civil Procedure Rules, including, in favour of exclusion, the tendency of the evidence to prolong the trial or to confuse the jury,[45] and against exclusion, the stronger the probative value of the evidence.[46]

The issue may arise, however, not at the stage of admissibility at trial,[47] but at the stage of amendment of pleadings to allow allegations of similar conduct in the past,[48] when the judge clearly has a discretion to weigh factors such as the difficulty of proof that such an amendment might create against the probative force of the allegations in the context of the case, or in relation to discovery, where inclusion of the allegations in the statements of claim is likely to be of critical importance.[49] Thus in *West Midlands Passenger Executive v Singh*,[50] the Court of Appeal accepted that statistical evidence of consistent employment practice in relation to particular ethnic groups was both necessary and relevant to prove discrimination, and an order for discovery was upheld.

The credibility of parties may be impugned by cross-examination about their bad character in much the same way as that of third-party witnesses.[51]

The exclusionary rules of the law of evidence play a very limited role in modern civil law, and it is certain that there are very many more examples of evidence of the character of a party being adduced inadvertently. Very occasionally, evidence of other misconduct is made admissible by statutory provision.[52]

CRIMINAL PROCEEDINGS

The admissibility of evidence of bad character both of witnesses, including the prosecutor,[53] and of the accused are governed by the terms of the Criminal Justice Act 2003, while that of good character remains governed by common law. This section will accordingly deal with the character of such parties both good and bad, so far as it relates to rebuttal of good character, leaving the principal provisions for the admissibility of the bad character of the accused, otherwise adduced either in chief and cross-examination, for fuller consideration in the next chapter. It is proposed to consider, in turn, the admissibility of evidence of the character of prosecutor, accused, and co-accused.

Prosecutor

By far the greatest accumulation of authority has accreted around the question of the admissibility of evidence and questioning as to the character of the complainant on an

---

[45] *O'Brien* (n35) [55].

[46] See *JP Morgan Chase Bank v Springwell Navigation Corp* [2005] EWCA Civ 1602, in which slight probative value was outweighed by the logistical difficulties to which admission would give rise.

[47] Or in seeking an injunction: see *Abbey National plc v JSF Finance and Currency Exchange Co Ltd* [2006] EWCA Civ 328.

[48] See *HIH Casualty & General Insurance Ltd v JLT Risk Solutions Ltd* [2006] EWHC 485, [2006] 1 CLC 499. [49] *EG Music v SF (Film) Distributors Ltd* [1978] FSR 121.

[50] [1988] 2 All ER 873. [51] See further 355.

[52] For example, Companies Directors' Disqualification Act 1986 s 6: see *Green v Secretary of State for Trade and Industry* [2006] EWHC 1739; Crime and Social Disorder Act 1998: see *Chief Constable of West Mercia Constabulary v Boorman* [2005] EWHC 2559, (2005) 169 JP 669.

[53] In the extended sense, including that of the complainant of a crime mentioned above.

allegation of rape or allied crimes. There are a number of reasons for this. One is that rape is rare in being a crime where the state of mind of the complainant is important; in evidential terms, her disposition may be relevant to the question of whether or not she consented. Sexual intercourse, whether or not consensual, most often takes place in private, and leaves few visible traces of having occurred. Evidence is often effectively limited to that of the parties, and much may depend upon the balance of credibility between them.[54] This has important effects for the law of evidence since it is capable of reducing the difference between questions going to credit and questions going to issue to vanishing point.[55] If the only issue is consent and the only evidence is the testimony of the complainant, the conclusion that she is unworthy of credit must be decisive of the issue. The difficulties caused by these factors recur in relation to much of the evidence used to resolve them. If it is sought to prove consent by evidence that the complainant is sexually promiscuous, it is likely to be just as difficult for the defence to rebut her denials of such promiscuity as it is for the prosecution to prove that she did not consent on the occasion in issue. If it is alleged that she has made a previous false allegation of rape, it is unclear how its falsity could satisfactorily be established.[56] In other words, the collateral issues in such cases are likely to prove particularly time-consuming, difficult to resolve, and confusing to the jury.

It is also likely to be more than usually unfair without warning to confront the complainant at the trial with isolated examples of her extrinsic sexual behaviour, since sexual activity tends to occur frequently, and it really would be tantamount to forcing her to defend her whole life in a way clearly less true than in relation to, say, allegations of crime. It has already been noted that the law has, in other respects, been influenced by the supposition that the testimony of complainants of sexual crimes may be tainted by considerations not obvious to juries. It should now be noted that juries in sexual cases may be influenced by considerations not intended by the law.[57] It must finally be remembered that the common law has developed during a period of rapidly changing sexual manners. Is it then at all surprising that the law should be confused and confusing, and latterly the subject of investigation and legislative reform?

Good character

One of the ingredients of rape is that the victim should have withheld consent to the sexual intercourse. In practice, it is rare for prosecution to proceed in the absence of

---

[54] Although it has been held in Canada to be wrong to present the issue to the jury in that way: *R v JHS* 2008 SCC 30, [2008] 2 SCR 152; in Australia, it has been held to be wrong to cross-examine the accused as to his knowledge of any reason why the complainant should lie: *Palmer v R* (1997) 186 CLR 499.

[55] See *R v Viola* [1982] 3 All ER 73, [1982] 1 WLR 1138; 77, 1143. See Seabrooke [1999] *Crim LR* 387, in which he suggests that it is the *significance* of the distinction that diminishes. This passage in the text has been widely accepted, sometimes in a stronger form, as in *R v Funderburk* [1990] 2 All ER 482, [1990] 1 WLR 587, 491, 594: see, in Australia, *Nicholls v R* [2005] HCA 1, 219 CLR 196 McHugh J; and in Ireland *People v Onumwere* [2007] IECCA 48, [2007] 3 IR 772, [9].

[56] In *R v Nagrecha* [1997] 2 Cr App Rep 401, this problem was sidestepped because the making of any complaint of a sexual nature was denied, so it was unnecessary to explore its falsity. This seems questionable, since the cross-examination was relevant only if the complaint were false. Multiple complaints may also damage the credibility of the complainant, even when some abuse has certainly occurred, if the view is taken that there are so many complaints that some are likely to be false, and it is difficult to determine which they are: see *R v S, B and C* [2003] EWCA Crim 3435.

[57] See Kalven and Zeisel *The American Jury* (1966) 249–54.

testimony from the complainant of such lack of consent.[58] As noted above, this issue is often characterized by a stark conflict of testimony between complainant and accused, with little other convincing evidence. In such cases, the accused has the benefit, as will be seen below, of calling evidence of his good character in the relevant respect. So despite the general rule that it is impermissible to call evidence to bolster the testimony[59] of a witness in advance[60] of any attack, it would be unfair not to allow the complainant to adduce evidence of her good character in this respect. It is certainly the case that the prosecution may in its account of the facts, tender evidence that it involved loss of virginity, even in a case in which the complainant was under the age of consent, and hence consent not strictly in issue.[61] Similarly, the prosecution may adduce evidence that the complainant's character is such that she would not indulge in sexual intercourse in the special circumstances alleged.[62] A further step, and the fullest discussion of the issue, occurred in *R v Amado-Taylor*,[63] in which the complainant was permitted to call[64] her boyfriend to testify to her strong religious belief, and to her having acted on it to resist his sexual advances. The court took the view that such evidence was relevant to the unlikelihood of her having consented to a sexual relationship with a slight acquaintance. The defence relied to some extent on the fact that the tenor of s 41 of the Youth Justice and Criminal Evidence Act 1999 is to narrow the extent to which the sexual disposition of the complainant is to be regarded as relevant to the disproof of lack of consent, but as the court pointed out, s 41(5)(a) does recognize that, at least in some cases, it may be so relevant, and as such adduced by the prosecution.

Similar principles apply outside the area of sexual offences, although the relevance of the evidence of good character of the victim of the crime may be regarded as less compelling, as in *R v G (R)*,[65] in which the trial judge allowed evidence of the peaceable disposition of the deceased victim of stabbing when self-defence was raised by the accused, and the Court of Appeal felt that the evidence was of minimal importance and should have been excluded by the exercise of the s 78 discretion.[66]

Bad character

Much of the significance of the position with regard to evidence of the complainant's good character relates to the opportunity that its admission confers on the accused to cross-examine, and to attempt to rebut it with evidence of bad character, and especially with evidence of specific incidents of sexual misconduct.[67] The extent to which such tactics

---

[58] See Ellison [2003] *Crim LR* 760 for discussion in the overlapping context of domestic violence.

[59] But in *R v DS* [1999] Crim LR 911, this was held not to prevent the prosecution from adducing evidence that one of the complainants of sexual abuse was a senior member of the Church of England.

[60] Cf *R v Beard* [1998] Crim LR 585. Since 1996, the accused has, in any case, been required to notify the prosecution of his general line of defence, so the attack will nowadays have been signalled in advance of actually being made.   [61] *R v Funderburk* (n55), distinguishing *R v Cargill* [1913] 2 KB 271.

[62] See e.g. *R v Riley* [1991] Crim LR 460 (presence of her child), in which the terminology of 'bolstering' seems to have been used.   [63] [2001] EWCA Crim 1898.

[64] No objection was made to her own testimony as to her previous virginity and religious belief, and the third party testimony to the same effect was partly justified by analogy.

[65] [2002] EWCA Crim 1056, [2003] Crim LR 43. See also, in Canada, *R v Scopelliti* (1981) 63 CCC 2d 481; *R v Soares* (1987) 34 CCC 3d 403; *R v Diu* (2000) 144 CCC 3d 481.

[66] Perhaps influenced by the consideration that the accused had a criminal record, which might then have had a prejudicial effect on the proceedings.

[67] For perceptive conceptual analysis, see Redmayne (2003) 7 *E&P*, 75.

should be permitted has been the subject of acute controversy for many years.[68] The vague and unconvincing criteria of the common law came under increasing attack, and laxity of interpretation permitting such cross-examination and rebuttal was widely regarded as an important factor inhibiting complainants from pressing their allegations, and from being prepared to testify in support of them. The matter was formally investigated by a special committee,[69] and the issue regulated by s 2 of the Sexual Offences (Amendment) Act 1976. That legislation had not precisely followed[70] the prescription of the Committee, especially in allowing a greater discretionary element, which empirical studies subsequently suggested was being applied too leniently.[71] Its approach was also significantly different from that adopted elsewhere in the common law, especially in North America.[72] These concerns led to further statutory reform in the shape of s 41 of the Youth Justice and Criminal Evidence Act 1999.[73] The twin aims of this legislation were to reduce the ambit of judicial discretion, and to extend coverage. The former was to be achieved by enacting a rule excluding evidence and cross-examination about the complainant's sexual behaviour,[74] except with the leave of the court, such leave to be given only subject to the detailed conditions set out. The latter was to be achieved by including other sexual behaviour with the accused, and by widening the range of offences subject to the provision to 'sexual offences'.[75] The form of the legislation proved to be highly controversial, and was heavily amended, especially in the House of Lords, before being enacted as s 41:[76]

(1) If at a trial a person is charged with a sexual offence, then, except with the leave of the court—

(a) no evidence may be adduced, and

(b) no question may be asked in cross-examination,

---

68 One of the earliest reported cases was *R v Hodgson* (1812) Russ & Ry 211. Legislation, so common as to have acquired the generic description of 'rape-shield', and case law proliferate unabated in all the common law jurisdictions. The secondary literature on this topic worldwide is, predictably enough, enormous. For a bibliography, see Kelly, Temkin, and Griffiths *Section 41: an evaluation of new legislation limiting sexual history evidence in rape trials*, Home Office Online Report 20/06.

69 Advisory Group on the Law of Rape Cmnd 6352 (the Heilbron Committee).

70 Largely reflecting opposition from lawyers in the House of Lords.

71 See Adler *Rape on Trial* (1987). A fuller list appears in Kibble [2000] *Crim LR* 274 fn 7.

72 Dicta of members of the Supreme Court of Canada in *R v Seaboyer* [1991] SCR 577 were especially influential.

73 For an account of its genesis, see Kibble (n71); for critical dispute about its merits, see Birch [2002] *Crim LR* 531, [2003] *Crim LR* 370 (largely anti) and Temkin [2003] *Crim LR* 217 (largely pro). It is worth comparing its provisions with those of ss 274, 275 of the Criminal Procedure (Scotland) Act, as substituted by the Sexual Offences (Procedure and Evidence) (Scotland) Act 2002, which has adopted a somewhat different formulation; see *DS v HM Adv* [2007] UKPC 36; and in Ireland *DC v DPP* [2005] IESC 77, [2005] 4 IR 281.

74 Defined by YJCEA 1999, s 42(1)(c) to include sexual experience (the term used in the 1976 Act), whether with the accused or anyone else, except that which is alleged to have taken place as part of the subject matter of the event constituting the subject of the charge. It may remain *experience* even though the complainant is totally passive: *R v V* [2006] EWCA Crim 1901, [20]; and *sexual* even if not so perceived by the victim: *R v Etches* [2004] EWCA Crim 1313, [6]. A disputed diary entry of a sexual nature is not 'sexual behaviour': *R v Lloyd* [2005] EWCA Crim 1111, [18]; nor, in the United States, is being in a 'committed romantic relationship': *People v Golden*, 10 March 2005.

75 As defined by s 62(1), as opposed to 'rape offences' as specified under the 1976 legislation, although the courts had applied the rules more widely by analogy: see *R v Funderburk* (n55).

76 Supplemented by YJCEA 1999, s 42, governing interpretation, and s 43, procedure.

by or on behalf of any accused at the trial, about any sexual behaviour of the complainant.

(2) The court may give leave in relation to any evidence or question only on an application made by or on behalf of an accused, and may not give such leave unless it is satisfied—

   (a) that subsection (3) or (5) applies, and

   (b) that a refusal of leave might have the result of rendering unsafe a conclusion of the jury or (as the case may be) the court on any relevant issue in the case.

(3) This subsection applies if the evidence or question relates to a relevant issue in the case and either—

   (a) that issue is not an issue of consent; or

   (b) it is an issue of consent and the sexual behaviour of the complainant to which the evidence or question relates is alleged to have taken place at or about the same time as the event which is the subject matter of the charge against the accused; or

   (c) it is an issue of consent and the sexual behaviour of the complainant to which the evidence or question relates is alleged to have been, in any respect, so similar—

      (i)   to any sexual behaviour of the complainant which (according to evidence adduced or to be adduced by or on behalf of the accused) took place as part of the event which is the subject matter of the charge against the accused, or

      (ii) to any other sexual behaviour of the complainant which (according to such evidence) took place at or about the same time as that event,

   that the similarity cannot reasonably be explained as a coincidence.

(4) For the purposes of subsection (3) no evidence or question shall be regarded as relating to a relevant issue in the case if it appears to the court to be reasonable to assume that the purpose (or main purpose) for which it would be adduced or asked is to establish or elicit material for impugning the credibility of the complainant as a witness.

(5) This subsection applies if the evidence or question—

   (a) relates to any evidence adduced by the prosecution about any sexual behaviour of the complainant; and

   (b) in the opinion of the court, would go no further than is necessary to enable the evidence adduced by the prosecution to be rebutted or explained by or on behalf of the accused.

(6) For the purposes of subsections (3) and (5) the evidence or question must relate to a specific instance (or specific instances) of alleged sexual behaviour on the part of the complainant (and accordingly nothing in those subsections is capable of applying in relation to the evidence or question to the extent that it does not so relate).

   …

(8) Nothing in this section authorises any evidence to be adduced or any question to be asked which cannot be adduced or asked apart from this section.

Before attempting an account of the way in which this provision has been received and interpreted, it is worth considering how far it has been affected by the Criminal Justice Act 2003. Section 100 legislates in relation to evidence of the bad character of non-defendants in terms wide enough to include prosecutors, and, in this context, complainants.[77] Section 112(3)(b)

[77] Who can be male, *R v Beedall* [2007] EWCA Crim 23, [21], but not victims of earlier sexual assaults relied upon only as evidence, *R v Maynard* [2006] EWCA Crim 1509, [24].

provides, however, that this provision does not affect 'the exclusion of evidence' under s 41 of the Youth Justice and Criminal Evidence Act 1999; s 41(8) of the Youth Justice and Criminal Evidence Act 1999 provides that the section does not authorize any evidence to be adduced or question asked under s 41 that would otherwise be inadmissible. Somewhat surprisingly, this combination of provisions has been held to lead to the application of both.[78]

It has been recognized that YJCEA 1999, s 41 is not easy to interpret or apply,[79] and it is still too early to be sure how such interpretation will develop, either as a matter of domestic law alone, or under the influence of the impact of the European Convention on Human Rights.

As noted above, the section was intended to curb the perceived excesses of cross-examination under the old law, and to this end, the provision adopts a number of devices. It requires a prior application to be made for leave to cross-examine,[80] some evidential basis to support such application,[81] that the matter relate to some specific, and specified, incident,[82] that it comply with any relevant exception to the general bar, that reasons for the decision be given, and most importantly, that it be of such weight in the circumstances of the case that refusal of leave might result in rendering a conviction unsafe. The last of these was stressed in *R v Mokrecovas*,[83] although its impact could be muted by the fact that it is necessary to show no more than that unsafety *might* result, which leaves plenty of scope for laxity, without providing much basis for any appeal against such a determination.

The prosecution may adduce any evidence that is part of the event which is the subject of the charge without the need to seek leave,[84] although it may sometimes be difficult to determine whether or not this is the case.[85] It also seems to be contemplated that the prosecution may adduce evidence of other sexual behaviour,[86] although, in such a case, it would need leave. In *R v Singh*,[87] in which the appeal was in respect of a retrial, the prosecution deliberately modified its presentation of the case for the retrial so as to preclude

---

[78] *R v V* (n74), [25].

[79] *R v Winter* [2008] EWCA Crim 3, [32]. It is surprising that, in *R v Whitworth* [2002] EWCA Crim 2425, [19], the court regarded s 41 as reflecting the common law prior to its passage.

[80] See new Pt 36 of the Criminal Procedure Rules, substituted by Sch 2 of the Criminal Procedure (Amendment No 2) Rules 2006.

[81] See *R v T and H* [2001] EWCA Crim 1877, [2002] 1 All E R 683, [41], in which this was stressed; see also *R v AM* [2009] EWCA Crim 618, [25] (sufficient); *R v Evans* [2009] EWCA Crim 2668, 11] (insufficient); *R v Davarifar* [2009] EWCA Crim 2294, [11] where the issue was whether the falsity of an earlier complaint was 'reprehensible'.

[82] See *R v Darnell* [2002] EWCA Crim 176, [44]. So preventing automatic leave to cross-examine about earlier prostitution: see *R v White* [2004] EWCA Crim 946, (2004) 148 SJLB 300, [12]; or evidence of reputation for promiscuity from being adduced purportedly to prove belief in consent.

[83] [2001] EWCA Crim 1644, [2002] 1 Cr App Rep 226.

[84] Because it falls outside the definition of sexual behaviour in s 42(1)(c); it would presumably extend to the sort of preliminaries with which *R v Turner* [1944] KB 463, [1944] 1 All ER 599 was concerned.

[85] See *R v Soroya* [2006] EWCA Crim 1884, (2006) 150 SJLB 1054, in which the complainant had, admittedly falsely, claimed to be a virgin as a means of attempting to deter the accused.

[86] YJCEA 1999, s 41(5)(a). It will be rare for the prosecution to seek to adduce such evidence, but it is not inconceivable, for example to draw a contrast between circumstances in which consent has been forthcoming in the past, and those constituting the present charge. One of the principal recommendations in Kelly, Temkin, and Griffiths *Section 41: an evaluation of new legislation limiting sexual history evidence in rape trials*, Home Office Online Report 20/06 is that this should be more tightly regulated.

[87] [2003] EWCA Crim 485.

cross-examination under YJCEA 1999, s 41(5)(a). If rebuttal is sought on this basis, it is immaterial that it relates principally to credibility.

The principal conditions for granting leave are set out in YJCEA 1999, s 41(3). The first of these is that the issue is not one of consent. The two main defences under which consent is not in issue are those under which the accused denies the commission of the act, and those under which he admits the act, but asserts his belief in the complainant's consent. It might be thought that the latter is particularly corrosive, since it is hard to imagine situations in which the accused alleges consent, but not his belief in such consent. Such an argument is, however, no longer tenable in the light of the judgment of the House of Lords in *R v A (No 2)*,[88] in which it was made clear that, in order for belief in consent to be in issue for this purpose, it must be clearly viable on the facts.[89] It may also be remarked that, unless this view were taken, s 41(4) would lose much of its effect, since the credibility of the complainant is unlikely to be relevant to the accused's belief.[90] The Court of Appeal has expressed its determination not to allow a lax construction of s 41(3)(a) to undermine the main thrust of the provision.[91]

Where consent is in issue, the court has taken a restrictive view of the contemporaneity required for the purposes of s 41(3)(b), although it will be observed from the definition of sexual behaviour that it must not amount to part of the events charged.[92] It seems that the interval is to be measured in hours, rather than in days or weeks.[93] Section 41(3)(c) largely replicates the reasoning for the admission of 'similar fact' evidence against the accused under the old law.[94] It too was restrictively interpreted in *R v A (No 2)* to prevent its use to evade the operation of the definition of 'sexual behaviour' in s 42, to the extent that it covers sexual behaviour on another occasion with the same person with no more similarity than that. On the other hand, an allegation of intercourse on a previous group occasion with the same two males, and in the same order,[95] and a previous act with the same individual in the same unusual circumstances,[96] have been regarded as being so justified.

---

[88] [2001] UKHL 25, [2002] 1 AC 45, [2001] 3 All ER 1.

[89] [35]; thus not, for example, in a situation in which the complaint is one of a violent assault to secure penetration, and the defence is one of enthusiastic participation by the complainant in an act unaccompanied by the slightest suggestion of violence: see also *R v R* [2003] EWCA Crim 2754, [14], and in Scotland, *Blyth v HM Adv* [2005] HCJAC 110, 2005 SCCR 710, and for commentary McEwan [2006] *Crim LR* 969.

[90] And might even be regarded as operating conversely, in the sense that the more credible the complainant, the more plausible any defence based on belief in her alleged intimation of consent.

[91] *R v Mokrecovas* (n83), yet in *R v Bahador* [2005] EWCA Crim 396 the court seemed prepared to contemplate leave being given in relation to allegations of a previous encounter, which may have given grounds for belief in the *likelihood* of *future* consent, but see the strong statement of O'Connor LJ in *R v Barton* (1987) 85 Cr App R 5, at 13: 'There is a difference between believing that a woman is consenting and believing that a woman will consent if advances are made to her.' Endorsed by the Court of Appeal in *R v Winter* (n79), [28].

[92] Although it must relate to a relevant issue as defined in YJCEA 1999, s 42(1)(a), which may be argued to extend to issues raised by the circumstances of a particular case rather than be limited by the formal definition of the offence: see *R v Darnell* (n82) [42].

[93] *R v A (No 2)* [2001] UKHL 25, [2002] 1 AC 45, Lord Hope, [82] relying in part on the explanatory note, although Lord Slynn, [12] was prepared to allow a little more leeway.

[94] Ibid [83]: see 9th edn of this work, ch 8 pt 1, for further elaboration of the old rule.

[95] (n89), [25] (reference is actually made to s 41(5) but it is clear that s 41(3) was intended).

[96] Generously interpreted in *R v Tahed* [2004] EWCA Crim 1220, [2004] 2 Cr App R 551, [15] (sexual position sufficiently unusual).

It will be noted that both conditions applying where consent is in issue refer to evidence *about* sexual behaviour, and in a number of cases, it has been alleged that a line of questioning about previous complaints, especially complaints of rape by other persons, or on other occasions, is not about sexual behaviour, but rather about statements relating to such sexual behaviour. In many cases, however, this will amount to an attempt to put the claimant's credibility in issue by alleging the falsity[97] of such other complaints, notwithstanding that an irrebuttable denial of falsity is anticipated.[98] This possibility was recognized as a danger in *R v T*, but it was argued that the need to show an evidential justification for the grant of leave to ask the question would be sufficient to meet the danger. There appears, however, to be some circularity in this reasoning, since leave is required only in relation to questions about sexual behaviour,[99] yet *R v T* itself acknowledges that questions relating to complaints of sexual misbehaviour are not necessarily *about* sexual behaviour.[100] It has been held that the mere extent of previous complaints is insufficient,[101] but the presence of circumstantial support for falsity, such as reference to claims under the Criminal Injuries Compensation Scheme, might be enough.[102] If despite some degree of falsity cross-examination will reveal other sexual behaviour, s 41 is engaged,[103] and the Court will be astute to detect attempts to exploit this to evade its application.[104]

The fullest and most authoritative judicial[105] consideration of the construction of the provision as a whole was made in *R v A (No 2)*, in which the House of Lords was confronted by a case in which the accused alleged consent, and sought to ventilate the issue that the parties were then[106] in an ongoing sexual relationship. The House of Lords took the view that, as a matter of common sense, such evidence was capable of being relevant[107] to the issue of consent, and that the Act had adopted too restrictive an approach.[108] It held that, in view of s 3 of the Human Rights Act 1998, it was necessary, and possible, to read

---

[97] Including the misattribution of the perpetration of an act that did occur: see *R v C and B* [2003] EWCA Crim 29, [27].

[98] In *R v T* (n81), [40]–[41]. Such anticipation may turn out to be false, as in *R v Nagrecha* (n56), in which the complainant instead denied making the previous complaint. There must be an unequivocal assertion of falsity: *R v TW* [2004] EWCA Crim 3103, [8].

[99] At least under the Youth Justice and Criminal Evidence Act 1999; but it might be possible to argue that leave will be required under s 100(4) of the Criminal Justice Act 2003, since s 112(3) of the Criminal Justice Act 2003 preserves s 41 only so far as it relates to the exclusion of evidence by the Criminal Justice Act 2003, and the requirement to seek leave could be regarded differently, as they appear to have been treated in *R v Stephenson* [2006] EWCA Crim 2325.

[100] Although if the alleged falsity relates only to the issue of consent, the question will be about sexual behaviour whether the allegation is true or false: see *R v Archer* [2003] EWCA Crim 2072, [14].

[101] *R v Etches* (n74), [10].

[102] *R v Garaxo* [2005] EWCA Crim 1170, [14]; but see *R v V* (n74), [28] on the significance of failure to cooperate with the police in relation to a previous complaint.

[103] *R v Evans* (n81), [18] (one of complaints admitted to be true).   [104] See *R v Winter* (n79), [25].

[105] For academic consideration based on surveys of practitioners and assessment of overseas comparators, see Kibble [2005] *Crim LR* 190, 263, in which the case for a stronger discretionary element is presented, and Kelly, Temkin, and Griffiths *Section 41: an evaluation of new legislation limiting sexual history evidence in rape trials*, Home Office Online Report 20/06, in which the case for limiting the discretionary element still further is presented.

[106] It was alleged that consensual intercourse had last taken place some seven days earlier.

[107] See also *R v T* (n81), [25], in which the court distinguishes 'normal' and statutory relevance.

[108] See Lord Slynn, [10], Lord Steyn, [31], Lord Clyde, [136], Lord Hutton, [152].

into s 41(3)(c) a requirement that expanded its ambit to allow cross-examination under its provisions if to exclude it would be unfair to the defendant:[109]

The effect of the decision today is that under section 41(3)(c) of the 1999 Act, construed where necessary by applying the interpretative obligation under section 3 of the Human Rights Act 1998, and due regard always being paid to the importance of seeking to protect the complainant from indignity and from humiliating questions, the test of admissibility is whether the evidence (and questioning in relation to it) is nevertheless so relevant to the issue of consent that to exclude it would endanger the fairness of the trial under article 6 of the Convention.

To the extent that fairness to the accused as guaranteed under Art 6 was a motivating factor, it may have been exaggerated, since in *Oyston v United Kingdom*,[110] the European Court of Human Rights refused even to consider a claim under the SO(A)A 1976 that the accused had been denied a fair trial on account of his having been prevented from cross-examining the complainant about her sexual history, despite his own witnesses having been so cross-examined.[111]

The effect of this decision remains to be fully elaborated. In *R v R*,[112] it was used to justify cross-examination as to sexual intercourse with the accused more than four months earlier, and 11 months later than the date of the intercourse constituting the charge. In *R v White*,[113] it was suggested that its primary application was to cases in which the same two individuals had been involved on each occasion, and it was denied that the effect of *A (No 2)* or the Human Rights Act 1998 would have significant impact elsewhere.[114] The result was to disallow questioning about the previous convictions of the victim for prostitution. This view found support from *R v Mokrecovas*, in which the court, while allowing questioning about the circumstances prevailing at the time in order to show motive for a false complaint, insisted upon eliminating from them an express allegation of sexual activity with a third party.[115] It seems to be becoming accepted that one of the effects of the decision in *A (No 2)* has been to import considerations of proportionality, and to disallow cross-examination when the sexual element is of little importance in the circumstances of the case. Thus in *R v Bahador*,[116] in which the issue was belief in consent, the relevant sexual behaviour was eclipsed by other subsequent circumstances as generating such belief, and in *R v X*,[117] in which the issue was consent, it added little to other admitted facts. In *R v Soroya*, it was even suggested[118] that s 78 would be available here to exclude the prosecution evidence, and so avoid any injustice in the application of s 41 in this context.

---

[109] Lord Steyn, [46]. It seems not to have been argued that so to read s 41(3) deprives the second condition in s 41(2) of any significant effect.

[110] App 42011/98, 22 January 2002.

[111] For different statutory provisions in Scotland (Sexual) Offences (Procedure and Evidence) Act 2002 ss 274, 275) and their compatibility with the European Convention, see *MM v HM Adv* 2005 1 JC 102, [2004] SCCR 658.   [112] (n89), [34].

[113] (n82), [35].

[114] Although this restriction was qualified in *R v Hamadi* [2007] EWCA Crim 3048, [21].

[115] (n91), [19].   [116] [2005] EWCA Crim 396.

[117] [2005] EWCA Crim 2995; cf *R v F* [2005] EWCA Crim 493, [2005] 1 WLR 2848, in which the underlying facts were disputed.

[118] (n85), [28]. But see *R v F* (n117), [29], endorsed in *R v Miah and Uddin* [2006] EWCA Crim 1168, (2006) 150 SJLB 702, [30], denying the operation of discretion once relevance is determined.

Much less attention has been devoted to the interpretation of s 41(5) which, reasonably enough, permits evidence or cross-examination in relation to matters adduced by the prosecution itself, and when different counts are intertwined may have far-reaching effects on credibility.[119] It has, however, been held that matters raised by the prosecution in answer to questions in cross-examination do not normally count as evidence *adduced* by the prosecution.[120]

It is worth noting that erroneous refusal of cross-examination under s 41 will not necessarily be fatal to a conviction, if the court believes that the allegations put to the witness would be denied, and the jury directed that the matter should be disregarded in arriving at its verdict.[121]

Outside the ambit of s 41, the admissibility of evidence of bad character is governed by s 100 of the Criminal Justice Act 2003, which applies to all persons other than the defendant, not excepting parties in the extended sense applied here.[122] It has been stressed that it is to be interpreted as a new provision, and not according to the old common law.[123] It seems that the interpretation may, however, in relation to the bad character of a complainant, or the victim of an assault,[124] reflect the approach taken with regard to the bad character of the accused to be discussed in the following chapter.[125]

Under the new provisions, leave is required before the character of the prosecutor can be attacked,[126] but where it is given, provided that the other conditions to be discussed below have been satisfied,[127] cross-examination going either to issue or credibility seems to be allowed,[128] and in *R v Griffiths* a rather broad view was taken of non-sexual conduct affecting the credibility of a sexual complainant.[129] Opinions have differed as to the extent to which mere allegations of misconduct are admissible.[130] It has been suggested that when the credibility of a complainant has been attacked, it may not, but ought to, be susceptible of rebuttal by evidence of credibility.[131]

---

[119] As in *R v F* [2008] EWCA Crim 2859, [25].

[120] *R v Hamadi* [2007] EWCA Crim 3048, [21], unless necessary to ensure a fair trial when the evidence sought to be rebutted has not been deliberately elicited by the defence.

[121] *R v Martin* [2004] EWCA Crim 916, [2004] 2 Cr App R 354.

[122] In *R v S* [2006] EWCA Crim 1303, [2006] 2 Cr App R 437, the appellate court disagreed with the trial court as to whether the complainant's non-sexual record was admissible as going to credibility (even if interpreted more widely than propensity to be untruthful) or as to issue under s 100; see also, in Australia, *R v Cakovski* [2004] NSWCCA 280, 149 ACR 21.   [123] *R v Garnham* [2008] EWCA Crim 266, [12].

[124] *R v Goddard* [2007] EWCA Crim 3134.

[125] In *R v S* (n122), the distinction made in *R v Hanson* [2005] EWCA Crim 824, [2005] 1 WLR 3169 between propensity for dishonesty and credibility was applied, and in *R v Garnham*, [13] its further elaboration in *R v Campbell* [2007] EWCA Crim 1472, [2007] 2 Cr App R 361, [24].

[126] And if it is not sought for tactical reasons complaint on some other basis that the complainant's bad character has not come out is unlikely to succeed: *R v Renda* [2005] EWCA Crim 2826, [2006] 2 All ER 553 (*Razaq*), [77].

[127] In *R v Renda* (n126) (*Osbourne*) [57], the evidence of the complainant's bad character was not sufficiently important.   [128] *Renda* (n126) (*Razaq*), [82]; but see *R v S* (n122).

[129] [2007] EWCA Crim 2468, [10] (drug-taking, differing in this assessment from the trial judge).

[130] In *R v Bovell* [2005] EWCA Crim 1091, [2005] 2 Cr App R 401, [21], the relevance of an allegation that was subsequently withdrawn was doubted, but this dictum was itself doubted in *R v Edwards and Rowlands* [2005] EWCA Crim 3244, [2006] 3 All ER 882, [1](vii). Both courts agreed on the undesirability of engaging in satellite litigation, and it may be significant that in the former the misconduct was of the complainant, governed by s 100, while in the latter it was of the defendant, and governed by s 101.

[131] *Davarifar* [2009] EWCA Crim 2668, [11].

Accused

The most common situations involving evidence of the bad character of the accused are those in which it is adduced in chief by the prosecution, or in cross-examination of the accused. These are now governed by the Criminal Justice Act 2003 and will be considered in the next chapter. Those provisions do not, however, affect the adduction of evidence of the good character of the accused, or of the co-accused. They will be considered here, along with those provisions of the Criminal Justice Act 2003 most apposite to[132] the rebuttal of such evidence. This section is concerned with those cases in which the accused adduces evidence of his own good character, and the extent to which that opens the way to cross-examination, or rebutting evidence, and cases in which the accused seeks to adduce evidence, or cross-examine, as to the bad character of his co-accused.

Good character

The accused has been permitted to adduce evidence of his own good character from very early times.[133] Questions arise as to the interconnected issues of the precise purpose for admitting such evidence, the type of evidence to be permitted, and the effect of such evidence when admitted. Evidence of the good character of the accused could be admitted because it goes to the issue of guilt or innocence, because it supports the credibility of the accused, or simply so as to predispose the jury in the accused's favour. Since such evidence was admitted long before the accused became a competent witness, it is clear that, in origin at least, it was not admitted to support his credibility as a witness. In the leading case of *R v Rowton*,[134] only Baron Martin was at all inclined to accept that it was admitted simply so as to predispose the jury in favour of the accused. So far as relevance to an issue is concerned, the process of reasoning was explained in *R v Stannard*:[135]

...the object of laying it before the jury is to induce them to believe, from the improbability that a person of good character should have conducted himself as alleged, that there is some mistake or misrepresentation in the evidence of the prosecution, and it is strictly evidence in the case.

It has been held that elementary fairness requires that the jury be directed, not as a matter of discretion, but as one of practice, of the significance of the accused's good character.[136] Both a propensity and a credibility direction are required if the issue of the accused's character has been raised,[137] unless to do so would, in the circumstances, amount to an insult to common sense.[138]

The issue could be raised by calling evidence of good character, by putting questions asserting it, or at the request of the defence;[139] the judge is not bound to raise the issue

---

[132] Especially CJA 2003, s 101(1)(e) and (f), and their elaboration in ss 104 and 105.

[133] See *R v Turner* (1664) 6 State Tr 565, 613; *R v Harris* (1680) 7 State Tr 926, 929.

[134] (1865) 34 LJMC 57, 65.   [135] (1837) 7 C & P 673, 674.

[136] *R v Aziz* [1996] AC 41, [1995] 3 All ER 149; *Randall v R* [2002] UKPC 19, [2002] 1 WLR 2237, [32].

[137] Especially by evidence suggesting that it might be bad: see *R v A* (13 May 2004, unreported), CA.

[138] Thus in *R v Young* [2004] EWCA Crim 3520, the credibility limb was inappropriate because the accused had lied extensively in interview, and the propensity limb because there was clear evidence of his involvement in crime of the relevant type.

[139] But, in Australia, not by reply to an improper question: *R v Norfolk* [2002] WASCA 118, 129 ACR 288.

of his own motion,[140] nor to solicit evidence to enable him to give a direction.[141] In the absence of such evidence there is no basis for giving such direction,[142] although very occasionally the omission to call such evidence may help to render s conviction unsafe.[143] The judge may also refrain from responding to an extra-curial assertion of good character traits that is before the jury, when he knows that the accused in fact has previous convictions that would prevent a good character direction from being given,[144] and presumably a similar discretion would apply, if the accused were entitled only to a qualified direction, but might then be exercised differently.[145] Conversely, the judge may wish to give such a direction upon a corrective basis, when the prosecution adduces evidence that might be taken to indicate the accused's bad character.[146] The accused may now testify, and in *R v Bellis* Lord Widgery CJ said that 'possession of a good character is primarily a matter which goes to credibility'.[147] If the accused fails to testify, he is still entitled to have evidence of his good character considered as relevant to the issue,[148] a view since re-emphasized.[149] If an extra-curial mixed statement has been admitted, the accused is entitled to a direction as to his good character in relation to the exculpatory part.[150] In *R v Fulcher*,[151] this was held also to be true of wholly exculpatory extra-curial statements that were reflected by the defence at a trial, but Lord Steyn's remarks in *R v Aziz* appear deliberately to have been cast so as not to go so far, and it is submitted that it would be a dangerous step to extend the rules applicable to testimony to such statements, which may themselves not be evidence in the case.[152] In *R v Vye*, the Court of Appeal clarified the law by stating it in three propositions:[153]

(1) A direction as to the relevance of his good character to a defendant's credibility is to be given where he has testified or made pre-trial answers or statements.

(2) A direction as to the relevance of his good character to the likelihood of his having committed the offence charged is to be given whether or not he has testified, or made pre-trial answers or statements.

(3) Where defendant A of good character is jointly tried with defendant B of bad character (1) and (2) still apply.

---

140 *Barrow v State* [1998] AC 846.   141 *R v Prayag* (1991) The Times, 31 July.

142 *R v Daniel* [2007] UKPC 39, [36]; *R v Muirhead* [2008] UKPC 40, [26].

143 *R v Bull* [2007] EWCA Crim 5, [9]; *R v Maye* [2008] UKPC 36, [21]; *Muirhead* (n142) [38].

144 *R v Thorpe* [1996] 1 Cr App Rep 269.

145 Thus in *R v Condron* [2004] EWCA Crim 556, [13], such omission was not fatal when agreed statements were before the jury. In Australia, it has been held that the court has no power to indicate in advance how such a discretion might be exercised: *TKWJ v R* [2002] HCA 46, 212 CLR 124.

146 *Guevara v R* [1996] CLY 1386 (identification from batch of photographs produced by police).

147 [1966] 1 All ER 552n, [1966] 1 WLR 234, 552, 236; see also *Berry v R* [1992] 2 AC 364, [1992] 3 All ER 881.

148 *R v Bryant*; *R v Oxley* [1979] QB 108, [1978] 2 All ER 689. In Australia, it now seems clear that the accused is entitled to a direction that does not explicitly exclude either ground: see *R v Murphy* (1985) 63 ALR 53, 64; *R v Palazoff* (1986) 23 ACR 86, especially 96.

149 *R v Berrada* (1989) 91 Cr App Rep 131n.

150 *R v Aziz* (n136).

151 [1995] 2 Cr App Rep 251.

152 For failing to satisfy the conditions in s 120 of the Criminal Justice Act 2003.

153 [1993] 3 All ER 241, [1993] 1 WLR 471, 248, 479. Approved, explained, and applied in *R v Aziz* (n136).

Such a direction is to be given[154] even though the accused admits having told lies to the police,[155] admits having been arrested for a similar offence,[156] pleads guilty to a lesser crime arising from the same facts,[157] or to a second count arising from the same facts, and even when he has previous convictions for old,[158] different,[159] and trivial offences.[160] It should not be made conditional upon resolution of disputed background evidence that might cast doubt on the true character of the accused.[161] It is immaterial that the co-accused in question has attempted to cast the blame on another co-accused by running a cut-throat defence.[162] If the accused admitted significant dishonesty,[163] or serious criminal conduct of a gravity similar to that charged,[164] then no direction would be appropriate,[165] unless it occurred as part of the course of conduct within which the crime charged occurred.[166] It was held in *R v Cain*[167] not to prevent a direction on the good character of one co-accused when the convictions of another were already before the trier of fact, and a third co-defendant had not adverted at all to his character. Where the accused has a caution[168] but no convictions, the judge has discretion whether to give a qualified direction,[169] or to refrain altogether.[170] The mere fact that evidence of previous convictions has been excluded does not automatically entitle the accused to a good character direction.[171] The form of the direction is naturally left largely within the discretion of the judge in the light of the circumstances of the trial,[172] who is bound to direct the jury straightforwardly, without sarcasm,[173] and not in the form of rhetorical questions.[174] It is best to adopt the form suggested by the Judicial Standards Board,[175] but variation is not necessarily fatal.[176] If the judge decides that a full direction is appropriate, he should

---

[154] A conviction may be quashed if it is not, even if by inadvertence no application has been made. In other jurisdictions, it has been felt anomalous and unsatisfactory to make such a direction mandatory: see, in Australia, *Melbourne v R* [1999] HCA 32, (1999) 198 CLR 1; in New Zealand, *R v Falealili* [1996] 3 NZLR 664.

[155] As in *R v Kabariti* (1990) 92 Cr App Rep 362.

[156] *Arthurton v R* [2004] UKPC 25, [2004] 2 Cr App R 559, [4].

[157] As in *R v Teasdale* [1993] 4 All ER 290; but see the limitation placed upon this decision in *R v Challenger* [1994] Crim LR 202.

[158] Especially if spent: *R v MacDonald* (25 March 1999, unreported), CA; but not necessarily: *R v Mentor* [2004] EWCA Crim 3104, [2005] Cr App R (S) 33.

[159] *R v Payton* [2006] EWCA Crim 1226, (2006) 150 SJLB 741.

[160] *R v Durbin* [1995] 2 Cr App Rep 84, even ones involving dishonesty. See also *R v Gray* [2004] EWCA Crim 1074, [2004] 2 Cr App. R 498.   [161] *R v Butler* [1999] Crim LR 835.

[162] *R v Aziz* (n136), 53H, 158j.   [163] *R v Buzalek and Schiffer* [1991] Crim LR 115.

[164] *R v Zoppola-Barraza* [1994] Crim LR 833.

[165] Although it still might be given in the judge's discretion: *R v Burnham* [1995] Crim LR 491. And if one is given, the court is likely to be more generous towards it: *R v Akram* [1995] Crim LR 50.

[166] *R v Durbin*, (n160).

[167] [1994] 2 All ER 398. See also *R v Shepherd* [1995] Crim LR 153. If the accused does testify, he is presumably entitled to have his good character considered on both grounds.

[168] Even though a conviction rather than a caution would by the time of trial be spent: *R v Sabahat* [2001] EWCA Crim 2588.   [169] *R v Martin* [2000] 2 Cr App Rep 42.

[170] As in *R v Maillett* [2005] EWCA Crim 3159.

[171] *R v Lawson* [2006] EWCA Crim 2572, [2007] 1 Cr App R 178,[40].

[172] The Judicial Studies Board's specimen direction, as set out in Munday [1997] Crim LR 247, 251, has remained little changed. It seems that an English court would be no more inclined than the Australian, in *R v Jackson and Hakim* (1988) 33 ACR 413, to discriminate between a direction that good character made guilt 'less likely' or 'unlikely'.   [173] *R v Berrada* (n149).

[174] *R v Lloyd* [2002] 2 Cr App Rep 355, 360.   [175] *R v Scranage* [2001] EWCA Crim 1171.

[176] *R v M* [2007] EWCA Crim 1182, [20].

not direct the jury that they have discretion to disregard it.[177] The judge may qualify the direction in cases in which the good character is somewhat blemished, but not to the extent of depriving the accused of entitlement to such a direction completely,[178] nor should he diminish the force of the direction simply because the good character consists of the absence of previous convictions,[179] or because the commission of the crime was spontaneous, rather than premeditated.[180] If the accused testifies, he is normally entitled to have his good character considered on both grounds.[181] Failure to direct properly, or at all,[182] is likely to be fatal, however strong the case against the accused,[183] unless conviction would have been inevitable had it been given, which is most unlikely[184] in any case where credibility is in issue[185] on a fundamental matter between the accused and the prosecution.[186]

When the only possible purpose was relevance to the issue, it made good sense to restrict the evidence of character to those aspects relevant to the nature of the charge. Thus, when the accused was charged with treason, it was held that evidence of his good character should not be general, but limited to his character for loyalty and as being peaceable.[187] The rule seems, however, to have been disregarded both before 1898,[188] and after.[189] It was accepted by all of the judges in *R v Rowton* that such evidence could not consist of particular examples of good acts, since it did not follow that the accused never acted otherwise.[190] It was impossible to maintain such a rule consistently in practice, once it was accepted that answers to questions in cross-examination could constitute evidence of good character, since such questions invariably condescend to particularity.[191] Nevertheless, the rule

---

[177] *R v M (CP)* [2009] EWCA Crim 158, [2009] 2 Cr App R 54 (spent convictions for quite different offences).   [178] *R v Durbin* (n160).

[179] *R v Waring* [2001] EWCA Crim 1674. See also, in Australia, *R v Wedd* [2000] WASCA 273, (2000) 115 ACR 205.   [180] *R v Fitton* [2001] EWCA Crim 215, [7].

[181] *Paria v State* [2003] UKPC 36, (2003) 147 SJLB 537 (credibility direction given in provocation case but held even there that propensity direction also necessary); but see *Teeluck v State* [2005] UKPC 14, [2005] 1 WLR 2421, [39]; *Singh v State* [2005] UKPC 35, [2005] 4 All ER 781 (propensity direction given but held that credibility direction also necessary).

[182] It is generally immaterial that because of inadvertence or incompetence, no direction has been sought: *Sealey and Headley v State* [2002] UKPC 52, [30], [41], but see cases cited above n 181; cf *Teeluck v State* (n181), in which different results were reached as between two co-accused in this situation.

[183] But see *R v Bhola* [2006] UKPC 9, [17]; *R v Smith* [2008] UKPC 34, [30].

[184] See *R v Goss* [2003] EWCA Crim 3208 for a case in which credibility was not in issue; *R v Gilbert* [2006] UKPC 15, [2006] 1 WLR 2108, in which circumstantial evidence was overwhelming.

[185] And where there is a stark conflict of testimony unlikely to be corrected by direction to disregard inadmissible inconsistent evidence that has been wrongly admitted: *Arhturton v R* [2004] UKPC 25, [2005] 1 WLR 949, [31].

[186] *Sealey* (n182), [34]. This case is very near the limit, and two of the Committee dissented on this point on the facts.   [187] *R v Turner* (1817) 32 State Tr 957, 1007.

[188] See *R v Burt* (1851) 5 Cox CC 284 (evidence of general good character on a charge of receiving); for judicial recognition of widespread abuse in the older law, see *R v Jones* (1809) 31 State Tr 251, 310.

[189] See *R v Savory* (1942) 29 Cr App Rep 1 (good character as railway porter on a charge of indecent assault); for judicial recognition of widespread abuse in the newer law, see *R v Butterwasser* [1948] 1 KB 4, [1947] 2 All ER 415; 6, 416.

[190] (n134), 67; although in *R v Williamson* (1807) 3 C & P 635, Lord Ellenborough CJ permitted a male midwife charged with manslaughter to adduce evidence of his kind and skilful attention to other women.

[191] See *R v West* (1890) 112 CCC Sess Pap 724 for a particularly harsh example in which the negative answer given by a police witness, when asked by counsel for the defence whether anything was known against the accused, was held to amount to evidence of good character sufficient to permit rebuttal.

still retains sufficient vitality in this respect to have prevented a man accused of homosexual offences from adducing evidence of particular heterosexual acts as evidence of his proclivities.[192]

The matter for decision in *R v Rowton*, as will be seen below, related to the type of evidence that could be adduced in rebuttal of good character, but by parity of reasoning, the majority held that a witness to the good character of the accused could speak only to the accused's reputation, and not to his personal opinion of the accused's disposition. The court confessed its unfamiliarity with any practice in this area and even admitted the rule to be anomalous and illogical. It is also arguable that it confused general evidence of character, with which it was concerned, with evidence of general character, with which the principal authorities cited to it were concerned. Nevertheless, the limitation, in this context at least, of evidence of character to signify reputation has not, so far, been overruled.[193] No detailed analysis of such reputation evidence has been attempted in England, but it was suggested by Wigmore[194] that it should extend to reputation in any relevant field,[195] and need not be confined to reputation in the local community. Given the tendency to apply the rule to issue, as well as to credibility, this seems good sense,[196] although if it is taken to imply a narrowing of possible sources of information, then there must be an increased danger of conflict with the rule against hearsay.[197] Nor has much attention been devoted here to the question of how much need be done to constitute evidence of good character.[198] As noted above, it was in one case held to apply when a question was asked in cross-examination of a prosecution witness about the absence of convictions.[199] This has stimulated distinctions in South Australia between negative good character,[200] good character, and positive good character.[201] This seems needlessly elaborate.

The final question here relates to the effect of the evidence when adduced. It was long considered that its effect was for the jury to take it into account only when otherwise left in

---

[192] *R v Redgrave* (1981) 74 Cr App Rep 10. See also, in Australia, *R v Zaidi* (1991) 57 ACR 189; but cf, in Canada, *R v Aylward* (1992) 71 CCC (3d) 71. In *R v Mohan* [1994] 2 SCR 9, the court refused to accept evidence of a novel distinction of bad character profiles adduced by the accused.

[193] For a modern antipodean assessment, see *Donaldson v R* [2007] WASCA 216, 176 ACR 488.

[194] [245] et seq, a view accepted in many American jurisdictions; see also Federal Rules of Evidence, r 803(21).

[195] For example, among business associates.

[196] It has been adopted in Canada: see *R v Levasseur* (1987) 35 CCC (3d) 136.

[197] The borderline could not have been very far away in *Levasseur* (n196), in which the witness testified on the basis of his own limited knowledge and that of 15 business acquaintances with whom he had discussed the accused's reputation in business matters.

[198] See further 346.

[199] See also *R v Lopatta* (1983) 35 SASR 101, in which a question was asked of a prosecution witness as to whether the accused was a good person. In New Zealand, absence of convictions has not been unequivocally accepted as evidence of good character: *R v Falealili* [1996] 3 NZLR 664, in which it was roundly condemned by Thomas J.

[200] Absence of convictions, suggested distinction in *R v Mandica* (1980) 24 SASR 394, 406. In *R v W* [1994] 2 All ER 872, [1994] 1 WLR 800 it was, however, agreed that, in order to avoid a possible inference of commission of similar crimes to that charged, two minor offences of a different character could be admitted, but the accused, not presented to the jury as a man of good character. In that case, he was held not to be entitled to a direction distinguishing between effects on credibility and propensity.

[201] Doing good works in the community, canvassed by the trial judge, as reported in *R v Palazoff* (1986) 43 SASR 99, 111.

doubt.[202] It was then claimed in *R v Bliss Hill*[203] that this reduced its effect to nil, since if the jury was in doubt, the accused was in any event entitled to be acquitted. This is unconvincing because there must be a point at which the jury requires only the slightest extra evidence to feel the reasonable doubt sufficient to acquit the accused, and that surely must have been the situation contemplated.[204] It should also be noted that good character may sometimes be relevant to sentence, despite not being listed among the factors to be taken into account.[205]

Bad character

At common law it was settled[206] that the bad character of the accused could be adduced or elicited by the prosecution only when the accused had put his character in issue. It was not enough for him to have attacked the character of the witnesses for the prosecution:[207]

I do not see on what principle it can be said, that if a man does not go into the box and put his character in issue, he can have evidence against him of previous bad character when all that he has done is to attack the witnesses for the prosecution. The reason is that by attacking the witnesses for the prosecution and suggesting that they are unreliable, he is not putting his character in issue; he is putting their character in issue.

The problem at common law was to determine when the accused had put his character into issue.[208] The most obvious way was to call witnesses to testify to his good character; indeed if character meant reputation, it was not clear how the accused could testify to his own good character. It was, however, held that rebuttal could not be shut out or restricted by confining the evidence of the accused's good character to a particular period,[209] or trait.[210]

The rebuttal of evidence of good character by adducing evidence of the accused's bad character has now been assimilated with the rules relating to cross-examination of the accused as to his bad character, and both are dealt with in c 1 of Pt 11 of the Criminal Justice Act 2003. As noted above, it is proposed here to consider only those parts of these provisions most obviously relevant to these matters, leaving the remainder to be discussed in the following chapter.

CJA 2003, s 99(1) abolishes the rules governing the admissibility of evidence of bad character, and whatever reservations may be harboured as to the applicability of that provision in relation to exclusionary rules, it clearly does away with the rules permitting rebuttal of evidence of good character by evidence of bad. The one exception to this abolition is retention of the rule permitting proof of bad character by adducing evidence of reputation.[211] As noted above, there seem to be strong arguments against this rule, and the Law Commission was distinctly unenthusiastic about its retention.[212]

---

[202] See *R v M* (1994) 72 ACR 269 for a modern direction to this effect.

[203] (1918) 13 Cr App Rep 125. Reaffirmed in *R v Brittle* (1965) 109 Sol Jo 1028. See also *R v Falconer-Atlee* (1973) 58 Cr App Rep 348, 358; *R v Tarrant* (1981) 34 OR (2d) 747; *R v Lawrence* [1984] 3 NSWLR 674.

[204] This may account for the persistence of the older form of direction: see *R v Islam* (1969) 113 Sol Jo 185.   [205] *R v Simmons* [2006] EWCA Crim 1259, [13].

[206] Approved in Canada, *R v A (WA)* (1996) 112 CCC (3d) 83; in New Zealand, *R v Kino and Mete* [1997] 3 NZLR 24.   [207] *R v Butterwasser* (n189).

[208] See *R v Gadbury* (1838) 8 C & P 676; *R v Redd* [1923] 1 KB 104 (no intention to elicit such evidence).

[209] *R v Shrimpton* (1851) 2 Den 319.   [210] *R v Winfield* (1939) 27 Cr App Rep 139.

[211] CJA 2003, s 99(2).

[212] Law Com No 273 [4.79]. It seems to have been retained because of the recommendation in Law Com 245 [8.132], but even there no detailed consideration of the rule was essayed.

The principal avenue for the admission of evidence of the accused's bad character to rebut evidence of good would appear to be that in CJA 2003, s 101(1)(f), to correct a false impression given by the defendant, which is amplified in s 105:

(1) For the purposes of section 101(1)(f)—

  (a) the defendant gives a false impression if he is responsible for the making of an express or implied assertion which is apt to give the court or jury a false or misleading impression about the defendant;

  (b) evidence to correct such an impression is evidence which has probative value in correcting it.

(2) A defendant is treated as being responsible for the making of an assertion if—

  (a) the assertion is made by the defendant in the proceedings (whether or not in evidence given by him),

  (b) the assertion was made by the defendant—

    (i) on being questioned under caution, before charge, about the offence with which he is charged, or

    (ii) on being charged with the offence or officially informed that he might be prosecuted for it,

    and evidence of the assertion is given in the proceedings,

  (c) the assertion is made by a witness called by the defendant,

  (d) the assertion is made by any witness in cross-examination in response to a question asked by the defendant that is intended to elicit it, or is likely to do so, or

  (e) the assertion was made by any person out of court, and the defendant adduces evidence of it in the proceedings.

(3) A defendant who would otherwise be treated as responsible for the making of an assertion shall not be so treated if, or to the extent that, he withdraws it or disassociates himself from it.

(4) Where it appears to the court that a defendant, by means of his conduct (other than the giving of evidence) in the proceedings, is seeking to give the court or jury an impression about himself that is false or misleading, the court may if it appears just to do so treat the defendant as being responsible for the making of an assertion which is apt to give that impression.

(5) In subsection (4) 'conduct' includes appearance or dress.

(6) Evidence is admissible under section 101(1)(f) only if it goes no further than is necessary to correct the false impression.

(7) Only prosecution evidence is admissible under section 101(1)(f).

It is first necessary to note that this provision, in common with the other gateways to the admission of evidence of the bad character of the accused, applies not only to cross-examination, but also to the adducing of evidence in chief, or in rebuttal. Although the evidence is adduced to *correct* a false impression, this does not prevent its use in chief, since the false impression can be conveyed by acts, such as cross-examination of prosecution witnesses, which can occur before the close of the prosecution case, or, which contrary to the old law, under s 105(2)(b) have been given in the course of pre-trial questioning.[213]

---

[213] As in *R v Spartley* [2007] EWCA Crim 1789 (denial of previous trouble with police or involvement with drugs), and *R v Chable* [2009] EWCA Crim 496 (denial of improper use of knives).

S 105, like most of the other gateways, derives from the report of the Law Commission,[214] but, also like them, will operate in a much more stringent form than that which the Commission envisaged, or intended. The terminology of correcting a false impression is derived from that report.[215] Part of its motivation was to clarify the law, and in particular, the triggering of such a rebuttal. It cannot be denied that the old law lacked clarity. In part, this derived from the very expansive view[216] taken of character that, at least in this respect, was regarded as indivisible in extent,[217] and unlimited in duration.[218] It was uncertain how far it was put in issue by reference to the accused's employment,[219] business[220] or religious practice,[221] or marital status,[222] by pointed reference to the bad character of others,[223] or even by looking respectable in court.[224] It was generally agreed that the accused should have been responsible for the reference, thus excluding statements elicited by questions from the prosecution,[225] spontaneous and unexpected statements volunteered by defence witnesses,[226] or matters inseparable from an answer to the charge.[227]

The basic triggering conditions set out in CJA 2003, s 105(2) correspond closely to those to be found in cl 10 of the Law Commission's draft bill. They differ, however, in being more stringent so far as they differ, and more significantly in the environment in which they are to operate, in particular the absence of any requirement to seek the leave of the court before adducing the evidence,[228] and the modification or absence of the further qualifying conditions that the Law Commission regarded as necessary in the interests of justice.[229] In the triggering condition (s 105(2)(d)), the Act weakens the subjective intent to elicit the assertion of good character by a question, by adding the objective possibility of its being apt or likely to do so, apparently whether intended to do so or not. The Act fails to reproduce the Law Commission's requirement that evidence admitted under this head have *substantial* probative value in correcting the false impression, allowing any probative value at all, however little.[230] In one of the earliest cases to be decided under the new provision, a spent conviction was admitted.[231] Still more importantly, the Act altogether omits the Law Commission's condition that such evidence either carry no risk of prejudice, or if it do, the interests of

---

[214] Law Com 273 Pt XIII, and draft bill cl 10.

[215] Where it was itself adopted in response to an article by Seabrooke in [1987] Crim LR 231, although the bulk of his article was devoted rather to the rules relating to the response to attacks by the cross-examined party on the character of others.

[216] But see *PGM v R* [2006] NSWCCA 310, 164 ACR 426 for an example of denial that an answer in cross-examination amounted to evidence of good character, but which it is submitted would certainly come within the bounds of false impression here.

[217] *R v Winfield* (1939) 27 Cr App Rep 139 (charge of indecency, evidence of good character in sexual matters, rebuttal by reference to convictions for offences of dishonesty); endorsed by the House of Lords in *Stirland v DPP* [1944] AC 315, [1944] 2 All ER 13.

[218] *R v Shrimpton* (n209), and even capable of being projected back from a time after the commission of the offence to character at the time of the offence: *R v Wood* [1920] 2 KB 179.

[219] *R v Powell* [1986] 1 All ER 193, [1985] 1 WLR 1364.   [220] *R v Stronach* [1988] Crim LR 48.

[221] *R v Ferguson* (1909) 2 Cr App Rep 250 (attendance at Mass).

[222] *R v Coulman* (1927) 20 Cr App Rep 106 Swift J during argument.

[223] *R v Lee* [1976] 1 All ER 570, [1976] 1 WLR 71.   [224] See Law Com 273, [13.5].

[225] *R v Stronach* (n220).   [226] *R v Redd* [1923] 1 KB 104.

[227] *R v Ellis* [1910] 2 KB 746, 5 Cr App Rep 41.

[228] Nothing in the Act corresponds to the enacting words of cl 2(1) of the Law Commission's draft bill.

[229] Law Com 273 [13.8], [13.29–36].

[230] It is not possible to imply that the value be substantial partly because here there is deviation from the Law Commission's draft, while elsewhere, a requirement that probative value be substantial has been retained, for example in s 100(1)(b).   [231] *R v Amponsah* [2005] EWCA Crim 2993.

justice nevertheless require its admission.[232] The odd fixation with implicit representation of good character by dress or appearance is catered for explicitly by s 105(4) and (5).

It has been suggested[233] that, under the new provisions, what amounts to a false impression is 'fact-specific', tending to preclude the development of coherent principles in the area. In that case, the accused suppressed relevant qualifications to his true assertions about his current and earlier employment. He was forced to concede these qualifications in cross-examination, but such a form of withdrawal was regarded as insufficient to come within the ambit of s 105(3).

It should also be noted that s 105(6) restricts rebuttal to the nature of the false impression created,[234] and so changes the common law under which character was indivisible for such purposes.[235]

The issue of discretionary exclusion under the common law or s 78 of the Police and Criminal Evidence Act 1978 will be considered further in the next chapter. Its application in this context was mentioned in *R v Amponsah*,[236] but left unresolved. It will be seen that the arguments are generally well balanced, although it is perhaps worth mentioning that, in this particular context, a number of the matters influencing the use of the discretion in the old law no longer apply.[237] It was suggested[238] in *R v Assani* that in an appropriate case, it might be influenced by the factors applied to offences committed by children in s 108 of the Criminal Justice Act 2003.

Finally, it is worth considering the implications of the change of focus from rebutting evidence of good character to correcting a false impression. Under the old law, it was possible in theory, even if difficult in practice, to determine merely from the evidence tendered whether or not it was evidence of good character and, if it were, to permit an attempt to rebut it, the efficacy of which was for the jury to determine. Under the new provisions, it appears to be a condition of admissibility that the impression be false, but its falsity can hardly be determined in advance of any attempt to rebut it. It appears that such a condition will require the judge to determine, at least provisionally, the falsity of the impression that the evidence conveys.[239] It remains to be seen how this will be interpreted when the accused tenders irrefutable evidence of good character—for example, in a case of a charge of a sexual offence against a child, that he has a completely clean formal criminal record, yet the prosecution seeks to adduce evidence of his bad reputation in the community. The problem is that if the impression created is categorized as being that he has no criminal record, it can be determined in advance that it is true; if it is categorized as being that he is the sort of person who is unlikely to commit the offence, it cannot be determined in advance that it is false. The very existence of other gateways indicates that a false impression of innocence will be insufficient,[240] but short of that, everything

---

[232] Clause 10(4), which, together with cl 10(8), sets out the factors to be taken into account in making such a determination. Vestigial traces of these conditions are to be found only in the requirement in s 105(4) that rebuttal of impression by conduct be considered just, and in the limitation in the extent of the evidence admitted through this gateway in s 105(6).

[233] *R v Renda* [2005] EWCA Crim 2826, [2006] 2 All ER 555, [19].

[234] See *R v Weir* [2005] EWCA Crim 2866, [2006] 2 All ER 570 (*Somanathan*) [43].

[235] *R v Winfield* [1939] 4 All ER 164, 27 Cr App R 139.   [236] (n231), [20].

[237] Such as the absence of any intention to raise the issue, or the fact that it brought the whole of the accused's bad character into play.   [238] [2008] EWCA Crim 2563, [16].

[239] In other contexts, such as the admissibility of confessions, the law has gone to some lengths to distinguish questions for the judge from those for the jury.

[240] And so held in *Weir* (n234) (*Somanathan*), ibid.

will depend upon the hazard of construction of the impression sought to be created. It may sometimes prove difficult, and largely a matter of degree, to distinguish between a vehement expression of innocence and furnishing a false impression of some more particular aspect of the commission of the crime as charged.[241] It is particularly difficult to discern the impression sought to be created when it is to be derived from an ambiguous answer under cross-examination to a bipartite question, the denial of only one part of which is prone to give the relevant false impression.[242]

Nor should it be ignored that the 'simplification' of this part of the law has, in moving away from *Butterwasser*, brought into contention a whole range of new issues as to whether the words alleged to have given the false impression were used at all, or if they were in what context, and with what intonation. Under the old law the judge would have been able to rely upon his own senses to resolve them; under the new, he might well be presented with the perhaps imperfect recollection, of a less than impartial witness whose testimony, or even documentation where it exists, might be fiercely controverted.

Co-accused

Another area partly governed by common law rules is that dealing with evidence of the character of a co-accused. Here, too, the position is that the admissibility of evidence of good character is governed by the common law, but evidence of bad character in rebuttal is governed by the provisions of the Criminal Justice Act 2003.

Good character

It will be extremely rare for one co-accused to seek to adduce evidence of the wholly good character of his co-accused.[243] It is very much more common for the accused to adduce evidence of his own good character,[244] in particular by comparison with that of his co-accused in a situation in which each is alleging that the crime was committed solely by the other, often described in the vernacular as a 'cut-throat' defence. Just occasionally, this may involve stressing some qualification of the bad character of the co-accused.[245]

Bad character

The old law relating to the admissibility of evidence of the bad character of one co-accused, either by way of evidence in chief or cross-examination, and emanating either from the prosecution or the other co-accused, had become extremely complex.[246] It had common law[247] and statutory components;[248] it related sometimes to issue,[249] sometimes to credit,

---

241   As in *R v Chable* (n213).

242   As in *R v Good* [2008] EWCA Crim 2923.

243   Although it is not inconceivable, for example if joint participation is alleged and the co-accused has a particularly good character that the other seeks to stress, perhaps himself having a bad character that he does not wish to expose to attack.   244   And so subject to the conditions described above.

245   Thus in *R v Bracewell* (1978) 68 Cr App Rep 44, the accused testified to the inexperience as a burglar of his co-accused so as to show that he was the more likely of the two to have panicked.

246   It was little better in Scotland: see *Barnes v HM Adv* 2001 JC 61, [2000] SCCR 995.

247   Often relating to the nature of the evidence of character capable of being adduced, for example propensity, specific acts, or reputation.

248   Principally in s 1(f)(iii) of the Criminal Evidence Act 1898.

249   As in *R v Miller* [1952] 2 All ER 667, 36 Cr App Rep 169, in which a prosecution witness was asked whether the crimes of which the defendant had been charged had never taken place when one of his co-accused was in

and sometimes to both;[250] and it raised questions of how far prosecution and co-accused could avail themselves of opportunities open to the other.[251] Sometimes the attacked co-accused had put his character in issue,[252] and sometimes not. The position was also prone to change as the trial proceeded.[253]

These difficulties made jury directions cumbersome and complex, and ran the risk of their being more perplexing than clarifying. It is hardly surprising that an attempt was made to remedy the situation as part of the general reform of the law relating to the admissibility of evidence of bad character in Pt 11 of the Criminal Justice Act 2003.

One of the basic principles of the bad character provisions is their assimilation of the rules of admissibility for evidence in chief and cross-examination.[254] The application of that principle in this context has removed one of the major sources of confusion. A more minor theme has been the segregation of evidence adduced by the prosecution and by the defence. This accounts for the separation of the rules governing the admissibility of evidence of the accused's bad character by the prosecution to rebut attacks on another in s 101(1)(g), to be considered in the next chapter, from the rules governing the admissibility of such evidence by a co-defendant governed by s 101(1)(e), and considered here.[255] Evidence of a co-accused's bad character elicited from a prosecution witness comes within this 'gateway'.[256]

Since the definition of bad character excludes evidence 'having to do with the facts of the offence with which the defendant is charged',[257] there is nothing in the Act to prevent a co-accused from presenting evidence that his co-accused alone committed the offence charged.[258] Section 101(1)(e) comes into play only if he wishes to support that proposition by evidence of the co-accused's bad character.[259]

Two significant differences from the general rules governing the admission of such evidence through other gateways are apparent. First, the evidence has here to meet an enhanced standard of *substantial probative* value,[260] while still retaining the requirement in the principal gateway[261] for prosecution evidence that it relate to an important matter in issue.[262] Second, s 101(3), which enjoins exclusion of evidence having such an adverse

---

prison; or as in *R v Lowery* [1974] AC 85, [1973] 3 All ER 662, in which one co-accused of murder proposed to adduce expert psychiatric evidence of the greater propensity of his co-accused to commit such a crime.

[250] As in *R v Randall* [2003] UKHL 69, [2004] 1 All ER 467, [21].

[251] As in *R v Seighley* (1911) 6 Cr App Rep 106.   [252] As in *Lowery* (n249), and *Bracewell* (n245).

[253] In *R v Bracewell* (n245), one co-accused was not permitted to cross-examine a prosecution witness about the other's violence; but was then allowed to cross-examine the co-accused about it, once that co-accused had made overt comparison between the characters of the two co-accused; in *R v Sullivan* [2003] EWCA Crim 764, (2003) 147 SJLB 299, the prosecution was not permitted to adduce evidence of one co-accused's bad character in chief, but his co-accused was allowed to do so once the first had, contrary to his earlier assurances, attacked him. See also *R v Rafiq* [2005] EWCA Crim 1423, [17](v).

[254] See Munday [2005] *Crim LR* 624.

[255] As stressed in *R v Edwards and Rowlands* (n130), [24], but in *R v Bovell* (*Dowds*), it was the prosecution who sought admission of the evidence to rebut the attack on the co-accused, and so it was dealt with under gateway (g), with some consideration of gateway (f) (false impression).   [256] (n255).

[257] CJA 2003, s 98(a).

[258] As in *R v Passos-Carr* [2009] EWCA Crim 2018 (where this was conceded to be an important issue between them, but, surprisingly, not one of 'substantial probative value').

[259] For example, by evidence of his bad reputation, or of misconduct showing his bad disposition.

[260] Decisive in *R v Assani* (n238), [17].   [261] Section 101(1)(d).

[262] Although no supporting explanation of the nature of an important matter between defendants corresponding to that for important matters between prosecution and defence, as supplied by s 103(1), appears

effect of the fairness of the proceedings that the court ought not to admit it, applies to the prosecution gateway in s 101(1)(d), but not to the co-accused's gateway in s 101(1)(e). However, since this issue is prone to surface only during the course of the trial it may well be the case that notice of intention to adduce or elicit the evidence will not have been given at the due time under the Criminal Procedure Rules, which then brings into play the judge's undoubted discretion to admit the evidence despite the breach.[263] It may well be the case that the very limited scope for discretionary exclusion in the case of the co-accused will lead to higher standards of relevance.[264] It seems also that the use of bad character of the co-accused under this gateway to impugn the credibility of the other may also be more readily admitted than for the prosecution under gateway (d).[265] It seems clear that the court is applying between co-accused a much more liberal view than as between prosecution and defence. It is curious that if the character of the co-accused, while bad, falls outside the bad character provisions of the Criminal Justice Act 2003 on account of the restricted definition of bad character in s 98, there is scope for discretionary exclusion either at common law, or under s 78 of the Police and Criminal Evidence Act 1984.[266]

Section 104 constitutes a somewhat vestigial[267] elaboration of this gateway, providing that:

(1) Evidence which is relevant to the question whether the defendant has a propensity to be untruthful is admissible on that basis under section 101(1)(e) only if the nature or conduct of his defence is such as to undermine the co-defendant's defence.

(2) Only evidence—

(a) which is to be (or has been) adduced by the co-defendant, or

(b) which a witness is to be invited to give (or has given) in cross-examination by the co-defendant, is admissible under section 101(1)(e).

Although this particular gateway is closer to the recommendations of the Law Commission than some, like most of them, it dilutes the safeguards proposed, in particular by omitting the requirement to take into account a number of carefully elaborated[268] factors relevant to the assessment of the probative value of the evidence. It is, however, possible that the court will have recourse to many of them in determining that the probative value is substantial, although it is likely to take a generous view of the latitude to be allowed to a co-accused to

---

in s 104(1), the explanatory provision for s 101(1)(e). The only guidance comes from s 112(1), which defines it as being 'of substantial importance in the context of the case as a whole'.

263 As in *R v Musone* [2007] EWCA Crim 1237, [56], where there was a deliberate decision not to give notice so as to ambush the co-accused; and *R v Jarvis* [2008] EWCA Crim 488, where the co-accused was taken by surprise when the prosecution failed to avail itself of its opportunity to adduce or elicit evidence of the accused's bad character.

264 Cp the distinction between levels of violence under this provision in *R v Lawson* (n171) with that taken under gateway (d) in *R v Brima* [2006] EWCA Crim 408, [2007] 1 Cr App R 316, [40].

265 Cp *R v Rosato* [2008] EWCA Crim 1243, [21] under this gateway with the restricted view taken by Lord Phillips CJ in *R v Campbell* (n125) [31] in relation to gateway (d).

266 So exercised in *R v Smith* [2007] EWCA Crim 2105, [21]–[23], *R v Downer* [2009] EWCA Crim 1361 (also issue of relevance of conviction of co-accused following guilty plea to different offence arising from same incident); cf *R v Rehman* [2009] EWCA Crim 1944 (discretion to exclude evidence of co-accused's conviction for same offence not exercised).

267 Certainly by comparison with cl 5 the Law Commission's draft bill, although the main principle has been retained.   268 See the Law Commission's draft bill cl 5(2).

make his defence that the offence was committed by the co-accused alone or with some other third party. It seems that only where a co-accused's stance amounts to no more than a denial of participation with another is the court likely to conclude that the case falls short of amounting to an important issue between them.[269]

The most substantial analysis so far of this gateway appeared in *R v Edwards and Rowlands*, in which the police entered a house in the belief that a drugs transaction was taking place between a courier whom they had seen enter the house, and the occupant. Two packages of drugs were found with the fingerprints of the occupant upon them, together with other paraphernalia consistent with drug dealing, and large sums of cash. The courier's house also contained a firearm and ammunition. Each of the accused advanced an innocent explanation: the occupant that the courier had brought the drugs into the house without his knowledge or permission; and the courier that he had nothing to do with the drugs on the premises, and was there for an innocent, indeed laudable, reason.[270] Both co-accused had previous convictions and the occupant sought to cross-examine the courier on his. These were old, and for dissimilar offences.

It was argued that the courier's defence had not undermined that of the occupant, and that the nature of the convictions rendered them irrelevant. On the first point, the court looked at the case as a whole, and seems to have taken the view that, so long as one of the co-accused sought to implicate the other, that constituted an important issue between them. This seems odd, since it means that any co-accused can secure the admission of his co-accused's bad character, simply by raising a defence inculpating that co-accused, even though the co-accused has not attacked him in any way. On the second point, the court clearly had reservations as to the relevance of the convictions. It noted that the reference to the significance of age in s 101(4) in diminishing the relevance of convictions for the purposes of exclusion under s 101(3) did not apply directly, but felt that it nevertheless constituted a factor to be taken into account in determining relevance. Here, none of the previous convictions had any real relevance to issue, and only one, for handling, much to credibility. While the court seems to have taken the view that this gateway applies both to bad character as indicating propensity and untruthfulness,[271] it remains difficult to see, given that the convictions here could relate only to untruthfulness, how the courier's defence did go beyond mere denial and otherwise amount to an undermining of the occupant's defence.

Any such issue was, however, put beyond doubt by a conjoined decision,[272] in which the previous convictions were for offences of violence. The oddity there was that the trial judge had refused permission for the prosecution to adduce the evidence under s 101(1)(d) because it was insufficiently relevant, but then allowed a co-accused to adduce exactly the same evidence the next day under s 101(1)(e), despite the stronger test of relevance there set out. The Court of Appeal appears to have considered the trial judge to have been over-generous in relation to exclusion under 101(1)(d), and that such generosity could not be allowed to affect a more correct approach to the later provision. This raises the old question of how far the prosecution can rely on evidence of one co-accused's bad character, when it

---

[269] *R v Edwards and Rowlands* (n130), [1] (vi)(c) referring back to *R v Varley* [1982] 2 All ER 519, 75 Cr App R 242.   [270] He advanced no explanation for the occupant's attempt to inculpate him.
[271] See [1](vi)(b), explaining that s 104(1) does not have the effect of limiting the gateway to evidence indicating untruthfulness.   [272] *R v Edwards and Rowlands* (n130), (*McLean*), [51].

has been adduced or elicited by the other pursuant to section 101(1)(e). It seems likely that, in view of dicta in *R v Highton*[273] distinguishing sharply between admissibility through a gateway, a matter for the judge's decision or discretion, and use once admitted, a matter for the judge's direction, that the latter depends entirely on relevance to the case for the prosecution. Such a view is also consistent with the desire for simplicity in jury direction. It might, however, be thought rather more difficult to sustain the converse proposition that evidence admitted for the prosecution under s 101(1)(d) against one of the co-accused could be utilized by the other, since the required probative value for such a use would have needed to be greater to satisfy the conditions of s 101(1)(e). It is, however, submitted that the same conclusion is likely to be reached, bearing in mind the availability of s 101(3) to exclude for unfairness in this situation, the reluctance of the court in *R v Edwards and Rowlands* to attach much importance to the required difference in probative value, and the need for simplicity in direction that arises whichever side is seeking to take advantage of admissibility at the hands of the other.

It is ominous for the coherent development of the law that in both cases the court should have adopted so consciously broad-brush an approach,[274] depending heavily upon the 'feel' of the trial judge,[275] especially when in *Edwards and Rowlands* (*McLean*) that feel seems to have vacillated from day to day.

SECTION 2. THE CHARACTER OF WITNESSES

Although much of the law relating to the character of witnesses applies generally, the Criminal Justice Act 2003 has introduced a new statutory regime for evidence of the bad character of non-defendants in criminal proceedings.[276] Since the common law still applies to witnesses in civil proceedings, and since it was influenced by rules then in common between civil and criminal proceedings, it has been necessary to retain some reference to pre-2003 criminal cases, but it must be recognized that much of their importance is now confined to evidence in civil proceedings.[277] In the remaining part of this section, it has also become necessary, on account of CJA 2003, s 100, to distinguish between the position in civil and in criminal proceedings.

CHARACTER OF PARTY'S OWN WITNESS

Civil proceedings

Good character

Evidence explicitly commending the good character of a party's own witness[278] is rarely led, even though as going to the credibility of the witness, a matter that is automatically

---

[273] [2005] EWCA Crim 1985, [2006] 1 Cr App R 125, [10].

[274] See [1](v) declaring fine toothcomb analysis of the gateway to be unlikely to be helpful.

[275] See [1](viii)(b).   [276] CJA 2003, s 100.

[277] And of diminished importance along with the general status of the law of evidence in civil proceedings.

[278] Except in cases, considered elsewhere in this chapter, in which the witness is a party to the events in issue, such as the accused or a complainant.

in issue, it might logically be thought material and relevant. Thus in *R v Turner*, in which the dispute related to the intention of the accused, Lawton LJ said: 'In general evidence can be called to impugn the credibility of witnesses but not led in chief to bolster it up.'[279] The rule applies equally to cases in which there is a conflict of testimony on a question of fact. In *R v Robinson*,[280] it was said in general terms that 'the Crown cannot call a witness of fact and then, without more, call a psychologist or psychiatrist to give reasons why the jury should regard that witness as reliable'. Such a procedure is regarded as usurping the function of the jury.

It is nevertheless common for a party to present his witnesses with as respectable an appearance as possible,[281] and introductory questions are commonly asked about the employment and marital status of the witness so as to enhance such an impression. Very occasionally, reference is made to the good character of a witness as justifying reliance upon his evidence, both in criminal[282] and in civil proceedings.[283] If the impression conveyed in this way is totally false, it may be sufficiently serious to provide grounds for a successful appeal,[284] or even, if it emerges after an appeal, for the conviction of a lower court to be quashed by certiorari.[285] It may even expose counsel to a wasted costs order.[286]

Bad character

The court accepts that, in general, a party tenders a witness as capable of being believed. If a party tenders a witness whose character may be impugned, for example by proof of previous convictions, the court expects candour. In general, a party is neither inclined, nor permitted, to impeach the credibility of his own witness,[287] not even when the witness is the opposing party.[288] This rule is enshrined in the Criminal Procedure Act 1865 to the extent that it prohibits a party from impeaching his own witness 'by general evidence of bad character',[289] and was defended by the Criminal Law Revision Committee, largely on the basis that a party should not be in a position to intimidate a witness into testifying, perhaps falsely, in his favour.[290] This argument fails to cover the situation in which a party might learn only after a witness has testified adversely just why he should have chosen to do so.[291] For this reason, the rule has been condemned as unconstitutional in the

---

[279] [1975] QB 834, [1975] 1 All ER 70; 842, 75; see also Lord Ellenborough CJ in *Bamfield v Massey* (1808) 1 Camp 460, 460, 461. See further, 306, on the use of scientific means to accomplish this.

[280] [1994] 3 All ER 346, 352. See also *R v Nelson* [1982] Qd R 636, in which the evidence was adduced by the defence. [281] See Cmnd 4991, [135].

[282] See e.g. *R v Kemp* [1995] 1 Cr App Rep 151, 152.

[283] See e.g. *Orchard v South Eastern Electricity Board* (n18); 578, 104.

[284] *Meek v Fleming* [1961] 2 QB 366, [1961] 3 All ER 148, in which the court was deliberately left with the impression that a police witness, sued for assault, had retained the rank of chief inspector, when he had in fact been demoted to sergeant for being concerned with the presentation of false evidence to a court.

[285] *R v Knightsbridge Crown Court, ex p Goonatilleke* [1986] QB 1, [1985] 2 All ER 498.

[286] *R v P* [2001] EWCA Crim 1728, [2002] 1 Cr App Rep 207.

[287] As noted, 308. See also III Wigmore [896].

[288] See *Scott v Sampson* (1881) 8 QBD 491, 498; *Skender v Barker* (1987) 44 DLR (4th) 106, 125.

[289] Section 3, 312. Section 112(3)(a) of the Criminal Justice Act 2003 explicitly preserves the operation of this provision.

[290] Cmnd 4991, [162]–[4]. These arguments were rejected by the Australian Law Reform Commission, Research Paper No 8 'Manner of Giving Evidence' ch 9.

[291] See Lord Denman CJ in *Dunn v Aslett* (1838) 2 Mood & R 122.

United States, at least as concerns the accused in a criminal trial,[292] and has been widely abrogated by statute.[293] It clearly cannot be applied to a hostile witness in its full rigour. Apart from the statutory provision for inconsistent statements dealt with in the previous chapter, the rules relating to the impeachment of hostile witnesses are still governed by the common law in other respects. It seems clear that the witness cannot be impeached by evidence of convictions or discreditable acts unconnected with his testimony, so far as those matters are not governed by the statutory prohibition against general evidence of bad character, which must still be understood in its common law sense of reputation.[294] Nor may he be cross-examined about his general veracity. It is, however, equally clear that he can be cross-examined about his means of knowledge, and general capacity. It is slightly less certain whether or not he can be cross-examined about possible bias against the party calling him, but the better view is that he may be so cross-examined.[295]

Criminal proceedings

Good character

The rules relating to good character are unaffected, at least directly,[296] by the provisions of the Criminal Justice Act 2003.

Bad character

Evidence of the bad character of anyone other than the defendant himself is governed in criminal proceedings by the provisions of s 100 of the Criminal Justice Act 2003, but those provisions are mainly concerned with situations in which the bad character is relevant to issue, in the sense of showing that a third party, who might or might not be a witness, was the real criminal. They have, however, also been held to extend to credibility, partly by reference to the explanatory notes, and partly on the basis that there would otherwise be an unacceptable lacuna in the provisions.[297]

If a prosecution witness has convictions, thus tending to undermine the case for the prosecution, there is now[298] a primary statutory obligation to disclose them in advance, and to inform the jury of them at the outset.[299] In such cases, the party asks the court to accept the testimony of the witness despite his bad character. It very occasionally happens that a party seeks to prove the bad character of his own witness in order to enhance his credibility on a particular matter, and there appears to be no objection to this.[300] He may

---

[292] *Chambers v Mississippi* 410 US 285, 294 (1973), although this view has been rejected in Canada: see *R v Williams* (1985) 44 CR (3d) 351.

[293] See, e.g. r 607 of Federal Rules (following the Model Code and Uniform Rules).

[294] *R v Rowton* (n134).

[295] Despite dicta to the contrary in *Fenton v Hughes* (1802) 7 Ves 287, 290, and in *R v Ball* (1839) 8 C & P 745, 746; the point seems settled by *R v Chapman* (1838) 8 C & P 558, 559; *Dunn v Aslett* (1838) 2 Mood & R 122, 123, and *Melhuish v Collier* (1850) 15 QB 878, 890.

[296] They may be affected indirectly by a perceived need to avoid conveying a false impression that will trigger correction by evidence of bad character admitted under the provisions of s 101(1)(f) of the Criminal Justice Act 2003.   [297] *R v Weir* (n234) (*Yaxley-Lennon*), [73].

[298] Criminal Procedure and Investigations Act 1996, s 3. See in Scotland *HM Adv v Murtagh* [2009] UKPC 35, and ongoing statutory reform, Criminal Justice and Licensing (Scotland) Bill 2009.

[299] *R v Taylor: R v Goodman* [1999] 2 Cr App Rep 163, unless requested not to do so by the defence.

[300] It occurred in *R v Brophy* [1982] AC 476, [1981] 2 All ER 705 (membership of IRA to support allegation of police misconduct), and in Australia on a similar basis in *R v von Rijssen* (1995) 77 ACR 566.

not, however, impugn the general character of his own witness.[301] In *R v Ross* it seems to have been accepted that the witness's character is divisible, and that if his evidence relates to a matter extrinsic to the subject matter of the convictions it is not discredited by reference to them.[302]

In the case of a party's own witness, any necessity to adduce evidence of his bad character would be most likely to be allowed by agreement of the parties pursuant to CJA 2003, s 100(1)(c).[303]

CHARACTER OF OPPONENT'S WITNESS

It is so unlikely[304] to occur that there is no occasion to discuss adducing evidence of the good character of an opponent's witness, so this section will be concerned only with the ways in which such a witness may be discredited. On account of the Criminal Justice Act 2003, which applies only to criminal proceedings, it is, however, necessary to divide discussion between civil and criminal proceedings. Discussion of the character of the accused himself, even when he testifies on his own behalf, will be considered in the following chapter.

An opponent's witness may be discredited in a wider variety of ways than one's own. In addition to demonstrating lack of knowledge or capacity and inconsistent statements, it is possible to raise his previous convictions, discreditable conduct, bias, corruption, or lack of veracity.[305] There are, however, two general restrictions. The first is that the matter must be relevant, at least to the witness's credibility,[306] although this sometimes seems rather notional. If it is relevant only to credit, the general rule is that evidence may not be adduced to rebut the witness's denial. Thus in *R v Cargill*,[307] in which the accused was charged with a sexual offence against a child, he was not permitted to adduce evidence to rebut her denial of being a prostitute, despite the fact that she had, in error, been allowed to assert in chief that she was a virgin. Since she was a child, consent was not in issue, and her prostitution, even if it could be proved, was relevant only to credit. The second general restriction is that the judge has the duty to prevent questioning of an unduly offensive, vexatious, or embarrassing character,[308] and to prevent the process of the court from being abused to torture witnesses by oppressive cross-examination.[309] His powers in this respect have been enhanced by the discretion conferred upon him by Pt 32.1 of the Civil Procedure Rules to control the evidence to be adduced, including

---

[301] Criminal Procedure Act 1865 s 3, which is explicitly retained by Criminal Justice Act 2003, s 112(3)(a).

[302] [2007] EWCA Crim 1457, [31].

[303] In which case, CJA 2003, s 100(4) dispenses with the need to seek the leave of the court.

[304] Although it is not quite impossible, for example if there is more than one opponent, and there is some advantage in having one rather than the other found liable.

[305] Although the Bar's Code of Conduct, and the Law Society's Code for Advocacy restrain questions that are 'merely scandalous or calculated only to vilify, insult, or annoy'.

[306] In *R v Humphreys and Tully* [1993] Crim LR 288, questions simply showing association with criminals were rejected on this basis.   [307] (1913) 8 Cr App Rep 224.

[308] *Vassiliades v Vassiliades* (1941) 18 Cyprus LR 10, 22, Lord Wright; *Wong Kam-Ming v R* [1980] AC 247, [1979] 1 All ER 939; 260, 946, Lord Edmund-Davies. See also *Fanjoy v R* (1985) 21 DLR (4th) 321.

[309] *Re Mundell* (1883) 48 LT 776, 778; *R v Brown* [1998] 2 Cr App Rep 364. See also, in Canada, *R v Walker* (1994) 90 CCC (3d) 144, in which the cross-examination was of the accused, who there attracts no special protection when testifying.

the discretion to disallow cross-examination on evidence of bad character.[310] It is now convenient to consider the different ways of attacking the character of an opponent's witness. Convictions, which are the subject of an explicit statutory rule, will be considered first. They can be regarded as affecting credit only on the basis that they show the witness in a generally unfavourable light. Since the same light is shed by equally discreditable conduct which does not happen to have become the subject of a conviction, it is necessary to consider also evidence of that character. Traditionally, bias in the sense of underlying and undue sympathy or hostility felt by the witness towards a party, has been regarded as relevant to credit, and has been distinguished from corruption, in the sense of more specific interference with testimony, typically by way of bribery. Finally, there is a special technique of the common law permitting an attack upon the general veracity of a witness. For convenience of exposition,[311] these will be considered separately, but similar principles underpin them all.

It is worth noting that even a mistaken decision not to allow cross-examination of a witness's bad character at the instance of the accused may not lead to a conviction being automatically regarded as unsafe, when such a decision would, under the provisions[312] of the Criminal Justice Act, have allowed the accused to be cross-examined as to his, perhaps more devastating, record.[313]

Convictions[314]

Civil proceedings

It was rare for witnesses who had convictions to be regarded as competent to give evidence at common law.[315] The question became important only after the passage of the Evidence Act 1843. It was considered by the Common Law Commissioners, who recommended in 1853 that cross-examination be confined to 'offences which imply turpitude and want of probity, and more especially absence of veracity—as for instance, perjury, forgery, obtaining money or goods under false pretences and the like'.[316] For

---

[310] See e.g. *Watson v Chief Constable of Cleveland* [2001] EWCA Civ 1547.

[311] Some scepticism of the value of such division was expressed in *R v TM* [2004] EWCA Crim 2085 [34].

[312] Especially s 101(1)(g).   [313] This contributed to the decision in *R v Bovell* (n130), [23].

[314] In some situations, adjudications of disciplinary tribunals seem to be assimilated to convictions: see e.g. *R v Edwards* [1991] 2 All ER 266, [1991] 1 WLR 207, 275, 216; but this may lead to difficulty, since such adjudications are unaffected by the provisions of either s 6 of the Criminal Procedure Act 1865, of s 11 of the Civil Evidence Act 1968, or of s 74 of the Police and Criminal Evidence Act 1984, which apply in the relevant respects only to convictions. Cf *R v Dick* [1982] Tas R 282. In Canada, convictions have been held to comprehend those in which an appeal is still pending: *R v Watson* (1996) 108 CCC (3d) 310 (although there the conviction had relevance both to issue and to credit, in other ways as well). The convictions must be those of the accused himself for the purpose of this rule: *R v Dupuis* (1995) 98 CCC (3d) 496 (not his father's); *R v Kino and Mete* (n206) (not those of a non-testifying co-accused). Cautions involve an admission of guilt, but are not caught by the legislation referring to convictions, and so do not become spent, but they may nevertheless be regarded as militating against a good character direction, and even sometimes as having more force than extant convictions: see *R v Sabahat* (n168), [11]. Foreign convictions may be proved so as to prevent a good character direction: see e.g. *R v Mauricia* [2002] EWCA Crim 676, [2002] 2 Cr App Rep 377; and may be so used even if they could not be so used in the jurisdiction concerned: see *R v El-Delbi* [2003] EWCA Crim 1767, (2003) 147 SJLB 784.

[315] In *Bugg v Day* (1949) 79 CLR 442, 467, Dixon J, dissenting on this point, took the view that, at common law, questions had to be restricted to convictions for offences involving the veracity of the witness.

[316] Second Report of Her Majesty's Commissioners for Inquiry into the Process, Practice and Pleading in the Superior Courts of Law (1853), 21.

some reason, this limitation was not included in the ensuing statutory provision, which now reads:[317]

If, upon a witness being lawfully questioned as to whether he has been convicted of any…misdemeanour and he either denies or does not admit the fact, or refuses to answer, it shall be lawful for the cross-examining party to prove such conviction.

Whatever the reason for enacting the statute in so broad a form, it was generally taken to authorize cross-examination about any previous conviction.[318] In civil proceedings, a spent conviction can be put to a witness at the discretion of the court when it is relevant to an issue, including credit, when justice cannot otherwise be done,[319] although such a conclusion should not be reached without consideration also of the prejudice it may cause. In *Thomas v Metropolitan Police Comr*,[320] two spent convictions for minor offences were admitted on this basis, despite going no more than marginally to credit, because the issue depended on a conflict of testimony, and the Court of Appeal was reluctant to interfere with the trial judge's exercise of his discretion.

Section 6 of the Criminal Procedure Act 1865 itself provides for proof of the conviction if the witness should deny it,[321] thus constituting an explicit statutory exception to the general rule that denial of a collateral matter cannot be rebutted.[322]

Criminal proceedings

The Criminal Law Revision Committee recommended the requirement of an explicit link between the conviction and the credibility of the witness, leaving the interpretation of such provision to the courts without further guidance. It is to be regretted that no such provision has yet been included in any subsequent legislation[323] in England.[324] The Criminal Justice Act 2003 retained s 6 of the Criminal Procedure Act 1865, subject only to minor amendment[325] recognizing the increased possibility of convictions being proved against the accused in chief. It seems that any greater stringency introduced by the Criminal Justice Act 2003, restricting the use of convictions against the accused's credit to those demonstrating 'untruthfulness' rather than general dishonesty,[326] has not been

---

[317] Criminal Procedure Act 1865, s 6 (as amended). The Canada Evidence Act 1985, s 12 is in similarly wide terms: see *R v Watkins* (1992) 70 CCC (3d) 341. For historical background, see Ladd (1936) 4 U Chi LR 69.

[318] In *Clifford v Clifford* [1961] 3 All ER 231, [1961] 1 WLR 1274; 232, 1276, Cairns J: 'It has never, I think, been doubted that a conviction for any offence could be put to a witness by way of cross-examination as to credit, even though the offence was not one of dishonesty.' In *R v Latimer* [1988] 11 NIJB 1, a witness's credibility was attacked by cross-examination about the theft of a pound of butter 19 years before; *R v Sweet-Escott* (1971) 55 Cr App Rep 316, 320.   [319] Rehabilitation of Offenders Act 1974, s 7(3).

[320] [1997] QB 813, [1997] 1 All ER 747.

[321] The marginal note to the section suggests that it was principally designed to facilitate such proof.

[322] Under the old law, a false denial could always provide the basis for a charge of perjury: *R v Baker* [1895] 1 QB 797. See, now, *R v Sweet-Escott* (n318). See also *R v Livingstone* [1987] 1 Qd R 38.

[323] Cmnd 4991, paras 159–61, draft bill, cl 10(1). In Canada, it has been held that the dishonesty of the basis for the conviction trumps the triviality of the sum involved: *R v Turlon* (1989) 70 CR (3d) 376.

[324] In the United States, r 609 of the Federal Rules of Evidence was amended in 1990 so as to subject convictions used under it to impeach witnesses other than the accused to the general balancing test in r 403. In Australia, under the provisions of the Evidence Act 1995 (NSW), convictions are not regarded as necessarily relevant to credibility: *R v Galea* [2004] NSWCCA 227, 148 ACR 220, [117]; cf *R v Burns* [2003] NSWCCA 30, 137 ACR 557.   [325] Into the form quoted above: Sch 37 Pt 5.

[326] *R v Hanson* [2005] EWCA Crim 824, [2005] 2 Cr App Rep 299, [13].

carried over to third-party witnesses. Thus in *R v Osbourne*,[327] the Court of Appeal refused to overturn the trial judge's determination that an offence of violence could be proved against a defence witness testifying that no violence had been inflicted by the defendant on the complainant, on the basis that the jury was entitled to know the character of the witness so testifying.

As noted above, s 100 does require *substantial* probative value to a matter that is of *substantial* importance in the context of the case as a whole. In *R v Yaxley-Lennon*,[328] a caution for possession of drugs was held on this basis to deserve a jury direction to disregard.

It should be noted that, although convictions that are 'spent' under the provisions of the Rehabilitation of Offenders Act 1974 are technically admissible in criminal proceedings,[329] the court, as a matter of practice, requires leave to be sought before permitting cross-examination on such convictions.[330] Cross-examination is subject to the discretion of the judge to disallow such questioning, a discretion recommended to be exercised as benevolently to the accused as possible,[331] only as a last resort if justice can be done in no other way,[332] and less generously than in cases of live convictions.[333] This has been applied where cases of assault depended upon a conflict of testimony[334] as to which party was the aggressor, when one had spent convictions for dishonesty and violence.[335] It seems that a good character direction should now be given, although failure to give such a direction is not necessarily fatal, and should not normally[336] be qualified in respect of spent convictions.

Discreditable acts

Civil proceedings

If the character of a testifying[337] witness is relevant to the issue, then he may be cross-examined about it, and any denial rebutted, and in such a case, the judge should be

---

[327] *R v Renda* (n126), [59].

[328] *R v Weir*, (n234), [74]; see also *Renda* (n126), *(Rafiq)*, [74], in which a prosecution witness's caution was not so regarded.

[329] Section 7(2)(a), and 25-year-old convictions have been permitted to be put to an accused person aged under 50: *R v Bailey* [1989] Crim LR 723.

[330] *Practice Note* [2002] 3 All ER 909, [2002] 1 WLR [6.6]. Non-compliance with its predecessor was, however, not necessarily fatal to a conviction: *R v Smallman* [1982] Crim LR 175. It was suggested in *R v Lawler* (1999) unreported, CA, 6 May that the earlier Practice Direction was made ultra vires as conflicting with the express exclusion of criminal proceedings by the Act, but this view was rejected by the court, and that view seems to have been endorsed by the reissue of the Direction, although the prospect of further revision was also indicated.

[331] *R v Nye* (1982) 75 Cr App Rep 247. See also *R v O'Shea* [1993] Crim LR 951. Now see also *Practice Direction* [2002] 3 All ER 909, [6.4].

[332] See broad dicta in *R v Hastings Justices, ex p McSpirit* (1994) The Times, 23 June, 162 JP 44.

[333] *R v Lawrence* [1995] Crim LR 815.

[334] And even in its absence when the accused's account was otherwise before the court: *R v Whelan* [1996] Crim LR 423.

[335] *R v Paraskeva* (1982) 76 Cr App Rep 162; *R v Evans* (1992) 156 JP 539; but see *R v Sabahat* (n168), in which a direction was qualified in respect of a caution that had it been a conviction, would have been spent.

[336] *R v MacDonald* (n158), CA. Presumably subject to exception in cases where the significance of the old offence was so remarkable as to render the good character direction absurd.

[337] See above, for discussion of evidence of the character of the co-accused, and below, for that of a non-testifying third party.

particularly careful to ensure that the jury understands that the evidence may be regarded as going both to credit and to issue.[338]

The traditional rule of the scope of cross-examination and rebuttal was laid down by Lawrence J in *Harris v Tippett*:[339]

I will permit questions to be put to a witness as to any improper conduct of which he may have been guilty for the purpose of trying his credit; but, when the questions are irrelevant to the issue on the record, you cannot call witnesses to contradict the answers he gives.

There are thus two issues: first, whether cross-examination about the discreditable matter is to be allowed at all; second, if it is, whether a denial can be rebutted. These will be considered in turn.

If the question imputes a crime of which the witness has not been convicted,[340] he may claim the benefit of the privilege against self-incrimination so as to refuse to answer.[341] Subject to that, and to the judge's discretion to disallow improper questions, cross-examination about discreditable acts was widely permitted.[342] The width and tone[343] of such cross-examination caused some disquiet, which was not wholly stilled by a new Rule of Court made in 1883.[344] Principles governing the discretion to disallow cross-examination to credit were propounded by Stephen, incorporated into the Indian Evidence Act, and endorsed by Sankey LJ in *Hobbs v Tinling & Co Ltd*,[345] to the effect that (i) questions are proper only when answers would seriously impair the credibility of the witness; (ii) questions are improper if they relate to matters so remote in time or of such a character that, if true, they could not seriously impair the credibility of the witness; and (iii) questions are improper if there is a substantial disproportion between the importance of the imputation against the witness's character and the importance of his evidence to the issue to be decided.[346]

As will be seen below, it has now been accepted in criminal proceedings,[347] and in civil proceedings in other jurisdictions,[348] that a more liberal approach to rebuttal has been adopted, and it is submitted that, in the light of the increased case-management powers

---

[338] *R v Arcangioli* [1994] 1 SCR 129.   [339] (1811) 2 Camp 637, 638.

[340] If the witness has been charged, but not yet convicted, Canadian authority distinguishes between witnesses for the defence of whom the question may not be asked because there is nothing to discredit the witness, and witnesses for the prosecution whose credibility may be affected by the desire to curry favour with the prosecuting authorities: *Titus v R* [1983] 1 SCR 259.

[341] In the early nineteenth century, he could invoke an analogous privilege in respect of questions the answers to which would disgrace him.

[342] Although it must be the matter put in cross-examination itself, and not a false denial alone which impugns the credibility of the witness: *Spenceley v De Willott* (1806) 7 East 108.

[343] See, in Australia, for modern concern about the tone of cross-examination on such matters: *R v Power and Power* (1996) 87 ACR 407, 416.

[344] Order 36, r 38, not carried over into the new rules in 1965. The rules of the bar do, however, set out appropriate principles: see *R v Guney* [1998] 2 Cr App Rep 242, 259D.   [345] (n26), 51.

[346] These principles still allow considerable latitude to a cross-examiner: see *R v Longman and Richardson* [1969] 1 QB 299, [1968] 2 All ER 761, in which it was put to a witness not only that she was generally unreliable, but that she was a drunkard, suffered from hallucinations, entertained groundless fears, was a prostitute, and a deliberate perjurer, and, in the words of the court, her whole history and background were brought out.   [347] See *Tiwari v State* [2002] UKPC 29, [28]; see further below, 362.

[348] See, in Australia, *Natta v Canham* (1991) 104 ALR 143.

of the judge under the Civil Procedure Rules, a similar liberality may be expected here,[349] and rebuttal allowed when the issue is central and does not raise the spectre of prolonged, and expensive, ventilation.

Criminal proceedings

The same rules regulating the use of the bad character of witnesses other than the accused and complainants in sexual cases apply in criminal proceedings as were stated in *Hobbs v Tinling*, although courts seem sometimes to have been more reluctant to enforce them to the disadvantage of the defence.[350] For this reason, the Law Commission proposed statutory control on the admissibility of evidence of the bad character of witnesses other than the defendant.[351] These proposals have now been enacted as s 100 of the Criminal Justice Act 2003, although it may be questioned how far those proposals have taken the law beyond the position reached at common law, which will first be outlined.

Common law

In *R v Edwards*,[352] the Court of Appeal considered how far it was proper to cross-examine a police witness about previous improprieties to the effect that there was systematic perversion of justice, that some officers had been the subject of criminal or disciplinary processes in relation to the falsification of evidence, and that acquittals had been secured in cases in which the witnesses had testified. The court rejected the first line of attack as too remote,[353] accepted the second only to the extent that the proceedings had culminated in adverse findings,[354] and the third only where there was no other reasonable explanation for the acquittal than a determination that the witness must have been lying.[355] It is dubious how far a witness may be asked about criticisms of his testimony made by a judge in earlier proceedings, whether or not an acquittal resulted.[356]

Attention has been focused on this problem by high-profile investigations into improper practices in particular units of the police force,[357] and, in the view of a Lord Chief Justice,

---

[349] It seems to have been accepted in *Scott v Chief Constable of South Yorkshire* [2006] EWCA Civ 598, [19] that complaints against a policeman leading only to 'advice' could be put to him in cross-examination, despite being of slight weight even to credibility.

[350] *R v Longman and Richardson* (n346) was a particularly egregious example.

[351] Law Com 273 Pt IX.   [352] (n314).

[353] See also *R v Irish* [1995] Crim LR 145. It is not obvious why this reverse similar fact argument was rejected so perfunctorily.

[354] Although this was more restrictive than the statutory view in the Criminal Evidence Act 1898, s 1(f), under which it seems to have been assumed that charges might impugn credit, and which appears inconsistent with the ruling of the House of Lords in *R v Z* [2000] 2 AC 483, [2000] 3 All ER 385 that acquittals can be adduced as evidence of guilt on the basis of having been unjustified.

[355] See the discussion of *R v Thorne* (1977) 66 Cr App Rep 6; *R v Cooke* (1986) 84 Cr App Rep 286. The earlier cases of *R v Hay* (1983) 77 Cr App Rep 70 and *R v Doosti* (1985) 82 Cr App Rep 181; the later cases of *R v Lewis* (1992) The Guardian, 9 April; *R v Lucas* [1993] Crim LR 599; and *R v Gale* [1994] Crim LR 208 should also be considered. See, in Scotland: *MacDonald v HM Adv* [2004] SCCR 100, 2003 GWD 40–1074.

[356] See, in Australia, *Roberts v Western Australia* [2005] WASCA 37, 152 ACR 346, in which adverse remarks by a judge in earlier civil proceedings in connection with the very matter in issue in the criminal proceedings were held allowable in cross-examination.

[357] Reported cases have referred to the investigations of the West Midlands Serious Crime Squad, the Stoke Newington drugs squad, and the Rigg Approach Flying Squad. The principles apply generally to professional misconduct: see *R v Guney* (n344), 260A.

an inclination to construct defences especially to take advantage of such suspicion.[358] The first conclusion in *Edwards*, that the court will not entertain cross-examination based on generalized[359] allegations against the officers of a unit, has largely been endorsed,[360] and was explained in *R v Guney* on the basis that it is unfair to cross-examine about the misconduct of another, and that there is a danger of a bandwagon effect when a multiplicity of unproved[361] allegations is put to a police officer.[362] It is sometimes necessary to distinguish between those officers who were involved in malpractice, and those who were merely aware of it, and failed to report it. This raises the issue of the extent to which unproved allegations can be put to a police officer, or reliance placed upon the failure of a prosecution in which he has been heavily involved. In *R v Edwards*, the court looked carefully at the circumstances of each allegation and each unsuccessful case.[363] It must be recognized that acquittal does not necessarily lead to the conclusion that any particular prosecution witness[364] was lying; still less success of an appeal against conviction;[365] and perhaps least of all a decision not to proceed with a prosecution. It has nevertheless been accepted that if, on analysis of the earlier case, it appears that doubt as to the credibility of the police officer in a relevant respect accounted for failure to prosecute successfully, then that may be put in cross-examination.[366] Given the recognition[367] in *R v Guney* of a culture of discreditable behaviour, solidarity, and misplaced loyalty in some police units, this seems remarkably limited. The impact of any police impropriety upon the credibility of a witness subjected to it will also need consideration, and in some cases, very serious impropriety has been regarded as having insufficient effect in the context of the evidence as a whole,[368] especially where the impropriety occurred long after,[369] and there is some independent support for the evidence of the discredited officer. Similar considerations may apply to non-police witnesses.[370]

---

[358] Lord Taylor CJ in the 1994 Tom Sargent lecture (1994) NLJ, 28 January, 127.

[359] Although if sufficiently clearly established, it is unnecessary that the misconduct take exactly the same form, for example subornation of perjury in one case and fabrication of evidence in another: see *R v Malik* [2000] 2 Cr App Rep 8.

[360] See *R v Guney* (n344); *R v Crook* [2003] EWCA Crim 1272; *R v Stephens* [2003] EWCA Crim 2085; *R v Mills and Poole (No 2)* [2003] EWCA Crim 1753, [2003] 1 WLR 2931; but cf *R v Maxine Edwards* [1996] 2 Cr App Rep 345; *R v Whelan* [1997] Crim LR 353; *R v Twitchell* [2000] 1 Cr App Rep 373; *R v Zomparelli (No 2)* (23 March 2000, unreported), CA.

[361] The court must also be alert to suggestions that allegations against an officer have been deliberately shelved until after he has testified in a given case: see *R v Llewellyn and Gray* [2001] EWCA Crim 1555, [28] (requiring positive evidence to sustain such an allegation).

[362] There may be more resistance to putting unproved allegations to independent witnesses, especially those for the defence: see *R v Jeneson* [2005] EWCA Crim 1984, [59].

[363] In *R v Twitchell* (n360) it was stressed that in relation to other adjudications reliance should be placed only upon proved facts, bearing in mind that appellate courts do not normally find facts.

[364] The same applies to key lay prosecution witnesses: *R v H* (1990) 90 Cr App Rep 440.

[365] *R v Guney* (n344), 262C.

[366] See *R v Beattie* (1996) 89 ACR 393 for a similar decision in Australia under the provisions of the Evidence Act (NSW) 1995.
[367] 261A.

[368] See *R v Mills and Poole (No 2)* [2003] EWCA Crim 1753, [2003] 1 WLR 2931, [76], in which a Detective Inspector had threatened a potential defence witness with arrest if he attended the trial, but had denied doing so, and implied that he had tried to persuade the witness to testify for the prosecution, but it was held that this did not in its context amount to such an abuse of process as to justify setting aside the conviction.

[369] *R v Deans* [2004] EWCA Crim 2123, [37].

[370] See *R v Pedder* [2004] EWCA Crim 2094 (medical expert criticized by the court on a different basis in earlier case); *R v Carr* [2008] EWCA Crim 1283 (witness member of one of two feuding families); *R v McDonald* 219 CCC3d 369 (2007) (close family member).

If a question is allowed then, as stated above, the rule used to be that the witness's denial could not be rebutted on a purely collateral matter, but here, as elsewhere, there are now signs of a more liberal approach to rebuttal,[371] certainly in criminal cases.[372] Thus in *R v Busby*,[373] it was suggested that a police witness for the prosecution had fabricated an oral confession and threatened a potential witness for the defence so as to prevent him from testifying. Both allegations were denied by the police officer, and the defence proposed to call the man who had been threatened to rebut the denial of a threat. The judge refused, applying the traditional collateral matter rule, but the Court of Appeal quashed the conviction on the basis that the defence should have been allowed to rebut the denial because it went to a fact in issue. This seems quite contrary to the decision in *Harris v Tippett*,[374] and to most tests for the distinction between credit and issue.[375] It should be noted that the argument was that the testimony of someone who would tamper with potential witnesses in the way alleged was likely to be unreliable, and ought not to be believed in conflict with the testimony of the accused, who alleged that the witness's evidence of an oral confession was fabricated. It was not suggested that there was any special animus against the accused,[376] or that the witness's testimony had been secured by corruption. A similar approach is also apparent in the Divisional Court's agreement[377] that 'a matter going to the credit of a witness in a criminal case cannot be said to be collateral to the vital issue...especially where...the witness in question provides the only evidence upon that issue'. This is especially likely to be the case where the issue arises in a sexual case, where there is a clear conflict of evidence as to the truth of an allegation about sexual contact in private.[378] It remains the case, however, that in cases in which rebuttal may be time-consuming, confusing, and inconclusive, rebuttal is less likely to be allowed.[379] So too the more remote the issue from the central issues of the

---

[371] This passage was cited with apparent approval, and applied in *R v Nagrecha* (n56), and *Tiwari v State* (n347), [28]. See also, in Canada, *Aalders v R* [1993] 2 SCR 482; *R v R (D)* [1996] 2 SCR 291, 313. It has, however, been stressed in Australia that a proper foundation for rebuttal must be laid: *Nicholls v R* (n55).

[372] Though the suggestion in *R v Funderburk* (n55); 486, 591 that there is a separate category permitting rebuttal in cases in which the police have gone to improper lengths to secure a conviction was explicitly rejected by Lord Lane CJ in *R v Edwards* (n314), 274, 215.

[373] (1981) 75 Cr App Rep 79. See also *R v Mendy* (1976) 64 Cr App Rep 4, in which a witness's denial that he had received an improper communication to assist his testimony for the accused was permitted to be rebutted.

[374] (n339). Although Pattenden has questioned the degree of inconsistency: see [1992] *Crim LR* 549, 551.

[375] Various formulations were advanced in *A-G v Hitchcock* (1847) 1 Exch 91, 99. See *R v Funderburk* (n55); and further extensive discussion by the High Court of Australia in *Nicholls v R* (n55).

[376] *Busby* (n373) was nevertheless characterized as a case of bias in *Edwards* (n314); but if so, it is bias in an extended sense overlapping this category, a view endorsed by Wolchover in [1992] *Crim LR* 863, 865.

[377] In *R v Knightsbridge Crown Court, ex p Goonatilleke* (n285), 11. For further examples of liberality, see also *R v Marsh* (1985) 83 Cr App Rep 165; *R v Barton* (1986) 85 Cr App Rep 5, 13. For an Australian application to the credibility of a sexual complainant by reference to other sexual relations between the parties, see *Bannister v R* (1993) 10 WAR 484; but see also *Hickman v R* (1993) 60 SASR 415, in which the issue upon which credibility depended was too remote from the facts in issue.

[378] *R v Nagrecha* (n56): in such a case, denial of a previous disputed complaint of sexual contact is especially likely to be permitted to be rebutted; although in *Tiwari v State* (n347) [29], a much wider range of issues depending upon a conflict of credibility was regarded as susceptible to a similar approach. See also *R v David R* (16 July 1999, unreported) (in which the evidence related to collusion to make false complaints); *R v Willshire* (13 December 1999, unreported), CA.

[379] In *R v S* [1992] Crim LR 307, the Court of Appeal distinguished between an attempt to rebut the denial that an allegation of rape was false by readily controvertible evidence such as consent, and by effectively incontrovertible evidence, such as proof of absence abroad.

trial, the less the court will be inclined to allow rebuttal.[380] The Court of Appeal has said[381] it needs to be 'of such probative force and so important in the overall context of the case that in the properly informed judgment of the trial judge there would be a danger of a miscarriage if such evidence were not permitted.'

Criminal Justice Act 2003

The Law Commission's aim was to emphasize the enhanced standard of relevance required of the bad character evidence of non-defendants, whether it went to issue or to credit. To that end, s 100 of the CJA 2003 was enacted:

(1) In criminal proceedings evidence of the bad character of a person other than the defendant is admissible if and only if—

   (a) it is important explanatory evidence,

   (b) it has substantial probative value in relation to a matter which—

      (i) is a matter in issue in the proceedings, and

      (ii) is of substantial importance in the context of the case as a whole, or

      (iii) all parties to the proceedings agree to the evidence being admissible.

(2) For the purposes of subsection (1)(a) evidence is important explanatory evidence if—

   (a) without it, the court or jury would find it impossible or difficult properly to understand other evidence in the case, and

   (b) its value for understanding the case as a whole is substantial.

(3) In assessing the probative value of evidence for the purposes of subsection (1)(b) the court must have regard to the following factors (and to any others it considers relevant)—

   (a) the nature and number of the events, or other things, to which the evidence relates;

   (b) when those events or things are alleged to have happened or existed;

   (c) where—

      (i) the evidence is evidence of a person's misconduct, and

      (ii) it is suggested that the evidence has probative value by reason of similarity between that misconduct and other alleged misconduct, the nature and extent of the similarities and the dissimilarities between each of the alleged instances of misconduct;

   (d) where—

      (i) the evidence is evidence of a person's misconduct,

      (ii) it is suggested that that person is also responsible for the misconduct charged, and

      (iii) the identity of the person responsible for the misconduct charged is disputed, the extent to which the evidence shows or tends to show that the same person was responsible each time.

---

[380] In *R v Neale* [1998] Crim LR 737, this was taken to the extent of excluding rebuttal of lies alleged to have been made by the complainant in other parts of the same complaint on which the accused was charged, but against his wife, who had not been charged, even though these complaints were of the same general character as those made against the accused, and had a sexual context.

[381] *R v Letts and Chung* [2007] EWCA Crim 3282, [34].

(4) Except where subsection (1)(c) applies, evidence of the bad character of a person other
      than the defendant must not be given without leave of the court.

It will be seen that this section imposes a requirement that the leave of the court be
obtained,[382] and that the evidence of bad character be of substantial probative value to
a matter that is in issue in the proceedings. It is clear from the discussion, examples, and
notes in the Law Commission's report that it envisaged the same test applying both to
matters at common law regarded as going to issue and to credit. In part, it was inspired
by a need to ensure parity between the ability to attack a witness's character, which was
regarded as in practice very wide, and the prosecution's ability to attack the accused's
character, which was regarded as very restricted. It is disturbing that, by enacting CJA
2003, s 100 in essentially the same form as that recommended by the Law Commission,
while at the same time making the admission of evidence of the accused's bad character
much less restricted than the Commission's recommendations; the result may have been
not to achieve the balance aimed at by the Law Commission, but to have arrived at another
unbalanced result, this time against the interests of the accused. The Law Commission
spent some time in explaining that its proposals in this respect to limit the range of evidence capable of being adduced by the accused in his defence were compatible with the
European Convention on Human Rights, but the imbalance mentioned above may be
regarded by some to have tipped the situation over into incompatibility. Now these provisions are in force, they seem likely to be tested for such compatibility.

    One consequence of the enhanced probative value required for the evidence to be
admitted in the first place is that rebuttal of a denial will become almost automatically
allowed, since the matter will already have been determined to be of such significance to
an issue of substantial importance in the context of the case as a whole in order to have
been adduced at all.

Bias[383]

Civil proceedings

This topic remains governed by the common law. Bias was more important under the
old law when incompetence on account of interest was widespread. If a wife was totally
incompetent to testify for a spouse, it was not unnatural for a court to allow a witness to
be asked whether she was the mistress of the party for whom she was testifying, and even
for her denial to be rebutted.[384] In the modern law, it is quite clear that many witnesses,
such as parties and their close relatives, are likely to be biased, and there is no special need
to bring this out. In some cases, it may not be obvious, and it is then perhaps desirable to

---

[382] Although this may not necessarily imply a discretion to exclude if the conditions in s 100 are held to
have been satisfied: *R v Riley* [2006] EWCA Crim 2030, [19]. No leave is required in respect of allegations
of improper conduct 'in connection with the prosecution of the offence' within s 98(b): *R v Ibrahim* [2008]
EWCA Crim 880, [2008] 4 All ER 208, [124].

[383] It seems that, in the United States, generic bias is included: see Park (1996) 67 *U of Col LR* 747 (analysis
of cross-examination about racial bias of police witness in the *OJ Simpson* case). In *R v Jeneson* (n362), [60]
the term 'partiality' was used.

[384] See *Thomas v David* (1836) 7 C & P 350. In *R v Longman and Richardson* (n346), a witness was even
permitted to be called to rebut the testimony of a mistress that she was afraid of her paramour.

make the true position clear by permitting rebuttal of a denial,[385] but not if the evidence is peripheral.[386] It seems similarly reasonable in a case in which some special factor is present in addition to foreseeable bias, such as the information passed to the accused's husband while he was waiting outside the court before giving his evidence in his wife's favour in *R v Mendy*,[387] to allow it to be brought out, once again by rebuttal of a denial. The English courts have not had reason to consider the question of whether an admission of bias for one reason lets in evidence of bias for another reason; the Supreme Court of Victoria has held that it does not.[388]

Criminal proceedings

This, too, is now governed by s 100 of the Criminal Justice Act 2003 discussed above. It seems unlikely to make much difference to the law as it had already developed.

Corruption

Civil proceedings

Here too the common law still governs. Corruption requires separate treatment from bias, if only because the bias cases have been expressly distinguished as constituting a separate area.[389] The scope for an allegation of corruption is limited because, if the corruption were attempted by a party to the proceedings, it could in any event be proved as a form of admission by conduct.[390] The whole area was reviewed in *A-G v Hitchcock*,[391] in which a witness for the prosecution in an excise case was cross-examined as to whether he had said that he had been offered a bribe to testify, impliedly falsely, for the prosecution. The prosecution argued that his denial of so saying could not be rebutted because it was a collateral matter, and more collateral than his denial of the actual receipt of a bribe would have been, which, they argued, could not have been rebutted either. The defence argued that the matter was not completely extrinsic. The court held that the denial could not be rebutted because the question was collateral in the sense that, even if it could be shown that the witness had said that he had been offered a bribe, it would constitute no disparagement of him. This, however, would seem to make the question not merely collateral, but wholly irrelevant. His denial of having said he had been offered a bribe might indeed disparage him if false, but it was already well established by 1847 that it was impermissible to make an irrelevant allegation merely in the hope of securing a false denial, which could be rebutted so as to discredit the witness.[392] It seems hard to contend that saying that a bribe has been offered in any way reveals that one has been accepted. In such a situation, the man who has accepted a bribe will either keep quiet if he is speaking to a stranger, or confide that he has accepted it if speaking to a close friend. The only man who will openly admit to all and sundry that

---

[385] As in *R v Phillips* (1936) 26 Cr App Rep 17, in which relations between the accused and his wife and children had become poisoned. See also, in Australia, *R v Harrington* [1998] 3 VR 531; *R v LSS* [2000] 1 Qd 546.

[386] *R v Young* [1995] Crim LR 653. [387] *R v Mendy* (n373).

[388] *Bakopoulos v General Motors Holdens Pty Ltd* [1973] VR 190 (although it allowed evidence of more extreme bias than had been admitted).

[389] In *A-G v Hitchcock* (n375), 100. The connection remains close since the offer of a bribe is some evidence of the bias of the offeror. In *R v TM* (n311), [34], the term 'partial' was preferred to 'bias' in this context. In *Nicholls v R* (n55), the High Court chose not to distinguish bias and corruption.

[390] *Moriarty v London, Chatham and Dover Rly Co* (1870) LR 5 QB 314. [391] (n375).

[392] *Spenceley v De Willott* (n342).

he has been offered a bribe is one who implies that he has rejected it. It seems that, if the issue relates to the solicitation of a bribe by the witness, rebuttal is permitted.[393] In *A-G v Hitchcock*, the court had been careful not to accede to the full width of the argument advanced by the prosecution, although it is hard to fit the case of an actual bribe into the formulations of the various tests for the distinction between collateral and crucial issues propounded by the different judges. It may, however, be the case that here too the only test had become the importance of the allegation in the context of the case.

Criminal proceedings

This certainly seems to have been the view of Lord Hewart CJ in criminal proceedings in *R v Phillips*,[394] in which the question was whether the denial of the child victims of alleged incest by their father that they had been schooled by their mother could be rebutted.[395] It is conceivable that some witnesses may become so tainted as to become impervious to cross-examination, even when denials can be rebutted, and in such a case, there may be no alternative but to preclude their testimony altogether.[396]

It seems that the offer of a bribe will not be collateral, even though rejected, certainly where it is argued that other witnesses may have been offered similar bribes. In such a situation, the offer of a bribe may be adduced, and rebutted.[397]

If expectations of financial reward for testimony have been aroused and denied, and documentation that could rebut that denial been improperly not disclosed to the defence, it will invalidate a conviction, even after a plea of guilty.[398] On the other hand, mere suspicion of improper collaboration between a witness and police officers, with a view to indirect financial reward via the media, has not been regarded as sufficient.[399] Nor does it seem likely that rebuttal will be allowed where the relevant witness's credibility is peripheral,[400] or sufficiently discredited otherwise.[401]

The advent of CJA 2003, s 100 seems only to have consolidated the law as it had developed at common law, as described above.

Lack of veracity

Civil proceedings

From the very beginning of the modern law of evidence, it has been possible to call a witness to swear that the opponent's witness cannot be believed upon his oath.[402] It was established that the impugning witness must speak from his personal knowledge,[403] but that he could not refer

---

[393] *Jackson v Thomason* (1861) 8 Jur NS 134; *R v Denley* [1970] Crim LR 583; *R v Aldridge* (1990) 20 NSWLR 737. Cf *R v Umanski* [1961] VLR 242. Any solicitation of a bribe by a witness for the prosecution must be disclosed to the defence: *R v Rasheed* (1994) 158 JP 941.   [394] (1936) 26 Cr App Rep 17.

[395] The rebuttal was to have been by two women to whom they had admitted that this was so, but it is not clear why this would not have been inadmissible as hearsay. In *R v S* (1988) 39 ACR 288, in which a denial of an allegation of corruption was rebutted, surrebuttal of that rebuttal was permitted.

[396] The Ontario Court of Appeal divided on this issue in *R v Buric and Parsniak* (1996) 106 CCC (3d) 97.

[397] *R v TM* (n311), [36].   [398] *R v Matthew Smith* [2004] EWCA Crim 2212.

[399] *R v Steele, Whomes, and Corry* [2006] EWCA Crim 195.

[400] *R (Boston) v Criminal Cases Review Commission* [2006] EWHC 1966 (Admin), [36].

[401] *R v Letts and Chung* [2007] EWCA Crim 3282, [35] (where the alleged corruption related to assistance with the witness's immigration status).   [402] Wigmore traces the rule back to 1664.

[403] *Trial of O'Connor* (1798) 26 How St Tr 1192, 27 How St Tr 32.

to particular events to justify his belief.[404] The pattern of the question moved from the general to the more particular, by asking first: 'Have you the means of knowing what the general character of the witness is?'; and then: 'From such knowledge of his general character, would you believe him on oath?'[405] It was not necessary that the witness have personal knowledge of false testimony by the witness,[406] and even if he did, he would not be allowed to refer to it under the ban on collateral matters.[407] The rule was reconsidered in *R v Brown and Hedley*[408] in the light of the decision in *R v Rowton*[409] that a witness could not express his personal opinion of the accused's character in rebuttal of a character witness called by the accused. The reasoning of the court was not wholly satisfactory, but the outcome was to endorse the existing practice, and to condense the questioning to elicit a simple asseveration that the impugning witness would not believe the opponent's witness on his oath.[410] It became very rare in practice for this cumbersome, anomalous, and unconvincing exercise to be conducted.[411]

Criminal proceedings

Its continued availability was, however, endorsed by a unanimous House of Lords in *Toohey v Metropolitan Police Comr*,[412] and most subsequent development took place in criminal cases. In *R v Richardson and Longman*,[413] strenuous efforts were made to impugn the credibility of a key witness for the prosecution. The defence called a witness in the hope that he would testify that this witness could not be believed on her oath if she were frightened, and her own evidence was that she was frightened of the accused. The trial judge allowed the witness to be asked if he were aware of her reputation for veracity, and whether he would believe her on oath. After a caution from the trial judge, the witness replied that, in certain particulars, she could be believed, whereupon the judge intervened to prevent any qualification of that statement, although the witness had got so far as to indicate that he wished to make some qualification. Nor, despite counsel's persistence, would the trial judge allow the witness to be asked to give an opinion of her credibility on oath on the basis of his personal knowledge of her. It was held that the further question should have been permitted, and a witness allowed to express his opinion of the veracity of another on the basis both of the general reputation for veracity, and of his personal knowledge, of the impugned witness. No final view was expressed about the intervention to prevent qualification, although the court seemed to incline to the view that qualification is impermissible if it is adduced only as a means of introducing in chief particular reasons for the qualification, although cross-examination about such reasons is permissible. It should also be noted that the party tendering the witness is not entitled to anticipate attack in court on this basis, and gets its rebuttal in first, as that is indistinguishable from inadmissible 'oath-helping'.[414] It is to be hoped that s 99 of the Criminal Justice Act 2003 will be accepted to have rid the law of this decrepit survival.[415]

---

[404] *R v Rudge* (1805) Peake Add Cas 232, a decision of Lawrence J who also presided in *Harris v Tippett* (n339).   [405] See *Mawson v Hartsink* (1802) 4 Esp 102.

[406] *R v Bispham* (1830) 4 C & P 392.   [407] *R v Hemp* (1833) 5 C & P 468.

[408] (1867) 10 Cox CC 453 (a better report than (1867) 1 CCR 70).   [409] (n134).

[410] See also *R v Watson* (1817) 2 Stark 116, 152 for this form of question.

[411] None of the Lords of Appeal, nor any of the counsel, in *Toohey* [1965] AC 595, [1965] 1 All ER 506, could recall its ever having happened.   [412] (n411).

[413] [1969] 1 QB 299, [1968] 2 All ER 761.   [414] *R v Beard* (n60).

[415] Despite having been affirmed, (without reference to s 99), to be 'alive and well in England' by an enlarged Court of Appeal in *R v BDX* [2009] VSCA 28, [41].

That rule is to be distinguished from the situation in which a witness's lack of veracity is imputed to some specific medical or mental condition.[416] In *Toohey v Metropolitan Police Comr*,[417] the accused was charged with assault, and wished to call medical evidence that the victim, who had testified for the prosecution, was suffering from hysteria. The courts below refused to permit such evidence.[418] In the House of Lords, counsel did not seek to support that decision, and it was overruled, the rule being held to be that:[419]

Medical evidence is admissible to show that a witness suffers from some disease or defect or abnormality of mind that affects the reliability of his evidence. Such evidence is not confined to a general opinion of the unreliability of the witness, but may give all the matters necessary to show not only the foundation of and the reasons for the diagnosis but also the extent to which the credibility of the witness is affected.

It seems clearly right that such evidence should be before the jury, and the possibility in these circumstances of prolonging the trial unduly is remote. There is some danger of attempts to influence the jury's assessment of the credibility of a witness by calling medical evidence to prove matters within the jury's normal competence, such as the propensity of some witnesses, who could perfectly well tell the truth, to tell lies.[420] Such cases are best dealt with on the basis of the relevance of the evidence, and the proper function of expert witnesses.[421] Some forms of attack, although on their face medical, may promote prejudice, such as cross-examination of complainants of sexual offences about their psychiatric history.[422] The rule in *Toohey* applied just as much to evidence adduced by the prosecution as by the defence.[423] Expert testimony as to the effect of a marginal mental condition upon a witness's veracity is more likely to be received when it is offered to rebut testimony that the witness should not be believed on oath,[424] than where it is offered in advance of any attack.[425] It seems that such medical evidence is now more likely to be received,[426] even in the absence of direct examination of the subject by the testifying witness.[427] In *R v Richard W*, the court was careful to distinguish medical evidence tending to identify a relevant condition from evidence more directly going to the credibility of the witness's testimony.[428]

Although not strictly relevant to impugning the testimony of an opponent's witness by medical evidence, it is convenient to consider here the question of how far a statement

---

[416] See Pattenden [1986] *Crim LR* 92; *Murphy v R* (1989) 86 ALR 35; *R v Kliman* (1996) 107 CCC (3d) 549, 564, correcting just such confusion by the trial judge.   [417] (n411).

[418] In reliance upon *R v Gunewardene* [1951] 2 KB 600, [1951] 2 All ER 290.   [419] 609, 512.

[420] See *R v Ashcroft* [1954] Qd R 81, 85; *R v MacKenney* (1980) 72 Cr App Rep 78.

[421] See Chapter XI. The attempt in *R v MacKenney* (n420) to limit the decision in *Toohey* (n411) to total incapacity to tell the truth appears to be inconsistent with the last sentence of Lord Pearce's speech quoted above.   [422] Ellison (2009) 13 *E&P* 28.

[423] *R v Eades* [1972] Crim LR 99. And has been held in Australia to be capable of being led in chief: *Coombes v Bessell* (1994) 4 Tas 149.

[424] As in *R v Taylor* (1986) 31 CCC (3d) 1 (allegation of sexual abuse by borderline schizophrenic).

[425] As in *R v B* [1987] 1 NZLR 362 (allegation of sexual abuse by slightly retarded 12-year-old).

[426] See *R v Mackenney (No 2)* [2003] EWCA Crim 3643, [2004] 2 Cr App R 32, [15], relying in part on the greater liberality towards the admissibility of evidence about the condition of the accused at the time of making a disputed confession: see *R v Ward* (1993) 96 Cr App Rep 1; thus evidence rejected as inadmissible at the first trial in 1980 was regarded as admissible by 2003, and led to a different outcome.

[427] Ibid, [16].

[428] [2003] EWCA Crim 3490, [24]. See also, in Scotland, *Mackay v HM Adv* 2004 SCCR 478.

tendered by the prosecution can be discredited by medical evidence of the condition of the maker at the time that the statement was made. It has been argued above[429] that the court has, at least, a discretion to reject a confession made by an accused person suffering at that time from mental instability. Under s 76 of the Police and Criminal Evidence Act 1984, a confession may be excluded if it were obtained in consequence of anything done that was likely, in the circumstances existing at the time, to render a confession unreliable. It might well be argued that to question a mentally disturbed person was so likely.[430] In such cases, it would seem right that the defence should be able to adduce medical evidence of the accused's condition at such a time.[431] Such evidence has been admitted in Commonwealth jurisdictions.[432] To the extent that *Toohey* is relied upon to justify these decisions, it is somewhat questionable whether it goes so far.[433] In these cases, the accused himself often testifies inconsistently with his confession, and it would appear that the expert evidence could be regarded as simply bolstering the testimony of the accused in the way criticised by the Court of Appeal in *R v Turner*.[434]

Since the medical condition of the witness, even if it causes him to lie, can hardly be regarded as evidence of misconduct, it falls outside the definition of bad character in CJA 2003, s 98, and so precludes the operation of s 100 in this context.[435]

SECTION 3. THE CHARACTER OF THIRD PARTIES

Sometimes a key figure in a case, or even the alleged alternative perpetrator of a crime is not the defendant or the co-accused, a victim or even a witness, but a third party.[436] If such third party is not called as a witness, questions arise as to the extent to which the character of such a person may be explored.

CIVIL PROCEEDINGS

A more generous view tends to be taken of the possible scope for attacking the character of third parties in civil proceedings than in criminal, partly because of the absence of any established discretion to avoid prejudice to one accused of a crime.[437] It seems that the only test is relevance, subject to the general power of the court to control proceedings and to prevent their abuse.

---

[429] 210.

[430] As recognized by the prescription of a mandatory direction to the jury of the need for caution in convicting upon such a basis: Police and Criminal Evidence Act 1984, s 77.

[431] Expert medical evidence of the accused's condition at the time of confessing adduced to impugn its reliability was admitted in *R v Powell* [1980] Crim LR 39, and held admissible in *R v Ward* [1993] 2 All ER 577. It was rejected in *R v Weightman* (1990) 92 Cr App Rep 291, in which the relevant condition was held not sufficiently beyond the comprehension of normal people.

[432] See *Sinclair v R* (1947) 73 CLR 316; *Jackson v R* (1962) 108 CLR 591; *Phillion v R* [1978] 1 SCR 18 (although this aspect of the case was not the subject of the appeal); *Murphy v R* (1989) 86 ALR 35.

[433] See *R v McKay* [1967] NZLR 139, 153.

[434] (n279); 842, 75. See also *R v Moore* [1982] 1 NZLR 242.

[435] As in *R v Hall-Chung* [2007] EWCA Crim 3429, 50 SJLB 1020, [21].

[436] But there must be some plausible evidence to connect the third party to the issues before his bad character can be adduced: see, in Canada, *R v Grandinetti* 2005 SCC 5, [2005] 1 SCR 27.

[437] *Hurst v Evans* [1917] 1 KB 352, 355.

CRIMINAL PROCEEDINGS

R v Murray[438] demonstrated that, here too, relevance appeared to be the key, but was more rigorously interpreted. In that case, evidence[439] of the bad character of a third party,[440] whose conduct was alleged to have frightened the accused into reckless driving, was held admissible on that count, but not on another relating to unlawful wounding of a passenger in the third party's car after the vehicles had stopped, here alleged as self-defence. Perhaps the driver's record was regarded as too remote from the accused's fear of the driver's passenger.[441] It has been suggested in Canada that the degree of probative force of such evidence need not be so great when adduced by the defence because of the lower onus upon the accused merely to raise a reasonable doubt, and because there is no prejudice to balance against such reduced probative force.[442] It may be accepted that s 100 of the Criminal Justice Act 2003 merely fortifies this result.

---

[438] [1995] RTR 239.   [439] To be elicited by cross-examination of a police prosecution witness.

[440] Although the convictions were mainly for offences of dishonesty, with offences of violence or in respect of driving offences in a very minor key.

[441] See also *R v Gadsby* [2005] EWCA Crim 3206 (attempted murder by burning, in which an old conviction for a quite different sort of arson by a third party, with access to the premises in question, was held inadmissible).

[442] *R v A (GJ)* (1989) 70 CR (3d) 298 (where expert defence evidence was admitted to show the phenomenon of 'transference', by which a child might accuse an innocent person of a perpetrated crime rather than her own father, supported by evidence of the perpetration of acts very similar to those in question, perpetrated by the father in the past on other daughters).

VIII

BAD CHARACTER OF
THE ACCUSED

This chapter complements Chapter VII, and its subject matter is now almost wholly governed by the provisions of Pt XI c 1 of the Criminal Justice Act 2003.[1] The origins of that legislation will be considered first, then its structure, the gateways it provides for admissibility, followed by the briefest mention of other statutes, and concluding with a brief appraisal.

SECTION 1. ORIGINS OF THE MODERN LAW

This section will comprise, first, the nature of the problem of the admission of evidence of the bad character of the accused; then attempts at reform, at common law, by recommendations of law reform bodies, and by legislation; an indication of the principal forms of continuing dissatisfaction; and finally the intentions and techniques designed to remedy them.

NATURE OF THE PROBLEM

It is hardly surprising to find that the issue of the admissibility in evidence of the accused's bad character has always been regarded by both prosecution and defence as being of vital importance in criminal proceedings. The reason is simply that such evidence is believed to be very influential in its effect upon a jury.[2] It is likely both to help prove the guilt of the accused, and to prejudice the jury against him. The prosecution justifiably seeks its

---

[1] Some parts of which, concerned with rebuttal of good character of the accused, the use of bad character in relation to a co-accused, and the bad character of non-defendants, have already been considered in Chapter VII. There are, in addition, a few statutory provisions, authorizing the admission of such evidence, which have been left unaffected by the Criminal Justice Act 2003, since s 99(1) purports to abolish only the common law rules governing the admissibility of evidence of bad character in criminal proceedings. For further detail of the old law, see previous editions of this work.

[2] This commonly held belief is largely confirmed by the results of such empirical investigation as has been possible given the straitjacket imposed by s 8 of the Contempt of Court Act 1981: see Law Com Con Pap No 141 App D, as supplemented by Law Com No 273 (Cm 5257, 2001) App A. In *R v Bills* [1995] 2 Cr App Rep 643, a conviction was quashed because the jury attempted to change its verdict after hearing for the first time of the accused's record at the sentencing stage; in *R v Johnson* [1995] 2 Cr App Rep 1, the Court of Appeal thought that there was no case to answer without the disputed evidence, but that with it, a conviction was inevitable.

inclusion for the former purpose, and the defence equally justifiably seeks its exclusion for the latter reason.[3]

An exclusionary rule was established by the beginning of the nineteenth century, and stated in recognizably modern terms in *R v Cole*:[4]

...in a prosecution for an infamous crime, an admission by the prisoner that he had committed such an offence at another time and with another person, and that he had a tendency to such practices, ought not to be admitted.

Its application was uncertain throughout the nineteenth century,[5] and first considered by a final appellate court in *Makin v A-G for New South Wales*,[6] with guidance provided by Lord Herschell in cryptic and vague terms. It comprehended situations in which evidence was relevant by way of the alleged repetition of very similar conduct in the past by the accused;[7] situations in which previous commission was less clearly attributable to him, but the number of such cases in which he was one of few possible participators made coincidence implausible;[8] and situations where there was direct evidence of the commission of relevant acts by the accused, or his presence at the scene of the crime, but contested issues as to his intent,[9] or the nature of his involvement in relation to the crime charged.[10] Despite the complexity of the problem, and the imprecision of Lord Herschell's language, attempts were made to construe it as if it were a statutory provision, which generated still further layers of uncertainty.

It is hardly surprising given the difficulty of the problem, and deficiencies of attempts to provide a solution, that similar problems afflicted the entirely new situation of determining the limits of cross-examination upon bad character when the accused was first made generally competent to testify in his own defence by the Criminal Evidence Act 1898, perhaps exacerbated by parliamentary perception of the general hostility of cross-examination at that time. What emerged was, in broad terms, a ban on cross-examination relating to the commission of crimes, convictions, charges, or evidence of bad character,[11] unless such evidence were admissible to show guilt,[12] rebutted a claim for good character,[13] or amounted to retaliation for an imputation upon the character of the prosecutor or his witnesses,[14] or for an attack upon another accused charged with the same offence.[15] The drafting of the provision was complex, and its relationship to the terms of the abolition of the privilege of self-incrimination obscure.[16]

---

[3] It was accordingly extremely rare, but not quite unknown (see e.g. *R v McKenzie* [1991] Crim LR 767), for a conviction to be upheld despite the wrongful admission of such evidence, or in the face of a misdirection as to its relevance; but for an exception, see *R v B (CR)* [1990] 1 SCR 717. On the other hand, the mere knowledge by the jury from sitting in a different case of the association of the accused with those convicted on that occasion was not necessarily fatal: *R v BM* [2003] EWCA Crim 2952.

[4] As reported in Phillips *Evidence* (1814), 69. The trial judge's original note is appended to the judgment in *R v Sims*, as reported in [1946] KB 531, 544.

[5] Compare the reasoning in the poisoning cases of *R v Geering* (1849) 18 LJMC 215, *R v Winslow* (1860) 8 Cox CC 397, and *R v Hall* (1887) 5 NZLR 93, for example. Nor did these varieties exhaust the possibilities; in the infamous case of *Neill Cream*, the evidence of other poisonings was admitted by Hawkins J 'as corroboration': Shore *Trial of Neill Cream* (1923), 154.

[6] [1894] AC 57. For additional facts and social background, see Palmer (1993) 67 *Law Inst J* 1171.

[7] As in *R v Straffen* (n62).   [8] As in *R v Robinson* [1952] 2 All ER 334.   [9] As in *R v Cole*.

[10] As in *R v Ball* (n22).

[11] Section 1(f).   [12] Section 1(f)(i).   [13] Section 1(f)(ii) first limb.

[14] Section 1(f)(ii) second limb.   [15] Section 1(f)(iii).   [16] Section 1(e).

In both situations, the law was regarded as capable of leading to injustice to the accused, and was mitigated by discretion to exclude evidence the prejudicial effect of which exceeded its probative value.[17]

ATTEMPTS AT REFORM

Common law

It is somewhat tendentious to describe the process of the common law as an attempt to reform the law, but there seems little doubt that towards the end of the twentieth century the House of Lords was trying to establish a more satisfactory basis for it. Thus in *DPP v Boardman*, an authoritative restatement of principle was attempted.[18] The accused schoolmaster was charged with homosexual offences against some of his pupils, a few of the incidents as described by the youths indicating that the accused envisaged playing the passive role. Their Lordships all held the evidence to have been rightly considered relevant and cross-admissible to counts involving that characteristic. The speeches are inconsistent in some aspects of their reasoning, but unanimous in requiring the 'similar fact' evidence, as it was then called, to be more than barely relevant to guilt.[19] This decision was accepted elsewhere by the highest courts in the Commonwealth,[20] but in England the courts increasingly took the view that the restrictions on admissibility in chief of evidence of the bad character of the accused had been too tightly restrained by the formulation in *Boardman*. This led both to some redefinition of the scope of the rule, and to a series of decisions in the House of Lords,[21] having the broad effect of eroding the protection it offered against the admissibility of such evidence. In addition, it became increasingly common to side-step any restrictions on admissibility by categorizing the evidence as 'background' material assisting only in the understanding of the situation in which the events constituting the charge occurred.[22]

[17] In the case of evidence in chief, it became uncertain whether this was a supplementary discretion or inherent in the inclusionary exception to the exclusionary rule: see e.g. *R v Clarke and Hunt* [2002] EWCA Crim 2948, [70].

[18] [1975] AC 421, [1974] 3 All ER 887. See also commentaries by Hoffmann (1975) 91 *LQR* 193; Cross [1975] *Crim LR* 62; Tapper (1975) 38 *MLR* 206.

[19] It should be 'of close or striking similarity' (Lord Morris, 441, 895); 'striking similarity' (Lord Wilberforce, 444, 897); 'striking resemblance' (Lord Hailsham, 455, 907); 'exhibit very striking peculiarities' (Lord Cross, 460, 911); and 'be uniquely or strikingly similar' (Lord Salmon, 462, 913). The phrase 'striking similarity' is derived from *R v Sims* [1946] KB 531, [1946] 1 All ER 697 ; 540, 701.

[20] See *Sutton v R* (1984) 152 CLR 528 (Australia); *R v Hsi En Feng* [1985] 1 NZLR 222 (New Zealand); *R v Robertson* [1987] 1 SCR 918 (Canada).

[21] *DPP v P* [1991] 2 AC 447, [1991] 3 All ER 337 (relaxation of enhanced relevance required by *Boardman*); *R v H* [1995] 2 AC 596, [1995] 2 All ER 865 (presumption of truth of allegations of previous bad character); *R v Christou* [1997] AC 117, [1996] 2 All ER 927 (no rule of severance because evidence on one count inadmissible on another); *R v Z* [2000] 2 AC 483, [2000] 3 All ER 385 (permission to use evidence of bad character despite acquittal of accused on charges involving the use of such evidence).

[22] *R v Pettman* (2 May 1985, unreported), CA, could be regarded as the origin of such a line of argument, although it might be argued that it was inherent in the decision of the House of Lords in *R v Ball* [1911] AC 47 (incestuous behaviour and inclination of the accused at an earlier time admitted to prove the crime of incest at a later date), and of the High Court of Australia in *O'Leary v R* (1946) 73 CLR 566 (assaults at earlier time during a series of brawls culminating in the events constituting the crime charged).

Statutory provision

Perhaps the longest running and most contentious piece of law reform in this area was making the accused competent to testify in his own defence in criminal proceedings. The issue was first seriously raised in the late 1850s and subsided in England, many bills and some legislation later, only with the passage of the Criminal Evidence Act 1898, s 1(f).[23] It took the courts some time to construe its internal structure,[24] how far it was limited to credit,[25] the meaning of its terminology,[26] and the extent to which it was subject to any exclusionary discretion.[27] It was also necessary to enact formal amendment to correct the application of the provision as between co-accused.[28]

Proposals for legislative reform

At no stage in its development was this area of the law regarded with admiration or enthusiasm. The first sustained attack was made by the Criminal Law Revision Committee in its comprehensive 11th Report,[29] renewed in more recent times by the Law Commission in a consultation paper,[30] and some years later in its final report.[31]

The law of evidence in criminal proceedings was referred to the Criminal Law Revision Committee in 1964,[32] although its final report was not submitted until 1972. It found this part of the subject 'far the most difficult of all the topics we have discussed'.[33] The Committee proposed no radical change, and, in particular, retention of the general division in the then current law between evidence of bad character adduced in chief, and in cross-examination of the accused.[34] It did, however, propose the repeal and replacement of the relevant provisions of the Criminal Evidence Act 1898. Here it felt that the conflict between majority and minority in *Jones*, on the relation between s 1(e) and 1(f), needed to be resolved, which it proposed to do by adopting both views, namely by exposing the testifying accused to cross-examination about any matter relevant to guilt, including any evidence admissible in chief,[35] and by permitting cross-examination on any matter already

---

[23] For an account of this history, see Tapper in Tapper (ed) *Crime, Proof and Punishment* (1981).

[24] See *Jones v DPP* [1962] AC 635, [1962] 1 All ER 569 (relationship of enacting part and exceptions, including privilege against self-incrimination); *R v Anderson* [1988] QB 678, [1988] 2 All ER 549 (refinement of *Jones*).   [25] See *Maxwell v DPP* [1935] AC 309; *R v McLeod* [1994] 3 All ER 254, [1994] 1 WLR 1500.

[26] See *Maxwell v DPP* above (effect of acquittal of previous offence on meaning of 'charge'; *Stirland v DPP* [1944] AC 315, [1944] 2 All ER 13 (meaning of 'charge')).

[27] See *Selvey v DPP* [1970] AC 304, [1968] 2 All ER 497 (when invoked against prosecution); *Murdoch v Taylor* [1965] AC 574, [1965] 1 All ER 406 (when invoked against co-accused); *R v Britzman and Hall* [1983] 1 All ER 369, [1983] 1 WLR 350, 374, 355 (guidelines for direction).

[28] Criminal Evidence Act 1979 (from 'charged with the same offence' to 'charged in the same proceedings').   [29] Cmnd 4991, (1972).

[30] *Evidence in Criminal Proceedings: Previous Misconduct of a Defendant* (1996). For detailed appraisal, see Roberts, McEwan, and Darbyshire [1997] *Crim LR* 75, 93 and 105.

[31] *Evidence of Bad Character in Criminal Proceedings* (Cm 5257, 2001). For detailed appraisal, see Mirfield (2002) 6 *E&P* 141; McEwan [2002] *Crim LR* 180.

[32] The law of evidence in civil proceedings was simultaneously referred to the Law Reform Committee. The Conservative government, then coming to the end of its term, hoped thereby to pre-empt part of the attraction of the new Law Commission proposed to be established by the Labour Party if it secured power, since among the topics it proposed to refer to it was the whole of the law of evidence.   [33] [70].

[34] Although the effect of its amendment and codification of the existing law was to some extent designed to reduce the differences between the two situations.

[35] Thus, as noted above, achieving a greater measure of coherence between admissibility of bad character in chief, and in cross-examination.

adduced in evidence. It also felt that the ambiguity of the term 'character' should be eliminated, and proposed to do so by eschewing use of the generic term, and instead, in its draft provisions, referring to 'disposition', 'reputation', or 'credibility' as appropriate.

The Committee was deeply divided as to its policy in relation to the cross-examination of the accused who made imputations. It canvassed numerous objections, including the anomalies of treating admissibility in chief and in cross-examination differently, and also in so treating cases in which the impugned individual had, and had not, testified for the prosecution. It was concerned that the risk of exposing his own bad character would inhibit the accused in deploying his true defence, and might turn the trial into a tactical battle, akin to a game.[36] In the end, it opted to permit cross-examination of a testifying defendant,[37] but only to impair credibility, because both prosecution and defence should equally be able to test the credit of the other side's witnesses.

The Committee's proposals attracted some criticism on account of its policy, some on account of its method, which was strictly non-empirical,[38] and some on account of the complication of its draft provisions. The proposals were never enacted in the form recommended by the Committee since other provisions of its draft bill encroaching on the right to silence were then still politically unacceptable. The significance of this report in establishing an agenda for change should not however, be underestimated.

In 1994 the whole issue of character evidence in criminal proceedings was referred to the Law Commission, and its Consultation Paper was published in May 1996,[39] containing very full and generally persuasive analysis and criticism of the then existing law. Its robust statement[40] of principle included the promotion of simplicity, and the exclusion of any evidence for which no coherent instructions as to weight and use could be given to juries or magistrates.

It differed from the Criminal Law Revision Committee both in its overall policy and in its method. It explicitly disavowed the Committee's equation of the desirability of convicting the guilty and acquitting the innocent, by regarding the latter as taking priority.[41] It also made some attempt to use empirical studies.[42] It followed the lead of the Committee, however, in keeping separate the rules relating to admissibility of evidence of previous misconduct in chief and in cross-examination, which it justified on the basis that the latter is directed more to credibility, the decision is made later in the trial process in a different evidential context, and is directed to show character at a different time.[43] Its suggestions and preferences for reform were, however, overtaken by the final report, which took a rather different approach.

Reform of this area had figured as an issue in the general election of 2001, the manifesto of the winning Labour Party committing to preservation of the rash of decisions of the House of Lords in the previous decade or so[44] on the admissibility of evidence of bad character in chief. Meanwhile, the issue had been mentioned in a number of policy papers,[45]

---

[36] For a particularly striking example in Australia, see *TKWJ v R* [2002] HCA 46, 212 CLR 124.

[37] But only where the imputation went beyond the facts of the case and was intended merely to attack credibility. [38] For spirited defence of the Committee in this respect, see Cross [1973] *Crim LR* 400.

[39] Response was required urgently, presumably with a view to a bill being included in the Queen's speech for the next session of Parliament. [40] [1.14].

[41] [13]. [42] See [1.20] et seq. [43] [1.35]. [44] nn21, 22.

[45] For example, *Criminal Justice: The Way Ahead* (Cm 5074, 2001).

and in the far-reaching Auld Report into criminal procedure.[46] The general tenor of such opinion favoured increased reliance upon the ability of juries to deal with evidence of the accused's bad character, and placed some emphasis on securing a different balance between the interests of victims and society more generally, and those of the accused. On the other hand, the delay and change of government had led to a new context, in the shape of the enactment of the Human Rights Act 1998 with its promotion of the influence of the European Convention on Human Rights on English law.

The most significant difference from the two previous reports was determination to assimilate to a much greater extent the law relating to the use of bad character[47] evidence in chief and in cross-examination. Another important extension lay in the interpretation of the terms of reference to embrace all evidence of bad character, whether or not of the accused or co-accused.

It promoted an approach based on degrees of relevance, and rejected one based on prohibited categories, or certainly a prohibited category of propensity. It devoted some attention to the scope of the rule, and in particular to the difficulty of distinguishing between 'background' evidence, which lay outside the exclusionary rule, and that for other misconduct, which was subject to it. Like the Consultation Paper, it devoted more of its elaboration of the defects of the law to the rules relating to the use of such evidence in cross-examination than to its use in chief, and also like its predecessor, it saw reliance on discretion to avoid the worst effects of the provision not only as a telling indictment of it, but also as an unsatisfactory method of mitigation. It rejected as justifications for the general-approach arguments based on comparative credibility,[48] fairness,[49] or deterrence of unjustified attack.[50] It remained troubled by the anomaly that the sanction of use of the accused's record operated only against a *testifying* accused.[51] It noted that not only was the law inconsistent, but that prosecution practice, for example in determining whether or not itself to bring out the misconduct of its own witnesses,[52] was also inconsistent.

DISSATISFACTION

It is proposed here to retrace some of the ground covered above, but also to amplify a few of the main areas of difficulty and dissatisfaction that emerged during the development of this area of the law of evidence. The areas mentioned below in no way seek to be

---

[46] *Criminal Courts Review* (2001). Although in view of the then imminent publication of this final report, no firm recommendations for reform of this area of the law were propounded.

[47] It is interesting to note the change from refusal to use the phrase 'bad character' in the 11th Report to the reference to 'misconduct' in the Consultation Paper, and then finally to 'bad character' in the final Report. Much of the more popular discussion had been cast in terms of evidence of 'convictions'.

[48] The imputation might not affect credibility, and its rebuttal might well not be used by the jury only to weaken the credibility of the accused, whatever direction were given.

[49] Because it might let in evidence that was more prejudicial than probative to rebut a true and necessary part of the defence.

[50] Partly because it would be ineffective in preventing attack where the accused had no record, taking the view that this was better remedied by direct provision.

[51] On the basis of the rule in *R v Butterwasser* [1948] 1 KB 4, [1947] 2 All ER 415, notwithstanding the pressure upon the accused to testify imposed by s 35 of the Criminal Justice and Public Order Act 1994.

[52] So relieving the accused of the need to do so, and so to bring himself within the ambit of retaliation.

comprehensive, but may provide some perspective for evaluation of the provisions of the Criminal Justice Act 2003 to be elaborated in the next part of this chapter.

It must initially be confessed that there is little hard empirical evidence of the operation of the old law. The very first recommendation of the Royal Commission on Criminal Justice was that s 8 of the Contempt of Court Act should be amended so as to allow research into the reasoning of juries. It has not been, and may never be, implemented. In its absence, attempts to reform, or to appraise, this area of the law struggle in a sea of ignorance.[53] Simulations have the obvious defect that those participating in them know that they are simulations,[54] so impinging on the behaviour of participants.[55] Quite apart from lack of access to the jury, it is also the case that there is a dearth of empirical research and accessible statistical analysis,[56] for example on such matters as the incidence of testimony by the accused, or the incidence of re-offending or of serial or differential law-breaking.

Scope

As noted above, there was an increasing tendency to remove evidence described as 'background' from the impact of the basic exclusionary rule. Although this discussion was usually confined to the admissibility of such evidence in chief, it also applied where similar factors underlaid the debate about the relationship of ss 1(e) and 1(f) of the Criminal Evidence Act 1898 in the context of cross-examination. At first, a narrow approach was adopted under which only those matters so closely connected that the very facts in issue could not be understood at all without reference to them were included, but almost inevitably the idea of background was extended to matters that merely assisted the understanding of the facts in issue, such as the relationship between the parties as they had developed over the years, and it became highly problematic where the line between background and relevance was to be drawn.

Another difficult problem of scope related to the application of the inclusionary 'similar facts' exception to evidence that, while it undoubtedly showed bad conduct on other occasions, was nevertheless not introduced or used on that account. Thus, if a car were stolen in order to commit a robbery, the fact of such stealing is relevant to whether the person who stole it was involved in the robbery, but as a piece of ordinary evidence rather than as illustrating the accused's disposition to crime. It would be just as probative to show that the accused solicited a consensual loan of the car for the same purpose.[57]

It was also claimed at times that the 'similar facts' rule was not engaged when the reasoning process went, not from the disposition of the accused to commit crimes such as the one charged to his having committed the one actually charged, but rather in the other direction from his having committed the actual crime charged to his having the disposition to commit such crimes.[58] Thus, in relation to *Makin*, it was argued that the accuseds'

---

[53] Most especially on the real incidence of prejudice, and the effectiveness of directions. But see *R v Smith* [2005] UKHL 2, [2005] 2 AC 176, [11] for a rare reported insight into what one member claims to have transpired in the jury's deliberations.

[54] Which are difficult to stage in even a remotely similar way to the conduct of a real trial.

[55] It may be thought that this might also apply to patent observation of real juries.

[56] Despite the admirable Crown Court Survey conducted by the Royal Commission, and the questionnaires used and research commissioned by the Law Commission in preparing its final report.

[57] In these situations, there is scope for bowdlerization of the evidence, perhaps by formal partial admission. See, for a similar approach in the United States, *Old Chief v United States* 519 US 172 (1997).

[58] Similar reasoning justifies the aggregating approach to identification.

commission of the crime charged stemmed from the statistical incidence of the deaths of children in houses the accused had occupied, and that their disposition to commit such crimes played no part in the argument to show that they had done so in any one case.[59]

If such cases did fall outside the rule, they escaped being subject to any enhanced standard, and were admitted on a basis of no more than simple relevance, subject only to rarely exercised discretionary exclusion. As noted in the previous chapter, this unembellished standard already applied to evidence of bad character of the accused adduced by a co-accused, and to evidence of the bad character of third parties adduced by the accused.

Test

The test eventually adopted for the admission of evidence of the accused's bad character in chief was roughly[60] that it should be more probative than prejudicial. As noted above, one of the complaints advanced against the rule was that this formulation was too vague to give much guidance. Sometimes it was claimed that previous convictions, for example, were in themselves of no relevance at all,[61] but this view was rather inconsistent with authorities such as *R v Straffen*.[62] It certainly seemed that a different view was taken of relevance in different contexts.[63] The courts generally ignored attempts of commentators to dissect and label various elements of probative force, or different forms of prejudicial effect. It could indeed be argued that the test, as formulated in terms of weighing probative force against prejudicial effect, was incoherent. It was clear that 'prejudicial effect' must mean more than that the admission of the evidence would tend to lead to an increased chance of conviction, and it was usually accepted that it meant that the trier of fact would attach more weight to the evidence than it deserved. The problem is that the weight it deserved was nothing other than its true probative force, so any notion of weighing prejudicial effect against probative force must already have taken place in order to determine that the evidence was prejudicial at all. It was also remarked that the concepts of prejudicial effect and probative value were left undeveloped in the case law, and, operating as they did in the different realms of emotion and logic, resisted convincing comparison with each other.[64] The result was in effect to leave the application of the rule at the mercy of the court's instinctive reaction.[65]

Procedure

If, however, the test for admissibility was nevertheless to be one of the balance of probative force and prejudicial effect, there were procedural difficulties, since the application of

---

[59] Although the counterargument is that a statistical premise can lead only to a statistical conclusion, in this case, that the Makins killed most of the children, and that the necessary linkage to the particular death was accomplished only by way of an argument relying upon the disposition indicated by the statistical conclusion.   [60] Minor differences of formulation appeared in the cases.

[61] See Lord Hailsham LC in *DPP v Boardman* (n18), 451, 904.

[62] [1952] 2 QB 911, [1952] 2 All ER 657, in which about the only evidence apart from Straffen's propensity was his being in the general area where the crime had been committed, and so having had an opportunity to commit it.

[63] Compare, for example, the strict view taken of relevance in *R v Slender* [1938] 2 All ER 387 with the lax view taken in *R v West* [1996] 2 Cr App Rep 374.

[64] Memorably categorized by Mirfield as an attempt to balance 'apples and Thursdays': (2002) 6 *E&P* 141, 148.

[65] It is symptomatic that the number of murder cases in which the evidence has been excluded is very small indeed.

these concepts in the context of a trial might involve the determination of matters of fact, which were, in general, the province of jury rather than judge. The problem was exacerbated by those very facts governing admissibility being, in many cases, effectively indistinguishable from those that the jury would ultimately have to determine in order to arrive at its verdict.

Matters were complicated by the fact that, even when some misconduct of the accused was irrelevant to some other misconduct, he might nevertheless be charged with both on the same indictment if there was sufficient connection between them.[66] Matters were capable of further complication and unfairness when more than one person was tried in the same trial, and evidence admissible against one not strictly admissible under the similar fact rules against another, but might nevertheless be prejudicial to him.

Nor did the position remain static during the trial itself. As further evidence emerged, sometimes quite different from what was initially expected, evidence of other misconduct, which seemed initially admissible, or inadmissible, might change from one category to the other.

Then the whole pattern of the trial was capable of being itself affected by the perceived operation of the rules. For example, the accused with a bad record might choose not to advance his true defence,[67] or might choose not to testify.[68] Nor was this vital decision an easy one since the disparity between the rules governing evidence in chief and evidence in cross-examination[69] meant that the decision to testify had to be taken in ignorance of whether cross-examination would be allowed. It was also the case that, even if a particular question in cross-examination about other misconduct were not permissible, it might not be obvious to prosecuting counsel that it would not be allowed, and a damaging and disallowable question might be put without the accused having had an opportunity to protest in advance in the absence of the jury, perhaps placing the accused in the difficult position of either protesting after the event and running the risk of the jury's attention having become concentrated on the inadmissible evidence, or not protesting and so allowing it to have been heard without demur despite its inadmissibility.

Discretion

This whole subject was considered in Chapter IV above, but it may be re-emphasized here that, in this vital area, it introduced inconsistency and uncertainty, and, to the extent that it was explicitly invoked, removed whole swathes of the area from effective appellate control. This was particularly unfortunate in an area in which emotions run high, and when trials are often conducted without adequate preparation, without ready recourse to authority, and sometimes at a relatively low level, both in terms of the experience of the advocates and the competence, or even fairness, of the tribunals.

---

[66] Indictment Rules 1971, r 9, which is subject to discretionary control under s 5(3) of the Indictments Act 1915, but which operates on different principles from those governing only the admissibility of evidence.

[67] Rebuttal by reference to the bad character of the accused was permissible, even though an attack on a prosecution witness was completely true: see *R v H* [2003] EWCA Crim 1300, [19].

[68] In *Ebanks v R* [2006] UKPC 11, [2006] 1 WLR 1660, [17], it was stressed that any decision not to testify should be recorded in writing, and signed.

[69] And especially the heavy use of judicial discretion to mitigate the severity of the operation of the rules.

Consequences

There were also a number of unfortunate by-products of the old rules, in terms of the logistics of trials, their collateral impact, and the dangers they could pose more generally to the criminal system.

Since the focus is on *other* misconduct of the accused, it may often happen that its investigation and presentation will have the effect of increasing the expense, and prolonging the duration, of a trial. These factors will become more serious, the longer the period over which the alleged misconduct occurred.[70] Then there is the paradox that the more central the allegation of other misconduct to proof of guilt, the more attention will need to be devoted to its correct determination, and the greater the chance of distracting the jury from the matters upon which it is required to arrive at a verdict.

Where the other misconduct has itself already been tried,[71] it creates some risk of inconsistency; where it is concurrently being tried,[72] it creates some risk of anomaly; where it has not been tried or charged,[73] it creates some risk of abuse of process by prior publicity.

Quite apart from such effects, the ready use of previous misconduct could have the result of distorting the criminal process by increasing the power of the police to manipulate the investigation of crime both in selection of suspects, and their treatment under interrogation. Nor does undue reliance upon previous convictions promote policies of rehabilitation.

In many such situations, there is an obvious danger of unfairness, and since the passage of the Human Rights Act 1998, an increasing likelihood of recourse to the European Court of Human Rights, with still greater risks of prolonging the criminal process, and whenever such recourse were successful, of bringing the English system into disrepute, or in extreme cases, of causing further distortion if particular parts then require hasty adaptation in the light of such decisions.

DESIGN

Although the Law Commission had appended draft legislation drafted to implement its recommendations, that draft was not enacted[74] for a number of reasons. As noted above the whole issue had become embroiled in the political process, and much of the lay debate had been cast in crude terms of the aim of increasing the extent of the admissibility of the accused's criminal convictions. While it is true that there had been reluctance[75] under the old law to admit evidence of convictions in chief,[76] this reflected the absence of probative force of the bare record, when what was required was similarity of factual detail.

Nevertheless, the drive to achieve this aim caused some distortion of the debates in parliament, sometimes by dictating acceptance of other areas of amendment, from those

---

[70] As will the likelihood of achieving an accurate result.

[71] Whether resulting in conviction or acquittal.

[72] Different counts in the indictment, or a joint trial.

[73] Allegations of commission of other crimes.

[74] Although interestingly an amendment to substitute it for the government bill as it had become, was defeated only at its very final stage in the House of Commons.

[75] See *DPP v Kilbourne* [1973] AC 729, [1973] 1 All ER 440, where the whole case turned on the admissibility of similar allegations in different counts, and the accused's convictions for similar offences seem to have been ignored.   [76] As opposed to cross-examination.

presenting a credible threat to the passage of the legislation if their chosen amendments were rejected. It also dictated a tougher attitude to the interests of the accused, and a more generous one to the interests of the prosecution than had inspired the final report of the Law Commission, which had sought a more even balance between them. Ironically enough the polarization of the debate, and the strength of the opposition to the use of convictions, compelled the government to abandon the form of its original bill constituting them as a separate gateway to admissibility, although the government's determination to expand admissibility in that respect determined a further amendment to make specific, and complex, reference to the admissibility of convictions in relation to the principal gateway to admissibility, namely an important matter in issue between the defendant and prosecution.

One of the principal aims of the Law Commission had been to clarify the law, by assimilating the rules both relating to the bad character of the accused with that of other participants, such as witnesses or co-accused, or third parties where their bad character was relevant, and by assimilating the rules relating to the admission of evidence of bad character whether adduced in chief, in cross-examination, or in rebuttal. It further sought to eschew any undue technicality both in the substance of the law by the use of ordinary language,[77] and procedurally by making evidence of the accused's bad character admissible by the prosecution without the need for application to the court in every case.

It is, however, rarely the case that departure from a carefully drafted form arrived at after considerable preparation and consultation, and then amendment on a continuing basis during parliamentary passage, contributes to clarity and coherence. Thus, in the very first case to consider the new provision, the Court of Appeal was driven to bemoan its complexity and its drafting.[78]

SECTION 2. STRUCTURE OF THE MODERN LAW

As noted above, although inspired and informed by the recommendations of the Law Commission, the new provisions of Part 11 c 1 of the Criminal Justice Act 2003 depart in both letter and spirit from those recommendations in significant respects. They were intended to replace both common law and most existing general statutory provisions. Their purpose was judicially described in one early case as being:[79]

...to assist in the evidence based conviction of the guilty, without putting those who are not guilty at risk of conviction by prejudice.

In another, their passage was described as 'a sea-change',[80] and it was asserted that:[81]

...the important change is that whereas previously evidence of the defendant's propensity to offend in the manner now charged was prima facie inadmissible, now it is prima facie admissible.

---

[77] *R v Bullen* [2008] EWCA Crim 4, [29].

[78] *R v Bradley* [2005] EWCA 20, [2005] 1 Cr App Rep 397, [38]; apparently accepted as the standard view soon after in *R v Isichei* [2006] EWCA Crim 1815, [32].

[79] *R v Hanson* [2005] EWCA Crim 824, [2005] 2 Cr App Rep 299, [4].

[80] While recognizing that some of the concepts of the old law would still be applicable, and the result often the same; for similar terminology but a different approach to the use of the old law see *R v Saleem* [2007] EWCA Crim 1923, [23].   [81] *R v Chopra* [2006] EWCA Crim 2133, [2007] 1 Cr App R 225, [12].

Subsequent experience seems to have borne out this effect as the then Lord Chief Justice noted in the opening words of his judgment in the important case of *R v Campbell*:[82]

Prior to the Criminal Justice Act 2003 it was rare for a jury to be given details of a defendant's previous criminal record. Since that Act has come into force it has become much more common.

It is now proposed to discuss first the general framework, concepts and procedure embodied in the Act before going on to the detail of the various gateways to admissibility.

FRAMEWORK

The broad outline of the Law Commission's recommendation that the old law should be abolished and replaced, and the accused's bad character defined and admitted on the same basis, and through a number of defined gateways, whether in evidence in chief or in cross-examination,[83] subject only to limited exclusionary conditions, was retained, although as will be seen there was considerable variation in detail; some induced by change of policy, and some by the hazard of parliamentary passage.

It is useful to begin by reciting CJA 2003, s 101(1), the principal provision setting out the 'gateways' for the admissibility of evidence of the defendant's bad character:

In criminal proceedings evidence of the defendant's bad character is admissible if, but only if—

(a) all parties to the proceedings agree to the evidence being admissible,

(b) the evidence is adduced by the defendant himself or is given in answer to a question asked by him in cross-examination and intended to elicit it,

(c) it is important explanatory evidence,

(d) it is relevant to an important matter in issue between the defendant and the prosecution,

(e) it has substantial probative value in relation to an important matter in issue between the defendant and a co-defendant,

(f) it is evidence to correct a false impression given by the defendant, or

(g) the defendant has made an attack on another person's character.

These provisions were brought into force, somewhat prematurely,[84] in December 2004. The new rules were, despite some unhelpful drafting, held to apply to all trials[85] that commenced after that date, irrespective of proceedings being already in train,[86] or of their taking the form of a rehearing after reference from the Criminal Cases Review Tribunal of a case initially determined under the old rules.[87]

Section 99 abolished all common law rules governing the admissibility of evidence of bad character in criminal proceedings.[88] Most general statutory provisions relating to the

---

[82] [2007] EWCA Crim 1472, [2007] 2 Cr App Rep 361, [1].

[83] Although the Law Commission's draft exclusion of propensity to be untruthful from matters in issue between prosecution and defence (cl 8(5)) was reversed by its express inclusion in the Act (s 103(1)(b)), at least in the vast majority of cases.

[84] No transitional provisions, as promised, had been drafted, and no judicial instruction, as arranged, had been undertaken.　　　　　　　　　　　　　　　　　　[85] And *Newton* hearings.

[86] *R v Bradley* (n78), [34].　　　[87] *R v Campbell* [2006] EWCA Crim 1305, (2006) 150 SLB 1527.

[88] Although s 99(2) preserved the common law rule relating to proof of reputation as a means of proving bad character, and rules excluding bad character evidence on other grounds are preserved by s 112(3)(c).

admissibility of evidence of bad character were also repealed.[89] While it is clear that the intention was to substitute the new provisions relating to the admissibility of evidence of bad character for the old, this was a curious way of doing it, since the target was obviously the old rules of *inadmissibility* of evidence of bad character,[90] and it is clear that the most substantial rule of the old law relating to evidence of bad character, namely that it was admissible if relevant and not excluded by a rule of inadmissibility, has in fact been retained.[91] The abolition only of *rules* of admissibility further left obscure the position relating to exclusion by discretion,[92] or under rules of practice.[93]

CONCEPTS

The most important concept is that of bad character itself, which the Act defines in s 98 as:

…evidence, of, or of a disposition towards, misconduct on…[a person's] part, other than evidence which—

(a) has to do with the alleged facts of the offence with which the defendant is charged, or

(b) is evidence of misconduct in connection with the investigation or prosecution of that offence.

This is supplemented by the definition of misconduct in s 112(1) to mean:

The commission of an offence, or other reprehensible behaviour…

In the Law Commission's draft bad character had been differently defined,[94] and the two conditions had been specified as those where exceptionally leave to adduce the evidence of bad character did not need to be sought. It is important to note that the function of s 98 is to exclude what it contains from the definition of bad character, both for the purposes of the admissibility of the evidence of the bad character of the accused or co-accused sought by the prosecution or co-accused under the gateways specified in s 101, and that of witnesses or third parties, usually sought by the accused under s 100. This means that evidence within the conditions specified in s 98 is admissible, not under the terms of the Act but under the old conditions applying before its passage, principally at common law, since the abolition of the rules of inadmissibility by s 99 is itself governed by the terms of s 98. It was nevertheless at first held that evidence falling outside this definition will be admissible 'without more ado'.[95] This was soon corrected by its propagator's simply changing the

---

[89] Sch 7, Pt 5.

[90] The distinction between rules of admissibility and of inadmissibility is recognized elsewhere in the Act: see s 62(9), was emphasised in *R v Y* [2008] EWCA Crim 10, [2008] 2 All ER 484, [47], and further endorsed in *R v O* [2008] EWCA Crim 463, [29].

[91] See *R v Highton* [2005] EWCA Crim 1985, [2006] 1 Cr App Rep 125 (*Van Nguyen*), [42]; *Weir* [2005] EWCA Crim 2866, [2006] 2 All ER 570 (*Somanathan*), [36]; *R v Bullen* (n77), [29].

[92] See Police and Criminal Evidence Act 1984 s 82(3). Nor has s 78 of that Act been either repealed, or by contrast to s 126(2) in relation to hearsay, explicitly retained. See further, 618.

[93] See *Practice Note* [2002] 3 All ER 904 (use of spent convictions).

[94] In cl 1 as 'evidence which shows or tends to show that – (a) he has committed an offence, or (b) he has behaved, or is disposed to behave, in a way that, in the opinion of the court, might be viewed with disapproval by a reasonable person'.

[95] *R v Edwards and Rowlands* [2005] EWCA Crim 3244, [2006] 3 All ER 882, [1](i); *Weir* (n91) (*Manister*), [95].

rule from '*will* be admissible without more ado' to '*may* be admissible without more ado'.[96] Under the revised formulation, evidence of the accused's reprehensible behaviour may, if inadmissible under the Act, perhaps remain governed by the enhanced relevance requirement of the common law, and certainly may be excluded if more probative than prejudicial. In *R v Fox*, the trial judge regarded the evidence as admissible either at common law if s 98(a) applied, or under s 101 if it did not, without much discrimination between them. The Court of Appeal held this too cavalier an approach, instead requiring careful consideration of which was to apply, and the proper direction in either case.[97] It took a narrow view of the scope of s 98(a), restricting it to evidence of actus reus rather than mens rea. It also took the view that where it did exclude the other statutory provisions, the common law still applied, as suggested above.[98] Because of the application of the definition to the operation of both s 100 and s 101 as indicated above, neither a broad nor a narrow interpretation will always tend to further the interests of prosecution or accused. Occasionally, evidence can be relevant only if it does show bad character.[99]

It is proposed to examine first the notion of what amounts to 'reprehensible' behaviour, and then the operation of s 98, including the meaning to be attached to its two conditions.

Exactly what counts as 'reprehensible' conduct for these purposes remains obscure.[100] The difficulty stems from the need to cater for conduct not itself necessarily constituting an offence, and the rejection during parliamentary passage of the Law Commission's circumlocution. In *R v Campbell* it was equated with 'blameworthy', although some may think that has a different nuance of meaning. Perhaps the most extensive interpretation so far is the suggestion that conduct is reprehensible even though, when tried for it, the accused was found unfit to plead,[101] which must surely raise at least the possibility that it was unintended. That it extends well beyond criminality is illustrated by the finding that female promiscuity can be enough.[102] On the other hand, a sexual relationship between a man aged 34 and a girl aged 16 has been thought not reprehensible, nor remarks of that man to a girl aged 15 indicating sexual interest.[103] This striking contrast between the categorization of male and female sexuality[104] suggests that conventional stereotyping, however unjustified, may play a role. Simply having been found in the vicinity of a crime, arrested, and having refused to make a witness statement,[105] has been held not to be reprehensible, and nor has an exaggeration by a witness of violence by a schoolteacher for the purposes of s 100.[106] In *R v Osbourne*[107] an allegation of shouting at a partner was not regarded as sufficiently 'reprehensible' on a charge of murder, perhaps[108] suggesting the application

---

[96] *R v Watson* [2006] EWCA Crim 2308, [19].

[97] [2009] EWCA Crim 653, [33]; cf *R v Marsh* [2009] EWCA Crim 2696, [46] where another constitution of the Court of Appeal seemed to adopt the position criticized in *Fox*.   [98] [30], [34].

[99] As in *Weir* (n91) (*He and He*), [120] (as between co-accused).

[100] See further and fuller, Munday [2005] *Crim LR* 24, Goudkamp (2008) 12 *E&P* 116.

[101] *R v Renda* [2005] EWCA Crim 2826, [2006] 1 Cr App Rep 380, [24]; cf *R v Davarifar* [2009] EWCA Crim 2294, [11] where personality problems leading to a possibly false sexual complaint were regarded as making it dubiously reprensible.   [102] Ibid (*Ball*), [35].

[103] *Weir* (n91) (*Manister*), [94], [97].

[104] Despite the rather closer connection between rampant male sexuality and violence.

[105] *Weir* (n91) (*He and He*), [118].   [106] *R v V* [2006] EWCA Crim 1901, [41].

[107] [2007] EWCA Crim 481, [34].

[108] The evidence was, however, tendered as explanatory evidence under gateway s 101(c), and perhaps for that reason was more strongly linked than otherwise to the nature of the offence charged.

of a scale varying with the seriousness of the offence charged. Ostensibly neutral conduct has been held 'reprehensible' as merely the observable part of a larger clearly reprehensible whole.[109] This seems questionable when the inference is of the very same conduct with which the accused is on trial.

The terminology and operation of s 98 has been regarded as difficult,[110] no doubt partly because the whole section had had to be drafted for the first time to cater for the departure from the Law Commission's scheme, partly because it had been subjected to amendment during parliamentary passage, and partly because of an apparently deliberate attempt to use non-technical language[111] such as 'has to do with' and 'connected with'. If read literally, without regard to its origins, context or extent, it might be thought to describe relevance either to issue or credit at trial, but so to read it would deprive this whole part of the Act of effect, since it is fundamental that only relevant evidence is admissible. So it must be given a more limited meaning;[112] the difficulty is to establish just how limited.

Such little authority as there is[113] has mainly concerned the interpretation of s 98(a). It seems clear that the Law Commission had had in mind misconduct which formed part of the crime charged,[114] and was relevant as background or circumstantial evidence, or difficult to disentangle from the crime itself, such as in the case of a bank robbery that the thief stole a car as a get-away vehicle, or assaulted customers as well as staff of the bank in the course of the robbery. Complication is created in its application to cases where there are co-accused, either because the bad character has to do with the case against only one of the two co-accused,[115] or where the evidence is of the bad character of one, when it does have to do with the issue involving the other on the defence argument, but not on that of the prosecution.[116] An attempt to construe the opening words of s 98 so as to eliminate cases in which the evidence was to be relevant only otherwise than circumstantially was rejected in *R v Wallace*, despite finding some support from the Judicial Studies Board in its suggestions for direction of the jury.[117] It has thus been circumscribed as needing to be part of the res gestae,[118] or to have taken place at the same time and location as the crime itself.[119] It is rather more startling to find that such contiguity may be sufficient as well as necessary.[120] The time component seems to have varied from case to case, sometimes apparently needing to be 'contemporaneous',[121] sometimes 'reasonably contemporaneous',[122] sometimes enough to have occurred two days earlier or later,[123] and sometimes to have occurred in the 'aftermath' of the crime charged.[124]

---

[109] *R v Rossi* [2009] EWCA Crim 2406.

[110] See *R v Edwards and Rowlands* (n95) [19]; *R v Wallace* [2007] EWCA Crim 1760, [38]; *R v Lewis* [2008] EWCA Crim 424, [13] ('notoriously').

[111] Said in *R v Tirnaveanu* [2007] EWCA Crim 1239, [23] to be 'a fact specific exercise involving the interpretation of ordinary words'. [112] Ibid. [113] Ibid, [22].

[114] As in *DPP v Agyemang* [2009] EWHC 1542 (driving while disqualified shown memorandum of previous conviction resulting in that disqualification). [115] As in *R v AJR* [2006] EWCA Crim 3196, [19].

[116] As in *R v Lewis* (n110), [13] where the complication seems to have excited the Court's use of an alternative, and, it is submitted, plainly erroneous, justification. [117] (n110), [36]–[39].

[118] *R v Lowe* [2007] EWCA Crim 3047, [18](a). [119] *Tirnaveanu* (n111), [23] ('some nexus of time').

[120] *R v Machado* [2006] EWCA Crim 837, [16]. [121] Ibid, [13].

[122] *R v McNeill* [2007] EWCA Crim 2927, [14]. [123] Ibid, [15].

[124] *R v McKintosh* [2006] EWCA Crim 193, [24].

Since s 101 contains gateway (c) dedicated to explanatory evidence of bad character, and in relation to gateway (d) expressly[125] admits evidence going beyond that of propensity, it is difficult[126] to construe the meaning of s 98 exclusively from that of s 100 and s 101. If there is an overlap between evidence having to do with the alleged facts of the offence, and evidence relevant under one of the gateways specified in s 100 or 101, which is to prevail, and does it matter? It can be argued that it does not, since even if s 98 were to apply exclusively it would not as indicated above, prevent inadmissibility on the basis of irrelevance, or under s 78 of the Police and Criminal Evidence Act 1984.[127] It is not, however, completely clear that in this context relevance under the old law was exactly the same as relevance under the new, and it is clear that the new legislation brings with it a completely new apparatus of notices, for leave, and stopping for contamination which did not apply in exactly the same way under the old law. For example, it could be argued that if the accused were to allege that the crime with which he is charged, say causing a death by dangerous driving, were committed by a prosecution witness, say another driver involved in the incident, such an allegation would clearly come within s 98(a), so take him outside the provisions of s 100, and preclude the necessity to seek leave to tender evidence of that driver's bad character. So loosely worded a provision may also provide a bolt-hole for those disinclined to wrestle with the complexities of the more detailed provisions of this part of the Act, and of the rules and procedures it prescribes. It is accordingly submitted that it may be dangerous to take an extended view of the ambit of s 98(a), especially when a restricted view is taken of the exclusionary rigour of the common law. Sometimes the Court seems close to holding that any evidence relevant to facts in issue is 'to do with' them, and hence admissible without reference to the 'gateways';[128] and sometimes that any evidence relevant to showing that a prosecution witness is telling the truth about the alleged facts is similarly automatically relevant.[129]

S 98(b) is cast in similarly vague terms, especially in the use of the term 'in connection with'. This part of the provision has so far hardly surfaced at all, except to have been said[130] by the Lord Chief Justice to have been clearly applicable so as to eliminate any need for one co-accused to seek leave under s 100 to attack a co-accused and his solicitor on the basis that they had sought to pressure him into supporting that co-accused's defence.

PROCEDURE

Because, the substance of the provisions now differs so radically from that of the old common law, it has been necessary to devise new procedures, and for the courts to spell out their detailed operation. Since these are matters of general application it is proposed to mention them first, before going on to consider the substance of individual 'gateways'. This

---

[125] S 103(1) 'include'.

[126] Cf Rix LJ, *Tirnaveanu* (n111), [24] 'there is a potential overlap'; Rix LJ, *R v McNeill* (n122), [16] 'evidence within the exception of section 98(a), and *therefore* not...within the bad character provisions of the 2003 Act' (emphasis supplied).

[127] Now recognized as equivalent in effect to s 101(3) of the Criminal Justice Act 2003 despite the different terminology: *R v Tirnaveanu* (n111), [28].

[128] As in *R v Lewis* (n110), [13], although the Court found it unnecessary to make a final determination.

[129] As in *R v McKintosh* (n124), [24].

[130] *R v Ibrahim* [2008] EWCA Crim 880, [2008] 4 All ER 208, [124].

somewhat arbitrary selection of topics will include matters concerning leave to adduce evidence of bad character; the use of the voir-dire and, more generally, means of proof of such bad character, including the problem of avoiding satellite litigation; multiple counts and cross-admissibility; exclusion of evidence of bad character as unfair or contaminated; direction of the jury; and the approach to appeal and review.

Leave and notice

Deliberately departing from the recommendations of the Law Commission for the form of definition adopted in the Act, leave to adduce evidence of his bad character is not required in the case of the *accused*, despite its retention in relation to the bad character of others. On the other hand, *notice* of intent to adduce evidence of the accused's bad character is required,[131] and elaborated in the provisions of the Criminal Procedure Rules, which require the prosecution to notify the defence of its intention to do so in detail,[132] and notably to specify the particular gateway, the relevance of the evidence, and in the case of convictions, whether the fact, or facts, of the conviction are relied upon.[133] It is in fact frequently treated, and referred to, as an application.[134] Given the danger of 'satellite' litigation,[135] the Court of Appeal has warned against routine prosecution[136] applications,[137] or the adoption of devious tactics to secure relevance,[138] but has instead urged compliance with the spirit as well as the letter of the requirements.[139]

It was said in *Hanson* that where the evidence is of convictions it may be necessary to give no more than a list, allowing the nature of the crime to indicate its relevance to the accused's propensity. It seems also that any notice should not only indicate the 'gateway' invoked, but that in the most common case of (d) should distinguish between relevance to issue and to credibility, which can cause difficulty when the evidence is capable of going to both.[140] The amount of detail required will be considered further below in relation to the means of proof of the basis for allegations of bad character.

The rules specify[141] that the prosecutor give notice of intention to adduce or elicit evidence of the accused's bad character in a specified form no more than fourteen days after committal,[142] although the court may waive the requirement as to form, or vary the time limit.[143] It has been stressed that justice will normally demand strict adherence to these limits so as to give the accused a chance to consider, and to respond by way of application to prevent the admission of the evidence.[144] It has also been remarked[145] that an incidental advantage of serving notice is that it automatically clarifies the issues, and may save time

---

[131] S 111(2). Although it seems not to have been given in *R v Marsh* (n97), despite assuming admissibility under s 101(1)(a).

[132] Thus necessitating the making, retention, and accessibility of such detail: *R v Bovell and Dowds* [2005] EWCA Crim 1091, [2005] 2 Cr App R 401, [2].

[133] *R v Hanson* (n79), [17]. Similar considerations apply to the co-accused in relation to gateway (e): see *R v Edwards and Rowlands* (n95), [1](ii).

[134] In *R v McNeill* (n122), [9] 'notice' and 'application' are used synonymously.

[135] So described in *R v Edwards and Rowlands* (n95) (*Smith*), [86]; see further, 406.

[136] Or co-accused: *R v Edwards* [2005] EWCA Crim 1813, [2006] 1 Cr App Rep 31, [1](ii); or defence, *R v Hanson* (n79), [17]. [137] *R v Hanson* (n79), [4].

[138] *R v Renda* (n101) (*Ball*), [38]. [139] *R v Letts and Chung* [2007] EWCA Crim 3282, [21].

[140] As it did in *R v Culhane and Chin* [2006] EWCA Crim 1053. [141] CPR 35.4.

[142] In the most common case. [143] Ibid 35.8.

[144] *R (Robinson) v Sutton Coldfield Magistrates' Court* [2006] EWHC 307 (Admin), [16]–[17].

[145] *R v Tirnaveanu* (n111), [39].

and expense. Nevertheless, complete failure to give notice before the opening of the prosecution case has been allowed,[146] even when the evidence is sought to be adduced by the prosecution in retaliation for departure by the accused from his case as disclosed.[147] It has sometimes been commended,[148] and sometimes a late plea may so change the whole basis for the relevance of evidence of bad character as to require the notice to be reconsidered.[149] Because some of the 'gateways' depend upon events during the course of the trial, such as making an attack on another or conveying a false impression, it has been suggested that the time limits for such eventualities be examined,[150] although some robust opinions have categorized waiting for such triggers before service of the notice as 'absurd'.[151]

The availability of the power to vary the limits has lent support to the general inclination to sanction breach of the rules by the prosecution so long as no prejudice or injustice can be detected,[152] which may well be the attitude when the court feels that the evidence would certainly have been admitted had proper notice been served.[153] Conversely, the Court may sometimes refrain from criticism when there is a different reason for excluding the evidence.[154] Perhaps the most far-reaching manipulation of the notice provisions was made in *R v Musone*, where the Court of Appeal conjured up a previously prohibited discretion to disallow the admission of evidence of the bad character of one co-accused by another, on the basis that failure to give notice had there amounted to deliberate ambush.

Proof of bad character

In the old law the fact of conviction was often used to discredit witnesses in cross-examination, but because of the enhanced relevance required for evidence in chief, underlying facts were then usually necessary. Assimilation of the rules for the use of evidence of the accused's bad character in cross-examination and in chief has thus created problems, immediately exposed in *R v Hanson*,[155] where it was accepted that sometimes under the new law a list of previous convictions would be sufficient, no doubt reflecting the abandonment of any enhanced standard of relevance.[156] On the other hand in relation to credit a more refined standard is required in the new law,[157] and this was reflected in *Hanson's* further discrimination of dishonesty from untruthfulness.[158] In cases where the underlying facts of a conviction, or any other example of bad character, were relied upon, the rules required the Crown in its notice to specify the circumstances and means of proof of the evidence. In *Hanson* it was hoped that this would generally be the subject of admission, and:[159]

Even where the circumstances are genuinely in dispute, we would expect the minimum indisputable facts to be thus admitted. It will be very rare indeed for it to be necessary for the judge to hear evidence before ruling on admissibility under this Act.

---

[146] *R v Culhane* (n140); *R v Wallace* (n110), [40] (on account of confusion about the effect of s 98(a)).
[147] *R v Delay* [2006] EWCA Crim 1110 (where the notice was oral).
[148] *R v Wilson* [2008] EWCA Crim 134, [23].
[149] *R v Bullen* (n77), [27] (late plea of manslaughter at murder trial previously expected to turn on self-defence).   [150] *R v Letts and Chung* (n139), [21].
[151] *R v Ullah* [2006] EWCA Crim 2003, [18].   [152] As in *R v Culhane and Ching* (n140), [25].
[153] *R v Wallace* (n110), [40].
[154] As in *R v Urushadze* [2008] EWCA Crim 2498, [19], (very late oral notice).   [155] (n79), [17].
[156] See the distinction between similar fact evidence under the old law and propensity under the new drawn in *R v Hewlett* [2008] EWCA Crim 270, [24].
[157] As explained in *R v Lawson* [2006] EWCA Crim 2572, [2007] 1 Cr App R 11, [32].
[158] *R v Hanson* (n79), [13].   [159] [17].

It immediately emerged that the apparently straightforward realm of convictions might sometimes lead to dispute; even as to whether those proffered really were those of the accused.[160] It has been stressed that even a conviction is not itself bad character, but merely evidence of it, a status unavailable to mere unproved charges.[161] Similarly, the basis of the convictions might well be challenged.[162] The position is still worse in the absence of the 'launch pad' of a conviction, most clearly summarized by Toulson LJ in *R v McKenzie*:[163]

Without such a launch pad, proof of the previous alleged misconduct requires the trial of a collateral or satellite issue as part of the trial of the defendant for the offence with which he is charged. Trials of collateral issues have the dangers not only of adding to the length and cost of the trial, but of complicating the issues which the jury has to decide and taking the focus away from the most important issue or issues.

He also pointed out the paradox that proof of the relevant bad character is stronger the more previous incidents there are; but at the same time the more such incidents, the greater these dangers of distraction. Similarly, the further the previous misconduct from a formal charge, and the more ancient it is, the more difficult it is likely to be to prove.

Although many factual issues may arise in relation to the evidence of previous misconduct it is relatively rare for a voir dire to be thought necessary.[164] A number of other expedients have been followed or recommended, including ventilation at a preparatory hearing,[165] making a conditional decision to admit the evidence,[166] and deferring any decision until a triggering condition has occurred.[167] The advantage of considering the matter early is that it may help to precipitate a plea, and so avoid a trial at all; the disadvantage is that until all the evidence is in, it is difficult to assess its precise relevance and force. Nor should the amount of such evidence be underestimated. In one case[168] with two co-accused they had over a hundred previous convictions between them, of which just under half were admitted after the judge's ruling. The amount of time at trial and length in the judge's summing-up may be overwhelming,[169] and become a major reason for prolonging a trial.[170]

The two basic methods of proving previous misconduct are oral evidence of witnesses, especially in sexual cases, of complainants, and documents either used in previous proceedings or summarizing such evidence.[171] Attempts have sometimes been made to use material from the Police National Computer system, but then there is a danger that detail

---

[160] As in *R v Burns* [2006] EWCA Crim 617, [2006] 2 Cr App R 264, [17]; *R v Lewendon* [2006] EWCA Crim 648, [2006] 1 WLR 1278.   [161] *R v Hussain* [2008] EWCA Crim 1117, [13].

[162] As in *R v Humphris* [2005] EWCA Crim 2030, (2005) 169 JP 441, [18]; *R v Ainscough* [2006] EWCA Crim 694, (2006) 170 JP 517, [19].   [163] [2008] EWCA Crim 758, [23].

[164] *R v Hanson* (n79), [17] (convictions); *R v Maynard* [2006] EWCA Crim 1509, [10] (non-convictions). One was held in *R v Weir (Yaxley-Lennon)*, (n91) [64].

[165] *R v Steen* [2007] EWCA Crim 335, [2008] 2 Cr App R 380, [8]; although such issues are sometimes overlooked at that stage: see *R v O'Dowd* [2009] EWCA Crim 905, [71].

[166] *R v Lamaletie and Royce* [2008] EWCA Crim 314, [10].

[167] *R v Card* [2006] EWCA Crim 1079, [2006] 3 All ER 689, [23]; *R v Gyima and Adjei* [2007] EWCA Crim 429, [40]; *R v Hewlett* (n156), [23].   [168] *R v Culhane and Chin* (n140), [10] (48 out of 109).

[169] As in *R v O'Dowd* (n165), [74] (16 out 42 trial days, and 148 pages out of 434).

[170] Ibid, [2] (the trial lasted over six months).

[171] Including the use of reports of previous civil proceedings: *R v Hogart* [2007] EWCA Crim 338.

of criminal method often amounts to hearsay.[172] In the case of convictions the relevant provisions of the Police and Criminal Evidence Act 1984 may be more appropriate.[173]

Occasionally the use of the oral evidence of a complainant excites objection on account of the difficulty of assessing the credibility of such a witness, perhaps years after the commission of the relevant act, in the absence of further contemporary records and the disappearance of the sort of material usually apt for mounting cross-examination. In *R v Woodhouse*[174] the defence felt unable to admit the underlying facts of a caution some twelve years earlier for such reasons.

Attempts to prove the matters by oral evidence can also cause problems; for example, those witnesses may themselves be unsatisfactory. It may also happen that where the evidence is to be derived from some result of a previous trial other than a conviction, that second-order questions may arise about the quality of the evidence of the matters relied upon.[175] It may also be the case that to call the oral evidence only of a complainant may be unfair if there are other possible witnesses, whose testimony is equivocal and neither party is anxious to call.[176] In *R v Nguyen*[177] where some witnesses were unsatisfactory the Crown deliberately decided not to proceed to trial in respect of that alleged incident, but was then permitted to use it as bad character evidence in support of its case in respect of a later incident, and to prove the earlier incident by other more satisfactory witnesses.

It has been stressed that the court's function is to act as an arbiter only of the admissibility of evidence of bad character, and not as an assessor of its weight.[178] This is, however, liable to exception if the evidence is so weak as to be 'inherently incredible',[179] or if the rest of the evidence is so weak that the evidence of bad character constitutes virtually the whole of the prosecution case.[180]

Cross-admissibility[181]

When an indictment contains more than one count against the accused, three different, but related, issues may arise. First, whether the indictment can be severed so that they are tried separately; secondly, if not, whether the evidence on one count is admissible on another; and thirdly, if it is, how it may be used. The first of these is governed by the old law, unaffected by the new legislation.[182] The House of Lords took a strict view of the undesirability of severing an indictment, despite evidence on one count being under

---

[172] As in *R v Humphris* (n162); it will rarely be the case that these can be overcome by the invocation of the inclusionary discretion in s 114(1)(d) of the Criminal Justice Act 2003, *R v Z* [2009] EWCA Crim 20, [24]; but see *R v Steen* (n165), [15] (not cited in *R v Z*).

[173] Ss 73, 74 as suggested in *Humphris*, (n162),[7]; *R v O'Dowd* (n165), [71].

[174] [2009] EWCA Crim 498, [16]; in *R v Steen* (n165), [12] similar considerations prevented agreement to the underlying facts of a previous conviction.

[175] Thus in *R v O'Dowd* (n165) one of the three trials had resulted in an acquittal, and another in a stay for abuse of process (on the basis of contamination of the very witness tendering evidence of it at the current trial).

[176] As in *R v Maynard* (n164) (defence prevented from calling witness); *R v Loughman* [2007] EWCA Crim 1912 (defence reluctant to call witness).   [177] [2008] EWCA Crim 585.

[178] *R v Highton* (n91), [10].   [179] *R v Edwards and Rowlands* (n95) (*Smith*), [82].

[180] *R v Highton* (n91), [10].   [181] See further Fortson and Ornerod [2009] *Crim LR* 313.

[182] See *R v Koc* [2008] EWCA Crim 77, [29] (severance of trials of different offenders}.

the exclusionary rule inadmissible on the other. This matter is governed by Indictment Rules 1971, r 9,[183] which provides that:

Charges for any offences may be joined in the same indictment if those charges are founded on the same facts, or form or are part of a series of offences of the same or similar character.

It will be noted that this provision applies only to joinder of charges, and can thus extend only to part of the field, since often there is no more than one formal charge.[184] Nor can it be regarded simply as a subset of similar fact cases since it can apply to a series of offences even though evidence of some is inadmissible on others on such a basis.[185] The general provision is, however, qualified by a discretionary power to sever an indictment conferred by s 5(3) of the Indictments Act 1915:

Where before trial, or at any stage of a trial, the court is of opinion that a person charged may be prejudiced or embarrassed in his defence by reason of being charged with more than one offence in the same indictment, or that for any other reason it is desirable to direct that the person should be tried separately for any one or more offences charged in the indictment, the court may order a separate trial on any count or counts of such indictment.

It was authoritatively affirmed in *R v Christou*[186] that this discretion of the trial judge is unconstrained, and in particular that there is no rule[187] or presumption in favour of severance in sexual cases in which the evidence on one count is inadmissible on the other. Factors mentioned[188] as relevant for consideration were how discrete were the facts, the impact of ordering separate trials on the accused and on the victim, and, most importantly, whether the judge believed that fair joint trial could be achieved by suitable direction of the jury.[189]

If separate counts remain, the second issue, of their admissibility under the new legislation, needs analysis, especially since the courts regard it as having become more difficult.[190] S 112(2) provides that:

Where a defendant is charged with two or more offences in the same criminal proceedings, this Chapter (except section 101(3)) has effect as if each offence were charged in separate proceedings: and references to the offence with which the defendant is charged are to be read accordingly.

It has been explained[191] that the consequence is that the evidence of bad character as defined by the Act tendered to prove each charge must be considered separately,[192] and

---

[183] See *Ludlow v Metropolitan Police Comr* [1971] AC 29, [1970] 1 All ER 567, and commentary from an Australian perspective by Weinberg in (eds) Campbell and Waller *Well and Truly Tried* (1982). For the view in the United States, see *Zafiro v United States* 506 US 534 (1993).

[184] It was pointed out in *R v Williams* [1993] Crim LR 533 that it is not necessary to include an incident as a charge in an indictment in order to secure the admission in evidence of the details relating to it, if they are relevant and otherwise admissible.   [185] See *R v Cannan* (1991) 92 Cr App Rep 16.

[186] [1997] AC 117, [1996] 2 All ER 927. Lord Hope, 130, 937 made it clear that the rule is the same in Scotland.

[187] In New Zealand, there appears to be a rule that cases in which there is little nexus beyond the identity of the victims, separate sexual offences by different offenders should be severed: *R v D and S* [1996] 2 NZLR 513.   [188] 129D, 937b.

[189] For problems still capable of occurring in this regard, see *R v Dye* [2003] EWCA Crim 2424, [2004] 1 Cr App Rep 206; *R v Carman* [2004] EWCA Crim 540.

[190] *R v Wallace* (n110), [3]; *R v Freeman and Crawford* [2008] EWCA Crim 1863, [2009] 1 Cr App R 137, [17].

[191] *R v Chopra* (n81), [14].

[192] Perhaps unless the charges constitute no more than 'a single book of many parts, but with a consistent theme', *R v Doncaster* [2008] EWCA Crim 5, [22].

admitted only on the basis of coming within one of the gateways. Difficulty has arisen on account of the diversity of forms of relevance, thus in some cases the evidence on each count, if believed, demonstrates the accused's propensity to commit the relevant crime;[193] in others it may do no more than establish the possibility of the accused's involvement, but in enough instances for it to be unlikely to have arisen by coincidence;[194] or contamination of the evidence of the complainants on the different counts, whether guilty by deliberate fabrication,[195] or innocent by unconscious influence as a result of pre-trial discussion.[196]

If both hurdles have been surmounted, attention focuses on the use to be made of the evidence. An expansive view has been taken. Thus evidence on one count admitted under one gateway can be used for any purpose to which it is relevant, on the basis that once admitted there should be no restriction on use, in this respect taking over[197] the law first established in relation to the use of convictions.[198] The purport of the evidence must be established, however, as this will determine its relevance under different gateways,[199] and it was suggested in *R v Campbell* that it would rarely be useful to consider relevance to credit separately, despite the terms of the standard direction.[200] Irrelevance under one gateway is not determinative of relevance under another, even when the conditions for the latter are more stringent.[201] Similarly, the definition of propensity in s 103 applies not only for the purposes of gateway (d), but also for the purposes of the other gateways, although it should be remembered that propensity is not the only form of relevance.[202]

PROTECTION OF THE ACCUSED

Because of the ever-present danger of prejudice in admitting evidence of the bad character of the accused, the Law Commission required such evidence to satisfy what it described as an 'interests of justice' test, according to which such evidence would be admitted only if there were no risk of prejudice, or that the interests of justice *required* the evidence nevertheless to be admissible depending on its probative value, the other evidence in the case, and its importance for the case as a whole.[203] No such strong inclusionary conditions appear in the main provisions[204] of the Act.[205] Nevertheless, given the power of evidence of the bad character of the accused to create prejudice, in the sense of unduly increasing the likelihood of his being found guilty, it was thought desirable to build some protection into the legislation. This includes protection against the use of contaminated evidence, some

---

193 As in *R v Chopra* (n81).   194 As in *R v Wallace* (n110).

195 As alleged in *R v Freeman and Crawford* (n190).

196 Alleged as possible in *R v Lamb* [2007] EWCA Crim 1766, [38].   197 *R v Wallace* (n110), [42].

198 *R v Highton* (n91), [22]; *R v Campbell* (n87), [25]. This also applies under s 100, despite the indication there in the wording of concentration on propensity alone: *Weir* (n91) (*Yaxley-Lennon*), [73].

199 In *R v Leaver* [2006] EWCA Crim 2988, once it had been agreed between the parties and accepted by the judge that the purport of a previous conviction was propensity to degrade women, it could not be used to show violence or lack of credibility.   200 [30], [41].

201 *R v Edwards and Rowlands* (n95) (*McLean*), [52]: irrelevant for (d), but relevant for (e).

202 *R v McAllister* [2008] EWCA Crim 1544, [13] (not itself a multiple count case).

203 See e.g. LC 273 (Cm 5257, 2001) draft bill cl 8(3)(b).

204 But see s 108(2)(b), in which it plays some role in relation to the admission of convictions committed when the defendant was a child.

205 Not even in relation to the bad character of others than the accused.

protection against the use of evidence which may render the trial unfair, and a requirement to direct the jury carefully on the proper use of the evidence.

Contamination

Section 107 confers upon the trial judge a new supplementary[206] statutory continuing power to stop a case on finding that the evidence of bad character is contaminated:

(1) If on a defendant's trial before a judge and jury for an offence—

  (a) evidence of his bad character has been admitted under any of paragraphs (c) to (g) of section 101(1), and

  (b) the court is satisfied at any time after the close of the case for the prosecution that—

    (i) the evidence is contaminated, and

    (ii) the contamination is such that, considering the importance of the evidence to the case against the defendant, his conviction of the offence would be unsafe,

the court must either direct the jury to acquit the defendant of the offence or, if it considers that there ought to be a retrial, discharge the jury.

…

(5) For the purposes of this section a person's evidence is contaminated where—

  (a) as a result of an agreement or understanding between the person and one or more others, or

  (b) as a result of the person being aware of anything alleged by one or more others whose evidence may be, or has been, given in the proceedings,

the evidence is false or misleading in any respect, or is different from what it would otherwise have been.

This provision appears to have been included to meet concern expressed by the House of Lords under the old law.[207] It was there thought highly unlikely that such contamination would occur, and be apparent on the papers.[208] The court is similarly concerned here to limit the range[209] and application[210] of this form of protection, which explicitly excludes evidence admitted under gateways (a) and (b). It is, however, disturbing to find any countenance at all to the use of contaminated evidence. Such disturbance becomes more acute, the tighter the definition of contamination. There has so far been little guidance on that, but in *Renda*, it was held not to encompass evidence that had been wrongly admitted as a conviction, but only on the mistaken acquiescence of counsel that it should be so categorized.[211]

Because this provision does require the trial judge to make an assessment of fact, it has been held that the judge should, where possible, postpone a ruling until the close of the case when all the facts will be in, but must then give it very serious consideration, especially when there is internal evidence from the testimony that it has been suggested by someone else.[212] Even if a firm finding that as a result of pre-trial discussion evidence *is* different as required by s 107(5) cannot be sustained, it was held in *R v Lamb* still to be

---

[206] Section 107(4). [207] *R v H* [1995] 2 AC 596, [1995] 2 All ER 865. [208] See, 379.
[209] *R v Bradley* (n78), [31] excluding its applications from Newton hearings and cases tried by magistrates.
[210] *Renda* (n101), [27] castigating its use as a means of reiterating rejected arguments for inadmissibility under one of the gateways. [211] Ibid. [212] *R v Card* (n167), [28].

necessary to direct the jury carefully where such discussion *might* have led to innocent contamination.[213] Paradoxically a more general jury direction seems to be all that is necessary if the allegation is of wrongful contamination.[214]

If the trial judge orders a retrial in preference to directing an acquittal, such a retrial cannot, for that reason, be objected to as an abuse of process, since such an objection would be tantamount to an appeal against the original decision.[215]

Unfairness

The principal provision is s 101(3), clearly modelled on s 78 of the Police and Criminal Evidence Act 1984:

The court must not admit evidence under subsection 1(d) or (g) if, on an application by the defendant to exclude it, it appears to the court that the admission of the evidence would have such an adverse effect upon the fairness of the proceedings that the court ought not to admit it.

In the case of convictions, this is supplemented by s 103(3) in relation to those of the same description or category under s 103(2):

Subsection (2) does not apply in the case of a particular defendant if the court is satisfied, by reason of the length of time since the conviction or for any other reason that it would be unjust for it to apply in his case.

It is worth noting at the outset that s 101(3) differs in form from s 78 in that it makes exclusion on satisfaction of the conditions mandatory,[216] but only in form, since it cannot be supposed that any judge, having determined for the purposes of s 78 that the admission of the evidence would make the trial so unfair that it ought not to be admitted, would go on to do so.[217] It has accordingly been held that, while s 101(3) involves a balancing exercise, it does not amount to the exercise of a discretion.[218] The exercise under s 103(3) was said in *Hanson* to be similar in determining whether the admission of a conviction was just. In both cases, the court was bound to take into account the degree of similarity[219] between the events showing the defendant's bad character and those with which he was now charged,[220] the respective gravity of the past and present offences,[221] and the strength of the rest of the prosecution case.[222] Although, as noted above, the court is not primarily concerned with the weight of the evidence of bad character, it may exclude such evidence if it is 'inherently incredible'.[223] There has also been some indication that collusion between witnesses to different events might lead to the exclusion of their evidence,[224] although this seems to fall squarely within s 107, discussed above. On the other hand, the length of the

---

[213] (n196), [57].   [214] *R v King* [2008] EWCA Crim 3177, [29].   [215] Ibid, [22].

[216] As noted in *R v Hanson* (n79), [10].

[217] See *R v Chalkley* [1998] QB 848, [1998] 2 All ER 155; Auld LJ, 874D, 178d.

[218] *R v Weir* (n91) (*Somanathan*), [46]; the impropriety of so referring to it was not, however, alone enough to allow the appeal in *R v McMinn* [2007] EWCA Crim 3024, [5].

[219] Although it need not be so high as to be 'striking' as at one time required under the old law: see *R v Clements* [2009] All ER (D) 261 (different form of sexual offence inadmissible).

[220] Whether or not within the same description or prescribed category.

[221] Although without any indication of what this entails, or even which way it inclines.

[222] Here on the basis that the weaker the rest of the case, and greater the reliance to be placed on the accused's bad character, the more likely it was to be excluded under this provision.

[223] *R v Edwards and Rowlands* (n95) (*Smith*), [52].   [224] *R v Weir* (n91) (*Somanathan*), [39].

previous record,[225] and the closer its similarity to the offences charged,[226] the less likely it is to be excluded. Two matters relevant to exclusionary discretion under the old law have cropped up under the Act. Thus the intention of the accused in casting an imputation on his co-accused is, under the Act, to be disregarded;[227] but springing an allegation on the accused without warning is relevant.[228]

As s 101(3) itself makes clear, it is to be taken into account only on the application of the[229] defendant.[230] It will also be seen that neither of these provisions applies to gateways other than (d) and (g), thus begging the question of whether there is any similar machinery for exclusion under other gateways. The most obviously eligible candidate is s 78 of the Police and Criminal Evidence Act 1984. A complication is the specification for the purposes of s 101(3) of only gateways (d) and (g), together with the conspicuous absence of any explicit saving of the operation of s 78 in this[231] chapter of Pt 11. The contrary argument would be that, since s 99(1) purports to abolish only common law rules of admissibility, and as s 78 has not been explicitly repealed for the purposes of c 1, it follows that a common law *discretion*[232] and a *statutory* provision have not been abolished, and continue in force. It can further be argued that the exclusion of evidence on the basis that its admission would be more prejudicial than probative, or would make the proceedings so unfair that it ought not to be admitted, does not amount to exclusion on the grounds that it is evidence of bad character, and is thus preserved by s 112(3)(c).[233]

Although no definitive decision has been made by the Court of Appeal, the Chief Justice stated that, in its provisional view,[234] s 78 of the Police and Criminal Evidence Act 1984 does continue to apply to the other gateways, and recommended trial judges to act upon that basis.[235] Here too part of the reason is to help preserve decisions from attack under Art 6 of the European Convention,[236] although that article seems unable otherwise to generate discretionary exclusion.[237] On the other hand, there seems little inclination to protect the accused by a process of bowlderizing the evidence of bad character so as to leave out the most prejudicial and least probative detail.[238]

True discretionary control has, however, been applied where one co-accused deliberately ambushed another in omitting to give notice under the rules, by failure to apply the

---

[225] *R v Hanson* (n79), [26], although it was held in *R v McMinn* (n218), [8] that a single three-year-old conviction was not 'demonstrably' unfair.   [226] *R v Edwards* (n136) (*Chohan*), [76].

[227] *R v Bovell* (n132) (*Dowds*), [32].   [228] *R v Weir* (n91) (*Somanathan*), [40].

[229] Section 103(3) refers to 'a particular defendant', but the reason for the change of terminology is not apparent.

[230] Although no such wording appears in s 103(3), with the apparent result that the court may there take the point of its own initiative.

[231] By contrast with the explicit saving in c 2 in relation to hearsay in s 126(2) of both s 78 and the exclusionary discretion at common law, fortified by the explicit limitation of that saving to c 2.

[232] It should be noted that an exclusionary discretion is needed only in the case of a rule of admissibility.

[233] The government's spokeswoman in the House of Lords specifically affirmed its view that this provision did preserve the operation of s 78: see Official Report Vol 654, col 1988 (19 November 2003). In *R v Maitland* [2005] EWCA Crim 2145, [21], the Court of Appeal refused to express a view on what it described as so controversial an argument.

[234] It had been left more open in *R v Amponsah* [2005] EWCA Crim 2993, [20].

[235] *R v Highton* (n91), [13]; see also *R v Weir* (n91) (*Somanathan*), [44] in relation to gateway (f).

[236] Ibid, [14].   [237] *R v Musone* [2007] EWCA Crim 1237, [2007] 1 WLR 2467, [52].

[238] *Edwards* (n136) (*Chohan*), [74], [75].

discretion to dispense with such conduct,[239] contrasting with its application to permit the prosecution to adduce bad character evidence despite not serving notice, and even intimating that it did not intend to adduce the evidence.[240]

Direction

Taken together, the matters mentioned above confer considerable importance on the trial judge's directions in relation to bad character.[241] It is not enough to tell the jury that it is entirely for them to decide what to do with the evidence.[242] The admissibility of evidence of bad character is capable of changing in the light of developments at the trial, and the judge must keep it constantly under review. If at a later stage, for this reason, or because of an earlier mistaken ruling, he feels at the end of the case that the evidence is inadmissible, he can direct the jury to disregard[243] it.[244] Given the comprehensive coverage of the new provisions, and the prejudice that evidence of the accused's bad character can create[245] it has been held, even when adduced by the accused himself,[246] that the trial judge must draw the threads together[247] and direct the jury[248] carefully, and moderately,[249] on the way in which evidence of the bad character of the accused should be used:[250]

The important question that a court must consider, when deciding what help may need to be given to the jury in summing up, is the relevance of the evidence which was admitted. If the evidence has been admitted for a particular purpose, the jury may, depending on the circumstances, need to be told how they should use that evidence and the issue to which it goes.

The concept of relevance has not only been carried over from the old law, but is now of paramount importance.[251] It must be considered, not in the abstract by the mechanical and unthinking repetition of a standard direction,[252] but in the context of the precise issues that arise,[253] which may be determined by the defence raised,[254] or issues of fact conceded,[255] by the accused. It may also be wise to direct the jury on the non-use of bad character derived otherwise than from evidence adduced by the parties.[256]

The relevance of the evidence of bad character should be explained in detail in the context of the case as a whole, and if it amounts to little more than background, that must be

---

[239] *R v Musone* (n237) [60].   [240] *R v Moran* [2007] EWCA Crim 2947, [37].

[241] *R v Edwards and Rowlands* (n95), [1](iv).   [242] *R v Lafayette* [2008] EWCA Crim 3238, [25].

[243] Or even if such disregard is merely implicit in his direction: see *Edwards and Rowlands* (n95), [28].

[244] *R v Weir* (n91) (*Yaxley-Lennon*), [75], even though there only a majority verdict.

[245] Described in *R v Clarke* [2008] EWCA Crim 651, [25] as 'obvious'.

[246] As in *R v Harper* [2007] EWCA Crim 1746, [12].   [247] *R v O'Dowd* (n165), [82].

[248] Magistrates need not, however, rehearse their full reasoning, *R (Wellington) v DPP* [2007] EWHC 1061 (Admin).   [249] *R v Clarke* (n245), [27].

[250] *R v Tirnaveanu* (n111), [32].   [251] *R v Bullen* (n91), [29].

[252] *R v Campbell* (n87), esp [22], [36], [37].

[253] In *R v Leaver* [2006] EWCA Crim 2988, once it had been agreed between the parties and accepted by the judge that the purport of a previous conviction was propensity to degrade women, it could not be used to show violence or lack of credibility; in *R v Clarke* (n245) the evidence did not go to the principal issue of the distinction between murder and manslaughter.

[254] *R v Bullen* (n91), (late abandonment of defence of self-defence); but sometimes abandonment does not remove a possible defence, as in *R v Rees* [2007] EWCA Crim 1837 (of provocation).

[255] *R v Whitehead* [2007] EWCA Crim 2078, [5] (driving speed).

[256] *R v Wilson* [2008] EWCA Crim 134 (sight of court list on which the accused's name included in relation to a separate case); *R v Culhane and Chinn* (n140), [18] (concern that evidence admitted to issue might be used for credit).

made clear.[257] The purport of the evidence must be established, as this will determine its relevance under different gateways,[258] Although, indeed because, evidence once admitted under any gateway may be used for the purposes of another, it is not necessary to explain the gateways, but becomes still more important to explain their relevance,[259] and to give an appropriate direction.[260] Irrelevance under one gateway is not determinative of relevance under another, even when the conditions for the latter are more stringent.[261] More generally where the court has assured counsel that it will direct in a particular way, it should do so.[262] The judge should also normally direct the jury that the evidence of bad character should not be regarded as decisive in itself,[263] and that its relevance be to an *important* matter in issue if admitted under the gateway of s 101(1)d).[264] In cases where the relevance of the evidence to issue is circumstantial rather than via propensity, there seems to be some division as to whether it is necessary so to direct the jury.[265]

Most difficulty has arisen over the distinction between relevance to issue and to credit in the sense of propensity to untruthfulness. In the important case of *R v Campbell* the Lord Chief Justice explained that:[266]

Whether or not a defendant is telling the truth to the jury is likely to depend simply on whether or not he committed the offence charged. The jury should focus on the latter question rather than on whether or not he has a propensity for telling lies.

It may nevertheless sometimes occur that a distinction needs to be made, and in such cases the direction must ensure that where relevance is to untruthfulness,[267] the jury be directed not to use it for issue, and perhaps more rarely where relevance is to issue,[268] that there be no suggestion that it may also be regarded as going to untruthfulness.

Appeal and review

In the earliest detailed guidance to the application of the bad character provisions[269] of the Criminal Justice Act 2003 in *R v Hanson* Rose LJ affirmed that:[270]

If a judge has directed himself or herself correctly, this Court will be very slow to interfere with a ruling either as to admissibility or as to the consequences of non compliance with the regula-

---

[257] *R v Highton* (n177) (*Van Nguyen*), [43]; *R v Kumar* [2005] EWCA Crim 3549, [22].

[258] In *R v Leaver* (n253), once it had been agreed between the parties and accepted by the judge that the purport of a previous conviction was propensity to degrade women, it could not be used to show violence or lack of credibility. [259] *R v Campbell* (n87), [38].

[260] *R v Murphy* [2006] EWCA Crim 3408, 19].

[261] *Edwards and Rowlands* (n95) (*McLean*), [52]: irrelevant for (d), but relevant for (e).

[262] *R v Highton* (n91), [22].

[263] *R v Edwards* (*Chohan*) (n136), [77] (commended by the Court of Appeal as a model direction).

[264] *R v Garnham* [2008] EWCA Crim 266, [16].

[265] Cp *R v Campbell* (n87), [40], *R v Tirnaveanu* (n111), [38]. [266] (n87), [30].

[267] *R v Meyer* [2006] EWCA Crim 1126, [22] (convictions for violence after guilty plea irrelevant to credit); cf *R v Lafayette* (n242), [50] (where (d) and (g) appear to have been confusingly interchanged).

[268] As tendered in *R v Culhane and Chinn* (n140), [18].

[269] Subject to some doubt in the case where the bad character is adduced by a co-accused under s 101(1)(e): *R v Reed and Williams* [2007] EWCA Crim 3083, [37], although much the same considerations seem to apply to the categorization of the issue as 'substantial'.

[270] [2005] EWCA Crim 824, [2005] 1 WLR 3169, [15]. See also *R v Awaritefe* [2007] EWCA Crim 706, [33]–[35]. The same approach is taken when the prosecution appeals against a decision of the magistrates by way of case stated: *DPP v Chand* [2007] EWHC 90 (Admin), [9].

tions for the giving of notice of intention to rely on bad character evidence. It will not interfere unless the judge's view as to the capacity of prior events to establish propensity is plainly wrong, or discretion has been exercised unreasonably in the *Wednesbury*...sense....

Judge LJ forcefully re-emphasised this view in *R v Renda* by assimilating fact-specific judgments to discretion, and assigning their determination to the trial judge, by way of his 'feel' for the case, deploring the creation of 'authority' from such rulings, and devolving at least primary responsibility to trial courts.[271] It is difficult to reconcile such an approach with the obligation to provide reasons for any ruling on issues of admissibility and reasons for exclusion imposed by s 110 of the Criminal Justice Act 2003,[272] with the general rule laid down in *Renda* itself on the effect of a concession in cross-examination on whether a false impression had been given,[273] and more generally with the later proposition 'that the Court of Appeal Criminal Division is the appropriate court in which the correctness of the judge's decision should be questioned.'[274]

So light an appellate rein is worth some further exploration, distinguishing situations in which the application of discretion by the trial judge has been reversed; those in which the appellate court has applied its own view in the absence of any exercise of discretion by the trial judge; and those in which it has eschewed the language of review, and apparently exercised its own discretion, but then arrived at a conclusion agreeing with the result achieved by the trial judge.

The first case to overturn a trial judge's ruling on such an issue appears to have been *R v Murphy*,[275] where the Court of Appeal, while recognizing the limitations on its powers in these respects expressed in previous authorities,[276] nevertheless held the trial judge's determination of the relevance of an old conviction to the issues at trial to have been 'plainly wrong',[277] and allowed the appeal. In *R v McKenzie* the Court of Appeal was also prepared simply to disagree in one instance while agreeing in another with the trial judge's assessment of admissibility, without in either invoking dyslogistical adverbial support.[278] More recently, in *R v McAllister* the Court of Appeal felt free to overrule the trial judge on the application of the discretion under s 101(3), partly because the trial judge failed to explain the reasons for her decision.[279] In effect in these cases the Court of Appeal simply substituted its own 'feel' for the case, and exercised its own discretion or judgment on a matter of fact for that of the trial judge.

Notwithstanding the justification for limited control on the basis of lack of appellate opportunity for direct observation of the trial, such lack has on occasion failed to deter

---

[271] (n101), [3]. See also *R v Rossi* (n109), [22 referring to the judge's 'very wide discretion' to admit evidence of bad character.]

[272] Itself explicitly endorsed elsewhere in *R v Renda*, (n101), [60], at least in relation to a determination in favour of the defence. It is, however, sometimes ignored; see e.g. *R v Clarke* [2006] EWCA Crim 3427, [23]; *R v Awaritefe* [2007] EWCA Crim 706, [25].   [273] [21].

[274] [27].

[275] (n260), see [14]. In *R v Griffiths* [2007] EWCA Crim 2468 (where there is no explicit reference to any limitation of powers) the Court of Appeal, [12] seems to have thought it enough that the evidence excluded by the trial judge *might well have been considered relevant by the jury* and that its exclusion made the verdict unsafe.   [276] Citing *R v Hanson* and *R v Renda*.

[277] [17]. See also *R v Williams* [2007] EWCA Crim 211, [48]; *R v Smith* [2007] EWCA Crim 2105, [25], in both of which the Court of Appeal found the exercise of discretion at the trial to have been clearly wrong.

[278] [2008] EWCA Crim 758, (2008) 172 JP 377.

[279] (n202), [34]. Other factors included reliance on matters found 'not proven' and the need to minimize satellite litigation.

the Court from exercising its own discretionary and judgmental control when the trial court has failed even to attempt to exercise any at all. In *R v Gyima and Adjei* the Court of Appeal was quite specific in asserting: first, that the relevant condition was 'a question of fact for the trial judge'; second, that the trial judge made 'no express finding of fact'; and third that it 'found no difficulty in making such a finding itself'.[280] While in *R v Lamaletie and Royce*[281] the Court of Appeal took the view that although the application of s 101(1)(g) had been argued at trial to be inapplicable as a matter of rule, and not as one of discretion under s 101(3), it was nevertheless able to agree with what it predicted the trial judge's ruling would have been, had the defence instead been rested on that basis.

In a number of cases the Court of Appeal has agreed with the trial judge about the admission of the evidence, by the exercise of discretion or some fact-specific judgment, but in upholding his decision has failed to advert to the limited basis for its review, and instead appeared merely to record its own similar view of the relevant factors, which is somewhat confusing, and quite unnecessary, if it really is exercising only a limited power of review. In *R v Watson* the Court went out of its way to assert that the trial judge's decision in relation to the common law[282] had to be made 'by the exercise of his judgment in the light of all the information he had about the trial', but then went on to record that 'from all the information we have, we are of the view that the trial judge was quite right in reaching the conclusion he did'.[283] That certainly sounds more like positive agreement on appeal than reluctance to overturn on review.

In many cases the determination of the trial judge has been upheld by the appellate court on the basis that any mistake has not rendered the conviction unsafe.[284] While the vagueness of this condition has caused considerable difficulty,[285] its significance is indirect. It does not itself render the rules of admissibility more vague, but rather reduces any pressure to sharpen their accuracy.

A similar approach has also been made in a number of cases to the assessment of credibility of a witness, which might well be thought still more clearly to be the prerogative of the trial judge. In *R v Musone* the Court of Appeal was unable to accept the principal reasons for rejecting the defence hearsay advanced by the judge, but upheld his fall-back provision finding a new discretion to reject such evidence in the Criminal Procedure Rules, and then went beyond review to express its agreement with the substance of the trial judge's decision to exclude.[286] It is somewhat paradoxical that while elsewhere matters of law seem to be assigned to the exclusive control of the trial Court, these matters of fact should be determined against the defence by an appellate tribunal without seeing the witnesses at all.

It has further been held that no appeal is likely to succeed after a plea of guilty, even though precipitated by a finding of admissibility of evidence of the accused's bad

---

[280] (n167), [24]–[25].

[281] [2007] EWCA Crim 314, [9]. See also *R v Reid and Rowe* [2006] EWCA Crim 2900, [23], where, after accepting that no discretion arose either under s 101(3) or s 78 of the Police and Criminal Evidence Act 1984 (because the evidence was not adduced by the prosecution), the Court of Appeal still thought it appropriate to indicate its view that the evidence should not have been excluded on a discretionary basis.

[282] Discretion to depart from the normal rule against investigation of collateral matters.

[283] [2006] EWCA Crim 2308, [31].

[284] The new criterion for the exercise of the old proviso as introduced by the Criminal Appeal Act 1995.

[285] And led to a now postponed proposal for further statutory amendment.   [286] (n237), [64].

character.[287] So also the Court of Appeal has generally been reluctant to allow appeals for mere breach of the rules in the absence of a showing of real prejudice[288] incapable of cure by procedural steps,[289] or remedial directions.[290] Nor is it prepared to intervene to exercise any exclusionary discretion in the absence of explicit application by the defence.[291]

SECTION 3. GATEWAYS

This section will mention all of the gateways specified for the admission of evidence of the bad character of the accused in CJA 2003, s 101(1), although only cursorily in the case of those discussed in the previous chapter.

AGREEMENT OF THE PARTIES

It is likely to be rare[292] for all of the parties to agree to the admission of evidence of the defendant's bad character, except perhaps for evidence falling within the next gateway. Within the Law Commission's scheme, these two gateways were treated simply as two situations in which it was not appropriate to require leave to be sought. It is perhaps just conceivable that a defendant might prefer the evidence to be led in chief by agreement with the prosecution through this gateway, rather than himself to do so either by leading the evidence, or by raising the matter in cross-examination of a prosecution witness.

A feature of the empirical research on juries carried out by Professor Lloyd Bostock for the Law Commission was that it not only confirmed the expectation that evidence of the convictions for similar crimes by the accused was likely to lead to a greater chance of his being found guilty, but that it also demonstrated the unexpected result that evidence of a dissimilar conviction was more likely to have the opposite result,[293] so perhaps on that basis the defendant would be happy to acquiesce in such evidence being led.[294]

CHOICE OF THE DEFENDANT

It might also be thought rather rare for the defendant to wish to adduce evidence of his own bad character, but sometimes the exigencies of the situation are such that the defendant sees some advantage in it. In *Jones v DPP*, the accused needed to establish an alibi, and first gave one that could be proved to be false, which he explained as having been given because he had been in trouble with the police. Subsequently, still needing to rely upon an alibi, he claimed to have been with a prostitute at the relevant time.

Another result shown by Professor Lloyd Bostock was that, if the previous conviction were for indecent assault of a child, the prejudicial effect was especially strong. But even

---

287 *R v Hanson* (n79), [29].   288 *R v Edwards* (n136) (*Duggan*), [42].

289 *R v Edwards* (n136) (*Fysh*), [32].

290 *R v Hanson* (n79) (*Gilmore*), [37] (possible extension of time).   291 *R v Highton* (n91) [23].

292 But see *R v Hussain* (n161), [7] (all agreed on admissibility of convictions of co-accused running cut-throat defences); *R v Marsh* (n97) (inferred from lack of objection).   293 LC 141, App D.22.

294 Although, since this result seems most likely to be explained on the basis that the use of convictions in a different area is unfair, such acquiescence might well be counterproductive.

in this situation the accused may want to adduce the evidence, as in *B v R*,[295] where the accused, most ill-advisedly, thought it would assist his defence on a charge of sexual abuse of his daughter to refer to his previous conviction for just such an offence as an explanation of why she might be making up a false charge this time.

It was also pointed out by some respondents to the Law Commission that, where the accused's bad character is relatively innocuous in the context of the trial, he might prefer to put it in rather than leave the jury to speculate about it.[296] He might also choose to do so where he considers that his own character, while bad, is less likely to indicate guilt than that of a person he alleges was the true criminal.[297]

IMPORTANT EXPLANATORY EVIDENCE

As noted above,[298] the old law had elaborated a rather ill-defined category of the admissibility of background evidence that evaded the normal criteria of admissibility for evidence of bad character. The Law Commission was particularly concerned to restrain abuse in this area. It is indicative of the tenor of much of this part of the legislation that none of the Law Commission's proposed safeguards in terms of detailed criteria, enhanced relevance, and strong discretionary control are reflected in gateway (c), or its vestigial elaboration in s 102:

For the purposes of section 101(1)(c) evidence is important explanatory evidence if—

(a) without it, the court or jury would find it impossible or difficult properly to understand other evidence in the case, and

(b) its value for understanding the case as a whole is substantial.

It was said in *R v Davis* that this gateway should be applied with great care, and that it should not be used as an easier route for letting in evidence properly to be admitted under one of the other 'gateways',[299] most often as propensity evidence under 'gateway' (d), or to correct a false impression under 'gateway' (f). It should also be borne in mind that it operates only when it does not 'have to do with the facts of the offence,'[300] which many of the cases under the old law clearly did. This leaves a narrow ambit for 'gateway' (c). It is also tightly drawn in making its conditions cumulative,[301] and in the statement of its conditions, so that it might well be hard[302] to point to pieces of particular evidence to which they apply.

IMPORTANT ISSUE BETWEEN DEFENDANT AND PROSECUTION

This is the core gateway, designed to replace the major part of both the similar fact rule and the Criminal Evidence Act 1898 so far as issues between the prosecution and the defence are concerned.[303] It is proposed to start with the overall pattern of the provision, comparing it, in this respect, with the recommendations of the Law Commission; then to discuss

---

[295] (1992) 175 CLR 599.   [296] LC 273, [6.25].

[297] As under the old law in *R v Bracewell* (1978) 68 Cr App Rep 44.   [298] 377.

[299] [2008] EWCA Crim 1156, [2009] 2 Cr App R 306, [36].

[300] Noted in *R v Edwards and Rowlands* (n95), [1](i).

[301] Noted in *R v Beverley* [2006] EWCA Crim 1287, [7].

[302] Although accomplished in *R v Edwards (Chohan)* [2005] EWCA Crim 1813, [2006] 1 Cr App R 31, [75].

[303] Said in *R v Bradley* (n78), [12] to represent the most radical departure from the old law.

its substance distinguishing between bad character as going to propensity, or otherwise to issue, and as going to credibility, so far as these matters can be distinguished.

In defining the gateway, section 101(1)(d) specifies that the matter in issue should be important, although this qualification is not repeated in the heading[304] of s 103, which adds a little elaboration. In this dual provision, it differs from the pattern adopted by the Law Commission under which evidence of bad character going to issue, and such evidence going to credibility, were governed by separate clauses. The justification for such separation was that the issues will usually arise at different times and in a different state of the evidence, and given the concern of the Law Commission to ensure that detailed factors were set out to assist the determination of the balance of probative value and prejudicial effect, different factors needed to be set out.[305] The difference between the care and stringency of the conditions set out by the Law Commission, and the vestigial elaboration to be found in the provisions of the Act, is indicative of a very different spirit.

Where the evidence of bad character went to issue, the Law Commission required enhanced relevance by reference to *substantial* probative value,[306] and the satisfaction of a second stringent condition that the court be satisfied:

(a) that, in all the circumstances of the case, the evidence carries no risk of prejudice to the defendant, or

(b) that, taking into account the risk of prejudice, the interests of justice nevertheless require the evidence to be admissible in view of—

   (i) how much probative value it has in relation to the matter in issue,

  (ii) what other evidence has been, or can be, given on that matter, and

 (iii) how important the matter is in the context of the case as a whole.

The Law Commission further required regard to the various factors it had listed as governing the general probative value of evidence of bad character in this context.[307]

In stark contrast, s 103 provides that:[308]

(1) For the purposes of section 101(1)(d) the matters in issue between the defendant and the prosecution include—

(a) the question whether the defendant has a propensity to commit offences of the kind with which he is charged, except where his having such a propensity makes it no more likely that he is guilty of the offence;

(b) the question whether the defendant has a propensity to be untruthful, except where it is not suggested that the defendant's case is untruthful in any respect.

(2) Where subsection (1)(a) applies, a defendant's propensity to commit offences of the kind with which he is charged may (without prejudice to any other way of doing so) be established by evidence that he has been convicted of—

(a) an offence of the same description as the one with which he is charged, or

(b) an offence of the same category as the one with which he is charged.

---

[304] Which coheres with the pattern for issues between co-defendants, but not with that for explanatory evidence, where 'important' does appear in the heading of s 102, the elaborating provision.

[305] It should, however, be noted that the substance of cl 8 of the Law Commission's draft bill relating to credibility does reappear in s 106 in the guise of an attack upon the character of another.

[306] Clause 8(2).   [307] Clause 5(2).

[308] For doubts about the usefulness of the official explanatory notes as a guide to the interpretation of this provision, see Munday [2005] *Crim LR* 337.

(3) Subsection (2) does not apply in the case of a particular defendant if the court is satisfied, by reason of the length of time since the conviction or for any other reason, that it would be unjust for it to apply in his case.

(4) For the purposes of subsection (2)—

(a) two offences are of the same description as each other if the statement of the offence in a written charge or indictment would, in each case, be in the same terms;

(b) two offences are of the same category as each other if they belong to the same category of offences prescribed for the purposes of this section by an order made by the Secretary of State.

(5) A category prescribed by an order under subsection (4)(b) must consist of offences of the same type.

(6) Only prosecution evidence is admissible under section 101(1)(d).

One of the most significant features of this provision is its severity by contrast to s 100 in relation to evidence of the bad character of others than the accused, and especially the terseness of s 103(1), explaining that this formula covers propensity to commit offences of the kind charged, 'except where his having such a propensity makes it no more likely that he is guilty of the offence'. This qualification, so far from being a safeguard, is so stringent in its exemption that it will hardly ever be capable of establishment,[309] given minimal ingenuity by the prosecution. It might be thought that such a rejection shows no more than distaste for the complexity of the elaboration proposed by the Law Commission, but this cannot be the explanation, since that very complexity *is* required in s 100(3) in relation to the bad character of a non-defendant. The result is not only to turn the existing law on its head, by making the conditions to be satisfied for the prosecution to adduce bad character evidence less, rather than more, rigorous than those to be applied to its use against other persons who are not being tried; but by its deliberate substitution of the vestigial and severe elaboration in s 103(1)(a) for the extended and careful elaboration in cl 5(2), it seems to have weakened still further the standard of relevance under the existing law. The court was thus, in *R v Randall*, inclined to accept that a witness's identification of a man as a burglar was supported, not only by one conviction in similar circumstances, but by others of far less statistical significance.[310] Such a difference between the rules applying to the bad character of the accused and of all other witnesses also contradicts the policy of the Law Commission to achieve a measure of simplicity, and fairness, and far from having adopted the uniform approach it proposed, has reinstated different, but converse, tests for the admission of bad character in the two different situations.[311]

The Criminal Justice Bill had included evidence of convictions as a separate gateway,[312] but in the course of passage, they lost that distinct and direct route, and were instead accommodated here. It will, however, be seen that the enormous width of the definition of

---

[309] But see *Beverley* (n301), (n[8] doubting the relevance even of a conviction in the same category, also for possession of drugs with intention to supply, but in very different circumstances.

[310] [2006] EWCA Crim 1413, [11].   [311] See e.g. [9.14].

[312] It is significant that most of the public attention to the issue before and during the passage of the legislation was dominated by reference to the admissibility of convictions: see e.g. the government's White Paper *Justice for All*, Home Office 2002.

relevance to both issue[313] and credibility in subs (1) means that little has been altered by that change.

These provisions have generated a deluge of case law, which it will be convenient to discuss separately in relation to issue and credibility.

Issue

It has become clear that the provision covers not only cases where the reasoning is via propensity, but also where it is circumstantial. In the latter case its relevance may be to establish the accused's commission of the actus reus on the basis that all of the crimes were likely to have been committed by the same person, and the accused was connected with all of them;[314] or his mens rea where the act is established but issues arise as to intent;[315] or sometimes both.[316] An important difference between these two routes is that if the evidence is relevant only via propensity, then the prior misconduct, and its *capacity*[317] to show the relevant propensity, must be established by the prosecution to the ordinary criminal standard.[318] However, if the route is circumstantial it would defeat the whole basis of the reasoning if that standard were required of any individual example of misconduct standing alone.[319] A difficulty is that if the misconduct is sufficiently similar to ground propensity reasoning, then even though its initial admissibility were determined by the circumstantial route, it can if believed to the requisite standard, theoretically be used to show propensity, so potentially complicating jury directions.[320]

The parentheses in ss 103(2) make it clear that propensity to commit crimes of the relevant sort can be established, as under the old law, by much more than evidence of previous convictions, or the commission of criminal offences,[321] and the same applies in relation to the circumstantial route. This is capable of raising a very serious risk of satellite litigation[322] when the misconduct is disputed even if derived from convictions or cautions, and still more when derived from the facts underlying acquittals, stays, 'not proven' or other foreign verdicts, or allegations.[323] Similarly, it has been held that the facts of offences alleged, but not proved because of the accused's unfitness to plead at the time of trial, are admissible under gateway (g),[324] on the basis of reasoning equally applicable to (d). It has been definitively decided that the mere fact that the evidence consists of unproved allegations is immaterial to admissibility,[325] and relevant only to use by the jury.[326]

---

[313] Where they may postdate the matters in issue: *R v Adenusi* [2006] EWCA Crim 1059.

[314] As in *R v Wallace* (n110), [37]; *R v McAllister* (n202), [25]; *R v Freeman and Crawford* (Crawford) (n190), [25].   [315] As in *R v Saleem* (n80), [37] (rebutting innocent presence).

[316] As in *R v Chopra* (n81) (both touching patient, and intent in so touching).

[317] *R v Brima* [2006] EWCA Crim 408, [39].   [318] See *R v O'Dowd* (n165), [65].

[319] Clearly explained in *R v McAllister* (n202), [18].   [320] Ibid, [27].

[321] Affirmed in *R v Weir* (n91) [7]. In *R v S* [2006] EWCA Crim 756, [2006] 2 Cr App R 341, [12], cautions were held to come within s 98.

[322] Resulting in appeals being allowed in *R v McAllister* (above n202), and still more spectacularly in *R v O'Dowd* (n165).

[323] Although these origins may affect the operation of discretion, *R v Edwards and Rowlands* (n95), [1](vii).   [324] *R v Renda* (n101), [24].

[325] Although also perhaps relevant to the exercise of discretion: *R v Edwards and Rowlands* (n95) [1](vii).   [326] *R v Edwards and Rowlands* (95) (*Smith*), [81].

Much of the law has, however, concerned the use of convictions,[327] and in that respect, the statute has been supplemented, pursuant to ss 4(b), by order[328] establishing categories of offences of theft and sexual offences against persons under the age of 16. The Act thus specifies relevant convictions as those for an offence of the same description, or of the same category, as the one charged.[329] This is then amplified[330] by defining offences as being of the same description if the statement on a charge sheet or indictment would be in identical terms, or as being in the same category by reference to such categorization in an order to be made by the Secretary of State. It is far from clear exactly how easy such categorization will prove to be. The matter is made a little more mysterious by s 103(5), which provides that such a category must consist of offences of the same type. Needless to say, 'same type' is not defined. Presumably, this is intended to provide some check upon the discretion of the Secretary of State, but if a court can, and must for the purposes of such a check, determine whether offences are of the 'same type', it is not quite clear why the intervention of the Secretary of State in performing such categorization is necessary at all. The whole area was first considered extensively by the Court of Appeal in *R v Hanson*.[331] Perhaps the most significant guidance was denial, even when offences were categorized as being of the same description, that this was either necessary, *or sufficient*, to justify admission.[332] It still depended upon the convictions establishing propensity, and that propensity being relevant to the accused's guilt. Thus the allegation of no more than a propensity to acquire the property of others for gain,[333] or to commit sexual offences,[334] are far too broad, and a propensity to know what theft is, and to perceive its occurrence is incomprehensible.[335] It was suggested that no minimum number of events was appropriate.[336] So far as age is concerned,[337] this relates to the time of those events.[338] Considerations of relevance and age interact, so older and more relevant convictions[339] may be preferred to newer but less relevant ones.[340] In one case, however, the trial judge seems to have imposed an upper limit of twenty years, however relevant the convictions were.[341] If the perpetrator were young at the relevant time, it seems that should be taken into account, although it will have less impact when there are subsequent occurrences of the same type.[342] It may also be necessary to bear in mind that the accused may have spent considerable periods of time in

---

[327] Which include foreign convictions: *R v Kordasinski* [2006] EWCA Crim 2984, [2007] 1 Cr App R 238 [65].   [328] SI 2004/3346.

[329] CJA 2003, s 103(2). Arson of dwellings and vehicles were treated as sufficiently similar in *R v Jan* [2006] EWCA Crim 2314, [30].   [330] CJA 2003, s 103(3)–(5).

[331] (n79).   [332] [8]. See also *R v Johnson* [2009] EWCA Crim 649, [20].

[333] *R v Tully and Wood* [2006] EWCA Crim 2270, [26].   [334] *R v Clements* (n219).

[335] *R v Urushadze* (n154), [23].

[336] Although one would rarely be sufficient: see also *R v Murphy* (n260), 17] (single conviction for possession of firearms not enough to establish propensity to use firearms twenty years later).

[337] Specifically mentioned as a factor relevant to the exercise of exclusionary discretion in subs (3).

[338] Applied by analogy to the events where matters other than conviction were relied upon: see *R v Edwards and Rowlands* (95) (*Smith*), [74].

[339] In *R v Hanson* (n79) (*P*), [50] it was immaterial that a relevant conviction was spent under the Rehabilitation of Offenders Act 1974. See also *R v Amponsah* (n234), [19].

[340] *R v Edwards* (n136) [16] (the reasoning applies to this gateway as much as to (g)); in *R v Tangang* [2007] EWCA Crim 469, [17] a two-week gap between offences of the same type of fraud strengthened the evidence of propensity.   [341] *R v Edwards* (n136) (*Fysh*), [24].

[342] *R v Edwards* (n136) (*Chohan*), [72]; and cf *R v Renda* (n101) (*Razaq*), [76] (although there the bad character of a complainant, and a caution rather than a conviction).

prison, so diminishing the mitigation to be attached to mere passage of time.[343] Because of the stress on relevance, the facts underlying the conviction are more important than its formal title, or the sentence imposed,[344] so also the closer the factual circumstances, the more relevant the conviction is likely to be.[345] If an offence contains distinguishable elements, a propensity showing only one of them remains admissible.[346] It should further be noted that convictions for events occurring subsequent to those the subject matter of the trial may still be relevant, and admissible.[347]

Where the facts, as opposed to the fact, of a conviction are vital, there may well be difficulty in establishing them by admissible evidence, especially if they are old. For this reason, an appropriate amendment was made[348] to s 74 of the Police and Criminal Evidence Act 1984, which then, by operation of s 75, permits reference to 'the contents of the information, complaint, indictment or charge-sheet on which the person in question was convicted'.[349] This was designed to meet the criticism that evidence of a bare conviction would be unhelpful, and might be unduly prejudicial. Foreign convictions may be proved under the provisions of s 7 of the Evidence Act 1851.[350]

Credibility[351]

Under the old law, virtually any conviction was regarded as relevant to credibility.[352] In *Hanson*, however, the Court of Appeal construed the modern provisions differently, and refused to regard even offences involving dishonesty as automatically establishing a propensity to be untruthful. It required reference to such matters as whether there had been a denial of the commission of the earlier offence, a plea of not guilty, or some element of untruthfulness inherent in the matters there charged.[353] This view was endorsed in subsequent cases, and in some regarded as beyond argument,[354] although distinguishing propensity to untruthfulness from credibility.[355] A still more radical approach was adopted by the Lord Chief Justice in *R v Campbell*:[356]

The question of whether a defendant has a propensity for being untruthful will not normally[[357]] be capable of being described as an *important* matter in issue between the defendant and the prosecution. A propensity for untruthfulness will not, of itself, go very far in establishing the

---

[343] In *R v O'Dowd* (n165) the accused had spent many years in prison between the earliest misconduct relied upon and the date of the offence, during which period his opportunities to commit heterosexual rape were limited.

[344] *Hanson* (n79), [12]. Although in cases of doubt, the sentence may indicate the facts underlying the conviction, as in *Atkinson* (n259).   [345] *Edwards* (n136) (*Chohan*), [76].

[346] *R v Harris* [2009] EWCA Crim 434, [25] (stabbing to secure sex, convictions for use of knife, but none for sexual offences).   [347] *Edwards* (n136) (*Duggan*), [44]; *R v Adenusi* [2006] EWCA Crim 1059, [13].

[348] Schedule 37 Pt 5.

[349] Suggested in *R v O'Dowd*, (n165), [71] as a means of avoiding resort to excessive satellite litigation.

[350] *R v Kordasinski* (n327), [66].

[351] For full and perceptive analysis see Mirfield [2009] *Crim LR* 135.

[352] So construing s 6 of the Criminal Procedure Act 1865.

[353] [13]. Affirmed in *Edwards* (n136), [33]; see also *Edwards and Rowlands* (n95) (*Enright and Gray*), [104]. This approach finds some support in the official explanatory notes. Such a view has been rejected in New Zealand: *R v Wood* [2006] 3 NZLR 743.

[354] *R v Meyer* (n267), [22]; a position there accepted by the prosecution, [1]; see also *R v Awaritefe* (n270), 24].

[355] [22], in the sense of going to issue despite resolution depending upon the comparative reliability of the accounts given by complainant and accused.   [356] [30], original emphasis.

[357] Even in cases where it may, it will be because it goes to issue; see *R v Blake* [2006] EWCA Crim 871, [25].

commission of a criminal offence. To suggest that a propensity for untruthfulness makes it more likely that a defendant has lied to the jury is not likely to help them.

This seem to emasculate s 103(1)(b) to virtual[358] impotence, a result which should be recognized in directing the jury about use of convictions admitted as going to issue.[359] This approach fails to cohere with that adopted in relation to the untruthfulness of prosecution witnesses under the provisions of s 100,[360] or in the event of such an attack, of the attacking accused under 'gateway' (g).[361]

In relation to convictions especially, the balance of research,[362] and even anecdote[363] recounted by the Law Commission, suggests that the danger of prejudice is extremely high. Nor should the degree to which such further use of convictions in respect of which the defendant has served his sentence might discredit, and distort, the fairness of the whole system of criminal justice be lightly dismissed.

There has so far been little indication of matters other than conviction that might affect credibility, except the rejection in *R v Purcell and Christopher*[364] of an outrageous suggestion that a plea of not guilty might indicate a propensity to lie.

Important issue between co-defendants
This was discussed in Chapter VII.[365]

False impression
This was also discussed in Chapter VII.[366]

Attack on another[367]
The final gateway for admission of evidence of the bad character of the defendant is when he has attacked the character of someone else. Under the old law, this constituted the second limb of s 1(3)(ii) of the Criminal Evidence Act 1898, sometimes characterized as a case of 'tit for tat'.[368] It was thought unfair if the accused attacked a prosecution witness for being of bad character in a particular respect, while having exactly the same character defect himself, and that it was misleading to allow the jury to decide between the two

---

[358] In *R v Belogun* [2008] EWCA Crim 2006, [23] *R v Campbell* was distinguished in order to allow in a previous conviction for fabricating a defence when here it was alleged the defence was also fabricated.

[359] *R v McDonald* [2007] EWCA Crim 1194, [25]; although such misdirection is not necessarily fatal: *R v Foster* [2009] EWCA Crim 353, [18].

[360] *R v Renda (Osbourne)* (n101), [59]; *R v Stephenson* [2006] EWCA Crim 2325, [27]; but see *R v S* [2006] EWCA Crim 1303, [2007] 1 WLR 63, [11]–[12]; see further 354.

[361] *R v Lamaletie and Royce* (n166), [15]–[17]; cp *R v Renda (Osbourne) (Razaq)* (n101), [73], in which emphasis was placed upon not guilty pleas having been made at the previous trials resulting in conviction. See further 348.

[362] LC 141, [9.14] mentions Dutch research in which 100 per cent of judges who had heard the accused's convictions in advance went on to convict him, when only 27 per cent of those who had no prior knowledge convicted, the rest of the evidence being identical.

[363] Thus para 14.33 recounts a judge's account of a case involving two co-defendants, which found it proved against the one whose previous convictions had been disclosed, despite the fact that the evidence against the other who was acquitted was much stronger.   [364] [2006] EWCA Crim 1264, [24].

[365] 349.   [366] 345.

[367] For more detailed analysis, see Munday [2006] *Crim LR* 300. For a novel approach to one aspect of this topic in Scotland, see *DS v HM Adv* [2007] UKPC 36.

[368] See e.g. LC 273, [1.9]; [12.10]. See also *R v McLeod* (n25), 264g.

without knowing that this was the case. It was defective in a number of respects. It hindered the accused with a bad record from advancing true defences denying or mitigating the commission of the crime, or attributing commission to a third party. To the extent that the rationale depended upon a fair comparison between accuser and accused, it inhibited attack on prosecution witnesses,[369] while leaving defence witnesses open to exactly similar attack.[370] It was all the more damaging since the definition of what amounted to an attack was vague, and the retaliatory use of the accused's bad record extended to all convictions, however close to the subject matter of the case, irrespective of their not having been admitted, often being inadmissible, in chief, and theoretically going only to credit. There were two mitigating factors in the old law. First, the accused could evade the exposure of his record, by not testifying; and second, if he did, the courts developed a practice of discretionary refusal of allowing the accused's bad character to be adduced if they thought it unfair.

The Law Commission was aware of these defects, and sought to alleviate them; but once again the Act departed from the Law Commission's proposals. The Law Commission distinguished sharply between incriminatory and credibility gateways to admissibility, but the CJA 2003 did not. It would have been possible to regard the comparative credibility of the prosecution witnesses and those for the defence as merely one type of important issue between them. Despite the credibility of the defendant being covered by that gateway,[371] a further gateway was felt necessary to cater for attacks of this sort.

The Law Commission adopted the same position for attacks on credibility as for issue, namely that enhanced probative value should be required, that in order to make that assessment a detailed list of factors must be considered, and that there should be an overriding requirement, in all cases of possible prejudice, that the interests of justice should require admission, with the relevant factors to be taken into account for this purpose being set out in detail.[372] Once again, the whole of that detail was omitted from s 101(1)(g), and the supplementary s 106, which provides:

(1) For the purposes of section 101(1)(g) a defendant makes an attack on another person's character if—

   (a) he adduces evidence attacking the other person's character,

   (b) he (or any legal representative appointed under section 38(4) of the Youth Justice and Criminal Evidence Act 1999 (c 23) to cross-examine a witness in his interests) asks questions in cross-examination that are intended to elicit such evidence, or are likely to do so, or

   (c) evidence is given of an imputation about the other person made by the defendant—

      (i) on being questioned under caution, before charge, about the offence with which he is charged, or

      (ii) on being charged with the offence or officially informed that he might be prosecuted for it.

---

369 Because this would expose the accused's bad character.
370 Because this would not expose the accuser's bad character.
371 Abundantly clear from the reference in CJA 2003, s 103(1)(b), to the propensity of the defendant to be untruthful.   372 Law Commission's bill cl 9.

(2) In subsection (1) "evidence attacking the other person's character" means evidence to the effect that the other person—

(a) has committed an offence (whether a different offence from the one with which the defendant is charged or the same one), or

(b) has behaved, or is disposed to behave, in a reprehensible way; and "imputation about the other person" means an assertion to that effect.

(3) Only prosecution evidence is admissible under section 101(1)(g).

It is unfortunate that this provision[373] of the new legislation has been construed much more in line with the provisions of the old law.[374] Despite some weak recognition of formal change,[375] the old law has been overwhelmingly endorsed.[376] It might have been thought that an attack on a prosecution witness need not have been made a separate 'gateway' from that for an important issue between prosecution and defence described above,[377] but the need to avoid such redundancy has been regarded as justifying a more expansive interpretation of this gateway.[378] Thus it remains the case that the admissibility of the accused's bad character is still triggered, despite the attacking element being an integral element of the defence,[379] despite the attack being inadvertent,[380] despite its not being false in any way,[381] and despite its having been determined by the Court to be in the interests of justice for it to have been made, since leave is required under s 100 to launch such an attack,[382] although this requirement seems often to have been ignored.[383] As under the old law, however, mere allegation of consent as a defence to rape seems still not by itself to amount to such an attack,[384] but will if it is alleged that witnesses for the prosecution have colluded to present a false story.[385] The range of attack has also been extended under the new provisions to take in attacks upon non-complainants and non-witnesses, although it has been said that discretion may provide some protection.[386]

Not only have the new provisions reinforced the defects of the old law, they have also diminished its alleviations. The most notable respect is that the gateway applies even when the accused chooses not to testify, but has made his attack in an earlier statement.[387] It is true that the statement must 'be in evidence', but this may include its being put in evidence not by the accused but by the prosecution against the wishes of the defence, at least if such a procedure were more than a ruse for getting evidence of the accused's bad

---

[373] But not for (f) (false impression).   [374] *R v Hanson* (n79), [14].

[375] *R v Bahanda* [2007] EWCA Crim 2929, [16].

[376] *R v Singh* [2007] EWCA Crim 2140 [8]; *R v Lamaletie and Royce* (n166), [8], [15]; *R v Hearne* [2009] EWCA Crim 103 [10].

[377] Overlap was recognized in *R v Lamaletie and Royce* (n166), [13], [14]. There is no overlap with 'gateway' (e) on account of the limitation to prosecution evidence, although this seems often to have been overlooked, as in *R v Bovell (Dowds)* (n132), [30];see also *R v Lewis* (n110), [13] (limitation also ignored in relation to 'gateway' (f) so as to create overlap with (e)).   [378] *R v Singh* (n376), [9].

[379] Ibid, [8].   [380] *R v Bovell (Dowds)* (n132), [32].

[381] *R v Renda (Osbourne and Razaq)* (n101).

[382] Invocation rendered the admission of the accused's bad character in *R v Bovell* (n132), [23] and *R v Edwards (Fysh)* (n136), [34] ('inevitable'), and in *R v Highton (Carp)* (n91), [51] ('irresistible').

[383] It was not referred to in *R v Hanson (P)*, (n79) or *R v Renda (Ball)*, (n101), and only obliquely in *R v Singh* (n376), [6] ('properly put' to the complainant).   [384] *R v Renda* (n101) *(Ball)*, [34].

[385] *R v Hanson* (n79) *(P)*, [49]; R v *Edwards* (n136) *(Fysh)*, [34].

[386] *R v Nelson* [2006] EWCA Crim 3412, [14]–[16].

[387] Section 106(1)(c) applied in *R v Renda* (n101) *(Ball)*, [35].

character admitted.[388] The gateway is not, however, appropriate for a case where the attack appears in the witness statement of a prosecution witness, but is not relied upon in chief, but adduced only in cross-examination by a co-accused.[389] Nor is there now any vestige of the old limitation of effect to credibility, since once admitted the evidence of the accused's bad character can be used for any purpose for which it is relevant.[390] It is true that there is here a discretion to exclude such evidence under s 101(3), although it seems not yet to have been exercised decisively in this context.

SECTION 4.   OTHER STATUTORY PROVISION

As noted above, CJA 2003, s 99(1) purported to abolish only the common law rules relating to the admissibility of evidence of bad character, several provisions explicitly preserve other statutory provisions in the area, and Sch 37, Pt 5 is selective in its specification of statutory provisions to be repealed.[391]

Nevertheless, by far the most important previous statutory provision, s 1(3) of the Criminal Evidence Act 1898, has been repealed, and the provisions that remain are of little general importance.

Two[392] statutes abrogate the rules discussed in this section in the particular circumstances to which they apply: namely, s 1(2) of the Official Secrets Act 1911, and s 27(3) of the Theft Act 1968.

Section 1(1) of the Official Secrets Act 1911 (as amended by the Official Secrets Act 1920) punishes various forms of spying prejudicial to the state. Section 1(2) provides that it shall not be necessary to show that the accused person was guilty of any particular act tending to show a purpose prejudicial to the safety or interests of the state and, notwithstanding that no such act is proved against him, he may be convicted if, from the circumstances of the case, or his conduct, or his known character as proved, it appears that his purpose was a purpose prejudicial to the safety or interests of the state. The wording of this subsection shows that evidence of the accused's misconduct may be given, although relevant only because it shows that he is the kind of man whose purpose in doing certain acts might be of the type proscribed by the statute.

The Law Commission recommended that, so far as OSA 1911, s 1(2) dealt with the means rather than the object of proof, it should be dealt with under the rules it recommended to govern bad character. Since the section has not been repealed by the Criminal Justice Act 2003, it must remain in force, and will be subject to the new rules, although, as noted above, they are considerably more stringent than those recommended by the Law Commission, which the Commission had assumed in abstaining from recommending repeal of this provision.

Section 27(3) of the Theft Act 1968, reads as follows:

Where a person is being proceeded against for handling stolen goods (but not for any offence other than handling stolen goods), then at any stage of the proceedings, if evidence has been

---

388   *R v Nelson* (n386), [19].   389   *R v Assani* [2008] EWCA Crim 2563, [18].
390   *R v Highton* (n91), [10].   391   Some are repealed only in part.
392   For an Australian example, see Crimes Act (Victoria) 1958, s 47A, considered by the High Court in *KRM v R* [2001] HCA 11, 206 CLR 221. There are other statutes that exceptionally allow proof of other convictions for limited purposes: see e.g. Social Security Administration Act 1992, s 120.

given of his having or arranging to have in his possession the goods the subject of the charge, or of his undertaking or assisting in, or arranging to undertake or assist in, their retention, removal, disposal or realisation, the following evidence shall be admissible for the purpose of proving that he knew or believed the goods to be stolen goods:

(a) evidence that he has had in his possession, or has undertaken or assisted in the retention, removal, disposal or realisation of, stolen goods from any theft taking place not earlier than twelve months before the offence charged; and

(b) (provided that seven day's notice in writing has been given to him of the intention to prove the conviction) evidence that he has within the five years preceding the date of the offence charged been convicted of theft or handling stolen goods.

The subsection re-enacts, with some significant differences,[393] s 43(1) of the Larceny Act 1916, which, in its turn, re-enacted s 19 of the Prevention of Crimes Act 1871.

It has proved so unpopular with English judges as to be given a highly restricted interpretation.[394] In particular, there has been concern to restrict its application to proof of guilty knowledge,[395] and, despite the apparently mandatory language, the court has invested itself with, and applied, discretion to exclude evidence should there be any danger of this restriction being undermined.[396] Similar motives have led to the application of a strictly literal construction being placed upon the ambit of the evidence admitted under the provision. Thus, in the case of s 27(3)(a), it has been determined that no surrounding detail of the previous possession can be adduced beyond the barest description of the relevant goods.[397] Similarly, in relation to s 27(3)(b), no more than the formal details of the relevant conviction may be adduced, corresponding to those certified under the provisions of s 73(2) of the Police and Criminal Evidence Act 1984. This permits little more than a brief description of the goods,[398] and the result of the case. Here, too, there is a discretion to exclude the evidence if it seems likely to be unfairly prejudicial. It has been argued[399] that this effort has been counterproductive, since the elimination of detail makes it very difficult for the jury to evaluate the true significance of the evidence, and gives rise to the possibility of exacerbating the very prejudice that it is designed to eliminate. The prosecution is in no way hampered, since it can adduce any detail that is sufficiently relevant under the ordinary similar facts rules that the provision supplements, while the accused has no

[393] On which, see the Eighth Report of the Criminal Law Revision Committee (Cmnd 2977, 1966), paras 157–9.

[394] It is no more popular in its local form in Australia: see *R v Cresswell* (1987) 8 NSWLR 56, in which faint ambiguity in the drafting of the starting point for time beginning to run was resolved in favour of inadmissibility.

[395] *R v Wilkins* (1975) 60 Cr App Rep 300; *R v Bradley* (1979) 70 Cr App Rep 200. It cannot be used to undermine the accused's general credibility: see e.g. *R v Duffas* (1993) The Times, 19 October.

[396] *R v Herron* [1967] 1 QB 107, [1966] 2 All ER 26; see above 199.

[397] *R v Wood* (1987) 85 Cr App Rep 287, preferring *R v Bradley* (1979) 70 Cr App Rep 200 to *R v Smith* [1918] 2 KB 415.

[398] Until the decision of the House of Lords in *R v Hacker* [1995] 1 All ER 45, [1994] 1 WLR 1659, no detail at all of the stolen goods had been permitted: see, in New Zealand, *R v Brosnan* [1951] NZLR 1030, 1039.

[399] By Smith, in his note in the *Criminal Law Review* on *R v Bradley* [1980] Crim LR 173, and Munday [1988] *Crim LR* 345.

ready means to avoid the prejudice, since it would hardly help his cause to draw attention to the variety and versatility of his previous criminal conduct.[400]

The Law Commission recommended repeal of this provision, partly because its retention would be otiose in the light of its other recommendations.[401] It would appear to be still more otiose under the enacted provisions of the Criminal Justice Act 2003, but, perhaps surprisingly, has been omitted from the provisions listed for repeal under the Schedule.

SECTION 5.   APPRAISAL[402]

Reform of this area of the law sought to consolidate its sources, to clarify its rules, to simplify its procedures, and to improve its operation. How far has it succeeded in so doing?

CONSOLIDATION

The aim was to substitute one single set of statutory provisions for the combination of statutory and common law rules, discretions, and practices which had previously prevailed. To that end the common law rules were to be abolished, and evidence of bad character governed only by these statutory provisions. Unfortunately, the terminology for abolishing the common law was flawed,[403] and in particular it has been accepted that basic concepts like relevance remain,[404] although whether unchanged is somewhat less clear. Similarly, although the principal general statute, the Criminal Evidence Act 1898, has been repealed, other statutory provisions remain unrepealed, or repealed only in part.[405] Even in the case of repealed provisions some parts of the common law interpretation of those provisions seems to have been retained, while other parts have not. Thus the common law interpretation of what was once s 1(f)(ii) of the Criminal Evidence Act has been retained so far as it related to attack on the character of others,[406] but rejected so far as it related to response to evidence of good character.[407] It was also left unclear how far some important statutory provisions operative in this area applied despite neither explicit retention nor repeal. S 78 of the Police and Criminal Evidence Act 1984 thus seems to have survived, although its relationship to explicit discretions and similarly worded provisions in the new provisions remains mysterious.[408] Reference to Codes extraneous to the legislative provisions remains necessary for some purposes, such as procedural rules governed by the Criminal Procedure Rules and guidance as to direction of juries by the forms promoted by the Judicial Standards Board.[409] Perhaps most significant of all, s 98 of the Act defines

---

[400] The Law Commission in Law Com No 273, [11.55], rec 15, recommended its repeal, as did the Criminal Law Revision Committee, and as occurred in 1973 in the State of Victoria. Such a course would have left this situation to the operation of the ordinary rules.

[401] Law Com 273 [11.55], rec 15, draft bill cl 20(3)(b).

[402] Based upon consideration only of reported cases. Most of the points summarized below have appeared earlier in this chapter, or its predecessor. A rather limited empirical study by the Ministry of Justice *Research into the impact of bad character provisions on the courts* MoJ Res Ser 5/09 (March 2009) came to a very different conclusion, although it had no data on the operation of the old law with which to compare the impact of the new.

[403] S 99, 383.

[404] *R v Bullen* (n77), [29].   [405] 410.   [406] *R v Lamelitie* (n166), [8].

[407] *R v Renda* (n101), [19].   [408] *R v Highton* (n91), [13]; *R v Moran* (n240), [36].

[409] Cp *R v Hanson* (n79), [18]; *R v Campbell* (n87), [37]–[43].

its area of operation to exclude from its operation in the very vaguest of terms evidence otherwise satisfying the Act's criterion of misconduct, but 'having to do with the facts of the case', or 'connected with' their investigation or trial. This has left it quite uncertain what is excluded, whether it is wholly excluded, and what rules apply to it, to the extent that it is excluded.[410]

CLARIFICATION

The aim was to make the law more comprehensible, for lawyer and juror alike. It sought to accomplish this by the use of less technical terms, by the dissection of admissibility into discrete sub-rules, each with its own expository clause, and by the casting of rules in forms closer to that of the terminology of their underlying policies. Unfortunately, the use of a new terminology, or re-use of an old,[411] requires elucidation, and it was ominous that in the very first case to arise in relation to the new provisions, it was complained that there had been insufficient time to train the judiciary,[412] and that it was felt necessary to deliver sometimes as many as five composite judgments at a time[413] to illustrate the operation of the Act. The combination of non-technical language and the multiplication of sub-rules has also led to potential overlapping,[414] and there has been a number of examples of appellate courts differing from trial courts as to the correct rule to apply,[415] or sometimes simply getting it wrong themselves.[416] While it is possible to use terms in common use in legislative provisions, this is often at the expense of clarity in their connotation. At the most general level, terms such as fairness can be understood, but this may well be at the expense of dispute as to just what fairness requires in a given situation, say in a three-cornered case involving prosecution, and two mutually hostile co-accused.[417] Similarly, instead of a provision allowing bad character to be admitted in response to the adduction or elicitation of evidence of good character, the new provisions refer to evidence apt to convey a false impression. The difficulty and ambiguity inherent in the latter notion is patent. Where new terms have been coined, such as 'reprehensible' behaviour, interpretation has proved difficult and inconsistent. It is hard to believe that practitioners now have confidence in their ability to predict admissibility.

SIMPLICITY

It was hoped that the new law would be simple to operate, by providing for admissibility without needing leave of the court, and by avoiding the need for voir dire or appeal, so giving trial judges a freer hand. The decision on leave was, however, taken between receipt of the Law Commission's recommendations and the passage of the Act, and applied only to evidence of the bad character of the accused, thus exacerbating difference from the rules applying to the admissibility of evidence of others. Since simplicity of operation was also

---

[410] *R v Watson* (n96), [19].   [411] *R v McAllister* (n202), [22].
[412] *R v Bradley* (n78), [38]–[39], the provisions were said to be 'conspicuously unclear', the language 'obfuscatory' and the legislation 'perplexing'.   [413] *R v Weir* (n91); *R v Renda* (n101).
[414] *R v Bovell and Dowds* (n132), [32] ('gateways' (f) and (g).   [415] *R v Lamelitie* (n166), [14].
[416] *R v Lewis* (n110), (assuming 'gateway' (g) to enable one co-accused to adduce evidence of the other's bad character); *R v Z* (n21), [27] (assuming s 116(4) to apply to evidence admitted under s 116(2)(a)).
[417] Such as *R v Musone* (n237).

designed to avoid delay and adjournment it was necessary also to provide for notice to the accused of an intention to adduce or elicit evidence of bad character, and for the accused to be able to apply to exclude the evidence. This is in practice regarded, and described, as a system of application and counter-application.[418] Many of the changes in the legislation have introduced new factual conditions for admissibility, some of them capable of being very close to the issues ultimately to be decided by the jury, for example in the area of false impression. It has not been possible to avoid the resolution of such preliminary issues by securing agreement in a number of high-profile cases, and it has proved difficult to establish the underlying facts even of convictions,[419] and still less of acquittals, stayed proceedings, or mere allegations. This has, of necessity, led to proliferation of satellite litigation, one feature of which has been doubt about the interaction of the means of establishing such facts and those of the issues crucial to the offences being tried.[420] If it was hoped to avoid recourse to appellate tribunals by restricting their intervention to one of review, this seems not to have succeeded either in terms of the number of cases being reported at the appellate level, or in the abstention of such courts from reversing decisions in some cases, even though all of the matters relevant to the exercise of a discretion[421] or making a fact-sensitive judgement[422] had been rehearsed at trial. In effect this attempt to substitute admission for admissibility seems to have led to greater pressure upon the direction of juries, and some inconsistency in the appellate courts towards the use of standard directions to secure uniformity of approach. Any failure of clarity in the rules of admissibility is likely to inhibit agreement between the parties, and restriction of appeal to prolong argument at trial.

IMPROVEMENT

Few doubt that the result of the introduction of the new provisions has increased rather than reduced complexity,[423] and that it has spawned more satellite litigation.[424] It seems[425] to have led to the increased use of evidence of the accused's bad character as the government intended, but since the criterion under the old law was that such evidence was admissible unless more prejudicial than probative, it is not self-evident that the result has been an improvement in justice.

---

[418] R v McNeill (n122), [9].   [419] R v Burns, R v Lewendon (n160).

[420] R v Freeman and Crawford (n190), [20].   [421] R v O'Dowd (n165), [61] (s101(3)).

[422] R v Murphy (n260); in R v McKenzie (n163) the Court of Appeal upheld the decision of the trial judge on the evidence of one event, and rejected it on another.

[423] R v Isichei [2006] EWCA Crim 1815, [32].   [424] R v O'Dowd (n165), [2].

[425] R v Chopra (n81), [12]; R v Campbell (n87), [1].

IX

PRIVILEGE[1]

A witness is 'privileged' when he may validly[2] claim not to answer a question, or to supply information relevant to the determination of an issue in judicial proceedings. Because the effect is to deprive the tribunal of relevant evidence, powerful arguments are required for such rules, and the modern law has reduced their number and scope,[3] although balanced by an increase in status,[4] now further elevated by construction of the European Convention on Human Rights.[5] Only types of privilege are sufficiently important to require discussion here: the privilege against self-incrimination; legal professional privilege; privilege for statements made without prejudice as part of an attempt to settle a dispute; and a privilege derived from the former for statements made to a conciliator. A few preliminary observations are also necessary.

As the privilege is that of a particular person or class, matters covered by it may always be proved by the evidence of other witnesses.[6] Parke B once said:[7]

Where an attorney entrusted confidentially with a document communicates the contents, or suffers another to take a copy, surely the secondary evidence so obtained may be produced. Suppose the instrument were even stolen, and a correct copy taken, would it not be reasonable to admit it?

It was on the authority of Parke B's remark that the Court of Appeal allowed copies of proofs of witnesses with notes on the evidence in a former claim brought by the claimant's predecessor in title to be put in by the defendant in *Calcraft v Guest*,[8] the originals having been handed over by the defendant's solicitor to the claimant to whom they belonged. Such secondary evidence cannot, however, be used if it consists of, or is derived from, a

---

[1] See generally, Thanki (ed) *The Law of Privilege* (2006); for an Australian emphasis, McNichol *Law of Privilege* (1992).

[2] Some evidential basis for refusal to answer is required; it is not enough, for example, that the witness might be put in personal jeopardy by doing so: *The Coca Cola Co v Gilbey* [1996] FSR 23. See also *S v Sithole* 1991 (4) SA 94.

[3] Recommendations to this effect in the 16th Report of the Law Reform Committee (Cmnd 3472, 1967) and in the 11th Report of the Criminal Law Revision Committee (Cmnd 4991, 1972) were largely implemented in Civil Evidence Act 1968, s 16, and Police and Criminal Evidence Act 1984, s 80 (9). Even in the United States, there has been strong resistance to the creation of new heads of privilege: see *University of Pennsylvania v Equal Employment Opportunity Commission* 493 US 182, 188 (1990).

[4] See e.g. *Brannigan v Davison* [1997] AC 238, 249D (against self-incrimination); *R v Derby Magistrates, ex p B* [1996] AC 487, [1995] 4 All ER 526; 507D, 541a (legal professional privilege).

[5] See *Saunders v United Kingdom* (1996) 23 EHRR 313; *Heaney and McGuiness v Ireland* (2001) 33 EHRR 12 (privilege against self-incrimination); and for commentary, Emmerson, Ashworth and Macdonald *Human Rights and Criminal Justice* (2007) 15.68–15.100.

[6] See also, in Australia, *Bond v Tuohy* (1995) 128 ALR 595; cf, in Canada, *Del Zotto v The Queen* (1997) 147 DLR (4th) 457.   [7] *Lloyd v Mostyn* (1842) 10 M & W 478, 481–2, in the course of argument.

[8] [1898] 1 QB 759.

document brought into court by an opponent, or his legal representative, and then improperly obtained.[9] No recommendation was made upon this matter by early Law Reform reports,[10] nor has there been subsequent statutory provision. The matter is thus left to the general common law relating to the admissibility of improperly obtained evidence, under which the rules in England generally favoured admissibility more than some other common law jurisdictions, and very much more than the United States.[11]

Secondly, the personal nature of privilege means that a party will not necessarily be entitled to succeed on an appeal, or obtain an order for a new trial, when the claim to privilege of his own, or his opponent's, witness has been wrongly rejected or accepted in the court below.[12] There is express authority for this view in a case in which the witness had unsuccessfully invoked the privilege against self-incrimination,[13] and practically all the decisions of appellate courts in which the judge's ruling on a question of privilege has been varied, or reversed, relate to issues in which the person claiming the privilege was a party to, and not merely a witness in, the proceedings. Many of them are concerned with the disclosure of documents, or requests for further information, since the issue of privilege is often raised before the trial.

Thirdly, according to English law, no adverse inference should normally be made from claiming privilege,[14] although it is hard to believe that, in practice, none is ever drawn.[15] It is interesting that refusal to answer on the basis of privilege is one of the circumstances excepted[16] from the authorization of comment and the drawing of adverse inferences from failure to answer a question under the Criminal Justice and Public Order Act 1994.

Lastly, privilege involves withholding information from the court at the expense of what may be abstract justice to one of the parties.[17] It follows that there should be good cause, plainly shown, for the existence of any privilege,[18] and it remains to consider whether this is always true. The crucial question is whether some interest protected by the privilege is

---

9 *ITC Film Distributors v Video Exchange Ltd* [1982] Ch 431, [1982] 2 All ER 241. If there has been no impropriety in obtaining such a document, it may apparently be used: see *Bell Cablemedia plc v Simmons* [2002] FSR 551 (privilege against self-incrimination); *R v Tompkins* (1977) 67 Cr App Rep 181 (legal professional privilege); for a more restrictive view in New Zealand, see *R v Uljee* [1982] 1 NZLR 561.

10 Cmnd 3472, [32]. The Committee assumed that secondary evidence of a privileged document could be given, however it had been obtained; see also *Waugh v British Railways Board* 1980] AC 521, [1979] 2 All ER 1169; 536, 1177.

11 See further Chapter X. The Report of the Law Reform Committee referred to r 26 of the Uniform Rules, which conferred very wide protection on the privilege holder; there is no equivalent in the Federal Rules, under which privilege is governed by the common law.

12 *Greenan v HM Adv* [2006] HCJAC 80, 2006 SCCR 658, [12].   13 *R v Kinglake* (1870) 22 LT 335.

14 *Wentworth v Lloyd* (1864) 10 HL Cas 589, 590–2; for commentary, see Young (1991) 65 ALJ 412. The contrast with r 233 of the Model Code is striking: 'if a privilege to refuse to disclose, or a privilege to prevent another from disclosing, matter is claimed and allowed, the judge and counsel may comment thereon, and the trier of fact may draw all reasonable inferences therefrom'; but this rule was not adopted by the Uniform Law Commissioners: see Uniform Rules, r 39. In *Oxford Gene Technology v Affymetrix Inc* [2001] RPC 18, and *Sayers v Clarke Walker* [2002] EWCA Civ 645, [2002] 3 All ER 490, [16], *Wentworth v Lloyd* was approved by the Court of Appeal, whereas in *Murray v United Kingdom* (1996) 22 EHRR 29, [47], the European Court of Human Rights seemed quite prepared to contemplate the drawing of adverse inferences from silence, equating it with the privilege against self-incrimination in the relevant passage. See also, in Australia, *Thompson v Bella-Lewis* [1997] 1 Qd 429.

15 *Den Norske Bank v Antonaos* [1991] QB 271, 296; *Compagnie Noga D'Importation et Exportation SA v ANZ Banking Group Ltd* [2007] EWHC 85 (Comm), [41].   16 Section 35(5)(a).

17 This may be extremely important in separate criminal proceedings against those co-accused: see *R v Swick* (1997) 150 DLR (4th) 566.   18 VIII Wigmore 67.

more significant than the administration of justice. It is nevertheless important also to consider potentially legitimate claims to privilege. The influence of public opinion should not be ignored. The proper administration of justice may encompass the rejection of relevant evidence unduly offensive to contemporary public opinion. It follows that that which was the subject of privilege in one generation should not necessarily be privileged in the next, and vice versa.

SECTION 1. THE PRIVILEGE AGAINST SELF-INCRIMINATION[19]

The privilege against self-incrimination originated in the unpopularity of the Star Chamber, where those charged with an offence were interrogated on oath. This contributed to the rule that the accused could not testify in a criminal case, and the idea that no one could be obliged to jeopardize his life, or liberty, by answering questions on oath came to be applied to all witnesses in all proceedings in the course of the seventeenth century. In the narrowest sense, the privilege operates to permit a witness in legal proceedings to refuse to answer questions the answers to which may tend to incriminate him by exposing him to subsequent criminal proceedings. The common law was said by Lord Diplock[20] to have been stated, so far as offences and penalties provided by the law of England are concerned, in s 14 of the Civil Evidence Act 1968 as:

(1) The right of a person in any legal proceedings other than criminal proceedings to refuse to answer any question or produce any document or thing if to do so would tend to expose that person to proceedings for an offence or for the recovery of a penalty.

This narrow sense has, however, come under conflicting pressures on the one hand from those who think the privilege a bastion of human freedom from oppression by the state, to be construed expansively:[21]

The privilege against compulsory self-incrimination is part of the common law of human rights. It is based on the desire to protect personal freedom and human dignity. These social values justify the impediment the privilege presents to judicial or other investigation. It protects the innocent as well as the guilty from the indignity and invasion of privacy which occurs in compulsory self-incrimination; it is society's acceptance of the inviolability of human personality.

And on the other, from those who think it an obstruction to the administration of justice, to be construed restrictively:[22]

It is difficult to see any reason why in civil proceedings the privilege against self-incrimination should be exercisable so as to enable a litigant to refuse relevant and even vital documents which

---

[19] VIII Wigmore (McNaughton revision), paras 2250–1 contains a classic statement of the history and rationale of the rule. See also Morgan (1949) 34 *Minn LR* 1; Levy *Origins of the Fifth Amendment* (1968). For modern approaches, see McNair (1990) 10 *OJLS* 66; and from a US perspective, see Helmholz et al *The Privilege Against Self-Incrimination* (1997). See also MacCullough (2006) 26 *Leg St* 211 for discussion of the rationale in relation to competition law, and more generally Redmayne (2007) 27 *OJLS* 209.

[20] *Rio Tinto Zinc Corp v Westinghouse Electric Corp* [1978] AC 547, [1978] 1 All ER 434, 636, 464.

[21] Murphy J in *Pyneboard Pty Ltd v Trade Practices Commission* (1983) 152 CLR 328, 346. In *R v White* [1999] 2 SCR 417, 438, it was described as an 'over-arching principle', and applicable however minor the charge. [22] Lord Templeman in *Istel Ltd v Tully* [1993] AC 45, [1992] 3 All ER 523, 53, 530.

are in his possession or power and which speak for themselves.... I regard the privilege against self-incrimination exercisable in civil proceedings as an archaic and unjustifiable survival from the past when the court directs the production of relevant documents and requires the defendant to specify his dealings with the plaintiff's property or money.

Given such conflicting pressures, and the intervention of the legislature in support of the increasing role of the state in social affairs, it is hardly surprising that the contours of the privilege should be somewhat uncertain.[23] It is desirable first to consider the scope of the privilege, then the procedure by which it is invoked, and finally the inroads into it made by statute.

SCOPE OF THE RULE

A number of different matters require consideration. It is clear that the privilege extends beyond mere permission not to answer while testifying to entitlement not to comply with pre-trial process to compel production by way of disclosure, but it is questionable exactly which pre-trial processes[24] qualify for protection.[25] This merges with a second question how far the privilege extends to different forms of self-incrimination. A final issue relates to the range of deleterious consequences, beyond personal exposure to criminal prosecution, which the privilege protects. These will be considered separately, despite some overlap.

Range of application

One area of pressure has been to extend the privilege further and further before the occasion of testifying. It is useful to distinguish here between pre-trial civil and criminal proceedings,[26] given the perhaps differential impact of the European Convention after the Human Rights Act 1998. The discretion to stay civil proceedings arising from the same facts pending criminal, is unaffected by the Convention; the privilege itself neither bars civil proceedings, nor furnishes a defence.[27]

Civil proceedings

There is no doubt that the privilege can be claimed at the stage of disclosure and inspection;[28] indeed, that is the stage when it most commonly would be claimed. Speedy interim action must sometimes be taken in civil cases, often *ex parte*, especially by way of search

---

[23] Nor that the limits should be differently drawn in different jurisdictions, and liable to fluctuate: see e.g. for hints of the prospect of further fluctuation in the United States, Justices Thomas and Scalia in *US v Hubbell* 530 US 27 (2000), 56.

[24] It may also be claimed in post-trial ancillary proceedings: *A v A; B v B* [2000] 1 FCR 577, 600.

[25] It cannot be used as a defence or stay to a claim for summary judgment on the basis that any defence would incriminate: *V v C* [2001] EWCA Civ 1509, [2002] CPR 8. It has, however, been held in Australia that to claim the privilege in such circumstances does not disqualify the tender of other evidence: *In the marriage of Atkinson* (1997) 136 FLR 347.

[26] Bearing in mind that some civil proceedings attract the same concerns as criminal: see e.g. *Pickering v A-G* [2001] 2 NZLR 324 (writ of arrest), and in *C Plc and P v Home Secretary* [2007] EWCA Civ 493, [33] it was said that the rule operated identically in both contexts. Most crimes involve the commission of civil wrongs, and it is sometimes advantageous to pursue the former: see Christopher (2008) 158 *NLJ* 1558.

[27] *Mote v Secretary of State for Work and Pensions* [2007] EWCA Civ 1324; for similar reasoning in Ireland, see *Wicklow County Council v O'Reilly* [2006] IEHC 273, [2006] 3 IR 623.

[28] As in *Istel Ltd v Tully* (n22).

orders and freezing injunctions. Although the privilege clearly applies at that stage,[29] it has recently been modified by judicial decision to bring it more closely into line with its operation in criminal cases. In *C plc and P v Home Secretary*,[30] it was determined that its operation should be restricted to evidence *elicited* by compulsory process, and should not apply to evidence existing independently of that process,[31] even though its existence was so compulsorily revealed. Accordingly, even though in that case material from a computer had been surrendered under a search order to an expert, subject to a claim for the protection of the privilege, it was held that pornographic images, possession of which was prima facie criminal, could be passed on to the police.[32]

It seems that proceedings to inquire into the means to pay taxes preliminary to a committal order for that failure may attract the privilege.[33] In some jurisdictions, the privilege has been held to apply to various pre-trial procedures to gather evidence for civil proceedings.[34] In England, the privilege has been held not to apply in proceedings to disqualify a company director,[35] although in Australia, the High Court has affirmed more generally that it cannot be contended that the privilege is inherently incapable of application in non-judicial proceedings.[36] In Canada, it has been held that pre-trial investigation of a formally criminal, but essentially administrative, nature falls outside the protection offered by the privilege.[37]

Criminal proceedings

One of the effects of the European Convention has been to subvert the possibility of distinguishing between the rules defining the range of compulsory disclosure, and the operation of the privilege within those boundaries. Thus in *Heaney and McGuinness v Ireland*,[38] it was held that legislation imposing an obligation to provide information subject to a penalty for failing to do so was in breach of Art 6 in destroying 'the very essence of the privilege against self-incrimination'. This is a very strong decision, since the legislation in question was inspired by the threat of terrorism, there was no suggestion of procedural violation of

---

[29] So long as it has not been waived, perhaps merely by failure to claim it: *O Ltd v Z* [2005] EWHC 238 (Ch),[70].

[30] (n26).

[31] Collins LJ was more dubious about this, while agreeing in the result.

[32] Nor was it material, or in breach of any implied undertaking, that the images had nothing whatever to do with litigation in which the search order was made.

[33] *R v Highbury Corner Magistrates, ex p Watkins* [1992] RA 300 (although there no privilege arose because the question involved no risk of incrimination, leading only to such committal). The freedom of questioning about affairs relevant to tax assessment from the constitutional protection of the privilege was affirmed in Canada in *Re 462657 Ontario Ltd* (1989) 62 DLR (4th) 666.

[34] In Australia, to questioning with a view to instituting disciplinary proceedings against a police constable: *Police Comr v Justin* (1991) 55 SASR 547; or a customs officer: *Re Comptroller-General of Customs* (1992) 107 ALR 480. In Canada, to compulsory statements to insurers after a motor accident: *R v Spyker* (1990) 63 CCC (3d) 125.

[35] *R v Secretary of State for Trade and Industry, ex p McCormick* [1998] BCC 379; *Re Westminster Property Management Ltd* [2001] 1 All ER 633.

[36] *Pyneboard Pty Ltd v Trade Practices Commission* (n21), 341.

[37] *Thomson Newspapers Ltd v Director of Investigation and Research* [1990] 1 SCR 425. The position in Canada has been highly influenced by the impact and drafting of the Canadian Charter of Rights and Freedoms. Purely disciplinary proceedings have still been held to fall outside the range of those in which the privilege operates: *R v Wigglesworth* [1987] 2 SCR 541; *Knutson v Saskatchewan Registered Nurses' Assoc* (1990) 75 DLR (4th) 723.

[38] (2001) 33 EHRR 12; applied in *Shannon v United Kingdom* (2006) 42 EHRR 660.

the trial of the offence of withholding the information, and the accused had been acquitted of the substantive offence of which they were suspected, to which the information withheld had related.[39] The court relied upon its earlier decision in *Funke v France*,[40] in which similar legislation in France, penalizing the withholding of documents relating to bank accounts suspected of being used to evade tax, had been held to violate Art 6. If taken literally, and applied widely, the combination of these two decisions would cripple the administrative, and especially fiscal, powers of a modern state, which requires a flow of information from the subject to the state, and would very significantly impede criminal investigation. It seems therefore that there must be some limitation upon the width of application of these decisions. Some qualification, albeit obiter, could be found in the further decision of the European Court of Human Rights in *Saunders v United Kingdom*.[41] There, the accused was charged with offences of fraud in the course of a company takeover, part of the evidence for which was a transcript of exculpatory[42] answers given under statutory compulsion to inspectors commissioned[43] to investigate the circumstances of the takeover. Although the ultimate decision was that this use did violate Art 6, it was pointed out that no complaint was made of the fairness of the investigation by the inspectors, which the court appeared to regard as immune on the basis of being an independent administrative inquiry, enlisting the very significant justification that any other view would 'in practice unduly hamper the effective regulation in the public interest of complex financial and commercial activities'.[44]

This accorded with the elaborate rules for English criminal proceedings defining the extent of such compulsory powers so far as real evidence is concerned. They permit the gathering of real evidence, such as the sound of a person's voice,[45] or samples from a person's body,[46] subject only to obedience to the normal rules relating to trespass and assault,[47] untrammelled by the privilege against self-incrimination.[48] Indeed, in such

---

[39] Membership of a terrorist organization.   [40] (1993) 16 EHRR 297.

[41] (1996) 23 EHRR 313.

[42] Or so intended, although they became inculpatory in the light of other evidence by the time of the criminal proceedings.   [43] Pursuant to s 432(2) of the Companies Act 1985.

[44] Even in *JB v Switzerland* (2001) 3 ITLR 663, in which the court sought to distinguish the exclusion of documents from that of physical samples, the court was careful, [63], to avoid expressing a view on whether documents could be required for the purposes of securing a correct tax assessment, and in *Allen v United Kingdom* (2002) 35 EHRR CD 289, it was said that 'the privilege against self-incrimination cannot be interpreted as giving a general immunity to actions motivated by the desire to evade investigation by the revenue authorities'. This was applied to investigation by the Office of Fair Trading under the Competition Act 1998 in *Office of Fair Trading v Unnamed Defendants* [2003] EWHC 1042 (Comm), [2003] 2 All ER (Comm) 183.

[45] *R v Deenik* [1992] Crim LR 578.

[46] *R v Apicella* (1985) 82 Cr App Rep 295, and see Easton [1991] *Crim LR* 18, with particular reference to DNA testing. The rule is similar in the United States: *Schmerber v California* 384 US 757 (1966) confines the privilege, even in the case of an accused, to evidence of a testimonial or communicative nature, but this is, of course, subject to the rights accorded to an accused by the constitutional provision against unreasonable searches. It has, however, been suggested that, in some circumstances, the privilege could be invoked in relation to an order to produce a child addressed to its mother: *Baltimore Department of Social Service v Bouknight* 493 US 549 (1989).

[47] Or any more specific rules and regulations, such as the Code of Practice, or the Family Law Reform Act 1969 in relation to blood samples: see above, 54.

[48] The coherence in this respect between European Human Rights Law and English law was noted and approved by the Court of Appeal in *A-G's Reference (No 7 of 2000)* [2001] EWCA Crim 888, [2001] 2 Cr App Rep 286.

cases, it seems that adverse comment could be made upon, and adverse inferences drawn from, the accused's exercise of his rights of refusal.[49] Section 36 of the Criminal Justice and Public Order Act 1994 makes more general provision to this effect:

(1) Where—

    (a) a person is arrested by a constable, and there is—

        (i) on his person; or

        (ii) in or on his clothing or footwear; or

        (iii) otherwise in his possession; or

        (iv) in any place in which he is at the time of his arrest, any object, substance or mark, or there is any mark on any such object; and

    (b) that or another constable investigating the case reasonably believes that presence of the object, substance or mark may be attributable to the person arrested in the commission of an offence specified by the constable; and

    (c) the constable informs the subject that he so believes, and requests him to account for the presence of the object, substance or mark; and

    (d) the person fails or refuses to do so,

then [the court may draw such inferences from the failure or refusal as appear proper].

The European Court of Human Rights has, however, rejected all attempts to harden the dicta in *Saunders* into unequivocal restrictions on the ambit of the privilege. It has rejected the limitation in *R v Hertfordshire County Council, ex p Green Industries Ltd*[50] to *use* of compulsorily obtained information in subsequent criminal proceedings.[51] It has also rejected any rigid distinction between obtaining material by coercion of the will or by other means, and between pre-existing or independent materials and evidence generated by the effect of the coercion.[52] It seems that the Court prefers a more open-ended approach:[53]

Whether a particular applicant has been subject to compulsion to incriminate himself and whether the use made of the incriminating material has rendered criminal proceedings unfair will depend upon an assessment of each case as a whole.

In *Jalloh v Germany*, where emetics had been used on the subject against his will to recover ingested drugs, the criterion was whether the 'very essence' of the privilege had been violated, and a three-step analysis proposed:[54]

[T]he Court will have regard, in turn, to the following factors: the nature and degree of compulsion used to obtain the evidence; the weight of the public interest in the investigation of and

---

[49] At common law, see *R v Smith* [1985] Crim LR 590; or by specific statutory provision, see Family Law Reform Act 1969, s 23 (blood tests).

[50] [2000] 2 AC 412, [2000] 1 All ER 773. This decision antedated the application of the Human Rights Act 1998, but was nevertheless required to construe the European Convention as the relevant legislation gave effect to a European Directive.   [51] Especially in *Shannon* (n38) where *Green* was cited.

[52] *O'Halloran and Francis v United Kingdom* (2007) 46 EHRR 397, [54] (thus rejecting the broad application of obiter dicta to that effect in *Saunders v United Kingdom* (n5)). It is interesting that in *Brown v Stott* [2003] 1 AC 681, [2001] 2 All ER 97, Lord Bingham seemed to turn the argument on its head by arguing that since the privilege did not according to dicta in *Saunders v UK* apply to real evidence, neither should it apply to statements functionally equivalent to real evidence, such as an admission of a high blood alcohol level.

[53] *Saunders* (n5), [70].   [54] (2007) 44 EHRR 667, [117].

punishment of the offence at issue; the existence of any relevant safeguards in the procedure; and the use to which any material so obtained is put.

The issue is further clouded by the European Court's refusal to separate issues of the right to silence, and the presumption of innocence from those relating to the privilege against self-incrimination as traditionally understood in this jurisdiction.[55] Thus in England the facts of *Jalloh* would more appropriately be considered in the context of improperly obtained evidence, and the possible use of discretionary exclusion.[56]

The result is a mass of conflicting case-law driven by the factual basis of each case, stressing, and sometimes rejecting, different factors. It is possible to do little more here than to indicate the range of those factors, many of them interrelated, grouped under their relationship to the occasion of application, the sort of material involved, the form of pressure, and a miscellany of possible further considerations.

Occasion

Although some cases have apparently endorsed a distinction between preliminary administrative and criminal procedures,[57] especially in relation to taxation[58] or regulation,[59] this is not always decisive.[60] Sometimes the privilege is denied in relation to specific offences of failing to supply information as opposed to being claimed in subsequent criminal proceedings,[61] but it is more often allowed and the fact that no further proceedings are already under way,[62] or possible,[63] or of which the accused has been acquitted,[64] is immaterial. Particular difficulty may be occasioned in distinguishing demands for administrative information, which are likely, if false, to precipitate extraneous fiscal, disciplinary, or criminal proceedings, and those which are more clearly the initial stages of a criminal process.[65] In this connection it might well seem that requiring the owner of a vehicle to identify the driver at a time when an offence was committed, especially when failure to do so would itself constitute a criminal offence, would amount to the early stages of such a prosecutorial process, but both in the European Court[66] and in the Privy Council[67] the privilege has there been held not to apply.[68]

Materials

Because of the imprecision of focus of the privilege in the jurisprudence of the European Court a wide variety of materials is capable of being encompassed: general statements of

---

[55] *Weh v Austria* (2005) 40 EHRR 37, [39] refers to all three. For discussion and dissent about similar overlapping in Canada, see *R v Singh* 2007 SCC 48, [2007] 3 SCR 405.

[56] As recognized in *R v S and A* [2008] EWCA Crim 2177, [22]; see further 507.

[57] *Fayed v UK* 18 EHRR 393, [62]; *Saunders* (n5), [67]; and domestically more robustly *Green* (n50).

[58] *Abas v Netherlands* [1997] EHRLR 418; *Allen v UK* (2002) 35 EHRR CD 289; and domestically more robustly *R v Allen* [2001] UKHL 45, [2002] 1 AC 509.   [59] *Weh v Austria* (n55); *O'Halloran v UK* (n52).

[60] *Funke* (n40); *JB v Switzerland* (n44) (taxation).

[61] *King v UK* (2003) unreported ECHR 8 April, [2].   [62] *Shannon* (n38).   [63] *Funke* (n40).

[64] *Heaney* (n5).   [65] See *IJL v UK* (2001) 33 EHRR 225, [100].

[66] *Weh* (n55); *O'Halloran* (n52) (both in relation to use of the compelled answer and to conviction for the offence of failure to answer). For contrasting North American reactions to this problem, cp *Byers v United States* (1971) 402 US 424 (no breach); *R v White* [1999] 2 SCR 417 (breach).

[67] *Brown v Stott* [2001] 2 LRC 612, [2003] 1 AC 681.

[68] Although perhaps more for the extrinsic factors mentioned 423.

fact;[69] answers to specific enquiries;[70] testimony to some formal tribunal;[71] production of documents;[72] production of things; submission to searches or examinations, or alcohol testing;[73] and even searches against the will of the subject, such as enforced disgorgement. Any connection with the privilege against self-incrimination as understood here seemed to be lost when in *Saunders v UK*[74] the privilege was extended to false exculpatory statements, if circumstantially supportive of the prosecution case, although interestingly it was said in *Allen v UK*[75] that the privilege did not protect lies.

Pressure

This variety of forms of material inevitably determines the choice of form of pressure used to induce it. Sometimes the pressure is itself authorized, or even required, for example in the compulsory process used to secure information relating to the basis for assessment of taxes,[76] or for investigating allegations of abuse of status.[77] Sometimes the pressure is improper or illegal.[78] Sometimes the degree of pressure may be relevant, thus in *Brown v Stott* the House of Lords stressed[79] that there was a single question,[80] not necessarily incriminating,[81] sanctioned by no more than a moderate penalty for refusal to answer.[82] In some cases[83] the Court's assessment of the pressure has been influenced by the availability of other means to secure the information not amounting to self-incrimination.

Other factors

A multitude of further factors may influence the ascription of the privilege, reflecting the infinite variety of factual settings within which the privilege may operate. The following examples have been culled from the rampant case-law, but represent only a small proportion of those considered to date. First, in motoring identification cases[84] some influence has been placed on the accused's having voluntarily undertaken an activity known to be regulated by the measures alleged to amount to breach of the privilege. Secondly, although it has been denied that the seriousness of the crime to which the material relates is significant, and the privilege has been upheld in relation to charges of the most serious[85] nature, *Jalloh* seems to belie this in its second criterion quoted above, which some[86] of the dissenters in *O'Halloran* thought to have influenced the result. Thirdly, the strain on administrative resources crippled by the unavailability of compulsory disclosure seems likely to have influenced the results in some of the taxation and regulatory cases. Fourthly, some cases have focused on the transparency and accountability of the application of the particular form of compulsion in issue.[87] Finally, and closely related to the last of these, stress has

---

[69] As in *Allen* (n58) (sources of income for tax assessment) (non-infringing).
[70] As in *Heaney* (n5) (infringing); *O'Halloran* (n52) (non-infringing).
[71] As in *Shannon* (n38) (infringing); *IJL* (n65) (non-infringing).
[72] As in *Funke* (n40) (infringing).   [73] As in *Brown v Stott* (n67) (unopposed, non-infringing).
[74] (n5), [71].   [75] (n58).   [76] As in *Funke* (n40).   [77] As in *Saunders* (n5).
[78] As in *Jalloh* (n54).   [79] (n67).
[80] *Heaney* (n5) upheld the privilege despite there being only one question.
[81] *Funke* (n40) upheld the privilege despite the questions not being incriminating.
[82] *JB v Switzerland* (n44) upheld the privilege despite there being only a moderate penalty.
[83] *Funke* (n40), [57]; *Jalloh* (n54), [77].   [84] *Brown v Stott* (n67); *O'Halloran* (n52), [57].
[85] *Heaney* (n5), [57].   [86] Judges Pavlovschi and Myjer.
[87] As in *Teixeira de Castro v Portugal* (1999) 28 EHRR 101, [17].

sometimes been placed on the compensating protective measures. A difficulty here has been the sometimes very strict view taken by the European Court of the adequacy of such measures. In English law such compensation was not generally available at common law, but has been a feature of modern statutory provisions, especially since the decision in *Saunders*. Now that the whole position has been re-opened by the more recent decisions in the European Court the efficacy of such provisions to prevent breach has become more doubtful. This will be discussed later in more detail, but it is worth mentioning here that in *Shannon* the European Court held[88] it not enough to ban only the use of information so obtained in subsequent proceedings, if it could still be used in those proceedings in any way to discredit the maker.

The current situation in England is that in the light of all of these conflicting factors it is difficult to discern clear rules,[89] and preferable for trial courts to deal with the matter as one of discretion.[90] The relevant matters were said to include:[91] (i) the true benefit of the material sought, taking into account the availability of other means of access, staged disclosure and appropriate redaction; (ii) the need for convincing justification; (iii) the gravity of the sanction; (iv) the risk of prosecution; and (v) the power to exclude under s 78 of the Police and Criminal Evidence Act 1984.

The privilege applies to proceedings in the Coroner's Court.[92] It also applies at all curial stages of the criminal process.[93] It is further available in relation to ancillary orders sometimes made to secure enforcement of other orders in criminal proceedings, such as a disclosure order to assist with a restraint order made pursuant to s 77 of the Criminal Justice Act 1988.[94]

Range of incrimination

The focus now shifts to the range of issues where questioning might be regarded as triggering the privilege. These include: first, the extent to which the question must go towards establishing the relevant criminality; second, the extent to which a question criminating another can be objected to, especially, a spouse or under some form of vicarious responsibility; and third, any special rules applicable to fiduciaries.

---

[88] (n38), [40].   [89] Pending clarification from the Supreme Court.

[90] *R (Malik) v Manchester Crown Court* [2008] EWHC 1362 (Admin), [78], accepting the approach in *R v Central Criminal Court, ex p Bright* [2001] 2 All ER 244, [2001] 1 WLR 662.

[91] *Malik* (n90), [79]–[84].

[92] Coroners' Rules 1984, SI 1984/552, r 22(1); *R v Coroner, ex p Alexander* [1982] VR 731. See also *R v Zurlo* (1990) 57 CCC (3d) 407, considering the impact of the Canadian Charter of Rights and Freedoms on this situation.

[93] When taking compulsory depositions under s 97A of the Magistrates Courts Act 1980, *R (CPS) v Bolton Magistrates' Court* [2003] EWHC 2697 (Admin), [2005] 2 All ER 848, [24], on the voir dire, and at the post-verdict sentencing stage; on the last, see, in the United States, *Powell v Texas* 492 US 680 (1989). But not in South Africa to compulsory questioning to assist a foreign government investigating a crime on its territory: *Thatcher v Minister of Justice and Constitutional Development* 2005 (4) SA 543.

[94] *Re O (Restraint Order)* [1991] 2 QB 520, [1991] 1 All ER 330. It should be noted that the now-customary condition restraining further use of the material in evidence, recommended in *Re O* as a means of circumventing the problem, does not prevent its use in cross-examination to credit: *R v Martin and White* [1998] 2 Cr App Rep 385.

Indirect incrimination

The rule extends beyond answers[95] directly incriminating the witness to those that might be used as a step towards obtaining evidence against him,[96] and so make a prosecution more likely. In *R v Slaney*[97] a witness giving evidence at a prosecution for criminal libel in a newspaper advertisement when asked whether he knew the provenance of the advertisement, answered in the affirmative, but Lord Tenterden CJ upheld his objection to stating the name of the writer of the letter:

You cannot only not compel a witness to answer that which will criminate him, but that which tends to criminate him: and the reason is this, that the party would go from one question to another, and though no question might be asked, the answer of which would directly criminate the witness, yet they would get enough from him whereon to found a charge against him.

Although the answer must incriminate, it may be capable of doing so by doing no more than adding to the material already available for use by the prosecution, and extending to that which might induce it to launch a prosecution[98] but not to the revelation of further detail relating to a crime to which he has already pleaded guilty.[99] It has similarly been held in Australia that to be asked to provide information already in the public domain cannot amount to self-incrimination, the privilege having been impliedly waived.[100]

Incrimination of another

In civil cases, s 14(1)(b) of the Civil Evidence Act 1968 extended the privilege to questions tending to criminate a spouse. The Criminal Law Revision Committee recommended a similar rule for witnesses in criminal proceedings, excepting only the accused and his spouse,[101] although no such rule has yet been enacted. Despite old dicta to the contrary, it is uncertain whether the privilege extended so far at common law.[102] Thus in *R v Pitt*[103] it was held that a spouse should be advised that, if she chose to testify for the prosecution, she would be treated like any other witness. In such circumstances, she can be treated as hostile. All of this would be quite futile if she could nevertheless claim a privilege against incriminating her spouse. It need hardly be added that there is no privilege against incriminating

---

[95] It does not extend to an order for the subsequent disclosure of an incriminating statement obtained voluntarily, and filed in the court without objection: *Re L* (1995) The Times, 25 April.

[96] In *Sociedad Nacional de Combusiveis de Angola UEE v Lundqvist* [1991] 2 QB 310, [1990] 3 All ER 283; 325, 292, Staughton LJ was inclined to limit it to matter capable of constituting evidence in the case, even though not alone conclusive, but in *R v S and A* [2008] EWCA Crim 2177, [24] the key to encrypted incriminating material on a computer was regarded as capable of protection by the privilege. In the United States, it is immaterial that the witness claims complete innocence if the answer is capable of raising suspicion: *Ohio v Reiner* (2001) 532 US 17.

[97] (1832) 5 C & P 213. See also *Short v Mercier* (1851) 3 Mac & G 205, 217, Lord Truro.

[98] *Den Norske Bank ASA v Antonatos* (n15), 289A, 89a.

[99] *R v Khan* [2007] EWCA Crim 2331, [30]; and in Scotland, *Greenan v HM Adv* (n12), [11].

[100] See *Registrar of the Supreme Court of South Australia v Zappia* [2003] SASC 276.

[101] Cmnd 4991, [169].

[102] Dicta of Bayley J in *R v All Saints, Worcester Inhabitants* (1817) 6 M & S 194, 201; cf Lord Diplock in *Rio Tinto Zinc Corp v Westinghouse Electric Corp* (n20), 637, 465: 'At common law...the privilege against self-incrimination was restricted to the person claiming it and not anyone else.' For a contrary view, see Lusty (2004) 27 *UNSWLR* 1; endorsed in *Callanan v B* [2004] QCA 478, 151 ACR 287, although not extended to de facto spouses. See also *S v Boulton* [2006] FCAFC 99.   [103] [1983] QB 25, [1982] 3 All ER 63.

strangers.[104] In England, there seems to be no doubt that the privilege can be claimed by any entity having legal personality,[105] but this is not the case in North America,[106] nor in Australia.[107]

In *Rio Tinto Zinc Corp v Westinghouse Electric Corp*, the question of the extent to which an individual director could claim the privilege in relation to material that might incriminate his company was raised. It was not necessary for their Lordships to express a final view on this question, which they felt required further consideration, since if some such privilege were not recognized, that of the company might be rendered nugatory.[108]

Fiduciaries

In some old cases, it was suggested that, as a party could validly contract not to exercise the privilege against another, and by simply choosing to act as a fiduciary impliedly put himself in the same position.[109] Attempts to invoke this doctrine in modern cases have been uniformly unsuccessful,[110] and affirmation of the basic premise has been conspicuously withheld.

Range of effects

There are a number of possible unpleasant effects to which an answer might expose a witness. The central case is conviction of a crime under the law of the forum.[111] On the other hand, a witness cannot claim to be privileged from answering questions on the ground that the answers will expose him to civil liability,[112] either at the suit of the Crown, or of

---

[104] *R v Minihane* (1921) 16 Cr App Rep 38.

[105] *Triplex Safety Glass Co Ltd v Lancegaye Safety Glass (1934) Ltd* [1939] 2 KB 395, [1939] 2 All ER 613; *Rio Tinto Zinc Corp v Westinghouse Electric Corp* (n20).

[106] *United States v White* 322 US 694 (1944); *Braswell v United States* 108 S Ct 2284 (1988); *R v NM Paterson & Sons Ltd* [1980] 2 SCR 679; *R v Amway Corp* [1989] 1 SCR 21.

[107] *Environment Protection Authority v Caltex Refining Co Pty Ltd* (1993) 178 CLR 477; Evidence Act 1995, s 187(2), although the witness can claim protection personally, and it is immaterial that his personal protection overlaps that of the corporation. Neither can the privilege against exposure to a penalty (or a forfeiture, see *Re Warden: ex p Roberts* (1997) 18 WAR 379) be so claimed in respect of documents, either in response to a notice to produce: *Trade Practices Commission v Abbco Iceworks Pty Ltd* (1994) 123 ALR 503; or on discovery: *Trade Practices Commission v CC (New South Wales) Pty (No 4)* (1995) 131 ALR 581.

[108] In *Kensington International Ltd v Congo* [2007] EWHC 1632, [47] Gross J was opposed to any extension of the privilege in this way, at least when the claimant could not be considered the alter ego of the corporation, while the Court of Appeal remained neutral, [2007] EWCA Civ 1128, [73]. It is clear that an individual not authorized to speak on behalf of the corporation cannot invoke the privilege on behalf of the corporation: *Walkers Snack Foods Ltd v Coventry County Council* [1998] 3 All ER 163. Cf *Upjohn & Co v United States* 449 US 383 (1981) for the position in the United States, and *R v Nova Scotia Pharmaceutical Society* (1990) 73 DLR (4th) 184 for that in Canada.

[109] *Green v Weaver* (1827) 1 Sim 404; *Chadwick v Chadwick* (1852) 22 LJ Ch 329; *Robinson v Kitchin* (1856) 21 Beav 365. See generally Grevling in Rose (ed) *Consensus ad Idem* (1996), 38.

[110] See *Rank Film Distributors Ltd v Video Information Centre* [1982] AC 380, [1980] 2 All ER 273, in which the point was defeated by a majority in the Court of Appeal, and not even argued in the House of Lords; *Tate Access Floors v Boswell* [1991] Ch 512, [1990] 3 All ER 303; *Mirror Group Newspapers plc v Maxwell* [1993] Ch 1, [1992] 2 All ER 856. See also, in Australia, *Reid v Howard* (1995) 184 CLR 1.

[111] For a straightforward example unalloyed by statutory intervention, see *United Norwest Co-operatives Ltd v Johnstone* (1994) The Times, 24 February. Perjury is probably an exception: see *per* Arbour J in *R v Noël* [2002] SCC 67, [2002] 3 SCR 433, [26].

[112] Even for fraud: *Shierson v Rastoghi* [2002] EWCA Civ 1624, [2003] 1 WLR 586; although it may sometimes be taken into account in relation to discretionary control of its proceedings by the court.

any other person.[113] Nor will exposure to other unpleasant consequences be enough,[114] such as rendering the witness liable to bankruptcy,[115] or to professional disciplinary proceedings,[116] but there are a number of other possibilities that need to be mentioned.

Liability to conviction in a different jurisdiction

The few authorities dealing with this question at common law tended to conflict, both here,[117] and elsewhere.[118] In the light of such uncertainty, the Privy Council in *Brannigan v Davison*[119] relied upon principle[120] in stressing that no sovereign[121] state could contemplate its domestic law being frustrated by the law of another expressed through the operation of the privilege. This applied whether or not the privilege related to evidence of a crime already committed, or where the foreign legislation made the tendering of such evidence itself a crime.[122] By statute in the United Kingdom, s 14(1)(a) of the Civil Evidence Act 1968, expressly confines the privilege to 'criminal offences under the law of any part of the United Kingdom and penalties provided for by such law'.[123] Even then the court retains discretion, at least in respect of disclosure,[124] and its exercise may be influenced by the prospect of incrimination under foreign law.[125] The precise delimitation of the discretionary powers of the court at common law was left unresolved[126] in *Brannigan v Davison*.

---

[113] Witnesses Act 1806. Liability for civil contempt will suffice: *R v K* [2009] EWCA Crim 1640, [2010] 1 Cr App R 44, [42].

[114] In the United States, not loss of a prisoner's privileges: *McKune v Lile* (2002) 536 US 24; nor, in New Zealand, chance of early release: *Burke v Superintendent of Wellington Prison* [2003] 3 NZLR 206.

[115] *Re XY, ex p Haes* [1902] 1 KB 98.

[116] See *Re Fang and College of Physicians and Surgeons of Alberta* (1985) 25 DLR (4th) 632; *Re Johnstone and Law Society of British Columbia* (1987) 40 DLR (4th) 550; *Re Prousky and the Law Society of Upper Canada* (1987) 41 DLR (4th) 565, although in Canada, the position has been much affected by the Canadian Charter of Rights and Freedoms, which these decisions construe. In the United States, the privilege has been held not to extend to protect a foreign bank account from compulsory disclosure: *Doe v United States* 487 US 201 (1988); nor to prevent the accused from being shown to be 'a sexually dangerous person': *Allen v Illinois* 478 US 364 (1986).

[117] Cf *King of the Two Sicilies v Willcox* (1851) 1 Sim NS 301, and *Re Atherton* [1912] 2 KB 251, 255, with *United States of America v McRae* (1867) 3 Ch App 79.

[118] Cf, in Australia, *Adstream Building Industries Pty Ltd v The Queensland Lime and Cement Co Ltd (No 4)* [1985] 1 Qd R 127 with *FF Seeley Nominees v El Ar Initiations (UK) Ltd* (1990) 96 ALR 468, 472, 473; and, in the United States, *United States v (Under Seal)* (1986) 794 F 2d 920 (1986) (4th Cir) with *Mishima v United States* (1981) 507 F Supp 131, now resolved by the Supreme Court against the privilege: see *United States v Balsys* 524 US 666 (1998). [119] (n4); for commentary see Pattenden (1997) 2 Int J Ev & Pr 44.

[120] It approved the statement of it in *Murphy v Waterfront Commission of New York Harbour* 378 US 52 (1964), 55.

[121] It recognized that modification might be necessary to accommodate internal operation within federal jurisdictions.

[122] A similar result was achieved in this respect in Canada, in *Spencer v R* [1985] 2 SCR 278, and in the United States, in *United States v Field* 532 F 2d 404 (1976).

[123] There was a corresponding provision in cl 15(1)(a) of the draft bill attached to the 11th Report of the Criminal Law Revision Committee, but not yet been enacted.

[124] And in relation to revelation pursuant to a freezing injunction: *A-G for Gibraltar v May* [1999] 1 WLR 998.

[125] *Arab Monetary Fund v Hashim* [1989] 3 All ER 466, [1989] 1 WLR 565. In *Levi Strauss & Co v Barclays Trading Corp Inc* [1993] FSR 179, it was not regarded as a sufficient answer that to disclose would effectively deprive the party of his privilege against self-incrimination elsewhere. [126] 251D.

Liability to the imposition of a penalty[127]

The rule that a witness cannot be obliged to answer a question if the answer would expose him to the risk of a penalty seems to have originated in the doctrine that equity would not assist a common informer by making an order for discovery in his favour. This rule survived the Judicature Acts.[128] Proceedings for penalties, as opposed to compensation,[129] became virtually obsolete, but the Law Reform Committee considered that the privilege should continue so long as penalties are recoverable in some civil proceedings.[130] The category of penalties in respect of which the privilege may be claimed was later augmented by accession to the European Union, since penalties imposed for breach of the terms of the EEC Treaty, and of Council Regulations, have been held to qualify.[131] It has further been held that penalties for civil contempt come within the category of those in respect of which the privilege can be claimed, and that there is nothing in the wording of s 14 of the Civil Evidence Act 1968 to the contrary.[132] This is, however, subject to the qualification that, where the order could have been made in one set of contempt proceedings, a second set cannot be frustrated by the privilege on the basis that they might expose the party to a penalty in the first set,[133] at least where it is no more than a technicality that there are formally two sets of proceedings.[134] The European Court of Human Rights adopts its own autonomous view of what amount to criminal proceedings, and it was held in *King v Walden*[135] that the system of imposing penalties for incorrect tax returns would be included.

PROCEDURE

The privilege strictly applies only to answering; not to prevent the relevant question being asked.[136] The judge will often warn a witness that he is not obliged to answer criminating questions, but there is no rule of law to this effect,[137] and ignorance of his rights does not

---

[127] For learned exegesis of the concept of a penalty in this context, citing extensive English common law authority, see *Rich v Australian Securities and Investments Commission* [2003] NSWCA 342, 203 ALR 671; but see also reversal by the High Court on the facts, [2004] HCA 42.

[128] *Hunnings v Williamson* (1883) 10 QBD 459; *Martin v Treacher* (1886) 16 QBD 507.

[129] *Adams v Batley* (1887) 18 QBD 625.   [130] Sixteenth Report, [13].

[131] *Rio Tinto Zinc Corp v Westinghouse Electric Corp* (n20). It is also important where regulations are enforced by the imposition of penalties, often by a commission or tribunal: see *Pyneboard Pty Ltd v Trade Practices Commission* (n21); although, in Australia, this has been mitigated by extension of the exclusion of corporate persons from the benefit of this aspect of the privilege in exactly the same way as with regard to exposure to ordinary criminal prosecution: *Trade Practices Commission v Abbco Ice Works Pty Ltd* (n107).

[132] *Bhimji v Chatwani (No 3)* [1992] 4 All ER 912, [1992] 1 WLR 1158, preferring the dicta of Lord Denning MR in *Comet Products UK Ltd v Hawkex Plastics Ltd* [1971] 2 QB 67, [1971] 1 All ER 1141; 74, 1144 to the decision of Walton J in *Garvin v Domus Publishing Ltd* [1989] Ch 335, [1989] 2 All ER 344.

[133] *Crest Homes plc v Marks* [1987] AC 829, [1987] 2 All ER 1074, 859, 1082.

[134] So not in *Cobra Golf Ltd v Rata* [1998] Ch 109, [1997] 2 All ER 150, in which the two sets of proceedings were separate, and the search order in the second used to secure evidence for committal in the first.

[135] [2001] STC 822, [71]. Although it was also held that the Hansard letter procedure was proportionate, and not in breach of Art 6. This may now need reconsideration in the light of the decision in *R v Gill and Gill* [2003] EWCA Crim 2256, [2003] 4 All ER 681. For the position in Canada, see *R v Jarvis* 2002 SCC 73, [2002] 3 SCR 757.

[136] *Allhusen v Labouchere* (1878) 3 QBD 654, 660. Contrast the introductory words of the now-repealed Criminal Evidence Act 1898, s 1(3).

[137] Although it has been said that a judge should warn a witness of the absence of the privilege: *R v Pitt* [1983] QB 25, [1982] 3 All ER 63; and in Canada, once the accused has indicated his possible commission of a further crime he must be readvised of his right to counsel: *R v Sawatsky* (1997) 150 DLR (4th) 750.

prevent the court from utilizing a witness's evidence in the instant case, or in subsequent criminal proceedings brought against him.[138]

The practice when someone claims the privilege was established in *R v Boyes*.[139] The witness's mere statement that his answer might have this effect is insufficient, although on oath, even if bona fide, and claimed on legal advice.[140] The court must determine from all the circumstances and the nature of the evidence that the witness is called to give, that there is reasonable ground to apprehend danger to him from his answer.[141] There must be no nice balancing of odds;[142] the judge must come to the conclusion that such danger is real, and appreciable with reference to the ordinary operation of law in the ordinary course of things, and not a danger of an imaginary and insubstantial character, having reference to some extraordinary contingency so improbable as not to deter a reasonable man.[143]

If a witness has already made himself liable to a criminal prosecution by an admission, his refusal to answer may be held not to be bona fide,[144] or a form of waiver.[145] If the offence was of a trifling nature, or committed many years ago, a court might be inclined to regard the danger as too insubstantial to allow the plea to succeed. It will also be responsive to diminution of particular dangers in the light of changes of practice, and alert to the risk of defendants seeking to avoid civil liability by exaggerating dangers of prosecution,[146] especially where the offence to which the privilege is claimed to apply is overshadowed by others to which it does not.[147] Perhaps surprisingly, the House of Lords has held an informal assurance by the prosecuting authorities of the absence of any intention to rely upon materials discovered in any subsequent criminal proceedings enough to dispel danger, and to avert the operation of the privilege.[148]

The burden of showing the danger real is borne by the claiming witness. If discharged, the court will not be deterred from upholding the privilege by commercial inconvenience. Thus in *Rank Film Distributors Ltd v Video Information Centre*, in which the defendant claimed the privilege to defeat the application of a search order summarily requiring him

---

[138] *R v Coote* (1873) LR 4 PC 599. Cf *S v Lwane* 1966 (2) SA 433. For the stage in the proceedings at which the objection should be taken, see *Spokes v Grosvenor Hotel Co* [1897] 2 QB 124; *A J Bekhor v Bilton* [1981] QB 923, [1981] 2 All ER 565. It seems that a warning is not mandatory in relation to incrimination under foreign law: *R v Bateman and Cooper* [1989] Crim LR 590.

[139] (1861) 1 B & S 311; *Kensington International Ltd v Republic of Congo* (n108), [33].

[140] *R (CPS) v Bolton Magistrates' Court* (n93), [25].

[141] *Triplex Safety Glass Co Ltd v Lancegaye Safety Glass (1934) Ltd* (n105), approved in *Rio Tinto Zinc Corp v Westinghouse Electric Corp* (n20). The claimant bears the evidential burden of showing this: *Sociedad Nacional de Combustiveis de Angola UEE v Lundqvist* (n96); and is unlikely to discharge it when the claim is inconsistent with his own affidavit which remains unretracted: *Downie v Coe* (1997) The Times, 28 November.

[142] *Re Westinghouse Electric Corp Uranium Contract Litigation NDL Dock 235* [1977] 3 All ER 703, 726.

[143] As in *Boyes* (n139) (possibility of impeachment after pardon).

[144] *Brebner v Perry* [1961] SASR 177, in which various English authorities are mentioned.

[145] *Registrar Court of Appeal v Craven* (1994) 120 FLR 427; although testifying voluntarily has been held in Australia not to amount to waiver, so the privilege can be claimed when a witness is testifying in chief: *Lewis v Nortex Pty Ltd* [2002] NSWSC 1192, 217 ALR 719.

[146] *Rank Film Distributors Ltd v Video Information Centre* (n110); 441, 80.

[147] *Khan v Khan* [1982] 2 All ER 60, [1982] 1 WLR 513; *Renworth Ltd v Stephansen* [1996] 3 All ER 244.

[148] *AT & T Istel Ltd v Tully* (n22): see (1993) 109 LQR 48. For a similar result in Australia, see *Saffron v Federal Comr of Taxation* (1992) 109 ALR 695, relying in part upon some dicta of Lord Diplock in *R v McDonald* [1983] NZLR 252, 255. An undertaking by a private party has even been held sufficient in Ireland: *M v D* [1998] 3 IR 175.

to furnish certain information about his infringement of copyright in video films, the danger of a criminal charge of conspiracy to defraud was very real. The House of Lords upheld the claim for privilege, even though it accepted that the result of so doing would be the practical destruction of the usefulness of search orders.[149]

Anything that a person was wrongly compelled to say after he had claimed his privilege was treated as having been said involuntarily, with the result that it was inadmissible in subsequent proceedings brought against him,[150] but the provisions and, to some extent, the construction of statutes have prevented this result from being reached in a number of cases. Where incriminating material has been inadvertently disclosed to the other party, the privilege cannot be invoked to prevent its subsequent use in evidence in the criminal proceedings.[151] Failure to claim the privilege may sometimes be construed as waiver, and bar a subsequent claim.[152]

STATUTORY PROVISION[153]

Although some statutes endorse this privilege quite explicitly,[154] it is more common to find statutory abridgement, usually designed to facilitate effective extracurial investigation.[155] Some such statutes have a draconian effect. Their effect is to abolish the privilege for all purposes wherever they apply. In such cases, the obligation to supply the relevant information is unqualified, and in *R v Scott*, the court declined to imply a common law proviso that the answers could not be used in subsequent criminal proceedings against the provider.[156] The explanation was that:[157]

When the legislature compels parties to give evidence accusing themselves, and means to protect them from the consequences of giving such evidence, the course of legislation has been to do so by express enactment.

---

[149] See Lord Fraser, 445, 83. It was thought necessary to enact s 72 of the Supreme Court Act 1981 to restore the position, although, in New Zealand, a similar result was achieved at common law: see *Thorn EMI Ltd v Kitching and Busby* [1984] FSR 342. For a similarly stringent approach in the context of freezing injunctions, see *Sociedad Nacional de Combustiveis de Angola UEE v Lundqvist* (n96).

[150] *R v Garbett* (1847) 1 Den 236; it is not obvious that this result can be reconciled with s 76(2) of the Police and Criminal Evidence Act 1984. *Obiter dicta* to the same effect in *R v Coote* (1873) LR 4 PC 599 have, however, been used in New Zealand to assist the court to resist a claim to the privilege on an application for a search order because it made the chance of criminal proceedings being brought more remote: *Thorn EMI Video Ltd v Kitching and Busby* [1984] FSR 342.

[151] *Bell Cablemedia plc v Simmons* (n9). There is here no prima facie confidentiality as there is in relation to legal professional privilege.

[152] *Compagnie Noga D'Importation et Exportation SA v ANZ Banking Group Ltd* (n15), [32].

[153] An attempt to replace the full protection of the privilege with partial protection otherwise than by statutory provision was rejected in *Den Norske Bank v Antonatos* (n15); 285, 85, and 295, 94.

[154] See e.g. the Consumer Protection Act 1987, s 47(2); Social Security Fraud Act 2001, s 1(5) (both of which extend to the incrimination of a spouse); Nationality, Immigration and Asylum Act 2002, s 139(1), Pensions Act 2004, s 310.

[155] Bankruptcy legislation goes back to the earliest times; in 1820 Lord Eldon held that it prevailed over the privilege against self-incrimination: *Ex p Cossens* (1820) Buck 531, 540, and it is so construed also in Scotland, *McLennan* [2005] SCLR 563. Such legislation has been held constitutional in Ireland: *Re National Irish Bank Ltd (No 1)* [1999] 3 IR 145, and in Australia, *Barnes v Boulton* [2004] FCA 1219, [30], [37]–[41].

[156] Above, although there has been a trickle of authority to the contrary: see e.g. *R v Savundra and Walker* (1968) 52 Cr App Rep 637, 644 (but see *R v Harris* [1970] 3 All ER 746, [1970] 1 WLR 1252); *R v Central Criminal Court ex p Bright* [2001] 2 All ER 244, [118].   [157] Lord Campbell, 60.

The pattern of such legislation may be illustrated by one of the more far-ranging examples of the genre,[158] s 13 of the Fraud Act 2006, which provides that:

(1) A person is not to be excused from—

    (a) answering any question put to him in proceedings relating to property, or

    (b) complying with any order made in proceedings relating to property,

    on the ground that doing so may incriminate him or his spouse or civil partner of an offence under this Act or a related offence.

(2) But, in proceedings for an offence under this Act or a related offence, a statement or admission made by the person in—

    (a) answering such a question, or

    (b) complying with such an order,

    is not admissible in evidence against him or (unless they married or became civil partners after the making of the statement or admission) his spouse or civil partner.

(3) "Proceedings relating to property" means any proceedings for—

    (a) the recovery or administration of any property,

    (b) the execution of a trust, or

    (c) an account of any property or dealings with property,

    and "property" means money or other property whether real or personal (including things in action and other intangible property).

(4) "Related offence" means—

    (a) conspiracy to defraud;

    (b) any other offence involving any form of fraudulent conduct or purpose.

Such a provision, restricting the use to which the statement may subsequently be put, is sometimes referred to as conferring 'use immunity', and as reflecting a balance of interests struck by Parliament, not to be construed restrictively.[159]

The rigour of the general rule under which there was no such provision was well illustrated by development in the law relating to intellectual property. In order to secure the elimination of 'piracy' in respect of copyright in such things as recordings and computer programs, the courts developed a special summary procedure, the search order, requiring a defendant to provide materials and to answer enquiries. Given the operation of criminal sanctions in the area, compliance with such orders could lead to self-incrimination and, as noted above, in *Rank Film Distributors Ltd v Video Information Centre*,[160] the House of Lords upheld the privilege at common law. Almost immediately, legislation was enacted as s 72(1) of the Supreme Court Act 1981 to abrogate the privilege, but providing a measure of use immunity.

This technique of abrogation can, however, sometimes lead to difficulty in establishing the range of proceedings in respect of which the material so obtained cannot be used.[161] It

---

[158] An extended form of s 31 of the Theft Act 1968, partly responding to criticism in *Sociedade Nacional de Combustiveis de Angola UEE v Lundqvist* (n96), 338, 302j.

[159] *Kensington International Ltd v Republic of Congo* (n108), [36].   [160] (n110).

[161] As in *Kensington International ltd v Congo* (n108), [37]–[67], *JSC BTA Bank v Ablyazov* [2009] EWCA Civ 1124. Some legislation provides very narrowly defined immunity: see Terrorism Act 2000, s 10. In Australia, these considerations have inhibited judicial attempts to modify the privilege, and cast doubt

should also be noted that the abrogation of the privilege may be wider than its restoration in such proceedings.[162] Nevertheless, it was regarded as better than acceptance of the old regime, and pleas were made for its general application.[163] A government Consultation Paper recommending such a measure was published in July 1992.[164] That paper suggested a switch from the then current operation of the privilege that it regarded as leading to injustice and uncertainty to a system based on what it described as 'secondary privilege'.[165] This would simply withdraw the privilege in civil proceedings, but provide that information so divulged could not be used in subsequent criminal proceedings.[166] This secondary privilege would, in principle, exclude documents on the basis that the privilege is least justifiable in relation to the production of material that existed before the commencement of the civil proceedings.[167] All would, however, remain available to be used in a prosecution for perjury,[168] and to discredit the witness if he testified inconsistently with it[169] in any subsequent criminal proceedings.[170] The mechanism would not require the claim to privilege to be made before the attempted use of the information in the subsequent criminal proceedings,[171] and would be determined by the judge at the criminal trial.

The paper recognizes that to bestow a secondary privilege in this way could lead to abuse, for example by a collusive civil claim designed to insulate information from use in an apprehended prosecution. It was partly to meet this danger that the paper suggested that the privilege should exclude pre-existing documents, and it is proposed also that the secondary privilege should not apply to statements or admissions relied upon by the claimant in the precedent civil proceedings.

Although, as its title suggests, the paper is principally concerned with the operation of the privilege in civil proceedings, it suggests that there is no reason for its proposals not to apply to witnesses, apart from the accused, in criminal proceedings.[172]

No final paper seems to have been published, and matters were somewhat overtaken by the decision of the European Court of Human Rights in *Saunders v United Kingdom* that compulsorily obtained material might infringe Art 6 of the European Convention if used in subsequent criminal proceedings. Although convictions obtained under the old

---

on stratagems to evade it: see *Reid v Howard* (n110); *Australia Securities and Investments Commission v Michalik* [2004] NSWSC 909, 211 ALR 285.

[162] The abrogation extends to materials discovered while the restoration is limited to admissions and statements.   [163] *Sociedade Nacional de Combustiveis de Angola UEE v Lundqvist* (n96).

[164] Consultation Paper *The Privilege Against Self-Incrimination in Civil Proceedings* (Lord Chancellor's Department, 1992).

[165] [30]. The less radical alternative proposal is that existing secondary privilege provisions be consolidated and applied to all proceedings involving an allegation of dishonesty.

[166] See Financial Services and Markets Act 2000, s 174 for an example of a modern statute adopting this approach.

[167] [11], although the recommendation goes further in proposing the exclusion from the secondary privilege of all documents, except those recording the civil proceedings, since to exclude those would subvert the secondary privilege altogether.   [168] Or in contempt proceedings: [19].

[169] This appears to be the situation at common law where an order has been made forbidding direct use of compulsorily disclosed material: *R v Martin: R v White* [1998] 2 Cr App Rep 385.

[170] The paper devoted little attention to the privilege relating to the imposition of a penalty.

[171] [20]–[22].

[172] [24]. The application of similar immunities to the accused has been extensively discussed in Canada: see e.g. *BC Securities Commission v Branch* [1995] 2 SCR 3. The relaxation in s 59 of the Youth Justice and Criminal Evidence Act 1999 is confined to the accused.

regime, with the assistance of such compulsorily obtained evidence, have been upheld despite this decision,[173] the decision precipitated legislative change. First, a Guidance Note from the Attorney-General sought[174] to prevent prosecution use of such material; and second, more extensive statutory amendment to confer a measure of use immunity was made to a number of statutory provisions.[175] Initial indications are that such provisions will not be interpreted in an over-restrictively technical way,[176] but as noted above,[177] serious doubts remain about compliance with the European Convention.

It should, however, be noted that this is only a small selection of the number of statutory provisions for the compulsory garnering of information, and in cases in which the use of the material is of a more administrative nature, and more remote from the likelihood of eliciting directly incriminating material, no change has been made; as noted by Lord Hoffmann in *R v Hertfordshire County Council, ex p Green Industries Ltd*,[178] the matter is ultimately one of the construction of the relevant statute,[179] taking into account both the policy of the statute, and the particular variety of the right to silence sought to be protected.[180]

The net result is that, if information has been lawfully obtained pursuant to those statutory provisions,[181] and there is no restriction on the use which can be made of the information, the person giving it cannot object to its being used in evidence against him either on the ground that such use would infringe his privilege against self-incrimination, or because the information would not have been given voluntarily.[182] In the case of the co-accused, a problem has emerged, as it seems that answers compulsorily given by one such co-accused may be used as evidence against another, and such use may be regarded as unfair.[183]

There are a number of important provisions of this character in the Children Act 1989,[184] designed to secure statements from parents and carers in order to facilitate the best treatment of the child. The protection offered there is extensive, in that it limits subsequent use in evidence to proceedings for perjury. Perhaps for that reason, it has been interpreted restrictively so as not to protect statements made in advance of proceedings in

---

[173] Notably in *R v Lyons* [2002] UKHL 441, [2003] AC 976, in which Saunders himself was one of the appellants.

[174] Although it appears not to have been widely known or applied: see e.g. *R v Faryab* [1999] BPIR 569.

[175] Youth Justice and Criminal Evidence Act 1999, s 59, and Sch 3, amending eleven specific statutes and four orders, including s 434 of the Companies Act 1985, which had been the offending provision in *Saunders* (n5).   [176] See e.g. *R v Sawtell* [2001] BPIR 381.

[177] 424.   [178] [2000] 2 AC 412, [2000] 1 All ER 773.

[179] There s 71(2) of the Environmental Protection Act 1990.

[180] As distinguished by Lord Mustill in *R v Director of the Serious Fraud Office, ex p Smith* [1993] AC 1, [1992] 3 All ER 456.

[181] In Australia, it has been held that where a statute also provides reasonable excuse as a defence, this should be brought to the attention of the subject of the questioning as a condition of overriding the privilege: *Work-cover Authority of New South Wales v Seccombe* (1998) 43 NSWLR 390.

[182] *R v Scott* (1856) Dears & B 47; *R v Coote* (1873) LR 4 PC 599; *Customs and Excise Comrs v Harz* [1967] 1 AC 760, [1967] 1 All ER 177; *George v Coombe* [1978] Crim LR 47.

[183] *R v Sweetbaum* (2003) unreported Cr Ct, which will effectively inhibit use of this procedure in the vast majority of such cases in which there is more than one potential accused: see Hood (2003) 153 *NLJ* 1140.

[184] Sections 48, 50, and 98. In *Re Y and K* [2003] EWCA Civ 669, [2003] 2 FLR 273, [35] it was said that the existence of such a clause in no way affected the compellability of the relevant witness.

court,[185] nor where there is no more than a remote chance of the maker being charged with an ancillary offence,[186] and that such statements can be disclosed,[187] and used, to discredit their maker, at least if the maker is not the alleged principal offender.

It should be noted that protection can rarely be derived in this area from the provisions of the Police and Criminal Evidence Act 1984 relating to proper procedures to be observed by those charged with the duty of investigating offences, since here the primary focus is principally concerned with administration and regulation rather than prosecution.

Where the privilege has been abrogated, it may nevertheless be just, and within the discretion of the court, to stay contemporaneous civil proceedings, so that the criminal proceedings can be completed without such encroachment upon the accused's position.[188] It will often[189] be better to defer any civil proceedings until after the termination of related criminal trials.[190]

The number and effect[191] of these abrogations of the privilege, especially as they relate not only to the investigation of serious offences, such as infringements of s 1 of the Official Secrets Act 1911,[192] but also to matters like taxation, gambling, and road traffic[193] derogate from the view that the privilege is a fundamental principle of English law.

It seems now to have been accepted[194] that the Canadian Charter of Rights and Freedoms has colonized the privilege against self-incrimination in that jurisdiction by enacting, in s 11(c), that a person accused of crime may not be compelled to testify, and in s 13, that a witness may not have incriminating evidence used against[195] him in subsequent proceedings.[196] Contrary to some early indication,[197] it seems unlikely that the ambit of the privilege will be extended by reference to s 7 of the Charter, since so expanded a concept is not regarded as a 'principle of fundamental justice' in Canada.[198] In civil proceedings, a witness can rely only upon the protection offered by the Charter against use of his testimony in any subsequent proceedings.[199]

---

[185] *Re C (a minor) (care proceedings: disclosure)* [1997] Fam 76.

[186] *Re K (minors)* [1994] 3 All ER 230, [1994] 1 WLR 912. The same view was taken by the Supreme Court of Canada in *R v Kuldip* [1990] 3 SCR 618.

[187] Family Proceedings (Amendment No 4) Rules 2005 (SI 2005/1976).

[188] *Jefferson Ltd v Bhetcha* [1979] 2 All ER 1108, [1979] 1 WLR 898. See, for a similar approach in Australia, *Kirk v Australian Federal Police Comr* (1988) 81 ALR 321; and in Canada, *Saccamanno v Swanson* (1987) 34 DLR (4th) 462.   [189] But not always: see *Mote v Secretary of State for Work and Pensions* (n27).

[190] As urged by Lord Diplock in *R v IRC, ex p Rossminster* [1980] AC 952, [1980] 1 All ER 80; 1012, 94.

[191] In the United States, since the decision of the Supreme Court in *Counselman v Hitchcock* 142 US 547 (1892), it has become more common for abrogation of the privilege to lead to complete immunity from prosecution for the relevant offence rather than merely to the inadmissibility in it of evidence so obtained.

[192] See s 6 of the Act of 1920, under which it is an offence to withhold information from a duly authorized officer of police.

[193] On the whole subject, see Heydon (1971) 87 *LQR* 214; and as it relates to corporations, McCormack (1993) *JBL* 425.   [194] *Thomson Newspapers v Director of Investigation and Research* (n37).

[195] Nor may a witness so testifying be cross-examined as to knowledge of the privilege so as to impugn credibility: *Jabarianha v R* [2001] SCC 75, [2001] 3 SCR 430.

[196] The exegesis of this concept has proved problematical: see e.g. *R v Dubois* [1985] 2 SCR 350; *R v Mannion* [1986] 2 SCR 272.

[197] *RL Crain v Couture and Restrictive Trade Practices Commission* (1983) 6 DLR (4th) 478.

[198] *Thomson Newspapers* (n37), see also *R v McKinlay Transport Ltd* (1987) 48 DLR (4th) 765. This reflects long experience of s 5 of the Canada Evidence Act, which merely provided use immunity.

[199] *Caisse Populaire Laurier d'Ottawa Ltee v Guertin (No 2)* (1983) 150 DLR (3d) 541; *Saccamanno v Swanson* (1987) 34 DLR (4th) 462.

SECTION 2. LEGAL PROFESSIONAL[200] PRIVILEGE[201]

The central case is a communication passing between lawyer and client about ongoing litigation, which need not be given in evidence or disclosed by the client and, without the client's consent, may not be given in evidence or disclosed by the legal adviser. Its scope is, however, broader than that in extending between lawyer and client to legal advice outside the context of ongoing litigation, and within that context, now often described as 'litigation privilege',[202] to communications by lawyer or client with third parties, or to documents 'created'[203] for litigation, and not communicated to anyone. The distinction was decisive in *Re L (a minor)*,[204] and regarded as settled in later authority,[205] despite occasional expressions of doubt.[206] It is convenient, first, to describe the privilege between lawyer and client for the purpose of furnishing legal advice, despite many of the characteristics of this branch being shared by the litigation branch, then to consider some special features of the latter, before going on to describe some general exceptions, and finally, examining claims made for extension to relationships other than lawyer and client.

A statutory formulation[207] of the privilege stated by the Police and Criminal Evidence Act 1984, s 10(1) provides that:

(1) Subject to subsection (2) below[208] in this Act 'items subject to legal privilege' means—

    (a) communications between a professional legal adviser and his client or any person representing his client made in connection with the giving of legal advice to the client;

---

[200] Lord Wilberforce criticized this label as inaccurate because the privilege is that of the client: *Waugh v British Railways Board* (n10); 531, 1172; see also *AM & S Europe v EC Commission* [1983] QB 878, [1983] 1 All ER 705; 894, 718, and 910, 730. The expression nevertheless continues to be used, and subsists in some 61 statutory provisions: see e.g. Political Parties and Elections Act 2009, s 2. In some other statutes, one of the two adjectives is omitted: 'professional privilege' appears in four provisions, the most recent in 2002; 'legal privilege' in 126, the most recent in 2009 (as indicated by searches on LEXIS conducted in December 2009).

[201] See also Auburn *Legal Professional Privilege: Law and Theory* (2000); Pattenden *The Law of Professional–Client Confidentiality* (2003).

[202] *Re Highgrade Traders Ltd* [1984] BCLC 151 (a search in December 2009, LEXIS indicated 288 cases (but no statutory provisions) in which this phrase had been used). In Australia, the Evidence Act 1995 distinguishes two varieties of client legal privilege: s 118 for legal advice, and s 119 for litigation; in Canada, it was suggested in *Minister of Justice v Blank* 2006 SCC 39, [2006] 2 SCR 319 that the incidents and rationale of the two were so different that they might better be regarded as two distinct privileges (despite the further finding that the relevant legislation comprehended both in its term 'solicitor–client privilege').

[203] *Per* Bingham LJ in *Ventouris v Mountain* [1991] 3 All ER 472, [1991] 1 WLR 607, 476c, 611H. A translation of a document is not 'created' for this purpose, nor is a photocopy: *Sumitomo Corp v Credit Lyonnais Rouse Ltd* [2001] EWCA Civ 1152, [2002] 4 All ER 68, [2002] 1 WLR 479, [46].

[204] [1997] AC 16, [1996] 2 All ER 78. Adopted in Australia in the Evidence Act (Cwth) 1995, ss 118, 119.

[205] *Three Rivers DC v Bank of England* [2003] EWCA Civ 474, [2003] QB 1556, where its origin was traced, and legal advice privilege found much more obscure in its incidents.

[206] See Lords Nicholls and Mustill dissenting in *Re L* (n204); and Lord Carswell in *Three Rivers DC v Bank of England (No 5)* [2004] UKHL 48, [2005] 1 AC 610, [105].

[207] For a slightly different formulation, see Proceeds of Crime Act 2002 s 330(10). See also the formulation in Australia in Pt 3.10 Div 1 of the Evidence Act 1995; although this deals in terms with the operation of the privilege only at the trial stage, it seems that similar rules will be applied at other stages: see *Towney v Minister for Land and Water Conservation for NSW* (1997) 147 ALR 402, approving earlier cases to that effect. [208] This refers to communications for a criminal purpose: see further 458.

(b) communications between a professional legal adviser and his client or any person representing his client or between such an adviser or his client or any such representative and any other person made in connection with or in contemplation of legal proceedings and for the purposes of such proceedings; and

(c) items enclosed with or referred to in such communications and made—

(i)   in connection with the giving of legal advice; or

(ii) in connection with or in contemplation of legal proceedings and for the purposes of such proceedings; when they are in the possession of a person who is entitled to possession of them.

This has been authoritatively stated[209] to reproduce the common law.[210] In s 10(1)(c), 'made' refers to items enclosed or referred to, and not to the communication itself.[211]

LEGAL ADVICE PRIVILEGE

This part of the privilege will be taken to focus upon the rule of evidence that confidential communications passing between legal adviser and client in a relevant legal context, with a view to giving or securing legal advice, are privileged so far as the client is concerned, but may be frustrated by the admissibility of secondary evidence. Each of these components requires some discussion below, although not necessarily in that order.[212]

Rule of evidence[213]

In England, the rule was traditionally regarded as a rule of evidence, and applied only to prevent compulsory disclosure either before,[214] or in the actual course of judicial,[215] or quasi-judicial, proceedings.[216] Its observation by lawyers is presumed in the absence of evidence to the contrary.[217] Elsewhere in the Commonwealth, the extension of the rule to proceedings not falling within so strict a category, or in respect of earlier and more peripheral activities relevant to such proceedings, has been the subject of intense judicial debate, elevating it into something more nearly resembling a basic constitutional

---

[209] *R v Central Criminal Court, ex p Francis & Francis* [1989] AC 346, [1988] 3 All ER 775; 392, 797.

[210] Cp 16th Report of the Law Reform Committee 'Privilege in Civil Proceedings' Cmnd 3472 (1967), [17].

[211] It has even been applied to a sample of blood prepared for submission to a prospective expert witness: *R v R* [1995] 1 Cr App Rep 183.   [212] Much applies to both branches of the privilege.

[213] In *Three Rivers (No 5)* [2004] UKHL 48, [2005] 1 AC 610 Lord Scott, [26], categorized this issue as sterile.

[214] Under the provisions of s 54 of the Criminal Justice and Police Act 2001, it also generates an obligation to return any legally privileged material obtained by a power of seizure under the Act.

[215] Even then the privilege will not operate to prevent disclosure of communications relating to legal advice on other unrelated proceedings, for example when the personal liability to tax of a solicitor is in question: *R v IRC, ex p Taylor (No 2)* [1990] 2 All ER 409.

[216] See Diplock LJ in *Parry-Jones v Law Society* [1969] 1 Ch 1, [1968] 1 All ER 177; 9, 180. But in *AM & S Europe v EC Commission* (n200) 895, 896, and 719, 720, Advocate-General Warner seemed to suggest that there was no reason not to apply the Commonwealth approach, as exhibited in the *West-Walker* and *Shell Canada* cases (nn220 and 226), to the construction of English statutes.

[217] *R (Faisaltex Ltd) v Crown Court at Preston* [2008] EWHC 2832 (Admin).

principle, expressed in the rhetoric of rights.[218] In Australasia,[219] after some uncertainty[220] and despite some dissent,[221] the doctrine was extended beyond the law of evidence strictly defined. Its capacity to apply in derogation of valid search warrants, by the application of very strict principles of construction to the relevant empowering legislation, led to some encroachment.[222] In Canada, similar steps have been taken, and some of the Canadian cases were influential in Australia.[223] In one,[224] a search warrant was quashed because it was directed to the seizure of documents subject to privilege, and in another the principle underlying the privilege was applied to regulate the opening of mail passing between a solicitor and his client, who was in prison.[225] It now seems well established there also that the legal effects of the relationship between solicitor and client extend beyond the protection from disclosure in legal proceedings of relevant communications that pass between them.[226] So far, however, the doctrine appears not to have been extended so far as to protect communications that implicate third parties.[227] The position is nevertheless far from being fully worked out in Canada, and further development seems inevitable.[228]

This view of the status of the privilege was resoundingly echoed here in Lord Taylor's speech in *R v Derby Magistrates' Court, ex p B*:[229]

Legal professional privilege is thus much more than an ordinary rule of evidence, limited in its application to the facts of a particular case. It is a fundamental condition on which the administration of justice as a whole rests.

He went on to describe it as a fundamental human right, protected by the European Convention on the Protection of Human Rights and Fundamental Freedoms, although

---

[218] *Sorby v Commonwealth* (1983) 152 CLR 281, 314, Brennan J.

[219] For example, Deane J in *A-G for The Northern Territory v Maurice* (1986) 161 CLR 475, 490.

[220] See *Crowley v Murphy* (1981) 34 ALR 496; *O'Reilly v Comr of State Bank of Victoria* (1983) 153 CLR 1; *Baker v Campbell* (1983) 153 CLR 52; and in New Zealand, *IRC v West-Walker* [1954] NZLR 191; *Rosenberg v Jaine* [1983] NZLR 1.   [221] Most notably from Brennan J.

[222] See especially *Baker v Campbell* and *Rosenberg v Jaine* (n220); *Cockerill v Collins* [1999] 2 Qd 26. Now magnified by substitution of 'dominant' for 'sole' purpose as the test: *Esso Australia Resources Ltd v Federal Comr of Taxation* [1999] HCA 67, 201 CLR 49.

[223] Although the privilege remains more pervasive in Canada: see *Minister of Correctional Services v Goodis* 2006 SCC 31, [2006] 2 SCR 32; *Privacy Commissioner of Canada v Blood Tribe* 2008 SCC 44, [2008] 2 SCR 574.

[224] *Re Borden and Elliot v R* (1975) 70 DLR (3d) 579; in England, this seems to have been achieved by statutory intervention: *R v Southampton Crown Court, ex p J and P* [1993] Crim LR 962; in Australia, see *Horowitz, Bilinsky & Spinak v Condie, Woods, Jones & Corby* (1989) 41 ACR 285.

[225] *Solosky v R* [1980] 1 SCR 821, without, however, going so far as to sever all evidentiary connection, with the result that the claim was disallowed.

[226] *Descoteaux v Mierzwinski* (1982) 141 DLR (3d) 590 (here too the discussion was strictly obiter and did not govern the actual result); *Re Ontario Securities Commission and Greymac Credit Corp* (1983) 146 DLR (3d) 73; *Re Director of Investigation and Research and Shell Canada Ltd* (1975) 55 DLR (3d) 713. See also Kasting (1978) 24 *McGill LJ* 115; Chasse (1977) 36 *CRNS* 349.

[227] *Re Gowling and Henderson and R* (1982) 136 DLR (3d) 292, in which some doubt was expressed upon the general policy of expansion of the privilege at the expense of the public interest in the detection and successful prosecution of criminal activities.

[228] The privilege was described as a 'fundamental policy of the law' in *Privacy Commissioner of Canada v Blood Tribe Department of Health* (n223), [11].

[229] [1996] AC 487, [1995] 4 All ER 526; 507D, 540, 541.

admitting that no argument had been heard to that effect.[230] This sits somewhat uneasily with insistence that the privilege is compatible with unfairness,[231] but has been accepted by the House of Lords,[232] and applied so as to permit being overridden[233] only by express statutory[234] provision or necessary implication. It was further recognized in *R v Secretary of State for the Home Department, ex p Daly*,[235] where its breach was invoked to strike down prison regulations permitting the reading of legal correspondence during searches in their absence of inmates' cells. On the other hand, breach, even when malicious, gives rise to no tortious remedy.[236]

Legal adviser[237]

In England, at common law, the term 'legal adviser' means solicitors or barristers,[238] or to those shown to be reasonably believed by the client to be so,[239] proof of which lies upon the party so asserting.[240] Counsel's opinion taken by a solicitor is privileged either because counsel counts as the client's legal adviser, or because he is the alter ego of the solicitor.[241] The privilege extends to communications to salaried legal advisers in that capacity.[242] This has been explained on the basis that they are professionally qualified, members of

---

[230] At 507G, 541d. For criticism of so exalted a view of the status of the privilege, see Tapper (1997) 1 *Int J of Evidence and Proof* 5.   [231] *Paragon Finance plc v Freshfields* [1999] 1 WLR 1183, [2000] CPR 81.

[232] *R (Morgan Grenfell) v Special Comr of Income Tax* [2002] UKHL 21, [2003] 1 AC 563, [2002] 3 All ER 1, [7]; but see Lord Hobhouse's acid scepticism, [43]. In *B v Auckland District Law Society* [2003] UKPC 38, [2003] 2 AC 736, Lord Millett expressed a similar view, although he admitted, [55], that a final court of appeal in a common law jurisdiction would be free to adopt a different policy. See also *R (Prudential plc) v Special Commissioner of Income Tax* [2009] EWHC 2494 (Admin). [72].

[233] Nor waived, *Expandable Ltd v Rubin* [2008] EWCA Civ 59, [38].

[234] Not indirectly by general rule-making provision: *General Mediterranean Holdings v Patel* [1999] 3 All ER 673, [2000] 1 WLR 272 (CPR); *R (Kelly) v Warley Magistrates' Court* [2007] EWHC 1836 (Admin) (CrPR). Although a mitigation mentioned in the latter (preventing use of witnesses unless details have been provided in advance) has now appeared by way of 2008 Amendment to rule 3.10 of the CrPR.

[235] [2001] UKHL 26, [2001] 2 AC 532, [2001] 3 All ER 433.

[236] *Watkins v Home Office* [2006] UKHL 17, [2006] 2 AC 395.

[237] The rule stated below applies to communications with a foreign legal adviser and to cases in which the litigation contemplated is foreign: *Re Duncan, Garfield v Fay* [1968] P 306, [1968] 2 All ER 395. It also extends to proceedings under the rules of the European Union Community: see *AM & S Europe v EC Commission* (n200); and is recognized by the European Convention on Human Rights: *Foxley v United Kingdom* (2000) 31 EHRR 637. In Canada, it extends to advice from a lawyer from another province even though not entitled to practice in the province where the privilege is claimed: *Gower v Tolko Manitoba Inc* (1999) 181 DLR (4th) 353.

[238] Including those chosen and remunerated by a third party, for example by an insurer for an insured: *Brown v Guardian Royal Exchange Assurance plc* [1994] 2 LlR 325; cf, in New Zealand, *R v H* [2000] 2 NZLR 257; and in Australia with or without a practising certificate, *Commonwealth v Vance* [2005] ACTCA 35, 158 ACTR 47.   [239] *Calley v Richards* (1854) 19 Beav 401.

[240] *Dadourian Group Int Inc v Simms* [2008] EWHC 1784 (Ch).

[241] *Bristol Corp v Cox* (1884) 26 Ch D 678. See also *Koowarta v Bjelke-Petersen* (1988) 92 FLR 104, in which claims for public policy immunity in respect of cabinet documents failed, but a claim in respect of counsel's opinion succeeded. Neither an accountant, *Comr of Taxation v Pratt Holdings Pty Ltd* [2003] FCA 6, 195 ALR 717, nor an auditor, *789TEN Pty Ltd v Westpac Banking Corp* [2005] NSWSC 123, 215 ALR 131, so consulted is so regarded in Australia.

[242] *Alfred Crompton Amusement Machines Ltd v Customs and Excise Comrs (No 2)* [1972] 2 QB 102, [1972] 2 All ER 353; 129, 376 (this point was neither raised nor questioned in the subsequent proceedings in the House of Lords). See also, in Canada, *Campbell and Shirose v R* [1999] 1 SCR 565; and in Australia, including advice by the Director of Public Prosecutions irrespective of whether the government advised was a party to the relevant litigation, *Health Insurance Commission v Freeman* (1998) 158 ALR 267. For a more

professional bodies with disciplinary powers to enforce their rules, and owe a duty to the court.[243] Legal professional privilege has also been extended by statute to patent,[244] and trademark,[245] agents, to licensed conveyancers,[246] and to authorized advocates and litigators.[247] It is not otherwise enough that someone without formal legal professional qualification is performing the functions of a legal adviser, such as an accountant,[248] a legal aid officer in a prison,[249] a probation officer,[250] a personnel consultant in an industrial dispute,[251] or a tax consultant.[252] Nor does the privilege extend to internal documents of bodies determining the provision of legal aid, since they do not directly offer legal advice.[253]

It should be noted, however, that there may sometimes be an alternative route to the suppression of the evidence on the basis of public policy.[254]

Communication

The privilege applies only to communications;[255] a solicitor can be obliged to disclose the identity of his client,[256] or potential client,[257] and the privilege does not prevent the

restricted view in the EU see *Akzo Nobel Chemicals Ltd v Commission of the European Communities* [2008] All ER (EC) 1.

[243] *New Victoria Hospital v Ryan* [1993] ICR 201, 203.

[244] Copyright, Designs and Patents Act 1988, s 280, enlarging the privilege previously bestowed by Patents Act 1977 to include non-litigious communications. For the situation in Australia, see *Sepa Waste Water Treatment Pty Ltd v JMT Welding Pty Ltd* (1986) 6 NSWLR 41; for liberal construction of similar legislation in New Zealand, see *Frucor Beverages Ltd v Rio Beverages Ltd* [2001] 2 NZLR 604.

[245] Trade Marks Act 1994, s 87, reversing the position at common law: see *Dormeuil Fréres SA v Dormière Menswear Ltd* [1983] RPC 131.   [246] Administration of Justice Act 1985, s 33.

[247] Courts and Legal Services Act 1990, s 63.

[248] *R (Prudential plc) v Special Commissioner of Income Tax* (n232).

[249] *R v Umoh* (1986) 84 Cr App Rep 138, although in some circumstances immunity may be available on grounds of public policy, or the evidence may be excluded in criminal proceedings, by way of discretion under s 78 of the Police and Criminal Evidence Act 1984, if the fairness of the proceedings might be jeopardized by its admission.   [250] *R v Secord* [1992] 3 NZLR 570. See also *R v Walker* (1992) 74 CCC (3d) 97.

[251] *New Victoria Hospital v Ryan* (n243), distinguishing *M & W Grazebrook Ltd v Wallens* [1973] 2 All ER 868.

[252] Notwithstanding the European Convention on Human Rights: *Home or Away v Commrs of Customs and Excise* (5 April 2002, unreported) VADT.

[253] See, in Canada, *Jobb v Dept of Justice* (1999) 173 DLR (4th) 739.

[254] *Evans v Chief Constable of Surrey* [1988] QB 588, [1989] 2 All ER 594; see further, 488. The policies there governing communications between police and DPP resembled those applied here. In *Goodridge v Chief Constable of Hampshire* [1999] 1 All ER 896, it was held that the issue should be determined by analogy to a private legal adviser in the circumstances of each case. Elsewhere, they have been held to fall within it: see, in Australia, *A-G (NT) v Kearney* (1985) 158 CLR 500; *Waterford v Commonwealth of Australia* (1987) 163 CLR 54. In Australia also communications conveying legal advice by DPP to government departments are privileged perhaps even though ultra vires, if reasonably believed to be within the powers of the Director: *Grofam Pty Ltd v Australia and New Zealand Banking Group Ltd* (1993) 117 ALR 669.

[255] Including secondary evidence of such communication: *Financial Services Compensation Scheme Ltd v Abbey National Treasury Services Plc* [2007] EWHC 2868 (Ch), [9].

[256] *Bursill v Tanner* (1885) 16 QBD 1; the same is true in Ireland: *Miley v Flood* [2002] 1 IR 50; although for an exception in Australia, see *Federal Comr of Taxation v Coombes (No 2)* (1998) 160 ALR 456, and for consideration of statutory amendment, *Z v New South Wales Crime Commission* [2007] HCA 7, 231 CLR 75. See Morrick (1980) 124 *Sol Jo* 303 for possible qualification to allow for the operation of the privilege against self-incrimination.   [257] *Police v Mills* [1993] 2 NZLR 592.

disclosure of facts observed[258] by either party in the course of their relationship as client and legal adviser.[259] In *Brown v Foster*,[260] for instance, it was held that a barrister who saw a book produced at the trial of his client could testify in subsequent proceedings, without the client's consent, on the question of whether it contained a particular entry when he previously saw it at the preliminary examination. The two concepts ran together in *R (Howe) v South Durham Magistrates' Court*,[261] in which a solicitor had acted for two clients with the same name, and was held compellable to identify the former client, and to produce notes of interview when there was no other way of proving that it was the first and not the second who had been disqualified from driving. In *Conlon v Conlons Ltd*,[262] the defence to a claim for damages for personal injury alleged that the claimant had agreed to accept a sum in full settlement. In his reply, the claimant denied that his solicitor had been authorized to settle the claim, and it was held that he could be obliged to answer an interrogatory as to whether he had authorized his solicitor to negotiate a settlement. If settlements made before the issue of a claim form are to be binding, the client's instruction to his solicitor in this regard ought to be held to be outside the rule relating to legal professional privilege, for a solicitor has no implied authority to conclude negotiations at that stage, although he may bind his client by doing so later.

If a third party is consulted by a legal adviser for the purposes of litigation, perhaps as a potential witness, a question may arise as to the extent to which privilege can be claimed in respect of communications to him.[263] Since there is no property in a witness,[264] the third party is compellable. He is then free to testify, subject only to the ordinary operation of legal professional privilege, which will not protect documents submitted to him for expert advice, and not otherwise protected.[265] It is dubious how far the old privilege in respect of witness statements can survive the modern practice of requiring disclosure[266] in advance of trial.[267]

---

[258] Or coming into the possession of the lawyer: see *R v Murray* (2000) 144 CCC3d 289 (pre-existing videotapes amounting to evidence of the crime removed from the client's premises by his lawyer at the client's request); but not, in Australia, a telephone number divulged on a confidential basis for the purpose of securing legal advice by its use: *Minister for Immigration v Hamdan* [2005] FCAFC 113, 143 FCR 398.

[259] *R v Jack* (1992) 70 CCC (3d) 67 (client's attitude towards husband as manifested during interview for advice on separation, when husband subsequently tried for wife's murder).

[260] (1857) 7 H & N 736; *Re Cathcart, ex p Campbell* (1870) 5 Ch App 703.

[261] [2004] EWHC 362, [2005] RTR 4. So far as the solicitor had been present in court during the trial of the first client, it was said that he was testifying not as a solicitor, but just like any other witness of the proceedings.   [262] [1952] 2 All ER 462.

[263] It has been held that legal professional privilege will not itself provide a basis for restraining disclosure of such communications by the supplier: *W v Egdell* [1990] Ch 359, [1990] 1 All ER 835. The Criminal Justice Act 2003, s 35, requires the defence to disclose the names and addresses of any experts consulted by the defence. It was held in *HM Adv v Wilson* 2001 SCCR 663 that it did not amount to a breach of the European Convention for the prosecution then to call such witnesses to testify.

[264] *Harmony Shipping Co SA v Davis* [1979] 3 All ER 177, [1979] 1 WLR 1380. See also *Trade Practices Commission v Ampol Petroleum (Victoria) Pty Ltd* (1994) 126 ALR 111 (transcripts provided to witnesses at preceding statutory examination).

[265] *R v King* [1983] 1 All ER 929, [1983] 1 WLR 411, although it seems that it will protect his expression of opinion derived from an object provided to him for the purposes of legal advice: *R v R* (n211). See also *R v Ward* (1980) 3 ACR 171. For suggestion of radical reduction of privilege in this context, see Edis (2007) 27 CJQ 40.   [266] See 278.

[267] See *Trade Practices Commission v Ampol Petroleum (Victoria) Pty Ltd*, (n264) commenting on *Re Strachan* [1895] 1 Ch 439. Cf *Carbone v National Crime Authority* (1994) 126 ALR 79.

Confidentiality and waiver

Confidence lies at the very heart of legal professional privilege.[268] In order to attract privilege, the communications passing between legal adviser and client must be intended to pass in confidence.[269] That confidential character may be lost by waiver,[270] express or implied, or by accident. It may sometimes be important to distinguish between waiver of confidence and waiver of privilege. Thus where otherwise privileged documents have already been revealed, and their return, or an order to restrain their use, is sought, the relevant considerations relate to property[271] or confidence.[272]

Legal professional privilege may always be waived by the client. While making the advice public would certainly amount to waiver, it seems that more limited disclosure, seeking to exclude the claimant, will not do so.[273] The fact that a conversation between a client and his solicitor takes place in the presence of a third party does not necessarily amount to a waiver,[274] although it will no doubt usually be held to exclude confidentiality.[275] If a presumptively privileged document is offered to an opponent to read, the privilege is waived whether or not he reads it.[276] An agreement to waive the privilege attaching to a medical report will not, however, be implied from the acceptance of the opposite party's unconditional production of his medical report.[277]

It is here necessary to distinguish between the situation at different stages. The extent of pre-trial waiver may be determined by the party making it,[278] except that it is always

---

[268] Bingham LJ in *Ventouris v Mountain* (n203); 475, 611. In Australia this is much less clear in relation to litigation privilege, see *Southern Equities Corp Ltd v West Ausralian Government Holdings Ltd* (1993) 10 WAR 1v. See also in Canada *City of Windsor v MFP Financial Services Ltd* (2004) 247 DLR (4th) 640. Under the European Convention confidentiality is likely to be considered under art 8, as in *Wieser v Austria* (2008) 46 EHRR 1353 (and a lawyer's office for these purposes is a 'home').

[269] *Gardner v Irvin* (1879) 4 Ex D 49, 53; *Webster v James Chapman & Co* [1989] 3 All ER 939, 944. See also *A-G for The Northern Territory v Maurice* (n219), 490.

[270] In Canada, it has been held that privilege may be waived by reference to legal advice in the statement of a party's defence, even though no explicit revelation of the advice has been made: *Campbell and Shirose v R* (n242). [271] *B v Auckland District Law Society* (n232), [70].

[272] *GE Capital Commercial Finance Ltd v Anglo Petroleum Ltd* [2004] EWCA Civ 315, [2004] 2 BCLC 662, [23].

[273] *Gotha City v Sothebys* [1998] 1 WLR 114. In such a case, privilege may attach to a summary or extract from the original advice: *USP Strategies plc v London General Holdings Ltd* [2004] EWHC 373. See also, in Australia, *Mann v Carnell* [1999] HCA 66, 201 CLR 1; and in New Zealand, *C-C Bottlers Ltd v Lion Nathan Ltd* [1993] 2 NZLR 445. In Australia, however, if the party making such disclosure does so in order to secure an advantage in the litigation, he may still be taken to waive the privilege by making it: *Goldberg v Ng* (1994) 185 CLR 83.

[274] *A Local Authority v B* [2008] EWHC 1017 (Fam), [2009] 1 FLR 289 (appropriate adult present at interview in police station between child suspected of crime and his solicitor). In *R v Atkinson* [1990] 2 NZLR 513, a conversation between two men at a solicitor's home when he was absent, but in the presence of his secretary, was held not to qualify on this basis.

[275] As in *R v Sharp* [2003] NSWSC 1117, 143 ACR 344; *Sullivan v Ministry of Fisheries* [2002] 3 NZLR 721 (whispered advice during interrogation).

[276] *Argyle Brewery Pty Ltd v Darling Harbourside* (1993) 120 ALR 537.

[277] *Causton v Mann Egerton (Johnsons) Ltd*, [1974] 1 All ER 453, [1974] 1 WLR 162. For consideration of the impact of the CPR and associated protocols in this area, see *Carlson v Townsend* [2001] EWCA Civ 511, [2001] 3 All ER 663.

[278] *Lyell v Kennedy (No 3)* (1884) 27 Ch D 1, 24. Although evidence of the underlying facts proving such waiver may be adduced by the party seeking to rely upon it, *R v Hall-Chung* [2007] EWCA Crim 3429, [16].

necessary to reveal enough of the material so as not to mislead.[279] So long as the material disclosed is fairly severable from that which is suppressed, its disclosure will not waive privilege in that which has been suppressed,[280] although there may sometimes be difficulty in determining what is the whole of which the matter disclosed is a part.[281] At the stage of discovery under the old law, subject to this qualification, it was made clear that privilege could attach to, and validly be claimed for, part of a document only.[282] It may also have been possible to waive the privilege for legal advice, without waiving it for that in respect of litigation.[283]

Difficult questions may arise as to the extent of any implied waiver by reliance[284] upon a document in the preparation and presentation of a case, either civil[285] or criminal.[286] Waiver does not necessarily extend to all otherwise privileged documents dealing with any matter merely mentioned in such a document.[287] Simple reference to a privileged document in an affidavit will thus not necessarily amount to waiver,[288] but more extensive reliance may well do so.[289] The fact that the final version of a document will become public does not prevent earlier drafts from remaining privileged.[290]

Privilege may be waived by the legal adviser, even though acting under a mistake, and against the client's interests and wishes.[291] It may not, however, be waived by an adviser acting ultra vires.[292] Such waiver may be implied from failure by the adviser to assert

---

[279] Described in *Dunlop Slazenger Int Ltd v Joe Bloggs Sports Ltd* [2003] EWCA Civ 901, [11] as being against 'cherry picking'. In patent cases in which experiments otherwise subject to privilege are disclosed, such waiver applies also to 'work-up' experiments: *Mayne Pharma Pty Ltd v Debiopharm SA* [2006] EWHC 164 (Pat), [2006] FSR 37 (rejecting the analogy of earlier drafts of expert reports employed by Laddie J in *Electrolux Northern Ltd v Black & Decker* [1996] FSR 595).

[280] *R v Secretary of State for Transport and Factortame Ltd* (1997) 9 Admin LR 591.

[281] As in *Fulham Leisure Holdings Ltd v Nicholson Graham & Jones* [2006] EWHC 158 (Ch), [2006] 2 All ER 599.

[282] *GE Capital Corporate Finance Group v Bankers Trust Co* [1995] 2 All ER 993, [1995] 1 WLR 172, Hoffmann LJ in highly persuasive *obiter dicta*; endorsing the approach of Saville J in *The Good Luck* [1992] 2 Lloyd's Rep 540, eulogizing that of McPherson J in *Curlex Manufacturing Pty Ltd v Carlingford Australia General Insurance Ltd* [1987] 2 Qd R 335, and distinguishing *Great Atlantic Insurance Co v Home Insurance Co* [1981] 2 All ER 485, [1981] 1 WLR 529; *The Sagheera* [1997] 1 Lloyd's Rep 160. It seems that the same is true under the Civil Procedure Rules: see CPR 31.19(3), Practice Direction 31, [6.1].

[283] *George Doland Ltd v Blackburn Robson Coates & Co* [1972] 3 All ER 959, [1972] 1 WLR 1338; but see *General Accident Fire and Life Assurance Corp Ltd v Tanter* [1984] 1 All ER 35, [1984] 1 WLR 100.

[284] In *Brennan v Sunderland City Council* UKEAT/349/08 [2009] ICR 479, [67] reference and reliance were subsumed in a general test of fairness in determining waiver.

[285] *Expandable Ltd v Rubin* (n233).   [286] As in *R v Muhammed Ahmed* [2007] EWCA Crim 2870.

[287] *General Accident Fire and Life Assurance Corp Ltd v Tanter* (n283). See also *A-G for The Northern Territory v Maurice* (n219), in which the High Court of Australia insisted that the test was whether use of part only of the material, or even oblique reference to it, would be unfair or misleading; and see *R v Muhammed Ahmed*, [23].

[288] *Tate and Lyle International Ltd v Government Trading Corp* [1984] LS Gaz R 3341.

[289] *Equiticorp Industries Group Ltd v Hawkins* [1990] 2 NZLR 175.

[290] *Jackson v Marley Davenport Ltd* [2004] EWCA Civ 1225, [2004] 1 WLR 2926 (earlier drafts of expert report).

[291] *Great Atlantic Insurance Co v Home Insurance Co* (n282), 494, 539. The same may apply to any waiver made under the ostensible authority of the client's legal adviser: see *Causton v Mann Egerton (Johnsons) Ltd* (n277); but see *Frank Truman Export Ltd v Metropolitan Police Comr* [1977] QB 952, [1977] 3 All ER 431; 957, 436. See also *R v CKC* (1987) 62 CR (3d) 131, in which privilege was held not to have been waived in Canada when a report was disclosed by counsel as part of an unauthorized plea bargain.

[292] *GE Capital Commercial Finance Ltd v Anglo Petroleum Ltd* (n272).

privilege.[293] It may be waived by the supply of otherwise privileged material to an expert who testifies upon its basis,[294] or to the prosecution who may then use it for the purposes of cross-examination of the accused,[295] or co-accused.[296] It is not waived by consenting to an order allowing disclosure by subsequent order of a court.[297] Waiver may be implied from the use of a privileged document in court,[298] for example by its use for the purposes of cross-examination,[299] or to refresh a witness's memory whether in court or out.[300] In *R v Wilmot*,[301] the accused sought to rebut a suggestion of recent fabrication of a particular claim, and it was held that it in no way trenched upon the privilege that the judge remarked upon the accused's failure to waive his privilege and call his solicitor to prove an earlier manifestation of the claim. Privilege may, however, be lost if the accused in a criminal case, in an attempt to avoid any adverse inference under the provisions of the Criminal Justice and Public Order Act 1994, expatiates[302] upon the nature of the legal advice that induced him to remain silent.[303] The extent of any such waiver becomes then a matter of fairness, especially in not misleading,[304] and in criminal proceedings the material remains subject to discretionary exclusion under s 78 of the Police and Criminal Evidence Act 1984.[305]

A client impliedly waives privilege in respect of any matter in which he commences a claim against his legal adviser, but such waiver does not extend to unrelated matters in respect of which the adviser acted,[306] nor to cases in which the client sues not his legal adviser, but other advisers, even though part of the same team,[307] nor to communications with other legal advisers, even in respect of the same matter.[308]

---

[293] *Spedley Securities Ltd (in liq) v Bank of New Zealand* (1991) 26 NSWLR 711, 729.

[294] As in *Clough v Tameside and Glossop Health Authority* [1998] 2 All ER 971. For full Australian discussion of this issue, including the English authorities, see *Sevic v Roarty* (1998) 44 NSWLR 287.

[295] *R v Cottrill* [1997] Crim LR 56.   [296] *R v Ungvari* [2003] EWCA Crim 2346, [68].

[297] *British American Tobacco (Investments) Ltd v USA* [2004] EWCA Civ 1064, [32].

[298] But not from disclosure in advance under the provisions of RSC Ord 38, r 2A, if any intention to adduce the document in evidence is subsequently disavowed: *Vista Maritime Inc v Sesa Goa* [1997] CLC 1600. See Passmore (1998) NLJ 1366 for comparison with *Clough v Tameside* (n294).

[299] *Nea Karteria Maritime Co v Atlantic and Great Lakes SS Co (No 2)* [1981] Com LR 138. See also *Buttes Gas and Oil Co v Hammer (No 3)* [1981] QB 223, [1980] 3 All ER 475, 268, 502 (unaffected on this point by subsequent proceedings).

[300] *Mancorp Pty Ltd v Baulderstone Pty Ltd* (1991) 57 SASR 87 (although the court has more discretion in relation to the production of a privileged document so used than in the case of an unprivileged one).

[301] (1988) 89 Cr App Rep 341.

[302] Privilege is not waived simply by stating that silence was maintained on the advice of a solicitor: *R v Bui* [2001] EWCA Crim 1, [39]. See also, in New Zealand, *Miller v IRC* [1999] 1 NZLR 275, 297.

[303] *R v Bowden* [1999] 4 All ER 43, [1999] 1 WLR 823. See also *R v Wishart* [2005] EWCA Crim 1337.

[304] *R v Loizou* [2006] EWCA Crim 1719, (2006) 150 SJLB 1187, [79], although it seems that, in Australia, inconsistency between maintenance of the privilege, and what has been disclosed, is now sometimes regarded as having superseded fairness as the criterion: see *Mann v Carnell* (n273).

[305] *R v Hall-Chung* (n278), [19].   [306] *Lillicrap v Nalder & Son* [1993] 1 All ER 724.

[307] *Nederlandse Reassurantie Groep Holding NV v Bacon & Woodrow* [1995] 1 All ER 976, [1995] 2 LlR 77.

[308] *Paragon Finance plc v Freshfields* (n231). For commentary, see Auburn (2000) 63 *MLR* 104 (anti) and Mathieson and Page (2000) *NZLJ* 355 (pro). This is sometimes described as a 'putting in issue' exception, or waiver, but was resoundingly rejected in *Farm Assist Ltd v Secretary of State for Environment, Food and Rural Affairs* [2008] EWHC 3079 (TCC) and *Digicel (St Lucia Ltd) v Cable and Wireless Plc* [2009] EWHC 1437 (Ch)); and in New Zealand in *Shannon v Shannon* [2005] 3 NZLR 757.

Attempts are sometimes made to infer waiver from accidental disclosure by one side to the other. In modern litigation, with voluminous documentation,[309] severe pressure of time, and the extensive use of unqualified staff,[310] such accidents are highly prone to occur. It seems that, where it is obvious to the party seeking to use a document that it must have been disclosed in error, then no question of waiver can arise,[311] and the question becomes one of practicality and the ability of the court to override the normal incidents of privilege by a protective injunction.[312] If, however, a reasonable recipient could believe that privilege was being waived, then the fact that a mistake had indeed been made is irrelevant, and the privilege is lost.[313] Under the Civil Procedure Rules, the consequences of inadvertent disclosure and inspection are specifically placed under the control of the judge.[314]

Privilege may be claimed at an interim stage of the proceedings, but waived at trial.[315] Nor is the privilege waived by reference in interim proceedings to only so much of the document as demonstrates that it is indeed subject to privilege, since this would defeat the purpose of a motion to prevent the use of such material by the opponent at trial.[316] Otherwise, the same principles apply to interim deployment as to deployment at the trial.[317]

It should also be noted that waiver applies only for the purposes of the proceedings, or part of the proceedings,[318] in which the privilege was waived. Thus documents handed over to the police by the claimant in a civil suit, for the purpose of prosecuting the defendant in that suit, remained privileged in the civil suit.[319] The same applies to civil proceedings, even to the extent of different actions between the same parties.[320]

The law recognizes a category of common interest privilege, for example as a joint tenant or as one of several victims of a common calamity.[321] Where it applies, any privy party

---

309   For example, in *USA v Philip Morris Inc* [2004] EWCA Civ 330, [2004] 1 CLC 811, forty million documents had been subject to disclosure in the American proceedings.

310   In *Transamerica Computer Co v IBM Corp* 573 F 2d 646 (9th Cir, 1978), no fewer than 1,138 privileged documents were inadvertently disclosed when 17 million pages had had to be vetted in three months. The problem prompted further amendment of the Federal Rules of Civil Procedure in the United States with effect from 1 December 2006.

311   *Guinness Peat Properties Ltd v Fitzroy Robinson Partnership* [1987] 2 All ER 716, [1987] 1 WLR 1027; *Derby & Co Ltd v Weldon (No 8)* [1990] 3 All ER 762, [1991] 1 WLR 73. See also *Kenning v Eve Construction Ltd* [1989] 1 WLR 1189, in which the relevant document had to be disclosed for a different reason. The position in New Zealand is the same: *National Insurance Co Ltd v Whirlybird Holdings Ltd* [1994] 2 NZLR 513.

312   See further, 449.

313   *Pizzey v Ford Motor Co* [1994] PIQR P15; *Breeze v John Stacy & Sons Ltd* [2000] Cf Rep 77.

314   CPR 31.20, although the principles remain the same: *Al Fayed v Metropolitan Police Comr* [2002] EWCA Civ 780, [18].

315   Although at peril as to costs: *Buttes Gas and Oil Co v Hammer (No 3)* (n299); *Somerville v Australian Securities Commission* (1993) 118 ALR 149.

316   *Def American Inc v Phonogram Ltd* (1994) The Times, 16 August.

317   *Dunlop Slazenger Int Ltd v Joe Bloggs Sports Ltd* (n279).

318   *Goldman v Hesper* [1988] 3 All ER 97, [1988] 1 WLR 1238, in which legal professional privilege attaching to documents put forward on taxation of costs was waived for that purpose only irrespective of whether produced under order of the court or voluntarily: *Bourns Inc v Raychem Corp* [1999] 3 All ER 154, [1999] CLC 1029. This procedure now appears in CPD [40.14], and was endorsed as compliant with Art 6 of the European Convention in *South Coast Shipping Co v Havant BC* [2002] 3 All ER 779, (2002) 1 Costs LR 98, [32].

319   *British Coal Corp v Dennis Rye Ltd (No 2)* [1988] 3 All ER 816, [1988] 1 WLR 1113. Distinguished in Canada in *Bone v Person* (2000) 185 DLR (4th) 335, in which it was the claimant who had made the unqualified disclosure.   320   *Bourns Inc v Raychem Corp* (n318). See also CPR 31.20.

321   *Buttes Gas and Oil Co v Hammer (No 3)* (n299). In Australia, in *Farrow Mortgage Services Pty Ltd v Webb* (1996) 132 FLR 466, the Federal Court of Appeal distinguished common interest from joint retainer.

may claim the privilege[322] against an outsider, but not against a privy,[323] and only for communications made during any common interest,[324] not after it has ended,[325] or is in abeyance.[326] Communication between such privies does not automatically amount to waiver, and the privilege cannot be waived by one, without the authority of the other. In cases of joint retainer of solicitors, the agreement establishing the retainer may explicitly waive privilege between the joint retainers.[327]

It is also worth noting that failure to waive may prevent a party from succeeding on a motion to strike out, since further material may be forthcoming if a subsequent waiver is in fact made.[328]

Legal advice in a relevant legal context

This first head of legal professional privilege was the later to gain full recognition by the courts, for it was not until *Greenough v Gaskell* was decided in 1833[329] that it was held that the privilege attached to communications between client and legal adviser, absent any contemplated litigation. In that case, Lord Brougham said:[330]

If the privilege was confined to communications connected with suits begun, or intended or expected or apprehended, no-one could safely adopt such precautions as might eventually render any proceedings successful, or all proceedings superfluous.

Although the privilege under consideration applies to communications made with the object of retaining a solicitor's services even if they are not in fact retained, the relationship of solicitor and client must at least be contemplated, and the communications must be fairly referable to that relationship: 'The mere fact that the person speaking is a solicitor and the person to whom he speaks is his client affords no protection.'[331] It has been held to cover information communicated by the solicitor to the client for the purpose of tendering advice, despite the information emanating from a third party, being passed on as received, and there being no litigation in prospect.[332] It does not, however, include communications to a client from his opponent's solicitor,[333] since such a communication is hardly likely to

---

[322] Under both advice and litigation branches: *Svenska Handelsbanken v Sun Alliance and London Insurance plc* [1995] 2 Ll R 84.

[323] *Cia Barca de Panama SA v George Wimpey & Co* [1980] 1 Lloyd's Rep 598, 614.

[324] Which may be tested by whether or not it would be proper for both parties to retain the same solicitors: see *USP Strategies plc v London General Holdings Ltd* [2004] EWHC 373 (Ch), [14].

[325] *Talbot v Marshfield* (1865) 2 Drew & Sm 549. Or when made before any common interest existed: *R v Trutch* [2001] EWCA Crim 1750, [22].

[326] *Leif Hoegh & Co A/S v Petrolsea Inc* [1993] 1 Lloyd's Rep 363.

[327] *Brown v Guardian Royal Exchange Assurance plc* (n238) (notwithstanding the possibility of subsequent conflict of interest). In Australia, privilege can be waived more readily by a party in common interest with another than where there is joint interest as a result of joint retainer: *Patrick v Capital Finance* [2004] FCA 1249, 211 ALR 272, [23].

[328] *Creative Resins International Ltd v Glasslam Europe Ltd* [2005] EWHC 777 (QB).

[329] (1833) 1 My & K 98; some would say not until the judgment of Lord Selbourne in *Minet v Morgan* (1873) 8 Ch App 361.   [330] 103.

[331] *Minter v Priest* [1930] AC 558, 568 *per* Lord Buckmaster. The mere fact that a solicitor advising trustees is himself a trustee does not exclude the privilege: *O'Rourke v Darbishire* [1920] AC 581. In Australia, in *Global Funds Management (NSW) Ltd v Rooney* (1994) 36 NSWLR 122, it was held, after consideration of the older English cases, that a bona fide and reasonable belief in the existence of the relationship will suffice so long as the belief persists.   [332] *Re Getty (Sarah C) Trust* [1985] QB 956, [1985] 2 All ER 809.

[333] Even when the eventual opponents had retained the same solicitor: *Perry v Smith* (1842) 9 M&W 681.

convey legal advice,[334] although if such a communication contemplates settlement of a dispute, it may be within the protection conferred by the privilege to be described in the next section of this chapter. Nor does it extend to communications to a third party informing him of a claim to be made against him.[335]

While it is possible in a few cases for the content of advice to be inferred from the form of communications between lawyer and client not ostensibly conveying legal advice,[336] or for the advice to be inextricably intertwined with the extrinsic material,[337] this is likely to be rare, and such documents as records of attendance will not normally attract the privilege,[338] nor will their disclosure waive privilege in any underlying associated privileged material.[339] In *C v C*,[340] the threatening way in which the client behaved in the course of arguing about the solicitor's retainer was held to fall outside the privilege.

The precise extension of the privilege was determined by the decision of the House of Lords in the leading case of *Three Rivers v Bank of England (No 5)*.[341] The issues were narrowed by concession and previous decision to whether or not advice from solicitors to their clients upon the presentation of evidence in a non-adversarial legal context was privileged, even though not constituting advice as to legal rights and duties. It was held unanimously that it was, in part because of the difficulty in distinguishing issues of presentation from other aspects of legal advice, especially in public law areas.[342] The ambit of a 'relevant legal context',[343] although crucial to the decision, was not defined, but merely illustrated.

It has also been determined that even though a given retainer is in part for tendering legal advice of the requisite character to attract privilege, not all advice passing between the solicitor and client in relation to it is automatically privileged,[344] perhaps especially in the case of a long-running and far-extending retainer.[345] In such a case, each communication should be considered individually.[346]

Privilege of client

At common law,[347] legal professional privilege in both of its aspects is that of the client,[348] although it also extends to communications by the client's agent[349] to the clerk or other

---

[334] *Hadley v Baddock* [1987] WAR 98.

[335] *CHC Software Care Ltd v Hopkins & Wood* [1993] FSR 241.   [336] See *Rosenberg v Jaine* (n220).

[337] As in *Churton v Frewen* (1865) 2 Drew & Sm 390.

[338] *R v Manchester Crown Court, ex p Rogers* [1999] 4 All ER 35, [2001] 1 WLR 832. See also *Packer v Deputy Comr of Taxation* [1985] 1 Qd R 275 (bill of costs); *Re Merit Finance and Investment* [1993] 1 NZLR 152. In Canada, fee statements are presumed to be within the range of the privilege: *Maranda v Richer* 2003 SCC 67, [2003] 3 SCR 193; ; but see *Ministry of the Attorney-General v Mitchinson* (2005) 251 DLR (4th) 65.

[339] *Lake Cumbeline Pty Ltd v Effem Foods Pty Ltd* (1994) 126 ALR 58.

[340] [2001] EWCA Civ 469, [2002] Fam 42.   [341] (n213).

[342] Carrying a clear danger of subverting the distinction between litigious and non-adversarial legal process, and so threatening the distinction between advice and litigation privilege.

[343] The term was taken from the judgment of Lord Taylor CJ in *Balabel v Air India* [1988] Ch 317, [1988] 2 All ER 246.   [344] Notwithstanding the decision in *Balabel* (n343).

[345] *City of Montreal v Foster Wheeler Power Co Ltd* 2004 SCC 18, [2004] 1 SCR 456, [41].

[346] *USA v Philip Morris Inc* (n309), [79].

[347] But a number of statutes, such as the Friendly Societies Act 1992, s 62(7), extend privilege to legal advisers that is not available to their clients.

[348] *Wilson v Rastall* (1792) 4 Term Rep 753; *CHC Software Care v Hopkin* (n335); *Nationwide Building Society v Various Solicitors (No 2)* (1998) The Times, 1 May. See Higgins (2008) 27 CJQ 377 arguing for re-examination of the extent of privilege in the case of corporate clients.

[349] See *Mudgway v New Zealand Insurance Co Ltd* [1988] 2 NZLR 283, in which the agent was not an employee but a third party acting as *agent*, and so distinguished from a true third party. In Canada, the

subordinate of the adviser, and vice versa.[350] It may even, in an exceptional case, apply in favour of the client against his agent.[351] It enures for the benefit of his successors in title[352] with regard, for instance, to documents handed over by him,[353] and the Court of Appeal accordingly held that the original of the proofs and notes on evidence with which the case of *Calcraft v Guest*[354] were concerned were privileged from production. The fact that they had been brought into existence for the purposes of a particular claim, which had been concluded, was treated as immaterial. Lindley MR stated this conclusion in terms of a general rule:[355] 'once privileged, always privileged'; nor is it necessary that subject matter or parties be identical.[356] In *Schneider v Leigh*,[357] the claimant had sought damages for personal injuries against a company, whose solicitor obtained the usual medical report—a document covered by ordinary litigant's privilege. The report was made by the defendant, and the claimant contended that it libelled him. It was held that the defendant could claim no privilege with regard to his report. This case illustrates what Lord Atkin once described as the 'double nature' that problems relating to professional privilege may assume. First, there is the question of whether the document or statement need be put in evidence—a general question of adjectival law; second, there is the question of whether the occasion on which the statement (*ex hypothesi* before the court) was published is an occasion of absolute or qualified privilege—a question with which the substantive law of defamation is concerned.[358] On facts such as those of *Schneider v Leigh*, a claim for qualified privilege might ultimately succeed, although the claims of professional privilege failed. It seems

police are not regarded as clients, employees, or agents of the Crown in relation to the protection of advice from government lawyers: *R v Gray* (1992) 74 CCC (3d) 267; the position appears to be different in Australia: *Dunesky and Bay Wool Pty Ltd v Elder* (1992) 60 ACR 459.

[350] But, in Canada, it has been held that the Crown does not act as agent or trustee for native Indians within its care for the purpose of denying privilege to communications between the Crown, and its legal advisers, in relation to native title litigation: *Samson Indian Band v Canada* (1995) 125 DLR (4th) 294.

[351] See *Burcher v Bradford Hospitals NHS Trust* (28 September 2001, unreported) EAT, in which the agent took notes of a meeting at which he was seeking legal advice on behalf of his employer, but was refused access to the notes on the basis of privilege when he subsequently sued his employer for wrongful dismissal, although this seems somewhat inconsistent with the approach to disputes between client and legal adviser: see further, 461.

[352] And so may be waived by his personal representative: *Chant v Brown* (1849) 7 Hare 79; *Re Molloy* [1997] 2 Cr App Rep 283; or by his trustee in bankruptcy: *Re Konigsberg (a bankrupt)* [1989] 3 All ER 289, although a different view is taken in some other jurisdictions: see in Canada, *Re Bre-X Minerals* (2001) 206 DLR (4th) 280; in Australia, *Worrell v Woods* [1999] FCA 242, 163 ALR 195 (explicitly refusing to follow *Re Konigsberg*); and in the United States, the Supreme Court, while holding that, in the case of corporations, the trustee in bankruptcy could waive, ostentatiously declined to consider whether the same rule applied outside the corporate context: *Commodity Futures Trading Co v Weintraub* (1985) 471 US 343, 356. Special rules apply in the case of wills, where the evidence of what transpired between solicitor and client may be decisive in determining who the successor is, with the result that privilege will not normally apply to prevent the solicitor from testifying as to his instructions, and the circumstances in which they were conveyed: *Russell v Jackson* (1851) 9 Hare 387, 392. See also, in the United States, *Swidler & Berlin v United States* (25 June 1998, unreported); and for a similar view in Canada, in relation to wills, see *Geffen v Goodman Estate* [1991] 2 SCR 353.

[353] *Minet v Morgan* (n329); followed in *Crescent Farm (Sidcup) Sports Ltd v Sterling Offices Ltd* [1972] Ch 553, [1971] 3 All ER 1192. For fuller analysis see Loughrey [2007] *JBL* 778.   [354] (n8).

[355] In Canada, see *Minister of Justice v Blank* (n202), in which it was held that litigation privilege terminates at the conclusion of the relevant litigation.   [356] *The Aegis Blaze* [1986] 1 Lloyd's Rep 203.

[357] [1955] 2 QB 195, [1955] 2 All ER 173.   [358] *Minter v Priest* (n331), 579.

that the result would be different if the claim against the witness were in respect of the very same subject matter in the original litigation.[359]

If a lawyer swears that a question cannot be answered without disclosing communications made to him professionally by his client, his oath is conclusive unless it appears from the nature of the question that the privilege cannot be applicable.[360] There is little case law on this subject due, no doubt, to the fact that the issue of legal professional privilege is most frequently raised in connection with pre-trial disclosure of documents that the judge has power to inspect.[361]

Privilege may, however, be claimed by one not strictly a client of the legal adviser where common interest privilege arises.[362] In the case of corporate bodies, no privilege can be claimed against shareholders,[363] except in respect of material coming into existence in the course of, and for the purpose of, hostile litigation between the shareholders and the corporation.[364] In this context also, it is important to distinguish between legal advice obtained, or sought,[365] personally and corporately by directors of a corporate body.[366] It seems that within a corporation it is necessary to identify some subset of employees as the client.

A very restrictive, and odd, definition of the client in earlier proceedings[367] by the Court of Appeal in this regard contributed to the difficulties of the *Three Rivers* litigation, and approval of it was conspicuously withheld[368] by the House of Lords in the latter.[369]

At common law, the rule was clear that legal professional privilege did not attach to documents or things that had come into existence before the relationship of solicitor and client had become established, even though submitted to a legal adviser for his advice,[370] or sent by him to a third party in connection with litigation.[371] The privilege was regarded as that of the client, and if the document or thing were not protected in the hands of the client, it could not attract protection merely by being submitted to a legal adviser.[372] The rule is now stated by the Police and Criminal Evidence Act 1984.

---

[359] *Lee v South West Thames Regional Health Authority* [1985] 2 All ER 385, [1985] 1 WLR 845.

[360] *Morgan v Shaw* (1819) 4 Madd 54.

[361] A power that the majority of the High Court of Australia in *Grant v Downs* (1976) 135 CLR 674 felt should be exercised more readily: see CPR 31.19(6)(a).

[362] 444. Carefully distinguished in *Re Teleglobe Communications Corp* 493 F3d 345 (CA3, 2007) from joint privilege.

[363] *Woodhouse & Co Ltd v Woodhouse* (1914) 30 TLR 559; *CAS (Nominees) Ltd v Nottingham Forest plc* [2001] 1 All ER 954.

[364] Then even material created under a joint retainer: *Commercial Union Assurance Co v Mander* [1996] 2 LlR 640. See also in Australia, *Yunghanns v Elfic Pty Ltd* [2000] VSC 113, 1 VLR 92; and in New Zealand, *Gemini Personnel Ltd v Morgan and Banks* [2001] 1 NZLR 14.

[365] *South Australia v Barrett* (1995) 64 SASR 73.

[366] See e.g. *GE Capital Commercial Finance Ltd v Sutton* [2003] EWHC 1648, and Loughrey (2005) 9 *E&P* 183; for a particularly clear exposition of the position in the United States, see *Re Grand Jury Investigation No 83–30557* 577 F Supp 777 (ND Ga, 1983).   [367] *Three Rivers (No 5)* (n205).

[368] Since the point had become moot, and leave to appeal in the earlier proceedings had been refused.

[369] Lord Scott [48], Lord Rodger [49], Baroness Hale [63], and Lord Carswell [118].

[370] *R v Peterborough Justices, ex p Hicks* [1978] 1 All ER 225, [1977] 1 WLR 1371 (forged power of attorney deposited for legal advice in relation to impending prosecution).

[371] *R v King* [1983] 1 All ER 929, [1983] 1 WLR 411 (document sent by defence to handwriting expert to use for comparison with prosecution documents in connection with impending prosecution). This case disapproved comments in *Frank Truman Export Ltd v Metropolitan Police Comr* (n291), and endorsed the criticism of them made in the 5th edn (1979) of this work.

[372] Now Police and Criminal Evidence Act 1984 s 10(1)(c).

Other confidential material passing between solicitor and client, although not protected by this privilege,[373] is nevertheless subject to a special procedure to secure access under the Police and Criminal Evidence Act 1984.[374]

Secondary evidence

A legal adviser owes a twofold duty to his client with regard to confidential communications: first, he must claim privilege for them in legal proceedings; second, he must not disclose their contents to anyone without the client's consent.[375] A problem may occur when those contents have become known to a third party who wishes to prove them in litigation against the client. The disclosure may have been due to the adviser's wilful or negligent breach of duty; to accident; or to the wrongful act of a third party. The information sought to be proved in the litigation may be the outcome of oral communication or the previous reading of a document, but more often than not it will be contained in a copy of a privileged document. In *Calcraft v Guest*,[376] the Court of Appeal allowed copies of proofs of witnesses with notes on the evidence in a former claim brought by the claimant's predecessor in title to be put in by the defendant. In that case, the originals had accidentally fallen into the defendant's hands, but the principle of the decision applies to all methods of obtaining. It overlaps with the rule that has already been mentioned in Section 2 of Chapter IV and to which further reference is made in Section 3 of Chapter X, that illegally and improperly obtained evidence is admissible if it is relevant. Thus in *Re Briamore Manufacturing*,[377] in which inadvertent disclosure of privileged documents was made, its receiver made notes and copies of some, but the mistake was discovered before receipt of a request for copies of all, which was refused. It was held to be futile[378] to maintain such refusal since, as a result of *Calcraft v Guest*,[379] the mistaken receiver could use all of his secondary evidence at the trial, and it was clearly preferable to have it conducted on the basis of the best evidence, namely the original documents.

One exception to the principle of *Calcraft v Guest* occurs when a document subject to legal professional privilege brought into court by one party, is improperly obtained by his opponent, and then sought to be put into evidence by the wrongdoer. In *ITC Film Distributors v Video Exchange Ltd*,[380] Warner J restrained the use of documents obtained in such a way on the basis that the interests of the proper administration of justice so required. This restriction does not, however, apply when the potential user has obtained

---

[373] Ibid. s 14(2).

[374] See *R v Central Criminal Court, ex p Francis & Francis* (n209); *R v Inner London Crown Court, ex p Baines & Baines* [1988] QB 579, [1987] 3 All ER 1025. See also Intrusive Surveillance Code of Practice [2.4], [2.6].

[375] For the stringency of this duty, see *per* Lord Millett *Bolkiah v KPMG* [1999] 2 AC 222, [1999] 1 All ER 517; 235G, 527f. It applies also to any interpreter who is used to assist with the provision of legal advice: *Bozkurt v Thames Magistrates' Court* [2001] EWHC Admin 400, [2002] RTR 246, [18].   [376] (n8).

[377] [1986] 3 All ER 132, [1986] 1 WLR 1429. *R v Cottrill* [1997] Crim LR 56 is another (prosecution allowed to adduce in cross-examination of the accused as a previous inconsistent statement one supplied to them by his former solicitors).

[378] It is not futile if the secondary evidence is incomplete, and the fact that an application is made strongly suggests that the party making it has not got all that he wishes: see *Hooker Corp Ltd v Darling Harbour Authority* (1987) 9 NSWLR 538.   [379] Which was conceded to apply.

[380] (n9). Where the police seek to use intercepted privileged communications between the accused and his lawyer, it amounts to a breach of the Convention on Human Rights: *S v Switzerland* (1991) 14 EHRR 670.

the document without impropriety. Thus in *R v Tompkins*,[381] a note that the accused had written to his counsel was found on the floor of the courtroom during an adjournment and handed to prosecuting counsel who then used it to devastating effect in cross-examination.

By far the most common occurrence is that in which there is no impropriety,[382] but in which, under the pressure of litigation, a privileged document is disclosed in error. If *Calcraft v Guest* stood alone, there would be little question but that privilege would be lost, and secondary evidence of the privileged material admissible. But it does not stand alone. In *Lord Ashburton v Pape*,[383] the defendant, a bankrupt, obtained possession of correspondence passing between Lord Ashburton and his solicitor, taking copies before he returned it. Lord Ashburton sought, and eventually secured, an unqualified injunction against any use being made of those copies on the general ground that equity will act to restrain a breach of confidence. It was unclear exactly how these two rules related to each other.[384] The matter was clarified by the Court of Appeal, as explained in *Webster v James Chapman & Co*. The issue is governed by the principle of *Ashburton v Pape* so long as any relief is practicable, that is, until the documents have been used, or otherwise relied upon, in the relevant litigation.[385] It is not necessary to commence separate proceedings; an application can be made at any time. It seems that this relief depends upon purely equitable considerations, and is largely unaffected by the potential application of the privilege. Even in a case in which the privilege is established, it may be outweighed by the public interest in the proper administration of justice, for example where evidence has been forged and is proposed to be used in an attempt to mislead the court.[386] The judge should take into account both any degree of impropriety in obtaining or using the material, and, on the other hand, the importance to the administration of justice of securing and using as much relevant evidence as possible. Familiar equitable principles, such as the effect of delay, may apply. The main influence of the privilege may reside in the undesirability of subverting the rule limiting professional privilege for confidential communications to those made in connection with legal advice or litigation. It is necessary also to consider the question of any implied waiver when any carelessness leading to disclosure is that of a party in conducting the very litigation in which the document is to be used.[387] In some

---

381 (1977) 67 Cr App Rep 181. See also *Re Girouard and the Queen* (1982) 138 DLR (3d) 730; but in New Zealand, it has been held that a policeman could not testify to a conversation between a solicitor and his client that he had, without impropriety, overheard: *R v Uljee* (n9), a decision preferred to *Tompkins* (n9) in *obiter dicta* by Nourse LJ in *Goddard v Nationwide Building Society* [1987] QB 670, [1986] 3 All ER 264; 686, 272.

382 Although in *English and American Insurance Co Ltd v Herbert Smith & Co* [1988] FSR 232, the Vice-Chancellor intimated that, to peruse plainly confidential material known at the time to be privileged, was not entirely innocent, even though received in error. Such material should be returned to the sender without further scrutiny, and if scrutinized, the adviser should no longer continue to act: *Ablitt v Mills & Reeve* (1995) The Times, 25 October.   383 [1913] 2 Ch 469.

384 See Tapper (1972) 35 *MLR* 83; Heydon (1974) 37 *MLR* 601.

385 In *Shaw v Harris (No 1)* (1992) 3 Tas R 153, this principle was applied to documents secured without impropriety from the courtroom. Even that is no longer decisive under CPR 31.22, which deals with this very situation, and invests the judge with a wide discretion.

386 As in *ISTIL Group Inc v Zahoor* [2003] EWHC 165 (Ch), [2003] 2 All ER 252, [112]. For discussion of the issue in Australia, see *DPP (Cwth) v Kane* (1997) 140 FLR 468.

387 In Australia, this situation has been held to fall outside the concept of implied waiver: *Kingston v State Fire Commission* (1995) 8 Tas R 152.

situations, extrinsic duties may compel disclosure to the party seeking to use the information, and in such cases, neither privilege nor the equity to restrain use can be invoked. Nor may the equitable duty prevail against the interest of the Crown in conducting a public prosecution.

The resultant law can be criticized on two grounds: first, the contrast between *Calcraft v Guest* and *Lord Ashburton v Pape* makes the client's success in getting evidence excluded depend on the date at which he found out that he was the victim of a wrong-doer; second, the distinction between public prosecutions and other legal proceedings is unjustified. If they can be answered, the answer to the first criticism seems to be that trials at which it was claimed that the contents of a confidential document ought not to be put in evidence, although no previous injunction had been obtained, would be unduly protracted by the collateral inquiry into the circumstances in which the document was obtained; the answer to the second criticism may be that, in criminal proceedings, the accused receives as much protection as he should receive from the law of privilege in the strict sense, and it would be going too far to afford him the protection afforded by the law of confidentiality.

LITIGATION[388] PRIVILEGE[389]

This second head of legal professional privilege was distinguished only later from that for legal advice. Its contours are obscure: partly because it was distinguished later; partly because the two overlap, since the central case of legal advice is indeed advice rendered in connection with ongoing litigation;[390] and partly because the culture of litigation is currently changing.[391] The traditional position at common law was that litigation was conducted in a wholly adversary fashion, with nothing revealed to an opponent except the statement of claim and pleadings. Thereafter, little further[392] disclosure of a party's case took place until witnesses were called to testify to prove the allegations upon which the pleadings were premised. It was axiomatic that law and *not* evidence was to be pleaded. Inroads were made upon this procedure in the nineteenth century, when some incidents[393] of the very different form of trial in Chancery were engrafted on to the old common law system.[394]

---

[388] The extent to which this extends to 'quasi-litigation' such as statutory and non-statutory tribunals, and to witnesses giving evidence to such tribunals, was canvassed in *Three Rivers District Council v Bank of England (No 6)* [2004] EWCA Civ 218, [2004] QB 916, [31]–[37]. In Canada proceedings before a coroner do not sustain this branch: *Hudson Bay Mining and Smelting Co v Cummings* (2006) 272 DLR (4th) 419.

[389] While by no means identical, this head of privilege resembles that isolated in the United States as 'lawyers' work product': see *Hickman v Taylor* 329 US 495 (1946). Its differentiation from legal advice privilege by Lord Denning MR in *Buttes Gas and Oil Co v Hammer (No 3)* (n299); 243, 474 was described as orthodox by Bingham LJ in *Ventouris v Mountain* [1991] 3 All ER 472, [1991] 1 WLR 607; 482a, 617D.

[390] Indeed, in *Re Barings plc* [1998] Ch 356, [1998] 1 All ER 673, Scott VC favoured the view that litigation privilege is effectively a subset of legal advice privilege, although he acknowledged binding authority to the contrary.

[391] See Lord Donaldson MR in *Mercer v Chief Constable of Lancashire* [1991] 2 All ER 504, [1991] 1 WLR 367; 508,373. This change largely dictated the tenor of the Civil Procedure Rules, and in *Three Rivers (No 5)* (n213), [29], Lord Scott favoured re-examination of the scope of litigation privilege.

[392] Although clarification was permitted by way of requests for particulars.

[393] Especially pretrial discovery. Scepticism was sometimes expressed in Chancery as to the competence of the common lawyers to handle these doctrines: see Jessel MR in *Anderson v Bank of British Columbia* (1876) 2 Ch D 644, 654.

[394] See Williams (1990) 9 *Civ JQ* 139, to which the editor is greatly indebted in this section.

It remained the case, however, that a party's 'brief' remained immune from discovery, since its revelation would have been completely contrary to the adversarial system of litigation then employed.[395] The strength of this view is encapsulated in the words of James LJ in *Anderson v Bank of British Columbia*[396] that:

...as you have no right to see your adversary's brief, you have no right to see that which comes into existence merely as the materials for the brief.

Thus communications with potential witnesses by lawyer,[397] or by client for onward communication to his lawyer,[398] and the lawyer's own documentary preparation for the litigation in prospect, remain immune from discovery.[399] Matters are, however, changing, and litigation is conducted to a much greater extent with cards on the table.[400] For example, an expert report[401] must now disclose the instructions upon the basis of which it was created,[402] and witness statements of fact upon which it relies must also be disclosed.[403] Three aspects of litigation privilege will be considered here: the extent to which a lawyer's own work in preparation for litigation can be shielded from his client's opponent; the protection afforded to communications with third parties within the context of litigation; and the question of communication with an opponent.

The legal adviser's own work

There is no doubt that this has to be protected to some extent to make adversarial litigation a feasible proposition. The question is really one of how far it extends. It seems that the essential criterion is whether or not the particular disclosure is likely to reveal the structure of the resister's case. It has been held that disclosure of a selection of pieces of evidence may be protected upon such a basis.[404] This may necessitate the drawing of highly technical

---

[395] In *Re Strachan* [1895] 1 Ch 439, Lindley LJ said 'our rules of evidence and of discovery are not based upon the theory that it is advantageous to let each side know what the other can prove, but rather the reverse'. It is significant that this view was explicitly rejected on account of the new practice of litigation in *Trade Practices Commission v Ampol Petroleum (Victoria) Pty Ltd* (n264).

[396] (n393), 656. The statement was *obiter dictum*, but strong for that very reason, since it was made without any impulsion from the exigency of the litigation in question.

[397] *Curling v Perring* (1835) 2 My & K 380. Including negotiations for granting immunity to a prosecution witness: *R v King* [2007] 2 NZLR 137.

[398] *Linstead v East Sussex, Brighton and Hove Health Authority* [2001] PIQR P356 (witness statement prepared by client); and in Australia, *Saunders v Comr of Australian Federal Police* (1998) 160 ALR 469 (aide-mémoire prepared by client in preparation for meeting with legal advisers).

[399] Unaffected by the advent of the Human Rights Act 1998: see *Linstead* (n398) [22].

[400] Contrasted by the district judge in *Khan v Armaguard Ltd* [1994] 3 All ER 545 with the older 'adversarial cat-and-mouse' approach, and said by Woolf LJ in *B v John Wyeth & Brother Ltd* [1992] 1 All ER 443, 447 to be one where the cards are placed on the table *face up*. It is interesting to note that even within the EU, a strict view is being taken of when access to documents required for the purposes of litigation may be refused: *Interporc Im-Und Export gmbh v EC Commission* [1998] 2 CMLR 82, [49].

[401] For a stimulating and perceptive account of the whole area, see Pattenden (2000) 4 *E&P* 213.

[402] CPR 35.10(4); although this does not extend to earlier drafts: *Jackson v Marley Davenport Ltd* (n290). The position is different in Australia: see *Sevic v Roarty* (n294). See Edis (2007) 26 CJQ 40 arguing for abolition of privilege in relation to expert witnesses.

[403] *Malcolm Electroplating Group v West Midlands PTE* (2 April 2003, unreported) LT.

[404] *Lyell v Kennedy (No 3)* (n278); *Dubai Bank Ltd v Galadari (No 7)* [1992] 1 All ER 658. The continued validity of this line of authority has been doubted in Australia: see *Bond v JN Taylor Holdings Ltd* (1992) 57 SASR 21, 46.

distinctions.[405] It may also lead to some unpalatable results if all of the incidents of legal advice privilege are to be applied to it.[406] The impact of the compulsory disclosure of witness statements remains contentious, and some consider that a new category of privilege is required to regulate just what can, and cannot, be done with such disclosed statements before their adduction in evidence,[407] or in consequence of their preparation, or service, in different litigation, sometimes between different parties.[408] No privilege attaches to a purely objective note of evidence[409] taken in open court, but an opponent can obtain disclosure of such a note only in exceptional cases.[410]

Communications with third parties[411]

An important distinction between legal advice and litigation heads arises from the fact that, when litigation is not contemplated, communications between the adviser and third parties to enable him to obtain information before giving his opinion are not normally privileged. This was decided in the leading case of *Wheeler v Le Marchant*,[412] where the defendant was obliged to produce reports made to his solicitor by a surveyor about property that became the subject of litigation, the litigation not having been contemplated when the reports were made. Cotton LJ observed that such documents had hitherto been protected only when made in contemplation of some litigation, and he did not consider that all communications between a solicitor and a third person in the course of advising clients ought to be protected. Both client and legal adviser can act through an agent, and it is often a difficult question whether the communication was between client and legal adviser through an agent, in which case, legal advice privilege is apposite and litigation need not be contemplated, or whether the intermediary is not to be regarded as the alter ego of client or legal adviser, in which case, the availability of the privilege depends upon the contemplation of litigation.[413]

For communications between client or legal adviser and third parties to be privileged, there must be a definite prospect of litigation in contemplation by the client, and not a

---

[405] As in *Lyell v Kennedy (No 3)* (n278) in which it was recognized that a reference in a report to 'the tomb of George Duncan' might have to be treated differently from a reference to 'the tomb of *the said* George Duncan'.

[406] See *Dingle v Commonwealth Development Bank of Australia* (1989) 91 ACR 239, in which Pincus J remarked that, on the 'once-privileged always privileged basis', it would mean that witness statements taken by a legal adviser for A in litigation between A and B, never shown to A or used in the litigation, could be insulated from use in litigation between total strangers entirely at A's whim.

[407] See Grainger (1995) 145 *NLJ* 961, 1062. The obligation is expressed in CPR 32.4(2) unqualified by any new privilege, although the judge is invested with a considerable measure of control over how it may subsequently be used: see CPR 32.12.

[408] As in Australia in *Australian Competition Commission v Cadbury Schweppes Pty Ltd* [2009] FCAFC 32, see Pobjoy (2009) 28 *CJQ* 46.

[409] But any annotations for the purposes of the action will be privileged, so conceded in *Imerman v Tchenguiz* [2009] EWHC 2902, (QB), [10]; see in Ireland in *MFM v PW* [2001] 3 IR 462.

[410] *Comfort v Department of Constitutional Affairs* (2005) 102(35) LSG 42.

[411] The privilege extends to communications passing between the members of a business organization or government department and its salaried permanent legal advisers: *Alfred Crompton Amusement Machines Ltd v Customs and Excise Comrs (No 2)* (n242) (the point was not argued before the House of Lords); there can be little doubt that this would be true of confidential communications in order to obtain legal advice simpliciter.

[412] (1881) 17 Ch D 675.

[413] See *C-C Bottlers Ltd v Lion Nathan Ltd* (n273).

mere vague anticipation of it;[414] it is not, however, necessary that a basis for claim should have arisen,[415] nor is it essential that the third party should anticipate litigation.[416] This was re-examined in *USA v Philip Morris Inc*,[417] where the Court of Appeal recognized that it was difficult to express the idea precisely, but intimated that a mere possibility was not sufficient, although it was not necessary that the likelihood of litigation exceed 50 per cent.[418] The communication must have been made, or the document brought into existence,[419] for the purpose of enabling the legal adviser to advise or act in the litigation. Normally this gives rise to no particular difficulty. A mere request for information, unaccompanied by any suggestion that it is required for legal advice, is clearly not privileged, however probable the litigation may have been at the time of the request.[420] Where information is sought from a party to the ultimate litigation there is no need to disclose an intention to institute litigation,[421] although a positive misrepresentation may bar a subsequent claim for privilege.[422] There have been, however, a number of troublesome borderline cases in which the communication was made for more than one purpose, and it was difficult to say much more with regard to the decisions in these cases than that they showed that the utilization of the communication in litigation must have been one of its main purposes, even though the client may have intended to settle the claim without litigation if he could.[423]

Examples of material that had been held not to be privileged include: reports made to the directors of a railway company simply for the purpose of conveying information even if litigation were contemplated;[424] information supplied by a member of a trade union to officials of the union to enable them to decide whether to refer his claim for wrongful dismissal to the union's solicitor for legal action;[425] and the report of a private inquiry into an accident, aimed primarily at preventing the recurrence of such an event,[426] especially when required by a company rule.[427] Examples falling on the other side of the line include: reports of an accident made to the director of a company to be placed before the company's solicitors;[428] and correspondence by the Transport Commission with its servants concerning the cause of an accident intended to be placed before the Commission's solicitors.[429]

---

[414] *Bray on Discovery*, cited by Lord Denning MR in *Alfred Crompton Amusement Machines Ltd v Customs and Excise Comrs (No 2)* (n242) 130, 377.   [415] *Bristol Corp v Cox* (n241).

[416] *Di Pietrantonio v Austin Hospital (Heidelberg)* [1958] VR 325.   [417] (n309).

[418] [68]. It further distinguished, [72], between cases where the litigation was apprehended by a potential party, and by a potential third party.

[419] In *R v R* (n211), the ambit of the privilege was extended to an expert opinion based upon a sample of blood provided by the client through his legal advisers, to the expert for the purpose of supplying an expert opinion (which was not, in fact, used).

[420] *Anderson v Bank of British Columbia* (n393) (an odd decision on the facts).

[421] Especially where there is a pre-existing duty to supply the information: *Plummers v Debenham Plc* [1986] BCLC 447, 459.   [422] *LFEPA v Halcrow Gilbert & Co* [2004] EWHC 2340, [2005] BLR 18, [18].

[423] *Ogden v London Electric Rly Co* (1933) 149 LT 476.

[424] *Woolley v North London Rly Co* (1869) LR 4 Cf 602.

[425] *Jones v Great Central Rly Co* [1910] AC 4.

[426] *Longthorn v British Transport Commission* [1959] 2 All ER 32, [1959] 1 WLR 530; *Warner v Women's Hospital* [1954] VLR 410.

[427] *West London Pipeline and Storage Ltd v Total UK Ltd* [2008] EWHC 1729 (Comm).

[428] *Southwark Water Co v Quick* (1878) 3 QBD 315; *Ankin v London and North Eastern Rly Co* [1930] 1 KB 527.

[429] *Seabrook v British Transport Commission* [1959] 2 All ER 15, [1959] 1 WLR 509; *Britten v FH Pilcher & Sons* [1969] 1 All ER 491.

In *Alfred Crompton Amusement Machines Ltd v Customs and Excise Comrs (No 2)*,[430] the company notified the Commissioners in 1967 that it was dissatisfied with the agreed formula under which it had been paying purchase tax. The prescribed procedure in the event of disagreement was that the Commissioners should state their opinion concerning the basis on which purchase tax was payable and, if this was not accepted, the taxpayer could proceed to arbitration. The Commissioners expressed their opinion in 1968 and the parties proceeded to arbitration. Both the Court of Appeal and House of Lords took the view that the Commissioners had reasonably anticipated arbitration after receipt of the company's notification of dissatisfaction with the agreement in 1967. The Commissioners claimed legal professional privilege in respect of: first, communications with their salaried legal advisers in order to obtain advice; second, communications with their legal advisers in order to obtain evidence for the anticipated arbitration; third, internal communications with their officers and agents concerning the proper assessment of the purchase tax payable by the company; and fourth, documents received in confidence from third parties concerning the market value of machines sold by the company. There was no argument in the House of Lords with regard to the first set of communications, so the decision of the Court of Appeal that they were privileged stands; the House held that privilege attached to the second set, even if it were assumed that litigation had to be anticipated to found it; but the majority held that the third and fourth sets were not subject to legal professional privilege, because they came into existence for one single purpose—to assist the Commissioners to form an opinion about the basis on which purchase tax should be paid by the company, and not for the dual purpose of enabling an opinion to be formed and resisting the company's contentions in the arbitration. It was held that the third and fourth sets of communications ought not to be disclosed in the public interest, a matter that is considered in the next chapter.

Having regard to the decision under the third and fourth heads, everything said in the House about dual or multiple purpose communications was obiter, but the majority favoured a restrictive view with regard to the recognition of privilege in such cases. In *Waugh v British Railways Board*,[431] the House of Lords was unanimous in approving a 'dominant' purpose test,[432] and overruling previous decisions of the lower courts to the extent of any inconsistency. Their Lordships felt that a restrictive 'sole purpose' test would go too far in denying privilege for communications the overwhelming purpose of which was litigation, but for which some other minor purpose could be discovered. Lord Russell, who initially favoured that test, was eventually persuaded that it would mean that it would be virtually impossible ever to raise a claim for privilege on this basis. None of their Lordships anticipated any difficulty in applying a test of dominance, which is familiar in other branches of the law.[433] The asserting party bears the burden of proving the

---

[430] (n242). See also *Silver Hill Duckling Ltd v Minister of Agriculture* [1987] IR 289.

[431] (n10) (an accident report case).

[432] For detailed exegesis in Australia, and that where purposes are equal neither can be dominant, see *Commissioner of Taxation (Cth) v Pratt Holdings Pty Ltd* [2005] FCA 1247, [30].

[433] It was subsequently applied to documents made in the course of an inquiry into the conduct of the police under s 49 of Police Act 1964 following a complaint and threat of legal action: *Neilson v Laugharne* [1981] QB 736, [1981] 1 All ER 829 (cf *Konia v Morley* [1976] 1 NZLR 455, in which the same result was reached even on the basis of the older test), and to reports on the cause of a suspicious fire commissioned by the solicitors to the insurers of the relevant premises: *Re Highgrade Traders Ltd* (n202). In Australia, a 'sole purpose' test was adopted by a majority of the High Court in *Grant v Downs* (1976) 135 CLR 674, but this

necessary basis for the privilege, usually in the form of a disclosure statement, to which the old reluctance to allow cross-examination continues to apply.[434]

A problem may arise in relation to original documents that are not subject to the privilege because themselves not made in contemplation of litigation, but which are then copied for the purpose of litigation.

In cases in which copies of documents held by third parties have been made specifically for the litigation in respect of which disclosure is sought, the privilege has been upheld.[435] If, however, the originals would have been unprivileged in the hands of the opponent, then merely copying them for the purposes of the litigation should not shield them from discovery.[436] It now seems that, in England, privilege is not available for copies of unprivileged documents, whether the original is in the hands of the client,[437] or third party,[438] and even though the copy has been made for the purpose of securing legal advice in the litigation.[439] This position acknowledges the inconvenience of distinguishing for these purposes between original and copy in the age of the photocopier, fax, and computer.[440] It has also been suggested[441] that it ignores the importance of *communication with a lawyer* in the definition of the privilege, and concentrates unduly on the status of the document. It is submitted that this criticism is misplaced, since it promotes the anomaly of distinguishing between the communication of an unprivileged original to a lawyer for advice, which must on any view be produced, and the communication of a copy for that purpose, which is not to be produced, and all of this made in a context in which the distinction has become impractical in the light of modern copying technology. It may also be dangerous by putting a premium on the disappearance of the original. Legal effect depends upon the content of the original document, and the provenance of the means of proof seems strictly secondary. If production of the original by the lawyer cannot be refused, it is hard to understand why his production of a copy should be treated differently.

Communications with opponent

It seems a truism to say that privilege cannot be claimed for communications passing between one party and another, or his agent, but the cases show that problems can

---

was rejected in s 119 of the Evidence Act 1995, and then at common law by a majority of the High Court in *Esso Australia Resources Ltd v Comr of Taxation of the Commonwealth of Australia* [1999] HCA 67, 201 CLR 49, at both trial and pre-trial stages. The dominant purpose test applies in Canada: see *Edgar v Auld* (2000) 184 DLR (4th) 747; New Zealand, *Guardian Royal Exchange Assurance of New Zealand Ltd v Stuart* [1985] 1 NZLR 596; and South Africa, *A Sweidan and King (Pty) Ltd v Zim Israel Navigation Co Ltd* 1986 (1) SA 515.

[434] *West London Pipeline and Storage Ltd v Total UK Ltd* (n427), [90].

[435] *The Palermo* (1883) 9 PD 6; *Watson v Cammell Laird & Co (Shipbuilders and Engineers) Ltd* [1959] 2 All ER 757, [1959] 1 WLR 702. See also *Hodgkinson v Simms* (1988) 55 DLR (4th) 577, in which the court applied the principle to a single document. It is unclear that the reasoning of these cases can survive the more general endorsement of disclosure by third parties in CPR 31.17.

[436] *Chadwick v Bowman* (1886) 16 QBD 561.

[437] *R v Board of Inland Revenue, ex p Goldberg* [1989] QB 267, [1988] 3 All ER 248, in which the privilege was, in fact, allowed, but the case was held in *Dubai Bank Ltd v Galadari* [1990] Ch 98, [1989] 3 All ER 769, 108, 775 to have been wrongly decided.   [438] *Dubai Bank* (n437).

[439] *Lubrizol Corp v Esso Petroleum Ltd* [1992] 1 WLR 957. Different views prevail elsewhere: see, in Australia, *Federal Police Comr v Propend Finance Ltd* (1997) 188 CLR 501; and in Canada, *Regional Municipality of Ottawa-Carleton v Consumers' Gas Co Ltd* (1990) 74 DLR (4th) 742.

[440] *Lubrizol Corp v Esso Petroleum Ltd* (n439), 961.   [441] By McHugh J in *Propend* (n439), 552.

arise. In *Grant v South Western and County Properties Ltd*,[442] the claimant caused a tape recording to be made of a conversation between himself and one of the defendants, and it was held that he could not claim privilege from the obligation to disclose the recording. So far as the defendant was concerned, there was no intention that it should be placed before the claimant's solicitor; so far as the claimant himself was concerned, what he said to the defendant could not be privileged. From the point of view of the privilege, the recording was the equivalent of a letter and copy letter exchanged between the parties. Conversely, the mere intention to place into the hands of an opponent a document received from an expert in the course of preparing for litigation is not sufficient to displace the privilege if the legal adviser changes his mind, and never does despatch the document.[443]

In *Baker v London and South Western Rly Co*,[444] a case in which executors were claiming damages for personal injuries to the deceased, the defendants alleged that their medical officer had visited him and negotiated a settlement. The officer's report was held unprivileged. The decision seems to have been correct on its particular facts because, subject to the without prejudice rule, there is no reason why privilege should attach to discussions aimed at achieving a settlement.[445] The judgment suggests that privilege could never attach to an agent's report about an interview with the opposite party, but subsequent authority reveals that statements taken from the victim on behalf of a potential defendant for the purpose of laying them before his solicitor are privileged in accident cases.

In *Feuerheerd v London General Omnibus Co*,[446] the claimant mistakenly believed that she was speaking to her solicitor about the accident in which she had sustained her injuries, when she was in fact being interrogated by the company's claims manager. It was held that the defendants could claim privilege for the statement, as a documentary record made for the purpose of laying it before their solicitors. The Court of Appeal laid stress on the fact that the manager acted in good faith. Had he not done so, the claim to privilege would presumably have failed on the ground that the defendants could not take advantage of their agent's wrong.[447] There was no discussion of the effect of the claimant's mistake as to the person to whom she was speaking. Subject to this point, there is no obvious reason why the victim's statement should be differentiated from those of other witnesses taken on behalf of a potential defendant shortly after the occurrence of an accident. A cynic is entitled to ask why, if the victim does not take the precaution of getting a copy of his statement at the time it was made, he should have a right to its production at a later stage in order to trim his evidence accordingly.[448]

---

[442] [1975] Ch 185, 199. See also *Telebooth Pty Ltd v Telstra Corp Ltd* [1994] 1 VR 337.

[443] *Derby & Co Ltd v Weldon (No 9)* [1991] 2 All ER 901, [1991] 1 WLR 652.

[444] (1868) LR 3 QB 91.

[445] Neither litigation privilege, nor that for without-prejudice negotiations, is waived by disclosure of a mere attendance note recording the fact of a conversation with an opponent's legal adviser: *Parry v News Group Newspapers Ltd* [1990] NLJR 1719.   [446] [1918] 2 KB 565.

[447] Although it might have been argued that, if a person may steal a document and put it in evidence, there is no reason why evidence should not be given of what occurred at any interview obtained by deception.

[448] See the judgment of Thesiger J in *Britten v F H Pilcher and Sons Ltd* (n429). See also Cotton LJ in *Kennedy v Lyell* (1883) 23 Ch D 387, 404. In Australia, see *Aydin v Australian Iron and Steel Pty Ltd* [1984] 3 NSWLR 684; *Hadley v Baddock* (n334).

EXCEPTIONS[449]

There are a number of exceptional situations[450] in which material that would otherwise be privileged must be disclosed for reasons of policy. There are similarities in the policies that determine the exclusion at common law[451] of communications to facilitate the commission, or evasion from detection, of crime and fraud; those to establish the innocence of the accused; or to those that are claimed in the course of a dispute between client and legal adviser.[452] These will be considered first, and then a residual category of cases in which there has been some statutory intervention.

Communications to facilitate[453] crime or fraud[454]

In the leading case of *R v Cox and Railton*,[455] the Court for Crown Cases Reserved decided that, if a client applies to a lawyer for advice intended to guide him in the commission of a crime or fraud, the legal adviser being ignorant of the purpose for which his advice is wanted, the communication between the two is not privileged.[456] Accordingly, a solicitor was compelled to disclose what passed between the prisoners and himself when they consulted him with reference to drawing up a bill of sale that was alleged to be fraudulent. As Stephen J pointed out when delivering the judgment of the court, if the law were otherwise, a man intending to commit treason or murder might safely take legal advice for the purpose of enabling himself to do so with impunity, and the solicitor to whom the application was made would not be at liberty to give information against his client in order to frustrate his criminal purpose.[457] If the lawyer participates in the criminal purpose, he ceases to act as a lawyer.[458] Stephen J concluded that the court must judge whether the evidence is admissible on the special facts of each particular case, and every precaution should be taken against compelling unnecessary disclosures. It has been held not enough, in Canada, that a party consults a lawyer as to his course of action, and then on the basis of the advice commits what turns out to be a crime.[459]

---

[449] Some authorities would deny that there are any real exceptions to the privilege, and that the situations described below, to the extent that they are allowed, merely fall outside the ambit of the privilege: see Lord Taylor CJ in *R v Derby Magistrates' Court, ex p B* (n4); 508, 509, 542d—'no exception should be allowed to the absolute nature of legal professional privilege, once established'. See also McHugh J in *Carter v Managing Partner of Northmore Hale Davy & Leake* (1995) 183 CLR 121, at 163, '...the so-called exceptions to the doctrine are in truth not exceptions at all'. This may be no more than a matter of semantics, since it is quite clear that the ambit of communication with a legal adviser, which may be disclosed, notwithstanding the privilege, cannot be foretold, in advance of any such consultation, with much accuracy.

[450] Wu argues in (2005) 24 *CJQ* 246 that claims in restitution for money paid under mistake of law should constitute another.

[451] Although the first now also finds statutory expression in the Police and Criminal Evidence Act 1984, s 10(2).

[452] In Canada, there is also an exception where suppression may endanger public safety: *Jones v Smith* [1999] 1 SCR 455 (applied there in a situation resembling that in England of *W v Egdell* (n263)).

[453] The exclusion applies also to communications that themselves amount to criminal offences: *C v C* [1993] 4 All ER 690.   [454] See generally Newbould (1990) 53 *MLR* 472.

[455] (1884) 14 QBD 153.

[456] In Australia, the converse situation in which the lawyer, but not the client, has the fraudulent intent also comes within the exception: *Clements, Dunne & Bell Pty Ltd v Comr of Australian Federal Police* [2001] FCA 1858, 188 ALR 515, [220].   [457] Cf *R v Smith* (1915) 11 Cr App Rep 229.

[458] In *Gemini Personnel Ltd v Morgan and Banks Ltd* (n364), this was regarded as a key consideration in determining whether the situation fell entirely outside the privilege, or constituted an exception to it.

[459] *Campbell and Shirose v R* (n242).

The doctrine of *R v Cox and Railton* has been applied to civil cases[460] in which fraud[461] was alleged, and it has since been stressed that there should be prima facie evidence[462] that it was the client's intention to obtain advice substantially[463] in furtherance of his criminal or fraudulent purpose before the court will consider whether the situation comes within the exception to the rule relating to professional privilege.[464] It seems that the manufacture of fraudulent evidence,[465] or in the case of conveyancing transactions, the object of depriving a creditor of his security,[466] are enough, and opinions have differed as to whether a mere mis-statement of the purpose for seeking a loan will suffice.[467] It was decided in *Kuwait Airways Corp v Iraqi Airways Co*[468] that, in principle, the exception applies as much to litigation as to advice privilege, although where the allegation relates to the very matters in dispute in the litigation, the court will require very strong evidence,[469] since otherwise, as Hoffmann J remarked in *Candler v Church*,[470] a party need only allege fraud in bringing proceedings to secure sight of the whole of his opponent's brief. Where the issue is independent of the matters in dispute, weaker evidence will suffice.[471] The exception will not apply to an allegation of fraud in securing legal aid in respect of launching proceedings.[472] Still less is the privilege likely to be lost in respect of communications with their legal advisers by innocent assignees of goods obtained by the fraud of third parties.[473]

In its codification of the law relating to police powers of search, the Police and Criminal Evidence Act 1984, s 10(2) provides a statutory version of this limitation upon the privilege: 'Items held with the intention of furthering a criminal purpose are not items subject

---

[460] *Williams v Quebrada Railway, Land and Copper Co* [1895] 2 Ch 751; *Gamlen Chemical Co (UK) Ltd v Rochem Ltd (No 2)* (1979) 124 Sol Jo 276.

[461] Or abuse of statutory power: see, in England, *Dubai Aluminium Co Ltd v Al Alawi* [1999] 1 All ER 703, [1999] 1 WLR 1964; and in Australia, *Freeman v Health Insurance Commission* (1997) 157 ALR 339. It is also enough in Australia that the object was to circumvent UN sanctions: *AWB Ltd v Cole (No 5)* [2006] FCA 1234; but not to prevent the disclosure of tax avoidance communications: *Kennedy v Wallace* [2004] FCAFC 337, 213 ALR 108. Trespass and conversion would not, however, be enough: see *Dubai Aluminium*, 707h. In New Zealand, the fraud must be not merely technical, but involve actual dishonesty: see *Gemini Personnel Ltd v Morgan and Banks Ltd*, (n364).

[462] The strength of the evidence required may vary with the circumstances and the nature of the proceedings: *Derby & Co Ltd v Weldon (No 7)* [1990] 3 All ER 161, [1990] 1 WLR 1156. In *Buttes Oil Co v Hammer* (n299); 246, 486f, Lord Denning MR required the evidence to be strong, and of obvious fraud, a test found to have been passed in *Walsh Automation (Europe) Ltd v Bridgeman* [2002] EWHC 1344 (QB) (employee setting up rival company to employer). It seems that it need not come dehors the allegedly fraudulent document, which the court may inspect to determine its purpose: *R v Governor of Pentonville Prison, ex p Osman* [1989] 3 All ER 701, [1990] 1 WLR 277; *Seamar Holdings Ltd v Kupe Group Ltd* [1995] 2 NZLR 274. On the other hand, it has been held in Australia that it must be raised by admissible evidence: *Australian Federal Police Comr v Propend Finance Pty Ltd* (n439).

[463] *Royscott Spa Leasing Ltd v Lovett* [1995] BCC 502.

[464] *O'Rourke v Darbishire* (n331); *Bullivant v A-G for Victoria* [1901] AC 196.

[465] *Re David Agmashenebeli* [2001] CLC 942; *ISTIL Group Inc v Zahoor* (n386).

[466] *Barclay's Bank plc v Eustice* [1995] 4 All ER 511, [1995] 1 WLR 1238.

[467] See *Nationwide Building Society v Various Solicitors* [1998] NLJR 241, disapproving *Birmingham Midshires Mortgage Services Ltd v Phillips* [1998] PNLR 468.

[468] [2005] EWCA Civ 286, [2005] 1 WLR 2734.

[469] See also *Dubai Aluminium Co Ltd v Al Alawi* (n461). [470] [1987] NLJ Rep 451.

[471] *Kuwait Airways* [2005] EWCA Civ 286, [2005] 1 WLR 2734, [42](3), citing and perhaps reading down *R (Hallinan, Blackburn Gittings & Nott) v Crown Court at Middlesex Guildhall* [2004] EWHC 2726 (Admin), [2005] 1 WLR 766. [472] *R v Snaresbrook Crown Court, ex p DPP* [1988] QB 532, [1988] 1 All ER 315.

[473] *Banque Keyser Ullmann SA v Skandia (UK) Insurance Co Ltd* [1986] 1 Lloyd's Rep 336.

to legal privilege.' In *R v Central Criminal Court, ex p Francis & Francis*,[474] the majority of the House of Lords took the view that this provision had left the rule unaffected, and, in particular, that its reference to the intention with which documents were held was capable of referring to the intention, not of the adviser, but of the client, with the result that documents[475] held innocently by a solicitor remain outside the protection of the privilege if the client's intention is fraudulent. It seems that the restriction to 'furthering a criminal purpose' is probably no more restrictive than the position at common law in its reliance upon the concept of 'fraud', which in this context had been held not to extend to every act or scheme that was unlawful, such as, for example: an inducement of breach of contract;[476] an unsolicited letter to a client advising him that certain conduct could lead to his being prosecuted;[477] or a conveyance without consideration designed to defeat creditors.[478] It seems that, in order to determine whether documents fall within this exception, the judge himself is entitled to inspect them.[479]

Since fraud unravels all confidence, the legal adviser need not await a claim by a third party, but may himself initiate proceedings.[480]

Information tending to establish innocence

In *R v Barton*, an exception was suggested in favour of the accused in criminal proceedings, who required access to otherwise privileged materials to establish his defence,[481] analogous to a similar exception to public interest immunity.[482] Such an exception has, however, now been rejected by the highest courts both in England, in *R v Derby Magistrates ex p B*,[483] and in Australia, in *Carter v Managing Partner of Northmore Hale Davy & Leake*.[484] The English case involved a prosecution for murder in which two men were involved, one of them then tried and acquitted. The second was then charged with the murder, and sought access to the first's communications with his lawyer in advance of the first trial.[485] It was a strong case for the exception, since the first party whose communications were sought was no longer in jeopardy,[486] having been acquitted of the very crime. The House of Lords nevertheless rejected the suggested exception,[487] largely on the ground that, to allow an exception that it felt would lead to a balancing exercise in every case, would run counter to the general policy of legal professional privilege, which it saw as encouraging private

---

[474] (n209).

[475] Especially if forged: *R v Leeds Magistrates' Court, ex p Dumbleton* [1993] Crim LR 866.

[476] *Crescent Farm (Sidcup) Sports Ltd v Sterling Offices Ltd* [1972] Ch 553, [1971] 3 All ER 1192.

[477] *Butler v Board of Trade* [1971] Ch 680, [1970] 3 All ER 593.

[478] See *Re Konigsberg (a bankrupt)* [1989] 3 All ER 289, [1989] 1 WLR 1257.

[479] *R v Governor of Pentonville Prison, ex p Osman* (n462).

[480] *Finers v Miro* [1991] 1 All ER 182, [1991] 1 WLR 35.

[481] [1972] 2 All ER 1192, [1973] 1 WLR 115; accepted here in *R v Ataou* [1988] QB 798, [1988] 2 All ER 321, in Canada, in *R v Dunbar and Logan* (1982) 138 DLR (3d) 221 (but even there the evidence must be shown to be unavailable otherwise, and the test is a stringent one: see *R v Brown* 2002 SCC 32, [2002] 2 SCR 185); and in New Zealand, in *R v Craig* [1975] 1 NZLR 597; but rejected in Australia, in *R v Connell (No 2)* (1992) 8 WAR 148; and effectively, in South Africa, in *S v Safatsa* 1988 (1) SA 868.   [482] See, 492.

[483] [1996] AC 487, [1995] 4 All ER 526; for criticism, see Tapper (1996) 1 *E&P* 5.

[484] (1995) 183 CLR 121, although largely resurrected there by s 123 of the Evidence Act 1995.

[485] Which there were good reasons to suspect might have indicated his commission of the crime for which he had been acquitted.

[486] This preceded modification of the double jeopardy rule by the Criminal Justice Act 2003: see, 100.

[487] And overruled both *Barton* [1972] 2 All ER 1192, [1973] 1 WLR 115 and *Ataou* (n481).

citizens to consult lawyers, secure in the knowledge that their communications would remain forever inviolate. It is arguable that this reasoning confuses the balancing necessary to establish a *general* rule of exception with the balancing necessary to derogate from an established rule in a *particular* case, and underplays the number of situations in which what transpires in the course of communication with a lawyer, either to seek legal advice or to prepare for litigation, may be revealed contrary to the expectations, and against the wishes and interests of the client.

Although there is no reason to doubt that privilege may be successfully pleaded on behalf of the client of a solicitor called by the prosecution in a criminal case,[488] we shall see that the client's right to confidentiality as against third parties in respect of the contents of a letter written to him by his solicitor may have to yield to the Crown's right to prove them in a public prosecution.[489]

Disputes between clients and legal advisers

Since the whole point of legal professional privilege is to encourage the fullest possible disclosure between legal adviser and client, it follows that no privilege can arise between them, but only with respect to disclosure to a third party. The client may not therefore make a claim against his legal adviser, and at the same time take advantage of legal professional privilege to the adviser's disadvantage. It seems that even here, however, the privilege is recognized to exist and to inhere in the client, but if he fails to waive it, then he exposes himself to adverse inference.[490] If the privilege is waived, for example by suing a former solicitor, privileged material in the hands of subsequent legal advisers is unaffected.[491] This constraint applies not only to litigation formally between client and legal adviser, but may extend to other cases in which the interests of solicitor and client are clearly opposed.[492] This constraint is, in England, firmly rooted in fairness between lawyer and client, and if the client is suing a third party, then the privilege remains intact.[493] So, too, if a third party is suing a client's lawyer, the privilege remains intact, and if not waived may well prevent a wasted costs order from being made.[494] If the interests of different clients with a joint interest in litigation themselves become temporarily opposed, then legal advice tendered during such estrangement loses its privilege as against a third party in the main dispute, so long as such estrangement and separate advice persists.[495] Similar considerations may also apply to cases in which a third party in conflict with the client is entitled to disclosure from the legal adviser.[496] For similar reasons, privilege cannot be claimed between those already

---

[488] As it was in *R v Ataou* (n481).   [489] *Butler v Board of Trade* (n477).

[490] *Ridehaulgh v Horsefield* [1994] Ch 205, [1994] 3 All ER 848.

[491] *Paragon Finance plc v Freshfields* (n231) overruling *Hayes v Dowding* [1996] PNLR 578, and doubting *Kershaw v Whelan* [1996] 2 All ER 404, [1996] 1 WLR 358. See also *Goldberg v Ng* (n273).

[492] As in *R v Charbonneau* (1992) 74 CCC (3d) 49 (in which the legal adviser was charged with an alleged attempt to pervert the course of justice by persuading the client to commit perjury in separate proceedings. The client was a willing witness for the prosecution in the attempt proceedings against his erstwhile adviser, but sought to invoke the privilege to avoid cross-examination.)

[493] *Nederlandse Reassurantie Groep Holding NV v Bacon & Woodrow* (n307).

[494] As confirmed by the House of Lords in *Medcalf v Weatherill* [2002] UKHL 27, [2003] 1 AC 120, [2002] 3 All ER 721.   [495] *Leif Hoegh & Co A/S v Petrolsea Inc* (n326).

[496] *Brown v Guardian Royal Exchange Assurance plc* (n238) (the entitlement arose under a contract of which the client was fully aware and to which he raised no objection); but for a strict approach to the construction of such a contract, see, in New Zealand, *Nicholson v Icepak Coolstores Ltd* [1999] 3 NZLR 475.

under a mutual duty of disclosure[497] to each other.[498] The right to disclosure persists after the common interest has terminated, even despite a subsequent conflict of interest.[499]

Statutory exclusion

There are few, if any, statutes[500] abrogating[501] legal professional privilege by express reference,[502] and implied abrogation will be hard to establish.[503] In this respect, there is a striking contrast with the privilege against self-incrimination.[504] One area in which it has arisen, and caused difficulty, relates to the provision of s 1 of the Children Act 1989 that 'the child's welfare shall be the court's paramount consideration'. This matter was considered at length by the House of Lords in *Re L (a minor) (police investigation: privilege)*[505] in the context of a claim to privilege to prevent revelation to the police of a doctor's report on the death of a child,[506] prepared for the purpose of care proceedings. The majority took the view that, however absolute the privilege might be in relation to legal advice, its litigation branch could not operate to suppress the disclosure of evidence[507] that would, in other circumstances, be privileged, when in care proceedings the best interests of the child would be promoted by disclosure. The majority view would have prevented disclosure on the basis of the privilege, which it regarded as applicable in both of its branches as an 'absolute' rule.

---

[497] Right to disclosure *inter se*, and to prevent disclosure to third parties, were described in *Winterthur Swiss Insurance v AG (Manchester) Ltd (In Liq)* [2006] EWHC 839 (Comm), [79], in terms of 'sword' and 'shield'.

[498] *Brown v Guardian Royal Exchange Assurance plc* (n238) (joint retainer); *Dockrill v Coopers & Lybrand* (1994) 111 DLR (4th) 62 (partners).

[499] See *Winterthur* (n497) [81]; the precise extent of the survival of the right of access once a conflict has arisen may, however, depend upon the construction of the contractual term under which the common interest has been so created, [74], and may not exist at all if the contract has been repudiated: *Commercial Union Assurance plc v Mander* [1996] 2 Ll R 640.

[500] See *R v IRC, ex p Taylor (No 2)* [1990] 2 All ER 409 for consideration of the Taxes Management Act 1970, s 20, under which it is preserved for legal advisers, but only when so acting, and not in relation to their position as taxpayers. As noted, 438, attempted abrogation by the CPR was struck down in *General Mediterranean Holdings v Patel* (n234).

[501] It has even been suggested that any attempt to do so might be incompatible with the European Convention on Human Rights: see *R (Morgan Grenfell Ltd) v Special Comr of Income Tax* (n232) [39]. The privilege may, however, yield to a more pressing public interest under s 42 of the Freedom of Information Act 2000.

[502] See the extraordinary lengths to which Sch 1AA to the Taxes Management Act 1970 goes to preserve legal professional privilege, even in a provision substantially aimed at documents in the possession of legal advisers. In Australia in *Osland v Secretary, Department of Justice* [2008] HCA 37, 234 CLR 275 in considering an explicit power the High Court held that inspection by the judge should be undertaken before refusing access.

[503] *Morgan Grenfell* (n232), distinguishing or overruling cases to the opposite sense; *Bowman v Fels* [2005] EWCA Civ 226, [2005] 4 All ER 609, in which s 328 of the Proceeds of Crime Act 2002 was construed, after particularly detailed consideration, so as not to apply to legal advisers so acting. See also in Australia: *Yuill v Corporate Affairs Commission* (1990) 20 NSWLR 386. By contrast in *Criminal Lawyers' Association v Minister of Public Safety and Security* (2007) 220 CCC3d 343 it was held unconstitutional *not* to allow abrogation.   [504] See *Re Compass Airlines Pty Ltd* (1992) 109 ALR 119.

[505] (n204).

[506] Commissioned by the child's mother, who authorized the disclosure to the doctor of the materials in the case upon which the report had been based.

[507] The majority was careful to avoid describing this as an exception to, or as overriding, legal professional privilege.

The majority took the view that litigation privilege operated differently in non-adversarial proceedings, assimilating care proceedings to wardship proceedings[508] for this purpose. The minority rejected the sharpness of the distinction between legal advice and litigation privilege, arguing that proceedings involving children are often extremely contentious,[509] and resting ultimately on the absolute nature of legal professional privilege in both of its principal branches as a bulwark of a fair trial. The rejection of this proposition by the majority must cast some doubt upon the validity of some of the more extreme remarks in the *Derby Justices* case.[510]

Jones v G D Searle & Co Ltd[511] shows that s 33 of the Limitation Act 1980 is a clear instance of a statutory exception to the rule of legal professional privilege, for the claimant was required to answer an interrogatory inquiring whether the legal advice he had received was favourable or unfavourable. The section empowers the court to give leave to bring a claim out of time having regard to a number of factors affecting the delay, including the nature of the advice received. It has, however, become increasingly common to preserve the privilege by express provision,[512] and in criminal cases, the Police and Criminal Evidence Act 1984 has not only insulated material covered by the privilege from the issue of search warrants, but has also invalidated all previous legislation to the extent of any inconsistency.[513] The strongest recent example of implied abrogation is represented by *Re McE* where the House of Lords held that the omission of explicit preservation of the privilege by the Regulation of Investigatory Powers Act, together with explicit reference to surveillance of legally privileged conversations in the Code of Practice supplementing the legislation, was sufficient.[514]

Given the strong aversion to abrogation of this privilege so far as compulsory disclosure or use in evidence is concerned, attention has been diverted to the extent to which it inhibits the operation of compulsory powers of search when there is a possibility that privileged material may be found. Difficulties exposed by case law in this regard should now be resolved by express statutory provision.[515]

THE CLAIMS OF OTHER RELATIONSHIPS

The distinction between professional privilege and the protection of confidentiality lies at the root of the present law concerning disclosure by doctors and priests of statements made by a patient or penitent. There is no doubt that voluntary disclosure of such matters

---

[508] See *Re A (minors) (disclosure of material)* [1991] 2 FLR 473. It is interesting that, in New Zealand, in *R v H* (n238), the Court of Appeal felt that the privilege did not apply in the same way where the legal adviser was appointed by the court rather than the client, as is often the case with the legal representation of children.

[509] Although such an argument seems to invest the word 'adversarial' with its popular, rather than with its technical, meaning, as the minority itself recognized.

[510] But see *S County Council v B* [2000] 2 FLR 161 for the converse view of its relation with the reasoning in *Re L* (n204).   [511] [1978] 3 All ER 654, [1979] 1 WLR 101.

[512] See e.g. Data Protection Act 1998, Sch [7 10]; Proceeds of Crime Act 2002, s 330(6)(b); Enterprise Act 2002, s 196(1).   [513] Section 9(2).

[514] [2009] UKHL 15, [2009] 1 AC 908. It was also, Lord Phillips dissenting, held sufficient to prevail over earlier statutory provisions authorizing professional consultations in private.

[515] Criminal Justice and Police Act 2001, s 50, and Sch 1: see *Bates v Chief Constable Avon and Somerset Police* [2009] EWHC 942 (Admin).

would be restrained by injunction. There is equally no doubt that, in England,[516] such statements are not privileged from compulsory disclosure in court by the person to whom they are made. For this reason, it may be doubted whether an injunction would ever extend to compulsory disclosure in court, but this has not been the subject of case law to date.[517] The problem is simply whether the equivalent of legal professional privilege, which covers confidential communications between client and legal adviser in the course of obtaining advice, should be extended to other relationships.

It is hardly surprising that privilege should, at different times, have been claimed for confidential communication between friends,[518] documents in the possession of an accountant,[519] auditor,[520] or banker[521] relating to his client's affairs, and even for information supplied to a pursuivant of the Royal College of Heralds.[522] All of these claims have been unsuccessful in England[523] at common law.[524]

It is necessary only to add a few remarks on the subject of the non-recognition by the law of privilege of the relationship between priest and penitent, and physician and patient. There are, however, two points that should be stressed before this is done. In the first place, although law rather than discretion may be in control 'if it comes to the forensic crunch', the court has always had a discretion to disallow questions unless they are relevant and necessary, or such as to serve a useful purpose in relation to the proceedings in hand;[525] second, it is a mistake to suppose that the choice lies between a privilege of complete secrecy on the one hand, and on the other hand, compulsory disclosure without restriction. It is possible, and sometimes desirable, that the claimant to the privilege should decline to produce documents or give evidence until so ordered by the court. Such a course is contemplated by statute and approved by the cases. Thus, s 7 of the Bankers' Books Evidence Act 1879 assumes that an application will be made to the court for an order for inspection

---

[516] It is interesting that in New Zealand, in *R v Rapana* [1995] 2 NZLR 381, the court was prepared to use the broad provision of s 35 of the Evidence (Amendment) Act No 2 1980 in favour of confidential communications to supplement the more narrowly phrased medical privilege in s 33 in the case of a communication to a psychotherapist.

[517] An injunction may, however, be granted to prevent such disclosure to a foreign court: *XAG v A bank* [1983] 2 All ER 464, [1983] 2 Lloyd's Rep 535.   [518] *Duchess of Kingston's Case* (1776) 20 State Tr 355.

[519] *Chantrey Martin & Co v Martin* [1953] 2 QB 286, [1953] 2 All ER 691. There would be no obligation to disclose if the documents were the client's property, but that is not the result of the law of privilege. See also, in Canada, *Minister of National Revenue v Tower* (2003) 231 DLR (4th) 318.

[520] *Price Waterhouse v BCCI Holdings (Luxembourg) SA* [1992] BCLC 583.

[521] *Robertson v Canadian Imperial Bank of Commerce* [1995] 1 All ER 824, PC.

[522] *Slade v Tucker* (1880) 14 Ch D 824. See also *Jones v Great Central Rly Co* (n425) (trade union official). So far as bankers are concerned, their contractual duty is not to disclose the state of their customer's account without his consent, except under order of the court or pursuant to a public duty: *Tournier v National Provincial and Union Bank of England* [1924] 1 KB 461. See also *R v Daye* [1908] 2 KB 333.

[523] In Australia, see *R v Young* [1999] NSWCCA 166, 46 NSWLR 681 for extensive discussion of the considerations relevant to establishing a special privilege at common law for the non-disclosure of communications made by complainants in sexual cases under a sexual assault communication privilege; in Canada, a special statutory privilege in s 278 of the Canadian Criminal Code, preventing the disclosure of psychiatric records of complainants in sexual cases to the accused, was upheld as constitutional in *R v Mills* [1999] 3 SCR 668.

[524] A circumscribed statutory privilege was invested in respect of banking records in s 175(5) of the Financial Services and Markets Act 2000.

[525] *A-G v Mulholland* [1963] 2 QB 477, 489, and 492, Lord Denning MR and Donovan LJ, respectively. Any such discretion is enlarged by the broad and indeterminate powers conferred by CPR 32.1.

of a banker's books, and in *R v St Lawrence's Hospital*,[526] Lord Goddard CJ approved the refusal of medical officers to disclose their communications with the visitors to a hospital under the Mental Deficiency Acts without an order of the court. When such an order is made, it can be on such terms as, for example, that no use will be made of the information disclosed outside the particular proceedings before the court.[527] Non-compliance with the order would constitute a contempt of court,[528] but it must be admitted that there are circumstances in which disclosure, even on the most stringent terms as to dissemination of the information, is abhorrent to the witness. He may consider himself inadequately protected by the discretion of the court simply because there are cases in which the question is both relevant and, from the point of view of the party putting it, necessary.

Priest and penitent

A possible case for the creation of a new privilege is that of the Roman Catholic priest called upon to testify with regard to that which took place in the confessional.[529] There is very little English judicial authority on the subject, but such as there is, supported by all relevant text writers, is to the contrary.

Were the problem to arise in an acute form in practice, most judges would probably sympathize with Best CJ when he said: 'I, for one, will never compel a clergyman to disclose communications made to him by a prisoner; but if he chooses to disclose them I shall receive them in evidence.'[530]

A privilege is conferred on penitential communications by statute in various parts of the Commonwealth,[531] and in most American states,[532] but both the Law Reform Committee and the Criminal Law Revision Committee are opposed to any change here.[533]

---

[526] *R v St Lawrence's Hospital, Caterham Statutory Visitors, ex p Pritchard* [1953] 2 All ER 766, 772. A statute may affect the terms upon which an order for discovery may be made: see *McIvor v Southern Health and Social Services Board* [1978] 2 All ER 625. See also *Church of Scientology of California v Department of Health and Social Security* [1979] 3 All ER 97.

[527] See the order in *Chantrey Martin & Co v Martin* (n519). In wardship and custody proceedings, there may be disclosure to the court, leaving it to the discretion of the judge to decide whether there should be any disclosure to the parties: see e.g. *Official Solicitor of the Supreme Court v K* [1965] AC 201, [1963] 3 All ER 191; *Re M* [1973] QB 108, [1972] 3 All ER 321. The number of such cases may be increasing: see *Science Research Council v Nassé* [1980] AC 1028, [1979] 3 All ER 673 (anti-discrimination legislation); *Campbell v Tameside Metropolitan Borough Council* [1982] QB 1065, [1982] 2 All ER 791 (psychologists' reports on children).

[528] Even in the absence of a special order, it amounts to contempt to use a document obtained by discovery for any purpose ulterior to the purposes of the litigation in which it was obtained: *Harman v Secretary of State for the Home Department* [1983] 1 AC 280.

[529] The usual claim is that the privilege is that of the penitent, but it is sometimes said that it should belong to the priest alone, as distinct from being exercisable by him on behalf of an absent person.

[530] *Broad v Pitt* (1828) 3 C & P 518 (obiter). A clergyman was obliged to disclose an admission of adultery made in conversation by a friend in *Normanshaw v Normanshaw and Measham* (1893) 69 LT 468.

[531] In Australia, such a privilege has a statutory basis as s 127 of the Evidence Act 1995; in Canada, the privilege depends upon a balancing exercise: *Jones v Attorney General for British Columbia* (2007) 286 DLR (4th) 66; in New Zealand, see *R v Howse* (1983) 1 CRNZ 32; *R v L* [1998] 2 NZLR 141 (construing such a confession strictly).

[532] It has also been accepted in the Federal courts without the benefit of statute: *Mullen v United States* 263 F 2d 275 (1958).

[533] Sixteenth Report of the Law Reform Committee, [46]–[47]; 11th Report of the Criminal Law Revision Committee, [272]–[275]. Even so, the police have given an informal undertaking not to conduct intrusive surveillance in such a way as to infringe the secrecy of the confessional: Intrusive Surveillance Code of Practice [2.3].

Physician and patient[534]

There is more judicial authority on the subject of communications between doctors and their patients than there is on statements made to clergymen. It is uniformly against the existence of any privilege,[535] although privacy concerns have dictated some reserve in compelling disclosure, especially in advance and to anyone other than a medical practitioner.[536] The problem is much more likely to arise in practice than that which relates to statements made to clergymen, for these are likely to be relevant to litigation only when they constitute admissions, and in many cases, no one will know whether they were made, whereas questions concerning medical treatment are both more likely to arise in a law suit, and more likely to be the subject of such knowledge as could warrant the calling of a doctor as a witness.

In the United States, the Federal Rules of Evidence leave the creation of new privileges to the common law, and the Supreme Court in *Jaffee v Redmond*[537] so acted for those engaged in psychotherapy. This matter is also dealt with by statute in various parts of the Commonwealth,[538] but both the Law Reform Committee and the Criminal Law Revision Committee were against any change in the English law.[539]

In the enacted legislation, it has been found necessary to include exceptions. Not only is there a tendency to confine medical privilege to civil proceedings, a restriction that some would advocate for priest and penitent, but it has also been found desirable to impose special limitations in civil cases. Examples are actions for medical negligence brought by a patient against his doctor, cases in which the patient's sanity is in issue, and claims by the patient in respect of personal injuries, the nature, duration, extent or effect of which is in issue. In the case of medical, and especially psychiatric, evidence, there are obvious dangers in according to the patient complete control over the disclosure of information relating to his medical condition, and it has been held that the doctor cannot be inhibited by considerations of confidentiality from discharging his duty to the community.[540]

A doctor, like a clergyman, may be able to rely on some other head of privilege or exemption, such as that which relates to negotiations between estranged spouses, or the possible protection from disclosure on the ground of public interest of communications with the Minister relating to the National Health Service.[541] It is also possible that, in some situations, it would be unfair within s 78 of the Police and Criminal Evidence Act 1984 to use statements made to a doctor, but it would be unwise to prescribe conditions under which this might be the case.[542]

---

[534] When the claim to privilege is made, it is always treated as that of the patient.

[535] *Duchess of Kingston's Case* (n518); *R v Gibbons* (1823) 1 C & P 97; *Wheeler v Le Merchant* (1881) 17 Ch D 675, 681; *Garner v Garner* (1920) 36 TLR 196; *Hunter v Mann* [1974] QB 767, [1974] 2 All ER 414; *R v Smith* [1979] 3 All ER 605, [1979] 1 WLR 1445; *Campbell v Tameside Metropolitan Borough Council* (n527).

[536] *OCS Group Ltd v Wells* [2008] EWHC 919 (QB).

[537] 518 US 1 (1996). Legislation enacting such privileges exists in many states.

[538] For the position in Canada, see *Smith & Nephew v Glegg* 2005 SCC 31, [2005] 1 SCR 724; in Australia, the Evidence Act 1995 makes no provision for a medical privilege, although a few states have one.

[539] Sixteenth Report of the Law Reform Committee, paras 48–52; 11th Report of the Criminal Law Revision Committee, [276].

[540] *W v Egdell* (n263); *R v Crozier* [1991] Crim LR 138. If necessary, the court will stay proceedings upon condition that a claimant waives his right to confidentiality: *Nicholson v Halton Hospital NHS Trust* [1999] PIQR P310.   [541] 66 LQR 92.

[542] See *R v McDonald* [1991] Crim LR 122.

While special restrictions are put upon access to some confidential material falling short of being the subject of legal professional privilege by the Police and Criminal Justice Act 1984, these apply for the protection of the adviser, not of the subject, and thus voluntary disclosure by the medical adviser is not liable to the subject's control by a claim in the nature of privilege.[543]

Conclusions

In a much-quoted paragraph,[544] Wigmore mentioned four preconditions of a privilege of the lawyer–client type.[545] They are that:

(1) the communications must originate in a confidence that they will not be disclosed;

(2) the element of confidentiality must be essential to the full and satisfactory maintenance of the relationship between the parties;

(3) the relationship must be one that in the opinion of the community ought to be sedulously fostered;

(4) the injury that would inure to the relationship by the disclosure of the communication must be greater than the benefit gained through the correct disposal of the litigation.

Wigmore had no doubt about the compliance of the lawyer–client privilege with these conditions. He was unsympathetic to medical privilege and suggested that, in its case, preconditions (2) and (4) are not fulfilled, while he thought that there might be some uncertainty with regard to precondition (3) in the case of the priest–penitent privilege, with which he was sympathetic. Some would disagree on both points. It remains to be seen how far the position will be affected by the new powers of discretionary exclusion conferred by the CPR.

Identity of informant

It has been recognized as being contrary to public policy[546] to require the names of informants to the police, or to some other bodies conducting similar functions, to be revealed in civil proceedings. An allied privilege has occasionally been claimed by journalists.[547] The privilege differs from the professional privileges considered above in that the claim is not normally made in respect of the content of the communication, which has usually been revealed already,[548] and in the absence of any clear recognition that the privilege belongs to the informant, and not to the journalist himself. Such a privilege is recognized in some other jurisdictions,[549] but at least in an absolute form, has been rejected here.

---

[543] *R v Singleton* [1995] 1 Cr App Rep 431 (here the adviser was a dentist). [544] [2285].

[545] In *Slavotych v Baker* [1976] 1 SCR 254, 260, Spence J expressed approval of this approach, but his remarks were obiter, and subsequently criticized by McLachlin (later Chief Justice of the Supreme Court of Canada) (1977) 11 UBCLR 266. [546] Chapter X, Section 1.

[547] *A-G v Clough* [1963] 1 QB 773, [1963] 1 All ER 420; *A-G v Mulholland* (n525). See also *McGuiness v A-G of Victoria* (1940) 63 CLR 73; *Wran v Australian Broadcasting Commission* [1984] 3 NSWLR 241; *Independent Commission against Corruption v Cornwall* (1993) 116 ALR 97.

[548] In *Moysa v Alberta (Labour Relations Board)* (1989) 60 DLR (4th) 1, the unsuccessful claim related to information conveyed by the journalist to a known party.

[549] It is recognized in many United States jurisdictions; for an extensive discussion, see *Branzburg v Hayes* 408 US 665 (1972). In Canada it seems that the privilege is unlikely to protect documents which are themselves part of the criminal act: *R v National Post* 290 DLR (4th) 655 (2008).

The question was considered by the House of Lords in *British Steel Corp v Granada Television Ltd*.[550] A confidential document belonging to the claimants came into the hands of the defendants, and was knowingly used as part of a television programme. The claimants secured an order for the return of the documents, but the defendants mutilated them so as to try to conceal any indication of the identity of their supplier. The claimants then sought an order for the revelation of his identity. It transpired that an undertaking to respect the anonymity of the source had been given. The majority of Their Lordships was quite clear that journalists had no privilege akin either to that of lawyer and client, or in respect of the non-disclosure of their sources of information akin to that of the police. It was said that such a privilege would:[551]

...place journalists (how defined?) in a favoured and unique position as compared with priest-confessors, doctors, bankers, and other recipients of confidential information and would assimilate them to the police in relation to informers.

This decision caused some disquiet in the media of communication, and a new statutory privilege was created in an attempt to assuage it:

No court may require a person to disclose, nor is any person guilty of contempt of court for refusing to disclose, the source of information contained in a publication for which he is responsible, unless it be established to the satisfaction of the court that disclosure is necessary in the interests of justice or national security or for the prevention of disorder or crime.[552]

This statutory privilege draws additional support from Art 10 of the European Convention, guaranteeing freedom of expression, of which compulsory disclosure of a journalist's sources has been construed to amount to prima facie breach.[553] There too, however, the freedom is qualified, and Art 10(2) provides:

The exercise of these freedoms, since it carries with it duties and responsibilities, may be subject to such formalities, conditions, restrictions or penalties as are prescribed by law and are necessary in a democratic society, in the interests of national security, territorial integrity or public safety, for the prevention of disorder or crime, for the protection of health or morals, for the protection of reputation or rights of others, for preventing the disclosure of information received in confidence, or for maintaining the authority or impartiality of the judiciary.

In *Goodwin v United Kingdom*, while the European Court of Human Rights recognized that a margin of appreciation existed for national courts in the first instance, it held the value of press freedom to be high, and to require a very strong showing of necessity to justify compulsory disclosure:[554]

Having regard to the importance of the protection of journalistic sources for press freedom in a democratic society and the potentially chilling effect an order of source disclosure has on the exercise of that freedom, such a measure cannot be compatible with Article 10 of the Convention

---

[550] [1981] AC 1096, [1981] 1 All ER 417.

[551] Lord Wilberforce, 1171, 457. See also Viscount Dilhorne, 1181, 465; Lord Fraser, 1196, 476; Lord Russell concurred.

[552] Contempt of Court Act 1981, s 10, partly in an attempt to implement Art 10 of the European Convention on Human Rights. For exegesis see Costigan [2007] *Pub L* 464. Much the same result seems to have been reached in Canada as a matter of the construction of s 2 of the Canadian Charter of Rights and Freedoms: see *The Citizen v Coates* (1986) 29 DLR (4th) 523.

[553] *Goodwin v United Kingdom* (1996) 22 EHRR 123.   [554] [39], [40].

unless it is justified by an overriding requirement in the public interest.... As a matter of general principle, the "necessity" for any restriction on freedom of expression must be convincingly established.

The House of Lords has subsequently held that s 10 and Art 10 should be construed congruently.[555] It has become quite clear that the burden of justifying disclosure is upon the party seeking it, and that even after a justification for disclosure under s 10 or Art 10(2) has been established, there remains a discretion in the court to refuse it.[556] Nevertheless, it has proved possible to establish such a need for disclosure in a number of recent cases, such as *Ashworth* itself, in which the content of the communication was confidential medical records,[557] where the motivation of the source[558] may have been significant. In *Financial Times Ltd v Interbrew SA*,[559] where it was confidential business information, disclosure of which had significant financial consequences both private and public in the context of a takeover bid, the English court ordered disclosure, but the European Court of Human Rights found breach of article 10.[560]

In *Secretary of State for Defence v Guardian Newspapers Ltd*,[561] Lord Diplock pointed out that the requirement of necessity for disclosure was mandatory, and it has been further explained that administrative convenience is insufficient.[562] It seems that, where an end, such as the assessment of damages, can be achieved without disclosure, but by other means, such as a firm jury direction, the availability of such means removes any necessity for disclosure.[563] It is, however, also worth noting that failure to disclose the identity of a source may weaken very substantially the weight of the content of the communication, should it be relied upon in court.[564] It is not, however, enough to prevent disclosure automatically that the issue arises during proceedings to secure interim orders.[565] In the case of prosecution of crime, it has been held that the reference is to crime in general, and not to a specific crime, so there is no need to demonstrate that some particular crime will be prevented by disclosure,[566] nor that disclosure would necessarily prevent the commission of further crime,[567] if it would have that tendency. In the case of the interest of the administration of justice, the concept is to be construed narrowly,[568] typically referring

---

[555] *Ashworth Hospital Authority v MGN Ltd* [2002] UKHL 29, [2002] 4 All ER 193, [38].

[556] *Re Insider Dealing Inquiry* [1988] AC 660, [1988] 1 All ER 203, 703, 208. See also, in Ireland, *Burke v Central Independent Television* [1994] 2 IR 61, in which disclosure might have endangered the lives of the sources.   [557] Themselves receiving special protection under Art 8 of the European Convention.

[558] In a number of recent cases, including *Ashworth* (n555), the direct source to the journalist is an intermediary to whom the transgressor transmits the relevant material, and an interesting sequel to the *Ashworth* case was that, after revelation of the identity of the intermediary, a further action was instituted seeking disclosure of the identity of his sources, to which different considerations were held to be applicable from those in *Ashworth*: see *Mersey Care NHS Trust v Ackroyd* [2007] EWCA Civ 101.

[559] [2002] EWCA Civ 274, [2002] 2 LlR 229.   [560] (2009) The Times 16 December.

[561] *Secretary of State for Defence v Guardian Newspapers Ltd* [1985] AC 339, [1984] 3 All ER 601, 350, 607.

[562] In the *Insider Dealing* case (n556), 704, 208, the meaning was said by Lord Griffiths to lie between being 'indispensable' and 'useful or convenient', and capable of being paraphrased as 'really needed'.

[563] *Maxwell v Pressdram Ltd* [1987] 1 All ER 656, [1987] 1 WLR 298.

[564] *R v Secretary of State for the Home Department, ex p Al Fayed* [2001] Imm AR 134.

[565] *Michael O'Mara Books Ltd v Express Newspapers plc* [1998] EMLR 383.

[566] *Insider Dealing* (n556), 705, 209.   [567] See also *X v Y* [1988] 2 All ER 648.

[568] See *John v Express Newspapers* [2000] 3 All ER 257, [2000] 1 WLR 1931, in which the court was not prepared to use its discretion to permit disclosure, even in defence of legal professional privilege.

to proceedings in a court of law,[569] including proceedings to secure interim orders,[570] or proceedings to identify a tortfeasor,[571] although there must be evidence of some intention to initiate such proceedings.[572] The privilege in respect of police informants[573] cannot be claimed to the prejudice of the defence in criminal case. There is no such expressed limitation here, and as noted above, the accused would bear the burden of establishing grounds for disclosure.

SECTION 3. STATEMENTS MADE WITHOUT PREJUDICE[574]

In civil proceedings,[575] in an attempt[576] to settle a dispute,[577] parties frequently make statements 'without prejudice'. The contents of the statement then cannot be put in evidence[578] without the consent of both parties, the case being one of joint privilege.[579] The statements sometimes relate to the offer of a compromise, and, were it not for the privilege, they would often constitute significant items of evidence on the ground that they were admissions. Obviously, it is in the public interest that disputes should be settled and litigation reduced to a minimum,[580] and so favours enlarging the cloak under which negotiations may be conducted without prejudice,[581] although it has been suggested that the passage of the Human Rights Act 1998 now requires the policy to be more restrained.[582] The privilege

---

[569] (n561); 350, 607.   [570] *Guardian Newspapers Ltd* (n561).

[571] *X Ltd v Morgan-Grampian (Publishers) Ltd* [1991] 1 AC 1, [1990] 2 All ER 1; or if appropriate a criminal: see *Ashworth v MGN Ltd* (n555), [53].

[572] *Handmade Films (Productions) Ltd v Express Newspapers plc* [1986] FSR 463.

[573] Chapter X, Section 1.

[574] For the history of this privilege, see Vaver (1974) 9 UBCLR 85. It appears in statutory form in Australia in the Evidence Act 1995, s 131, and for exegesis, see *GPI Leisure Corp Ltd (In Liq) v Yuill* (1997) 42 NSWLR 225.

[575] No comparable privilege appears to attach here to statements made in criminal proceedings in the course of 'plea bargaining', at least in the absence of any explicit claim: *R v Hayes* [2004] EWCA Crim 2844, [2005] 1 Cr App R 557, cf in Canada; *Re Delorme v R* (2005) 198 CCC3d 431. The EU has recommended extension to mediation, COM (2004) 718.

[576] With or without the assistance of a mediator: *Reed Executive plc v Reed Business Information Ltd* [2004] EWCA Civ 887, [2004] 4 All ER 942, [17].

[577] One of the principal concerns of the Woolf Report, reflected in the Civil Procedure Rules Pt 36, was the creation of an environment more conducive to settlement, and CPR 36.19 explicitly applied without-prejudice offers to the new regime.

[578] It is uncertain upon whom the burden of demonstrating the application of the privilege falls: see *Carman v Cronos Group SA* [2006] EWHC 1324 (Ch), [12].

[579] No waiver is to be implied notwithstanding CPR 31.6 from inclusion of a document in a list for standard disclosure: *Galliford Try Construction Ltd v Mott MacDonald Ltd* [2008] EWHC 603 (TCC), [23].

[580] Difficult questions may arise as to the extent to which litigation can be severed in the course of negotiation, and how far without-prejudice correspondence, in arriving at a partial settlement, can be protected: see *Tomlin v Standard Telephones & Cables Ltd* [1969] 3 All ER 201, [1969] 1 WLR 1378 (holding that a without-prejudice statement on contribution could be adduced, even though the attempted full settlement failed on the issue of quantum). See also *Lukies v Ripley (No 2)* (1994) 35 NSWLR 283 for a full discussion of policy in this context.

[581] Such an aim lies at the core of the new regime of civil procedure, and received the accolade of the Lord Walker in *Ofulue v Bossert* 2009] UKHL 16, [2009] 1 AC 990 [57].

[582] *Prudential Assurance Co Ltd v Prudential Assurance Co of America* [2002] EWHC 2809 (Ch), [26]–[28].

is accepted to have two strands: the first based on public policy most evident in cases in which the privilege applies despite not having been explicitly invoked; the second where it has been so invoked, depending upon the implied agreement of the parties. Questions may arise as to the scope and effect of the privilege, issues that often overlap.

SCOPE

This privilege has been authoritatively stated to be 'founded on the public policy of encouraging litigants to settle their differences rather than litigate them to a finish'.[583] The detail represents no more than a number of illustrations of that guiding principle. It follows that literal use of the phrase 'without prejudice' is no more than indicative that evidence[584] so prefaced may be intended to lead to the settlement of a dispute,[585] and thus protected.[586] It is certainly immaterial that a different formulation is adopted, or the words used elsewhere than at the beginning of a document.[587] It is even unnecessary to use the words, or any equivalent,[588] if it is clear from the surrounding circumstances that the evidence is part of a continuing negotiation,[589] whether or not part of a mandatory process,[590] or obtained pursuant to one.[591] If negotiations for a settlement during which without-prejudice documents pass between the parties fail, either party is then free to open subsequent correspondence between them over the objection of the other, and despite the fact that such subsequent correspondence itself seeks to negotiate a settlement.[592] Any such change in status must be intimated clearly, and if so, it then becomes immaterial that the recipient fails to understand its significance, or is unwilling to accept it.[593] In the absence of any such termination, the privilege will continue to apply in closely related disputes.[594] Where joint experts are instructed to report under the Civil Procedure Rules, the content of their discussions can be revealed only by agreement between the parties.[595]

---

[583] By Lord Griffiths in *Rush & Tompkins Ltd v Greater London Council* [1989] AC 1280, [1988] 3 All ER 737; 1299, 739. To which Walker LJ in *Unilever plc v The Proctor & Gamble Co* [2001] 1 All ER 783, 789, 790, added the further basis of implementation of the express or implied agreement of the parties that no such disclosure be admissible. See also Hoffmann J in *Muller v Linsley* [1996] PNLR 74, 77; Neuberger J in *Hodgkinson & Corby Ltd v Wards Mobility Services Ltd* [1997] FSR 178, 190.

[584] The rule applies to both oral and documentary statements.

[585] Invocation of a private grievance procedure was held in *BNP Paribas v Mezzotero* [2004] IRLR 508 (EAT) not to amount to initiation of a dispute for the purposes of the rule.

[586] *South Shropshire District Council v Amos* [1987] 1 All ER 340, [1986] 1 WLR 1271; 344, 1277.

[587] *Cory v Bretton* (1830) 4 C & P 462.

[588] But see *Prudential Assurance Co Ltd v Prudential Assurance Co of America* (n582)', [18]–[21], where omission of the words in negotiations largely intended to prevent a dispute arising, influenced the decision that the evidence was not privileged under this rubric.

[589] *Paddock v Forrester* (1842) 3 Man & G 903, where heading of the first letter in a series invested later ones with the privilege, and *Oliver v Nautilus SS Co* [1903] 2 KB 639, where so labelling a later one invested an earlier with the privilege.

[590] *Jackson v Ministry of Defence* [2006] EWCA Civ 46 (joint settlement meeting as part of special experimental scheme). [591] *Rabin v Mendoza & Co* [1954] 1 All ER 247, [1954] 1 WLR 271.

[592] *Dixons Stores Group Ltd v Thames Television plc* [1993] 1 All ER 349.

[593] *Cheddar Valley Engineering Ltd v Chaddlewood Homes Ltd* [1992] 4 All ER 942, [1992] 1 WLR 820.

[594] *Instance v Denny Brothers Printing Ltd* [2000] FSR 869 (closely related parties in relation to dispute about similar patents overseas).

[595] CPR 35.12(4). But see *Aird v Prime Meridian Ltd* (2006) unreported CA, 21 December, in which a joint report, not otherwise entitled to privilege, did not become entitled to protection simply because it had been used in a failed attempt at mediation.

Use of the phrase 'without prejudice' is inefficacious, whether used to describe a meeting[596] or stated in a document,[597] if the meeting or document is not made as part of a genuine attempt to negotiate a settlement. Thus, a threat to pursue an admittedly false claim, made under the rubric, will not be privileged, although designed to force settlement of a related dispute.[598] Similarly, an unequivocal admission of the matters in issue may be received, even though made under the rubric in the context of negotiation, although an English court may be more alert than some others[599] to find such equivocation.[600] There may also be some reluctance to exclude evidence in situations of significant social importance.[601] Another difficult situation arises in relation to a simple statement of a legal claim so headed. If the document contains no other hint of any intention to negotiate, it will be insufficient,[602] but the court will be astute to detect such an intention,[603] and it is certainly not the case that a letter first intimating a dispute can never be made without prejudice.[604] Although the privilege can be invoked in attempt to preclude litigation altogether,[605] it does not extend to meetings between parties with some common cause, designed to improve their prospects in any litigation which might ensue.[606] The privilege protects all relevant statements made in a genuine attempt to negotiate a settlement, and is not confined to admissions.[607]

It has become very much more common to attempt to settle disputes informally without initial recourse at least to the courts,[608] and many of the schemes of conciliation and mediation being adopted include, in their rules, references to such negotiations being conducted on a 'without prejudice' basis.[609]

EFFECT

If the privilege can be established, it is sometimes uncertain exactly what it prohibits. It seems clear that it can prevent use, not only by parties to the relevant negotiation, but also

---

[596] As in *BNP Paribas v Mezzotero* (n585).

[597] As in *Re Daintrey, ex p Holt* [1893] 2 QB 116 (declarations of bankrupt declaring inability to pay so headed).

[598] *Hawick Jersey International Ltd v Caplan* (1988) The Times, 11 March. See also *Greenwood v Fitt* (1961) 29 DLR (2d) 260; *Cedenko Foods Ltd v State Insurance Ltd* [1996] 3 NZLR 205. Such situations have been categorized as ones of 'unambiguous impropriety', but this concept is, in this jurisdiction at least, strictly confined: see *WH Smith Ltd v Colman* [2001] FSR 91. It is not enough merely to show a serious and substantial risk of prejudice: *Berry Trade Ltd v Moussavi* [2003] EWCA Civ 715, (2003) 100(29) LSG 36.

[599] See, in Australia, *Davies v Nyland* (1974) 10 SASR 76, 91, adopting the view of Wigmore; *J A McBeath Nominees Pty Ltd v Jenkins Development Corp Pty Ltd* [1992] 2 Qd 121.

[600] See e.g. *Savings and Investment Bank v Fincken* [2003] EWCA Civ 1630, [2004] 1 All ER 1125.

[601] As in *BNP Paribas v Mezzotero* (n585) (allegations of sexual or racial discrimination).

[602] *Buckinghamshire County Council v Moran* [1990] Ch 623, [1989] 2 All ER 225.

[603] To be determined objectively, and not conclusively by evidence of the party making the statement that he did not intend to negotiate: *Pearson Education Ltd v Prentice Hall India Private Ltd* [2005] EWHC 636 (QB), [2006] FSR 8, [22].

[604] *South Shropshire District Council v Amos*, (n586); *Schering Corp v Cipla Ltd* [2006] EWHC 2587 (Ch).   [605] *Framlington Group Ltd v Barnetson* [2007] EWCA Civ 502, [34].

[606] *Stax Claimants v Bank of Nova Scotia Channel Islands Ltd* [2007] EWHC 1153, [29].

[607] *Unilever plc v The Procter & Gamble Co* (n583), explicitly overruling, 797e, the supposed old rule in *Kurtz v Spence* (1888) 5 RPC 161 that threats could never be so protected.

[608] See Practice Direction Pre-Action Protocol 2009, [8], requiring evidence that ADR has been considered as an alternative to litigation.

[609] See e.g. *Smiths Group PLC v George Weiss* [2002] EWHC 582 (Ch) (mediation under the Arbitration and Commercial Initiative (ACI) scheme).

by other parties.[610] A party to negotiations to settle a dispute might well be inhibited from making damaging admissions if he knew that they could be used by a different adversary. Similarly, solicitors for the parties may claim privilege for statements made in letters written on their clients' behalf in proceedings in which they are sued personally;[611] but the statement in respect of which privilege is claimed must have some bearing on negotiations for a settlement.[612] It may sometimes be difficult to determine what is in dispute, and whether a statement in the course of negotiations is an admission of the truth of a disputed matter. In *Bradford & Bingley BS v Rashid*,[613] the House of Lords was unable to agree on such matters in the context of an attempt to use negotiations[614] to settle an effectively undisputed debt as an acknowledgement, so as to prevent the claim being time-barred, despite being unanimous in the result that they could be so used.

It seems that by analogy with the position in relation to legal professional privilege, if a statement which would have been protected from disclosure by the privilege nevertheless comes into the hands of a third party it remains admissible, at least for the prosecution, in a subsequent criminal prosecution,[615] although use in such circumstances by a third party in subsequent unrelated civil proceedings is more doubtful.[616]

In *Unilever v Proctor & Gamble*, Robert Walker LJ stressed that the privilege was subject to numerous exceptions, and listed eight, while disavowing that the list was comprehensive.[617] Even when genuinely made in the context of a negotiation, it seems that a statement can be put in evidence for some purpose not directly linked to the truth of the statement,[618] such as to identify the handwriting of a party,[619] to prove the severance of a joint tenancy,[620] to show notice of the exercise of an option,[621] or to show, in the context of a subsequently disputed settlement, that it was false.[622] Thus if the negotiations succeed,

---

[610] *Rush & Tompkins v Greater London Council* (n583). By analogy with the operation of CPR 36.19, it was, however, held in *Gnitrow Ltd v Cape plc* [2000] 3 All ER 763 that, while the same rule does not apply to settlements involving third parties, the terms of such settlement, when relevant, should not be disclosed until after a decision had been determined on liability. For a still broader view in Australia, see *Mercantile Mutual Custodians Ltd v Village/Nine Restaurants and Bars Pty Ltd* [2001] 1 Qd 276.

[611] *La Roche v Armstrong* [1922] 1 KB 485.

[612] *Field v Comrs of Railways for New South Wales* (1957) 99 CLR 285, in which the authorities are reviewed.

[613] [2006] UKHL 37, [2006] 4 All ER 705. Some members distinguished sharply between the undisputed debt and negotiations for its repayment; others between definitive and hypothetical admissions; Lord Hoffmann's distinction between use of the statement as evidence of an acknowledgement, and as *being* an acknowledgement was rejected as too subtle in *Ofulue v Bossert* (n581), [95]. All thought that the solutions they rejected would lead to difficulty in borderline cases. The protection is not limited to admissions. See also in New Zealand, *Cooper v van Heeren* [2007] 3 NZLR 783.

[614] The relevant letters were not explicitly marked 'without prejudice'.　　[615] *R v K* (n113), [72].

[616] Ibid, [64].

[617] Note 546, 793d. In addition to those mentioned here, often in different terms, he includes use to prove that an agreement to settle was made; to show that such an apparent agreement should be set aside for fraud; to found an estoppel; to reveal an 'unambiguous impropriety; in striking-out proceedings on the basis of delay; and in proceedings seeking to demonstrate attempts to mitigate loss.

[618] In *Re Anglo American Insurance Co Ltd* [2002] BCC 715, Neuberger J contrasted the existence and the contents of the negotiations for this purpose.　　[619] *Waldridge v Kennison* (1794) 1 Esp 143.

[620] *McDowell v Hirschfield Lipson & Rumney and Smith* [1992] 2 FLR 126.

[621] *Tenstat Pty Ltd v Permanent Trustee Australia Ltd* (1992) 28 NSWLR 625.

[622] *Muller v Linsley* (n583), but only as between the parties themselves, excluding third party without-prejudice statements, *Cumbria Waste Management Ltd v Baines Wilson* [2008] EWHC 786 (QB), [24].

and constitute a binding contract, this may be proved, and interpreted,[623] by the use of without-prejudice material.[624] It has also been said that it is permissible to refer to such statements, and the dates upon which they were made, in order to establish laches.[625] On the other hand, no such reference can be made upon an application to secure costs.[626] These decisions may be reconciled upon the basis that, in the former, it was not necessary to do more than establish the context within which the letters were written, whereas in the latter, reliance had to be placed upon the contents of the documents as admissions. Similar considerations have caused difficulty in relation to disputes about the taxation of costs. The general rule is that negotiations made without prejudice cannot be taken into account when considering questions of costs.[627] This principle has, however, been eroded to the extent that the court will permit a sort of hybrid 'without prejudice' statement to be made, which reserves the right to refer to it,[628] but only on questions of costs.[629] The reason for this is simply that such an erosion is more likely to promote speedy settlement.[630] It has further been held[631] that there is no exception to this privilege by close analogy with the rule in *R v Cox and Railton*,[632] since here the question relates not to the propriety of an underlying transaction, but to the procedure for vindicating it, and different principles apply.[633] Nor is it possible to import the notion of waiver from legal professional privilege, since where 'without prejudice' privilege exists, it is essentially joint.[634] A party may nevertheless not use part of without-prejudice negotiations as part of his case on a pre-trial application, and still restrain his opponent from using other parts of the same otherwise privileged material for his own purposes.[635] Even though disclosure is not limited to documents that are admissible in evidence, it does not extend to those covered by this branch of privilege, and even if disclosure should take place, it still does not necessarily amount to acquiescence in use of such material in evidence.[636]

---

[623] *Oceanbulk Shipping and Trading SA v TMT Asia Ltd* [2009] EWHC 1946 (Comm), [33].

[624] *Tomlin v Standard Telephones and Cables Ltd* (n580).

[625] By Lindley LJ in *Walker v Wilsher* (1889) 23 QBD 335, 338. See also *McFadden v Snow* (1951) 69 WN NSW 8, in which it was decided in Australia that such a statement could be referred to in order to rebut an inference of an admission by otherwise apparent silence.

[626] *Simaan General Contracting Co v Pilkington Glass Ltd* [1987] 1 All ER 345, [1987] 1 WLR 516.

[627] *Walker v Wilsher* (n625), applied to arbitrations in *Stotesbury v Turner* [1943] KB 370, and affirmed in the light of the CPR in *Reed Executive plc v Reed Business Information Ltd* (n576), [34].

[628] This is indeed the model adopted by Civil Procedure Rule 36.19 for P 36 offers. It seems that the reservation must be made explicitly: see, in Australia, *In the marriage of Steel* (1992) 107 FLR 143.

[629] *Calderbank v Calderbank* [1976] Fam 93, [1975] 3 All ER 333; *Cutts v Head* [1984] Ch 290, [1984] 1 All ER 597. See also, in Ireland, *Ryan v Connolly* [2001] IR 697. This no longer applies in family law finance proceedings: Family Proceedings (Amendment) Rules, SI 2006/352; see further, Hodson (2006) 36 *Fam L* 276.

[630] See generally Civil Procedure Rules, Pt 36.

[631] *Forster v Friedland* (1992) LEXIS, 10 November.   [632] (1884) 14 QBD 153.

[633] As explained in *Chandler v Church* [1987] NLJ Rep 451; *Derby & Co Ltd v Weldon (No 7)* (n462); 170, 1174–5.

[634] There may, however, be implied joint waiver, for example in the course of satellite litigation relating to the privileged occasion: see *Hall v Pertemps* [2005] EWHC 3110 (Ch), [16].

[635] *Rabin v Mendoza & Co* [1954] 1 All ER 247, [1954] 1 WLR 271. See also, in Australia, *Trade Practices Commission v Arnotts Ltd* (1989) 88 ALR 69, at 74–5. Nor, for the reasons given above, does disclosure imply waiver: *Somatra Ltd v Sinclair, Roche & Temperley* [2000] 2 Ll R 673.

[636] *Smiths Group PLC v Weiss* [2002] EWHC 582 (Ch). For a somewhat similar case of vacillation between the parties in Australia, see *Chapman v Allan and Draper* (1999) 74 SASR 274.

SECTION 4. WITHOUT-PREJUDICE NEGOTIATIONS BETWEEN ESTRANGED SPOUSES

This emerged from the womb of 'without prejudice' statements as an independent privilege.[637] If a solicitor were consulted by both husband and wife, professional privilege might attach to statements made to him by either of them, so that he might not disclose them in subsequent matrimonial proceedings without the consent of the maker.[638] The ordinary law concerning without-prejudice statements applies to negotiations between the parties personally, or between their solicitors, which take place with a view to compromising a matrimonial cause. With the greater emphasis in the modern law relating to the family and children upon the concept of conciliation,[639] it was necessary to protect also statements made to a conciliator, and the law was developed in a series of cases.[640] It has been held[641] that the effect of this privilege is different from that described in the previous section of this chapter, partly on account of the greater concern of the law to prevent the breakdown of marriage than the onset of litigation, and partly because of the paramount consideration of the well-being of children.

In particular, these have operated, so far as the former is concerned, for the protection not only of statements made in a sincere effort to achieve reconciliation, but for all statements made in the course of such meetings designed to accomplish that end. Thus threats, which might not be protected as 'without prejudice' statements,[642] could perhaps be shielded under this head. On the other hand, the paramount need to secure the well-being of children dictates a narrow exception from the general rule in relation to statements that 'clearly indicate that the maker has in the past caused or is likely in the future to cause serious harm to the well-being of a child'.[643]

The precise limits of this new privilege have still to be determined, and it is not clear whether older limitations to the scope of the privilege survive. It has been suggested that the privilege should be that of the mediator, at any rate when he is a marriage guidance officer, but the Law Reform Committee was against the creation of a statutory privilege for court welfare officers and marriage guidance counsellors.[644] No privilege attached in affiliation proceedings to a statement made by the respondent to a case worker acting for an adoption society,[645] nor to a report prepared by a court welfare officer.[646]

---

[637] *D v National Society for the Prevention of Cruelty to Children* [1978] AC 171, [1977] 1 All ER 589; 226, 236, and 601, 610; *Re D (Minors)* [1993] Fam 231, [1993] 2 All ER 693. The possibility of a further sibling privilege for mediation being in gestation was raised in *Brown v Rice* [2007] EWHC 625 (Ch), [20].

[638] *Harris v Harris* [1931] P 10.

[639] Expansively defined to include reconciliation and mediation in addition to conciliation *stricto sensu*.

[640] Including *McTaggart v McTaggart* [1949] P 94, [1948] 2 All ER 754; *Mole v Mole* [1951] P 21, [1950] 2 All ER 328; *Pool v Pool* [1951] P 470n, [1951] 2 All ER 563; *Henley v Henley* [1955] P 202, [1955] 1 All ER 590n; *Theodoropoulas v Theodoropoulas* [1964] P 311, [1963] 2 All ER 722; *Pais v Pais* [1971] P 119, [1970] 3 All ER 491. See also, in New Zealand, *G v R* [1981] 2 NZLR 91.   [641] In *Re D* (n637).

[642] *Kitcat v Sharp* (1882) 48 LT 64.

[643] *Re D (Minors)* (n637), 241, 699. For a similar exception in Australia, see *Hutchings v Clarke* (1993) 113 ALR 709; for its limits see *Re Marriage of Day* (1994) 115 FLR 450; and for criticism of defects in its statutory form, see *Re W and W* [2001] Fam CA 216, 164 FLR 18.   [644] Sixteenth Report, paras 39, 40.

[645] *R v Nottingham Justices, ex p Bostock* [1970] 2 All ER 641, [1970] 1 WLR 1117.

[646] *Re H (conciliation: welfare reports)* [1986] 1 FLR 476. See, in Australia, *In the marriage of Wardle* (1990) 100 FLR 107; in Canada, *Re Child Welfare Act, Brysh v Davidson* (1963) 42 DLR (2d) 673; but in New Zealand, see *G v R* (n640), in which a new head of privilege was recognized in this situation.

X

PUBLIC POLICY

Relevant evidence must be excluded on the ground of public policy when it concerns certain matters of public interest considered to be more important than the full disclosure of facts to the court, and when it relates to miscellaneous matters connected with litigation. These subjects are discussed in the first two sections of this chapter. Evidence that has been illegally obtained, considered in Section 3, is not usually discussed under the head of public policy. Although there is no comparably strict general exclusionary rule, it is increasingly the case that the courts[1] recognize the existence of an exclusionary discretion, governed in part by weighing the public interest in the conviction of guilty criminals against the public interest in the preservation of basic civil liberties.[2]

This topic is made more difficult by the wide variety of situations to which it can be considered to apply. An important distinction is between application at the stage of disclosure, and application at trial.[3] In the former, it is difficult to distinguish rules applying generally to disclosure, and those peculiar to public interest. It is also necessary to distinguish between claims for inspection by the court, and for actual production. A wide spectrum of public interests may be urged in favour of immunity, some of them apparent upon the face of the documents, and others apparent only to those possessing intimate acquaintance with the operation of the public service, and with the psychology of those who work in it, or supply it with information. A final complicating factor is that, while in many cases a party may share the public interest concerned, and be instrumental in ensuring that it is brought to the attention of the court, this will not necessarily be so. The court must itself always be alert to the possibility of such an interest being involved. Such a possibility may be very hard to detect where the claim does depend upon knowledge of esoteric, and perhaps secret, aspects of the conduct of affairs of state.

Before considering some of the major varieties of claim, it is worth mentioning the impact of the factors set out above upon the terminology of this branch of the law, upon the question of waiver, and upon the admissibility of secondary evidence of excluded matter.

This topic was once called 'Crown privilege'. The reasons for change were stated by Lord Simon as long ago as 1942:[4]

The withholding of documents on the ground that their publication would be contrary to the public interest is not properly to be regarded as a branch of the law of privilege connected with

---

[1] Both those in the United Kingdom and the European Court of Human Rights: see *Osman v United Kingdom* (1998) 29 EHRR 245, [147]–[154] (immunity from suit).

[2] In this, adopting policies already familiar in other Commonwealth jurisdictions such as Australia: *Bunning v Cross* (1978) 141 CLR 54, 74.

[3] It is generally desirable that the tribunal conducting the trial, at whatever level, should itself determine initial disclosure involving public interest immunity: *R (CPS) v Acton Youth Court* [2001] EWHC Admin 402, [2001] 1 WLR 1828.

[4] *Duncan v Cammell Laird & Co Ltd* [1942] AC 624, 641. See also *Rogers v Secretary of State for the Home Department* [1973] AC 388, [1972] 2 All ER 1057.

disclosure. 'Crown privilege' is for this reason not a happy expression. Privilege, in relation to disclosure, is for the protection of the litigant and could be waived by him, but the rule that the interest of the state must not be put in jeopardy by producing documents which would injure it is a principle to be observed in administering justice, quite unconnected with the interests or claims of the particular parties in litigation, and, indeed, is a rule on which the judge should, if necessary, insist even though no objection is taken at all.

In *Rogers*, Lord Simon thought the term 'privilege' properly applicable only to a claim that could be waived. This was reasserted by Lord Fraser in *Air Canada v Secretary of State for Trade (No 2)*: 'Public interest immunity is not a privilege which may be waived by the Crown or by any party.'[5] At first sight, this view might seem inconsistent with dicta of Lord Cross in *Alfred Crompton Amusement Machines Ltd v Customs and Excise Comrs (No 2)*,[6] that where claimed to protect the interests of third parties in the confidentiality of information supplied to public authorities, the privilege can be waived. There is, however, no real inconsistency. Before waiver can take place, there must be some claim based upon public interest to be waived. It is material to the determination of that question whether or not the suppliers of information are willing for it to be revealed. It may well, in many cases, be hard to demonstrate a public interest in keeping information secret on behalf of those quite willing for it to be revealed, if that is the only basis for the claim.[7] In such a case, the correct analysis is not that a valid public interest claim is waived, but that no public interest is ever established.[8] It should also be remembered that, as the immunity is claimed in the public interest, any waiver can be made only by someone representing that public interest, and not by a stranger.[9]

In similar fashion, where the archive of an international organization was accorded inviolability on the same basis as a diplomatic mission, the House of Lords held that no objection could be taken to the use in litigation of documents that had been voluntarily communicated to third parties.[10] The act of communication prevented such documents from any longer attracting immunity, and the situation should be distinguished from deliberate waiver for the purposes of litigation. In these circumstances, it is sometimes said, where consent has been given to the release of the relevant information, and a fortiori where it has in fact been released, that the claim for immunity is not waived, but rather evaporates.[11]

Nor is the question of the admissibility of secondary evidence free from confusion. The general rule was stated many years ago by Bayley J: 'If the document cannot, on principles of public policy be read in evidence, the effect will be the same as if it was not in evidence, and you may not prove the contents of the instrument.'[12] It is important to understand

---

[5] [1983] 2 AC 394, [1983] 1 All ER 910; 436, 917; *Carey v The Queen in right of Canada* [1986] 2 SCR 637, 653; *Fletcher Timber Ltd v A-G* [1984] 1 NZLR 290, 291. The same rule does not necessarily apply to statutory versions: see *Babcock v A-G of Canada* 2002 SCC 57, [2002] 3 SCR 3 (Canada Evidence Act 1985, s 39).

[6] [1974] AC 405, [1973] 2 All ER 1169, 434, 1185. See also *Peach v Metropolitan Police Comr* [1986] QB 1064, [1986] 2 All ER 129; 1071, 131 (applying the same view to statements made to the police in the course of an internal inquiry).

[7] It might sometimes even be regarded as contrary to the public interest that information should be withheld when its suppliers wished it to be revealed.

[8] As suggested by Brightman LJ in *Hehir v Metropolitan Police Comr* [1982] 2 All ER 335, [1982] 1 WLR 715; 341, 723; approved by Lord Woolf in *R v Chief Constable of West Midlands, ex p Wiley* [1995] 1 AC 274, [1994] 3 All ER 420; 299A, 440d.   [9] *Wiley* (n8), 298G, 440b.

[10] *Shearson Lehman Bros Inc v Maclaine Watson Co Ltd (No 2)* [1988] 1 All ER 116, [1988] 1 WLR 16.

[11] *Multi-Guarantee Co Ltd v Cavalier Insurance Co* (1986) The Times, 24 June.

[12] *Cooke v Maxwell* (1817) 2 Stark 183, 186. See also Lynskey J in *Moss v Chesham UDC* (1945) 109 JP 167, cited by Simon (1955) CLJ 62: 'if it is contrary to public interest to produce the original documents, it must

that this prohibition is limited to secondary evidence of the documents, and does not necessarily, or even often,[13] extend to secondary evidence of the matters dealt with in the documents. Indeed, it is often a reason for upholding public interest immunity that the information contained in the relevant documents adds nothing to information in the hands of the parties that they may adduce in evidence without constraint.[14] This is not, however, to deny that, where the claim is based upon the vital importance of the contents of some documents, a national defence secret for example, any oral evidence of the matter in question might be prohibited.

It may thus be appreciated that, while there are clear analogies between claims for private privilege and those under consideration here, there are nevertheless important distinctions emphasized by the currently fashionable terminology of 'public interest immunity'.[15] Sometimes other private privileges[16] are asserted supplementary to public interest immunity. Any tendency to exploit the overlap in an attempt to resuscitate arguments based on candour, following the government's acceptance[17] of the recommendations of the Scott Report,[18] was deprecated by Scott VC in *Re Barings plc*,[19] and even argument by analogy rejected by the Privy Council in *Mount Murray Country Club v Macleod*.[20]

The most important part of public interest immunity is that of state interest, discussed in the early part of Section 1. Before referring to matters of detail, it would be well to emphasize the devastating effect that exclusion of such evidence can have on the substantive rights of litigants. It may render it totally impossible for them to rely on matters that would otherwise have constituted an unanswerable claim or a complete defence. It is particularly unacceptable when the entity seeking to suppress is party to the litigation, and most unacceptable of all when that party is the Crown, and the litigation, a criminal prosecution in which the information, or document, is vital to the defence.[21] In those circumstances, and in the aftermath of the Human Rights Act 1998, it is hardly surprising that the courts have eschewed fixed and firm rules of immunity in favour of a more flexible, case-specific approach balancing the public interest in suppression against the public interest of fair proceedings.[22] This extends to cases where the subject seeks information to enable him to rebut prosecution evidence.[23]

[S]ome derogation from the golden rule of full disclosure may be justified but such derogation must always be the minimum necessary to protect the public interest in question and must never imperil the overall fairness of the trial.

---

be equally contrary to public interest to produce copies which the maker of the document has kept for his own information'.

[13] *Wiley* (n8), 306G, 447d.

[14] See *Air Canada v Secretary of State for Trade (No 2)* (n5), 442, 920, per Lord Wilberforce (available documents 'primary'; those for which immunity was claimed 'secondary').

[15] For criticism of the new terminology of public interest immunity, see *R v Young* (1999) 46 NSWLR 681, 693 (full consideration of the criteria for establishing a new category of public interest immunity, separate from private privilege regarding records of psychiatric counselling of victims of sexual assaults).

[16] Most often legal professional privilege.

[17] See the Attorney-General's paper *Public Interest Immunity*, laid before the Houses of Parliament in December 1996.

[18] *Report of the Inquiry into the Export of Defence Equipment and Dual-Use Goods to Iraq and Related Prosecutions* (1996) vol IV, pt 5, sect K, ch 6.   [19] [1998] 1 All ER 673, 689.

[20] [2003] UKPC 53, [2003] STC 1525, [31]–[34].

[21] As in the *Matrix Churchill case*, which precipitated the Scott inquiry.

[22] *R v H and C* [2004] UKHL 3, [2004] 2 AC 134, [18].

[23] *Aamer v Secretary of State for Foreign and Commonwealth Affairs* [2009] EWHC 3316 (Admin).

It is, however, disturbing to note that claims for public interest immunity appear to be burgeoning, in particular in criminal cases,[24] that their resolution may affect not least the appearance of doing justice,[25] and that knowingly false claims have been advanced.[26]

SECTION 1. MATTERS OF PUBLIC INTEREST

This category has broadened and is capable of modification by the courts, as Lord Hailsham remarked in *D v National Society for Prevention of Cruelty to Children*: 'The categories of public interest are not closed and must alter from time to time whether by restriction or extension as social conditions and social legislation develop.'[27] On the other hand, the court will not lightly create a new class-based public interest since, as Lord Woolf said in *R v Chief Constable of West Midlands, ex p Wiley*, 'the recognition of a new class-based public interest immunity requires clear and compelling evidence that it is necessary'.[28] The tide of opinion seems also to be running towards increasingly open government.[29] Although the initiative has come from central government, its resonance may be felt in surrounding areas.[30] Lord Hailsham spoke in the context of an extension of public interest outside the confines of central government, concerning a claim for preservation of the anonymity of a supplier of information. That consideration raises the question of the underlying basis for this immunity. It is sometimes raised because the public interest demands that a particular *piece* of information not be revealed, and sometimes, because it demands that a particular *source* of information remain inviolate. Such demands are not, of course, mutually exclusive. The basis of claim may also affect the procedure for determining it, and, in particular, the desirability of the court's inspecting the relevant document in order to assist its decision. It is best to examine, first, the considerations and procedure that govern the clearest cases, those in which vital interests of state are affected,[31] and then to go on to consider how far the principles that apply there extend to less vital interests, such as material relating to parliamentary proceedings, to the police, to local government, and to matters of a confidential nature.[32] It is finally necessary to consider how far the rules extend to criminal cases.

No distinction is drawn between cases in which the Crown, or a government department, is a party to the proceedings, and those in which the parties are private citizens, or corporations. The former class of case has, however, increased since the Crown Proceedings Act 1947, and although an order for disclosure may be made against the Crown under s 28, it is expressly made subject to this doctrine of public policy.

---

[24] See Abrams The Guardian, 2 December 2003, and in *R v West* [2005] EWCA Crim 517, [4] ascribed by the trial judge to the growth of intelligence-led policing.

[25] Thus in *R v Templar* [2003] EWCA Crim 3186, [24] the Court of Appeal expressed concern that, during the trial, the judge retired to his room with prosecuting counsel alone on no fewer than 36 occasions.

[26] As vehemently criticized in *R (Al-Sweady) v Secretary of State for Defence* [2009] EWHC 1687 (Admin). For similarly flagrant overclaiming, see also in Canada, *Clerk of the Privy Council v Pelletier* ((2005) 253 DLR (4th) 435; and in Australia *Victoria v Brazel* [2008] VSCA 37, 181 ACR 562.

[27] [1978] AC 171, [1977] 1 All ER 589; 230, 605.   [28] (n8); 305, 446.

[29] See the Freedom of Information Act 2000, although this does not appear to diminish the range of material subject to public interest immunity at common law.

[30] As envisaged in the Attorney-General's 1996 paper *Public Interest Immunity* sect 4.6.

[31] In which the claim must be made by someone holding a very high office.

[32] In which the claim may be made by those in a much more humble position.

While the only basis for immunity from disclosure in the English courts is the public interest of the United Kingdom,[33] and the interests of a foreign state are not, in principle, alone sufficient,[34] two possible qualifications might be made. The first is that now as a member of the European Union, similar considerations apply to confer immunity in respect of the interests of organs of the Community, including the European Commission.[35] The second is that government may regard its own interests as affected, and so certify, by judicial disregard of the public interests of a foreign state.[36] This is particularly likely where the foreign state is a confidential source of vital information very[37] likely to dry up if revealed. It should also be noted that the discretionary power of the court extends to refusing to issue letters of request in relation to evidence seeking to impugn the motives of a foreign legislature.

VITAL INTERESTS OF STATE

The importance of particular pieces of information or classes of source to the interests of the state must obviously vary, not only from subject to subject, but also from time to time. There can be no clearly defined line between cases where such vital interests are at stake, and those where they are not. It is now recognized that many factors are involved, and such recognition has contributed to the current practice of assessing the relative importance of the policies suggesting suppression, and those favouring disclosure. Some particular pieces of information are of so important a nature at some times that it is hard to see how any contravening policy in favour of the administration of justice could outweigh them. Thus in *Asiatic Petroleum Co Ltd v Anglo-Persian Oil Co Ltd*,[38] the defendants, acting under the direction of the Board of Admiralty, refused to produce a letter to their agent on the ground that it contained information concerning the government's plans with regard to one of the Middle Eastern campaigns of the First World War. The information had, of course, been given to the defendants by the Board of Admiralty under the seal of the strictest security, but as Swinfen-Eady LJ observed:[39]

The foundation of the rule is that the information cannot be disclosed without injury to the public interests, and not that the documents are confidential or official, which alone is no reason for their non-production: the general public interest is paramount to the interests of the suitor.

The defendant's objection was upheld, and a similar principle successfully invoked in *Duncan v Cammell Laird & Co Ltd*,[40] where the defendants to a claim for damages for negligence in the construction of a submarine were directed by the Admiralty to object to the production of numerous documents in their possession as government contractors.

---

[33] Devolution may now present problems: see *Al-Megrahi v Her Majesty's Advocate and the Lord Advocate* [2008] HCJAC 15, 2008 SCCR 358.

[34] *Buttes Gas and Oil Co v Hammer (No 3)* [1981] QB 223, [1980] 3 All ER 475; a principle said to be even stronger in Ireland: *W v Ireland* [1997] 2 IR 141.

[35] *Hasselblad (GB) Ltd v Orbinson* [1985] QB 475, [1985] 1 All ER 173. See also *WWF UK v Commission* [1997] ECR II-313.

[36] The protection of a foreign central bank was sufficient in *Koo Golden East Mongolia v Bank of Nova Scotia* [2007] EWCA Civ 1443.

[37] *R (Mohamed) v Secretary of State for Foreign and Commonwealth Affairs* [2009] EWHC 2549 (Admin).

[38] [1916] 1 KB 822.

[39] 830.   [40] (n4).

The structure of submarines is clearly a matter that affects national security, and ought to be kept secret while the country is at war, as in that case.[41]

In both cases, the interest of the state would have been threatened by disclosure of the particular information contained in the relevant documents. All claims in this category are based on the damage to a vital public interest that disclosure will cause. It was formerly accepted that documents falling within certain, rather ill-defined,[42] classes were automatically exempt from disclosure upon this basis.[43] It became impossible to sustain such a view once courts began to adopt a balancing approach towards, and inspect for themselves, documents falling into such prime examples of such classes as Cabinet documents,[44] and those relating to the secret security services.[45] In *Commonwealth v Northern Land Council*,[46] the High Court of Australia distinguished between documents prepared for consideration by the Cabinet, and notes of the actual discussions and decisions of the Cabinet. The latter were regarded as particularly sensitive, and liable to be disclosed only in the most exceptional situations, highly unlikely ever to arise outside the context of criminal proceedings in which they might, just conceivably, be essential to establish the truth about a very serious offence.[47] This matter is occasionally the subject of direct statutory intervention.[48] The United Kingdom government has now declared,[49] in the Attorney-General's important paper *Public Policy Immunity*,[50] that as a matter of practice it will no longer claim suppression solely upon a document's membership of a given class. Instead, it will, in all cases, seek to show in detail in the certificate, or affidavit, the nature of the damage that disclosure

[41] The public interest in the security even of such pieces of information is ephemeral, and could hardly prevail once the campaign had been fought, or the design of the submarine become common knowledge; cf *R v Abbott* [2003] EWCA Crim 350, [25] denying that the passage of time eroded class-based immunity for confidential records. In *Turek v Slovakia* (2007) 44 EHRR 861, [115] it was held that even this exception did not survive a complete change of the political regime.

[42] The general lack of definition was noticed in *Victoria v Brazel* (n26), [19].

[43] See e.g. Lord Reid in *Conway v Rimmer* [1968] AC 910, [1968] 1 All ER 874; 952, 888; Lord Salmon in *Rogers v Secretary of State for the Home Department* (n4); 412, 1071.

[44] See e.g. in England *Air Canada v Secretary of State for Trade (No 2)* (n5); 432, 915; in Australia, *Sankey v Whitlam* (1978) 142 CLR 1; in New Zealand, *Environmental Defence Society Inc v South Pacific Aluminium Ltd (No 2)* [1981] 1 NZLR 153; in Canada, the matter is now governed by s 39 of the Canada Evidence Act: see *Babcock v A-G of Canada* (n5); and in the United States, *Nixon v United States* 418 US 683 (1974) (criminal); *Cheney v Dist Ct for Dist of Columbia* 542 US 367, 124 S Ct R 2576 (2004) (civil). In Canada, the same approach has been utilized in relation to the oral evidence of a Cabinet minister: *Smallwood v Sparling* (1982) 141 DLR (3d) 395, but see *Re Mulroney and Coates* (1986) 27 DLR (4th) 118. In Ireland, this result was achieved only by constitutional amendment: see *Irish Press Publications Ltd v Minister for Enterprise and Employment* [2002] 2 IR 110.

[45] See e.g. in Australia, *Alister v R* (1983) 154 CLR 404; in Canada, *Re Henrie and Security Intelligence Review Committee* (1988) 53 DLR (4th) 568, and in New Zealand, *Choudry v A-G* [1999] 2 NZLR 582. In England, the courts have shown more reluctance in relation to this category: see *Balfour v Foreign and Commonwealth Office* [1994] 2 All ER 588, [1994] 1 WLR 681 (in which documents relating to the security services were unsuccessfully required for the prosecution of a claim for unfair dismissal). The Security Services themselves seem to have adopted a more robust approach: see Scott Report vol III [G18.40].

[46] (1993) 176 CLR 604.

[47] Normally required by the defence to establish innocence; but still more exceptionally to support an allegation against a member of the Cabinet.

[48] For example, Parliamentary Commissioner Act 1967, s 8(4); Health Service Commissioners Act 1993, s 12(5). In these circumstances, the only sanction for refusal becomes political: see *Minister of Energy v Auditor General of Canada* [1989] 2 SCR 49. See also Canada Evidence Act, ss 37–39.

[49] It accepted the recommendation of the Scott Report vol IV ch 6 [K.1] that legislation was undesirable in this area.

[50] Section 4.1.

will be likely to cause.[51] It should nevertheless be noted that, in some cases, the damage to the public interest may be incremental, and that it does not necessarily follow that a document innocuous on its face can never qualify for suppression.

The operation of the new system is illustrated[52] in the paper in the three areas of national security, internal governmental discussion and advice, and international relations. The paper also sets out the way in which it is envisaged that the new regime will operate in practice. This builds upon the procedure set out most clearly by Bingham J in *Air Canada v Secretary of State for Trade (No 2)* at first instance,[53] and upon the approach adopted by Lord Woolf in *R v Chief Constable of West Midlands, ex p Wiley*.[54]

When the question first arises, usually at the stage of pre-trial disclosure,[55] it will be for the minister to consider whether a claim to immunity arises at all. It is envisaged that this will occur much less often under the new regime: partly because of the elimination of class claims; partly because of the use of editing, so as to eliminate material damaging to the relevant aspect of the public interest, while releasing those parts of the document necessary for the aspect of public interest concerned with the administration of justice;[56] and partly because the disclosure provisions of the Criminal Procedure and Investigations Act 1996[57] should better reveal issues relevant in criminal proceedings. The burden of this decision will also be reduced by the use of sampling techniques in relation to repetitive documents, provided that the techniques for such sampling are stated in the relevant certificate. The decision must, however, normally be made at ministerial level,[58] although the minister need not be the most senior in line,[59] and where the decision relates to a previous administration, the permanent secretary to the ministry may act.[60] It is also envisaged in the Attorney-General's paper[61] that, exceptionally, a minister will not be involved because a department is not headed by a minister, or where the court is content for the matter to be raised by an affidavit from an official, or even simply raised by counsel. It is to be hoped that little use will be made of these exceptions, since the best guarantee that claims will be made only in the most serious cases is to insist upon direct ministerial involvement. Officials might well be inclined to make claims on behalf of their departments that they would not wish to take to a minister. It is expected that the minister will, in future, be given

---

[51] Ibid, s 4.5.   [52] These categories are not intended to be exhaustive.

[53] [1983] 1 All ER 161, 164. Although his judgment was reversed on one point, his general approach was endorsed both by the House of Lords and by the Court of Appeal, by which he was described as an acknowledged authority upon the subject.   [54] (n8).

[55] See the Civil Procedure Rule 31.19, and Practice Direction 31, for detail of the current procedure. Similar principles applied to interrogatories, and will presumably extend to requests for further information under Pt 18 of the Civil Procedure Rules. See also *Whitlam v ACP Ltd* (1985) 73 FLR 414, 417.

[56] As recommended by Lord Woolf in *Wiley* (n8) 307A, 447f, in which he also canvasses other possibilities, such as the provision of information rather than a particular document, or a summary, or restricted, disclosure (despite his reluctance to disclose to counsel but not client), or by assurances or other forms of cooperation between counsel. For an example of heavy editing to avoid complete suppression, see *Three Rivers District Council v Bank of England* [2002] EWHC 2735 (Comm).   [57] See further, 280.

[58] Especially in any class claim, *Amaryllis Ltd v HM Treasury* [2009] EWHC 1666 (TCC), [44].

[59] In *Burmah Oil Co Ltd v Bank of England* [1980] AC 1090, [1979] 3 All ER 700, the claimant was the Chief Secretary of the Treasury, who although of Cabinet rank was subordinate to the Chancellor of the Exchequer; also in that case, it was regarded as appropriate for the Attorney-General to present the argument for immunity, even to the extent of arguing before the House of Lords without being made a party. In *Continental Reinsurance Corp (UK) Ltd v Pine Top Insurance Ltd* [1986] 1 Lloyd's Rep 8, 12, a junior and non-Cabinet minister was accepted as appropriate.   [60] As in *Air Canada* (n5).

[61] Section 2.4.

adequate time to make this decision, and have access to legal advice.[62] It was made clear in *Wiley*[63] that the minister should claim only if he is satisfied that there will be substantial danger in disclosure, or if he is uncertain. In either case, the certificate or affidavit must explain the nature of the apprehended danger as fully as possible, consistent with not pre-cipitating it, and may also claim immunity in respect of oral evidence of the documents. If the government is not a party, nor closely involved, it is open for one of the parties to seek a certificate from the government.[64] The question may, in any event, always be raised by a party, or by a witness, and should be taken by the court on its own initiative whenever it appears to arise.[65]

If a claim is made, it must then be subject to review by the court. Its first task is to estab-lish that the information or document for which the claim is made is indeed relevant, and in this context, it has been held that this means that it must be shown by the claimant that the document sought was not only relevant to the dispute, but also that it would assist his own case.[66] In *Air Canada*, the documents in question related to fixing landing fees at Heathrow airport. The plaintiffs contended that the Secretary of State had acted upon criteria different from those specified by the relevant statutory provision, and sought dis-closure of relevant documents that included some Cabinet papers, and documents relating to meetings held between the Secretary of State and his advisers, and between the advisers. The plaintiff was not in a position to demonstrate that these documents would support his case, and even if they did, it was felt that they could add nothing to other evidence of the matters in question, already available to the plaintiffs. This point, one of disclosure[67] rather than evidence, was decisive.

The problem for the party seeking disclosure is that, because of the requirements of English law[68] as reiterated in *Air Canada*, he has to show that the documents are very likely to assist his case before he has had any opportunity to see them.[69] Under the Civil Procedure Rules,[70] a party who believes that disclosure has been defective may apply for specific disclosure, but must adduce evidence to justify the claim.[71] While perfectly rea-sonable to prevent 'fishing', it would not seem unreasonable to put the burden of showing that the documents need not be disclosed upon the party who usually possesses them, and refuses disclosure.[72]

---

[62] Section 2.3.   [63] (n8).

[64] In *Buttes Gas and Oil Co v Hammer (No 3)* (n34), such an application was made, but was unsuccessful.

[65] *Rogers v Home Secretary* (n4); 400, 1065. It is permissible for the question to be raised on appeal without notice as it was in the *Buttes Gas* case (n34). The failure of a party to challenge the certificate is no admission of the truth of its contents: *Sethia v Stern* (1987) The Independent, 30 October.

[66] It would now usually need to fulfil the criteria set out in CPR 31.6.

[67] Discovery, as it was then called.

[68] It is significant that in jurisdictions with different rules of discovery there seems less inclination to refuse inspection upon any such basis, even in the case of higher state documents: see, in New Zealand, *Fletcher Timber Ltd v A-G* (n5), 293; and in Canada, *Carey v The Queen in right of Canada* (n5), 194. In Australia refusal requires more justification in criminal cases: *Australian Crime Commission v Magistrates' Court Victoria* [2007] VSC 297, 173 ACR 572, [15]–[21].

[69] In criminal cases where documents have been seized, relevance is a matter for the investigator, and cannot be delegated to a special advocate: *Faisaltex Ltd v Chief Constable of Lancashire Constabulary* [2009] EWHC 1884 (QB), [26].

[70] CPR 31.12.

[71] Practice Direction 31 [5.2]. See also, in Australia, *CTC Resources NL v Australian Stock Exchange Ltd* [2000] WASCA 19, (2000) 22 WALR 48.

[72] Held to breach ECHR equality provisions in *Turek v Slovakia* (n41), [116].

Once a claim has been made upon such a basis, or if the judge discerns such an interest himself, for example where the Crown is not a party,[73] the judge's task is to compare the public interest in the administration of justice secured by disclosure with that set out in the certificate, or discerned by the court, in favour of suppression.[74] In striking a balance, the court will take into account factors such as the seriousness of the claim for which disclosure is sought,[75] whether or not the government is itself a party or alleged to have acted unconscionably,[76] the relevance of the particular evidence to the dispute,[77] taking into account other possible sources of evidence,[78] and on the other side, the nature of the state's interest,[79] and the length of time that has elapsed since the relevant discussion took place.[80] In one Canadian case, the fact that the government had set up the relevant Royal Commission before which the evidence was sought to be tendered was regarded as favouring admissibility.[81] Only if the court is doubtful about the balance, or provisionally in favour of disclosure, will it seek to inspect.[82] In the latter, it would normally inspect to confirm its provisional view before ordering disclosure, and, in the case of a lower court, would postpone disclosure pending appeal.[83] It is important to distinguish the separate questions of whether the document should be inspected by the court, and whether it should be disclosed to the other party. These questions arise at different stages of the reasoning process, and must not be run together.[84]

[73] CPR 31.19(1) is careful to refer to a 'person' rather than to a 'party'. See also CPR 31.19(6)(b).

[74] The existing law on public interest immunity is preserved by CPR 31.19(8). The Rules affect only procedure.

[75] Thus in *Henrie* (n45), the fact that it related to security clearance so as to permit promotion within the government service was thought insufficiently compelling.

[76] See *Burmah Oil* (n59), 1128, 720. See also *Sankey v Whitlam* (n44), 56; *Carey* (n5), 673; *Koowarta v Bjelke-Petersen* (1988) 92 FLR 104. In these circumstances, there is a danger that justice will not be done because the interest of the government has been assimilated to that of the state, and a certainty that it will not have been seen to be done.

[77] See *Hospitals Consolidated Fund of Australia v Hunt* (1983) 76 FLR 408.

[78] An important consideration in *Air Canada* (n5); it was, however, decided in Australia in *Adelaide Brighton Cement* (1999) 75 SASR 209 that it is not a condition for disclosure that the case be unprovable without access to the evidence.

[79] Preferring disclosure of discussion even at the highest level if the subject was of commercial rather than security matters: see *Hospitals Consolidated Fund of Australia v Hunt* (1983) 76 FLR 408. In the United States, there is a special 'deliberative process' immunity for intragovernmental communications: see *NLRB v Sears Roebuck & Co* 421 US 132 (1975); but it is strictly confined, *Department of Interior v Klamath Water Users* 532 US 1 (2001).

[80] *A-G v Jonathan Cape Ltd* [1976] QB 752, [1975] 3 All ER 484; 770, 496. See also *Sankey v Whitlam* (n44), 41, 42.

[81] *Re The Queen and the Royal Commission into the Donald Marshall Junior Prosecution* (1988) 51 DLR (4th) 705.

[82] Inspection by the court is sometimes allowed by a party despite his claim for immunity: see Lord Wilberforce in *Burmah Oil* (n59), 1116, 711 citing *Tito v Waddell* [1975] 3 All ER 997, [1975] 1 WLR 1303, and *Barty-King v Ministry of Defence* [1979] 2 All ER 80, [1979] STC 218.

[83] In *Burmah Oil* (n59), Lord Keith said, 1136, 727, that a judge should not undertake even inspection without allowing time for appeal, but invoked Lord Reid in *Conway v Rimmer* (n43) as authority, yet Lord Reid referred only to production. In *Air Canada* (n5), Bingham J accordingly proposed the procedure stated in the text, approved by Lord Fraser.

[84] See, under the old law, *Continental Reinsurance Corp (UK) Ltd v Pine Top Insurance Ltd* [1986] 1 Lloyd's Rep 8; see now the Civil Procedure Rules Pt 31, which clearly distinguishes disclosure and inspection.

The court's power to inspect applied even under the old law to documents of vital state interest, such as Cabinet papers.[85] This became clearer when it was recognized that the power to inspect was not limited to cases in which the court was doubtful whether the documents really fell within the public interest claimed, but also extended to cases in which the doubt was whether or not that claim overbalanced the countervailing public interest in the administration of justice. A further advantage of inspection is that it may enable partial disclosure of documents. Sometimes the most relevant parts can without distortion be severed from those whose disclosure would be overly inimical to vital interests of state,[86] or to supply a summary of their contents rather than complete original documents.[87] It is also possible, in some cases, for the courts to restrict disclosure to the legal advisers of the parties,[88] or, even in civil claims,[89] to a special advocate representing but separate from the non-state party,[90] to order proceedings to be held in camera,[91] and to impose orders restricting the reporting of proceedings;[92] and may well choose to do so if the alternative is the abandonment of the trial.[93] Another method, at first approved by the House of Lords,[94] extending an innovation devised[95] in the context of cases involving police informers, was to permit disclosure only to a special security-cleared advocate, who could then argue the case on behalf of the accused, but without further contact with him after disclosure of the sensitive information. Although at first apparently approved, for some cases at least, by the European Court of Human Rights in *Chahal v United Kingdom*,[96] the procedure was held to prevent a fair trial when the material withheld from the accused prevented him from knowing enough of the allegations against him to be able to mount an effective defence.[97] The House

---

[85] See, under the old law, e.g. Lord Fraser in *Air Canada* (n5), 432, 915; but see *Balfour v Foreign and Colonial Office* (n45); see now CPR 31.19(6)(a). See, in Ireland, *McDonald v Radio Telefís Éireann* [2001] 1 IR 355.   [86] See e.g. Lord Keith in *Burmah Oil* (n59), 1135, 726.

[87] As in *R v Hansford* [2006] EWCA Crim 1225 (accompanied there by an admission of truth, since the evidence helped the accused); held not to be a breach of the ECHR in *Botmeh and Alami v UK* (2008) 46 EHRR 659.

[88] *Church of Scientology of California v Department of Health and Social Security* [1979] 3 All ER 97, [1979] 1 WLR 723, although it seems that the court should not discriminate between counsel and solicitors: *WEA Records Ltd v Visions Channel 4 Ltd* [1983] 2 All ER 589, [1983] 1 WLR 721. In *Baker v Paper Sacks* [1995] CLY 4119, the restriction was to a party's medical advisers.

[89] *Al Rawi v Security Service* [2009] EWHC 2959.

[90] See *Secretary of State for Home Affairs v AE* [2008] EWHC 132 (Admin); although this procedure remains controversial.

[91] In the very case that enunciated the general obligation for courts to sit in public, it was recognized that they could sit in camera if the administration of justice so required: *Scott v Scott* [1913] AC 417. This inherent power has been supplemented in certain cases by explicit statutory provision, e.g. Official Secrets Act 1920, s 8(4). Appeals against any such decision may also be heard in camera: Criminal Procedure Rules 2005 r 67.2, held to be compatible with the European Convention in *R (A) v Crown Court at Central Criminal Court* [2006] EWCA Crim 4, [2006] 2 All ER 1.

[92] Contempt of Court Act 1981, s 11, stilling doubts vented in *A-G v Leveller Magazines Ltd* [1979] AC 440, [1979] 1 All ER 745. See also *Times Newspapers Ltd v R* [2007] EWCA Crim 1925.

[93] *R v Wong Yam* [2008] EWCA Crim 269.

[94] *Secretary of State for the Home Office v MB* [2007] UKHL 46, [2008] 1 AC 440.

[95] See further Ip [2008] Pub L 717.   [96] (1996) 23 EHRR 413, (1996) 1 BHRC 405.

[97] *A v United Kingdom* (2009) 26 BHRC 1, [220]. But see in Canada, *Charkaoui v Canada* 2007 SCC 9, [2007] SCR 350, [55].

of Lords has now somewhat reluctantly agreed to apply that ruling domestically,[98] and it has so been applied in subsequent cases.[99]

It is always the case that documents compulsorily disclosed under Pt 31 of the Civil Procedure Rules should be used only for the purposes of the litigation in question, and not for any ulterior purpose,[100] even after being put in evidence in open court.[101] There is no general public policy to prevent disclosure[102] of documents acquired by compulsory process, for example by liquidators to prosecutors or regulatory authorities,[103] or conversely, from prosecutors or regulatory authorities to liquidators,[104] although no disclosure will be ordered without giving the party affected a chance to be heard.[105]

REPORTS OF PROCEEDINGS IN PARLIAMENT

Questions have arisen about immunity from use in evidence[106] of reports of Parliamentary proceedings. It was settled in 1688[107] that proceedings in Parliament ought not to be questioned in any court, although statements in parliament can be used to assist construction of statutory provisions,[108] or more generally to determine the purpose for which a statute was enacted.[109] At common law, this privilege cannot be waived either by an individual member, or by the House.[110] In *Church of Scientology v Johnson-Smith*,[111] this was interpreted

---

[98] *Secretary of State for the Home Department v AF (No 3)* [2009] UKHL 28, [2009] 3 All ER 643.

[99] *BM v Secretary of State for the Home Department* [2009] EWHC 1572 (Admin) (modification of control order); *K Tariq v Home Office* (2009) unreported EAT 16 October; *Secretary of State for the Home Department v AS* [2009] EWHC 2564 (Admin) (sufficient disclosure for effective instructions); *Secretary of State for the Home Department v BC* (2009) unrep QBD 11 November. Repatriation may involve different considerations: *RB v Secretary of State for the Home Department* [2009] HL 10, [2009] 4 All ER 1045.

[100] CPR 31.22(1). For the practice under the old law, see *Riddick v Thames Board Mills Ltd* [1977] QB 881, [1977] 3 All ER 677. The ban even extended to closely related proceedings against the same defendants: *Miller v Scorey* [1996] 3 All ER 18, [1996] 1 WLR 1122.

[101] *Harman v Home Office* [1983] 1 AC 280, [1982] 1 All ER 532. This case is particularly significant, since the material revealed had been the subject of a claim to public interest immunity, and the documents had been ordered to be produced only after inspection by the judge: *Williams v Home Office* [1981] 1 All ER 1151. The extent of this obligation was accorded a most conservative construction under the old law: see *Apple Corp Ltd v Apple Computer Inc* [1992] 1 CMLR 969; *Singh v Christie* (1993) The Times, 11 November; *SmithKline Beecham Biologics SA v Connaught Laboratories Inc* [1999] FSR 284; and now made subject to explicit judicial control, CPR 31.22(3).

[102] As opposed to use in evidence, from which it was sharply distinguished in *R v Hertfordshire City Council, ex p Green* [2000] 2 AC 412, [2000] 1 All ER 773, following the decision of the European Court of Human Rights in *Saunders v United Kingdom* (1996) 23 EHRR 313, and noting the implementation of its policy in Sch 3 to the Youth Justice and Criminal Evidence Act 1999: see further above, 432.

[103] *Re Headington Investments* [1993] Ch 452, [1993] 3 All ER 861.

[104] *Wallace Smith Trust Co Ltd v Deloitte, Haskins & Sells* [1996] 4 All ER 403.

[105] *Soden v Burns* [1996] 3 All ER 967, [1996] 1 WLR 1512.

[106] Different rules may apply to pre-trial disclosure or search: see *Crane v Gething* [2000] FCA 45, (2000) 169 ALR 727, [46].

[107] Bill of Rights 1688, Art 9. See also US Const Art I cl 6.1: *United States v Johnson* 383 US 169 (1966).

[108] *Pepper v Hart* [1993] AC 593, [1993] 1 All ER 42, *Rv Secretary of State for the Home Department, ex p Brind* [1991] 1 AC 696, [1991] 1 All ER 720; in *Toussaint v Att-Gen for St. Vincent & The Grenadines* [2007] UKPC 48, [2008] 1 All ER 1, local legislation requiring the Speaker's permission for such use was held unconstitutional.

[109] *Three Rivers District Council v Bank of England (No 2)* [1996] 2 All ER 363, especially if there were a European dimension.

[110] *Hamilton v Al Fayed* [2001] 1 AC 395, 405.   [111] [1972] 1 QB 522, [1972] 1 All ER 378.

broadly to exclude the use of such reports in evidence to impugn the motives and intentions of members in any proceedings. It seems to be the case that the judge should, as in other public policy situations, intervene himself if the point is not taken by the parties.[112] In an extreme case in which it would be impossible to adjudicate without access to such excluded material, the court may stay an action, but it is normally immaterial that the claim is brought by a member of the body concerned, and the material required by way of defence.[113]

LOCAL GOVERNMENT MATTERS

Immunity is granted, and granted only, in the public interest. If no public interest is asserted, but merely an interest of a local authority, it will not be accepted as alone justifying immunity.[114] Sometimes, however, a matter of national concern raising a clear public interest is entrusted to a local authority. It is not then conclusive against the recognition of immunity that the claim is made by the local authority, even though unsupported by an affidavit from a minister.[115] Still less is it conclusive in favour of immunity that the question arises in wardship proceedings.[116] Thus in *D v National Society for the Prevention of Cruelty to Children*, the House of Lords recognized, obiter, such a claim in relation to information given to the local authority to enable it to discharge its statutory duties in relation to the care of children.[117] It is, however, likely to be rare that a claim for public interest immunity, raised only by a local authority, and supported by affidavits not from ministers, but local professional advisers, will prevail against the public interest in the administration of justice,[118] especially in a case in which the documents are of the utmost significance to the outcome of the litigation for which they are required,[119] or in which different official bodies take opposing views in relation to disclosure.[120] In this area, as elsewhere, the principles laid down in *Air Canada* regarding balancing for both inspection and disclosure are appropriate,[121] and more than mere relevance is required before disclosure of social service files will be ordered.[122] It should be noted that the decision remains one for the judge, even though a local official may have given assurances of confidentiality to the supplier of the relevant information.[123]

---

[112] See *R v Murphy* (1986) 64 ALR 498.

[113] *Prebble v Television New Zealand Ltd* [1995] 1 AC 321, [1994] 3 All ER 407; where the evidence is required by a member to defend a defamation claim, the position has been amended by statute both in England by the Defamation Act 1996, s 13, and in Australia, by the Parliamentary Privileges Act 1987.

[114] *Blackpool Corp v Locker* [1948] 1 KB 349, [1948] 1 All ER 85, as interpreted by Lord Edmund-Davies in *D v National Society for the Prevention of Cruelty to Children* (n27); 245, 618.

[115] The procedure is set out in *Re C (child cases: evidence and disclosure)* [1995] 1 FLR 204.

[116] *Re M (A Minor)* [1990] 2 FLR 36, disapproving *Re S* [1987] Fam 199.

[117] *Re D (infants)* [1970] 1 All ER 1088, [1970] 1 WLR 599, is similar, but *Campbell v Tameside Metropolitan Borough Council* [1982] QB 1065, [1982] 2 All ER 791; 1077, 798, shows its strictly confined ambit.

[118] Access by guardians *ad litem* is governed by s 42 of the Children Act 1989, and overrides any claim to public interest immunity: see *A Metropolitan Borough Council v JJ* [2003] EWHC 976 (Fam).

[119] In cases involving the sexual abuse of children, local protocols govern the disclosure of local authority records, and it is common for relevance to be decided by lawyers acting for the local authority: see e.g. *R v Abbott* (n41), [26]. For North American attitudes, see, in Canada, *R v O'Connor* [1995] 4 SCR 411; and in the United States, *Pennsylvania v Ritchie* 480 US 62 (1993).

[120] As in *Re G (a minor) (social worker: disclosure)* [1996] 2 All ER 65, [1996] 1 WLR 1407.

[121] *Re M* (n116).   [122] *R v Reading Justices, ex p Berkshire County Council* [1996] 1 Cr App Rep 239.

[123] *Re G (welfare report: disclosure)* [1993] 2 FLR 293.

POLICE MATERIALS[124]

Despite the fact that the police are not strictly to be regarded as an emanation of the state, it has been common[125] to accord public policy immunity to some, at least, of the information and documents held by them. Information may come into the hands of the police either in the course of an internal inquiry, or from outside the police force in the ordinary course of police business.[126] Other materials may be generated by the police themselves in either pursuit, or indeed independently. It seems clear that rules both of privilege, and of public interest immunity apply differently in criminal proceedings,[127] and for this reason, the discussion here is divided between public interest immunity for policing material as it applies in civil and criminal proceedings.

Civil proceedings

These are mainly claims against the police, although, on occasion, members of the police force themselves seek to pursue proceedings in relation to matters arising in connection with their work.[128] *Conway v Rimmer*,[129] the genesis of much of the modern law on the whole topic of public interest immunity, is more typical. In that case, the appellant had been a probationary police constable. He was accused by a fellow probationer of stealing a cheap torch, and was ultimately prosecuted by the respondent, a superintendent in that police force. The prosecution was unsuccessful, but the appellant was dismissed from the police force. He brought a claim for malicious prosecution, and sought disclosure of probationary reports upon him, made both before and after the allegations of theft, and of a report to the Director of Public Prosecutions about the circumstances. The Home Secretary claimed Crown privilege upon the basis that disclosure would injure the public interest. The House of Lords rejected the claims in respect of ostensibly routine documents such as the probation reports, or in the case of the report to the Director of Public Prosecutions after the occasion of the prosecution had passed. It was relevant that the documents were of crucial importance to the outcome of the case.[130]

More often, the issue concerns information coming to the police from external sources. The facts of *Rogers v Secretary of State for the Home Department*[131] make a neat transition. An applicant for a gaming licence was unsuccessful. Subsequently, he came into possession of a copy of a letter written to the Gaming Board by a police officer in relation to his application, which, he alleged, contained defamatory statements. He sought to prosecute the officer for criminal libel, and served witness summonses upon the Secretary of the Gaming Board and the relevant chief constable to testify, and to produce relevant documents, including the original letter. The summonses were set aside by the Divisional

---

124 It was explicitly denied in Australia in *R v Robertson, ex p McAuley* (1983) 71 FLR 429, 438 that police materials are sufficiently homogenous to constitute a class to which immunity can attach.

125 *Conway v Rimmer* (n43); Lord Reid, 953G, 889D ('never doubted').

126 In *Spigelman v Hocken* (1933) 50 TLR 87, a claim was made for completely routine witness statements made to the police after a road accident.

127 *R v Brown; R v Daley* (1987) 87 Cr App Rep 52, 57 ('always accepted'). But see *R v Robertson* (n124). It has also been recognized by statute: see Iron and Steel Act 1982, s 33(1). Some statutory provisions of a like character, such as the Regulation of Investigatory Powers Act 2000, s 17, which prohibits any evidence or cross-examination on certain sensitive matters, apply indifferently to civil and criminal proceedings alike.

128 As in *Ex p Coventry Newspapers Ltd* [1993] QB 278, [1993] 1 All ER 86, where defamation was alleged by police officers.   129 See also *Konia v Morley* [1976] 1 NZLR 455.

130 They were requested by both parties.   131 (n4).

Court. The House of Lords upheld this decision, not on the basis that the letter was a policy document, but because its production might jeopardize the working of the public service. The House was impressed by the fact that the police, in responding to inquiries from the Gaming Board, and the Board itself, depended upon the provision of information from members of the public, and that such sources might be threatened if protection from disclosure could not be guaranteed.

An example of materials generated by the police outwith the course of an inquiry or investigation occurred in *Goodwin v Chief Constable of Greater Manchester*,[132] in which the plaintiffs sought discovery of a police operations manual in support of their claim for personal injuries suffered in the course of operations of the sort included in the manual. There, the claim failed because of insufficient demonstration of the need for disclosure of the manual. Police information relating to the identity of its informers[133] constitutes one of the most sensitive categories of material, and the strong view was expressed by Lord Diplock in *D v National Society for the Prevention of Cruelty to Children*[134] that:

> By the uniform practice of the judges which by the time of *Marks v Beyfus*, (1890) 25 QBD 494, had already hardened into a rule of law, the balance has fallen on the side of non-disclosure except where upon the trial of a defendant for a criminal offence disclosure of the identity of the informer could help to show that the defendant was innocent of the offence. In that case, and in that case only, the balance falls on the side of disclosure.

It has even been held that the police would be open to a claim for damages if they did disclose the identity of an informer.[135]

The extreme severity of that view in civil proceedings has not, however, prevailed. Indeed, it was never completely justified, since in *Marks v Beyfus* itself civil actions for malicious prosecution were explicitly equated with criminal cases in which the accused sought disclosure to demonstrate his innocence. It was subsequently decided in *Savage v Chief Constable of Hampshire*[136] that, if the informer himself were content for his name to be disclosed, and no greater public interest was at stake, disclosure be allowed, thus effectively introducing a balancing test.[137] The balancing test has now been adopted on a more general basis,[138] and applied even in a case in which the informer did not wish his identity to be disclosed.[139] It remains, of course, the case that the interest in disclosure is likely to be less strong in a civil case in which the party seeking it is merely claiming damages, than in criminal proceedings in which disclosure is necessary to secure acquittal.[140]

---

[132] [1993] PIQR P187. See also *Carnduff v Rock* [2001] EWCA Civ 680, [2001] 1 WLR 1786, where an informer was suing for remuneration, and it was felt that ventilation would expose police operations unduly.

[133] This category is not self-evident, and includes many different categories of persons and different relationships to the police, for judicial recognition of which, see *R v Agar* [1990] 2 All ER 442, 90 Cr App Rep 318; 444g, 320. In Canada, see *R v Gordon* (1999) 136 CCC 3d 64 (excluding from category material witnesses to crime and agents provocateurs); *R v Babes* (2000) 146 CCC 3d 465 (excluding members of public acting under directions of police).   [134] (n27).

[135] *Swinney v Chief Constable of Northumbria* [1997] QB 464, [1996] 3 All ER 449.

[136] [1997] 2 All ER 631, [1997] 1 WLR 1061.   [137] See also *Carnduff v Rock* (n132).

[138] Partly in view of the influence of the European Convention on Human Rights.

[139] *Chief Constable of Greater Manchester v McNally* [2002] EWCA Civ 14, [2002] 2 Cr App Rep 617, although one of the considerations was that the party seeking disclosure already knew the identity of the alleged informer.

[140] As noted in *Powell v Chief Constable of North Wales* (2000) The Times, 11 February; see also *Law Society v Karim* (2005) unreported Ch, 5 July.

In civil proceedings, the first hurdle is to demonstrate that the documents sought relate to the cause of action, and that their inspection is necessary to dispose fairly of it. Some of the cases seeking information from the police have fallen at this stage, rendering any consideration of public interest immunity strictly irrelevant.

Claims have been made[141] by complainants for documentation arising in the course of the police complaints procedure[142] to assist with civil litigation arising from the subject matter of the complaints. The view was taken that public interest immunity should be claimed wherever it might conceivably arise, so as to pass the relevant decision on to the court. This view was criticized in the Scott Report,[143] and overruled in *R v Chief Constable of the West Midlands, ex p Wiley*.[144] Judicial review[145] was sought of the refusal of the chief constables[146] to give an undertaking that complaints material[147] would not be used in the preparation of defences to civil claims alleging police misconduct. In the House of Lords,[148] both applicants and the chief constables agreed that complaints material was not, as a class, entitled to public policy immunity,[149] and eventually even the Police Complaints Authority agreed.[150] Although perhaps to some extent weakened by the absence of argument to the contrary, the House of Lords expressed its unanimous adherence to the view that no class immunity extended to police complaints procedure material, and overruled the cases[151] asserting the contrary. It was conceded that, in some cases, a 'contents' claim might be made for particular pieces of complaints material, and the possibility of a 'class' claim for a sub category, such as the report of the officer investigating a complaint, was not totally excluded.[152] It has indeed since been accepted.[153] That acceptance has itself since been confirmed, opining rather ominously that, in the case of routine reports, the claim can be made at a low level within the police force.[154] Indeed, despite the Attorney-General's paper disavowing class claims in relation to government documents, this was subsequently said to correspond to the government's thinking.[155] It does, however, seem, even in such cases, that the threshold test to secure inspection by the judge was no higher

---

[141]   Including *Neilson v Laugherne* [1981] QB 736, [1981] 1 All ER 829; *Hehir v Metropolitan Police Comr* (n8); *Halford v Sharples* [1992] 3 All ER 624, [1992] 1 WLR 736; *Makanjuola v Metropolitan Police Comr* [1992] 3 All ER 617 (decided in 1989).

[142]   The earlier cases were concerned with the procedure established by the Police Act 1964, s 49, and the later with that under Pt IX of the Police and Criminal Evidence Act 1984. A different system was introduced under the Police Act 1996, and is itself scheduled for replacement by a new Police Reform Bill.

[143]   Vol III [G18.52] et seq.   [144]   (n8).   [145]   And injunctions against its use.

[146]   Two appeals were consolidated.

[147]   In *Halford v Sharples* (n141), this category had been extended to internal complaints as well as to complaints from the general public under s 49 of the Police Act 1964.

[148]   But not before, since *Neilson v Laugherne* (n141) was binding up to the level of the Court of Appeal.

[149]   The Attorney-General declined to intervene.

[150]   Although it still wished to assert public interest immunity in a number of different narrower respects.   [151]   *Neilson, Hehir*, and *Makanjuola* (all n 141).

[152]   Lord Woolf, with whom all of the other judges agreed in the result, was inclined against such a claim, but on this Lord Slynn and Lord Lloyd expressly reserved their view. In *R (Green) v Police Complaints Authority* [2004] UKHL 6, [2004] 2 All ER 209, it was also held that even where public interest immunity did not apply, it did not mean that disclosure need take place to the complainant during the hearing of the complaint, notwithstanding Art 2 of the European Convention on Human Rights.

[153]   *Taylor v Anderton* [1995] 2 All ER 420, [1995] 1 WLR 447.

[154]   *O'Sullivan v Metropolitan Police Comr* (1995) 139 SJLB 164.

[155]   *Kelly v Metropolitan Police Comr* (1997) The Times, 28 August.

than that for discovery in general.[156] This may serve to prevent suppression of such reports as a matter of routine.

The House of Lords offered support for the views expressed in earlier cases that a 'class' claim in this area can be no more than provisional, both as to inspection by the court,[157] and to liability to disclose to the applicant when the administration of justice so dictates in relation to a particular document.[158] It was also remarked that the balance between different aspects of the public interest may change as the factual basis of the case develops.[159] It also seems that this aspect of public policy may be overridden by the administration of justice, not only where that operates in favour of the accused, but occasionally against his interests, for example in the best interests of a child.[160]

As noted above, the matter was raised in *R v Chief Constable of the West Midlands, ex p Wiley* by way of an application for judicial review of the decisions of the chief constables, and for an injunction to prevent use of immune material. The House of Lords thought it better that the matter normally be raised in the civil proceedings for which the material was required. In *Bennett v Metropolitan Police Comr*,[161] the procedural context was the still more unusual one of a claim against the relevant minister for impropriety in the consideration of whether to make a claim for immunity. It is significant that, although the point was not finally determined, it was held arguable that the minister is under a duty to weigh the aspect of the administration of justice against that of suppression of a class[162] of police documents before making a claim. The facts of that case reveal the vital importance of continuing judicial control over the actions of the executive in this matter, since it was evident that no damage would be done to any wider interest than the preservation of an agency of government[163] from an embarrassing disclosure.

Disclosure of police information to family courts has also caused some concern, reflected in the design and pilot operation of a special protocol to govern the issue.[164]

Criminal proceedings[165]

It has already been noted that a claim to public interest immunity may be overridden when the evidence may enable the accused to resist an allegation made by the Crown or to

---

[156] *Goodridge v Chief Constable of Hampshire* [1999] 1 All ER 896, [1999] 1 WLR 1558.

[157] *R v Backhouse* [1993] Crim LR 69.

[158] See e.g. *Makanjuola v Metropolitan Police Comr* (n141), 623; *Ex p Coventry Newspapers Ltd* [1993] QB 278, [1993] 1 All ER 86; 289, 93; *Taylor v Anderton* (n153).

[159] A point also stressed in *R v Bower* [1994] Crim LR 281.

[160] See *Re M (care proceedings: police videos)* [1995] 2 FLR 571, in which police videos, which would normally have been subject to public interest immunity, were made available for use in care proceedings involving a different child. [161] [1995] 2 All ER 1, [1995] 1 WLR 488.

[162] There, communications with overseas police forces.

[163] The Crown Prosecution Service's employment of a stratagem to evade the unwelcome absence of an extradition treaty with the relevant jurisdiction.

[164] O'Connor and Dixon *Disclosure of Police Information in Family Proceedings: A qualitative evaluation of the pilot protocol* (March 2006). See also *Working Together to Safeguard Children* (DfES, 2006), and below, 497, for disclosure of other confidential records to family courts.

[165] For a full account of the position immediately before the passage of Pt 1 of the Criminal Procedure and Investigations Act 1996, see the Scott Report (n18) vol IV, pt 5, sect K.6.

establish his innocence.[166] In relation to public interest immunity, it was stated by a Lord Chancellor that:[167]

...if medical documents, or indeed other documents, are relevant to the defence in criminal proceedings, Crown privilege should not be claimed.

It was made clear that the rule was far-reaching, and applied even to prosecutions for minor offences. It should, however, be noted that the reference is to the practice of claiming Crown privilege, and not to its non-existence as a matter of law. Indeed, such existence is rather presumed by the form of the statement, and may well be necessary, since it can hardly be supposed that there are no means of preventing disclosure of the most vital national secrets just because they are relevant to the defence of one accused of some most trivial[168] offence. On the other hand, it also seems clear that, in cases in which the liberty of the claimant is at stake,[169] the public interest in the administration of justice will weigh very heavily in the balance,[170] although it may be outweighed if the relevance of the material is at best peripheral.[171] It was officially expected that the occasion for claiming public interest immunity in criminal cases would be much diminished by Pt 1 of the Criminal Procedure and Investigations Act 1996.[172]

It is useful to distinguish in this context evidence relating to the identity of informers as such from that relating to the location of places of observation.[173]

Identity of informers[174]

Here, too, the general rule is relaxed in favour of the defence, as Lord Simon of Glaisdale recognized in *Rogers v Home Secretary*:[175]

Sources of police information are a judicially recognised class of evidence excluded on the grounds of public policy *unless their production is required to establish innocence in a criminal trial.*

Since the rule exists for the protection of informers,[176] it cannot, without further justification, be applied to prevent the informer himself from adducing evidence of his having

---

[166] 489. The rules apply in the ordinary way to evidence required by the prosecution: see *R v King* [1983] 1 All ER 929, [1983] 1 WLR 411; 931, 414.

[167] 197 HL Official Report (5th series) col 745, quoted by Lord Reid in *Conway v Rimmer* (n43); 942, 881.

[168] See the converse in *R v Clowes* [1992] 3 All ER 440, 95 Cr App Rep 440, in which the *seriousness* of the charge militated against suppression.

[169] Although not once liberty has been lost, as in the case of someone already a prisoner: *Mulkerrins v Price Waterhouse Coopers (a firm)* [2003] UKHL 41, [2003] 4 All ER 1.

[170] *R v Governor of Brixton Prison, ex p Osman* [1992] 1 All ER 108, [1991] 1 WLR 281; 116, 288.

[171] *Re Manda* [1993] Fam 183, [1993] 1 All ER 733; *Morrow, Geach and Thomas v DPP* [1994] Crim LR 58.   [172] See Attorney-General's paper *Public Interest Immunity* (1996) [2.5] et seq.

[173] Exposition is made difficult since, in some cases, the nature of the issue leads to vestigial reporting, even of the grounds for allowing an appeal years after an initial conviction, as in *R v Doubtfire* [2001] 2 Cr App Rep 209.   [174] See in Canada *Named Person v Vancouver Sun* 2007 SCC 43, [2007] 3 SCR 252.

[175] (n4); 407, 1067 (emphasis supplied), citing *R v Hardy* (1794) 24 State Tr 1076; *Hennessy v Wright* (1888) 21 QBD 509; *Marks v Beyfus* (1890) 25 QBD 494. See also *Roviaro v United States* 353 US 53 (1957) for a similar approach in the United States.

[176] The strength of this interest is indicated in *Swinney v Chief Constable of Northumbria* [1997] QB 464, [1996] 3 All ER 449, in which the Court of Appeal decided that the police are under a duty of care to keep an informer's identity confidential.

performed such a role,[177] although this may lead to difficulty in the case of co-accused in which different attitudes are adopted.[178] It seems likely that the English courts would, as in New Zealand, offer no protection under this rule to someone deliberately providing false information as a form of harassment.[179]

The earliest cases[180] involved vital state interests, and were resolved in favour of the application of the privilege. In less important situations, the cases diverged,[181] and in the leading case of *Marks v Beyfus*,[182] it was regarded as a matter for discretion[183] by the judge at the trial. It was for the defence to show[184] that disclosure was necessary for the proper presentation of the defence case.[185] The judge should take into account the nature of the information to be revealed, and its importance to the accused's defence.[186] For example, if the defence were that the accused was inveigled into a compromising situation by a particular third person, the fact that the third person was an informer with a motive for so behaving ought not to be suppressed.[187] Here, too, the law distinguishes between different types of informer,[188] and in *R v Davis*,[189] the suppression of the fact that the informant was both participating, and in receipt of a reward, accounted for the appeal being allowed. Nor is it permissible for the police routinely to withhold the telephone numbers of those making 999 calls, even though the defence seeks disclosure so as to identify the callers.[190] Once the court has ruled in favour of disclosure, a consequential decision by the prosecution to abandon the case is not a ground for the court to reverse its decision.[191] The court has not, however, been prepared to countenance 'fishing' expeditions, and has refused to lift the immunity when the accused did not know the identities of potential informers,[192] or adduced no evidence of their having 'planted' incriminating material,[193] or where the

---

[177] *R v Denton* [2002] EWCA Crim 272.   [178] As in *R v Adams* [1997] Crim LR 292.

[179] *R v Strawbridge* [2003] 1 NZLR 683.

[180] *R v Hardy* (n175); *R v Watson* (1817) 32 State Tr 1; *R v Cobbett* (1831) 2 State Tr NS 789; *R v O'Connor* (1843) 4 State Tr NS 935.

[181] In *A-G v Briant* (1846) 15 LJ Ex 265, disclosure was not compelled, while in *R v Richardson* (1863) 3 F & F 693, and *Webb v Catchlove* (1886) 3 TLR 159, it was. See also *Thomson v Neilson* 1900 8 SLT 147.

[182] (n175), 498. The position seems not to be materially different in Ireland: see e.g. *DPP v Special Criminal Court* [1999] 1 Ir 60.

[183] *R v Hallett* [1986] Crim LR 462 emphasized that it was not truly a matter of discretion since, once the judge found the relevant condition to be established, he was bound to allow the evidence to be given or questions to be asked.

[184] *R v Hennessey* (1978) 68 Cr App Rep 419, 426. Preliminary negotiations between counsel may be called for, and these must be conducted with delicacy and accuracy: see *R v Smith* (1997) The Times,19 December.

[185] This formulation of the test seems to have been adopted in *R v Williams* [1988] Crim LR 113.

[186] In a number of jurisdictions, a distinction is made between relaxation of the immunity when it helps the defence directly, but not when it might merely show that a warrant was unlawfully obtained: see *Hilton v Wells* (1985) 59 ALR 281; *R v Hunter* (1987) 57 CR (3d) 1; *McCray v Illinois* 386 US 300 (1967).

[187] *R v Williams* (n185); *R v Agar* (n153); *R v Reilly* [1994] Crim LR 279; cf *R v Menga and Marshalleck* [1998] Crim LR 58.

[188] See *R v Agar* (n153), 444g, 320; Home Office Guidelines for handling informants reproduced in *R v Patel* [2001] EWCA Crim 2505, [12]. For criticism of lack of differentiation, see *Fitt v United Kingdom* (2000) 30 EHRR 480, [53].   [189] [2001] 1 Cr App Rep 115; [66], [72]; see also *R v Patel* (n188) [56].

[190] *R v Heggart* LEXIS 30 November 2000, CA.

[191] *R v Vaillencourt* [1993] Crim LR 311. In that case, the prosecution's decision was made even though the initial order for discovery was limited to counsel.

[192] But see *R v Baker* [1996] Crim LR 55, in which disclosure was ordered although the defence believed that there had been no informer, and the application was designed to expose that situation.

[193] *R v Farrell* [2002] EWCA Crim 1223.

identity of the informer was on a correct analysis irrelevant to the defence.[194] The court should be alert to the manufacture of defences fabricated just so as to raise claims of public interest immunity.[195] Nor should immunity be withdrawn when the defence is 'manifestly frivolous and doomed to failure',[196] to which the failure of the accused to answer questions, or to submit a defence, or to testify at trial, may well contribute.[197]

Editing so as to conceal the identity of the informer is a hazardous undertaking, since it may be far from clear just which details will reveal it.[198] Where the material emanates not from the prosecution but from a third party, it has been held that public policy will be still less likely to be overridden by the need to protect the accused.[199]

The law relating to pre-trial disclosure by prosecution to defence was put on a statutory footing by Pt 1 of the Criminal Procedure and Investigations Act 1996,[200] specifically subject to withholding material on the basis of public policy.[201] In general, it is for the court to decide this matter, so notice must be given to the defence, indicating at least the category of the material, and allowing scope for representations by the defence.[202] Some situations are so sensitive that they would be compromised even by informing the accused that information was not being disclosed on the basis of the public interest,[203] in which case an *ex parte* application is inevitable.[204] In such a case, it is still more crucial that the evidence submitted to justify this step be both full[205] and scrupulously accurate,[206] even though the House of Lords has now determined that the trial judge is not entitled to rely upon information so revealed otherwise to assist the case for the prosecution.[207]

This procedure[208] has been subjected to critical examination by the European Court of Human Rights. In *Rowe and Davis v United Kingdom*,[209] the prosecution had failed to disclose the identity of a witness as an informer to the trial judge, and the appeal allowed because it rendered the trial unfair, and had not been saved by eventual revelation to the appellate court.[210] The court was particularly concerned that the accused

---

[194] As in *R v Dearman and Southgate* [2001] EWCA Crim 2022, [11]; *R v Dervish* [2001] EWCA Crim 2789, [2000] 2 Cr App Rep 105, [37].   [195] *R v Agar* (n153); *R v Turner* [1995] 2 Cr App Rep 94.

[196] As it was put in *Agar* (n153). Similarly an appeal will not be allowed when disclosure could not have made the slightest difference to the result: *R v Iroegbu* [2003] EWCA Crim 2317, [29].

[197] As it seems to have done in *R v Farrell* (n193).   [198] *R v Leipert* [1997] 1 SCR 281.

[199] *Re Barlow Clowes* [1992] Ch 208, [1991] 4 All ER 385.

[200] Afforced by the Crown Court (Criminal Proceedings and Investigations Act 1966) Disclosure Rules 1997, adopting the recommendations made in the government's Consultation Paper *Disclosure* Cm 2864 (1995).

[201] Sections 3(6), 7(5), 8(5), 9(8), and 21(2). Some amendment has been made to the procedure in magistrates' courts: see s 14 and *R (CPS) v Acton Youth Court* (n3).

[202] This must be full and accurate, whether tendered on a voir dire, at the trial, or pursuant to a claim for abuse of process: *R v Early* [2002] EWCA Crim 1904; [2003] 1 Cr App Rep 288. Similar procedures in respect of an appeal were detailed in *R v McDonald* [2004] EWCA Crim 2614, (2004) 148 SJLB 1218.

[203] And convictions can be quashed on such a basis without informing the accused of the reasons: *R v Doubtfire* (n173).

[204] *R v Davis* [1993] 2 All ER 643, [1993] 1 WLR 613. The court disapproved of disclosure to counsel on the basis that no further disclosure would take place to solicitor or client. This position was endorsed in the Attorney-General's *Guidance on the Disclosure of Information in Criminal Proceedings* (2000).

[205] *R v Patel* (n188), [52].   [206] *R v Jackson* [2000] Crim LR 377.

[207] (n22), [42] overruling *R v Joe Smith* [2001] 1 WLR 1031, [2001] 2 Cr App Rep 1.

[208] Although not in its most extreme form, in which the defence is not even notified of an application.

[209] (2000) 30 EHRR 1. See also *Atlan v United Kingdom* (2002) 34 EHRR 833.

[210] A conclusion subsequently endorsed by that court in *R v Davis* [2001] 1 Cr App Rep 115, [60]. See also *Dowsett v UK* (2004) 38 EHRR 41 (in which the Court of Appeal did not inspect the undisclosed material).

had no opportunity to make representations on the evidence presented to the judge. While not imposing an absolute obligation of disclosure to the accused, it did insist that any restriction on the defence be proportionate, and counterbalanced by procedural safeguards.[211] Its limits were tested in *Jasper v United Kingdom*,[212] in which the very same judges who had been unanimous in *Davis* split nine to eight to uphold the procedure in a case in which disclosure had been made to the trial judge.[213] It may therefore be worth noting that, in this case, the informer did not testify, so it might be said that equality of arms was preserved; that the *category* of withheld material was disclosed;[214] that a summary of what it contained was disclosed; that the trial judge inspected it; that he retained the discretion under s 78 to exclude material that would render the trial unfair; that the defence was able to make submissions about the non-disclosed material; that disclosure was kept under review for the remainder of the trial; that the trial judge directed the jury that an informer had been involved; that, if the material had helped the defence, he would have ordered its disclosure; and finally, that the whole conduct of the trial had been the subject of further review by the Court of Appeal. Even then, the decision was reached by a paper-thin majority.[215] It was thus hardly surprising that, in the next decision of the European Court of Human Rights to examine the issue, *Edwards and Lewis v United Kingdom*,[216] the court fastened on to the distinction that in that case there might have been reliance upon an undisclosed matter in the determination by the trial judge of an issue of fact, so as to hold the process unfair in the sense of 'inequality of arms'. Support was there expressed for the appointment of special independent counsel to redress this inequality,[217] but the House of Lords in *R v H; R v C*[218] has expressed doubts about the adoption of such a solution, at least in anything other than the most exceptional case.[219] It has been held unnecessary for the judge to recuse himself when he is confident that, despite having seen undisclosed material, he will be able to avoid using it in his determination of an issue within his own exclusive domain.[220]

Where relevant material has been secured by surveillance authorized under the Regulation of Investigatory Powers Act 2000, the rigorous exclusion of judicial appraisal of such authorization by s 91(10) will not only preclude investigation of the lawfulness of obtaining it, but will also preclude disclosure to support judicial appraisal of its

---

[211] [54]. It had been urged that a special counsel procedure, introduced to meet earlier criticisms of procedure in the United Kingdom by the European Court of Human Rights in *Tinnelly v United Kingdom* (1998) 27 EHRR 249, might have been appropriate.

[212] (2000) 30 EHRR 441; and in the companion case of *Fitt v United Kingdom* (n188).

[213] Rather than belatedly to the Court of Appeal as in *Davis* (n210). Although a somewhat fuller opportunity for the Court of Appeal to make an *ex parte* ruling was upheld in *R v Botmeh and Alami* [2001] EWCA Crim 2226, [25].   [214] That it related to a source of information.

[215] Some of the dissentients felt that it might be fairer to have the *ex parte* proceedings conducted by a judge other than the trial judge.   [216] (2003) 15 BHRC 189, [57].

[217] For some detail of this procedure see *Secretary of State for the Home Department v AE* [2008] EWHC 132 (Admin), [2008] ACD 35.   [218] (n22), reinforced by the recent decisions in terrorist cases, 485.

[219] Although recommended in 2001 in general terms by the Auld Review of Criminal Courts, [193], [194], the contrary view was expressed in 2003 by Butterfield J in his review of criminal proceedings by Customs and Excise, 264, and his view was approved by the House of Lords (n22), [22]. It was further decided in *R v B; R v G* [2004] EWCA Crim 1368, [2004] 1 WLR 2492, that partial inadvertent disclosure made this still more undesirable. See also Rea (2004) 148(11) *SJ* 314, for the suggestion of an agreed protocol to meet some of the objections.   [220] *R v Dawson* [2007] EWCA Crim 822, 151 SJLB 432, [58].

admissibility, thus effectively sidelining the operation of s 78 of the Police and Criminal Evidence Act 1984 in this context.[221]

Location of observation point

A more dubious step has been extension from protecting the identity of informers to that of the location of premises used as police observation points. In *R v Rankine*, it was said that:[222]

…the reasons which give rise to the rule that an informer is not to be identified apply with equal force to the identification of the owner or occupier of premises used for surveillance *and to the identification of the premises themselves*. The cases are indistinguishable, and the same rule must apply to each.

It is submitted that the words emphasized above do not constitute a separate basis for protection, but are subordinate to the consideration of protecting the identity of the owner or occupier. If taken as an independent basis, the reasoning could easily be extended to the protection of methods of surveillance. Such further extension was attempted in *R v Brown and Daley*,[223] where the police refused to describe cars used for surveillance. As the court pointed out, such an extension would distort the reason for the rule, and destroy the analogy with the case of informers. The critical difference is that, in the case of an informer, the prosecution must elect either to take the direct benefit of the informer's information by calling him to testify, in which case, his identity is revealed and he is available for cross-examination, or to secure only indirect benefit from his information by using it to find evidence that they can then adduce without revealing his identity. If the extension to the identity of observation posts were to be accepted, the prosecution would be able to secure the direct benefit of evidence observed from the post while at the same time insulating that evidence from any effective cross-examination by suppressing all indication of its location. Since this information will normally be necessary for such cross-examination, it is to be hoped that the occasions for applying the analogy to informers, and suppressing the information, will be rare. In particular, it has been said necessary for the prosecution to satisfy the court of a particular need for the observation post, and for anonymity, before suppression would even be considered.[224] Some erosion of these conditions has, however, taken place, with the rules relating to identification posts being equated with those relating to informers, without consideration of more than the similar motives for reluctance to be identified.[225] It now seems that more restrictions will be placed on the evidence that can be given,[226] less basis required for reluctance to be located,[227] and application allowed in more trivial cases.[228] In neither the case of an informer, nor of an owner of an observation

---

[221] *R v GS* [2005] EWCA Crim 887.

[222] [1986] QB 861, [1986] 2 All ER 566; 867, 570, emphasis supplied.   [223] (n127).

[224] *R v Johnson* [1989] 1 All ER 121, [1988] 1 WLR 1377.

[225] See *R v Hewitt; R v Davis* (1991) 95 Cr App Rep 81; cf, in Canada, *R v Lam* (2000) 148 CCC 3d 379.

[226] *Blake v DPP; Austin v DPP* (1992) 97 Cr App Rep 169 (refusal even to identify where the crime was observed to have been committed); *R v Grimes* [1994] Crim LR 213 (bearing of crime from post suppressed).

[227] *Blake v DPP; Austin v DPP* (n226) (no special reason for apprehension); *R v Grimes* (n226) (ascertained by telephone call rather than personal visit).

[228] *Blake v DPP; Austin v DPP* (n226) (indecency in churchyard).

point, should the defence be permitted to exploit the exception as a substitute for discovery.[229] Nor should an order ever be made *ex parte*.[230]

CONFIDENTIAL MATTERS

It was stated quite clearly by Lord Cross in *Alfred Crompton Amusement Machines Ltd v Customs and Excise Comrs (No 2)* that: '"Confidentiality" is not a separate head of privilege, but it may be a very material consideration to bear in mind when privilege is claimed on the ground of public interest.'[231] This proposition had impeccable historical credentials,[232] and was reaffirmed by the House of Lords.[233] It is necessary to restate it on account of the later approach to public interest immunity exhibited in the quotation from Lord Hailsham's speech in *D v National Society for the Prevention of Cruelty to Children*, with which this section of the chapter began. The judgments in the Court of Appeal in that case exhibited the conflicting views then current. On the one hand, Lord Denning's view that breach of confidence was a sufficient basis for making a claim for immunity from disclosure on the basis of public interest, and would prevail unless overbalanced by the public interest in the administration of justice. On the other, the view of the majority that the categories of public interest immunity were strictly limited to the sorts of claim on behalf of central government recognized in the past. The House attempted to steer a middle course. The case arose from the visit, without prior warning, by an inspector of the NSPCC to the home of the mother of a young child. It transpired that the visit was to investigate an allegation that the child had been ill treated. There was no evidence of such ill treatment, and no subsequent proceedings were set in train. The mother was most upset by the incident, and eventually brought a claim for negligence against the NSPCC for its conduct, pursuant to which she sought discovery of all relevant documents in its possession, some of which would be very likely to reveal the identity of the society's informant. The society sought an order that no such documents should be discovered. This application was dismissed by the master, upheld by the judge, and dismissed by the majority of the Court of Appeal, but only over the dissent of Lord Denning. It may be noted that there could be no reasonable doubt that such documents existed, and that they would assist the plaintiff's case. It is also the case that the plaintiff was interested only in the identity of the informant, and that the society relied upon no certificate or affidavit from any official in support of its claim that it would be contrary to the public interest to make such a revelation to the plaintiff. Nor was the issue capable of being disposed of simply as a matter for the discretion of the judge at the stage of discovery. The case was accepted, and discussed, by the House of Lords on the basis that it affected the law of evidence,[234] in the sense that the decision involved also

---

[229] *R v Robertson* (1983) 21 NTR 11.

[230] *R v Guildhall Justices, ex p DPP* (1983) 78 Cr App Rep 269.

[231] (n6); 433, 1184. It may also influence the form and conditions of disclosure: *Three Rivers District Council v Bank of Credit and Commerce International* [2002] EWHC 2309.

[232] See VIII Wigmore [2286].

[233] For example, *D v National Society for the Prevention of Cruelty to Children* (n27); 238, 612; *Science Research Council v Nassé* [1980] AC 1028, [1979] 3 All ER 673; 1080, 691; and held to remain good law in *Amaryllis Ltd v HM Treasury* (n29), [52], notwithstanding the decision of the ECJ in *Varec SA v Etat Belge* (C-450/06, 14 February 2008).

[234] See Lord Diplock, 219, 595, Lord Hailsham, 221, 600, and Lord Simon, 241, 615.

the range of questions that could be put at the trial of the action. The unanimous view of the House was that it could not be regarded as fatal that no arm of central government was involved, so long as the defendant's claim were capable of subsumption under a head of public policy, at least analogous to one previously recognized. In the particular case, it was felt that there was clear analogy to the public policy of preserving from disclosure in civil proceedings the identity of informants to the police. This option may not, however, be available to all of those giving a guarantee of confidentiality,[235] not even disciplinary tribunals.[236] In the area of confidential material[237] garnered and created by social workers, there is an increasing movement toward disclosure for the purposes of family proceedings.[238] Even where witnesses were encouraged to testify, by reference to the use immunity qualifying the statutory abrogation of the privilege against self-incrimination in s 98(2) of the Children Act 1989,[239] it was held that details of their evidence could be supplied to the police.[240] Such an analogical approach opens up the field of public interest immunity just because the closeness of the necessary analogy is left for subsequent development.[241] The facts of the case demonstrate that the analogy may be close enough, even though no organ of central government is involved, and notwithstanding the absence of official certification of any public interest.[242]

The House regarded the role of confidence as being essentially confirmatory, in the sense that it is unlikely that the argument for refusing disclosure of any statement made otherwise than in confidence would ever be supported by a public policy so strong as to override the public interest in the proper administration of justice.

The ambit of this extension of public interest immunity was soon afterwards explored in two discrimination cases, eventually heard together by the House of Lords.[243] In both

---

[235] *Re G (A Minor) (Social Worker: Disclosure)* 1970] 2 QB 643, [1970] 3 All ER 546.

[236] *Wakefield v Channel Four Television Corporation* [2006] EWHC 3289 (QB).

[237] Quite apart from public interest immunity, such issues may involve the application of Art 6 of the European Convention on Human Rights in relation to disclosure to a party to litigation, and the application of the common law of confidence: see *Samuel R v W Primary Care Trust* [2004] EWHC 2085 (Fam).

[238] See McGrath [2006] *Fam L* 40; although it may be doubted whether the further pressure for greater reporting of such proceedings is necessarily helpful: see DCA Consultation *Confidence and Confidentiality: Improving Transparency and Privacy in Family Courts* (CP 11/06). For more restrictive conditions in Canada, see *Hawley v Fearn-Stewart* (2003) 233 DLR (4th) 160.

[239] Although use of such statements to impair credibility remains possible: *Re X Children* [2007] EWHC 1719 (Fam), [2008] 1 FLR 589, [50], and sometimes information derived from such statements, as in *Re M (Disclosure to Police)* (n116). Use may also be permitted in the criminal proceedings as part of a victim impact statement; for the quantification of damage by the Criminal Injuries Compensation Authority; and for the guidance of social workers, *Re X Children* [2008] EWHC 242 (Fam), [2008] 3 All ER 958.

[240] *Re C (A Minor) (Care Proceedings: Disclosure)* [1997] Fam 76, [1996] 2 FLR 725; the factors to be taken into account in striking the balance are helpfully summarized. Many of these issues are now covered by national protocol on the exchange of confidential information, the Protocol of Judicial Case Management in Public Law Child Act Cases, and governmental guidance: see *Reading BC v A et al* [2006] EWHC 1465 (Fam), [2007] 1 All ER 293, [97].

[241] Occasionally statutory, see Child Maintenance and Other Payments Act 2008 s 39.

[242] This may, however, be relevant to the burden of proof that Lord Edmund-Davies in *D* (n27), 246, 619 regarded as being borne by the party resisting disclosure, apparently at the standard of the balance of probabilities, by contrast to his view in *Burmah Oil* (n59) 1127, 719 and repeated in *Air Canada* (n5) at 442, 922, that the burden in those cases, where there was such a certificate, was borne by the party seeking disclosure, and at an apparently high standard ('the scales must come down decisively').

[243] *Science Research Council v Nassé, Leyland Cars (BL Cars Ltd) v Vyas* [1980] AC 1028, [1979] 3 All ER 673.

cases, discrimination was alleged in relation to employment; in both, the claimant sought disclosure of confidential reports upon the successful applicants; and in both, disclosure was ordered at a lower level, but denied by the Court of Appeal. One of the respondents rested its case upon a claim for public interest immunity. This was rejected by the whole House. Most of Their Lordships were concerned to point out that there was no such analogy to a recognized form of public interest immunity as there had been in *D v National Society for the Prevention of Cruelty to Children*. It was pointed out that the interest of the employers, even though one was a public body, was of a private and not a public nature. Nor was Parliament's expression of public policy in setting up the relevant Commissions compatible with public interest immunity that would effectively prevent discharge of their statutory functions. It is perhaps least likely of all that the courts will recognize public interest immunity in an area that has been excluded from the limited scope of private privilege, such as that of banking documentation.[244] It seems that sometimes, however, the courts have themselves developed practices of automatically refusing disclosure to particular types of document, such as records of case conferences in relation to wards of court.[245] They may also insist upon the prior satisfaction of procedural guaranties of fairness.[246]

It might be thought that the Human Rights Act 1998, giving further force to rights to privacy and confidentiality in the shape of Art 8(1) of the European Convention on Human Rights, would alter the position radically, were it not for the width, and vagueness, of the qualifications in Art 8(2). It should also be noted that these provisions operate overwhelmingly in the private and domestic sphere. It does seem, however, that they will reinforce the trend towards balancing already discernible before 1998.

It had been held, in the light of *D v National Society for the Prevention of Cruelty to Children*, that refusal of disclosure should never be automatic, but taken only after a balancing exercise has been conducted,[247] and one, even in adoption proceedings, undertaken subject to a strong presumption in favour of disclosure.[248] A similar view has been taken in relation to the disclosure of social welfare documents sought by the police with a view to bringing criminal proceedings,[249] or by the defence with a view to defending them.[250] One relevant factor is whether the ward himself is seeking disclosure, especially after attaining his majority.[251] The seeker of the information must be sufficiently specific in identifying the relevant documents to avoid any suggestion of a fishing expedition.[252] Medical

---

[244] See e.g. *Kaufman v Crédit Lyonnais Bank* (1995) 7 Ad R 669; *Price Waterhouse v BCCI Holdings (Luxembourg) SA* [1992] BCLC 583.

[245] In this case, the confidentiality is that of the court administering the ward's affairs, rather than that of the ward personally.

[246] *R (TB) v Combined Court at Stafford* [2006] EWHC 1645 (Admin), [2007] 1 All ER 102 (opportunity for person whose confidence is at risk to make representations).

[247] *Re M (a minor) (disclosure of material)* (n116).

[248] *Re D (adoption reports: confidentiality)* [1996] AC 593, [1995] 4 All ER 385, Lord Mustill, 609A, 393a; for some qualification in the light of the Human Rights Act 1998, see *Re B (disclosure to other parties)* [2001] 2 FLR 1017, [66].

[249] *Re W (minors) (social worker: disclosure)* [1998] 2 All ER 801, [1999] 1 WLR 205, in which the seriousness of the allegation against the parent was regarded as a reason for, rather than against, disclosure.

[250] *Re Z (Children) (Disclosure: Criminal Proceedings)* [2003] EWHC 61, [2003] 1 FLR 1194.

[251] *Re Manda* (n171).

[252] *Re X* [1992] Fam 124, [1992] 2 All ER 595. For a useful procedural device to avoid difficulty in this context, see Rodwell [1998] *Crim LR* 332.

records are often regarded as particularly confidential,[253] although to refuse disclosure
automatically would, in much the same way as mentioned above in relation to banking
records, undermine the limitation of private professional privilege to legal matters.[254] Nor
is there much point in refusing advance disclosure of records subject to a subpoena duces
tecum at the trial.[255] In exceptional circumstances, there may even be a compelling reason to disclose medical,[256] or police,[257] records held in confidence on account of a greater
public interest,[258] such as the safety of others,[259] or the administration of justice.[260] Such
decisions as to disclosure, especially where balancing is involved, should be taken by the
court,[261] and not by the parties, even when those parties are local authorities or professional bodies.[262]

Despite dicta in *D v National Society for the Prevention of Cruelty to Children* tending to elide the distinction between private privilege and public interest immunity in
some respects, the House clearly reaffirmed that any immunity based upon public interest cannot be waived by the parties, and must be taken by the court even if not explicitly
claimed by one of them.[263] On the other hand, a court may be more prepared to protect the confidentiality of documents secured by compulsory process,[264] such as pre-trial

---

[253] And have, for the purposes of the Police and Criminal Evidence Act 1984, s 12, been construed as
extending beyond records of medical treatment to those of dates of attendance at a hospital: see *R v Cardiff
Crown Court, ex p Kellam* (1993) 16 BMLR 76. Legislation exists in some Commonwealth jurisdictions,
usually by according a private, and hence waivable, privilege to the patient; for comparison with the situation in England, see Temkin (2002) 61 *Camb LJ* 126. Such legislation has survived constitutional challenge
in Canada: see *R v Mills* [1999] 3 SCR 668, construing Canadian Criminal Code, ss 278.1–278.91; see in
Australia, Evidence Act 1995 (Cwth), s 130, and similar provisions protecting therapeutic communications
relating to complainants of sexual crimes, clearly construed as creating a new form of public interest immunity in *R v Young* [1999] NSWCCA 166, (1999) 46 NSWLR 681; *Question of Law Reserved (No 1 of 2000)*
[2000] SASC 205, (2000) 113 ACR 272.   [254] See in Canada, *M (A) v Ryan* [1997] 1 SCR 157.
[255] *Dunn v British Coal Corp* [1993] ICR 591.
[256] *W v Egdell* [1990] Ch 359, [1990] 1 All ER 835; *R v Kennedy* [1999] 1 Cr App Rep 54. Although this will
almost never be required in relation to confidential medical records of third parties: see *A v X & B* [2004]
EWHC 447, QB. The European Court of Human Rights will be more ready to permit disclosure for use only
in criminal proceedings: see *Z v Finland* (1998) 25 EHRR 371. Once even limited disclosure is made for the
purposes of legal proceedings, its maker will become exposed to cross-examination upon undisclosed matters: *Re B (Children)* [2003] EWCA Civ 786, [2003] 2 FLR 813.
[257] *Hellewell v Chief Constable of Derbyshire* [1995] 4 All ER 473, [1995] 1 WLR 804.
[258] See in Australia reluctance to override statutory requirements of confidentiality by reference to considerations like the paramount interest of a child in care proceedings: see *Mallia v Collins* (1993) 115 FLR 35;
Piras v Thaisawat (1993) 115 FLR 79.   [259] *Re M (child abuse: police videos)* (n160).
[260] *Rowe v Fryers* [2003] EWCA Civ 655, [2003] 1 WLR 1952, which may include disciplinary proceedings: *Woolgar v Chief Constable of Sussex* [1999] 3 All ER 604, [2000] 1 WLR 25; *A Health Authority v X* [2001]
EWCA Civ 2014, [2002] 2 All ER 780; and care proceedings, *Re C* (29 November 2001, unreported).
[261] Although a preliminary decision on relevance may be delegated to counsel for a local authority:
W (G) v W (E) [1997] 1 Cr App Rep 166; and see *Maddock v Devon County Council* [2004] EWHC 3494, in
which disclosure of confidential local authority records to a university in relation for an applicant for admission to a social work course was said not to require prior application to the court.
[262] *A Health Authority v X*, (n260) [25], and preferably by the trial judge. But see *H v N* [2002] EWCA Civ
195, [2002] EMLR 425, and comment by Hyam (2002) 152 *NLJ* 1129.
[263] Lord Wilberforce, 1067, 681; Lord Edmund-Davies, 1074, 686; Lord Fraser, 1082, 693.
[264] Although it will be reluctant to impede the work of a statutory inquiry: *Mount Murray Country Club v
Macleod (Assessor of Income Tax)* (n20); or foreign proceedings in which there is an obligation of disclosure:
Bank of Crete SA v Koskotas (No 2) [1993] 1 All ER 748, [1992] 1 WLR 919; especially if there is an allegation
of fraud: *Pharaon v Bank of Credit and Commerce International* [1998] 4 All ER 468; cf *Tabbah v Eronat*
[2002] EWCA Civ 950.

discovery[265] or disclosure,[266] than those divulged voluntarily,[267] for example in an arbitration,[268] at least when disclosure is sought from the body holding the documents as a result of that process.[269] It nevertheless remains the case that:[270]

A court can release or modify the implied undertaking, or give leave to disclose material subject to it, if it concludes that to do so would be in the overall public interest.

It has also been held that there is no general principle of allowing claims for all documents divulged in confidence to a regulatory body.[271] In principle, as in the case of private privilege, the right to claim or waive resides in the person to whom the confidence is owed, and not the person who owes it.[272] It should also be noted that the privilege persists only so long as the document or information remains confidential, and is lost when it is made public,[273] for example when a statement made under caution to the police is read out in open court.[274]

SECTION 2. MISCELLANEOUS MATTERS CONNECTED WITH PREVIOUS LITIGATION

Judges cannot be compelled to give evidence concerning cases tried by them, and more or less closely analogous rules exist concerning the evidence of arbitrators, mediators, jurors, or barristers.

EVIDENCE OF JUDGES

This subject was authoritatively re-examined by Lord Woolf MR in *Warren v Warren*.[275] He cited the dicta of Cleasby B in *Buccleuch (Duke) v Metropolitan Board of Works*,[276] who said:

With respect to those who fill the office of judge it has been felt that there are grave objections to their conduct being made the subject of cross-examination and comment (to which hardly any

---

[265] *Riddick v Thames Board Mills* [1977] QB 881, [1977] 3 All ER 677.

[266] *Taylor v Serious Fraud Office* [1999] 2 AC 177, [1998] 4 All ER 801.

[267] *Derby v Weldon* (1988) The Times, 20 October; see, in Canada, *Schwartz v Schwartz Estate* (2000) 189 DLR (4th) 79. Although contrary arguments can be based upon the need to encourage candid voluntary disclosure, as intimated by Lord Browne-Wilkinson in *Re Arrows (No 4)* [1995] 2 AC 75; aff'd *sub nom Hamilton v Naviede* [1994] 3 All ER 814, 101F, 826f.

[268] *Shearson Lehman Hutton Inc v Maclaine Watson Co Ltd* [1989] 1 All ER 1056, [1989] 2 Ll R 570.

[269] Thus in *Lonrho plc v Fayed (No 4)* [1994] QB 775, [1994] 1 All ER 870, copies of tax returns were not immune in the hands of the taxpayer; see also, in Australia, *Pooraka Holdings Pty Ltd v Participation Nominees Pty Ltd* (1989) 52 SASR 148.   [270] *A v A; B v B* [2000] 1 FLR 701, 720.

[271] *Kaufmann v Credit Lyonnais Bank* (1995) 7 Ad LR 669, disagreeing with *MGN Pensions Trustees v Invesco Asset Management Ltd* (14 October 1993, unreported).

[272] *Price Waterhouse v BCCI Holdings (Luxembourg) SA* (n244).

[273] The onus of showing that such a document has not become public rests upon the party so asserting: *Barings plc (in liq) v Coopers & Lybrand* [2000] 3 All ER 910, [53].

[274] *Bunn v British Broadcasting Corp* [1998] 3 All ER 552, under the new civil procedures now extended to documents read out of court by the judge, which would, if read in court, have been covered by this exception: *SmithKline Beecham Biologicals SA v Connaught Laboratories Inc* [1999] 4 All ER 498. For an example of the operation of this procedure where there has been a confidentiality agreement, see *Lilly Icos Ltd v Pfizer Ltd* [2002] EWCA Civ 02, [2002] 1 All ER 842. It is immaterial that it has been covertly recorded: *Chairman and Governors of Amwell School v Dogherty* (2006) unreported EAT, 16 June.

[275] [1997] QB 488, [1996] 4 All ER 664.

[276] (1872) LR 5 HL 418, 433. A subpoena may be issued against a magistrate's clerk to bring and produce notes of proceedings before the magistrates.

limit could be put) in relation to proceedings before them; and, as everything which they can properly prove can be proved by others, the courts of law discountenance and I think I may say prevent them being examined.

Although this makes no distinction of rank between judges,[277] Lord Woolf explicitly recognized that magistrates are treated differently.[278] Despite the last quoted sentence, he held judges to be competent, but not compellable,[279] witnesses to all matters relating to, and resulting from, the performance of their judicial functions.[280]

EVIDENCE OF ARBITRATORS

So far as arbitrators are concerned, it is settled that they can be compelled to give evidence with regard to occurrences at the arbitration, and to state what matters were included in the submission, but they must not be asked questions about the reasons for their award.[281] Such a limitation may be justified on the ground that the evidence would be irrelevant, as the reasons for an award could only be material at the hearing of an application to have it set aside, but in the absence of such proceedings the award must be treated as final.[282]

EVIDENCE OF MEDIATORS

As mediation becomes more common, issues have begun to arise relating to evidence from mediators, and in *Farm Assist Ltd (In Litigation) v Secretary of State for the Environment, Food and Rural Affairs (No 2)*[283] it was held that a mediator could be compelled to testify

---

[277] Masters of the Supreme Court are judges for this purpose. Elsewhere, members of various tribunals have by legislation been assimilated to judges: see in Australia, *Herijanto v Refugee Review Tribunal* [2000] HCA 16, (2000) 170 ALR 379; in Canada, *Cherubini Metal Works Ltd v Att-Gen for Nova Scotia* (2007) 282 DLR (4th) 538.

[278] For the position of magistrates' clerks, see *McKinley v McKinley* [1960] 1 All ER 476, [1960] 1 WLR 120. Quasi-judicial offices, such as that of an inspector presiding over a planning appeal, seem likely to be assimilated to the position of magistrates: *Jones and Jones v Secretary of State for Wales* (1995) 70 P & CR 211.

[279] Nor can disclosure be claimed of in camera discussion, even between members of a professional disciplinary tribunal: *Roylance v General Medical Council* [2000] 1 AC 311; or such material used if obtained clandestinely: *Chairman and Governors of Amwell School v Dogherty* (n274). See also, in New Zealand, *Air New Zealand v Commerce Commission* [2004] 3 NZLR 550.

[280] Which, in Canada, have been held to informal conferences in the judge's chambers: *Edwards v A-G of Canada* (1999) 182 DLR (4th) 736. The Supreme Court of Canada has also held the exemption from compellability to extend beyond strictly judicial to administrative matters, such as the reasons for the composition of a particular court: *MacKeigan v Hickman* [1989] 2 SCR 796; for a different approach in New Zealand, see *Tau v Durie* [1996] 2 NZLR 190. In Canada, a more literal view has been taken, and the rule extended to make judges incompetent: *Ermina v Minister of Citizenship and Immigration* (1998) 167 DLR (4th) 764. In Hong Kong, an affidavit has been received from a High Court judge who had chaired a tribunal as to the events that had taken place when one of the other members of the tribunal was accused of wrongdoing in relation to those proceedings: *Cheung v Insider Dealing Tribunal* [1999] 3 HKLRD 254.

[281] *Buccleuch's* case (n276), applied to a member of a medical board under the National Insurance (Industrial Injuries) Act 1946, in *Ward v Shell Mex and BP Ltd* [1951] 2 All ER 904, and to the PIA Ombudsman and his staff in *Brooks v Reliance Mutual Ltd* Ind, 3 November 1997.

[282] It was noted by Hoffmann LJ in *Land Securities plc v Westminster City Council* [1993] 4 All ER 124, [1993] 1 WLR 286 that, where an award is relevant in *other* proceedings, then the rule in *Hollington v Hewthorn & Co Ltd* [1943] KB 587, [1943] 2 All ER 35 applies: see further, 118.

[283] [2008] EWHC 2079 (TCC), (2009) BLR 399. Cp in Canada; *Rudd v Trossacs Investment Inc* (2006) 265 DLR (4th) 718.

to words said before her, notwithstanding her objection that she had no recollection of the proceedings. This is a strong decision since the mediation agreement contained an express prohibition of the mediator testifying in relation to the underlying dispute, and there was also a confidentiality clause in the ensuing settlement agreement. It was further held that the mediator could not herself claim the benefit of without prejudice privilege.

EVIDENCE OF JURORS

The traditional rule was that jurors might not give evidence[284] of discussions that took place in the jury box or jury room concerning the cases in which they had been[285] acting.[286] Nor could third parties testify to what they had learned from jurors about such matters.[287] The exclusionary rule was confined to evidence of discussions concerning their verdict that took place between the jurors, but extended beyond matters disclosure of which would contravene s 8(1) of the Contempt of Court Act 1981.[288]

The rule still permitted evidence of matters extrinsic[289] to discussion. Accordingly, in *Ellis v Deheer*,[290] a new trial was ordered on the ground that some jurors had not been present in court when their verdict was announced, and it is probable that the fact that one of the jurors did not understand English would be a good ground for setting aside their verdict. As Lord Atkin observed, finality is a good thing, but justice is better.[291] In later cases it was held that a verdict could be quashed when it was discovered that the jurors had used necromancy for assistance,[292] and in another when it was found that the verdict announced in court did not correspond with the actual decisions of the jurors.[293] In such a case any objection by a juror should be made immediately.[294]

---

[284] Disclosure of deliberations by a juror otherwise than to the court amounts to contempt contrary to s 8(1) of the Contempt of Court Act 1981: see *A-G v Scotcher* [2005] UKHL 36, [2005] 3 All ER 1.

[285] It seems, however, that they may be questioned as a body in open court about cases in which they *are* acting so as to determine whether or not they should be discharged: *R v Orgles* [1993] 4 All ER 533, [1994] 1 WLR 108, approved in *R v Marron* [2006] EWCA Crim 3304. See also Criminal Procedure Rules Consolidated Jury Direction IV.42.7 seeking to ensure that alleged impropriety is dealt with before the trial has ended.

[286] Nor may they be questioned by the judge about any matter with which such deliberation is inextricably entangled: *R v Smith* [2005] UKHL 2, [2005] 2 AC 176, [20]; nor in Canada, where the basic rule was held constitutional in *Pan v R* 2001 SCC 42, [2001] 2 SCR 344, can they be compelled to testify before a public inquiry set up to consider wrongful convictions: *Re Morin* (1997) 154 DLR (4th) 146.

[287] *R v Connor; R v Mirza* [2004] UKHL 2, [2004] 1 All ER 925. Although material found in the jury room after its deliberations may be taken into account in determining whether to quash a verdict on the basis of the presence of extrinsic material: *R v Karakaya* [2005] EWCA Crim 346, [2005] 2 Cr App R 77; the position is the same in Australia: *R v K* [2003] NSWCCA 406, (2003) 144 ACR 468 (also an Internet search).

[288] *R v Miah; R v Akhbar* [1997] 2 Cr App Rep 12, held compatible with the European Convention on Human Rights in *Miah v United Kingdom* (1998) 26 EHRR CD199.

[289] Although this distinction may be problematic: *R v Adams* [2007] EWCA Crim 1, [180] (oral evidence from jurors as to remarks indicating bias); *R v Hood* [1968] 2 All ER 56, 52 Cr App Rep 265 (affidavit evidence of juror's knowledge of accused previous convictions); in both held extrinsic. The same distinction, and the same difficulty, apply in Australia: see *R v Minarowska* (1995) 83 ACR 78, 85.   [290] [1922] 2 KB 113.

[291] *Ras Behari Lal v R* (1933) 102 LJPC 144, disapproving in the Privy Council the decision of the Court of Criminal Appeal in *R v Thomas* [1933] 2 KB 489.

[292] *R v Young* [1995] QB 324, [[1995] 2 Cr App R 379 (outside the formal deliberations there).

[293] *R v Charnley* [2007] EWCA Crim 1354.

[294] *R v Moran* [2007] EWCA Crim 2947 (pressure to concur).

Even where the matter in question does not relate directly to the deliberations of the jury, different views have been taken of juror compellability.[295]

EVIDENCE OF ADVOCATES

There are obvious reasons why an advocate should not give evidence against his own client in a case in which he is acting, not least on account of problems with legal professional privilege. Advocates are nevertheless technically compellable, and may be compelled if there is no other practicable means to prove an issue.[296] They are also competent to testify in favour of their own clients, but this is also undesirable on account of the confusion caused by the change of role, and possible inhibition of the vigour of cross-examination, so it has been suggested that this too should be undertaken only if absolutely necessary,[297] and that the rules of etiquette of the Bar be amended to reflect that view.[298]

SECTION 3. IMPROPERLY OBTAINED EVIDENCE

The problem hitherto was simply whether relevant evidence was inadmissible because it had been obtained improperly: for example, by a crime, tort, breach of contract, or an infringement or evasion of official regulations, typically one of the Codes of Practice. The short answer was that confessions could not be admitted if they were obtained by oppression, or made in consequence of anything said or done likely in the circumstances to render them unreliable;[299] subject to that important qualification, there was no other clear exclusionary rule, certainly not at common law.[300]

Partly as a result of the passage of the Human Rights Act 1998, and partly as a result, more generally, of the jurisprudence of the European Court of Human Rights, it has become necessary also to consider the issue of whether a trial can be regarded as fair if improperly obtained evidence is tendered.[301] Even before the enactment of this legislation, it had been recognized by the House of Lords in *R v Khan*[302] that comparative study was

---

[295] *R v Valentine* (29 March 1996, unreported) CA (competent); in Scotland, *Gray v HM Advocate* 2005 SCCR 106 (competent at appellate stage);in Canada *R v Budai* (1999) 180 DLR (4th) 565 (competent at appellate stage) (in all evidence of sexual affair between juror and accused); cp *R v Adams* (n289), [169] (witness summons to reluctant juror to testify at appellate stage, although leave of court before interviewing juror desirable).

[296] As in *R (Howe) v South Durham Magistrates' Court* [2004] EWHC 362; the rule is the same in Canada: *R v Elliott* (2003) 181 CCC3d 118.

[297] For reluctance in Canada, see *R v 1504413 Ontario Ltd* (2007) 230 CCC3d 193; but see *Ramdhanie v State* [2005] UKPC 47, [2006] 1 WLR 796, [15], in which the Board deplored the absence of evidence from trial counsel on the hearing of an appeal.

[298] *R v Jacquith and Emode* [1989] Crim LR 508, 563. The rules now reflect this view, subject only to the qualification in [608(a)] that a barrister may refrain from withdrawing from a case in which he is obliged to testify, if to do so would jeopardize his client's interests.

[299] Police and Criminal Evidence Act 1984, s 76.

[300] Although it had been established in *R v Preston* [1994] 2 AC 130, [1993] 4 All ER 638 that no reference could be made to a warrant to intercept telecommunications in connection with the Interception of Communications Act 1985, which achieved a similar result.

[301] See *R v Togher* [2001] 3 All ER 463, [2001] 1 Cr App Rep 457; 472, 467.

[302] [1997] AC 558, [1996] 3 All ER 289; 583, 302.

valuable, and in *R v DPP, ex p Kebilene*[303] that a more purposive approach to interpretation should be adopted in relation to the fundamental rights and freedoms enshrined in the Convention. A further consequence of the increased importance in English law of the European Convention on Human Rights has been its effect[304] of inducing a switch from a primarily common law approach, supplemented by administrative rules, to a requirement for statutory authorization.[305] Such statutes define the conditions under which official incursions into privacy may be made, and often determine, sometimes indirectly, the way in which the fruits of such incursions can be used, including their use in evidence.

Even within the strict confines of English law, it has become necessary also to consider whether such evidence, although technically admissible, should be excluded as a matter of the operation of the discretion conferred by s 78 of the Police and Criminal Evidence Act 1984. It is further possible to discern, in the relevant case law, increasing attention to the possibility of staying proceedings for abuse of process.[306]

Because of the rule excluding involuntary confessions, the issue of the admissibility of real evidence obtained as a result of such a confession was considered at common law, and dealt with specifically in the Police and Criminal Evidence Act 1984. It will be convenient to deal with that legislation first, and then to consider other varieties of improperly obtained evidence, before drawing some more general conclusions.

FACTS DISCOVERED IN CONSEQUENCE OF INADMISSIBLE CONFESSIONS

Section 76 of the Police and Criminal Evidence Act 1984 provides:

(4) The fact that a confession is wholly or partly excluded in pursuance of this section shall not affect the admissibility in evidence—

(a) of any facts discovered as a result of the confession; or

(b) where the confession is relevant as showing that the accused speaks, writes or expresses himself in a particular way, of so much of the confession as is necessary to show that he does so.

(5) Evidence that a fact to which this subsection applies was discovered as a result of a statement made by an accused person shall not be admissible unless evidence of how it was discovered is given by him or on his behalf.

(6) Subsection (5) above applies—

(a) to any fact discovered as a result of a confession which is wholly excluded in pursuance of this section; and

(b) to any fact discovered as a result of a confession which is partly so excluded, if the fact is discovered as a result of the excluded part of the confession.

These provisions were intended to clarify what had become a particularly unsatisfactory and unsettled area of the common law. Section 76(4) followed the recommendations of

---

[303] [2000] 2 AC 326, [1999] 4 All ER 801; 375, 839.   [304] In this context, especially that of Art 8.
[305] First apparent in the passage of the Interception of Communications Act 1985 as a response to the decision of the European Court of Human Rights in *Malone v United Kingdom* (1984) 7 EHRR 14.
[306] For fuller academic study, see Choo *Abuse of Process and Judicial Stays of Criminal Proceedings* (1993).

the 11th Report of the Criminal Law Revision Committee,[307] and was consistent with the reasoning of the Royal Commission on Criminal Procedure.[308] Section 76(5), however, adopted the minority view of the Criminal Law Revision Committee.[309]

The effect of s 76(4) was intended to preserve the position established in the old case of *R v Warickshall*,[310] in which a woman who was charged as an accessory after the fact to theft, and as a receiver of stolen goods, was improperly induced to make a confession, in the course of which she said that the property in question was in her lodgings where it was, in fact, found. The court held that the exclusion of a confession 'forced from the mind by the flattery of hope, or by the pressure of fear' was not based on any breach of public faith that might be involved in its reception, but was due to the fact that the confession comes in so questionable a shape, when it is to be considered as evidence of guilt, that no credit ought to be given to it. But:[311]

... this principle respecting confessions has no application whatever as to the admission or rejection of facts, whether the knowledge of them be obtained in consequence of an extorted confession or whether it arises from any other source; for a fact, if it exist at all, must exist invariably in the same manner whether the confession from which it derives be in other respects true or false. Facts thus obtained, however must be fully and satisfactorily proved without calling in the aid of any part of the confession from which they may have been derived.

It was immaterial that the 'fact' that was discovered was a document.[312] The Criminal Law Revision Committee also took the view that other forms of evidence derived indirectly from an inadmissible confession should be permitted. A confession may be of evidential value because it shows that its maker writes, speaks, or expresses himself in a particular way and thus helps to identify him as the culprit. For example, in *R v Voisin*,[313] the accused was convicted of the murder of a woman, part of whose body was found in a parcel in which there was also a piece of paper with the words 'blady belgiam'. The accused had been asked by a police officer if he had any objection to writing down the two words 'bloody Belgian', and had replied 'Not at all'; he had written down 'Bladie Belgiam'. The accused appealed unsuccessfully against his conviction on the ground, among others, that this writing ought to have been rejected as he had not been cautioned before being asked to write the words down. There was no question of an inadmissible confession, but it seemed to the Criminal Law Revision Committee that, if the words had been written in an inadmissible confession, it would be right that they should be admissible for the purpose of showing that the accused writes, speaks, or expresses himself in a particular way; s 76(4) so enacted.

It can be argued that, in exactly the same way, it ought to be possible to rely upon an otherwise inadmissible confession to show that it was the accused who provided the information leading to the discovery of the relevant facts, or to show his knowledge of some independently verifiable circumstance.[314] The latter possibility seems to have aroused little, if any, judicial discussion, was specifically rejected by the Criminal Law Revision

---

[307] Cmnd 4991, [68], draft bill cl 2(5)(a) and (c).   [308] Cmnd 8092, [4.123f].

[309] [69]. The Royal Commission did not descend to this level of detail.

[310] (1783) 1 Leach 263, reaffirmed in *R v Berriman* (1854) 6 Cox CC 388.   [311] 264.

[312] *R v Leatham* (1861) 8 Cox CC 498. The extremely unsatisfactory case of *R v Barker* [1941] 2 KB 381, [1941] 3 All ER 33, which appeared to assimilate false accounts with a confession of false accounting, and which was overturned on its facts by Finance Act 1942, s 34 (see now Taxes Management Act 1970, s 105), was rejected by the House of Lords in *R v Allen* [2001] UKHL 25, [2002] 1 AC 509.

[313] [1918] 1 KB 531, [1918–19] All ER Rep 491.   [314] See Andrews [1963] *Crim LR* 15, 77.

Committee, and is not provided for in PACE.[315] The former situation has aroused more concern. In some cases in which the location of the facts found in consequence of the otherwise inadmissible confession was less indicative of the accused's guilt than in *Warickshall*, the court permitted the prosecution to testify that it was the accused whose statement revealed the location of the goods.[316] This practice was endorsed by a majority of the Criminal Law Revision Committee, and a provision included in its draft bill.[317] No such provision was, however, made in the Police and Criminal Evidence Act 1984, presumably upon the ground that to admit such evidence would tend to subvert the exclusion of the confession itself.[318]

A question might be raised as to whether facts permitted to be proved under PACE 1984, s 76(4) might nevertheless be excluded under the discretion in s 78. While there is no indication in s 78 that it does not apply to such facts, and s 78 has, in other contexts, been used to secure the discretionary exclusion of evidence made admissible by other specific provisions of the Police and Criminal Evidence Act 1984,[319] the issue has not yet been tested here, but there is no reason to suppose that the decision of the Privy Council in *R v Todd*[320] that such a discretion can be applied would not be accepted, notwithstanding the statutory differences.

In *Gafgen v Germany* it was held that inhuman[321] treatment of the accused leading to confession and the subsequent discovery of real evidence did not automatically lead to the admission of such evidence rendering a trial unfair, but only to a balancing exercise.[322]

EVIDENCE PROCURED BY IMPROPER[323] MEANS

Torture[324] is the most egregiously improper means of procuring evidence, and the exclusion of evidence so obtained has been re-emphasized by the House of Lords,[325] and its

---

[315] It is, however, possible that the words would be construed to apply to use of the form of the confession to show the accused's mental state at the time of making it: see, for permission of such use in Canada, *R v Edgar* (2000) 142 CCC 3d 401 (self-serving parts of mixed statements for the accused); *R v Fournier* (2000) 143 CCC 3d 341 (for the prosecution).

[316] *R v Grant* (1801) and *R v Hodge* (1794) 2 East PC 658. Practice was far from consistent: for different approaches, see *R v Griffin* (1809) Russ & Ry 151; *R v Gould* (1840) 9 C & P 364; *R v Garbett* (1847) 2 Car & Kir 474, 490; *R v Berriman* (n310). [317] [69], cl 2(5)(b).

[318] In Scotland, no part of an inadmissible confession can be received however much of it is confirmed: *Chalmers v HM Adv* 1954 JC 66; in Canada, the same result has probably been achieved under the Canadian Charter of Rights and Freedoms: *R v Black* [1989] 2 SCR 138; but see *R v Sweeney* (2000) 148 CCC 3d 247. In Australia, it was held in *R v Scott, ex p A-G* [1993] 1 Qd R 537 that the discretion to exclude such parts of a confession is governed solely by considerations of fairness to the accused, and is unaffected by considerations relevant to the exclusion of real evidence, as enunciated in *Bunning v Cross* (n2).

[319] See *R v O'Connor* (1986) 85 Cr App Rep 298, applying it to evidence of a conviction admissible under s 74. See further, 114. [320] [2008] UKPC 22.

[321] Torture, from which this treatment was contentiously distinguished, would have led to a different result. [322] (2009) 48 EHRR 253, [105].

[323] Including those improper under the law of the jurisdiction where they take place, but only if they ride 'roughshod' over the local law, and still excluded here only on the same basis as evidence improperly obtained under English law: *R v Redmond* [2006] EWCA Crim 1744, [2009] 1 Cr App R 335.

[324] To be distinguished from merely inhumane or degrading treatment, governed by more lenient rules; for the distinction, see Convention against Torture art 16; *Republic of Ireland v United Kingdom* (1978) 2 EHRR 25; *Selmouni v France* (1999) 29 EHRR 403, [101], stressing that the definition is adaptable to new practices.

[325] *A v Secretary of State for Home Department* [2005] UKHL 71, [2006] 2 AC 221. For academic discussion of the background, see Pattenden (2006) 10 *E&P* 1, and (2006) 2 EHRLR special number.

use condemned even in a special tribunal otherwise freed from constraint in the use of evidence.[326] It is to be regretted that some signs of peripheral crumbling of the stringency of this exclusion are beginning to emerge,[327] and to be hoped that resistance to hiding its incidence by means of claims for public interest immunity will continue.[328]

The modern law[329] in less heinous situations stems from the decision of the Privy Council in *Kuruma, Son of Kaniu v R*,[330] an appeal from Kenya, applying English law. The accused had been convicted of being in unlawful possession of ammunition, discovered during a search of his person by a police officer below the rank of those so permitted to search. Although it referred the case to the Colonial Secretary on other grounds, the board was of opinion that the evidence had been rightly admitted. Its view was that, if evidence is relevant, it does not matter how it was obtained. Their Lordships made it plain that they were not qualifying the law with regard to the admissibility of confessions in any way whatsoever. This strict view was qualified by discretion, to exclude evidence from a criminal trial if the strict rules of admissibility would operate unfairly against the accused, illustrated by the example of a document obtained by a trick.[331] The House of Lords subsequently decided[332] in *R v Sang*[333] that any such discretion was much more circumscribed than such dicta suggested, and applied only in respect of evidence obtained from the accused[334] after the commission of an offence. The reference to trickery was taken to refer to situations in which the accused was so induced to deliver up a document, or a piece of real evidence, contrary to the principle underlying the privilege against self-incrimination, and thought also to underlie the exclusion of involuntary confessions.[335] So narrow a view of the discretion proved to be unpalatable, and a late amendment to the Police and Criminal Evidence Act 1984[336] introduced a new statutory formulation in s 78 that:

In any proceedings the court may refuse to allow evidence on which the prosecution proposes to rely to be given if it appears to the court that, having regard to all the circumstances, including the circumstances in which the evidence was obtained, the admission of the evidence would have such an adverse effect on the fairness of the proceedings that the court ought not to admit it.

---

[326] Such prohibition has here the status of a constitutional principle: see Lord Bingham, [51]; and confers an absolute non-derogatable right under the European Convention on Human Rights: *Chahal v United Kingdom* (1996) 23 EHRR 413, [79]. See also *General Comment No 2* (2008) 46 EHRR SE 120.

[327] *Mustafa v US* [2008] EWHC 1357, [41] (indirect use); *OO v Secretary of State for the Home Department* [2009] UKHL 10, [2009] 4 All ER 1045 (acceptance of risk of torture in jurisdiction seeking extradition).

[328] Above 478.

[329] For both civil and criminal proceedings, see *R v Senat* (1968) 52 Cr App Rep 282 below; in Ireland, where constitutional protection is absent: *Universal City Studios Inc v Mulligan* [1999] 3 IR 392; in Canada, where s 24 of the Charter does not apply: *Schmeiser v Monsanto Canada Inc* 218 DLR (4th) 31, [70].

[330] [1955] AC 197, [1955] 1 All ER 236.

[331] Formulated in those terms by Lord Goddard CJ in *Kuruma*; 204, 239.

[332] Although technically obiter outside the area of entrapment, it has been highly persuasive: see Lord Roskill in *Morris v Beardmore* [1981] AC 446, [1980] 2 All ER 753; 469, 767; *R v Adams* [1980] QB 575, [1980] 1 All ER 473; *Cameron v Charles Simpson Motors* [1980] CLY 2630.

[333] [1980] AC 402, [1979] 2 All ER 1222.

[334] It was unclear how far it applied to evidence obtained from the accused's premises: see above, 202.

[335] It is not clear how this doctrine could be reconciled with the decision in *R v Derrington* (1826) 2 C & P 418, in which a letter obtained from the prisoner by the turnkey, under a false promise that he would post it, was admitted in evidence for the prosecution. Cf *R v Pamenter* (1872) 12 Cox CC 177.

[336] For a fuller account of its genesis, see Grevling (1997) 113 *LQR* 667.

Despite the vagueness of its terms, and the lack of logical progression from the unfairness of the means of obtaining the evidence to the unfairness of the proceedings in which it is adduced,[337] it became widely accepted that the discretion provided by s 78 was at least as wide as the common law discretion mentioned in *R v Sang*,[338] and in practice, it thereafter dominated the area.[339] There have even been signs of its transformation into an inclusionary discretion,[340] perhaps influenced by increasing stress on account being taken of fairness to the prosecution as well as to the defence.

The situation has more recently been transformed by the impact of the European Convention on Human Rights, and especially of Art 6 providing the right to a fair trial,[341] and of Art 8 providing for a right to privacy.[342] The enactment of the Human Rights Act 1998, and particularly the provision in s 3 requiring domestic legislation to be read in a manner compatible with Convention rights, has enabled the Court of Appeal to resolve some tension in this area between its previous decisions[343] by determining, in *R v Togher*,[344] that the Court of Appeal retained the power[345] to allow an appeal on the basis that a conviction had been obtained by improper conduct, capable of extending not only to cases of abuse of process, but to those in which evidence had been obtained improperly. There remains, however, considerable flexibility, and consequent uncertainty, in determining exactly what forms of impropriety will justify judicial intervention, whether by excluding evidence at trial, or by allowing an appeal.[346] Thus, although it was stated in *R v Francom*[347] that the English test of the safety of a conviction was not identical to the ECHR test of fairness of trial, nevertheless, in some cases, the two issues would be approached in 'exactly the same way',[348] without any precise indication of when that would be the case. Similar confusion reigns as to the relationship between the English criteria for the operation of the exclusionary discretion under s 78, and the ECHR criteria of fairness under Art 6.[349] It is

---

[337] See *DPP v Marshall* [1988] 3 All ER 683, and the temptation mentioned by Staughton LJ in the Court of Appeal in *R v Latif* [1995] 1 Cr App Rep 270, 278D.

[338] Preserved by s 82(3) of the Police and Criminal Evidence Act 1984, despite which the majority of the High Court of Australia remarked, in *Ridgeway v R* (1995) 184 CLR 19, 35, that s 78 amounted to the legislative reversal of the reasoning in *R v Sang* (n333).

[339] See Lord Nolan in *R v Khan* (n302); 578E, 298f, endorsing the view of Lord Taylor CJ below. In *R v Horseferry Road Magistrates' Court* [1994] 1 AC 42, [1993] 3 All ER 138, it was said by Lord Griffiths, 61A, 149g, to have enlarged the exclusionary discretion.

[340] See its formulation by Simon Brown LJ in *R v Bailey* [1993] 3 All ER 513, 97 Cr App Rep 365; 520j, 372; by Lord Taylor CJ in *R v Smurthwaite; R v Gill* [1994] 1 All ER 898, 98 Cr App Rep 437; 903a, 440; by Lord Bingham CJ in *R v Staines* [1997] 2 Cr App Rep 426, 443B (referring to the decision in *R v Khan* (n302)).

[341] In terms unqualified.

[342] As qualified by Art 8(2). See *Perry v United Kingdom* (2003) 39 EHRR 76 for application to installing covert recording devices, although at a previous hearing use of the evidence so obtained had been held not to violate Art 6. For a general assessment of the evidential implications of Art 8, see Ormerod [2003] *Crim LR* 61; see also, in New Zealand, *R v Shaheed* [2002] 2 NZLR 377, rejecting a prima facie exclusionary presumption in case of breach of the Bill of Rights in favour of a balancing test.

[343] Especially between *R v Chalkley* [1998] QB 848, [1998] 2 All ER 155, and *R v Mullen* [2000] QB 520, [1999] 2 Cr App Rep 143. [344] (n301).

[345] Despite the change to a single criterion for allowing an appeal that it be 'unsafe' introduced by the Criminal Appeal Act 1995.

[346] And within such a decision on whether to quash a conviction or to order a retrial under the provisions of s 7 of the Criminal Appeal Act 1968. [347] [2001] 1 Cr App Rep 237, 248.

[348] 249. See also *R v Togher* (n301) 468, 463.

[349] Although in *R v Sanghera* [2001] 1 Cr App Rep 299, 304, the Court of Appeal approved the view that invocation of Art 6.1 could not succeed if the application of s 78 would not.

clearly the case that the operation of s 78 by the trial judge, before the trial has terminated, must be different from that of Art 6, which amounts to a determination of whether the trial, considered as a whole,[350] has been fair. One justifies action; the other evaluates it.

Although it has been held that the use in evidence of material obtained by a breach of Art 8 does not automatically amount to a breach of Art 6,[351] nor of s 6 of the Human Rights Act 1998,[352] the court's determination that such breach has occurred has been a catalyst for statutory intervention in a number of areas. Article 8 provides:

(1) Everyone has the right to respect for his private and family life, his home and his correspondence.

(2) There shall be no interference by a public authority with the exercise of this right except such as is in accordance with the law and necessary in a democratic society in the interests of national security, public safety or the economic well-being of the country, for the prevention of disorder or crime, for the protection of health or morals, or for the protection of the rights and freedoms of others.

A general principle of interpretation is that rights are to be construed broadly,[353] and exceptions narrowly.[354] As a result, enabling provisions have to pass through a number of hoops in order to qualify under Art 8.2. First, they must be in accordance with the law, which has been interpreted to mean in accordance with a publicly accessible code, preferably one with legislative force;[355] second, they must accord with basic legal values;[356] and third, they must be necessary, in the sense of being both the least restrictive means of dealing with the problem, and proportional to its magnitude.

It is further worth noting that the emphasis in the Convention on the activities of public bodies and servants accentuates[357] the possibility of different rules applying to public and private impropriety.[358] A further consequence of this concentration on public bodies is that, in a number of cases, there is some tension between the desire of those bodies to use the fruits of their action at trial, and their reluctance to divulge any detail of the methods used to obtain them, especially in advance of trial.

---

[350] An element that the ECHR regards as particularly important: see *Klass v Germany* (1978) 2 EHRR 214.

[351] *Khan v United Kingdom* (2001) 31 EHRR 1016, [29]–[40]; *PG and JH v United Kingdom* (2001) 31 EHRR 1016, [76]–[81]; in both, over strong dissenting opinions on this very point.

[352] *R v Button* [2005] EWCA Crim 516, [21].

[353] *Niemetz v Germany* (1992) 16 EHRR 97, [29]–[30].   [354] *Klass v Germany* (n350), [42].

[355] A rule now accepted by the government of the United Kingdom: see the concession of this point in *Lewis v United Kingdom* (2004) 39 EHRR 213, [18].

[356] See *Klass v Germany* (1978) 2 EHRR 214, [49]; *Halford v United Kingdom* (1997) 24 EHRR 523, [61]; the Convention contains in its Preamble reference to 'the rule of law', and regards it as of fundamental importance in the interpretation of its provisions: *Golder v United Kingdom* (1975) 1 EHRR 524, [34].

[357] Although it also exists in English law, in distinguishing between surveillance conducted by the police, and their knowledge and use of surveillance conducted, in breach of Art 8, by private individuals: *R v Rosenberg* [2006] EWCA Crim 6, [18].

[358] Although there is occasionally some overlap, as in *DPP v Bignell* [1998] 1 Cr App Rep 1, QBD (police officers misusing official facilities for private purposes); *R v Sargent* [2001] UKHL 54, [2003] 1 AC 347 (engineer misusing telecommunications facilities for private purposes); in Canada, *Insurance Company of British Columbia v Suska* (2008) 296 DLR (4th) 257 (state performed functions through private contractor). In *R v Holford* [2001] 1 NZLR 385, the Court of Appeal required the conduct of private investigators to be 'outrageous' before regarding a case based upon evidence obtained by illegal means by them as an abuse of process.

Impropriety can take many forms, but a number of different clusters can be discerned, and will be used as a framework for discussion, although it is recognized that the divisions adopted here are neither exclusive, nor exhaustive. Statutory procedures now apply[359] in an increasing number of areas, generally with a more prescriptive effect.

Improper[360] searches[361]

The traditional English view was laconically expressed by Crompton J in *R v Leatham*,[362] when he said: 'It matters not how you get it if you steal it even, it would be admissible in evidence.' Thus in *Jones v Owen*,[363] a constable searched the appellant illegally and found a quantity of young salmon in his pocket. This evidence was held to be admissible on a charge of unlawful fishing, Mellor J expressing the view that:

It would be a dangerous obstacle to the administration of justice if we were to hold, because evidence was obtained by illegal means, it could not be used against a party charged with an offence.

These views have persisted. Crompton J's dictum was cited in *Kuruma's* case, and it will be recollected that *Calcraft v Guest*,[364] the leading authority on the admissibility of secondary evidence of privileged documents, was decided on a similar principle.[365] In *R v Khan*,[366] the House of Lords took into account, in relation to the placing of listening devices on private premises,[367] trespass to, and slight damage of, private premises, the possibility that this might have amounted to criminal damage, and breach of privacy, but nevertheless concluded[368] that, 'as a matter of English law, evidence which is obtained improperly or even unlawfully remains admissible'. Sometimes breach of the precise formulation of the rules relating to breath, urine, or alcohol levels, or to the retention of properly obtained fingerprints or DNA samples, leads to the exclusion of reliable real evidence discovered as a result.[369] This normally involves a special test,[370] and may necessitate an arrest in order to accomplish it. It seems that even if the test is conducted only after, and in consequence

---

[359] Sometimes indirectly, as where statutory provision is made for the operation of a code of practice.

[360] See dispute in Canada about the extent of common law police powers of search: *R v Clayton* 2007 SCC 32, [2007] 3 SCR 725.

[361] This category includes improper use of material properly obtained in the first place. The notion of a search may itself be problematic: cf decisions in the United States and Canada on thermal imaging: *Kyllo v US* 533 US 27 (2001) (is); *R v Tessling* 2004 SCC 67, [2004] 3 SCR 432 (is not); and on use of sniffer dog: *Illinois v Caballes* 543 US 405, 125 S Ct R 834, (2005); *Darby v DPP* [2004] NSWCA 431, 150 ACR 314 (both is not); *R v Kang-Brown* 2008 SCC 18, [2008] 1 SCR 456 (is); or even sniffer police officer, *R v Rajaratnam* (2006) 214 CCC3d 547, but see *R v Janvier* (2007) 227 CCC3d 294. [362] (n312), 501.

[363] (1870) 34 JP 759. [364] [1898] 1 QB 759, and see 415.

[365] Admissibility of unlawfully obtained evidence obtains as much in civil as in criminal proceedings, subject to the new exclusionary discretion in CPR 32.1: see *Silversafe Ltd v Hood* [2006] EWHC 1849 (Ch), [2006] STI 1988, [52].

[366] (n302). This result is in accord with that arrived at in the different constitutional and legislative context in the United States: *Dalia v United States* 441 US 238 (1979); and in Canada: *Lyons v R* (1985) 14 DLR (4th) 482; but not in Australia: *Coco v R* (1994) 120 ALR 415.

[367] Although the police were conceded to have been acting in general in accordance with procedures approved by Parliament. [368] 578A, 298a. Subject only to discretionary power to exclude.

[369] But even here there is a developing tendency to eschew technicality: see *Jones v DPP* [2003] EWHC 1729 (Admin), (2003) 167 JP 481. See also, in Australia, *Police v Astley* (1997) 69 SASR 319.

[370] The precise specification of which may lead to inability to use reliable real evidence: see *Evans v DPP* (1996) The Times, 30 May.

of, an illegal[371] arrest,[372] the evidence is nevertheless admissible in subsequent proceedings for driving with excess alcohol in the body.[373] A sample is admissible notwithstanding that the device used to obtain it had not been duly approved,[374] or the specified procedure ignored.[375] Nor is it relevant that the substance found is used in relation to a different offence from that for which its use was originally envisaged.[376] If evidence is obtained illegally to the knowledge of counsel, it seems that it should be mentioned to the court on an interim application, since that may be relevant to the exercise of the judge's discretion.[377] In *ITC Film Distributor v Video Exchange Ltd*,[378] in which the material in question was found to have been obtained by means of a contempt of court, it was, however, held that it should not be admitted.[379] The combination of these approaches leads to the conclusion that, in England, illegally obtained evidence is admissible as a matter of law, provided that it involves neither a reference to an inadmissible confession of guilt, nor the commission of an act of contempt of court.[380]

It remains to be considered how far this result is mitigated by the exercise of discretion under s 78. In the case of real evidence obtained by an illegal search, the position seems to be that, while the discretion may be taken into account, it is exceedingly difficult to persuade a court to exercise it. In *R v Fox*,[381] the House of Lords regarded it as justifying the refusal of the magistrates to exercise their discretion to exclude the evidence that the police had acted 'in good faith, and that the specimen itself had been obtained without inducement, threat,... trick or other impropriety'. Similarly, it has not been exercised to exclude an intimate sample taken from a prisoner wrongly informed that he was bound to submit,[382] nor a non-intimate sample obtained after police in riot gear had entered the suspect's police cell and made it clear that force would be used if he resisted,[383] nor the observation of illicit electricity connections within a dwelling house secured by the threat of forcible entry,[384] and not even the contents of the accused's mouth disgorged only after forcible interference with a suspect's breathing.[385] It is then hardly surprising to find that

---

[371] Or even prohibited: *DPP v Wilson* [2009] EWHC 1988 (Admin).

[372] A fortiori after slight delay in providing access to a lawyer: *Causey v DPP* [2004] EWHC 3164, (2005) 169 JP 331.

[373] *R v Fox* [1986] AC 281, [1985] 3 All ER 392. To be distinguished from the offence of refusing a test, since the conditions may there require that the arrest be lawful: *Morris v Beardmore* (n332).

[374] *Criminal Proceedings Against Lemmings* [1998] All ER (EC) 604.

[375] *R (CPS) v Wolverhampton Magistrates' Court* [2009] EWHC 3467 (Admin).

[376] *R v Kelt* [1994] 2 All ER 780, [1994] 1 WLR 765.

[377] See *Memory Corp v Sidhu* [2000] 1 WLR 1443, [2000] FSR 921.

[378] [1982] Ch 431, [1982] 2 All ER 241.

[379] The same applies where, although the document may have been obtained perfectly lawfully, for example on discovery, its use in different proceedings would amount to contempt: Waller LJ in *Riddick v Thames Board Mills Ltd* [1977] QB 881, [1977] 3 All ER 677; 911, 702.

[380] This statement of the law was explicitly approved by the Court of Appeal in *R v Khan* [1995] QB 27, [1994] 4 All ER 426; 37B, 434c.

[381] (n373), 290, 395. Section 78 had been enacted, but not brought into force, at the relevant time. It was, however, approved in *DPP v Kennedy* [2003] EWHC 2583 (Admin), 168 JP 185, in which the breach was purely technical. See in Australia *Parker v Comptroller-General of Customs* [2007] NSWCA 348, 243 ALR 574.   [382] *R v Apicella* (1985) 82 Cr App Rep 295.

[383] *R v Cooke* [1995] 1 Cr App Rep 318.   [384] *R v Stewart* [1995] Crim LR 500.

[385] *R v Hughes* [1994] 1 WLR 876, 99 Cr App Rep 160; for the same result in New Zealand, see *R v Roulston* [1998] 2 NZLR 468, but for a different one in the ECHR, see *Jalloh v Germany* (2007) 44 EHRR 667 (which is likely to prevail here).

breach of an international convention[386] relating to the treatment of those with diplomatic immunity,[387] or breach of foreign law,[388] have not sufficed. The possibility that this might occur was not, however, rejected completely, if there were sufficient bad faith and flagrant enough breaches of the Code on the part of the searchers. *R v Nathaniel*,[389] in which the police not only failed to follow the statutory instruction to destroy the DNA profile, but, in failing to do so, broke the assurance under which they had secured the accused's agreement to provide it, is one of the few cases[390] in which such an argument has succeeded.

As noted above, this part of the law has increasingly been made subject to statutory provision. It is now the case that the powers of the police to search, to seize, and to store are closely regulated by statute,[391] and in many cases, those very statutes[392] include rules affecting the admissibility of such materials in evidence. *R v Nathaniel* was just such a case. The relevant provisions of the Police and Criminal Evidence Act 1984 were subsequently amended, and the amended version constituted the basis for the decision of the House of Lords in *A-G's Reference (No 3 of 1999)*.[393] There, too, a DNA sample had been retained in accidental breach of the relevant provision,[394] and in this case, its use led to the taking of a new sample that it was proposed to put in evidence. The relevant provision[395] prevented the use in evidence of the first improperly retained sample, and also prevented its use for the purposes of any investigation. It was accordingly argued by the accused that the new sample could not be put in evidence, as it had been obtained by the use of the first sample for the purposes of investigation. The House of Lords relied upon the principle of *Kuruma's* case as ameliorated by the exclusionary discretion under s 78 to reject this view, and to hold that evidence obtained as a result of an illegal process should not be excluded as a matter of rule.[396] It further relied upon the decision of the European Court of Human Rights in

[386] Even though given statutory force in the United Kingdom by the Diplomatic Privileges Act 1964.

[387] *R v Khan, Sakkarevej and Pamarapa* [1997] Crim LR 508, in which *R v Fennelley* [1989] Crim LR 142, one of the few cases to have excluded real evidence obtained by breach of the Code of Practice, was disavowed.

[388] *R v Hardy* [2003] EWCA Crim 3092, although following dicta in *R v Khan* (n302); 581H, 301g, such a breach was regarded as a matter that could be taken into account in the exercise of the discretion under s 78.

[389] [1995] 2 Cr App Rep 565. Although the result seems to have been inspired by incompetence rather than dishonesty, and was achieved despite the decisive nature of the evidence in relation to the serious crime of rape. See also *R v Weir* (26 May 2000, unreported), CA; in New Zealand, *R v Hanna* [2004] 3 NZLR 301. For a similar approach to fingerprint retention in Australia see *R v Sarlija* [2005] ACTSC 120, 158 ACR 125.

[390] *R v Veneroso* [2002] Crim LR 306, exposing a lacuna in s 17 of the Police and Criminal Evidence Act 1984, is another. See also *R v Allen* [2001] UKHL 25, [2002] 1 AC 509, [2001] 4 All ER 768, [35], in which Lord Hutton seems to suggest that the provision of a document constituting the commission of an earlier offence on the basis of a Hansard warning might be excluded on this basis.

[391] Supplemented by Code of Practice A under s 67 of the Police and Criminal Evidence Act 1984 (as amended). Although the common law still applies to the extent that it has not been repealed, either expressly or by necessary implication: see *R v Metropolis Police Comr, ex p Rottman* [2002] UKHL 20, [2002] 2 AC 692. The court is also reluctant to extend either the common law, *R (Hewitson) v Chief Constable of Dorset Police* [2003] EWHC 3296 (Admin), or the statutory provisions, *Khan v Commissioner of Police for the Metropolis* [2008] EWCA Civ 723 to fill any gaps.

[392] Often by way of Codes of Practice made under them, such as Codes A and B, the scope of the latter of which was given a liberal interpretation in *R v Sanghera* [2001] 1 Cr App Rep 299; cf, in Canada, *R v Law* [2002] 1 SCR 227.   [393] [2001] 2 AC 91, [2001] 1 All ER 577.

[394] Police and Criminal Evidence Act 1984, s 64.   [395] PACE, s 64(3B).

[396] In relation to DNA this may not survive the decision in *S and Marper v United Kingdom* (2009) 48 EHRR 1169.

Khan[397] to hold that such use, given the availability of the exclusionary discretion,[398] did not render the trial unfair so as to amount to breach of Art 6 of the Convention.

From the time of the decision of the House of Lords in *Khan* onwards, there has been a deluge of legislative activity, progressively widening the authorization of official incursions into private life in the interest of law enforcement.[399] Part III of the Police Act 1997 was designed to provide a legislative framework for the implantation of bugging devices on private property. The Code of Practice[400] made under it expressly provides for the retention of product 'for the purposes of future civil or criminal proceedings'.[401] The Regulation of Investigatory Powers Act 2000 was a more comprehensive measure[402] replacing the Interception of Communications Act 1985, but dealing also with surveillance, and the use of human intelligence sources. It is noteworthy that s 81(5)[403] seems to preserve the right to use material obtained by such methods in legal proceedings. Further extension took place in the Criminal Justice and Police Act 2001,[404] to some extent providing legislative approval for the conduct found to have been improper in *R v Chesterfield Justices, ex p Bramley*,[405] and that found to have been improper at the level of the Court of Appeal in *A-G's Reference (No 3 of 1999)*.[406] Then, in reaction to a perceived increased threat of terrorism,[407] further extension of powers to disclose information for the purposes of criminal proceedings was made in the Anti-Terrorism, Crime and Security Act 2001.[408] This is a particularly far-reaching incursion, since it applies not only to terrorist, but to all crimes; requires no more than that a criminal investigation be in existence, irrespective of whether there is any evidence to justify it, or reason for suspicion; and expressly provides for the use of such material in evidence.

Many other common law jurisdictions seem readier to exclude evidence obtained by improper searches. In Scotland, the discretion is inclusionary.[409] Illegally obtained evidence is excluded in the absence of an excuse for its reception.[410] There are even signs

---

[397] (2001) 31 EHRR 1016.

[398] Rather ignoring the weakness of this means of protection, bearing in mind the infrequency of its exercise in this context.

[399] Including the Police Act 1997 Pt III; the Terrorism Act 2000; the Regulation of Investigatory Powers Act 2000; the Criminal Justice and Police Act 2001; and the Anti-Terrorism, Crime and Security Act 2001. The courts seem unlikely to take a restricted view of the ambit of the powers of search under such provisions, and the use of material so obtained in evidence: see *R v Hundal and Dhaliwal* [2004] EWCA Crim 389, [2004] 2 Cr App R 307.   [400] Made under s 101 of the PA 1997.

[401] Paragraph 2.34.

[402] Held in *R v Lawrence* [2002] Crim LR 584 to be compatible in these respects with the European Convention: see also Mirfield [2001] *Crim LR* 91.

[403] Together with the absence of any equivalent of the obligation to exclude intercepted material from evidence imposed by s 17.   [404] See Wasik [2001] *Crim LR* 931, 944–6.

[405] [2000] QB 576, [2000] 1 All ER 411 (removing from searched premises for sifting elsewhere, material containing potentially legally privileged documents): s 50.   [406] Above: s 82.

[407] This threat may well render more serious impropriety capable of being regarded as 'proportionate': see *R v Hundal* (n399), [20].   [408] Section 17; Sch 4.

[409] But does not apply outside the rather restricted notion of a search: *Howard v HM Adv* [2006] HCJAC 21, 2006 SCCR 321.

[410] *Lawrie v Muir* 1950 JC 19; *Morrison v O'Donnell* 2001 SCCR 272. For a case in which the Scots courts would have been prepared to receive illegally obtained evidence because of the danger that the accused would destroy the evidence against him, see *Hay v HM Adv* 1968 JC 40. This aspect of Scottish law was regarded as compatible with the European Convention on Human Rights in *Hoekstra v HM Adv (No 6)* 2002 SCCR 135.

that the discretion may exist under Scots law in civil cases,[411] while there was no parallel development in English procedure.[412]

In Canada, as noted above, the position is now governed by the Charter of Rights and Freedoms.[413] This has adopted a position intermediate between the English[414] rule that evidence is in principle admissible however it has been obtained, subject only to an exclusionary discretion, and the old American rule that illegally obtained evidence should, in principle, be excluded. The Canadian compromise is to exclude evidence obtained in breach of the Charter, but only if its admission is likely to bring the administration of justice into disrepute. It is obvious that such a position requires detailed elaboration, and the Supreme Court of Canada has been deluged with appeals to this end. The leading case is still *R v Collins*,[415] which seems broadly to regard the administration of justice as brought into disrepute more by evidence secured by conscripting the accused against himself[416] than by other forms of illegality,[417] or trickery.[418] The test also recognizes that the administration of justice may sometimes also be brought into disrepute by the exclusion of reliable evidence,[419] and that the good faith of the police,[420] or even the obnoxious reaction of the suspect,[421] may cure any technical illegality from this point of view.[422] The test does not, however, apply in its full rigour to administrative, as opposed to investigative acts, so not to the actions of a coroner in determining the cause of death,[423] nor where the breach is in respect of a third party.[424]

By contrast, in Australia,[425] the position is determined by the common law:[426]

On the one hand there is the public need to bring to conviction those who commit criminal offences. On the other hand there is the public interest in the protection of the individual from unlawful and unfair treatment. Convictions obtained with the aid of unlawful and unfair acts may be obtained at too high a price. Hence the judicial discretion.

---

[411] *Rattray v Rattray* 1897 25 R 315; *Maccoll v Maccoll* 1946 SLT 312.

[412] At common law, but see *L v L* [2007] EWHC 140 (QB), [2007] 2 FLR 171, [115] indicating possible loosening, irrespective of the discretion now provided under CPR 32.2.

[413] Supplemented by a more general exclusionary discretion: *Buhay v R* [2003] SCC 30, [2003] 1 SCR 631, [40]. For the position under the New Zealand Bill of Rights, see *R v Shaheed* (n342).

[414] It also represented the previous position in Canada: see *R v Wray* (1970) 11 DLR (3d) 673.

[415] [1987] 1 SCR 265, in which Lamer J set out the principles according to which s 24(2) of the Charter was to be construed, restated in *R v Law* [2002] SCC 10, [2002] 1 SCR 210, [33] as comprising three categories: (1) the effect of admission on the fairness of the trial; (2) the seriousness of the misconduct; and (3) the effect on the administration of justice.

[416] A concept extended to include the illegal obtention of constituent parts of the human body and its contents: see *R v Therens* [1985] 1 SCR 613 (breath); *R v Dersch* [1993] 3 SCR 768 (blood); *R v Stillman* (hair, saliva, mucous samples, and dental impressions); *R v Greffe* [1990] 1 SCR 755 (contents of rectum). It also applies to fingerprints obtained after an illegal arrest: *R v Feeney* [1997] 2 SCR 13.

[417] Although, in *R v Golden* [2001] SCC 83, [2001] 3 SCR 679, the Supreme Court took into account the fact that the circumstances of the strip search conducted there were especially demeaning, and even that such searches were conducted disproportionately on non-white citizens.

[418] *R v Van Nguyen* (2002) 161 CCC3d 433 (DNA from chewing gum supplied by police, and discarded after use by the accused).

[419] See the division of the Supreme Court on this point in *R v Mann* 2004 SCC 52, [2004] 3 SCR 59.

[420] Or other infringer of Charter principles: see *R v Lerke* (1986) 25 DLR (4th) 403.

[421] See *Tremblay v R* [1987] 2 SCR 435.   [422] *Sieben v R* [1987] 1 SCR 295.

[423] *R v Colarusso* [1994] 1 SCR 20.   [424] *R v Edwards* [1996] 1 SCR 128.

[425] For full and illuminating discussion of the area in New Zealand, see *R v Williams* [2007] NZCA 52, [2007] 3 NZLR 207.
      [426] *R v Ireland* (1970) 126 CLR 321, 335.

The notions of public policy and fairness are combined in this statement. The former is predominant in Ireland:[427] 'I am disposed to lay emphasis not so much on alleged unfairness to the accused as on the public interest that the law should be observed in the investigation of crime.' It is interesting that, in *King v R*,[428] a similar policy was found by the Privy Council to underlie the common law discretion.

Perpetration of illegal acts[429]

Sometimes, the impropriety occurs not in searching for evidence, but in inducing, or even participating in, the commission of the crime charged, often described as entrapment. In *R v Looseley: A-G's Reference (No 3 of 1999)*,[430] Lord Nicholls explained that:

It is simply not acceptable that the state through its agents should lure its citizens into committing acts forbidden by the law and then seek to prosecute them for doing so.

As Lord Nicholls observed, there are a number of variable factors to be considered in any such situation, and a variety of legal means of control. It remains the case that, in England,[431] and in most other common law jurisdictions,[432] entrapment does not amount to a defence.[433] It will most often be inconsistent with a substantive defence.[434] It was also held in *R v Sang* that such a rule would be undermined by the exclusion of evidence obtained of a crime committed in such circumstances,[435] and entrapment was regarded as affecting only sentence.[436] Since that decision, a new discretion to exclude has been created by s 78 of the Police and Criminal Evidence Act 1984, and the remedy of staying proceedings for abuse of process has been developed at common law,[437] most relevantly for this context in *R v Latif; R v Shahzad*.[438] The courts are also bound[439] to take into account the jurisprudence of the European Court of Human Rights, where the leading decision is *Texeira de Castro v Portugal*.[440] That court will also intervene to ensure that the procedure for determining any such issue is fair, and that the prosecution should not be permitted to refuse to disclose relevant information to the defence on the basis of public interest without appropriate safeguards.[441] The issue of disclosure is, however, likely to be particularly sensitive and important in this situation, and the English courts have adopted a flexible

---

[427] *People (A-G) v O'Brien* [1965] IR 142, 160.

[428] [1969] 1 AC 304, 319F. The search must not have constituted 'conduct of which the Crown ought not to take advantage'.   [429] For fuller discussion, see Ashworth [2002] *Crim LR* 161.

[430] [2001] UKHL 53, [2001] 4 All ER 897, [1] (hereafter *Looseley*).

[431] *R v McEvilly* (1973) 60 Cr App Rep 150; *R v Mealey* (1974) 60 Cr App Rep 59, approved in *R v Sang* [1980] AC 402, [1979] 2 All ER 1222, 432A, 1226e.

[432] See in Australia, *Ridgeway v R* (n338), 30; in Canada, *Mack v R* [1988] 2 SCR 903, 947; and in New Zealand, *R v Katipa* [1986] 2 NZLR 121, 125. Although sometimes it may be in the United States, see *United States v Russell* 411 US 423, 435 (1973).

[433] In part, as explained by Lord Scott in *Looseley* (n430), [125], since if it were, it might generate a demand for disclosure of police practice in the course of such operations.

[434] *R (Edwards) v Criminal Cases Review Committee* [2008] EWHC 2389 (Admin).

[435] 433D, 1227f.

[436] Lord Diplock, 432. See *R v Shannon* [2001] 1 WLR 51, [2001] 1 Cr App Rep 168 for an example of such mitigation. It was also envisaged in *Sang* (n333) that judicial criticism of police methods was appropriate.

[437] It is interesting to note that its application was explicitly denied by Lord Scarman in *Sang* (n333), 455.   [438] [1996] 1 All ER 353, [1996] 1 WLR 104.

[439] Human Rights Act 1998, s 2(1)(a).

[440] (1998) 28 EHRR 101, applied and extended in *Khudobin v Russia* (2009) 48 EHRR 523.

[441] *Edwards and Lewis v United Kingdom* (n216), [57].

approach,[442] eschewing rigid rules, although they are unlikely to order disclosure where failure has caused no prejudice to the accused.[443] They will also require an adequate evidential basis to support a claim that a request for extradition is vitiated by entrapment.[444]

Further impetus for change had been provided by the reasoning of the High Court of Australia in *Ridgeway v R*,[445] in which it was said[446] that 'the basis in principle of this discretion lies in the inherent or implied powers of our courts to protect the integrity of their processes'. There, as in *Latif*, the case embodied a classical 'sting' operation, whereby the police acting through undercover agents infiltrated a drug-smuggling operation, and cooperated in the illegal importation of drugs into Australia in order to secure an arrest within the jurisdiction. The accused was charged with possession of the illegally imported drugs.[447] The element of illegal importation caused the problem. It had to be proved,[448] because it was an essential element of the offence, yet it had been committed by the police themselves. This stuck in the craw of the majority. It held that, where commission of an offence has been procured by agents of the state, it would be in only a rare case[449] that prosecution would be appropriate.[450] The remedy involved a stay of the proceedings for abuse of the process of the courts. Much of the discussion in the case considers the relationship of such a remedy to that of the discretionary exclusion of evidence.

These matters have now been ventilated here in twin appeals to the House of Lords in *Looseley*. Both cases involved the use of undercover police agents to provide evidence of drug dealing, and in both cases, the undercover agents solicited the supply of drugs. In one case, the solicitation, having been successful, was repeated on two further occasions, and in the other, it was secured on the sole occasion in part by the agents' supply of cheap, purportedly contraband, cigarettes. The House of Lords, in its review of the law, distinguished more sharply than before between the remedy of staying proceedings for abuse of process, or as Lord Hoffmann preferred 'to prevent abuse of executive power',[451] and that of excluding evidence.[452] It regarded entrapment as most appositely remedied by the former, ideally before the trial, since the essence of the claim is that there should be no prosecution

---

[442] *R v H and C* (n22), [33].   [443] See e.g. *R v Nicholls* [2005] EWCA Crim 1797, [40].

[444] *Jenkins v USA* [2005] EWHC 1051 (Admin), [32].

[445] (n338). See further Grevling (1996) 112 LQR 401. For comparative judicial analysis of *Ridgeway* and *Looseley* see *Robinson v Woolworths Ltd* [2005] NSWCA 426, 158 ACR 546.

[446] 31, the reference is to the *Bunning v Cross* (n2) discretion.

[447] Contrary to s 233B(1) Customs Act 1901 (Cwth).

[448] It would not have had to be proved under state offences of possession of illegal substances, and the majority, rather surprisingly in view of their apparent outrage at the procedure in the Commonwealth prosecution, regarded prosecution for such offences as not merely tolerable, but even to justify quashing the convictions for the Commonwealth offences.

[449] For example, where there was no high level involvement, and the officers actually involved had been punished.

[450] Although such a view was not shared either by the legislatures that passed 'Controlled Operations' legislation *Ridgeway* (n338) in the Commonwealth with retrospective effect, upheld in *R v Nicholas* (1998) 193 CLR 173, but see *Gedeon v NSW Crime Commission* [2008] HCA 43, 236 CLR 120 striking down an application of the NSW legislation; or by the courts that swiftly proved astute to distinguish it: see e.g. *R v Kokosi* (1995) 64 SASR 319 (see also Criminal Law (Undercover Operations) Act 1995 (SA)); *R v Salem* (1997) 96 ACR 421 (NSW); *R v Haughbro* 135 FLR 415 (ACT); *R v Te* [1998] 3 VR 566.   [451] [40].

[452] An important difference is that an appellate court can adopt its own independent view in abuse cases, but in s 78 cases is restricted to review of the trial judge's exercise of his discretion: see *R v Harmes and Crane* [2006] EWCA Crim 928, [54].

for the crime at all having regard to the state's involvement in its commission.[453] It was nevertheless recognized that s 78 could also be invoked in this context, perhaps where the factual basis of the claim became clear only during the trial, although even then the appropriate conditions would remain those for granting a stay rather than those for excluding evidence.[454] It was also recognized that there could be some cases in which the nature of the entrapment might be such as to taint the evidence of the agent.[455]

It remained to determine upon what basis such control by the court should be exercised, since it was apparent that, in some situations, it is not improper for the agents of the state to cooperate in the commission of a crime.[456] Lord Nicholls set out three elements relevant to such a determination. First, he thought that the nature of the crime to be investigated was relevant, with 'victimless' crimes, such as drug dealing, particularly eligible for such an approach, just because it would be so difficult to secure evidence of their commission otherwise. Second, he was concerned that, in general, the police should have definite grounds for suspicion,[457] and should not merely engage in random testing of the virtue of the community.[458] It seems clear that the suspicion need not be of a particular individual,[459] and that such methods would be appropriate where the suspicion was of the likelihood of the commission of crime in a particular area, or presumably of a particular type of crime.[460] He also regarded previous convictions as some, but by no means an infallible,[461] indication of whether such suspicion might be held to be reasonable. Third, he recommended regard to the nature of the police involvement in the crime in the light of the nature of the crime, and the vulnerability of the accused. Thus more active and persistent involvement by the agent would be justified in relation to a serious crime to be perpetrated by a hardened, and astute, potential actor. In many situations, it would not be objectionable for the police agent to act as an ordinary customer of a particular trade,[462] whether criminal or not.

A number of these elements were further elaborated by Lord Hoffmann, who seemed particularly anxious to disavow the availability of simple rules of thumb in such cases, such as that the agent should never take an active role in the commission of the crime,[463] or that the predisposition of the accused to commit a crime was decisive.[464] As if to emphasize the

---

[453] Lord Nicholls, [17].   [454] Lord Hoffmann, [44].

[455] At [43] approving dicta of Potter LJ in *R v Shannon* (n436), 187, 68.

[456] Test purchases are often statutorily authorized: see e.g. Licensing Act 2003 s 152(4); Criminal Justice and Police Act 2001, s 31.

[457] Conversely, it is immaterial that the very same person has already been charged with offences of the same type, if the police suspect that similar offences are continuing to be committed: *R v Brett* [2005] EWCA Crim 983.

[458] For example, by leaving a wallet abandoned in a crowded city centre, as in the example of unacceptable conduct mentioned by Lamer J in the leading Canadian case of *Mack v R* (n432), 957.

[459] Indeed, the more the suspicion is centred on a particular known individual, the less need there might be thought to go beyond more conventional forms of evidence-gathering.

[460] *Williams v DPP* [1993] 3 All ER 365, 98 Cr App Rep 209, in which a load of cigarettes was left apparently unattended in an area where theft from vehicles was rife might seem to satisfy these criteria, but nevertheless comes very close to random virtue testing.

[461] Neither a necessary nor a sufficient condition according to Lord Hoffmann, [68].

[462] Although in a case such as *Nottingham City Council v Amin* [2000] 2 All ER 946, [2000] 1 WLR 1071, this involved imagining the ordinary customer to flag down a cab even though its light was not illuminated.

[463] [69]. As had been argued on the basis of some of the dicta in *Teixeira de Castro* (n440).

[464] [68]. Contrary to the view in the United States, where entrapment can constitute a defence.

complexity of the determination, the appeal was denied in one of the two cases before the House of Lords, in which there was no more than persistent solicitation of a sort to which a drug dealer is regularly exposed,[465] but allowed in the other, in which there was only one supply, denial of normal involvement in the supply, and the unusual counter-offer of cheap cigarettes, generating demand for the return of a favour.

Many of these issues should be resolved by insistence upon close adherence to the Codes of Practice under the Regulation of Investigatory Powers Act, especially in relation to authorization, although there is some danger of undermining such insistence by reluctance to allow appeals.[466]

Although in any modern criminal[467] case it is the state that conducts the ultimate prosecution, it sometimes happens that the entrapment of the accused has already been accomplished by private individuals[468] before any agents of the state become involved. Two such cases[469] in England, both involving the same entrapper,[470] were unsuccessful: one in securing the exclusion of the evidence under s 78, and the other in having the proceedings stayed for abuse of process. The latter distinguished 'commercial' and 'executive' entrapment, and regarded as over-lenient an earlier view[471] that there was no difference between them. It is interesting to note that the leading European case on abstention from intervention on matters of admission of evidence under national rules, *Schenk v Switzerland*,[472] also involved private individuals rather than agents of the state.

In all of these cases, it was an inherent part of the plan that the relevant crime should be committed. Sometimes it is not intended to go so far, but to stop short at the point at which evidence of an intention to commit the crime has been gathered with a view to prosecution for an inchoate offence. Here, again, there has been reluctance to employ the discretion in s 78 to exclude the evidence. Thus in *R v Smurthwaite; R v Gill*,[473] the court refused to exclude evidence secured by an undercover police officer posing as a contract killer. The court did, however, accept that the role of the police as agents provocateurs was a relevant consideration to weigh in the balance, although it was felt that no precise guidance could, or should, be given on the operation of s 78 in this area.[474]

---

[465] See also *R v Byrne* [2003] EWCA Crim 1073, in which it was not enough that the accused had not been targeted as a dealer, and that she was merely attempting to assist someone she thought suffering withdrawal symptoms, if she would have supplied drugs to anyone in that situation.

[466] As in *R v Harmes and Crane* (n452).

[467] Some domestic disciplinary proceedings are, for these purposes, akin to criminal proceedings, and there is also likely to be more reluctance to stay on the basis of entrapment by private persons: *Council for the Regulation of Health Care Professionals v GMC* [2006] EWHC 2784 (Admin), (2006) 92 BMLR 153 (by journalists); see in Canada, *College of Optometrists v SHS Optical Ltd* 2008 ONCA 685, 300 DLR (4th) 548.

[468] Who would themselves in many cases be guilty of incitement or conspiracy: see generally Hofmeyr [2006] *Crim LR* 319.

[469] In *R v Shannon* (n436) an application to the ECHR was rejected as 'manifestly ill-founded', (n472), [71]; *R v Hardwicke and Thwaites* [2001] Crim LR 220.

[470] A journalist who claimed in *Shannon* (n436) to have been responsible for no fewer than 89 successful prosecutions.   [471] In *R v Morley and Hutton* [1994] Crim LR 919.

[472] (1988) 13 EHRR 242. But the ECHR does not rule out the possibility that private entrapment might trigger breach of Art 6: *Shannon v UK* (n472).

[473] (n340); see also, after the passage of the Human Rights Act 1998, *R v Paullsen* [2002] EWCA Crim 3109; *R v Rajkuma* [2003] EWCA Crim 1955, stressing that the Codes of Practice for police interviewing do not apply in this situation.

[474] See also *R v Governor of Pentonville Prison, ex p Chinoy* [1992] 1 All ER 317, in which the entrapment related to crimes under foreign law for which extradition was sought.

Improper interception or recording of communications[475]

Evidence of communications encouraged by the police and then intercepted were not automatically inadmissible as such at common law.[476] It makes no difference that such communications[477] have been recorded electronically, nor that the recording device has been placed by an illegal act, even on the premises of a third party,[478] nor that the opportunity to plant it has been secured by deception.[479] It is immaterial that the police arrange an elaborate charade to deceive the accused into believing[480] that their conversations in a cell are not being recorded.[481] In such a case, it is also irrelevant to the exclusion of evidence so obtained that the whole object of the stratagem is to circumvent the accused's explicit invocation of his right to remain silent in the face of police questioning, or to withhold a voice sample,[482] or that a cell mate is introduced whom the police believe will seek to persuade the accused to confess.[483] It has been held that a merely technical breach of the Code of Practice for Police Questioning,[484] or of the guidelines issued by the Home Office in 1984 on the Use of Equipment in Police Surveillance,[485] would not suffice to exclude. Nor does it seem that the use of such equipment, even after arrest, is to be regarded as so much in breach of the spirit of the Codes as to trigger the exclusionary discretion in s 78 of the Police and Criminal Evidence Act 1984.[486] One of the few cases in which evidence derived from surveillance has been excluded under the s 78 discretion involved a more serious breach of the spirit of the Code of Practice, in that the police had, in bad faith, so arranged facilities for prisoners to be interviewed by their legal advisers that such conversations could be overheard.[487] Only in the case of letters, messages, and telephone calls

---

[475] See further Mirfield [2001] *Crim LR* 91; Ormerod and McKay [2004] *Crim LR* 15.

[476] *R v Derrington* (n335), where a letter obtained from the prisoner by the turnkey, under a false promise that he would post it, was admitted in evidence for the prosecution. Similarly, in *R v Keeton* (1970) 54 Cr App Rep 267, it was irrelevant that the accused assumed that a telephone call to his wife from the police station would not be intercepted and put in evidence.

[477] For special difficulties relating to email, see *R (NTL Group Ltd) v Ipswich Crown Court* [2002] EWHC 1585 (Admin).

[478] As in the leading case of *R v Khan* (n302). The same applies in civil proceedings to the use of covert video surveillance on private premises obtained by trespass, and in breach of Art 8 of the European Convention on Human Rights: *Jones v University of Warwick* [2003] EWCA Civ 151, [2003] 3 All ER 760, [2003] 1 WLR 954 (although a court may award substantial damages for such an incursion in separate proceedings, see (2003) The Times (Law Supp) 25 March 2003); privacy can be protected by restricting access to any playing of the recording: *XXX v YYY* (9 April 2003, unreported). For a similar result in Scotland, see *Martin v McGuiness* 2003 SLT 1136, 2003 SCLR 998.

[479] *R v Chalkley* (n343); this was also true in *Jones* (n478).

[480] Despite having been warned by their own lawyers that just such a stratagem was likely to be tried by the police.   [481] *R v Bailey* (n340) in which many of the earlier cases are reviewed.

[482] *PG and JH v United Kingdom* (n351), in which these decisions had been taken on legal advice.

[483] *R v Roberts* [1997] 1 Cr App Rep 217 (34 solicitations were made); cf, in Australia, *R v Juric* [2002] VSCA 77, 129 ACR 408.   [484] *R v Bailey* (n340), 522, 374.

[485] *R v Mason* [2002] EWCA Crim 385, [2002] 2 Cr App Rep 628, [58].

[486] *R v Bailey* (n340), 524, 375; *R v Mason* (n485), [64]. Although it might well fall foul of the European Convention on Human Rights: see *Doerga v Netherlands* (2005) 41 EHRR 45; but see also *Dudley v HMA* 2003 JC 53, 2003 SLT 597. In Australia, see *R v Chimirri* [2002] VSC 555, 136 ACR 381.

[487] *R v Grant* [2005] EWCA Crim 1089, [2006] QB 60, in which proceedings were stayed as an abuse of process, despite the absence of prejudice to the accused. Such an interception would also be in breach of the European Convention on Human Rights: *S v Switzerland* (1991) 14 EHRR 670. It is significant that deception of a legal adviser in addition to the accused was the basis for the exclusion under s 78 of a confession in *R v Mason* (485), and in *PG and JH v United Kingdom* (n351), in which a conversation with a solicitor had been

made from police premises is there provision in the Code of Practice for warning the suspect that the call may be overheard.[488] It should be noted, however, that the whole system has been affected by the Regulation of Investigatory Powers Act 2000, and the Codes of Practice made under it.[489] This sort of interception of communications[490] may combine elements of covert surveillance, intrusive surveillance, and the use of human intelligence sources,[491] together with interference with property authorized under Pt III of the Police Act 1997.[492] From the point of view of the admissibility in evidence of the product of such methods, it seems that a common regime of putative admissibility applies,[493] subject only to control under the exclusionary discretion in s 78 of the Police and Criminal Evidence Act 1984.[494] It is immaterial that the authorization for the surveillance makes no reference to the use of the product in evidence.[495] Given that evidence from covert eavesdroppers is regarded as admissible,[496] the fact that the communication has been recorded electronically can hardly be regarded as doing anything other than adding credibility to the evidence.[497] Any attempt to secure legally professionally privileged material is not, however, to be permitted,[498] at least in the absence of explicit statutory authorization.[499]

overheard, it was stressed that the police officer stopped listening when he realized its nature, and it was not attempted to use it in evidence. Similarly, in *Brennan v United Kingdom* (2001) 34 EHRR 507, the fact that a police officer insisted on overhearing the accused's first interview with his solicitor, for security reasons, was regarded as amounting to an infringement of Art 6(3)(c) of the European Convention on Human Rights. Nor should the police seek to use a clerk in a solicitors' office as an informant: *R v Robinson* [2002] EWCA Crim 2489, 146 SJLB 256 (2002).

[488] Code C, [5.7] reversing the previous position as determined in *R v Keeton* (n476).

[489] Section 71. Separate Codes deal with: Interception of Communications and Accessing Communications Data; Covert Surveillance; The Use of Covert Human Intelligence Sources; Investigation of Electronic Data Protected by Encryption etc.

[490] The scale is massive, with some 1,800 warrants for telephone interception issued in 2005–06.

[491] As defined in Regulation of Investigatory Powers Act 2000, s 26.

[492] All four seem to have occurred in *PG and JH v United Kingdom* (n351).

[493] See Regulation of Investigatory Powers Act 2000, s 81(5); draft Code of Practice on Covert Surveillance [1.4]. It may be necessary to change these to reflect the critical views of the European Court of Human Rights in *Liberty v UK* (2009) 48 EHRR 1.

[494] The availability of which in this context has been regarded by the European Court of Human Rights as satisfying the requirements of art 6 of the European Convention: *Khan v United Kingdom* (n302), [38]; *PG and JH v United Kingdom* (n351), [79]; *Chalkley v United Kingdom* (2003) 37 EHRR 30.

[495] *R v Kelly and Andrews* [2007] EWCA Crim 1715, [66]–[68].

[496] And even when unauthorized, has been held in Scotland not necessarily in breach of Art 8: *Gilchrist and Quinn v HMA* 2005 1 JC 34, [2004] SCCR 595. It may be excluded in Canada if allied to denial of access to counsel: *R v Smith* (2008) 229 CCC3d 117.

[497] The situations were explicitly equated in *R v Bailey* (n340); 523, 374; and in *R v Bailey* [2001] EWCA Crim 733, [9], it was noted that memory could be refreshed in the case, where the statement had been both heard and recorded. Presumably, as in *R v Fliss* [2002] SCC 16, [2002] 1 SCR 535, in Canada, this would be limited to cases of genuine refreshment, and not extend to cases of past recollection recorded.

[498] See *R v Robinson* (n487), condemning a police operation using a solicitor's clerk as an informant, citing in support *R (Daly) v Secretary of State for the Home Department* [2001] UKHL 26, [2001] 2 AC 532, and paras 3.5 and 3.6 of the Code of Practice relating to the use of covert intelligence sources.

[499] *Re McE* [2009] UKHL 15, [2009] 4 All ER 335, where a majority of the House of Lords found covert surveillance of interviews between suspects and solicitors and medical advisers capable of authorization under the Regulation of Investigatory Powers Act 2000, and its Codes of Practice. In exceptional cases it seems unlikely that the European Court of Human Rights would take a different view: see *Weber and Saravia v Germany* (2008) 46 EHRR SE 47 (monitoring journalistic communication), although in an apparent attempt to pre-empt criticism an enhanced approval mechanism has already been introduced: SI 2009/3404. See in Canada *R v Doiron* (2007) 221 CCC3d 97.

The interception of telephone calls, having been declared by the European Court of Human Rights to require guarantees against abuse,[500] was first subjected to statutory control by the Interception of Communications Act 1985, perhaps designed[501] to prevent the use of intercepted material from being used in evidence.[502] The drafting of this legislation led to great difficulty of interpretation,[503] and it has now been replaced by Pt I of the Regulation of Investigatory Powers Act 2000. This legislation applies to the interception[504] of communications carried by a public, or now a private, telecommunications system.[505] It does not, however, apply to the use of a device that is capable of overhearing one end of a telephone message as part of the sounds made in a particular location.[506] Under both the old law,[507] and the new,[508] revelation of anything disclosing the authorization of interception is prohibited.[509] To the extent that this depended upon the view that the scope of retention of intercepted material under the ICA 1985 was limited to the detection and prevention of crime, and excluded its prosecution,[510] it is confirmed in RIPA 2000.[511] To the extent that it depended upon a strict obligation to destroy material not so authorized for retention,[512] it has been modified by s 18(7), which disapplies s 17(1) for limited purposes.[513] This remains a controversial issue, and legislative authorization of the admissibility of the

---

[500] *Malone v United Kingdom* (n305).

[501] ICA 1985, s 2(2), as interpreted in *R v Preston* (n500), 169, 669.

[502] A different approach was, however, taken in the Intelligence Services Act 1994, s 2(2)(a)(iv). Both the Security Service Act 1996, s 1(1) and the Police Act 1997, s 93(2)(a) use the terminology of the Interception of Communications Act 1985, s 2(2), although they lack any equivalent to s 9 of that Act positively forbidding reference to intercepted communications, and will, it now seems likely, be treated as permitting use of product, subject only to the exclusionary discretion in s 78, which can consider the validity of any purported authorization: *R v Templar* (n25), [14].

[503] It had to be considered by the House of Lords on no fewer than five separate occasions in *R v Preston* (n500); *R v Effik* [1995] 1 AC 309, [1994] 3 All ER 458; *Morgans v DPP* [2001] 1 AC 315, [2000] 2 All ER 522; *R v P* [2002] 1 AC 146, [2001] 2 All ER 58; *R v Sargent* (n358).

[504] It does not apply to recording by one party to the conversation, even when that person is an undercover police officer: *R v Hardy* [2002] EWCA Crim 3012, [2003] 1 Cr App Rep 30.

[505] Thus evading the difficulties under the 1985 legislation exposed in *Halford v United Kingdom* (n356), and *R v Effik* (n503). It makes no distinction between wired and wireless communication. See also, in New Zealand, *Moreton v Police* [2002] 2 NZLR 234. There is no bar on questioning to establish whether interception is public or private: *A-G's Ref (No 5 of 2003)* [2003] EWCA Crim 1632, [2003] 1 WLR 2902.

[506] *R v E* [2004] EWCA Crim 1243, 148 Sol Jo LB 537 provided that it has not been implanted for that particular purpose: see Code of Practice on Covert Surveillance [3.15]. This accords with the old law: see *R v Smart and Beard* [2002] EWCA Crim 772 [68].   [507] Interception of Communications Act 1985, s 9.

[508] Regulation of Investigatory Powers Act 2000, s 17; so construed in *A-G's Ref (No 5 of 2003)* (n505).

[509] After some vacillation, it was finally decided under the old law, in *Morgans v DPP* (n503), that this prohibition applied to lawful and unlawful interception alike, and that it applied to the use of the content of such interception as well as to information as to its provenance. If, however, evidence was obtained indirectly as a result of an illegal interception, but which could be put in evidence quite independent of it without prejudice to the accused, then it was not excluded: *R v Sargent* (n358), [36]. In Canada cross-examination as to the authorization is subject to leave: *R v Pires* 2005 SCC 66, [2005] 3 SCR 343.

[510] As decided in *Preston* (n500).

[511] RIPA 2000, 5(3)(b), s 81(5), although the latter destroys the generality of the reasoning that prevailed in *Preston* (n500).   [512] Interception of Communications Act 1985, s 6.

[513] See Mirfield [2001] *Crim LR* 91, 96–8 for criticism on the basis that this may create disparity between prosecution and defence, and be vulnerable to attack under Art 6 of the European Convention on Human Rights.

fruits of interception, as in most foreign jurisdictions,[514] is an active possibility for the future,[515] but currently, even though lawful under s 3,[516] is explicitly excluded from the operation of s 17(1).[517] Where interception is consented to by sender or receiver, it is governed by the regime applying to directed surveillance,[518] and its admission governed by the operation of the s 78 exclusionary discretion. Under the old law, where a telephone call was recorded by one of the parties to it in an attempt to secure evidence, one of the considerations relating to the operation of s 78 was the extent to which that method had been employed to evade the restrictions of the Code of Practice on Police Questioning.[519]

The new Act applies only to interception in the United Kingdom, and probably, like its predecessor, will be interpreted so as not to exclude evidence from interception overseas, whether lawful,[520] or not,[521] in the jurisdiction in which it took place.[522] It was reaffirmed by the House of Lords in *R v P*[523] that this view had survived the passage of the Human Rights Act 1998, and that, even though the result of the statutory regime may be to exclude intercepted material, there is no principle of English, or indeed European Convention, law to that effect.

A clearer distinction is made in the new Act between data representing the contents of a communication, and that representing the fact of the communication.[524] The latter is less sensitive than the former, and is made subject to a quite separate regime under Pt II C II of the Act. Communications data may under this chapter be obtained, or disclosed, in a wider range of cases than contents data.[525] No equivalent to s 17 applies to such authorization, although as the overlap between the two sets of purposes is at the more serious end of the

---

[514] In Australia, failure to adduce such fruits requires explanation: see *R v Lao* [2002] VSCA 157, 137 ACR 20. In Canada, see *R v Mapara* 2005 SCC 23, [2005] 1 SCR 358; *R v Chow* 2005 SCC 24, [2005] 1 SCR 384; in *R v Rowe* ((2006) 208 CCC3d 412 it was held that the conscience of the court would be more shocked by exclusion than admission of a taped communication to a private individual acting on behalf of the police.

[515] *Intercept as Evidence: A Report* (Cm 7760, 2009), [25].

[516] Section 4 includes special authorizations for hospitals and prisons, evading the problems that arose under the old law in *R v Allen* [2001] EWCA Crim 1027. [517] Section 17(4).

[518] By a combination of ss 3(2), 26(4)(b) and 48(4), thus evading the difficult problems raised under the old law in *R v Rasool* [1997] 4 All ER 439, [1997] 1 WLR 1092.

[519] Thus in *R v H* [1987] Crim LR 47, in which the accused had already been arrested and questioned, a further telephone call from the alleged victim seeking to elicit incriminating remarks was held to be inadmissible, whereas in *R v Jelen and Katz* (1989) 90 Cr App Rep 456, in which matters were at a much earlier stage, evidence of a call was not excluded, although had an interview been conducted the accused would have had to be cautioned. A similar view seems to prevail in Australia: see *R v Dewhirst* [2001] VSC 172, (2001) 122 ACR 403. [520] *R v Aujla* [1998] 2 Cr App Rep 16.

[521] As in *R v Governor of Pentonville Prison, ex p Chinoy* (n474), although perhaps only if the illegality abroad would not have triggered exclusion under s 78 if it had taken place here.

[522] In Canada, a distinction is drawn between the acts of Canadians outside the jurisdiction, which are governed by the Charter, and the acts of foreigners, which are not: *Harrer v R* [1995] 3 SCR 562; in the United States, the evidence will be admissible even though the acts are performed in the foreign jurisdiction by US citizens: *United States v Verdugo-Urquidez* 494 US 259 (1990).

[523] (n503), despite the ingenious argument that, since there was recognized here to be no necessity to use domestic-intercepted material, it could hardly be necessary to use foreign. This argument failed in part on the basis that the most it could show would be breach of Art 8, which does not govern admissibility in an English court.

[524] In cases of hacking into multiple computers the distinction becomes difficult to draw, as shown in *Morgans v DPP* above (n503), 332–3, 537–9. [525] Cf s 5(3) (contents) and s 22(2) (communications).

spectrum, it is not clear why the more rigid statutory exclusion applies to authorization of interception of content only, while that of communications is left to the common law of public interest immunity.

Although illegally obtained recordings are as admissible in civil proceedings as they are in criminal,[526] it has been held that the fact of such illegality must be disclosed to the judge, if they are to be adduced in evidence.[527]

Deception[528]

Many of the situations considered above include elements of deception, and this final residual category is intended to encompass principally those in which the deception is primarily designed to generate evidence of offences that have already been committed, otherwise than by improper searches, or the use of electronic interception of communications. The clearest example in modern English law[529] is provided by *R v Christou*,[530] where the police engaged in an elaborate long-running operation to secure evidence of theft, by operating a shop that bought and sold jewellery.[531] The Court of Appeal took the view that the evidence obtained from this operation in the form of video and aural recordings, including evidence of incriminating conversations with the undercover operators, and real evidence in the shape of fingerprints, was admissible. It was regarded as important that the operation had no precise targets,[532] and that there was no attempt to subvert the operation of the Codes of Practice by the simple expedient of pretending not to be police officers.[533] This aspect of the decision was underlined soon afterwards by the decision in *R v Bryce*,[534] in which evidence of an incriminating conversation between an undercover police officer and the accused was excluded under the s 78 discretion, since the operation did subvert the Codes. In particular, the police already had reason to suspect the accused, they asked questions going critically to guilt, and they failed to secure any adequate recording of the alleged statements.[535] Similarly, if the undercover agent plays too active a part in eliciting the evidence, it is more likely to be excluded.[536]

---

[526] In *R v Senat* (n329), 287, the Lord Chief Justice said their use was an everyday occurrence in the divorce court. Nor, at that time, was there any exclusionary discretion in civil proceedings.

[527] *St Merryn Meat Ltd v Hawkins* [2001] CPR 116.   [528] See further Ashworth 114 *LQR* 108 (1998).

[529] Extremely elaborate deceptions seem to be practised in Canada: as in *R v Grandinetti* [2005] 1 SCR 27; and have been copied in Australia, *Tofilau v R* [2007] HCA 39, 231 CLR 396.

[530] [1992] QB 979, [1992] 4 All ER 559. For a different approach to this very situation in Canada, see *R v Castro* (2001) 157 CCC 3d 255.

[531] The shop offered market rates, and the trial judge's view that the offences had already been committed seems to have been accepted, so as to rebut allegations of entrapment. This is, however, dubious in view of the charges of handling, and the court's own later treatment, 991G, 567b, of allegations of facilitation of crime.

[532] See 989A, 564h: 'the trick was not applied to the appellants; they voluntarily applied themselves to the trick'. See also *R v Lin, Hung and Tsui* [1995] Crim LR 817, in which the accused were targeted by the undercover officers, but in respect of a different crime.

[533] 991C, 566h. Although breach alone will not necessarily be enough to trigger the discretion, even when it results in there not being an objective record of what had been said: see *R v Edwards* [1997] Crim LR 348.

[534] [1992] 4 All ER 567, 95 Cr App Rep 320.

[535] Which the accused denied (even if unconvincingly).

[536] As in *R v Hall* (2 March 1994, unreported), and *R v Stagg* (14 September 1994, unreported), in both of which undercover female police officers exploited the sexual predilections of the male suspects as a means of eliciting the evidence. Cf *R v Kennedy* [1998] Crim LR 739, in which an element of enticement of a prisoner to speak by psychiatrists and a probation officer was held insufficient.

It is extremely common for the police to seek evidence of a crime by attempting to deceive the suspect into believing that an undercover police officer, or a member of the public, is a secure confidant for the suspect, and then to record any incriminating statements or admissions that he might make.[537] In England, although it has repeatedly been denied that any general principles operate, it seems that evidence obtained in this way has been more likely to be admitted than in many other Commonwealth jurisdictions.[538] In *R v Roberts*,[539] the police had good reason to believe that one of two suspects would attempt to persuade the other to exculpate him, and in so doing inculpate himself. They accordingly, and covertly, fitted recording devices in the suspects' cells. The resulting admissions were held to be admissible, and the trial judge's decision not to exclude them under the s 78 discretion was upheld, despite the fact that both had been charged with the relevant offences, and the accused had asserted his right to remain silent. On the other hand, the court went out of its way to stress several factors in the situation with the implication that, if they had been different, they would have militated in favour of exclusion. In particular, the court emphasized its belief that the second suspect was not in active collusion with the police,[540] that they still harboured hopes of convicting him, that they were concerned to recover a firearm that had been used, that proper authority had been obtained for the installation of recording apparatus into the cells, and that neither of the suspects knew that the cells were so fitted out.[541] This decision may be contrasted with decisions,[542] and even legislation,[543] elsewhere, although it must be stressed that, in some jurisdictions, there are relevant constitutional differences, and in none is there anything approaching the detailed guidance provided here by the Codes of Practice for interviews known to be by or on behalf of the police.

---

[537] In Canada, see *R v Liew* [1999] 3 SCR 227, and where the more unusual situation of the undercover policeman disparaging the accused's lawyer in the hope that he would not then seek legal advice has also been accepted: *United States of America v Burns* (1997) 117 CCC 3d 454.

[538] But see now in the High Court of Australia, *Tofilau v R* (n529); *Em v R* [2007] HCA 46, 232 CLR 67; *Carr v Western Australia* [2007] HCA 47, 232 CLR 138 (in both police knew that accused wrongly believed that confessions unrecorded, and would not otherwise have confessed).

[539] [1997] 1 Cr App Rep 217.

[540] In *Allan v R* [2004] EWCA Crim 2236, (2004) 148 SLJB 1032, this factor was decisive on a subsequent reference, following the decision of the European Court of Human Rights in *Allan v United Kingdom* (2003) 36 EHRR 12, in determining that Art 6 was breached when an informer was placed by the police in the same cell as the accused, with instructions to press him for all he could get, especially when the informer had an end of his own to serve, and the police had interviewed the accused in such a way as to make it more likely that the accused would speak. Some reliance was placed on the situation in Canada; see briefly below.

[541] The Court of Appeal was, however, [120] and [121], more dubious of the relevance of the factors of whether a deal had been done with the police, and how early the information was elicited in the investigation.

[542] It is possible to do no more than indicate the trend of the most important recent decisions. In Australia, discretion has been exercised to exclude evidence elicited by an undercover police officer from a suspect who had been charged, and under the Judges' Rules was entitled no longer to be questioned in the absence of a caution; but not in another case, in which the evidence was secured by an associate of the accused whom the police expected to attempt to persuade the accused to exculpate him: *R v Swaffield*; *Pavic v R* (1998) 151 ALR 98; in Canada, evidence secured by means of conversation with an undercover police officer in a police cell has been admitted under the Charter: *R v Liew* (n537); in New Zealand evidence obtained by an exchange of text messages with the victim, unknown by the accused to be controlled by the police, was admitted in *R v Ross* [2007] 2 NZLR 467; in the United States, no caution was required in the case of an undercover police officer posing as a fellow criminal in respect of a conversation recorded in a cell: *Illinois v Perkins* 496 US 292 (1990).   [543] For example, Criminal Law (Undercover Operations) Act 1995 in South Australia.

Although it has been denied that there should be any set form for warning the jury about cell confessions,[544] the Privy Council has also emphasized that, in such cases, it is incumbent on the trial judge carefully to explain the ways in which such evidence may be tainted, and its proper weight.[545]

The Regulation of Investigatory Powers Act 2000, and the Codes of Practice made under it have now provided some statutory and regulatory underpinning. Section 26 defines three forms of surveillance, most of which will involve a certain amount of deceit of the accused, at least in the sense that he is being observed or recorded unaware.[546] The three principal forms of such surveillance[547] are directed surveillance, intrusive surveillance, and the use of covert human intelligence sources. Intrusive surveillance covers cases in which a device or a person is concealed on residential premises, or in a vehicle.[548] Directed surveillance covers cases[549] in which the process is likely to reveal private information about a person, and has been mounted for the purposes of a specific investigation, otherwise than an immediate response to the situation. A covert human intelligence source may be an undercover agent or a member of the public, and the information may be recorded in any form. All that is required is that the source have a personal relationship with another, which he uses to disclose information discovered in it. It should be noted that it is the *use* of such a source that is regulated under the Act,[550] which involves soliciting the source to act in the manner required, thus excluding from the ambit of the Act purely spontaneous communication of information.

In none of these cases is there any attempt to render the product obtained by such conduct inadmissible in evidence; indeed, such use is often a prime aim of such activity. This means that the normal rules as to the exclusion of evidence under s 78 of the Police and Criminal Evidence Act 1984[551] apply as much here as elsewhere. So too do the overriding requirements of a trial fair under Art 6 of the European Convention on Human Rights. Codes of Practice[552] both attempt to guide the operations of the police, and to provide a basis for a claim to bring the system within the protection of Art 8(2) of the European Convention, as a lawful and necessary measure of protection. The system imposes detailed rules for authorization of surveillance, graduated according to the nature of the place at which it is mounted,[553] and the type of material expected to be found.[554] It also requires documentation in writing, both of the original authorization, and of such matters as payments to informants, as well as the retention of material to the extent required by the Criminal Procedure and Investigations Act 1996. It remains to be determined whether or not the system so established will be held to satisfy the requirements of the European

---

[544] *Pringle v R* [2003] UKPC 9, [30].

[545] *Benedetto v R* [2003] UKPC 27, [2003] 2 Cr App Rep 390, [35].

[546] RIPA 2000, s 26(9). Thus surveillance by publicly situated CCTV cameras falls outside the ambit of the Act.   [547] As defined by RIPA 2000, s 26.

[548] RIPA 2000, s 26(4)(a) excludes tracking devices in cars, and s 26(5) includes surveillance by devices that, while not so installed, are capable of providing information of the same quality.

[549] Falling outside the definition of intrusive surveillance.

[550] As defined in RIPA 2000, s 27(7)(b).   [551] Above, 203.   [552] Made under RIPA 2000, s 71.

[553] A more elaborate procedure of authorization is required for intrusive surveillance: ss 32, 35.

[554] Higher level authorization is thus required where confidential material, including that subject to legal professional privilege, is expected to be encountered: see *Bates v Chief Constable of Avon and Somerset* [2009] EWHC 942 (Admin).

Convention, although some commentators have expressed their doubts.[555] The absence of special rules of admissibility is mirrored by a similar absence of special rules preventing disclosure of prosecution evidence under the provisions of the Criminal Procedure and Investigations Act 1996.[556] Since police operational methods, the identities of informants, and the location of covert surveillance points might be prejudiced by the use of such material, the normal rules of public interest immunity law apply to enable discretionary suppression of such details.[557]

CONCLUSIONS

This part of the law of evidence is marked by a stark clash between opposing popular reactions: on the one hand, abhorring the acquittal of the demonstrably guilty;[558] on the other, deploring the development of a 'police state'.[559] To exclude relevant and reliable real evidence seems to pander to the one; to aggrandise the powers of search and surveillance of the police, while excluding responsibility for, or public scrutiny of, the exercise of those powers, seems to acquiesce in the other.

At one time, the common law world seemed sharply divided between the polar opposites of the law of the United States and of England. In the United States, the issue was a matter of constitutional law, and took the form of an exclusionary rule of evidence, barring the use of illegally obtained evidence, and of other evidence derived from it.[560] In England, it was a matter of common law, admitting all relevant and reliable evidence irrespective of its provenance,[561] and relying only upon collateral means of restraining official misconduct.[562] Other jurisdictions occupied intermediate positions, with those of Ireland,[563] and Scotland,[564] somewhere near the centre, operating on a much more discretionary basis. In some such situations, in which there is an overriding discretion to exclude material that will bring the law into disrepute, there is a danger of transforming the position into one at

---

[555] For example, Gillespie (2000) 5 *Web JCLI*; Mirfield [2001] Crim LR 91. The Scottish equivalent was held in *HM Advocate v Higgins* [2006] HCJ 05, 2006 SCCR 305 not to allow the use of evidence obtained unfairly (by placing the suspects in adjoining cells and covertly recording their conversation).

[556] Above, 280.   [557] Above, 488.

[558] As Cardozo J put it in *The People v Defoe* 242 NY 413 (1926): 'A room is searched against the law, and the body of a murdered man is found. If the place of discovery may not be proved, the other circumstances may be insufficient to connect the defendant with the crime. The privacy of the home has been infringed, and the murderer goes free.' A sentiment echoed in this country by Lord Nolan in *R v Khan* (n302), 302: 'It would be a strange reflection on our law if a man who has admitted his participation in the illegal importation of a large quantity of heroin should have his conviction set aside on the grounds that his privacy had been invaded.'

[559] As Holmes J put it in *Olmstead v United States* 277 US 438 (1926): 'It is desirable that crimes should be detected, and to that end too all available evidence should be used. It is desirable that the government should not itself foster and pay for other crimes, when they are the means by which the evidence is to be obtained... We have to choose, and for my part I think it a less evil that some criminals should escape than that the government should play an ignoble part.' A similar sentiment was expressed here by Lord Nicholls in *R v Looseley* (n430), [1]: 'courts ensure that executive agents of the state do not misuse the coercive, law enforcement functions of the courts and thereby oppress citizens of the state'.

[560] *Mapp v Ohio* 367 US 656 (1961).   [561] *R v Leatham* (n312).

[562] *R v Mills and Lemon* [1947] KB 297, [1946] 2 All ER 776 (judicial exhortation); *Treadaway v Chief Constable of West Midlands* (1994) The Times, 25 October (civil damages).

[563] *People (A-G) v O'Brien* (n427) (inclusionary discretion in constitutional cases and exclusionary discretion in others).   [564] *Lawrie v Muir* 1950 JC 19 (general inclusionary discretion).

which there is, in effect, an inclusionary discretion, sometimes justified in terms of crude popular reaction.[565]

It is doubtful whether such an analysis was ever much more than a caricature of the real position in any jurisdiction. Constitutional provisions are inevitably expressed in highly general terminology subject to judicial interpretation, and official action in a modern state requires some legislative basis. It is certainly the case that the positions in the United States and in England have moved closer together in recent times, with increasing qualification of the exclusionary rule in the one,[566] and the burgeoning development of an exclusionary discretion in the other.[567]

The impact of the Human Rights Act 1998 bringing the provisions of the European Convention on Human Rights into play in England could be seen as a further move in the direction of the old position in the United States, as a form of constitutional guarantee against official misconduct in this area. Yet this too is a document of a high degree of generality, and so vagueness, of terminology, interpreted by an ever-shifting body of judges from a multitude of different jurisdictions, each with its own institutions, procedures, and culture. The rights it contains are highly qualified, explicitly[568] or implicitly.[569] Yet, paradoxically, its interpretation has supported[570] a possible route out of the impasse of popular reaction indicated above. One of the principal flaws in the traditional position in the United States was the high importance attached to the exclusion of evidence as a means of checking the excesses of the agents of the state;[571] one of the principal flaws in the traditional position in England was the ineffectiveness of the collateral means recommended to restrain such excesses.[572] A more promising response has been provided by the development of detailed guidance for the agents of the state, in the shape of legislation, and of codes of practice for individual areas of official activity.[573] Such codes have both provided detailed guidance for officials, and by their insistence on documentation, a firmer basis for judicial control of such action. In its insistence on the provision of such a framework in order for such official action to be accorded the status of a lawful response, the European Convention on Human Rights has had a significant catalytic effect.

---

[565] Thus in *R v Fliss* (n497), the Supreme Court found a breach of the Charter of Rights and Freedoms, but nevertheless refused to exclude the evidence on the basis that *exclusion* would be more likely to bring the law into disrepute than *inclusion*; for sophisticated discussion of this issue, see Mirfield *Silence, Confessions and Improperly Obtained Evidence* (1997) 368–70.

[566] See e.g. *United States v Leon* 468 US 897 (1984); *Hudson v Michigan* 547 US 586 (2006); *Herring v United States* 129 S Ct R 695 (2009).

[567] Including the extension of s 78 to cater for abuse of process in addition to the exclusion of evidence, 206.   [568] Article 8.

[569] Article 6.

[570] *Malone v United Kingdom* (n305), which precipitated the Interception of Communications Act 1985, was roughly contemporaneous with the passage of s 66 of the Police and Criminal Evidence Act 1984 authorizing the promulgation of detailed Codes of Practice for police in this area.

[571] See Oakes (1970) 37 *Un of Chi LR* 665.

[572] In many cases, the use of evidence elicited by illegal means, which precipitated pleas of guilty, severely restricting judicial examination of such means, although the boundaries may have been relaxed a little after the decision in *R v Togher* [2001] 3 All ER 463, [2001] 1 Cr App Rep 457.

[573] For example, the various Codes made under s 71 of the Regulation of Investigatory Powers Act 2000.

XI

OPINION[1]

The law relating to evidence of opinion is less developed in the United Kingdom than in North America where, over a century ago, Thayer said: 'the quantity of decisions on the subject is most unreasonably swollen'.[2] Half a century later, Wigmore claimed that, so far as the United States was concerned, the rule 'had done more than any other rule of procedure to reduce our litigation towards a state of legalized gambling'.[3] In England, the reported decisions on the subject are comparatively few, and it is difficult to believe that the exclusionary rule gives rise to very much trouble in practice. There are, however, some theoretical difficulties, and some residual problems in criminal cases.[4] In the area of procedure, however, Lord Woolf concluded that the development, and cost, of a system of expert witnesses[5] was one of the principal blemishes upon the process of litigation, and recommended radical procedural reform, which was implemented in Pt 35 of the Civil Procedure Rules, which has now generated a greater body of case law, and itself already required amendment.[6]

This chapter will first consider the rationale of the rule, and especially the nature of its relationship to the rules excluding hearsay, which is to be examined in greater detail in the chapters that follow. The operation of the rule will then be illustrated, together with the two areas of expert and non-expert opinion in which there are exceptions, and the final section will deal with reform of the rule.

SECTION 1. RATIONALE OF THE RULE

STATEMENT OF THE RULE

A witness may not give his opinion on matters calling for the special skill or knowledge of an expert unless he is an expert in such matters, and may not give an opinion on other

---

[1] See generally, Hodgkinson *Expert Evidence: Law and Practice* (3rd edn, 2009); Dwyer *The Judicial Assessment of Expert Evidence* (2009); Woolf Report *Access to Justice* (1996) ch 13; the Civil Procedure Rules Pt 35; Code of Guidance on Expert Evidence (2001); Auld Review of Working of Criminal Courts (2001), ch XI, paras 129–51.

[2] *Preliminary Treatise on Evidence at the Common Law* 525. By 1990, 86 per cent of trials in California heard expert testimony, and, on average, there were 3.3 experts per trial: Gross (1991) *Wisc LR* 1113, 1119.

[3] VII Wigmore, 27.

[4] Unaffected by the passage of the Civil Evidence Act 1972, which enacted the principal recommendations of the Law Reform Committee's 17th Report.

[5] In *Parkin v Bromley Hospitals NHS Trust* [2002] EWCA Civ 478, [2002] CPR 44, 16 different types of expert witness gave evidence.

[6] It was also felt that greater use could be made of expert assessors in a wider variety of situations, and to that end, procedures were put in place by CPR 35.15, occasionally augmented by judicial decision: see e.g. *The Global Mariner v Atlantic Crusader* [2005] EWHC 380 (Admlty), [2005] 1 LlR 699 (Dwyer [2006] *CJQ* 219).

matters if the underlying facts can be stated without reference to it in a manner equally conducive to the ascertainment of the truth.[7]

There are thus two broad spheres of evidence of opinion. The first concerns matters calling for specialized skill or knowledge. In this sphere, the only questions are whether the subject of inquiry does raise issues calling for expertise, and whether the witness is a qualified expert. This part of the rule is exclusionary only in the sense that the testimony of non-experts is excluded on matters calling for a specialist. In the residuary non-expert sphere, evidence of opinion will be excluded if the subject is one with regard to which fact and inference can conveniently be kept separate. In *R v Robb*,[8] these two spheres overlapped in relation to the identification of the voice of the accused on the telephone, with expert opinion admitted from an auditory specialist, and evidence of composite fact admitted from police officers who had become familiar with the voice of the accused.[9]

NATURE OF OPINION

'Opinion' means any inference from perceived facts, and the law on the subject derives from the general rule that witnesses must speak only to that which they themselves perceived. English law assumes that inferences, and their underlying facts can be sharply distinguished.[10] The drawing of inferences is said to be the function of the judge or jury, while it is that of a witness to state facts. But the law recognizes that, so far as matters calling for special knowledge or skill are concerned, judges and jurors are not necessarily equipped to draw true inferences from facts stated by witnesses. A witness is therefore allowed to state his opinion about such matters, provided he is expert in them. It is, however, necessary to distinguish as carefully as possible between the legitimate expression of opinion, and its application to an assumed set of facts. Thus in *HG v R*[11] while it would have been permissible for a psychiatrist to express an opinion as to whether a child's behaviour indicated that it had been sexually abused, it was inappropriate for him to express an opinion that the abuse had been perpetrated by a particular person at a particular time.

Although the distinction between fact and inference is relatively straightforward, there are borderline cases.[12] The statement that a car was being driven on the left side of the road is essentially one of fact,[13] while the assertion that a particular piece of driving was

---

[7] See *Sherrard v Jacob* [1965] NI 151, 157, Lord MacDermott.   [8] (1991) 93 Cr App Rep 161.

[9] The accused did not testify so the jury did not have sufficient opportunity to hear his voice live in court; whereas in *R v Hersey* [1998] Crim LR 281, in which there was no auditory record but a witness testified to recognizing the accused's voice at the time of the crime, and confirmed it on a staged voice comparison, expert evidence was not admitted.

[10] In *R (Harris) v Secretary of State for the Home Department* [2007] EWHC 3218 (Admin), [37] the distinction was said to be metaphysical. For an alternative approach based upon the disputability of an assertion, see Cox J in *R v Perry (No 4)* (1982) 28 SASR 119, 123.   [11] [1999] HCA 2, (1999) 197 CLR 414.

[12] Which may become more significant in the light of pressure to restrict evidence of opinion: see *Kirkman v Euro Exide Corp* [2007] EWCA Civ 66.

[13] Although, even there, the statement may verge on opinion if the witness did not have a clear view, or if the car were near the centre of the road, or if the relevant point of time were not precisely that of the observation.

negligent is equally a matter of inference from observed facts. Statements concerning speed, temperature, or the identity of persons,[14] things,[15] and handwriting are, however, indissolubly composed of fact and inference. Similarly, a witness's view of what another would do in certain circumstances is a matter of opinion, but his view of what he himself would do is a matter of fact.[16] The law makes allowances for such cases, by permitting witnesses to state their opinions with regard to matters not calling for special knowledge whenever it would be virtually impossible for them to separate their inferences from the facts on which those inferences are based.

Courts try to avoid receiving evidence from witnesses as to the very matter that the judge or jury has to decide, largely because litigants are entitled to have their disputes settled by a judge, with or without a jury, and not by the statements of witnesses. If witnesses are allowed too readily to express an opinion concerning an ultimate issue, there is a risk that the jury will be unduly influenced, yet it must always be free to reject even unanimous expert evidence, for example if it rejects the facts upon which it is based.[17] Even when receiving expert evidence, judges have tended to prevent witnesses from stating their opinion on an ultimate issue, such as the reasonableness of a covenant in restraint of trade,[18] the validity of a patent, or the construction of a document: 'The admission of the opinion of eminent experts upon the issues leads to the balance of opinions and tends to shift responsibility from the bench or the jury to the witness box.'[19] The exclusion of opinion evidence on the ultimate issue is something of a fetish, and has been explicitly relaxed for civil proceedings by s 3 of the Civil Evidence Act 1972.[20]

REASONS FOR EXCLUDING EVIDENCE OF OPINION

There have traditionally[21] been two main and two subsidiary reasons for the exclusion of evidence of opinion falling within the rule as stated above. The two main reasons are

[14] See *Kirkman v Euro Exide Corp* (n12) distinguishing a treating doctor who could give evidence of the fact of what he would have recommended, from a subsequently consulted doctor (who could give evidence only of opinion). In *R v Stockwell* (1993) 97 Cr App Rep 260 the court distinguished between a clear case of identification from a photograph where the jury could decide for itself as a matter of fact, and the case where the accused had been disguised and expert evidence of opinion was appropriate. See also *R v Clare; R v Peach* [1995] 2 Cr App Rep 333, in which a security video film was short and confused, and a police officer acquired expertise by studying it, and was permitted to testify as an expert in the interpretation of that film. This is not unlike the expertise of the audio typist in *Hopes and Lavery v HM Adv* 1960 JC 104. In *R v Clarke and Hunt* [2002] EWCA Crim 2948, [65], it was, however, denied that a police officer who had acquired familiarity with the appearance of a number of relevant persons was giving expert opinion evidence when identifying one of them on a blurred CCTV image; see also, in Australia, *R v Griffith* (1995) 79 ACR 125.

[15] See e.g. *R v Barker* (1988) 34 ACR 141, in which it was denied that a police officer's evidence that pipes were of the type used for smoking marijuana was opinion rather than fact.

[16] *Allstate Life Ins Co v ANZ Banking Pty Ltd* (1996) 136 ALR 627.   [17] *R v Ratti* [1991] 1 SCR 68.

[18] *Haynes v Doman* [1899] 2 Ch 13.

[19] *Joseph Crosfield & Sons Ltd v Techno-Chemical Laboratories Ltd* (1913) 29 TLR 378, 379.

[20] But no similar statutory relaxation has been made for criminal proceedings, contrary to the recommendation of the Criminal Law Revision Committee: see Cmnd 4991, [270], and draft bill, cl 43 (1972). See further 539.

[21] In modern times, the expense of opinion evidence has sharpened their force: see *Gumpo v Church of Scientology Religious Education College Inc* [2000] CPR 38.

founded on the principle that evidence of opinion is excluded when its reception would not assist, and might even mislead, the court. In the first place, it is said that opinion evidence is irrelevant,[22] and this is largely true of non-expert opinion on a subject requiring expertise, as well as opinion evidence concerning matters that do not call for expertise, although some writers prefer to say that the evidence is insufficiently relevant to be admissible.[23] Secondly, it is said that the reception of opinion evidence would usurp the functions of the jury. To the extent that this suggests that the witness might undesirably indicate what factual evidence was accepted or rejected, the danger can be avoided by stressing the hypothetical basis for any opinion;[24] to the extent that it suggests an opinion might be unduly influential, it will be discussed below.

The two subsidiary reasons for the rejection of certain kinds of evidence of opinion are that a witness who merely expresses his opinion[25] cannot be prosecuted for perjury,[26] and the danger that its reception might indirectly evade other exclusionary rules. The first is of some antiquity,[27] but has weakened, since the general rule of witness immunity has been said to have less weight in relation to experts,[28] and prevents neither professional disciplinary proceedings in respect of sufficiently flawed expert evidence tendered in court,[29] nor the liability of an expert witness for costs occasioned by such evidence.[30] The second is stronger, but has been little mooted by judges. The exclusionary rules most likely to be indirectly infringed by the reception of opinion evidence are those excluding irrelevant matter or hearsay, and those limiting the reception of the findings of other tribunals. Witnesses can always be cross-examined on the grounds for their opinions, and, if they seem irrelevant, the evidence can be ignored. The relationship of opinion to hearsay requires separate consideration.

RELATION TO THE HEARSAY RULE

The basic rule excluding opinion has the same origin as the hearsay rule —every witness must be able to say that he had seen or heard that to which he deposes. He must have been 'oyant' and 'voyant',[31] but the two rules are now distinct, although the same item of evidence may occasionally call for a consideration of both.

---

[22] Goddard LJ in *Hollington v F Hewthorn & Co Ltd* [1943] KB 587, [1943] 2 All ER 35, 595, 40.

[23] Cowen and Carter *Essays on the Law of Evidence* 169.

[24] Although a long hypothetical tracking all of the alleged facts may itself be prejudicial: see *R v Ryan* (1993) 80 CCC (3d) 514.

[25] He may be prosecuted for perjury in respect of false evidence as to his qualifications: see *R v Bates* (2008) unreported Bristol Cr Ct April 2008.

[26] And is not liable for negligence in respect of expert evidence tendered in court or contained in a witness statement: *Stanton v Callaghan* [2000] QB 75, [1998] 4 All ER 961; even if he has dishonestly misrepresented his expertise in order to secure appointment: *Raiss v Palmano* [2001] PNLR 540, [21].

[27] *Adams v Canon* (1621) 1 Dyer 53b.   [28] *Stanton v Callaghan* (n26), 91C, 974d.

[29] *GMC v Meadow* [2006] EWCA Civ 1390, [2006] 3 FCR 447.

[30] *Phillips v Symes* [2004] EWHC Civ 654, [2006] 34 All ER 838 (which may also be visited on the calling party); *Balmoral Group Ltd v Borealis (UK) Ltd* [2006] EWHC 2531 (Comm).

[31] Thayer *Preliminary Treatise on Evidence at the Common Law* 523.

An opinion is generally admissible only[32] if based upon facts that will be proved by admissible evidence,[33] or have been admitted.[34] So it may not be based upon hearsay, unless it can be admitted notwithstanding the rule excluding hearsay.[35] It may be useful to summarize these situations.[36] In some cases, the opinion may be based upon statements that fall within an exception to the hearsay rule.[37] In civil proceedings, the matter is now governed entirely by statute, as will be explained in Chapter XIII. Thus, if an expert relies for his opinion upon facts related to him by a third party who had observed them, this would provide a sufficient foundation for the admissibility of his opinion.[38] A more usual situation is one in which the opinion is based upon expertise, in part derived from hearsay material, which may indeed be incorporated into the expert's evidence, notwithstanding that he has no personal knowledge of its factual basis, and which may either be in the form of general works of reference,[39] particular studies,[40] or information gleaned from others in the course of professional life.[41] In *R v Zundel*,[42] it was necessary to prove the basic facts of the Holocaust. The court took the view that, while judicial notice[43] might be taken of

---

[32] An expert must accept the court's finding of fact as the basis for an opinion: *Re J (A Child)* (2007) The Times 17 August (Fam).

[33] See e.g. *R v Edwards* [2001] EWCA Crim 2185, in which both prosecution and defence were prevented from tendering opinion based on anecdotal accounts from drug takers as to the amounts they consumed; in Ireland, a medical expert can rely upon out-of-court statements by the parties in forming his opinion, but not on those of third parties: *FP v SP* [2004] 2 IR 280; for procedure in Australia, see *Daniel v Western Australia* [2000] FCA 858, 178 ALR 542. Some disquiet has been expressed in New Zealand upon the pressure that this may exert on the accused to testify: *R v Rongonui* [2000] 2 NZLR 385, [64]; and conversely, about manipulation by parties who are aware of what will be to their advantage: *R v Rapira* [2003] 3 NZLR 794.

[34] See *R v Jackson* [1996] 2 Cr App Rep 420, in which this is strongly suggested as a means of saving expense, and see the suggestions of the Law Commission, 549. It is important that any admission be not only of the fact that the evidence involves expertise, but also of the facts upon which it is based: *Lenaghan v Ayrshire and Arran Health Board* 1994 SC 365.

[35] This is occasionally effected by statute: see the Terrorism Act 2000, s 108 allowing the opinion of senior police officers to be admitted for the purposes of helping to establish membership of a terrorist organization, although this now applies only to Northern Ireland. See for a similar provision, and the model, in the Republic of Ireland, Offences Against the State Act 1939, s 52.

[36] See, further, Pattenden [1982] *Crim LR* 85. The situation was generally approved by the Law Commission in Law Com No 245 *Evidence in Criminal Proceedings: Hearsay and Related Topics* (Cm 3670, 1997) [9.8], rec 32.

[37] Now expanded by the possibility of discretionary admissibility under s 114(1)(d) of the Criminal Justice Act 2003.

[38] Section 127 of the Criminal Justice Act 2003 makes specific provision for the admissibility of such preparatory work in criminal proceedings: see Howard [2009] *Crim LR* 415. The same result has been obtained in Scotland under the provisions of s 281(2) of the Criminal Procedure (Scotland) Act 1995: *Bermingham v HMA* 2005 1 JC 17, 2004 SLT 692.

[39] *Rowley v London and North Western Rly Co* (1873) LR 8 Exch 221 (mortality tables). See also *Borowski v Quayle* [1966] VR 382 (standard pharmaceutical guide).

[40] *H v Schering Chemicals Ltd* [1983] 1 All ER 849, [1983] 1 WLR 143; 853, 148 (research studies into drug). See also *R v Abadom* [1983] 1 All ER 364, 76 Cr App Rep 48 (statistics of refractive index of samples of glass).

[41] *English Exporters (London) Ltd v Eldonwall Ltd* [1973] Ch 415, [1973] 1 All ER 726, 420, 730 (general knowledge of property values derived from reports of transactions conducted by others); although it has since been held that there is now more scope for disclosure of the individual valuations that have been relied upon, just so as to promote the possibility of cross-examination: *Newman v Hatt* [2001] RVR 307. See, in Australia, *Pownall v Conlan Management Pty Ltd* (1995) 12 WALR 370.   [42] (1987) 35 DLR (4th) 338.

[43] See further, 78.

such a notorious matter based upon historical treatises, it was better[44] to prove it by calling expert witnesses who could themselves rely upon historical treatises,[45] and contemporaneous documents of the sort relied upon by historians. An opinion will not be admissible if it is based upon more specific hearsay not falling under any such exception,[46] although the dividing line between generic and specific hearsay may occasionally prove difficult to draw with any precision. If the opinion is not solely based upon inadmissible hearsay, then the statements may be proved not as evidence of their truth, but as an additional basis for the opinion.[47]

SECTION 2. OPERATION OF THE RULE

In so far as it is exclusionary, two classes of case are contemplated in the formulation of the rule in the previous section, and it is hardly surprising that there should be but few reported decisions falling within the first class. Where the rule does operate to exclude opinion, it does so both for the prosecution and the defence,[48] and there is no discretion to permit the use of otherwise inadmissible opinion, merely because it would assist a co-accused in the presentation of a 'cut-throat' defence.[49]

LACK[50] OF EXPERTISE

A litigant would normally have to be in desperate straits before he thought of calling a witness, who was not an expert on the matter in question, to give his opinions on a subject involving special skill or knowledge.[51] This may have been the position of counsel for the defence in *R v Loake*,[52] when he applied to the Court of Criminal Appeal for leave to call fresh evidence in support of the accused's plea of insanity. Among the witnesses he wished to call were a friend of the accused, who saw him three days before the crime was committed and formed the opinion that he was insane, together with a magistrate who had come to a similar conclusion after visiting the prisoner in his cell. The court disposed of the

---

[44] Because an expert witness could be cross-examined, and because of the undesirability of establishing by judicial notice a major part of the prosecution case.

[45] Such use of treatises constitutes an acknowledged exception to the hearsay rule.

[46] See *Eldonwall* (n41) and *Borowski* (n39), in each of which some bases for the opinion were excluded for this reason; *Mobil Oil Corp v Registrar of Trademarks* (1983) 51 ALR 735 (excludes opinion survey evidence in trademark case).   [47] *R v Abbey* [1982] 2 SCR 24, 138 DLR (3d) 202.

[48] Expert evidence for the defence was rejected in *R v Barnes* [2005] EWCA Crim 1158, despite being the only evidence available after a considerable search, and it was pointed out, [46], that even if such defective evidence were admitted it would carry little weight.   [49] *R v Theodosi* [1993] RTR 179.

[50] If expertise exists, questions of credibility go to weight and not to admissibility: *Bates v Chief Constable of Avon and Somerset* [2009] EWHC 942 (Admin), [22]; and statutory provisions authorizing experts are subject to a permissive construction: *R (CPS) v Sedgemoor Magistrates* [2007] EWHC 1803 (Admin).

[51] Although it may be hard to separate such cases from those in which a witness tendered as an expert is held to have inappropriate or insufficient expertise: see *Seyfert v Burnaby Hospital Society* (1986) 27 DLR (4th) 96 (emergency physician inappropriate to testify to qualities required of emergency physician); *Gaudiuso v Walker* (1989) 56 DLR (4th) 355 (doctor competent to testify to medical examination but not to theory of scientific tests used); *R v Anderson* [2000] VSCA 16, (2000) 111 ACR 19 (distinguishes between doctors who did and did not have expertise in determining whether wounds were self-inflicted).

[52] (1911) 7 Cr App Rep 71.

application so far as these witnesses were concerned by saying that the friend's evidence was clearly inadmissible, and the magistrate was not an expert. Non-experts may be asked to state whether they consider a person with whom they are well acquainted to be sane, but this has been said to be no more than a 'compendious mode of ascertaining the result of the actual observation of the witness, from acts done, as to the habits and demeanour' of such person.[53] There was no suggestion that either of the proposed witnesses in *Loake's* case were at all intimately acquainted with the accused. It has also been held[54] that, where psychiatric harm is alleged, it is not enough to rely upon the evidence of the subject, but it is necessary to call appropriately qualified expert evidence.[55]

UNNECESSARY EXPERTISE

An expert's opinion is admissible to furnish the court with scientific information which is likely to be outside the experience and knowledge of a judge or jury. If on the proven facts a judge or jury can form their own conclusions without help, then the opinion of an expert is unnecessary. In such a case if it is given dressed up in scientific jargon it may make judgment more difficult. The fact that an expert witness has impressive scientific qualifications does not by that fact alone make his opinion on matters of human nature and behaviour within the limits of normality any more helpful than that of the jurors themselves; but there is a danger that they may think it does.

These words[56] provide a clear explanation of the basis of the second limb of the exclusionary rule. Evidence of opinion on matters not calling for expertise is generally excluded because, like the evidence of non-experts on matters calling for expertise, it does not help the court. At best, it is superfluous,[57] and it could be a cause of confusion. Its rejection is sometimes tied to an interpretation of the substantive law that removes the matter to which the evidence relates from those that are in issue.[58] The court should be careful not to take too restricted a view of the issues so as to exclude the expert opinion.[59] It may, however, be rejected where there is an alternative route to determining the issue, and both parties have tendered false expert evidence.[60]

In *R v Chard*,[61] the Court of Appeal held the judge rightly to have excluded medical evidence concerning the intention, at the material time, of someone charged with murder, where there was no question of his being insane or suffering from diminished

---

[53] Parke B in *Wright v Doe d Tatham* (1837) 4 Bing NC 489, 543–4. Cf *R v Davies* [1962] 3 All ER 97, [1962] 1 WLR 1111.

[54] *R v Morris* [1998] 1 Cr App Rep 386 (in which the support of a general medical practitioner was not enough to raise the issue).

[55] By statute under s 4(6) of the Criminal Procedure Insanity Act 1964 to justify a finding of unfitness to plead: see *R v Borkan* [2004] EWCA Crim 1642; (but *not* fitness to plead, *R v Ghulam* [2009] EWCA Crim 2285).

[56] Lawton LJ in *R v Turner* [1975] QB 834, 841, cited with approval by Lord Wilberforce in *DPP v Jordan* [1977] AC 699, [1976] 3 All ER 775; 718, 779b.

[57] Thus in *R v Land* [1999] QB 65, [1998] 1 All ER 403, it was held that the jury did not require expert assistance to determine the age of a child depicted in a photograph.

[58] As in *R v Coles* [1995] 1 Cr App Rep 157, in which the evidence of a psychiatrist was admissible only on the basis, which was rejected, that subjective foresight of risk was necessary in a prosecution for manslaughter.   [59] *R (Bull) v Northampton Justices* [2009] EWHC 1768 (Admin).

[60] *Zabihi v Janzemini* [2009] EWCA Civ 851.   [61] (1971) 56 Cr App Rep 268.

responsibility.[62] A judge and jury are as competent as a psychiatrist to form an opinion about the past intention of a normal[63] man. On similar grounds, it has been held that expert evidence is inadmissible to explain the ordinary meaning of words such as 'obscene or indecent',[64] or 'calculated to deprave or corrupt',[65] or perhaps 'severe impairment',[66] when used in a modern general Act of Parliament, or the phrase 'following the settlement' in a contract of insurance.[67] Expert opinion may never be received on a question of domestic law,[68] or forensic procedure.[69] Still less should it be allowed to force a view of the application of the relevant law upon the trial judge.[70]

R v Turner, the case from which the passage quoted above is taken, is more controversial on account of the problem of reconciling it with the decision of the Privy Council in *Lowery v R*.[71] Turner unsuccessfully pleaded provocation in answer to a charge of murder of his girlfriend, whom he alleged that he had killed in a fit of rage caused by her sudden confession of infidelity. He appealed on the ground that the judge had wrongly refused to allow him to call a psychiatrist. This witness would have sworn that the accused was not mentally ill; that he had a deep relationship with the girl, which was likely to cause an explosive outburst of rage at her confession; and that his subsequent behaviour showed profound regret at what he had done. The Court of Appeal held that no evidence was required for the first of these matters, which was undisputed, and that jurors do not need a psychiatrist to tell them how ordinary people who are not suffering from mental illness are likely to react to the stresses and strains of life. This would appear to provide a basis for reconciling this decision with *Lowery v R*, where Lowery and King were charged with a murder that must have been committed by either, or both, of them, and the Privy Council held that the judge had properly allowed King to call a psychiatrist to swear that he was less likely to have committed the crime than Lowery. Juries do not need to be told that normal men are liable to lose control of themselves when their women admit to infidelity, but they do require assistance to help them determine which of two accused has the more aggressive personality. Another factor could have been that Lowery had put his character in issue, the psychiatric evidence then being admissible to impugn the credibility of his testimony. Unfortunately, no guidance was provided on the subject from the Court of Appeal, which contented itself with saying that *Lowery's* case was decided on its special facts.[72]

---

[62] In *R v Gilfoyle* [2001] 2 Cr App Rep 57, a psychological profile of the victim of murder was similarly rejected as fresh evidence on appeal.

[63] It may be admissible in the case of an abnormal person: see *R v Makoare* [2001] 1 NZLR 318.

[64] *R v Stamford* [1972] 2 QB 391, [1972] 2 All ER 427.

[65] *R v Anderson* [1972] 1 QB 304, [1971] 3 All ER 1152. For possible exception, see *DPP v A and BC Chewing Gum Ltd* [1968] 1 QB 159, [1967] 2 All ER 504.   [66] *R v Hall* (1987) 86 Cr App Rep 159.

[67] *Royal Insurance Australia Ltd v Government Insurance Office of New South Wales* [1994] 1 VR 123.

[68] *Prigmore v Welbourne* [2003] EWHC 3259.   [69] *Re M-M (a Child)* [2007] EWCA Civ 589, [15].

[70] *LB of Hackney v Rottenberg* [2006] EWHC 166 (Admin), [20] (whether noise a statutory nuisance); *Esure Insurance Ltd v Direct Line Insurance plc* [2008] EWCA 842 (likelihood of consumer confusion when trademarks similar).   [71] [1974] AC 85, [1973] 3 All ER 662: see Pattenden [1986] *Crim LR* 92.

[72] It would probably be a mistake to regard *R v Turner* as closing the door to the admissibility of psychiatric evidence on behalf of the accused in all cases of provocation, especially having regard to changes in the substantive law on the subject: indeed, some encouragement to the tendering of such evidence seems to have been offered in *R v Ahluwalia* [1992] 4 All ER 889, 96 Cr App Rep 133, 898, 141. For a similar approach to self-defence in Canada, see *R v Lavallee* [1990] 1 SCR 852.

In England, there has been little inclination to extend the category of those in respect of whom expert psychiatric testimony may be received. Thus in *R v Henry*,[73] such evidence was held inadmissible in relation to a borderline mental defective; in *R v Weightman*,[74] to an abnormal and histrionic, but not mentally ill or handicapped individual;[75] and in *R v Loughran*,[76] to a young man with female characteristics, on the basis that it could show no organic or psychiatric link to his claimed impotence. Such evidence may, however, be admitted in the case of an otherwise normal person who is temporarily suffering from an abnormal condition having an impact upon his mental state.[77] Some slight flexibility in this formulation has, however, been exploited to admit such evidence outside these strict limits in the case of the young. A distinction has been drawn[78] between evidence that attacks the credibility of an out-of-court statement tendered by the prosecution,[79] and that which supports the credibility of the oral testimony of a witness.[80] This is largely attributable to the procedural prohibition on bolstering a witness.[81] Where the credibility of a witness is in issue, expert evidence is not automatically excluded,[82] but its use needs to be restrained by a strict doctrine of necessity.[83] In most cases, the court will not require outside assistance to enable it to determine whether or not a witness is credible,[84] although it may be helped by expert evidence as to the nature of a syndrome that may cast doubt on such credibility.[85] In Canada, there seems to have been wider extension still to permit expert opinion on such evidential issues as the likelihood of pre-trial recantation,[86] of pre-trial lapse of memory,[87] of the difference between visual and verbal memory,[88] or even of the unlikelihood of the witness having been coached,[89] at least in relation to child complainants of sexual abuse by an adult.[90]

---

[73] [2005] EWCA Crim 1681, [2006] 1 Cr App R 118. See also, in Australia, *R v Hoogwerf* (1992) 63 ACR 302; in Canada, *Roy v R* (1988) 62 CR (3d) 127; in New Zealand, *R v B* [1987] 1 NZLR 362.

[74] (1990) 92 Cr App Rep 291.

[75] The general rule was stated to be that an intelligence quotient of less than 70 was required to justify the admissibility of expert psychiatric evidence of credibility. In *R v Antar* [2004] EWCA Crim 2708, the Court of Appeal allowed an appeal on this basis despite the trial judge's scepticism about the quoted figure in view of the accused's educational attainments. [76] [1999] Crim LR 404.

[77] As in *R v Toner* (1991) 93 Cr App Rep 382, in which starvation had induced hypoglycaemia, although in Australia no comparable exception has been made for alcoholics: *R v Haidley and Alford* [1984] VR 229.

[78] In *R v Robinson* [1994] 3 All ER 346, 98 Cr App Rep 370.

[79] Citing *R v Raghip* (1991) The Times, 9 December; *R v Ward* [1993] 2 All ER 577, [1993] 1 WLR 619, in which expert psychiatric evidence was admitted to throw doubt upon the veracity of confessions made by mentally handicapped individuals. Although such an expert must rest his opinion on established fact: see *R v Lee* (1991) 42 ACR 393.

[80] As in *Robinson* (n78) in which the expert opinion was tendered to show that the complainant was too defective to have understood enough to be suggestible, and insufficiently creative to be capable of fantasy about the incident in question. [81] See, 326.

[82] It may be more readily admitted in rebuttal when expert evidence has been admitted on the issue: *HMA v A* 2005 SCCR 593, 2005 SLT 975; cf *Campbell v HMA* 2004 SCCR 220, 2004 SLT 397, in which expert evidence discrediting testimony was held admissible, but not that bolstering it. For a modern appraisal, see Ward (2009) 13 *E&P* 83.

[83] *Re M and R (minors)* [1996] 4 All ER 239, 253h; *Re CB and JB* [1998] 2 FCR 313.

[84] The evidence of the same expert on recovered memory was accepted, with some qualification, [47], in *R v H: R v G* [2005] EWCA Crim 1828, [2006] 1 Cr App R 195, rejected in *R v Snell and Wilson* [2006] EWCA Crim 1404. [85] *R v Richard W* [2003] EWCA Crim 3490, [24].

[86] *R v P (C)*. [87] *R v C (RA)* (1990) 78 CR (3d) 390. [88] *R v R (D)* [1996] 2 SCR 291.

[89] *R v Manahan* (1990) 61 CCC (3d) 139.

[90] Although in *R v Parrott* 2001 SCC 3, [2001] 1 SCR 178, it was held better to determine the competency of a child by calling it on the voir dire than by the use of expert opinion. In New Zealand, s 23G of the

In some Australian cases, emphasis has been placed upon the difference between expert psychiatric evidence in relation to testimony for the purpose of testing its credibility, and in relation to out-of-court statements for the same purpose, or as going to an issue in the case.[91] In a somewhat similar fashion, a distinction has also been made between the rejection of expert evidence as to the sincerity of views expressed by individual members of the public in response to a survey, and its acceptance as the expert's opinion of the public's view, even though derived from perusal of the results of the survey.[92]

In England, the Youth Justice and Criminal Evidence Act 1999 makes some inroad into this position, in its explicit endorsement of the use of expert evidence to help determine the competence of witnesses,[93] and whether to make a special measures direction.[94]

ULTIMATE ISSUE

A considerable body of authority once asserted that evidence of opinion may not be proffered on an ultimate issue. This rule was supposed to apply both to expert,[95] and to lay,[96] opinion, and both to civil,[97] and to criminal, proceedings.[98] So far as the rule is justified upon the basis that it prevents usurpation of the function of the trier of fact, it was condemned by Wigmore as 'a mere bit of empty rhetoric',[99] since the trier of fact is always free to reject the guidance offered by the opinion,[100] although where such opinions, especially if unanimous, are rejected, the judge must give convincing reasons,[101] most especially in a serious case where he goes beyond the schedule of findings submitted by the tendering party.[102] The justification appeared to confuse the admissibility of evidence with its having conclusive weight. It may be for this reason that some recent overseas authority has formulated the rule in different terms, as excluding opinion only on the application of an essentially legal standard, such as that of negligence or incapacity to marry:[103]

When a standard, or a measure, or a capacity has been fixed by law, no witness whether expert or non-expert, nor however qualified, is permitted to express an opinion as to whether the person or the conduct, in question, measures up to that standard; on that question the court must instruct the jury as to the law, and the jury draw its own conclusion from the evidence.

Evidence Act 1908 deals with the admissibility of expert evidence in this context explicitly: for exegesis, see *R v Aymes* [2005] 2 NZLR 376.

[91] *R v Barry* [1984] 1 Qd R 74.

[92] *Ritz Hotel Ltd v Charles of the Ritz Ltd* (1988) 15 NSWLR 158, 175. In England, such evidence has been held not to be expert, nor even opinion: *Reckitt & Colman Products Ltd v Borden Inc (No 2)* [1987] FSR 407.

[93] YJCEA, s 54(5).   [94] YJCEA, s 20(6)(c).

[95] See, for example, *North Cheshire and Manchester Brewery Co v Manchester Brewery Co* [1899] AC 83, 85.   [96] See, for example, *R v Davies* (n53).

[97] See above.   [98] *R v Wright* (1821) Russ & Ry 456, 458.

[99] *Evidence* (Chadbourn rev) [1920].

[100] In *Armstrong v First York Ltd* [2005] EWCA Civ 277, [2005] 1 WLR 2751, the Court of Appeal emphasized that a trial judge could accept the evidence of a claimant, despite being unable to find any flaw in the contrary evidence of a competent and honest expert.

[101] *Re W (A Child)* [2005] EWCA Civ 649, [2005] 2 FCR 277, [92].

[102] *Re G and B (Children)* [2009] EWCA Civ 10.

[103] *Grismore v Consolidated Products Co* 5 NW 2d 646, 663 (1942), approved in *R v Tonkin and Montgomery* [1975] Qd R 1, 42. See also *R v Palmer* [1981] 1 NSWLR 209.

The rule has now been abandoned in England.[104] In civil cases, its abolition was recommended by the Law Reform Committee in its 17th Report,[105] and implemented by s 3 of the Civil Evidence Act 1972:

(1) Subject to any rules of court made in pursuance of Part I of the Civil Evidence Act 1968 or this Act, where a person is called as a witness in any civil proceedings, his opinion on any relevant matter on which he is qualified to give expert evidence shall be admissible in evidence.

(2) It is hereby declared that where a person is called as a witness in any civil proceedings, a statement of opinion by him on any relevant matter on which he is not qualified to give expert evidence, if made as a way of conveying relevant facts personally perceived by him, is admissible as evidence of what he perceived.

(3) In this section 'relevant matter' includes an issue in the proceedings in question.

The operation of this provision was conveniently, and convincingly, explained in *Barings plc v Coopers & Lybrand*,[106] where the court explained that, while expert evidence would no longer be excluded simply because it went to an ultimate issue, relevance remained necessary, in the sense of helpful to the tribunal of fact, and that especially in cases in which the issue related to the practice of a specialized and regulated profession, expert evidence of that practice would be helpful.[107] It would be otherwise if the evidence were no more than that the defendant had shown himself incompetent in applying the standards expected.[108]

The Criminal Law Revision Committee recommended a similar step for criminal proceedings,[109] but it has not yet been enacted.[110] The continuance of the rule was, however, questioned in *DPP v A and BC Chewing Gum Ltd*,[111] and in *R v Stockwell*,[112] the Court of Appeal adopted the view expressed in a previous edition of this text that the expert should be permitted to give his opinion on an ultimate issue,[113] subject only to a direction

---

[104] For explicit approval of this view in three quite different contexts, see *Glaverbel SA v British Coal Corp* [1995] RPC 255 (obviousness of 'invention'), 277; *Re M and R* (n75), 250j (credibility of witnesses); *Routestone Ltd v Minories Finance Ltd* [1997] 1 EGLR 123, 127L (satisfaction of professional standard of performance). For a similar view in Australia, see *Farrell v R* [1998] HCA 50, (1998) 194 CLR 286 (credibility of witness).

[105] Cmnd 4489, conclusions (1) and (2). On the basis that, in the case of non-expert opinion, the relaxation applied only to compendious statements of fact and opinion perceived by the testifying witness.

[106] [2001] Lloyd's Rep Bank 85.

[107] Strong reliance was placed upon remarks of Evans LJ in *United Bank of Kuwait v Prudential Property Services* [1995] EGCS 190. In Australia, the standard has been expressed more strictly as when 'absolutely necessary': *Wright and Samuels v McLeod* [1969] SASR 256, 261.

[108] So distinguishing remarks of Oliver J in *Midland Bank Trust Co v Hett, Stubbs and Kent* [1979] Ch 384, [1978] 3 All ER 571, and *Bown v Gould & Swayne* [1996] PNLR 130.

[109] Clause 43 of the draft bill annexed to its 11th Report (Cmnd 4491).

[110] Section 30 of the Criminal Justice Act 1988, which deals with expert reports contains no such, or even similar, provision.   [111] (n65).

[112] (n14), 265 (in which the issue was the identity of a disguised man in a security video recording, and an expert in facial mapping was permitted to testify to his being the accused).

[113] Cf *R v Jeffries* [1997] Crim LR 819, in which the old rule seems to have been applied; but see also the critical commentary by Birch. For the similar position in North America, see, in the United States, Federal Rules Evidence, 704; and in Canada, *Grant v R* [1982] 2 SCR 819.

to the jury that it be not bound to accept the expert's opinion.[114] Depressingly, the Auld Report detected some signs of abuse of this development.[115]

PROCEDURE

As a result of the scathing criticism of the system of expert witnesses in civil proceedings in the Woolf Report, procedure in civil proceedings has been revolutionized in the Civil Procedure Rules.[116] In very broad outline, the thrust of the change is to attempt to limit the ambit, and cost, of expert evidence.[117] It starts by stressing that:[118] 'Expert evidence shall be restricted to that which is reasonably required to resolve the proceedings.' It seeks to promote this result by requiring the leave of the court before expert evidence can be tendered at all,[119] puts significant pressure upon the parties to agree to instruct a single joint expert,[120] and empowers the court to cap the fees that may be recovered,[121] although where there are significantly different schools of expert thought, no such pressure will be applied.[122] The whole point of this is to make the system open and transparent, so there is no scope for one side to have a private conference with such an expert.[123] Even if a single

---

[114] Though this need not be in any particular form, and its omission is not an automatic ground for allowing an appeal: *R v Fitzpatrick* [1999] Crim LR 832; but see *R v Ugoh* [2001] EWCA Crim 1381.

[115] Chapter XI, [133] (by deliberately instructing 'expert' opinion on matters as close to the ultimate issue as possible). Nor should it be used to ratchet up the standard of liability: *Stewart v Coulson* [2009] EWHC 704, [5].   [116] CPR, Pt 35.

[117] Which has been robustly defended from attack on human rights grounds: *Daniels v Walker* [2000] 1 WLR 1382, 1387; cf *H v France* (1989) 12 EHRR 74; for comparison between common and civil law approached to expert evidence, see Verkerk (2009) 13 *E&P* 167. For attempts to restrict legal aid for experts in family cases, see Mahoney (2008) 38 *Fam L* 1046.

[118] CPR 35; further strengthened by the October 2009 amendment introducing 35PD para 7 specifying the relevant considerations.

[119] CPR 35.4(1). Nor can this discretion be fettered by agreement between the parties: *Parkin v Bromley Hospitals NHS Trust* [2002] EWCA Civ 478, [2002] CPR 44, [38]. For application to issues of causation in low-impact collision cases, in which there has been inconsistency, see now *Casey v Cartwright* [2006] EWCA Civ 1280, (2006) 150 SJLB 1331.

[120] CPR 35.7. Nor is it likely to be easy to persuade the court to agree to the use of a private expert witness in the event of dissatisfaction with the joint report: *Peet v Mid-Kent Healthcare Trust* [2001] EWCA Civ 1703, [2002] 3 All ER 688, stiffening the criteria stated in *Daniels v Walker* (n117), and amplified in *Cosgrove v Pattison* [2001] CPLR 177. But neither may it be impossible if there are good reasons, especially in a case involving large sums: *Austen v Oxford City Council* (17 April 2002, unreported) QBD; or permanent separation from a child, *Re B* [2007] EWCA Civ 556, [2007] 2 FLR 979; after other steps to resolve the issue have failed: *Layland v Fairview Homes* [2002] EWHC 1350 (Ch), [2003] CPLR 19, [30]; or in a case of apparent expert bias, *Saunder v Birmingham CC* (2008) unreported EAT 21 May. It should be noted that CPR 35.8(1) permits separate instructions by each party to a single joint expert: see *Yorke v Katra* [2003] EWCA Civ 867.   [121] CPR 35.4(4).

[122] *Oxley v Penwarden* [2001] CPLR 1 or where there is difficulty in distinguishing between expert witnesses and witnesses of fact *S v Chesterfield NHS Trust* [2003] EWCA Civ 1284 (Admin).

[123] *Childs v Vernon* [2007] EWCA Civ 305, [18]. If a party instructs an expert, and subsequently receives leave to discard that evidence and to instruct a new expert, then, at that stage, the original report can be required by the opponent: *Beck v Ministry of Defence* [2003] EWCA Civ 1043, [2004] PIQR P1, [24], whether or not the disclosing party remains in the litigation, *Shepherd Neame v EDF Energy Networks* [2008] EWHC 123 (TCC), or had been commissioned before the proceedings commenced, *Carruthers v MP Fireworks Ltd* (2007) unreported Bristol CC 26 Jan. Such a condition applies to early drafts, and in no way derogates from legal professional privilege by making its waiver a condition for approval of such substitution, so as to discourage 'expert-shopping': *Vasiliou v Hajigeorgiou* [2005] EWCA Civ 236, [2005] 3 All ER 17.

joint expert[124] is not appointed,[125] there is provision for the exchange of information[126] and reports,[127] which can then be used by the other party,[128] and for the court to direct discussion between the experts.[129] It is envisaged that expert evidence will normally be tendered in the form of a written report,[130] that written questions will be addressed to, and answered by, the expert before the hearing,[131] and that, at least on the fast or small claims track,[132] attendance for cross-examination will be ordered only if the court believes it to be necessary in the interests of justice.[133]

For similar reasons, it has been provided[134] that advance notice must be given of the intention to adduce expert evidence in criminal proceedings,[135] an opportunity provided to examine the factual basis for any such evidence of opinion,[136] and, even when avowedly independent, the chance to call expert evidence in rebuttal.[137] It is within the discretion of the judge in a criminal trial to determine that a given field of expertise is irrelevant or unhelpful, and accordingly to refuse to allow it to be called.[138]

Measures broadly similar to those contained in the CPR for the purposes of civil proceedings were incorporated as a new Pt 33 in the Criminal Procedure Rules.[139] The

---

[124] Nor should other professionals involved with litigation, such as clinical case managers, be assimilated to experts for these purposes: *Wright v Sullivan* [2005] EWCA 656, [2006] 1 WLR 172.

[125] Acquiescence in the choice of an expert is not the equivalent of the selection of a joint expert, and in such a case the instructing party retains privilege in relation to the report: *Carlson v Townsend* [2001] EWCA Civ 511, [2001] 3 All ER 663.   [126] CPR 35.9.

[127] Practice Direction 35, [2(1)] provides that expert reports are to be addressed to the court and not to the instructing party, but it seems that if not joint, expert reports may still attract privilege: *Sage v Feiven* [2002] 7 CL 45; as do earlier drafts of reports where no explicit permission is required to tender the final version: *Jackson v Marley Davenport Ltd* [2004] EWCA Civ 1225, [2004] 1 WLR 2926.   [128] CPR 35.11.

[129] CPR 35.12. Exceptionally, it may be necessary for a third expert to be appointed to justify the replacement of an expert who is alleged to have modified his view improperly at such a discussion: *Stallwood v David and Adamson* [2006] EWHC 2600 (QB), [2007] 1 All ER 206.

[130] CPR 35.5(1), which must contain an acknowledgement of the duty to the court, and an enhanced statement of truth, 35PD.3, which must state the substance of all material instructions that are not privileged (CPR 35.10), and include material supplied with the instructions to the extent that the absence of such material would render the instructions inaccurate or incomplete: *Lucas v Barking, Havering & Redbridge Hospitals Trust* [2003] EWCA Civ 1102, [2003] 4 All ER 720 (the practical effect of the broad meaning of instructions in this decision is that privilege may be claimed in relation to material supplied to the expert, unless its disclosure is necessary to render his statement of instructions accurate or complete).

[131] CPR 35.6 (now required to be proportionate). These are limited to clarification, but an extended meaning seems to have been given to the concept: see *Mutch v Allen* [2001] EWCA Civ 76, [2001] CPR 77. Answers form part of the final report. Once an expert's method of valuation has been agreed between the parties, there should be no further application to the court: *Bruce v Carpenter* [2006] All ER (D) 405 (Nov).

[132] Although such cross-examination of joint experts is common in the Family Division: *Re S* (n157), [10].

[133] CPR 35.5(2). Although where that occurs, it is desirable that any supporting literature relied upon by the expert should be available in court: *Breeze v Ahmad* [2005] EWCA Civ 192, [2005] 4 All ER 1.

[134] Police and Criminal Evidence Act 1984, s 81; Crown Court (Advance Notice of Expert Evidence) Rules 1987 SI 1987/70 (L 2), as amended by SI 1997/700 (L 6); Magistrates' Courts (Advance Notice of Expert Evidence) Rules 1997 SI 1997/705 (L11).

[135] Or, in the case of the defence, notice of the name and address of any expert consulted even, or especially, when such expert is not to be called to give evidence: Criminal Justice Act 2003, s 35; despite the reluctance of the Auld Report to move in such direction: ch XI, [149].

[136] If no such notice or opportunity is given or afforded the evidence can be adduced only by leave of the court.   [137] *R v Sunderland Justices, ex p Dryden* (1994) The Times, 18 May.

[138] *R v Hersey* (n9).

[139] They supplement guidance provided under the auspices of the Attorney-General to expert witnesses instructed by the prosecution in the wake of his investigation of 'shaken-baby syndrome' cases in February 2006.

principal differences are that there is not the same emphasis on the restriction of expert evidence in criminal proceedings, there is a clear requirement to furnish details of the facts, and their provenance, upon which the opinion is based,[140] and the encouragement to the use of joint experts applies only as between co-defendants,[141] rather than as between prosecution and defence.

SECTION 3. EXCEPTIONS TO THE RULE

EXPERT OPINION[142]

Courts have acted on the opinion of experts from early times. In 1553, Saunders J said:[143]

If matters arise in our law which concern other sciences or faculties we commonly apply for the aid of that science or faculty which it concerns. This is a commendable thing in our law. For thereby it appears that we do not dismiss all other sciences but our own, but we approve of them and encourage them as things worthy of commendation.

But the early expert was often a member of the jury, and there was no question of his opinion being disregarded by that body. Expert witnesses began to play their modern role in the eighteenth century.[144]

The facts upon which an expert's opinion is based must be proved by admissible evidence, and he should be asked in chief what those facts are.[145] If he observed them, he may testify to their existence, but, when the facts in question are dependent upon ordinary human powers of perception, the expert may be contradicted by a lay witness, as when an expert and an eyewitness give different estimates of the speed of a vehicle.[146] A doctor could not state what a patient told him about past symptoms as evidence of the existence of those symptoms because that would infringe the rule against hearsay, but he could give evidence of what the patient told him[147] in order to explain the grounds on which he came to a conclusion with regard to the patient's condition.[148] In these cases, an opinion based solely upon uncorroborated statements by the patient is not automatically inadmissible,

---

[140] Reflecting the continuing power of the hearsay rule in criminal cases.

[141] Although even there, the matter is discretionary, and is presumably most unlikely to be ordered when the co-defendants are running 'cut-throat' defences.

[142] See Learned Hand (1901) 15 *Harv LR* 40. For a statutory definition of an expert, see Social Security Act 1998, s 6. For extended consideration, see Redmayne *Expert Evidence and Criminal Justice* (2002).

[143] *Buckley v Rice-Thomas* (1554) 1 Plowd 118, 124.   [144] *Folkes v Chadd* (1782) 3 Doug KB 157.

[145] *R v Turner* (n56), 840. See also *R v Abbey* (1982) 138 DLR (3d) 202.

[146] As in *Coopers Payen Ltd v Southampton Container Terminal Ltd* [2003] EWCA Civ 1223, in which the trial judge's resolution in favour of the eyewitness against the opinion of the single joint expert was overturned. If an expert offers an opinion as a layman, and not as an expert, this must be brought to the attention of the jury: *R v Cook* [1982] Crim LR 670.

[147] An assessment of medical condition does not necessarily require personal examination but may be made by observation alone: *R v Mackenney* [2003] EWCA Crim 3643, [2004] 2 Cr App R 32, [16].

[148] A statement explicitly approved in *R v Bradshaw* (1985) 82 Cr App Rep 79, 83; *Ramsay v Watson* (1961) 108 CLR 642; *Leis v Gardner* [1965] Qd R 181; *Leonard v British Columbia Hydro and Power Authority* (1965) 49 DLR (2d) 422. Modern statutory intervention has vastly extended the situations in which such hearsay is admissible.

but is likely to be of very little weight, and the jury should be instructed appropriately.[149] In general, expert evidence requires support from extrinsic material.[150]

The functions of expert witnesses were succinctly stated by Lord President Cooper in *Davie v Edinburgh Magistrates*,[151] when he said:

> Their duty is to furnish the judge with the necessary scientific criteria for testing the accuracy of their conclusions, so as to enable the judge or jury to form their own independent judgment by the application of these criteria to the facts proved in evidence.

The Court of Session repudiated the suggestion that the judge or jury is bound to adopt the views of an expert, even if they should be uncontradicted, because 'The parties have invoked the decision of a judicial tribunal and not an oracular pronouncement by an expert',[152] although in such a case, the judge must state his reasons.[153] This case reaffirmed the view that an expert might adopt statements made in scientific works as part of his testimony, and portions of such works might be put to him in cross-examination. To this extent, they may be used as evidence in the case, but the judge is entitled to form an opinion on the basis of other parts of the book.[154] Although the judge or jury is bound to come to an independent view, it may occasionally be necessary for a judge, having heard expert evidence and considered it to be evenly balanced,[155] to decide on the basis of the burden of proof.[156] The judge must not, however, simply substitute his own view for that of an expert,[157] and if there is nothing in the case to contradict unanimous expert evidence in favour of the accused, the trier of fact is not entitled to reject it.[158] In most serious cases where expert opinion is crucial to the outcome, it should neither be accepted[159] nor rejected without the most careful examination, especially if there is a gap in the expertise;[160] but nor should the

---

[149] *R v Bradshaw* (n148), ibid. See also *Lortie v R* (1986) 54 CR (3d) 228.

[150] *EPI Environmental Technologies Inc v Symphony Plastic Technologies plc* [2004] EWHC 2945 (Ch), [2005] 1 WLR 3456, [76]. But it is not necessarily fatal that an opinion is based in part on a mistake of fact: *R (China) v Secretary of State for the Home Department* [2009] EWCA Civ 81.   [151] 1953 SC 34, 40.

[152] 1953 SC 34, 40. See also *Re B (a minor) (care: expert witnesses)* [1996] 1 FLR 667, applying these remarks in the context of child care, but requiring reasons for disagreement with a unanimous expert view. Still less can it be argued that, where complicated expert opinion is divided, the trier of fact must be speculating in preferring one view to the other, even when it decides rapidly: *R v Cutts* [2003] EWCA Crim 28, [19].

[153] *Re M (child residence)* (2002) The Times, 24 July, in which it was held that the trial judge should not have rejected the unanimous opinion of three medical experts simply on his own view derived from the witness's demeanour. See also the caution required by the Supreme Court of Canada to reject unanimous expert medical opinion in *R v Molodowicz* [2000] 1 SCR 420.   [154] *Collier v Simpson* (1831) 5 C & P 73.

[155] In some situations, it will be preferable not to allow the case to go to trial, where reputable expert witnesses are fundamentally opposed to each other: *R v Cannings* [2004] EWCA Crim 1, [2004] 1 All ER 725, [178]. Although mere conflict between experts does not by itself justify acquittal: *R v Anthony* [2005] EWCA Crim 952, [81]; it is certainly necessary in such a case for the competing arguments to be set out in the summing-up: *R v Suratan* [2004] EWCA Crim 1246.

[156] *Pickford v Imperial Chemical Industries plc* [1998] 3 All ER 462, [1998] 1 WLR 1189; 473, 1200; cf *Sewell v Electrolux Ltd* (1997) The Times, 7 November.

[157] *Dover District Council v Sherred* (1997) 29 HLR 864, least of all in the absence of the expert: *Re S (A Child)* [2007] EWCA Civ 356, [4].

[158] *R v Bailey* (1961) 66 Cr App Rep 31, not even when it relates to an issue first decided on contrary expert evidence many years before: *Re Johnson* [2002] EWCA Crim 1900, [16]. See also *R v Hall* (1988) 36 ACR 362; *Towne Cinema Theatres Ltd v R* (1985) 18 DLR (4th) 1 (community standard of obscenity).

[159] *Re B (A Child)* [2008] EWCA Civ 1547; [2009] 2 FLR 14. But a party is on appeal bound by an expert report not contested at trial: *Re M (Children)* [2007] EWCA Civ 1363.

[160] *R v Holdsworth* [2008] EWCA Crim 971.

judge 'cherry-pick' by treating conflict between experts as entitling him to accept one part of one expert's opinion while rejecting the rest, and the whole of the other.[161]

The testimony of an expert is likely to carry more weight, and more readily relate to an ultimate issue, than that of an ordinary witness. It is thus understandable that higher standards of accuracy and objectivity should both be required,[162] and *seem*[163] to be provided. The obligations of an expert witness in these respects were helpfully summarized by Cresswell J in *The Ikarian Reefer*,[164] in the course of which he remarked that: 'An expert witness should provide independent assistance to the Court by way of objective unbiased opinion in relation to matters within his expertise.... An expert witness in the High Court should never assume the role of an advocate.'[165] These remarks would appear applicable a fortiori in relation to forensic scientific evidence tendered by the prosecution in a criminal case.[166] It has also been emphasized that an expert in a case involving children bears a heavy responsibility to be as objective as possible, and to make clear the extent to which his opinion was based on hypothesis, especially when it departs from a consensus view.[167] This view of the role of the expert has received emphatic expression[168] in r 35.3 of the Civil Procedure Rules:[169]

(1) It is the duty of experts to help the court on the matters within their expertise,

(2) This duty overrides any obligation to the person from whom they have received instructions or by whom they are paid.

No useful purpose would be served by an endeavour to enumerate the matters that have been treated by the courts as requiring a sufficient degree of specialized knowledge to

---

[161] *Y (Sri Lanka) v Secretary of State for the Home Department* [2009] EWCA Civ 362, [34].

[162] See Laddie J in *Autospin (Oil Seals) Ltd v Beehive Spinning* [1995] RPC 683.

[163] See Lord Wilberforce in *Whitehouse v Jordan* [1981] 1 All ER 267, [1981] 1 WLR 246, 276, 256, thus making it questionable whether a personal friend should act as an expert witness in civil proceedings: *Liverpool Roman Catholic Archdiocese Trustees v Goldberg (No 2)* [2001] 4 All ER 950, [2001] 1 WLR 2337. An appearance of bias will not normally bar a witness from appearing as an expert in criminal proceedings, if otherwise qualified,, but may diminish the weight of his opinion, *R v Stubbs* [2006] EWCA Crim 2312, as explained in *Leo Sawrij Ltd v North Cumbria Magistrates* [2009] EWHC 2823 (Admin). Any material suggesting lack of independence should, however, be disclosed in advance, perhaps by amendment of the CPR requirement of a declaration of truth: see *Toth v Jarman* [2006] EWCA Civ 1028, [2006] 4 All ER 1028 note, [120]. See in Ireland *Galvin v Murray* [2001] 1 IR 331. For management and analysis of expert bias, see Dwyer (2007) 27 CJQ 57, 425.

[164] *National Justice Compania Naviera SA v Prudential Assurance Co Ltd* [1993] 2 Lloyd's Rep 68, 81. CPR 35 has been said to embody these obligations, and to make clear that they are now owed to the court: *Stevens v Gullis* [2000] 1 All ER 527.

[165] Nor should an advocate, such as a guardian *ad litem*, assume the role of an expert for the purpose of expressing an opinion on a child's veracity: *Re N (a minor) (sexual abuse: video evidence)* [1996] 4 All ER 225, 236d.

[166] See Ormerod [1968] Crim LR 240; Roberts and Willmore *The Role of Forensic Science Evidence in Criminal Proceedings* Roy Com Res St No 11 (1993) ch 4.

[167] *Re AB (a minor)* [1995] 1 FLR 181. The desirability of reference to the consensus view was also stressed in the context of medical negligence in *Sharpe v Southend Health Authority* [1997] 8 Med LR 299.

[168] Although the rules impose no specific sanction for breach in *Pearce v Ove Arup Partnership* [2002] 25(2) IPD 25011, Jacob J [61] was prepared to refer to his professional association an expert he considered in breach.

[169] See also in Scotland, *Preece v HM Adv* [1981] Crim LR 783; in New Zealand, *R v Tihi* [1990] 1 NZLR 540, 548.

render expert evidence admissible.[170] They have included medical and scientific questions, the meaning of technical terms, questions of commercial practice or market value, the provisions of a foreign system of law, and the identity of a person's handwriting—a subject that is discussed in Chapter XV. These areas are in constant flux. Some areas become commonplace, and judicial notice more appropriate than the requirement of expert testimony;[171] once-established fields may become obsolete,[172] and new areas arise, with the progress of human knowledge and technological prowess. At one time, a conservative approach requiring the field of expertise to have become generally accepted was widely adopted.[173] This is now regarded as too stultifying, that test having now been rejected in its jurisdiction of origin,[174] and increasingly disregarded elsewhere.[175] The better, and now more widely accepted, view is that, so long as a field is sufficiently well established to pass the ordinary tests of relevance and reliability,[176] then no enhanced test of admissibility should be applied, but the weight of the evidence should be established by the same adversarial forensic techniques applicable elsewhere. It has, however, been recommended that a Forensic Science Advisory Council be established to review potential new areas of forensic expertise.[177]

Even if a field of expertise is well established, the guidance it provides must also be sufficiently relevant to a matter in issue.[178] If the court comes to the conclusion that the subject of investigation does not require a sufficient degree of specialized knowledge to call for the testimony of an expert, evidence of opinion will be excluded, unless the case is one in which non-expert opinion is admissible.[179] Thus in *R v Mackenney*,[180] a psychologist

[170] See *Re Pinion, Westminster Bank Ltd v Pinion* [1965] Ch 85, [1964] 1 All ER 890; 98, 891. See also *Scottish Shire Line Ltd v London and Provincial Marine and General Insurance Co Ltd* [1912] 3 KB 51, 70, and *Carter v Boehm* (1766) 3 Burr 1905.

[171] See, in relation to proof of the ordinary operation of computers: *R v Shephard* [1993] AC 380, [1993] 1 All ER 225; 387, 231.

[172] See, in relation to voice identification: *R v O'Doherty* [2002] NI 263, [2003] 1 Cr App Rep 77, [31]. Although there may still be some reluctance to accept evidence in recently developed fields of expertise in cases referred to the Court of Appeal by the Criminal Cases Review Commission a long time after the initial decision: see e.g. *R v Moloney* [2002] NI 263.

[173] Heavily influenced by the American case of *Frye v United States* 293 F 1013 (1923).

[174] In *Daubert v Merrell Dow Pharmaceuticals Inc* 509 US 579 (1993). See also *General Electric Co v Joiner* 522 US 136 (1997); *Kumho Tire Ltd v Carmichael* 526 US 137 (1999), making it clear that *Daubert* applies to all expert opinion, and is to be interpreted flexibly.

[175] See e.g. in Canada, *R v Diffenbaugh* (1993) 80 CCC (3d) 97, 106; in England, *R v Robb* (n8), 166.

[176] In *R v Mohan* [1994] 2 SCR 9, evidence of a novel, and exclusive, categorization of sexual offenders fell at these fences. See also *R v DD* 2000 SCC 43, [2000] 2 SCR 275, and, for an even more outrageous example, *R v J-LJ* 2000 SCC 51, [2000] 2 SCR 600.

[177] By the House of Commons Science and Technology Committee in *Forensic Science on Trial* HC 96–1 (2005), [173].

[178] *R v Tilley* [1985] VR 505 accepted stylistic analysis as a sufficiently well-developed field, but denied that it was appropriate to apply it to the material available. See also *R v Watson* [1987] 1 Qd R 440, 465.

[179] See *United States Shipping Board v The St Albans* [1931] AC 632, now further reinforced by the Civil Procedure Rules Pt 35; but see, on the qualification, *R v Hersey* (n9), in which lay opinion identifying a voice was admitted, but expert evidence relating to the difficulty of doing so, excluded.

[180] (1981) 76 Cr App Rep 271. See also *R v Smith* [1987] VR 907 (in which evidence of a psychologist was rejected on the question of the reliability of eye witness identification); *Hersey* (n9) (in which the rejection related to the reliability of voice identification). These conclusions seem not to have been contradicted by the reversal of the decision in *Mackenney* in the subsequent reference to the Court of Appeal in [2003] EWCA Crim 3643, [2004] 2 Cr App R 32; see the valuable comments by Roberts (2004) 8 *E&P* 215.

was not permitted to give evidence of his opinion of the likelihood of a witness telling lies. He was not medically qualified and, even if he had been, the only evidence he could have given related not to the incapacity of the witness to tell the truth,[181] but to his disinclination to do so, which the jury was able, and indeed bound, to decide for itself. Much the same approach is being increasingly taken towards questions of the application of standards well within the knowledge of the court, such as those to be expected of a solicitor,[182] although it is important for the court to preserve an open mind, and not to exclude the expert evidence inflexibly when it can be of help.[183]

It is for the judge to determine,[184] preferably on the documents rather than on a voir dire,[185] whether the witness had undergone such a course of special study or experience as will render him expert in a particular subject,[186] and it is not necessary for the expertise to have been acquired professionally. In *R v Silverlock*,[187] for example, the Court for Crown Cases Reserved considered that a solicitor might be treated as an expert in handwriting even if he had acquired his knowledge as an amateur. Most of the reported cases on the subject of a witness's skill are concerned with evidence of foreign law discussed in Chapter XVI. Specialization is a matter of degree, but the area of expertise should not be taken at too high a level of abstraction.[188] It is, however, not necessary for a doctor to have specialized in studies concerned with the rate at which the blood destroys alcohol before he can give evidence on such a subject, based on analysts' tables,[189] a stenographer who has familiarized herself with the contents of a tape recording may be treated as a temporary expert,[190] a police officer's experience in investigating traffic accidents may make him an expert for the purpose of reconstructing a particular motor accident[191] or for testifying

---

[181]   Which is permissible: *Toohey v Metropolitan Police Comr* [1965] AC 595, [1965] 1 All ER 506. See also *Re J (a minor)* [1984] Fam Law 308.

[182]   See *Bown v Gould & Swayne* (n108); in New Zealand, *Bindon v Bishop* [2003] 2 NZLR 136; in Australia, *O'Brien v Gillespie* (1997) 41 NSWLR 549.

[183]   See the especially helpful analysis of Evans LJ in *United Bank of Kuwait v Prudential Property Services Ltd* (n107).

[184]   See *R v Bonython* (1984) 38 SASR 45 for a particularly clear exposition of the issues to be considered by the judge in determining the admissibility of expert opinion.

[185]   *R v G* [2004] EWCA Crim 1240, [2004] 2 Cr App R 638, [32]. It is open to the judge to remove a witness's expert status in the course of the trial if he deems it necessary: *R v Skingley and Barrett* (1999) unreported CA, 17 December.

[186]   Under Civil Procedure Rule 35.4 identification of expert and relevant field of expertise must be made in advance.   [187]   [1894] 2 QB 766; *R v Bunnis* (1964) 50 WWR 422. Cf *Clark v Ryan*.

[188]   So membership of a similar, but different, profession may not be enough: see e.g. *Sansom v Metcalf Hambleton & Co* (1997) 57 Con LR 88 (evidence of structural engineer inadmissible against chartered surveyor).

[189]   *R v Somers* [1963] 3 All ER 808, [1963] 1 WLR 1306; *R v Richards* [1974] 3 All ER 696, [1975] 1 WLR 131. A biologist working as a forensic DNA analyst who frequently testified as an expert was permitted to give a statistical evaluation of DNA evidence in *R v Fisher* (2003) 179 CCC3d 138, despite having no statistical qualification.

[190]   *Hopes and Lavery v HM Adv* (n14). See also *R v Clare; R v Peach* (n14), in which a police officer acquired expertise in identifying those shown on a security video film by studying it, and was permitted to testify as an expert in the interpretation of that film.

[191]   *R v Oakley* [1979] RTR 417; *R v Murphy* [1980] QB 434, [1980] 2 All ER 325.

to the normal dosage of a drug addict,[192] and a professional enhancer and interpreter[193] of videotape evidence may be considered expert, even if using relatively unsophisticated techniques.[194] But experience in driving does not make a bombardier an expert on the subject of the capabilities of someone charged with dangerous driving.[195] Addiction to a drug may give sufficient experience to permit credence to be given to the addict's identification of a substance as that drug.[196]

An expert's testimony may be vulnerable on account of previous judicial criticism of his deployment of it in a previous case, or because of perceived conflict of interest, but such matters, unless extreme, go more to weight than to admissibility.[197]

NON-EXPERT OPINION

When, in the words of an American judge,[198] 'the facts from which a witness received an impression were 'too evanescent in their nature to be recollected, or too complicated to be separately and distinctly narrated', a witness may state his opinion or impression. He is better equipped than the jury to form it, and it is impossible for him to convey an adequate idea of the premises on which he acted to the jury:[199]

Unless opinions, estimates and inferences which men in their daily lives reach without conscious ratiocination as a result of what they perceived with their physical senses were treated in the law of evidence as if they were mere statements of fact, witnesses would find themselves unable to communicate to the judge an accurate impression of the events they were seeking to describe.

There is nothing in the nature of a closed list of cases in which non-expert opinion evidence is admissible. Typical instances are provided by questions concerning age,[200] speed,[201] weather, handwriting, and identity in general. Proof of handwriting, is discussed in Chapter XV, but a word may be said here about identification. When a witness says, 'That is the man I saw the other day', pointing to someone in court, or 'That is the man whose wedding I attended', pointing to a figure in a photograph,[202] or, 'That is a copy of a picture of which I have seen the original',[203] there is clearly a sense in which it is true to say that he is expressing an opinion. He is not simply narrating what he has perceived in the past; but the perception on which his statements are founded cannot be conveyed to the jury in the

---

[192] *White v HM Adv* 1986 SCCR 224; *R v Hodges and Walker* [2003] EWCA Crim 290, [2003] 2 Cr App Rep 247, irrespective of the unreliability of the sources of information: see *R v Ibrahima* [2005] EWCA Crim 1436, [30] (drug counsellor). In Australia, police evidence as to the sort of pipes used by drug addicts has been regarded as evidence of fact and not opinion at all: *R v Barker* (1988) 34 ACR 141.

[193] But not one of the depicted persons as an expert as such on the nature of what was depicted: *R v TA* [2003] NSWCCA 191, 139 ACR 30.

[194] *R v Briddick* [2001] EWCA Crim 984. See also *Westminster City Council v McDonald* [2003] EWHC 2698 (Admin) (absence of scientific acoustic measurement); *R v Atkins* [2009] EWCA Crim 1876 (no statistical database for visual mapping).

[195] *R v Davies* (n53). See also *Seyfert v Burnaby Hospital Society* (n51); *Gaudiuso v Walker* (n51).

[196] *R v Chatwood* [1980] 1 All ER 467, [1980] 1 WLR 874.

[197] *R v Pedder* [2004] EWCA Crim 2094, [17] (criticism); *R v Stubbs* (n163), [59] (conflict). The position is similar in Australia: see *R v Li* [2003] NSWCCA 290, 139 ACR 281.

[198] Gibson J cited in VII Wigmore, 12.

[199] Seventeenth Report of the Law Reform Committee, [3].   [200] *R v Cox* [1898] 1 QB 179.

[201] Road Traffic Regulation Act 1984, s 89.   [202] *R v Tolson* (1864) 4 F & F 103.

[203] *Lucas v Williams & Sons* [1892] 2 QB 113.

same way that the premises for, or against, an inference of negligence can be narrated. In *Fryer v Gathercole*,[204] in order to prove the publication of a libellous pamphlet to friends of a female witness, she was allowed to swear that she received a pamphlet from the defendant, lent it to friends in succession, and put her name on it when it was ultimately returned to her. She said that she believed the pamphlet returned by the last borrower to be identical with that received from the defendant, but she could not swear to this fact because it was possible that another pamphlet had been substituted for the original. Pollock CB disposed of an objection to the effect that her evidence was mere opinion by saying 'There are many cases of identification where the law would be rendered ridiculous if positive certainty were required from witnesses', and Parke B said, in the course of the argument; 'In the identification of person you compare in your mind the man you have seen with the man you see at the trial. The same rule belongs to every species of identification.' Every fact on which the identification is based cannot be satisfactorily given in evidence.

In some cases, a non-expert witness has been allowed to give evidence of opinion on a subject on which expert testimony would have been admissible. Acquaintances of a person whose sanity is in issue may be asked whether they consider him sane, but this is not so much a demand for an opinion as a 'compendious mode of ascertaining the result of the actual observations of the witness'. Did the witness observe any action by the accused characteristically associated with persons of dubious sanity? Similarly, in *R v Davies*,[205] the Courts Martial Appeal Court held that, on a charge of drunken driving, a non-medical witness might state that he formed the impression that the accused had been drinking, but it was said that he must state the facts on which that impression was based, and it was also held that the witness ought not to have been allowed to add that he believed the accused to be unfit to drive, although an expert could have testified to this effect. In an interesting decision in South Africa,[206] it has been held that lay eyewitness evidence of a collision between motor vehicles was to be preferred to expert evidence reconstructing the collision from physical traces alone,[207] unless it were completely incredible.

In *R v Beckett*,[208] the accused was charged with maliciously damaging a plate-glass window worth more than £5. The fact that the window was worth more than £5 was an essential ingredient of the offence, and it was held to have been proved by the statement of an assistant superintendent of the post office, who swore that the window was worth more than £5. In cross-examination, it became clear that his evidence was largely based on hearsay, but the Court of Criminal Appeal upheld the conviction on the footing that the case was proved by the witness's statement of his personal opinion as to the value of the window. The basis of the admissibility of this evidence was not considered by the court, and the decision is perhaps open to question on the ground that it raises insoluble problems of degree. Is it confined to non-expert opinion concerning the value of commonplace objects? If so, what are commonplace objects? Does it apply where the witness opines that the value of an article exceeds a specified sum by a considerable amount? If so, what is a

---

204   (1849) 13 Jur 542.
205   (n53). See also *Croft v Jewell* [1993] PIQR P270; *Sherrard v Jacob* (n7); *R v German* [1947] 4 DLR 68; *Burrows v Hanlin* [1930] SASR 54; *R v McKimmie* [1957] VLR 93; *R v Spooner* [1957] VLR 540; *R v Kelly* [1958] VLR 412; *A-G (Rudley) v James Kenny* (1960) 94 ILTR 185 (77 LQR 166); *Blackie v Police* [1966] NZLR 910; *Grant v R* [1982] 2 SCR 819.   206   *Motor Vehicle Assurance Fund v Kenny* 1984 (4) SA 432.
207   As noted, 546, this is a subject sometimes thought only marginally of a sufficient status to be appropriate for the admission of expert testimony.   208   (1913) 8 Cr App Rep 204.

considerable amount? But *R v Beckett* was cited in a South Australian case, in which it was said that the court may always act on non-expert opinion as to value when no specialized knowledge is required.[209]

SECTION 4. REFORM OF THE RULE[210]

Reform of the rule in England was first considered in detail by the Law Reform Committee in its 17th Report 'Evidence of Opinion and Expert Evidence'.[211] The Report was, however, somewhat conservative in its approach, and rejected radical reform, for example for a switch to a system of court experts.

Some further measures of reform were implemented, such as rules enabling the limitation of numbers of experts,[212] to direct that a 'without prejudice' meeting of experts take place in advance of the trial,[213] and those enabling expert reports to be used in criminal proceedings without the necessity for the expert to testify orally.[214]

As described above, despite such reform, pressure continued to build, and Lord Woolf in his interim report identified the cost and partisan nature of much expert evidence as one of the principal defects of the system of civil litigation,[215] finding concern about it second only to that relating to discovery.[216] He found, however, that recommendations designed to limit the use of expert evidence aroused more opposition than those in any other area,[217] especially in relation to the use of single experts.[218] The final recommendations[219] were accordingly somewhat more muted, and, as seen, still do not make the use of single experts mandatory. In relation to criminal proceedings some earlier recommendations have now been implemented in the new Criminal Procedure Rules. Unease about the reliability of expert evidence has, however, persisted,[220] and the Law Commission has issued a consultation paper with a view to further reform.[221] It may consider the use of an Australian 'hot-tub' approach under which opposing experts question each other.[222] It may be expected that pressure for reform will continue to be felt as scientific knowledge and technique continues to advance, and to become used ever more widely. It must necessarily be the case that the increase of knowledge of the average juror cannot be expected to keep up with such scientific progress, so the need for expert guidance will continue to grow.[223] It may also be the

---

[209] *Wise v Musolino* [1936] SASR 447. In some cases, judicial notice may be taken that the value of an object exceeds the specified sum or evidence of its purchase price might suffice.

[210] For comparative appraisal by several members of the judiciary of different approaches to reform in a number of jurisdictions, see 23 *Civ JQ* 367–410.   [211] Cmnd 4489 (1970).

[212] RSC Ord 38, r 4.

[213] RSC Ord 38, r 38. Further encouragement to such meetings, and to the submission of agreed joint reports has been provided by the grant of immunity from suit to the expert in respect of such agreement: *Stanton v Callaghan* (n26).   [214] Criminal Justice Act 1988, s 30.

[215] *Access to Justice: Interim Report* (1995) [3.7].   [216] Paragraph 23.1.

[217] *Access to Justice: Final Report* (1996) [13.5].   [218] Paragraph 13.16.

[219] Recommendations 156–73.

[220] See House of Commons Science and Technology Committee 7th Report *Forensic Science on Trial* (25 July 2005).

[221] *The Admissibility of Expert Evidence in Criminal Proceedings in England and Wales* CP 190 (April 2009).

[222] See Edmond (2008) 27 CJQ 51; although in England experts are reluctant to criticize each other's opinions: *Re W (Threshold Criteria)* [2007] EWCA Civ 102, [2007] 2 FLR 98.

[223] Significant changes were introduced in the latest revision of CPR 35 coming into force in October 2009.

case that, with the provisions mentioned above for advance disclosure, the role of experts in the conduct of legal proceedings will become more diversified, and some experts used not so much as witnesses whose reports will need to be disclosed, but simply as advisers to the parties whose work will attract litigation privilege,[224] and be immune from such disclosure.[225]

[224] For some indication that this is occurring, see (2000) *IHL* May 86. It may not be possible to recover costs if the prior approval of the court has not been secured.

[225] This is already commonplace in the United States.

XII

HEARSAY IN GENERAL

The hearsay rule is one of the most complex and most confusing of the exclusionary rules of evidence. Lord Reid said that it was 'difficult to make any general statement about the law of hearsay which is entirely accurate'.[1] Both its definition, and the ambit of exceptions to it were unclear. It led to the exclusion of much reliable evidence, and, on that account, exceptions were created ad hoc, often without full consideration of their implications. In this jurisdiction,[2] at long last, the situation has changed. Fundamental statutory reform has now been implemented in both civil[3] and criminal proceedings.[4] This permits shorter and simpler discussion of the topic in a work of this nature: some general matters relating to hearsay at common law, remain useful as a background and foundation to understand the new statutory provisions for civil[5] and criminal[6] proceedings, which will then be separately mentioned.

The first section of this chapter will consider, in outline, the definition, rationale, development and reform of the hearsay rule at common law; the second will examine more closely the scope of the rule, implied assertions, res gestae, the rule against narrative, and the extent to which admissions constitute an exception to the rule.

SECTION 1. THE NATURE OF THE RULE

This section contains a short statement of the hearsay rule at common law, explains why such an exclusionary rule was thought necessary, and then indicates the tenor of its development and reform.

STATEMENT

According to the rule against hearsay at common law, as formulated in Chapter I, a statement other than one made by a person while giving oral evidence in the proceedings was

---

[1] *Myers v DPP* [1965] AC 1001, [1964] 2 All ER 881; 1019, 884.
[2] Not only in England, but in most Commonwealth jurisdictions. The United States alone among major common law jurisdictions seems more conservative; see 49 *Hastings LJ* 477 et seq (1998).
[3] Civil Evidence Act 1995.
[4] Criminal Justice Act 2003, Pt 11, ch 2, largely adopting the recommendation of the Law Commission in Law Com No 245 *Evidence in Criminal Proceedings: Hearsay and Related Topics* Cm 3670 (1997).
[5] This will include those matters in which the rule remains the same for both civil and criminal proceedings.
[6] This will include also confessions, treated separately from admissions in general, which will be treated in this chapter, but also extending more widely into non-hearsay issues involved in the overlapping area of police questioning, and inferences from pre-trial silence.

inadmissible as evidence of any fact stated.[7] The rule applied to all kinds of statement, whether made orally, in writing, or by conduct,[8] and equally to hearsay of all degrees.[9] It was less clear how far it extended to assumptions of fact inferred from words or deeds. This formulation conflates two common law rules: the rule that the previous statements of the witness who is testifying were inadmissible as evidence of the facts stated (sometimes spoken of as the 'rule against narrative', or the 'rule against self-corroboration'), and the rule that statements by persons other than the witness who is testifying were inadmissible as evidence of the facts stated (the rule against hearsay in the strict sense). At common law, there was only one clear exception to the first rule: an informal admission proved against the party who made it.[10] In Chapter VI it was said that, at common law, the previous consistent statements of witnesses were usually inadmissible as evidence of consistency although inconsistent statements might be proved, not as evidence of the facts stated, but in order to cast doubt on the witness's testimony. It was also shown that previous consistent statements might be proved by way of exception to the general exclusionary rule in the case of complaints of sexual offences, statements forming part of the res gestae, statements rebutting a suggestion that the witness's testimony was a recent invention, and sundry statements of the accused. In these cases, the witness's previous statements were not, strictly speaking, received as evidence of the facts stated, and therefore not received under exceptions to the rule against hearsay. There were, however, many common law exceptions to the rule against hearsay in the strict sense.

The law of evidence distinguishes between a witness's statements of fact and opinion. This should be reflected in a complete formulation of the common law rule against hearsay. A full version of that adopted in this book should therefore read 'any statement other than one made by a person while giving oral evidence in the proceedings is inadmissible as evidence of any fact or opinion stated'. This chapter is primarily concerned with the common law rule against hearsay in the strict sense. It has never been fully formulated judicially,[11] but most authorities concur in the view that:[12]

Evidence of a statement made to a witness by a person who is not himself called as a witness may or may not be hearsay. It is hearsay and inadmissible when the object of the evidence is to establish the truth of what is contained in the statement. It is not hearsay and is admissible when it is proposed to establish by evidence, not the truth of the statement, but the fact that it was made.

---

[7] Documents may, however, be placed before the jury by agreement between the parties, and taken into consideration by it, without becoming evidence in the case, and so not becoming subject to the hearsay rule: see e.g. *R v Opwa-Otto* [2004] EWCA Crim 251, [17].

[8] *Chandrasekera (alias Alisandiri) v R* [1937] AC 220, [1936] 3 All ER 865 (signs made by woman dying as a result of her throat being cut); although it is not always recognized at trial: see *R v Perciballi* (2001) 154 CCC (3d) 481 (statement that third party pointed out telephone boxes).

[9] That is, irrespective of the number of intermediate communicators between the original source and the testifying witness.

[10] The exception of the admission has been described as the only 'clear' one, because of the possibility that previous statements of witnesses received as part of the res gestae are received as evidence of the facts stated.

[11] It, is however, defined for the purposes of the Civil Evidence Act 1995 by s 1(2)(a), and effectively, as indicated by the rubric, for the purposes of the Criminal Justice Act 2003 by s 114(1), as supplemented by s 115. A definition similar to that proposed above, which appeared in earlier editions of this work, was explicitly approved by the House of Lords in *R v Sharp* [1988] 1 All ER 65, [1988] 1 WLR 7; 68, 11.

[12] *Subramaniam v Public Prosecutor* [1956] 1 WLR 965, 969.

This crucial distinction was overlooked by the trial judge in the case from which these words are quoted. The appellant was charged with being in possession of firearms without lawful excuse, and his defence was that he was acting under duress of threats uttered by Malayan terrorists. The judge would not allow the accused to state what had been said by the terrorists, and the Judicial Committee advised that the conviction should be quashed, because the reported assertions were tendered as original evidence and ought to have been received as such.[13]

RATIONALE

The development of the hearsay rule coincided with the stabilization of a recognizably modern form of trial. Whether the exclusion of hearsay was based upon distrust of the abilities of the jury to evaluate it, or upon faith in the power of cross-examination, or both,[14] it remains to be seen what frailties required such elaborate precautions.[15] Their examination may help to explain the basis for the development of the rule.

It is helpful to start by contrasting the reasoning process involved in the acceptance of direct testimony with that involved in the acceptance of hearsay.[16] If a witness testifies to a relevant event that he has himself observed, say 'that X existed', the trier of fact is invited to accept that the witness did perceive X, that he has remembered correctly what he perceived,[17] that there is no ambiguity in his relation of X to the court, and that he is sincere in his testimony. Sincerity may be promoted by the sanction of the oath and the prospect of prosecution for perjury, but the principal guaranties for these factors are provided by the witness's availability for cross-examination to probe into them. Ultimately the trier of fact must be satisfied both that the witness believes that X existed, and that his belief is justified.

It is obvious that any danger in accepting these conclusions is multiplied when hearsay is tendered. In such cases, the trier of fact must be satisfied that the witness believes he heard a third party say 'X exists'; that the witness's belief was justified; that the third party believed that X existed; and that the third party's belief was justified. This must be done in the absence of any safeguard from the ordinary conditions of testimony[18] in relation to the third party; in the absence of any opportunity to probe the third party by cross-examination; and despite the diminution of the value of these safeguards in relation to the testifying witness, on account of the severance of any direct link between his testimony and the proposition that the trier of fact is invited to support as a result of it. A direct witness, who asserts that X existed, can be cross-examined much more fruitfully about his

---

[13] For a similar oversight by a trial judge, see *R v Willis* [1960] 1 All ER 331, [1960] 1 WLR 55; and for one by magistrates, see *Woodhouse v Hall* (1980) 72 Cr App Rep 39.

[14] The history of the rule has generated significant debate and dispute. For a modern indication of thinking, from an American perspective, see Friedman [1998] *Crim LR* 697, 700–5.

[15] Such frailties have led to convictions being regarded as obtained contrary to basic principles of justice, even in jurisdictions with a totally different tradition and form of trial, when dependent upon evidence from anonymous informants: see further, 233.

[16] For a graphic exposition of the basis of the hearsay rules, see Graham (1982) 5 *Un of Ill LR* 887.

[17] Scientific investigation into these factors is presented and evaluated in the Australian Law Reform Commission's Research Paper No 3 *Hearsay Evidence* (1981) ch 2.

[18] Namely, that the third party did not speak on oath, and was not liable to prosecution for perjury if he were lying.

perception and memory of X of which he claims experience, than the hearsay witness, who merely testifies that he heard a third party say 'X exists', can be cross-examined about what he claims he heard.

It was largely because of the increased dangers of misperception, forgetfulness, ambiguity, and insincerity, coupled with the decreased effectiveness of conventional safeguards, that hearsay was regarded as so particularly vulnerable as to require a special exclusionary rule.[19] Because dangers of ambiguity and insincerity relate to the existence of belief, while those of misperception and forgetfulness relate to its reflection of reality, some commentators explicitly utilized the difference between them in their definition of hearsay.[20] Because cross-examination is often supposed to be more effective in relation to perception and memory, the diminution of such dangers in particular circumstances was often used to help to justify special exceptions.[21]

It should be noted that it was possible to explain many of the results of the hearsay rule by reference to the somewhat different confrontation principle: namely, that a party, and especially the accused, was entitled to confront his opponents as an essential element of a fair trial. Such a rule is embodied in the European Convention on Human Rights,[22] and in the Constitution of the United States.[23] Although such a rule applies under different conditions, and must be made subject to different exceptions, there is significant overlap in the standard situation of the statement of an absent witness of the existence of a vital element in the case that cannot otherwise be proved.[24] It has provoked sharp disagreement between the European Court of Human Rights[25] and the English courts.[26]

In defining common law hearsay, implicit reference was made to the existence of these dangers in applying the exclusionary rule only to situations in which the out-of-court assertion was tendered for the truth of that which it asserted. If it were tendered merely as direct evidence of the fact of its having been asserted, or as circumstantial evidence of the belief of its auditor in the truth of the matter asserted, no question arose as to the sincerity,

---

[19] In *Teper v R* [1952] AC 480, [1952] 2 All ER 447; 486, 449, Lord Normand summarized the classic rationale for exclusion as being: 'It is not the best evidence and it is not delivered on oath. The truthfulness and accuracy of the person whose words are spoken by another witness cannot be tested by cross-examination, and the light which his demeanour would throw on his testimony is lost.' Such distrust lingers on, and may mitigate against the order of a new trial in which hearsay will predominate: see *Kent v M&L Management Ltd* [2005] EWHC 2546 (Ch), [15](vii).

[20] Lempert and Saltzburg *A Modern Approach to Evidence* (2nd edn, 1982) 357, 358.

[21] See e.g. United States Federal Rules of Evidence, r 803 (24) and r 804(b)(6).

[22] Articles 6(1), 6(3)(d).

[23] Sixth Amendment, often by American commentators traced back to *Raleigh's Trial* (1603) 2 St Tr 15. A dominant role has now been accorded to confrontation, at least in relation to 'testimonial' hearsay, by the Supreme Court in *Crawford v Washington* (2004) 541 US 36, 124 S Ct R 1354; for further exegesis, see *Davis v Washington; Hammon v Indiana* 547 US 813 (2006); for prospective support of such an approach, see Friedman (2004) *E&P* 1; and for retrospective criticism, see Ho (2004) *E&P* 147. It has not been regarded as so revolutionary as to be given retrospective effect: *Whorton v Bockting* 549 US 406, 127 S Ct R 1173 (2007); but has been interpreted so as to exclude from his trial for her murder of statements made by a wife killed by the accused: *Giles v California* 128 S Ct R 2678 (2008). For comparison with the position under the European Convention, see O'Brian 121 *LQR* 481 (2005).

[24] Indeed, in Scotland, it has been held that the admissibility of hearsay in criminal cases under s 259 of the Criminal Procedure (Scotland) Act 1995 is saved from breach of the Convention only by the provision in Scotland of the necessity for corroboration: see *HM Adv v Nulty* 2000 SCCR 431; *HM Adv v Beggs (No 3)* [2002] SLT 153.   [25] *Al-Khaweja and Tahery v R* (2009) 49 EHRR 1.

[26] *R v Horncastle* [2009] UKSC 14.

memory, or perception of utterance of the third party, and in many cases, there was little possibility of ambiguity. All four dangers were much more potent if the assertion were tendered to prove the truth of the matter asserted. Definitions of the type advanced here have been categorized as assertion-based definitions because of their concentration upon the role played by the assertion.[27] Other definitions, which stress the absence from the courtroom of the original source of the information, have been categorized as declarant-based definitions.[28] The principal reason for adopting the former approach was to cater for the assimilation of the exclusion both of the out-of-court assertions of third parties, and of those of the witness who is testifying.

It had also to be remembered that, if the hearsay rule were to be effective, it had to exclude circumstantial as well as direct inference. As Thayer put it:[29]

…the hearsay rule operates in two ways: (a) it forbids using the credit of an absent declarant as the basis of an inference, and (b) it forbids using in the same way the mere evidentiary fact of the statement as having been made under such and such circumstances.

There would have been little point in excluding testimony that a named third party said 'X exists' for the purpose of showing directly that X existed, if the same testimony were nevertheless to be accepted as evidence that the third party *said* that X existed, perhaps coupled with testimony as to the third party's general high reputation for credibility, and then to permit the jury to infer on that basis that X existed. The analysis of testimony inviting this sort of circumstantial inference caused some difficulty in borderline cases. Occasionally, it led to the misclassification of non-hearsay as hearsay.[30] More often hearsay went unrecognized, and, if the definition had been more widely drawn, hardly any piece of testimony would have been completely free of its tentacles.

DEVELOPMENT

Parts of the rule were very ancient,[31] but like much of the law of evidence it began to crystallize in the late seventeenth century. Although apparently disregarded in some contexts,[32] it had become well established by the beginning of the nineteenth century, and was brought to prominence in the Dickensian saga of *Wright v Doe d Tatham*.[33] For some inexplicable reason,[34] that case turned on the admissibility of some letters written to a testator long before his death, tendered to rebut suggestions that he was a congenital idiot incapable of managing his affairs. In the course of the elaborate series of arguments and judgments that

[27] Park (1981) 65 *Minn LR* 423.

[28] See e.g., in South Africa, Law of Evidence (Amendment) Act No 45, s 4.

[29] Thayer *Legal Essays* (1907), 270. See also McHugh J in *Pollitt v R* (1992) 174 CLR 558, 620: 'The hearsay rule would be meaningless in practice if it prohibited a statement being used directly to prove a fact contained in a statement but allowed the statement to be used circumstantially to prove a state of mind from which could be inferred the existence of the very fact which could not be proved directly.' Cf Dawson and Gaudron JJ in the same case.

[30] See e.g. *R v Olisa* [1990] Crim LR 721; and more arguably *R v Irish* [1994] Crim LR 922.

[31] The rule allowing evidence of dying declarations as proof of the truth of their contents was shown by Thayer to antedate the exclusionary rule itself by some centuries.

[32] Such as low-level criminal prosecutions: see Langbein (1978) 45 *U of Chi LR* 263, 301.

[33] (1837) 7 Ad & El 313; aff'd (1838) 5 Cl & Fin 670. Other stages in the drama are reported in (1832) 2 Russ & M 1; (1834) 1 Ad & El 3 and (1837) 7 Ad & El 359.

[34] There was plenty of other much more direct evidence.

constitute the saga, many of the basic concepts and problems of hearsay[35] were ventilated. In the end, the letters were excluded.[36] The technicality of much of that discussion seems to have inhibited further development of the rule at common law, and it spluttered to an end soon afterwards.[37] Although sporadic efforts were made to create explicit exceptions in more modern times, the door was slammed shut by the declaration of Lord Reid in *Myers v DPP* that:[38]

If we are to extend the law it must be by the development and application of fundamental principles. We cannot introduce arbitrary conditions or limitations; that must be left to legislation: and if we do in effect change the law, we ought in my opinion only to do that in cases where our decision will produce some finality or certainty. If we disregard technicalities in this case and seek to apply principle and common sense, there are a number of parts of the existing law of hearsay susceptible of similar treatment... The only satisfactory solution is by legislation following on a wide survey of the whole field... A policy of make do and mend is no longer adequate.

Legislative reform of the rule had begun just as judicial moulding ceased at the end of the nineteenth century.[39] At first, it was limited to special situations, but when it was found that the results were acceptable, more general reform was mooted. Part of the reason for this was realization that the rule had been established to deal with an environment that had wholly changed,[40] and to cater for a system of the administration of justice that had also undergone considerable change.[41] This led to the realization that not all hearsay was unreliable, and that tribunals could cope with its assessment perfectly capably. Unfortunately, the tension between the technical rigidity of the rule and the need to do justice led to rather strained interpretation of basic concepts,[42] tending to undermine the whole edifice.

REFORM OF THE RULE[43]

Although Wigmore regarded the common law hearsay rule as the 'most characteristic rule of the Anglo-American law of Evidence—a rule which may be esteemed, next to jury trial, the greatest contribution of that eminently practical legal system to the world's methods

---

[35] And its interaction with evidence of opinion.

[36] Although, in the final stages, the strictly hearsay point was no longer being pressed.

[37] The last strong avowal of judicial ability to shape the rule came in *Sugden v Lord St Leonards* (1876) 1 PD 154, 241; the first strong denial in *Sturla v Freccia* (1880) 5 App Cas 623, 647.

[38] Note 1, 1021, 885. The comment was made in full knowledge, and approval, of the recommendations of the Law Reform Committee for wholesale reform of the rule, and probably in the expectation of their adoption by the Criminal Law Revision Committee, and speedy enactment thereafter.

[39] A clear example is the Bankers' Books Evidence Act 1879.

[40] Especially in reliance upon modern systems of record keeping in business, or more prosaically in the mobility and aggregation of populations. *Myers v DPP* (n1) was itself a case in which all turned on the accuracy of stored records, and in which oral testimony from those who had once had personal knowledge would have been valueless.

[41] Most notably by the demise of the jury in civil proceedings, and the disappearance of witnesses from the committal stage of criminal proceedings.

[42] See especially Ashworth and Pattenden (1986) 102 *LQR* 292; Birch in Smith P (ed) *Essays in Honour of JC Smith* 24 (1987); Pattenden (1993) 56 *MLR* 138.

[43] Different approaches to reform of the rule are extensively discussed in Law Reform Commission of Australia Research Paper No 9 *Hearsay Law Reform—Which Approach?* (1982).

of procedure',[44] not all views were quite so complimentary, with, for example, both Lord Reid[45] and Lord Diplock[46] judicially categorizing it as absurd.[47]

As mentioned above, the rule developed alongside that of the newer form of trial by jury, and was concerned to prevent its being undermined by the introduction of evidence that could not easily be tested by cross-examination in open court. Both of these justifications are now much weaker than once they were. The overwhelming majority of trials is now conducted without a jury, and a more literate and technologically advanced society provides, and depends upon, more reliable methods of keeping track of what has happened than can possibly be provided by the unassisted recollection of witnesses, even though exposed to cross-examination by an opponent. It remains true, however, that, in some circumstances, such records are not available, and the hearsay rule can then be utilized to prevent the deliberate dilution of proof by straining out the testimony of those with direct personal knowledge of relevant events, and by seeking to substitute for it the bland reportage of those who know only what they have been told by others.[48] The business of reform thus sought to prevent the rule from causing unnecessary difficulty, while at the same time preserving its efficiency.

This became a cause for concern across the whole range of legal proceedings, and in all common law jurisdictions.[49] This section will consider, first, the strategic choices for reform, then its accomplishment in this jurisdiction, subdivided into civil and criminal proceedings, and finally make brief comparison with reform elsewhere.

Strategic choices

Once reform of some sort has been decided upon, the major question is how extensive it should be, both as regards its width, in terms of the types of proceeding it should affect, and as regards its depth, in terms of the degree to which the rule should be changed. One of the defects of the rule as it had developed in English law was that it had become complicated by a patchwork of interpretation, modification, and reform, not always fully implemented, which led to differences between the operation of the rule in higher and lower courts, in civil and criminal proceedings, and sometimes between different forms of proceeding within those categories.

In England, the traditional approach was to distinguish sharply between the operation, and reform, of the rule in civil proceedings, and in criminal. The Law Commission accordingly worked upon the assumption[50] that the rules should continue to be different in civil and criminal proceedings, with more radical reform reserved for the former.

---

[44] V *Wigmore on Evidence* 1364.   [45] *Myers* (n1), 1019, 884.

[46] In *Jones v Metcalfe* [1967] 3 All ER 205, [1967] 1 WLR 1286; 208, 1291.

[47] See also *R v Gilfoyle* [1996] 1 Cr App Rep 302, 325: 'Although, in our opinion, the making of the statements in the present case was relevant and admissible under the existing complex hearsay rules, the fact that dubbing them "hearsay" sufficed to proscribe them from the jury's judgment is hardly likely to enhance public esteem of the criminal process.'   [48] See *R v Druken* (2002) 164 CCC (3d) 115.

[49] Even in the United States: see symposium on reform in 76 *Minn LR* 363–555 (1991).

[50] Law Com No 216, Cm 2321 (1993) [1.2] stressed that its consideration was restricted to the reform of the rule in civil proceedings because a separate reference was then pending in relation to criminal proceedings. The report on that reference Law Com 245, Cm 3670 (1997), did not explicitly consider adoption of the civil rules as such, but rejection was implicit in its eschewal of its radical options 2 and 3.

It was a matter of dispute whether civil proceedings before magistrates should be governed by the same rules as proceedings in the High Court.[51] The Civil Evidence Act 1995 provides for the same law to apply in both types of proceeding. There has been less explicit discussion in relation to reform in criminal proceedings as between those before magistrates, and those before judge and jury.[52] Despite the absence of explicit discussion, both the argument and definition in the reports both of the Criminal Law Revision Committee[53] and the Law Commission[54] envisaged proceedings[55] before magistrates, and before judge and jury, to be governed by the same rules, and the Criminal Justice Act 2003 so enacts.[56]

The problem of whether to apply the same rules within criminal proceedings to the defence in the same way as to the prosecution was the subject of explicit discussion by the Law Commission.[57] The view was taken that to have different rules[58] should be rejected, since, given the high standard required for conviction, it might lead to more unjust acquittals by permitting falsely manufactured evidence to tip the balance. It was also felt that it might lead to the anomaly that the prosecution would be entitled to cross-examine defence evidence that it could not itself have adduced in chief. Its final consideration was that any unfairness would be cured by the inclusionary residual discretion which it recommended. It should be remembered that both the common law exclusionary discretion, and its statutory counterpart,[59] operate only in favour of the defence.

These considerations relate only to the *general* rule. It does not follow that the rule will apply in exactly the same way to all types of civil or criminal proceeding,[60] to all types of evidence, to all types of issue, or in respect of all types of witness. Thus, the rule does not apply in the ordinary way to applications for interim remedies,[61] or to the use of transcripts in retrials of criminal proceedings ordered by the Court of Appeal.[62] Similarly, there has always been some relaxation in relation to some forms of evidence such as public documents.[63] In relation to different types of issue, statute now allows the admission of hearsay in connection with the upbringing, maintenance, or welfare of a child.[64] Numerous minor statutory exceptions apply to particular criminal proceedings.[65] The rule also applies

---

[51]   See Law Reform Committee 13th Report *Hearsay Evidence in Civil Proceedings* Cmnd 2964 (1966), [48]–[52]; Law Com No 216 (n50) [3.22]–[3.47].

[52]   Although some of the arguments in relation to civil proceedings relied upon the complexity in magistrates having to handle so many different versions of the rule, including one for criminal proceedings: see Law Com No 216 (n50) [3.23].

[53]   Eleventh Report Cmnd 4991, e.g. [246] and draft bill, cls 30(1), 45(1).

[54]   No 245 Cm 3670, e.g. [3.28] and draft bill, cls 1(1), 26(1).

[55]   So long as the strict rules of evidence apply.   [56]   Ss 114(1), 134(1).

[57]   [5.24], [8.136], [12.2]–[12.8].

[58]   Different in favouring greater exclusion of prosecution evidence; no one seems to have suggested a converse imbalance. The ECHR took a similar view in *Thomas v United Kingdom* (2007) 41 EHRR Supp 209.

[59]   Police and Criminal Evidence Act 1984, s 78; explicitly preserved by the Criminal Justice Act 2003 s 126(2).

[60]   See dicta, in Canada, suggesting a more relaxed approach to defence evidence in criminal proceedings: *R v Sheri* (2004) 185 CCC3d 155.

[61]   Affidavits are permitted, and required in certain cases, by the Civil Procedure Rules PD 25, [3.1].

[62]   Criminal Appeal Act 1968, Sch 2, [1], as substituted by s 131 of the Criminal Justice Act 2003.

[63]   See e.g. *Kennedy v Lyell* (1889) 14 App Cas 437; *R v Halpin* [1975] QB 907, [1975] 2 All ER 1124.

[64]   Children Act 1989, s 96, and SI 1993/621, building on the approach of the common law to adoption in *Official Solicitor v K* [1965] AC 201, [1963] 3 All ER 191.

[65]   See Law Commission Consultation Paper No 138 (1995), in which App C contains a non-exhaustive list of thirty.

differently to some types of witness, such as experts tendering the basis for their opinion.[66] So too the Criminal Justice Act 2003 relates only to criminal proceedings, with the result that its novel amendments,[67] exceptions,[68] and discretions,[69] do not apply elsewhere.

Reform in civil proceedings

General statutory change came first to civil proceedings in the form of the Evidence Act 1938, making some types of documentary hearsay admissible. That legislation was deliberately cast in cautious terms,[70] and effected no revolutionary change of attitude.[71] Such a change was, however, manifest in the proposal of the Law Reform Committee in its 13th Report, and the substantial and speedy enactment of its recommendations as the Civil Evidence Act 1968. The hallmark of this legislation was its radical approach in putting the admission of hearsay upon an overwhelmingly statutory basis.[72] The general approach was to place the matter more firmly in the hands of the parties allowing admission by consent, or in the absence of objection following the serving of notice. The Civil Evidence Act 1995 built upon these foundations.[73]

Alongside these overt reforms of the rules of admissibility, there has also been significant change in rules of procedure, militating in favour of greater pre-trial disclosure of evidence.[74] The Civil Procedure Rules Committee has even been accorded a power to modify the rules of evidence in the higher civil courts.[75]

Reform in criminal proceedings

Reform was slower here, influenced by concern not to prejudice the position of the accused. The matter was first generally considered by the Criminal Law Revision Committee in its 11th Report.[76] Its proposals were never enacted in England[77] in the form envisaged by the Committee, but it has since proved possible for the legislature to expand the admission of hearsay, most recently in the Criminal Justice Act 2003, although its provisions remain under risk of incompatibility with Art 6 of the European Convention on Human Rights, introduced to English law by the Human Rights Act 1998.[78]

Reform elsewhere

In a few jurisdictions, it has been possible to progress without legislation, by liberal judicial departure from the old constraints. The Supreme Court of Canada thus adopted what it describes as a 'principled' approach to the admission of hearsay,

---

[66] See e.g. *H v Schering Chemicals Ltd* [1983] 1 All ER 849, 853; *R v Abadom* [1983] 1 All ER 364, 76 Cr App Rep 48.   [67] For example, to the definition of 'statement' in CJA 2003, s 115.

[68] For example, for preparatory statements by third parties for use by experts in CJA 2003, s 127.

[69] For example, the 'safety valve' inclusionary discretion in CJA 2003, s 114(1)(d).

[70] See Lord Maugham LC (1939) 17 *Can BR* 475.

[71] See Report of the Committee on Supreme Court Practice and Procedure Cmnd 8878 (1953), [272]; 13th Report of Law Reform Committee Cmnd 2964 (1966), [11].

[72] Although much of the statute reproduced aspects of the common law, especially the exceptions enacted in s 9.   [73] Below Chapter XIII.

[74] 278.

[75] Civil Procedure Act 1997, Sch I, [4], although incidental only to procedural change, and not in derogation of fundamental human rights: *General Mediterranean Holdings v Patel* [1999] 3 All ER 673, [2000] 1 WLR 272.   [76] *Evidence: General* Cmd 4991 (1972) especially [224]–[271].

[77] Singapore was more receptive.   [78] See further 624.

admitting hearsay upon a sufficient showing of the reliability of, and necessity for, the evidence. It is noteworthy that this appears to be regarded as perfectly consistent with the Canadian Charter of Rights and Freedoms.[79] There were also signs[80] of such a development in Australia, before the passage of the Evidence Act (Cwth) 1995,[81] and in New Zealand.[82]

The most radical approaches to reform in most common law jurisdictions have been statutory, especially those implemented in South Africa and Scotland.

Canada

The Supreme Court of Canada never accepted the restrictive view of the House of Lords in *Myers v DPP*,[83] and found the legislature unwilling, or unable, to make a general reform of the hearsay rule.[84] Instead, it enthusiastically adopted what it described as 'a principled' approach to the admission of hearsay. This approach is taken by the court to have been initiated in *R v Khan*,[85] in which the prosecution was allowed to adduce hearsay emanating from a very young alleged victim of a sexual assault. In the following case of *R v Smith*, it was said that:[86]

Khan, therefore, signalled an end to the old categorical approach to the admission of hearsay evidence. Hearsay evidence is now admissible on a principled basis, the governing principles being the reliability of the evidence, and its necessity.

This reference to reliability, and necessity, was inspired by Wigmore's distillation of the justification for the creation of hearsay exceptions into this form. It was never intended by him to be applied directly to the outcome of cases, and predictably enough, the attempt to do so has led to difficulty.[87] It has been recognized that these concepts require judicial 'refinement',[88] that they are to be interpreted 'flexibly',[89] generally in accordance with

---

79   At least in a case in which there has been some provision for cross-examination at an earlier stage: see *R v Potvin* [1989] 1 SCR 525, which adopted such a view before this line of cases was subsequently approved in *R v Beck* (1996) 108 CCC (3d) 385.

80   See Mason CJ in *Walton v R* (1989) 166 CLR 283, 293: 'The hearsay rule should not be applied inflexibly...there will be occasions upon which circumstances will combine to render evidence sufficiently reliable for it to be placed before the jury for consideration and evaluation of the weight which should be placed upon it, notwithstanding that in strict terms it would be regarded as inadmissible hearsay.' See also Kirby P in *R v Astill* (1992) 63 ACR 148, 158: 'Reform, including judicial reform, of the hearsay rule appears to be both necessary and inevitable.'

81   Rather conservative in its admission of hearsay, and conservatively construed: see *Lee v R* [1998] HCA 60, (1998) 195 CLR 594; *R v Ambrosoli* [2002] NSWCCA 386, 133 ACR 461.

82   See Cooke CJ in *R v Baker* [1989] 1 NZLR 738, 741. For an approach residing somewhere between the Canadian and English, see *R v Manase* [2001] 1 NZLR 197. The admission of hearsay is not necessarily regarded as incompatible with the Bill of Rights: see *R v Cheprakov* [1997] NZLR 169, 173.

83   Note 1. Disapproved in *Ares v Venner* [1970] SCR 608.

84   Initiatives to that effect proposed by the Law Reform Commission of Canada in its *Report of Evidence* (1975), and the Federal/Provincial Task Force on Uniform Rules of Evidence (1982), were never implemented.

85   [1990] 2 SCR 531. It is, in fact, far from clear that this was intended as more than a limited ad hoc exception to the hearsay rule.

86   [1992] 2 SCR 915, 933 (telephone calls made by victim of murder shortly before her death).

87   There has been a vast increase in reported cases in this area.

88   *R v B (KG)* [1993] 1 SCR 740, 783.   89   *R v Hawkins* [1996] 3 SCR 1043, 1081.

other established rules of evidence,[90] and that a voir dire will normally be required.[91] A distinction was made between 'threshold' and 'substantial' application of these principles,[92] but has since been abandoned.[93] The new approach has been applied not only to hearsay in the strict sense, but also to cases where the witness is available to testify.[94] It has disturbed well-established rules relating to previous inconsistent statements,[95] competence of children,[96] of the mentally disturbed,[97] and of spouses,[98] and identification.[99] It was further extended to hearsay exceptions.[100] This would seem to mean that a voir dire will become necessary for every disputed piece of hearsay, a conclusion that certainly disturbed dissenters in the Supreme Court:[101]

I would not countenance the case-by-case application of the principled approach to statements falling within accepted exceptions to the rule against hearsay. Individual cases may illuminate or illustrate the need to modify a particular traditional exception, but every piece of evidence that falls within a traditional exception should not be subjected to the principled approach and the concomitant voir dire that it may entail. To do so would unnecessarily complicate the trial process and sacrifice experience, certainty and predictability in the name of the vague and uncertain mantra of principle.

Those who favour the wider admission of hearsay may accept increased imprecision when applied to the exclusionary rule, since it can only increase admissibility, but they will surely baulk at its application to exceptions, where it will decrease it. It is submitted that the doubts expressed in the quotation apply not just to its extension to exceptions, but to this whole development.[102]

The entirety of this jurisprudence was reviewed in *R v Khelawon*, which endorsed[103] the statement of the rule in *Mapara*, stressing that hearsay is presumptively inadmissible, but if, within a common law exception, presumptively admissible, subject to testing its reliability and necessity on a voir dire. In *Khelawon*, there were serious concerns about the reliability of the hearsay statement of a mentally disturbed inhabitant of a care home, whose statement was first made to a third party with a motive to encourage a complaint against the accused. The Supreme Court was particularly keen to overrule any suggestion of a sharp division between threshold and ultimate reliability, partly because it is so difficult to define them exclusively. No doubt in an effort to stem the tide of case law, the Supreme Court issued a single opinion, without any dissent. Unsurprisingly, it has failed

---

[90] *R v Couture* 2007 SCC 28, [2007] 2 SCR 516 (even so unsatisfactory a one as spousal incompetence). They may, however, be used to fill gaps left by statutory provision, as in *R v Lemay* (2004) 247 DLR (4th) 470 (S 31 of Canada Evidence Act).

[91] *R v Rockey* [1996] 3 SCR 829. Although it seems that no extrinsic evidence need be adduced: *R v WJF* [1999] 3 SCR 569, [41], and concession is permitted: *R v Campbell* (2002) 163 CCC (3d) 485.

[92] *R v UFJ* [1995] 3 SCR 764.   [93] *R v Khelawon* 2006 SCC 57, [93].

[94] B (KG) (n88), despite the obvious difficulty in such cases of establishing necessity, or, in cases of previous inconsistent statements, reliability.   [95] B (KG) (n88).

[96] *Rockey* (n88).   [97] *R v Parrott* [2001] 1 SCR 178.   [98] *Hawkins* (n89).

[99] *R v Tat* (1997) 117 CCC (3d) 481.

[100] *R v Starr* [2000] SCR 40. Such an extension had long before been anticipated, and deplored, by McHugh J in *Bannon v R* (1995) 185 CLR 1, 41. The Supreme Court subsequently stated it likely to be rare for a hearsay exception not to meet the criteria: *R v Mapara* 2005 SCC 23, [2005] 1 SCR 358, [37].   [101] [30].

[102] A view apparently shared by the New Zealand Court of Appeal: see *R v Manase* (n82), [16]— 'It has led the Canadian Courts to allow hearsay to be introduced in circumstances which depend on little more than the trial judge's subjective opinion that it would be desirable to let it in.'

[103] (n93), [42]; setting out [15] of *Mapara* (n100).

to halt the tide of litigation.[104] Its assimilation of the matters to be considered by the judge on the voir dire in relation to admissibility, and then again by the trier of fact in determining the result, seems more likely to encourage the issue to be raised twice.

South Africa

The Law of Evidence Amendment Act No 45 of 1988 provided an interesting new approach to the reform of the hearsay rule, making its admission in evidence in contested cases, in which the maker of the statement did not testify, wholly discretionary.[105] The provision is sufficiently short, and clear, to be quoted *in extenso*:[106]

(1) Subject to the provisions of any other law, hearsay evidence shall not be admitted as evidence at criminal or civil proceedings, unless,

   (a) each party against whom the evidence is to be adduced agrees to the admission thereof as evidence at such proceedings;

   (b) the person upon whose credibility the probative value of such evidence depends, himself testifies at such proceedings; or

   (c) the court having regard to—

      (i)   the nature of the proceedings;

      (ii) the nature of the evidence;

      (iii) the purpose for which the evidence is tendered;

      (iv) the probative value of the evidence;

      (v)   the reason why the evidence is not given by the person upon whose credibility the probative value of such evidence depends;

      (vi) any prejudice to a party which the admission of such evidence might entail;

      (vii) any other factor which should in the opinion of the court be taken into account,

   is of the opinion that such evidence should be admitted in the interests of justice.

(2) The provisions of subsection (1) shall not render admissible any evidence which is inadmissible on any ground other than that such evidence is hearsay evidence.

   ...

4) For the purposes of this section—

   "hearsay evidence" means evidence, whether oral or in writing, the probative value of which depends upon the credibility of any person other than the person giving such evidence;

   "party" means the accused or party against whom hearsay evidence is to be adduced including the prosecution.

As noted above the proposal is radical, at least in the British context, in applying equally to criminal and civil proceedings,[107] in applying to oral and documentary hearsay, and in

---

[104] See e.g. *R v TR* (2007) 220 CCC3d 37; (2008) *R v SS* 232 CCC3d 158; (2008) *R v Pasqualino* 233 CCC3d 319 (all in the Ontario Court of Appeal); in the relatively straightforward situation in *R v Goodstoney* (2007) 218 CCC3d 270 forty-eight appellate decisions had to be considered, nineteen of them of the Supreme Court of Canada.

[105] An approach that would have been welcomed by some distinguished American judges: see, for example, Justice Learned Hand as quoted in *Wigmore on Evidence* vol V, [1576].   [106] S 3.

[107] No doubt because juries are not used in South Africa either for civil or criminal proceedings. There is nevertheless still some reluctance to admit hearsay for the prosecution: see *S v Saat* 2004 (1) SA 593, 598C.

applying to hearsay in any degree. It appears also to abridge the common law exceptions to the hearsay rule, since the opening words seem to contemplate pre-existing statutory provisions only. It is interesting in its definition of hearsay, which makes no reference to the use to which the out-of-court statement is to be put, and in particular makes no reference to its being intended to prove the truth of the matters to which it relates. While it is just possible that this limitation may be construed from the reference to reliance upon the *credibility* of the out-of-court declarant, it is at least possible that it will be taken to encompass other out-of-court utterances, writings, or actions, the cogency of which depend upon the sincerity of speaker, writer, or actor.

A most important feature of the provision is the list of factors that the court is instructed to take into account in exercising its discretion. This simple and straightforward list seems ideally suited to the purpose of insulating the discretion from reversal on appeal,[108] but a cautious approach seems to be developing in criminal[109] proceedings.[110]

Scotland

In the same year as the South Africans made the admission of hearsay discretionary, the Scots took the radical step of abolishing the rule altogether in civil proceedings.[111] It is interesting that the two jurisdictions to make such moves are both ones in which there is some admixture of civilian law. It is noteworthy that Scottish common law was also more liberal than English in having a general rule admitting statements of deceased persons.[112]

It is particularly interesting that the Scottish Law Commission proposed a less radical measure of reform than that enacted. It took the view that it would be preferable to qualify its recommendation of abolition by conferring a power upon the court to refuse to admit the hearsay where it was both reasonable,[113] and practicable, for the maker to be called as a witness.[114] It was, at least in part, in reliance upon that qualification that the Commission felt emboldened to include within its recommendations hearsay of any degree, however remote.[115]

---

[108] The Appellate Division has nevertheless held that, as a matter of the admissibility of evidence, an appellate court is entitled to treat the exercise of discretion by the trial judge in this context as a matter of law, and to deal with an appeal on that basis: *McDonald's Corp v Joburgers Drive-Inn Restaurant Pty Ltd* 1997 (1) SA 1, 27. See also *S v Ndhlovu* 2002 (6) SA 305 for detailed exegesis of the provision, approval of the approach in *McDonalds*, and holding the statute constitutional.

[109] Cp in civil *Hlongwane v Rector, St Francis College* 1989 (3) SA 318; *Mdani v Allianz Insurance Ltd* 1991 (1) SA 184; *Skilya Property Investments (Pty) Ltd v Lloyds of London* 2002 (3) SA 765.

[110] In *S v Molimi* 2008 (3) SA 608 the Constitutional Court first noted that the provision was made expressly subject to other statutes, thus excluding the use of a co-accused's confession; and even interpreted its application to an admission extremely restrictively, by stressing the prejudicial effect of such evidence.

[111] There has been no such intention in relation to criminal proceedings: see Scottish Law Commission No 149 *Report on Hearsay Evidence in Criminal Proceedings* (1995) [2.11], [2.12]. A more limited relaxation of the rule was enacted as s 259 of the Criminal Procedure (Scotland) Act 1995, although even that provision makes admission automatic with no discretion to exclude: see *N v HM Adv* 2003 SLT 761, cp *HM Advocate v Khder* 2009 SCCR 187; and for general comment, Duff [2005] *Crim LR* 525, [2005] Jud Rev 1.

[112] See *Lauderdale Peerage Case* (1885) 10 App Cas 692; *Lovat Peerage Case* (1885) 10 App Cas 763.

[113] This is designed to cover both cases in which it is unreasonable on grounds of cost and trouble, and those in which it is unreasonable in terms of procedure, such as those in which the witness is in some sense an opponent.

[114] Scottish Law Commission No 100 *Evidence: Report on Corroboration, Hearsay and Related Matters* (1986), [3.40].

[115] Paragraph 3.52.

The legislation that ensued was starkly simple. Its effective provision is contained in the Civil Evidence (Scotland) Act 1988, s 2(1):

In any civil proceedings—

(a) evidence shall not be excluded solely on the ground that it is hearsay;

(b) a statement made by a person otherwise than in the course of proof shall be admissible as evidence of any matter contained in the statement of which direct oral evidence by that person would be admissible; and

(c) the court, or as the case may be the jury, if satisfied that any fact has been established in those proceedings, shall be entitled to find that fact proved by the evidence notwithstanding that the evidence is hearsay.

This appears to be the first legislation anywhere in the common law world to have abolished[116] the hearsay rule. The use of 'solely' in s 2(1)(a) ensures that the rule does not affect other exclusionary rules.[117] The Act applies to statements of opinion as well as to those of fact,[118] and of whatever degree. 'Document' is defined as in the English Civil Evidence Act 1968, and clearly extends to records emanating from computers. Transcripts of such records are admissible as copies, and are presumed to be accurate in the absence of evidence to the contrary.[119] It departs from the recommendations of the Scottish Law Commission in dispensing with the elaborate notice procedure it required to try to preserve the testimony of a witness whom it was practicable and reasonable to call. There is, however, still one line of escape from so completely radical a change. Section 4 permits an additional witness to be called by either party before the start of closing submissions, so, if the maker is available, his presence for cross-examination can be secured, although only with the leave of the court. If a witness is called, then any previous statements, whether consistent or inconsistent, can be put to him, and as such become evidence in the case. Further provisions of the Act[120] provide for the automatic admissibility of the records of any business or undertaking.[121] Following the explicit recommendations of the Scottish Law Commission, no distinction at all is made between the admissibility of records from computers, and those from any other devices. Rather oddly, the Act explicitly preserves the admissibility of statements as evidence of the fact that the statement was made, although it is hard to see when this will be relied upon. Provision is explicitly made for the admission of negative hearsay, but only in the case of business records,[122] so presumably, if a private person keeps a meticulously detailed diary of appointments, the absence of an entry will not be evidence that there was no appointment as may well have been claimed.

Part of the reason for taking so radical an approach was that it seemed to have caused little, or no, difficulty in those non-judicial proceedings in which hearsay is admitted.[123] So far, there is no evidence that this measure has caused such mischief either.

---

[116] This was the terminology deliberately adopted by the Scottish Law Commission for its own more qualified proposal.

[117] Although it does not preserve rules of incompetence: *T v T* 2000 SCLR 1057, a case that contains a full, and fascinating, description of the genesis and policy of this reform by Lord Rodger.

[118] CE(S)A 1988, s 9.   [119] CEA 1968, s 6.   [120] CEA 1968, s 5.

[121] Defined widely enough to include trades, professions, and both local and national governmental institutions.   [122] Section 7.

[123] SLC No 100, [3.14].

SECTION 2. THE SCOPE OF THE RULE

Because the rule has now become almost wholly statutory, and more relaxed, there is now less need, or opportunity, to exploit legal technicality in order to hold that the exclusionary rule does not apply to particular categories of utterance, document, or conduct, but nevertheless some attention still has to be paid to the scope of the rule, since statutory reform[124] has chosen to define hearsay for the purpose, using terminology that has acquired a substantial patina of interpretation.[125]

Discussion can, however, now be considerably curtailed, since it is inconceivable that the courts will, either in civil or in criminal cases, countenance a situation in which the clearest non-hearsay and hearsay evidence is admitted, but that, falling into some indeterminate penumbra between these extremes, excluded.[126]

In this section, a number of the old frontier areas will be reviewed, including statements admitted on the basis that they have been made,[127] statements forming part of the res gestae,[128] previous consistent statements, and admissions.

STATEMENTS AS FACTS

One of the most difficult issues in the old law was the determination of when statements were admitted, not as evidence of the truth of what they stated as such, but as a basis for grounding a relevant inference, alleged not to depend upon their being true. It was on this basis that operative statements were admitted. A very clear example of the distinction was provided by the American case of *Johnson v Hansen*,[129] in which the rent for a farm was half of the crop, and the crop was stored in a barn divided into two equal segments. The tenant was heard to say to the landowner, indicating one end of the barn: 'That part of the crop is yours.' This was an operative statement when first made, since it designated the part of the crop that was the landowner's, but any later statement of the same words, for example because the landowner had forgotten which end of the barn had been indicated, would have been hearsay. In other words, the statement that one part of the crop was the landowner's *was made true* by its first utterance, but its *truth was affirmed* by subsequent repetition.[130] In such cases, the statement is itself in issue, but sometimes it is merely relevant to a fact in issue. In *Ratten v R*, the accused was charged with the murder of his wife,

---

[124] This includes the Criminal Justice Act 2003.

[125] The Law Commission itself envisaged that reference would continue to be made to existing authority defining the boundary of hearsay: Law Com No 216, [4.6], [4.35] (for the purposes of civil proceedings), and Law Com No 245, [7.41] (for the purposes of criminal proceedings), stating only that boundary problems will be *reduced*, an implied assertion that they will not disappear entirely.

[126] See *R v Singh* [2006] EWCA Crim 660, [2006] 2 Cr App R 201, [14]; *R v MK* [2007] EWCA Crim 3150, (2008) 172 JP 538, [17].

[127] Including such issues as statements as real evidence, as operative facts, and implied assertions.

[128] To a considerable extent overlapping the previous category.

[129] 201 NW 322 (Min, 1924); see also *R v Jones* [2006] SASC 189, 161 ACR 511, [13]–[42].

[130] English parallels are provided by *Stobart v Dryden* (1836) 1 M & W 615 (attestation as fact rather than statement); *Re Wright, Hegan v Bloor* [1920] 1 Ch 108 (distinction between appointment being void because it was *said* to be a fraud on a power or because it *was* a fraud on a power).

and it became important to establish just when, to what effect, and by whom, a telephone call had been made from the house in which the death took place. The disputed evidence was that of a telephone operator who testified to having received a call from the deceased, asking for the police in a distressed voice. Lord Wilberforce expressed the view that the evidence of the call having been made was not hearsay:[131]

The mere fact that evidence of a witness includes evidence as to words spoken by another person who is not called is no objection to its admissibility. Words spoken are facts just as much as any other action by a human being. If the speaking of words is a relevant fact, a witness may give evidence that they were spoken. A question of hearsay only arises when the words are relied on 'testimonially', ie as establishing some fact narrated by the words.

The situation is more problematic when the statement is relevant to the state of mind of its hearer,[132] or of its speaker.[133] Disputes often arose as to the relevance of the state of mind, and the contiguity of hearsay exclusion seems sometimes to have led to a very strict view of relevance, so as to permit exclusion of the evidence on that basis, without resolution of the more complex hearsay issues.[134]

A cognate problem existed with identifying statements. This may be illustrated with one of the less celebrated issues in *Myers v DPP*.[135] That was a car-ringing case, and involved comparison between the combination of the number stamped into cylinder blocks and others. No question was raised as to whether the number stamped into the block was hearsay, since it identified the car to which the other numbers were merely attached. The problem arose when the identifying feature was itself a statement of fact, whether what it was identifying was the nature,[136] provenance,[137] or ownership of goods,[138] the date of a document,[139] or the relationship,[140] or identity,[141] of a person.

---

[131] [1972] AC 378, [1971] 3 All ER 801, 387, 805.

[132] As in *Subramaniam v Public Prosecutor* (n12), in which the question was whether a man had been acting under duress, and it was proposed to adduce evidence of the threats made to him by terrorists.

[133] As in *Woodhouse v Hall* (n13), in which the question was whether a statement offering immoral services was evidence that they were supplied.

[134] As in *R v Blastland* [1986] AC 41, [1985] 2 All ER 1095, in which statements indicating the knowledge of a third party of the detail of commission of a murder, at that time not public knowledge, were held irrelevant to the issue of whether it was committed by him, or by the accused. For a more relaxed view in Australia, see *R v Ung* [2000] NSWCCA 195, (2000) 173 ALR 287 (implied statement of knowledge of one party to prove knowledge of another).   [135] Note 1, 1019, 884D.

[136] In *R v Fizzell* (1987) 31 ACR 213, the court rejected a forensic scientist's evidence of analysis that she had performed, because she had relied upon the sample having been correctly taken and labelled by an absent assistant prior to her analysis; cf *R v Orrell* [1972] RTR 14. See also *Holmden v Bitar* (1987) 47 SASR 509 (labels on tins of paté); *R v Lenaghan* [2008] NZCA 123 (label on box of proprietary drugs).

[137] Compare *Patel v Comptroller of Customs* [1966] AC 356, [1965] 3 All ER 593 (label on sacks of coriander as 'Produce of Morocco'), with *Comptroller of Customs v Western Electric Co Ltd* [1966] AC 367, [1965] 3 All ER 599 (stamp on plastic implement 'Made in Denmark').

[138] *R v Brown* [1991] Crim LR 835 (name in book); cf *Daniels v Western Australia* [2000] FCA 413, (2000) 173 ALR 51 (not labels on exhibits in a museum).

[139] *R v Cook* (1980) 71 Cr App Rep 205. There is considerable early authority on the use of postmarks to establish the date of posting. Similar considerations arise in relation to the use of the URL in relation to an email message: see *R v Mawji* [2003] EWCA Crim 3067, [2003] All ER (D) 285 (Oct); and to the use and location of mobile telephones: see *R v Singh* (n126).

[140] *R v Benz* (1989) 168 CLR 110 ('my mother is sick').

[141] *R v McCay* [1991] 1 All ER 232, [1990] 1 WLR 645 (at identification parade).

This issue often overlapped with another problem that caused great difficulty, frequently categorized as the problem of implied assertions. This concerned the extent to which circumstantial inference could be based upon the statements of third parties without breach of the rule. This was considered in the leading case of *R v Kearley*.[142] In that case, the police conducted a raid on premises from which it was suspected that the accused was dealing in drugs. While on the premises, they intercepted ten telephone calls seeking the supply of drugs, some referring to past transactions, and opened the door to seven callers who were also seeking drugs. The prosecution proposed to adduce evidence of the fact of these calls, and the terms of what transpired during them, in order to prove that the accused was in the business of supplying drugs from the premises. This evidence was admitted by the trial judge, and his decision upheld by the Court of Appeal. A further appeal to the House of Lords was allowed by a majority of three to two. The speeches of the majority all stressed the irrelevance of the calls as direct evidence of the state of mind of the callers, and Lord Ackner went so far as perhaps to make any question of hearsay *obiter dictum*:[143]

An oral request for drugs to be supplied by the defendant, not spoken in his presence or in his hearing, could only be evidence of the state of mind of the person or persons making the request, and since his or their state of mind was not a relevant issue at the trial, evidence of such a request or requests, however given, would be irrelevant and therefore inadmissible. The jury would not be entitled to infer from the fact that the request(s) was made that the appellant was a supplier of drugs.

It will be apparent from what I have already stated that the application of the hearsay rule does not, on the facts so far recited fall for consideration. The evidence is not admissible because it is irrelevant.

The acid test for this view is whether the evidence would have been admissible if testified to directly by the callers, and Lord Oliver, in particular, makes it crystal clear that it would not.

The hearsay point arises only if the calls are treated as implied assertions of the basis for the beliefs of the callers which led them to make their requests, namely that the accused was a dealer. All three members of the majority were clear that implied assertions were just as susceptible to the operation of the hearsay rule as express assertions. Lord Ackner thought it only reasonable:[144]

If…the simple request or requests for drugs to be supplied by the appellant, as recounted by the police contains in substance, but only by implication, the same assertion, then I can find neither authority nor principle to suggest that the hearsay rule should not be equally applicable and exclude such evidence. What is sought to be done is to use the oral assertion, even though it may be an implied assertion, as evidence of the truth of the proposition asserted. That the proposition is asserted by way of necessary implication rather than expressly cannot, to my mind, make any difference.

Lord Bridge[145] and Lord Oliver[146] had more qualms about the policy, but nevertheless felt constrained[147] to come to the same decision. This result opened a chasm between the rather

---

[142] [1992] 2 AC 228, [1992] 2 All ER 345. Rejected in Australia, *Abrahamson v R* (1994) 63 SASR 139, 142; *R v Nguyen* [2008] ACTSC 40, 184 ACR 207, [23]; and New Zealand, *R v Holtham* [2008] 2 NZLR 758.
[143] 254, 363. See also Lord Bridge, 243, 353; and Lord Oliver, 263, 370.   [144] 255, 364.
[145] 249, 359.   [146] 268, 375.
[147] Induced by the tenor of the decision in *Wright v Doe d Tatham* (n33), and less plausibly by that in *R v Blastland* (n134).

technical rule in England, and the position arrived at elsewhere in the Commonwealth in this context.[148] It is ironic that the situation in the United States, which is the same in its result as that in the rest of the Commonwealth, was used by Lord Bridge to justify his contrary view, on the basis that it had there been achieved only by express provision in the Federal Rules of Evidence.[149]

Although it has been categorically stated[150] that the decision in *Kearley* has been set aside by the Criminal Justice Act 2003, in all such situations, careful directions to the jury as to the relevance and use of the evidence might still be required.[151]

No question of hearsay was thought to be involved if a statement was adduced as demonstrably false.[152] Thus in *A-G v Good*, in which a wife's untrue statement that her husband was away from home was received on the issue of whether he intended to defraud his creditors, Garrow B said:[153]

The doubt on the present occasion has originated in calling that hearsay evidence which has no approximation to it. The answer is received as a distinct fact in itself, to be compared and combined with other facts;...Suppose an unreasonable time had intervened between the demand of entrance and the opening of the door...is not that a circumstance to be inquired into with a view to the fact under investigation...

So too in *Mawaz Khan v R and Amanat Khan*, in which it was alleged that a false alibi had been concocted by two co-accused. Lord Hodson said of the statement:[154]

...they can without any breach of the hearsay rule be used, not for the purpose of establishing the truth of the assertions contained therein, but for the purpose of asking the jury to hold the assertions false and to draw inferences from their falsity.

Questions of implied assertion also arise when a negative is sought to be proved from failure to state a positive, in situations in which one might be expected. In the old law, the admissibility of such evidence was regarded as compatible with the exclusion of hearsay.[155] It is envisaged that such evidence continues to be admissible under the new statutory regime,[156] even without explicit[157] general[158] provision.

---

[148] For example, in *R v Firman* (1989) 52 SASR 391, rehearsing much antipodean authority, but not mentioned in *Kearley* (n142); see now *R v Abrahamson, R v Nguyen* (above n142).

[149] Citing *United States v Zenni* 492 F Supp 464 (1950) in its construction of 801(a).

[150] *Singh* (n126), [14] fortified by the House of Lords' refusal of leave to appeal on this point certified by the Court of Appeal; see also *R v MK* (n126) (factually identical to *Kearley*, hence also accepting relevance).

[151] *R v John-Akpaette* [2005] EWCA Crim 1784, [15].

[152] These situations fall outside the statutory definitions: see Civil Evidence Act 1995, s 1(2)(a); Criminal Justice Act 2003 s 114(1); although, as will be seen below, it was held in *R v Z* [2003] EWCA Crim 191, [2003] 2 Cr App Rep 173 that such a statement is governed by the rules relating to confessions, so far as the implication to be drawn from its falsity is concerned.   [153] (1825) M'Cle & Yo 286a, 290.

[154] [1967] 1 AC 454, 462.

[155] *R v Shone* (1982) 76 Cr App Rep 72; *R v Muir* (1983) 79 Cr App Rep 153; *R v Harry* (1988) 86 Cr App Rep 105.   [156] See Law Com No 216, [4.40]; Law Com No 245, [7.10]–[7.12].

[157] Such provision is made elsewhere: see Civil Evidence (Scotland) Act 1988, s 7; United States Federal Rules of Evidence, 803(7), (10).

[158] Provision is made for the proof of the absence of entries in public and business records: Civil Evidence Act 1995, s 9(3).

Assertions may sometimes be made by conduct rather than in words, either because speech is impossible,[159] or because conduct is more graphic and effective.[160] Such assertions were, and remain,[161] hearsay. It may also be noted that conduct has occasionally been regarded as equivalent to a statement, and susceptible to the hearsay rule.[162] This view has rarely been applied in England,[163] and despite the general endorsement of *Wright v Doe d Tatham* in *Kearley v R*, no reference was made to these dicta.[164] It is submitted that evidence of such conduct is admissible, if relevant, without reference to the hearsay rule.

RES GESTAE STATEMENTS

Partly on account of the injustice caused by the inflexibility of the hearsay rule, an unsatisfactory[165] inclusionary exception[166] was created at common law for statements so closely intertwined with the events in issue as to amount to part of what was going on. The general abrogation of the rule in civil cases has eliminated any need for it there, but it has been retained in criminal proceedings,[167] and applied in *R v C*.[168] It should be noted, however, that the now stricter definition of hearsay should reduce the need for reliance upon it. Thus in *Teper v R*, a bystander at the scene of a fire had been heard to exclaim at the oddity of the owner of the premises driving away. Such a statement would not fall within the new limited definition of hearsay,[169] and there would be no need to rely upon this exception. The need for it is still further reduced by the Criminal Justice Act 2003, s 116, making general provision for the admissibility of hearsay statements by unavailable witnesses.[170]

[159] As in *Chandresekara v R* [1937] AC 220, [1936] 3 All ER 865, in which a woman, whose throat had been cut, used sign language to indicate the identity of her assailant.

[160] As in *Li Shu-ling v R* [1989] AC 270, [1988] 3 All ER 138, in which a crime was re-enacted.

[161] Civil Evidence Act 1995, s 13; Criminal Justice Act 2003, s 135(2).

[162] Most famously by Parke B in *Wright v Doe d Tatham* (n33), 387.

[163] See e.g. *Manchester Brewery v Coombs* (1900) 82 LT 347 (voluntary conduct); *R v Turner* [1975] QB 834, [1975] 1 All ER 70, 840, 73 (involuntary conduct).

[164] Such conduct falls outside current statutory provision: see Civil Evidence 1995, s 1(2)(a); Criminal Justice Act 2003, s 114(1).

[165] In *Ratten v R* (n131), Lord Wilberforce remarked, 388, 806 that: 'The expression "res gestae," like many Latin phrases, is often used to cover situations insufficiently analysed in clear English terms.'

[166] Not only to the hearsay rule, where its existence can cloud the clarity of exceptions: see *Mills v R* [1995] 3 All ER 865, [1995] 1 WLR 511 (dying declarations); *Hamill v HM Adv* 1999 SCCR 384 (co-conspirators); but to other exclusionary rules also, such as those relating to evidence indicating bad disposition. The court has a discretion to exclude res gestae statements, even if they fulfil all of the relevant conditions, if the inability to cross-examine a potentially available witness is likely to render the trial unfair: *A-G's Reference (No 1 of 2003)* [2003] EWCA Crim 1286, [2003] 2 Cr App Rep 453, [21].

[167] Criminal Justice Act 2003, s 118(1) 4, adopting the final view of the Law Commission, Law Com Consultation Paper No 138 (1995), [11.57], departing from its earlier recommendation of abolition in its consultative paper. For criticism of such retention, see Ormerod [1998] *Crim LR* 301, and for devastating criticism of the whole technique, see Munday (2008) 124 *LQR* 46.

[168] [2007] EWCA Crim 3463, [15] (although apparently in such a way as to minimize the overlap with hearsay).

[169] Criminal Justice Act 2003, s 115(3), because it would not have been uttered with the intention of causing belief in its truth.

[170] This would have removed the need to rely upon res gestae in such leading cases as *R v Bedingfield* (1879) 14 Cox CC 341 (see Wilde [2000] 4 E & P 107); *Ratten v R* (n131); and *R v Andrews* [1987] AC 281, [1987] 1 All ER 513. The same result applies in Australia under the provisions of the Evidence Act 1995: see *R v Polkinghorne* [1999] NSWCCA 704, (1999) 108 ACR 189.

The Act identifies the rule for the purpose of its preservation according to a classification adopted in previous editions of this work:[171]

Any rule of law under which in criminal proceedings a statement is admissible as evidence of any matter stated if—

(a) the statement was made by a person so emotionally overpowered by an event that the possibility of concoction or distortion can be disregarded,

(b) the statement accompanied an act which can be properly evaluated as evidence only if considered in conjunction with the statement, or

(c) the statement relates to a physical sensation or a mental state (such as intention or emotion).

Since the aim of this section is to *preserve* the common law, it seems that no dispositive significance should be attached to the verbal formulation, which seems, in some respects, narrower, and in others, wider, than the common law jurisprudence indicates.

Statements relating to a relevant event

The reasoning here is that some statements are inspired by events to such an extent as to reduce substantially the chance of error.[172] It seems that the statement must be roughly contemporaneous[173] with the event, and made in circumstances of such involvement in it as to diminish the dangers of concoction,[174] mistake,[175] or distortion.[176] This exception has most often been used to indicate the identity of the criminal,[177] but is sometimes used for other purposes.[178]

It seems immaterial that the statement is elicited by questioning, so long as the principle of 'spontaneity' can be held to have been satisfied. Perhaps the analogy of the instigation of complaints in sexual cases may be thought apposite.[179] Spontaneity will partly be a function of the intrinsic excitement of the event, partly of the declarant's degree of involvement in it, and partly of the separation in time between the event and the declaration.[180]

---

[171] CJA 2003, s 118(2)(4). Subject only to elision of physical sensation and mental state into one category.

[172] Although it has been suggested that such involvement is more likely to increase that danger: see Hutchins and Slesinger (1928) 28 *Col LR* 432, but the English Law Commission felt the formulation of the condition sufficient to cater for this.

[173] *R v Newport* [1998] Crim LR 581. It may, however, be either earlier (as in *Ratten v R* (n131)), or later (as in *R v Andrews* (n170)), than the crime charged.

[174] *Ratten v R* (n131); this was the basis for rejection in Canada in *R v QD* (2005) 199 CCC3d 490.

[175] *R v Nye and Loan* (1977) 66 Cr App Rep 252. The Law Commission rejected this form of disqualification: see Law Com No 245, [8.120].

[176] *R v Andrews* (n170) to which list *R v Lawson* [1998] Crim LR 883 appears to have added fabrication and dishonest motive, although it is hard to see why these were not covered by concoction. In Australia in *R v Cooper* [2007] ATSC 74, 175 ACR 94 a telephone call made by a child of eight was held admissible as res gestae, irrespective of the child's competence.

[177] As in *R v Andrews; R v Turnbull* (1984) 80 Cr App Rep 104 (in both cases identification of the attacker by the victim who later died); *R v Glover* [1991] Crim LR 48 (in which the statement emanated not from the victim, but from the accused, and was reported by a third party); *R v Kelly* [2005] EWCA Crim 730 (in which it was in issue whether it emanated from the accused or another).

[178] As in *R v Bedingfield; Ratten v R* (to defeat defence of suicide, or accident); *R v Boyle* (6 March 1986, unreported) (to show that a clock was taken without victim's consent).   [179] See, 302.

[180] In Canada, proneness of the class of witness to concoct has been taken into account in relation to the acceptability of a given temporal separation between event and declaration: *R v Khan* (1988) 44 CCC (3d) 197, 210.

In one case,[181] in which the event was no more than a collision causing damage to a coach driven by the declarant, his identification of the accused as the other driver some twenty minutes later was not regarded as sufficiently spontaneous. If these conditions are taken into account by the trial judge, an appellate court is unlikely to interfere with his decision. It must be stressed, however, that where the declarant is available as a witness, he should normally be called, and not only is the statement likely to be excluded if there is any suspicion of an attempt deliberately to shield a witness from cross-examination, but even when a witness is not present, owing to the incompetence of the prosecution, the same attitude is likely to be adopted.[182] On the other hand, the doctrine can be used when the prosecution has taken all reasonable steps to secure the attendance of a witness, but he has simply failed to appear.[183]

Statements accompanying a relevant act

More than 150 years ago, Parke B spoke of 'proof of the quality and intention of acts by declarations accompanying them' as an exception to the rule against hearsay that has been recognized from very early times on the ground of necessity, or convenience.[184] The rule was stated by Grove J to be that:[185]

Though you cannot give in evidence a declaration per se, yet when there is an act accompanied by a statement which is so mixed up with it as to become part of the res gestae, evidence of such a statement may be given.

Thus in *Walters v Lewis*,[186] the defendant was allowed to call a witness to say that he had heard the defendant's wife say 'this money is to pay for the sheep' when handing it over to a servant. The purpose of the evidence was simply to explain the nature of the wife's act.[187] The danger of permitting the manufacture of evidence looms up at this point, and it may be thought that *Lister v Smith*[188] illustrated it by making no distinction between evidence of the statement of a testator, at the time of making a formally valid codicil, and at other times, that he did not intend it to take effect.[189] The difference between the two situations is that, when the words are uttered at the time of the act they explain, they can be regarded as part of that act that is independently relevant, but when they are uttered separately, they can have no purpose other than to make an assertion about the quality of the earlier act. For this reason, the exception was strictly confined by conditions that the act be independently relevant,[190] that the words be contemporaneous,[191] and that they be spoken by the actor.[192]

---

[181] *Tobi v Nicholas* (1987) 86 Cr App Rep 323. See also *Re Plumbers and Gasfitters* (1987) 72 ALR 415, 434.
[182] Ibid.
[183] *Edwards and Osakwe v DPP* [1992] Crim LR 576.   [184] *Wright v Doe d Tatham* (n33), 384.
[185] *Howe v Malkin* (1878) 40 LT 196.   [186] (1836) 7 C & P 344.
[187] It was regarded as irrelevant that the absent third party was an incompetent witness. See also *R v Lord George Gordon* (1781) 21 State Tr 485 (words uttered during riot); *Hayslep v Gymer* (1834) 1 Ad & El 162 (words accompanying delivery of money).   [188] (1863) 3 Sw & Tr 282.
[189] The evidence would now be admissible under the Civil Evidence Act 1995, or the Criminal Justice Act 2003.
[190] See the rejection of an attempt to justify the admission of the words used in *R v Kearley* (n142) on the basis that they accompanied the act of telephoning.
[191] See Lord Denman CJ in *Peacock v Harris* (1836) 5 Ad & El 449: '[A] contemporaneous declaration may be admissible as part of a transaction, but an act done cannot be varied or qualified by insulated declarations made at a later time.'
[192] *Howe v Malkin* (1878) 40 LT 196.

Statements of a relevant physical sensation or mental state

Physical sensation

A person's statements concerning his contemporaneous physical sensation were admissible at common law as evidence of that fact. In *Gilbey v Great Western Rail Co*, Cozens-Hardy MR entertained no doubt that:[193]

Statements made by a workman to his wife of his sensations at the time, about the pains in his side or head, or what not—whether the statements were made by groans, or by actions, or were verbal statements—would be admissible to prove these sensations.

The Master of the Rolls also held that the workman's assertion of the cause of his condition was inadmissible at common law, and his view of the law on both points is well supported.[194] For example, as long ago as 1846, it was said:[195]

If a man says to his surgeon 'I have a pain in the head', or 'in such a part of my body', that is evidence, but if he says to the surgeon. 'I have a wound', and was to add 'I met John Thomas who had a sword and ran me through the body with it', that would be no evidence against John Thomas.

The statement must not relate to a past state of body, though a little latitude has to be allowed:[196]

Surely 'contemporaneous' cannot be confined to feelings experienced at the actual moment when the patient is speaking. It must include such a statement as 'Yesterday I had a pain after meals'.

It has been held in Australia to be immaterial that the person who experienced, and declared, the symptoms at the time does not testify, although available to do so.[197] There is plainly force in Wigmore's view that, in such a case, the contemporary statements of the witness as to his symptoms are likely to be more reliable than his later recollection of them in the witness box.[198]

Mental state

A person's declaration of his contemporaneous state of mind, or emotion, was admissible at common law as evidence of the existence of such state of mind, or emotion. The reason for this exception to the hearsay rule was usually regarded as being that a person's statements are the best, and sometimes the only, means of demonstrating his state of mind. To that extent, even direct statements of state of mind, comprehending such states as knowledge, memory, belief, opinion, intention, and emotion, could be accepted notwithstanding any technical hearsay objection.[199] The danger of undermining the hearsay rule in this situation is plain, and the law's response was, first, to require fairly strict

---

[193]   (1910) 102 LT 202.

[194]   *Aveson v Lord Kinnaird* (1805) 6 East 188; *R v Johnson* (1847) 2 Car & Kir 354; *R v Conde* (1867) 10 Cox CC 547; *R v Gloster* (1888) 16 Cox CC 471.   [195]   *R v Nicholas* (1846) 2 Car & Kir 246, 248, Pollock CB.

[196]   Salter J in *R v Black* (1922) 16 Cr App Rep 118.

[197]   *R v Perry (No 2)* (1981) 28 SASR 95; *Batista v Citra Constructions Pty Ltd* (1986) 5 NSWLR 351.

[198]   This point may largely be met under the Criminal Justice Act 2003 by generous construction of s 120(6).

[199]   In some situations, the line between hearsay and original evidence is very fine in this area. In Australia, a more relaxed view has prevailed in the aftermath of *Walton v R* (n80): see e.g. *R v Matthews* (1990) 58 SASR 19; for New Zealand, see *R v Baker* (n82).

contemporaneity,[200] and second, to impose strict limitations upon what the declaration was permitted to prove. Thus in *Thomas v Connell*,[201] it was held on appeal that a bankrupt's statement that he knew he was insolvent was admissible to prove his knowledge of that fact at the time when he made a payment to the defendant, but not the fact of the insolvency, and this point was emphasized by Parke B when he said:

If a fact be proved aliunde, it is clear that a particular person's knowledge of that fact may be proved by his declaration...and under the impression that such evidence was admissible after proof of the fact to which it related, I postponed the reception of such declaration in a cause of *Craven v Halliley* tried by me at York until after the fact was proved.

The converse was held in *R v Gunnell*,[202] in which it was decided that a statement that a fact exists is not admissible as evidence of the knowledge of the recipient of such a statement that the fact exists. In that case, the issue was whether the fact of Gunnell's fraud was known before his examination in bankruptcy. If it had not previously been disclosed, he could take advantage of a special statutory defence. The prosecution called one, Marshall, to testify that another, Andrews, had told him of Gunnell's fraud before the date of the examination, and that hence it had not been disclosed, in the sense of made known for the first time, during the bankruptcy proceedings themselves. It can be seen that the inference that it had been disclosed rested upon double hearsay: what Gunnell told Andrews, and what Andrews told the witness. It is not, however, clear why the exception to the hearsay rule cannot be applied twice. Each speaker is declaring or demonstrating his own state of mind, namely his 'knowledge' of Gunnell's fraud. It may be true that information acquired at third hand is generally less cogent than information acquired at second hand, but it is not clear that it is different in kind. The real question should have been whether, on the construction of the statute, it had become so remote as to be accounted rumour rather than knowledge. An unusual, but it is submitted correct, application of the rule in *R v Pangallo*[203] admitted evidence of the accused's statement that he had heard voices in his head, not to prove that they existed, but that he believed he had heard them.

Such questions are particularly acute in relation to the states of mind of knowledge, memory, and belief. The court must be specially sensitive to avoid infringement of the hearsay rule, and scrupulous to inhibit inference of the underlying fact, known, remembered, or believed. In some cases, such as *Thomas v Connell*, the issue directly involves the relevant state of mind. It is more tricky if it is merely argued that the state of mind is relevant to facts in issue. The problem is well illustrated by the case of *R v Blastland*.[204] The accused was charged with the murder of a young boy with whom he admitted having homosexual relations early on the evening of the boy's murder, although he denied otherwise harming him in any way. He claimed that a third man had been lurking nearby, and so implied that another had the opportunity to commit the crime. His description of the man agreed with that of a local homosexual who was interviewed by the police, and in

---

[200] *R v Vincent, Frost and Edwards* (1840) 9 C & P 275; *R v Petcherini* (1855) 7 Cox CC 79; *R v Kay* (1887) 16 Cox CC 292.

[201] (1838) 4 M & W 267.

[202] (1866) 16 Cox CC 154.   [203] (1989) 51 SASR 254.

[204] (n154). See also *R v Roberts* (1984) 80 Cr App Rep 89, a case very similar on its facts. In Australia, see *R v Zullo* [1993] 2 Qd R 572 (*Blastland* cited); in Canada, see *R v Luke* (1993) 85 CCC (3d) 163 (*Blastland* not cited).

relation to whom statements were taken from others. Those statements were made available to the defence, and the accused wished to adduce evidence that the third man had made statements indicating his knowledge of the killing before it had become public. The House of Lords held evidence of such knowledge inadmissible, adopting a very narrow view of its relevance. It was suggested that, because there were a number of innocent explanations of the acquisition of that knowledge, it would be no more than speculative to infer that it had been acquired in the course of the commission of the crime, and it thus had insufficient relevance to any issue in the case. The court was further struck by the anomaly that would be created by the rule that a direct 'confession' of guilt by the third party would be inadmissible.[205] If such a statement were to be admitted, it would be tantamount to allowing evidence to prove indirectly that which could not be proved directly. This is the classic argument against allowing circumstantial undermining of the hearsay rule. It is, however, certainly arguable, especially in the case of someone accused of so heinous a crime, that little harm would have been done by admitting the evidence, allowing its cogency to be attacked by reference to the alternative innocent explanations, and leaving its ultimate weight to be determined by the jury.[206]

Declarations of intention need special consideration because proof of intention is required in very many different legal contexts, and is generally regarded as being particularly difficult to establish without reference to its declaration by the person in question. This view was very clearly expressed by Mellish LJ in *Sugden v Lord St Leonards*:[207]

... wherever it is material to prove the state of a person's mind, or what was passing in it, and what were his intentions, there you may prove what he said, because that is the only means by which you can find out what his intentions are.

This is an exaggeration, since intention very often is proved in the absence of any express declaration of it by the relevant party. It is a curious phenomenon that declarations of intention are more prone to be used to establish the performance of the act intended, than are declarations of knowledge, memory, or belief, perhaps because the clash with the hearsay rule is less overt. The phenomenon is surprising, because it can hardly be doubted that the inference to the commission of the act from a statement of intention to perform it is more precarious than the inference of commission from a statement of memory of having performed it. Given equal sincerity in either case, it is more likely that something will occur to frustrate a sincere intention to act than that memory of having acted will be mistaken. Of course, in either case, there will be considerable variation in reliability, depending upon the distance in time between the statement and the act, its ease of accomplishment, and different degrees of detail of the act intended or remembered.

Since there is usually little question but that the existence of intention can be proved by way of express declaration, whether by exception to the hearsay rule or as original evidence, the focus of attention must again concentrate on the relevance of the utterance. In the case of declarations of intention, questions may be raised in relation to the persistence of any such intention, and to its eligibility to prove the commission of the act intended.

---

[205] As hearsay, not falling within any exception to the rule at common law. It is noteworthy that just such 'confessions' had been made at various stages by the third man, although subsequently retracted.

[206] In many cases, such evidence would be admissible under s 116(2)(e) of the Criminal Justice Act 2003, on the basis that such a witness fails to testify in whole, or in part, on account of fear.   [207] (n37), 251.

Occasionally, the statement may be one of lack of intention, as in *R v Gregson*,[208] in which the accused asked his friends what he could do with drugs in excess of the amount he believed he had been buying for his own use, tendered to show that he did not possess intending to supply.

In *Robson v Kemp*,[209] Lord Ellenborough said, 'If the declarations of the bankrupt had been made before his act (a fraudulent assignment) they may show with what intention it was done'; in *Re Fletcher, Reading v Fletcher*,[210] Cozens-Hardy MR said, 'It is common practice, particularly in criminal cases, to prove intention at a particular time by words and acts at a subsequent date.' A's declaration of intention on 1 January is received as testimonial evidence of that fact under an exception to the rule against hearsay, and the existence of the intention is then treated as an item of circumstantial evidence to prove the continuance of the intention up to 1 February, or its antecedent existence on 1 December. Obviously, a point will be reached at which A's intention on 1 January is so remote as to be irrelevant to the question of his intention at another time, and, equally clearly, it is impossible to lay down rigid rules to determine when that point will be reached.

It remains to be considered whether a declaration of intention to perform an act is admissible to prove that the act was performed. It should first be noted that, in criminal cases, it seems that the prosecution can so prove statements of intent by the accused, for example on a charge of murder that the accused threatened to kill the deceased.[211]

In civil proceedings, the problem was mainly discussed in relation to wills. The leading case was *Sugden v Lord St Leonards*,[212] in which the testator was known to have taken great care in drafting his will, but after his death, all that remained in the box thought to contain it were a number of codicils, and holograph notes, apparently made at the time of drafting it. His daughter, who had acted as housekeeper, was, however, able to remember its terms, and her version of the will was accorded probate. On appeal, the question arose of what use could be made of the pre-testamentary[213] declarations of the testator, principally deduced from his holograph notes. It was held by the majority[214] of the five-judge court that such pre-testamentary declarations were admissible as proof of the contents of the will. This decision found little favour with the House of Lords, and was said in *Woodward v Goulstone* to have reached 'the very verge of the law, and was not to be extended'. Some support for it can be found in earlier decisions[215] relating to disputes about the terms of executed wills, and in the light of the criticisms of the House of Lords,[216] its effects probably extended no further.

---

[208] [2003] EWCA Crim 1099, [2003] 2 Cr App Rep 521.   [209] (1802) 4 Esp 233.

[210] [1917] 1 Ch 339, 342.

[211] *R v Ball* [1911] AC 47, 68; *R v Williams* (1986) 84 Cr App Rep 299. See also *Plomp v R* (1964) 110 CLR 234; *R v Andrews* [1987] 1 Qd R 21; *R v White* (1989) 41 ACR 237.   [212] (n37).

[213] He had in addition made post-testamentary declarations of the contents of the will, and these were also held admissible evidence of its contents. The pronouncements of the court as to both categories were, however, regarded as unnecessary for its decision, and thus strictly, no more than *obiter dicta*: see Lord Cockburn CJ, 224; Jessel MR, 243; Mellish LJ, 250.

[214] Lord Cockburn CJ, with whom Baggalley JA and James LJ agreed; Jessel MR thought that, even then, they were admissible only as circumstantial evidence; Mellish LJ was prepared to admit them only to corroborate other evidence.

[215] See *Doe d Shallcross v Palmer* (1851) 16 QB 747; *Johnson v Lyford* (1868) LR 1 P & D 546.

[216] (1886) 11 App Cas 469, 485. Although there are a few cases in which such evidence seems to have been admitted without argument on this point: see *Marshall v Wild Rose (Owners)* [1910] AC 486 (declaration that deceased workman was going on deck to get some air); *Tracey v Kelly* (1930) WC & Ins Rep 214 (declaration

In criminal cases, the English authorities were in some disarray. Evidence of a declaration of intention to visit the accused, who was subsequently accused of murdering the declarant, was excluded in two Old Bailey cases, once[217] by Lord Cockburn CJ on the basis 'that it was only a statement of intention which might or might not have been carried out'. On the other hand, in *R v Buckley*,[218] a declaration by a policeman that he was going to observe the suspected criminal activities of the man accused of his murder was admitted by Lush J on assize.[219] In that case, however, no question of hearsay was raised. The issue has since been considered only sporadically. In *R v Thomson*,[220] an appeal against conviction for abortion on a woman who had died before trial, it was held that her statement of intention to perform the operation herself had been rightly excluded as evidence for the defence, together with her later assertions that she had procured her own miscarriage. The reception of such later assertions as testimonial evidence of their truth would have been an obvious infringement of the hearsay rule, and it may have been felt, much as was argued in *Blastland*,[221] that it would be anomalous to allow in the declarations of intention to prove indirectly what more direct assertions were not allowed to prove.[222]

There is no more modern English case in which the issue has been squarely addressed.[223] It was considered by the High Court of Australia in *Walton v R*.[224] The accused was charged with the murder of his wife, after having lured her into meeting him in the local town centre. After receiving a telephone call in which she declared that the caller was her husband, she said that she intended to meet him in the town centre. The High Court admitted evidence of such declarations, despite any hearsay element, as original evidence of her intentions, from which the jury could draw appropriate inferences, although they could not use them as direct testimonial evidence of her having met her husband at the appointed place. In so admitting the declarations of intention, the High Court appears to have accepted a famous line of American authority stemming from *Mutual Life Insurance Co v Hillmon*.[225] In that case, insurance had been taken out on Hillmon's life, and a claim was made in respect of a man killed in the wilds of Colorado. The defendants claimed that the body was not that of Hillmon, but that of one Walters, who had written letters declaring his intention of accompanying Hillmon on the relevant trip. At the trial,[226] the judge excluded

---

that leaving room to relieve call of nature). See also *Dobson v Morris* (1985) 4 NSWLR 681 (declaration of destination of journey); *Italiano v Barbaro* (1993) 114 ALR 21 (declaration of intention to stage car accident); in which the question was considered.

[217] *R v Wainwright* (1875) 13 Cox CC 171. See also *R v Pook* 172.   [218] (1873) 13 Cox CC 293.

[219] After consulting his colleague Mellor J.   [220] [1912] 3 KB 19.   [221] (n204).

[222] Considerations of just such an anomaly led the majority in *Sugden v Lord St Leonards* (n37) to apply the same rules as to both pre- and post-testamentary declarations. In all of the cases mentioned above, the statement would now be admissible under s 116 of the Criminal Justice Act 2003.

[223] In *R v Moghal* (1977) 65 Cr App Rep 56, dicta suggested that a declaration of intent to kill by the principal offender, as conceded by the prosecution despite her previous acquittal, would have been admissible at the trial of an alleged accomplice, although these dicta were doubted by the House of Lords in *Blastland* (n154), 60, 1104.

[224] (n80); see Odgers (1989) 13 *Crim LJ* 201. See also *R v Hendrie* (1985) 37 SASR 581, in which the victim's declaration of intention to have repairs done to her bedroom by the accused was admitted to explain the absence of a struggle in any other part of the house, her raped and murdered body having been found in the bedroom.   [225] 145 US 284 (1892).

[226] In fact, the third trial, the jury having disagreed at the first two, and there were a further three, the last of which also found in favour of the claimant, only to be reversed by the Supreme Court. The issue was finally settled in the widow's favour by the insurance companies.

these letters as hearsay, but the Supreme Court of the United States held[227] that they were admissible as relevant original evidence of Walters' intentions. Despite subsequent criticism of this decision by the Supreme Court,[228] and by other eminent American judges,[229] it has been extended to allow such declarations of intention to implicate second parties, and to permit proof of declarations as to past facts in interpretation of such declarations.[230] It is, however, generally recognized in the United States that the admission of declarations for such purposes can be permitted only by way of exception to the hearsay rule.[231] Such extensions were also involved in the reasoning accepted in *Walton*, although without the invocation of any special exception.[232]

Despite the importance of this issue to criminal proceedings, the Law Commission devoted little space to its consideration, and appears to have recommended its retention largely to facilitate proof of fear for the purposes of s 116(2)(e).[233]

PREVIOUS STATEMENTS BY TESTIFYING WITNESSES

As noted earlier in this chapter, and explained in more detail in Chapter VI above, at common law previous statements of witnesses, whether consistent or inconsistent with the witness's testimony, were normally inadmissible, and to the extent to which they were admissible, were not admitted as evidence of the truth of the assertions contained in them. These rules largely[234] reflected the common law's preference for oral trials. In civil proceedings, this preference persists only in procedural rules, designed to ensure the tendering of oral evidence when it is necessary, but not otherwise.[235] Although this pattern was recommended for criminal proceedings by the Criminal Law Revision Committee,[236] and largely[237] adopted in Scotland,[238] it was rejected by the Law Commission.[239] Its recommendations distinguish between the rules relating to previous statements inconsistent, and consistent, with the witness's testimony,[240] which it is helpful to reflect here.

---

[227] For an account of the genesis of this decision, see Maguire (1925) 38 *Harv LR* 109.

[228] By Cardozo J in *Shephard v United States* 290 US 96 (1933).

[229] By Traynor J in *People v Alcalde* 148 P 2d 627 (Cal, 1944), 633.

[230] *United States v Annunziato* 293 F 2d 373 (2nd Circ, 1961).

[231] See Federal Rules of Evidence, r 803(3).

[232] For illustrations of the problems to which this gives rise, see *R v Macrae* (1995) 80 ACR 380; *T v R* (1998) 20 WAR 573; *R v Hytch* [2000] QCA 315, (2000) 114 ACR 573. In *R v Bull et al* [2000] HCA 24, (2000) 201 CLR 443, the majority rather pointedly failed to endorse some of the reasoning in *Walton* (n80). In most of these situations, including that in *Walton*, the statement would now be admissible in England under s 116 of the Criminal Justice Act 2003. Unsurprisingly *R v Starr* [2000] SCR 40, has not solved the problem in Canada: see *R v Maciel* (2007) 219 CCC3d 516.   [233] [8.125] and [8.126].

[234] Other factors include the saving of time, cost, and complication; and fear of concoction.

[235] Now under the provisions of the Civil Evidence Act 1995, and rules of court: see further Chapter XIII.

[236] Eleventh Report Cmnd 4991, [236], [249], draft bill, cl 31(1)(a).

[237] For documentary statements by competent witnesses, authenticated, and adopted by the maker as evidence for the trial.

[238] Criminal Justice (Scotland) Act 1995, s 18; Criminal Procedure (Scotland) Act 1995, s 260.

[239] Law Com No 245, [10.34].

[240] Statements that are partly consistent, and partly inconsistent, are treated as if wholly inconsistent for these purposes.

Previous inconsistent statements

S 119 of the Criminal Justice Act 2003 has accepted the robust view that a previous inconsistent statement, either accepted by the witness, or proved against the witness under the
provisions of the Criminal Procedure Act 1865, should be admitted as evidence of the
truth of its contents.[241] Although the effect of this recommendation relates primarily to
the effect of the evidence, it also extends admissibility in the case of co-accused to previous
statements of a testifying co-accused whose previous statement implicated his co-accused,
even though his testimony does not. It should be further noted that a second order effect
is that, in such a case, other previous statements consistent with the testimony, but *ex
hypothesi* inconsistent with the previous inconsistent statement, will also become admissible as evidence of the truth of their contents.[242]

Previous consistent statements

Given that the general admission of previous consistent statements as evidence of their
truth might lead to needless proliferation of evidence,[243] the Criminal Justice Act 2003
admits such statements only in a number of discrete situations.

Previous statements of complaint

As noted above,[244] there was, at common law, an ancient and anomalous exception permitting proof of the terms of a recent complaint of a sexual offence. The Law Commission
felt that there was virtue in widening the admissibility of previous complaints to apply to
any form of offence, on the basis that the court would generally benefit from the ability
to consider the terms of the earliest statement made by the complainant about the alleged
offence. The Law Commission also proposed removal of the condition that the complaint
be unassisted,[245] and required merely that it be made as soon as reasonably possible. When
admitted, such a statement would constitute evidence of the truth of its contents.[246] These
proposals were accepted and are encapsulated in s 120(7):[247]

(7) The third condition is that—

  (a) the witness claims to be a person against whom an offence has been committed,

  (b) the offence is one to which the proceedings relate,

  (c) the statement consists of a complaint made by the witness (whether to a person in
      authority or not) about conduct which would, if proved, constitute the offence or
      part of the offence,

---

[241] See Law Com No 245, [10.87]–[10.101]. This approach constituted a prime focus in the White Paper
Justice for All: see [4.62]. In Australia, a similar provision has been strictly construed, and excluded from
application in conjunction with the exception for confessions, thus preventing the use of a third party's
recanted statement of the accused's confession as evidence of the accused's guilt: *Lee v R* (n81).

[242] Section 119(2); although, in such a case, they will merely reinforce the testimony.

[243] Law Com No 245, [10.30]–[10.34], despite the court's inherent power to exclude irrelevant evidence,
as applied to previous consistent statements in *R v Tooke* (1990) 90 Cr App Rep 417, and the new discretion
to exclude on this basis in s 126(1)(b).   [244] 301.

[245] So as to become a matter of weight.

[246] Although if in the form of a written statement, and as such an exhibit, to be made available to the jury
only with the leave of the court: s 122, which will require justification: see *R v Hulme* [2006] EWCA Crim
2899, [25].

[247] Subject to conditions relating to the maker testifying, the evidence being admissible if tendered in
testimony, and acknowledged and authenticated by its maker.

(d) the complaint was made as soon as could reasonably be expected after the alleged conduct,

(e) the complaint was not made as a result of a threat or promise, and

(f) before the statement is adduced the witness gives oral evidence in connection with its subject matter.

Previous statements to rebut suggestions of fabrication

The Law Commission recommended[248] a further exception to the hearsay rule for previous consistent statements of witnesses designed to rebut any suggestion of subsequent fabrication, thus retaining the old common law exception, but altering the formal effect of such admission, bringing the law into line with that applicable in civil proceedings under the provisions of s 6(2) of the Civil Evidence Act 1995, and achieving coherence in this respect with its recommendations as to previous inconsistent statements. Section 120(2) accordingly provides:

If a previous statement by the witness is admitted as evidence to rebut a suggestion that his oral evidence has been fabricated, that statement is admissible as evidence of any matter stated of which oral evidence by the witness would be admissible.

Previous statements of identification

Despite the dictum of Lord Morris in *Sparks v R*[249] that 'There is no rule which permits the giving of hearsay evidence merely because it relates to identity', the law had come very close to creating one in its treatment of previous acts of identification of persons,[250] either on identification parades,[251] or by way of assisting with graphic representations of a criminal,[252] or even as an adjunct to a dying declaration.[253] It had, however, developed no comparable rules for the identification of objects.[254] The Criminal Justice Act 2003 now provides,[255] as an alternative to the process of creative definition that had previously disfigured this area of the law, a special exception to the hearsay rule for previous statements of witnesses that identify or describe a person, object, or place.

Previous statements of matters reasonably forgotten

The common law rules relating to the refreshment of memory were complex, technical, and applied inconsistently. In some cases, previous statements that might well have

---

[248] Law Com No 245, [10.41]–[10.45], rec 34.   [249] [1964] AC 964, [1964] 1 All ER 727, 981, 735.

[250] Including self-identification by a circular use of the exception for admissions: *R v Ward* [2001] Crim LR 316.

[251] As in *R v Osbourne and Virtue* [1973] QB 678, [1973] 1 All ER 649; *R v McCay* (n141). Cases in which the rule has been invoked in this context seem to turn more on the acceptability of dock identification: *R v Fergus* [1992] Crim LR 363; *R v Hussain* [1998] Crim LR 820.

[252] As in *R v Percy Smith* [1976] Crim LR 511; *R v Cook* [1987] QB 417, [1987] 1 All ER 1049; *R v Constantinou* (1989) 91 Cr App Rep 74. For the position in Australia under the Evidence Act (Cwth) 1995, see *R v Gee* [2000] NSWCCA 198, (2000) 113 ACR 376. See also the analysis by the Supreme Court of Canada in *Starr v R* [2000] SCC 40, [2000] 2 SCR 144.   [253] *R v Elliott* [2000] Crim LR 51.

[254] See e.g., on the identification of cars, *R v Kelsey* (1982) 74 Cr App Rep 213; *R v Townsend* [1987] Crim LR 411; and on the identification of objects, *R v Fizzell* (1987) 31 ACR 213 (label on sample in forensic laboratory); cf *R v Orrell* (n136). In Scotland, a remarkably cavalier approach has been tolerated: see e.g. *Dryburgh v Scott* 1995 JC 75; *Allan v Ingram* 1995 SLT 1086.

[255] Section 120(5); see Law Com No 245, [10.46]–[10.52], rec 35.

refreshed the memory of the witness, or even without doing so would have had value, were excluded for technical reasons; in others, similar such statements were admitted, even though they could not credibly have refreshed anyone's memory. There was inconsistency between the general run of cases dealt with under this rule, and the special case of identification mentioned above. The Act accordingly creates a further exception for cases where a testifying witness made a statement when the matters stated were fresh in the memory of the witness,[256] is now able to assert that the statement was made and is believed to be true, and that the witness reasonably does not now remember the matter in sufficient detail to be able to testify to it.

It should be noted that there remains some illogicality in requiring the witness to testify to his belief in the truth of matters of which he may have no present recollection at all.[257]

ADMISSIONS

Although admissions are often said to be received on account of the unlikelihood of a person saying something to his disadvantage,[258] it can also be argued that the adversarial nature of litigation plays a part and the reason resides rather in the absurdity of a party seeking to assert his own unreliability except when speaking on oath, or the fact that he had no opportunity to cross-examine himself.[259] The exception was extended to include inextricable exculpatory parts, of otherwise inculpatory statements.[260] In general, it operated only against the party making it,[261] and against him only in a representative capacity if so made.[262] If the party had no personal knowledge of the matter admitted, then the admission was worthless.[263] In civil proceedings, no special rules are any longer required to cater for informal admissions against interest, and the common law has been expressly superseded by statutory provision.[264] In the case of formal admissions, for example on

---

[256] CJA 2003, s 120(6). This phrase appears in Evidence Act (Cwth) 1995, s 64(3), and in Australia has been construed to connote a different standard from the contemporaneity required under the old res gestae rule: *Commonwealth v McLean* (1996) 41 NSWLR 389.

[257] As in *R v Thomas* [1994] Crim LR 745 (cited by the Law Commission in fn 81 to [10.67]), in which a little girl had no recollection at all of the events, and was not at all assisted in her recollection by reading her earlier statement. It might have been better to have imposed as a condition that the witness has no reason to believe the statement to have been false.

[258] *R v Hardy* (1794) 24 State Tr 199, 1093; *R v Sharp* (n11), 68, 11.

[259] Morgan *Basic Problems of Evidence* (1962), 266, cited by Smith [1995] *Crim LR* 280, 282.

[260] *Harrison v Turner* (1847) 10 QB 482. See also Birch [1997] *Crim LR* 416.

[261] As in *Morton v Morton, Daly and McNaught* [1937] P 151, [1937] 2 All ER 470 (leading to the conclusion that it was proved that A had sexual relations with B, but not that B had them with A). The Civil Evidence Act 1995 would now prevent such a result in civil proceedings, but the same absurd conclusion might be necessitated in an incest prosecution today, if the parties were relevantly related.

[262] *Legge v Edmonds* (1855) 25 LJ Ch 125, 141 (statement in personal capacity not binding when suit in representative capacity); but oddly not conversely: *Stanton v Percival* (1855) 5 HL Cas 257 (statement in representative capacity did bind when sued in personal capacity).

[263] *Comptroller of Customs v Western Electric Co Ltd* (n137); 371, 601. This applies where both a subjective intent and objective state of affairs need to be demonstrated, e.g. in a prosecution for handling, in which an admission may be capable of proving belief that the goods were stolen without proving that they really were: *R v Korniak* (1983) 76 Cr App Rep 145.

[264] Civil Evidence Act 1995, s 7(1), (CPR 14.15) permits a party to resile from an admission, and the conditions under which this will be allowed were set out by the Court of Appeal in *Sollitt v DJ Broady Ltd* [2001] CPLR 259.

the pleadings, although the court may not simply disregard them if it believes them to be wrong, the proper course is to permit an amendment of the pleadings before considering their truth further.[265] In criminal proceedings, the use of an admission against its maker, or in relation to a co-accused,[266] will mainly be considered in Chapter XIV. The only issues to be considered here relate to the use of informal admissions by third parties, as evidence in criminal proceedings. First, there is the question of the use of third-party admissions of guilt to exculpate the accused, and, second, the use of third-party admissions to inculpate the accused on a theory of vicarious effect.

Exculpatory third-party admissions

The long-established rule of the common law was that statements by third parties confessing to the crime with which the accused is charged are inadmissible hearsay, whether tendered in chief,[267] or put in cross-examination.[268] Indeed, so strong was the rule that, in *R v Blastland*,[269] not only was leave to appeal against its application refused, but that result was then, as noted above,[270] used as a lever to exclude evidence of the accused's state of mind as circumstantial evidence. It should also be noted that, even if the maker of the confession had died before the trial, the statement would not have been admissible as a statement against interest.[271] The one crack in the edifice was furnished by dicta in a thin trickle of cases[272] in which it seems that a factor reinforcing the doubts about a conviction felt by the Court of Appeal was that a third party had confessed.

The Criminal Justice Act 2003 has retained this rule, although its impact will be softened by the reduced scope, and expanded exceptions to the rule to be discussed in more detail in Chapter XIV below, and it seems to have been envisaged that any remaining injustice might be remedied by the new inclusionary discretion.[273]

Vicarious admissions

The question of how far the admissions of one party can inculpate another is more a matter of substantive law, and of relevance, than anything else, and will be discussed here only in connection with admissions by co-conspirators.[274] The general rule was that admissions by those in privity with a party to litigation could be given in evidence against him. 'In privity' was not a technical term; it included predecessors in title,[275] referees,[276] all manner

---

[265] *Loveridge v Healey* [2004] EWCA Civ 173, [2004] CPR 30.

[266] In some cases, an admission will not only inculpate its maker, but also exculpate the co-accused seeking its admission. [267] Reaffirmed in *R v Turner* (1975) 61 Cr App Rep 67.

[268] *R v Windass* (1989) 89 Cr App Rep 258; *R v Gray and Evans* [1998] Crim LR 570. [269] (n204).

[270] 576.

[271] *Sussex Peerage Case* (1844) 11 Cl & Fin 85. The rule has been changed by statute in Australia: see Evidence Act (Cwth) 1995, ss 65(2)(d), 65(7)(b). See also *R v Bannon* (1995) 185 CLR 1; and in the United States, by Federal Rule 804(3)(b) (although corroboration is required); see also *Chambers v Mississippi* 410 US 295 (1973). In Canada, see *R v O'Brien* [1978] 1 SCR 591.

[272] *R v Cooper* [1969] 1 QB 267, [1969] 1 All ER 32; *R v Hails* (6 May 1976, unreported), CA; *R v Wallace and Short* (1978) 67 Cr App Rep 291. See also *R v Beckford and Daley* [1991] Crim LR 833, in which the same approach was adopted in relation to the confession of a co-accused there held to be inadmissible.

[273] Law Com No 245, [8.97]–[8.99]. [274] For more detail, see Spencer (2007) E&P 106.

[275] As in *Falcon v Famous Players Film Co* [1926] 2 KB 474.

[276] As in *R v Mallory* (1884) 13 QBD 33.

of agents, and a few miscellaneous cases' but not necessarily associated entities, such as other departments of government.[277]

Statements made by an agent within the scope of his authority to third persons during the continuance of the agency could be received as admissions against his principal in litigation to which the latter was a party.[278] So far as the reception of admissions was concerned, the scope of authority was a strictly limited conception. It was sometimes said that the agent must be authorized to make the admission, but that was a confusing statement, for admissions were often received although no one was expressly, or impliedly, authorized to make them. A better way of putting the matter is to say that the admission must have been made by the agent as part of a conversation, or other communication, that he was authorized to have with a third party. The authority to have such conversations, or make such communications, was frequently not coterminous with an authority to act on behalf of the principal,[279] a point that had an important bearing on the limited extent to which an employee's admissions concerning acts done by him in the course of his employment could, as such, be proved against his employer.[280]

The statement of the agent that was tendered as an admission had, on the preponderance of authority, to have been made to a third person, not to the principal.[281] It was necessary to prove the existence of the agency before the admissions of the agent could be received against the principal.[282] It was sometimes possible to imply the existence of the agency from the surrounding circumstances,[283] especially if an incorporate entity was to be bound.[284] It was not sufficient, at common law,[285] to rely upon the agent's own statements of that fact, because they were hearsay.[286] The agent could, of course, give evidence of the making of any operative statement without infringing the rule.

The statement tendered as an admission must have been made by the agent during the continuance of his agency.[287] Relatively few agents have authority to speak about past

---

[277] *Olupitan v Director of the Assets Recovery Agency* [2008] EWCA Civ 104, [28] (defendant not bound by concession made by CPS in separate criminal proceedings).

[278] This has been left unaffected by the new Civil Procedure Rules: see *Salter v McCarthy* [2002] 12 CL 39. But if such admissions are sought by questioning the agent in the course of such litigation, an objection by the principal automatically terminates any authority: *Bond Media Ltd v John Fairfax Group Pty Ltd* (1988) 16 NSWLR 82.

[279] See *Scott v Fernhill Stud Poultry Farm Pty Ltd* [1963] VR 12, holding a company not bound by a director's admissions; *Shears v Chisholm* [1994] 2 VR 535 for the converse.

[280] Cf *Kirkstall Brewery Co v Furness Rly Co* (1874) LR 9 QB 468 with *Great Western Rly Co v Willis* (1865) 18 CBNS 748.   [281] *Re Devala Provident Gold Mining Co Ltd* (1883) 22 Ch D 593.

[282] *G (A) v G (T)* [1970] 2 QB 643, [1970] 3 All ER 546; *R v Evans* [1981] Crim LR 699. See also *Maxwell v IRC* [1959] NZLR 708.

[283] *R v Turner* (n163) (acting as barrister representing a party); cf *Wagstaff v Wilson* (1832) 4 B & Ad 339 (acting as party's attorney insufficient), and *R v Evans* (n282) (acting as clerk to party's solicitor insufficient). See also *Smart v Popper and Casswell* (1987) 26 ACR 140 (solicitor representing client who was present in court).

[284] Reply signed by employee in company's name to enquiry addressed to the company and delivered to its premises: *Barnet LBC v Network Sites Ltd* [1997] JPL B90; cf *R v Natesan and Subramaniam* (1996) 88 ACR 444 (individual directors not bound by employee's admission).

[285] In appropriate circumstances, it is now possible to invoke the Civil Evidence Act 1968: see *G (A) v G (T)* (n282); where the only reason for not doing so was that the proceedings took place in the magistrates' court.

[286] *R v Evans* (n282). *Edwards v Brookes (Milk) Ltd* [1963] 3 All ER 62, [1963] 1 WLR 795 cannot be supported to the extent of any inconsistency after *Myers v DPP* (n1).

[287] *Peto v Hague* (1804) 5 Esp 134; *The Prinses Juliana, Esbjerg (Owners) v Prinses Juliana (Owners)* [1936] P 139, [1936] 1 All ER 685.

transactions, and, once an agent's employment as such had ceased altogether, he could have had no authority to do so.

It seems that the requirement of personal knowledge applied in the case of admissions by agents like that of admissions by parties, but this was subject to the proviso that an agent, such as a solicitor, who was instructed to pass on information, need not have accepted it in any way, and yet his statement could be evidence against his principal.[288] It seemed to be the case that, if an agent for a principal gathered information, and made an admission based on such information, the principal would be bound unless there was some overt qualification, or disclaimer.[289]

These old common law rules provided the background to the treatment of the statements of conspirators[290] in criminal proceedings,[291] which has been expressly preserved in the Criminal Justice Act 2003.[292] The admissions[293] of one conspirator are receivable against the other if they relate to an act done in furtherance of the conspiracy,[294] but not otherwise.[295] Thus in *R v Blake and Tye*,[296] the co-accused were charged with a conspiracy to pass goods through the customs without paying duty. Tye had made entries incriminating Blake as well as himself in two books. In one, the entry was a necessary part of the fraud; in the other, it was made solely for the purposes of record, and for Tye's convenience. It was held that the first entry was admissible against Blake as something tending to the advancement of the common object, but the second constituted evidence against Tye alone, because it was not concerned with the disposal of the plunder. In determining whether there is such a common purpose as to render the acts, and extra-judicial statements, done or made by one party in furtherance of the common purpose evidence against the others, the judge may have regard to these matters, although their admissibility is in

---

[288] *The Actaeon* (1853) 1 Ecc & Ad 176. See, in New Zealand, *R v Harris* [1998] 1 NZLR 405; and in Australia, *R v Caratti* [2000] WASCA 279, (2000) 22 WAR 527.

[289] *Welsbach Incandescent Gas Lighting Co v New Sunlight Incandescent Co* [1900] 2 Ch 1. See also *Claiborne Industries Ltd v National Bank of Canada* (1989) 59 DLR (4th) 533; *Juken Nissho Ltd v Northland RC* [2000] 2 NZLR 556.

[290] It is unnecessary for a conspiracy to be formally charged, if the allegation is one of joint participation in a criminal enterprise. Nor is it material that a conspirator is communicating with a third party: *R v Platten* [2006] EWCA Crim 140, [45].

[291] This passage was approved in *R v Walker* [2007] EWCA Crim 1698, [32]. See further Smith [1996] *Crim LR* 386, [1997] *Crim LR* 333.

[292] CJA 2003, s 118(1), (6), (7). Law Com No 245 deals with the matter rather perfunctorily in [8.130]–[8.132].

[293] Even if not strictly admissions, statements by conspirators may be circumstantially relevant: see *R v Jones* [1997] 2 Cr App R 119, 129, approving a passage in an earlier edition of this work, and itself approved in *Singh* (n126), [15]. See also the alternative ground advanced, but not determined, in *R v Hulme and Maguire* [2005] EWCA Crim 1196, [26].

[294] Even acts done after the principal object of the conspiracy has been accomplished may be in furtherance of it, e.g. those done to avoid detection or conviction: *Conway v R* [2000] FCA 461, (2000) 172 ALR 185, [256]; as may those relating to an earlier object in the case of a continuing conspiracy if amounting to support for it: *Hulme and Maguire* (n293), [25].

[295] Although it should be noted that, in many cases, out-of-court assertions and actions of conspirators may be admissible as circumstantial evidence of a conspiracy quite independently of reliance upon any admission, express or even implied.

[296] (1844) 6 QB 126; it may sometimes be difficult to distinguish a record relating to the past, and a continuing tally of an ongoing conspiracy: see *R v Sofroniou* [2009] EWCA Crim 1360, [49].

issue, as well as to other evidence.[297] This doctrine is obviously liable to produce circularity in argument:[298]

Since what A says in B's absence cannot be evidence against B of the truth of what was said unless A was B's agent to say those things, how can one prove that A was B's agent to say them by showing what A said?

The answer is that the agency may be proved partly by what A said in the absence of B, and partly by other evidence of common purpose. It makes no difference which is adduced first, but A's statements will have to be excluded if it transpires that there is no other evidence of common purpose: it is another instance of conditional admissibility.[299]

In England, this view of the law was accepted without cavil, or much elaboration.[300] In other jurisdictions, questions have arisen both as to the standard that the extrinsic evidence of conspiracy should reach, and whether the question, once having been decided by the judge so as to admit the evidence, should be subject to reconsideration by the jury. Since there is little difference here between the preliminary question and the final issue, namely whether the accused was party to the conspiracy, it would be futile to require the preliminary issue to be decided upon proof beyond reasonable doubt. The better view is that the judge should decide[301] the preliminary issue on a prima facie basis.[302] The one qualification is that it should not be so insubstantial as to be capable of being 'swept away' by the supporting hearsay.[303] It is submitted that, since the evidence has been admitted upon such a basis, it is unnecessarily confusing for the jury to be given an opportunity to reject it upon the application of a different standard of proof from that which they will have to be instructed to apply to the ultimate question of guilt, or innocence, of participation in the conspiracy,[304] although at that stage, it will be appropriate to warn the jury of the dangers posed by any admissible hearsay.[305]

The rule under consideration is not confined to charges of conspiracy, as it is based on implied agency, and would apply, for example, to charges of aiding and abetting, even though the secondary party was not charged, perhaps to all charges involving a common

---

[297] *Ahern v R* (1988) 165 CLR 87.   [298] *R v Mayet* 1957 (1) SA 492, 494.

[299] *Tripodi v R* (1961) 104 CLR 1; *Ahern* (n297), 104.

[300] *R v Donat* (1985) 82 Cr App Rep 173, 179; *R v Governor of Pentonville Prison, ex p Osman* [1989] 3 All ER 701, [1990] 1 WLR 277; *R v Windass* (n268). It has, however, influenced attitudes against the use of convictions for conspiracy under s 74 of the Police and Criminal Evidence Act 1984: see, 114.

[301] In the United States, the Federal Rules of Evidence permit hearsay, including the hearsay of the alleged co-conspirators, to be used in the determination of that preliminary question: Federal Rules of Evidence, rr 104(a), 1101(d)(1); *Bourjaily v United States* 483 US 971 (1987).

[302] Used for some other issues of fact upon which the admission of evidence depends: see *R v Robson and Harris* [1972] 2 All ER 699, [1972] 1 WLR 651; for an example of failure to meet it, see *R v Williams: R v Davies* [1992] 2 All ER 183, [1992] 1 WLR 380. In *Ahern v R* (n297) the High Court of Australia preferred the term 'reasonable evidence' to 'prima facie case', but thought there to be no real distinction of meaning; for an example of failure to meet it, see *R v Kalajdic* [2005] VSCA 160, 157 ACR 300. See also *R v Masters, Richards and Wunderlich* (1992) 26 NSWLR 450. In New Zealand, *R v Qiu* [2007] 2 NZLR 433, [24] explicitly rejected the standard of the balance of probabilities; but it is used in the United States: *Bourjaily v United States* (n301).

[303] *R v Evans* [2005] EWCA Crim 3542, [49], referring to *R v Barham* [1997] 2 Cr App R 117.

[304] *R v Platten* (n290), [27]. This seems the predominant view in other common law jurisdictions: see *Ahern* (n297) (Australia); *R v Walters* [1989] 2 NZLR 33 (New Zealand, explicitly endorsing *Ahern*); and *Bourjaily* (n301) (United States). But Canada adopts a different view: *R v Carter* [1982] 1 SCR 938; *R v Barrow* [1987] 2 SCR 694; *R v Sutton* (1999) 140 CCC (3d) 336.   [305] *R v Jones* [1997] 2 Cr App Rep 119.

purpose,[306] and even to civil proceedings;[307] it is in relation to conspiracy trials that the rule may operate most oppressively. If there is a series of counts charging separate offences, and a concluding count alleging conspiracy, evidence may be admissible against all of the accused on the last count, although it would not be admissible against more than one of them on any of the separate counts.[308] The evidence often takes the form of directions given, and acts done, by the other parties, which can take a much broader form when there is a conspiracy charge than when the charge relates to one specific transaction.[309] It remains to be seen whether it will pass the scrutiny of the European Court of Human Rights if there considered.

[306] The Criminal Justice Act 2003 employs the rubric of 'common enterprise' to describe the rule it is retaining in s 118(2) 7. See in Australia, *Tripodi* (n299); in Canada, *R v Carter* (n304), and after the new approach to hearsay, *R v Chang* (2003) 173 CCC (3d) 397; in New Zealand, *R v Tauhore* [1996] 2 NZLR 641.

[307] *Italiano v Barbaro* (n216).

[308] *R v Griffiths* [1966] 1 QB 589, [1965] 2 All ER 448; but see criticism by Smith [1995] *Crim LR* 47.

[309] See *R v Gray; Liggins; Riding, and Rowlands* [1995] 2 Cr App Rep 100, and the gloss put upon it in *R v Murray, Morgan and Sheridan* [1997] 2 Cr App Rep 136.

XIII

HEARSAY IN CIVIL PROCEEDINGS

As previously noted, the hearsay rule has little, or no, exclusionary effect in civil proceedings in the modern law. Section 1 of the Civil Evidence Act 1995 proclaims that:

> (1) In civil proceedings evidence shall not be excluded on the ground that it is hearsay.

This certainly permits discussion to be abbreviated, but it does not permit it to be altogether abrogated. It has been clearly held that such a rule is compatible with the European Convention on Human Rights:[1]

...the use of the Civil Evidence Act 1995 and the rules in cases under the first part of s 1 are not in any way incompatible with the HRA.

Doubts have nevertheless been raised as to whether the Act does achieve the result proclaimed, and on any basis, there are procedural differences between the methods of adducing different forms of hearsay under the provisions of the Act. Consideration of the effect of the Act in changing the law will constitute the first, and more important, section of this chapter.

Section 1 of the Act goes on to provide:[2]

> (2) In this Act—
>
> > (a) 'hearsay' means a statement made otherwise than by a person while giving oral evidence in the proceedings which is tendered as evidence of the matters stated; and
> >
> > (b) references to hearsay include hearsay of whatever degree.
>
> (3) Nothing in this Act affects the admissibility of evidence admissible apart from this section.
>
> (4) The provisions of sections 2 to 6 (safeguards and supplementary provisions relating to hearsay evidence) do not apply in relation to hearsay evidence admissible apart from this section, notwithstanding that it may also be admissible by virtue of this section.

These provisions indicate that some of the existing rules relating to the admissibility of hearsay in civil proceedings remain in force, and consideration of them will occupy the second section of the chapter.

---

[1] *R v Marylebone Magistrates' Court, ex p Clingham* [2002] UKHL 39, [2003] 1 AC 787, [35], endorsing the view of the Divisional Court in [2001] EWHC Admin 1, [11].

[2] The definition in s 1(2) is repeated as CPR 33.1.

SECTION 1. THE CIVIL EVIDENCE ACT 1995

This Act implements the recommendations of the Law Commission in its report *The Hearsay Rule in Civil Proceedings*.[3] Although the two previous pieces of general legislation[4] had attempted to revolutionize the admissibility of documentary hearsay in civil proceedings, they had been bedevilled by excessive caution, and cumbersome procedures, with the result that hearsay was very often admitted only by agreement between the parties, and despite any formal difficulty, an approach, in part at least, inspired by judicial distaste for the exclusion of relevant evidence in civil proceedings on technical grounds alone.[5] The new approach of the Law Commission was to extend admissibility, while using procedural measures, and considerations of weight, to prevent abuse. It should also be noted that increased readiness to permit video-linking has reduced the necessity to rely upon hearsay.[6] This section will consider first the admissibility, and then the means of proof of hearsay in civil proceedings.

ADMISSIBILITY

Notwithstanding the bold claim in the very first subsection of the Act quoted above, it has been argued[7] that the Act has failed to achieve that effect on account of its restrictive definition of hearsay in s 1(2)(a) in terms of 'a statement'.[8] Exactly the same argument was also raised in relation to criminal proceedings in *R v Singh*, in which it was roundly rejected on the basis of words indicating abolition of the old hearsay rule.[9] Notwithstanding slight differences between the drafting of the relevant provisions, it is quite inconceivable that the admission of such evidence should be more restricted in civil than in criminal cases. It is thus submitted that no more should be heard of this argument.

The remaining aspects of general admissibility can be considered shortly. It is clear from the definition in s 1(2)(a), and from the terms of s 6, that the new rule of admissibility applies both to third party hearsay, and to previous statements of a witness. In the latter case, as much as in the former, such admissibility operates to prove the truth of the matter stated.[10] Section 1(2)(b) makes it quite explicit that admissibility extends to hearsay of any degree.[11]

---

[3] Law Com No 216, Cm 2321 (1993). The Act follows the draft bill appended to the report very closely, adding only a single clause relating to the admissibility of Ogden tables that had been recommended in a separate Law Commission Report *Structured Settlements and Interim and Provisional Damages* (Law Com No 224 (1994)).   [4] Evidence Act 1938; Civil Evidence Act 1968.

[5] See e.g. Balcombe LJ in *Ventouris v Mountain (No 2)* [1992] 3 All ER 414, [1992] 1 WLR 887; 426b, 899: 'The modern tendency in civil proceedings is to admit all relevant evidence, and the judge should be trusted to give only proper weight to evidence which is not the best evidence.'

[6] See *Polanski v Condé Nast Publications Ltd* [2005] UKHL 10, [2005] 1 All ER 945, [68].

[7] By Ockleton, in his annotation of the Act in *Current Law Statutes*.

[8] Support might be enlisted: first, from the formulation of s 1(4), which could be read to suggest that some hearsay may not be made admissible by the section, although it is submitted that the alternative of construing 'may' as the subjunctive equivalent of 'is' is preferable both as a matter of grammar, and of policy; second, from the definition of 'statement' in s 13 as 'any representation of fact or opinion', although this too is capable of being read as equivalent to 'representing any fact or opinion', subject to appropriate grammatical manipulation of the form of the definition.   [9] [2006] EWCA Crim 660, [2006] 2 Cr App R 201, [14].

[10] Although only if proved under s 1, as authorized by s 6(5): see *Denton Hall Legal Services v Fifield* [2006] EWCA Civ 169, [2006] LlR Med 251, Buxton LJ, [77]; but see Stockdale (2006) 156 *NLJ* 751.

[11] So eliminating the tortuous reasoning in *Ventouris v Mountain (No 2)* (n5) under the old law.

It is worth emphasizing that one great advantage over the previous law in this respect is the treatment of information in electronic form, so far as possible, in exactly the same way as any other form of information.[12] The extremely cumbersome procedures of the CEA 1968 have been jettisoned without specific replacement, and expansive definitions of 'records',[13] 'statement', 'document', and 'copy'[14] adopted, clearly with a view to including electronic forms, and even automatic generation and reproduction.

Hearsay is inadmissible where the maker of the statement would have been incompetent.[15] It is odd that this section is much more explicit in applying both to the original supplier of information, and to subsequent conduits of it, than that relating to attendance for cross-examination under s 3. It is also worth noting that the proviso to s 5(2) prevents the admission of evidence relating to any matter as to which a denial by the declarant, if he had testified in person, would have been conclusive. This remains different from the situation in criminal proceedings.

The rule of admissibility extends to all civil proceedings, including proceedings in the magistrates' court,[16] the Crown Court,[17] and in tribunals, but only so far as the court or tribunal applies the strict rules of evidence,[18] either as a matter of rule, or by agreement between the parties.[19] Although, as pointed out in Chapter I above, there is a myriad of rules of evidence, applying in different combinations to different courts, types of proceeding, and stages, the courts can be relied upon to find a sensible and satisfactory route through the maze, and there appear to be no examples of other tribunals applying *stricter* exclusionary rules than the ordinary courts.

MEANS OF PROOF

The scheme of the legislation is to distinguish between information, which is governed by notice provisions, and special procedures for assessing and testing weight, and documents containing such information, the means of proof of which are, in some cases, alleviated.

Since one of the main defects of the 1968 Act had been identified as the cumbersome nature of the notice procedure required under it, every effort has been made to simplify the procedure here. CEA 1995, s 2(1) requires no more than an informal notice of the intention to rely on hearsay evidence, and an obligation to provide further particulars upon request. This added little to the previous requirement upon a party under the old

---

[12] Afforced by the Electronic Signatures Regulations 2002, SI 2002/318, implementing the European Electronic Signatures Directive 1999/93/EC. For a fuller account, see Saxby (ed) *Encyclopedia of Information Technology Law* ch 11.   [13] Section 9(4).

[14] Section 13.

[15] A child is regarded as competent if it would have been permitted to testify unsworn.

[16] See Magistrates' Courts (Hearsay Evidence in Civil Proceedings) Rules 1999, SI 1999/681.

[17] In relation to antisocial behaviour proceedings: *R v Wadmore and Foreman* [2006] EWCA Crim 686, (2006) 170 JP 406, [37]. It was noted in *R (Cleary) v Highbury Corner Magistrates's Court* [2006] EWHC 1869 (Admin), [2007] 1 ALL ER 270, [32] that there is some inconsistency between the time limits required under the Anti-Social Behaviour Act 2003, and by the Magistrates' Court (Hearsay Evidence in Civil Proceedings) Rules 199.   [18] So not in wardship proceedings in the High Court.

[19] Section 11. See also the reference in s 12 to arbitration proceedings. Just occasionally the parties may agree to limit the forms of evidence to be used to resolve a dispute: see *A-G for the Falkland Islands v Gordon Forbes Construction (Falklands) Ltd (No 2)* [2003] BLR 280, [2003] JCLR 9 (contemporary records).

procedure to supply witness statements to an opponent,[20] and it is now explicitly provided that the delivery of a witness statement satisfies the notice requirement.[21] It is put further within the control of the parties by permitting them to exclude the obligation by agreement, or for the party in whose favour it is intended to operate to waive it. Provision is also made for rules excluding particular classes of proceedings from the obligation, and for varying the requirements.[22] The effect of failure to give notice is significantly weakened by the consideration that such failure will be visited not by inadmissibility, but by re-ordering proceedings, sanctions by way of costs, and by authorizing adverse inference as to weight.

It remains the case that, in case of conflicting evidence, the court is likely to require cross-examination where that is possible,[23] and one further safeguard to be mentioned here is that s 3 makes provision for rules of court under which a party against whom hearsay is to be tendered may call the maker of the statement to attend as a witness, for his statement to stand as his evidence in chief, and for him to be cross-examined.[24] In *R (Cleary) v Highbury Corner Magistrates' Court*[25] it was regarded as contrary to the spirit, but not the letter, of this provision to tender hearsay from an unidentified witness. It should be noted that the reference is only to the maker of the statement, and does not appear to extend to intermediaries in the chain of supply of remote hearsay.[26] A party who has served a notice may nevertheless refrain from either tendering the evidence,[27] or calling the witness, and in such a case, cross-examination of the maker of the statement will not be possible, since there will be no primary evidence to cross-examine. If such a witness refuses to testify, the court has power to exclude the hearsay statement under the discretion conferred by Pt 32.1 of the Civil Procedure Rules, but this is likely to be exercised only in a most exceptional case.[28]

Although previous statements of witnesses, to be used under the provisions of CEA 1968, s 6 are not explicitly exempted from notice procedures, they are clearly less appropriate.[29] Fuller notice may be required in relation to the use of admissions as such under s 7(1), but none is required in relation to other common law exceptions preserved by s 7.[30]

---

[20] RSC Ord 38, r 2A; see further, 278.　　[21] CPR 33.2.

[22] Section 2(2). It is not envisaged that these powers will be used to impose a more stringent set of requirements than those under the current law, although there is no formal prohibition on their doing so.

[23] As in *Long v Farrer & Co* [2004] EWHC 1774 (Ch), [2004] BPIR 1218.

[24] In *Douglas v Hello! Ltd* [2003] EWCA Civ 332, (2003) 147 Sol Jo LB 297, it was held that a party could cross-examine his own uncalled witness on a statement that his opponent was seeking to rely upon as hearsay.

[25] (n17), [30]. Although in *M v DPP* [2007] EWHC 1032 (Admin) in just such a case the Court was prepared to excuse failure to serve notice. In *Wear Valley DC v Robson* [2008] EWCA Civ 1470 the admission of hearsay in this situation was approved without any suggestion of notice having been served.

[26] This appears to be borne out by the use of the same form of words in CPR 33.4, which implements the statutory provision. Where the party originally tendering the hearsay withdraws reliance upon it, then, although any other party may take over the statement, they cannot then require the original party to tender the maker for cross-examination: *Society of Lloyds v Jaffray* (2000) The Times, 3 August.

[27] In *The Green Opal* [2003] 1 LIR 523, it was held that an expression of intention to rely on the served statement did not amount to tender, even though the statement had, at that stage, been read in advance by the judge. Tender was held to be possible only after the opening of the case for the tenderer.

[28] *Polanski v Condé Nast Publications Ltd* (n6), [78]; in such a case, it is not being excluded as hearsay, but because its maker has refused to testify, so there is no breach of s 1(1); cf *R (Brooks) v Parole Board* [2003] EWHC 1458 Admin, [47], in which unwillingness to testify reinforced the decision to admit it.

[29] Any necessary procedural steps will be handled under the provision of s 6(2)(a), requiring the leave of the court before such statements are adduced.

[30] Namely published works, public documents, records, and evidence of reputation.

The principal counter-balance for expansion of admissibility is intended to be closer attention to weight,[31] and the Act not only permits any relevant circumstance to be taken into account, but goes on to mention a number of particular considerations:[32]

(a) whether it would have been reasonable and practicable for the party by whom the evidence was adduced to have produced the maker of the original statement as a witness;

(b) whether the original statement was made contemporaneously with the occurrence or existence of the matters stated;

(c) whether the evidence involves multiple hearsay;

(d) whether any person involved had any motive to conceal or misrepresent matters;

(e) whether the original statement was an edited account, or was made in collaboration with another for a particular purpose;

(f) whether the circumstances in which the evidence is adduced as hearsay are such as to suggest an attempt to prevent proper evaluation of its weight.

Since these criteria are not exclusive,[33] and relate to weight rather than to admissibility, there will be no attempt to construe them rigidly, and they should achieve their purpose of highlighting the sorts of considerations, and weaknesses, that the trier of fact should attempt to take into account, and canvass in the judgment.[34] It should be noted that the Act includes no preference for non-hearsay, so there is no obligation upon the court to defer consideration of hearsay until after it has decided whether the non-hearsay evidence is sufficient to determine the outcome.[35] Because of the possibility of requiring a witness to be called, it is quite proper, where no such request has been made, for a party to rely upon hearsay rather than to call the witness to testify.[36] This remains different from the position in criminal proceedings.[37]

Where hearsay is contained in a document, then the means of proof are simplified by the provisions of s 8,[38] which permits production of original or copy,[39] subject only to whatever form of authentication the court deems appropriate. In the case of records[40] of[41]

---

[31] Including the contemplation of some relevant evidence having no weight at all: s 4(1). See also, in Scotland: *TSB (Scotland) plc v James Mills (Montrose) Ltd (in receivership)* 1992 SLT 519.

[32] Section 4(2).

[33] See e.g. *R v Secretary of State for Home Affairs, ex p Fayed* [2001] Imm AR 134 (fact that origin of hearsay statement was a journalist's undisclosed source).

[34] *Moat Housing Group-South Ltd v Harris* [2005] EWCA Civ 287, [2005] 4 All ER 1051, [140].

[35] *Solon South Wales Housing Association v James* [2004] EWCA Civ 1847, [2005] HLR 24, [14]; cf *Moat Housing* (n34), [136].

[36] Nor is the judge required to intervene: *Ryell v Health Professions Council* [2005] EWHC 2797 (Admin), [46].   [37] Cf Criminal Justice Act 2003, s 124(2)(b).

[38] Following the form of s 27 of the Criminal Justice Act 1988, which appeared to have worked perfectly satisfactorily.   [39] At whatever remove.

[40] Although the form of a 'record' is given a wide definition, no explicit attempt is made to resolve the dispute in the old law as to the definition of a record itself: see *Savings and Investment Bank Ltd v Gasco Investments (Netherlands) BV* [1984] 1 All ER 296, [1984] 1 WLR 271; itself approved in *R v Governor of Pentonville Prison, ex p Osman* [1989] 3 All ER 701, [1990] 1 WLR 277. Compare the more liberal approach in *Campofina Bank v ANZ Banking Group* [1982] 1 NSWLR 409.

[41] In Australia, a similarly phrased provision was construed liberally to include private records of an employee about his business activities: *Standard Chartered Bank of Australia Ltd v Antico* (1993) 36 NSWLR 87. See also *Duncan Davis Pty Ltd v Hurstbridge Abattoirs (Australia) Pty Ltd* [1995] 1 VR 279, in which a personal diary containing prices was held to be a 'book of account' under the local legislation.

businesses or public authorities,[42] certification procedures are specified in s 9(2), although the court is also given full power to dispense with them if it thinks fit.[43] In the case of such records, an omission may be received in evidence.[44]

SECTION 2. OTHER PROVISIONS

As noted above, the Act seeks to expand admissibility, and to that end, has chosen not to affect existing relaxation of the rule.[45] It further specifically preserves a number of common law[46] and statutory rules[47] having such an effect. Some of these have accreted a body of authority and interpretation, and will briefly be mentioned below.[48]

PUBLIC DOCUMENTS

Section 7(2) provides that:

The common law rules effectively preserved by s 9(1) and (2)(b) to (d) of the Civil Evidence Act 1968, that is, any rule of law whereby in civil proceedings—

(a) published works dealing with matters of a public nature (for example, histories, scientific works, dictionaries and maps) are admissible as evidence of facts of a public nature stated in them,

(b) public documents (for example, public registers, and returns made under public authority with respect to matters of public interest) are admissible as evidence of the matters stated in them, or

(c) records (for example, the records of certain courts, treaties, Crown grants, pardons and commissions) are admissible as evidence of facts stated in them,

shall continue to have effect.

Published works

Little need be said about the first of the above rules, which is also applicable to criminal proceedings. It is not difficult to think of historical facts that could be proved in a contemporary court of law only by recourse to the works mentioned, and Lord Halsbury was merely stating the dictates of common sense when he said: 'Where it is important to ascertain ancient facts of a public nature, the law does permit historical works to be referred to.'[49] It was by analogy with those dictates that the report of the engineer responsible for the construction of the Thames tunnel, made in 1844, was admitted in 1904 as evidence of the nature of the soil above it in *East London Rly Co v Thames Conservators*.[50] It is regrettably true that a higher degree of technicality had been allowed to creep into this branch of the law,[51] but the conversion of the common law rule into a statutory provision cannot, of itself, effect any change in this regard.[52]

---

[42] Broadly defined in CEA 1968, s 9(4). [43] CEA 1968, s 9(5). [44] CEA 1968, s 9(3).
[45] CEA 1968, s 1(3). [46] CEA 1968, s 7(2), (3). [47] CEA 1968, s 14.
[48] The formulation dealing with the common law exceptions considered in parts A and B has been repeated in s 118(1) of the Criminal Justice Act 2003. [49] *Read v Bishop of Lincoln* [1892] AC 644, 653.
[50] (1904) 90 LT 347. The report had become part of the technical expertise of the relevant witness.
[51] See e.g. *A-G v Horner (No 2)* [1913] 2 Ch 140. [52] CEA 1968, s 9(6).

Public documents

Statements in public documents are generally admissible evidence of the truth of their contents.[53] The common law has also been retained in virtually identical terms to those set out above for the purposes of criminal proceedings by the Criminal Justice Act 2003.[54] But since the rule operates more often in civil proceedings than in criminal, and there seem to be no special considerations applying to its operation in criminal proceedings, it is principally considered here. It has been retained largely on account of being presupposed by some of the statutory provisions that are also being retained.[55] Many of the statements contained in such documents would be admissible in civil proceedings under the provisions of s 1 of the Civil Evidence Act 1995, but the advantage of proving such a document under this exception is that the notice, and weighing, provisions associated with proof under s 1 do not then apply. Its nature, rationale, and scope will be mentioned here.

Nature

The most succinct formulation of this exception to the hearsay rule is that of Phillimore J in *Wilton & Co v Phillips*:[56] 'A public document coming from the proper place or a certified copy of it is sufficient proof of every particular stated in it.' In *Re Stollery, Weir v Treasury Solicitor*,[57] Scrutton LJ expressed the opinion that this was simply a restatement of the law laid down in the leading cases of *Irish Society v Bishop of Derry*,[58] and *Sturla v Freccia*.[59] Some limit must, however, be placed upon the generality of Phillimore J's statement, in view of the explanation of *Bird v Keep*[60] adopted in *Re Stollery, Weir v Treasury Solicitor*. In *Bird v Keep*, it was held that a death certificate was inadmissible evidence of the cause of death mentioned therein on information supplied by a coroner.[61] This conclusion was technically *obiter dictum*, because the Court of Appeal considered that the cause of death was sufficiently proved by other evidence, but it was justified in *Re Stollery* on the ground that, as the registrar of births, deaths, and marriages is bound by statute to record the verdict of a coroner's jury, and as that verdict was inadmissible evidence of the facts on which it was based, it would be absurd to treat the registrar's certificate as any proof of this particular fact. Such a certificate does, however, constitute evidence of the date, as well as the fact of the birth, marriage, or death recorded,[62] and, as was decided by the Court of Appeal in *Re Stollery*, a birth certificate may constitute a link in the evidence relating to the marriage of the parents of the child whose birth is recorded. A birth certificate is likewise evidence of the paternity of the person named therein as the father.[63]

---

[53] In the United States, the matter is governed by the Federal Rules of Evidence, r 803 (8)(c), which has been held to encompass opinion as well as fact, if based upon factual findings: *Beech Aircraft Corp v Rainey* 488 US 153 (1988).   [54] CJA 2003, s 118(2).

[55] Law Com No 216, [4.32].   [56] (1903) 19 TLR 390.   [57] [1926] Ch 284, 318.

[58] (1846) 12 Cl & Fin 641.   [59] (1880) 5 App Cas 623.   [60] [1918] 2 KB 692.

[61] *Bird v Keep* (n60) was followed in *Chapman v Amos* (1959) 18 DLR (2d) 140.

[62] *Wilton & Co v Phillips* (n56); *Re Goodrich's Estate, Payne v Bennett* [1904] P 138; *Brierley v Brierley and Williams* [1918] P 257. Statements of opinion are now admissible under the Civil Evidence Act 1995, and would include a doctor's statement of the cause of death.

[63] *Jackson v Jackson and Pavan* [1964] P 25, [1960] 3 All ER 621. See also *Carlton and United Breweries Ltd v Cassin* [1956] VLR 186 (statement of age on marriage certificate evidence of that fact).

Rationale

The rationale of this broad exception to the hearsay rule was explained by Parke B in *Irish Society v Bishop of Derry* as being that:[64]

In public documents, made for the information of the Crown, or all the King's subjects who may require the information they contain, the entry by a public officer is presumed to be true when it is made, and it is for that reason receivable in all cases, whether the officer or his successor may be concerned in such cases or not.

To the extent that this reason rests upon the reliability of the documents, it was amplified by Lord Blackburn in *Sturla v Freccia*:[65]

In many cases, entries in the parish register of births, marriages and deaths, and other entries of that kind, before there were any statutes relating to them, were admissible, for they were 'public' then, because the common law of England making it an express duty to keep the register, made it a public document in that sense kept by a public officer for the purposes of a register, and that made it admissible.

This reasoning is just as capable of applying to foreign public documents as to English, and it was so extended by Lord Selbourne in *Lyell v Kennedy*:[66]

Foreign registers of baptisms and marriages or certified extracts from them are receivable in evidence in the courts of this country as to those matters which are properly and regularly recorded on them when it sufficiently appears (in the words of Mr Hubbock's learned work on evidence) that they 'have been kept under the sanction of public authority and are recognised by the tribunals of the country' (ie of the country where they are kept) 'as authentic records'.

If these reasons cannot be demonstrated to apply, then the courts will reject the document as evidence of the truth of what it asserts. Thus in *Sturla v Freccia*,[67] the report of a committee appointed by the Genoese government on the fitness of a candidate for the post of consul, which contained a statement of his age, was rejected as evidence of that fact. The grounds on which the House of Lords held that the evidence should be rejected were that the report was not made under a strict duty to inquire into all the circumstances it recorded, it was not concerned with a public matter, it was not intended to be retained, and it was not meant for public inspection. A word must be said about each of these matters, which may be treated as the usual prerequisites of a document's admissibility as a public document, although the last appears in the forefront of Lord Blackburn's description, which has been quoted on a number of subsequent occasions. He said he understood:[68]

…a public document to mean a document that is made for the purpose of the public making use of it, and being able to refer to it. It is meant to be where there is a judicial or quasi-judicial duty to inquire, as might be said to be the case with the bishops acting under the writs issued by the Crown.

---

[64] (1846) 12 Cl & Fin 641, 668, 669.

[65] (n59), 644. In *R v Halpin* [1975] QB 907, [1975] 2 All ER 1124, it was suggested that it would have been more accurate if Lord Blackburn had spoken of registers of baptisms, marriages, and burials, because the parish officer would not have had personal knowledge of births and deaths, and was under no duty to enquire into their occurrence.

[67] (n59).   [68] 643, 4.   [66] (1889) 14 App Cas 437, 448–9.

This is probably the definition most often repeated, and it is worth amplifying some of its elements.

(a) Public duty to inquire and record

It has been said that the admissibility of a register depends on the public duty of the person compiling it to make an entry after satisfying himself of the truth of the statement.[69] The duty must be imposed on a public official in that capacity. Surveys made under private authority have been held to be inadmissible, although they were kept in a public office,[70] and baptismal registers kept by Nonconformists or Quakers were inadmissible as evidence of the facts stated at common law.[71] Even if a duty to report to a public authority is imposed upon an official by statute, his report will not constitute proof of the truth of its contents if made solely in order to provide a check upon himself.[72] Nor is it enough to make a report in anticipation of an official request.[73]

(b) Public matter

It was recognized in *Sturla v Freccia* that a matter may be public although it is not the concern of the entire community. Accordingly, the court rolls of a manor have been received as evidence of a custom,[74] but entries in a corporation's books were sometimes rejected at common law, because they did not concern a public matter.[75] It is, however, doubtful whether this is something with regard to which any high degree of precision can be achieved. In *R v Halpin*,[76] it was held that a company's file of statutory returns, kept in the register of companies, was admissible evidence that the appellant was a director at the material time because, under modern conditions, it is sufficient if one person (the officer making the return) has a duty to satisfy himself as to the facts stated, and another (the registration officer) has a duty to record those facts.

(c) Retention

If a document is brought into existence for a temporary purpose, it cannot be received under this head. Thus in *Heyne v Fischel & Co*,[77] it was held that records, compiled by the post office showing the times at which telegrams were received, were inadmissible as there was no intention that they should be retained for public inspection, and Crown surveys were rejected on account of their temporary purpose in *Mercer v Denne*.[78]

---

[69] Erle J in *Doe d France v Andrews* (1850) 15 QB 756. A gratuitous annotation to an official record is thus inadmissible: *Re Simpson* [1984] 1 NZLR 738 (annotation on death certificate that the deceased's issue had been adopted).

[70] *Daniel v Wilkin* (1852) 7 Exch 429. The surveys would now be admissible under s 1 of the Civil Evidence Act 1995.

[71] *Re Woodward, Kenway v Kidd* [1913] 1 Ch 392. In so far as they are not admissible by virtue of some other statute, they would now be admissible under s 1 of the Civil Evidence Act 1995: *Re H's Estate* [1949] VLR 197.   [72] *Merrick v Wakley* (1838) 8 Ad & El 170.

[73] *Newbold v R* [1983] 2 AC 705, although such a report would now be admissible in England under s 117 of the Criminal Justice Act 2003.   [74] *Heath v Deane* [1905] 2 Ch 86.

[75] *Hill v Manchester and Salford Waterworks Co* (1833) 5 B & Ad 866.

[76] (n65). Applied in Australia to the Annual Report of a public company: *Residues Treatment and Trading Co Ltd v Southern Resources Ltd* (1989) 52 SASR 54, 83.   [77] (1913) 30 TLR 190.

[78] [1905] 2 Ch 538; see also *White v Taylor* [1969] 1 Ch 150, [1967] 3 All ER 349.

(d) Public inspection

The possibility that the public may refer to the document undoubtedly enhances the credibility of its contents;[79] the decision in *Lilley v Pettit*,[80] which turned on this requirement, may be thought to justify Professor Baker's comment that:[81]

Accessibility of the public to documents should never have been raised from the status of an additional reason for admitting official records to that of a condition of admissibility.

Lilley v Pettit was a case in which a woman was prosecuted for making a false statement with regard to the paternity of her child, in entering it as that of her husband. The prosecution tendered in evidence the regimental records of the army unit in which her husband had been serving abroad at all material times, but the Divisional Court held them to be inadmissible, because they were not kept for the use and information of the public, who had not got access to them. Accordingly, the prosecution failed. The result is surprising, but the principle on which it was reached was already deeply embedded in our law,[82] and subsequently adopted by the Privy Council.[83]

Scope

It is clear from the cases mentioned above that there are several different kinds of public document. Wigmore distinguished between registers, returns, and certificates.[84] Apart from its convenience from the point of view of exposition, it may have practical significance, because the general conditions of admissibility that have just been enumerated undoubtedly undergo some modification when applied to different species of public document. In the case of registers, it may be fatal to the reception of the entry to prove that it was not made promptly,[85] or in accordance with the prevailing practice relating to the keeping of the register.[86] Any excess of jurisdiction would be fatal to some types of return.[87] There would, however, be no point in endeavouring to lay down hard-and-fast rules, inferred from the cases, concerning the further conditions of admissibility that may have to be satisfied in the case of certain public documents, for each decision is highly dependent on its specific facts, and has lost much of its force since the passage of the 1995 legislation.

Records

This rule, which is applicable also in criminal proceedings, requires no special comment.

---

[79] But if this were the reason for the rejection of certificates, issued under the Drug Trafficking Act 1986, as evidence of their contents, in *R v Boam* [1998] Crim LR 205, it is unconvincing since the accuracy of the statements derived from their resulting from judicial inquiry, which seems a much better guarantee of accuracy.

[80] [1946] KB 401, [1946] 1 All ER 593. Cf *Andrews v Cordiner* [1947] KB 655, [1947] 1 All ER 777, an affiliation case in which regimental records were admitted under the Evidence Act 1938, as they would be under the Act of 1968. [81] Baker *The Hearsay Rule* 137.

[82] See e.g. *A-G v Horner (No 2)* (n51).

[83] *Thrasyvoulos Ioannou v Papa Christoforos Demetrious* [1952] AC 84, [1952] 1 All ER 179; see also *R v Kaipianen* (1954) 17 CR 388. Admissibility under CEA 1995, s 1 has now resolved most of the problems.

[84] V Wigmore [631] f.   [85] *Doe d Warren v Bray* (1828) 8 B & C 813.

[86] *Fox v Bearblock* (1881) 17 Ch D 429; *Doe d Davies v Gatacre* (1838) 8 C & P 578.

[87] *Evans v Taylor* (1838) 7 Ad & El 617.

REPUTATION

Section 7(3) provides that:

The common law rules effectively preserved by s 9(3) and (4) of the Civil Evidence Act 1968, that is any rule of law whereby in civil proceedings

(a) evidence of a person's reputation is admissible for the purpose of establishing his good or bad character, or

(b) evidence of reputation or family tradition is admissible—

(i) for the purpose of proving or disproving pedigree or the existence of the marriage, or

(ii) for the purpose of proving or disproving the existence of any public or general right or of identifying any person or thing,

shall continue to have effect in so far as they authorise the court to treat such evidence as proving or disproving that matter.

Where any such rule applies, reputation or family tradition shall be treated for the purposes of this Act as a fact and not as a statement or multiplicity of statements about the matter in question.

It is important to distinguish between the establishment of reputation and the use made of it when established. Reputation is established by a witness's evidence concerning the sayings and doings of a plurality of people. Accordingly, it has been said that a witness may not narrate a single person's statement of either the fact reputed, or reputation, unless it is the pedigree declaration of a member of the family with regard to a genealogical issue.[88] There is, therefore, no question of an infringement of the rule against hearsay, so far as the establishment of reputation is concerned, but that rule would be infringed whenever reputation were tendered as evidence of the facts reputed. If a witness depose to a tradition concerning the existence of a public right prevailing in the community, or the neighbourhood's treatment of a couple as man and wife, he is recounting the express, or implied, assertions of a number of other people, in order to establish the truth of that which was asserted.

This distinction is recognized in the final sentence quoted above, so as to make it clear that the notice provisions do not apply to every statement relied upon by the witness to justify his testimony as to reputation.

Nothing need be said about evidence of character, but reference must be made to the matters of pedigree, and public or general rights, mentioned in s 7(3) because, at common law, they are the subject of technical requirements, some of which will very probably be held to have survived the Act.

Pedigree

At common law, there is an exception to the hearsay rule under which the oral, or written, declarations of deceased persons, or declarations to be inferred from family conduct, are, subject to the conditions of admissibility mentioned below, admissible as evidence of pedigree. The evidence often takes the form of direct assertions of fact, as in the ancient case

---

[88] *Shedden v A-G* (1860) 30 LJPM & A 217.

of *Goodright d Stevens v Moss*[89] in which the question was whether a child was the legitimate offspring of its parents (since deceased), and Lord Mansfield admitted the parents' declarations, proved by the persons to whom they were made, to the effect that the child was born before their marriage. Such declarations would now, like any other first-hand hearsay statement, be admissible under s 1 of the 1995 Act.

The common law conditions of admissibility of pedigree statements or, to employ the more usual word 'declarations', are that:

(i) the declarant should have been dead;

(ii) the declarations should relate to a question of pedigree, i.e. have a genealogical purpose;[90]

(iii) the declarant should have been a blood relation, or the spouse of a blood relation, of the person whose pedigree is in issue;[91] and

(iv) the declaration should have been made before the dispute in which it is tendered had arisen.[92]

All these conditions are now irrelevant so far as declarations of fact, as distinct from reputation, are concerned, provided they can be rendered admissible under s 1. For example, the issue being A's legitimacy, A's mother writes to B from America to say that she has heard of the dispute, and may as well state the truth, viz, that she never married A's deceased father; the mother's statement is admissible under s 1 as of one otherwise than while giving evidence. If the issue is whether the defendant to a claim for breach of contract is an infant, an affidavit sworn by his deceased father in relation to another case is admissible, although the question is not one of pedigree.[93] If the issue is which of the twins C and D is the elder, the statement of a deceased nurse that she was present at the birth, and marked C's foot as that of the first born, may be proved under s 1.[94]

It is therefore only in a very restricted sense that s 7 can be said to have preserved this common law exception to the hearsay rule. A statement tending to establish family reputation, or tradition, which would, but for the Act, have been admissible for the purpose of proving pedigree, is admissible by virtue of s 7 only if the common law conditions of admissibility are satisfied. Accordingly, if A could prove that B, a deceased retainer of the X family, had told him that, according to the family tradition, X's grandfather was illegitimate, it seems that, although the statement would be inadmissible by virtue of s 7, it would still be admissible if tendered under s 1.

Public or general rights[95]

At common law, an oral, or written, declaration by a deceased person concerning the reputed existence of a public, or general, right is admissible as evidence of the existence of

---

[89] (1777) 2 Cowp 591; *Murray v Milner* (1879) 12 Ch D 845; *Re Turner, Glenister v Harding* (1885) 29 Ch D 985.

[90] *Haines v Guthrie* (1884) 13 QBD 818; cf *Hood v Beauchamp* (1836) 8 Sim 26, and *Shields v Boucher* (1847) 1 De G & Sm 40.

[91] *Johnson v Lawson* (1824) 2 Bing 86; *Shrewsbury Peerage Case* (1858) 7 HL Cas 1, 23; *Berkeley Peerage Case* (1811) 4 Camp 401. On problems of legitimacy and legitimation, see *Hitchens v Eardley* (1871) LR 2 P & D 248; *Re Jenion, Jenion v Wynne* [1952] Ch 454, [1952] 1 All ER 1228; *Re Perton Pearson v A-G* (1885) 53 LT 707; *Re Davy* [1935] P 1, followed in *Battle v A-G* [1949] P 358. See also *Monkton v A-G* (1831) 2 Russ & M 147; *B v A-G* [1965] P 278, [1965] 1 All ER 62. [92] *Berkeley Peerage Case* (n91).

[93] Cf *Haines v Guthrie* (n90). [94] Cf *Johnson v Lawson* (n91).

[95] Except where admissibility under the Civil Evidence Act is being considered, what is said under this head could apply in criminal proceedings.

such right, provided the declaration was made before the dispute in which it is tendered had arisen, and, in the case of a statement concerning the reputed existence of a general right, provided the declarant had competent knowledge.

A public right is one affecting the entire population, such as a claim to tolls on a public highway,[96] a right of ferry,[97] or the right to treat part of a river bank as a public landing place.[98] Declarations by deceased persons tending to prove or disprove the existence of such rights are admissible at common law, and evidence of this nature is received on cognate questions, such as the boundaries between counties and parishes,[99] and the question of whether a road is public or private.[100]

A general right is one that affects a class of persons, such as the inhabitants of a particular district, the tenants of a manor, or the owners of certain plots of land. Examples are rights of common,[101] the rights of corporations,[102] and a custom of mining in a particular district.[103] The distinction from public rights is not precise, and if important, only because it has been said that no evidence of competent knowledge of the subject matter of the reputed right on the part of the declarant is necessary when the right is public because 'in a matter in which all are concerned, reputation from anyone appears to be receivable; but of course it would be almost worthless unless it came from persons who were shown to have some means of knowledge as by living in the neighbourhood, or frequently using the road in dispute'. If, however, the alleged right is a general one, such as a mining right under certain land, 'hearsay from any person wholly unconnected with the place in which the mines are found, would not only be of no value, but probably altogether inadmissible'.[104]

A far more crucial distinction is that between public, or general, rights, on the one hand, and private rights on the other hand, for the latter cannot be proved by evidence of reputation.[105] But here, again, the distinction is none too precise: all that can be said is that a public, or general right must be enjoyed by the claimant as a member of the public, or as a member of some clearly defined class. Evidence of a reputation is admissible when private and public rights coincide, as when the boundaries between two estates are coterminous with those between two hamlets.[106]

The common law conditions of admissibility of hearsay statements concerning reputed public or general rights are:

(i)   the death of the declarant;

(ii)   that the declaration should have been made before the dispute in which it is tendered;[107] and

---

[96] *Brett v Beales* (1830) 10 B & C 508.   [97] *Pim v Curell* (1840) 6 M & W 234.

[98] *Drinkwater v Porter* (1835) 7 C & P 181.

[99] *Brisco v Lomax* (1838) 8 Ad & El 198; *Evans v Rees* (1839) 10 Ad & El 151.

[100] *R v Bliss* (1837) 2 Nev & PKB 464.   [101] *Evans v Merthyr Tydfil UDC* [1899] 1 Ch 241.

[102] *Davies v Morgan* (1831) 1 Cr & J 587.   [103] *Crease v Barrett* (1835) 1 Cr M & R 919.

[104] *Crease v Barrett* (n103); see also *Rogers v Wood* (1831) 2 B & Ad 245. Even in the case of a general right, the declarant need not be proved to have been resident in the neighbourhood: *Duke of Newcastle v Broxtowe Hundred* (1832) 4 B & Ad 273.

[105] *R v Antrobus* (1835) 2 Ad & El 788; *Talbot v Lewis* (1834) 1 Cr M & R 495; *Lord Dunraven v Llewellyn* (1850) 15 QB 791 (see *Evans v Merthyr Tydfil UDC* [1899] 1 Ch 241 for the limits of this decision); *White v Taylor* [1969] 1 Ch 150, [1967] 3 All ER 349.   [106] *Thomas v Jenkins* (1837) 6 Ad & El 525.

[107] *Berkeley Peerage Case* (n91); the fact that the declaration was made to provide against future controversy does not affect its admissibility, nor does the existence of a general motive to misrepresent: *Moseley v Davies* (1822) 11 Price 162; but see the judgment of Joyce J in *Brocklebank v Thompson* [1903] 2 Ch 344, in which, however, the remarks about interested persons were obiter.

(iii)   that the declaration should concern the reputed existence of the right, as opposed to a particular fact from which the existence of the right may be inferred.[108]

This last requirement marks a great distinction between the admissibility of pedigree declarations, and the admissibility of declarations concerning public, or general, rights. In the case of each, the declarant must be dead, and the statement must have been made before the dispute arose; but, whereas proof of reputation is merely one way of establishing pedigree by hearsay at common law, it is the only way of doing so in the case of public, or general, rights.

All the above conditions must be fulfilled if evidence of the reputed existence of such rights is to be admissible by virtue of s 7 of the Civil Evidence Act 1995; but is this true of a statement that can, by virtue of s 7(3), be treated as a statement of fact, and thereby rendered admissible by virtue of s 1? For example, if A, formerly the oldest inhabitant of a village, were to write from America, after a dispute had arisen concerning rights of common, stating that, according to the tradition that had prevailed in the village community, those rights were enjoyed only by the occupiers of certain lands, could A's statement be received under s 1 as one made otherwise than while giving oral evidence? It is submitted that the answer is positive, because the exclusion of statements made after a dispute has arisen is a common law restriction on the reception of hearsay under a particular exception to the hearsay rule, and has suffered the same fate as other restrictions on the admissibility of hearsay evidence at common law. Evidence of reputation is second-hand hearsay, and now admissible under s 1.

A further difficult question relates to the effect of the Act on the third common law condition of admissibility: that the declaration should concern the reputed existence of the right, as opposed to a particular fact from which it might be inferred. This has produced decisions of breathtaking absurdity. For example, in *Mercer v Denne*,[109] the issue was whether the fishermen of Walmer had a customary right of immemorial antiquity to dry their nets on part of the foreshore. In support of the contention that the custom could not have existed throughout the relevant period, a survey, depositions, and old maps were produced. They showed that the sea had run over the portion of foreshore in respect of which the customary right was claimed, but they were rejected, because they amounted to statements of particular facts, and had nothing to do with the reputed existence of the custom. Is the condition of admissibility under consideration simply a common law restriction on the reception of hearsay under an exception to the general rule excluding such evidence, or is it an independent rule, which can equally well be described as one of evidence, or substantive law, which has survived the partial abolition of the hearsay rule in civil cases? Perhaps it would be rash to predict the courts' answer to this question, but it is to be hoped that *Mercer v Denne*, and the congeries of similar decisions, have not survived the Civil Evidence Act 1995. The survey, depositions, and old maps appear to have been documents in which statements were made by persons who could, if living, have given direct oral evidence with regard to the condition of the foreshore.

Whatever view may ultimately be taken by the courts on the matters mentioned above, some of the absurd results of past decisions will be avoided for the future, so far as rights of way are concerned, on account of the provisions of the Highways Act 1980, s 32. The

[108]   *R v Lordsmere (Inhabitants)* (1866) 16 Cox CC 65 (conviction for non-repair as evidence road public).
[109]   (n78); see also *R v Bliss* (n100); *R v Berger* [1894] 1 QB 823; *A-G v Horner (No 2)* (n51).

section provides that any map, plan, or history of locality is admissible to show whether a way has or has not been dedicated as a highway, or the date on which such dedication took place. Such weight is to be given to the above documents as the court considers justified by the circumstances, including the antiquity of the document, the status of the person by whom it was made, its purpose, and the custody in which it was kept, or from which it was produced.

CHILDREN

In part to avoid anomaly by comparison with wardship proceedings, in which the strict rules of evidence[110] did not apply, s 96 of the Children Act 1989 empowered the Lord Chancellor to make orders admitting hearsay in any civil proceedings in connection with the upbringing, maintenance, or welfare of a child.[111] In 1993, he ordered[112] that:

> 2. In—
>   (a) civil proceedings before the High Court or a county court; and
>   (b) (i)   family proceedings, and
>   (ii) civil proceedings under the Child Support Act 1991 in a magistrates' court,
>
>   evidence given in connection with the upbringing, maintenance or welfare of a child shall be admissible notwithstanding any rule of law relating to hearsay.

Despite such provisions, anomalies will remain so long as the hearsay rule is retained in English law for any purposes at all.[113]

COMPANY LITIGATION

Under the old law, hearsay was admissible only under the terms of the Civil Evidence Act 1968, by agreement of the parties, or under a statutory provision. It was thus prima facie odd[114] that, in proceedings to wind up companies, the courts came to rely upon hearsay in reports made by inspectors, despite their fulfilling none of these criteria.[115] The use of such a report can be justified upon the basis of the professionalism of the compilers of such a report, despite their lack of first-hand knowledge, especially when it has been considered sufficient for an independent official to act upon, and when the defendant who does have such first-hand knowledge has had ample opportunity to attempt to refute any statements it contains. The fig leaf relied upon to cover its technical inadmissibility was an *implied* statutory exception.[116] It extended both to applications to wind the company up, and to

---

[110] Including the hearsay rule: see *Official Solicitor v K* [1965] AC 201, [1963] 3 All ER 191.

[111] For a similar result in Ireland, see *Southern Health Board v CH* [1996] 1 ILRM 219.

[112] SI 1993/621.

[113] *Re C (hearsay evidence: contempt proceedings)* [1993] 4 All ER 690 revealed that anomaly remained even in relation to the evidence of children. The modern law still stops short of total abolition of the sort accomplished by the Scots in the Civil Evidence (Scotland) Act 1988, s 2: see Cm 2321 (1993).

[114] See doubts expressed by Staughton LJ in *Re Rex Williams Leisure Ltd* [1994] Ch 350, [1994] 4 All ER 27, 369c, 42a.   [115] *Re Koscot Interplanetary (UK) Ltd* [1972] 3 All ER 829.

[116] Unconvincingly derived from the terms of the 1968 Act, and the relevant rules made under it; but approved in principle in *Secretary of State for Business Enterprise and Regulatory Reform v Aaron* [2008] EWCA Civ 1146.

disqualify a director.[117] In the latter case, it applied whether, under s 7 of the Company Directors Disqualification Act 1986, the hearsay were adduced by the Official Receiver, or the Secretary of State;[118] whether the application were made under s 7, or under s 8;[119] and to both finding of primary fact and evaluation.[120]

AFFIDAVITS[121]

It has been long established that, where evidence is given in the form of an affidavit, it may be based on information and belief. The urgency of applications so supported often precludes the possibility of discovering, and obtaining access to, original sources of information. Even before the passage of s 1(2)(b) of the Civil Evidence Act 1995 applying its provisions to evidence of every degree, it had been held that such statements could themselves be based upon hearsay statements.[122]

INQUESTS

Rule 37 of the Coroners Rules 1984 provides a special Code for the admission of hearsay at inquests, and was held in *R (on the application of Paul and Ritz Hotel Ltd) v Assistant Deputy Coroner of Inner West London*[123] to preclude a Coroner from admitting disputed hearsay on his own initiative without a witness being called.

---

[117] *Re St Piran Ltd* [1981] 3 All ER 270, [1981] 1 WLR 1300.
[118] *Re Rex Williams Leisure Ltd* (n114).
[119] *Secretary of State for Trade and Industry v Ashcroft* [1998] Ch 71, [1997] 3 All ER 86.
[120] *Official Receiver v Stojevic* [2007] EWHC 1186 (Ch).
[121] See the Civil Procedure Rules, especially CPR 32.15.
[122] *Deutsche Rückversicherung AG v Walbrook Insurance* [1994] 4 All ER 181, [1995] 1 WLR 1017 (unaffected on this point by the dismissal of an appeal, [1996] 1 All ER 791), declining on this point to follow *Savings and Investment Bank Ltd v Gasco Investments (Netherlands) BV* (n40).
[123] [2007] EWHC 2721 (Admin).

XIV

HEARSAY IN CRIMINAL PROCEEDINGS[1]

Since 1984, this subject has been transformed[2] from one primarily determined by common law rules into one dominated by statute,[3] ultimately enacting proposals of the Law Commission.[4] In contrast to the position in civil proceedings, a basic rule excluding hearsay has been formally retained in criminal,[5] although subject to redefinition,[6] considerable relaxation,[7] and elaboration in various respects. The position of the accused, and especially the great importance of the huge exception from the exclusionary rule for confessions, dictates a different approach, both to the reform, and to the exposition of this area of the law of evidence. This chapter will consider, first, the relevant provisions of the Criminal Justice Act 2003, and then the rules relating to confessions,[8] and closely related rules, such as those concerned with police questioning, and the right of silence. It should be noted that some topics, strictly speaking within the scope of the title of this chapter, are considered elsewhere, such as the admissibility of previous statements of a witness, whether consistent, or inconsistent, which appeared in Chapters VI and XII, res gestae statements and admissions in Chapter XII, public documents in Chapter XIII, and the Bankers' Books Evidence Act in Chapter XV.

---

[1] Including those in magistrates' courts: *R (Crown Prosecution Service) v City of London Magistrates' Court* [2006] EWHC 1153 (Admin); and under the Criminal Procedure (Insanity) Act 1964 s 4A: *R v Chal* [2007] EWCA Crim 2647.

[2] Principally by Pt 7 of the Police and Criminal Evidence Act 1984, Pt 2 of the Criminal Justice Act 1988, and Pt 11 c 1 of the Criminal Justice Act 2003, s 118(2) of which abolished all of the common law rules apart from those preserved in terms by the statute.

[3] Described in *R v Athwal* [2009] EWCA Crim 789, [61] as a 'comprehensive code'.

[4] Law Com No 245 *Evidence in Criminal Proceedings: Hearsay and Related Topics* Cm 3670 (1997). For commentary, see Tapper [1997] *Crim LR* 771.

[5] Criminal Justice Act 2003, s 114(1). Many of the old common law exceptions have also been explicitly preserved by s 118.   [6] CJA 2003, s 115.

[7] Including admission by agreement of all of the parties to the proceedings: CJA 2003, s 114(1)(c); and at the discretion of the court if determined to be in the interests of justice that it be admitted: CJA 2003, s 114(1)(d), quite apart from expansion of the exceptions.

[8] The existing common law was explicitly preserved by CJA 2003, s 118, and the principal relevant sections of the Police and Criminal Evidence Act 1984 left unrepealed; indeed, supplemented by s 128, with a new s 76A dealing with the use by one co-accused of the confession of another.

SECTION 1. THE GENERAL POSITION UNDER THE CRIMINAL JUSTICE ACT 2003

As long ago as 1965, in *Myers v DPP*,[9] Lord Reid recommended wholesale statutory revision of the law of hearsay. It finally occurred for criminal proceedings in the shape of ch 2 of Pt 11 of the Criminal Justice Act 2003. In this section, it is proposed, first, to consider those provisions, and then to deal with s 9 of the Criminal Justice Act 1967, which, however important it may be in practice, requires less attention here, and which has now been supplemented by more general provision for the admission of hearsay by agreement of all parties to the proceedings.[10] It will be necessary to discuss the basic policy of the reform, to some extent reflected in its new definition of hearsay, the general exception, special exceptions for business documents and previous statements of witnesses, the impact of discretion, and provisions relating to the authenticity and weight of hearsay. The Act also preserved a number of common law exceptions, and complements a number of statutory exceptions, which will then be outlined. Finally, reference needs to be made to the impact upon these provisions of the European Convention on Human Rights.[11]

POLICY

The legislation adopted the rejection by the Law Commission of a policy of free admission of hearsay in criminal cases,[12] despite the advantages of simplicity, and coherence, that such a policy would have promoted.[13] Such rejection was based on fears both about the quality of such evidence, which it was felt might confuse triers of fact, and its quantity, which it was felt might overwhelm them. Neither argument seems very persuasive. Every human being deals with hearsay in his everyday decisions and judgements without undue difficulty, and it would seem to be much easier for a jury to apply such common skills than to engage in the convoluted reasoning induced by the inadmissibility of hearsay, under which evidence is to be accepted for some purposes but not for others, and against some people but not against others, which no one would dream of adopting for any purpose at all outside the compulsion of the courtroom,[14] and which is capable of leading to illogicality, and demonstrably inconsistent conclusions. Nor is there much in the point that witnesses might be thus insulated from damaging cross-examination,[15] since provision could

---

[9] [1965] AC 1001, 1022, [1964] 2 All ER 881, 1022, 886. See further, 566.

[10] Criminal Justice Act 2003, s 114(1)(c). See also s 132(4) permitting rules to be made whereby such agreement is presumed from the service of notice to adduce hearsay statements, in the absence of objection by counter-notice; and *Williams v Vehicle and Operators Service Agency* [2008] EWHC 849 (Admin) (agreement inferred from lack of objection, at least in the case of a legally represented party). Consent given only on account of an erroneous ruling on the admission of other evidence can be disregarded: *McEwan v DPP* [2007] EWHC 740 (Admin), [23].   [11] As introduced by the Human Rights Act 1998.

[12] Law Com No 245, [6.16].   [13] See Law Com No 245, [6.4]–[6.7].

[14] See Law Com No 245, [4.33], and Tapper (1990) 106 *LQR* 441, 450 for more elaborate exemplification of this point.

[15] Although this may well have occurred in *R v Santharatnam* [2007] EWCA Crim 2687, [24].

easily be made, as in civil cases, for the opponent to require the attendance of a witness.[16] So far as quantity is concerned, it is submitted that advocates will be well aware of the danger of antagonizing the court by adducing vast amounts of only marginally helpful material. Even if they are not, the CJA 2003 made specific provision for the discretionary exclusion of hearsay, the admission of which would result in a disproportionate waste of time,[17] and made no inroad in this respect in the court's inherent control of its own procedure.[18] A further subsidiary reason for rejection seems to have been concern that a policy of free admissibility might infringe Art 6(3)(d) of the European Convention on Human Rights, guaranteeing the accused the right to 'examine or have examined witnesses against him'.[19]

The CJA 2003 similarly accepted the Law Commission's rejection of a purely discretionary approach to the admission of hearsay.[20] At one point,[21] it suggests that such a system might lead to arbitrary justice. It may be noted that an effectively discretionary system, disguised by the use of such vague terms as 'necessary' or 'reliable' hearsay, has not been particularly successful where it has been attempted.[22]

The preferred solution is the rather messy[23] one of retention of a general rule of inadmissibility,[24] but according to a narrow definition of hearsay, subject to broad exceptions, and to both inclusionary, and exclusionary, discretions. It has been described as being deeply obscure,[25] and to have generated unintended and unanticipated consequences.[26]

DEFINITION

As noted above,[27] one of the key problems with hearsay has been its definition, in particular the extent to which out-of-court utterances can be used circumstantially rather than testimonially, and the related problem of distinguishing between such use and implied assertions, which the House of Lords in *R v Kearley*[28] insisted on assimilating with direct or intended assertions, and as falling within the exclusionary rule.

One of the most important features of the new regime is the way in which this problem has been tackled, and in particular, the attempt to narrow the ambit of hearsay, and hence the width of the exclusionary rule. The method ultimately[29] chosen to accomplish this purpose makes statements other than those made in oral evidence inadmissible to prove the

---

[16] Such a system would be close to that described, and also rejected, by the Law Commission as the 'best evidence' option.   [17] CJA 2003, s 126(1).

[18] As CJA 2003, s 126(2)(b) recognizes.

[19] Law Com No 245, [6.10], citing *Saidi v France* (1993) 17 EHRR 251. See further below 624.

[20] Law Com No 245, [4.28]–[4.31], [6.33]–[6.37]. Although the general inclusionary discretion in s 114(1)(d) is capable, if expansively construed, of undermining this decision: see further, 615.   [21] [4.31].

[22] Notably in Canada: see further, 560.

[23] For confusion by a trial judge, and inability of the Court of Appeal to do other than order a re-trial, see *R v McLean* [2007] EWCA Crim 219, [2008] 1 Cr App R 155; for contradictory results by trial judges in a series of re-trials, see *R v Scorah* [2008] EWCA Crim 1786, [28].

[24] This terminology is confusing, given the existence of an inclusionary discretion, making all hearsay capable of being admitted in criminal proceedings upon satisfaction of the relevant conditions.

[25] *R v Singh* [2006] EWCA Crim 660, [2006] 2 Cr App R 201, [14].

[26] *R v Z* [2009] EWCA Crim 20, [1].   [27] 554.   [28] [1992] 2 AC 228, [1992] 2 All ER 345.

[29] In its initial Consultation Paper, the Law Commission proposed, in ch XVI, [16], a definition in terms of intended assertions, adopting the terminology of the Federal Rule 801(a) in the United States, but this was amended in the final report to the formulation adopted in the Criminal Justice Act 2003.

truth of the matters stated except under the terms of the Act, thus transferring the burden of definition to the term 'statement':[30]

> (2) A statement is any representation of fact or opinion made by a person by whatever means; and it includes a representation made in a sketch, photofit or other pictorial form.

> (3) A matter stated is one to which this Chapter applies if (and only if) the purpose, or one of the purposes, of the person making the statement appears to the court to have been—

>> (a) to cause another person to believe the matter, or

>> (b) to cause another person to act or a machine to operate on the basis that the matter is as stated.

This was intended to make it quite clear that the purpose of the statement is to be considered rather than its form, and excludes statements not intended to assert *the matter sought to be proved*[31] by adducing the statement,[32] and, even when in assertive form, those for which there was no purpose of inducing belief in the matter asserted,[33] like private entry in a personal diary.[34] It also quells any fear that conduct not intended to assert anything could be excluded as hearsay.[35] It is further worth noting that the statement has to emanate from a person,[36] and hence representations made in documents emanating from machines, adduced to prove something other than the truth of a statement previously entered into them by a human being, do not amount to hearsay.[37] Given retention of an exclusionary rule for first-hand hearsay, it is natural to exclude more remote hearsay.[38] This is largely accomplished by the requirement in CJA 2003, s 116(1)(a) that oral evidence of the maker would have been admissible of the matter, which is to be understood as applying to admissibility without the assistance of a hearsay exception.[39] Specific allowance is, however, made in s 127 for the use of statements made by collaborators in the preparation of expert evidence for criminal investigation or proceedings. It is also worth noting that a subtle change in the drafting[40] makes it clear that it embraces statements of opinion, as well as of fact.

---

[30] Ss 115(2) and (3).

[31] It is submitted that in *R v Leonard* [2009] EWCA Crim 1251, [36] this was overlooked as the statement adduced there would have yielded the inference sought to be proved, whether true or false.

[32] Like most of the statements in *R v Kearley* (n28); see *R v Singh* (n25).

[33] Like the statement in *Teper v R* [1952] AC 480, [1952] 2 All ER 447.

[34] As in *R v N* [2006] EWCA Crim 3309; *R v Knight* [2007] EWCA Crim 3027 .

[35] Like the examples given by Baron Parke in *Wright v Doe d Tatham* (1837) 7 Ad & El 313.

[36] Such a person, and any other within a relevant chain of transmission, must also satisfy standard requirements of competence: CJA 2003, s 123.

[37] Preserving the previous law: see *R v Dodson* [1984] 1 WLR 971, (1984) 79 Cr App Rep 220. Although where the output depends upon the accuracy of information entered into the machine, that must still be shown to be accurate, subject to a presumption of proper set-up and calibration: CJA 2003, s 129.

[38] Except in relation to business documents, and previous statements of witnesses, and subject to the agreement of the parties, or to a specific inclusionary discretion taking into account likelihood of reliability and the interests of justice: CJA 2003, s 121; see *R v Xhabri* [2005] EWCA Crim 1335, [2006] 1 Cr App R 413, [39].   [39] By operation of CJA 2003, s 121(1).

[40] From 'fact' in the Criminal Justice Act 1988, to 'matter' in the Criminal Justice Act 2003: see especially s 127(1).

GENERAL EXCEPTION

The Act's most important extensions of the ambit of the general exception to the hearsay rule[41] are to apply it to oral statements as well as to statements in documents, and in most cases, to make such hearsay automatically admissible upon satisfaction of the relevant conditions. It is proposed first to mention the substance of the relevant conditions, and then the means of proving them.

Conditions

These are based on the conditions for statements in documents under the old law, but subject to some modification. One matter of clarification mentioned above is that, in the general case, only first-hand hearsay is admissible,[42] whether or not conditions triggering exceptions would apply to the remote statement, or statements.[43] Subject to that, the unifying feature of this general exception, reflected in the rubric to CJA 2003, s 116, is that the human source of the information[44] be unavailable to testify because of falling within one or other of the states mentioned below.[45]

Dead

This exception is cast in similar terms to that in the CJA 1988,[46] and causes no special difficulty.[47] It is, however, worth noting that the extension to oral hearsay brings with it the demise of even the theoretical possibility of the use of the old common law exceptions contingent upon the death of the declarant, including dying declarations, which effectively was the only type ever invoked in recent times.[48]

Unfit

Here, the terminology has changed very slightly in referring to unfitness to *be* a witness rather than to *attend* as one. The change of terminology reflects the interpretation of the old law, under which an amnesiac was held so unfit.[49] It is worth noting that this provision is rarely likely to be invoked in relation to mental condition, since the reference here is to unfitness at the time of trial, and, since unfitness at the time of making the statement is explicitly governed by CJA 2003, s 123,[50] it will normally apply only to those who become mentally unfit after making the statement, but before the trial.

---

[41] As formerly embodied in Pt II of the Criminal Justice Act 1988. For fuller exposition, see previous editions of this work.

[42] As noted 605, a different position applies in relation to the exceptions for business documents, and previous statements of witnesses.

[43] CJA 2003, s 121(1)(a). The position under the old law was uncertain: see Law Com No 245, [8.25].

[44] Referred to as the maker of the statement.

[45] Unless the person seeking to adduce the evidence, or someone acting on his behalf, has brought about the satisfaction of the condition in order to prevent the person giving oral evidence in the proceedings: CJA 2003, s 116(5).   [46] CJA 1988, s 23(2)(a).

[47] Even of compatibility with Art 6 of the European Convention: see, 624.

[48] It was considered in *R v Lawson* [1998] Crim LR 883.

[49] *R v Setz-Dempsey* (1994) 98 Cr App Rep 23.

[50] Which itself represents a change from the old law, under which the incompetence of the maker was subject to exclusion by discretion rather than rule: see *R v AS* [2004] EWCA Crim 1294, [2004] 1 WLR 3218.

Abroad

The terminology of this condition repeats that of CJA 1988, s 23(2)(b) in requiring both that the person be abroad, and that it be not reasonably practical to secure his attendance, and is[51] interpreted in much the same way.[52] The two conditions were held to operate cumulatively, and the defence had to be allowed to test their satisfaction.[53] It should be noted that the first was construed to apply to physical, rather than jurisdictional, presence outside the United Kingdom, and so not to a resident diplomat.[54] On the other hand, a witness physically outside the United Kingdom could be said to attend if his evidence were taken by video link, although not if taken on commission abroad, despite the opportunity to cross-examine.[55] The second condition, however, refers not to inability to attend, but to *secure* attendance, and may be satisfied by the recalcitrance of a witness outside the United Kingdom.[56] Reasonable practicality implies assessing the likely effectiveness of taking normal steps to secure the attendance of the witness, and considering in relation to such a judgment the importance of the evidence, the degree of prejudice to the defence if it is admitted, and the expense and inconvenience involved in securing attendance.[57] There is no longer[58] any explicit requirement to apply the additional requirements of s 9(4) of the Crime (International Co-operation) Act 2003, but such matters may well influence the application of any discretionary control.

Unfound

This condition also repeats the terminology of the previous legislation,[59] here requiring both that the witness cannot be found and that such steps as reasonably practicable to find him have been taken, and it too can be expected to be construed in the same way. The impracticality requirement was held satisfied in *R v Lockley and Corah*,[60] where testimony alleging a confession by one co-accused during an aborted trial was recorded in a transcript, and the witness then absconded from an open prison and could not be found by the police. Some disquiet has been expressed about the inadequacy of prosecution attempts to find, or secure attendance of, sometimes key witnesses.[61]

In some ways, this condition may become more important under the new law than under the old, now that the exception extends to oral hearsay. It is for that reason that CJA 2003, s 116(1)(b) requires that the maker should be identified to the court's satisfaction as

---

[51] See *R v C and K* [2006] EWCA Crim 197.

[52] Subject only to relevant discretions considered as a second stage, being now s 126 of the Criminal Justice Act 2003, and s 78 of the Police and Criminal Evidence Act 1984, supplanting ss 25 and 26 of the Criminal Justice Act 1988.   [53] *R v Elliott* [2003] EWCA Crim 1695, [18].

[54] *R v Jiminez-Paez* (1994) 98 Cr App Rep 239.   [55] *R v Radak* [1999] 1 Cr App Rep 187.

[56] *R v French and Gowhar* (1993) 97 Cr App Rep 421. Once these conditions have been satisfied there is no need to consider also those specifically related to fear: *R v Bailey* [2008] EWCA Crim 817, [45].

[57] *R v Castillo* [1996] 1 Cr App Rep 438; *R v Yu* [2006] EWCA Crim 349. The seriousness of the offence has not been considered an independent factor: *R v Coughlan* (1999) unreported CA, 2 March.

[58] Sch 37 Pt 6.   [59] CJA 1988, s 23(2)(c).

[60] [1995] 2 Cr App Rep 554. The report exhibits some confusion between s 23(2)(c) and parts of those in subss (2)(b) and (3).

[61] *R v Williams* [2007] EWCA Crim 211, [42] (sole independent eye-witness); *R v Kamuhuza* [2008] EWCA Crim 3060, [21] (scenes of crime officer); *R v Adams* [2007] EWCA Crim 3025, [2008] 1 Cr App R 430, [13] (not key).

a condition of admissibility. This is designed to enhance the operation of ss 123 and 124, relating to the capability and credibility of the statements of their makers.

Afraid[62]

The problem of intimidation is now better recognized,[63] and perceived to be growing.[64] It has accordingly[65] generated more elaborate statutory treatment than the other conditions:

116(2) The conditions are—

...

> (e) that through fear the relevant person does not give (or does not continue to give) oral evidence in the proceedings, either at all or in connection with the subject matter of the statement, and the court gives leave for the statement to be given in evidence.

> (3) For the purposes of subsection (2)(e) "fear" is to be widely construed and (for example) includes fear of the death or injury of another person or of financial loss.

> (4) Leave may be given under subsection (2)(e) only if the court considers that the statement ought to be admitted in the interests of justice, having regard—

> (a) to the statement's contents,

> (b) to any risk that its admission or exclusion will result in unfairness to any party to the proceedings (and in particular to how difficult it will be to challenge the statement if the relevant person does not give oral evidence),

> (c) in appropriate cases, to the fact that a direction under section 19 of the Youth Justice and Criminal Evidence Act 1999 (c 23) (special measures for the giving of evidence by fearful witnesses etc) could be made in relation to the relevant person, and

> (d) to any other relevant circumstances.

It should be noted that, in relation to this, unlike the other conditions, the principle of automatic admissibility does not apply.[66] It seems that this was because, unlike the other conditions, it is essentially a mental state, and capable of being feigned by those who wish to make a false statement, and to avoid cross-examination upon it.[67] The provision also operates in a new environment, not only of the special measures explicitly mentioned, but also of the new s 119, which explicitly enables previous inconsistent statements to be used as evidence of their truth, and thus removes any possible anomaly between the use of

---

[62] See *R v Devine* 2008 SCC 36, [2008] 2 SCR 283 for the application of the Canadian approach to this situation.

[63] It has been addressed directly by s 51 of the Criminal Justice and Public Order Act 1994, and ss 54 and 55 of the Criminal Procedure and Investigations Act 1996.

[64] See Home Office White Paper *Speaking Up for Justice* (1998) ch 4, Annex A 111–29; *Justice for All* (2002) [2.28]–[2.34]; *R v Davis and Ellis* [2006] EWCA Crim 1155, [2006] 4 All ER 648, [8]; see also Youth Justice and Criminal Evidence Act 1999, s 17, providing for special measures directions for intimidated witnesses.

[65] Although the Law Commission's initial view was that it would be satisfactorily catered for under the other conditions, bearing in mind that witnesses who can be found can be subpoenaed: CP 138 [11.21].

[66] Although failure to provide detail, or of police investigation, is not necessarily decisive: *R v Boulton* [2007] EWCA Crim 942, [35].

[67] Law Com No 245, [8.48]. See *R v Santharatnam* (n15), [28] (evidence of feigning emerged only after trial).

previous statements of witnesses who fail to testify at all or in part,[68] and those of hostile witnesses who testify deliberately falsely.[69]

An extensive interpretation is urged of the nature of the fear,[70] although precise definition is deliberately avoided. As under the old law, it may be assumed that the fear need not be reasonable,[71] nor relate to the maker himself,[72] nor that it need be related either to the accused,[73] or even to the offence being tried.[74] The fear may be indirect, and the test is clearly subjective, but it still needs to be established by credible evidence, although that will normally be documentary since to require oral testimony would be to court the very dangers feared.[75]

An important difference from the old law under CJA 1988, s 23 is that the statement need no longer be one made to those investigating offences, and hence can clearly be applied to defence witnesses who have become fearful, perhaps of the police, after providing an initial statement.[76] Here, too, it is necessary to bear in mind the new environment in which names and addresses of potential defence witnesses are required to be disclosed to the prosecution in advance.[77]

Admissibility depends also upon the exercise of the court's inclusionary discretion,[78] which explicitly mentions fairness in view of the difficulty of challenging the evidence if not given orally, but is made open-ended in that any relevant circumstances can be taken into account.[79] Thus in *CPS Durham v CE*,[80] admissibility was refused in relation to a witness statement of a fearful, and mentally weak, complainant of rape, where the statement would have been the sole or main evidence of absence of consent. No complaint of failure to explore the possibility of taking special measures[81] to secure the voluntary attendance of a witness is likely to succeed unless raised at trial,[82] and sometimes such measures are likely to be inapplicable.[83]

It has been stressed[84] that, in any such case, the court should not be too readily convinced that the accused is truly in fear,[85] and that the provisions of Art 6 of the European Convention should be taken very seriously.

---

[68] In these respects, adopting the position under the old law: *R v Jennings and Miles* [1995] Crim LR 810 (although present in court, the witness refused to testify at all on account of fear); *R v Ashford Justices, ex p Hilden* [1993] QB 555, [1993] 2 All ER 154 (the witness began to testify, but broke off on account of fear).

[69] Although this too had been achieved as a matter of construction under the old law: *R v Waters* (1997) 161 JP 249.

[70] Likely to be construed as under the old law to be required to remain operative: *R v H, W and M* [2001] Crim LR 815.   [71] *R v Acton Justices, ex p McMullen* (1990) 92 Cr App Rep 98.

[72] Made explicit in *R v Doherty* [2006] EWCA Crim 2716, [18].

[73] *R v Wood and Fitzsimmons* [1998] Crim LR 213; *R v Rutherford* [1998] Crim LR 490.

[74] *R v Martin* [1996] Crim LR 589.

[75] *R v Davies* [2006] EWCA Crim 2643, (2006) 150 SJLB 1288, [14].

[76] As claimed in *R v Lloyd* (2004) unreported CA, 18 November, although held not to have been proved.

[77] Criminal Justice Act 2003, ss 34 and 35, inserting new ss 6C and 6D into the Criminal Procedure and Investigations Act 1996.   [78] As under the old law: see *R v Lobban* [2004] EWCA Crim 1099.

[79] In *Smith v R* [2008] UKPC 34, where the discretion was exclusionary the Privy Council adopted the view expressed in *Scott v R* [1989] AC 1242, [1989] 2 All ER 305, who thought its exercise would be rare in this situation.   [80] [2006] EWCA Crim 1410.

[81] Whether or not those mentioned by s 116(4)(c).

[82] *R (Robinson) v Sutton Coldfield Magistrates' Court* [2006] EWHC 307 (Admin), [2006] 4 All ER 1029, [37].   [83] As in *R v Davies* (n75), (in which the witnesses and the accused knew each other well).

[84] *R v Arnold* [2004] EWCA Crim 1293, (2004) 148 SJLB 660, [30]; see further, 625.

[85] Especially where medical evidence is equivocal, and no consideration has been given to alternative measures: *R (Meredith) v Harwich Magistrates' Court* [2006] EWHC 3336 (Admin).

MEANS OF PROOF

The general rule in English law is that the party adducing evidence must prove any necessary preconditions by admissible evidence,[86] normally on oath,[87] and subject to cross-examination whether called by prosecution or defence,[88] and they cannot be inferred,[89] nor mere lip service paid to their satisfaction,[90] even though this often means that a voir dire must be held to avoid prejudice to the accused,[91] or an adjournment to promote the interests of justice.[92] It has been held, however, that, if such evidence is recorded in a document, that document must be proved by admissible evidence in the normal way, and cannot prove itself.[93] It is far from clear why CJA 2003, s 133 cannot be employed for this purpose. It is certainly the case that the condition of absence can be applied twice: first, in relation to inability of the maker of the statement to attend, and second, in relation to the inability of the witness testifying to such inability to attend. Proof must rise to the appropriate standard, namely proof beyond reasonable doubt in the case of the prosecution, and proof on the balance of probabilities in the case of the defence. These rules have been retained subject to the one exception that, where it is alleged that a condition should not be regarded as satisfied because brought about by the person adducing the evidence, then the burden of proof of such an allegation should be on the party making the allegation, rather than the burden of its negation being imposed on the party seeking to adduce the evidence.[94]

If something has been formally excised from a statement admitted under s 116, then the court should not pay regard to that matter, even if it appears in some other piece of evidence.[95]

BUSINESS DOCUMENTS

The business document exception in CJA 1988, s 24 seemed to have worked very well in principle, and its substance has been retained, subject to a few drafting amendments, in the form of CJA 2003, s 117:

(1) In criminal proceedings a statement contained in a document is admissible as evidence of any matter stated if—

   (a) oral evidence given in the proceedings would be admissible as evidence of that matter,

---

[86] Not by hearsay: see *Neill v North Antrim Magistrates' Court* [1992] 4 All ER 846, [1992] 1 WLR 1220. It may, however, be possible for a police officer to observe the fear of such a person who declares it, and in such cases, the evidence will be admissible to prove such fear without requiring the attendance of the declarant, as in *R v Denton* [2001] 1 Cr App Rep 227.

[87] But see *R v Jennings and Miles* (n68), in which it was said to have been realistic for counsel not to have taken the point that the witness had not been sworn, and *R v Greer* [1998] Crim LR 572, in which the court upheld a decision made upon such a basis despite the point having been taken. It is far from clear why this departure from normal methods should be tolerated, since it adds a further layer of denial of cross-examination, which might make the exercise of the ultimate exclusionary discretions still more difficult.

[88] *R v Wood and Fitzsimmons* (n73) (fear); *R v Elliott* [2003] EWCA Crim 1695 (disability).

[89] It has been suggested in New Zealand that fair trial considerations under human rights provisions require rigorous examination of conditions under which cross-examination of a key witness will be avoided: *R v M* [1996] 2 NZLR 659.

[90] *R v Coughlan* (1999) unreported CA, 2 March; *R v Reith* (2000) unreported CA, 7 April.

[91] *R v Nicholls* (1976) 63 Cr App Rep 187; *R v Case* [1991] Crim LR 192; *R v Jennings and Miles* (n68). See *R v Lobban* (n78) for some of the problems engendered by these rules under the old law.

[92] *R (Crown Prosecution Service) v Uxbridge Magistrates' Court* [2007] EWHC 205 (Admin).

[93] *R v Belmarsh Magistrates' Court, ex p Gilligan* [1998] 1 Cr App Rep 14.   [94] CJA 2003, s 116(5).

[95] *Huggins v DPP* [2006] EWHC 1376 (Admin), [13].

    (b) the requirements of subsection (2) are satisfied, and

    (c) the requirements of subsection (5) are satisfied, in a case where subsection (4) requires them to be.

(2) The requirements of this subsection are satisfied if—

    (a) the document or the part containing the statement was created or received by a person in the course of a trade, business, profession or other occupation, or as the holder of a paid or unpaid office,

    (b) the person who supplied the information contained in the statement (the relevant person) had or may reasonably be supposed to have had personal knowledge of the matters dealt with, and

    (c) each person (if any) through whom the information was supplied from the relevant person to the person mentioned in paragraph (a) received the information in the course of a trade, business, profession or other occupation, or as the holder of a paid or unpaid office.

(3) The persons mentioned in paragraphs (a) and (b) of subsection (2) may be the same person.

(4) The additional requirements of subsection (5) must be satisfied if the statement—

    (a) was prepared for the purposes of pending or contemplated criminal proceedings, or for a criminal investigation, but

    (b) was not obtained pursuant to a request under section 7 of the Crime (International Co-operation) Act 2003 (c 32) or an order under paragraph 6 of Schedule 13 to the Criminal Justice Act 1988 (c 33) (which relate to overseas evidence).

(5) The requirements of this subsection are satisfied if—

    (a) any of the five conditions mentioned in section 116(2) is satisfied (absence of relevant person etc), or

    (b) the relevant person cannot reasonably be expected to have any recollection of the matters dealt with in the statement (having regard to the length of time since he supplied the information and all other circumstances).

(6) A statement is not admissible under this section if the court makes a direction to that effect under subsection (7).

(7) The court may make a direction under this subsection if satisfied that the statement's reliability as evidence for the purpose for which it is tendered is doubtful in view of—

    (a) its contents,

    (b) the source of the information contained in it,

    (c) the way in which or the circumstances in which the information was supplied or received, or

    (d) the way in which or the circumstances in which the document concerned was created or received.

This provision retains categorization of admissibility in this area by reference to business,[96] rather than duty.[97] Given the expansive definition, however, and the inclusion of s 116 for

---

[96] As in s 24 of the Criminal Justice Act 1988. Defined widely enough to include court records, as in *R v Lockley and Corah* [1995] 2 Cr App Rep 554, 559; police custody records, as in *R v Hogan* [1997] Crim LR 349; and perhaps even to foreign customs records, as canvassed in *R v Dyer* [1997] Crim LR 442.

[97] As previously in s 68 of the Police and Criminal Evidence Act 1984.

first-hand hearsay, this is unlikely to cause any difficulty.[98] It has been used to allow proof of statements in decisions of the civil courts, quite contrary to the position under the old law.[99] Although the statement should have been admissible in the mouth of some witness at some stage, and must have been supplied by someone with personal knowledge,[100] there is no restriction upon the length of the chain of supply so long as every subsequent reception takes place in the course of business.[101] It should be noted that intermediate reception need not be in documentary form. The whole aim of this legislation is to allow inferences from documents in the absence of oral testimony, and accordingly, as under the old law, the court is likely to admit documents appearing to fulfil the relevant conditions, and then leave it to those objecting to make out their case, whether the evidence be real,[102] or documentary.[103]

In contrast to the position in some other jurisdictions,[104] no explicit provision is made in relation to statements of negative purport. The reasoning here was that the change to the definition of statement would accomplish this, since omissions will normally not be intentional, and hence not purposive, thus falling outside the scope of exclusion under s 114(1).

As under the old law, in the case of documents prepared for the purposes of criminal proceedings,[105] it is necessary to establish either one of the conditions under CJA 2003, s 116(2) for the admissibility of non-business documents, or that the relevant person cannot reasonably be expected to remember the relevant details.[106] Where a witness remembers, and can reasonably be expected to remember, some, but not all, of the details of a statement, those parts may be considered separately from the remainder, and admitted under this provision.[107]

One change from the approach of the old law is that, under the new, the discretion to exclude business records is contained within the same section. This is largely because it was originally intended to dispense with discretionary exclusion altogether, and to make admission automatic, but the Law Commission had second thoughts.[108] It took the view that, in certain cases, the court should be able to direct that a business record should be regarded as too unreliable to admit.

To some extent, the factors specified in CJA 2003, s 117(7) for consideration in deciding to direct inadmissibility reflect those governing the exercise of the reciprocating exclusionary,[109] and inclusionary,[110] discretions under the old law. Although both old and new pieces of legislation appear to require the judge to attend to the contents of

---

[98] All subsequent reference in this part to 'business' is intended to refer to the extended meaning. For an attempt to exclude police documents from the ambit of s 24(1), see McEvoy [1993] *Crim LR* 480, and further discussion with Smith, [1994] *Crim LR* 426.   [99] *R v Hogart* [2007] EWCA Crim 338, [22].

[100] Which militates against the use of records of criminal method derived from the Police National Computer, when they have been compiled by staff without personal knowledge of their truth: *R v Humphris* [2005] EWCA Crim 2030, (2005) 169 JP 441.

[101] In *Maher v DPP* [2006] EWHC 1271 (Admin), (2006) 170 JP 441, a note from one member of the public to another of a miscreant car registration number failed to meet this criterion, despite being later supplied to the police.   [102] *R v Foxley* [1995] 2 Cr App Rep 523.

[103] *Vehicle and Operator Services Agency v George Jenkins Transport Ltd* [2003] EWHC 2879.

[104] Such as Australia, under Evidence Act (Cwth) 1995, s 69; and the United States, by Federal Rules of Evidence, r 803(7).

[105] See *West Midlands Parole Board v French* [2008] EWHC 2631 (Admin), [47], said to be consistent with the approach under the old law in *R v Bedi and Bedi* (1992) 95 Cr App R 21.

[106] *R v Kamuhuza* (n61) (details relating to fingerprints at scene of crime).

[107] *R v Carrington* (1993) 99 Cr App Rep 376.   [108] See Law Com No 245, [8.74]–[8.77].

[109] Criminal Justice Act 1988, s 25.   [110] Criminal Justice Act 1988, s 26.

the statement in order to decide how to exercise this discretion, it was regarded as sufficient under the old law to do so in general terms, without reading the statement in full.[111] Nor was it regarded as mandatory to consider it at all.[112] It should be noted that this discretion may be exercised in favour of the defence,[113] if it is seeking a direction to exclude a prosecution statement under s 117(6), and in such a case, the conditions for the exercise of this power, like the old inclusionary discretion,[114] seem likely to need to be established only on the balance of probabilities. It was further held there that, in such a case, it is not necessarily decisive that the statement is of crucial importance to the defence. As under the old law, it remains possible that, in some situations, evidence that is relevant to the accused's defence will be excluded if the court directs such exclusion.[115] As under the old law, it is not a sufficient reason to refuse to admit the evidence that there is live evidence to prove the same matter.[116] In exercising its discretion, the court is entitled to take into account the strength of the evidence, for example where identity[117] is in issue,[118] that the circumstances are such that mistake is extremely unlikely,[119] or conversely, that they make the evidence suspicious.[120] So too the court was likely to attach weight to the independence of the witness, in deciding to exercise its discretion.[121] In other words, the court was likely to focus upon the likelihood of cross-examination being effective, and whether the effect could be achieved in other ways.[122] It was certainly a relevant consideration that, under different available procedures, cross-examination by the accused could have been secured.[123] On the other hand, where it could not, the discretion to include was unlikely to be exercised.[124] It is as yet uncertain how much of this will be taken over into the new law, although now that the direction relates only to business documents, and is certainly drafted in different terms, perhaps it will be disregarded altogether in favour of constructing a completely new edifice upon such different foundations.

---

[111] *R v Ashford Justices, ex p Hilden* [1993] QB 555, [1993] 2 All ER 154.

[112] *R v Acton Justices, ex p McMullen* (1990) 92 Cr App Rep 98; *R v Samuel* [1992] Crim LR 189.

[113] *R v Bailey* (n56), [35].   [114] *R v Patel* (1993) 97 Cr App Rep 294.

[115] For an example of such exclusion under the admittedly different conditions of the old law, see *R v W* [1997] Crim LR 678.

[116] *R v Xhabri* (n38), [42]. It may indeed insulate such hearsay from being found to infringe Art 6 of the European Convention.   [117] Of a car in *Maher v DPP* (n 101).

[118] Which, in itself, may justify special caution: *R v McCoy* [1999] All ER (D) 1410, CA, [25]; *R v Hardwick* [2001] EWCA Crim 369, [17].   [119] *Maher v DPP* (n101), [20].

[120] In *R v Lockley and Corah* [1995] 2 Cr App Rep 554, the statements consisted of a disputed cell confession, as reported by a woman who had a strong motive for ingratiating herself with the authorities, and who was self-confessedly dishonest.   [121] *R v Denton* (n86), [37].

[122] In *R v Dragic* [1996] 2 Cr App Rep 232, it was suggested that disputed identification could be supported by an alibi; in *R v Martin* [1996] Crim LR 589, that counsel would be just as effective by making criticisms of the quality of the evidence in argument; and in *R v Thompson* [1999] Crim LR 747, that the prosecution conceded the mental defects of the absent witness. But see *R v Radak* [1999] 1 Cr App Rep 187, in which it was said that procedural rather than substantive concerns should prevail; and in Scotland, *McPhee v HM Adv* [2001] SCCR 674.

[123] See *R v Radak* [1999] 1 Cr App Rep 187, in which the evidence should have been taken on commission abroad.

[124] *R v M* [2003] EWCA Crim 357, [2003] 2 Cr App Rep 332, in which the prejudiced accused was unfit to plead, and establish, his own case, and rebuttal of the statement would have been extremely difficult, despite the fact that its maker was a flawed witness.

PREVIOUS STATEMENTS OF WITNESSES

The relevant provisions of the Criminal Justice Act 2003[125] were considered more fully in Chapter VI, especially in connection with the use of a witness's previous consistent statements, even without an explicit affirmation of belief in his having made it, and his belief in its truth, to rebut suggestions of fabrication[126] and to refresh memory by statements in documents,[127] and, subject to such affirmation, to support complaints of the commission of offences[128] against the maker,[129] and the identification of persons, objects, or places.[130] A wholly new extension in the latter category is, however, to admit a previous statement if:[131]

...the statement was made by the witness when the matters stated were fresh in his memory but he does not remember them, and cannot reasonably be expected to remember them, well enough to give oral evidence of them in the proceedings.

Some difficulty in directing the jury is apparent when there are a number of previous statements,[132] and it will be interesting to see how much use will be made of so open-ended an exception to the exclusionary rule. There has been some reluctance to use it in conjunction with a declaration of hostility to evade the problem of dealing with reluctant witnesses, at least in relation to domestic violence.[133]

The CJA 2003 also makes explicit provision[134] for the use of pre-recorded video evidence of witnesses, other than the accused, in substitution in whole, or in part,[135] for the testimony of the witness as to those matters. Such substitution requires an operative direction by the court,[136] and may be made only upon the satisfaction of a number of conditions, namely: that the maker be called as a witness in an offence capable of being tried on indictment; that the witness claims to have witnessed relevant events; that he has had his account recorded on video at a time when those events were fresh in his memory, and likely to have been significantly better than they would be at the time of the trial, and he is at the trial prepared to assert the truth of that account; and that the recording is played at the trial in accordance with any conditions specified in the court's direction. It is further provided that the use of the recording be in the interests

---

[125] Principally ss 119, 120.   [126] CJA 2003, s 120(2).

[127] CJA 2003, s 120(3). Statements by others used to refresh memory are dealt with by s 139.

[128] No longer limited to sexual offences.

[129] CJA 2003, s 120(7), (8). Applied in *R v Xhabri* (n38), [35].

[130] CJA 2003, s 120(5). This was designed to remove the anomaly in the old law between previous verbal descriptions by witnesses, and photofit representations made under their direction, and to prevent further anomaly between previous statements identifying persons, and those identifying objects, such as cars by reference to their registration numbers.   [131] CJA 2003, s 120(6).

[132] *R v Billingham and Billingham* [2009] EWCA Crim 19, [2009] 2 Cr App R 341.

[133] *R v C* [2007] EWCA Crim 3463, [12].

[134] CJA 2003, ss 137, 138. These provisions did not appear in the Law Commission's draft bill, but adopt, and apply more generally, the principles first developed in relation to the recording of evidence of children: see further, 237.

[135] CJA 2003, s 138(3) confers a special discretion in relation to the admission of part only of a pre-recorded statement taking into account, on the one hand, possible prejudice to the defendant in admitting a partial account, and on the other, the desirability of admitting all, or most, of such a statement despite any such prejudice.   [136] CJA 2003, s 137(1)(f).

of justice, and that the following factors be taken into account in making any such judgment:[137]

(a) the interval between the time of the events in question and the time when the recorded account was made;

(b) any other factors that might affect the reliability of what the witness said in that account;

(c) the quality of the recording;

(d) any views of the witness as to whether his evidence in chief should be given orally or by means of the recording.

A new entitlement[138] to use previous inconsistent statements as evidence of their truth was another matter considered more fully in Chapter VI.[139] This is reflected in a preference for automatic admissibility for evidence coming within the statutory exceptions,[140] subject only to discretionary exclusion in the case of evidence that was more prejudicial than probative, or unfair within the provisions of s 78 of the Police and Criminal Evidence Act 1984.

DISCRETION[141]

The Law Commission started from the position that discretion should be limited, especially any inclusionary discretion.[142] It felt, however, that such a position would be too inflexible, and that there might well be unforeseeable examples of hearsay that it would be in the interests of justice to admit.[143] This led to a number of provisions[144] in the Criminal Justice Act 2003 bestowing an inclusionary discretion. The first is the general residuary discretion in s 114(1)(d) to allow hearsay that the court finds in the interests of justice to admit. The Law Commission envisaged this as a very *limited* exception.[145] It was, however, hard to see that this was reflected by its completely open-ended drafting, and with no sanction for misuse. It might have been possible to argue that its impact was limited by the explicit inclusion of further discretions, such as that in s 116(2)(e) for those declining to testify through fear,[146] or still more, the further explicit inclusionary discretion for multiple hearsay, which would otherwise be inadmissible under the terms of s 121(1)(c), if:

The court is satisfied that the value of the evidence in question, taking into account how reliable the statements appear to be, is so high that the interests of justice require the later statement to be admissible for that purpose.

If explicit provision were required even for cases in which the interests of justice were so strong as to *require* the admission of the evidence, it might well have been taken to suggest that the operation of a general inclusionary discretion cast in less stringent terms must have been intended to operate only as a necessary, but not as a sufficient, condition

---

[137] CJA 2003, s 137(4).   [138] CJA 2003, s 119(1).   [139] 317.

[140] Which was also the position for common law exceptions under the old law.

[141] See Munday (2007) 171 *JP* 276.

[142] The fullest analysis is in its Consultation Paper No 138, [9.6]–[9.25].

[143] Third-party confessions was an example.

[144] Quite apart from those mentioned below, CJA 2003, s 132(5) bestows discretion to admit hearsay, despite failure to comply with procedural requirements prescribed by rules of court.

[145] Law Com No 245, [6.49] (original emphasis).   [146] Here guidelines are provided in s 116(4).

of admissibility.[147] It is also worth noting that whereas an exclusionary discretion works against a soft-edged general rule making relevant evidence admissible, an inclusionary discretion works against hard-edged limited exceptions to that general rule, especially in this context where the exceptions are statutory, and carefully drafted. In consequence, it has sometimes been uncertain whether the application is made under the inclusionary discretion or the statutory exception;[148] at others the guidelines for the inclusionary discretion have been attributed to the statutory exception.[149] Nevertheless, a loose interpretation was adopted from the beginning.[150] Thus in *R v Xhabri*,[151] the Lord Chief Justice was prepared to apply the inclusionary discretion as an alternative to the specific hearsay exception in s 120(4) for previous consistent statements, and even for the specific inclusionary discretion in s 121(1)(c) for double hearsay. It should be noted, however, that, in this case, the original supplier of the information, and complainant, testified, and was thus available for cross-examination. It has also been used without qualm to admit the statement of an incompetent child under three years' old.[152]

Several reservations have been advanced against taking a wide view of the operation of the discretion. It has been held that it should not be applied to overturn common law rules preserved by s 118;[153] that it should not be applied to evade the operation of specifically drafted exceptions, such as those in s 116;[154] that it should not be applied to remedy defects in the prosecution preparation of its case;[155] and argued that it should not apply against the interests of the defence as rigorously as those of the prosecution.[156] None of these has been universally accepted. The most comprehensive, and persuasive rejection of many appears in *R v Y*, where the confession of a third party was held admissible against the accused, despite the preservation of the common law's rules of admissibility in s 118.[157] It was emphasized[158] that s 114(1)(d) provides an independent statutory route to admissibility, and that a statute overrules the common law. It was said[159] that s 118 preserves only rules of admissibility, not rules of inadmissibility.[160] It was also forcefully stated[161] in *Sak v CPS* that any disqualifying failure of prosecution preparation would need to be quite egregious. The argument that admissibility is to be interpreted differently against the defence was also rejected[162] in *R v Y*.

---

[147] Although *R v Walker* [2007] EWCA Crim 1698, [30] claimed that satisfaction of reliability for the purposes of s 114(2) mandated also that of the higher standard; *R v Scorah* (n23), [32] took the approach in the text.   [148] *R v Gyima* [2007] EWCA Crim 429, [18].

[149] *R v Adams* [2007] EWCA Crim 3025, [2008] 1 Cr App R 430, [15].

[150] *Maher v DPP* (n101), [15] ('with a measure of common sense and realism').   [151] (n38), [36].

[152] *R v SJ* [2009] EWCA Crim 1869.

[153] *R v Ibrahim* (2007) unreported Cr Ct 4 June; *R v Natheeswaran* [2009] EWCA Crim 295, [16] (although neither the provisions of s 114, nor the contrary decision in *R v Y* [2008] EWCA 10, [2008] 2 All ER 484, [48] seem to have been noticed here).

[154] *R v O'Hare* [2006] EWCA Crim 2512, [30]; see also *R v Finch* [2007] EWCA Crim 36, [2007] 1 WLR 1685, [24]; *R v Z* (n26), [20]; *R v Mohammed Khan* [2009] EWCA Crim 86, [15]; *R v DT* [2009] EWCA Crim 1213, [25]–[28].   [155] *McEwan v DPP* (n10), [18].

[156] *R v Y* (n153), [49](ii).   [157] See also *R v Lynch* [2007] EWCA Crim 3035 (118(1).4 res gestae).

[158] [48].   [159] [47].

[160] Ironically *after* the passage of the Act, resulting from this interpretation of s 14(1)(d), the distinction has become drastically diluted.

[161] [2007] EWHC 2886 (Admin), [25] per Thomas LJ; [20] Dobbs J is more restrained,

[162] [53]; see also *O'Hare* (n154), (defence hearsay excluded).

Admissibility under the inclusionary discretion is one thing; admission another.[163] S 114(2) provides , guidelines for the latter:[164]

In deciding whether a statement not made in oral evidence should be admitted under subsection (1)(d), the court must have regard to the following factors (and to any others it considers relevant)—

(a) how much probative value the statement has (assuming it to be true) in relation to a matter in issue in the proceedings, or how valuable it is for the understanding of evidence in the case;

(b) what other evidence has been, or can be, given on the matter or evidence mentioned in paragraph (a);

(c) how important the matter or evidence mentioned in paragraph (a) is in the context of the case as a whole;

(d) the circumstances in which the statement was made;

(e) how reliable the maker of the statement appears to be; how reliable the evidence of the making of the statement appears to be;

(f) whether oral evidence of the matter stated can be given and, if not, why it cannot;

(g) the amount of difficulty involved in challenging the statement;

(h) the extent to which that difficulty would be likely to prejudice the party facing it.

It has been noted that, like much such guidance, the factors are capable of pointing in different directions.[165] Nor is the meaning always absolutely clear.[166] In *R v Taylor* the Court shied away from an interpretation requiring the trial judge to investigate, hear evidence,[167] and reach a conclusion on each of these factors,[168] Instead he need make only an overall judgment, partly to avoid prolonging and complicating trials. His decision may survive his having made no reference at all to the guidelines.[169] This will also have the consequence of limiting the scope for appeal. The Court has, however, occasionally reversed a discretionary decision,[170] and sometimes itself exercised the discretion, when an attempted exercise had miscarried.[171]

Although it is clear that s 114(1)(d) provides an independent route to the admission of hearsay, it is not surprising that it is, like the exclusionary discretion of s 78 of the Police and Criminal Evidence Act 1984, used as a secondary safety-net for the various hearsay exceptions in this part of the Criminal Justice Act 2003. It has thus supplemented primary reliance on s 115,[172] s 116,[173] s 117,[174] s 118,[175] and s 120.[176] It has also been relied upon in the elucidation of s 121.[177] Although the criteria for the application of the inclusionary discretion have been distinguished from those apposite to the operation of the statutory

---

[163] As stressed in *R v Y* (n153), [57] rejecting conflation based on *R v McLean* [2007] EWCA 219, [2008] 1 Cr App R 155.   [164] In *R v SJ* (n152) the trial judge misinterpreted them as going only to weight.
[165] *McLean*, [26].
[166] In *R v Walker* (n147), [23] the word 'appears' in condition (e) and (f) was questioned.
[167] But if he does it must be based only on material available to both parties: *Ali and Hussain v Revenue and Customs Prosecutions Office* [2008] EWCA Crim 146, [32].
[168] *R v Taylor* [2006] EWCA Crim 3132, [2006] 2 Cr App R 222, [38], [39].
[169] *R v Steen* [2007] EWCA Crim 335, [2008] 2 Cr App R 380.
[170] *McEwan v DPP* (n10); *R v Scorah* (n23); *R v Z* (n26).   [171] *Maher v DPP* (n101).
[172] *R v Isichei* [[2006] EWCA Crim 1815, [41].
[173] *R v Gyima* (n148); *R v Williams* [2007] EWCA Crim 211.
[174] *Maher v DPP* (n101); *R v Kamuhuza* (n61).   [175] *R v Walker* (n147).   [176] *R v Xhabri* (n38).
[177] *R v Athwal* (n3).

exceptions on the basis that the former is concerned with reliability justifying admission and the latter with conditions for admissibility,[178] factors influencing the latter may contribute to the resolution of the former.[179] Thus in *R v Z* factor (g) was noted[180] as connoting inability to give evidence, cohering with the conditions in s 116. So too the justifications offered for reading down discretionary *admissibility* mentioned above, may also come into play in determining discretionary admission.[181]

The CJA 2003 explicitly preserved the exclusionary discretions present in the old law in s 126(2):

Nothing in this Chapter prejudices—

(a) any power of a court to exclude evidence under section 78 of the Police and Criminal Evidence Act 1984 (c 60) (exclusion of unfair evidence), or

(b) any other power of a court to exclude evidence at its discretion (whether by preventing questions from being put or otherwise).

The earlier subsection had supplemented such existing discretions with a new one to exclude evidence on the basis of waste of time.[182] In criminal proceedings the court may refuse to admit a statement as evidence of a matter stated if—

(a) the statement was made otherwise than in oral evidence in the proceedings, and

(b) the court is satisfied that the case for excluding the statement, taking account of the danger that to admit it would result in undue waste of time, substantially outweighs the case for admitting it, taking account of the value of the evidence.

This additional discretion was included partly because of the increased admissibility of, especially oral, hearsay under these provisions, and because the existing exclusionary discretions operate only to exclude evidence adduced by the prosecution. It is also significant that the much broader exclusionary discretion for documentary hearsay under the old law[183] has not been retained, although there is, as mentioned above,[184] a new, and more limited, discretionary power to direct the exclusion of business records.[185] Retention of the exclusionary discretion of s 78 allows some control over automatic admission under sections 116 and 118.[186] It has also, somewhat surprisingly, been regarded as appropriately considered even after finding the conditions of s 114(2) satisfied.[187]

AUTHENTICATION

As noted in Chapter XII, the hearsay rule was developed in a very different context from that of modern times. At a time when most litigation was based on personal dealings, it made sense to concentrate on the credibility of human beings, but in the modern world,

---

[178] *R v Williams* (n61), [29]; *R v Gyima* (n148), [29].   [179] *R v Y* (n153), [59].

[180] (n26), [24]. [27] invoking s 116(4)(b) in relation to the statement of a dead person seems not to accord with the plain meaning of the provision.

[181] In *R v Cole and Keet* [2007] EWCA Crim 1924, [2008] 1 Cr App R 5, [7] it was said that the exclusionary discretion under s 78 and the inclusionary discretion in s 114 would be unlikely to have different effects.

[182] Section 126(1), a less elaborate equivalent to United States Federal Rule of Evidence 403.

[183] Criminal Justice Act 1988, s 25.   [184] 612.

[185] In *Maher v DPP* (n101), [24] failure to exclude under this provision was thought to mandate inclusion under s 114(1)(d) or even the higher test in s 121(1)(c).

[186] Although in *R v Pulley* [2008] EWCA Crim 260, [22], [27] s 114(2) was, it is submitted wrongly, regarded as appropriate.   [187] *R v SJ* (n152), [23], [37].

where much litigation arises from business dealings, it is reasonable to seek to place more stress on the reliability of the systems used by such businesses to record information about such dealings.[188]

The Criminal Justice Act 2003 reflects this, in providing for the means of proving statements in documents:[189]

Where a statement in a document is admissible as evidence in criminal proceedings, the statement may be proved by producing either—

(a) the document, or

(b) (whether or not the document exists) a copy of the document or of the material part of it, authenticated in whatever way the court may approve.

It is worth noting that, in terms, this is a more limited provision than its predecessor[190] in omitting the last phrase that there explicitly authorized such authentication, irrespective of the number of removes between original and copy. The omission may reflect the greater need for restriction on multiple hearsay, now that the legislation authorizes the admission of more, and especially oral, hearsay. Little seems lost, since there is no explicit restriction on the court's power to authenticate.

In an increasing number of situations, reliance is placed on automatically produced records as circumstantial evidence, and so far the courts have adopted a liberal approach to authenticity so far as ascription of such records is concerned.[191]

COMMON LAW EXCEPTIONS[192]

Given the extension of admissibility to oral hearsay, generally to that of deceased persons, and narrowing the definition of hearsay excluded under the rule, there is much less need for the preservation of common law exceptions. The CJA 2003 accordingly abolishes all except those expressly preserved.[193] Most of those that have been preserved have already been considered as fully as necessary, and only a few marginal comments will be offered here.

Public information

Section 118(1) of the Criminal Justice Act 2003 adopts the wording used to preserve the same common law exceptions for civil proceedings by s 7(2) of the Civil Evidence Act 1995, and may be expected to be construed in the same way.[194] One addition has been made here:

…evidence relating to a person's age or date or place of birth may be given by a person without personal knowledge of the matter.

---

[188] Nowadays 'readwrite' would be more fitting a name than 'hearsay' (or 'seedo').
[189] Section 133.   [190] Criminal Justice Act 1988, s 27.
[191] See *R v M* [2003] EWCA Crim 3067 (email); *Davis and Ellis* (n64), [122] (mobile phone use); *R v Bailey* [2008] EWCA Crim 817 (internet chatroom).
[192] Including closely related new statutory exceptions, such as that for preparatory statements for use by an expert.
[193] Section 118(2). Preservation does not, however, import aspects of the old law incompatible with the new: *R v O* [2006] EWCA Crim 556, [2006] 2 Cr App R 405. It seems incoherent to 'preserve' exceptions to a very differently defined exclusionary rule.   [194] See further, 591.

This is practically helpful, and seems unlikely to prove troublesome, but it does seem to have been smuggled into the Act without much discussion, and it is far from clear that it really did exist at common law.[195]

Reputation

This consists of two parts: the first dealing with reputation as to good or bad character; the second, with family matters, such as pedigree, the existence of a marriage, or personal identity.

Character

So far as the first is concerned the wording repeats that of s 7(3) of the Civil Evidence Act 1995 regarding the substance of the evidence, although it omits the explicit qualification found there that the reputation is to be treated as a fact rather than as a multiplicity of statements about the matter reputed. Issues of character, and especially of bad character, are generally much less significant in civil proceedings than in criminal, so it is far from clear that the preservation of this rule should have been accepted for criminal proceedings in the absence of substantial argument.[196] In fact, the rule justifying the admissibility of reputation originated in the execrated case of *R v Rowton*,[197] where witnesses in rebuttal of good character evidence adduced in favour of the accused were not permitted to state their own view of his character in sexual matters, but to testify only to his reputation for such matters. Part of the trouble with the rule lies in the nature of the evidence being so endorsed. Evidence of reputation, general or specific, is thoroughly unconvincing.[198] It necessarily rests upon hearsay, gossip, and rumour, and permits a witness without perjury to state something that he believes to be unjustified, and which he knows will be used as the foundation for an inference that he believes to be false. It is uncomfortable to have to rely upon a rule defended by the Supreme Court of the United States only on the ground that 'to pull one misshapen stone out of the grotesque structure is more likely simply to upset its present balance between adverse interests than to establish a rational edifice'.[199] It is hardly surprising to find that the rule has been roundly condemned by commentators,[200] ignored in practice,[201] and rejected as a model for the construction of the once much more important provisions of the Criminal Evidence Act 1898.[202] It is hard to justify its retention by the Criminal Justice Act 2003, especially in view of the otherwise wholesale jettisoning of the old law as to character.[203]

---

[195] It seems to have appeared for the first time in the list of retained common law provisions in Law Com No 245, [8.132].

[196] Law Com No 245, [8.132] simply remarked that the rules recommended there for preservation serve useful purposes, and that there seemed no serious difficulties.   [197] (1865) Le & Ca 520, 34 LJMC 57.

[198] And especially unconvincing in relation to sexual disposition: see *R v Profit* [1993] 3 SCR 637. But cf *R v Marr* (1989) 90 Cr App Rep 154.   [199] *Michelson v United States* 335 US 469, 486 (1948).

[200] See Stephen *History of Criminal Law* (1882) vol 1, 450: 'The decision [in *Rowton* (above, 367)] settled the law, but in practice it is impossible to act upon it, and it may be doubted whether it is desirable to try to do so.'

[201] See e.g. *R v West* (1890) 112 CCC Sess Pap 724, in which the rebuttal consisted in part of evidence of the accused's known association with criminals.

[202] See *R v Dunkley* [1927] 1 KB 323, 329. It was also subjected to penetrating and convincing criticism in New Zealand in *R v Ravindra* [1997] 3 NZLR 242.   [203] Section 99.

Family matters

Here, the wording is substantially identical[204] to that of s 7(3)(b) of the Civil Evidence Act 1995.[205]

Res gestae[206]

The redefinition of hearsay and expansion of statutory exceptions has reduced the range of cases to which the old common law exception could apply, and it has been cogently argued[207] that the few remaining cases could all be catered for under the inclusionary discretion conferred by CJA 2003, s 114(1)(d). Given the complexity and imprecision of the old law, it is indeed disappointing to find it retained with so little positive argument in its favour,[208] especially as it has been abolished for civil proceedings by the Civil Evidence Act 1995.[209]

Admissions

As recommended by the Law Commission,[210] the CJA 2003 explicitly preserved the old law in these areas,[211] namely the basic law relating to confessions[212] and admissions, including vicarious admissions, and, most relevantly in criminal proceedings, the special provisions for statements inculpating the accused made by parties to a common enterprise.[213]

Expertise[214]

The rules retained here are those permitting experts to rely upon matters of professional expertise, or technical information, even though they have no first-hand knowledge of them. It should be noted that these have now been supplemented by a new exception[215] for statements prepared for the use by experts in criminal investigations or proceedings, for example by junior assistants to the principal expert. In some cases, the defence may wish to cross-examine such an assistant, and the mechanism for enabling this in appropriate cases is that, under current, and enhanced,[216] disclosure provisions,[217] notice must be given of the intention to rely upon such a statement, setting out details of the makers of such a state-

---

[204] Subject to the omission of the qualification as noted in (i) above.   [205] See further above, 597.

[206] For persuasive criticism see Munday (2008) 172 *JP* 348.   [207] By Ormerod [1998] *Crim LR* 301.

[208] In relation to different strands of the rule, the Law Commission remarked in Law Com No 245, that: [8.121] 'its fears had been allayed' (statements reacting to events); [8.124] it was 'not aware of any injustice caused by it' (statements accompanying acts). Some more positive argument is made for statements describing physical, or mental, state, but in the case of identified witnesses, such statements could be admitted under the new statutory exceptions, or in other cases, would fall outside the definition as not having been uttered with the required purpose.

[209] Thus contributing to potential anomaly in the increasing number of cases in which civil and criminal proceedings ensue in respect of the same matter.   [210] Law Com No 245, recs 18, 26, and 27(7).

[211] CJA 2003, s 118(1).

[212] Including tacit confessions: see *R v O* [2005] EWCA Crim 3082. Subject only to a new s 76A inserted into the Police and Criminal Evidence Act 1984 by s 128, to provide for the use of confessions by a co-accused, and to the effect of s 114(1)(d) on third party confessions, 616. The whole topic of confessions will be considered in the next section of this chapter.   [213] Discussed, 583.

[214] See further Chapter XI, Section 1.

[215] CJA 2003, s 127. Even under the old rules, it was possible to infer a chain of continuity between provision of sample and evidence of its ultimate analysis: see *Khatibi v DPP* [2004] EWHC 83, (2004) 168 JP 361.

[216] By Pt 4 of the Criminal Justice Act 2003.

[217] Principally, by rules authorized by the statutory provisions mentioned in s 127(7).

ment and the work performed by them. Any party may then apply to the court to direct that it is not in the interests of justice that the statement should be admitted under the provisions of CJA 2003, s 127, and the matters to be considered are to include:[218]

(a) the expense of calling as a witness the person who prepared the statement;

(b) whether relevant evidence could be given by that person which could not be given by the expert;

(c) whether that person can reasonably be expected to remember the matters stated well enough to give oral evidence of them.

If, as may sometimes be the case, the assistant cannot be expected to remember the detail, then his statement would be admissible under the more general provisions for business documents in s 117(5)(b).

STATUTORY EXCEPTIONS

From 1772 onward, the legislature has enacted various exceptions admitting hearsay in criminal proceedings, usually to a rather limited extent, and in a limited context.[219] All statutory exceptions are explicitly preserved by CJA 2003, s 114(1)(a). It is not appropriate in a work of this character to discuss such provisions in detail, but two of the more general, and important, such provisions are worth mentioning. It should also be noted that the Criminal Justice Act 2003 repealed Sch 2 to the Criminal Procedure and Investigations Act 1996, which had formerly permitted the admissibility of depositions before magistrates. This provision had attracted cogent academic criticism,[220] and its repeal had been recommended by the Law Commission.[221]

Bankers' Books Evidence Act 1879[222]

Although statements in such books would invariably be admissible under the business records exception in s 116 of the Criminal Justice Act 2003, it was not thought necessary to repeal this legislation.

Criminal Justice Act 1967, s 9

Upon the fulfilment[223] of specified conditions, this section provides that agreed statements of facts may be admitted in evidence at any criminal trial to the same extent, and with the same effect, as oral evidence.[224] The principal conditions are that the statement should be signed, and contain a declaration of the maker's knowledge that it was made subject to penalties in the event of its being used in evidence, if the maker knew it to be false, or did not care whether it was true; that a copy should have been served on the opposite party;

---

[218] CJA 2003, s 127(5).

[219] Appendix C to Law Com CP No 138 contains a professedly incomplete list of some 32 such exceptions extant in 1995.   [220] See Munday (1997) *NLJ* 821, 860.

[221] Law Com No 245, rec 21.   [222] See further, 673.

[223] It is vital that they are fulfilled meticulously: *Paterson v DPP* [1990] RTR 329. If the conditions were not fulfilled, the statement was nevertheless admissible under s 23 of the Criminal Justice Act 1988, although in that case it would be subject to a warning as being of lesser weight than oral testimony: *R v Millen* [1995] Crim LR 568. It will now presumably be admissible by agreement of the parties under s 114(1)(c) of the Criminal Justice Act 2003.   [224] *Ellis v Jones* [1973] 2 All ER 893.

and that no notice of objection should have been received from that party within seven days. Where such evidence is admitted, it has the same status as oral evidence, and the jury should not, because of no more than a conflict with oral evidence, be instructed to prefer the latter.[225] It is also possible for the parties to agree to the reception of such a statement at, or before, the trial, although the provisions with regard to service of a copy of the statement, and non-receipt within seven days of notice of objection, have not been fulfilled.

If a defendant wishes to challenge such evidence, he should serve notice under s 9(2)(d), and if he challenges it at the trial without doing so, the court may order an adjournment, and may charge him with the costs.[226] It is important to preserve the orality of criminal proceedings, and maintenance of the rule in *Browne v Dunn*[227] that the defence case should be put to the witnesses for the prosecution in cross-examination wherever possible. These considerations still permeate the modern law, as indicated by rules for notice and counter-notice under CJA 2003, s 132.

WEIGHT

One striking difference from the provisions of the Civil Evidence Act 1995 is that the Criminal Justice Act 2003 contains no provision quite comparable to s 4, setting out considerations relevant to the weight to be attached to hearsay admitted under the Act. This can be attributed to a number of factors. First, in relation to the operation of the new inclusionary discretion CJA 2003, s 114(2) specifies a number of factors to be taken into account,[228] many of them concerned with weight, especially those explicitly referring to probative value, the circumstances in which the statement was made, the reliability of the maker and of the evidence of the statement's having been made, the reasons for not adducing oral evidence, and the difficulty of challenging it. Second, there was already discretion to exclude prosecution evidence the prejudicial effect of which exceeded its probative value, or which was unfair in criminal proceedings, while no such general discretion existed in 1995[229] in civil proceedings. Third, s 126(1)(b) confers a new discretion to exclude evidence the weight of which is insufficient to justify the time spent in hearing it. Fourth, the two new exceptions for the admission of statements made by those witnesses who are unavailable through fear,[230] and for business records,[231] are both qualified by the need for leave, or exclusion, by direction, the guidelines for both of which incorporate consideration of weight.[232] Fifth, s 125 confers a new power to stop the case where hearsay adduced by the prosecution is so unconvincing that any conviction based upon it would be unsafe. Sixth, the jury is the trier of fact in criminal proceedings in the higher courts, and so provisions relating to weight would have to be conveyed by the judge's direction to the jury, which many consider already overloaded and over-regulated.[233] The old law itself became more relaxed in this respect,[234] although some form of warning was nevertheless

---

[225] *R v Mitchell* [1995] Crim LR 146.

[226] *Lister v Quaife* [1983] 2 All ER 29, [1983] 1 WLR 48; although if this is not done, and the trial proceeds in the absence of the prosecution witnesses, the trier of fact is not bound to accept the truth of their statements.
[227] (1893) 6 R 67; see, 314.

[228] Recited, 617.   [229] Although now see CPR 32.1.2, discussed further, 212.
[230] CJA 2003, s 116(2)(e).   [231] CJA 2003, s 117.   [232] CJA 2003, s 116(4); 117(7).
[233] See Law Com No 245, [11.33]–[11.35].
[234] Cp *R v Cole* [1990] 2 All ER 108, [1990] 1 WLR 865; *R v Greer* [1998] Crim LR 572.

still required,[235] and attention to be directed to any inconsistency with other evidence,[236] at least where the evidence was vital to the prosecution case.[237] There seems to be no pressing reason to depart from such an approach.

Specific provision is, however, made for ensuring the competence of the maker of the statement,[238] and for testing his[239] credibility:[240]

(2) In such a case—

    (a) any evidence which (if he had given such evidence) would have been admissible as relevant to his credibility as a witness is so admissible in the proceedings;

    (b) evidence may with the court's leave be given of any matter which (if he had given such evidence) could have been put to him in cross-examination as relevant to his credibility as a witness but of which evidence could not have been adduced by the cross-examining party;

    (c) evidence tending to prove that he made (at whatever time) any other statement inconsistent with the statement admitted as evidence is admissible for the purpose of showing that he contradicted himself.

(3) If as a result of evidence admitted under this section an allegation is made against the maker of a statement, the court may permit a party to lead additional evidence of such description as the court may specify for the purposes of denying or answering the allegation.

This provision, within its context, clearly allows such a maker to be discredited by the use of inconsistent statements, and it should be noted that it specifically allows both for proving collateral matters that would, at common law, not to have been put in cross-examination of a witness who denied them, and for adducing evidence to rehabilitate the maker, subject to the leave of the court.

EUROPEAN CONVENTION ON HUMAN RIGHTS

The shadow of the European Convention affected the light in which the Law Commission considered its recommendations, as evidenced by its devotion of a separate chapter to its impact in both Consultation Paper[241] and final Report,[242] and in its endorsement and then rejection of one fundamental proposal.[243]

It is generally agreed that the key provision is Art 6 of the Convention, headed 'Right to a Fair Trial', and more particularly Art 6.3(d):

Everyone charged with a criminal offence has the following minimum rights.

...

    (d) to examine or have examined witnesses against him and to obtain the attendance and examination of witnesses on his behalf under the same conditions as witnesses against him.

---

[235] Said in *R v Blok* (1999) unreported CA, 18 February to be satisfied so long as the jury was directed that the evidence was not agreed, and its information provider had not been subjected to cross-examination, and in *R v Hardwick* [2001] EWCA Crim 369, not to be in any predetermined form, but adapted to the facts of the individual case.   [236] *R v Gavin* (2000) unreported CA 3 May.

[237] *R v Curry* [1998] 2 Cr App Rep (S) 410. Munday pointed out in (1997) 141 JP 691 that the specimen direction in the Judges' Bench Book echoes the form of direction recommended in relation to s 13 of the Criminal Justice Act 1925 in *Scott v R* [1989] AC 1242, [1989] 2 All ER 305.

[238] CJA 2003, s 123. Extended by s 124(3) to the use of additional evidence.

[239] CJA 2003, s 124(4) extending to any intermediaries.   [240] CJA 2003, s 124.

[241] Con Pap No 138, pt V.   [242] Law Com No 245, pt V.

[243] To disallow convictions based upon hearsay alone.

It is immediately apparent that this provision is loosely drafted, and gives rise to many ambiguities, and matters of contention. The scheme of the Human Rights Act requires[244] a court to take into account[245] opinions[246] of the European Court of Human Rights, opinions[247] or decisions[248] of the Commission, and decisions of the Committee of Ministers.[249] It is dubious how helpful, consistent, and unequivocal such guidance is likely to be.

It is nevertheless clear that these minimum rights apply only to the accused in criminal proceedings, and so, in relation to the admission of hearsay, seem incompatible with the general approach of the Law Commission, which favoured application of the same rules to prosecution and defence.[250]

Although the European Court of Human Rights had approved the general scheme of the exclusion of hearsay in English criminal proceedings,[251] it was apparent from decisions before the incorporation of the Convention into English law, that English[252] courts took the clear view that there was no presumptive incompatibility between the admission of hearsay against the accused under the exceptions to the rule in the Criminal Justice Act 1988, and the right to a fair hearing guaranteed by the Convention.[253] In one of the co-joined appeals in *R v Al-Khawaja*[254] the same view was taken of Part 2 of Chapter 11 of the Criminal Justice Act 2003,[255] and the position regarded as sufficiently settled for neither the Court of Appeal nor the House of Lords to give leave to appeal to the latter.

Any such complacency was, however, shattered by reference to the European Court of Human Rights which allowed both appeals on the basis that where the statement is the sole or decisive element in the decision,[256] the attendance of the witness is a minimum condition for a fair trial, even where as in one of these cases the witness had died before the trial, and in the other was too fearful to testify.[257] This view was based upon the Court's earlier pronouncement that:[258]

…where a conviction is based solely or to a decisive degree on depositions that have been made by a person whom the accused has had no opportunity to examine or to have examined, whether during the investigation or at the trial, the rights of the defence are restricted to an extent that is incompatible with the guarantees provided by Article 6.

Such a view was so subversive, not only of the modern hearsay rule, but also of the abolition of corroboration requirements, that when the issue arose again in *R v Horncastle*, reaction came in the unanimous judgment first of a very strong five-member Court of Appeal,[259] and then of a seven-member Supreme Court, reasserting the previously understood English position. The reasoning of the European Court of Human Rights was exposed to withering attack on the basis of its failure to distinguish adequately between the anonymity and

---

[244] Section 2(1).   [245] Which, it should be noted, does not impose an obligation to accept.
[246] Judgments, decisions, declarations, and advisory opinions.   [247] Under Art 31.
[248] Under Arts 26, 27(2).   [249] Under Art 46.   [250] Law Com No 245, [12.2]–[2.8] rec 48.
[251] *Blastland v United Kingdom* (1987) 10 EHRR 528.
[252] Scottish courts initially took a more expansive view of the effects of Art 6, but felt constrained to rein back: see *Campbell v HM Adv* 2004 JC 1, 2003 SCCR 779. Other common law jurisdictions such as Canada, Australia and New Zealand took a similar view, although the United States became more restrictive: see 554.
[253] *R v Gokal* [1997] 2 Cr App Rep 266, especially 278 et seq; *R v M* (n124); *R v Sellick* [2005] EWCA Crim 651, [2005] 1 WLR 3257, [35]; *R v Cole and Keet* (n181).
[254] [2005] EWCA Crim 2697, [2006] 1 All ER 543.
[255] Those sections relating to previous statements of witnesses fall outside the reach of Art 6.
[256] Which was conceded.   [257] *Al-Khawaja v United Kingdom* (2009) 49 EHRR 1.
[258] *Luca v Italy* (2003) 36 EHRR 807, [40].   [259] [2009] EWCA 964, [2009] 4 All ER 183.

absence of witnesses, vacillation on the existence of exceptions,[260] and the width of its definition of 'decisive' to amount to little more than bare relevance. It was felt that too little
weight had been attached both to the autonomy of member states so far as issues of admissibility are concerned, especially when criminal procedures vary so much between common
and civil law jurisdictions; and too little deference to the care and crafting of the relevant
provisions of the English legislation designed to guarantee a fair trial.[261]

The position under the European Convention remains unsettled, however, with an
appeal in *Al-Khawaja* now pending before the Grand Chamber, which will have to respond
to the arguments and views expressed in *Horncastle*.

SECTION 2. CONFESSIONS, SILENCE, AND POLICE QUESTIONING

This part of the chapter is mainly concerned with the single largest exception to the hearsay rule, that for confessions of the accused, in connection with which it is convenient to
consider also the evidential value of inferences from the accused's silence, and in relation
to both, the Codes of Practice relating to different aspects of police investigation, which is
often a component in the exercise of the judge's discretion to exclude evidence.[262]

CONFESSIONS[263]

This part will concentrate upon the substance of the law embodied in s 76 of the Police and
Criminal Evidence Act 1984.[264] The Law Commission did not propose[265] major reform of
the rules relating to confessions, although it did recommend[266] the fresh approach to the
problem of confessions made by one of several co-accused, now s 76A of the Police and
Criminal Evidence Act 1984.[267] Before examining s 76 in detail, it is useful to consider
briefly the development and rationale of the old law relating to confessions.

Development

The Police and Criminal Evidence Act 1984 defines a confession to include 'any statement wholly or partly adverse to the person who made it, whether made to a person in

---

[260] There is some acceptance of the view in *Sellick* (n253) that cases where the accused is responsible for
the absence of the witness may be an exception, and endorsement of further exceptions in cases with 'special
features,' such as *SN v Sweden* (2004) 39 EHRR 13, [2002] ECHR 3409/96.

[261] Strongly supported by Annex 4 to the judgment of the Supreme Court specifying precisely how that
domestic law would have operated in the leading nineteen decisions of the ECHR to achieve similar, or
sometimes stronger protection for the accused.

[262] See also: generally on the exclusionary discretion, 196 above; on the discretion to exclude real evidence, 511 above; and for the conduct of identification parades, 704 below.

[263] This enormous topic has, in the past, been the subject of a number of monographs, among them Joy
On Confessions (1842), still an important historical source. For a stimulating and perceptive view of the
whole area, see Mirfield *Silence, Confessions and Improperly Obtained Evidence* (1997).

[264] Influenced by, but not wholly in accord with, the recommendations of the 11th Report of the Criminal
Law Revision Committee Evidence: General Cmnd 4991 (1972), 34–47, draft bill, cl 2.

[265] Law Com No 245, [8.84]–[8.92], rec 18.

[266] Law Com No 245, [8.93]–[8.96], rec 19, draft bill, cl 17 inserting a new s 76A into the Police and
Criminal Evidence Act 1984.   [267] Inserted by s 128 of the Criminal Justice Act 2003.

authority or not and whether made in words or otherwise'.[268] When made otherwise than by a witness while testifying in court, it amounts to hearsay as defined in this work. It thus prevented use of an out-of-court confession against anyone other than its maker.[269] If, on a joint trial of A and B, the guilt of A depends upon the guilt of B, and that guilt is established by B's confession, it has been held that B's confession is not, as such, being used against A for these purposes.[270] If made by a testifying witness, it does not cease to be admissible against an incriminated party merely because the circumstances of making it would have rendered an earlier statement to the same effect inadmissible against its maker if tendered as an out-of-court confession.[271]

The origin of the exclusionary rule is to be found in the mid-eighteenth century, and achieved its first clear and authoritative formulation in the case of *R v Warickshall*:[272]

...a confession forced from the mind by the flattery of hope, or by the torture of fear, comes in so questionable a shape when it is to be considered as the evidence of guilt, that no credit ought to be given to it; and therefore it is rejected.

It is interesting to note that the court went out of its way to assert that the rationale of the rule was based entirely on considerations of credit, having first denied quite explicitly that it depended upon any 'regard to public faith'. In origin, the rule had little or no connection with the privilege against self-incrimination.[273] That doctrine had developed a century or so earlier, in reaction to the oaths required by the Courts of High Commission and Star Chamber. The line between judicial proceedings in which that doctrine came to flourish and extracurial investigations was, however, blurred by the investigatory functions of magistrates, which were not clearly, or finally, distinguished until after the establishment of a regular police force, and the passage of the Indictable Offences Act 1848.[274]

Between the end of the eighteenth century and the middle of the nineteenth, the rules excluding confessions were elaborated in a series of judgments at first instance. The conditions of that period were described by Lord Hailsham as:[275]

...a time when the savage code of the 18th century was in full force. At that time almost every serious crime was punished by death or transportation. The law enforcement officers formed no disciplined police force and were not subject to effective control by the Central Government Watch Committee or an inspectorate. There was no legal aid. There was no system of appeal. To crown it all the accused was unable to give evidence on his own behalf and was therefore largely at the mercy of any evidence, either perjured or oppressively obtained, that might be brought against him. The judiciary were therefore compelled to devise artificial rules designed to protect him against dangers now avoided by other and more rational means.

---

[268] Section 82(1).   [269] Even when made by a co-accused: *B v DPP* [2002] EWHC 2930 (Admin).

[270] *R v Hayter* [2005] UKHL 6, [2005] 2 All ER 209; cp *Persad v Trinidad* [2007] UKPC 51, [2007] 1 WLR 2379, where the Privy Council refused extension to cases where the guilt of one connoted the innocence of another.   [271] *R v Jamieson and Hobden* [2003] EWCA Crim 193, [20].

[272] (1783) 1 Leach 263, 263, 264.

[273] See Wigmore (1891) 5 *HLR* 71, and Morgan (1949) 34 *Minn LR* 1.

[274] The form of caution established by that legislation had an impact upon the attitudes of the judiciary to confessions secured by the police: see *R v Baldry* (1852) 2 Den 430. There is a persistent tendency to formalize, and to judicialize, the rules applicable to the earlier stages of investigation; strikingly demonstrated by the current law relating to the Codes of Practice.

[275] *DPP v Ping Lin* [1976] AC 574, [1975] 3 All ER 175, 600, 182. See also the remarks of Lord Diplock in *R v Sang* [1980] AC 402, [1979] 2 All ER 1222, 436, 1230.

By mid-century, not without some grave judicial misgivings, it was accepted that, in the words of Baron Parke:[276]

By the law of England, in order to render a confession admissible in evidence, it must be perfectly voluntary; and there is no doubt that any inducement in the nature of a promise or of a threat held out by a person in authority vitiates a confession.

Thereafter, the formulation of the rule remained relatively constant,[277] but became more and more rigid as a developing case law filled out the interstices of the definition by the determination of particular disputes. In England, this prevented the rule from extending beyond inducements in the shape of threats or promises,[278] although these were often construed with some ingenious generosity. This meant that, in order to accommodate the exclusion of confessions obtained by the use of reprehensible police methods, not on any view involving the use of either promises or threats, it was necessary to develop rules of practice.[279] Since the evolution of such a rule of practice could hardly be left to the vagaries of dozens of uncoordinated decisions, the scene was set for the promulgation of the English Judges' Rules, attempting to encapsulate a set of rules of fair police practices, although without the sanction of automatic enforcement. It also meant that, in order to provide for exclusion in the most egregious cases of malpractice, it was ultimately necessary[280] to amplify the formulation of the exclusionary rule to include a reference to oppression.[281] Conversely, the consequence of construing individual decisions on particular facts as rules of law was that some forms of words, which many felt could hardly have induced the most timorous of suspects to confess falsely, became automatic warrants for exclusion.[282] The basic roots of the technicality in which the law had become enmeshed were reduced in *DPP v Ping Lin*.[283] The effect was to emphasize that the question of the exclusionary test was one of fact, especially one of causation, to be construed on a common-sense basis and necessarily determined without reference to authority, just because everything depended upon the particular circumstances in which the particular suspect was placed.[284] In this way, the judge could approach the question just as it would be approached by a jury, whose function in this situation he was unusually, but unavoidably, assuming.

---

[276] *R v Baldry* (1852) 2 Den 430, 444.

[277] The leading authorities were *R v Thompson* [1893] 2 QB 12, and *Ibrahim v R* [1914] AC 599.

[278] In Australia, the courts were more prepared to take a wider and less blinkered view of the impediments to voluntariness: see *Cornelius v R* (1936) 55 CLR 235, in which Dixon J explicitly contrasted the position in England. See also *Wan v United States* 266 US 1 (1924), for a similar statement of the American position by Justice Brandeis.

[279] The basic principles appeared during the nineteenth century: see *Peart v R* [2006] UKPC 5, [2006] 1 WLR 970, [18]; and were judicially recognized by 1905: see *R v Knight and Thayre* (1905) 20 Cox CC 711, Channell J.   [280] But see *DPP v Ping Lin* (n275); 606, 188, Lord Salmon.

[281] It was first introduced here by Lord Parker CJ in his judgment in *Callis v Gunn* [1964] 1 QB 495, [1963] 3 All ER 677; 501, 680, and shortly afterwards, incorporated as part of principle (e) of the introduction to the new Judges' Rules of 1964. It may represent an attempt to make explicit in English law the prohibition of torture included in 1950 as Art 3 of the European Convention on Human Rights.

[282] Here, too, some jurisdictions avoided such consequences by robust intervention, thus the colony of Victoria, as early as 1857, enacted a provision providing that only inducements 'really calculated' to cause untrue admissions were to lead to exclusion, now Evidence Act 1958, s 149.

[283] [1976] AC 574, [1975] 3 All ER 175.

[284] Or perhaps reasonably believed that he was placed: see *DPP (Cwth) Ref No 1 of 1996* [1998] 3 VR 217, canvassing whether someone testifying under compulsory process before a tribunal wrongly believed to have jurisdiction could be said to have confessed voluntarily.

Rationale

The House of Lords declined to speculate in *Ping Lin*[285] upon exactly what basis the exclusion of involuntary confessions was to be justified. A number have been suggested, both in relation to the rules excluding involuntary confessions, and to the exercise of exclusionary discretions that apply to confessional statements, and to other evidence obtained by illegal means, itself sometimes regarded as being governed by analogous policies. The general ground for accepting admissions, that what a party says against his own interests may be presumed to be true, has not always been accepted in relation to confessions. Thus Wigmore cites the same eminent English judge, asserting first in 1798 that 'confession is a species of evidence which, though not inadmissible, is regarded with great distrust',[286] and in 1820, that 'confession generally ranks high, or I should say, highest in the scale of evidence'.[287] This discrepancy is plausibly enough explained[288] on the basis that, when satisfactorily established to have proceeded from a genuine motive, and to have been accurately recorded, a confession may well be worthy of the highest esteem, but just because this is the case, such high regard will also be sought by the less scrupulous for statements that merely purport to satisfy these conditions. In contested criminal cases, given that the accused is present in court, has pleaded not guilty, and has retracted his purported confession, there must always be a possibility that the statement falls into the latter category.[289] It is for this reason that some form of corroboration has been suggested,[290] and the need for a warning to the jury to take great care, and to look for supporting evidence, endorsed by the Royal Commission on Criminal Justice.[291] It has also played some part in the development of rules for the aural and video recording of confessions, although in most jurisdictions,[292] failure to perform such recording is not automatically fatal to admissibility.[293]

The old requirement that a confession be 'voluntary' may be regarded as demanding satisfaction of quite different rationales.[294] *Warickshall* stressed the need for the confession to be creditworthy, and, to that end, distinguished sharply between the making of an oral statement that might, or might not, be false, and the finding of objects that it assumed to be automatically cogent, although such evidence rarely proves much in the absence of testimony, or other circumstantial evidence. In *Baldry*, the court was anxious to point

---

[285] By Lord Morris, 595, 178, and by Lord Salmon 607, 188.

[286] Sir William Scott in *Williams v Williams* (1798) 1 Hag Con 299, 304.

[287] *Mortimer v Mortimer* (1820) 2 Hag Con 310, 315.

[288] See also *R v Maynard* (1979) 69 Cr App Rep 309, 312.

[289] See Cave J in *R v Thompson* (n277), 18. In Canada, in recognition of confessions being technically hearsay, the reliability limb of the local hearsay rule has been applied: *R v Moore-McFarlane* (2001) 160 CCC (3d) 493.

[290] And accepted by the High Court of Australia in *R v Mackinney and Judge* (1992) 171 CLR 468.

[291] Cmnd 2263, [4.56]–[4.87], and recs 89–90. See also the Commission's Research Study No 13 'Corroboration and Confessions: The Impact of a Rule Requiring That No Conviction Can Be Sustained on the Basis of Confession Evidence Alone'.

[292] In those where it is, the legislation has been difficult to draft and has led to difficulty: see, in Australia, *Kelly v R* [2004] HCA 12, 218 CLR 216; *Nicholls v R* [2005] HCA 1, 219 CLR 196.

[293] They were not so regarded in relation to Northern Ireland by the European Court of Human Rights in *Brennan v United Kingdom* (2001) 34 EHRR 507, [53].

[294] It has been argued that a 'voluntariness' rationale still underlies the modern statutory law: see Bicak (2001) 65 J Crim L 85. It remains the test in Canada: see *R v Spencer* 2007 SCC 11, [2007] 1 SCR 500.

out that involuntary confessions are not presumed to be false,[295] but that it is nevertheless dangerous, from the point of view of the administration of justice, to admit them. *Ibrahim* referred to the rule as one of policy, but abstained from elaborating the nature of that policy.

Some cases, at the same time as clarifying the operation of the rule, have suggested a more diffused basis for it in policy. Thus one further strand intertwined with reliability in the current approach, and to be discerned both in Lord Reid's speech in *Harz and Power*,[296] and in Lord Diplock's in *Sang*,[297] is that of the basis for the privilege against self-incrimination, a vindication of the right of the individual not to be subjected to official pressure to condemn himself.[298] This rationale, concerned so closely with the rights of the accused at his trial,[299] seems to exemplify what has been called the 'protective principle'.[300] It is clearly intended to be distinguished from what the Criminal Law Revision Committee referred to as the 'disciplinary principle', the thrust of which is more to deter improper police practices than to protect the rights of the accused. Yet this principle itself found some expression, for example, in *Wong Kam-ming v R*, Lord Hailsham said:[301]

...any civilised system of criminal jurisprudence must accord to the judiciary some means of excluding confessions or admissions obtained by improper methods. This is not only because of the potential unreliability of such statements, but also, and perhaps mainly, because in a civilised society it is vital that persons in custody or charged with offences should not be subjected to ill treatment or improper pressure in order to extract confessions.

The generality and instrumentality of these words suggest that Lord Hailsham's principal concern was with the control of police behaviour.[302] Indeed, the rationale is sometimes put on a still higher plane, and, quite irrespective of the deterrent force of a decision upon police practice, related to the court's expression of abhorrence for the methods used. Thus in *King v R*, Lord Hodson expressed the view of the Privy Council by saying:[303]

This is not, in their opinion, a case in which evidence has been obtained by conduct of which the Crown ought not to take advantage. If they had thought otherwise they would have excluded the evidence even though tendered for the suppression of crime.

This view has received even stronger support in Australia, where the High Court has explicitly rejected a fair play rationale in favour of such a view: 'It is not fair play that is

---

[295] In *Burns v R* (1975) 132 CLR 258, 262, the High Court of Australia was equally insistent that voluntary confessions were not to be presumed to be true.   [296] [1967] 1 AC 760, [1967] 1 All ER 177; 820, 184.

[297] [1980] AC 402, [1979] 2 All ER 1222; 436, 1230. The passage is somewhat difficult to interpret since after mentioning the principle *nemo debet prodere se ipsum* in relation to the justification for modern confession law, Lord Diplock relates it to the discretion to exclude, going on to describe that, as a sanction upon the improper conduct of the prosecution, contrasting it with the power only to secure a fair trial, and denying the existence of any comparable sanctioning power in relation to obtaining any other evidence.

[298] See also *R v Keenan* [1990] 2 QB 54, [1989] 3 All ER 598, 62, 603, in which the modern law under s 76 of the Police and Criminal Evidence Act 1984 is ascribed to such a rationale; for its influence in Canada, see *R v Singh* 2007 SCC 48, [2007] 3 SCR 405.

[299] Or occasionally otherwise, as in *R (U) v Metropolitan Police Comr* [2002] EWHC 2486 (Admin), [2003] 3 All ER 419, in which a caution was offered on the basis of a confession secured without warning the accused that the consequence would entail an entry on the register of sexual offenders.

[300] See Ashworth [1977] *Crim LR* 723.   [301] [1980] AC 247, [1979] 1 All ER 939; 261, 946.

[302] For a still more explicit reference to this rationale, see *R v Trump* (1979) 70 Cr App Rep 300, 303.

[303] [1969] 1 AC 304, [1968] 2 All ER 610; 319, 617.

called in question in such cases but rather society's right to insist that those who enforce the law themselves respect it.'[304] It should be noted that, in both of these cases, the issue related to the discretion to exclude real evidence secured after breach of proper procedure, and in *Bunning v Cross*, was said 'not to entrench upon the quite special rules which apply to the case of confession evidence'. Yet it can hardly be argued today that a weaker justification is required to restrain the application of pressure to human beings to force them to confess, than is required to prevent intrusion into private property. The further step of explicit extension to disputed confessions was taken by the High Court of Australia in *Cleland v R*,[305] in accordance with the position that the discretion to exclude had always been wider in Australia than in England,[306] but not so different in the result from the position in Scotland.[307] It should be noted that, under modern English law, discretionary exclusion under s 78 of the Police and Criminal Evidence Act 1984 extends to means of obtaining evidence having an adverse effect upon the fairness of the proceedings, a provision that has been explicitly held to extend to confessions.[308] In Canada, this area, like so much of the law of evidence, was affected by the advent of the Canadian Charter of Rights and Freedoms. Under Art 24(2) of the Charter, any evidence in breach of the rights guaranteed by the Charter must be excluded 'if it is established that, having regard to all the circumstances, the admission of it in the proceedings would bring the administration of justice into disrepute'. This will, in many cases, operate in relation to confessions by way of breach of the right to counsel guaranteed under the Charter.[309]

The explicit rejection of such rationales is as significant as their espousal has been as an indication of the uncertainty of the law in this area. In *R v Warickshall*, the court was clear that:[310]

It is a mistaken notion that the evidence of confessions and facts which have been obtained from prisoners by promises or threats, is to be rejected from a regard to public faith: no such rule ever prevailed.

In stark contrast when, in *Wong Kam-ming v R*, counsel for the respondent began his argument by expressing the reliability principle, he was sharply upbraided by Lord Diplock with the assertion that such an argument was contrary to authority.[311] Nor do the views in *R v Sang* support a general disciplinary policy in this area, for, as expressed by Lord Diplock:[312]

It is no part of a judge's function to exercise powers over the police or prosecution as respects the way in which evidence to be used at the trial is obtained by them. If it was obtained illegally there will be a remedy in civil law; if it was obtained legally but in breach of the rules of conduct of the police, this is a matter for the appropriate disciplinary authority to deal with. What the judge at the trial is concerned with is not how the evidence sought to be adduced by the prosecution has been obtained, but with how it is used by the prosecution at the trial.

---

[304] (1978) 19 ALR 641, 659.   [305] (1982) 151 CLR 1.

[306] Justified by Murphy J, 17 on the basis of the lower standard of proof for the voluntariness of a confession in Australia.   [307] *Cleland v R* (1983) 151 CLR 1, Gibbs CJ, 8.

[308] *R v Mason* [1987] 3 All ER 481, [1988] 1 WLR 139; 484, 143H.

[309] *R v Manninen* [1987] 1 SCR 1233. For full judicial consideration of the relation of the Charter to the rationales of the confession rule, see *R v Oickle* [2000] SCC 38, [2000] 2 SCR 3. It has been suggested that the constitutions of many Caribbean jurisdictions present similar opportunities: see O'Brien and Carter [2000] 4 *Int J Ev & Pr* 45.

[311] [1980] AC 247, 251.   [310] (n272).

[312] (n297); 436, 1230. See also *R v Delaney* (1988) 88 Cr App Rep 338, 341.

It should be noted that, by excluding confessions from this reasoning, Lord Diplock was countenancing just that split between the rationales in respect of police methods in obtaining confessions, and in obtaining other evidence, that was rejected by the High Court of Australia in *Cleland v R*.[313] Lord Diplock's view distinguished sharply, and perfectly understandably, between police practice in inducing speech, and in searching premises. It is less clear how Lord Fraser and Lord Scarman, who extended discretionary exclusion to some searches, could subscribe to the same rationale. It is hard to see why it is worse for the police to search the accused's premises improperly than so to search those of anyone else. If anything, the former seems *less* iniquitous. The current view was stated by Lord Griffiths in *Lam Chi-ming v R*:[314]

... the most recent English cases established that the rejection of an improperly obtained confession is not dependent only upon possible unreliability but also upon the principle that a man cannot be compelled to incriminate himself and upon the importance that attaches in a civilised society to proper behaviour by the police towards those in their custody.

The overall rationale for admission, taking into account discretionary exclusion,[315] is now rested on fairness:[316]

The criterion for admission of a statement is fairness. The voluntary nature of the statement is the major factor in determining fairness. If it is not voluntary, it will not be admitted. If it is voluntary, that constitutes a strong reason in favour of admitting it, notwithstanding a breach of the Judges' Rules; but the court may rule that it would be unfair to do so even if the statement was voluntary.

Police and Criminal Evidence Act 1984

This legislation still governs the admissibility of confessions,[317] and requires detailed consideration. Questions arise as to its extent, its conditions for admissibility, and its effect.

Extent

Section 76 of the Police and Criminal Evidence Act 1984 establishes its extent by providing:

> (1) In any proceedings a confession made by an accused person may be given in evidence against him in so far as it is relevant to any matter in issue in the proceedings and is not excluded by the court in pursuance of this section.

This is supplemented by s 82, which states that:

> (1) 'confession' includes any statement wholly or partly adverse to the person who made it, whether made to a person in authority or not, and whether made in words or otherwise.

---

[313]   (1983) 43 ALR 619.   [314]   [1991] 2 AC 212, [1991] 3 All ER 171; 220, 179.

[315]   Which has itself developed dramatically in recent years: see *R v Hussein* [2005] EWCA Crim 31, [48], [59].

[316]   *Peart v R* (n279), [24]; subsequently endorsed in *Williams v R* [2006] UKPC 21, in which, [26], fairness is described as 'the sovereign requirement'.

[317]   Although, even if admissible as a confession, such a statement may not satisfy more precise rules, such as that for a signature even though the confession is of the fact so certified: *Mawdesley v Chief Constable of Cheshire* [2003] EWHC 1586 (Admin), [2004] 1 All ER 58.

Two sets of issues arise as to the extent of these provisions, the first relating to formal, and the second, to procedural, delimitation. These will be considered in turn.

Formal delimitation

In the first category, it is necessary to elucidate the notion of a 'statement': whether it extends to matters of opinion as well as those of fact, the precise extent of the phrase 'made in words or otherwise', and how far, if at all, purely exculpatory statements are caught by the words 'wholly or partly adverse'.

There is, in this Part of the Act, no further definition of 'statement', by contrast to the preceding Part, in which it is defined in accordance with the definition in the Civil Evidence Act 1968.[318] That definition, as amended, now includes an expression of opinion, so it is reasonable to construe 'confession' here as excluding any expression of opinion.

It will be noticed that, to amount to a confession, any statement must be, at least in part,[319] adverse to its maker. Questions have arisen as to the position with regard to a statement wholly exculpatory in intention and apparent effect when made, but which, by the time of trial, has become damaging to the accused, either because it can be shown to be false, or because it is inconsistent with the defence raised at the trial.[320] The inadmissibility of such a statement derived some support from the reasoning in *Lam Chi-ming v R*, in which Lord Griffiths said that:[321]

...it is surely just as reprehensible to use improper means to force a man to give information that will reveal he has knowledge that will ensure his conviction as it is to force him to make a full confession. In either case a man is being forced into a course of action that will result in his conviction: he is being forced to incriminate himself.

This is consistent with the decision in *R v Treacy*[322] that an inadmissible confession cannot be used as a previous inconsistent statement for the purpose of discrediting its maker. It also coheres much better with the attitude of the European Court of Human Rights in its treatment of the privilege of self-incrimination, which, in *Saunders v United Kingdom*,[323] it explicitly extended to statements intended to exculpate. The view attracted powerful academic support,[324] and similar reasoning has been used elsewhere.[325]

After some vicissitudes, it was, however, unanimously rejected by the House of Lords in *R v Hasan*,[326] and such rejection regarded as compatible with the European Convention.[327] Despite indubitable difficulty in determining whether a statement, when made, is adverse

---

[318] Section 72(1).   [319] For difficulties of definition of 'mixed' statements see, 306.

[320] In *R v Toothill* [1998] Crim LR 876, the statement, which may well have been false, was intended to exculpate, but because of lack of knowledge of the relevant branch of the criminal law, in fact supplied one of the essential elements of the charge.

[321] [1991] 2 AC 212, [1991] 3 All ER 172; 222, 179. See also *R v Ismail* [1990] Crim LR 109.

[322] [1944] 2 All ER 229. The Supreme Court of Canada came to the same result in *Cook v R* [1998] 2 SCR 597, and in *R v G (B)* [1999] 2 SCR 475, applied the reasoning to a second confession confirming a prior inadmissible one. In *R v Mason* (1995) 15 WAR 165, however, a false exculpatory statement was admitted to discredit the accused because inconsistent with two earlier inculpatory statements, which had themselves been excluded because improperly obtained.   [323] (1996) 23 EHRR 313, [71].

[324] Elliott and Wakeham [1979] *Crim LR* 428; Mirfield (n263), 54–8; Pattenden (1999) 3 *E&P* 217.

[325] See, in the United States, *Miranda v US* 384 US 436, 477 (1966); in Canada, *Piché v R* [1971] SCR 23; in Australia, *R v Horton* (1998) 45 NSWLR 426.   [326] [2005] UKHL 22, [2005] 2 AC 467.

[327] [62]. Partly in reliance on the availability of the exclusionary discretion in s 78 of the Police and Criminal Evidence Act 1984.

to the accused, this approach seems better adapted to the statutory wording, and to common understanding. As trenchantly remarked in *R v Pearce*,[328] 'a denial does not become an admission because it is inconsistent with another denial'.

The most common relevance of a false denial is to show consciousness of guilt.[329] Such consciousness may also be shown by such things as making false,[330] or evasive,[331] statements, remaining silent when speech could have been expected,[332] refusing to supply a sample of real evidence,[333] putting in a false notice of alibi,[334] attempting to suborn,[335] or kill,[336] witnesses, calling witnesses to give testimony known to be false,[337] or fleeing.[338] It is submitted that, unless the conduct can be regarded as indicating acceptance of an assertion made by another,[339] consciousness of guilt derived from such statements or conduct can amount only to circumstantial evidence, and cannot amount to hearsay.[340] In all such cases, it is admissible if relevant, irrespective of its motivation, save in so far as that it may so reduce the weight of such evidence as to suggest that it ought to trigger the exercise of the judge's discretion to exclude, because the prejudicial effect is likely to exceed probative value, a particularly likely situation here when the conduct or statement may have many other plausible explanations besides consciousness of guilt.[341] But where there is little such danger, it seems that the discretion to exclude will be less likely to be exercised in relation to statements intended to exculpate.[342] Such discretionary exclusion already applies to the kindred situation of police impropriety in securing statements for non-testimonial purposes, incapable upon any basis of being regarded as confessions, such as for voice comparison.[343]

It might be argued that this view deprives the second part of the expression 'in words or otherwise' of any meaning. It should, however, be noticed that the concluding words remain undeniably apt to cover evidence of admissions deduced from the conduct of the accused in the course of a re-enactment of the crime, orchestrated by the police.[344]

---

[328]   (1979) 69 Cr App Rep 365, 370.

[329]   The use of this terminology was criticized by the Supreme Court of Canada in *White v R* [1998] 2 SCR 72, [20].

[330]   *R v Knight* [1966] 1 All ER 647, [1966] 1 WLR 230; and see *R v Lucas* [1981] QB 720, [1981] 2 All ER 1008.   [331]   *Woon v R* (1964) 109 CLR 529.

[332]   *R v Chandler* [1976] 3 All ER 105, [1976] 1 WLR 585; and a fortiori assaulting an accuser: *Parkes v R* [1976] 3 All ER 380, [1976] 1 WLR 1251.   [333]   *R v Smith* (1985) 81 Cr App Rep 286.

[334]   *R v Rossborough* (1985) 81 Cr App Rep 139.

[335]   *Moriarty v London Chatham and Dover Rly Co* (1870) LR 5 QB 314.

[336]   *R v Tran* (2001) 150 CCC (3d) 481.   [337]   *R v Malone* [2006] EWCA Crim 1860, [62].

[338]   *R v Gay* [1976] VR 577.

[339]   In *R v Collins* [2004] EWCA Crim 83, [2004] 2 Cr App R 199, the court required an evidential basis before accepting that silence in the face of a lie told to the police by a co-accused in a joint interview amounted to adoption of the lie.

[340]   There is, of course, no doubt that it falls outside the definition proposed by the Law Commission.

[341]   This is consistent with the approach adopted in *R v Lucas* (n330), and in *R v Dowley* [1983] Crim LR 168, an appeal was allowed because the dangers had not been clearly enough spelled out.

[342]   See *R v Allen (No 2)* [2001] UKHL 45, [2002] 1 AC 509, [35]; *R v Gill* [2003] EWCA Crim 2256, [2003] 4 All ER 681.

[343]   See *PG and JH v United Kingdom* (2001) The Times, 19 October, ECHR (App 44787/98); *R v Piché* (1999) 136 CCC (3d) 217.

[344]   *Li Shu-ling v R* [1989] AC 270, [1988] 3 All ER 138. Also accepted elsewhere: see *Collins v R* (1980) 31 ALR 257; *R v Robert* (1996) 104 CCC (3d) 480; *S v Sheehama* 1991 (2) SA 860; *People v Dabb* 32 Cal 2d 491 (1948).

Procedural delimitation

These matters comprehend such issues as the extent to which the section applies to use of confessional material by the defence, and especially by a co-accused, how far it applies to statements made in other curial proceedings, to what extent it applies to magistrates, and the stage at which particular exclusionary rules apply.

At common law, statements made by third parties confessing guilt were inadmissible as hearsay when adduced by the accused in chief.[345] They may now be admissible if they satisfy the conditions established by the Criminal Justice Act 2003.[346]

The wording of s 76 of the Police and Criminal Evidence Act 1984 originally distinguished between its general application to all confessions made by an accused person, and the special restrictive conditions that applied only to those put in evidence by the prosecution. The result appeared to be that one co-accused might himself adduce the confessions of another without regard to the restrictive conditions laid down, but this proved problematic, culminating in the decision of the House of Lords in *R v Myers*.[347] There the co-accused's confession could have been excluded under the s 78 discretion for breaches of the Code of Practice, and for this reason was not adduced by the prosecution.[348] It was held that this confession could be adduced by the exculpated co-accused, over the objection of the other. So it seemed to be the position that a co-accused might be entitled to adduce, or to cross-examine,[349] on the basis of such a confession, despite the objection of the inculpated co-accused, and however much prejudice it caused that co-accused. The position remained unclear if it fell foul of s 76, and on this point there was some disagreement in *Myers*.[350]

Although there was no discretion to exclude evidence that is otherwise admissible tendered by the defence,[351] it was held in *R v Rogers and Tarran*[352] that the discretion to exclude evidence tendered by the prosecution at a joint trial could be invoked on account of prejudice to the co-accused other than that against whom it is tendered.

The Criminal Justice Act 2003 modified the situation[353] by inserting[354] a new s 76A in the Police and Criminal Evidence Act 1984, which effectively applies exactly the same

---

[345] *Sussex Peerage Case* (1844) 11 Cl & Fin 85. The same rule applies in Australia: see *Re Van Beelen* (1974) 9 SASR 163; *R v Bannon* (1995) 185 CLR 1; but not in Canada: *R v O'Brien* (1977) 76 DLR (3d) 513; or the United States, Federal Rule 804(3)(b) requiring corroboration, and see *Chambers v Mississippi* 410 US 295 (1973).

[346] See further, 606.

[347] [1998] AC 124, [1997] 4 All ER 314. *Myers* was itself rejected in Australia in *Question of Law Reserved (No 3 of 1997)* (1997) 70 SASR 555.

[348] It is less clear why a confession in identical terms to a third party, not in any way governed by the Code, was not adduced.

[349] *R v Jamieson and Hobden* [n271], [30].

[350] Between Lord Hope and Lord Slynn. See also Mirfield (n263) 220 (in a passage written before the decision of the House of Lords in *Myers* (n347)).

[351] *R v Miller* [1952] 2 All ER 667; 36 Cr App Rep 169, 669, 171; *Murdoch v Taylor* [1965] AC 574, [1965] 1 All ER 406. Or even if tendered by the prosecution if its effect is to exculpate one of the co-accused, and he objects to the invocation of discretion for this purpose: *Lobban v R* [1995] 2 All ER 602, [1995] 1 WLR 877. This is a strong decision, since there was no case to answer against the co-accused, and it was only by accident that he had not already been excluded from jeopardy, and in such a case the confession would clearly be inadmissible, as in *R v Campbell* [1995] 1 Cr App Rep 522.

[352] [1971] Crim LR 413.

[353] *R v Nazir* [2009] EWCA Crim 213, [19].

[354] Section 128(1), acting upon Law Com No 245, paras 8.93–8.96, rec 19.

rules to confessions[355] adduced by the co-accused[356] to those adduced by the prosecution, subject only to the application of the lower standard of proof on the balance of probabilities to matters to be proved by the defence. The effect may, however, be different, since the discretion to exclude evidence at common law, and that under s 78, apply only to confessions upon which the prosecution proposes to rely,[357] and the defence need negate the conditions of s 76A on no more than the balance of probabilities. It has also been suggested[358] that s 76A may be too wide and too narrow, in that its application of the conditions of s 76 may prevent a co-accused from adducing evidence despite its being true, and may permit the use of evidence obtained in circumstances of such injustice that exclusionary discretion under s 78 would have been appropriate, had the prosecution sought to use it against its maker.

The next point to be made on the extent of the section relates to the question of the admissibility of confessions made in other proceedings, or at earlier stages of the same proceedings.[359] There is nothing in the wording of s 76 to suggest that it does not apply to statements made in the course of judicial proceedings just as much as to those not so made.[360] It would follow that the common law rules admitting statements made in other proceedings,[361] including those made only for the purposes of such proceedings,[362] pleas of guilty to associated offences,[363] and pleas of guilty that have been withdrawn,[364] will remain applicable, since it is inherently unlikely that the conditions for exclusion will be capable of being established in such situations.[365] Sometimes admissions may be made under compulsory process in other proceedings, and in *R v K* admissions of tax evasion made in ancillary domestic proceedings were thus excluded.[366]

The admissibility of statements on the voir dire has been more controversial. As noted earlier,[367] the position at common law seems to have been changed in some respects by

---

[355] Including the basis of a plea of guilty, subsequently permitted to be withdrawn: *R v Johnson* [2007] EWCA Crim 1651; although the admission of guilty pleas is subject to discretionary exclusion: *R v Smith* [2007] EWCA Crim 2105; and a strict view of its relevance was taken in *R v Girma* [2009] EWCA Crim 912, [64]–[66] and *R v Downer* [2009] EWCA Crim 1361.

[356] As widely defined in s 76A(1), excluding a co-accused who has pleaded guilty: *R v Finch* [2007] EWCA Crim 36, [2007] 1 WLR 1645.

[357] Although it seems that the determination may be postponed until the end of the case: *B and J v DPP* (21 May 2004, unreported), QBD.   [358] By Hartshorne (2004) *E&P* 165.

[359] The editor has relied heavily in this section upon Pattenden (1983) 32 *ICLQ* 812.

[360] Although confessional concessions made by counsel in opening may be withdrawn, and then become inadmissible: *R v Shalala* [2007] VSCA 199, 176 ACR 183.

[361] *R v McGregor* [1968] 1 QB 371, [1967] 2 All ER 267.

[362] *R v Hinchcliffe* [2002] EWCA Crim 837, [108].   [363] *R v Bastin* [1971] Crim LR 529.

[364] *R v Rimmer* [1972] 1 All ER 604, [1972] 1 WLR 268. It is not possible to appeal against a conviction following a guilty plea unless it is the product of a mistake, or has been induced by an erroneous ruling making acquittal legally impossible: *R v Thomas* [2000] 1 Cr App Rep 447. See also in Canada *R v Ford* (2000) 145 CCC (3d) 336.

[365] In *R v Scott* (1856) Dears & B 47, 58, Lord Campbell CJ said: 'Such an objection [involuntariness] cannot apply to a lawful examination in the course of judicial proceedings.' In *McGregor* (n361) also, the vigour of Lord Parker CJ's repudiation of the notion of the inadmissibility of a statement on oath in judicial proceedings points in the same direction. See also, in Australia, *R v Azar* (1991) 56 ACR 414, 418; *DPP(NSW) v Alderman* (1998) 104 ACR 116, 125. It has even been held irrelevant that such earlier proceedings were in fact invalid: *DPP's Ref (No 2 of 1996)* [1998] 3 VR 241.

[366] *R v K* [2009] EWCA Crim 1640, [2010] 1 Cr App R 44, although similar admissions were not excluded simply on the basis that they had been made in the course of a without prejudice meeting.

[367] 179–83.

the section. It is best to consider the matter in two stages: first, to consider to what extent admissions can be extracted on the voir dire; then to what extent they can be adduced at the trial. Section 76 makes no explicit reference to the propriety of asking about the truth or falsity of a confession on the voir dire,[368] so the matter is left to the common law. This is in a somewhat uncertain state.[369] In the case of such an issue being initiated by the prosecution, there was conflict between a decision of the Court of Criminal Appeal that such questioning was permissible,[370] and one of the majority of the Privy Council, that it was not.[371] In the case of the issue's being initiated by the defence, the House of Lords seems to have held that such questioning was proper.[372] This would probably have remained an academic issue at common law, in view of the further finding that no reference could be made to such an admission at the trial. On ordinary principles of statutory interpretation, however, this happy result was overturned by s 76, which applies to confessions in unrestricted terms, and makes them admissible at the instance of the prosecution in all cases, unless the conditions of subs (2) cannot be disproved.[373] But, as noted above, there is, in the case of an admission on the voir dire, every reason to suppose that such conditions will be held to be disproved. It would seem to follow that judicial confessions made at whatever stage are thus admissible. This effect appears to resurrect the conflict between *Hammond* and the majority view in *Wong Kam-ming*. In the first draft of the bill, as noted above, such a conflict was to have been resolved by a specific provision in favour of *Hammond* and the minority in *Wong Kam-ming*, but that provision was withdrawn, and the Act is now silent on the propriety of questions as to the truth or falsity of a confession on the voir dire.[374] On balance, it seems more likely[375] that the views of the majority of the Law Lords in *Wong Kam-ming* will prevail, especially as no disapproval of that decision was expressed by the House of Lords in *Brophy*.[376] It appears nevertheless that the general intention of *Wong Kam-ming* and *Brophy*, to protect the accused from damaging use at the trial of proceedings on the voir dire, has been frustrated by the drafting of the statutory provisions[377] so as

---

[368] The bill, as introduced, included a subsection specifically permitting such questioning, but it was withdrawn.

[369] Although in his dissenting speech in *R v Mushtaq* [2005] UKHL 25, [2005] 3 All ER 885, [16], Lord Hutton seemed to have no doubt that a confession on the voir dire could not be adduced (the majority view is silent on this point). [370] *R v Hammond* [1941] 3 All ER 318, 28 Cr App Rep 84.

[371] *Wong Kam-Ming v R* (n311).

[372] *R v Brophy* [1982] AC 476, [1981] 2 All ER 705. It is left unclear to what extent the questioning there did relate to an extrajudicial confession, and to what extent its adduction by the defence would permit cross-examination by the prosecution. In any event, the situation there was atypical, in that it was the defence that was alleging the confession to be true.

[373] 632. The same result was reached by the Supreme Court of Canada in *Boulet v R* [1978] 1 SCR 332, 350, and in none of *Hammond* (n370) *Wong Kam-Ming* (n311) nor *Brophy* (n372) was the question so much as raised. The regressive effect of voir dires into voir dires is surely to be avoided if at all possible.

[374] Commentators are not so much silent as divided: cp Murphy [1979] *Crim LR* 364; Arvay (1981) 23 *Cr LQ* 173.

[375] See *R v James* [2006] EWCA Crim 14, [2006] QB 588, reflecting on the precedential value of decisions of the Privy Council.

[376] It seems still permissible to ask the question in Australia: see *Frijaf v* R [1982] WAR 128; *R v Semyraha* [2000] QCA 303, 18 ACR 1; but not in South Africa: *S v De Vries* 1989 (1) SA 228.

[377] Mirfield argues in [1995] *Crim LR* 612 that the policies have been further frustrated by the pressures put upon the accused to testify by the Criminal Procedure and Investigation Act 1996. Although it was held, in *Thompson v R* [1998] AC 811, PC, that the rule that no reference should be made even to the decision on

to exclude confessions, only upon the satisfaction of conditions that judicial proceedings will rarely, if ever, satisfy in the United Kingdom.

'Proceedings' are defined by s 82(1) to mean criminal proceedings,[378] although no indication is given of whether that expression is meant to comprehend all stages of such proceedings at which evidence might be tendered.[379] It is clear that they comprehend proceedings before magistrates, and s 76(2) in its mandatory terms seems to have imposed an obligation upon magistrates to consider the admissibility of a confession as a separate preliminary matter in summary proceedings.[380] A different view was, however, taken in respect of an application to consider discretionary exclusion under s 78 as a preliminary matter.[381] The reasoning was based upon a supposed difference between the obligation under s 76(2) to take a decision on admissibility in advance of the evidence being tendered, and the decision under s 78, which could be taken at any time. It is doubtful, however, whether this view can survive the interpretation of ss 76 and 78 of the Police and Criminal Evidence Act 1984 in *R v Sat-Bhambra*[382] as referring only to the future, so that once the evidence has been adduced, their direct effect has been spent. The effect of any such view is, however, slight, since the judge may still discharge the jury, or direct it to disregard the confession, under his general discretionary powers, preserved by s 82(3) of the Police and Criminal Evidence Act 1984. In the case of summary trial, it has also been held that, if the accused's claim on s 78 involves nothing more than questions relating strictly to the disputed evidence, and does not otherwise introduce the substance of the charge, that fairness might dictate the claim being dealt with analogously to a claim under s 76.[383]

Conditions

Confessions were made admissible under the conditions set out in s 76:

> (2) If, in any proceedings where the prosecution proposes to give in evidence a confession made by an accused person, it is represented to the court that the confession was or may have been obtained—
>
> (a) by oppression of the person who made it; or
>
> (b) in consequence of anything said or done which was likely, in the circumstances existing at the time, to render unreliable any confession which might be made by him in consequence thereof,
>
> the court shall not allow the confession to be given in evidence against him except in so far as the prosecution proves to the court beyond reasonable doubt that the confession (notwithstanding that it may be true) was not obtained as aforesaid.

---

voluntariness on the voir dire had survived the new provisions (which were deemed to apply in the relevant jurisdiction).

[378] It seems that a police caution will not be invalidated if it is based on a confession that would have been inadmissible in proceedings in court: *R v Chief Constable of Lancashire, ex p Atkinson* (1998) 162 JP 275.

[379] Cf Criminal Evidence Act 1898, s 1.

[380] *R v Liverpool Juvenile Court, ex p R* [1988] QB 1, [1987] 2 All ER 668. It no longer applies in committal proceedings, and only in the most exceptional circumstances in extradition proceedings: *Fernandes v Governor of Brixton Prison* [2004] EWHC 2207 (Admin), [75]. See also *Police v Macklin* [1989] 3 NZLR 600.

[381] *Vel v Owen* (1987) 151 JP 510. See also *Carlisle v DPP* (1987) Lexis, 9 November.

[382] (1988) 88 Cr App Rep 55, intimating that the 1984 legislation had altered the procedure determined by *R v Watson* [1980] 2 All ER 293, [1980] 1 WLR 991.   [383] *Halawa v FACT* [1995] 1 Cr App Rep 21.

(8) …'oppression' includes torture, inhuman or degrading treatment, and the use or threat of violence (whether or not amounting to torture).

It is convenient to discuss these conditions under four headings: oppression; unreliability; causation; and burden of proof.

Oppression

This term entered English case law in this context only in the early 1960s,[384] was expansively construed in a number of cases,[385] and criticized for its imprecision.[386] It nevertheless received the endorsement of the legislature, as indicated above, although it provided only an inclusive definition, repeating the substantive form of the old Judges' Rules.[387] Its construction was considered by the Court of Appeal in *R v Fulling*.[388] A woman accused of fraud, at first, refused to make a statement to the police. She alleged that her interrogator had told her that her partner had been engaged in a sexual affair with the woman in the next cell. She claimed that this upset her, and that in her anxiety to get away from the police station, she then confessed. She contended that the confession should be excluded under s 76(2)(a), as having been obtained by oppression. The trial court rejected this view, and was upheld by the Court of Appeal on the basis that the Police and Criminal Evidence Act 1984 was a codifying Act, and to be construed without necessary reference to the old law. This was explained upon the basis that the newly extended grounds of exclusion on the basis of unreliability were sufficient to cover many of the situations previously within the wider old ambit of 'oppression'.[389] It is mystifying that no reference was made to the partial definition in s 76(8). Instead, the court applied a dictionary definition:[390]

Exercise of authority or power in a burdensome, harsh or wrongful manner; unjust or cruel treatment of subjects, inferiors, etc; the imposition of unreasonable or unjust burdens.

It drew attention to one of the quotations: 'There is not a word in our language which expresses more detestable wickedness than oppression.' The conclusion drawn from this reasoning was that it would be rare to establish oppression without some impropriety on the part of the interrogator. In this respect, it should be noted that the first phrase of the partial definition in s 76(8) appears also in Art 3 of the European Convention on Human Rights, and must now[391] be interpreted so as to conform with the accepted construction of that Convention.[392] The term 'violence' does not appear in the Convention, nor is it a term of art in English law. It seems possible that it will, because of its connection with the notion of torture in s 76(8), be construed as connoting a substantial application of force. It must certainly indicate more than a mere battery, as the legislature would presumably have used a term of art if to do so would have implemented its intention, and the requirement of so small

---

[384] *Callis v Gunn* [1964] 1 QB 495, [1963] 3 All ER 677; 501, 680.

[385] Among them, *R v Prager* [1972] 1 All ER 1114, [1972] 1 WLR 260, citing Sachs J in *R v Priestley*, but see (1967) 51 Cr App Rep 1.

[386] By the Royal Commission on Criminal Procedure, Cmnd 8092, paras 4.71 and 4.72.

[387] Although the Criminal Law Revision Committee had proposed to use the phrase 'oppressive treatment'.

[388] [1987] QB 426, [1987] 2 All ER 65; see commentary in [1987] All ER Annual Review 120.

[389] It is certainly difficult to construct realistic examples of oppression incapable of making a resulting confession unreliable.   [390] *Oxford English Dictionary* (3rd definition).

[391] Human Rights Act 1998, s 3.   [392] *Republic of Ireland v United Kingdom* (1978) 2 EHRR 25.

a degree of force would be prone to cause disputes in far too many perfectly reasonable, and acceptable, situations. It has been remarked that a procedure, such as compulsory interrogation, expressly instituted by the legislature, is unlikely to be regarded as oppressive.[393]

It is somewhat uncertain how far the effect of the conduct on the particular individual is to be taken into account under this head.[394] In the case of a mentally disturbed suspect, it seems that the fact that questioning might disturb him is irrelevant to the operation of the exclusionary conditions of s 76(2)(a), unless the asking of such questions was a deliberate attempt to exploit the suspect's mental condition,[395] although it may still aggravate other factors.[396] It is clear from the context that more than mere incarceration, or interrogation, in a police station is required to constitute oppression. The difficulty is to know exactly how much more. It seems that, if a deliberately unpleasant and uncomfortable technique is used in order to sap the will of the suspect, it will be held inherently oppressive.[397] Under the old law, such factors sometimes led to the exclusion of a confession as involuntary, especially if the actions of the police were unlawful.[398] Much may depend upon the notion of 'wrongful' in the dictionary definition adopted in *Fulling*. It seems that it is capable of applying to breaches of the Code of Practice for the interrogation of offenders, provided that they are sufficiently numerous and serious.[399] In *R v Davison*,[400] as in *Hudson*, they were further aggravated by failure to charge for the offence with which the interrogation was principally concerned, and the ground of oppression was held not to have been disproved.

It is for the judge to determine as a preliminary matter whether oppression has been disproved, but it was held by a majority of the House of Lords in *R v Mushtaq*[401] that, even then, the jury must be directed that, if it has a reasonable doubt about it, it should then not merely take that into account in its assessment of weight,[402] but disregard the confession altogether. It is dubious whether such a direction will really make much difference,[403] given that the jury will have heard the confession, and the centrality of its relevance will make it very difficult for the members to dismiss it entirely from their minds.

Unreliability

Although, as noted above,[404] the danger of unreliability was always regarded as one of the factors underpinning the development of the exclusionary rule for confessions in English

---

[393] *R v Seelig* [1991] 4 All ER 421, [1992] 1 WLR 148; 429, 159.

[394] It seems to have been decisive in *R v Gardner* [1986] CLY 1499, but that was decided before *Fulling* (n388), and may have been overinfluenced by the old law.

[395] *R v Miller* [1986] 3 All ER 119, [1986] 1 WLR 1191.

[396] As in *R v Paris* (1992) 97 Cr App Rep 99, 105.

[397] *Burut v Public Prosecutor of Brunei* [1995] 2 AC 579, [1995] 4 All ER 300; 593, 309e (in which the suspects were manacled, and hooded, while being interrogated). The unreported Hong Kong case of *Chan Lau* (1996) NLJ 1031 involved a suspect being suspended by his feet from a 16th-storey window until he confessed.

[398] *R v Hudson* (1980) 72 Cr App Rep 163 (uncomfortably hot); but cf *R v Hughes* [1988] Crim LR 519 (uncomfortably cold), in which it was thought more appropriate to consider the s 78 discretion. For the legal effect of cold in Canada, see *R v Hoilet* (1999) 136 CCC (3d) 449.

[399] For a particularly flagrant example, see *R v Paris* (1992) 97 Cr App Rep 99; cf *R v Beales* [1991] Crim LR 118; *R v Emmerson* (1991) 92 Cr App Rep 284, in which the misbehaviour of the police was more venial, and held not to amount to oppression.   [400] [1988] Crim LR 442.

[401] Applicable elsewhere and retrospectively when appropriate: *Wizzard v Jamaica* [2007] UKPC 21.

[402] [2005] UKHL 25, [2005] 3 All ER 885.

[403] Failure to give it left the result unaffected in *R v Pham* [2008] EWCA Crim 3182.   [404] 627.

law, it had never previously played a part in the formulation of the test for admissibility,[405] which had been traditionally cast in terms of 'voluntariness'.[406] The introduction of this notion into the English test for exclusion was recommended by the Criminal Law Revision Committee in its 11th Report.[407] It was not, however, endorsed by the Royal Commission on Criminal Procedure as a test for admissibility, but was simply to be regarded as an important matter going to the weight of those confessions obtained otherwise than by 'oppressive treatment'.[408] The Police and Criminal Evidence Act 1984 adopted the principle proposed by the Criminal Law Revision Committee, doing no more than broaden the nature of the conduct affecting reliability from 'threat or inducement'[409] to 'anything said or done'. Neither version limits such conduct to that performed by persons in authority.[410] The Criminal Law Revision Committee stressed that the test was not to be based upon the actual, but the potential, unreliability of a confession made in the relevant circumstances, which took into account such matters as the seriousness of the offence. It will be noted that s 76(2) refers explicitly to the 'circumstances existing at the time'. This seems to reflect the concern of the Criminal Law Revision Committee that the judge should try to recreate in his mind the conditions as they seemed to the accused at the moment of interrogation, although the Royal Commission was sceptical of the feasibility of such an exercise.[411] It seems that this provision will be interpreted in a manner similar to those already in force in New Zealand, and Victoria, where, despite minor differences of phraseology, the courts have regarded their respective provisions as referring to potential, rather than to actual, unreliability, and as requiring consideration of all the circumstances.[412]

In an apparent effort to encourage such an interpretation, s 76 makes explicit reference to the possibility of the confession being true despite its potential unreliability, and this view is further strengthened by the absence from the section as enacted of any authorization to ask about the truth, or falsity, of a confession. The reason for such concern was unease about the danger of the preliminary test for admissibility before the judge becoming one of whether or not a given confession is reliable, and, given such a test, that the jury would then infer that any confession proved before it, had already been considered by the judge to be reliable.[413] Given the lack of sophistication of some criminal proceedings, and the drafting of the section, which requires all relevant circumstances to be taken

---

[405] The state of Victoria has, however, had a test formulated in such terms since 1857, and New Zealand, since 1895.

[406] The old law has now been regarded as defective in this respect: see *R v Steel* [2003] EWCA Crim 1640, (2003) 147 SJLB 751, a reference of a pre-1984 case, in which it was pointed out that even then it was a breach of the Judges' Rules to interview a mentally handicapped suspect, and that, although such a breach did not amount to a condition precedent for allowing an appeal, a trial in which psychological evidence of the accused's mental handicap was suppressed was bound to have been unfair.   [407] Cmnd 4991, [65].

[408] This term is here used to connote the gamut of conduct regarded by the Royal Commission as justifying automatic exclusion.   [409] Draft bill, cl 2(2)(b).

[410] Although this remains part of the law of Canada, and was justified by the Supreme Court in *Hodgson v R* [1998] 2 SCR 449.

[411] Cmnd 8092, [4.72], although uttered in the context of oppression, it is just as applicable here. The increased use of video recording should ameliorate, although it will not eliminate, the problem.

[412] *Cornelius v R* (1936) 55 CLR 235; *R v Coats* [1932] NZLR 401, suggesting that the change in terminology in New Zealand in 1905 to 'in fact likely' from 'really calculated' was specifically designed to prevent an interpretation forcing admissibility upon the court whenever it believed the confession true.

[413] Although, paradoxically, the formulation of the new condition means it may logically infer even more strongly that he considers that it *could not* be unreliable.

into account, it was inevitable that the subtle difference between the tests to be imposed by judge and jury would become blurred. This was noted in *R v Tyrer*,[414] in which the Court of Appeal considered the trial judge to have come close to confusing these matters by taking into account, on the voir dire in relation to the confession of one co-accused, evidence given at the trial proper in relation to another co-accused, which indicated that the confession was probably true. It was, however, held that the voir dire should not be conducted in a vacuum. In some cases,[415] appeals have been allowed because trial judges have overtly posed the test in terms of reliability, as opposed to potential unreliability. It is asking a lot of a judge to hold that, even though he is quite sure that this confession made by this accused in these circumstances was reliable, it might, upon some hypothesis, not have been,[416] and should therefore, despite its actual reliability, be rejected, and the jury prevented even from considering it.

It should be noted that, in Victoria and New Zealand, the courts regard an unreliability test as in no way antithetical to the continued existence of a wide discretion to exclude on the ground of unfairness.[417] The Police and Criminal Evidence Act 1984, s 82(3) explicitly retained the existing discretion in England, but it was less generously interpreted than in Australia.[418] Two interlocking factors seem to have influenced subsequent development in England: first, the much more ready application of the discretion in s 78 to exclude evidence on the ground of 'unfairness', which was explicitly extended to apply to confessions;[419] and second, the extremely detailed guidance for the behaviour of the police provided by the Codes of Conduct given statutory force by Pt VI of the Police and Criminal Evidence Act 1984. The general tendency has been to take the Code as a rough guide to the likelihood of reliability, so that failure to comply is some indication of potential unreliability,[420] and compliance some indication of potential reliability. In some cases,[421] even though the relevant provision in the Code seems to relate only to reliability, and despite its breach not being held to have had sufficient potential to create unreliability for the purposes of s 76(2)(b), it has nevertheless been held to be sufficient to trigger discretionary exclusion under s 78.

Although in *R v Fulling*[422] it was stated that impropriety by the police is not a necessary condition to the establishment of potential unreliability under s 76(2)(b), the operation of this head is conditioned upon 'anything said or done',[423] which is likely, in the

---

[414]   (1990) 90 Cr App Rep 446.

[415]   For example, *R v Cox* [1991] Crim LR 276; *R v Kenny* [1994] Crim LR 284; *R v Sylvester* [2002] EWCA Crim 1327.

[416]   Although it was held by the Queen's Bench Divisional Court in *Re Proulx* [2001] 1 All ER 57, [46] that the words 'any confession' are to be interpreted to mean any such confession as the one actually made.

[417]   *R v Gardner* (1932) 51 NZLR 1648; *R v Larson and Lee* [1984] VR 559. In those jurisdictions, however, reliability operates positively to admit involuntary confessions that would otherwise be excluded, and in such cases, the discretion seems not to have been applied.   [418]   See 627.

[419]   *R v Mason* (n308); 484, 144.

[420]   But by no means conclusive: see *R v Delaney* (n312); or exclusive: see *DPP v Blake* [1989] 1 WLR 432, 89 Cr App Rep 179.

[421]   For example, *R v Howden-Simpson* [1991] Crim LR 49; *R v Haroon Ali* (24 November 1998, unreported) in which the statement contained a mixture of reliable and unreliable admissions.

[422]   [1987] QB 426, [1987] 2 All ER 65; 432, 70. See also *R v Brine* [1992] Crim LR 122; *R v Walker* [1998] Crim LR 211.

[423]   It is immaterial that the crux of the stimulus is constituted by an omission, such as failure to allow a period of rest: *R v Trussler* [1988] Crim LR 446; or to allow access to a solicitor: *R v McGovern* (1991) 92 Cr App Rep 228.

circumstances, to induce unreliability.[424] It should be noted that the test is objective in the sense that it is immaterial that the police are unaware of the factors inducing the potential unreliability,[425] or that they acted in perfect good faith.[426] If the mental condition[427] of the suspect is such that any statement he makes is likely to be unreliable, it might be thought that even the most innocuous remark might satisfy this requirement. Such a view was rejected by the Court of Appeal in *R v Goldenberg*,[428] in respect of the interviewing of a drug addict, who might have been desperate for release in order to satisfy his addiction, and in which it was emphasized that the stimulus must be external[429] to the suspect,[430] and likely to have an effect upon him.[431] On the other hand, it seems that, in the case of such a suspect, very little pressure may take the case over the line and into the area of potential unreliability.[432] It appears, indeed, that, where there is an inherent mental disorder, this may be enough to take any questioning by the police over the line of potential unreliability.[433] In such a case, after the unreliable parts of a confession have been excluded, there may not be enough left to justify conviction.[434] As noted above, breaches of the Codes of Practice may influence a court in deciding that oppression has not been disproved. It will, if anything, be easier to contend that potential unreliability under this head has not been disproved.[435]

---

[424] This is a fact-specific decision, unlikely to be illuminated by findings in other cases: *R v Wahab* [2002] EWCA Crim 1570, [2003] 1 Cr App Rep 232, [40]. [425] *R v Everett* [1988] Crim LR 826.

[426] *DPP v Blake* (1989) 89 Cr App Rep 179; or perhaps even one in which there was full compliance with a relevant Code of Practice: see *R v De Silva* [2002] EWCA Crim 2673, [2003] 2 Cr App Rep 74, [20], in which this was left open.

[427] Which may amount merely to a personality disorder: *R v Walker* (n147); and not amount to a recognized mental illness, but rather be any abnormality that might render a confession unreliable: *R v O'Brien, Hall and Sherwood* (2000) The Times, 16 February. [428] (1989) 88 Cr App Rep 285.

[429] It need not, however, emanate from the police, but can come from a third party: *R v Samuel* [2005] EWCA Crim 704, [45] (fellow prisoner); or even from the accused's own solicitor: *R v M* (12 June 2000, unreported); but not generally if the solicitor is acting properly: *R v Wahab* [2002] EWCA Crim 1570, [42]. See also *R v Walker* (n147), in which an inherent condition may have been aggravated by the voluntary act of the accused.

[430] This was thought to stem from the requirement of a causal link between stimulus and reaction, but it is not clear why self-stimulus cannot be causally linked to reaction, for example by taking hallucinogenic drugs.

[431] See also *R v Maguire* (1989) 90 Cr App Rep 115, in which statements made by a child questioned innocuously by a police officer, but in the absence of a responsible adult, were not rejected; *R v Crampton* (1991) 92 Cr App Rep 369, in which a heroin addict was suffering withdrawal symptoms, and despite police evidence that they would not have continued the interview if they had realized it; *R v Wahab* [2002] EWCA Crim 1570, in which the accused was anxious that family members not be charged with drug-related offences. On the other hand, in *R (on the application of Omar) v Chief Constable of Bedfordshire* [2002] EWHC 3060 (Admin) [2003] ACD 55, it was said that the prospect of a caution would not be enough, although in *Jones v Whalley* [2005] EWHC 931 (Admin), [9] (unaffected on this point by the appellate opinions) it was said to be overwhelmingly likely to lead to discretionary exclusion.

[432] See *R v Delaney* (n312), in which, while interviewing an educationally subnormal, and emotional, youth accused of a horrific assault on a small child, the police officers underplayed the seriousness of the matter, and emphasized the suspect's need for psychiatric help; in *R v McGovern* (n423), 232, such factors were said to be the 'background' to any submission.

[433] *R v Everett* [n425]; *R v Raghip* (1991) The Times, 9 December; *R v Ward* [1993] 2 All ER 577, [1993] 1 WLR 619; 641, 690. It should be noted that medical evidence of the accused's condition is not only admissible in determining the factual basis for such a submission, but positively required: *R v Ham* (1995) 36 BMLR 169; and to be strong enough to be truly relevant: *R v Heaton* [1993] Crim LR 593.

[434] *R v Haroon Ali* (n421). [435] See e.g. *R v Doolan* [1988] Crim LR 747.

It should finally be noted that the unreliability in question is the unreliability of the confession itself, and not of any recording of it, which raises different questions best dealt with under s 78.[436]

Causation[437]

It took some time before the old law arrived[438] at a satisfactory approach to causation: namely, that the judge should apply the spirit of the test in much the same way as it would be applied by a jury. In a mixed motive case, this would appear to require a determination of the dominant motive. Exactly the same approach is appropriate to the conditions imposed by s 76(2).[439] It should perhaps be noticed that there is a slight difference in the drafting of the two conditions, in that the first, relating to oppression, is introduced by the word 'by', whereas the second, which relates to unreliability, is introduced by the phrase 'in consequence of'. If anything should turn on that difference, it would presumably be to require less in the way of the demonstration of a causal link in the case of oppression, which may perhaps more readily be inferred, and where the law will be more anxious to mark its disapproval. Thus in *Burut v Public Prosecutor*,[440] the Privy Council required positive evidence from the prosecution to prove that the inherently oppressive first interrogation had not had a continuing effect on subsequent confessions.

It may often be necessary to determine whether an admission is made as a result of whatever has been said or done, or rather in recognition of the implausibility of previous statements, perhaps revealed by what has been said or done.[441] The words 'in consequence of', in relation to hypothetical reliability, were construed in *R v Samuel*[442] to be distinct from 'in the light of' in a case in which the alleged things said, or done, had been merely 'factored in', which appeared to mean that they were not dominant in the reasoning leading to the accused's decision to confess. A spontaneous confession seems admissible, however unreliable it may be in the light of the accused's mental or emotional state.[443] It may, however, in such circumstances, be excluded by the judge at his discretion,[444] and even if admitted, the weight to be attached to the confession of a person in such a state would obviously be small. It had become well established in the old law that a confession that, considered in isolation, appeared to satisfy the conditions for being voluntary, might nevertheless be excluded if preceded by an earlier involuntary confession. It would be so excluded if either the factors tainting the earlier confession continued to apply, or if the fact of having made such a confession could itself be regarded as precipitating its successor.[445] The situation has been elaborated in a series of cases. The question is one of fact. An early confession obtained in

---

[436] See the helpful commentary by Birch in [1991] *Crim LR* 624 upon the decision in *R v Chung* (1991) 92 Cr App Rep 314.   [437] See Mirfield [1996] *Crim LR* 554.

[438] In *DPP v Ping Lin* (n275); 602, 184; *R v Rennie* [1982] 1 All ER 385, [1982] 1 WLR 64.

[439] And has been so applied: see *R v Phillips* (1987) 86 Cr App Rep 18; *R v Crampton* (1991) 92 Cr App Rep 369; *R v Weeks* [1995] Crim LR 52.   [440] [1995] 2 AC 579, [1995] 4 All ER 300.

[441] As in *R v Tyrer* (n414).   [442] (n112), [45].

[443] *R v Goldenberg* (n428), 290. This appears to have been rejected by the Supreme Court in Canada after the Charter: *Brydges v R* [1990] 1 SCR 190.   [444] See, 179.

[445] *R v Smith* [1959] 2 QB 35, [1959] 2 All ER 193. See also *Missouri v Seibert* 542 US 630, 124 S Ct R 2601, (2004); *R v Wittwer* 2008 SCC 33, [2008] 2 SCR 235; *HM Adv v Docherty* 1981 JC 6; *R v Thomas* [2006] VSCA 165, 163 ACR 567. In *Gafgen v Germany* (2009) 48 EHRR 253, [107] the ECHR seems to have been easily convinced that there was no connection between an initial coerced confession, leading to the finding of real evidence, and a subsequent confession at trial.

breach of the Police and Criminal Evidence Act 1984, or the Codes of Practice, may well taint a later one,[446] but is less likely to do so if any breach was more accidental than deliberate,[447] or if legal advice were taken after the interview in respect of which the breach occurred,[448] or perhaps that later interviews still were barren.[449] It militates in favour of exclusion of the later confession if it were obtained without the presence of a legal adviser and succeeded an interview at which a legal adviser were present, and at which no confession were made. The principle has been said to depend upon whether the accused has, at the later interview, an informed and independent choice as to whether or not to repeat, retract, or remain silent.[450]

Burden of proof

At common law, it was for the prosecution to prove beyond reasonable doubt that a confession was voluntary.[451] Section 76(2) explicitly retains both incidence and standard. It also provides that the matter is to be tested whenever 'it is represented to the court' that one of the conditions has been satisfied. It has been held that merely to cross-examine so as to suggest the satisfaction of the invalidating conditions of s 76 is not sufficient.[452] This might have appeared to suggest that the court could no longer[453] take the point of its own motion, but any such argument has been pre-empted by explicit provision allowing such a course.[454] In most cases, of course, the defence will itself raise the point, usually with the prosecution informally, and before the trial, so that a disputed confession will not be opened before its admissibility has been tested. Breach of the provisions of the Codes of Practice requiring the documentation of action by the police may operate to prevent the prosecution from being able to negate the exclusionary conditions of s 76.[455] While it has been held that the prosecution bears no burden of disproof of unfairness for the purposes of s 78,[456] it seems that, if breaches are significant and substantial, then there is a prima facie breach of the standards of fairness set by Parliament.[457]

Effect

The principal intended effect of the legislation is to exclude[458] confessions as evidence of the truth of their contents, but this effect is qualified by further provisions also set out in s 76 as follows:

> (4) The fact that a confession is wholly or partly excluded in pursuance of this section shall not affect the admissibility in evidence—
>
> (a) of any facts discovered as result of the confession; or

---

[446] *R v McGovern* (n423), 234; but the conclusion is not inevitable: *R v Gillard and Barrett* (1990) 92 Cr App Rep 61, 65; *R v Ahmed* [2003] EWCA Crim 3627.   [447] *Y v DPP* [1991] Crim LR 917.

[448] *R v Hoyte* [1994] Crim LR 215 (a strong case, since it was merely presumed that legal advice would have been taken). It is not enough that there was merely an opportunity to take legal advice if it were not, in fact, taken: *R v Glaves* [1993] Crim LR 685.   [449] See *Y v DPP* (n447).

[450] *R v Neil* [1994] Crim LR 441.

[451] See *DPP v Ping Lin* (n275), 597 and 599, 178 and 180. The standard of proof had, however, been considered doubtful by the Criminal Law Revision Committee (Cmnd 4991, Annex 2, 213).

[452] *R v Liverpool Juvenile Court, ex p R* [1988] QB 1, [1987] 2 All ER 668.

[453] See the guidance provided in *Ajodha v The State* [1982] AC 204, [1981] 2 All ER 193; 222, 202.

[454] Section 76(3), in accordance with the Criminal Law Revision Committee's recommendation and draft bill: Cmnd 4991, [54], cl 2(3).   [455] *R v Delaney* (n312), 342.

[456] *Vel v Owen* (1987) 151 JP 510.   [457] *R v Walsh* (1989) 91 Cr App Rep 161165.

[458] Erroneous failure to exclude is not necessarily fatal, see *R v Noden* [2007] EWCA Crim 2050.

(b)   where the confession is relevant as showing that the accused speaks, writes or expresses himself in a particular way, of so much of the confession as is necessary to show that he does so.

(5)   Evidence that a fact to which this subsection applies was discovered as a result of a statement made by an accused person shall not be admissible unless evidence of how it was discovered is given by him or on his behalf.

These sections raise three matters that require to be mentioned: the admissibility of subsequently discovered facts; the limited circumstantial use that can be made of confessions; and the extent to which any part of an excluded confession may be given when it is confirmed by finding real evidence that it mentions. All three of these matters have already been considered.[459]

SILENCE[460]

At common law,[461] it was clear that a suspect could remain silent in the face of police questioning;[462] it was, however, not at all clear that such silence could be used as hostile evidence, or made the subject of adverse comment at a subsequent trial.[463] It should, however, be noted that, in certain situations, the stringency of any prohibition was mitigated. For example, if the accused and the person questioning him could be said to be on equal terms, a summing-up on the lines of Lord Atkinson's speech in *R v Christie*[464] might be appropriate. It is arguable that the presence of a solicitor equalizes the terms,[465] and this may provide a partial explanation of the decision in *R v Smith*,[466] in which the Court of Appeal allowed comment on the accused's refusal during such an interview to permit a sample of his hair to be taken for comparison with hair found on an incriminating object. It was also sometimes felt to be incumbent upon the court to make some comment in connection with a different rule, such as the presumption of knowledge arising from possession of recently stolen property.[467] Nor was it improper for the judge to emphasize both the nature of possible adverse inferences, and the prohibition upon drawing them.[468]

This part of the chapter will first set out the modifications made by statute, principally by the Criminal Justice and Public Order Act 1994, and then consider those provisions in more detail, in terms of their scope in relation to the nature of the pre-trial process involved, the form that any silence takes, the propriety of remaining silent, the form

[459]   See Chapter X, Section 3.

[460]   For judicial dissection of the concept of the right to silence, see *R v Director of the Serious Fraud Office, ex p Smith* [1993] AC 1, [1992] 3 All ER 456; 30, 31, 463, 464. For academic commentary, see Mirfield (n263); Birch [1999] *Crim LR* 769; Jackson (2001) 5 *E&P* 145; Dennis [2002] *Crim LR* 25. For strong affirmation of the right in Ireland, see *People v Bowes* [2004] 4 IR 223; in Canada *R v Turcotte* 2005 SCC 50, [2005] 2 SCR 519; and for full consideration by the Constitutional Court in South Africa, *S v Thebus* 2003 (6) SA 505.

[461]   For specific statutory modification, see e.g. Criminal Justice Act 1987, s 2, abridging this right in cases of allegations of serious fraud.   [462]   *Rice v Connolly* [1966] 2 QB 414, [1966] 2 All ER 649.

[463]   Such controversy continues to trouble superior courts elsewhere: see, in Australia, *Pavic and Swaffield v R* (1998) 192 CLR 159; in Canada, *R v Crawford* [1995] 1 SCR 858.

[464]   [1914] AC 545 (that, in some special circumstances, silence amounts to an implicit admission). See also *R v Collins* [2004] EWCA Crim 83, [2004] 2 Cr App R 199; *R v Tanasichuk* (2007) 227 CCC3d 446 (silence in face of lay accuser).   [465]   *R v Chandler* [1976] 3 All ER 105, [1976] 1 WLR 585.

[466]   (1985) 81 Cr App Rep 286.   [467]   *R v Aves* [1950] 2 All ER 330, 34 Cr App Rep 159; *R v Raviraj*.

[468]   *R v McNamara* (1988) 87 Cr App Rep 246, 253.

of direction that is appropriate, and last, the compatibility of these provisions with the European Convention on Human Rights.

Section 34 of the Criminal Justice and Public Order Act 1994[469]

Following a recommendation originally made in the 11th Report of the Criminal Law Revision Committee,[470] and despite its rejection by two subsequent Royal Commissions,[471] s 34 provides that:[472]

(1) Where, in any proceedings against a person for an offence, evidence is given that the accused—

    (a) at any time before he was charged with the offence, on being questioned under caution by a constable trying to discover whether or by whom the offence had been committed, failed to mention any fact relied on in his defence in those proceedings, or

    (b) on being charged with the offence or officially informed that he might be prosecuted for it, failed to mention any such fact,

    being a fact which in the circumstances existing at the time the accused could reasonably have been expected to mention when so questioned, charged or informed, as the case may be, subsection (2) below applies.

(2) Where this section applies—

    (c) the court, in determining whether there is a case to answer; and

    (d) the court or jury, in determining whether the accused is guilty of the offence charged,

    may draw such inferences from the failure as appear proper.

(2A) Where the accused was at an authorised place of detention at the time of the failure, subsections (1) and (2) above do not apply if he had not been allowed an opportunity to consult a solicitor prior to being questioned, charged or informed as mentioned in subsection (1) above.

(3) Subject to any directions by the court, evidence tending to establish the failure may be given before or after evidence tending to establish the fact which the accused is alleged to have failed to mention.

This section applies to all those charged with the duty of investigating offences, and complements, rather than replaces, the inferences available to be drawn at common law.[473]

---

[469] Described by Dyson LJ in *R v B* [2003] EWCA Crim 3080, [20] as 'a treacherous minefield'.

[470] Cmnd 4991, paras 28–52, draft bill, cl 1. Consolidated by the *Report on Right to Silence* Home Office 13 July 1989: see Zuckerman [1989] *Crim LR* 855; and promoted by Lord Lane CJ in *R v Alladice* (1988) 87 Cr App Rep 380, 385.

[471] Royal Commission on Criminal Procedure (1981) Cmnd 8092, [5.13]; Royal Commission on Criminal Justice (1993) Cm 2263, rec 82.

[472] Section 2A was inserted by the Youth Justice and Criminal Evidence Act 1999, ss 58(1), (2), 67, Sch 7, [8], and has been reflected in Annex C [2], reverting to the older form of caution in which the accused has requested legal advice that has not yet been furnished. This section is reinforced by further sections, relating in a broadly similar way to failure to account for ostensibly incriminating objects, substances, and marks (s 36); and failure to account for ostensibly incriminating presence in a particular place (s 37). For commentary, see Pattenden (1998) 2 *E&P* 141; Mirfield (n263) 238–81 (1997). Predictably enough the use of two forms of caution in different situations has led to confusion: see *R v Ibrahim* [2008] EWCA Crim 880, [2008] 4 All ER 208, [78].

[473] Section 34(5). For further detail of the common law, see earlier editions of this work.

It has itself subsequently been supplemented by the provisions of Pt I of the Criminal Procedure and Investigations Act 1996,[474] which imposed an obligation upon the accused to disclose the general nature of the defence, and details of any alibi.[475] Failure to do so is also sanctioned by the possibility of adverse comment, and inference.[476]

To a considerable extent, CJPOA 1994, s 34 mirrored recommendations earlier introduced in Northern Ireland,[477] and it became necessary to devise a new, and longer, form of caution.[478] It remains to be seen how these provisions are interpreted. It is arguable that little has been achieved, since the consensus of empirical research[479] shows that very few of those questioned in police custody ever have remained wholly[480] silent.[481] It has, indeed, been suggested that these provisions improved the lot of the suspect, since the discretion to exclude on the ground of fairness could extend to inferences from silence, if conditioned by defective disclosure, or non-disclosure, of the police case that the accused was required to meet.[482]

Section 34 was buttressed by ss 36 and 37 of the Criminal Justice and Public Order Act 1994.[483] These sections were not recommended in the 11 Report of the Criminal Law Revision Committee, and found their origin in the Republic of Ireland.[484] In broad, and crude, outline, they permit adverse inferences against a suspect[485] who fails, when taxed by an investigator,[486] to offer an explanation of objects or marks, on his person, on his clothes, or in his possession, or, at the place of his arrest,[487] or under similar conditions,[488]

---

[474] See also Chapter VI. The Terrorism Act 2000, s 109 contains a similar provision to s 34, except that it dispenses with the need to show reliance upon the fact in the accused's defence.

[475] Section 5. Now further amplified by s 33 of the Criminal Justice Act 2003: see above, 33.

[476] Section 11(3).

[477] Criminal Evidence (NI) Order 1988, SI 1988/1987 (NI 20); see Jackson [1991] *Crim LR* 404.

[478] Suspended pending the arrival of requested legal advice. The current form still reminds the suspect of his right to remain silent, while warning him of the dangers of doing so. This can cause problems in cases in which the suspect is, at the same time, being interviewed in respect of a special statutory offence that carries different consequences if he remains silent, as in *R v Customs and Excise Comrs, ex p Mortimer* [1998] 3 All ER 229, [1999] 1 WLR 17. See also *Heaney and McGuiness v Ireland* (2001) 33 EHRR 264.

[479] Home Office Research Study 199 *The Right of Silence: the impact of the Criminal Justice and Public Order Act 1994* (2000) Table 3.2 shows that the incidence of total silence declined from 10 per cent to 6 per cent, and that of partial silence from 13 per cent to 10 per cent after the passage of the Act.

[480] Answering some questions did not invest failure to answer others with special significance: *R v Henry* [1990] Crim LR 574.

[481] Silence is a more opaque concept than is generally assumed, and certainly does not equate to failing to make a sound when questioned. Both making and failing to make sounds may be quite unrelated to the questioning: see *Yisrael v District Court of New South Wales* (1996) 87 ACR 63, 67.

[482] Zuckerman 144 *NLJ* 1104 (1994).

[483] It seems that, to the extent of an overlap, s 34 is likely to prevail: see *R v Turner* [2003] EWCA Crim 3108, [2004] 1 Cr App Rep 305, [16].

[484] Criminal Justice Act 1984, ss 18, 19. They came into English law via Northern Ireland, but it should be noted that, in origin, they were confined to trials for a limited range of offences; that they are subject to a constitutional guarantee of proportionality: *Heaney v Ireland* [1996] 1 IR 244; *Rock v Ireland* [1997] 3 IR 484; *Re National Irish Bank Ltd (No 1)* [1999] 3 IR 145 (reliance may invalidate confession); and that proposals to apply them generally, as in England, have encountered significant resistance in the Republic. They may also fall foul of the European Convention on Human Rights, as indicated by *Heaney and McGuiness v Ireland* (n478), condemning s 52 of the Irish Offences Against the State Act 1939, which provides a criminal sanction against those refusing to divulge information upon request by the police.

[485] Who must, under these two provisions, have been arrested.

[486] It is enough for the offence to be specified in general terms: *R v Compton* [2002] EWCA Crim 2835.

[487] CJPOA 1994, s 36.

[488] There is, however, an enigmatic difference in the tense of the opening words.

fails to offer an explanation[489] of his presence at the scene of the crime at about the time of its commission.

Some safeguard was afforded by CJPOA 1994, s 38(3), which provides that a case to answer or a conviction may not be based *solely*[490] on adverse inferences under the scheme. As noted above,[491] it is only in relation to s 35 that the inference cannot count towards a case to answer.

Interviews[492]

It should be noted that the conditions under which CJPOA 1994, s 34 operates to permit an adverse inference are somewhat confined. It applies only to failures when being questioned[493] at interviews with those charged with the duty of investigating offences,[494] and then only when the interview is conducted under caution with a view to discover whether a crime has been committed,[495] and if so by whom,[496] or to rebut fresh evidence despite a prior intimation of silence, supported by the presentation of a prepared written statement.[497] It has now been settled, however, that the Code permits the accused to be offered the opportunity to advance an explanation,[498] despite sufficient evidence to charge, and if no explanation is forthcoming, then that failure can be the subject of adverse comment.[499] If a fact is mentioned otherwise than on the specified occasions, it will not prevent the adverse inference from being drawn.[500]

Nature of silence

It applies also only if the accused fails to mention a fact *relied on in his defence*.[501] The concept of reliance on a fact is not intrinsically clear, but in *R v Webber*,[502] the House of

---

[489] This should be explicit, and not left to be inferred from the accused's general response: *R v Compton* (n486).

[490] It is not absolutely clear that the prosecution cannot add together adverse inferences from more than one of the sections: see Mirfield (n263) 269, but it is submitted that the better view is that it may not. The same presumably applies to the accumulation of inferences from different instances of silence within the same category.

[491] 44.

[492] See further, 660. In the United States, Miranda warnings are required only for those in custody, and a narrow view is sometimes taken of that status, as in *Yarborough v Alvarado* 541 US 652, 124 S Ct R 2140, (2004).

[493] It is not enough to refuse to be questioned: *R v Johnson and Hind* [2005] EWCA Crim 971, [31].

[494] Section 34(4) expands the scope of s 34(1) in this respect; cf the Police and Criminal Evidence Act 1984, s 67(9), 659.

[495] Section 34(1)(a). It also applies to similar failures upon being charged, or informed of possible prosecution: s 34(1)(b). These operate independently, and the refusal of an adverse inference from silence at an improper interview does not necessarily prevent an adverse inference at the charge stage: *R v Dervish* [2001] EWCA Crim 2789, [2002] 2 Cr App Rep 105.

[496] The person interrogated need not be the principal, still less only, suspect.

[497] *R v Ali Sed*, [77].

[498] But, if the form of the interview precludes any realistic opportunity for the accused to speak, no adverse inference can be drawn from his failure to do so: *R v Hillard* [2004] EWCA Crim 837, [2004] All ER (D) 41 (Mar).

[499] *R v Elliott* [2002] EWCA Crim 931, in which the conflicting earlier authority is reviewed. The matter was clarified by the 2002 amendment to Code C, [11.6].

[500] *R v O* [2000] Crim LR 617. Code C, [11.4] requires any prior interview significant statements or silences to be put to the suspect, and Note 11A emphasizes that this may also be done at later stages in the interviewing process.

[501] In *T v DPP* [2007] EWHC 1793 (Admin), [26] Hughes LJ helpfully spells out the proper sequence of reasoning.

[502] [2004] UKHL 1, [2004] 1 All ER 770, [34].

Lords adopted an expansive construction under which an adverse inference is permitted not only where a new fact is put in evidence by the defence, but also when, at trial, the accused advances an exculpatory explanation of the prosecution case by putting suggestions to their witnesses in cross-examination premised on the existence of facts not previously mentioned, whether or not the cross-examined witness accepts it. Some support for this broad interpretation may be found in the explicit provision in CJPOA 1994, s 34(2)(c), permitting the use of an adverse inference to establish a case to answer. It does, however, appear to conflict with the terminology of s 34(3), which, in this connection, refers to 'evidence to establish the fact'. The House of Lords rather unconvincingly disregarded this subsection as being concerned only with timing, and thus not dispositive. The House of Lords excluded from this expansive interpretation, however, failure to mention matters seeking merely to probe the prosecution case, matters not known to exist at the relevant time,[503] and matters that are accepted to be true,[504] or for which the prosecution is simply put to its proof.[505] Where the theory of the defence depends upon particular facts failure to mention them will be sufficient.[506] It often happens that a short initial statement by a suspect is contradicted by a later fuller and more considered one. Where the later one contains facts not mentioned in the earlier the statements are inconsistent, and may well technically trigger an adverse inference under s 34, even though once both statements are before the jury it is evident that its decision will assess their relative probative value. In such cases it has been suggested[507] that there is no need to apply s 34, and so formalize the reasoning process.

As noted above, s 34(2)(c) explicitly allows failure to mention such a fact to be taken into account in determining whether or not the accused has a case to answer. If it is to be so used, it must be determined before the matter comes before the jury, which implies that the accused must seek exclusion of evidence of the silence altogether, yet the Court of Appeal has regarded this as applicable only in a quite exceptional situation.[508] It has been recommended that the prosecution should content itself initially with establishing that the accused did remain silent during interview,[509] and wait for the case to develop, before arguing for an adverse inference.

If the accused initially fails to mention a fact, but then does so subsequently, the initial silence may be made the subject of adverse comment,[510] and although it should then be made clear that it is only the initial failure that is being commented upon, failure to do so is not necessarily decisive.[511] So, also, if the accused first mentions something, is then

---

[503] [22], endorsing *R v Nickolson* [1999] Crim LR 61, in which, at the time of the interview, the accused did not know enough of the case that would be made against him at trial to meet it specifically in advance with a fact that he then mentioned when confronted with the previously unknown issue; see also *R v B(MT)* [2000] Crim LR 181.   [504] [28], endorsing *R v B* [2003] EWCA Crim 3080, [16].

[505] [23] and [24].

[506] *R v Esimu* [2007] EWCA Crim 1380, [13] (that the accused had worked in a car wash advanced to explain the presence of his fingerprints on the back of false number plates on a stolen car).

[507] By Hughes LJ in *R v Maguire* [2008] EWCA Crim 1028, [11].

[508] *R v Condron and Condron* [1997] 1 WLR 827, [1997] 1 Cr App Rep 185; 837A, 196E. See also *R v Argent* [1997] 2 Cr App Rep 27, 31D–F.

[509] Although in *R v Griffin* [1998] Crim LR 418, the Court of Appeal, somewhat surprisingly, felt that it was not necessarily more prejudicial than probative for the prosecution to read, even at that early stage, the questions to which no answer had been vouchsafed.

[510] *R v Betts and Hall* [2001] EWCA Crim 224, [2001] 2 Cr App Rep 257, [31]; *R v Daly* [2001] EWCA Crim 2643, [2002] 2 Cr App Rep 201.   [511] *R v Flynn* [2001] EWCA Crim 1633, [77].

cautioned, fails to mention it again in interview, but relies upon it at trial, no adverse inference from the silence at interview is appropriate.[512]

It has become common for the accused to tender a prepared statement at interview,[513] and to refuse to answer questions. Such a course may be dangerous if the statement is less complete than, or inconsistent with, the accused's case at trial,[514] but the judge should not instruct the jury to draw an adverse inference under s 34 unless the accused relies on facts not set out in the prepared statement.[515] The section makes it clear that the adverse inference relates to reliance in the defence upon undisclosed facts, and not upon silence per se.[516]

If the accused fails to admit an important part of the prosecution case at his interview, but then does subsequently admit it at the trial, no adverse comment may be made on the failure, although such comment may be made upon the failure to advance at the interview any exculpatory facts that are then relied upon at the trial.[517] It is not the case, nor compatible with the European Convention, that the accused be compelled to make all of his admissions when first interviewed by the police. It does, however, now[518] seem that he is required to make all of the denials upon which he proposes to rely at the trial, however central they are to the prosecution case, and however inevitable in all the circumstances. It may indeed be true that, then, the accused's failure to mention the fact becomes unreasonable only upon the hypothesis that the case against him has been made out, which is the proposition that the adverse inference is deployed to support, and hence makes it futile. Since the inference is futile rather than misleading, however, it is hard to see how it could be very prejudicial to the accused, and the converse rule would require the quashing of a conviction because a futile inference had not been precluded, which seems perverse.

It should be noted that the section requires only that the fact be mentioned, not that all of the detail relied upon at the trial should have been stated, so it seems sufficient that the bare bones of the matters relied upon have been indicated.[519]

---

[512] *R v Johnson* [2005] EWCA Crim 3540, [16].

[513] If tendered later, it is likely to be inadmissible as a previous consistent statement, and impotent to prevent an adverse inference under s 34, however much it anticipates the defence raised (unless there is a suggestion of later fabrication): *R v Lowe* [2003] EWCA Crim 3182, [22].

[514] *R v Turner* (Dwaine) [2004] EWCA Crim 3108, [2004] 1 All ER 1025, [25]; *R v Faisal Mohammad* [2009] EWCA Crim 1871, [25].   [515] *R v Knight* [2003] EWCA Crim 1977, [2004] 1 Cr App Rep 117.

[516] As emphasized in *R v Turner* [2003] EWCA Crim 3108, [2004] 1 All ER 1025.

[517] *R v Betts and Hall* [2001] EWCA Crim 224, [2001] 2 Cr App Rep 257, [33]; the apparent denial of this in *Daly* (n510), [10] is best interpreted as relating only to the exculpation. It may sometimes be difficult also to distinguish between the fact itself, and the way it is proposed to be used.

[518] *R v Webber* [2004] UKHL 1, [26], disapproving *R v Mountford* [1999] Crim LR 575, and *R v Gill* [2001] 1 Cr App Rep 160.

[519] *R v McGarry* [1999] 1 Cr App Rep 377. This accords with the accused's obligation to disclose only the nature of his defence under s 5 of the Criminal Procedure and Investigations Act 1996. But see *Averill v United Kingdom* (2000) 31 EHRR 36, in which the accused's failure to amplify, or repeat, his brief initial statement of his alibi was made the subject of 'very strong' adverse inference by the trial judge, without explicit condemnation by the European Court of Human Rights. See also *R v Robinson* [2003] EWCA Crim 2219, in which it was insufficient that the accused merely said that he would rely on self-defence, refusing to supply any more detail at that stage.

Propriety of silence

A more generic condition may be implied from the considerations that the matter must be one that it would have been reasonable to expect the accused to mention,[520] and that only *proper* inferences can be drawn. The boundaries of reason and propriety remain to be fully clarified. It has nevertheless emerged that merely to assert that refusal to mention facts was maintained on legal advice[521] will not, by itself, be sufficient, even though offered for other than merely tactical reasons.[522] The accused is put in something of a dilemma in this situation, since it has been held both that it will rarely be sufficient to refer only to legal advice in the abstract, but also that any elaboration of the basis of the advice[523] will amount to a waiver of legal professional privilege,[524] which might well have fatal consequences.[525] If the defence is alleged to be a recent fabrication, that imputation can be resisted by reference to a previous statement to a solicitor,[526] but the court will be reluctant to extend this exception.[527] A claim of badly advised silence, because the adviser had a conflict of interest,[528] is unlikely to succeed in the absence of waiver.[529] Nor is it necessarily sufficient that the police hold back some information[530] in their possession from the suspect.[531] It has, indeed, been stated[532] that the only obligation is that the police should not actively mislead the suspect. In *R v Condron and Condron*,[533] the court approached the problem of what was reasonable from the opposite direction, and held that the jury should be directed

---

[520] It has been argued that CJPOA 1994, s 34 should not be construed in normative terms of whether it is reasonable that the accused *should* speak, but in non-normative terms of whether it is reasonable to expect him *to* speak: Leng (2001) 5 *E&P* 240; but see *R v Essa* [2009] EWCA Crim 43, [15] effectively rejecting such an approach.

[521] Not even when it is alleged that the adviser had a conflict of interest on account of representing also a co-accused: *R v Hill* [2003] EWCA Crim 1179. As noted, 649, amendment to Code C inhibits adverse inference from silence prior to the provision of requested legal advice.

[522] *R v Condron and Condron* (n508). In this respect, following the Northern Irish approach: see Jackson [1995] *Crim LR* 587.

[523] Even when offered by the solicitor at the time and subsequently put in evidence at the trial by the prosecution, *R v Hall-Chung* [2007] EWCA Crim 3429, 50 SJLB 1020, [16], although such an advantage should not be sought as a matter of course, [19].

[524] It seems unlikely that the accused will be prevented from testifying to the advice on account of the hearsay rule: see *R v Davis* [1998] Crim LR 659. If he refrains from calling the solicitor, then it may be dangerous for the direction to speculate on the explanation for that: see *R v Khan* [2001] EWCA Crim 486, [25]. It is, however, a matter for the accused's own decision, and he should not be put under pressure in the form of intervention by the judge to induce him to waive any privilege: *R v Wood* [2002] EWCA Crim 2474.

[525] *R v Bowden* [1999] 1 WLR 823; *R v Roble* [1997] Crim LR 449. In *R v Condron and Condron* (n508), this prospect was regarded as so dire that the defence should be warned of its impending danger by the judge, and certainly the accused should not be badgered by counsel, or by the court, to waive it: *R v P* [2002] EWCA Crim 1388.

[526] As in *R v Wilmot* (1989) 89 Cr App R 341, 351; *R v Wishart* [2005] EWCA Crim 1337, [19].

[527] See *R v Loizou* [2006] EWCA Crim 1719, (2006) 150 SJLB 1187, [84].

[528] Although such a conflict may lead to an unfair trial if the adviser fails to withdraw: see *R v Pearson* [2005] EWCA Crim 1412, [55].   [529] *R v Hill* [2003] EWCA Crim 1179.

[530] Including information about the status of an undercover officer: *R v Edwards* [1997] Crim LR 348.

[531] In *R v Roble* (n525), an extreme failure to disclose was posited, and although in *R v Argent* (n 459) the court seemed more sympathetic to the argument that the accused was reasonable in meeting silence with silence, it still felt, and indeed held, that an adverse inference was justified despite less than full, or usual, disclosure there by the police.

[532] *R v Imran and Hussein* [1997] Crim LR 754, the line between actively misleading and deliberately failing to disclose seems somewhat chimerical.

[533] (n508).

that an adverse inference should be drawn only if subsequent fabrication of the fact relied upon were the *only* rational explanation for such failure. This seemed remarkably generous to the suspect, since it requires little ingenuity to suggest some possible alternative explanations, and it is hardly surprising that it has now been reined back, principally by requiring 'soundly based objective reasons for silence, sufficiently cogent and telling to weigh in the balance against the clear public interest in an account being given by the suspect to the police'.[534]

It is clearly difficult to generalize in this area, and in *R v Argent*, Lord Bingham CJ was anxious to stress the wide range of factors to be taken into account, and the balance between the subjective elements of factors peculiar to the particular accused, and the objective element of what is in principle reasonable. In the case of legal advice, he did, however, make it clear that it is not the competence of the advice, or the genuineness of the accused's belief in it, but the reasonableness of the accused in relying upon it that is crucial.[535] It seems that it will often be reasonable for a young person,[536] or a mentally vulnerable adult,[537] to rely upon such advice.

As mentioned above, it has become common for an accused person to provide a prepared written statement for the police, and then to refuse to answer questions about it, asserting that this is done on legal advice. It was determined in *R v Knight* that it was possible for such a strategy to prevent any adverse inference, provided that the accused does not depart from the prepared statement at his trial, and provided that a credible reason for the provision, and acceptance, of such legal advice were adduced. The court remarked that the object of the section was to secure an early explanation of the line of defence, not submission to cross-examination on it by the police in advance of the trial. The court's view was that the strength of the explanation was best determined by the jury at the trial, and that cross-examination at the trial was preferable. The court remarked that, if the accused avoided such cross-examination by refusal to testify, then an adverse inference could be drawn under s 35.[538] The court was clear[539] that, in cases in which the accused, having provided such a statement, was otherwise silent before, and at, the trial, only the adverse inference under s 35 would be appropriate.

Form of direction

If the conditions for drawing an inference are not satisfied, either at common law or under the Act, then it may be desirable that the jury should be so instructed.[540] Since the

[534] *R v Howell* [2003] EWCA Crim 1, [2003] EWCA Crim 01 [24]. This was endorsed in *R v Knight* [2003] EWCA Crim 1977, [2004] 1 Cr App Rep 117, and held compatible with the decision, and dicta, in *R v Betts and Hall* [2001] EWCA Crim 224, [2001] 2 Cr App Rep 257.

[535] *R v Hoare and Pierce* [2004] EWCA Crim 784, [54]; endorsed in *R v Beckles* [2004] EWCA Crim 2766, [2005] 1 All ER 705, [47], noting that this view was to be made explicit in the Judicial Studies Board model direction. [536] As in *R v P* [2002] EWCA Crim 1388.

[537] As in *R v V* [2005] EWCA Crim 581, (2005) 149 SJLB 301. [538] See further, 44.

[539] [12], although this remark was obiter since the accused had testified in *Knight* (n534). In cases in which no such statement is tendered, it seems unlikely that a s 34 inference can be avoided by subsequent choice not to testify. See also *R v A* [2003] EWCA Crim 3554.

[540] *R v McGarry* [1998] 3 All ER 805, [1999] 1 Cr App Rep 377; *R v Bowers, Taylor and Millan* (1999) JP 33; but see *R v Leon La Rose* [2003] EWCA Crim 1471; *R v Brizzalari* [2004] EWCA Crim 310, [57]. Failure to give such a direction may not be fatal: see *R v Hussein* [2007] EWCA Crim 859; and it was recognized in *R v Sylvester* [2002] EWCA Crim 1327, [14] that the plethora of directions often required in quite simple cases run the risk of confusing the jury. It may also be questioned whether a direction not to take silence into

conditions are obscure in meaning, and difficult to construe, the Judicial Studies Board has devised, and repeatedly revised,[541] a model direction.[542] The court has expressed its anxiety that such directions, even in simple cases, have to be so long and complex as to exalt unduly the importance of any adverse inference.[543] While not determinative, it has been held that a trial judge should depart from the model to the least possible degree,[544] and that the key features must appear.[545] Such a direction must be especially sensitively drafted when the accused has been advised to remain silent by his lawyer.[546] It may also need to be very strong if the evidence of silence has been in some way prejudicial.[547] It is highly desirable that the form of the direction should be discussed between the trial judge and counsel so as to minimize the volume of appeals.[548]

The jury should first be directed as to the terms, and meaning, of the caution.[549] Thereafter, the essential features are that the jury must be satisfied that there is a case for the accused to meet;[550] that guilt is not to be inferred directly from silence, but only by way of the credibility of the accused's defence;[551] and that no adverse inference should be drawn if the accused's explanation is plausible,[552] or in relation to any matter mentioned before the interview at which it was not.[553] The possibility of contamination[554] should be mentioned in the case of multiple complaints.[555] The judge should direct the jury that it is for the prosecution to prove those matters upon which they rely as justifying the drawing of an adverse inference.[556] Where the reason for failing to mention a matter is to preserve a lying denial of something else, it is probably better to give neither a *Lucas*, nor a s 34,

---

account can ever be effective so far as the jury is concerned, although failure to give it may be very effective in providing a promising ground for appeal.

[541] See *R v Beckles* (n535), [33]; see *R v Boyle and Ford* [2006] EWCA Crim 2101, (2006) 150 SJLB 1151, [36] for the form of direction as at 26 August 2006.

[542] The annotation adopts the advice offered in *R v Gill* [2001] 1 Cr App Rep 160, 165, that such a direction should be discussed with counsel before being delivered.

[543] *R v Bresa* [2005] EWCA Crim 1414, [4]; in *R v Bashier and Razak* [2009] EWCA Crim 2003, [41] simplification was explicitly approved.

[544] *R v Kennedy and Hill* [2001] EWCA Crim 998, [36]; *R v Turnbull* [2001] EWCA Crim 2244. But see *R v Morgan* [2001] EWCA Crim 445, [38] for a more relaxed view; and in *R v Everson* [2001] EWCA Crim 896, [23] the elision of two paragraphs of the model direction was tolerated.   [545] *R v Bresa* (n543), [41].

[546] *R v Moshaid* [1998] Crim LR 420. See *R v Bresa* (n543), [49] for a suggested model in cases in which waiver has not been made.

[547] As it was held to have been in *R v Griffin* [1998] Crim LR 418. See also *R v Pointer* [1997] Crim LR 676.   [548] See e.g. *R v Hillard* (n498) [17].

[549] *R v Allan* [2004] EWCA Crim 2236, (2004) 148 SJLB 1032, [70]; although it is not an absolute requirement that the jury be directed explicitly that the accused is entitled to remain silent: *R v Lowe* [2007] EWCA Crim 833, [19].

[550] *R v Doldur* [2000] Crim LR 178, taking into account defence as well as prosecution evidence; *Allan* (n549), [86].

[551] *R v Turnbull* [2001] EWCA Crim 2244, [7]. For this reason, the standard direction includes reference to the facts not mentioned that are subsequently relied upon: see *R v Chenia* [2002] EWCA Crim 2345, [2004] 1 All ER 543; although when the list would be very long, it might be favourable to the accused to abbreviate the reference: *R v Kennedy and Hill* [2001] EWCA Crim 998, [31]; and in *R v Boyle and Ford* (n541), [44], it was said that it was positively beneficial that no such direction was given.

[552] *R v Milford*, [57]; *R v Petkar* [2003] EWCA Crim 2668, [2004] 1 Cr App Rep 270, [60]–[63].

[553] *R v Allan* (n549), [75].

[554] More especially in the case of innocent contamination: *R v Shukla* [2006] EWCA Crim 797, [41].

[555] *R v Alan* [2003] EWCA Crim 3461, although failure will not necessarily be decisive: *R v Shukla* (n554), [42].   [556] Ibid, [84].

direction, but if the latter is given, it should emphasize that explanation as an alternative explanation for the silence.[557] If such a direction has been given in relation to lies, it is unlikely that an appeal will succeed on the basis of a faulty direction on silence in relation to the very same matter.[558] In this context, it should be remembered that mere conflict between a statement at interview, and its contradiction at trial, is not enough either to constitute a lie or silence, and no special direction is required.[559]

There is no doubt that this provision has caused great difficulty, as witnessed by the volume of case law that it has generated, and perhaps in consequence, the Court of Appeal has suggested that it be relied upon only when 'the merits of an individual case *require* that that should be done'.[560]

Human rights

It has been questioned how compatible these provisions are with the European Convention on Human Rights.[561] Although the European Court of Human Rights has upheld convictions supported by adverse inferences from silence under the comparable Northern Ireland provisions,[562] in the course of its judgments, it took the opportunity to refer to the right of silence, and privilege against self-incrimination, as 'generally recognised international standards which lie at the heart of a notion of fair procedure under Art 6'.[563] The court also takes a very strong position on access to legal advice,[564] and indeed allowed the appeals in both cases on that basis. These cases establish that, while making an important contribution to the fairness of proceedings, the right to silence is not regarded by the European Court of Human Rights as absolute. It is accordingly necessary to determine when deprivation will be held to be in breach of the Convention, and when it will not. Especially after the implementation of the Human Rights Act 1998, this determination must be guided by the decisions both of the European Court of Human Rights, and of domestic courts.

Some claims in the name of human rights have been very broad. Thus, the procedural suggestion in *R v Mushtaq*[565] that the jury was a public authority subject to the Convention independent of the other constituents of the court, and the more substantial proposition in *R v Allen*[566] that to secure tax returns by compulsory process amounted to breach of its provisions, have been roundly, and, it is submitted, rightly, rejected.

---

[557] *R v Stanislas* [2004] EWCA Crim 2266, [13]–[16]. The position had been earlier anomalous: see further Grevling in Mirfield and Smith (eds) *Essays for Colin Tapper* (2003) 1.

[558] See *R v Petkar* (n532), [89]; *R v Adetoro* [2006] EWCA Crim 1716 (in which the *Lucas* direction had been erroneous).   [559] *R v Shukla* (n554), [53].

[560] *R v Brizzalari* (n540), [57] (emphasis supplied).

[561] Emmerson and Ashworth *Human Rights and Criminal Justice* (2nd edn, 2007) paras 15.115–15.119; Munday [1996] *Crim LR* 370.

[562] *Murray v United Kingdom* (1996) 22 EHRR 29, [65], in which the rest of the case against the accused was very strong; *Averill v United Kingdom* (2001) 31 EHRR 839, [50] (in which the Northern Ireland equivalent of s 36 was in issue).

[563] The court seems very reluctant to accept that the seriousness of offences, or the difficulties of securing convictions, makes encroachment on these rights a proportional response: *Saunders v United Kingdom* (1997) 23 EHRR 313, [74]; *Heaney and McGuiness v Ireland* (n478), [58].

[564] Which dictated the changes to domestic practice in the form of the insertion of the new s 2A into s 34 Criminal Justice and Public Order Act 1984, and the 2002 amendments to Code C.

[565] (n369), [52].

[566] (n342), [30]. This decision was upheld by the European Court of Human Rights: *Allen v United Kingdom* (2002) 35 EHRR CD 289.

It remains the case that, at least in the past,[567] there has been divergence between the requirements of the Convention, and the approach of domestic courts, illustrated quite clearly by the decision in *Condron v United Kingdom*,[568] in which the European Court of Human Rights deliberately rejected the reasoning of the Court of Appeal.[569] At that time, the English court went only so far as to require that the adverse inference should not be the *sole* reason for conviction, while the European Court thought that neither should it be the *main* reason.[570] In that case, the accused had been advised by their solicitor to remain silent as, in his view, they were suffering from symptoms associated with withdrawal from drugs. The European Court took the view that the jury should have been positively directed to take into account the fact that the silence was maintained on legal advice. While the Court of Appeal had regarded as merely 'desirable' a direction to the jury to draw an adverse inference only if they rejected the plausibility of such a reason, the European Court held it to be essential. On the other hand, both courts agreed that, where the accused relied upon the content of the legal advice given to him, it did not amount to a breach of any Convention right for him to be cross-examined about it.

It has also been held that a violation is more likely to be found in respect of a direction to draw an adverse inference from silence than of one that omits to provide a caution against drawing such an inference, when it is inappropriate for the jury to do so.[571]

QUESTIONING SUSPECTS

This topic was put on a new footing by the Police and Criminal Evidence Act 1984, and the Codes of Practice issued thereunder.[572] Their application, and interpretation, has generated much modern case law.[573] The whole subject was reviewed by the Royal Commission on Criminal Justice in 1994;[574] some of its recommendations were implemented in the Criminal Justice and Public Order Act 1994, the Codes were revised in 2002 to meet the strictures of the European Court of Human Rights, and the whole area has been scheduled for reform.[575] It is proposed to give here, first, a brief account of the development of the modern law, and then a short summary of its operation, distinguishing special rules that apply to questioning children, the mentally vulnerable, and spouses.

Development

During the nineteenth century, the police gradually assumed the major responsibility for the detection, apprehension, and questioning of those suspected of the commission of

---

[567] Although the differences have narrowed with the changes in the model direction since *Condron* (n508), the European Court of Human Rights has still required a stronger direction on the possibility of an innocent explanation for silence, and on the need to stress the way in which silence is relevant than the Court of Appeal: see e.g. *Beckles v United Kingdom* (2002) 36 EHRR 13. In *R v Howell* (n534), [25] the Court of Appeal expressed the view that the current English position is consistent with that of the ECHR as stated in *Condron* and *Beckles*.   [568] (2001) 31 EHRR 1.

[569] In *R v Condron and Condron* (n508).

[570] This has now been remedied in the Judicial Studies Board's model direction.

[571] *R v Francom* [2001] 1 Cr App Rep 237.

[572] As recommended by the Royal Commission on Criminal Procedure (1981) Cmnd 8092.

[573] Within five years, described in *R v Keenan* (n298); 59, 601 as a 'flood'.   [574] Cm 2263.

[575] The current review is considering among other matters the whole status of the Codes, and the extension of post-charge questioning.

crimes. They were also expected to collect evidence for, and to initiate, most prosecutions in England and Wales, but given the combination of stringency, and uncertainty, surrounding the exclusion of incriminating statements made to persons in authority, it became necessary for the judges to issue a set of Judges Rules to guide the police.[576] The general scheme was that admissibility continued to be governed by the general law relating to confessions, but it was still possible for the trial judge to exclude evidence obtained as a result of a breach of the Judges' Rules at his discretion.[577] The Police and Criminal Evidence Act 1984, as noted above, in s 76, adopted a less stringent test for inadmissibility, but in s 66, prescribed the publication of Codes of Police Practice in relation to search and seizure, and to detention, treatment, questioning, and identification.[578] Since then, as noted above,[579] the situation has been directly affected by the imposition of formal sanction upon failure to mention when questioned matters later relied upon at trial, or to explain suspicious marks, or presence at the scene of a crime. It has also been affected indirectly by an obligation[580] to disclose the nature of the defence, and any alibi, in advance of trial.[581]

Operation

The Codes of Practice are designed to regulate the rights of a suspect to communication with third parties, to legal advice and to medical treatment, and to provide guidance to the police on such things as the conduct of searches, the administration of a caution, the provision of interpreters, and, in all cases, the compilation of adequate documentation of what occurs.[582] It is worth considering in more detail the questions of access to legal advice, to whom and when the Codes apply, their guidance, and the effects of breach of their provisions by the police.

Access to legal advice[583]

The right of access to a solicitor in a police station[584] was always so fundamental a part of the scheme of the Police and Criminal Evidence Act 1984[585] that a court was highly likely

---

[576] First in 1912, but supplemented and revised over the years.   [577] See, 209.

[578] Replacing the old Judges' Rules; the value of a legislative scheme has been endorsed in New Zealand: *R v Mitchell* [1996] 3 NZLR 302, 305. In some jurisdictions, the courts have themselves had to construe the principles from case law: see e.g. the encapsulation of the rules applicable in New South Wales into 11 (non-exhaustive) propositions in *R v Plevac* (1995) 84 ACR 570, 580.   [579] 647.

[580] Under the Criminal Procedure and Investigations Act 1996: see above, 280.

[581] Although these sanctions have been alleviated for the benefit of those who have requested, but not yet received, legal advice.

[582] They do not apply to statements which themselves constitute offences: *DPP v Lawrence* [2007] EWHC 2154 (Admin), [2008] 1 Cr App R 147.

[583] See Police and Criminal Evidence Act 1984, s 58; Code C especially paras 3.1(ii), 6 *passim*. The need for such access is well illustrated by the Canadian case of *R v Burlingham* [1995] 2 SCR 206, in which the accused misunderstood the legal implications of the offer made to him by the police to induce him to confess. It is also necessary in Canada to remind the suspect of his right to legal advice if he indicates the possible commission of other offences: *R v Sawatsky* (1997) 150 DLR (4th) 750.

[584] But not necessarily at home: *RSPCA v Eager* [1995] Crim LR 59 (in the US *Miranda* warnings are so required); *US v Craighead* [2008] USCA9 354 (21 August 2008); or when interviewed elsewhere by a trading standards officer: *Beale v UK* (2005) 40 EHRR Supp SE6.

[585] And of some other jurisdictions, such as Canada, see *R v Lewis* (2007) 219 CCC3d 427 construing s 10(b) of the Canadian Charter; but it is not a common law right, and does not exist in Northern Ireland: *R v Chief Constable of the RUC, ex p Begley* [1997] 4 All ER 833, [1997] 1 WLR 1475.

to exercise its discretion to exclude a confession[586] obtained after wrongful refusal of such access,[587] even retrospectively,[588] and to construe the grounds[589] for proper refusal of such access narrowly.[590] The need for such access has been repeatedly stressed by the European Court of Human Rights, and has underpinned a succession of successful appeals to the court.[591] The court has concerned itself not only with the provision of access, but also with its quality in terms of speed,[592] and conduct.[593] The right may, however, be derogated from by statutory provision, and in *Re McE*[594] the House of Lords construed the Regulation of Investigatory Powers Act 2000 to have authorized the possibility of covert surveillance of the provision of such advice, subject to the specified conditions.

In *R v Alladice*,[595] however, the court was able to disregard a breach of these provisions on the basis that the suspect asserted, on the voir dire, not that in the absence of legal advice he had spoken instead of remaining silent, but that he had not confessed at all. It will be rare for that to be regarded as a sufficient reason, as the accused might still be prejudiced in the subsequent proceedings, since he will be less able to corroborate his account of what has taken place.[596] If the refusal of access does not influence the accused's decision to speak, then the discretion to exclude will not be exercised,[597] although it has become more and more difficult to persuade the court that this has occurred.[598] Provision of access may indeed assist the prosecution, since legal advice can neutralize otherwise effective breaches of the Codes.[599]

Increased apprehension of terrorism has generated and emphasized statutory provision for 'safety interviews'[600] which the police may conduct in the absence of legal representation in order to obtain information to safeguard the public. The evidential consequences were considered at some length in *R v Ibrahim*.[601] Under the relevant provisions the old form of caution reminding the suspect of his right to silence, and the possibility of use

---

[586] But it may still draw an adverse inference from refusal to undergo a breath test, despite access to a lawyer having been requested, but not provided: *Whitley v DPP* [2003] EWHC 2512, (2004) 168 JP 350.

[587] Which includes failure to inform the accused of the presence in the station of a solicitor called on his behalf: *R v Franklin* (1994) The Times, 16 June. But see *R v Oliphant* [1992] Crim LR 40. In *Mohammed (Allie) v State* [1999] 2 AC 111, the Privy Council even held that breach of a constitutional guarantee of a right to be informed of the right to consult a lawyer did not automatically lead to the exercise of the judge's discretion to exclude a confession made as a result. Nor is it likely that a statement secured under a foreign system denying access to legal advice will automatically be excluded in England: *R v McNab* [2001] EWCA Crim 1605, [2002] Crim LR 129.   [588] As in *R v James* [2008] EWCA Crim 1869.

[589] As set out in Police and Criminal Evidence Act 1984, s 58(8), Code C [6.6] and Annex B, as amended.

[590] *R v Samuel* [1988] QB 615, [1988] 2 All ER 135. In New Zealand a very strict view of purported waiver was taken in *R v Rogers* [2006] 2 NZLR 156.

[591] Initially, and influentially in inducing statutory change: *Murray v United Kingdom* (n562), [67]–[73] (silence). See also *Magee v United Kingdom* (2000) 31 EHRR 822 (confession).

[592] In *Averill v United Kingdom* (n519), [58], a 24-hour delay in allowing access to a lawyer was regarded as incompatible with Art 6; in *Gearing v DPP* [2008] EWHC 1695 (Admin) 1695, [22] 23 minutes was significant in the circumstances (although not enough to trigger s 78).

[593] In *Brennan v United Kingdom* (2002) 34 EHRR 507, [58]–[63], the fact that a police officer was present able to overhear what was said was found incompatible with Art 6.   [594] [2009] UKHL 15.

[595] (1988) 87 Cr App Rep 380.   [596] *R v Parris* (1988) 89 Cr App Rep 68.

[597] *R v Alladice* (1988) 87 Cr App Rep 380; but cf *R v Walsh* (457).

[598] *Simmons and Greene v R* [2006] UKPC 19, [25].

[599] *R v Dunn* (1990) 91 Cr App Rep 237 (presence inhibits false claims of fabrication); *R v Hoyte* [1994] Crim LR 215 (advice about inadmissibility of earlier statement following breaches frees subsequent repetition from taint).   [600] Terrorism Act 2000, and Code H introduced in 2006.

[601] (n472).

of anything he might say should have been used, but in fact the newer form indicating possible adverse inference from silence had been used. It was held that in the circumstances where the accused in fact advanced false exculpatory statements this had not led to injustice,[602] and that the absence of legal representation had been immaterial since no complicated legal or factual issues arose.

Range of application

If these provisions conferring a right to legal advice are to be effective, it becomes increasingly important to regulate any other contact between the police and the suspect. Two issues need to be considered: first, whether the investigator is a person to whom the provisions of the Code apply; second, whether the occasion is one to which they apply. They will be considered separately.

Person

The Codes of Practice address themselves to 'police officers',[603] but s 67(9) of the Police and Criminal Evidence Act 1984 extends their ambit to other persons 'charged with the duty of investigating offences or charging offenders'.[604] Code C has thus been applied to other investigators, both official,[605] and private.[606] Nor is it possible to evade the provisions of the Code merely by acting under cover,[607] or through an 'agent or stooge'.[608] On the other hand, it does not apply to foreign investigators,[609] to psychiatrists when attempting to determine whether the accused is fit to plead,[610] to probation officers compiling a sentence report,[611] to prison officers used only as searchers,[612] or to headteachers.[613] In such cases, the only question is one of the effect of the procedure on the fairness of the proceedings,

---

[602] At least to justify the exclusionary discretion of s 78.

[603] Whether or not at the time acting in the roles mentioned in s 67(9): *R v Sparks* [1991] Crim LR 128 (policeman sitting in station with eventual accused, but as friend). It should also be noted that interviews are now sometimes carried out by civilian 'approved persons', which has been reflected by use of the word 'interviewer' in the newer drafts of the Codes.

[604] A similar limitation applies at common law in Australia, where it was determined that private citizens who had arrested children for stealing from a supermarket need not follow the procedures that bound the police in interviewing children: *H v Hill* (1993) 112 FLR 353.

[605] See *R v Seelig* [1991] 4 All ER 429, [1992] 1 WLR 149 (inspector under Companies Act 1985); *R v Okafor* [1994] 3 All ER 741, 99 Cr App Rep 97; *R v Weerdesteyn* [1995] 1 Cr App Rep 405; *R v Senior* [2004] EWCA Crim 454, [2004] 3 All ER 9 (Customs officers); *R v Souter* [1995] Crim LR 729 (military police); *R v Devani* [2007] EWCA Crim 1926 (prison officers, but not support staff); and see *R v Doncaster* [2008] EWCA Crim 5, [33] (not tax inspectors prior to referring case for consideration of prosecution).

[606] See *R v Twaites and Brown* (1990) 92 Cr App Rep 106 (company's internal investigators) cp *R v Welcher* [2007] EWCA Crim 480; *R v Bayliss* (1993) 98 Cr App Rep 235 (store detective); *Joy v Federation Against Copyright Theft Ltd* [1993] Crim LR 588 (Federation's investigator); *RSPCA v Eager* [1995] Crim LR 59 (RSPCA inspector), apparently equating having a duty with being charged with a duty. It was left open, in *R v Johnson* (n512), whether a company sergeant major fell into this category.

[607] *R v Bryce* [1992] 4 All ER 567, 95 Cr App Rep 320.

[608] *R v Roberts* [1997] 1 Cr App Rep 217, 232D. See, in Australia, *R v O'Neill* (1995) 81 ACR 458.

[609] *R v Quinn* [1990] Crim LR 581 (Irish police); *R v Konscol* [1993] Crim LR 950 (Belgian customs). See also, in Canada, *R v Terry* [1996] 2 SCR 207 (US police).   [610] *R v McDonald* [1991] Crim LR 122.

[611] *R v Elleray* [2003] EWCA Crim 553, [2003] 2 Cr App Rep 165.

[612] *R v Ristic* [2004] EWCA Crim 2107, (2004) 148 SJLB 942, [19].

[613] *G v DPP* [1997] 2 All ER 755, [1997] 2 Cr App Rep 78.

although the Code may nevertheless be used as an indicator of this.[614] Even where the Code does apply, this remains the decisive question, and failure to observe some aspects is unlikely to lead to exclusion. Thus, neither an under-cover policeman,[615] nor a customs officer on first encounter,[616] is required to administer a caution, nor is a private investigator working in a private residence bound to follow minutely the provisions as to recording that apply to police officers interrogating suspects in a police station.[617] The European Court of Human Rights has been prepared to distinguish, in some respects, between investigators who have no special power of arrest, and the police.[618]

Occasion

Any questioning[619] of a suspect[620] designed to obtain admissions of guilt[621] of an offence,[622] or to establish its commission,[623] will constitute an 'interview', and require the suspect to be cautioned,[624] however informal and unpremeditated the situation,[625] even if it encom-

---

[614] Thus in *R v Smith* [1994] 1 WLR 1396, 99 Cr App Rep 233, it was held that, although the Bank of England's supervisor of a banking institution fell outside the ambit of s 67(9), a statement was nevertheless to be excluded because of shortfalls from Code C, even though not strictly applicable.

[615] *R v Christou* [1992] QB 979, [1992] 4 All ER 559 (so long as this is not used as a subterfuge to evade the restrictions of the Code); cf, in Canada, *R v Grandinetti* 2005 SCC 5, [2005] 1 SCR 27; nor need he follow the provisions of the Code if his aim is not so much the investigation of past offences, as to secure evidence of future plans: *R v Lin, Hung and Tsui* [1995] Crim LR 817.

[616] *R v Shah* [1994] Crim LR 125, unless he already has reasonable grounds to suspect the commission of an offence: *R v Nelson and Rose* [1998] 2 Cr App Rep 399; but in some such cases at least it is permissible to ask questions relating to possession of the baggage in question: *R v Senior* (n605). See, in Australia, *R v Raso* (1993) 115 FLR 319.   [617] *Stilgoe v Eager* (1994) The Times, 27 January.

[618] *Beale v UK* (n584).

[619] If no questions are asked, but the police merely listen and note down information, then it is not an interview within the Code: *R v Menard* [1995] 1 Cr App Rep 306. This seems likely to be a rare occurrence, and any suggestion that it has occurred will need rigorous scrutiny. In Canada, in *R v Mishra* (2004) 191 CCC3d 399, a stratagem of two police officers conversing in the hearing of the accused, with the view of eliciting an admission, was held not to amount to questioning in breach of the Charter.

[620] Before suspicion, the Codes do not apply, and in a number of cases the defence paradoxically argues that there was enough ground for suspicion to require a caution: see *R v Shillibier* [2006] EWCA Crim 793, [60], in which it was also revealed that the police divide non-suspects into a number of categories, some of them receiving a diminished form of caution; *R v Perpont* [2004] EWCA Crim 2562, (2004) 148 SJLB 1372 (not enough to ground suspicion that accused had enquired at airport desk about a drug smuggler); *Sneyd v DPP* [2006] EWCA Crim 560 (Admin), (2006) 170 JP 545 (only *after* breath test that enough suspicion of drink-driving offence); *R v Rehman* [2006] EWCA Crim 1900 (unrevealed prior intelligence of drug smuggling).

[621] It does not include contact designed to secure the accused's cooperation in the course of an ongoing investigation: *R v De Silva* [2002] EWCA Crim 2673, [2003] 2 Cr App Rep 74, [22].

[622] Under English law, although even in relation to a foreign offence in extradition proceedings evidence obtained by means 'outraging civilised values' may still be excluded by discretion: see *Fernandes v Governor of Brixton Prison* (n380), [80].

[623] *R v Cheb Miller* [2007] EWCA Crim 1891 (to seek reason for carrying knife).

[624] See Code C, [11.1A]; *Batley v DPP* (1998) The Times, 5 March. Blood alcohol testing is explicitly excluded from being an interview, and its administration, pending the provision of legal advice does not constitute a breach of Art 6 of the European Convention on Human Rights: *Campbell v DPP* [2002] EWHC 1314 (Admin), [2004] RTR 64. Failure to administer a caution cannot necessarily be retrieved by subsequently putting the statement so made to the accused after a caution: *R v Webster* (12 December 2000, unreported CA), [18].

[625] *R v Absolam* (1988) 88 Cr App Rep 332; *R v Keenan* (n298). Code C [11.1] requires interviews after arrest normally to take place in a police station.

passes no more than one question.[626] The sequence of questions is to be treated as a whole for this purpose.[627] It has been said[628] not to be within the spirit of the Act or Code to give 'interview' a restricted meaning.[629] Code C has, indeed, been revised so as to apply some of its requirements, such as those relating to recording,[630] outside even this extended sense of 'interview'.[631] It may be preferable to adopt such an approach rather than to adopt an unduly rigid approach to the interpretation of the Code.[632] It should further be noted that the revised form of the Code was designed to clear up some of the confusion that had been created by the original provisions.[633] Although the structure and terms of the amendment are far from clear, it has been held that their general tenor is to enlarge, rather than to constrict, the concept of an 'interview'.[634]

Conduct of questioning

As noted above, the Code starts to govern questioning as soon as the police officer has grounds for suspecting the person questioned of having committed a[635] crime;[636] thereafter, as soon as the police officer decides to arrest the suspect, he must normally conduct any further questioning only at a police station,[637] and once the police officer believes that a prosecution should be brought, and that there is sufficient evidence for it to succeed, he must cease questioning.[638] Some of the most beneficial features of the Codes are their insistence upon the provision of documentation of what has occurred between the police and the accused,[639] as much, if not more, outside, rather than within, the confines of the police station. It has been said that the importance of these rules can scarcely be overemphasized.[640] Despite doubts in some quarters as to its efficacy,[641] automatic recording of interviews relating to indictable offences has been made mandatory.[642] The Code contains detailed guidance as to the care and treatment of suspects, and in many ways, guarantees the observation of these rules by allocating supervision to separate custody officers, and as noted above, by

[626] *R v Ward* (1993) 98 Cr App Rep 337.

[627] *R v Weekes* (1993) 97 Cr App Rep 222.   [628] *R v Matthews* (1989) 91 Cr App Rep 43, 47, 48.

[629] See also in Australia *Carr v Western Australia* [2007] HCA 47, 232 CLR 138.

[630] As in *R v Miller* [1998] Crim LR 209, in respect of spontaneous remarks.

[631] Code C, [11.13]. It should be noted that the court regards changes to the Code as indicative of a new standard of fairness for the purposes of s 78: see *R v Ward* (1993) 98 Cr App Rep 337.

[632] As indicated in *R v Marsh* [1991] Crim LR 455, although such flexibility seems more appropriate not so much to the question of breach, as to the consequences of any such breach.

[633] See e.g. *R v Maguire* (1989) 90 Cr App Rep 115. The problem of impracticality, identified in *R v Parchment* [1991] Crim LR 626, was solved by the redrafted [11.10].

[634] *R v Cox* (1992) 96 Cr App Rep 464, 470. See also *R v Goddard* [1994] Crim LR 46.

[635] Where the accused is suspected of more than one crime, he must be told in respect of which he is being questioned: *R v Kirk* [1999] 4 All ER 698, [2000] 1 WLR 567.

[636] But it does not require the police to disclose all of their evidence at this stage: *R v Rosenberg* [2006] EWCA Crim 6, [25].

[637] Paragraph 11.1, subject only to delay on account of danger to evidence or persons, the risk of alerting others, or hindering the recovery of property. For criticism of any attempt to abuse this exception, see *R v Khan* [1993] Crim LR 54.   [638] Paragraph 11.6, see further, 660.

[639] Recording has been required of spontaneous remarks at the conclusion of a formal interview after the tape has been turned off: *R v Scott* [1991] Crim LR 56. See also, in Australia, on the value of recording: *R v Stewart* (1993) 2 Tas R 274; *R v Smith* (1996) 86 ACR 398.

[640] *R v Canale* [1990] 2 All ER 187, 91 Cr App Rep 1; 190, 5.

[641] Extending to video as well as to audio recording: see McConville [1992] *Crim LR* 532.

[642] SI 1991/2686. Video recording is now governed by Code F. In Australia, some difficulty has arisen in construing the comparable provisions: see *Pollard v R* (1992) 176 CLR 177.

provision for documentation. Even so, complaints of breach of the provisions of the Codes are often made, and the sanctions for any such breach are considered below.

Effects of breach

The Royal Commission on Criminal Procedure was unhappy about reliance upon the use of an exclusionary discretion as the primary sanction for breach of the Code,[643] and the early drafts of the Police and Criminal Evidence Bill contained no explicit reference to any such discretion, although *R v Sang* provided common law authority for its existence in relation to 'admissions and confessions and generally with regard to evidence obtained from the accused after the commission of the offence'.[644] At a late stage in its passage, new and explicit provision was made in the 1984 Act for such a discretion:[645]

(1) In any proceedings the court may refuse to allow evidence on which the prosecution proposes to rely to be given if it appears to the court that, having regard to all the circumstances in which the evidence was obtained, the admission of the evidence would have such an adverse effect upon the fairness of the proceedings that the court ought not to admit it.

(2) Nothing in this section shall prejudice any rule of law requiring a court to exclude evidence.

It should be noted that subs (2) is designed to preserve the exclusionary rule set out in s 76. This was necessary because this section, unlike the clause it replaced, is of general application, and applies across the whole range of the law of evidence in criminal proceedings.[646] Nor does this new discretion derogate from the common law discretion[647] discussed in *Sang*, since s 82(3) provides that:

Nothing in this Part of this Act shall prejudice any power of a court to exclude evidence (whether by preventing questions from being put or otherwise) at its discretion.

Section 78 was expressed in such vague terms that it was hard to anticipate how it would be applied.[648] There was, indeed, some warrant for regarding s 76 as constituting an exclusive new codification of the rules relating to confessions, but as noted above, any such view was rejected at an early stage in *R v Mason*.[649] Although, as also noted, the Codes of Practice have been accepted as providing some indication of the satisfaction of the conditions of admissibility under s 76, their implementation has mainly been by way of triggering the exercise of the discretion to exclude conferred by s 78.

In many, if not most, cases, discretionary exclusion is held in reserve in case a claim under s 76 should fail.[650] The principal differences between the two sections are that exclusion under s 76 is by rule,[651] and that under s 78 by discretion. In the case of s 76, the burden of disproof of the relevant conditions is always on the prosecution, whereas under

---

[643] An ingenious attempt by a solicitor to bring a civil action in respect of denial of access to his client was rejected in *Chief Constable of Kent v Rixon* (2000) The Times, 11 April, but the possibility of such an action being brought by the client was canvassed, [22]. [644] [1980] AC 402, [1979] 2 All ER 1222, 437, 1231.

[645] Section 78. [646] 'Proceedings' are defined as criminal proceedings by s 82(1).

[647] Indeed, in *Thompson v R* [1998] AC 811, the Privy Council approved the remarks of Lord Taylor CJ in *R v Christou* [1992] QB 979, [1992] 4 All ER 559 that there is no difference between them in this context.

[648] See remarks to this effect in *R v Keenan* (n298), 62, 603. [649] (n308), 484, 144.

[650] See e.g. *R v Delaney* (n312), 340; *R v McGovern* (n423), 235.

[651] In *R v Chung* (1991) 92 Cr App Rep 314, 323, the Court of Appeal declared its greater readiness to review the decision because it had been arrived at under s 76 as well as s 78.

s 78, the incidence of burden of persuading the court to exercise its discretion is neutral, and does not require the court to make a finding on each matter of fact to be taken into consideration, in deciding whether the admission of the evidence would make the proceedings sufficiently unfair.[652] It has been held that it is not for the judge to exclude under s 78 on his own initiative in the absence of argument by the defence that he should do so.[653] Procedurally, s 78 presents serious difficulties to the judge, who has to exercise his discretion before all the evidence and relevant information is before him, and in particular whether the accused will testify, however the discretion is exercised.[654] This presents further problems on appeal, when the court has to put itself in the position of the trial judge, and ignore any such matters, even though they have, by then, been revealed.[655]

The relationship between breaches of the Codes, and the operation of s 78, have come before the Court of Appeal in two main contexts: first, in which the trial judge has found no breach of the Codes, and has not otherwise excluded the evidence under his discretion; second, those in which the trial judge has found breach of the Codes, but has declined to excluded the evidence by his discretion.[656] The Court of Appeal is, in principle, more likely to intervene in the former situation, in which the judge may not have addressed his mind to the exercise of the discretion at all,[657] or only upon a hypothetical basis.[658]

In either case, review of the trial judge's exercise of discretion is a limited exercise, determined by *Wednesbury* principles, and not by those appropriate to erroneous determinations of law or fact.[659] It might also have been thought that in no case could unfairness not resulting in unreliability of outcome be regarded as sufficient to allow an appeal after the amendment of the Criminal Appeal Act 1968, but this still awaits final resolution.[660]

In *R v Walsh*,[661] the Court of Appeal took the view that any breach of the Codes[662] impairs the fairness of the proceedings, although it also pointed out that s 78 seems, by the use of the phrase '*such* an adverse effect', to contemplate some situations of venial unfairness insufficient to justify the exclusion of evidence thereby obtained because the

---

[652] *Re Saifi* [2001] 4 All ER 168, [2001] 1 WLR 1135, [59]. In Australia, the burden is borne by the accused: see *MacPherson v R* (1981) 147 CLR 512, 519, 520; *Cleland v R* (1982) 151 CLR 1, 19, 20, in which Deane J applied the same principle to the *Bunning v Cross* discretion.   [653] *R v Raphaie* [1996] Crim LR 812.

[654] These difficulties are explained at some length in *R v Keenan* (n298); they have been alleviated by the increased pre-trial disclosure of the nature of the defence required under Pt 5 of the Criminal Justice Act 2003.   [655] *R v Parris* (1988) 89 Cr App Rep 68.

[656] Or determined that the confession has not been caused by the breach, as in *Simmons and Greene v R* (n598), [25].

[657] In *R v Parris* (1988) 89 Cr App Rep 68, the trial judge appears to have been under the impression that he was obliged to consider s 78 only if satisfied that a breach of the Code had been shown.

[658] See *R v Samuel* [1988] QB 615, [1988] 2 All ER 135.

[659] *Thompson v R* [1998] AC 811. See further, 194. In Scotland, fairness plays a larger role, and appeals have been allowed on the basis that the issue of fairness ought not to have been left to the jury: *Harley and Roche v HM Adv* 1995 SCCR 595.

[660] Cf *R v Mullen* [2000] QB 520, [1999] 2 Cr App Rep 143, allowing pre-trial acts not leading to an unreliable outcome at trial to be sufficient, with *Simmons and Greene* (n598), in which even iniquitous refusal of access to legal advice was held ineffective in the absence under the local provisions of 'any miscarriage of justice'.

[661] (n457), 163, emphasis supplied.

[662] A similar approach has been taken to refusal of a voir dire to attempt to establish a breach: *R v Rehman* (n620), [27].

effect is not adverse enough.[663] Any breach should be 'significant and substantial',[664] and while bad faith might exalt into that category behaviour that might otherwise fall short, the converse did not follow. If there was significant, and substantial, unfairness, directed against the complainant,[665] then it would be sufficient to justify[666] discretionary exclusion whether or not there were bad faith. The basic problem is that the Codes of Practice cover a multitude of topics, occurring at different stages in the investigation and prosecution of crime, and it is far from obvious that all can be brought within the precise terms of s 78. Conversely, there may well be other matters that are not dealt with under the Codes, which should trigger such an exclusionary discretion.[667] It has been held, in Australia, that such a discretion should be employed to exclude from the record of a confession any lengthy argumentative assertions of guilt made by the interrogators.[668]

Special cases

The Code of Practice is also concerned to prevent statements being taken from juveniles, the mentally ill, the mentally handicapped, those incapacitated by drink or drugs, non-English speakers,[669] or the deaf, except upon the satisfaction of appropriate conditions, just because they may be unreliable.[670] Accordingly, breach of the Code in relation to such matters has led to discretionary exclusion under s 78.[671] The discretion conferred by s 78 also provides a means whereby statements spontaneously[672] blurted out by those so disadvantaged may be excluded.[673] Special mention may be made of the rules relating to children, the mentally impaired, and spouses.

---

[663] See also *R v Parris* (1988) 89 Cr App Rep 68, 72; *R v Rajakuruna* [1991] Crim LR 458. But see *R v Fennelley* [1989] Crim LR 142, in which it is hard to see why failing to tell a man why he was being searched so impaired the fairness of the proceedings as to lead to the exclusion of the real evidence so found. For a clear case of a breach regarded as insignificant, see *R v Courtney* [1995] Crim LR 63 (note of answer not shown by Customs officer to accused when clear that he would make no further statement).

[664] And in cases in which the matter is considered on a reference by the Criminal Cases Review Commission, the court is entitled to take into account both breaches of the Code as it was at the time of the trial, and what would now amount to breach of the revised form of the Code, so long as the relevant breaches are sufficient to render the trial unfair: *R v Allen* [2001] EWCA Crim 1607, [36]. See also *R v Ward* (1993) 98 Cr App Rep 337.   [665] *R v Roberts* (n608).

[666] But would not mandate it: *R v Armas-Rodriguez* [2005] EWCA Crim 1081, [17].

[667] See *R v Woodall* [1989] Crim LR 288, in which there appears neither to have been a breach of the Code, nor any unfairness in obtaining the admission, but its use was nevertheless regarded as making subsequent proceedings unfair since it had been volunteered 'off the record', and no subsequent reference had been made to it until the first day of the trial; in *R v Pall* (1992) 156 JP 424, it was indicated that a caution should be given after arrest, but before a voluntary statement, even though the Code is silent as to this situation.

[668] *R v Kallis* [1994] 2 Qd R 88.

[669] Code C, [13]. Although a somewhat cavalier approach appears to have been taken in *Leong v Customs and Excise Comrs* (4 April 2002, unreported) VADT, in contrast to a more solicitous approach in Australia in *Kiah v R* [2001] NTCCA 1.   [670] See Cmnd 8092, [4.133].

[671] *R v Fogah* [1989] Crim LR 141 (juvenile, and no appropriate adult); *Timothy v DPP* [1989] Crim LR 893 (drunkenness, though a note of a request for a specimen of breath was not excluded); but see *R v Clarke* [1989] Crim LR 892 (deaf, but discretion not exercised because the condition was not known to the police).

[672] A wholly spontaneous statement has been held not to amount to an 'interview': *R v Menard* (n619).

[673] Cf *R v S and J* (1983) 32 SASR 174.

Children[674]

In the case of children, Code C makes special provision for the presence during the interview of an appropriate adult,[675] who may be a parent, social worker, or failing them, any responsible adult over the age of 18 and not a police officer, or person employed by the police.[676] The appropriate adult[677] should act as more than an observer, and should be informed of his role in advising the child of any unfair conduct by the police, and in assisting communication.[678] It should be recognized that children[679] are likely to be especially vulnerable, and that unfairness may be triggered at an earlier stage than in the case of an adult.[680]

Under the new regime for reprimanding, and warning, children introduced by the Crime and Disorder Act 1998, it has been held unfair for a confession to be secured without provision of full information of the effect of the warning, such as inclusion of the name of the person so confessing on the register of sexual offenders.[681]

The mentally vulnerable[682]

Code C also prescribes a special regime for such persons,[683] requiring the attendance at interview of an appropriate adult,[684] except in situations of urgency.[685] Despite this apparently mandatory requirement, s 77 of the Police and Criminal Evidence Act 1984 prescribes,[686] in the case of the mentally handicapped,[687] a special warning to the jury against convicting on the basis wholly, or substantially,[688] of a confession, if it was made

---

[674] Described as 'juveniles', and defined in [1.5] as those persons who appear to be under the age of 17 in the absence of evidence to the contrary. It is submitted that the test is asymmetric, and that real age should prevail over apparent age in the case of those under 17, as in Australia: *R v T* [2001] NSWCCA 210.

[675] And in [3.13] for the person responsible for the welfare of the child to be informed of his arrest, and whereabouts.

[677] Exceptionally, there may be more than one.   [676] Paragraph 1.7(a).

[678] Paragraph 11.17, although if he does so act, it is not fatal that he has not been so informed: *H and M v DPP* [1998] Crim LR 653. For the position in Australia, see *R v H* (1996) 85 ACR 481.

[679] Or even those marginally over the age specified in the Code, which may be relevant to the exercise of the discretion to exclude under s 78: *R (DPP) v Stratford Youth Court* [2001] EWHC Admin 615, (2001) 165 JP 761, [11].   [680] See *Codona v HM Adv* 1996 SLT 1100.

[681] *R (U) v Metropolitan Police Comr* [2002] EWHC 2486 (Admin), [2003] 3 All ER 419, [2003] 1 Cr App Rep 447.

[682] This term is now used in Code C; different categorizations and more specific terminology apply in different situations.

[683] Paragraph 1.4 refers to the mentally disordered or otherwise mentally vulnerable, and is further defined in note 1G. Suspects are to be regarded as falling into this category if the custody officer has any suspicion, or is told in good faith, that they do, until the contrary is proved. Paragraph 3.16 requires diagnosis to determine whether this condition applies to be conducted as soon as possible.

[684] Paragraph 1.7(b); see also note 1D. For appraisal, see Hodgson [1997] *Crim LR* 785.

[685] Paragraph 11.1 and Annex B.

[686] Although in *R v Qayyum* [2006] EWCA Crim 1127 a sufficiently strong general direction was regarded as an adequate alternative.

[687] Defined by s 77(3) as those 'in a state of arrested or incomplete development of mind which includes significant impairment of intelligence and social functioning'. This has been interpreted as relating more to susceptibility to pressure than in terms of abstract ability as enumerated in tests: *R v Raghip* (1991) The Times, 9 December; *R v Kenny* [1994] Crim LR 284. It has been said to be wise for a judge to give such a warning in any borderline case: *R v Foster* [2003] EWCA Crim 178.

[688] So not if the effect of the confession is swamped by the rest of the evidence: *R v Campbell* [1995] Crim LR 157.

otherwise than in the presence of an independent person.[689] This seems to contemplate not only the tendering of statements obtained in breach of the Codes,[690] but also, in that situation, judicial abstinence from the exercise of any exclusionary discretion.[691] Indeed, in *R v Bailey*,[692] the court went further,[693] and prescribed a more detailed warning of the reasons for the mentally handicapped confessing falsely, and an examination of their possible effect in the light of the detailed facts of the case. It may sometimes be necessary to call evidence as to events at a relevant interview with a mentally vulnerable suspect, to determine whether any confession made in the absence of an appropriate adult is reliable.[694] The absence of an appropriate adult is also likely to affect the weight to be attached to any apparent waiver of legal advice,[695] and so lead to increased likelihood of breach of the European Convention on Human Rights.

Spouses

Although it was denied[696] in *R v L* that the police needed to warn a spouse of her non-compellability to testify against the other, it was suggested[697] that they should make it known that a spouse need not make a statement implicating the other.

---

[689] Not necessarily the same as an appropriate adult for the purposes of the Code: see *R v Lewis* [1996] Crim LR 260.

[690] In *R v Lamont* [1989] Crim LR 813, the Court of Appeal insisted upon such a warning being given in an appropriate case, and because it had not, was able to abstain from deciding whether the evidence should have been excluded altogether.

[691] There is some suggestion in *R v Moss* (1990) 91 Cr App Rep 371 that the discretion would more readily be exercised in relation to a series than to one interview in isolation. The suggestion that discretionary exclusion is mandatory in these circumstances was specifically rejected in *R v Law-Thompson* [1997] Crim LR 674. The more flagrant the breach of the Code, the more likely it is that the court will exercise its discretion to exclude: see *R v J* [2003] EWCA Crim 3309 (evidence that police deliberately disregarded warning that suspect was mentally impaired).   [692] [1995] 2 Cr App Rep 262.

[693] As s 77(1) explicitly allows.

[694] In *R v Nolan* [2006] EWCA Crim 2983, a case referred by the Criminal Cases Review Commission, it was noted, [23], how much more stringent this condition has become in recent years.

[695] *R v Aspinall* [1999] 2 Cr App Rep 115.   [696] [2008] EWCA Crim 973, [2009] 1 WLR 626, [31].

[697] [33].

XV

DOCUMENTARY EVIDENCE[1]

Darling J once said that a document is 'any written thing capable of being evidence', and he added that it is immaterial on what the writing may be inscribed.[2] It has now been accepted that there is no separate common law rule[3] requiring an original, but that all depends simply on the worth of the document in the circumstances.[4] There is, however, a common law rule equating all degrees of secondary evidence,[5] thus permitting oral evidence of the contents of a document, including its representation on the screen of a computer monitor.[6] The Civil Procedure Rules have clarified many issues that arose under the old law by their wide definitions of 'document' and 'copy'.[7]

This chapter contains three parts dealing in turn with the authentication, execution, and meaning of documents.

SECTION 1. PROOF OF THE CONTENTS OF A DOCUMENT

The old law contained arcane rules about the proof of the contents of documents of various sorts.[8] The modern law[9] is more straightforward, largely as a result of statutory intervention. The process started with the Bankers' Books Evidence Act 1879, and has largely kept pace with successive statutory inroads into the exclusionary effects of the hearsay rule, culminating in the wide definitions in s 13 of the Civil Evidence Act 1995:

…'document' means anything in which information of any description is recorded, and 'copy', in relation to a document, means anything onto which information recorded in the document has been copied, by whatever means and whether directly or indirectly.

---

[1] See generally Hollander *Documentary Evidence* (10th edn, 2006).

[2] *R v Daye* [1908] 2 KB 333, 340.

[3] Some legislation, e.g. Companies Act 1989, s 56, defines a document to include other forms, but permits conventional forms to be required for production.

[4] *Masquerade Music Ltd v Springsteen* [2001] EWCA Civ 563.

[5] In Australia, an enhanced copy remains a copy: *R v Giovannone* [2002] NSWCCA 323, 140 ACR 1, [57].

[6] See *R v Nazeer* [1998] Crim LR 750. See also, in Canada, *R v Lemay* (2004) 247 DLR (4th) 470 (supplementing defective microfiche provisions).

[7] CPR 31.4, adopting the definitions in Civil Evidence Act 1995, s 13. The Land Registration Act 2002, s 91(4) specifically regards an electronic form as 'a document in writing', and modified 'signed' to 'authenticated'. In the United States, the commentary to the amendments to the Federal Procedure Rules to cater for electronic information, which came into force on 1 December 2006, expresses some doubt about subsuming such material under the rubric of *documents*. [8] See older editions of this work.

[9] See also, in Australia, the simplifying provisions of Evidence Act 1995, Pts 2.2 and 4.3, and for commentary, see Magner (1995) 18 *UNSWLJ* 67.

In this respect the criminal law has sometimes moved ahead of the civil, and those definitions first appeared in the provisions of the Criminal Justice Act 1988.[10] It was also held
that any deficiencies in these definitions could be remedied by invocation of the old common law rules, as in *R v Nazeer*.[11] The Criminal Justice Act 2003, s 133 now permits the use
of copies in criminal proceedings, irrespective of the existence of the original, authenticated in any way approved by the court.

The main transformation represents an increasingly liberal attitude towards the reception of copies as sufficient proof of the contents of an original document. As noted in
Chapter XIII, the rules relating to the admissibility of documentary hearsay continue to
distinguish, in some respects, between business and public records, and others. This is
mirrored in the provisions for the means of proof, although it should be noted that these
provisions supplement, rather than supplant, existing means of proving documents.[12]
The simplicity of the new methods may, however, gradually render recourse to the older
means unnecessary. This section will consider, separately: proof under the new provisions
of statements in documents generally; proof of business, and public, records; procedure
under the Civil Procedure Rules; and some special considerations applying to public documents and to bankers' books.

PROOF OF STATEMENTS IN DOCUMENTS

The means of proving such documents is to be found for civil proceedings in s 8 of the Civil
Evidence Act 1995:[13]

(1) Where a statement contained in a document is admissible as evidence in civil proceedings, it may be proved—

   (a) by production of that document, or

   (b) whether or not that document is still in existence, by the production of a copy of that
   document or of the material part of it, authenticated in such manner as the court
   may approve.

(2) It is immaterial for this purpose how many removes there are between a copy and the
original.

One of the main reasons for the liberalization of the old rules was the development of new
technology under which copies were, in effect, duplicate originals, and the possibilities of
erroneous transcription were non-existent. The reform is not, however, limited to this situation, and it would be possible, if the court were satisfied of authenticity, for documents to
have been copied from memory at intermediate stages. The Law Commission considered
the less open-ended authentication provision to be found in the Scottish legislation,[14] but
since the 1988 provision had caused no difficulty, forbore to recommend any change.[15]
This seems sensible, since the Scottish provision would cause difficulty in the case of long

---

[10] Civil Evidence Act 1995, Sch 1, [12].   [11] (n6).   [12] Civil Evidence Act 1995, s 14(2).

[13] Itself reproducing s 27 of the Criminal Justice Act 1988, now replaced by Criminal Justice Act 2003
s 133: see further above, 658.

[14] Civil Evidence (Scotland) Act 1988, s 6, requiring the authentication to be by the person responsible
for making the copy. See also *ASIC v Rich* [2005] NSWSC 417, 216 ALR 320, for illuminating elaboration of
the concept of authentication of documents in Australia (unaffected on this point by the successful appeal).

[15] Law Com No 216 *The Hearsay Rule in Civil Proceedings* (Cm 2321, 1993), [4.37].

chains, old copies, and unidentifiable copiers, and for this reason, has had to be made subject to contrary direction.

Although the contrary has been suggested,[16] it is submitted that these provisions apply not only to cases in which the statements in the documents are to be used for the purpose of proving their truth, but also when they are operative, or required for some other purpose.

In view of the modelling of the provisions of the CEA 1995 upon the precedent set by s 27 of the Criminal Justice Act 1988,[17] it was surprising to find a rather radical change in the wording of the relevant provision for the admissibility of hearsay in criminal proceedings.[18] The Act retains the basic forms[19] of definition of 'document', and 'copy', but, without any argumentation, or justification; in the Law Commission's report, s 133 completely omits all reference to the immateriality of the number of removes between the original and the copy.[20] It is, of course, possible that this was simply thought unnecessary in view of the width of the definitions, and discretion as to authentication, but it is disturbing to find the hostage of formal deviation offered to the fortune of litigious desperation. It should be noted that authentication remains necessary, and may come into play when the evidence adduced results from an unexplained process of transcription, during which some detail may have been susceptible of alteration without leaving any obvious trace of having occurred.[21]

PROOF OF BUSINESS OR PUBLIC RECORDS

Although the Civil Evidence Act 1995 assimilated statements and records for the purposes of admissibility, it retained their separation for means of proof. It provides in s 9 that:

(1) A document which is shown to form part of the records of a business or public authority may be received in evidence in civil proceedings without further proof.

(2) A document shall be taken to form part of the records of a business or public authority if there is produced to the court a certificate to that effect signed by an officer of the business or authority to which the records belong. For this purpose—

    (a) a document purporting to be a certificate signed by an officer of a business or public authority shall be deemed to have been duly given by such an officer and signed by him; and

    (b) a certificate shall be treated as signed by a person if it purports to bear a facsimile of his signature.

(3) The absence of an entry in the records of a business or public authority may be proved in civil proceedings by affidavit of an officer of the business or authority to which the records belong.

(4) In this section–'records' means records in whatever form; 'business' includes any activity regularly carried on over a period of time, whether for profit or not, by any body (whether corporate or not) or by an individual; 'officer' includes any person occupying a responsible position in relation to the relevant activities of the business or public authority or in

---

[16] Commentary to *Current Law Statutes*.   [17] Law Com No 216 (n15), last sentence of [4.37].
[18] Law Com No 245 *Evidence in Criminal Proceedings: Hearsay and Related Topics* (Cm 3670, 1997).
[19] Merely abstaining from running them together, as s 13 of the Civil Evidence Act 1995 had done.
[20] There is a small number of other minor alterations of form.
[21] *R v Skinner* [2005] EWCA Crim 1439, [23] (decided under the old law, but applicable to the new).

relation to its records; and 'public authority' includes any public or statutory undertaking, any government department and any person holding office under Her Majesty.

(5) The court may, having regard to the circumstances of the case, direct that all or any of the above provisions of this section do not apply in relation to a particular document or record, or description of documents or records.

This provision is intended to allow the documents falling within it to prove themselves; that is, not to require even the open-ended process of authentication demanded of 'statements' in other forms of document. It was intended as a means of simplification,[22] justified positively, by routine reliance upon regularly recorded documents of this character by those most affected by them, and negatively, by the difficulty of providing authentication by human beings when the whole aim of modern business methods is to reduce the amount of human involvement in such documentation. Its reach is enhanced by the broad definitions in s 9(4).

It must be stressed that this provision merely secures admission of the documents; their effect will depend upon their weight,[23] and that, in its turn, will often depend upon the cogency of the evidence demonstrating the efficiency of the system of recording adopted. In an extreme case of unreliability, the court will be able to invoke the provisions of s 9(5) to exclude a document altogether. Secondary evidence of lost primary public records may be received.[24]

In criminal proceedings, most difficulties of proof were eliminated by s 27 of the Criminal Justice Act 1988, and are now expressed in s 133 of the Criminal Justice Act 2003.

THE CIVIL PROCEDURE RULES

These rules supplement the existing law by providing a simplified procedure that may reduce the need to rely upon older methods.[25] Section 14(2) of the Civil Evidence Act 1995 preserved all existing exceptions to the older rules restricting proof of the contents of documents, and in s 14(3), endorsed a number of specific statutory provisions.[26]

The new rules provide a much more liberal scheme for disclosure and inspection of documents in advance.[27] CPR 31.6 imposes a duty[28] upon a party to disclose:

(a) the documents on which he relies; and

(b) the documents which—

  (i) adversely affect his own case;

  (ii) adversely affect another party's case; or

---

[22] Law Com No 216 (n15), [4.38].

[23] See *Post Office Counters v Mahida* [2003] EWCA Civ 1583, [26], in which the secondary evidence, while admissible, was not regarded as sufficient to prove the amount of a debt, given that the party relying upon the evidence had destroyed the originals.

[24] *Miller-Foulds v Department of Constitutional Affairs* [2008] EWHC 3443 (Ch), [34].

[25] Under continuing review, see e.g. CPR 32(20) introduced in 2005 for notarial documents.

[26] Section 2, Documentary Evidence Act 1868; s 2, Documentary Evidence Act 1882; s 1, Evidence (Colonial Statutes) Act 1907; s 1, Evidence (Foreign, Dominion and Colonial Documents) Act 1933; and s 5, Oaths and Evidence (Overseas Authorities and Countries) Act 1963.

[27] In Pt 31. There are variations in relation to the different 'tracks'. In Canada material in electronic form has been excluded from the definition of 'document' for this purpose: *BMG Canada v John Doe* (2005) 252 DLR (4th) 342.

[28] In the standard case.

(iii) support another party's case; and

(c) the documents which he is obliged to disclose by a relevant practice direction.

This applies to documents that are, or have been under his control,[29] and which, in the case of those falling into the latter two categories listed above, he has discovered after making a reasonable search.[30] Only one copy of each document need be disclosed.[31] Disclosure is by list, indicating any documents for which a claim to withhold inspection is being made.[32] Rights are conferred to inspect, in addition, documents mentioned in a statement of case, witness statements, or summaries, affidavits, and subject to the provisions of CPR 35.10(4), expert reports.[33] Such a right entitles a party to a copy upon request.[34] It should be noted that provision is made for disclosure before proceedings start,[35] and from third parties.[36] Where documents have been disclosed to a party, he is taken to admit the authenticity of such documents unless he serves a notice requiring the document to be proved at the trial.[37]

It has already been remarked that the new rules amalgamate notices of reliance upon hearsay, and service of a witness statement.[38] It should, however, be mentioned that, in the case of other broadly documentary evidence, importantly including that which is receivable without further proof under s 9 of the Civil Evidence Act 1995, notice must be given of intention to use the evidence.[39] This is designed to give the other party a suitable opportunity to inspect the document,[40] and to agree to its admission without the necessity of formal proof; in default of such notice, the evidence is inadmissible.[41]

It should be stressed that the precise mode of operation of the new rules is uncertain, largely because of the wide discretionary power conferred upon the courts, especially by CPR 32.1(c), which authorizes directions as to 'the way in which evidence is to be placed before the courts'.[42] It is neither fruitful to speculate, nor possible to anticipate, just how these sweeping powers will be exercised. It was, however, held in *Mahida v Post Office Counters Ltd*[43] that the discretion to exclude evidence in civil proceedings implied the power to accept copies, even when the originals could not be produced owing to the fault of the party seeking to rely upon the copies. On the other hand, where a central issue turned on the correspondence of those copies to the original, the court felt that it would be unfair to determine it without access to the originals.[44]

PUBLIC DOCUMENTS

In *Mortimer v M'Callan*,[45] it was held to be unnecessary for originals of the books of the Bank of England to be produced. Alderson B said that, if they were not removable on the

---

[29] CPR 31.8.   [30] CPR 31.7.

[31] CPR 31.9, unless reliance is to be placed upon a different version.   [32] CPR 31.10.

[33] CPR 31.14.   [34] CPR 31.15(c).   [35] CPR 31.16.

[36] CPR 31.17. See also CPR 34.2(4)(b) authorizing the production of documents to the court in advance of the hearing on the direction of the court.

[37] CPR 32.19. See also CPR 34.2, which is directed to witnesses rather than to parties.

[38] CPR 33.2(1).   [39] CPR 33.6, specifically referring to plans, photographs, and models.

[40] See CPR 33.6(8).   [41] CPR 33.6(3), using the expression not receivable at a trial.

[42] For example, it seems still to be uncertain how far documents must be disclosed in intelligible form: *Paddick v Associated Newspapers* [2003] EWHC 2991 (QB), [26].   [43] [2003] EWCA Civ 1583.

[44] Where a reasonable explanation was, however, given for the absence of the original of an option agreement, a copy has been accepted even though the whole case turned on correspondence between the copy and the lost original: *Park Lane Ventures Ltd v Locke* [2006] EWHC 1578 (Ch).   [45] (1840) 6 M & W 58.

ground of public inconvenience, that was similar in to the case of physically immove-able things.[46] At common law, the contents of numerous public documents[47] could be proved by copies of various kinds, on account of the inconvenience that would have been occasioned by production of the originals. The mode of proving public documents is now governed by a host of statutes, and, it is possible to mention here only a few of more, or less, general application.

Private Acts of Parliament are, where necessary, proved by the production of a Queen's Printer's, or Stationery Office, copy.[48] Royal proclamations may be proved by production of a Queen's Printer's copy, or of the gazette containing them, or of a copy certified to be correct by the appropriate official.[49] Orders in Council and statutory instruments are proved in the same way.[50] Journals of either House of Parliament are proved by production of a Queen's Printer's copy.[51]

By-laws are proved under s 238 of the Local Government Act 1972, by the production of a printed copy, endorsed with a certificate purporting to be signed by the proper officer, containing details concerning the making, and confirming, of the by-law, and certifying that the document is a true copy.

Proclamations, treaties, and other acts of state of any foreign state, or British colony, may be proved either by examined copy, or by a copy authenticated with the seal of the foreign state or British colony.[52]

Records of the Supreme Court may be proved by production of any document sealed, or stamped with the seal or stamp, of the court.[53]

Records preserved in the Public Record Office are proved by copies certified by the Keeper of the Public Records,[54] and entries in registers that may be held on computer, kept in the Patent Office, are proved by copies certified by the Comptroller,[55] like those relating

---

[46] See also Pollock CB in *Sayer v Glossop* (1848) 2 Exch 409, 441.

[47] See 593, for a definition of a public document.

[48] Evidence Act 1845, s 3; Documentary Evidence Act 1882, equating Stationery Office copies with those of the Queen's Printer, or government printer, referred to in other statutes. Under s 3 of the Interpretation Act 1978, every Act is a Public Act to be judicially noticed as such, unless the contrary is expressly provided by the Act; it applies to Acts coming into force after 1890, and re-enacts an earlier provision applying to Acts passed since 1850. Generally speaking, therefore, it is unnecessary to produce any particular copy of a modern statute.

[49] Evidence Act 1845, s 3; Documentary Evidence Act 1868, s 2: see *West Midlands Parole Board v French* [2008] EWHC 2631 (Admin), [43]–[44].

[50] *R v Clarke* [1969] 2 QB 91, [1969] 1 All ER 924. Cf *Snell v Unity Finance Ltd* [1964] 2 QB 203, [1963] 3 All ER 50, suggesting judicial notice may be taken of all statutory instruments. In *R v Koon Cheung Tang* [1995] Crim LR 813, the Court of Appeal disapproved of objection to informal copies in the absence of any sug-gestion that they were wrong, and in *Hammond v Wilkinson* (2001) 165 JP 786, made it quite clear that any technical failure to prove them could be remedied after the formal closure of the prosecution case. In Ireland they must be proved: *People (DPP) v Cleary* [2005] 2 IR 189.   [51] Evidence Act 1845, s 3.

[52] Evidence Act 1851, s 7. Despite some technical difficulty, it appears that s 7 applies to the Republic of Ireland, as it applies elsewhere: see *R v McGlinchy* [1985] 9 NIJB 62.

[53] Supreme Court Act 1981, s 132.

[54] Public Records Act 1958, s 9; see also Public Records Act 1958 (Admissibility of Electronic Copies of Public Records) Order 2001, made under ss 8 and 9 of the Electronic Communications Act 2000, allowing admissibility of copies from an official website.

[55] Patents Act 1977, s 32, as substituted by the Patents, Designs and Marks Act 1986, Sch 1. The version held on the computer can be shown to be in error by extrinsic evidence: *Re European Patent (UK) 0469776 in the name of Eveready Battery Co Inc* [2000] RPC 852.

to companies, which may also be held on computer,[56] and may be proved by copies signed or sealed by the Registrar.[57]

Notices and directions made by the Home Secretary under the Terrorism Act 2000 are admissible in evidence, and deemed authentic, unless proved otherwise.[58]

Finally, two more general provisions may be noted: the effect of s 1 of the Evidence Act 1845 is that, when a statute permits a document to be proved by certified or sealed copy, it is unnecessary to prove certification or sealing; the production of the certified or sealed copy suffices. Under s 14 of the Evidence Act 1851, whenever any book or other document is of such a public nature as to be admissible in evidence on production from proper custody, and no statute exists that renders its contents provable by means of a copy, it may be proved by certified, or examined, copy. The upshot of these two provisions, together with those of numerous special statutes, is that a very large number of copy documents may be put in evidence on mere production to the court, without there being any question of accounting for the original, or proving the accuracy of the copy.

BANKERS' BOOKS

At common law, bankers' books, other than those of the Bank of England, are private documents; the inconvenience that would have been occasioned by the necessity of producing the originals as, and when, required for the purposes of any litigation was eliminated by the Bankers' Books Evidence Act 1879. Provided that the book is one of the ordinary ones of the bank, in its custody, the entry made in the ordinary course of business, and the copy examined against the original (all of which matters can be proved by the affidavit or the testimony of an officer of the bank),[59] a copy of an entry in a banker's book shall, in all legal proceedings, be received as prima facie evidence of such entry, and of the matters, transactions, and accounts therein recorded.[60] The application of these provisions has been very sensibly extended to modern forms of bookkeeping, such as microfilmed and computerized records.[61] This reform does not, however, extend beyond the form of the records to their substance, and it seems that copies of letters sent by the bank,[62] of cheques and paying-in slips,[63] or of records of meetings,[64] would still not be covered by the provisions. Under s 7, any party to a legal proceeding can apply, if necessary without notice, for an order that he be at liberty to inspect, and take copies of, any entries in a banker's books for the purpose of such proceedings.[65] This section, like the rest of the Act, applies to both civil

---

[56] Companies Act 2006, s 1114.   [57] Companies Act 2006, s 1085.

[58] Terrorism Act 2000, s 120.   [59] Sections 4 and 5.

[60] Section 3. The section creates an exception to the hearsay rule as to the transactions to which the entry relates: *Harding v Williams* (1880) 14 Ch D 197, questioned in argument in *Arnott v Hayes* (1887) 56 LJ Ch 844, 847; but see *Myers v DPP* [1965] AC 1001, 1028 and 1033. See also *Elsey v Taxation Comr of Commonwealth of Australia* (1969) 121 CLR 99.

[61] A new definition clause, s 9, substituted by the Banking Act 1979, Sch 6, has applied since 1982, although *Barker v Wilson* [1980] 2 All ER 81, [1980] 1 WLR 884 had already indicated the capacity of judicial intervention to achieve the same result. See also *ANZ Banking Group Ltd v Griffiths* (1988) 49 SASR 385; *R v Saffron* (1988) 36 ACR 262, 290.   [62] *R v Dadson* (1983) 77 Cr App Rep 91.

[63] *Williams v Williams* [1988] QB 161, [1987] 3 All ER 257.   [64] *Re Howglen Ltd* [2001] 1 All ER 376.

[65] Although obtaining such an order is not a condition precedent to putting a copy into evidence: *Wheatley and Penn v Comr of Police of the British Virgin Islands* [2006] UKPC 24, [2006] 1 WLR 1683 (the local statute is in identical terms to those of the English Act).

and criminal proceedings.[66] In civil proceedings, it is well established that the provision is to be applied according to the ordinary rules of disclosure,[67] and in particular, that it cannot be used to compel the revelation of incriminating matters.[68] There was no discovery in criminal proceedings, and, for many years, the application of the Act in such proceedings was left untested. In *Williams v Summerfield*,[69] it was, however, held that to apply the same ban on self-incrimination would frustrate the operation of the Act to criminal proceedings, and that an application could be granted upon conditions analogous to those applying to search warrants. The order is such a serious invasion of privacy that it should not be made without the most careful consideration, and the court granting it should satisfy itself that there is other evidence to support the charge,[70] and that the order is limited to entries strictly relevant, especially temporally, to the charge.[71] It is generally desirable that notice be given to anyone affected by an order,[72] although it should be noted that the account need not be that of a party to the proceedings, and may even be that of a person incompetent to testify.[73] These safeguards may, in some circumstances, lead courts to approve of action under these provisions in preference to those under less fastidious statutory provisions,[74] and in others, to construe such provisions with particular care to avoid inconsistency.[75] It remains to be seen how far the provisions of the Civil Evidence Act 1995, or of the Civil Procedure Rules,[76] will be permitted to supplant these provisions.[77]

SECTION 2.   PROOF OF THE EXECUTION OF PRIVATE DOCUMENTS

The statutes that enable the contents of public documents to be proved by copies also dispense with the necessity of proving that the documents have been properly executed. In the case of a public document, therefore, the mere production of the appropriate copy will suffice to put it in evidence, but something more than production is required in the case of a private document. The court will require to be satisfied by evidence that it was duly executed, unless it is more than twenty years old and comes from the proper custody, when there is a presumption of formal validity. Due execution of a private document is proved by showing that it was signed by the person by whom it purports to have been signed and,

---

[66]   Which, in Scotland, include a criminal petition: *Carmichael v Sexton* 1986 SLT 16n.

[67]   *Re Bankers' Books Evidence Act 1879, R v Bono* (1913) 29 TLR 635.

[68]   *Waterhouse v Barker* [1924] 2 KB 759.   [69]   [1972] 2 QB 512, [1972] 2 All ER 1334.

[70]   *R v Nottingham City Justices, ex p Lynn* (1984) 79 Cr App Rep 238. The court will be wary of a situation in which the charge is laid simultaneously with the application for the order, so as formally to satisfy the requirements of the section.

[71]   In *R v Marlborough Street Stipendiary Magistrate, ex p Simpson* (1980) 70 Cr App Rep 291, orders were quashed, largely on this basis. A party cannot necessarily prevent an order being made by proclaiming an intention to plead guilty: *Owen v Sambrook* [1981] Crim LR 329.

[72]   *R v Grossman* (1981) 73 Cr App Rep 302.

[73]   *R v Andover Justices, ex p Rhodes* [1980] Crim LR 644, in which this was, in fact, regarded as a further reason for making the order.

[74]   See *R v Epsom Justices, ex p Bell* [1989] STC 169; *R v Crown Court at Southwark, ex p Bowles* [1998] AC 641, [1998] 2 All ER 193.   [75]   *R v Crown Court at Lewes, ex p Hill* (1991) 93 Cr App Rep 60.

[76]   See *Re Howglen Ltd* [2001] 1 All ER 376.

[77]   The provisions of para 7(1)(b) of Sch 3 to the Prisoners and Criminal Proceedings (Scotland) Act 1993 were permitted to do so in *Lord Advocate's Reference (No 1 of 1996)* 1996 JC 152.

when necessary, that it was attested. Accordingly, proof of handwriting, and attestation, will be discussed before various presumptions applicable to documents are considered.[78] The section will conclude with a brief reference to a special provision permitting the use of electronic signatures.

PROOF OF HANDWRITING

There are three types of evidence of handwriting that call for discussion: testimonial evidence; opinion; and comparison.

Testimonial evidence

Testimonial evidence may take one of the following forms: the testimony of the person whose handwriting is to be proved; his admissible hearsay statement; the testimony of someone who saw the document executed (whether an attesting witness or a bystander); and an admissible hearsay statement of someone other than the person whose handwriting is in question. Nothing need be said with regard to any of these forms of testimonial evidence, except that it is usually unnecessary, in the first instance, for a witness to the signature to do more than swear that he saw someone sign in a particular name. The name will, in itself, be sufficient evidence of the identity of the signatory with the person whose handwriting is to be proved,[79] unless there are circumstances calling for investigation, or unless, perhaps, the name is a very common one.[80]

Opinion

Witnesses who have not seen the document in question written, or signed, may depose to their opinion that the writing is that of a particular person. Such opinion may be based upon the witness's acquaintance with the handwriting of the person in question through having seen him write on former occasions. It makes no difference whether these occasions were many, or few, and whether the signature was merely that of the signatory's surname without the addition of the Christian names appearing on the document before the court,[81] although these matters will affect the weight of the evidence.

It is unnecessary that the witness who thus deposes to his opinion should have seen the person whose writing is in question write at all, for it will be sufficient if he has received documents purporting to be written, or signed, by him,[82] and the capacity in which he has done so is immaterial, although this may affect the weight of the evidence:[83]

The clerk who constantly read the letters, the broker who was ever consulted upon them, is as competent to judge whether another signature is that of the writer of the letters, as the merchant to whom they were addressed. The servant who has habitually carried letters addressed by me to others has an opportunity of obtaining knowledge of my writing though he never saw me write or received a letter from me.

---

[78] The authenticity of documents that have been disclosed in civil proceedings is governed by CPR 32.19: see above. The due execution of a document might be formally admitted in a criminal case under s 10 of the Criminal Justice Act 1967.   [79] *Roden v Ryde* (1843) 4 QB 626.

[80] *Jones v Jones* (1841) 9 M & W 75.   [81] *Lewis v Sapio* (1827) Mood & M 39.

[82] *Harrington v Fry* (1824) 1 C & P 289.

[83] *Doe d Mudd v Suckermore* (1837) 5 Ad & El 703, 750, Lord Denman CJ.

There must, however, have been a sufficient opportunity for the witness to acquire such knowledge of the handwriting in question as to make it worthwhile receiving his evidence.[84]

Comparison

In some sense it is true to say that:[85]

All evidence of handwriting, except where the witness sees the document written, is in its nature comparison. It is the belief which a witness entertains on comparing the writing in question with an example in his mind derived from some previous knowledge.

Under s 8 of the Criminal Procedure Act 1865 handwriting may also be proved by comparison in a more specific sense. A document that is proved[86] to have been signed, or written, by the person whose handwriting is in issue is first produced, and this is compared with the writing[87] that is being considered by the court.[88] On the basis of such comparison, a handwriting expert may give evidence,[89] although the judge is entitled to reject it in the light of other evidence.[90] The rigour of the old law restricting a witness to testifying to points of comparison, rather than to the identity of two pieces of handwriting, has probably not survived s 3 of the Civil Evidence Act 1972.[91]

Although the evidence may be thought to be of less weight, an opinion with regard to the handwriting of the two documents may be given by a witness who is not an expert, or the document may be submitted to the court in order that the handwriting on each of them may be compared.[92] The document thus submitted to the jury for comparison with the one in dispute need not be relevant to the issues in the case in any other way,[93] and, if he gives evidence, the alleged writer may be asked to write in court for comparison with that on the disputed document.[94]

Conclusions based on comparison of handwriting by those who are not experts must obviously be treated with considerable caution, and the Court of Criminal Appeal has sometimes quashed convictions after examining two specimens of handwriting that had been submitted to the jury at the trial.[95] It is wrong[96] for a judge to invite the jury to make a comparison without the guidance of an expert, although, where they have to be allowed

---

[84] *R v O'Brien* (1911) 7 Cr App Rep 29; *Pitre v R* [1933] 1 DLR 417 (sight of two letters, and two postcards, insufficient).   [85] (n83), Patteson J.

[86] The section applies to civil and criminal cases, and in both instances, the standard of proof is the one normally appropriate to those proceedings: *R v Ewing* [1983] QB 1039, [1983] 2 All ER 645. See also *R v Sim* [1987] 1 NZLR 356.

[87] If the original has been lost, a facsimile may be used: *Lockheed-Arabia Corp v Owen* [1993] QB 806, [1993] 3 All ER 641.

[88] Which must itself be the document in dispute: *R v Nicholas* [1988] Tas SR 155.

[89] *R v Silverlock* (1894) 2 QB 766. It may be necessary to establish the basis of such expertise on a voir dire, although questions of methodology go to weight rather than to admissibility: *R v Bonython* (1984) 15 ACR 364.   [90] *Fuller v Strum* [2001] EWCA Civ 1879, [2002] 2 All ER 87.

[91] See also *R v Mazzone* (1985) 43 SASR 330, 339.

[92] In *R v Stephens* [1999] 3 NZLR 81, the Court of Appeal regarded such a procedure as inappropriate. See also, in Canada, *R v Tahal* (1999) 137 CCC 3d 206.

[93] *Birch v Ridgway* (1858) 1 F & F 270; *Adami v R* (1959) 108 CLR 605. It may even be an otherwise inadmissible confession: see *S v Duna* 1984 (2) SA 591.   [94] *Cobbett v Kilminster* (1865) 4 F & F 490.

[95] *R v Smith* (1909) 2 Cr App Rep 86; *R v Rickard* (1918) 13 Cr App Rep 40.

[96] The rule is less stringent in Australia: see *R v Burns and Collins* [2001] SASC 263, 123 ACR 226, [58], [59]: but stronger in New Zealand: *R v Stephens* [1999] 3 NZLR 81.

to consider exhibits, he cannot do more than warn them of the risks of comparison.[97] In Australia, the question has been raised of possible prejudice to the accused as a result of counsel asking the accused to provide a specimen by writing in court during cross-examination.[98] It has been held that a policeman who induced a prisoner to write while under arrest, in order that his handwriting might be compared with that on a threatening letter that he was alleged to have written, was a biased witness, and that his evidence of opinion based on a comparison ought not to have been submitted to the jury;[99] in *R v Harvey*,[100] it was said that the jury ought not to act on a comparison of the handwriting in books found in the possession of the prisoner with that on a document alleged to have been forged by him. These decisions may have turned on their special facts, for it appears to have been ruled in a later case that evidence by a policeman that he had seen the accused write for his own purposes pending trial was admissible.[101]

In spite of this variety of methods, there might be great difficulty in authenticating handwriting of any antiquity, and a presumption of due execution is also needed.

PROOF OF ATTESTATION

It is convenient to deal separately with proof of the attestation of wills, and other documents required by law to be attested.

Wills

If it becomes necessary to prove the due execution of a will, it is essential to call one of the attesting witnesses, if available. Before other evidence is admissible, it must be shown that all of the attesting witnesses are dead, insane, beyond the jurisdiction, or that none of them can be traced. This requirement holds good even if the execution can be proved by those who saw it, although they were not attesting witnesses, but the witness is treated as if he had been called by the court so he may be cross-examined by the party seeking to prove execution,[102] professional privilege cannot be claimed in respect of his previous statements to solicitors concerning execution,[103] and any other evidence may be given if he denies execution, or refuses to testify.[104]

If none of the attesting witnesses can be called for the reasons indicated in the previous paragraph, steps must be taken to prove the handwriting of at least one of them. This constitutes secondary evidence of attestation.

---

[97] *R v O'Sullivan* [1969] 2 All ER 237, [1969] 1 WLR 497; *R v Tilley* [1961] 3 All ER 406, [1961] 1 WLR 1309; *R v Smith* (1968) 52 Cr App Rep 648.   [98] *R v McCarthy and Martin* (1984) 14 ACR 73.

[99] *R v Crouch* (1850) 4 Cox CC 163. Perhaps this case is best regarded as turning on an analogy with those in which the answers to questions improperly put by policemen to prisoners in custody were rejected.

[100] (1869) 11 Cox CC 546.

[101] *R v McCartney and Hansen* (1928) 20 Cr App Rep 179. For further cases turning on the proof of handwriting, see *Lucas v Williams & Sons* [1892] 2 QB 113, and *R v Hope* (1955) 39 Cr App Rep 33. See also *R v Day* [1940] 1 All ER 402.

[102] *Oakes v Uzzell* [1932] P 19; *Re Webster, Webster v Webster* [1974] 3 All ER 822n, [1974] 1 WLR 1641 (general cross-examination by both parties permissible).

[103] *Re Fuld's Estate (No 2), Hartley v Fuld* [1965] P 405, [1965] 2 All ER 657.

[104] *Bowman v Hodgson* (1867) LR 1 P & D 362; *Re Ovens's Goods* (1892) 29 LR Ir 451, *Re Vere-Wardale, Vere-Wardale v Johnson* [1949] P 395, [1949] 2 All ER 250.

If evidence of handwriting is unobtainable, evidence of those who saw the will executed, or any other evidence from which an inference of due execution can be drawn, becomes admissible, but it seems that every effort must first be made to prove the handwriting of one of the attesting witnesses.[105] If a will is proved to have been in existence after the testator's death, a copy may be admitted to probate on proof that the original was signed by the testator, and bore the signature of two attesting witnesses,[106] although the person giving this evidence is unable to recollect their names.[107] It should, perhaps, be added that, when probate is sought in common form, the rigorous requirements as to proof of due execution to which reference has just been made do not apply.

Other attested documents

The comparatively few documents, other than wills, to the validity of which attestation is essential, may be proved by the testimony of one of the subscribing witnesses, but it is unnecessary to call any of them if the person wishing to prove due execution does not desire to do so. He may content himself with proving the handwriting of an attesting witness, and, if he is unable to do this, he may have recourse to other evidence. Section 3 of the Evidence Act 1938 provides that, in any proceedings, civil or criminal, an instrument to the validity of which attestation is requisite may, instead of being proved by an attesting witness, be proved in the manner in which it might be proved if no attesting witness were alive. By virtue of s 7 of the Criminal Procedure Act 1865 (which applies to civil and criminal cases), instruments to the validity of which attestation is not necessary may be proved as if there had been no attesting witnesses.

PRESUMPTIONS RELATING TO DOCUMENTS

Attestation, like handwriting, would not be easily proved in the case of a document of any antiquity, but practical difficulties are, in the main, obviated by the presumption of due execution that attaches to a document proved, or purporting to be, not less than twenty years old, provided it is produced from proper custody. 'Proper custody' is that which was reasonable, and natural, under the circumstances of the particular case. The other basic fact of the presumption—the age of the document—is prescribed by s 4 of the Evidence Act 1938 for criminal, and civil, cases. At common law, the period was thirty years.

Several other useful presumptions relating to documents may be mentioned. A document is presumed to have been executed on the date it bears;[108] alterations in a deed are presumed to have been made before execution, otherwise the entire deed might be avoided; but alterations in a will are presumed to have been made after execution because they would not invalidate the entire testament.[109] It is sometimes said that there is a presumption that a deed, even when less than twenty years old, was duly sealed,

---

[105] *Clarke v Clarke* (1879) 5 LR Ir 47.
[106] There is a presumption that both signed at the same time: *Bedwell v Stammers* (21 March 2003, unreported) Ch.
[107] *Re Phibb's Estate* [1917] P 93; *Re Webb, Smith v Johnson* [1964] 2 All ER 91, [1964] 1 WLR 509.
[108] *Anderson v Weston* (1840) 6 Bing NC 296.   [109] *Doe d Tatum v Catomore* (1851) 16 QB 745.

but this is not a presumption that is at all clearly established by the authorities.[110] On the other hand, a party may be estopped from denying that attestation took place in his presence.[111]

ELECTRONIC SIGNATURE[112]

Now that so many commercial documents are made, and transmitted, electronically, it has been thought necessary[113] to make formal provision for the admissibility of electronic 'signatures' to validate such documents. An appropriate provision was enacted as s 7 of the Electronic Communications Act 2000, and deliberately adopted a broad, and non-technical, definition of such a signature in subs (2):

For the purposes of this section an electronic signature is so much of anything in electronic form as—

(a) is incorporated into or otherwise logically associated with any electronic communication or electronic data; and

(b) purports to be so incorporated or associated for the purpose of being used in establishing the authenticity of the communication or data, the integrity of the communication or data, or both.

In addition, s 8 gives a broad power to the minister to modify the rules by statutory instrument.[114] The common law had already adopted a generous view towards the admissibility of material in electronic form, and as this provision supplements, rather than supplants, the common law, there is every reason to suppose that no insuperable difficulties will emerge. It remains the case that the automatic inclusion of the sender's email address in an electronic communication will not, without more, constitute a signature.[115]

It should also be noted that CPR 5.3 provides that:

Where any of these Rules or any practice direction requires a document to be signed, that requirement shall be satisfied if the signature is printed by computer or other mechanical means.

SECTION 3. ADMISSIBILITY OF EXTRINSIC EVIDENCE

The major problems with which this section is concerned are first, whether, once a transaction has been embodied in a document, evidence may be given of terms other than those it mentions, and, second, the extent to which evidence may be given of the meaning of the

---

[110] *Re Sandilands* (1871) LR 6 CP 411; *National Provincial Bank of England v Jackson* (1886) 33 Ch D 1, 11 and 14; *Re Balkis Consolidated Co Ltd* (1888) 58 LT 300.

[111] *Shah v Shah* [2001] EWCA Civ 527, [2001] 3 All ER 138.

[112] See further Mason *Electronic Signatures in Law* (2003); e-Signature LJ *passim*.

[113] See Electronic Signatures Directive 1999/93/EC, OJ L13 19 January 2001, 12, but see also Wright 'Electronic Signatures—not worth the paper they're written on?', explaining the Commission's disappointment at the implementation of this Directive.

[114] No such instruments appear to have been made at the time of editing.

[115] *Mehta v J Pereira Fernandes SA* [2006] EWHC 813 (Ch), [2006] 2 All ER 891, [30].

terms used in the document. In each instance, the problem is one of the admissibility of 'extrinsic evidence', an expression that means any evidence other than the document the contents of which are under consideration. It is often said to be 'parol evidence', no doubt because it usually takes the form of oral testimony, but it may consist of other documents.

THE CONCLUSIVENESS OF A DOCUMENT AS EVIDENCE OF THE TERMS OF THE TRANSACTION IT EMBODIES[116]

Statement and illustrations of the rule

Statement

Extrinsic evidence is generally inadmissible when it would, if accepted, have the effect of adding to, varying, or contradicting the terms of a judicial record, a transaction required by law to be in writing, or a document constituting a valid and effective contract, or other trans-action.[117] Most judicial statements of the rule are concerned with its application to contracts, and one of the best known is that of Lord Morris who regarded it as indisputable that:[118]

Parol testimony cannot be received to contradict, vary, add to or subtract from the terms of a written contract or the terms in which the parties have deliberately agreed to record any part of their contract.

Statements of this nature are best regarded as statements of the effect of the substantive law of merger, which is now based on the presumed intention of the parties.[119] If the court is satisfied that they effectively agreed to be bound by a written instrument, they are bound by its terms although unacquainted with them,[120] even though one of the parties believes that something said in the course of the negotiations is still binding. In such circumstances, it would be pointless to admit extrinsic evidence with regard to those negotiations, because it is irrelevant,[121] and a fortiori evidence of negotiations for other agreements.[122] Similarly evidence that one of the parties to a written agreement did not intend to be contractually bound is inadmissible.[123] In conveyancing, where certainty is at a premium, parol evidence is particularly unwelcome.[124] Evidence of antecedent negotiations is relevant, and admissible, if they retain their contractual effect, or legal significance, after the writing has been brought into existence. Such evidence is always admissible if tendered to establish the existence of a contract collateral to the writing, or the conclusion of a contract that is partly oral, and partly in writing. Evidence of antecedent negotiations is likewise admissible when relevant under provisions of the substantive law as the requirement, such as s 14(3) of the Sale of Goods Act 1979, which requires the buyer to make known to the seller that he relies on his skill and judgment.[125]

---

[116] See Stevens in Burrows and Peel (eds) *Contract Terms* (2007), 101.

[117] The position is similar in Scotland: *Smith v Mackintosh* 1989 SCLR 83.

[118] *Bank of Australasia v Palmer* [1897] AC 540, 545. See also *Goss v Lord Nugent* (1833) 5 B & Ad 58.

[119] See Wedderburn [1959] *CLJ* 58.   [120] *Parker v South Eastern Rly Co* (1877) 2 CPD 416, 421.

[121] *Lexmead (Basingstoke) Ltd v Lewis* [1982] AC 225, [1980] 1 All ER 978, 263, 1002 (unaffected on this point by the subsequent decision in the House of Lords).

[122] *Stroude v Beazer Homes Ltd* [2005] EWCA Civ 265, [2005] NPC 45.

[123] *Smith v Mansi* [1962] 3 All ER 857, [1963] 1 WLR 26.

[124] *WF Trustees Ltd v Expo Safety Systems Ltd* (1993) The Times, 24 May.

[125] *Gillespie Bros & Co v Cheney Eggar & Co* [1896] 2 QB 59; *Manchester Liners Ltd v Real Ltd* [1922] 2 AC 74, 85; *The Preload Company of Canada Ltd v The City of Regina* (1958) 13 DLR (2d) 305.

Illustrations

Judicial records

Once it has been drawn up, the order of a court is conclusive evidence of that which was directed by the judge. Steps may be taken to have clerical errors corrected, and there may be an appeal, but, in any other proceedings, extrinsic evidence of the terms of the decision would be irrelevant.

Transactions required by law to be in writing

Even when a transaction is required by law to be in writing, extrinsic evidence is admissible in aid of the interpretation of the document, but that does not constitute an infringement of the rule under consideration. Additional, or different, terms may not be proved by extrinsic evidence. In *Re Rees*,[126] a testator left part of his estate 'to my trustees absolutely, they well knowing my wishes concerning the same'. The Court of Appeal affirmed the judge's decision, reached without resort to extrinsic evidence, that, as a matter of construction, the estate was given on trust, and accordingly evidence showing that, in the events that had happened, the testator intended his trustees to take it beneficially was inadmissible because it would contradict the terms of the will as construed by the court.

Written contracts

In *Angell v Duke*,[127] the defendant agreed in writing to let a house to the claimant together with the furniture therein. The claimant tendered evidence that, before the execution of the writing, the defendant had orally agreed to send in additional furniture, but it was held that such evidence was inadmissible because, having once executed the writing, without making the terms of the alleged parol agreement part of it, the claimant could not afterwards set up that agreement. It would have contradicted the restriction of the written document to furniture already in the house.

The distinction between an addition, a variation, and a contradiction has not been discussed by the courts. With the possible exception of *Angell v Duke*, cases were treated primarily as ones in which an effort was made to give extrinsic evidence of additional terms. A case that was treated as one of attempted variation is *Re Sutro(L) & Co and Heilbut, Symons & Co.*[128] A written contract having provided for the sale of rubber to be shipped to New York, evidence of a practice under which the goods were dispatched by rail for part of the journey was held to be inadmissible. The admissibility of evidence of a variation of a written contract that has once been concluded is plainly dependent on the substantive law. If, having regard to the rules of consideration, the variation is effective, and if, having regard to statutory provisions such as s 2 of the Law of Property (Miscellaneous Provisions) Act 1989, it is enforceable, evidence of its terms will be received. When these conditions do not apply, such evidence will be irrelevant.

After the agreement had been reduced into writing, it is competent to the parties, at any time before breach of it, by a new contract not in writing, either altogether to waive, dissolve, or annul the former agreement, or in any manner to add to, or subtract from, or vary or qualify the terms of it, and thus to make a new contract, which is to be proved, partly by the written agreement,

---

[126] *Re Rees, Williams v Hopkins* [1950] Ch 204, [1949] 2 All ER 1003.
[127] (1875) 32 LT 320, but see [1959] CLJ 65–6; *Kaplan v Andrews* [1955] 4 DLR 553.
[128] [1917] 2 KB 348.

and partly by the subsequent verbal terms engrafted upon what will thus be left of the written agreement.

These words were spoken in a case[129] in which the claimant had agreed in writing to sell a number of lots of land to the defendant, and tendered evidence of a subsequent oral agreement discharging him from the duty of making a good title to one of the lots. The evidence was held inadmissible under the Statute of Frauds 1677,[130] but the court was clearly of opinion that evidence of the subsequent contractual variation, or discharge, of a written agreement is admissible in the ordinary case.[131]

Henderson v Arthur[132] and *Evans v Roe*[133] primarily turned on the question of whether extrinsic evidence could be received of terms contradicting those of a written agreement. In the former, a lease having been executed under which rent was payable in advance, the lessee was not allowed to give evidence of a prior undertaking by the lessor to accept rent in arrears; in the latter, evidence of a contemporaneous oral agreement that a written contract of service from week to week was to last for a year was rejected. Cases where a person has signed an agreement as 'owner',[134] or 'proprietor',[135] have excluded evidence that he was acting as agent for an undisclosed principal as contradicting the unambiguous statement in the agreement.[136]

Exceptions to, and cases falling outside, the rule

Cases of a subsequent variation, or discharge, of a written agreement may be treated as exceptions to the rule. Transactions required by law to be in writing may be discharged, or varied, by a parol contract, subject, in the case of a variation, to the requirements of relevant statutes, such as s 3 of the Law of Property (Miscellaneous Provisions) Act 1989.[137] Evidence tending to establish such a contract may be regarded as evidence varying, or contradicting, the terms of the original document. The same can be said of evidence varying, or discharging, a contract embodied in a document when writing is not a necessary condition of its validity, or enforceability. The following cases can be regarded either as exceptions to the rule or as falling outside it.

Public registers

Oral evidence has been received, and accepted, although establishing a different tonnage of a ship from that mentioned on the register of ships,[138] and a different proprietorship of a taxicab than that shown on the register of hackney carriages.[139] No reasons were given for the former decision; in the latter, the judgments were exclusively concerned with the

---

[129] *Goss v Lord Nugent* (1833) 5 B & Ad 58, Lord Denman CJ.

[130] See now s 2 of the Law of Property (Miscellaneous Provisions) Act 1989.

[131] A parol discharge as distinct from a variation was held effective in a case coming within s 4 of the Sale of Goods Act 1893 (now repealed), in *Morris v Baron & Co* [1918] AC 1.

[132] [1907] 1 KB 10. See also *Goldfoot v Welch* [1914] 1 Ch 213.   [133] (1872) LR 7 CP 138.

[134] *Humble v Hunter* (1848) 12 QB 310.

[135] *Formby Bros v Formby* (1910) 102 LT 116. This case, and *Humble v Hunter* (n134), were said to be no longer law by Scott LJ in *Epps v Rothnie* [1945] KB 562, [1946] 1 All ER 146; 565, 147 (*sed quaere*). The cases are discussed below: *Humble v Hunter* was held to be good law in *Murphy v Rae* [1967] NZLR 103.

[136] See the converse case of *Universal Steam Navigation Co v J McKelvie & Co* [1923] AC 492, and contrast *Automobile Renault Canada Ltd v Maritime Import Autos Ltd and Kyley* (1962) 31 DLR (2d) 592.

[137] *Morris v Baron & Co* (n131).   [138] *The Recepta* (1889) 14 PD 131.

[139] *Kemp v Elisha* [1918] 1 KB 228.

construction of the relevant statutes. So subject to the terms of the statute under which it is kept, it seems that the contents of a public register are not conclusive,[140] and extrinsic evidence affecting their truth admissible.

Cases concerning the validity or effectiveness of a written contract or other document

Extrinsic evidence is admissible to show that a written contract, or any other document, is void for mistake,[141] or illegality,[142] or for non-compliance with the provisions of a statute,[143] or voidable on account of a fraudulent or innocent misrepresentation.[144] It is also permissible to prove by extrinsic evidence that a deed, or written contract, unconditional on its face, was delivered as an escrow, or signed subject to a condition precedent to its effectiveness as in *Pym v Campbell*,[145] in which the defendants agreed in writing to buy an invention from the claimant, subject to the oral stipulation that the transaction was conditional on the approval of the invention by the defendant's engineer. Extrinsic evidence was received concerning this stipulation, and the fact that the invention had not been approved. Such evidence is also admissible to negate the implication of a warranty,[146] or to raise an equitable defence.[147] The rule under consideration can hardly be said to be infringed in any of the cases mentioned in this paragraph because it applies only to valid and effective transactions.

Consideration

Absence of consideration invalidates a simple contract in writing, and may always be proved by extrinsic evidence. The fact that a bill of exchange contains the words 'for value received' does not render evidence that it was an accommodation bill inadmissible in a relevant case relevant. When a deed contains no reference to consideration, or mentions nominal consideration, extrinsic evidence concerning real consideration has been held admissible. Thus in *Turner v Forwood*,[148] the claimant entered into an agreement under seal with a company and a director in which he assigned a debt due to him from the com-

---

[140] See e.g. British Nationality Act 1981, s 45, which makes certificates merely prima facie evidence of the matters entered on the registers, but conclusive of other matters not so entered. See also *R v Secretary of State for the Environment, ex p Simms* [1991] 2 QB 354, [1990] 3 All ER 490, construing ss 53 and 56 of the Wildlife and Countryside Act 1981 to the effect that, while a 'definitive' map was conclusive of its contents in independent proceedings, such status does not preclude the admission of inconsistent evidence in proceedings designed to correct the map itself.

[141] *Henkel v Royal Exchange Assurance Co* (1749) 1 Ves Sen 317; *Wake v Harrop* (1861) 7 Jur NS 710; *Cowen v Trufitt Bros Ltd* [1899] 2 Ch 309; *Roe v RA Naylor Ltd* (1918) 87 LJKB 958, 968 (*non est factum*); *Craddock Bros Ltd v Hunt* [1923] 2 Ch 136; *United States of America v Motor Trucks Ltd* [1924] AC 196.

[142] *Collins v Blantern* (1767) 2 Wils 341.

[143] *Campbell Discount Co Ltd v Gall* [1961] 1 QB 431, [1961] 2 All ER 104.

[144] *Dobell v Stevens* (1825) 3 B & C 623.

[145] (1856) 6 E & B 370; *Wallis v Littell* (1861) 11 CBNS 369; *Lindley v Lacey* (1864) 17 CBNS 578; *Davis v Jones* (1856) 17 CB 625; *Pattle v Hornibrook* [1897] 1 Ch 25, distinguished in *Smith v Mansi* (n123). See also *Frontier Finance Ltd v Hynes and Niagara Sewing Machine Co* (1956) 10 DLR (2d) 206. In *Re Tait* [1957] VLR 405, instructions for a will were admitted to show that a revocation clause was conditioned on the insertion of other clauses inadvertently omitted. [146] *Burges v Wickham* (1863) 3 B & s 669.

[147] *Martin v Pyecroft* (1852) 2 De GM & G 785, followed in *Scott v Bradley* [1971] Ch 850, [1971] 1 All ER 583; *Wake v Harrop* (n141).

[148] [1951] 1 All ER 746; *Clifford v Turrell* (1845) 1 Y & C Ch Cas 138 (affirmed 14 LJ Ch 390); *Frith v Frith* [1906] AC 254.

pany for £1,015 to the director in consideration of ten shillings, and it was held that oral evidence might be given of an antecedent agreement by the director to pay in full for the debt. The principle underlying such decisions appears to be that, as no consideration need, in general, be expressed in a deed in order that it should be effective, the parties may often be taken to have intended that their arrangements should be carried out partly by deed, and partly by parol. As a matter of conveyancing practice, it became usual to insert a nominal consideration in many deeds in order to avoid the implication of a use, so it was reasonable to infer that, so far as the intention of the parties was concerned, these cases were the same as those in which no consideration was inserted in a deed. There is no authority dealing with the admissibility of extrinsic evidence to vary real consideration stated in a deed. In *Turner v Forwood*, Lord Goddard CJ was not prepared to say that the principle applied by him was confined to cases in which nominal consideration was expressed in a deed, but, if the principle is extended, the question as to what undertakings are to be treated as part of the consideration would give rise to difficulty.

The real nature of the transaction

When it is relevant at common law or in equity, extrinsic evidence may be given of the real nature of any transaction, whether recorded in a document in pursuance of legal requirements, or at the instance of the parties. Thus evidence has been received to show that an apparent sale was really a mortgage,[149] and a secret trust could never be established without recourse to extrinsic means of proof.

Collateral undertakings, contracts partly oral, and partly in writing, or subject to usage

In *De Lassalle v Guildford*[150] the claimant made plain to his defendant landlord that he would not execute a lease unless the defendant gave a warranty concerning the healthy condition of the drains. Such warranty was given orally, and the lease duly executed. The lease did not refer to the state of the drains, but it was held that this fact did not prevent the adduction of oral evidence concerning the warranty. A court may, likewise, come to the conclusion that the parties intended their contract to be partly oral, and partly in writing, in which case, the oral parts may be proved by parol testimony. In *Harris v Rickett*,[151] the defendant was allowed to prove that a written agreement for a loan was accompanied by an oral stipulation that a bill of sale would be given. The claimant contended that the effect of this evidence was to add to, or vary, the writing, but Pollock CB said that: 'the rule relied on by the claimant only applies when the parties to an agreement reduce it to writing and agree or intend that writing should be their agreement'. A further example of the use of extrinsic evidence is provided by cases in which one party has been allowed to establish a trade usage, provided it is not inconsistent with the writing:[152]

[149] *Re Duke of Marlborough, Davis v Whitehead* [1894] 2 Ch 133.
[150] [1901] 2 KB 215; *Morgan v Griffith* (1871) LR 6 Exch 70; *Erskine v Adeane* (1873) 8 Ch App 756; *City and Westminster Properties (1934) Ltd v Mudd* [1959] Ch 129, [1958] 3 All ER 733. A possible distinction between this last case and *Angell v Duke* (n127) is that, in *Angell v Duke*, the lessee did not insist on the provision of further furniture being part of the consideration for his executing the lease. Cf *Couchman v Hill* [1947] KB 554, [1947] 1 All ER 103.   [151] (1959) 4 H & N 1.
[152] Coleridge J in *Brown v Byrne* (1854) 3 E & B 703. Cf *Krall v Burnett* (1887) 25 WR 305.

In all contracts, as to the subject-matter of which known usages prevail, parties are found to proceed with the tacit assumption of these usages, they commonly reduce into writing the special particulars of their agreement but omit to specify these known usages, which are included, however, as of course, by mutual understanding, evidence therefore of such incidents is receivable. The contract in truth is partly express and in writing, partly implied or understood and unwritten.

Memoranda

In some cases, after an oral contract has been concluded, a memorandum relating to the whole, or part, of the transaction is prepared by one of the parties, and handed to the other, which may then be treated as a mere memorandum, and, as it has no contractual effect, additional matter may be proved.[153] Whether the writing is to be treated thus, or whether it will be held to be not a memorandum, but a contractual document, depends on the intention of the parties, which must, lacking direct evidence, be ascertained by means of the inferences that a reasonable man would draw from the terms of the document, and surrounding circumstances. In *Hutton v Watling*,[154] in which a document providing for the sale of a business by the defendant to the claimant, and containing an option to purchase the land on which the business was carried on, was treated as contractual by the Court of Appeal, with the result that the defendant's evidence, in a claim, for specific performance of the option, that no option was given, was held to be inadmissible. The court treated the matter as one of construction, adding that:[155]

The true construction of a document means no more than that the court puts upon it the true meaning, being the meaning which the other party, to whom the document was handed or who is relying upon it, would put upon it as an ordinary intelligent person construing the words in a proper way in the light of the relevant circumstances.

The cases on collateral contracts, contracts partly oral, and partly in writing, contracts subject to usage, and memoranda raise the question whether, at least in its application to contracts, what is often called the parol evidence rule is anything more than an empty tautology.[156] If the law is simply that extrinsic evidence is inadmissible when the parties intended that a document should contain their entire contract, extrinsic evidence is naturally inadmissible because it is irrelevant. Cases such as *Hutton v Watling* show that the rule is not a tautology because the parties are bound by the terms of a document if a reasonable man would have considered the document to be a contractual one. This is so even if one of them thought that the contract contained additional terms not mentioned in the document, or that a clearly expressed term to which he had agreed bore a special meaning.[157]

The Law Commission, although at first inclined to recommend abolition of this rule, ultimately came to the conclusion that it had become too ineffective to cause serious

---

[153] As in *Bank of Australasia v Palmer* (n118).

[154] [1948] Ch 398, [1948] 1 All ER 803; *Stuart v Dundon* [1963] SASR 134.

[155] Lord Greene MR, 403, 805, respectively.

[156] See the discussion of this point in Treitel *The Law of Contract* (12th edn), 214.

[157] See the speech of Lord Denning in *London County Council v Henry Boot & Sons Ltd* [1959] 3 All ER 636, 641. The parties may be bound by terms to which they have agreed, although they both think the terms have a different meaning from that ultimately placed on them by the court.

difficulty, and that more disruption would probably be caused by formal abolition than by leaving it alone.[158]

EXTRINSIC EVIDENCE IN AID OF INTERPRETATION[159]

It was once said that:[160]

The admission of extrinsic circumstances to govern the construction of a written instrument is in all cases an exception to the general rule of law which excludes everything dehors the instrument.

But statements of this nature always had to be read with caution, for it would be impossible to interpret most documents if some extrinsic matter were not allowed to be proved. In modern times, this area of the law has become much less restrictive.[161]

The extent to which a document may be treated as conclusive as to the meaning of its terms is a question of degree. It can hardly ever be completely so, because some extrinsic evidence must be received, but the nature of such evidence, and the purposes for which it may be used in a case in which the meaning of a document is disputed, depends on the standard of interpretation by which the litigation must be decided. The competing standards will be considered first, and then, very briefly, their application to the special cases of commercial documents, and wills.

Standards of interpretation

Wigmore[162] spoke of four possible standards: the popular; the local; the common; and the individual. The popular standard refers to the ordinary meaning of words; the local standard refers to possible variations of the popular within a particular community, trade,[163] or religious sect; the common standard covers the sense in which the words were understood by both parties to a contract; while the individual standard is that of one party to a transaction, and is, in general, relevant only in cases of the construction of wills. Subject to the need to resort to extrinsic evidence in order to ascertain the persons, and things, covered by the words used, the application of the popular standard is a matter of exegesis, aided by judicial notice rather than evidence.[164] Judicial notice may be taken of some local, or trade, usages, but these are matters that usually have to be proved.[165] The application of the common, and individual, standards calls, in the

---

[158] Law Com No 154 (Cmnd 9700) (1986) Pt III. The term 'parol evidence rule', as used in this paper, is confined to the rule so far discussed in this section. The paper is not concerned with the rules discussed in Section 1, and in the remainder of this section.

[159] Since s 21 of the Administration of Justice Act 1982 implemented the recommendations of the 19th Report of the Law Reform Committee on the Interpretation of Wills (Cmnd 5301), it has been possible to eliminate much of the discussion of the old case law to be found in early editions of this work. The position in Australia was stated by the High Court in *Codelfa Construction Pty Ltd v State Railway Authority of NSW* (1982) 149 CLR 337.   [160] Plumer MR in *Colpoys v Colpoys* (1822) Jac 451.

[161] See *ICS Ltd v West Bromwich Building Society* [1998] 1 All ER 98, [1998] 1 WLR 896; Lord Hoffmann, 114e, 912F.   [162] [2458] and [2460].

[163] For an Australian example, see *Homestake Australia Ltd v Metana Minerals NL* (1991) 11 WAR 435.

[164] Thus, in the interest of certainty, a court is entitled to have recourse to previous judicial decisions on the construction of the same words elsewhere: *Crest Nicholson Residential (South) Ltd v McAllister* [2002] EWHC 2443, [2003] 1 All ER 46.

[165] Sometimes by expert evidence: see *Davis v Temco* [1992] CLY 2064.

absence of anything in the nature of a formal admission, for extrinsic evidence, which can be either circumstantial, or testimonial. Assuming that no exclusionary rules apply, the fact that the parties to a contract have a common objective may warrant an inference concerning the meaning they attached to certain clauses, just as the speech habits of a testator may justify a particular construction of the words used by him. The meaning of the contracting parties and the testator could also, subject to exclusionary rules, be proved in the one case by their direct oral evidence, and, in either case, by their out-of-court statements.

According to Wigmore, the application of each of the above standards should be, and to a large extent is, provisional. This means that extrinsic evidence in aid of interpretation may take a variety of forms, and be adduced for a number of different purposes varying with the facts of the particular case, but Wigmore did not deny the existence of restrictions on its admissibility. Such restrictions may, as a matter of law, rule out one or more of the standards that have just been mentioned.

Firstly, there was a general rule (subject to very limited exceptions) excluding statements of intention of the testator, or contracting parties, as evidence of the sense in which words were used by them in the relevant will, or written contract. In the case of wills, that general rule was abrogated by s 21 of the Administration of Justice Act 1982 for wills taking effect after 1 January 1983.

Secondly, the individual standard must always be inapplicable when the court is concerned with the construction, as opposed to the existence, avoidance, or rectification of a contract:[166]

The words used may, and often do, represent a formula which means different things to each side, yet be accepted because that is the only way to get agreement and in the hope that disputes will not arise. The only course there can be is to try to ascertain the natural meaning.

Contracts[167]

In *Prenn v Simmonds*, Lord Wilberforce re-emphasized the width of material that the law already admitted as an aid to construction, describing it as a matrix of facts:[168]

There is no need to appeal here to any modern anti-literal tendencies, for Lord Blackburn's well-known judgment in *River Wear Commissioners v Adamson* (1877) 2 App. Cas. 743, 763 provides ample warrant for a liberal approach. We must, he said, inquire beyond the language and see what the circumstances were with reference to which the words were used, and the object, appearing from those circumstances, which the person using them had in view.

He pointed out, however, that such width did not normally[169] extend to evidence of the negotiations leading up to the agreement,[170] not for technical reasons, but simply because

---

[166] Lord Wilberforce in *Prenn v Simmonds* [1971] 3 All ER 237, 241.

[167] Similar rules apply to notices: *Mannai Investment Co Ltd v Eagle Star Life Assurance Co Ltd* [1997] AC 749, [1997] 3 All ER 352, and even to conveyances, *Piper v Wakeford* [2008] EWCA Civ 1378; but not to contracts only partly in writing: *Maggs v Marsh* [2006] EWCA Civ 1058, [2006] BLR 395.

[168] (n166), 239i, 1384A.

[169] But even these may be considered in establishing the subject matter of the contract: see *Readers Digest Children's Publishing Ltd v Premier Books (UK)* [2002] EWHC 858, [31].

[170] Previous contracts are not automatically excluded as part of the negotiations for a new one: *Hill Casualty and General Insurance Ltd v New Hampshire Insurance Co* [2001] EWCA Civ 735, [2001] LL R 161, [83].

such evidence is likely to be unhelpful to the construction of the ultimately agreed draft.[171] Nor are the declarations by the parties of their subjective intent, or their subsequent actions, normally to be used as an aid to construction.[172] But the width of admissibility is now regarded as so broad that even these boundaries fail to apply to claims for rectification, and are regarded as far from settled, as stated by Lord Hoffmann in his first three numbered propositions in the *ICS* case:

(1) Interpretation is the ascertainment of the meaning which the document would convey to a reasonable person having all the background knowledge which would reasonably have been available to the parties in the situation in which they were at the time of the contract.

(2) The background which was famously referred to by Lord Wilberforce as the 'matrix of fact,' but this phrase is, if anything, an understated description of what the background may include. Subject to the requirement that it should reasonably be available to the parties and to the exception to be mentioned next, it includes absolutely anything which would have affected the way in which the language of the document would have been understood by a reasonable man.

(3) The law excludes from the admissible background the previous negotiations of the parties and their declarations of subjective intent. They are admissible only in an action for rectification. The law makes this distinction for reasons of practical policy and, in this respect only, legal interpretation differs from the way we would interpret utterances in ordinary life. The boundaries of this exception are in some respects unclear.

So liberal a view allows ample scope for the admissibility of evidence of the unreasonable result to which a given interpretation might lead,[173] since as Lord Reid remarked[174] in the *Wickman Tools* case, 'the more unreasonable the result the more unlikely it is that the parties can have intended it'. The force of this view was amplified still further by Lord Diplock in *Antaios Compania Naviera SA v Salen Redierna AB*:[175]

...if detailed semantic and syntactical analysis of words in a commercial contract is going to lead to a conclusion that flouts business commonsense, it must be made to yield to business commonsense.

In other words, commercial contracts are to be construed in the sense that a commercial person would understand them.[176] Similarly, it was stated[177] in *Wickman Tools* that

---

[171] Still less can terms of a draft agreement be regarded as binding in the absence of final agreement: *Bols Distilleries v Superior Yacht Services* [2006] UKPC 45, [2007] 1 WLR 12.

[172] *Wickman Machine Tools (Sales) Ltd v L Schuler AG* [1974] AC 235, [1973] 2 All ER 39, although, even in this respect, some exceptions are allowed, for example in relation to the construction of ancient documents, or ambiguous conveyances: *Ali v Lane* [2006] EWCA Civ 1532, [2006] 48 EGCS 231, [36]. In Australasia, it was held in *Sportsvision Australia Pty Ltd v Tallglen Pty Ltd* (1998) 44 NSWLR 103 that subsequent actions were admissible to identify the subject matter of the contract; and in *Posgold (Big Bell) Pty Ltd v Placer (Western Australia) Pty Ltd* [1999] WASCA 217, 21 WAR 350 and *Gibbons Holdings Ltd v Wholesale Distributors Ltd* [2007] NZSC 37, [2008] 1 NZLR 277, to resolve a latent ambiguity.

[173] To save costs the admissibility of such evidence should be considered in advance of trial: *Anglo-Continental Educational Group (GB) Ltd v Capital Homes (Southern) Ltd (2009)* [2009] EWCA Civ 218, [24].

[174] 251E, 45b.

[175] [1985] AC 191, [1984] 3 All ER 229; 201D, 233i. See *Folkes Group plc v Alexander and Lucas* [2002] EWHC (Ch) 51, [2002] 2 BCLC 254 for a recent application of this approach.

[176] *Sirius International Insurance Co v FAI General Insurance* [2004] UKHL 54, [2005] 1 All ER 191, [19].

[177] By Lord Wilberforce, 261D, 53e.

evidence of surrounding circumstances would be more readily admitted to resolve ambiguities, although ambiguity was not to be equated with mere difficulty of construction. If negotiations have resolved potential ambiguity, then they may to that extent, and for that purpose, be admissible as an aid to construction.[178] On the other hand, the mere fact that words are unambiguous will not shield their interpretation from evidence of surrounding circumstances when it is capable of showing that the clear words failed to express the intentions of the parties.[179]

In particularly strong and convincing obiter dicta the House of Lords in *Chartbrook Ltd v Persimmon Homes Ltd*[180] rejected use of the House's powers to overturn its own previous decisions in this context.

Wills

Most of the discussion of the admissibility of extrinsic evidence in aid of interpretation has been derived from learning devoted to the rules governing the interpretation of wills. It would hardly have made sense to insist upon strict formal rules for making wills, but then allow any vague expression to be interpreted in the light of informal statements of the testator. On the other hand, a succession of cases[181] exemplified the unsatisfactory nature of a system of rigid exclusionary rules, which often defeated the intentions of the testator completely.

For these reasons, the whole question of the interpretation of wills was referred to the Law Reform Committee, which reported in 1973.[182] The entire Committee favoured an extension of the use of extrinsic evidence to resolve ambiguities, misdescription, partial description, and equivocation. It was divided on how far to permit the use of direct evidence of the testator's dispositive intentions. The majority took the view that to allow it in all cases would go further than the rules applying to other documents, and would lead to uncertainty, expense, and delay.[183] This view was accepted, and s 21 of the Administration of Justice Act 1982 embodies it:

(1) This section applies to a will—

    (a) in so far as any part of it is meaningless;

    (b) in so far as the language used in any part of it is ambiguous on the face of it;

    (c) in so far as evidence, other than evidence of the testator's intention, shows that the language used in any part of it is ambiguous in the light of surrounding circumstances.

(2) In so far as this section applies to a will extrinsic evidence of the testator's intention may be admitted to assist in its interpretation.

This section should be read in conjunction with s 20, which extends the application of the equitable doctrine of rectification to wills, and thus allows words to be added to the probate, not, as before, merely to be omitted.

---

[178] See *Proforce Recruit Ltd v The Rugby Group Ltd* [2006] EWCA Civ 69, [36], in which Lord Nicholls' extrajudicial views were mentioned, (2005) 121 LQR 577.

[179] *Mannai Investment Co Ltd v Eagle Star Life Assurance Co Ltd* (n167), 779G; but see also *Melanesian Mission Trust Board v Australian Mutual Provident Society* [1997] 2 EGLR 128, PC, 129F, in which Lord Hope adopts a somewhat more stringent approach.   [180] [2009] UKHL 38, [2009] 1 AC 1101, [41].

[181] Including *Doe d Chichester v Oxenden* (1816) 3 Taunt 147; *Doe d Gord v Needs* (1836) 2 M & W 129; *Charter v Charter* (1874) LR 7 HL 364; *Higgins v Dawson* [1902] AC 1.

[182] Nineteenth Report (Cmnd 5301).   [183] Paragraph 54.

It is not intended that the section will enable a court to make a testator's will for him. Thus, it will not allow complete blanks to be filled in, nor, it is submitted, will it allow vestigial coding to be expanded.[184] The use, and limitations, of the new law were demonstrated in *Re Williams, Wiles v Madgin*,[185] in which a letter written by a testatrix to her solicitor explaining her intentions was admitted to help construe her will, but was unable to remedy the deficiency, which there was the omission of words of gift. The instructions indicated an order of preference of potential beneficiaries, but was of too vague and preparatory a nature to be regarded as more than instructions for a draft. It was held, however, that the letter could be used only to attempt to resolve the ambiguity justifying its admission, and not for any other purpose. The admissibility of this letter under the new provisions may be compared with the inadmissibility of counsel's opinion to help construe a settlement drawn up in consequence of it.[186]

The new section clearly retains the possibility of reference to the testator's direct statement of intention in cases of patent equivocation such as *Doe d Gord v Needs*,[187] to resolve the problem of misdescription, or incomplete description, thus adding to the evidence admissible if facts such as those of *Doe d Hiscocks v Hiscocks*,[188] or *Charter v Charter*,[189] were to recur. It would be of still more assistance in cases such as *Doe d Chichester v Oxenden*,[190] or *Higgins v Dawson*,[191] in which anything except direct evidence of the testator's intention would be admissible to demonstrate the ambiguity, and then, even including such direct evidence of intention, to resolve it.

It seems likely, and is to be hoped, that these provisions will achieve the aim of the Law Reform Committee to make this branch of the law simpler, and more logical. It has been seen that more satisfactory results would apparently have been achieved in the difficult problems thrown up by the old cases, and with the entry into force of these new provisions, it seems that a complicated, and confusing, chapter of the law of evidence can now be closed.

---

[184] As in *Clayton v Lord Nugent* (1844) 13 M & W 200, in which the letters K, L and M were used, and a key made, after the will was rejected.   [185] [1985] 1 All ER 964.
[186] *Rabin v Gerson Berger Assoc Ltd* [1985] 1 All ER 1041, [1985] 1 WLR 595.   [187] (n181).
[188] (1839) 5 M & W 363.   [189] (n181).   [190] (1816) 3 Taunt 147.   [191] (n181).

XVI

PROOF OF FREQUENTLY RECURRING MATTERS

This chapter describes different ways in which evidence may be given of certain matters that frequently have to be proved in litigation. Proof of handwriting and some documents, both private and public, was considered in the last chapter, together with the Bankers' Books Evidence Act 1879. Proof of foreign law, identity, birth, death, age, marriage and legitimacy, judgments, convictions, and other orders of the court will now be mentioned here. Reference will occasionally be made to judicial notice and presumptions, although it is not customary to describe them as means of proof. The possibility of a fact being admitted, formally or informally, should always be borne in mind.

SECTION 1. FOREIGN LAW[1]

Chapter IV noted that in English courts, foreign law is a question of fact[2] since 1920 to be decided by the judge,[3] and for appellate purposes not as a matter of domestic law.[4] Chapter IV explained that, in this context, 'foreign law' comprises the law of Scotland, of the British Commonwealth, and, to some extent, of Eire and Northern Ireland, as well as of a foreign country in the strict sense.[5]

The general rule is that foreign law must be proved by an expert witness,[6] who will, in a disputed or complicated case, testify on oath in the ordinary way. In routine cases, it is not uncommon for tender by affidavit, or under the Civil Evidence Act 1995.[7] The effect of the general rule is that foreign law cannot usually be the subject of judicial notice,[8] or, at common law, inferred from previous English decisions on the same subject,[9] still less from

---

[1] For a much fuller discussion and citation of authority, see Dicey, Morris, and Collins *Conflict of Laws* (14th edn, 2006) ch 9; Fentiman *Foreign Law in English Courts* (1998).

[2] Although in some respects of a special character: see *Arab Monetary Fund v Hashim (No 8)* (1994) 6 Admin LR 348.

[3] The same is true in Scotland: see *Armour v Thyssen Edelstahlwerke AG* 1989 SLT 182.

[4] *Egmatra AG v Marco Trading Corp* [1999] 1 Lloyd's Rep 862, construing Arbitration Act 1996, s 69.

[5] Customary international law is, however, regarded as part of the law of Scotland, and is thus not apt to be proved by an expert as a question of fact: *Lord Advocate's Reference (No 1 of 2000)* [2001] SLT 507, 512. In Canada, the issue of parliamentary privilege has been assimilated to foreign law for these purposes: *Goddard v Day* (2000) 194 DLR (4th) 551.

[6] It will be rare for the court to disallow the use of an expert for this purpose: see *Re E-B (Children)* [2002] EWCA Civ 1771.

[7] *Markes v Markes* (1955) 106 L Jo 75 (a decision on the Evidence Act 1938); *Kirsh v Kirsh* [1958] SASR 258.

[8] *Brenan and Galen's Case* (1847) 10 QB 492, 498; *R v Ofori and Tackie (No 2)* (1994) 99 Cr App Rep 223, 227.

[9] *M'Cormick v Garnett* (1854) 23 LJ Ch 777.

the production of foreign legal documents unsupported by any expert evidence.[10] Before the Civil Evidence Act 1972, it had to be proved afresh by an expert in each case. There are, however, certain cases in which foreign law is the subject of judicial notice, or something taken to have been established by a previous English decision, and there are also some special statutory provisions governing the proof of foreign law. These will be considered before reference is made to the question of the qualification of the expert when testifying in cases to which the general rule applies.

The burden of proof rests on the party asserting that foreign law differs from English law. This is sometimes, infelicitously, stated as a presumption that foreign and English law are the same,[11] although difficult questions may arise when only part of the relevant law has been proved.[12]

JUDICIAL NOTICE AND PREVIOUS DECISIONS

Judicial notice may be taken of notorious facts, and, in exceptional cases, the English courts have treated aspects of foreign law as matters of notoriety. A famous example is *Saxby v Fulton*,[13] in which judicial notice was taken of the fact that roulette is legal in Monte Carlo. Judicial notice might also be taken of the common law of Northern Ireland,[14] or of European Community law,[15] and the Supreme Court will take judicial notice of Scots law.[16] Under the Maintenance Orders Act 1950, s 22(2), judicial notice must be taken of the law with regard to maintenance orders in every part of the United Kingdom. It also seems to be settled that, once a statute passed in a British possession is properly before an English court, that court may construe the statute, with the result that a body of case law on the subject may be created.[17] The principal statute is the Evidence (Colonial Statutes) Act 1907, which is confined to British possessions, and it is not clear how far the English courts will construe foreign legislation without the guidance of an expert witness. There are cases in which the English courts appear to have done this, and their decisions are then, presumably, binding on other courts within the limits of the doctrine of precedent.[18] In principle, the function of an expert witness to foreign law is to provide an exposition of the foreign law, and not to apply it to the facts.[19]

---

[10] *R v Okolie* [2003] EWCA Crim 861.

[11] See e.g. *University of Glasgow v Economist* (1990) The Times, 13 July.

[12] See Briggs (2006) LMCLQ 1, commenting on *Neilson v Overseas Projects of Victoria Ltd* [2005] HCA 54.   [13] [1909] 2 KB 208. See also *Re Turner, Heyding v Hinchliff* [1906] WN 27.

[14] *Re Nesbitt* (1844) 14 LJMC 30, 33: see Nokes [1960] ICLQ 564.

[15] European Communities Act 1972, s 3.

[16] This is on account of the Court's appellate jurisdiction in civil cases. It is doubtful whether the Court would take judicial notice of Scots criminal law, should the question ever arise. The Court would take judicial notice of the law of Northern Ireland.

[17] *Re Sebba, Lloyds Bank Ltd v Hutson* [1959] Ch 166, [1958] 3 All ER 393. In *Mahadervan v Mahadervan* [1964] P 233, [1962] 3 All ER 1108, 240, 1113, it was said that an English court can construe a written foreign law once it is in evidence. Most of the decisions on this matter relate to countries to which the Evidence (Colonial Statutes) Act 1907 applies, although sometimes no reference is actually made to the Statute. See also *Shariff v Azad* [1967] 1 QB 605, [1966] 3 All ER 785.

[18] In *Re Cohn* [1945] Ch 5 (a provision in the German Civil Code).

[19] *Di Sora v Phillips* (1863) 10 HL Cas 624, 639. See also *Rouyer Guillet et Cie v Rouyer Guillet & Co* [1949] 1 All ER 244n. In Australia, see *United States Trust Co of New York v Australia and New Zealand Banking Group Ltd* (1995) 37 NSWLR 131.

Section 4(2) of the Civil Evidence Act 1972 permits the reception as evidence of foreign law of any previous determination by an English court of the point in question, provided it is reported in citable form,[20] and provided notice of intention to rely upon it has been given to the other parties to the proceedings.[21] The foreign law is to be taken to be in accordance with the determination unless the contrary is proved. It makes no difference whether the point was determined in civil, or criminal, proceedings, but foreign law may be proved in this way only in civil proceedings.[22]

OTHER STATUTORY PROVISIONS

Under the Evidence (Colonial Statutes) Act 1907,[23] copies of Acts, ordinances, and statutes passed by or under the authority of the legislature of any British possession shall be received in evidence by all courts of justice in the United Kingdom, if purporting to be printed by the government printer[24] without any proof given that the copies were so printed. The term 'British possession' means any part of Her Majesty's dominions exclusive of the United Kingdom.[25] It is clear that this statute enables an English court to receive a statute, or subordinate legislation, of a British possession in evidence on the mere production of a government printer's copy, but the Act of 1907 would not be much use if this were all that it has achieved, and it has been held in a number of cases that the English courts may construe the statute, acting on its provisions as so construed without anything in the nature of expert evidence.[26]

There has long been provision for ascertaining foreign law by special reference to a foreign court. Within the Commonwealth, this can be accomplished by the use of the British Law Ascertainment Act 1859.[27] Although the law to which it refers is strictly not 'foreign', of perhaps greater importance is the provision in Art 130u of the Treaty of Rome that any subordinate court of a member country of the European Community may, if it considers it necessary to give judgment, refer any question of the interpretation of Community law to the European Court for its opinion, and that any final court must do so. In *HP Bulmer Ltd v J Bollinger SA*,[28] the Court of Appeal set out guidelines to assist in determining when such reference was to be considered necessary, and for determining whether to exercise discretion to do so where it exists.

Although the Evidence (Foreign, Dominion and Colonial Documents) Act 1933 does not, strictly speaking, relate to the proof of foreign law, it contains useful provisions for cases involving a foreign element. Put very briefly, its effect is that Orders in Council may

[20] That is, in a report that could, if the question had been one of English law, have been cited as authority in any court in England or Wales.

[21] See CPR 33.7.

[22] There was a corresponding provision in the draft bill attached to the 11th Report of the Criminal Law Revision Committee, but it has never been enacted.

[23] See also the Colonial Laws Validity Act 1865, s 6.

[24] That is, the government printer of the possession.

[25] *Quaere* whether this statute still applies to all Commonwealth countries.

[26] *Jasiewicz v Jasiewicz* [1962] 3 All ER 1017, [1962] 1 WLR 1426.

[27] The comparable provision in relation to non-British law, the Foreign Law Ascertainment Act 1861, was never invoked, and consequently repealed in 1973.

[28] [1974] Ch 401, [1974] 2 All ER 1226. See also *Customs and Excise Comrs v ApS Samex (Hanil Synthetic Fiber Industrial Co)* [1983] 1 All ER 1042.

be made with regard to the proof, by authenticated copy, of extracts from public registers in the foreign jurisdiction to which the order applies. The certificate is not merely evidence of the contents of the register, but also evidence of the facts stated. The statute is very useful[29] in proving births, deaths, and marriages occurring abroad. In relation to marriage, it will generally dispense with the necessity of calling an expert in the relevant foreign law, in order to swear that the certificate would be accepted as evidence of the marriage in question in the courts of the foreign country. A number of Orders in Council have been made under the Act.

EXPERT WITNESS

In the case of proof of foreign law by an expert, the witness must be properly qualified. A judge, or regular practitioner, in the relevant jurisdiction is indubitably properly qualified,[30] but this was once thought both sufficient, and necessary, a condition. In *Bristow v Sequeville*,[31] a jurisconsult, adviser to the Prussian consulate in London, who had studied law in Leipzig, and knew that the Code Napoleon was in force in Saxony, was not allowed to give evidence concerning the Code. A number of cases departed from this rigid attitude over the years, and it seems that the Civil Evidence Act 1972, s 4(1) did no more than enact the common law in declaring that a person suitably qualified, on account of knowledge or experience, is competent to give evidence of foreign law, irrespective of whether he has acted, or is qualified to act, as a legal practitioner in the country in question.[32] Considerations as to weight were canvassed in *Glencore International AG v Metro Trading International Inc.*[33]

This begs the question of what constitutes a suitable qualification. It seems that practical experience will suffice, even though gained as businessman,[34] banker,[35] diplomat,[36] or Governor-General,[37] rather than as legal practitioner. A teacher of the law of the jurisdiction in question may be sufficiently qualified, although probably not a student.[38] Conversely, the evidence of a legal practitioner may be rejected if he cannot be shown to have practical experience.[39] There may indeed be room for argument as to what counts as practical experience.[40] A more lenient view used to be taken of the qualifications regarded as

---

[29] Assisted in proceedings related to entitlement to social security benefits by a rule of European law that courts must accept certificates, and similar documents, from other member states: *Dafeki v Landesversicherungsanstalt Württemberg* [1998] All ER (EC) 452, ECJ.

[30] *Baron De Bode's Case* (1845) 8 QB 208.   [31] (1850) 5 Exch 275.

[32] It is to be hoped that this is the case, since the recommendation of the Criminal Law Revision Committee in Cmnd 4991 draft bill, cl 44 that a similar provision be enacted for criminal proceedings seems not, so far, to have been enacted.   [33] [2001] 1 LlR 284, 300.

[34] *Vander Donckt v Thellusson* (1849) 8 CB 812.

[35] *Ajami v Customs Controller* [1954] 1 WLR 1405.   [36] *Re Dost Aly Khan's Goods* (1880) 6 PD 6.

[37] *Cooper-King v Cooper-King* [1900] P 65.

[38] *Brailey v Rhodesia Consolidated Ltd* [1910] 2 Ch 95 (reader in Roman-Dutch Law at Council for Legal Education); cf *Bristow v Sequeville* (n31) (a former student).

[39] *Cartwright v Cartwright and Anderson* (1878) 26 WR 684 (English barrister who had appeared in the Privy Council on Canadian appeals, but not in the relevant area of Canadian law).

[40] In *R v Brady* (1980) 57 FLR 198 (tax consultant operating schemes under the law of Liechtenstein, which he had studied only at second hand, entitled to give evidence on the general basis of the law, but not of its detailed application).

suitable, when there were particularly few witnesses,[41] although modern communications and relaxation of the hearsay rule should reduce the need for such leniency today.

The decision whether the proposed witness is properly qualified is made by the judge as a condition precedent to the admission of the evidence. In coming to a conclusion on a question of foreign law, the English courts may consider foreign statutes and decisions referred to by the expert witness, and if, but only if,[42] there is a conflict of expert testimony, the English judge must resolve it,[43] and is free to apply his own intelligence to do so.[44] In cases in which the relevant concepts of foreign law are sufficiently similar to those of English law for the judge to be able to employ his own legal training in determining their correct interpretation, and application, his decision is liable to reversal on appeal in much the same way as his determination of questions of domestic law.[45]

SECTION 2. EVIDENCE OF IDENTITY

Identity must be proved in a wide variety of situations. Most often it relates to the identity of persons,[46] but sometimes to the identity of objects.[47] In a sense, all litigation involves questions of the identity of persons, since the relevant order must relate to the same person implicated in the events upon the proof of which the order was made.[48] As the High Court of Australia has affirmed: 'evidence which may be relevant on the issue of identity is not necessarily evidence of identification'.[49] The most common situation of identification occurs in criminal cases in which it can be established that a crime has been committed, and witnesses are prepared to testify that they observed the accused in circumstances making it likely that he committed it. Sometimes, the presence of the accused[50] in a relevant place

---

[41] See *Direct Winters Transport v Duplate Canada Ltd* (1962) 32 DLR (2d) 278.

[42] *Bumper Development Corp Ltd v Metropolitan Police Comr* [1991] 4 All ER 638, [1991] 1 WLR 1362 (judge must accept a unanimous expert view). The same is true in Australia: see *James Hardie & Co Pty Ltd v Hall* (1998) 43 NSWLR 554.

[43] *Re Duke of Wellington* [1947] Ch 506, [1947] 2 All ER 854. In Australia, see *Bank of Valetta plc v National Crime Authority* [1999] FCA 791, (1999) 64 ALR 45, for justification, and application, of such a procedure.

[44] *A/S Tallinna Laevauhisus v Estonian State Steamship Line* (1946) 80 Ll LR 99, 107.

[45] *Macmillan Inc v Bishopsgate Investment Trust plc (No 4)* [1999] CLC 417, rejecting the view that an appeal could be allowed only if the trial judge's view was an impossible one.

[46] Or occasionally animals: see *Patterson v Howdle* 1999 SCCR 41.

[47] In *R v Browning* (1991) 94 Cr App Rep 109, 122, the Court of Appeal noted the different considerations that apply holding a *Turnbull* direction inappropriate, although reference should be made to any considerations diminishing potential reliability: *R v Hampton* [2004] EWCA Crim 2139, (2004) 148 SJLB 973, [51]. Care is nevertheless very necessary, especially in relation to the identification of mass-produced objects: see *Bond v MacFarlane* (1990) 102 FLR 38. In *Pfennig v R* (1995) 182 CLR 461, 127 ALR 99, a witness was given the opportunity to listen to the sound of eight cars including the suspect one, and identified it; but still the trial judge urged the jury to use the evidence only to show that the witness had heard a sound *like* that made by the accused's car. A specific identification warning was required of a lorry in Australia in *R v Clout* (1995) 41 NSWLR 312.

[48] For an expansive approach, see *R v Andrews* [1993] Crim LR 590, in which this feature is highlighted in Birch's commentary.

[49] *Festa v R* [2001] HCA 72, (2001) 208 CLR 593, [60]. See also *Watson v DPP* [2003] EWHC 1466 (Admin), (2003) 168 JP 116, in which an issue arose as to the fairness of evidence of confession of identity by one accused after the event of a driving offence.

[50] Slightly different considerations may apply to the identification of a third party accompanying the accused: see *R v Bath* (1990) 154 JP 849.

is controverted, but sometimes presence may be admitted, and the question is whether it was the accused, or others also present, who acted in a particular way.[51] Little attention seems to have been paid to negative evidence of identity, that is where a witness denies the identity claimed for a relevant participant, or cases in which the defence, rather than the prosecution, relies upon identification.[52] Identity can, of course, be equally central in civil cases, for example whether a particular claimant to an estate is the rightful heir,[53] or in extradition, where the standard of proof is now the balance of probabilities.[54]

Evidence of identity is at its most vulnerable when it purports to be based upon the identification by one human being of the features of another, whether those features are identified by sight, hearing, smell or, just conceivably,[55] touch, based upon an evanescent contact in the past. Sometimes, the past occasion has been captured in more permanent form, for example on a video or tape recording, in which case the jury may make its own identification, perhaps assisted by identification testimony from witnesses who have greater familiarity with the accused,[56] or from experts in the interpretation of real evidence, whether visual,[57] or aural.[58] Identification may also be accomplished by the use of circumstances, or by presumption. This section will consider identification by direct, circumstantial, and presumptive evidence separately, although the first is by far the most important.

DIRECT EVIDENCE

This part will first consider the reasons why direct evidence of identity poses particular problems, then the reactions of courts and law reformers to their perception of such problems. It will then go on to consider the modern law, mentioning, in turn, the different forms of identification, the question of the procedure for considering them, and finally, the proper direction to be given to the jury.

Special problems[59]

The Criminal Law Revision Committee stated in its 11th Report that:[60]

We regard mistaken identification as by far the greatest cause of actual or possible wrong convictions. Several cases have occurred in recent years when a person has been charged or convicted on what has later been shown beyond doubt to have been mistaken identification.

---

[51] It has been denied that this is an issue of identification at all: *R v Linegar* [2001] EWCA Crim 2404, [18]; or that a full *Turnbull* warning is required: *R v Oakwell* [1978] 1 All ER 1223, [1978] 1 WLR 32; *R v Slater* [1995] 1 Cr App Rep 584; or that *Forbes* [2001] 1 AC 473, [2001] 1 ALL ER 686 applies to compel a parade: *R v Conibeer* [2002] EWCA Crim 2059, on account of the dangers being somewhat different. But see also *K v DPP* [2001] EWHC 351 (Admin) for a different view, and further analysis by Roberts [2003] *Crim LR* 709.

[52] Some amelioration has, however, been allowed, both in England: see *R v Robinson* [2005] EWCA Crim 1940, [2006] 1 Cr App R 221, [15] (lower threshold for admission of voice identification); and in Australia: *R v Johnson* [2004] SASC 241, 147 ACR 151 (more muted warning of general dangers).

[53] As in the famous nineteenth-century case of the *Tichborne* claimant, a dispute that could now by genetic testing be settled immediately with complete certainty.

[54] See *Savvas v Italy* [2004] EWHC 1233 (Admin), [4].   [55] Taste does seem inconceivable.

[56] *Kajala v Noble* (1982) 75 Cr App Rep 149; *R v Fowden and White* [1982] Crim LR 588; *R v Grimer* [1982] Crim LR 674; *R v Caldwell and Dixon* (1993) 99 Cr App Rep 73. But not if the witnesses have no more previous knowledge of the accused than the jury itself: see *Leaney v R* (1989) 50 CCC (3d) 289.

[57] As in *R v Stockwell* (1993) 97 Cr App Rep 260; *R v Clarke* [1995] 2 Cr App Rep 425.

[58] As in *R v O'Doherty* [2002] NI 263.   [59] See Jackson [1986] *Crim LR* 203.

[60] Cmnd 4991 (1972) [196].

This was not, even then, novel. It was in consequence of a report[61] into the mistaken identification[62] of Adolph Beck that the Court of Criminal Appeal was established. Similarly, two miscarriages of justice on the basis of misidentification led to the establishment of Lord Devlin's Committee into all aspects of the law and procedure, relating to identification in criminal cases.[63] It has been established that the deficiencies of the old law sometimes led to the execution of those who should never have been found guilty.[64]

The reasons for such difficulty are apparent. A very substantial psychological literature[65] has demonstrated that the processes involved are riddled with weaknesses, from initial perception, to eventual recall. Articulation is particularly difficult, and suggestibility, both in the sense of accepting externally inspired suggestions, and in applying internal preconceptions, is high. These defects are compounded by the inability of conventional cross-examination to reveal their weaknesses. Identification is a largely internal, and isolated, process so, unlike other evidence, it resists probing based upon its coherence with the rest of the surrounding evidence. It is also usually sincerely believed in by the witness,[66] and the witness's view is more likely to be reinforced than weakened by the passage of time, or challenge.[67] The courts are generally reluctant to allow challenge based upon abstract or theoretical studies divorced from the facts of the instant case, and in this context, have refused to admit evidence designed to show the general weakness of evidence of identification.[68] The cumulative effect of these factors is to reduce probative value, while increasing prejudicial effect, given that, in this context, prejudice connotes adducing evidence that the jury[69] is likely to credit more than is warranted.

Problems are compounded when the variation between different situations is taken into account. For example, if the person identified is well known to the identifier, sometimes distinguished as recognition,[70] this might be regarded in many cases as decreasing the risk of misidentification,[71] except that there is a known tendency for an identifier to assimilate a perception to someone who is already known. The procedure for initial identification may also be suggestive,[72] for example in using photographs, or may reinforce an initially uncertain perception, for example by reference to an elicited description, or

---

[61] Cmnd 2315 (1905).   [62] By no fewer than 15 different women.

[63] HC Paper 338 (1976). For a similar exercise in Scotland, see Bryden Committee report on *Identification Procedure under Scottish Criminal Law* (Cmnd 7096, 1978).

[64] *R v Mattan* (1998) The Times, 5 March.

[65] Some of it is conveniently summarized in the Interim Report of the Australian Law Reform Commission No 26, Vol 1, [419]–[421] (1985).

[66] A factor emphasized in *R v Dickson* [1983] 1 VR 227, and echoed by the Privy Council in *Scott v R* [1989] AC 1242, [1989] 2 All ER 305 (in which it was said to be 'fundamental'), and *Reid v R* [1990] 1 AC 363, [1993] 4 All ER 95n. See also *R v Marshall* (2000) 113 ACR 190.

[67] See *R v Atfield* (1983) 25 Alta LR (2d) 97, 98.

[68] See *R v Smith* [1987] VR 907; cf Holdenson (1988) 16 *Melb ULR* 521; and in Canada, *R v McIntosh* (1997) 117 CCC 3d 385. But see *R v Roberts* [2000] Crim LR 183 for a more permissive view in relation to identification by voice.

[69] Although the same factors apply to all human beings, and in Australia, the same rules requiring careful direction have been held to apply to trial by judge alone: *Grbic v Pitkethly* (1992) 65 ACR 12.

[70] It has been remarked that, where the identification is of a person seen many years before, it savours more of recognition, and the procedures specified for identification cannot be applied in the same way: *R v Folan* [2003] EWCA Crim 908, (2003) 147 SJLB 477, [34].

[71] See *R v Caldwell and Dixon* (1993) 99 Cr App Rep 73, 77. See also *People v Stafford* [1983] IR 165.

[72] The Code of Practice does not apply at this stage, but it has been strongly recommended that a new set of provisions should be devised for it: *R v Hickin* [1996] Crim LR 584.

image.[73] Quite apart from anything else, physical conditions will vary greatly from one situation to another, and perceptive abilities from one person to another. Even in the case of a given individual, it is unlikely to be obvious, or known, how distorted perceptive faculties may become as a result of the stress, or trauma, or perhaps being the victim of, or even an eyewitness to, a particularly distressing event such as the commission of a brutal crime. It is sometimes suggested,[74] but by no means universally accepted[75] in the absence of any supporting evidence,[76] that identification by trained observers aware of potential need to justify it,[77] such as the police,[78] is likely to be more reliable than identification by others. Sometimes, special factors in the situation aggravate the difficulty of identification, for example when it is necessary to distinguish between identical twins.[79]

While failure to identify a person may be mistaken for similar reasons, or perhaps even by appreciation of these dangers, it does not follow that it should be subject to similar directions to the jury, which might indeed have the effect of reversing the burden of proof.[80]

There are also technical problems with the use of evidence of previous identification, since, if the testifying witness recognizes the accused in court as the criminal, then evidence of any previous act of identification might seem no more than a previous consistent statement, bolstering testimony; while if the testifying witness fails to recognize the accused in court,[81] evidence of previous identification might seem no more than a previous inconsistent statement, albeit now admissible as evidence of its truth.

Legal reaction

These problems are now better understood as a result of the development of psychological research into perception and recall. This increased awareness was first translated into intervention at a high judicial level in *People v Casey (No 2)*,[82] in which the Supreme Court of Ireland took the view that warning of the dangers of acting upon evidence of identification should always be given to the jury, and ordered retrial absent such warning. There, the purported identification was by a number of strangers to the accused, some of them victims, or children, or both, and in poor light and otherwise difficult conditions.

That approach was, however, rejected by the House of Lords in *Arthurs v A-G for Northern Ireland*,[83] significantly enough, a case in which the accused was well known to the identifying police witness. There was said to be no inflexible duty to warn, still less a requirement for corroborating material. The House of Lords left open whether a warning should be mandatory in a case in which the accused was previously unknown to the identifying witness,[84] but subsequently the Court of Criminal Appeal rejected any such view,[85] and the House of Lords refused leave to appeal.[86]

---

[73] See Roberts 71 *MLR* 331 (2008) for a normative rights based approach.

[74] See *R v Ramsden* [1991] Crim LR 295; *R v Tyler* (1993) 96 Cr App Rep 332; *R v Williams* (1994) The Times, 7 October.   [75] See *Reid v R* [1990] 1 AC 363, 392; *R v Smith* [2001] HCA 50, 206 CLR 650.

[76] *People (DPP) v O'Donovan* [2004] IECCA 48, [2005] 1 IR 385, [17].

[77] *R v Spittle* [2008] EWCA Crim 2537, [13].

[78] Or even bank clerks: *R v Hunter* [1969] Crim LR 262.

[79] See *R v Gornall* [2005] EWCA Crim 668, (2005) 149 SJLB 300 (in which they were successfully distinguished).   [80] *R v Speede* (1991) The Times, 4 April.

[81] As in *R v Ranger* (2003) 178 CCC3d 375.   [82] [1963] IR 33.   [83] (1970) 55 Cr App Rep 161.

[84] A position endorsed by Hailsham LC in *DPP v Kilbourne* [1973] AC 729, 740.

[85] *R v Long* (1973) 57 Cr App Rep 871.

[86] See also dicta of Gibbs J to the same effect in the High Court of Australia in *Kelleher v R* (1974) 131 CLR 534, 551.

Despite the duty to direct the jury in general terms on the strength of the prosecution case, many felt this insufficient. Some groups argued for a corroboration requirement,[87] and, in at least one case,[88] the still more stringent requirement that such corroboration should not itself consist of further identification evidence of the same character as that requiring corroboration. The Criminal Law Revision Committee, in its 11th Report, recommended a mandatory caution, but not any special form of words.[89] This recommendation was to apply, whether or not the accused was previously known to the witness, and irrespective of the number of acts of identification. The Devlin Committee went further, impelled to some extent by the fact that, in one of the cases that inspired its investigation,[90] such a general direction had been given, but without preventing a demonstrably wrong conviction. The Devlin Committee was thus inspired to make more radical recommendations. It resisted the suggestion of a corroboration requirement, partly because there frequently is corroboration in the evidence of other identifying witnesses, partly because corroboration had become enmeshed with technicality, and partly because of the burden that it would impose in clear cases.[91] Its recommendation was that the trial judge should, in every case, give a very strong direction to the jury that evidence of identification alone is not sufficient to satisfy the high burden of proof in criminal cases, and explain to it exactly why this is so. It recommended further that the jury be directed that only in exceptional circumstances would a conviction depending upon identification evidence be justified.[92] Like the Criminal Law Revision Committee, the Devlin Committee took the view that it was necessary for any such change to be introduced by statute.

That approach was overtaken by the highly influential decision of the Court of Appeal in *R v Turnbull*.[93] Since the Court of Appeal took the view that the direction of juries was a matter of practice, it felt competent to prescribe the proper direction. It took its cue from the recommendations of the Devlin Committee, and in particular, stressed the need for some explanation of the need for special caution in accepting evidence of identification.[94] It required the judge to direct the jury in some detail about the quality of the evidence of identification. It was in this stress upon quality that the court departed from the Devlin recommendations. It was not to countenance an automatic direction to acquit upon the basis of identification evidence alone, even in the absence of exceptional features in the Devlin sense, provided that the quality was good. It was indeed felt that the concept of exceptional features was undesirable, and for the very reason that commended it to the Devlin Committee, namely that it would be likely to generate a considerable corpus of precedent. The Devlin Committee welcomed this as being indicative, rather than definitive, but the Court of Appeal rightly feared the growth of excessive technicality.

These guidelines have precluded statutory intervention. The Royal Commission on Criminal Procedure did, nevertheless, recommend that identification procedures be made

---

[87] Submissions to this effect were received by the Devlin Committee from the Law Society, the British Legal Association, and the National Council for Civil Liberties.

[88] The submission of *Justice* to the Devlin Committee.

[89] Cmnd 4991 (1972), [199] and draft bill, cl 21.   [90] That of *Dougherty*: see Devlin Report, ch 2.

[91] [4.36]–[4.42]. As strikingly illustrated in Scotland in *BP v Williams* 2005 SLT 508, [2005] SCCR 234, in which the identification of the victims' father was thus prevented.

[92] For discussion of the Devlin Committee's Report, see Glanville Williams [1976] *Crim LR* 407.

[93] [1977] QB 224, [1976] 3 All ER 549, recently re-endorsed by the Privy Council in *Edwards v R* [2006] UKPC 23; (2006) 150 SJLB 570; and said to retain its full force in England: *R v Nash* [2004] EWCA Crim 2696, (2004) 148 SJLB 1249, [14].

[94] The more sincere the witness, the greater the need for caution: *R v Devlin* [1997] CLY 1152.

the subject of statutory regulation.[95] Section 66(b) of the Police and Criminal Evidence Act 1984 accordingly required the issue of a Code of Practice for the identification of suspects by police officers. It should be noted that, despite its title, this code deals in detail with identification by lay witnesses under the supervision of the police. The current version of this Code regulates procedures in most of the common situations to be mentioned in the next section.[96]

Different procedures for identification

The most common situation is identification by a witness, but exceptionally identification may be accomplished by the jury directly.

Identification by witnesses

There are many different procedures for identification by witnesses, depending upon the particular circumstances of a given case. Sometimes, the witness is able to describe the criminal in sufficient detail for a suspect to be identified, and sometimes such description is taken beyond words, and expressed by a drawing, or amalgamation of pre-recorded features in a so-called 'photofit'. A different technique is to show the witness a series of photographs, or video film, in the hope that the witness will be able to recognize one of those depicted as the criminal. Occasionally, a crime has been recorded on a security camera, which witnesses can inspect. Once a suspect has been initially identified by one of these methods, opportunity is often presented for confirmation of his identification by the relevant witness. Such confirmation is normally, and preferably, attempted by means of an identification procedure, which in England may take the form of video identification, parade, group identification, or confrontation, the least satisfactory form of such confrontation being one that takes place in court during the trial itself, frequently referred to as 'dock identification'. A little more will be said about the evidential repercussions of each of these approaches, bearing in mind that breach of the appropriate procedure will result in the exclusion of the evidence only if the breach is so serious as to trigger the judge's discretion to exclude under s 78, because the breach has had a sufficiently adverse effect on the fairness of the proceedings.[97]

Description

The Devlin Committee pointed out[98] that psychological research indicated that descriptions given by witnesses were likely to be a good deal more unreliable than acts of identification.[99] It nevertheless recommended that statutory provision be made for the police to

---

[95] Cmnd 8092 (1981), [3], [138].   [96] But not in all: see *R v Jones; R v Dowling* (1994) 158 JP 293.

[97] *R v Grannell* (1989) 90 Cr App Rep 149; but a qualified identification is unlikely alone be enough to trigger s 78 exclusion: [2002] EWCA Crim 1923, (2002) 99(38) LSG 33; *R v Rose* [2006] EWCA Crim 1720.

[98] [5.8].

[99] Although they may sometimes be decisive, and conclusive, where there is a very small number of suspects, as in *R v Byron* (1999) The Times, 10 March. It can be argued that an assertion that the criminal 'looked like' the accused falls short of an act of identification, and is more akin to an implicit description; in Australia, such evidence has been regarded as inadmissible: *R v Clune (No 2)* [1996] 1 VR 1, but not in Canada: *R v Rybak* 233 CCC3d 58 (2008), [121]; and in Scotland, where the witness asserted that two of the persons on a parade resembled the accused, was not regarded as contradicting a definite identification of one of them by another witness: *Kelly v HM Adv* [1998] SCCR 660.

secure a description from an identifying witness, and for the imposition of a duty to supply such description to the defence. In the case of a witness actually called by the prosecution to identify the accused, it recommended that such a description should itself become admissible in evidence.[100] In *R v Turnbull*,[101] the Court of Appeal recommended that any descriptions materially differing from the appearance of the accused should automatically be supplied to the defence, any other supplied upon request, and that the trial judge should specifically direct the jury as to any material discrepancy between such a description, and the actual appearance, of the accused.[102] The Code provides[103] that a description should be secured from an identifying witness, written down, and provided to the defence before any of the other procedures for identification is attempted. This is reinforced in relation to informal procedures for selection of suspects, but does not apply where it is impractical from the point of view of effective policing.[104]

Drawings or photofit compilations[105]

These techniques are designed to overcome the difficulty frequently experienced in trying to describe a criminal.[106] Instead, an artist attempts to draw to the witness's description, or, given that adequately competent artists are in short supply, someone,[107] assembles drawings or photographs of parts of a face, in the hope that, by trial and error, a representation will be obtained more satisfying to the witness, and more readily applied by investigators. In *R v Smith*,[108] one of the first English cases[109] to consider the point, it was argued that a sketch produced at the witness's behest was hearsay, like a dictated verbal description. Following some inconsistent rulings, it was resolved in *R v Cook*[110] that such a photofit picture infringed neither the hearsay rule, nor that against previous consistent statements, and was hence admissible, just like a photograph.[111] The matter was finally determined by s 120(5) of the Criminal Justice Act 2003, which renders admissible as evidence of its truth any previous statement identifying a person, object, or place.

Photographs

The problems of using photographs to assist the identification of offenders were thoroughly analysed by the High Court of Australia in *Alexander v R*.[112] A distinction was made between their use as an aid to detection by the police, and their use as evidence of

---

[100] [5.15].   [101] 228, 552.

[102] In *R v Nagah* (1991) 92 Cr App Rep 344, remarkable discrepancies contributed to quashing a conviction; in *R v Quercia* (1990) 60 CCC (3d) 380, they were decisive.   [103] Code D, [3.1].

[104] In *R v El-Hannachi* [1998] 2 Cr App Rep 226, it was held not to be practicable in urgent situations in which there is a danger of dispersion of possible suspects.

[105] Although mentioned in Code D, there is no detailed regulation of this practice, presumably on the basis that it is usually a more investigative than evidential procedure. For a comprehensive collation of United States authority: 42 ALR 3d 1217.

[106] For explicit judicial recognition of such difficulty, see *Adams v HM Adv* [1999] SCCR 188, 191.

[107] Nowadays perhaps using a computer: see *R v Darwiche* [2006] NSWSC 28, 166 ACR 28, [4].

[108] [1976] Crim LR 511.

[109] Although a drawing was admitted as early as 1817: see *R v Watson* (1817) 32 State Tr 1, 125.

[110] [1987] QB 417, [1987] 1 All ER 1049. Apparently accepted by Brooking J in *R v Hentschel* [1988] VR 362, but resolved to the contrary by s 59 of the Evidence Act 1995: see *R v Barbaro and Rovere* (2000) 112 ACR 551.

[111] It is rare to require the photographer to be called to testify: *Patterson v Howdle* [1999] SCCR 41.

[112] (1981) 145 CLR 395.

identification in court, recognizing that their use for the former purpose might infect their use for the latter.[113] It was pointed out that identification from photographs suffers from three defects: first, because it happens in the absence of the accused, there is no opportunity to see whether or not it has been conducted fairly, without prompting; second, because the act of picking out a photograph as resembling the criminal can subtly crystallize into firm recognition of the criminal at a subsequent stage;[114] and, third, because any revelation of initial identification by reference to photographs in the possession of the police may suggest the possession of a criminal record.[115] These defects work, to some extent, in a cumulative fashion, since it is difficult for the defence to expose the frailties of the procedure employed without at the same time drawing attention to the provenance of the photographs, and by inference to the accused's record.[116]

The proper procedure for the use of photographs in England is now set out in Annex E to Code D of the Codes of Practice, made pursuant to s 66 of the Police and Criminal Evidence Act 1984.[117] It provides that any showing of photographs must be supervised by an officer of the rank of at least sergeant, that only one witness at a time is to be shown the photographs, and that no fewer than 12 photographs should be shown in a batch.[118] The first description of the suspect must be recorded before the first photograph is shown, and once a positive identification has been made by one witness, the photographs should not be shown to others, but a parade or video identification should be attempted.

Even then, the showing of photographs must be recognized to weaken the strength of subsequent identification, despite a properly conducted parade.[119] It seems, however, that failure to comply with such practices will not itself automatically lead to the inadmissibility of such evidence.[120] Nor does it seem that a judge is necessarily bound to warn the jury of the danger of inferring a criminal record from the use of photographs,[121] or of the weakening of other identification evidence because of initial photographic identification, although such matters might well affect the general fairness of the direction to the jury on the question of identification.

Although there have been strong statements as to the inadmissibility of identifying photographs adduced in evidence, especially when they indicate possession of a criminal record,[122] it seems that such photographs are not, in all circumstances, inadmissible,[123]

---

[113] Initial identification from photographs should normally be followed by a formal identification procedure: Code D [3.12(i)]. See also, in Australia: *R v Cafaro* [2002] WASCA 208, 132 ACR 142.

[114] In England, Annex E to Code D requires the suspect, and his legal adviser, to be told of any such prior identification by reference to photographs when a parade, video, or group identification takes place subsequently. In Australia, such prior showing led to a conviction being quashed in *R v Marshall* (2000) 113 ACR 190, although this may be mitigated by the witness being available for cross-examination: *R v Stott* (2000) 116 ACR 15.   [115] See *R v Kitchen* [1994] Crim LR 684.

[116] For an account of, and justification for, a different method of using photographs that has some advantages over an identification parade, see *R v Murphy* [1996] 2 Qd 523.

[117] Some internal inconsistency in these provisions was criticized in *Kitchen* (n115).

[118] Similar procedures have been approved in New Zealand in *R v Tamihere* [1991] 1 NZLR 195, in which the law was said to be very similar to that in England; and in Australia, in *R v Britten* (1988) 51 SASR 567.

[119] *R v Dwyer and Ferguson* [1925] 2 KB 799.

[120] *R v Seiga* (1961) 45 Cr App Rep 220, and as decided in *Alexander* (n112) itself.

[121] *R v Lawrenson* [1961] Crim LR 398; *R v Seiga* (n120).   [122] *R v Lamb* (1980) 71 Cr App Rep 198.

[123] *R v Maynard* (1979) 69 Cr App Rep 309.

especially where the conduct of the defence had incited,[124] invited,[125] or agreed to[126] it. It is, however, likely that a judge would normally exercise his discretion to exclude unduly prejudicial evidence in many such cases, even as a matter of common law,[127] and quite apart from any breach of the Code of Practice, at least in relation to photographs clearly indicating the accused's possession of a criminal record.[128] If the photographs come from police custody, but not because the accused has a criminal record, a good character direction is appropriate.[129] On the other hand, if the photographs, even though coming from police custody, do not indicate their provenance, and have relevance, for example as explaining the failure of the identifying witness to pick out the accused on account of a recent change of appearance, then they may well be both admissible, and admitted.[130]

Film

The use of security cameras has become common, and the film may assist identification of the actors by being shown to those who might recognize them, such as the police.[131] It seems that, in such cases, there was no objection at common law to the use of covertly obtained video film for the purposes of expert comparison with the film taken at the time.[132]

Sometimes, the position is reversed, and the film shown in advance to facilitate recognition at the scene of the crime.[133] In *R v Clare; R v Peach*,[134] there were two videos: one taken of football supporters arriving for a match taken in good conditions, and one of a fracas taken in bad conditions by a security camera; the first used by the police to identify those shown in the second.

It has been suggested that specific provision should be made to regulate identification by reference to security films,[135] and it has been held that a warning should be given of the danger of identification even by the police from a security video seen only ten minutes before the relevant arrest.[136] So, too, it has been held that the prosecution will not be allowed to rely upon expert interpretation of a security film,[137] when it has refused the accused the opportunity of a live parade, at least where such a parade was a practicable possibility.[138] If recognition by the police from the film is admissible, it is not made

---

[124] In *R v Bleakley* [1993] Crim LR 203, the accused attacked the reliability of identification at a parade, subsequent to a successful identification by the witness from photographs.

[125] *R v Crabtree* [1992] Crim LR 65, in which the accused adduced the photographs himself.

[126] *R v Allen* [1996] Crim LR 426, in which the accused adduced evidence of his own bad record.

[127] In Australia, it seems that the *Bunning v Cross* discretion may also apply: see Gibbs CJ, and Stephen and Murphy JJ in *Alexander v R* (n112); *R v Burchielli* [1981] VR 611; *R v Shannon* (1987) 29 ACR 434.

[128] *R v Governor of Pentonville Prison, ex p Voets* [1986] 2 All ER 630, [1986] 1 WLR 470. See also *R v Coleman* (1987) 87 FLR 175.   [129] *Guevara v R* [1996] CLY 1386, PC.

[130] *R v Byrne and Trump* [1987] Crim LR 689.

[131] Although there is an obvious danger of prejudice in recognition by the police: *Cook v R* (1998) 126 NTR 17; and the police should certainly not testify as experts in the identification of the accused with the criminal depicted on the film using a stocking mask: *R v Griffith* [1997] 2 Qd 524.

[132] *R v Loveridge* [2001] EWCA Crim 973, [2001] 2 Cr App Rep 591.   [133] As in *R v Crabtree* (n125).

[134] [1995] 2 Cr App Rep 333.   [135] *R v Caldwell and Dixon* (1993) 99 Cr App Rep 73, 78.

[136] *R v Campbell* (1996) The Times, 20 February.

[137] Pending the establishment of a national database, it has been held that identification by imaging cannot be the subject of expertise: *R v Gray* [2003] EWCA Crim 1001.

[138] *R v Walker* (14 November 1994, unreported), CA. A parade may not be practicable for these purposes if the criminals wore stocking masks: see *R v Hookway* [1999] Crim LR 750. If a live parade is held, and a

inadmissible by the mere availability of the film to be played to the jury.[139] It is unfortunate that revisions of Code D still offer little guidance on this matter. In the light of one recent case,[140] it seems that some process of authentication of a film from which stills have been taken would be desirable.

Video identification

A different way of using this technology that has become more common has been to compile video recordings, including both the suspect, and other foils, to show to potential witnesses. The advantages of this technique, as opposed to the conventional identification parade, are that it eliminates any possibility of intimidation by the suspect, and may help surmount the problems of assembling enough suitable volunteers to attend ad hoc.[141] It is also far preferable to the practice condemned in *R v Johnson*[142] of allowing the investigating officer to show the victim a video taken of the accused in the vicinity around the time of the crime.[143]

This procedure[144] is governed by the revised Code D,[145] in which it is accorded preferential status, and to be conducted unless impracticable, or a live parade is both more practicable, and suitable.[146] The procedures prescribed by the Code apply as much to police witnesses as to others.[147] As elsewhere, it is not necessarily fatal that the Code has not been followed meticulously,[148] so long as the use of the evidence was fair, and an adequate direction given on failure to follow the Code. Thus in *Perry v United Kingdom*,[149] in which the accused was secretly filmed for this purpose, the European Court of Human Rights refused to intervene either on the basis of infringement of privacy, or the unfairness of trial. It is, however, quite wrong for the police to introduce a new technique inconsistent with the Code, and admitted to be blatantly unfair to the accused, just because of the difficulty of securing positive identification by following the Code.[150]

Identification parades

A properly conducted identification parade was previously accepted as being the least unsatisfactory method of confirming the identity of a suspect.[151] It remains an option,

---

positive identification ensues, it will not lead to the exclusion of expert analysis of the film in addition: *R v Briddick* [2001] EWCA Crim 984.

[139] *A-G's Reference (No 2 of 2002)* [2002] EWCA Crim 2373, [2003] 1 Cr App Rep 321.

[140] *R v Brady* (18 May 2004, unreported), CA (in which there were such serious doubts as to whether the relevant film was what it purported to be, that a conviction, even following a confession, was quashed).

[141] For convincing advocacy of the superiority of video identification over live parades, on account of the practical difficulties of the latter, see Tinsley [2001] 5 *E&P* 99. Sometimes, this advantage is ignored, as in *R v Blick* (2000) 11 ACR 326, in which the only bearded man depicted in the set shown was the accused.

[142] [1996] Crim LR 504.

[143] Especially when accompanied by prejudicial remarks from the investigating officer about previous dealings with the person depicted.

[144] Known as VIPER (Video Identification Parade by Electronic Recording), and now used also in Scotland; for Canadian practice, see *R v Beaulieu* 228 CCC3d 545.

[145] The detail is contained in Annex A.   [146] Code D [3.14].

[147] Code D, note 3A. See also *R v Nunes* [2001] EWCA Crim 2283.

[148] See *R v DPP* [2003] EWHC 3074 (Admin).   [149] (2003) 39 EHRR 76, [2003] Crim LR 281.

[150] *R v Marcus* [2004] EWCA Crim 3387 (in which the accused was of distinctive appearance, and when witnesses failed to identify from photographs edited so as to obscure the distinctive features, they were then asked to identify from the unedited photographs).

[151] But see McKenzie [1995] *Crim LR* 200, and Tinsley (n141).

its detailed operation is governed by Annex B to Code D,[152] and the Privy Council has re-affirmed that one should be held whenever it would serve a useful purpose.[153] Under previous versions of Code D, it became extremely contentious to determine to what extent the suspect could insist on a parade being held,[154] although failure to comply with any obligation to hold one was not necessarily fatal to a conviction,[155] nor conversely holding one when it fell within the exceptional cases noted below.[156] Despite the terminology of the Code, which appeared to make a parade mandatory whenever the suspect disputed his identification, it was recognized that, in some situations, to do so would be futile.[157] These conditions have now been spelled out in para 3.12 of Code D:

…an identification procedure shall be held unless it is not practicable or it would serve no useful purpose in proving or disproving whether the suspect was involved in committing the offence. For example when it is not disputed that the suspect is already well known to the witness who claims to have seen them commit the crime.

It is interesting that the further example of there being no reasonable prospect of identification by these means, which appeared in a previous version, has now been omitted.[158] It should, however, be noted that the failure by a witness to identify the accused does not preclude examination by the prosecution to explain the failure, nor the admission of relevant remarks made during the attempt to identify him.[159] Where the witness claims to have recognized the accused, a parade will be useful to establish whether such recognition is plausible, but not, in itself, as identification of the criminal.[160]

Code D applies only to cases of disputed identification, and the court has been reluctant to define this condition closely;[161] neither, although exemplified, is the term 'identification' explicitly defined in the Code. It may also be noted that the prosecution can always, if it chooses, rely upon evidence other than eyewitness identification to identify the accused with the offender, and in that case, it appears that failure to conduct a parade is unlikely to be fatal, however much the accused disputes being the perpetrator, and however available eyewitnesses may be.[162]

The rules provide that an identification procedure should take place as soon as possible, and that the suspect should be informed of his position under the Code, and provided

---

[152] It was suggested in *R v Burling* [2002] NSWCCA 298, 132 ACR 92 that, where there are two alternative suspects, both should stand in the same parade.

[153] *John v Trinidad and Tobago* [2009] UKPC 12, [14].

[154] Generating conflicting decisions in the Court of Appeal, finally resolved only by the House of Lords in *R v Forbes* [2001] 1 AC 473, [2001] 1 All ER 686.

[155] *R v Craven* [2001] 2 Cr App Rep 181, [93]. Not even when the futility applied to only one of two witnesses with similar opportunities to observe the suspect: *Hawksley v DPP* [2002] EWHC 852 (Admin).

[156] *R v Nolan* [2002] EWCA Crim 464.

[157] For a recent example, see *R (Marsh) v DPP* [2006] EWHC 1525 (Admin).

[158] Indeed, the procedure is to be made available only when the witness has expressed an ability to identify the subject, or there is a reasonable chance of their being able to do so.

[159] *R v George*, [35] and [38], although these may raise hearsay problems.

[160] *Goldson and McGlashan v R* (2000) 65 WIR 444, PC, Lord Hoffmann, 448; *R v Harris*, [33].

[161] *R v Montgomery* [1996] Crim LR 507. Such reluctance is not always extended to provisions of the Codes. It is indicated in [2.1], and has been held, however, that it relates only to visual identification, and not to identification by voice: *R v Gummerson and Steadman* [1999] Crim LR 680.

[162] *R v Rutherford and Palmer* (1993) 98 Cr App Rep 191 (possession of stolen property); *R v Montgomery* (n161) (handwriting); *R v Nicholson* [2000] 1 Cr App Rep 182 (confession and DNA evidence).

with a notice of it in writing. It seems, however, that, if the officer in charge has reason to believe that the suspect is unlikely to cooperate if so informed and supplied, that he can delay providing the information, or the prescribed notice. In the meantime, he is permitted to conduct a covert video identification. It is far from clear how compatible this provision is with the statement in the notice, or indeed with the European Convention on Human Rights, that the accused is entitled to refuse participation in a video identification, a parade, or a group confrontation.[163]

If the suspect refuses to participate in the procedure first offered,[164] he may make representations, and the officer may offer a different procedure, but if all the others are refused, the officer may ultimately resort to confrontation, for which the suspect's consent is not required. The rules also permit the suspect to object to the constitution of the parade, although the increasing use of video identification procedures has alleviated this sort of problem. While breach of the Code does not lead automatically to inadmissibility,[165] or in the absence of prejudice to abuse of process,[166] here, as elsewhere, cumulative breaches may,[167] sometimes on the basis of an *appearance*[168] of injustice. Acquiescence by the accused, or his advisers, in breach does not automatically cure it,[169] and still less the application of some other less satisfactory procedure by the prosecution.[170]

The prescribed procedure requires the witness to identify the suspect clearly during the course of the parade. Difficulty can occur if this is not done, or if the witness is subsequently unable, or unwilling, to identify the accused. As noted above, one of the advantages of a parade is that the suspect has an opportunity to monitor the fairness of the procedure. This is reduced to the extent that evidence may be admitted of events occurring out of his presence, especially when they are relied upon to contradict what did apparently occur. It sometimes happens that a witness, having failed to make a positive identification at the parade, becomes more certain later. The Code provides[171] that, in this situation, the suspect should be told, and consideration given to holding a second parade, although this presents difficulties. There is sometimes a suggestion of encouragement by the police, or by other witnesses, of such second thoughts, but in the absence of strong evidence to this effect, the court seems more inclined to admit the evidence, and to leave its assessment to the jury.[172]

The converse problem of a witness becoming less certain after an initially positive identification was[173] illustrated by the facts of *R v Osbourne and Virtue*.[174] Two ladies

---

[163] [2.21](iv).

[164] Mere refusal to be interviewed should not be construed as refusal to participate: *R v Johnson* (n52).

[165] See e.g. *R v Walters* [2001] EWCA Crim 1261 (presence of investigating officer); *R v McEvoy* [1997] Crim LR 887 (no parade when requested, and no good reason for denial, but case otherwise very strong).

[166] *R v Donald* [2004] EWCA Crim 965, [26].

[167] In *R v Miah* [2001] EWCA Crim 2281, two unexplained breaches were sufficient.

[168] See e.g. *R v Gall* (1989) 90 Cr App Rep 64 (opportunity for investigating officer to speak to witness just before parade); cf *R v Andrews* [1996] CLY 1380 (conversation between witnesses in uninterpreted Amharic shortly before parade); *R v Khan* [1997] Crim LR 584 (in which the investigating officer not only took advantage of the opportunity, but was also carrying in his pocket a current photograph of the accused, and the defect was held capable of correction by direction).

[169] *R v Higginson and Grainger* [2003] EWCA Crim 3319, [25].   [170] *R v Walker* (n138).

[171] Annex B, [20].

[172] See e.g. *R v Creamer* (1984) 80 Cr App Rep 248; *R v Willoughby* [1999] 2 Cr App Rep 82; *R v Walters* (n165).

[173] See *R v Gee* (2000) 113 ACR 376 for a similar situation in relation to prior identification by reference to a security camera film.   [174] [1973] QB 678, [1973] 1 All ER 649.

attended an identification parade, and allegedly identified the accused in the normal way. At the trial, however, one of them said that she could not remember identifying anyone, and the other said that the man she identified was not the accused. The officer supervising the parade was then called, and testified that they had, in fact, both identified the accused. His evidence was objected to, not as hearsay, but as contradicting the evidence of the ladies. This was unfortunate, since the evidence did raise difficult hearsay problems.[175] Although in *Sparks v R*[176] Lord Morris had declared that 'There is no rule which permits the giving of hearsay evidence merely because it relates to identity', it was hard to resist the view that there was such a rule, at least in relation to acts of identification at an identity parade,[177] as indicated by the admission of the evidence in *Osbourne's Case*.[178] The matter has, however, now been resolved by the passage of s 120(5) of the Criminal Justice Act 2003 expressly allowing previous statements of identity as an exception to the hearsay rule.[179]

The Code of Practice provides for the possibility that a witness may require more than the opportunity to inspect a static, and silent, line of human beings. In particular, it provides for them to be required to adopt a particular posture, to move, or to speak.[180] It also allows for the removal of items of clothing, such as a hat, and in those circumstances, given the availability of the discretion under s 78, it seems that a strict construction of the relevant provisions of the Code would be otiose.[181] It does, however, require the witness first to attempt to identify the criminal by appearance alone, since the parade has been assembled on that basis. Identification by voice[182] alone is particularly contentious,[183] since the human ear is generally less discriminating than the eye, and the aural abilities of people differ greatly,[184] and the area, not being regulated by Code D,[185] remains governed

---

[175] See Libling [1977] *Crim LR* 268, and Weinberg (1980) 12 *Melb ULR* 543. See also *R v Ward* [2001] Crim LR 316, in which the issue related to the application of the admission rule, when the admission was made in a statement of his identity as the accused by the criminal at the time, but subsequently denied by the accused to have been made by him. In *R v Adler* [2000] NSWCCA 357, (2000) 116 ACR 38, this situation was overlaid by voice identification.

[176] [1964] AC 964, [1964] 1 All ER 727, 981, 735.

[177] A similar approach would apply to other disputed out-of-court identification exercises such as perusal of photographs: see *R v Barbaro* (1993) 32 NSWLR 619.

[178] In *R v McCay* [1991] 1 All ER 232, [1990] 1 WLR 645, the admission of such evidence was said to have statutory authorization as a result of s 66 of the Police and Criminal Evidence Act 1984, and the terms of the Code of Practice governing identification, and especially Annex A, [7]. Such evidence is now widely admitted both as to visual, and aural, identification; and has been said to constitute a special exception: see *R v Cook* (n110); 425, 1051, 1052; see also *Frew v Jessop* 1990 SLT 396. In *R v Collings* [1976] 2 NZLR 104, 114, the Court of Appeal drew a distinction between statements that were part of the act of identification, and which were admissible, and those not part of it, which were rejected as inadmissible hearsay.

[179] But not in Canada: *R v Campbell* 207 CCC3d 18 (2006).

[180] It is undesirable to require those present to speak their names: *Ricketts v R* [1998] 1 WLR 1016. In Australia, it has been decided that to require the persons to speak so as to detect a linguistic defect is not the same as asking the witness to perform voice identification: *R v Evans* [2006] NSWCCA 277.

[181] See *R v Marrin* [2002] EWCA Crim 251, in which the removal of a hat by one member of the parade at the request of the witness was not fatal, although it was somewhat difficult to fit it into the relevant conditions.

[182] In *Pfennig v R* (n47), the possibility of identifying a car by its sound was treated still more cautiously.

[183] Different approaches have been taken by different states in Australia: see *R v Callaghan* [2001] VSCA 209, 124 ACR 126. See also, in Scotland, *Lees v Roy* 1990 SCCR 310; in New Zealand, *R v Waipouri* [1993] 2 NZLR 410.

[184] See Bull and Clifford 'Earwitness Testimony' in Heaton-Armstrong et al (eds) *Analysing Witness Testimony* (1999).

[185] Although the requirements of the Code should be applied suitably adapted: *R v Hersey* [1998] Crim LR 281. For fuller discussion, see Ormerod [2001] *Crim LR* 595.

by the common law. It is most useful in recognition cases,[186] and, where there is visual and circumstantial support, has been held to require a less stringent direction.[187] On the other hand, identification of the voice of a stranger is a slim basis upon which to justify the reception of prejudicial similar fact evidence in confirmation.[188] It may be especially prejudicial if the police claim to recognize the voice of the accused on the telephone on account of their extensive dealings with him.[189]

Group identification[190]

This involves the witness seeing the suspect among a group of other people, but not on a formal parade. Sometimes, the accused is assembled with others, and sometimes the witness observes a succession of individuals in a particular situation over a period of time. By comparison with a parade, there are disadvantages in the discrepancies between the attitudes, angles of view, and lighting of different people, and in the second case, the haphazard characteristics of the other people observed; an advantage is that people are seen behaving more naturally. Under the Code of Practice, group identification may be offered if the suspect refuses, or fails, to participate in a parade, or if the supervising officer thinks it more satisfactory, perhaps to avoid intimidation, and practicable. It is wrong for the police to pre-empt a parade by contriving group identification despite the accused having agreed to a parade,[191] or by using as arresting officer a constable, who had secured no more than a fleeting glance, to confirm his impression.[192] If, however, the accused agrees to group identification,[193] or if it occurs quite accidentally,[194] then it is unlikely that the evidence will be excluded for that reason. The Code provides that, so far as possible, the conditions applying to the composition of parades shall be applied to group identification.[195] A video recording may be taken of group identification, but it seems wrong to use it as evidence of identification made on such an occasion, and worse to use it after committal proceedings to try to improve the quality of the evidence of the identifying witness.[196]

---

[186] In *R v Davies* [2004] EWCA Crim 2521, [26], it is intimated that it will be very rare in recognition cases for purported *recognition* of either vestigial appearance, or voice, to be regarded as so weak as to be inadmissible. In *R v Korgbara* [2007] NSWCCA 84, 170 ACR 568 comparison of voice samples in different languages was allowed in the absence of expert evidence.

[187] *R v Callaghan* (n183), cp *R v Flynn and St John* [2008] EWCA Crim 970, [2008] 2 Cr App R 266.

[188] *R v Johnson* [1995] 2 Cr App Rep 41, in which the police played tapes of interviews with a number of different men to the victims of a masked man. Cf *Pfennig* (n47).

[189] Although this did not prevent reception of such evidence in Canada in *R v Williams* (1995) 98 CCC (3d) 160.

[190] The detail appears in Annex C to Code D. This term was applied differently in *R v O'Leary* [2002] EWCA Crim 2055 to a case in which the identification was of a group as a whole.

[191] *R v Nagah* (1991) 92 Cr App Rep 344. In Australia, see *R v Shannon* (n127).

[192] *R v Kensett* (1993) 157 JP 620.   [193] *R v Penny* (1991) 94 Cr App Rep 345.

[194] *R v Quinn* [1990] Crim LR 581; *R v Long* [1991] Crim LR 453.

[195] This was overlooked in *R v Ladlow* [1989] Crim LR 219, where the judge thought it permissible to include more than two suspects in a group, but not in a parade; and still more in *Tomkinson v DPP* [1995] Crim LR 60, where it was regarded as justifying group identification rather than a parade.

[196] *R v Smith and Doe* (1986) 85 Cr App Rep 197. It is interesting that no reference was made to *R v Cook* (n110), where Watkins LJ also delivered the judgment of the court.

Confrontation[197]

A confrontation between the witness and the suspect will be arranged only as a last resort,[198] if video, parade, or group identification is impracticable.[199] So strong is the objection, that the evidence is liable to be rejected even if the confrontation has been insisted upon by the accused.[200] The reason for this is that a confrontation in which the witness is asked 'Is this the man?' is somewhat analogous to a leading question.[201] Partly for this reason, it is desirable here, as elsewhere, for a description to be made by the witness in writing prior to the confrontation.[202] Provision is made in the code for confrontation through a one-way screen if necessary, although in such cases, only if the suspect is represented at the confrontation, or a video recording of it is made. If the accused succeeds on an objection to confrontation evidence, it is not open for him to attempt to reinstate it in respect of some witnesses, but not all.[203]

Dock identification

The least satisfactory method of all is to ask the witness to identify the man in the dock as the criminal.[204] It has all the disadvantages of a confrontation, and compounds them by being still more suggestive.[205] For these reasons, the Devlin Committee recommended that dock identification should become a purely formal matter, allowed only where identification had been made by a parade unless the judge took the view that to hold a parade would be impractical, or unnecessary.[206] It has been allowed when the accused has refused

[197] A confrontation is sometimes engineered otherwise than by the police: see *R v O'Leary* (1988) 87 Cr App Rep 387. If it is entirely accidental, the evidence will be admitted: *R v Campbell* [1996] Crim LR 500.

[198] Sometimes a form of confrontation occurs at an earlier stage, where witnesses to, or victims of, a crime are confronted with a man who has been arrested close to the scene of the crime, and asked to confirm that he is the criminal; for judicial criticism of this procedure, see *K v DPP* (n51)Admin, [35]; and for academic criticism, see Roberts (1999) 65 *J Cr L* 251, and Wolchover and Heaton Armstrong (2004) 3 *Arch News* 5 (suggesting that video identification will almost always be a more eligible alternative).

[199] *R v Ladlow* (n195) indicates the court's distaste for this method of identification, since the correct conduct of parades would have required some 231 parades over a bank holiday, and the conditions for a group identification could not strictly have been fulfilled, but still the convictions were quashed because confrontation had been preferred to either of these options. See also *R v Samms* [1991] Crim LR 197; in Ireland, *People v Duff* [1995] 1 IR 296; and in Canada, *R v Peazer* 200 CCC3d 1 (2005).

[200] *R v Joseph* [1994] Crim LR 48 (confrontation in cells, and no better than dock identification).

[201] It may also occur in prejudicial circumstances, as in *R v Williams* [2003] EWCA Crim 3200, (2003) 147 SJLB 1305, where the accused had been arrested, was in handcuffs, and surrounded by police beside a police van (although even then the identification was admitted).

[202] *R v Vaughan* [1997] NLJR 852 (the circumstances here were particularly suggestive).

[203] *R v Campbell* [1993] Crim LR 47.

[204] In *R v Conibeer* (n51), the Court of Appeal came close to directing the jury to ignore a dock identification.

[205] *R v Tricoglus* (1976) 65 Cr App Rep 16, in which the witness identified the accused in the dock despite having picked out someone else on a parade; and *People v Cahill and Costello* [2001] 3 IR 494, in which a parade had been refused, and confrontation unsuccessful. In *Pop v R* [2003] UKPC 40, 147 Sol Jo LB 692, the dock identification was wrongly stimulated by a leading question. See also *Davies and Cody v R* (1937) 57 CLR 170; *R v Hibbert* 2002 SCC 39, [2002] 2 SCR 445.

[206] The alternative of permitting the accused to stand elsewhere in the court, before the attempt at identification, was rejected as likely to be ineffective (such a technique had been adopted in one of the cases that had led to the Committee's being set up). The Criminal Law Revision Committee, in its 11th Report, had recommended its use only after successful identification at a parade: Cmnd 4991, [201].

a parade,[207] has failed to give prior notification of an issue of identification,[208] or in the magistrates' court to preserve police resources.[209] While in cases of genuine recognition, it might seem unnecessary to hold a parade, and sufficient simply to allow identification by the witness in court, this might depend upon how familiar the witness was with the accused before the offence took place,[210] and upon the strength of the supporting circumstantial evidence.[211] Where a witness does identify the accused in his evidence at the trial, it seems that evidence of a prior identification by him can be led.[212] A majority of their Lordships seems to have regarded such evidence as bolstering that of the witness: 'What was done and said out of court goes to show that the witness was able to identify at the time and to negative anything in the nature of an afterthought.'[213] It would be more consistent with principle to wait for some such attack to take place before permitting rebuttal in this way.

Although dock identification was held by the Privy Council in *Holland v HM Adv*[214] not automatically to make a trial unfair, it was said that a special warning of the increased dangers over other forms of identification should have been given,[215] and similarly so when the witness had previously failed to identify the accused at a parade.[216] In Canada, failure to make a dock identification, after a previous identification, has been held to require an appropriate jury direction as to its weakening effect.[217]

Identification by jury

If a crime has been recorded[218] on film, video, or sound recording, or by a still photograph, it may be possible[219] for the jury[220] to make its own identification of the criminal with the man on trial before them,[221] as, for example, in *Kajala v Noble*,[222] in which the incident

---

[207] In *R v John* [1973] Crim LR 113. It was allowed in Ireland when evidence from a parade resulting in a positive identification was excluded as being unconstitutional: *People v Cooney* [1997] 3 IR 205.

[208] *Karia v DPP* [2002] EWHC 2175 Admin, 166 JP 753.

[209] *Barnes v Chief Constable of Durham* [1997] 2 Cr App Rep 505. For criticism, see Watkin [2003] *Crim LR* 463.

[210] In *R v Fergus* [1992] Crim LR 363, one previous encounter together with hearsay as to the name of the person was held insufficient to make a dock identification satisfactory; cf *R v C and B* [2003] EWCA Crim 718, in which the witness had been at school with the persons recognized, and had merely needed to be told the name.

[211] *R v Demeter* [1995] 2 Qd R 626 (accused was overnight guest at house in which the offence took place).

[212] *R v Christie* [1914] AC 545. See, in Australia, *R v Fannon* (1922) 22 SR NSW 427; this has now been extended to cases in which the identifying witness is less than completely certain: *R v Jamal* [2000] FCA 1195, (2000) 116 ACR 45.   [213] Lord Haldane LC, 551.

[214] [2005] UKPC D1, 2005 1 SC (PC) 3. A dock identification has even been permitted after the witness was told that he had identified a foil at a previous parade: *Kerr v HM Adv* [2002] SCCR 275.

[215] Although not if the defence were that the witnesses were deliberately lying: *Capron v R* [2006] UKPC 34.   [216] Exacerbated by failures of disclosure by the prosecution.

[217] *R v Ranger* (n81).

[218] In many case the image is too unclear for interpretation in the absence of expert evidence: see *R v Faraz Ali* [2008] EWCA Crim 1522, [39]; for more general concern see Costigan [2007] *Crim LR* 5.

[219] But not in Scotland: *Donnelly v HM Adv* [2000] SCCR 861, 871E.

[220] In *R v Nikolovski* [1996] 3 SCR 1197, this was extended to a judge sitting as trier of fact, despite the failure of an eyewitness to accomplish the identification. It is submitted that it would have been better if an expert witness had been called in support, if only for the purposes of cross-examination.

[221] Although it seems that the accused is equally entitled not to present himself so as to prevent such an identification from being made: *R v McNamara* [1996] Crim LR 750.

[222] (1982) 75 Cr App Rep 149. Cf *Donnelly v HM Adv* (n219), 871E, in which the jury was forbidden to try to identify for itself without witness assistance, and *Smith v R* [2001] HCA 50, 206 CLR 650, in which witness assistance was inadmissible because the jury could identify for itself.

had been captured on a television camera as part of a news broadcast. Where all that can be seen on a visual representation of the crime is someone in disguise it is quite wrong to ask the accused to put on such disguise for the purposes of jury comparison.[223] In such cases, it is permissible for a witness to depose to the identity of the person depicted on the film, if for some reason or another it is desirable to supplement it.[224] This may even be done by an expert in the interpretation of photographic evidence, who can then testify to the identity of the accused despite having had no previous familiarity with him, and despite such identification being 'an ultimate issue'.[225] Discrimination of sound is much more difficult, and it will be rare for a court to leave a sound recording to the jury to compare with the voice of the accused.[226] If, however, the sound recording has been analysed by an expert, then it may be right for the recordings used by the expert to be submitted to the jury so as to assist their evaluation of his testimony.[227] It has now been held in Northern Ireland that expert acoustic evidence should always be tendered in addition to auditory evidence, where a recording is available.[228]

Procedure

Two procedural questions may arise about evidence of direct identification: first, whether the evidence should be allowed to go to the jury at all; second, if so, the proper direction to be given to the jury. The first involves the issue of whether a voir dire should be used in such cases, and the second of what, if any, warning should be given.

Voir dire

Under the old law, it was determined that a voir dire should never be held in relation to evidence of identity.[229] This followed from the analysis undertaken by the Court of Appeal in *R v Turnbull*,[230] which had determined that such evidence was either of such poor quality that the case should be withdrawn from the jury in the absence of any support, but if of better quality, or if supported, then the only question was one of weight rather than of admissibility, and there was no need for a voir dire. It was suggested in *R v Beveridge*[231] that the passage of s 78 of the Police and Criminal Evidence Act 1984 had transformed this situation in its enactment of a statutory discretion to exclude evidence likely to operate unfairly. Such a view was received coolly by the court, and apparently rejected in *R v Flemming*,[232] because identification evidence still differed from evidence of a confession admitted under s 76, in which a voir dire was appropriate, since s 76 imposes a persuasive burden of proof upon the prosecution in relation to admissibility, while s 78

---

[223] *Evans v R* [2007] HCA 59, 235 CLR 521, [27].

[224] *R v Fowden and White* [1982] Crim LR 588; *R v Grimer* (n56); *R v Caldwell and Dixon* (1993) 99 Cr App Rep 73. See also *Bowie v Tudhope* 1986 SCCR 205.

[225] *R v Stockwell* (n57). Nor need the expert evidence be especially technical: *R v Briddick* (n138), [19]. For discussion of facial mapping of persons depicted on CCTV footage, see Bromby (2003) 153 *NLJ* 302.

[226] See *Bulejcik v R* (1996) 185 CLR 375 for very full consideration of the problem; although it was allowed in *Neville v R* [2004] WASCA 62, 145 ACR 108. [227] *R v Bentum* (1989) 153 JP 538.

[228] *R v O'Doherty* (n58), remarking that modern techniques had rendered obsolete earlier views, such as those in *R v Robb* (1991) 93 Cr App Rep 161.

[229] *R v Walshe* (1980) 74 Cr App Rep 85, although it seems that voir dires were, in fact, sometimes held: see e.g. *R v Maynard* (n123). [230] (n93).

[231] (1987) 85 Cr App Rep 255.

[232] (1987) 86 Cr App Rep 32, rejecting the contrary practice adopted in *R v Leckie and Ensley* [1983] Crim LR 543.

does not. Given the unpopularity of holding a voir dire, this view seems likely to prevail in England.[233]

It has been emphasized that there is no incongruity between the decision in *R v Turnbull* that, if the evidence of identification is too poor, the issue should not be left to the jury, and that in *R v Galbraith*[234] that the judge should not usurp the function of the jury, and himself determine whether evidence is to be believed or not. In *Daley v R*,[235] Lord Mustill reconciled these decisions on the basis that identification evidence is unreliable not because of insincerity, which a jury can assess for itself, but, despite total sincerity, because of inherent weaknesses not necessarily appreciated, or capable of evaluation, by the jury.

Direction to the jury[236]

As noted above, the framework for such a direction was provided by *R v Turnbull*.[237] A judge should always[238] warn the jury of the special need for caution in relying on evidence of identification,[239] instruct them of the reason for giving such a warning, explain that this reflects actual experience of miscarriages of justice,[240] that multiple witnesses may be mistaken,[241] and highlight any particular[242] weaknesses in the instant case. There is something to be said for summarizing all of the identification together,[243] although in this, as elsewhere, the judge must have flexibility to mould the direction to the contours of the case.[244] This applies even though the evidence of identification is unchallenged.[245] A *Turnbull* warning is highly desirable even if the only issue is whether the identifying witness is sincere, and there is no real danger of mistake.[246] In cases of direct identification some of the features of a *Turnbull* direction will be inappropriate, but it should nevertheless

---

[233] But see *R v Kitchen* (n115), in which one was held. The situation may be more flexible in some jurisdictions in Australia: see *R v Hallam and Karger* (1985) 42 SASR 126; but not in those that have adopted the Evidence Act (Cwth) 1995, in which it has been rejected even for aural identification: see *R v Adler* (2000) 116 ACR 38.   [234] [1981] 2 All ER 1060, [1981] 1 WLR 1039.

[235] [1994] AC 117, [1993] 4 All ER 86.

[236] See Judicial Studies Board Model Direction No 30. In Canada, different principles apply to trial by judge alone, in which the judge is required to state his reasons for decision but not to give the equivalent of a jury direction: *R v Braich* [2002] SCC 27, [2002] 1 SCR 903.

[237] Its purport was approved by the High Court of Australia in *Domican v R* (1992) 173 CLR 555, 561.

[238] Unless the defence is of deliberate lying: see *Capron v R* (n215), or the evidence is not in dispute: *Dhanhoa v R* [2003] HCA 40, 217 CLR 1, [9]–[24].

[239] Including recognition: *R v Bentley* (1991) 99 Cr App Rep 342; *R v Bowden* [1993] Crim LR 379. It is still more necessary when there is some other flaw, such as failure to hold an identification parade: *Pop v R* (n205), [9]; or where, because the identification was by clothing, no parade was appropriate: *R v Haynes* [2004] EWCA Crim 390.   [240] *R v Nash* (n93), [8].

[241] *R v Melhado* [2009] EWCA Crim 1567, [23].

[242] Such as a parade following recent identification from photographs: *R v I* [2007] EWCA Crim 923, [2007] 2 Cr App R 316, [17]. It has, however, been held in Australia, it is submitted wrongly, that specific direction is not required on more generic identification weaknesses: see *R v Dodd* [2002] NSWCCA 418, 135 ACR 32 (cross-racial); *R v Nguyen* [2002] WASCA 181, 131 ACR 341 (voice).

[243] See *R v Trower* [2004] EWCA Crim 1533, [40].   [244] *Nash* (n93), [9].

[245] *Beckford v R* (1993) 97 Cr App Rep 409. See also *R v Courtnell* [1990] Crim LR 115; but cf *R v Bath* (n50).

[246] *Beckford v R* (n245); *Shand v R* [1996] 1 All ER 511, [1996] 1 WLR 67. Cases without a vestige of an identification issue will be very rare; but see *R v Courtnell*; *Shand v R*; *R v Cape, Jackson and Gardner* [1996] 1 Cr App Rep 191. *R v Beckles and Montague* [1999] Crim LR 148 was an unusual case in which the witness was wrong about two of the persons involved in an attack, but was regarded as incapable of being mistaken about three others, because they had admitted involvement (this point is unaffected by the lengthy subsequent history of this case).

be followed so far as possible, since all forms of identification are hazardous.[247] Especially strict directions may be necessary in relation to group[248] or dock identification[249] to the use of enhanced images from security films,[250] hypnotically induced identification,[251] and to the purported identification of voice.[252] A decisive single act of identification requires a particularly meticulous direction;[253] while a continuing series of identifications in a long-running saga of events may require less.[254]

Turnbull mandates direction closely to examine the circumstances in relation to each act of identification; and reminder of any specific weaknesses in the evidence, or of any breaches of the Code of Practice in the conduct of the technique of identification.[255] If, in the judge's view, the quality of the evidence of identity is good, he can leave it to the jury even in the absence of supporting evidence, subject always to a warning of the need for caution. If, in his view, the quality of the evidence is poor, he should withdraw the case from the jury unless there is some other evidence to support its accuracy.[256] The judge should identify which evidence can be relied upon as providing such support, and which cannot,[257] and draw to the attention of the jury any significant discrepancy between the witness's original description of the criminal, and the appearance of the accused.[258] In particular, he should explain that the accused's absence from the witness box can prove nothing,[259] although it may leave prosecution evidence uncontradicted,[260] and that a false alibi may be put forward for reasons unconnected with consciousness of guilt.[261] Such a direction should be given whether or not the Crown has sought to rely upon the failure of the alibi.[262] Where lies are relied upon to support evidence of identification, the direction recommended in *R v Lucas* should normally be given.[263] This guidance could, perhaps, be criticized for not indicating more clearly just how poor the evidence needs to be before a case should be withdrawn from the jury, and when a warning is sufficient.[264] It also failed to indicate whether further visual identification evidence could be relied upon as support. The answer to this was supplied in *R v Weeder*,[265] in which it was held that only high-quality identification evidence could provide support.

---

[247] *R v Dodson; R v Williams* [1984] 1 WLR 971, 79 Cr App Rep 220; *R v Blenkinsop* [1995] 1 Cr App Rep 7.
[248] See *R v Gorham* (1997) 68 SASR 505.   [249] See *R v Hibbert* (n205).
[250] *R v Briddick* (n138).   [251] *R v Baltovich* (2004) 191 CCC3d 289, [54]–[64].
[252] Comprehensively re-assessed in *R v Flynn and St John* (n187); see in Australia *R v Ong* [2007] VSCA 206, 176 ACR 366.   [253] *Edwards v R* [2006] UKPC 23, [27].
[254] *R v Giga* [2007] EWCA Crim 345, [29]–[31].
[255] *R v Quinn* [1995] 1 Cr App Rep 480; although if breach of the Code has not been relied upon in argument, and possible prejudice has been emphasized, failure to mention the breach may not be fatal: *R v Williams* (n201).   [256] *R v Fergus* (1993) 98 Cr App R 313.
[257] Although a failure to direct in this way, while to be deplored, is not necessarily fatal: *R v Akaidere* [1990] Crim LR 808.   [258] *Ricketts v R* (n180).
[259] Especially if a co-accused has testified: *R v Duncan* (1992) The Times, 24 July; although, after the advent of s 35 of the Criminal Justice and Public Order Act 1994, it was regarded in *R v Kelly* (1998) 162 JP 231 as weakening the accused's argument that failure to hold a parade was fatal to the safety of the conviction.
[260] The judge should be slow to emphasize this, especially where the rest of the evidence is weak: *R v Allan* (1990) The Times, 2 January.
[261] This was further emphasized in *R v Keane* (1977) 65 Cr App Rep 247; *R v Duncan* (n259). See also *R v Vincec* (1990) 50 ACR 203; *R v Dunn* (1990) 56 CCC (3d) 538.
[262] *R v Pemberton* (1993) 99 Cr App Rep 228.
[263] *R v Goodway* [1993] 4 All ER 894, 98 Cr App Rep 11.
[264] It was so criticized by Wilson J in the Supreme Court of Canada in *Mezzo v R* [1986] 1 SCR 802.
[265] (1980) 71 Cr App Rep 228.

It has been stressed that, when the jury is cautioned, it is wrong either to weaken the caution by putting counter-arguments,[266] or by failing to make it clear that the judge is himself endorsing, and not merely recapitulating, cautionary arguments put by the defence.[267] On the other hand, the judge is free to give a 'reverse' *Turnbull* direction in relation to false identification at a parade.[268] Where a parade has been wrongly[269] refused, it is appropriate to direct the jury that the accused has been deprived of the possibility of favourable evidence.[270]

It has been said[271] that: 'It would be wrong to interpret or apply *Turnbull* inflexibly.' It purports, after all, to offer no more than guidelines, and so flexible has this interpretation become that there are examples both of appeals being allowed despite an impeccable *Turnbull* direction,[272] and disallowed despite a quite inadequate *Turnbull* direction,[273] or without one at all.[274] It may also be emphasized that the effect of the direction is to be taken as a whole, and isolated departures, compensated for elsewhere, are unlikely to be fatal.[275] It is highly desirable for the judge to consult counsel about the form of direction he proposes, so as to minimize opportunities for error, and occasions for appeal.[276]

It should be noted that the judge's discretion to exclude evidence pursuant to s 78 of the Police and Criminal Evidence Act 1984 may be applied in respect of evidence of identification,[277] and occasionally, the judge will feel inclined to exercise his discretion only after initially permitting the evidence to be adduced. In such a case, he should do no less than direct the jury to disregard the evidence altogether. This might be thought too drastic a measure where the breach of Code D is venial, and in such cases, it seems that the judge is entitled not to direct the jury to disregard the evidence,[278] but rather to explain to them the reasons for regarding it with suspicion.[279] He should nevertheless explain any possible prejudice to the accused on account of breach of the Code.[280]

Even where the judge would have upheld a submission of no case on the identification evidence alone, he need not direct the jury of the necessity for it to find support.[281]

The *Turnbull* guidelines have been accepted in many Commonwealth jurisdictions,[282] but not in all.[283] Two situations that do not seem to require the full treatment are, first, those in which the real question is not whether or not someone was present on a particular

---

[266] *R v Keane* (n261).   [267] *Davis and Cody v R* (1937) 57 CLR 170, 182; *Domican v R* (n237), 564.

[268] *R v Trew* [1996] Crim LR 441 (the report in [1996] 2 Cr App Rep 138 does not include this issue).

[269] So not where the witness saw no more than the criminal's clothes: *R (Marsh)v CPS* [2006] EWHC 1525 (Admin), [9].   [270] *R v Pipersburgh and Robateau* [2008] UKPC 11, [17].

[271] By Scarman LJ in *R v Keane* (n261), 248; by the Privy Council in *Mills v R* [1995] 3 All ER 865, [1995] 1 WLR 511.

[272] *R v Pope* (1986) 85 Cr App Rep 201 (in which the court seemed remarkably unaware of black vernacular usage).   [273] *R v Clifton* [1986] Crim LR 399.

[274] *Freemantle v R* [1994] 3 All ER 225, [1994] 1 WLR 1347; *Shand v R* [1996] 1 All ER 511, [1996] 1 WLR 67.   [275] See, in Australia, *R v Zammit* [1999] NSWCCA 65, (1999) 107 ACR 489.

[276] *R v Stanton* [2004] EWCA Crim 490, [13].   [277] See *R v Quinn* (n194).

[278] Although he must give some explanation for admitting the evidence despite breach of the Code: *R v Allen* [1995] Crim LR 643.

[279] *R v Khan* [1997] Crim LR 584 (in which the investigating officer interviewed identifying witnesses before the parade, carrying in his pocket a photograph of the accused).

[280] *R v H* [2003] EWCA Crim 174, (2003) 147 Sol Jo LB 237, [38].

[281] *R v Ley* [2006] EWCA Crim 3063, [31].

[282] For example, in Australia, see *R v Duncan* (n259); in Canada, *Mezzo v R* (n264); in New Zealand, *Auckland City Council v Brailey* [1988] 1 NZLR 103.

[283] For example, New South Wales: see *R v De-Cressac* (1985) 1 NSWLR 381.

occasion, but whether they were performing a particular act,[284] and second, those in which the issue is not one of personal identification, but rather circumstantial identification.

CIRCUMSTANTIAL EVIDENCE OF IDENTITY

When there is no doubt that an act has been done, and the question is whether it was the act of a particular person, all relevant evidence is normally admissible in order to prove, or disprove, that fact.[285] Obvious instances are afforded by cases in which the criminal has left traces behind him. The fact that the crime was probably committed by a left-handed man and that the accused was left-handed, or any other physical or mental peculiarity exhibited by the criminal, may be shown to have been exhibited by the accused. This is, however, a branch of the law in which it is often necessary to have regard to the general prohibition on evidence that merely goes to show criminal tendencies, or a disposition to commit particular crimes on the part of the accused. From the point of view of relevancy, these should often be admissible, because they go to show that the accused was a member of a comparatively small class of which the criminal was also a member, but the prejudicial nature of the evidence will render it inadmissible, unless the tendency or disposition is of sufficient weight, and particular relevance, to a matter in issue in the proceedings.

Personal identity may be established by many factors other than that of name: obvious instances are provided by occupation, education, and mental, or physical, idiosyncrasies. In the *Lovat Peerage Case*,[286] it was held that the fact that an ancestor was reputed to have been guilty of manslaughter, coupled with the fact that a similar tradition prevailed with regard to the lineage of one of the claimants, was some evidence that the latter was the descendant of the former. The sole question with regard to the admissibility of circumstantial evidence of this nature is whether a particular characteristic is sufficiently rare, or a class sufficiently small, to make it worthwhile for the court to hear evidence tending to show possession of that characteristic or membership of that class.[287]

The most cogent circumstantial evidence of identity is likely to be evidence of fingerprints, or of DNA traces in relevant tissue. In practice, such evidence is likely to be conclusive.

PRESUMPTIVE EVIDENCE OF IDENTITY

Although it is highly exceptional for presumptions to operate against the accused in criminal cases at common law, such a presumption was made in Scotland in *Rollo v Wilson*,[288] in which the accused sought acquittal on the basis that the prosecution had failed to prove that he was the person summoned to appear in court, despite his having so appeared in answer to the summons. A similar result applies in England.[289]

---

[284] As in *R v Oakwell* (n51) (which in a crowd was the assailant); *R v Linegar* [2001] EWCA Crim 2404 (similar); *Auckland City Council v Brailey* [1988] 1 NZLR 103 (which of two people in a car was driving it); *Sharrett v Gill* (1992) 65 ACR 44 (a similar situation).

[285] For a particularly striking recent example see *Alabusheva v DPP* [2007] EWHC 264 (Admin).

[286] (1885) 10 App Cas 763.   [287] See II Wigmore, [386].   [288] 1988 JC 82.

[289] See further below, 720.

SECTION 3. BIRTH, AGE, DEATH, MARRIAGE, AND LEGITIMACY

BIRTH

There are four methods of proving birth. The most usual at the present day is the production of a certified copy of an entry in the register of births, which may be received as evidence of the facts stated under the public document exception to the hearsay rule.[290] The court will require some evidence identifying the person whose birth is in question with the person referred to in the birth certificate. This might take the form of a direct statement by the person in question, if he were testifying to the date or place of birth, although the evidence is, at best, hearsay, and at worst, pure guesswork. It could also be provided by someone who was present at the birth, or by the informant to the registrar; more often than not, the evidence of identity will be supplied by an affidavit in which the deponent, usually a member of the family of the person whose birth is in question, will depose to his, or her, belief that the person is, or was, the same person as the one referred to in the exhibited birth certificate. The testimony of someone present at the birth to that fact, its place, or date is a second, and separate, method of proving these matters. They may also be proved, in civil proceedings, by statements admissible by virtue of the Civil Evidence Act 1968, and in criminal proceedings, under exceptions to the hearsay rule relating to the declarations of deceased persons,[291] or perhaps under the provisions of the Criminal Justice Act 2003.

AGE

There are four ways in which a person's age can be proved: two of them depend on direct evidence, and two on the exceptions to the hearsay rule relating, respectively, to statements in public documents, and declarations of deceased persons.[292]

Direct evidence

A person's age may be proved by direct evidence: (a) by the testimony of those present at his birth; (b) by inferences from his appearance, which are permitted in special cases by certain statutes.[293] It is clearly rare that resort can be made to the first of these methods, and its use would often, to some extent, involve reliance on hearsay. Even the mother's evidence of the child's age might well be based on hearsay evidence of identity at the earliest stages of the child's life. The court is authorized by several statutes to act on inspection with regard to questions of age, but quite apart from these provisions, the general effect of which is to make the result of the inspection prima facie proof of age, such result would presumably be evidence of age in every case.[294] It would be a kind of real evidence, although, in many instances, it would not be sufficient for the court to act on it without more.

---

[290] Births and Deaths Registration Act 1953, s 34. See Chapter XV, Section 1. As to certified extracts from foreign registers, see the Evidence (Foreign Dominion and Colonial Documents) Act 1933, and as to births on board ship, the Merchant Shipping (Returns of Births and Deaths) Regulations 1979, made under s 75 of the Merchant Shipping Act 1970.   [291] Chapter XIV, Section 1.

[292] For a fuller account including reference to English authority see *Shah v Police* [2006] 2 NZLR 425.

[293] Children and Young Persons Act 1933, s 99; Criminal Justice Act 1948, s 80(3); Magistrates' Courts Act 1980, s 150(4).

[294] *Wallworth v Balmer* [1965] 3 All ER 721, [1966] 1 WLR 16.

Hearsay

Probably the most usual way of proving age is production of a birth certificate as evidence of the date of the birth specified therein under the public document exception to the hearsay rule.[295] Evidence of the identity of the person whose age is in question with the person named in the certificate will be required.

In criminal cases, age may be proved under the hearsay provisions of the Criminal Justice Act 2003. In these cases, too, it may be necessary to find some evidence identifying the person referred to in the statement with the person whose age is in issue.

DEATH

There are five ways in which a person's death may be proved. It is not necessary to refer to any of them in detail. The first, and most usual, is to rely on a death certificate, coupled with some evidence identifying the person named therein with the person whose death is in question.[296] Second, death may be proved by statements admissible under the Civil Evidence Act 1995, or the Criminal Justice Act 2003. Third, reliance may be placed upon the presumption of death.[297] Even where the presumption is inapplicable, the court may infer death from a protracted period of absence, the length of which will vary according to the facts of each case. The fourth, and fifth, ways are to rely either on the evidence of someone who was present at its occurrence, or of someone who is otherwise able to identify the corpse as that of the relevant person.

MARRIAGE

When a marriage is in issue, the first thing that has to be proved is a marriage ceremony. In certain cases, this may be presumed from proof of cohabitation, and repute. Subject to this further possibility, the person seeking to prove a marriage ceremony may rely on the same methods as those for proof of birth. Evidence may be adduced from someone who was present at the wedding,[298] and this is the method almost invariably adopted in matrimonial cases.[299] Declarations that a couple were married may be received in civil cases under the Civil Evidence Act 1995, or in criminal cases under the Criminal Justice Act 2003. The third, and most usual, method consists in the production of a marriage certificate, coupled with evidence identifying the persons mentioned in the certificate with those whose marriage is to be proved. When one is available, such evidence will generally be supplied by a party to the marriage. Whenever a certificate is available, the courts require it to be produced in addition to receiving the evidence of the parties as to the ceremony.

The second thing to be proved by someone seeking to establish a marriage is that the ceremony constituted a formally valid marriage. Generally speaking, it will have to be shown that a form recognized by the law of the place of celebration was adopted, but there

[295] Births and Deaths Registration Act 1953, s 34, and, as to foreign registers, the Evidence (Foreign, Dominion and Colonial Documents) Act 1933. See also Merchant Shipping (Returns of Births and Deaths) Regulations 1979.

[296] Births and Deaths Registration Act 1953, s 34; Merchant Shipping (Returns of Births and Deaths) Regulations 1979.   [297] See 134.

[298] This includes a party to the marriage.

[299] Statements may be received under the Civil Evidence Act 1995.

are exceptions in the case of marriages celebrated abroad.[300] If the ceremony took place in England, or Wales, the certificate is evidence of the marriage to which it relates,[301] but, in other cases, it will be necessary to produce expert evidence by a witness, or by affidavit of formal validity, according to the local law. This could be a costly requirement, and there are, accordingly, many exceptions.[302] In spite of the numerous exceptions to the requirement of proof of formal validity under the local law, the general rule remained, and it was often necessary to procure the attendance of an expert witness, or to obtain leave to read an affidavit by him to the effect that the certificate of the marriage would be recognized in the courts of the country in question.[303]

Because of such possibilities, exceptions to the requirement of proof by testimony, or affidavit, of the legal validity of a foreign marriage are of great importance. Under s 1 of the Foreign Marriage Order 1970, the celebration and validity of a marriage that took place outside England and Wales may be proved, in any matrimonial proceedings, by the production of appropriate certification from the United Kingdom consul in the relevant jurisdiction. In other cases, in which the existence, and validity, of the marriage is undisputed, reliance may be placed on the evidence of one of the parties, and the production of such a certificate, or certified copy, as a statement or record admissible by virtue of the Civil Evidence Act 1995, or the Criminal Justice Act 2003.

LEGITIMACY

In order to establish a child's legitimacy, reliance may be placed on the presumption of legitimacy. For this purpose, it is simply necessary to prove that the child was born, or conceived, during its mother's marriage to her husband, after which it is incumbent on those denying legitimacy to prove illegitimacy. Legitimacy may also be proved, in criminal cases, under exceptions to the rule against hearsay, notably that relating to pedigree declarations by deceased persons, perhaps under the Criminal Justice Act 2003, and, in civil cases, by statements admissible under the Civil Evidence Act 1995. It might also be proved by a statement in a public document, for the statements as to paternity in birth certificates are evidence of their truth. Finally, reliance might be placed on a declaration of legitimacy, which is a judgment *in rem* and therefore binding on the whole world. Nowadays, DNA evidence would be likely to be most convenient, and conclusive.

SECTION 4. JUDGMENTS AND CONVICTIONS

If the proof of judgments, and convictions, were not exhaustively covered by statutory provisions, it would be necessary to produce the actual record of the court, and to call evidence identifying the relevant parties with the person mentioned in the record. The different statutory provisions may be summarized for civil and criminal cases.

---

[300] For details, see Dicey, Morris, and Collins *Conflict of Laws* (14th edn).
[301] Marriage Act 1949, s 65.   [302] For further detail see previous editions of this work.
[303] *Todd v Todd* [1961] 2 All ER 881, [1961] 1 WLR 951 (Irish marriage).

CIVIL CASES

A sealed judgment of the Supreme Court is evidence without further proof.[304] Judgments of the Court of Appeal and High Court may be proved by production of an office copy made in the central office, or district registry.[305] Judgments of the county court may be proved by a certified copy of the entry in the registrar's book.[306] Judgments of the magistrates in civil matters are also proved by the production of a certified extract from the court book.[307] Foreign or colonial judgments may be proved by production of an examined copy,[308] or a copy sealed with the seal of the court, under the provisions of s 7 of the Evidence Act 1851. In all of the above cases, production of the relevant document will usually be sufficient to establish its authenticity, because the court will take judicial notice of the seal, or certificate, attached to the document, but oral evidence may be required to identify the parties to the judgment with the person whose rights the court is considering, or those through whom such persons claim. Evidence of this nature is, however, often rendered unnecessary by some kind of formal admission.[309]

CRIMINAL CASES

Proof of convictions in criminal cases has been revolutionized by the passage of the Police and Criminal Evidence Act 1984, s 73, which must be rendered in full:

(1) Where in any proceedings the fact that a person has in the United Kingdom been convicted or acquitted of an offence otherwise than by a Service court is admissible in evidence, it may be proved by producing a certificate of conviction or, as the case may be, of acquittal relating to that offence, and proving that the person named in the certificate as having been convicted or acquitted of the offence is the person whose conviction or acquittal of the offence is to be proved.

(2) For the purposes of this section a certificate of conviction or of acquittal—

(a) shall, as regards a conviction or acquittal on indictment consist of a certificate, signed by the clerk of the court where the conviction or acquittal took place, giving the substance and effect (omitting the formal parts) of the indictment and of the conviction or acquittal; and

(b) shall, as regards a conviction or acquittal on a summary trial, consist of a copy of the conviction or of the dismissal of the information, signed by the clerk of the court where the conviction or acquittal took place or by the clerk of the court, if any, to which a memorandum of the conviction or acquittal was sent; and a document purporting to be a duly signed certificate of conviction or acquittal under this section shall be taken to be such a certificate unless the contrary is proved.

(3) References in this section to the clerk of a court include references to his deputy and to any other person having the custody of the court record.

---

[304] Constitutional Reform Act 2005, s 55.

[305] Supreme Court Act 1981, s 132.   [306] County Courts Act 1984, s 12(2).

[307] Magistrates' Courts Rules 1981, rr 66 and 68.

[308] An examined copy is one examined against the original. As evidence of the examination is usually necessary, proof by examined copy is rare. Some cases are governed by separate statutory provision, e.g. Child Abduction and Custody Act 1985, s 22.

[309] Which is equally admissible in a criminal court: *R v Stokes* [1988] Crim LR 110.

(4) The method of proving a conviction or acquittal authorised by this section shall be in addition to and not to the exclusion of any other authorised manner of proving a conviction or acquittal.

This provision was recommended by the Criminal Law Revision Committee, and was adopted almost verbatim from the bill annexed to its 11th Report.[310] It permitted repeal or modification of a number of now obsolete provisions in relation to criminal proceedings,[311] and has been accepted[312] as additional to other ways of proving convictions, often, but not exclusively, by admission,[313] fingerprints, or the evidence of someone present in court at the time of the conviction in question. It is unclear why s 14 of Perjury Act 1911 has been retained, since it seems to add little to these provisions. There does, however, seem to have been a quite deliberate decision to retain, as additional methods, written statements admitted under the Criminal Justice Act 1967, s 9, and admissions under Criminal Justice Act 1967, s 10.

Under s 31 of the Road Traffic Offenders Act 1988, the endorsement of a licence is prima facie evidence of a conviction. This provision is in addition to the other statutory provisions dealing with the proof of previous convictions that have just been mentioned, but its object is to enable justices to determine sentence, and it does not supersede the other methods of proving convictions at the trial.[314]

Foreign convictions can be proved only as examined copies under s 7 of the Evidence Act 1851.[315]

If the apparent subject of the relevant conviction, including a foreign conviction, should deny that it relates to him, then this denial must be rebutted by evidence.[316]

---

[310] Cmnd 4991, Annex 1 cl 26.

[311] Evidence Act 1851, s 13; Criminal Procedure Act 1865, s 6; Prevention of Crimes Act 1871, s 18.

[312] *Pattison v DPP* [2005] EWHC 2938 (Admin), [2006] 2 All ER 317, [26], in which some confusion in the pre-existing case law was resolved in determining that, normally, coincidence of name, or other personal details, and absence of evidence to the contrary will be sufficient to establish that the memorandum of conviction relates to the accused.

[313] See *Barber v CPS*, in which an informal admission in police interview of the existence of a restraining order was allowed as evidence in the absence of production of the relevant order.

[314] *Stone v Bastick* [1967] 1 QB 74, [1965] 3 All ER 713, also requiring a certificate of disqualification to refer only to the offence in respect of which the disqualification was imposed.

[315] *R v Mauricia* [2002] EWCA Crim 676, [2002] 2 Cr App Rep 377.

[316] *Bailey v DPP* (1999) 163 JP 518. The same requirement would presumably apply to judgments. There is no special restriction on the form of evidence to accomplish this. In many cases, the prima facie evidence relating the conviction to the accused will be sufficient to prove that it relates to him, but it is ultimately a matter for the trier of fact: *R v Burns* [2006] EWCA Crim 617, [2006] 1 WLR 1273, [21].

INDEX

Printed and bound by CPI Group (UK) Ltd, Croydon, CR0 4YY